encyclopedia of the
DOCUMENTARY FILM

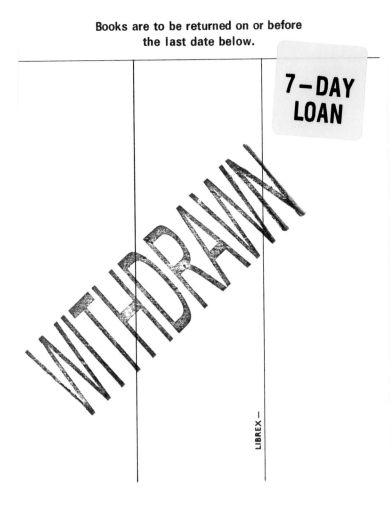

encyclopedia of the
DOCUMENTARY FILM

Volume 1
A–G
INDEX

Ian Aitken

editor

Routledge
Taylor & Francis Group
New York London

Published in 2006 by
Routledge
Taylor & Francis Group
270 Madison Avenue
New York, NY 10016

Published in Great Britain by
Routledge
Taylor & Francis Group
2 Park Square
Milton Park, Abingdon
Oxon OX14 4RN

Printed in the United States of America on acid-free paper
10 9 8 7 6 5 4 3 2 1

International Standard Book Number-10: 1-57958-445-4 (Hardcover)
International Standard Book Number-13: 978-1-57958-445-0 (Hardcover)
Library of Congress Card Number 2005046519

Library of Congress Cataloging-in-Publication Data

Encyclopedia of the documentary film / edited by Ian Aitken.
    p. cm.
  Includes bibliographical references and index.
  ISBN 1-57958-445-4 (set : alk. paper) -- ISBN 0-415-97637-5 (v. 1 : alk paper) -- ISBN 0-415-97638-3 (v. 2 : alk. paper) -- ISBN 0-415-97639-1 (v. 3 : alk. paper)
  1. Documentary films--Encyclopedias. I. Aitken, Ian.

PN1995.9.D6E53 2005
070.1'8--dc 22   2005046519

Taylor & Francis Group is the Academic Division of T&F Informa plc.

Visit the Taylor & Francis Web site at
http://www.taylorandfrancis.com

and the Routledge Web site at
http://www.routledge-ny.com

BOARD OF ADVISERS

LIST OF CONTRIBUTORS

Angela Aguayo
University of Texas at Austin

Ian Aitken
De Montfort University, and Hong Kong Baptist University

Jae Alexander
University of Southern Mississippi

Jessica Allen
Independent Scholar

Samara Allsop
Independent Scholar

Joshua Amberg
University of California, Los Angeles

Carolyn Anderson
University of Massachusetts, Amherst

Kevin Anderson
University of Massachusetts, Amherst

Richard Armstrong
British Film Institute

Isabel Arredondo
State University of New York, Plattsburgh

Michael B. Baker
Independent Scholar

Kees Bakker
Independent Producer of Documentaries

Charles Bane
Louisiana State University

Ilisa Barbash
Harvard University

Elke Bartel
Middle Tennessee State University

Stefano Baschiera
National University of Ireland, Cork

Gerd Bayer
University of Wisconsin, Whitewater

Philip Bell
University of New South Wales, Australia

Nitzan Ben-Shaul
Tel-Aviv University

Jeff Bergin
Independent Producer

Ina Bertrand
University of Melbourne

Robert Beveridge
Napier University

Daniel Biltereyst
Universiteit Gent, Belgium

Mira Binford
Quinnipiac University

Elizabeth Bishop
University of Texas at Austin

Jennifer Bottinelli
Kutztown University

Brett Bowles
Iowa State University

Melissa Bromley
British Film Institute National Film & Television Archive

John Burgan
Documentary Filmmaker

Andrew Burke
University of Winnipeg

Marina Burke
University College Dublin

Alan Burton
De Montfort University

Andreas Busche
Film Critic and Film Archivist

Lou Buttino
University of North Carolina, Wilmington

Jose Cabeza San Deogracias
Complutense University, Madrid

Michael S. Casey
Graceland University

Catalina Ceron
Independent Director and Producer of
Documentaries

Michael Chanan
University of the West of England

David Chapman
University of East London

Stephen Charbonneau
University of California, Los Angeles

Thomas Cohen
Rhodes College

Kathleen Collins
Indpendent Scholar

John Cook
Glasgow Caledonian University

Pat A. Cook
Brunel University

Sarah Cooper
University of Cambridge

John Corner
University of Liverpool

Kirwan Cox
Concordia University, Canada

Sean Cubitt
University of Waikato, New Zealand

Jacobia Dahm
Johannes Gutenberg-University, Germany and
Columbia University

Fergus Daly
University College Dublin

Jill Daniels
University of East London

Amy Darnell
Southern Illinois University, Carbondale

Jonathan Dawson
Griffith University

Rafael De Espana
University of Barcelona

Maria Elena De las Carreras-Kuntz
University of California, Los Angeles, and
California State University, Northridge

Annette Deeken
University of Trier, Germany

David Diffrient
University of California, Los Angeles

Caroline Dover
CAMRI (Communication & Media Research
Institute), University of Westminster

Dean Duncan
Brigham Young University

Sarah Easen
British Universities Film & Video Council

Suzanne Eisenhut
San Francisco State University

Jack Ellis
Northwestern University (emeritus)

Robert Emmons
Rutgers University, Camden

Leo Enticknap
University of Teesside, Middlesbrough, UK

Dino Everett
UCLA Film & Television Archive

Kirsty Fairclough
University of Salford

Tamara Falicov
University of Kansas

Seth Feldman
York University, Canada

Ramona Fotiade
University of Glasgow

Steven Foxon
Independent Scholar

Hugo Frey
University College, Chichester

Hideaki Fujiki
Nagoya University

Oliver Gaycken
University of Chicago

Jeff Geiger
University of Essex

Aaron Gerow
Yale University

Hal Gladfelder
University of Rochester

Paul Gleed
State University of New York at Buffalo

Marcy Goldberg
University of Zurich

Annie Goldson
Writer and Documentary Filmmaker

Ian Goode
University of Glasgow

Barry Keith Grant
Brock University, Canada

Leger Grindon
Middlebury College

Tom Grochowski
Queens College, City University of New York

Sapna Gupta
University of Calgary

Roger Hallas
Syracuse University

Ben Halligan
York St. John College, University of Leeds

Martin Halliwell
University of Leicester

Britta Hartmann
Universität der Künste Berlin

Vinzenz Hediger
Ruhr University, Bochum, Germany

Gillian Helfield
York University, Toronto, Canada

Walter Hess
Independent Scholar

Jeremy Hicks
Queen Mary College, University of London

Christine Hilger
University of Texas at Dallas

Jim Hillier
University of Reading

Roger Hillman
Australian National University

Lisa Hinrichsen
Boston University

Kay Hoffman
Haus des Dokumentarfilms, Germany

David Hogarth
York University, Canada

Bert Hogenkamp
Netherlands Institute for Sound and Vision /
Utrecht University

Bruce Horsfield
University of Southern Queensland

Kerr Houston
Maryland Institute College of Art

Amanda Howell
Griffith University

Robert Hunt
Webster University

LIST OF CONTRIBUTORS

Katherine Ince
University of Birmingham, UK

Michael Ingham
Lingnan University

Dina Iordanova
University of Leicester

Jeffrey Isaacs
University of Chicago

Gunnar Iversen
Trondheim University, Norway

D. B. Jones
Drexel University

Chris Jordan
Pennsylvania State University

Verónica Jordana
Independent Scholar

Uli Jung
University of Trier, Germany

Brett Kashmere
Concordia University, Canada

Alexander Kaufman
Purdue University

Misha Kavka
University of Auckland, New Zealand

Tammy A. Kinsey
University of Toledo

Michael Kogge
Fulbright Scholar in Iceland, 2000-2001

Yves Laberge
Film historian and Series Editor, Cinema et société, Les Presses de l'Université Laval

Suzanne Langlois
York University, Canada

Maximilian Le Cain
Independent Filmmaker and Writer

Charles Lee
St. Martin's College

Peter Lee-Wright
Southampton Institute

Neil Lerner
Davidson College

Jacquie L'Etang
University of Stirling, UK

Melinda C. Levin
University of North Texas

Jean-Luc Lioult
Université de Provence

André Loiselle
Carleton University

Alice Lovejoy
Yale University

David Lugowski
Manhattanville College

Catherine Lupton
Roehampton University of Surrey

Theresa C. Lynch
University of New Hampshire

David MacDougall
Australian National University

Misha MacLaird
Writer and Editorial Contractor

Wendy Maier
Oakton Community College

Joshua Malitsky
Northwestern University

Sunil Manghani
York St. John College, University of Leeds

Starr Marcello
Independent Scholar

Gina Marchetti
University of Hong Kong

Harriet Margolis
Victoria University of Wellington, New Zealand

Susan McFarlane-Alvarez
Georgia State University

Heather McIntosh
Pennsylvania State University

Luke McKernan
British Universities Film & Video Council

Tom McSorley
Canadian Film Institute and Carleton
University

Dhugal Meachem
Independent Scholar

Chris Meir
Concordia University, Canada

Martin Mhando
Murdoch University, Western Australia

Paul Miller
Davidson College

Ángel Miquel
Universidad Autónoma del Estado de Morelos,
Mexico

Akira Mizuta Lippit
University of California, Irvine

Julio Montero
Complutense University, Madrid

Albert Moran
Griffith University

James Moran
Emerson College, Los Angeles

Patrick Murphy
Independent Scholar, and York St. John
College, University of Leeds (emeritus)

Justine Nagan
University of Chicago

Caryn Neumann
Ohio State University

Abe Markus Nornes
University of Michigan

Harvey O'Brien
University College Dublin

Jules Odendahl-James
Southwestern Missouri State University

Tony Osborne
Gonzaga University

Derek Paget
University of Reading

Andreas Pagoulatos
Independent Scholar

Silke Panse
University of Kent

María Antonia Paz Rebollo
Complutense University, Madrid

Geraldene Peters
University of Auckland, New Zealand

Rod Phillips
Michigan State University, James Madison College

Shira Pinson
London Film School

Carl R. Plantinga
Calvin College

Wendy Pojmann
Johnson County Community College

Reza Poudeh
Texas Southern University

Jason Price
New York University

Paula Rabinowitz
University of Minnesota, Twin Cities

Charles Ramirez-Berg
University of Texas at Austin

Fernão Pessoa Ramos
Universidade de São Paulo

Laura Rascaroli
National University of Ireland, Cork

Richard Raskin
University of Aarhus, Denmark

Kokila Ravi
Atlanta Metropolitan College

Ramón Reichert
University of Art and Industrial Design, Linz,
Austria

Robert C. Reimer
University of North Carolina, Charlotte

John Riley
British Universities Film and Video Council

Churchill Roberts
University of Florida

Michael Robinson
Doc Films, Chicago

MJ Robinson
New York University

Jane Roscoe
Griffith University

Tom Ruffles
National Extension College, Cambridge, UK

Theresa Scandiffio
University of Chicago

Frank Scheide
University of Arkansas

Ralf Schenk
Film Historian

Paige Schilt
University of Texas at Austin

Jesse Schlotterbeck
University of Iowa

Alexandra Schneider
The Free University, Berlin

Steven Schneider
New York University

Danielle Schwartz
McGill University

Rada Sesic
International Documentary Film Festival
Amsterdam, and International Film Festival
Rotterdam

Jamie Sexton
University of Wales Aberystwyth

Sharon Shelton-Colangelo
Northwest Vista College

Kevin Sherman
San Francisco State University

Philip Simpson
Brevard Community College, Palm Bay Campus

James Skinner
University of Victoria, Canada

Belinda Smaill
Monash University

Ryan Smith
Clatsop Community College, Oregon

Beretta E. Smith-Shomade
University of Arizona

Gustavo Soranz
Independent Scholar

Pierre Sorlin
University of Paris, Sorbonne

Nicholas Stabakis
Independent Scholar

Eva M. Stadler
Fordham University

Sunny Stalter
Rutgers University

Cecile Starr
Film reviewer and film critic

D. Bruno Starrs
University of Melbourne

Matthias Steinle
Marburg University, Germany

Tracy Stephenson
Louisiana State University

Julianne Stewart
University of Southern Queensland

Martin Stollery
Southampton Institute

Dan Streible
University of South Carolina

Thomas Stubblefield
University of Illinois, Chicago

Richard Suchenski
Princeton University

Catherine Summerhayes
Australian National University

Yvan Tardy
De Montfort University

Thomas Tode
Independent scholar

Peter Urquhart
University of Nottingham

Trudi Van Dyke
William Paterson University & Rutgers
University

Roel Vande Winkel
Sint-Lukas Hogeschool, Belgium

Jennifer VanderBurgh
York University

Cristina Vatulescu
Society of Fellows, Harvard University

Joe Wagner
University of North Carolina, Greensboro

Alistair Wardill
Harrow College, UK

Charles Warren
Harvard University and Boston University

Gerlinde Waz
Filmmuseum Berlin

Mark Westmoreland
University of Texas at Austin

Catherine Wheatley
St. John's College, University of Oxford, UK

Helen Wheatley
University of Reading

Diane Wiener
University of Arizona

Danielle Williams
Auburn University

Deane Williams
Monash University

Gordon Williams
University of Wales, Lampeter

Keith Williams
University of Dundee

Ronald Wilson
University of Kansas

Sheena Wilson
University of Alberta, Canada

J. Emmett Winn
Auburn University

Mark J. P. Wolf
Concordia University, Wisconsin

Charles C. Wolfe
University of California, Santa Barbara

Alan Wright
University of Canterbury, New Zealand

John Young
University of Nottingham

CONTENTS

LIST OF ENTRIES A TO Z

THEMATIC LIST OF ENTRIES

Films

Abel Gance: Yesterday and Tomorrow
Act of God
Adolescents, The
American Family, An
Anais Nin Observed
Angela: Portrait of a Revolutionary
Ark, The
Ascent of Man
Aubervilliers

Back of Beyond, The
Basic Training
Bataille du Rail, La
Battle for Our Soviet Ukraine, The
Battle of Chile, The
Battle of China, The
Battle of Midway
Battle of Russia, The
Battle of San Pietro, The
Battle of the Somme
BBC: The Voice of Britain
Berlin: The Symphony of a Great City
Beruf: Neonazi
Black Box BRD
Blue Eyed
Bridge, The
Bronx Morning, A
Bumming in Beijing
Burden of Dreams
Burma Victory

Camera Natura
Canada Carries On
Cane Toads: An Unnatural History
Cathy Come Home
Chair, The
Chang
Chelsea Girls
Children at School

China!
Chronique d'un été
Chulas Fronteras
Churchill's Island
City, The
City of Gold
Close-Up
Coal Face
Comizi d'Amore
Contact
Cuba, Si!
Culloden

Dead Birds
Death of a Princess
December 7
Del Mero Corazón
Desert Victory
Diary for Timothy, A
Dinner Party, The
Divided World, A
Divine Horsemen
Dockers
Don't Look Back
Drifters

Eiffel Tower, The
Enough to Eat?
Enthusiasm
Eternity
Être et Avoir
Every Day Except Christmas
Exile and the Kingdom

Fall of the Romanov Dynasty, The
Family Portrait
Far from Vietnam
Farrebique
Finding Christa
Fires Were Started
First Love

THEMATIC LIST OF ENTRIES

Individuals: Directors and Producers

THEMATIC LIST OF ENTRIES

THEMATIC LIST OF ENTRIES

Individuals: Theorists and Thinkers

Individuals: Other

Production Companies, Organizations, Festivals, and Institutions

Scandinavia
Scotland
Southeast Asia
Spain
Switzerland

Underground/ Activist Documentary: Australasia/
   Oceania
Underground/Activist Documentary: Chile
United Kingdom
United Kingdom: Documentary Drama

West Indies and Caribbean

Yugoslavia (former)

General Topics and Concepts

Activist Filmmaking
Autobiography and documentary

Chicano Tradition
Cinemagazine

Docusoap

Globalization and Documentary Film

Mocumentary

News Magazines and Television Current Affairs
   Programming

Publicity and Public Relations

Realism, Philosophy and the Documentary Film
Reality Television
Reflexivity

Third Cinema

Video

Styles, Techniques, and Technical Issues

Acting
Animation

Camera Technology
Cinema Novo
Compilation
Computer Imaging

Computer Simulation
Digital video
Digitization
Distribution and Exhibition

Editing Techniques
Editing Technology

Film Stock
Found Footage

IMAX
Indexicality
Interactivity

Multimedia
Music

Narration

Production Processes

Sound
Spoken Commentary ("Voice of God")
Subjunctive Documentary

Videotape

Themes, Issues, and Representations

Aesthetics and Documentary Film: Poetics

Bosnian Documentary Movement

Deconstruction, Documentary Film and

Ethnographic Documentary Film

Falklands War
Fascist Italy
Fascist Spain
Feminism: Africa
Feminism: Critical Overview
Feminism: North America
Feminism: United Kingdom

Hitler and National Socialist Party
Homosexuality and Documentary Film
Human Rights and Documentary Film

Marxism
Modernism: Avant-garde and Experimental Early
   Silent European Documentary

INTRODUCTION

The documentary film can be regarded as the first genre of the cinema. During the 1890s, when the cinema came into existence, most viewers saw some kind of 'actuality' film. These early documentaries were often simple, single-shot affairs, showing newsworthy events, scenes from foreign lands, or everyday events. However, more fictional (or 'staged') actualities also began to be produced from the earliest years of the cinema, based on the special effects capacity of the cinema. An example here might be the Lumière brothers' *Arroseur arrose*, which appeared as early as 1895, but perhaps the most well known is Georges Melies' *A Trip to the Moon* (1902). Between 1895 and 1905 a number of identifiable genres of documentary film emerged, including 'topicals', 'travelogues', 'scenics', 'industrials', sports films, 'trick' films, 'fantsy' films, and films that used fictional reconstruction or staging in a variety of ways. These early genres of documentary film were quickly assimilated into existing modes of popular culture and entertainment and initially appeared in venues that used other, non-filmic, forms of performance such as acrobatics, song, and dance.

However, from quite early on, the value of documentary film as a form of promotion and persuasion was also recognised. For example, the 'industrials' were usually made by corporate businesses in order to promote their image. Examples include English 'industrials' such as *The Story of a Piece of Slate* (1904). Such films were primarily descriptive and expressed little if any opinion on the industrial processes they represented.

Later, the value of the documentary film as a form of social and political critique, ideology, and propaganda was quickly recognised, particularly so during World War I. During the war, all the participating countries embarked upon major programmes of propaganda production involving the use of the documentary film. The documentary moved out of the province of entertainment and private sponsorship and into the service of the state. Initially, government services were antipathetic and suspicious about this new medium that had emerged from the working classes and appeared to possess the worrying ability to show things that governments would prefer to keep well hidden, or, at least, maintain as the preserve of minority elites. As a consequence, strict controls were placed on documentary filmmaking during the war. For example, upon the outbreak of war, the War Office in England allowed cameramen to accompany the British Expeditionary Force (BEF) into France. A decisive victory had been expected, but when the BEF was forced to retreat from Mons and Ypres in late 1914, all newsreel permits were withdrawn and a blanket censorship was imposed. Nevertheless, important films were made during the war in all the participating countries. Perhaps the most important of these was the British film *Battle of the Somme* (1916). This film, striking for its images of life on the front line, had a considerable impact on its audience. Nevertheless, it was produced within the constraints of an extensive censorship system and would not have appeared if its representations were not acceptable to that system.

The documentary film did not really come into its own as a major and significant form of filmmaking until the 1920s. Before 1920, documentary films were largely 'un-authored', so to speak, and often rather simple in both form and aspiration. Despite the appearance of *Battle of the Somme*, few large-scale documentaries were made before 1920, and fewer of these can be regarded as historically, aesthetically, or politically important. However, the inter-war period in Europe was an age of ideology, and documentary film was soon put to the service of political promotion as well as artistic accomplishment.

One of the most important films in the history of the documentary film also appeared as early as 1922. It is difficult to exaggerate the historical impact of Robert Flaherty's *Nanook of the North*. Set in the far north of Canada, *Nanook of the North* presents compelling images of Eskimo life and reveals the startling potential of the documentary film for bringing the everyday world to life. This potential was not lost on early film theorists, who soon began to see documentary film as the principal means through which a genuine form of film art could be created, against the background of the accelerating domination of the medium by the mass-produced Hollywood feature film. Thus, André Sauvage regarded *Nanook of the North* as an example of 'pure cinema', by which he meant that Flaherty's film foregrounded the raw, visual naturalism that Sauvage believed to be at the heart of the aesthetic specificity of the medium.

Nanook was also an inspiration for the emergence of a number of hybrid documentaries that appeared in France and Germany during the 1920s. These films, which combined documentary with modernist form, include *Rien que les heures* (Alberto Cavalcanti, 1926) and *Berlin: die Symphonie der Grossstadt* (Walter Ruttmann, 1929). In addition to these films, *Nanook* also made it possible for Schoedsack and Coopers' *Grass* (1925) and *Chang* (1928) to appear, with their respective accounts of the tribulations of Iranian and Siamese peasant life and, less directly, Victor Turin's *Turksib* (1929), with its epic story of the building of the trans-Siberian railway. It was also in the Soviet Union that the second most important documentary film of the 1895–1945 period emerged: Dziga Vertov's *Man With a Movie Camera* (1929). As with *Nanook of the North*, it is difficult to exaggerate the importance this film has had, both in terms of the documentary film and in terms of film theory.

The 1930–1945 period marked another stage in the historical development of the documentary film, when individual authors began to emerge and documentary was put to increasing social and political use. In the United States, the Workers' Film and Photo League was formed, and committed (or socially concerned) films such as *Native Land* (Paul Strand and Leo Hurwitz, 1942) appeared. Similar organisations sprang up in Europe, and committed documentary filmmakers such as Joris Ivens, Henri Storck, Pare Lorentz, and Ivor Montagu also came to prominence. In Britain, John Grierson's documentary film movement made important films such as *Drifters* (1929) throughout the 1930s and 1940s and cultivated important filmmakers, such as Paul Rotha, Alberto Cavalcanti, Basil Wright, and Humphrey Jennings. Wright's *Song of Ceylon* (1934) and Grierson's *Drifters* remain impressive today for their command of aesthetic form and visual beauty. During the war the documentary film movement also played a role in developing a new genre: the dramatised documentary, exemplified by Jennings' *Fires Were Started* (1943).

After 1945, documentary film developed in a number of different directions. More clearly 'authored' but still socially concerned films began to appear, by such directors as Frederic Rossif, Karel Reisz, Lindsay Anderson, Georges Franju, and Alain Resnais. Of particular note is Resnais' *Nuit et brouillard* (1957, *Night and Fog*), with its stark and uncompromising portrayal of the Nazi death camps. Documentary genres were also developed further during this period. Chris Marker produced philosophical travelogues such as *Letter from Siberia* (1958), while the ethnographic film was taken to a new level of importance by Robert Gardner in *The Hunters* (1956) and *Dead Birds* (1963). Even more important in this respect was Jean Rouch, particularly his ground-breaking, reflexive *Chronicle of a Summer* (1961). The films of French filmmakers such as Rouch also influenced the development of the North American *cinéma vérité* movement and the films of Robert Drew, Richard Leacock, the Maysle Brothers, and others. Their work, in turn, influenced the filmmaking of Frederick Wiseman. Interview-based films, such as Marcel Ophuls' *The Sorrow and the Pity* (1970) and the British TV series *The World at War* (1974–1975) also made important advances within the field by tapping into historical experience in an often profoundly moving and discomforting manner. *The World at War* also broke new ground in telling the story of World War II from the perspective of ordinary people, rather than from the perspectives of the great and good.

During the period from the 1980s to the present, important documentary films and filmmakers continued to emerge. Important filmmakers of this period include Claude Lanzmann, Michael Moore, Errol Morris, Chris Marker, Jill Godmilow, Trinh T. Minh-ha, Barbara Kopple, Julia Reichert, Nick Broomfield, Molly Dineen, Peter Watkins, and many others too numerous to mention.

Perhaps the most significant development during this period was the gradual reeemergence of the documentary film as a mainstream cultural form and the creation of new, popular genres. Today, genres such as the docusoap, reality TV, the 'mockumentary', and others receive widespread broadcast coverage around the world and significantly increase the audience for the documentary film, turning it from the preserve of intellectuals and activists into yet another form of mass entertainment. Nevertheless, the recent success of a film such as *Farenheit 9/11* bucks this trend and returns documentary to its subversive roots. *Farenheit 9/11* also exemplifies a characteristic common to much recent documentary filmmaking: a tendency to indulge in a postmodern bricolage of technique, ranging from straight interview to fanciful reconstruction. Moore's film also illustrates another issue often set before documentary filmmakers: the issue of the impact of this genre of highly realistic and apparently persuasive cinema. Yet, despite its controversial character and public exposure, *Farenheit 9/11* did not derail George W. Bush's reelection campaign.

To some extent, documentary film theory has reflected more general trends within film theory. Early written attempts to assess the role and importance of the documentary film tended to focus on questions of realism, authorship, and social representation, reflecting the concerns of much so-called classical film theory. These include the work of Paul Rotha, Erik Barnouw, John Grierson, Basil Wright, and others. Later work by André Bazin and Siegfried Kracauer in the field of film theory also contained a strong documentary dimension.

However, from the 1970s onward, documentary film theory tended to adopt the concerns and intellectual orientations of theorists within the semiotic, structuralist, poststructuralist, and postmodernist camps of film theory. Perhaps it was inevitable that a medium such as documentary film would become a subject of criticism, on account of its supposed 'realism', given the 'antirealist' orientation of 'screen theory' and its derivatives. Given the general tendency of the period to dispense with 'master narratives' and a 'metaphysics of being', it was not surprising to find documentary film theory becoming increasingly preoccupied with the rhetoric and discursive patterns, the codes and interest-based practices of the documentary film, rather than more abstract questions of realism. Bill Nichols was something of a pioneer here, but he was quickly followed by others. This approach to understanding the 'rhetoric' of the documentary film also dominated documentary film theory in the 1980s and 1990s, often giving such theory a pronounced poststructuralist, postmodern, or relativist orientation. Within these approaches, it is the practical impact that documentary film and theory can have on behalf of the minority, or way in which documentary film deploys a post-colonialist, patriarchal, or heterosexist rhetoric, which is of particular import.

Since the early 1990s, however, the field of documentary film theory has broadened, reflecting the spirit of 'post-theory' in film theory. One crucial question affecting documentary film is the representation of history. Historical work on the documentary film has continued, and includes the work of Ian Aitken, Jack C. Ellis, Lewis Jacobs, Deane Williams, Thomas Waugh, and others. Questions of documentary film theory and history are also explored in the work of Charles Warren, Aitken, Derek Paget, William Rothman, Bert Hogenkamp, Philip Rosen, Vivian Sobchack, Michael Renov, and others. Questions of realism and reality in relation to the documentary film are also explored in works by Rosen, Renov, Winston, Anna Grimshaw, and Linda Williams. However, the issue of documentary film and its relation to questions of truth-value, objectivity and reference are rarely considered, though Winston has done so to some extent, and Aitken does in this Encyclopedia. Many of these writers, together with others such as Julia Lesage, Carl Plantinga, Bill Nichols and Trinh T. Minh-ha and Anna M Lopez, also continue to work in a framework informed by gender and postmodern theory.

Structure of the Encyclopedia

In attempting to achieve the requisite degree of comprehensiveness, the goal of this encyclopedia has been to encompass a wide range of different classificatory categories. The most common categories to appear in this work are those of individual films and filmmakers. Entries here range from short (500-word) pieces to much longer accounts of important films and filmmakers, such as *Nanook of the North* and Dziga Vertov.

In addition to this category, the encyclopedia also attempts to assess more broad-based documentary filmmaking traditions within nations and regions, or within historical periods. These are, in general, much longer pieces, ranging from 2,000 words to 7,000 words. Such entries attempt to sum up the most important developments in the documentary film in respective nations, regions, or historical periods. These entries may also prove to be particularly important in bringing to light new material and insights and in providing a rich source of information for future research.

These volumes also encompass a variety of theoretical areas such as deconstruction and feminism. Finally, a number of categories relating to style, technique, technology, production, distribution, exhibition, and other factors are included. All of these entries have a pronounced critical dimension: contributors have been encouraged to think hard about their entries and to interpret them insightfully. All entries also contain detailed empirical sections, such as biographies, bibliographies, and filmographies. Many of these are extensive and the product of considerable research.

INTRODUCTION

This encyclopedia provides a much-needed infrastructural support for the field of documentary film studies, and the material that it contains should provide the basis for many future research projects. The encyclopedia also enables the field to be considered, and even eventually theorised, as a totality. It is now, and for the first time, possible to make comparative studies of different national and regional documentary film traditions, and to create an overall 'map' of the field. This will prove an invaluable aid to future research.

Another function of the encyclopedia is to bring neglected authors, films, and geographical areas of production back into the light of analysis. English-speaking readers will, for example, discover here the names and details of many little-known documentary filmmakers from countries such as India, Bosnia, and China. In this respect, the encyclopedia will also play a particularly important role in bringing attention to bear on films and filmmakers from the former Soviet bloc of eastern European countries. Still another achievement of the Encyclopedia is to provide the opportunity for many contributors to write about the documentary film.

Many contributors to the encyclopedia are eminent scholars. Others are less well known, the representatives of a new generation of writers in the field. Many have produced admirably well-thought and well-researched entries. A smaller group of contributors are nonacademic, but bring their own personal experience to bear on the subject.

The field of documentary film studies is becoming an increasingly important area of study. Since the 1980s, a growing number of publications have appeared on the subject, and that subject has also begun to enjoy a greater presence within the academy. Standing conferences such as Visible Evidence and others also provide regular international forums for interested scholars to exchange ideas and research findings. The encyclopedia will aid this process of consolidation and advancement by making available a substantial corpus of critical writing and data that colleagues can draw upon.

Finally, I wish to thank the Board of Advisors of the encyclopedia for their generous help and advice during the course of this project.

IAN AITKEN

A

ABEL GANCE: YESTERDAY AND TOMORROW

Abel Gance: Yesterday and Tomorrow is the dubbed version of *Abel Gance, Hier et Demain,* produced by the Office de Documentation par le Film and directed by Nelly Kaplan.

In the 1960s, the motion picture rose to prominence as a key medium of expression. A newly focused and invigorated interest in the movies manifested itself both in new styles of filmmaking and the study of cinema's history. This generation questioned current cinematic conventions, watched old motion pictures, and identified with forgotten filmmakers and cinematic icons. An important outcome of this renaissance was a new appreciation for the art of the silent cinema. This audience was particularly receptive to *Abel Gance: Yesterday and Tomorrow,* which championed a rediscovered genius and his neglected silent masterpieces.

Nelly Kaplan, the director of *Abel Gance,* was in the vanguard of this new generation of film enthusiasts. Born in Buenos Aires in 1934, Kaplan abandoned her studies in economics at the University of Buenos Aires because of her fascination with film. She went to Paris as a representative of the Argentine Film Archive, and found employment as a film journalist writing for Argentine newspapers.

Shortly thereafter, in 1954, the 20-year-old met Abel Gance and worked as an actor, assistant director, and collaborator on a number of his film projects. A second unit camera operator on Gance's feature film, *Cyrano et d'Artagnan* (1963), Kaplan used footage of the 74-year-old filmmaker taken on the set to frame the flashback of his life and career in *Abel Gance: Yesterday and Tomorrow,* which was made that same year.

In this dubbed version of *Abel Gance, Hier et Demain,* an English speaker provides a first-person account of the filmmaker's story. Recognized as a great technical innovator as well as an artist, Gance tells us that he invented prototypes of Cinerama and stereophonic sound. As his cinematic achievements are identified, film clips support his claims. We see examples of Gance's use of montage in his 1921 *La Roue.* Yet, despite the quality of his cinematic innovations, Gance claims the studios were initially reluctant to support his style of filmmaking. With the advent of sound in film, the director was no longer encouraged to make silent films, which he preferred to make. When asked to work for Adolph Hitler during the war, he fled to Spain. Gance did not make another film for over 10 years.

1

Abel Gance: Yesterday and Tomorrow ends with Gance discussing his later work as a director, his disappointment with the current cinema, and his dreams of once again making sensational motion pictures in the future.

Abel Gance: Yesterday and Tomorrow presents its subject as a living treasure still capable of great work, one of the cinema's great innovators. Although her motives are understandable, Nelly Kaplan's narrowly focused concern that Gance be recognized as a hero of the cinema has its drawbacks. The constant emphasis on Gance's cinematic accomplishments to the exclusion of everything else prevents us from knowing him as a person. The limiting effect of off-screen narration, which could have been relieved by having Gance occasionally speak on camera, particularly accentuates our feeling of being distanced from the subject and prevents us from experiencing some sense of intimacy with Gance as a human being.

One way the interested viewer can get a better sense of Abel Gance, the person, is to watch the other important documentary on the filmmaker from this period. Kevin Brownlow's 1968 production of *Abel Gance: The Charm of Dynamite* centers on a trip Gance made to England in 1965. This documentary uses extensive interviews with the filmmaker to underscore the importance of his films. *Abel Gance: The Charm of Dynamite* also documents the beginning of Kevin Brownlow's lifelong pursuit of reconstructing *Napoleon*, a quest that confirmed *Napoleon* as one of the major accomplishments of the silent cinema.

Both *Abel Gance: Yesterday and Tomorrow* and *Abel Gance: The Charm of Dynamite* capture a 1960s cineaste's excitement in recognizing the art of a neglected major silent filmmaker. These documentaries also put Abel Gance in the select company of such maverick geniuses of the motion picture as D. W. Griffith, Erich Von Stroheim, Sergei Eisenstein, and Orson Welles. Lauded today for his innovative cinematic achievements, Gance ultimately was denied the freedom to make motion pictures the way he wished, as his iconoclastic vision could not be supported by the film industry.

FRANK SCHEIDE

See also **Kaplan, Nelly**

Selected Film

1962 *Abel Gance: Yesterday and Tomorrow*: Kaplan

Further Reading

Abel Gance, Hier et Demain [review], *Factual Films*, 20, no. 241, 1966, 626.

Abel Gance, Hier et Demain [review], "Current Non-Fiction and Short Films" in *Monthly Film Bulletin*, 34, no. 402, 1967, 411.

Daria, Sophie, *Abel Gance, Hier et Demain*, Paris: La Palatine, 1959.

Holmund, Chris, "The Eyes of Nelly Kaplan" in *Screen*, 37, no. 4, 1996, 351–367.

Kaplan, Nelly, *Napoléon*, London: BFI Publishing, 1994.

ACT OF GOD

One of the most controversial and innovative filmmakers of the British film renaissance of the 1980s, Peter Greenaway is a director of fiction films, documentaries, and TV programmes; a painter; and an author of essays and novels. His very distinctive poetic universe is characterized by a proliferation of details and references, and is driven by an encyclopaedic ambition. Fiction features such as *The Belly of an Architect* (1986), *Drowning by Numbers* (1988), and *The Pillow Book* (1996) alternate in his filmography with documentaries that, for their utter originality, are situated at the limits of the genre. He often employs the form of the documentary either to represent something true but futile, as in *Dear Phone* (1977), or *Water Wrackets* (1975), to tell a fictional story through absolutely neutral images a series of rivers and ponds. As Jorge Luis Borges does, Greenaway applies a scientific language to nonscientific topics, considering the language of science itself as articulated in essay writing, in Darwin's books, and in mathematical formulas as a form of narration.

Act of God is a 26-minute film made for Thames TV as part of a series produced by Udi Eichler. It consists of an investigation into the elusive nature of the phenomenon of lightning, through a series of filmed interviews with people who, from 1966 to 1980, were struck by lightning in various European locations. *Act of God* was presented at several international festivals, including Edinburgh, Chicago, and New York, and won prizes as Best Documentary at the festivals of Melbourne and Sidney. Made with his regular collaborator, musician Michael Nyman, *Act of God* is a documentary that, for its subject matter and aesthetic characteristics, is perfectly consistent with the filmmaker's artistic world and, in particular, with the obsessive cataloguing effort, which has always been at the core of his project. *Act of God*, in fact, confirms Greenaway's passion for taxonomy and categorization, which previously emerged, for instance, in the documentary *The Falls* (1980), the result of lengthy research carried out in the attempt at producing a sort of encyclopaedia of humanity, a gargantuan effort evocative of Borges.

In *Act of God*, Greenaway tries to classify and understand the most unclassifiable and unpredictable event on the face of the earth. Always looking for the point in which all the lines of the world converge and everything happens simultaneously, he searches for a mathematical formula for lightning, which he tries to extract from the numbers that recur in the different accidents, keeping into account the site, the date, and the precise time when the lightning struck, the weight and shoe size of the victim, and anything the subject was carrying or wearing at the time. Greenaway makes a list of all the numbers and objects, but also includes advice deriving from popular belief, thus ironically mixing and granting the same importance to science and to folklore, in tune with his postmodern stance.

Act of God is composed of 13 interviews with victims of lightning who are asked to describe in detail their experiences and the circumstances that preceded and followed the accident. Searching for a manifestation of God in the discovery of the presence of coherence even in the most absolutely indeterminate event, Greenaway is particularly interested in finding out whether and how intensely the victims believed that their accident had a religious meaning and saw it as a divine punishment. Finding that they did not, Greenaway suggests how these extraordinary instances have happened to ordinary people, who failed to interpret them as exceptional events, and tries to offer through the editing a sort of metaphorical interpretation of the stories told. These direct testimonies are intertwined with 10 apocryphal stories also related to lightning, narrated in voice-over, in which the focus is always on the site and date of the accident, the victim, and the objects that she or he was carrying. Greenaway consistently highlights the accidental nature of the events narrated in the made-up stories, and intertwines to them a series of references to literary and music works that refer to lightning, drawing attention to the recurrence of this natural phenomenon in Shakespeare's oeuvre.

The interviews of A*ct of God* are shot in a way that is utterly unique for a documentary. Every frame is composed by the filmmaker as if it were a painting, displaying a profound attention for location and background, and an obsessive research for symmetry between the body of the interviewee and the space that surrounds it. In some cases, Greenaway creates a game of shadows behind the interviewee's body; in other cases, he constructs an impressive depth of field through open doors and windows. In one interview made over the phone, Greenaway invents a shot with a strange perspective: a telephone handle in close-up looks unnaturally big, and from a window in the background the tops of some trees and a threatening sky are visible. Interviews are conducted both in interiors and in exteriors; when they are set outside, they are generally shot in gardens, always with an emphasis on the element of water (for instance, the rain is falling and the interviewee is under an umbrella, or water sprays out of a watering can, filling in the space between the camera lens and the interviewee). It must be noted that water is a recurrent presence in Greenaway's work, an ambivalent element, which is the object of innumerable associations and contradictions, loved by the director for its photogenic quality as well as for being a component of the human body that links us to the world. In *Act of God*, Greenaway suggests in fact the idea of the liquefaction of the body hit by lightning, in a sort of "water to water" (rather than "ashes to ashes") cycle.

The composition of the shots, the subject matter, and the music by Nyman make *Act of God* a product that is closer to video art than to traditional documentary. As always with Greenaway, the documentary is a language among other languages, to be deconstructed and reconstructed at will. Although the starting point is a real issue, the structure and visual quality of his documentary invite the spectator to doubt the reality of the testimonies, immersed as they are in an aesthetic surplus.

STEFANO BASCHIERA

Act of God (UK, Thames TV, 1980, 25 mins). Distributed by: Thames Television – British Film Institute. Produced by Udi Eichler for Thames Television. Directed and written by Peter Greenaway. Music by Michael Nyman.

Cinematography by Peter George. Editing by Andy Watmore. Filmed in: Devon, London, Lincolnshire, Germany, Surrey, Cardiganshire, Lancashire, Norway, Oxfordshire, Italy, Westmorland, Gwent.

Selected Film

1980 *Act of God*: director, writer

Further Reading

Ciecko, Anne T., "Peter Greenaway's Alpha-Bestiary Ut Pictura Poesis: *A Zed and Two Noughts*," *Post Script*, 12, no. 1, 1992, 37–48.

Hacker, Jonathan, and David Price, "Peter Greenaway" in *Take Ten: Contemporary British Film Directors*, New York: Oxford University Press, 1991, pp. 188–227.

Lawrence, Amy, *The Films of Peter Greenaway*, Cambridge: Cambridge University Press, 1997.

Pally, Marcia, "Order vs. Chaos: The Films of Peter Greenaway" in *Cineaste*, 18, no. 3, 1991, 3–8.

Steinmetz, Leon, and Peter Greenaway, *The World of Peter Greenaway*, Boston: Journey Editions, 1995.

ACTING

It may seem oxymoronic to discuss the role of acting in documentary film. It might be said, for example, that from the time film was invented there was an immediate distinction between the theater-influenced, narrative approach of Georges Méliès and the documentary approach of Louis Lumiere. Méliès used actors, while Lumiere began the documentary tradition by simply filming nonactors. But the issue of the status of acting reappears continually in the history of documentary film, and the simple distinction between actor and nonactor has proved untenable.

In the 1920s, Soviet filmmakers of both fiction and nonfiction film debated the relative importance of acting and editing in filmmaking. Lev Kuleshov's experiments in montage famously showed that an audience's perception of spatial relations can be manipulated through editing. If a shot of an actor in a theater is followed by a shot of an audience, we assumed the actor and audience are in the same theater; in other words, we assumed a spatial coexistence. But this spatial effect, often referred to as the Kuleshov effect, also demonstrated that contextual changes through editing can alter and control audience perception of an actor's performance. In his experiments, Kuleshov alternated identical, neutral shots of an actor's face with separate shots of a baby, a girl at play, a dead woman, soup, and nature scenes. The audience reportedly assumed not only that the actor and the other shots were spatially coexistent,

but that the actor's expression was different when it appeared after the soup than when it appeared after the dead woman. Pudovkin writes that the audience "raved about the acting of the artist. They pointed out the heavy pensiveness of his mood over the forgotten soup, were touched and moved by the deep sorrow with which he looked on the dead woman, and admired the light, happy smile with which he surveyed the girl at play. But we knew that in all three cases the face was exactly the same."

Such experiments led Soviet directors to aggressively assert the power of editing technique over the power of acting performance. To the extent that that assertion is true, it holds regardless of whether the acting performance occurs in a fiction film or in a documentary, but the assertion plays out in a variety of approaches toward editing and acting pursued by Soviet directors. Sergei Eisenstein's films usually staged quasi-documentary historical events in which actors often played typed, stereotypical roles. For Eisenstein, nuanced acting was less important that having the audience recognize that the actor represented a particular class or type of person. Once the audience recognized the desired type, a variety of effects and meanings could be produced through the juxtaposition of editing. Typage was also a means of rejecting the western star system.

Dziga Vertov, in contrast, developed the documentary genre by emphasizing nonrealistic editing and self-reflexivity, while remaining committed to nonfictive subjects and nonprofessional actors. Vertov claimed that filmmakers should intrude as little as possible on the lives of the subjects being filmed, thereby escaping bourgeois film conventions and capturing "film truth" (see entry for Vertov). In practice, of course, it was technically very difficult to avoid intruding on the subject who was being filmed. In *Chelovek s kinoapparatom* (1929) / *Man with a Movie Camera,* Vertov's man with a camera mounts a platform on a car, stands on top of it with a camera and full-length tripod, and has the driver motor around while he randomly films the passengers of cars that they encounter. It is clear that the people filmed in this manner aren't acting in the same way they would if the camera wasn't there. One can distinguish, then, between at least four types of behavior commonly seen by people on film and television:

1. The unaffected behavior of people filmed while they are unaware of being filmed (for example, the television show Candid Camera)
2. The affected behavior of people filmed who are acting for an audience rather than acting for the camera (one example is documentaries of people acting in a play or otherwise performing before live audiences—such actors may or may not be aware of being filmed)
3. The altered, self-conscious behavior of people suddenly aware (or, in the case of reality television, continually aware) that they are being filmed
4. The crafted behavior of professional actors who anticipate being filmed (in general, such acting is less documentary than numbers 1 through 3, although mock documentaries such as *Best in Show* use professional actors to simulate documentaries)

Vsevolod Pudovkin discusses the ways in which numbers 1 and 3 can be exploited. As an example of item 1, he would create real-life situations, place nonactors in the situations, and hope that their reactions would contain the elements he needed for his fiction film. He would, for example, praise nonprofessional actors on the set after they had ostensibly finished their scenes (and were, in their minds, not acting) and film the genuine emotions of joy and pride that he elicited. In this sense, he was documenting the nonacted reactions of persons after they attempted to act. But Pudovkin would then present the results not as a documen-

tary, but as a scene of an actor in a fictional film. Thus, instead of putting the footage of the praised, beaming actor in a documentary about people trying to act, the footage would be used in a fiction film to portray the glee of a young communist suddenly elected to office in a huge meeting. The audience of the film would thus actually be watching a documentary presented as an acted, fiction film.

In similar ways, Pudovkin used the self-conscious reactions of nonactors attempting to act (number 3, above). If a scene in a fiction film required self-conscious behavior, he would exaggerate the pressure felt by the actor of being on camera. The fictive or nonfictive status of such self-conscious acting is, however, less clear than number 1, which is more clearly nonfictive. Pudovkin used such self-conscious behavior for fiction film, but recently it has become a staple approach in "documentary" reality television.

In the later Italian neo-realist movement, directors reacted against many of the Soviet techniques concerning acting and editing. In his theoretical defenses and explications of neo-realist film, André Bazin agreed with Vertov's emphasis on nonprofessional actors and natural settings, but unlike Vertov and other Soviet directors, he deemphasized editing and asserted that the camera shot should respect the "actual duration of the event" (Bazin, 1971). Bazin argues that the authenticity of the nonprofessional actor in his or her real setting should dictate editing and meaning; meaning should not be constructed by editing in the manner exemplified by Kuleshov's experiments in montage. In the extreme case, neo-realist film would have no editing, and story time and discourse time would be identical (i.e., the entire duration of the event filmed would be identical to the length of the film). Indeed, it can be argued that Italian neo-realist films such as *Ladri di Biciclette* (1948) / *Bicycle Thief* are more "documentary" than Vertov's work, despite the fact that neo-realist film usually employs fictive plots. A neo-realist film of real people, in real settings, in real time is arguably less doctored than a film with the extensive editing employed by Vertov, Eisenstein, and Pudovkin.

The status of acting in documentary film arises again with cinema verité. The invention of small, portable cameras allowed filmmakers such as Jean-Luc Godard to shoot on location in restaurants, homes, and cars less obtrusively than Vertov could. Godard and other filmmakers in the cinema verité genre could thus play more easily with the four types of acting listed previously, because they had more control over whether or not to reveal the presence of the camera.

More recently, postmodern theories of performance drawn from the work of scholars such as Erving Goffman have questioned any hard distinction between fictive and nonfictive acting, claiming that all human behavior is role-playing of one sort or another. Recent films such as *American Splendor* (2003) elide the distinction between fictive and nonfictive acting by creating a mélange that includes real people; actors playing real people; drawings of real people as comic-book characters; real people appearing on television talk shows; staged versions of the same talk show with actors playing real people; and historical autobiography mixed with fictional scenes.

The plethora of reality television shows also plays with the distinction of fictive and nonfictive acting by taking "real" people and casting them in highly fanciful and artificial scenarios (deserted islands, staged marriages, and the like), or by taking "unreal" people (stars and celebrities) and showing them in mundane, "real" contexts (e.g., Paris Hilton in various blue-collar settings). Reality television also toys with the distinction between numbers 3 and 4 in the previous list by keeping people on camera so continuously that the novelty they associate with being recorded wears off. Such roles are an odd hybrid of professional acting and the stardom associated with it, and the naïve, unrehearsed behavior of neo-realism. Increasingly, such manipulations and blurring of real and fictive elements have undermined not only the distinction between acting and nonacting but have also helped undermine the broader distinction between documentary and nondocumentary film. The collapse of the latter, broader distinction is widelydiscussed in film theory, but seldom in the context of acting.

PAUL MILLER

See also **Bazin, André;** *Man with a Movie Camera;* **Vertov, Dziga**

Selected Films

1929 *Chelovek s kinoapparatom / Man with a Movie Camera*: Dziga Vertov, Dziga Vertov
1948 *Ladri di Biciclette / Bicycle Thief*: Vittorio De Sica, Cesare Zavattini
1960 *À bout de Souffle / Breathless*. Jean-Luc Godard, Jean-Luc Godard and Francois Truffault
2000 *Best in Show*. Christopher Guest, Christopher Guest and Eugene Levy
2003 *American Splendor*, Shari Berman and Robert Pulcini, Harvey Pekar

Further Reading

Bazin, André, *What Is Cinema?* vol. 2, Berkeley: University of California Press, 1971.

Benjamin, Walter, "The Work of Art in the Age of Mechanical Reproduction" in *Illuminations*, edited by Hannah Arendt, New York: Schocken, 1969.

Goffman, Erving, *The Presentation of Self in Everyday Life*, Garden City, NY: Doubleday, 1959.

Kuleshov, Lev, "Art of the Cinema" in *Kuleshov on Film: Writings of Lev Kuleshov*, edited by R. Levaco, Berkeley: University of California Press, 1974.

McDonald, Paul, "Film Acting" in *Film Studies: Critical Approaches*, edited by John Hill and Pamela Gibson, Oxford: Oxford University Press, 2000, pp. 28–33.

Naremore, James, *Acting in the Cinema*, Berkeley: University of California Press, 1988.

Pudovkin, V. I., *Film Technique and Film Acting*, translated by Ivor Montagu, London: Vision Press, 1958.

ACTIVIST FILMMAKING

For well over a century, nonfiction film has figured prominently in the public sphere as a powerful means of persuasion. In 1928, Stalin attempted to coordinate documentary film content with political goals. During World War II, the government of the United States heavily invested in documentary bugle-call films, designed to sell war to soldiers and teetering allies. The Nazi party had a documentary film unit, at times headed by Leni Riefenstahl, to bring highly aestheticized images of political practices to the masses (Barnouw :99–182). Recognized as a forceful means of persuasion, the documentary genre can aid the process of social change.

Using all the available means of persuasion and coercion at their disposal, social movements have collectively developed a diverse set of tactics and strategies to prompt social change—activist documentary film and video being one of the most understudied texts. Thus, there are several questions to be answered about the pragmatic functions of activist documentary film and video. What is activist documentary film and video? Documentary films that reflect the interests of social movements are important but to what end, and in what rhetorical situations are these strategies most effective for social change?

The manner in which activist documentary film is conceptualized in theoretical literature or in film reviews primarily qualifies the term "activist" with the intentions of the filmmaker and his or her ideological commitments outside of filmmaking. There is, however, another tendency to label documentary film as "activist" based on content. If the film mediates as political or moral controversy, the inclination is to label it "activist." However, such labels are fruitless if the film does not actually intervene in a larger public space to create active political agents that will extend and execute the political work initiated by activist documentary film and video. It is not enough for documentary to "be" activist; it must help in creating the space for activism and invested in producing material and cultural change.

Documentary film and video served various functions in the last century, often dictated by historical exigence. Since its inception, the documentary genre has begged the question of social change. John Grierson is widely noted as the father of documentary film and was the most vocal about the potential for documentary to create social change. He, like many of his contemporaries in the 1930s, began to question the expectations of what seemed like an illusory democracy in the United States. According to Grierson, social problems had grown beyond the comprehension of most citizens and their participation was nonexistent, apathetic, or perfunctory. At the same time, Grierson believed that the popular media could acquire leverage over ideas and actions once influenced by church and school. It became Grierson's mission to produce films that dramatized issues and their implications in a meaningful way. It was his hope that documentary could lead citizens through the political wilderness (Barnouw, 1993: 85). In line with Grierson efforts, the

Workers Film and Photo League was the first social movement to coordinate political dissent with the recording of a documentary text in the 1930s.

The activist documentary impulse was reinvigorated in the 1960s. However, the activist urge to coordinate documentary filmmaking with political protest morphed and changed. New strategies and technological innovation altered the manner in which filmmakers such as Fredrick Wiseman approached the documentation of social issues.

Reacting to an era of promoting cooperate interests, filmmakers of the 1960s began embracing the role as observer. The films of this period—often called *direct cinema*—were ambiguous, leaving conclusions to viewers, yet the content often poked into places that society was inclined to ignore or keep hidden. Fred Wiseman, lawyer turned filmmaker, was one of the most masterful documentarians of the direct cinema genre: "He selected institutions through which society propagates itself, or which cushion—and therefore reflect—its strains and tensions. All of his films became studies in the exercise of power in American Society—not at the high levels, but at the community level" (Barnouw, 1993: 244). In his film *Titicut Follies* (1967) he created a portrait of the Massachusetts Institute for the Criminally Insane. Although the state of Massachusetts attempted to block the film through legal action because of the fear of political embarrassment, Wiseman argued that if state institutions receive tax funds from citizens, then they have the right to know what happens in them. Hence, the process of documentary production could also be a valuable activist strategy.

The function of direct cinema was to bear witness and to place judgment in the hands of the audience. Although the activist moment for direct cinema is limited by the reluctance to be an advocate, the genre began to carve the way for vernacular discourse and the production of documentary films for the average working person. However, a new movement in activist documentary was mounting; the trend was percolating away from observation and toward intervention. Filmmakers came out from behind the camera and intervened in the world around them. In the early 1960s, heightened political crisis and the development of low-cost video technology created the breaking ground for a new population of filmmakers. This time, the people from the margins were making their own films and activists were creating their own media. It was the birth of activist documentary film and video movement.

According to Deirdre Boyle in her book *Subject to Change: Guerrilla Television Revisited,* the activist documentary video movement began with the development of lightweight, affordable, and portable video recording equipment in the early 1970s. This gave the baby boomers access to the resources to make their own brand of television (Boyle, 1997: VI). This "new brand of television," also called *guerilla television,* was part of a larger alternative media tide that swept across the country during the 1960s. For a generation that grew up in the shadows of the civil rights and anti-war movements, television had been the window to the world. Troubled by the political and social unrest of the 1960s, the guerrilla television movement focused on a utopian program to change the structure of information in America by creating a distinct parallel broadcast system: "Optimism about television and its dynamic impact not just on communications but on contemporary consciousness was seized by the first generation raised on television, who found . . . a euphoric explanation of themselves and their changing times [in television]" (Boyle, 1997: 13). Television, technological innovation, and the political unrest of the 1960s had redirected the potential of activist documentary to create social change. However, the political moment was potentially misguided. Instead of mobilizing around political issues, activists mobilized around video collectives whose objectives were to democratize access to technology. Political contestation was solved "not by directly assaulting the system—as in a political revolution—but by extending the unifying properties of electronic media to everyone" (Boyle, 1997: 31).

The liberating potential of this era of activist filmmaking is that (1) it gave legitimacy to groups at the margins of society but it also (2) exploded the rhetorical potentialities of documentary by foregrounding the ideas and speech of the film subjects. Unlike the earlier era of activist documentary film where the filmmaker—often the narrator—could manipulate footage to create his or her own arguments, the methodological commitments of direct cinema demanded that subjects speak for themselves:

> In the new focus on speech—talking people—documentaries were moving into an area they had long neglected, and which appeared to have surprising, even revolutionary impact. Since the advent of sound—throughout the 1930s and 1940s—documentaries had seldom featured talking people, except in brief static scenes.
>
> (Barnouw, 1993: 234)

Now, film subjects, with the help of technology that recorded synchronized sound and image, took significant interpretive control out of the hands of the editor. It was during this moment that the vernacular voice of marginalized communities began to take root in the documentary genre. Much of the activist documentary impulse reflected the technological innovations of the time. Inexpensive and portable recording equipment resulted in cameras occupying new spaces, from the streets to the bedroom. The legitimacy of these documentary works was found in the low-budget quality and arresting content. Aesthetically and in terms of content, there was little consideration for an audience outside of the given political context documented. However, the potential for documentary film and video to aid the process of social change would be tested again at the turn of the century.

The third wave of activist documentary began planting roots in the late 1980s. During this time there was a proliferation of union films that depicted a societal transition in worker-management relations. Films such as Barbra Kopple's *American Dream* (1990) were portraits of living with American workers through crisis. Community access channels in the rising cable market continued to produce an interesting range of activist programming from teaching media literacy through "Herbert Schiller Read the New York Times" to the expansion of parallel broadcast networks such as Paper Tiger TV.

Filmmaker Michael Moore developed one genre, a mixture of cinema verité guerilla documentary, and personal film essay. His works *Roger and Me* (1989) and *Bowling for Columbine* (2002) have played a significant role in contemporary activist documentary. However, Moore's work is strategically different from much of the activist documentary films that came before him. Unlike the second wave of activist documentary that characterized social change as a fight between surly commercial broadcasting and activist media, the new struggle for power is issue driven. In fact, much of contemporary activist media is at home in the slick world of corporate broadcasting that is dependent on maintaining a loyal viewership. Therefore, the strategy of third-wave activist documentary is to place films in major distribution houses for the maximum audience without compromising activist content.

What is specific about the third wave of activist documentary is that it coincides with the development of a new computer technology, the Internet. Much like the developments in recording technology and television drastically altered the project of activist documentary, the Internet provides a new addendum to the relationship between documentary film and social change. The Internet allows audience members to engage in cross-media use for civic purposes. Not only can viewers find out more about a social or political problem foregrounded in the documentary but they can also engage in political organizing on the Internet.

Another way that the public sphere and the Internet are being brought together with documentary video is through the resurgence of street tapes and activist video collectives. Activist Internet journalism developed roots in 1999 during the World Trade Organization (WTO) meeting in Seattle. The meeting of the WTO spawned one of the largest and most cohesively organized instances of social protests in recent decades. Tens of thousands traveled to Seattle from around the world to protest the WTO's meeting to discuss the possibility of further opening economic markets. The *Seattle Times* invited guest columnists such as U.S. Secretary of Commerce William Daley and Environmental Protection Agency Administrator Carol Browner to write for the paper, but the Internet-based Independent Media Center (IMC) was reporting a far different story.

On their Internet website, the Independent Media Center reported over 1 million hits during the WTO meeting while streamlining stories investigated by the IMC volunteers and captured with donated video and audio equipment. The volunteers—many of them WTO protestors themselves—logged around-the-clock footage of protest events and street interviews with everyone from black dress anarchists to the police. The stories emphasized the concerns of the protestors and functioned as a means to bear witness to the numerous acts of police brutally waged in an effort to control the crowds. Such stories included a "man who said he had been hit in the face with rubber bullets fired by police. Another [story] showed police firing canisters of

tear gas into a crowd" (salon.com). The images from the street reported by the Independent Media Center were reminiscent of a military invasion while the *Seattle Times* published stories from the Clinton Administration that justified the WTO meeting. The activist Internet video movement is a significant force that challenges the content and ideological commitments of a primary profit-driven media apparatus. This may become an invaluable and necessary agitational strategy to sustain the process of systematic social change.

Since the inception of nonfiction film at the turn of the twentieth century, documentary film has routinely played a supporting role to its more famous relative, fiction film. However, during the past century, documentary film has figured prominently in the public sphere as a powerful means of persuasion utilized by governments, rich patrons, academics, and working people alike. A myriad of historical and social contextual circumstances have situated the documentary genre in a unique historical exigence at the turn of the twenty-first century. As a result, activist documentary film and video are becoming a more visible and politically viable part of civic life. It is the third wave of the activist documentary impulse.

ANGELA J. AGUAYO

Selected Films

1967 *Titicut Follies*. Dir. Fred Wiseman
1968 *High School*: Dir. Fred Wiseman
1989 *Roger and Me*: Dir. Michael Moore
1990 *American Dream*: Dir. Barbra Kopple
2002 *Bowling for Columbine*: Dir. Michael Moore

Further Reading

Alexander, William, *Film on the Left: American Documentary Film from 1931–1942*, Princeton, NJ: Princeton University Press, 1981.

Barnouw, Eric, *Documentary: A History of the Non-Fiction Film*, New York: Oxford University Press, 1993.

Barsam, Richard M., *Nonfiction Film: A Critical History*, Bloomington, IN: Indiana University Press, 1992.

Boyle, Deirdre, *Subject to Change: Guerrilla Television Revisited*, New York: Oxford University Press, 1997.

Meikle, Graham, *Future Active: Media Activism and the Internet*, New York: Routledge, 2002.

Waldman, Diane, and Janet Walker, *Feminism and Documentary*, Minneapolis: University of Minnesota Press, 1999.

ADOLESCENTS, THE (A.K.A. THAT TENDER AGE)

(France, Brault, Rouch, 1964)

In 1964, at the height of the omnibus film phenomenon sweeping throughout Europe and parts of Asia, a four-part docudrama about the travails of the teenage years was jointly produced by Cinematografica, Les Films de la Pléiade, the National Film Board of Canada, and Ninjin Club. Released that year in Italy under the title *Le adolescenti*, in France and Canada as *La fleur de l'âge*, and in Japan as *Shishunki*, *The Adolescents* (as it eventually came to be known in the United States and Great Britain after a belated 1967 release) is a curious quartet, its many national affiliations and linguistically differentiated incarnations a product of the polyglot sensibilities of that era. With each of its four episodes helmed by a different director (Gian Vittorio Baldi, Michel Brault, Jean Rouch, and Hiroshi Teshigahara—all of whom had gained international notoriety by that time for their ability to wed documentary and fiction filmmaking), *The Adolescents* is, as its title implies, a *plural* text, one that deploys ruptures and discontinuities across a broad, indeed *global*, spectrum so as to point up similarities as well as differences between people based on national, cultural, racial, and ethnic backgrounds. Moreover, like other multidirector coproductions of the early 1960s, such as *L'Amour à vingt ans* (1962) / *Love at Twenty, Boccaccio '70* (1962), and *RoGoPaG* (1962), the film calls into question our critical dependency on the perhaps outmoded notions attending "auteurist cinema" (in particular, the idea that a single director puts his or her personal stamp on a film) even as its trumpets the individual talents of the contributing filmmakers. But, perhaps more importantly, it is plural insofar as it combines fiction and nonfiction aesthetics, thus collapsing distinctions between dramatic artifice and documentary verisimilitude, between narrative construct and unmediated reality.

The Adolescents is differentiated from the above mentioned and other omnibus films—besides its reliance on nonscripted action—is its overriding focus on youth. Although certainly not the first episode film to tap into the existential uncertainties and emotional problems faced by teenagers (Michelangelo Antonioni mined this rich thematic material as early as 1953, when he made *I vinti / The Vanquished*, a three-episode study of the moral bankruptcy and dehumanized behavior of Europe's postwar youth), *The Adolescents* provides a timely reminder of the generational and cultural schisms of the 1960s.

The only scripted episode is that of Gian Vittorio Baldi, who also served as one of the six producers of the film. His tale, "Fiammetta," concerns a 14-year-old Florentine girl (played by Micaela Esdra) whose father has recently passed away. Left to reminisce in her widowed mother's sprawling estate, Fiammetta spends her days moping about the tourist-filled mansion. Eventually, her sexual curiosity and growing awareness of her developing breasts are deflected onto her jealousy for her attractive mother, who is forced to give up her new lover and live a quiescent life alone with her demanding daughter. These interwoven themes of sexual curiosity and jealousy reemerge in the second episode, Canadian director Michel Brault's "Geneviève." The titular teen in this slim story is actually one-half of a female duo whose friendship is tested in a moment of indiscretion and dishonesty. Both Geneviève (Geneviève Bujold) and her companion Louise (Louise Marleau) are 17 years old, and their simultaneous sexual awakenings spark a silent rivalry during a winter carnival in Montreal. Having met a young man named Bernard (Bernard Arcand) the day before, Louise oversleeps and misses her early morning date to see him again. Geneviève steps in and takes her place, spending the day with Bernard while her friend remains blissfully unaware. Later, at the end of the date, Louise discovers the truth when she spies the two kissing; an impulsive yet tentative act on Geneviève's part—one that she steadfastly refuses to admit. Although the plot may sound trite, what energizes it is Brault's deft handling of space, and his judicious use of the wide-angle lens and mobile framing, which extends the social milieu of the two teens to include a panorama of "real" people doing "real" things.

The third story, Jean Rouch's contribution to *The Adolescents*, similarly revolves around the exploits of two girls. Titled "Marie-France et Véronique," this miniature psycho-drama—starring 16-year-olds Marie-France De Chabaneix and Véronique Duval—could be said to have paved the way for Eric Rohmer's *4 Aventures de Reinette et Mirabelle* / *4 Adventures of Reinette and Mirabelle*, another episodic, fragmented film whose main characters' emotional restlessness and perambulatory predispositions provide spectators with numerous opportunities to catch glimpses of Paris—a city that has been fetishized throughout the history of cinema, yet in Rouch's (and Rohmer's) work is portrayed in a subtle way. In "Marie-France et Véronique," Paris is an expressive backdrop against which this diametrically opposed duo make difficult choices in life and love before ultimately going their separate ways.

Followers of Rouch—a socially engaged anthropologist-documentarian sympathetic to the plight of marginalized dock workers, lumbermen, day laborers, vagabonds, and other fringe-dwellers populating postcolonial Africa—may be taken aback by his decision to focus neither on the dispossessed nor the diasporic, but instead on two well-to-do Parisians whose affluence affords them the luxury of grappling with such seemingly trivial issues as the need to escape boredom, family expectations, and marriages of convenience. But in delving into the everyday details of contemporary adolescence, the filmmaker gestures back to his first feature-length film, *Moi, un Noir* (1958) / *I, a Black*. That film focuses on three young men as they go about their daily routines in Treichville, a suburb of Abidjan in the Ivory Coast. Having emigrated from Niger to this so-called New York of West Africa, these laborers could effectively communicate a sense of rootlessness in improvised scenes that invite the spectator to ruminate on the effects of proletarianization and cultural imperialism. By the time he made his contribution to *The Adolescents*, Rouch had mastered not only the technical aspects of fiction and nonfiction filmmaking but also the thematic motif central to that film, which called for spontaneity on the young performers' parts as well as diegetic participation on the director's part.

The Adolescents is an important historical artifact capturing a decisive moment in the careers of all four directors, when "straight" documentary was giving way to fictional forms of cinematic discourse. For instance, Baldi, who drew on his training at the venerable Centro Sperimentale di Cinematografia in Rome when making such pro-proletariat documentaries as *Il pianto delle zitelle* (for which he took home the Venice Film Festival's Golden Lion in 1959), had begun segueing into short fiction during the early 1960s, when he contributed episodes to the omnibus films *Le italiane e l'amore* (1961) / *Latin Lovers* and *The Adolescents*. Although he continued to nurture his documentary roots and—as the organizer and director of the Istituto Italiano del Documentario—became close friends with Joris Ivens and John Grierson (with whom he cofounded the Associazione Internazionale del Film Cortometraggio e del Documentario), Baldi became increasingly ensconced in the world of fiction once he began overseeing the production of works by Pier Paolo Pasolini and Robert Bresson in the late 1960s.

Similarly, the multitasking Brault, one of the innovators behind the 1950s' "Candid Eye movement" in Canadian documentary who stepped behind the lens on such groundbreaking productions as *Les raquetteurs* (1958), *La lutte* (1961), *Golden Gloves* (1961), and *Pour la suite du monde* (1963), began to feel that fiction did not lie because it did not pretend to be the truth. Rouch was so deeply impressed by Brault's technical expertise and belief that the imagination was a necessary tool for penetrating reality that he proclaimed the Canadian to be the basis for French breakthroughs in cinema verité. Significantly, *The Adolescents*—released just one year before Brault left the National Film Board to found Nanouk Films—was made just a few months after his collaboration with friend Claude Jutra on the nondocumentary *À tout prendre* (1963), a film that suggests that Brault had indeed begun to question the ethical dimensions of documentary and shift into fictional modes of filmic discourse.

Like the other contributors to *The Adolescents*, Hiroshi Teshigahara had begun to feel that dramatic truth was as viable as documentary reportage, something to which the Japanese director's many films about artists and designers (such as *Hokusai* [1953], *12 Photographers* [1955], and *Ikebana* [1956]) only faintly attest. Made a few months before his haunting depiction of moral descent, *Suna no onna* (1964), / *Woman in the Dunes*, Teshigahara's "Ako" (sometimes referred to as "White Morning") is the fourth and final episode of *The Adolescents*, although it was cut from U.S. prints due to time constraints and has since been shown on its own as a short film in retrospectives.

DAVID SCOTT DIFFRIENT

See also **Brault, Michel; Rouch, Jean**

Further Reading

Betz, Mark, "Film History, Film Genre, and Their Discontents: The Case of the Omnibus Film" in *The Moving Image: Journal of the Association of Moving Image Archivists*, 2, 2001, 56–87.

Betz, Mark, "The Name Above the (Sub)Title: Internationalism, Coproduction, and Polyglot European Art Cinema" in *Camera Obscura*, no. 46, 2001, 1–44.

MacDougall, David, ed., *Transcultural Cinema*, Princeton, NJ: Princeton University Press, 1998.

Rouch, Jean, *Cine-Ethnography*, translated by Steven Feld, Minneapolis: University of Minnesota Press, 2003.

Ruby, Jay, ed., *The Cinema of Jean Rouch*, London: Harwood Academic Publishers, 1989.

AESTHETICS AND DOCUMENTARY FILM: POETICS

The term *poetic documentary* is usually applied to the study of a particular style of film with conscious or unconscious links to the modernist avant-garde of the 1920s and 1930s (Nichols, 2001), the naive romanticism of Robert Flaherty (Barsam, 1988), or the "prettifying" tendencies of the social problem films of the British Documentary Movement (Winston, 1995). However, both *poetry* and *poetics* are terms with deeper application to the study of documentary than initially seems obvious. The impulse to separate poetry from considerations of the real is characteristic of Western modes of thought descended from the Platonic ideal; however, it is worth remembering here that Aristotle did significant writing on poetics.

For Aristotle, poetry, like all art, was a form of imitation of life descended from man's primal desire to reproduce what he sees. In his *Poetics*, he concluded that there were three categories of imitation: those that portrayed men as better than they are, worse than they are, and as they are. It is easier to understand how this argument relates to the project of documentary given that, for Aristotle, poetry was integral to the development of a social conscience. These categories of imitation were closely related to a desire not merely for description but also to a desire for the betterment of humankind. If we recognize that documentary films constitute part of the human attempt to replicate, explicate, and transform the environment, we can see how the disciplines of poetry and documentary are related.

Joris Ivens saw the poetic and interpretative capacity of documentary as essential to its social value. For Ivens, the project of seeking direct connection with the audience imparts documentary film with the capacity to address important issues more clearly and honestly than narrative fiction. He wrote,

> A documentary film requires the development of the personality of the filmmaker, because only the personality of an artist separates him from commonplace actuality, from simple photography. A good filmmaker stands in the middle of the matter, in the middle of reality.
>
> (Ivens, 1931)

Identifying and analyzing the poetics of documentary can be seen as a defense of the paradox, from John Grierson, of "creative treatment of actuality." As much of the writing on subjectivity in documentary affirms the authorial voice, which many would see as a primary indicator of a "poetic" sensibility, is present as an aesthetic force even in a medium with such strong claims to referentiality. As Erik Barnouw (1993) writes, "Whether they [documentarists] adopt the stance of observer, or chronicler, or painter, or whatever, they cannot escape their subjectivity. They present their version of the world." Bill Nichols's concept of "voice" is also a theoretical signpost directing study of the utterances of the work of documentary to an identifiable, expressive presence that orders and arranges findings according to desire and disposition.

Jim Leach, drawing on Lindsay Anderson's critique of the work of Humphrey Jennings, lists three criteria that identify the "poetic" documentary: (1) the filmmaker's ability to develop a personal vision, (2) the absence of an omniscient voice-over or commentary and (3) the film's capacity to create a sense of private connection with the viewer in spite of the presence of a "public gaze." For Leach, the criterion of personal vision is probably the most troubling due to its associations with auteur theory, yet it is still a recognition of a disposition toward individual self-expression evident in the work of certain documentary filmmakers. The criterion of the absence of omniscient commentary seems to contradict this, but Leach explains that this absence refers to the manner in which "poetic" documentaries employ structural devices, such as ellipses and repetition, to create a space for the viewer's response. The sense of a "private eye," which he identifies as the third criterion, is concerned with how the process of connection between the viewer and the film can therefore be seen to "disturb the ideological continuity of the public sphere and to generate a psychological tension around the competing forces of association and dissociation, continuity editing and montage" (Leach, 1998).

Michael Renov delves more deeply into the ways in which poetics of documentary may be employed in analyzing the medium. He proposes four "fundamental tendencies" which, he claims, "operate as modalities of desire, impulsions which fuel documentary discourse" (Renov, 1993). His project is directed toward identifying and separating the impulses that fuel the desire to document; the constitutive principles that operate beneath the level of conscious action. His four fundamental tendencies are (1) to record, reveal, or preserve; (2) to persuade or promote; (3) to analyze or interrogate; and (4) to express. He examines these in terms of their operation within the documentary impulse as "modalities of desire" where each serves a different psychological/instinctual need.

The first tendency he refers to as "the most elemental of documentary functions"—a manifestation of the primal desire to mimic. The impulse to record, reveal, or preserve constitutes an element of our need to maintain our sense of self. The second tendency identifies the impulse seen in greatest force in rhetorical form, especially social documentaries such as those of Grierson and Pare Lorentz. These films are tempered by a propagative need that extends beyond physical recording, and is distinct from their coexisting desire to record, reveal, or preserve.

The third tendency may be seen to favor the exploration of lived experience—the need to penetrate filmed actualities and find in them matter with which to draw further conclusions concerning to the reality being portrayed. It is important that documentarians retain the ability to analyze and interrogate even the means of their own production (as in Nichols's reflexive mode), and that as an expression of desire, this is matched by the audience's curiosity about natural phenomena, events, history, and other subjects. Although Renov's fourth tendency, "to express," may seem out of place—being inherently linked to a project of concretizing the other impulses—he distinguishes "expression," or the desire to express oneself, as central to human experience, and a desire from which no documentary filmmaker is excepted.

HARVEY O'BRIEN

See also **Anderson, Lindsay; Barnouw, Erik; Flaherty, Robert; Grierson, John; Ivens, Joris; Jennings, Humphrey; Lorentz, Pare**

Further Reading

Aristotle, *Aristotle's Poetics*, translated by S.H. Butcher, New York: Hill and Wang, 1961 (reprinted 2000).
Barnouw, Erik, *Documentary: A History of the Non-Fiction Film* (2nd ed.), New York: Oxford University Press, 1993.
Barsam, Richard, *The Vision of Robert Flaherty*, Bloomington: Indiana University Press, 1988.
Ivens, Joris, "Notes on the Avant-Garde Documentary Film" in *Joris Ivens and the Documentary Context*, edited by Kees Bakker, Amsterdam: Amsterdam University Press, 1999.
Leach, Jim, "The Poetics of Propaganda" in *Documenting the Documentary: Close Readings of Documentary Film and Video*, edited by Barry Keith Grant and Jeannette Sloniowski, Detroit: Wayne State University Press, 1998.
Nichols, Bill, *Introduction to Documentary*, Bloomington: Indiana University Press, 2001.
Renov, Michael, "Towards a Poetics of Documentary" in *Theorizing Documentary*, edited by Michael Renov, New York: Routledge, 1993.
Winston, Brian, *Claiming the Real: The Documentary Film Revisited*, London: BFI, 1995.

AFRICA: DOCUMENTARY DRAMA

In Africa, the documentary drama film, like many other visual aids that were employed in the service of mass education in the 1970s and 1980s, elevated the documentary to the level of document. The documentary drama in Africa reveals historical and sociological documentation to have been at the heart of cinema culture during those decades. Notice the trend in the southern Africa region, with films such as *Borders of Blood* (Ebano Films) from Mozambique and *Flame* (Ingrid Sinclair, 1996) and *Everyone's Child* (Tsitsi dagarembga, 1996) from Zimbabwe that are based on closely documented historical environments.

Documentary drama, or docudrama, or fiction drama is variously defined. Essentially the genre refers to representations on film or video involving found stories that are dramatised for the purpose of passing a didactic message or a lesson. One can define *docudrama* as a cinematic outgrowth of documentary aesthetics of authoritative narratives premised on memory, representation, and found material (Goldfarb, 1995).

Documentaries remain the popular genre of films produced by Africans. African filmmakers were late entrants into the world of film due essentially to the colonial society's structures and strategies. Admittedly, African filmmakers were arguably different to colonial producers who saw in documentary a medium for "education," involving only the technical training of workers and peasants in order to make them understand new agricultural methods and modern products, health issues, and the new social relations (Smyth, 1989).

Colonial authorities went on to create educational film units that served as training grounds for future African filmmakers (Ukadike, 1994). Paulin Vieyra, Safi Faye, Oumarou Ganda, and Sarah Maldoror are good examples of future African filmmakers who came out of the colonial film units (Harrow, 1999). This insidious but extremely effective colonial educational structure was carried over into the postindependence period where nationalist regimes saw education as one of the pillars of development.

With independence, the documentary form, in its educational role, was hijacked to support the political strategies of postindependence regimes (Goldfarb, 1995). Pedagogy became ideology and politics; education became yoked to statist regimes of legitimisation and intervention into ordinary people's existence. This authoritarianism was clearly felt by filmmakers, leading to their tacit rejection of the "voice of god" style in documentary. This roundabout way led to the development of the documentary drama as a central cinema form in the continent. Moreover, this embrace of documentary drama satisfied audience desire for fictional narratives. This is essentially because most documentaries made during the colonial period were "suggestive" (Rouch in Levin, 1971).

Historically, however, the practice of the documentary drama in Africa can be found in the "scenarios" written specifically for educational films by colonial film units. In southern Africa, for example, films on health propaganda such as *Two Brothers* (South Africa, 1940) and those made within the Bantu Educational Kinema Experiment (BEKE, 1937–1939) worked toward either medicalising or bureaucratising social problems. Many of these films were comedies, a style that was often used to "good" effect during the colonial era. Under BEKE, over 35 short films were produced with the Bantu as a market and were shown across seven countries of the region with remarkable interest and ease (Smyth in Curan, 1993). The farcical nature of the narrative structure (Mr. Clever and Mr. Foolish) and acting lent themselves to emphasising the paternalistic and colonial perspective (Giltrow, 1986).

This can also be found in films such as *Daybreak at Udi* (Nigeria, 1950) and many others in Francophone, Lusophone, and even the former German Africa (Togo and Cameroon). What needs to be noted is that the films never did address the underlying socioeconomic structures that kept the problems current. They were marked by their paternalistic viewpoint and messages.

Early African filmmakers in each new nation endeavoured to educate their people in whatever the new regimes decided was important enough to be transmitted through the comparatively more expensive medium of film. This process led to a veritable propaganda genre that soon limited itself to newsreels about the leaders and regimes, but sometimes served a unifying role through making people in the nation acknowledge their identity in visual and ideological terms.

However, this was not to continue for long. Soon, African filmmakers realised that their audiences hankered after fictionally driven stories more than reality-based narratives, which led them to embracing the documentary drama genre. African filmmakers took the opportunity to speak of new subjects after independence, and the films produced allowed glimpses of liberation history and created a conscious interpellation of cultural interests.

African filmmakers also refined the genre itself. Filmmakers such as Sembene Ousmane used their creative and ideological prowess to clearly communicate, through reworked material, specific social messages. Ceddo (1976) and Camp de Thiaroye (1988) are typical examples of Sembene's employment of the creative treatment of reality.

There were, however, specific influences that helped build this genre and its acceptance among African filmmakers. These include Gillo Pontecorvo's *Battle of Algiers* (1966) and Lionel Rogosin's *Come Back Africa* (1956). These two documentary dramas were of critical importance to the theorisation and development of the genre in the continent, as they set the tone for the ideological perception of African narratives coming out of the colonial experience into nationhood. With *Battle of Algiers,* we find the enduring preoccupation by certain African filmmakers to tackle subjects according to "the theoretical positions of their auteurs"—consciousness-raising (Zacks, 1999).

With *Come Back Africa,* we find a lyrical structure that was to be reapplied in such major productions as Ruy Duarte's *Nellisita* (1982) and Ruy Guerra's *Mueda: Memoria e Massacre* (1979). Ruy Guerra's attempt to find a new language by a merging of orality and dramatisation reflects the contending space of documentary practice in Africa, which has led to the growth of documentary drama.

An excellent reflection of the status of documentary drama in Africa came in 1985 when the film *Arusi ya Mariamu* (Ng'oge and Mulvihill, 1985) was awarded the first OAU Award for a film that best expressed the idea of being African at FESPACO. This documentary drama was to set up the trend for the evaluation of the genre in the continent.

Indeed, many new styles of documentary drama are revealed through such films as *After the Wax* (Maviyane Davis, 1991), *The Ball* (Licino de Azevedo, 2002), and *Africa I Will Fleece You* (Jean-Marie Teno, 1992). These films mark a new approach to African filmmaking, one that is aware of the value of contextualising modes of production as well as "coherence in the discourse they [the filmmakers] choose to deploy" (Diawara, 1993).

MARTIN MHANDO

Further Reading

Bartlet, Olivier, *African Cinemas: Decolonising the Gaze*, London: Zed Books, 2000.

Cham, Mbye, and Imruh Bakari (eds.), *African Experiences of Cinema*, BFI, London, 1996.

Diawarra, M., *African Cinema: Politics and Culture*, Indianapolis/Bloomington: University of Indiana Press, 1993.

Giltrow, D. R., "Cinema with a Purpose: Films for Development in British Colonial Africa, 1925–1939," paper given at the African Studies Association Meetings, Canterbury, UK, 17–19 September 1986.

Givanni, June, (ed.), *Symbolic Narratives in African Cinema*, London: BFI, 2001.

Goldfarb, Brian, "A Pedagogic Cinema," *New Discourses of African Cinema*, Iris, no. 18, Spring 1995, 7–25.

Harrow, Kenneth, *African Cinema: Post-Colonial and Feminist Readings*, Asmarah: Africa World Press, 1999.

Hungwe, Kedmon, "Southern Rhodesian Propaganda and Education Films for Peasant Farmers, 1948–1955," *Historical Journal of Film, Radio and Television*, 11, no. 3, 1991, 232.

Mahoso, T., "Unwinding the African Dream on African Ground" in *Symbolic Narratives in African Cinema*, edited by June Givanni, London: BFI, 2001.

Russell, A., *African Cinema: A Bibliography*, London: Sage, 1998.

Smyth, R., *Journal of Film, Radio and Television*, 6, no. 4, 1986.

Smyth, R., "The Feature Film in Tanzania," *African Affairs*, July 1989.

Smyth, Rosaleen, "Movies and Mandarins: The Official Film and British Colonial Africa," in *British Cinema History*, edited by James Curan and vincent Porter, Weidenfeld and Nicolson, 1993, 129–143.

Tomaselli, Keyan, "Video, Realism and Class Struggle: Theoretical Lacunae and the Problem of Power," *Continuum*, 3, no. 2, 1990.

Ukadike, Frank, *Black African Cinema*, University of California Press, Los Angeles/London/Berkeley: 1994.

Zacks, S. "The Theoretical Construction of African Cinema," in *African Cinema: Post-Colonial and Feminist Readings*, edited by Kenneth Harrow, Asmarah: Africa World Press, 1999.

Africa. *See* **Documentary Drama: Africa; Feminism: Africa**

AG DOK

The German Documentary Association (Arbeitsgemeinschaft Dokumentarfilm)—AG DOK for short (www.agdok.de)—was founded on September 19, 1980, during the Duisburg Documentary Filmfestival by some mainly left-wing documentary filmmakers. In publicizing the "Duisburg Declaration," they were already trying to show the reasons why a strong pressure lobby was necessary: "Documentary filmmaking today is in a sorry state. Television has reduced the documentary film to journalism with pictures and for commercial cinema it does not exist at all. Faced with such a situation, we are no longer prepared to stand by and do nothing."

In the last 25 years, AG DOK has become the most important advocacy group for documentaries and independent filmmaking in Germany. Thomas Frickel, a politically committed documentary filmmaker himself, has headed the organisation since 1987. It has over 750 members. The association comprises numerous well-known German documentary filmmakers; winners of countless film, television, and festival awards. Five regional groups in Berlin, Hamburg, Köln, Frankfurt, and Munich enable direct contact and exchange through their activities. AG DOK is a professional organisation not only for filmmakers but also for authors, producers, cameramen and women, festivals organizers, and everybody who is interested in independent film, as well. It sees itself as the documentary lobby organisation in all debates on media policy and has successfully presented their position in official hearings (e.g., for film funding or on copyright laws). The goal is that the wide range of documentary forms, which have developed in the 1990s, should be present in the movie theatres as well as on television. It struggles for the recognition of the documentary film as an art form. In AG DOK's view, even a very long documentary by an acknowledged author should have its place in prime-time programming and not be pushed away to the specialized cultural channels. In the year 2000, AG DOK financed and published a study on slots for documentaries in German television. The association also commissions studies and legal reports on matters relating to independent film production. In addition, the organization argues in favour of better contractual conditions and against the position of public broadcasters who try to get more and more rights for less money or to not pay for the repetition of a program. Members can obtain legal advice free of charge and it offers professional help in lawsuits. AG DOK is very visible at media debates, conferences, and festivals to make its positions clear. With its initiative "German documentaries," an online database was founded with information on recent films and authors, which should become the important platform for efficient export and festival presentation of German documentaries. A catalogue is distributed every few years with the synopsis of films in English. AG DOK cooperates with international film festivals as well as institutions such as EDN (European Documentary Network, Copenhagen) to enable meetings and exchange with colleagues from other countries. A comprehensive manual with short biographies and selected filmogaphies of the members is published every two years, which is an important tool for getting in touch with the members.

In November 2000, the OnlineFilm AG was founded as a public company by 120 filmmakers and copyright owners, mainly organized in AG DOK. The goal was to build an online database and distribute German documentaries over the Internet by using recent digital tools. Unfortunately, this initiative was not too successful after the collapse of the new economy. But it shows that AG DOK is always trying to give the documentary a future perspective and to fight for it.

KAY HOFFMANN

Further Reading

Arbeitsgemeinschaft Dokumentarfilm e.V. (ed.), German Documentaries 1996–2002, Frankfurt 2002.

Arbeitsgemeinschaft Dokumentarfilm e.V. (ed.), Handbuch 2004, Frankfurt 2004.

Binninger, Susanne, and Stanjek, Klaus, Dokumentarische Sendeplätze im Deutschen Fernsehen (study for AG DOK), Frankfurt, 1999.

AGEE, JAMES

The American writer James Agee was one of the most significant contributors to the development of the documentary form in the United States in the mid-twentieth century. He offered no systematized theory of documentary film, and he was only peripherally involved in the industry—first as a reviewer in the 1940s, and then as a screenwriter for such films as *The African Queen* (1951) and *The Night of the Hunter* (1955). However, the publication of *Let Us Now Praise Famous Men* in 1941 and his collected writings in *Agee on Film* in 1958 are evidence of his importance to the history of the documentary. Agee argued that many documentaries in the 1930s and 1940s were as removed from reality as Hollywood movies, with the filmmaker often adopting a didactic and polemical approach to the subject. Agee's solution was to develop a hybrid form, or semidocumentary, that he believed would offer a truer record of experience than the "flat" presentation of life then currently presented in documentary films. He argued that propagandists had corrupted the documentary form in Germany and in the Soviet Union by degrading the film craft of Dziga Vertov and Sergei Eisenstein (arguing that by the 1940s it had become "posterish, opportunistic, and anti-human"), but he believed the form still held great promise in the United Kingdom and the United States.

Agee wrote extensively on British World War II films and newsreels in the early 1940s, applauding them for capturing the bravery of servicemen and offering a cathartic encounter with reality (calling them "the finest 'escapes' available"). He also praised poetic documentaries such as Robert Flaherty's *Nanook of the North* (1922), recommending it for its "beautiful simplicity," and *Man of Aran* (1934), which manages to convey the drama and nuances of human behavior in its portrayal of the daily struggle of Aran fishermen. He particularly liked the use of nonactors, which imparted a naturalness that would have been lacking, he believed, in actors' performances. Agee considered documentary no less a creative experience than fiction. As a modernist thinker, Agee was interested in the "musical coherence" of documentary film and wrote about the "real poetic energy" of its better exponents throughout his reviews for *The Nation* and *Time,* written between 1941 and 1948. This

kind of poetic realism, which cuts across generic boundaries, was popular among other American cultural producers such as Tennessee Williams, who developed a plastic form of theater in his dramatic work in the 1940s and 1950s, and later, the New Journalists, who attempted to blend factuality and fiction in their prose.

Agee's major work, *Let Us Now Praise Famous Men,* was derived from a feature article commissioned in 1936 by *Fortune* magazine, for which he was asked to document the lives of white tenant farmers in the South (the article never appeared in the magazine). His research was conducted in Hale County, Alabama. Agee wanted to interfere as little as possible in the lives of his subjects. He relied heavily on montage in the book, with Walker Evans's 60 photographs, literary and biblical allusions, poetic meditation, autobiographical reflection, newspaper reportage, and domestic anecdotes, creating a fragmented text that invites the reader to recognize the artifice involved in producing documentary. The result is a text that shuttles between detailed observation and a broader statement about poverty, deprivation, and human need that cuts across different modes of inquiry—a technique that accords with Agee's claim that he and Walker did not position themselves "as journalists, sociologists, politicians, entertainers, humanitarians, priests, or artists, but seriously." His radical documentary technique challenged the flat realist documentaries of the 1930s, as well as the conservative ideology of the southern Agrarians, with their emphasis on past glories at the expense of engaging with the present.

In light of Agee's disdain for certain modes of documentary technique, *Let Us Now Praise Famous Men* can be read as an attempt to create not only a semidocumentary but, as T. V. Reed argues, an "anti-documentary," marked by complexity and an apparent lack of structure. Because it is so difficult to classify, the book can be interpreted as a serious modernist intervention into the verbal and visual language of documentary, or even a playful postmodern pastiche of styles. In fact, its hybridity stems from Agee's interest in the same kind of affinity between documentary and art that is evident in his film criticism. Agee was more comfortable with photographic images than language in capturing "truth," arguing that words tend to be slippery, ambiguous, and often inaccurate. He describes the camera as belonging to an "absolute" realm: "an ice-cold, some ways limited, some ways more capable, eye, it is, like the phonograph record and like scientific instruments and unlike any other leverage of art, incapable of recording anything but absolute, dry truth." This emphasis on the absolute objectivity of photography echoes the American visual artist Paul Strand's statement in 1917 that "objectivity is the very essence of photography, its contribution and at the same time its limitation." For Agee, if handled "cleanly," photography could provide a documentary record unsurpassed in other media. However, he was aware that the artist's tendency to interfere with the subject, or to make aesthetic choices in terms of framing, would distort the truth of the moment or transform it into something else. In *Let Us Now Praise Famous Men*, Agee displays his modernist colors by insisting that "truth" lies in the photographic image, but he also goes beyond conventional documentary form by juxtaposing a range of texts and opening an interpretative space that encourages the reader to engage with the processes of composition.

MARGIN HALLIWELL

See also **Flaherty, Robert; *Man of Aran*; *Nanook of the North*; Vertov, Dziga**

Biography

James Agee was born in 1909 in Knoxville, Tennessee. He was raised in the Cumberland mountain region and used the topography of his childhood as the basis for his two autobiographical novels: *The Morning Watch* (1951) and the unfinished *A Death in the Family* (1957), for which he was posthumously awarded the Pulitzer Prize in 1958. Graduating from Harvard University, Agee became a feature writer for *Fortune* magazine. The research for one feature on sharecroppers in Alabama led to the publication of *Let Us Now Praise Famous Men* (1941) with the photographer Walker Evans. Agee published his first collection of poetry, *Permit Me Voyage*, in 1934 and spent the 1940s as a film reviewer working for *Time* and *The Nation*. In 1948 he worked as a scriptwriter in Hollywood, producing scripts for *The African Queen* (1951) and *The Night of the Hunter* (1955). Agee died in 1955 at the age of 45.

Selected Films

1949 *The Quiet One*: scriptwriter
1951 *The African Queen*: scriptwriter
1952 *Crin-Blanc* (Fr); *White Mane* (US): commentary
1952 *Face to Face*: scriptwriter and actor
1955 *The Night of the Hunter*: scriptwriter

Further Reading

Agee, James, *Agee on Film: Criticism and Comment on the Movies*, introduction by David Denby, New York: Modern Library, 2000.

Agee, James, and Walker Evans, *Let Us Now Praise Famous Men*, introduction by John Hersey, Boston, MA: Houghton Mifflin, 1988.

Böger, Astrid, *Documenting Lives: James Agee's and Walker Evans's* Let Us Now Praise Famous Men, Frankfurt: Peter Lang, 1994.

Coles, Robert, *Doing Documentary Work*, New York: Oxford University Press, 1997.

Reed, T. V. "Unimagined Existence and the Fiction of the Real: Postmodern Realism in *Let Us Now Praise Famous Men*," *Representations*, 24, 1988, 156–175.

Rufus, James, *Agee on Film: Five Film Scripts by James Agee*, Boston: Beacon, 1964.

Snyder, John J. *James Agee: A Study of His Film Criticism*, New York: Arno, 1977.

Stange, Maren, *Symbols of Ideal Life: Social Documentary Photography in America, 1890–1950*, New York: Cambridge University Press, 1989.

Stott, William, *Documentary Expression and Thirties Americma*, New York: Oxford University Press, 1973.

Ward, J. A. *American Silences: The Realism of James Agee, Walker Evans, and Edward Hopper*, Baton Rouge: Louisiana State University Press, 1985.

AGLAND, PHIL

Phil Agland is known to be an unusual filmmaker in the landscape of television documentaries. Agland's theory and techniques are often compared to those of a careful and detailed painter or a patient hunter. His films are often referred to as poetical and epical accounts of life.

Agland's first film, *Korup—An African Rain Forest*, was a five-year enterprise. Agland, a wildlife enthusiast, concerned about the plight of the endangered species in the rain forests, had ventured to make the documentary in an attempt to raise awareness of the problem. Despite having no cinematography experience and with a very small budget, he went into the depths of the rain forest in spells of three months over a period of five years. This endeavour resulted in a poetic film containing images never to be seen on screen before and in an award-winning documentary.

Since that time, Agland has turned his focus to people. He returned to Cameroon's rain forest to spend two years living among the Baka people with a small crew of two, filming *Baka—The People of the Rain Forest*. In the Western world, the Baka people are considered pygmies. Yet, Agland's impression was that this was in no way how the Baka perceived themselves. Agland's feelings were that the Baka's perception should be reflected in his camera work. Had he kept the camera on his shoulder, he would be filming the Baka from up high, giving cause to view them as pygmies. It was in the attempt to be truthful to the Baka's own image of their height that Agland developed what became his unique camera technique. Instead of perching the camera on the shoulder, Agland cradled the camera at waist height. This technique enabled him to film the Baka people from below their eye-level for a more intimate and nonpatronising viewpoint. Later on, Agland kept to this technique, claiming that by avoiding direct eye contact and by avoiding pointing the camera lens directly at his subject, he can minimise the presence of the camera.

Agland's theory is that in order to achieve genuine and intimate moments, the camera and crew should be as invisible as possible. He uses a radio microphone technique that enables the sound recordist to stay at a fair distance and away from the scene. This radio microphone technique not only enables removal of the sound recordist from the scene but it also eliminates the presence of a third and sometimes a fourth person holding a somewhat intimidating boom pole, minimising the crew to two members or sometimes even one. The invisibility, claims Agland, is crucial in this observant, unobtrusive type of documentary making, allowing the people in front of the camera to become oblivious to its presence.

Agland believes in observant documentaries rather than interview-based ones. His theory is that genuine stories or emotions will not emerge during an interview but rather in the small, sometimes insignificant and usually unpredictable moments in life; when the subjects are unaware of the camera and, hence, do not feel obliged to deliver or to satisfy. Agland also believe that the audience should feel part of the scene yet not in the middle of it. The centre of attention should be the story, the moment and the feelings within it rather than the camera or the audience. Agland therefore minimises his camera movements and often favours static camera shots.

Allowing for time and film stock is also a crucial aspect in Agland's careful work of portrayal. He avoids setting up situations and prefers to wait for moments and stories to emerge. Spending time with his characters allows them to get used to the presence of the camera and enables Agland to explore and capture rare and intimate moments in their lives. The structure and story are revealed throughout the filming process and during the editing period rather than in the scripting stage.

In his documentaries Agland creates scenes that follow the grammatical rules and language of a fiction film rather than adopting a documentary style of filming. Using a considerable coverage and carefully thought out editing ideas, both during and after filming, Agland creates rich and round scenes, covered with wide shots, close-ups and details and, hence, creating an illusion of fiction style multi-angled scenes.

Though his films appear not to be focusing on a specific place or a certain subject matter, Agland's passion and curiosity lie in people and in the small matters of life. Despite some views that would claim that Agland has an anthropologist's eye, Agland himself claims the very opposite. His aim is to emphasise the similarities between humans wherever they may live or come from; regardless of religion, cultural background or life circumstances. Agland strives to show the audience the familiar in the stranger on the screen.

Agland, therefore, comes back to the common subjects—family structure, sibling jealousy, parents' concern for their children, and the mutual need for attention and love. He deals with questions of age, health, and death as well as love, friendship, and community life. In *Baka—The People of the Rain Forest*, the focus of the film is four year old Ali and his family; his father's concern preparing him for life, his parents' relationship, and Ali's reaction to the newborn baby. Through these themes Agland explores the issues common to all humans and paints a portrait of what life is about, beyond the backdrop of place and time.

In *China: Beyond the Clouds* set in Lijang, a small rural town located in the southwestern region of China, it seems that Agland furthers his attempt to paint a rich and full portrayal of life. He creates an epic about the small, familiar details of life. Agland interlaces different stories; a loss of a child alongside a lifetime friendship, a juvenile crime in a small town alongside a young mother's struggle to heal her child who suffers from cerebral palsy. Maintaining a fine balance between the tragic and the comic in life, Agland offers a complex and multilayered picture.

In his only fiction film so far *The Woodlanders*, which is based on a nineteenth-century novel by Thomas Hardy, Agland challenges his audience to the same themes of finding the similarities beyond the differences by taking the audience on a journey to a different time, rather than to a far away place.

SHIRA PINSON

Biography

Born in Weymouth, England in 1950. Read Geography at Hull University, Yorkshire, England. 1982 Completed his first documentary film—*Korup—An African Rain Forest*. 1982–1986 Coproduced and Codirected a six hours series—*Fragile Earth*, associated with Michael Rosenberg of Partridge Films. 1987 completed *Baka—The People of the Rain Forest*. 1992 Executive Producer of *Turmid Hed—Sound Stuff* produced by Agland's company – River Films. 1994 completed a seven hours series *China: Beyond the Clouds* Produced by River Films for Channel 4. 1997 completed his first fiction feature *The Woodlanders* based on a novel by Thomas Hardy. 1999 completed *Shanghai Vice* a seven hours documentary Produced by River Films for Channel 4 and Discovery Communications. 2003 completed a three hours series *A French Affair* Produced by River Films for Channel 4.

Further Reading

Broadcast, July 30, 1999, p. 6.
Sight & Sounds, June 1999, p. 28.
Music from Movies, Spring 1999, p. 28.
Radio Times, February 27, 1999, p. 11.
Broadcast, February 26, 1999, p. 34.
Sight & Sounds, September 1998, p. 58.
Broadcast, September 11, 1998, p. 19.
Television, August / September 1998 pp. 12–13.
New-Zealand Film Music Bulletin, May 1998, p. 19.
Empire, March 1998, p. 48.
Neon, February 1998, p. 86.
Sight & Sounds, February 1998, p. 56.
Independent Eye, February 6, 1998, pp. 4–5.
Times, January 30, 1998, p. 33.
Variety, September 1, 1996, p. 28.
Variety, October 3, 1994, p. 54.
Financial Times, November 4, 1987, p. 25.
Listener, November 2, 1987, p. 42.
TV Times, October 31, 1987, pp. 18–19, 21.
Listener, October 29, 1987, p. 35.
Broadcast, October 19, 1984, p. 12.
Guardian, November 11, 1982, p. 12.
Broadcast, November 8, 1982, p. 12.
TV Times, November 6, 1982, pp. 26–27.

AKERMAN, CHANTAL

Like Pasolini, members of the French New Wave, Sembène, Kiarostami, and others, Akerman has found her own way to push the boundaries of film realism. She has made a number of creative observational films, or documentaries. Yet the fiction films, for which she is best known, repeatedly allow in, or call forth, a documented reality that turns the film inside out, or makes the viewer ask: Where is it really grounded, in imagination or in fact? In the third and final episode of *Je tu il elle* (1974), two young women make love in a bed, rendered in three long takes with three different fixed camera positions. Are the women acting? *Can* they be? In a way, it seems that the earlier part of the film—a woman at home writing and thinking, and then a road journey through the night—is brought to earth by this ultimate dose of reality. Everything must be judged by the standard set here. Everything previous seems, in retrospect, fanciful. In another way, the first part of the film seems an ordinary experience, tied to reality, waiting for the sexual and emotional explosion that goes beyond imagination. In Akerman's most acclaimed film, *Jeanne Dielman, 23 quai du Commerce 1080 Bruxelles* (1975), Delphine Seyrig gives a consummate, highly poised performance as the housewife, mother, and prostitute of the title. But the film has her assemble a meatloaf from scratch, or peel all the potatoes necessary for a meal, or wash all the dinner dishes, each action filling one extraordinarily long take with a fixed camera. The pure act, documented as such, takes over the film. *Les Rendez-vous d'Anna* (1978) begins with a long-running fixed shot of a railway platform, where a train arrives, a crowd of people leave it, and a woman enters a phone booth fairly far away from us, makes a call, and then leaves the area. Akerman is fond of the long distant look at a place, where the visual and aural environment seems to absorb people and their particular stories. Throughout this film, memories of 1930s and 1940s history, as well as personal problems of the present, struggle to find voice against the all-but-overwhelming documentation of Europe's cities, trains, train stations, and hotel rooms. In *Toute une nuit* (1982) the many characters, whose lives we see bits of in and around Brussels through a hot summer night, are never named, and their dialogue is largely inaudible; they are parts of the city and the atmosphere.

Akerman has said that she does not believe in the distinction between documentary and fiction. A film is made to project feelings and understanding, and the film may use an invented story and characters to do this, or it may take the world more or less as found, arranging a meeting of facts with what the filmmaker knows in her soul. Akerman's films without story and characters are perhaps best regarded in light of this denial of special documentary status, as personal, poetic works, which of course have the potential to reveal the world, to be true. *Hotel Monterey* (1972) is a silent film, giving us mostly fixed, long-held shots of the lobby area, elevator, hallways, and guest rooms of a modest old New York hotel, perhaps a residence for pensioners. People come and go in the shots, mysterious, ordinary, seemingly defined by their 1950s-ish attire and by the once stylish, now a bit desolate, clean atmosphere of this place they inhabit. The camera finds an abstract fascination in details of architecture or in the changing lights on an elevator-call panel, suggesting forces that shape people's lives, that may not usually be acknowledged, and that may not even be fully understandable. The silence adds to this sense of incomprehensible power in some things we see. Late in the film the camera begins moving forward and back in a hallway, peering out a window at the end, as if curious and seeking escape. In the film's final moments the camera is up on the roof, panning across the New York skyline and Hudson River. The outdoors, the daylight, and the vistas accentuate by contrast the lurid light, the hothouse quality, something even gothic about the hotel interior. The film becomes

a comment on the in-bred comforting worlds people make for themselves, or allow themselves, to live in.

Varied nonfictional work followed, including portraits of artists (choreographer Pina Bausch, pianist Alfred Brendel) and in *Aujourd'hui, Dismoi* (1982) a forum for older women to talk about their grandmothers and the Polish Jewish community that was obliterated or displaced by the Holocaust. Two of Akerman's most interesting observational films of the 1970s and 1980s show a great contrast in style. *News from Home* (1976) is a New York film kin to *Hotel Monterey*, this time with sound, giving us a succession of color shots of lonely alleys, streets busy with traffic and pedestrians, subway stations, subway cars with the camera inside among people, and a nearly empty diner restaurants at night. From time to time Akerman in voice-over reads letters from her mother in Brussels, at moments drowned out by the sounds of the city. The letters may be made up—but why be sceptical? or what difference does it make? With the reading there is a wonderful tension created between the pull of family ties, something going on in the head and heart, and what we otherwise see and hear in the film, evidence of the daughter artist confronting a multifarious new urban world, huge and forbidding, but where she can find an uncanny beauty. *Les Années 80* (1983) is about preparation for the making of Akerman's romantic musical *Golden Eighties* (1986). We see auditions and rehearsals, with Akerman's voice giving instruction from off screen. At one point the director appears in a recording booth to do her own version of one of the film's songs. We see acting and filmmaking prepared and executed. And the series of *Golden Eighties* fragments of scenes, some rough and very much in preparation, others perfected, takes us more and more into the world of the fiction film to come. The documentary, with its consciousness about performance, is another version of the fiction's exploration of the psychology of love and the moods of loss.

With *D'Est* (1993) Akerman's documentary work takes a serious turn into history and geography. This is her most impressive film in the observational mode and one of her very best films altogether, a grand two-hour study of eastern Europe and, mainly, Moscow, just watching and listening, offering no commentary and registering no one's words. Here, as a traveler, Akerman seems to find material she has always deeply known and understood, with which her filmmaking connects powerfully. The film opens with images of space—empty roads and intersections, and flat fields—and one never gets over the impression that human life in this East is lived against a background of emptiness. We see people sitting in their apartments, seeming to have agreed to pose for a portrait, exposing their somberness. Some eat a meal alone. And there are long mobile shots—one a full ten minutes—as if looking at an endless world, moving through the streets of Moscow taking in crowds waiting for buses, or moving through railway stations where crowds sit quietly on benches, bundled up in the cold, as if displaced from home and waiting forever. Much of the film is shot at night, with all its beauty and uncertainty, and most of the film in winter, where the physical world weighs heavily. It is a picture of life lived against the void, of a sameness with little sign of change. The many faces are intriguing, but do not show much; they acknowledge the camera, but only obliquely. People seem experienced and complex, but closed off. At the end of the film we are at a concert and hear a full solo cello piece by Boris Tchaikovsky, which is greeted with a strong ovation. This old-fashioned, soulful music, with some painful modernist twists, one feels could be playing inside the heads of all the people we see in the film.

Recent films of Akerman's continue to look at places and the cultures associated with them. *Sud* (1999) journeys across the American South, staring at the lush vegetation and the air's heat waves that surround all activity, and listens to people talk about poor lives and racial problems. The journey comes to an uneasy rest in Jasper, Texas, gathering information on the then recent murder by dragging of James Byrd, a black man, at the hands of whites. Twice, the camera, looking back at the road, travels over the route the man was dragged behind a truck. It is a simple, unnerving gesture, confronting the event in a way only film could do. *De l'autre côté* (2002) centers on the Mexican/U.S. border in the Sonoran desert/southern Arizona region. The problems of economically desperate Mexicans trying to cross into the United States come into the film in interviews and monologues, as do the attitudes of fearful white Americans. But the film mostly contemplates the *place*, the beautiful and threatening desert spaces, the skies in various light, the ugly endless border wall, the ramshackle buildings that have grown up in the region, and, viewed at night, the fence lights and search lights, roads or desert paths traversed by the camera like a migrant or the pursuer of migrants, barely revealing what is there, and

finally the view through the night-vision device of an airborne surveillance mechanism or weapon. Human pressures have made this place what it is, yet the place takes on a life of its own, as if it is a destiny that has drawn people into it. As always in Akerman, film registers an inhuman power of place and things, which, of course, is all too human.

CHARLES WARREN

Biography

Born in Brussels on June 6, 1950, Akerman was inspired to take up filmmaking after seeing Godard's *Pierrot le fou*. She studied for several months at the Belgian film school INSAS in 1967, completed her first film, *Saute ma ville*, in 1968, and won recognition when this was shown at the Oberhausen Short Film Festival in 1971. From 1971–1973, Akerman spent time in New York doing odd jobs, seeing avant-garde films, and making films. She won international acclaim for *Jeanne Dielman, 23 quai du Commerce, 1080 Bruxelles* in 1975, and was given a retrospective at the Venice Film Festival that year. With *Aujourd'hui, Dis-moi*, 1980, she began making films for television, which would sponsor much of her future documentary work. With *Hall de nuit*, 1991, she began writing plays, several of which were produced over the next decade. In 1995, her *D'Est* traveled to several museums in the United States and Europe. Two years later, she was given a retrospective at the Pesaro Festival in 1997. Akerman then taught filmmaking at Harvard University from 1997 to 1998. In 1998, she published *Une famille à Bruxelles*, a memoir/fiction centering on her mother, 1998. She used *De l'autre Côté* for an installation at Documenta 11, 2002.

Selected Films

1968 *Saute ma ville (Blow up My Town)*
1971 *L'Enfant aimé ou je joue à être une femme mariée (The Beloved Child, or I Play at Being a Married Woman)*
1972 *Hotel Monterey; La Chambre 1 (The Room, 1); La Chambre 2 (The Room, 2)*
1973 *Le 15/8; Hanging Out Yonkers 1973*
1974 *Je tu il elle (I You He She)*
1975 *Jeanne Dielman, 23 Quai du Commerce, 1080 Bruxelles*
1976 *News from Home*
1978 *Les Rendez-vous d'Anna (Meetings with Anna)*
1980 *Dis-moi (Tell Me)*
1982 *Toute une nuit (All Night Long)*
1983 *Les Années 80 (The Eighties); Un jour Pina m'a demandé (One Day Pina Asked Me); L'Homme à la Valise (The Man with the Suitcase)*
1984 *Lettre d'un cinéaste (Letter from a Filmmaker)*
1986 *Golden Eighties/Window Shopping; La Paresse (Sloth); Le Marteau (The Hammer); Letters Home; Mallet-Stevens*
1989 *Histoires d'Amérique (American Stories/Food, Family, and Philosophy); Les Trois derniéres sonates de Franz Schubert (The Last Three Sonatas of Franz Schubert);*

Trois strophes sur le nom de Sacher ("Three Stanzas on the Name Sacher" by Henri Dutilleux)
1991 *Nuit et jour (Night and Day)*
1992 *Le Déménagement (Moving In); Contre l'oubli (Against Forgetting)*
1993 *D'Est (From the East); Portrait d'une jeune fille de la fin des années 60 à Bruxelles (Portrait of a Young Girl at the End of the 1960s in Brussels)*
1996 *Un Divan à New York (A Couch in New York); Chantal Akerman par Chantal Akerman (Chantal Akerman by Chantal Akerman)*
1999 *Sud (South)*
2000 *La Captive (The Captive)*
2002 *De l'autre côté (From the Other Side)*
2004 *Demain, on déménage (Tomorrow We Move)*

Further Reading

Foster, Gwendolyn Audrey (ed.), *Identity and Memory: The Films of Chantal Akerman*, Trowbridge, Wiltshire: Flicks Books, 1999.

Halbreich, Kathy, and Bruce Jenkins et al., *Bordering on Fiction: Chantal Akerman's* D'Est, Minneapolis: Walker Art Center, 1995.

Indiana, Gary, "Getting Ready for the Golden Eighties: An Interview with Chantal Akerman," *Artforum*, 21, no. 10, 1983, 55–61.

Margulies, Yvonne, *Nothing Happens: Chantal Akerman's Hyperrealist Everyday*, Durham, NC and London: Duke University Press, 1996.

AKOMFRAH, JOHN

John Akomfrah was one of the founders of the Black Audio Film Collective in 1982, a group that went on to produce *Handsworth Songs* (1986). As a member of this cooperative, Akomfrah performed the role of director and writer alongside other writers and producers within a cooperative mode of production. The group's audiovisual practice was marked by a preference for discursive interrogation and recontextualization of archival documentary sources over documentary realism. After Black Audio ceased working as a collective in 1995, Akomfrah set up production of a company called Smoking Dogs with former members of Black Audio Lina Gopaul and David Lawson. The company produced television documentaries such as *Goldie: When Saturn Returnz* (1998) and *Riot* (1999) for United Kingdom's Channel 4 and *The Wonderful World of Louis Armstrong* as part of the *Omnibus* season for the BBC.

Akomfrah has frequently favored the documentary form as a means of formal innovation, while also making feature-length films that invoke the relation between drama and documentary. The resources of drama and archival documentary are called on as a means of articulating the diasporic experience in *Testament* (1988), whereas in *Who Needs a Heart* (1991), the combination is used to highlight the cultural politics of the 1960s and a figure rather overlooked by history in the form of Michael X. The style of documen-

tary demonstrated in *Handsworth Songs* involves a nonlinear structure, modernist techniques of juxtaposition and layering, and, in collaboration with Trevor Mathison, a dissonant and contrapuntal relation between sound and image. The interrogation of the relation between narrative, the poetic expression of diasporic memory, and the documenting of history in *Handsworth Songs* is recast via a female dramatic protagonist to Ghana in *Testament*. As a result, the referent for Akomfrah's filmmaking is not only black experience but also an ongoing exploration of form that looks into the problematic form of the bounded categories of fiction and nonfiction and simultaneously raises recurring questions concerning historiography. The concern with materializing history through documentary is underlined in *The Cheese and the Worm* (1996), featuring the historian Carlo Ginsberg and addressing Christianity, heresy, and witchcraft in Italy during the sixteenth century.

Akomfrah documents the diasporic experience of black British subjects in *Touch of the Tarbrush* (1991), which revisits J. B. Priestley's *English Journey* of 1933 as a starting point from which to enquire how the mixed race community of Liverpool describes its own routes to a hybrid identity. Here, Akomfrah fuses his personal and remembered history as a black English subject with the memories of some members of the mixed race community that is "rooted and located in Liverpool."

The expositional documentary and the tradition of surveying the condition of a particular place and time through history is annexed by Akomfrah in order to represent "the lives and histories that represent the hope for another England."

Akomfrah has produced work focused on significant cultural and political figures such as Malcolm X, Michael X, and Louis Armstrong. *Who Needs a Heart,* commissioned by Channel 4 in the United Kingdom, combines archival footage of the life of Michael X with a dramatic portrayal centered on a group of black people and white people who are caught up in the politics of black power and the culture of the 1960s. The dramatic element of the docudrama is supported by reportage. Diegetic sound and dialogue are frequently muted into silence and replaced by fragments of official voices denouncing the compromised life of Michael X. *Who Needs a Heart* emphasizes the problem of history as narrative and an approach to documenting a relatively undocumented political figure, where the outcome of historical knowledge and truth is rendered less secure and cannot be guaranteed.

Seven Songs for Malcolm X (1993) was produced for and broadcast by Channel 4 in the United Kingdom at the same time as the release in the UK of Spike Lee's film *Malcolm X* (1992). This documentary takes the form of a tableau, in which various black personalities and members of his family present a range of perspectives on Malcolm X. It is comprised of a combination of expositional testimonies, eyewitness accounts, archival footage, and dramatic reenactments. Sound is again used as a mechanism for drawing the viewer's attention to the relation between the different elements that constitute the documentary, and the different manifestations of Malcolm X within African-American culture.

In *The Mothership Connection* (1995), Akomfrah attempts to understand the African diasporic experience of displacement through the vehicle of science fiction and new technology. Connections are suggested between the musical sources of George Clinton and Sun Ra, the history of the blues, and science-fiction narratives of abduction and transportation. *The Mothership Connection* questions the boundaries that separate the history of the African diaspora from the scenarios of narrative fiction.

Akomfrah's documentary output spans both television and film. Productions for Black Audio, such as *Testament* (1988) and *Seven Songs for Malcolm X* (1993), were exhibited and awarded prizes at international film festivals—for example,

at the African Film Festival of Perugia, where *Testament* received the Special Jury Prize in 1989. In the United Kingdom, his films are generally either broadcast on television or receive a limited cinematic release. As a result, the critical context for Akomfrah's filmmaking is, somewhat problematically, a combination of the documentary tradition and European Art Cinema rather than the black communities in Britain (Gilroy, 1989).

Throughout the 1980s and 1990s, Akomfrah extended his reach beyond the context of black British experience, emphasizing the internationalism of the African diaspora. *Testament* (1988), *The Mothership Connection* (1995), and the *African Political Broadcasts* (1995) together represent a documenting of pan-African experience. Akomfrah's contribution to documentary represents both a formal interrogation of the materials and limits of documenting, and a significant contribution to the cultural representation of the black diaspora. Akomfrah, in collaboration with the members of the Black Audio Film Collective, opens up and places in doubt the language of documentary, while simultaneously exposing the gaps, silences, and blind spots of official, recorded history.

IAN GOODE

See also **Black Audio Film Collective;** *Handsworth Songs*

Biography

Born in Ghana in 1957 to parents who had met in England and had returned to Ghana, where Akomfrah's father was a member of the government under President Kwame Nkrumah. Raised in London. Attended Portsmouth Polytechnic, where he met some of the future members of Black Audio Film Collective. Returned to London and helped to establish Black Audio Film Collective in 1982. Formed Smoking Dogs production company in 1995 with Lina Gopaul and David Lawson. Member of PACT Cultural Diversity Panel (The Producers Alliance for Cinema and Television). Appointed governor on the board of the British Film Institute in October 2001.

Selected Films

1986 *Handsworth Songs* (director)
1988 *Testament* (director)
1991 *Who Needs a Heart* (director, writer)
1993 *Seven Songs for Malcolm X* (director, writer)
1996 *The Cheese and the Worm* (director)

Further Reading

Auguiste, Reece/Black Audio Film Collective, "Black Independents and Third Cinema: The British

Context," in *Questions of Third Cinema*, edited by Jim Pines and Paul Willemen, London: British Film Institute, 1989.

Diawara, Manthia, "The 'I' Narrator in Black Diaspora Documentary," in *Struggles for Representation. African American Documentary Film and Video*, edited by Phyllis Klotman and Janet Cutler, Bloomington & Indianapolis: Indiana University Press, 1999.

Gilroy, Paul, "Cruciality and the Frog's Perspective: An Agenda of Difficulties for the Black Arts Movement in Britain," *Third Text*, 5, 1989.

Marks, Laura, "Ghosts of Stories. Black Audio Film Collective's *Who Needs a Heart*," *Cineaction*, 36, February 1995.

Mercer, Kobena (ed.), *Black Film/British Cinema*, London: ICA, 1988.

Mercer, Kobena, *Welcome to the Jungle*, London: Routledge, 1994.

ALEXANDER, DONALD

Donald Alexander was a typical representative of the 1930s generation, which—shocked as it was by the human waste caused by the Depression—welcomed the social changes begun during the war and ending in the British Labour government's welfare program. After graduating from the University of Cambridge, he gained his first film experience in the South Wales coal fields in 1935. Using a borrowed 16mm camera, he and his companion filmed such typical sights as miners looking for coal high upon the slagheaps. Once the film was finished it was shown to Paul Rotha. He invited Alexander to be his assistant at Strand Films—an offer that was immediately accepted.

Rotha ensured that Alexander learned all the tricks of the trade by having him work with the company's more experienced staff. For *Today We Live*, commissioned by the National Council for Social Service, Alexander, acting as assistant to director Ralph Bond, personally reshot on 35mm stock the sequence from his novice film on the Tylorstown slagheap. The footage would be incorporated in countless historical documentaries.

In 1937, Alexander was ready for his first directorial assignment: *Eastern Valley*, about a substance farm for unemployed miners in Cwmavon, run by the Order of Friends. In his last prewar film, about the city of Dundee, he made use of the more complex narrative structure that would become so characteristic of his 1940s documentaries. The frame story for *Dundee* is provided by a group of people meeting by chance on the ferry crossing the Tay; each character is used to impart factual information to, and derive empathy from, the spectator.

In December 1940, Alexander was asked by Paul Rotha to return to London. In response to the plans of former Shell publicity officer, Jack Beddington [now head of Films Division at the Ministry of Information (MOI)], to involve outside units in the production program, Rotha had the idea of setting up a new unit. Its aim was making "films of social importance with an eye to the future" (Alexander), in line with the "war aims," presented in the very first issue of *Documentary Newsletter* (1940), which demanded that "the Educational system, Public Health Services, Child Welfare, the Housing Problem" be reviewed and reformed.

In 1941, Alexander was first introduced to Bridget (Budge) Cooper, who would soon become his (second) wife and close companion in film production. While working at Paul Rotha Productions (PRP), they tackled several social and health topics in films about day nurseries, rural local government, rehabilitation, female agricultural labor, and the contributions of West Indians to the war effort. But it was Cooper's *Children of the City* (1944), analyzing the social roots of child delinquency, that epitomized PRP's social approach to documentary. Alexander acted as the film's producer, but it was Rotha who got the credit. It was out of resentment against this and similar incidents that Alexander, Cooper, and eight others decided in 1944 to break away from PRP. They formed Documentary Technicians Alliance (DATA), a cooperative recognized by the Co-operative Productive Federation. Until his departure in 1950,

Alexander was annually elected as chairman by the DATA shareholder-employees.

To a large extent, the new unit was dependent on the MOI. When Labour won the 1945 general election by a significant majority, DATA felt proud in having contributed to this beginning of a new era through their films. However, Labour showed little concern for the documentary. It disbanded the MOI, replacing it with a common service department, the Central Office of Information. This remained the biggest sponsor of DATA, but its nongovernmental status proved a growing source of friction. By 1948, DATA, now employing more than 40 technicians, had changed its direction by looking for other sponsors such as the National Coal Board (for which it produced the monthly *Mining Review*) and the Steel Company of Wales.

In 1950, Alexander left DATA. The next year he was asked to take over the one-day-a-week job of Films Adviser at the National Coal Board (NCB). He discovered that there was a great need for technical, training, and safety films, and argued for the setting up of an in-house technical film unit. In 1953, the unit was operative. Over the years, the volume of its work increased and Alexander, whose NCB job gradually became a full-time one, had to hire more employees. It was his policy not only to give young people the chance to learn the trade but also to make sure that there would always be a place for those who had already "paid their dues" in documentary.

After a twelve-year stint at the NCB, Alexander decided to step down. He continued working for the Coal Board, and made several films, including *The 4 M's*, a film that NCB Chairman Alf Robens personally used in his presentations. In 1969, Alexander became Director of Audiovisual Aids at the

University of Dundee. Being back in his beloved Scotland offered him the chance to get involved in the (second) Films of Scotland Committee. In 1979, he retired from the University of Dundee. Donald Alexander died July 20, 1993.

BERT HOGENKAMP

See also **Documentary Technicians Alliance; Rotha, Phil**

Biography

Born in London, August 26, 1913. Graduated from St. John's College Cambridge, reading classics, and later modern and medieval languages, in 1935. Joined Strand Films in 1936 as an assistant. Joined Film Centre in 1939. Director at Paul Rotha Productions, 1941–1944. Founding member and first chairman of the film production cooperative Documentary Technicians Alliance (DATA), 1944–1950. Secretary of British Documentary, 1947–1949. Films Adviser to the Steel Company of Wales, 1950–1951. Films Adviser to the National Coal Board and later head of the NCB Film Unit, 1951–1963. Director of Audiovisual Aids at the University of Dundee, 1969–1979. Died near Inverness, Scotland, July 20, 1993.

Selected Films

1936 *Rhondda*: director, photographer
1937 *To-day We Live* (Bond, Ruby Grierson): assistant director
1937 *Eastern Valley*: director
1938 *Wealth of a Nation*: director
1939 *Dundee*: director
1944 *Children of the City* (Budge Cooper): producer
1948 *Here's Health*: director
1958–1962 *Experiment: Workstudy Experiment at Nafodynyrys Colliery*: producer, director, editor
1966 *The 4 M's*: director
1974 *Tayside*: treatment, written commentary

ALLÉGRET, MARC

Although often remembered as the long-time companion and protégé of eminent French novelist André Gide, Marc Allégret was also among the most prolific directors of his generation. Between 1927 and 1970, he made nearly 80 films, including fifteen documentaries clustered at the beginning and end of his career. His only two feature-length offerings were his most important: *Voyage au Congo / Travels in the Congo* (1927), a portrait of life in central Africa that played a seminal role in the emergence of cinematic ethnography, and *Avec André Gide / With André Gide* (1952), an affectionate retrospective of the writer's life and work.

In July 1925, Allégret and Gide embarked on a ten-month expedition across French Equatorial Africa. Allégret was in charge of all logistical details, foremost among which was crafting a written, photographic, and cinematic record of the journey. He had no formal training as a photographer or filmmaker, but he practiced extensively prior to the trip under the guidance of the renowned surrealist artist Man Ray. In contrast to both Robert Flaherty's influential *Nanook of the North* (1923) and Léon Poirier's hit *La Croisière noire / The Black Journey* (1926), Allégret wanted his film to be an objective record of African cultures that informed and explained rather than entertaining through adventure and exoticism. To that end, the first-time director deliberately excluded references to the trip itself, the many technical challenges he faced, his own presence behind the camera, and grotesque elements of African culture, such as the large wooden discs worn in the lips of Massa women.

Voyage au Congo presents scenes of daily life among eight distinct ethnic groups, focusing on agricultural practices, hunting and fishing techniques, architectural styles, and key collective rituals—all of which are carefully contextualized with didactic inter-titles (over 150 in the 80-minute montage that survives today) and detailed maps (ten in all). In so doing, Allégret rejected the sensationalism and racial stereotyping that had long characterized newsreel and documentary representations of so-called primitive cultures. Instead, the film promoted intercultural understanding by appealing to spectators' intellect and steeping them in knowledge. This approach, which reflects Gide's biting assertion that "the less intelligent the white man is, the dumber he perceives Blacks to be" was nothing short of revolutionary, for it revealed the potential of cinema as a legitimate ethnographic tool.

Perhaps most important, Allégret realized the impossibility of ever achieving total objectivity because of the inherently unequal power dynamic that exists between the filmmaker and his or her subjects. His travel diary, which first appeared in 1987 under the title *Carnets du Congo / Notebooks from the Congo,* charts the emergence of a precocious self-reflexivity that would inform the later work of anthropologists such as Michel Leiris, Jean Rouch, and Claude Lévi-Strauss. In order to minimize the contaminating impact of his presence,

Allégret shot much of the film with a long-range telephoto lens and whenever possible accustomed his subjects to the camera through repeated pantomime before taking any actual footage.

Whereas Gide's written accounts of the trip, *Voyage au Congo / Travels in the Congo* and *Retour du Tchad / Return from Chad*, sparked a national debate over colonial policy by exposing forced labour, crushing taxes, starvation, and insufficient medical care throughout central Africa, Allégret's film was more subtle in its politics, eschewing invective in favour of a primitivist aesthetic that celebrated African physical beauty, vitality, and moral purity. This brand of primitivism—which had its origins in the Enlightenment philosophers' critique of modern civilization and idealization of "natural man"—had a significant influence on French art (particularly sculpture and painting) throughout the 1920s as concerns over European decadence and the need for cultural rejuvenation intensified in the wake of the First World War.

In this regard, Allégret's footage of athletic competitions and dances is particularly striking. His long, graceful shots of contracting backs, arms, legs, and breasts create living, neo-classical sculptures reminiscent of the Renaissance. From today's perspective such scenes are disturbingly objectifying and voyeuristic, yet as an exercise in visual aesthetics and eroticism their appeal remains undeniable. Moreover, in the context of the late 1920s they constituted a powerful, if at root equally stereotypical, corrective to the widely held European prejudice that Blacks were ugly, brutish, and unworthy of artistic attention.

The film's potentially incompatible aesthetic and ethnographic dimensions in fact complement each other, culminating in a sixteen-minute segment that dramatized courtship and marriage customs among the Sara people near Lake Chad. Although the practices represented on screen are sociologically accurate, the story of a young couple who meet by the river, fall in love, and struggle to satisfy their families' demands is entirely fictional. As Allégret's *Carnets* reveal, he carefully managed all aspects of the production, from scouting picturesque locations and choosing his actors among the local population, to directing their movements on camera and writing the explanatory inter-titles. The result is a primitivist melodrama disguised as a documentary that uses the universal theme of love to inform European viewers about African cultural differences.

Although *Voyage au Congo* did not enjoy commercial success or have a substantial impact on popular mentalities, it received praise from critics and it launched Allégret's career as a filmmaker. During the following year he made short documentaries about native culture in Djerba, a small island off the coast of Tunisia, life in the region surrounding Tripoli, and a publicity film for the Belgian National Railroad Company. He then embarked on a successful career as a fiction film director, returning to documentary over twenty years later with *Avec André Gide*.

Released in early 1952 during a series of official ceremonies commemorating the first anniversary of Gide's death, the film was the first feature-length cinematic biography of a French writer. Its first two parts provide a historically contextualized overview of Gide's life and work through a smoothly edited montage of newsreel footage, photos, and voice-over narration. The narrative is accurate but highly selective and at times superficial, omitting major novels such as *Les Faux-Monnayeurs / The Counterfeiters* and *Les Caves du Vatican / Lafcadio's Adventures*, as well as allusions to Gide's homosexuality and its crucial place in his work.

The third and final section, shot in Gide's small Paris apartment during the last months of his life, is an intimate portrait that awkwardly attempts to humanize the Nobel Prize winner and to ensure his legacy for posterity. Rather than conveying nonchalance and spontaneity—as Allégret clearly intended by filming Gide reading aloud from his works in slippers and robe, playing with his grandchildren, and smoking at the kitchen table while reflecting on his career—this part of the film comes off as pretentious, transparently disguised hagiography. It is obvious that many scenes have been scripted, rehearsed, and edited in order to paint Gide as both the quintessential French intellectual whose genius enlightens the world and, quite inaccurately, as a devoted family man with whom everyone can identify. The film ends pointedly on that note as Gide paraphrases the final lines of *Thésée / Theseus*: "I have built my city, which is to say my writing. Through it my thought will live eternally."

In 1952, the film bitterly divided critics as Gide's work always had, eliciting lavish praise and sarcastic denunciation. Despite its obvious flaws, in retrospect *Avec André Gide* can be appreciated as the innovative forerunner of a film genre that is now a standard part of television programming. Also, despite its flaws, on a meta-textual level the film exemplifies Gide's penchant for self-reinvention and the growing role that cinema would play in shaping celebrity and public memory during the last half of the twentieth century. Allégret gave up fiction film in 1963 under the influence of the New Wave, whose exponents heavily criticized his traditional style. However, several years later he returned to directing with a series of well-crafted television documentaries based on the Lumière newsreel archives from the late nineteenth and early twentieth centuries.

In the end, Allégret's contribution to the development of documentary film is quantitatively modest but qualitatively significant for his pioneering experimentation with form and genre. Though *Avec André Gide* was an ambitious failure, *Voyage au Congo* stands as a masterpiece of early ethnographic cinema and the most influential film of Allégret's entire career.

BRETT BOWLES

See also **Voyage au Congo**

Biography

Born in Basel, Switzerland, 23 December 1900, son of a French Protestant pastor. Trip to England and beginning of lifelong relationship with André Gide, 1917–1918. Organized short-lived performing arts festival known as *Les Soirées de Paris*, 1924. Graduated from the prestigious Ecole des Sciences Politiques with a concentration in diplomacy, 1925. Traveled through central Africa with Gide, 1925–1926. Release of *Voyage au Congo* and emergence as a director, 1927–1939. Continued making fiction films in Nice during the Second World War, 1940–1945. Pursued various film projects in Switzerland and England, 1946–1950. Returned to France to make *Avec André Gide*, 1950–1951. Joined Cannes Film Festival Jury and received Chevalier des Arts et Lettres award, 1960. Named President of the Cinémathèque Française, 1966. Died in Paris, 3 November 1973.

Selected Films

1927 *Voyage au Congo / Travels in the Congo*: director
1927 *En Tripolitaine / Around Tripoli*: director
1928 *L'Ile de Djerba / The Island of Djerba*: director
1928 *Les Chemins de Fer Belges / The Belgian Railroad System*: director
1952 *Avec André Gide / With André Gide*: director
1952 *Occultisme et magie / Occultism and Magic*: director
1967 *Exposition 1900 / The 1900 World's Fair*: director
1967 *Lumière* [Lumière, part 1]: director
1968 *Lumière* [Lumière, part 2]: director
1968 *Début de siècle / Beginning of the Century*: director
1968 *Jeunesse de France / French Youth*: director
1968 *La Grande Bretagne et les Etats-Unis de 1896 à 1900 / Great Britain and the United States from 1896 to 1900*: director
1969 *L'Europe continentale avant 1900 / Continental Europe before 1900*: director

1969 *L'Europe méridionale au temps des rois* [*Southern Europe in the Time of the Kings*]: director

Further Reading

Allégret, Marc, "Voyage au Congo: Explications sur le film," in *Les Cahiers de Belgique*, 4 May 1928, 138–143.
———, *Carnets du Congo: Voyage avec André Gide*, edited by Daniel Durosay, Paris: CNRS Editions, 1993.
Durosay, Daniel, "Les images du *Voyage au Congo*: L'œil d'Allégret," in *Bulletin des amis d'André Gide*, 73, 1987, 57–79.
———, "Images et imaginaire dans le *Voyage au Congo*: Un film et deux auteurs," *Bulletin des amis d'Andre Gide*, 80, 1988, 9–30.
———, "Le document contesté: *Avec André Gide*, sa réception hier et aujourd'hui," *Bulletin des amis d'André Gide*, 98, 1993, 287–292.
———, "Analyse synoptique du *Voyage au Congo* de Marc Allégret avec l'intégralité des inter-titres," *Bulletin des amis d'André Gide*, 101, 1994, 71–85.
Geiger, Jeffrey, "Sightseeing: *Voyage au Congo* and the Ethnographic Spectacle," in *André Gide's Politics: Rebellion and Ambivalence*, edited by Tom Connor, New York: Palgrave, 2000, 111–130.
Gide, André, *Voyage au Congo*, suivi du *Retour du Tchad*, Paris: Gallimard, 1929.
Houssiau, Bernard, *Marc Allégret: Découvreur de stars*, Paris: Editions Cabédita, 1994.
Leprohon, Pierre, *L'Exotisme au cinéma: les chasseurs d'images à la conquête du monde*, Paris: J. Susse, 1945.
Putnam, Walter, "Writing the Wrongs of French Colonial Africa: *Voyage au Congo* and *Le Retour du Tchad*," in *André Gide's Politics: Rebellion and Ambivalence*, edited by Tom Connor, New York: Palgrave, 2000, 89–110.

ALVAREZ, SANTIAGO

Santiago Alvarez was not only the man who put Cuban documentary on the world map but he also was one of the most powerful and innovative documentarians in the history of cinema. Politically a supporter of Fidel Castro (he was once described as Castro's poet laureate for his loving film portrayals of the Cuban leader), his aesthetics were anything but conventional. Not only did Alvarez became a master of agitprop, whom many have compared with the Russian Dziga Vertov (although Alvarez himself knew nothing of Vertov's work until later), but he also extended the art of documentary in several directions. He did this through a highly personal style with huge visual impact, in which a rough-hewn lyricism was carried along by montage work that was often satirical or ironic, frequently using animated titles in place of commentary, and backed by the iconic use of music. In the 1950s, Alvarez worked as a record librarian in a television station, and he developed a keen sense of the possibilities of matching—and mismatching—music and images.

One of the founder members of the Cuban film institute ICAIC (Instituto Cubano de Arte e Industria Cinematográficas), which was set up in 1959 in the first year of the Revolution, Alvarez was already 40 years old when he was put in charge of the newsreel section and made his first short films. He once called himself a product of "accelerated underdevelopment" and was always grateful to the Cuban Revolution for making him a filmmaker and enabling him to fulfill his youthful dreams. Born in the working-class district of Colon in Old Havana, he was the son of immigrant parents from Spain. When he was 5 years old, his shopkeeper father was arrested for anarchist activities and spent two years in prison, while the young family struggled to survive on their own. Alvarez started working at the age of 15 as a compositor's apprentice, became active in the union of graphic arts workers, went to night school, and set up a students' association.

At the end of the 1930s, he went to the United States, working as a coal miner in Pennsylvania and as a dishwasher in New York. Back in Cuba in 1942, he joined the Communist Party and got a job in radio, and later in television. He also attended a film club in Havana run by the Young Communists, which became a recruiting ground for the new film institute. At ICAIC, he was put in charge of newsreels and quickly proceeded to turn them into a veritable art form, as well as a training ground for several generations of young filmmakers in how to make films quickly, cheaply, and using whatever materials were at hand. Perhaps it was his anarchist susceptibilities that gave his aesthetics their particular slant: a healthy disapproval of schools, conventions, and orthodoxy, together with a penchant for the deployment of pithy, intelligent, didactic montage. These susceptibilities rapidly induced him to discard the conventional language of the newsreel, and turn the format inside out. Instead of an arbitrary sequence of disconnected items, Alvarez combined them into a political argument, or turned them into single topic documentaries. He used this technique in the first of his films to win international awards, *Ciclón* (*Hurricane*) in 1963, and *Now* (1965), a denunciation of racial discrimination in the United States.

The newsreel job gave Alvarez the chance to film abroad, and here too he took a radical approach. In 1966, he accompanied Cuban athletes to the Pan-American Games in Puerto Rico, using the opportunity to turn out his longest film yet (thirty-four minutes), a biting satire of U.S. imperialism named after the ship that took them there, *Cerro Pelado*. ICAIC was still at this time filming newsreels on mute handheld 35mm cameras, but Alvarez was already at the height of his creative powers and using only a few inter-titles to convey basic information, eschewing a verbal voice-over and instead using music to narrate the events. At one point in *Cerre Pelado*, shots of a training center for Cuban counterrevolutionaries (as a caption describes it) are juxtaposed with a band arrangement of Rossini's "William Tell Overture," which naturally recalls the use of the same piece as the title music of the television series *The Lone Ranger*; thus Alvarez presents the counterrevolutionaries as imitation cowboys, an image both satiric and deflating. In 1967 came *Hanoi Martes 13* (*Hanoi, Tuesday 13th*), a lyrical and wordless forty-minute portrayal of what daily life was like in war-torn North Vietnam (Tuesday the 13th is the Spanish equivalent of Friday the 13th in English). Here, the music was an original score by Leo Brouwer, who was emerging as Cuba's most original film composer.

The same experimental approach produces both *LBJ* (1968), a stunning satire on U.S. political assassinations, and *79 Primaveras* (*79 Springtimes of Ho Chi Minh*, 1969), a deeply poetic tribute to the Vietnamese leader Ho Chi Minh. *LBJ* uses the three letters of President Johnson's initials to stand for Luther, Bob, and John—Martin Luther King and the two Kennedys—in a bold play on the strange coincidence that the corpses of these three men littered Johnson's ascent. Visually, the core of the satire is the image culled from a North American newspaper cartoon of Johnson as the incarnation of the Texan cowboy on his bronco. Alvarez doubles this up with Johnson as a medieval knight in armor astride his mount, reinforced with clips from two classic Hollywood genres—westerns and the his-

torical adventure—which appear distorted. (They came from wide-screen films that had been copied directly without using the appropriate lens to unsqueeze them.) The film is thus as much a deconstruction of the imagery of the mass media as of U.S. politics, in which assassination became an almost accustomed weapon that remained veiled in misinformation and mystery. Except for some linking animation and a few shots in the sequence on Martin Luther King, almost everything in this twenty-minute film is found material. As Alvarez put it himself, it was the U.S. blockade of Cuba that prompted this approach by denying Cuba access to new live material, so instead he raided the archives and used cuttings from newspapers and magazines.

One of his best-known films of these years, *Hasta la victoria siempre* (*Always Until Victory*) was made in only 48 hours, so it could be shown in the Plaza de Ia Revolución in Havana before Castro delivered his eulogy for Che Guevara. Less well known abroad are the films that Alvarez made on internal politics, including the forty-minute *Despegue a las 18:30* (*Take off at 18:00*, 1969), which confronted the failures of the Cuban economy, although it was made in a Guevara-like spirit of moral exhortation rather than as criticism. Even here, Alvarez eschews conventional narration in a long opening sequence that portrays the lines of potential customers at the food shops and the despondency of "No hay!" ("There isn't any!").

A series of longer films in the 1970s brought Alvarez's style back toward reportage. In *Piedra sobre piedra* (*Stone Upon Stone*, 1970), Alvarez goes to Peru to report on the radical military regime that had just restored diplomatic relations with Cuba, and is interrupted by a major earthquake, from which he draws a metaphor: an equation between the 60 seconds of the earthquake whose effects he films, and the earthquake of underdevelopment that lasted for 365 days a year. Then came three films that chronicled Castro's foreign tours of the 1970s (to Chile in 1971, Africa and Eastern Europe in 1972, and Africa again in 1977), where Alvarez developed a unique style of informal, observational filming that evidently took the Cuban leader's fancy. (Castro gave Alvarez a Russian Lada car for his sixtieth birthday.) *De América soy hijo* (*Born of the Americas*, 1972), the film of Fidel's visit to Chile, is by far the longest—195 minutes in the full version. The length is justified by taking the cue from Castro's oratory; Alvarez used Castro's speeches as entry points to sequences analyzing aspects of Latin American history and the Cuban experience, which Castro explained to his Chilean audiences, and a similar technique was used for *Y el cielo fue tomado por asalto* ("*. . . And Heaven Was Taken by Storm*"), which covers Castro's 1972 tour of ten different countries in just over two hours, except that here the interpolated sequences concerned the histories of the countries visited. As one commentator put it after a retrospective of Alvarez's work in London in 1980, these lengthy films have an easy pace and "a certain discursive quality which can be deceptively innocent"—especially *De América soy hijo*, which is "loose-jointed but powerful in its cumulative effect and its insistent contextualization of the Chilean situation" (Hood, 1980). At the same time, these films offer a rich collection of glimpses of Fidel Castro in a large variety of circumstances, both formal and informal. There is no denying that Castro greeting crowds and crowds greeting Castro can become repetitive, but such images are frequently offset by moments of individual interaction, such as an exchange he has with a working woman at a rally in Chile, or by the habit Alvarez has of leaving in the scenes that many editors would wish to leave on the cutting room floor (Castro fidgeting with the microphones on the podium in front of him, for instance).

Alvarez himself was a man of unflagging energy, until he was slowed by the onset of Parkinson's disease. His filmography is enormous. In the 1970s alone, important titles included two more films on Chile, *¿Como, por que y para que se asesina un general?* (*How, Why and What for Is a General Assassinated,* 1971), and *El tigre salto y mato, pero morira . . . morira* (*The Tiger Leaps and Kills But It*

Will Die . . . It Will Die, 1973), which are both rapid responses to events using a montage of library and archive images. Other notable achievements include the two-hour portrait of Vietnam, *Abril de Vietnam en el año del gato* (*April in Vietnam in the Year of the Cat*), commissioned by the Vietnamese to celebrate the thirtieth anniversary of the founding of the Democratic Republic, and *Mi hermano Fidel* (*My Brother Fidel,* 1977), an intimate portrait in which Castro meets a man of age 93 who had met the Cuban patriot José Martí when he was 11 years old, shortly before Martí was killed in battle.

Elected to the Cuban national assembly for the Havana district where he lived, Alvarez remained a significant figure at ICAIC, and in 1991, was one of the signatories of the unprecedented letter of protest with which ICAIC's film directors greeted the suppression of the controversial film *Alicia en el pueblo de Maravillas* (*Alice in Wondertown*) and the threat, later withdrawn, to merge ICAIC with Cuban television.

MICHAEL CHANAN

See also **LBJ**; *Now*; **79 Springtimes of Ho Chi Minh**

Biography

Born in 1919. Died May 20, 1998, in Havana, Cuba.

Further Reading

Chanan, Michael. *The Cuban Image,* BFI, 1984.
Hood, Stuart. "Murder on the Way," *New Statesman,* 18 April 1980.

AMERICAN BROADCASTING COMPANY

In 1960, documentary filmmakers Robert Drew, Richard Leacock, and D. A. Pennebaker convinced then United States Senators John F. Kennedy and Hubert Humphrey to allow the filmmakers access to every facet of their campaigns in Wisconsin for the Democratic Presidential nomination. Stressing the historical value of such a record, Drew promised the candidates that

nothing would be staged and no dramatic suggestions would be made. The filmmakers would simply observe and record. In the end, both candidates agreed. The final product, though occasionally flawed, is still astonishing to watch today. No film before or since has captured in such an illuminating way the thrills, triumphs, and exhaustion of a political campaign.

At the time, network television had strict policies regarding the broadcast of "outside" work, but *Primary* (1960) was telecast by several local stations. The film so impressed the board at the American Broadcasting Company (ABC) that it immediately offered a contract to Drew and his associates who were then employed and financed by Time, Inc. The result of the merger gave Drew, Leacock, and Pennebaker the financial backing needed to create some memorable documentaries and provided the group with an audience once the work was completed.

The first important film made by the group for ABC was *Yanki No!* (1960), a vivid and ominous picture of Latin American unrest and the rise of Fidel Castro. As they had with *Primary*, the filmmakers effectively captured the strife and struggles of people engaged in political warfare.

With *Crisis: Behind a Presidential Commitment* (1963), Drew and company returned to the United States to document then Governor of Alabama George Wallace's decision to deny two black students admittance to the University of Alabama. As President Kennedy urges the Governor to stand down, cries rise from both sides of the controversy. The film is fascinating and truly remarkable. Drew and company effectively captured all the elements and were given access to all principals involved: Governor Wallace, President Kennedy, Attorney General Robert F. Kennedy, and others. At the time, Alabama was the only state in the union that had not fully integrated its university system. The University of Alabama at Tuscaloosa approved the admission of the two students when Governor Wallace vowed to stand at the entrance and prevent the students from entering. The film creates real drama and tension as the viewer is witness to the plans of the federal government as it attempts to enforce the integration. Although at times Governor Wallace appears to know that he cannot win, he never denies access to the filmmakers. The filmmakers give an overpowering sense of history to the film as they make the participants very human by showing Robert Kennedy and George Wallace at home with their families. This documentary is one of the finest ever made and is a testament to the civil rights movement.

Although not as successful as *Crisis*, Drew and company's *The Chair* (1963) is an interesting look at capital punishment. The film follows attorney Louis Nizer and others in a crisis over an appeal involving a man sentenced to die in the electric chair. Although ABC aired the program, the pact between the network and the group was weakening. Sponsors were not always comfortable having their names associated with the politically charged documentaries. The network wanted to keep sponsors happy, but at the same time, it did not want to impose on the creativity of Drew and his team. The most interesting element of the series was its unpredictability. For the network to step in and begin dictating the course of the programs would defeat the purpose of having the program. But resistance from the sponsors continued and eventually a break was inevitable.

In 1963, Drew, Leacock, and Pennebaker joined the rest of the country and descended on the small town of Aberdeen, South Dakota. The Fischers, a young husband and wife, had recently produced quintuplets. All five children were happy and healthy and the news circled the world. Aberdeen, a small market town with an unstable economy, suddenly found itself famous. The Chamber of Commerce had meetings and began to plan for the long procession of tourists who would begin to visit the small town. Promotions were planned and souvenirs manufactured. Although solemn speeches about protecting the privacy of the Fischer family were delivered, the town council began to set up press conferences, banquets, parades, and reviewing stands. Corporations began to shower the family with gifts, and reporters and photographers flocked to the town and the Fischer's home. With Leacock in the director's chair for this project, the crew tried, as unobtrusively as they could, to film and record the family's reactions to their new lifestyle. The crew enlisted the help of Joyce Chopra to keep the story human and tried to remain conscious of the fact that they were part of the problem afflicting the Fischers.

When completed, *Happy Mother's Day* (1963) won awards at both the Venice and Leipzig film festivals. It also received airplay on European television and was widely discussed and debated in European film journals. However, it never made it to American television. ABC could not find a sponsor willing to support the film in its current state. The network felt that the Fischers were portrayed as victims at the hands of a merciless town that simply wanted to cash in on the children's fame. However, the quintuplets were such a big story that the network had to produce something from the efforts of Leacock. Using the same footage, the network edited out all shots that might suggest an overeager zeal on the town's part. Many of the mayor's more inane remarks were cut out, and the Chamber of Commerce meeting was eliminated entirely. All speeches made in defense of the privacy of the Fischers were retained, and any shot or sequence that implied that the town would not abide by these pronouncements were left on the cutting room floor. To fill in the noticeable gaps, a voice-over narration was added, and at other times, an on-camera newsperson provided statistics on the community and its business, and conducted interviews with town officials and hospital personnel. Retitled *The Fischer Quintuplets* (1963), ABC's version of the film became an assurance to viewers that when quintuplets are born in an American town, everyone in the country will rally around them to make sure all goes well. When aired, the program was sponsored by Beechnut baby foods.

No longer able to agree on the future of their programs, Drew, Leacock, and Pennebaker parted ways with ABC. The filmmakers went on to produce, together and separately, other important documentaries, including *Don't Look Back* (1966) and *Monterey Pop* (1968). Even when the group disbanded, they continued to carry on the techniques and style they had helped to develop. Even though ABC never really returned to the successful form of the early programs produced with the group, the network helped to pioneer a new genre: a regularly televised documentary series that dealt with current and up-to-date issues and that was, above all, real.

CHARLES BANE

Further Reading

Barnouw, Erik, *Documentary: A History of the Non-Fiction Film* (2nd ed., rev.), Oxford: Oxford UP, 1993.

Bordwell, David, and Kristin Thompson, *Film Art: An Introduction* (6th ed.), New York: McGraw-Hill, 2001.

Grant, Barry Keith, and Jeannette Sloniowski (eds.), *Documenting the Documentary: Close Readings of Documentary Film and Video*, Detroit: Wayne State University Press, 1998.

Jacobs, Lewis, *The Documentary Tradition* (2nd ed.), New York: Norton, 1979.

Nichols, Bill, *Introduction to Documentary*, Bloomington: Indiana University Press, 2001.

Quinlan, Sterling, *Inside ABC: American Broadcasting Company's Rise to Power*, Fern Park: Hastings House, 1979.

AMERICAN FAMILY, AN

(US, Gilbert, 1973)

The twelve-part 1973 PBS series *An American Family* marked the culmination of the direct cinema movement in the United States. Producer Craig Gilbert's decision to move his crew into the home, positioning living cinema in the living room of middle-class suburbia, and then broadcasting it into the living rooms of America, erased the divide between public and private, a recurrent dream of *cinéma vérité*. Instead of revealing the private moments of public figures as the Drew Associates had in *Primary* (1960), Alan and Susan Raymond reversed the logic, making public the very private rituals of bourgeois family life as found at 35 Wood Dale Lane, Santa Barbara, California, thus acknowledging it to be an institution as open to surveillance as that of welfare recipients. Joining direct cinema documentary methods with television sitcom format, *An American Family* created a hybrid that fascinated its viewers.

In Pat and Bill Loud, Gilbert found a family defined, because of their cultural, economic, and political centrality, by their lack of definition. Seemingly raceless and classless, they were nevertheless marked by changing sexual mores, divorce, and homosexuality. The serial exposure of the Loud family on television revealed the suburban home as a central institution of postwar, middle-class experience. Filmed over seven months, the saga of the Louds, "not *the* American family, but *an* American family," in the introductory words of Gilbert, begins with only the sketchiest background about the family prior to the moment of filming; the show, like all living cinema, features present-time experience shorn of sociological or historical context. The opening

credits focus the series: First the house appears, then, in succession, Bill, Pat, and each of the children frozen in the middle of doing some typical activity. Their portraits surround the house, which dominates the frame. The sun-drenched family home becomes a spectacle, a source of envy in a consumer culture. Incredibly successful, Bill has built his own business forging replacement parts for heavy-mining equipment, marketing his products worldwide. Thus his home is linked to a global economy that makes possible the expansive ranch house with a pool and ocean view and the comfortable lives of his wife and children, who pursue their interests, secure in the knowledge that he will foot the bill for dancing lessons, apartments in New York City, musical instruments, and a horse and stable.

Yet, for all his economic centrality, Bill is not the center of the home. Rather, Pat, his wife and mother of his five children, dominates and maintains the family, and the footage. In her early forties, she is always perfectly made-up, her hair neatly done, wearing matching outfits and strands of gold around her neck and wrists. During the first episode, which includes both the end of the

marriage (surrounded by friends, Pat tells Bill she is seeking divorce in the midst of drunken party at a restaurant) and the first day of filming, Pat is up at 6:30, poaching eggs and pouring mugs of coffee for her large family; however, the substance of the film is the emotional labor Pat expends in caring for her children. With the exception of the voluble and "flamboyant" Lance, her oldest son, the Loud children are barely articulate teenagers. They mumble about Michelle's horse, Delilah's tap dancing, Grant's band, Kevin's movies, and Lance's acting career.

The close monitoring that goes on in the Loud home (everyone checks in with the others about the day's activities, Lance calls long distance from New York frequently, parents discuss problems relating to their children) reflects the scrutiny of Alan and Susan Raymond's camera and microphone. It also typifies the emotional intensity of the postwar middle-class family. During the first episode, as the camera follows Lance unpacking after his move into New York's Chelsea Hotel, he describes his siblings. Kevin is "humane, the only one to buy presents for the others' birthdays." Delilah "lives a very Tammy existence, like Trisha Nixon with spice." Michelle is selfish and bratty, "made in the image of me," and Grant is "talented but arrogant." Summing up what will become clear over the course of the next eleven weeks, Lance's astute eye has been trained by gauging the emotional timbre of the home in which he was raised. The community he finds at the Chelsea Hotel, and continues to make in Copenhagen and Paris, becomes yet another form of this intimate social world.

This televised family saga codified a new political grammar, the rhetoric of celebrity. Both Lance and Pat launched careers from the series: Pat got her own talk show, and Lance became a minor star at Warhol's factory. HIV-positive since 1983, he died of complications from Hepatitis C in December 2001, as the Raymonds were filming his last days in a Los Angeles hospice.

PAULA RABINOWITZ

See also **Cinema verite**; **Drew Associates**; *Primary*

An American Family, The Loud Family (Top row: Lance, Michelle; Middle row: Kevin, Delilah, Grant; Front row: Pat, Bill), 1971.
[*Courtesy of the Everett Collection*]

An American Family (USA WNET/13, 1973, 720 mins.). Produced by Craig Gilbert. Jacqueline Donnet, coordinating producer, Susan Lester, associate producer. Director: Craig Gilbert. Camera: Alan Raymond; additional camera, Joan Churchill and John Terry. Sound: Susan Raymond; assistant sound, Tom Goodwin; additional sound, Peter Pilafian and Alber Mecklinberg.

Editor: Eleanor Hamerow (Episode 1); David Hanser, Pat Cook, and Ken Werner (Episodes 2–12).

Further Reading

Goulet, Ron (ed.), *An American Family*, New York: Warner Paperback Library, 1973.

Rabinowitz, Paula, *They Must Be Represented: The Politics of Documentary*, London: Verso, 1994.

Ruoff, Jeffrey, *An American Family: A Televised Life*, Minneapolis: University of Minnesota Press, 2002.

AMERICAN FILM INSTITUTE

After 1965 legislation passed during the Lyndon B. Johnson administration, the National Endowment for the Arts (NEA) was created, and a subsequent study for the NEA by the Stanford Research Institute identified the necessity of a film institute in America. As a result, the formation of the American Film Institute (AFI), a nonprofit organization, was announced on June 5, 1967. The United States was "one of the last of the major producing nations to establish such an organization," after "Britain, France, Italy and India" (Canby, 1967). Among other objectives, the AFI "was created to train the next generation of filmmakers and to preserve America's fast-disappearing film heritage" ("History of the AFI"). The AFI's initial funding budget of $5.2 million was divided equally between grants from the National Council of the Arts, the Motion Picture Association of America, the Ford Foundation, and fund-raising. Starting with one office in Washington, DC, the AFI expanded into numerous regional locations throughout the years and now has three additional central locations in Los Angeles, Orlando, and Silver Spring, Maryland.

There have been only two AFI directors since its inception. George Stevens, Jr., son of Hollywood director George Stevens, was named the first director in 1967. In 1980, Jean Picker Firstenberg became the second director and CEO, and remains at this post today. Actor Gregory Peck was the first chairperson of the original Board of Trustees. Other notables on the twenty-two member board included actor Sidney Portier (vice-chair), actress Elizabeth Ashley, experimental/documentary filmmaker Richard Leacock, Hollywood film directors Francis Ford Coppola and Fred Zinnemann, historian Arthur Schlesinger, Jr., and Jack Valenti, President of the Motion Picture Association of America.

The AFI originally started with four general goals—filmmaker training, film education, film production, and film archiving, but has expanded into countless film-related activities, including film festivals, special screenings, special awards, publication of books and reports on film topics, and so on. Among the many benefits to the film industry AFI has established and developed over the years are: the five-semester Master of Fine Arts (M.F.A.) program at the AFI Conservatory (1969), which is now a formally accredited educational institution; the AFI Filmmaker-in-Residence program (director John Cassavetes was the first in 1972); the AFI Lifetime Achievement Award (the first recipient was director John Ford in 1973); the Director's Workshop for Women (1974); acquisition of the AFI Conservatory campus in 1981 (four buildings on eight acres that was originally the Immaculate Heart College in Los Angeles); the AFI Los Angeles International Film Festival (beginning in 1987); the 7,000-square-foot AFI Showcase at Disney World in Orlando, Florida, (1996); the yearly AFI 100 Years Series listings (1998); and the *AFI Almanac* (2000).

The AFI is responsible for a profuse amount of publications concerning various film topics. Among the publications is the bimonthly *American Film* magazine (started in 1975). The AFI also publishes numerous reference volumes, which include the *AFI Catalog of Motion Pictures* and *Filmmakers on Filmmaking: The American Film Institute Seminars on Motion Pictures and Television* (edited transcripts of their seminars).

The institute has recently established the competitive SILVERDOCS: AFI/Discovery Channel Documentary Film Festival (2003), based out of their newly acquired and restored AFI Silver Theatre and Cultural Center in Silver Spring,

Maryland. Additionally, the AFI Conservatory has expanded its program to include education in previously ignored film disciplines (such as marketing and distribution) and to require internships for students in the original coursework disciplines of Cinematography, Directing, Editing, Production Design, Producing, and Screenwriting.

Today, the AFI's mission differs from its four original goals—it now emphasizes filmmaker training, presentation of the moving image to national and global audiences, preservation of the American film heritage, and redefinition of the moving image as digital technology advances, recently developing new activities related to advanced technology.

Although the AFI has been a valuable organization for film concerns in the United States, it has not existed without controversy and criticism throughout the years. Early criticism of the organization as it was forming included worries over strong Hollywood connections that might possibly deter benefits to other segments of the film industry—such as documentary, educational, and corporate filmmaking, as well as the youth and assumed inexperience of AFI Director George Stevens, Jr.'s leadership abilities in establishing the first programs for the institute. Additionally, beneficiaries of AFI production grants, educational fellowships, and internships in the first three years of its existence were mainly male. Even after pressure to grant more opportunities for women came from a Women for Equality in Media protest march and sit-in at the AFI West Coast headquarters in 1970, the AFI responded slowly to women's demands. It was not until a funding grant for $30,000 to $35,000 from Dr. Matilda Krim, a board member of the Rockefeller Foundation, came through in 1974 that the AFI Directors Workshop for Women (DWW) was finally developed and grew under the dedicated direction of Jan Haag. Nineteen women were chosen to participate. However, AFI funds were found to be inadequate for proper financing of the women's films. Reactions to the first DWW were mixed. Criticism of the workshop included issues such as selection of participants by committee rather than open applications, insufficient funding for the number of participants, and some participants who felt they were more knowledgeable about filmmaking than the instructors were. Completion of the films by the participating women was uneven and some films never received a public screening. One participant, scriptwriter Joanna Lee, dropped out early,

thus leaving eighteen in the group. Among the more notable, high-profile participants were Maya Angelou, Ellen Burstyn, Lee Grant, Margot Kidder, Lily Tomlin, and Nancy Walker. Today, the DWW is one of AFI's many solidly entrenched programs. Other recent discussion and criticism has stemmed from omissions or inclusions of certain films on the AFI 100 Greatest Movies list and the other listings that followed—perhaps the best evidence of the success the institute has had in generating a knowledgeable national audience of film lovers with a continuing interest in and passion for film and motion pictures.

D. JAE ALEXANDER

Further Reading

American Film (magazine), Los Angeles, CA: American Film Institute, 1975–present (bimonthly).

The American Film Institute Catalog of Motion Pictures Produced in the United States, various editions, 24 volumes, including indexes, Berkeley, University of California Press, 1971–1999, and New York: R. R. Bowker, 1971–1988.

Calta, Louis, "Academy a Regional Film Center," *New York Times*, 11 Novemmber 1973, 142.

Canby, Vincent, "Agency to Press Movies' Artistry," *New York Times*, 6 June 1967, L54.

Canby, Vincent, "George Stevens, Jr. Will Start U.S. Film Institute Next Week," *New York Times*, 10 June 1967, 26.

Cimmons, Marlene, "The Stevenses Commute for Two Causes," *Los Angeles Times*, 23 September 1973, X1+.

Crowther, Bosley, "Film Institute Outlook," *New York Times*, 7 June 1967, L40.

Crowther, Bosley, "A Hope for New Images," *New York Times*, 25 June 1967, sec. 2, 1+.

Grant, Lee, "AFI Showcase: Ready to Dip into Film Mainstream," *Los Angeles Times*, 10 March 1980, part VI, 2+.

Haag, Jan, "Dream of the Marble Bridge: The Founding of the Directing Workshop for Women of the American Film Institute—A History," http://janhaag.com/ESTheDWW.html.

Haag, Jan, "Re: First group of AFI women (fwd). E-mail to Jae Alexander. 1 April 2004.

"History of AFI, *American Film Institute* website: www.afi.com. (This website offers many links to various AFI informational webpages.)

McBride, Joseph (ed.), *Filmmakers on Filmmaking: The American Film Institute Seminars on Motion Pictures and Television, Volume 1*, Los Angeles: J. P. Tarcher, 1983. [Distributed by Houghton Mifflin Company, Boston.].

Murphy, Mary, "AFI Women: A Camera Is Not Enough," *Los Angeles Times*, 27 October 1974, Calendar: 1+.

Roberts, Steven V., "Young Filmmakers Find Study Haven," *New York Times*, 30 September 1969, L40.

Smith, Susan, "The AFI's Workshops for Women: An Assessment." *Los Angeles Times*, 13 September 1979, Part IV: 27+.

ANAIS NIN OBSERVED

(France, Snyder, 1974)

Released in 1973, *Anais Nin Observed* is one of a number of films directed by Robert Snyder that takes an intimate look at the lives and personalities of celebrated artists. Snyder describes his films as "voyages of discovery," and openly admits that he knew very little about Nin's life or works before he began the film. He was introduced to her in 1968, when filming *The Henry Miller Odyssey* (1974), and after a prolonged period of acquaintance she agreed to let him film her for a separate documentary, of which she would be the focus. The two films make up a kind of unofficial diptych: Nin not only features in the work on Miller, as he later would in the Nin documentary, but she also helped Snyder to edit the film, providing encouragement and advice, just as Miller spent a long time with Snyder editing *Anais Nin Observed*.

Snyder's film follows Nin through her daily life, as she takes tea, swims in her pool, works on her journal, and chats with friends. The vast body of the documentary consists of her conversations with Snyder, as well as with friends such as Frances Steloff and students from UCLA. Although frequently categorised as biography, *Anais Nin Observed*, like the majority of Snyder's works, makes no attempt to give a comprehensive historical account of Nin's life and works. The film is aimed rather at providing accessibility to the writer for an interested audience without the barriers of experts. It does not delve into her personal life, but is rather a mouthpiece for her musings on art, literature, and her own life. This is Anais Nin in her own words. She is, as the title states, observed.

To this end, the film sets out to reflect qualities of Nin's personality and work within its form. Snyder's signature as a documentary director, paradoxically, tends to consist of a deferral to the artistic stamp of the documentary's subject, with whom he works very closely. In this regard he calls to mind the many female critics of Anais Nin who have adopted her prose style, writing about her as she wrote about herself. The film echoes the quality in Nin's writings that the literary critic Edmund Wilson describes as "half . . . story, half dream"

and recreates the "special world, a world of feminine perception and fancy" that is the circumscribed universe that Nin's characters inhabit. His success in this area is due in no small part to the work of the film's director of photography, Baylis Glascock, who uses soft focus and filters to recreate the aura of mystery that surrounds Nin. Repeated shots of light catching on glasses and water create a lilting quality that echoes that of Nin's writing. The film is edited in slow rhythms; conversations are conserved in their actuality rather than edited for highlights, so that, for example, when Nin finishes a thought, and gazes off into the distance before beginning her next conversation, the pause resonates with Nin's careful, well-thought out intellect.

Snyder's film mirrors Nin's diary in other ways—a fact he comments on in his notes on the film. At the time of filming, Nin was editing her journals for publication. The editing of the film echoes the process by which Nin selects material from her books: "We could always pick up new material in the future and—together with material of our current film—make another one . . . that's how diaries work!" Nin refers to the diaries constantly within the film: They are, she says, her "cultural landscape," and she dips back into them daily. Snyder's film echoes this dialectic between past and present, opening with the contemporary Nin, before moving backwards to look at her past life and then forward again into the present (Snyder, 1976).

While *Anais Nin Observed* is unmistakably part of Snyder's oeuvre, at the same time we might consider it to be coauthored by Nin. The film is by no means an academic or historical study made *about* the subject, but is rather an experience *of* her: The director's authorship is in many ways secondary to Nin's, both in form and in content. In keeping with Miller's request for Snyder to "mythologise" her, the director gives a very positive portrayal of Nin that might not be as objective as a more conventional biography, such as Coky Giedroyc's *Spy in the House of Love—Anais Nin*, shown as part of the UK's Channel 4 *Arthouse* series on in the late 1990s. Snyder's film is certainly a lot more flattering, portraying Nin as gracious, unpretentious, and intelligent. Unlike Giedroyc's film and the numerous written biographies of Nin, there is little mention of her infamous sex life, and a great deal more emphasis is placed on her intellect and artistic merit. It is perhaps no coincidence that Nin agreed to the documentary at approximately the same time as Miller, Sherwood Anderson, and a group of other intellectuals were campaigning to have Nin nominated for the Nobel Prize for Literature. Until 1963, Nin was relatively unheard of as an author in the United States and had been very frustrated by it. In many ways, the film provides her with the artistic recognition that had so long eluded her.

As an objective history, Snyder's film certainly leaves gaps. Nin's husband, Rupert Pole, for example, who was sharing the house in which Nin was filmed (unbeknownst to her other husband, Hugo Guiler), is omitted from the film altogether, as if he never existed (probably for Guiler's sake!). But as a portrait of Anais Nin as she saw herself, or more importantly as she wanted others to see her, Snyder's film complements content with form elegantly. Through the film, Anais continues the constant process of seduction that has characterised her life and writing, reaching out to new audiences through the screen. In this respect, Snyder's documentary is an almost perfect replica of the diaries in intent and content. Even before the editing process begins, a great deal has been cut

out, leaving us as mystified as to who the real Anais Nin is as she has always wanted the world to be.

HELEN WHEATLEY

Anais Nin Observed (USA, Masters & Masterworks Productions, 1973, 60 mins.). Distributed by The Grove Press. Produced by Robert Snyder. Directed by Robert Snyder (Associate Director: R. A.Fitzgerald, Jr.). Cinematography by Baylis Glascock. Editing by R. A. Fitzgerald and Tom Schiller. Sound recording by John Glascock and Leslie Shatz. Re-recording by George Porter, Ryder Sound Services Inc. Colour by DeLuxe.

Selected Films

1973 *Anais Nin Observed* (dir. Robert Snyder)
1974 *The Henry Miller Odyssey* (dir. Robert Snyder)
1990 *Henry and June* (dir. Paul Kaufman
1998 *Anais Nin: A Spy in the House of Love* (dir. Coky Giedroyc)

Further Reading

Hollywood Reporter, 234, no. 17, December 1974, p. 4.
Both *Anais Nin Observed* and *The Henry Miller Odyssey* are complemented by books written by Snyder, which incorporate photo-stills and transcripts of interviews, some featured within the films and some not, along with Snyder's descriptions of the filming and musings on the subjects:
Snyder, Robert, *This Is Henry, Henry Miller from Brooklyn*, Chicago: Swallow Press Incorporated, 1975.
Snyder, Robert, *Anais Nin Observed*, Chicago: Swallow Press Incorporated, 1976.

ANDERSON, LINDSAY

Lindsay Gordon Anderson, a Scottish director, critic, and cofounder of the Free Cinema movement, played a seminal role in postwar British filmmaking. When Anderson entered the film world in 1947, British filmmakers had largely forsaken art for propaganda because of the utilitarian demands created by World War II. Accustomed to making movies that served a national purpose, British directors churned out works that, to Anderson's eyes, lacked aesthetic appeal. Preferring romanticism to realism, he urged docu-

mentarians to abandon the studios, abstain from sophisticated technology, and rediscover the freedom found in the harmony of expression and substance. His search for high art led him to direct low-budget documentaries in the 1940s and 1950s and to create the Free Cinema movement, which encouraged other filmmakers to slip out of their political and social chains. The naturalistic look at the working classes promoted by Anderson would culminate in the British new wave.

As an editor with the influential film magazine *Sequence* in the late 1940s and early 1950s, Anderson championed film as art and the director as the master of the medium. He argued that only the director was in a position to determine cinematic expression. On the basis of his reputation, he received a commission to make a series of industrial films for a Yorkshire conveyor belt company, Richard Sutcliffe Ltd. He accepted the offer because he wanted to learn how to make films and he believed that documentaries offered an avenue to larger projects. Anderson's first documentary, *Meet the Pioneers* (1948), focused on the firm's underground conveyor system that brought coal from the mines to the pithead in Yorkshire. This series of films share a characteristic common to Anderson documentaries, in that the subject is work itself, with the director focusing on how things are made and how processes are set in motion.

Anderson's first nonindustrial film, the thirty-minute *Wakefield Express* (1952), was commissioned to celebrate the one hundredth anniversary of the newspaper. Shot as usual with 16mm film, the documentary begins in typical Anderson fashion—not with background information, but with people. Although the history of the paper is provided, the director focuses on the work of producing an edition. Aiming to capture the dignity of ordinary Britons, Anderson follows a reporter as he interviews local people in search of stories, shows communal activities such as children playing, and has a final sequence of the paper going to press. Anderson was an admirer of Humphrey Jennings, and this film reflects Jennings's influence in its poetic style and focus on common subjects. By showing a reporter interviewing a 95-year-old woman, Anderson imitates Jennings's manner of linking person to person to show the relationship of the past to the present. Nothing about the film is impartial—another Anderson trait. The subjects frequently play to the camera, while the director does not attempt to hide his affection, respect, and occasional exasperation for the Wakefield community.

For his next film, Anderson collaborated with Guy Brenton, an Oxford acquaintance, to direct *Thursday's Children* (1953), about the Royal School for Deaf Children in Margate, UK. Named after the old nursery rhyme in which "Thursday-born children have far to go," the twenty-minute documentary follows Anderson's adage that to make a film, one must create a world. Immersing the viewer fully in the lives of the children, he shows them in their boarding school as they receive lessons and explains how they came to live away from their families. Without informing the filmmakers, the British Office of Information in New York submitted the film to the Motion Picture Academy and it won an Oscar for best short subject.

Not far from the deaf school was the most popular working-class amusement park in the south of England, called "Dreamland." Anderson paid it a visit, and was fascinated by exhibits such as "Torture Through the Ages" and "Famous Executions." He reacted harshly to the passivity of the audience in the face of the unimaginative diversions, sad exhibitions, and pitifully caged animals. It is his anger at the undemanding aesthetic criteria of the crowd that makes this documentary an aggressive criticism rather than the positive affirmation found in his other films. The thirteen-minute *O Dreamland* (1953) was the first film that Anderson directed with no other impetus other than his own wish to make it.

Every Day Except Christmas (1957) is a forty-minute portrait of the workers who sold fruit, flowers, and vegetables 364 days year in London's Covent Garden market. The bustling workers, who occasionally mug for the camera, were generally filmed in long shot or close-ups to show both their coordinated physical activity and their unique personalities.

Once Anderson developed a mastery of filmmaking, his impatience with the mediocrity and prescriptive narrative style of most British films of the era increased. To encourage social realist films and freedom for the filmmaker, Anderson helped develop the small Free Cinema movement. This British group presented six programs of films at the National Film Theatre from 1956 to 1959, including *O Dreamland* in 1956, *Wakefield Express* in 1957, and *Every Day Except Christmas* also in 1957. In the broadest sense, Free Cinema had two objectives: to show what it valued in the cinema, with the emphasis on the work of the young contemporary filmmakers, and to show films to encourage other similar films to be made. Anderson coined the phrase "Free Cinema," wrote most of the movement's propaganda, and directed the greatest percentage of documentaries in the programs.

Anderson always refused to give his definition of a documentary, arguing that the term limited discussion of the film in question. He cherished freedom, and his films both reflect and examine this concept. In all of his works, Anderson explores the ways in which subjects interact, and the ultimate impossibility of being subjective. Poetic and lacking technological tricks, his documentaries are unvarnished portrayals of British life during the mid-twentieth century.

CARYN E. NEUMANN

See also **Every Day Except Christmas**; **Jennings, Humphrey**

Biography

Born in Bangalore, India, to a South African mother and Scottish father in the Royal Engineers, April 17, 1923. Parents separated in 1926; moved to England with his mother. Graduated from Wadham College, Oxford University, reading classical studies, in 1942. Drafted into the Army, serving with the King's Royal Rifles as a clerk in India, 1943–1945. Graduated from Oxford with a Master of Arts in English, 1948. Cofounder and editor of *Sequence,* 1949–1951. Directed industrial films for Richard Sutcliffe, Ltd., the National Society for the Prevention of Cruelty to Children, the National Industrial Fuel Efficiency Service, and the Central Office of Information for the Ministry of Agriculture, Fisheries, and Food, 1948–1955. Wrote *Making a Film: The Story of "Secret People"* in 1952. Directed and acted in feature films and television commercials, 1963-1987. Wrote *About John Ford* in 1981. Died of a heart attack in Angoulême, Charente, Poitou-Charentes, France, August 20, 1994.

Selected Films

1948 *Meet the Pioneers* (director, editor, commentator)
1949 *Idlers That Work* (director, commentator)
1952 *Three Installations* (director, commentator)
1952 *Trunk Conveyor* (director, commentator)
1952 *Wakefield Express* (director)
1953 *Thursday's Children* (co-director)
1953 *O Dreamland* (director)
1955 *Green and Pleasant Land* (director and scriptwriter)
1955 *Henry* (director and scriptwriter)
1955 *The Children Upstairs*: (director and script-writer)
1955 *A Hundred Thousand Children* (director and scriptwriter)
1955 *£20 a Ton* (director)
1955 *Energy First* (director)
1955 *Foot and Mouth* (director and scriptwriter)
1957 *Every Day Except Christmas* (director)

Further Reading

Graham, Allison, *Lindsay Anderson*, Boston: Twayne, 1981.
Hedling, Erik, *Lindsay Anderson: Maverick Film-Maker*, London: Cassell, 1998.
Lambert, Gavin, *Mainly About Lindsay Anderson*, New York: Alfred A. Knopf, 2000.
Lovell, Alan, and Jim Hillier, *Studies in Documentary*, New York: Viking Press, 1972.

ANGELA: PORTRAIT OF A REVOLUTIONARY

(US, du Luart, 1971)

Angela: Portrait of a Revolutionary paints a picture of the educator Angela Davis from the point of view of one of her students at the University of California in Los Angeles in 1971. It explores the challenges Davis faced because of her political activism, and shows the consequences of her being a Communist. Shot entirely in black and white, this low-budget, student-produced documentary film is nonetheless ambitious. It tries to capture the essence of Angela Davis, lending a multidimensional view to the person behind the picture on the FBI's Ten Most Wanted poster. Yolande du Luart, the film's director, takes a sympathetic view of Davis, while at the same time presents the story from a number of different perspectives. The film is du Luart's attempt to legitimize Angela Davis personally, politically, and professionally.

Angela: Portrait of a Revolutionary begins with sound images of police car sirens combined with footage of Angela Davis's arrest in New York for her alleged involvement in the failed attempt to free Black Panther George Jackson, who was on trial for allegedly killing a prison guard at Soledad Prison in California. This scene is followed by a sound image of a cell door crashing shut against a totally dark screen. The camera then focuses on the Women's House of Detention on December 5, 1970, with a voice-over by Angela Davis stating that she is "now being held captive." Next, the camera focuses on still shots of her supporters rallying outside of the Women's House of Detention, carrying posters saying, "Free Our Sisters in the House of D" and "Free Angela Davis." Angela Davis is thus painted as a political prisoner, not a common criminal.

The film then flashes back in time to the autumn of 1969. The viewer is given an insider's look at Angela Davis, the academic, who is preparing for, and then teaching, a class in the philosophy department at UCLA. This scene is followed by one of two interviews with the Chairperson, Professor Donald Kalish, who is filmed in the middle of the screen behind his desk in his office, thus presenting an authoritative image. He discusses in a measured way why and how Professor Davis was hired, and he is quick to point out that her appointment was based on her outstanding academic credentials and the needs of the department.

Later in the film, Chairperson Kalish explains why the Board of Regents fired Professor Davis, and he concludes that it was because of her mem-

bership in the Communist Party. The film also includes a voice-over by Max Rafferty, a member of the Board of Regents, giving his rationale for her dismissal (Professor Davis had yet to earn her doctorate). It is important to note that the film uses more than one voice to tell the story. This use of multiple points of view ultimately gives credibility to Chairperson Kalish's account. He explains how Max Rafferty is misinformed about higher education, since a completed doctorate is not a requirement for the job of Assistant Professor in the early 1970s at UCLA. In addition, toward the end of the film, Angela Davis herself tells the story of her dismissal. This scene gives Davis ownership of her story. In sum, by illustrating her academic credentials and demonstrating the reasons for her dismissal, the film invites its audience to look at the politics behind the Board of Regents' decision.

Angela: Portrait of a Revolutionary also illustrates Davis's core beliefs. In it, Davis tries to spell out the difficulty of not only organizing a

Angela Davis: Portrait of a Revolutionary, Angela Davis, 1972.
[*Courtesy of the Everett Collection*]

movement for social change and equality but also struggling to maintain that movement. The film seeks to merge the political with the personal with a series of carefully spliced scenes that move between private spaces Davis occupies in her home and study, for example, and public spaces where she teaches, lectures, and gives political speeches. These scenes do justice to the idea that the personal and political cannot be separated. Finally, the film demonstrates how repression comes in many forms by linking the killing of two students at Jackson State College, the war in Vietnam, the killing of four white students at Kent State University, the trial in Connecticut of Bobby Seale, and the Soledad Brothers facing the gas chamber.

Other techniques include the use of sound images to remind viewers of what is not visually present (e g., police car sirens with gunshots ringing in the background while pictures of the bloody police raid on the Black Panther Party Office in South Central Los Angeles on December 8, 1969, are shown in still shots). This series of still shots serves to imprint police brutality of African Americans on the viewer's mind, especially since it is quickly juxtaposed with still shots of posters declaring "Feed Hungry Children" and "Free Breakfast for School Children," representing a Black Panther Party humanitarian initiative for inner-city poor children. By juxtaposing images of mainstream atrocities and Black Panther activism, not only are Davis's political views illustrated but also the notion that Jonathan and George Jackson and other Black Panthers are simple thugs who should be locked up, is challenged.

Angela: Portrait of a Revolutionary was little noted nor long remembered. Angela Davis herself, now a Professor of Social Consciousness at the University of California in Santa Cruz, neither owns a copy of it nor has she stayed in touch with its filmmaker, Yolande du Luart, who is now translating mysteries from French to English. Yet, to use a 1960s term, *Angela: Portrait of a Revolutionary* seems "relevant" to those interested in experiencing a pivotal moment in the life and work of the controversial and iconic Angela Davis, and in the production of student documentary films rooted in the political milieu of the early 1970s. Not only is the film Davis's story of struggle but it is also a political act in and of itself. In the end, it powerfully demonstrates the means and methods by which Angela Davis dedicated her life to the struggle against fascism and racism.

THERESA C. LYNCH

Angela: Portrait of a Revolutionary (USA, New Yorker Films Release, 1971, 60 mins.). Distributed by New Yorker Films. Produced by Mae Mercer. Directed by Yolande du Luart. Cinematography by Roger Andrieux and Lynn Merrick. Music by Yolande du Luart. Editing by Jacqueline Mappel. Sound direction by Nancy Dowd. Filmed in New York and California.

Further Reading

Davis, Angela, *Angela Davis: An Autobiography*, New York: Random House, 1974.

Davis, Angela Y., *If They Come in the Morning: And Other Political Prisoners*, New York: The Third Press, 1971.

——, *Women, Race and Class*, New York: Random House, 1981.

——, *Women, Culture, and Politics*, New York: Random House, 1984.

——, *Blues Legacies and Black Feminism: Gertrude "Ma" Rainey, Bessie Smith, and Billie Holiday*, New York: Pantheon Books, 1988.

ANIMATION

The art and freedom of animation and the realism and social purposes of the documentary would seem to be forever diametrically opposed, but in fact the two forms have often connected to great effect. In the discussion of documentary, animation has scarcely been mentioned. Bill Nichol's *Blurred Boundaries,* which "explores decisive moments when the traditional boundaries of fiction/nonfiction and truth/falsehood blur" (Nichols, 1994: 190) never visits animation. Nor have critics attended to the historical role that animation has played in the illustration or elucidation of actuality.

A precise definition of an animated documentary might be one where a larger part, perhaps over 50% of the work, is animated, where animation is defined as an illusion of movement created through manipulating objects or artwork at a certain number of frames per second, such as would satisfy the artistic aims of the filmmaker to reproduce an illusion of movement that is clearly not "actuality" (see also Strom, 1995: 362). Given that, it is effectively impossible to define documentary with an absolute precision (see Plantinga, 1997 passim).

It is clear that mere technical definitions will not suffice and that intention must be taken into account. Although there are few examples of animated films dealing with real happenings as they happen, nevertheless Norman McLaren's *Neighbours* (1953) and Saul Bass's *Why Man Creates* (1968) both won Oscars as Best Short Documentary.

If documentary intention were an adequate portmanteau definition for animated documentary, then Winsor McCay's attempt in 1914, *The Sinking of the Lusitania*, is an attempt to present a realistic (hand drawn) interpretation of the actual World War I tragedy that would certainly count as both animation and document. But then, Pathe's earlier attempts, such as *The Mont Pele Volcano* (Pathe, France, 1902) might also count (using models and a miniature 'sea') as animated documentary, except that it is not an interpretation of reality but an imitation of it undertaken with a clear intention to hoodwink the public.

In this broader definition, *Walking with Dinosaurs* (BBC, 1999), with its seamless melding of real scenery and CGI (Computer Generated Imagery), would also qualify. But in the end these are more like spectacles in the Grand Guignol (shock theatre) tradition of actuality-inspired melodramatic re enactment. Gunnar Strom notes:

> "when we see the film today we are struck by the authentic feeling of the drawings. However, it is much harder to accept the highly propagandistic content in the written text panels which provide extra information . . . In this film the animated scenes stand out as more authentic than the written text."

> (Strom 2001: 2)

It is upon this distinction between the "actual" and the "constructed" that the debate around the creative interpretation of actual events has circled. It is a dead end in philosophical terms. The argument is better advanced by looking at works where there is no attempt to distort, but rather a clear aim at emotional and artistic authenticity.

It is significant that, at the height of the work of the GPO Film Unit in Britain in the 1930s, documentary pioneer John Grierson actually raised money for the groundbreaking animator Len Lye to produce and screen highly experimental abstract color animations (although some used live action in much the same way as in surrealist films such as *Un Chien Andalou*). These short subjects, often illustrating a GPO subject, such as the proper addressing of mail, were greatly influential in animation circles rather than documentary ones. Nevertheless, they served a clear documentary, or educational, purpose.

Lye had developed a technique of painting designs onto raw film stock. Films such as *Colour Box* and *Rainbow Dance*, with jazzy modernist sound tracks, were very popular with audiences, including some specialist (film buff) American crowds, on Paul Rotha's publicity visit to the USA in 1937–1938. Lye's work was artistically most influential, though never penetrating the populist cinema chains to any extent. These films attracted great interest and comment and Lye was later to work at the Canadian National Film Board producing equally experimental animation.

Works that aim at a more personal view of the world and use animated techniques to reflect a realist vision are closer to any satisfactory definition of animated documentary, which mimics as precisely as possible the human actions presented on screen. The anecdote-based animations of Nick Park's Aardman studios from the 1970s onward clearly share the impulse to present small personal stories. More recent works to combine this documentary impulse and realist animation using animation as the illustrative medium are *Colours of My Father* (Canada, Joyce Berenstein, 1995) and *Cousins* (Australia, Adam Benjamin Eliot, 1998) which, like Nick Park, uses claymation.

Among the most remarkable and internationally successful "documentary animations" are the later works of Australian animator Dennis Tupicoff. *The Darra Dogs* (1993) combines personal reminiscence with realist and expressionist techniques, and *His Mother's Voice* (1998) deploys live actions overlaid with rotoscoped sketch animation to produce effects both naturalistic and hyper-real.

In taking as its text and audio track a recorded news interview with the mother of a youth shot by police during a bungled robbery interview, and building an animated narrative, in *His Mother's Voice*, Tupicoff has moved beyond the "authentic" power of his own suburban memories in *The Darra Dogs*, to create something both more particular and yet more universal, powerfully capturing the terrible moment when a parent realizes she has outlived her child. Using videotaped actors to enact the "actuality" sound track, in a style that recalls Russian Heroic realism, Tupicoff's *His Mother's Voice* marks out new territory for animation, a space that intersects with the traditional photographed realism of TV and film narratives, yet is powerful and politically subversive.

It is in these latter, highly personal works, rather than in the possibilities of a perfect mimicry of life that CGIs (computer generated images) offer, that the real achievements of animated documentary, or documentary in animation, truly lie.

JONATHAN DAWSON

See also: **GPO Film Unit; Grierson, John; Lye, Len; Pathe**

Further Reading

Nichols, Bill, *Blurred Boundaries*, Bloomington: Indiana University Press, 1994.

Plantinga, Carl R, *Rhetoric and Representation in Nonfiction Film*, Cambridge: Cambridge University Press, 1997.

Renov, Michale (ed.), *Theorising Documentary*, New York: Routledge. 1993.

Rosenthal, Alan, *The New Documentary in Action*, California: University of California Press, 1971.

Strom, Gunnar "Animasjon Film" in *Store Norske Leksikin*, Oslo: Aschhoug og Gylendal, 1995.

———, *The Animated Documentary — A Performing tradition*, Norsk: Medietidsskrift, 2001.

Sussex, Elizabeth, *The Rise and Fall of British Documentary*, London: Faber and Faber. 1976.

ANSTEY, EDGAR

Edgar Harold Macfarlane Anstey OBE, a documentary film director, producer, and critic, was perhaps one of the most versatile documentary filmmakers of the twentieth century, moving easily between the aesthetics of his time and its science.

Living in the shadow of John Grierson's desire to reshape society with ideals of social and ethical cohesion, Anstey was the only member of the Empire Marketing Board with a technical and scientific training, and he urgently felt a need to make technological processes comprehensible. Anstey instantly recognized the value of the informational film for the purpose of training and educating. He sought an opportunity to follow through this conception of the informational film, and worked on the report that brought into being the Shell Film Unit. He produced Shell's first film, *Airport* (1934, Roy Lockwood, UK), an observation of a day at Croydon Airport and the systematic examination and refurbishment of an aeroplane engine.

> The film lasted only seventeen minutes, but nothing could quite compare with aircraft, and everything associated with them, for excitement. Many people had never seen an aeroplane, yet everyone recognised the exotic glamour of flight. *Airport* informed, entertained and educated while simultaneously indicating Shell's own position in the vanguard of modernity.
>
> (Howarth, 1997)

Anstey shared John Grierson's view that documentary must both criticize the agents of state and represent the interests of the exploited worker. He became frustrated and unhappy with the rate of progress at Shell and resigned to pursue his ideology.

Anstey found his opportunity with the Gas, Light and Coke Company, and (along with Arthur Elton) brought to the screen *Housing Problems* (1935), which focused on the plight of a Stepney (in London's East End) slum-dweller. In doing so, he sparked a new approach to documentary filmmaking. *Housing Problems* marked the beginning of Anstey's long commitment to social change. The film was well-received, although Joris Ivens, a fellow documentary filmmaker, commented in hindsight:

> There have been cases in the history of documentary when photographers became so fascinated by dirt that the result was the dirt looked interesting and strange, not something repellent to the audience.
>
> In my opinion . . . *Housing Problems*, fell into this error of exotic dirt. You could not smell these London slums.
>
> (Ivens, 1969)

However, John Betjemen, film critic of the *Evening Standard*, praised this new style of filmmaking and in 1935 wrote movingly of these "films without sex." Betjemen came later to admire

Anstey's perceptive gifts as a critic with the BBC and *The Spectator*.

Grierson, too, later praised *Housing Problems,* and noted that both Anstey and Elton had "taken the documentary film into the field of social problems and keyed it to the task of describing not only industrial and commercial spectacle, but social truth as well" (Grierson, 1938).

Housing Problems convinced Anstey of the power of documentary, and he followed it with *Enough to Eat?* (1936), an examination of the problem of malnutrition. Pushing for social change, Anstey claimed the film was a contribution to ongoing national research on nutrition and nutritional issues. Its success can be attributed to the media coverage it received, rather than the quality of the filmmaking displayed. The *Catholic Herald*, for example, wrote on October 10, 1936:

> The film does not show the terrible ravages that undernourishment has created in England. Director Edgar Anstey has chosen the better method of revealing the tragedy of poverty and the consequent semi-starvation which is the result of a cheap diet chosen more for its filling qualities than for its nutritive value.

Like Grierson, Anstey believed that documentary could act as an effective medium of communication between the government and the working classes. During World War II, while at Film Centre, he made an abundance of films for the Ministry of Information to encourage more intensive cultivation of urban gardens and mixed farms throughout Great Britain.

It was during this time that the Scientific Film Association was formed. Anstey and Arthur Elton were convinced that film had a singular power to impart information. Anstey believed passionately that the scientist and the technologist shared the imagination and insight of the artist, and after the war he and Elton created the International Scientific Film Association to disseminate a wider corroboration of their outlook.

Anstey, like Grierson, had established himself at the forefront of documentary production. From the early 1940s he largely settled into the role of producer. His appointment as Films Officer and Producer in Charge to the British Transport Commission in 1949 allowed him to use his gifts and abilities to satisfy his vision for documentary film.

STEVEN R. FOXON

See also **British Transport Films; Documentary Film: Britain; Elton, Arthur; EMB Film Unit;** *Enough to Eat?***; GPO Film Unit;** *Granton Trawler***; Grierson, John;** *Housing Problems***;** *Industrial Britain***; March of Time; MOI WWII; Shell**

Biography

Born February 16, 1907, in Watford, England. Educated at Watford Grammar School and Birkbeck College, University of London. Married Daphne Lilly (Canadian documentary filmmaker NFBC) in 1949. Joined Grierson's Empire Marketing Board Film Unit after answering to an advertisement in the *Times* in 1931. Started the Shell Film Unit in 1934. Joined the March of Time Film Unit, initially as London Director of Productions, later Foreign editor in New York from 1936 to 1938. Member of the Board and Producer at Film Centre (UK), 1940–1948. Regular member of BBC radio program "The Critics," from 1949 to 1966. Organized and acted as producer-in-charge of British Transport Films from 1949 to 1974. In 1956 and in 1967, served as Chairman of the British Film Academy; President of the International Scientific Film Association from 1961 to 1963. Won an Academy Award for *Wild Wings* (1965) in 1966. Chairman, British Industrial & Scientific Film Association from 1969 to 1970. Board of Governors at the British Film Institute from 1974 to 1975. Chairman of Children's Film Foundation Production Committee from 1981 to 1983. Died September 25, 1987, in London, England.

Selected Films

1931 *Industrial Britain* (Editor)
1934 *Granton Trawler* (Editor)
1935 *Housing Problems* (Director/Producer [with A Elton])
1936 *Enough to Eat?* (Director)
1943 *Crown of the Year* (M.O.I., Associate Producer)
1947 *Caller Herrin'* (Scottish Home Dept., Producer)
1950 *Berth 24* (B.T.F., Producer)
1954 *Elizabethan Express* (B.T.F., Producer)
1957 *Journey Into Spring* (B.T.F., Producer)
1961 *Terminus* (B.T.F., Producer)
1965 *Wild Wings* (B.T.F., Producer)
1970 *Site in the Sea* (B.T.F., Producer)
1975 *Age of Invention* (B.T.F., Producer)

Further Reading

Gordon, Douglas, *Shell Films: The First Sixty Years*, London: Balding and Mansell, 1994.

Grierson, John, *Grierson on Documentary*, edited by Forsyth Hardy, London: Collins, 1946; New York: Harcourt Brace, 1947; revised edition, London: Faber, 1966, New York: Praeger, 1971; abridged edition, Faber, 1979.

Hardy, Forsyth, *John Grierson: A Documentary Biography*, London: Faber, 1979.

Howarth, Stephen, *A Century in Oil—The Shell Transport and Trading Company 1897–1997*, London: 1997.

Ivens, Joris, *The Camera and I*, Berlin: Seven Seas, 1969.

Roth, Paul, *Documentary Diary*, London: Seker and Warburg, and New York: Hill and Wang, 1973.

Sussex, Elizabeth, *The Rise and Fall of British Documentary*, Berkeley: University of California Press, 1975.

Tallents, Sir Stephen, *The Projection of Britain*, London: Faber, 1932 (reprinted 1955 Film Centre, UK).

ANTONIO, EMILE DE

Emile de Antonio is best known for his innovations in the approach to documentary filmmaking. His works engage viewers in pointed political discourse through the clever arrangement of images, historical footage, interviews, text, sound, and other elements compiled to create a story without the use of a narrator. Although he came to filmmaking in his forties and made relatively few major films, de Antonio is a significant figure in the history of documentary. Nearly all of his films are explorations of the Cold War, its legacies, and its effects on U.S. culture and values systems.

Perhaps the most fascinating thing about de Antonio's work is his challenge to the idea of truth being told about historical events. De Antonio is quite willing to accept that any story may have as many explanations and meanings given as it does witnesses. The notion of direct address of the witness championed by de Antonio is a simple principle with extremely complex implications for the understanding of history. This concept was well illustrated by his pioneering use of found footage. Television images are used to strengthen the inherent arguments about power and human nature that surface in his work.

De Antonio's first film was formulated in this way. *Point of Order* (1964) used historical footage of the McCarthy hearings to illustrate the trajectory of the tale. De Antonio employed distinctive editing techniques to create meaningful juxtapositions. He continued to explore the recontextualization of previously filmed material for the next few films, honing his skills in the compilation images. Although this is interesting as a formal technique, it is ever more intriguing when the content is considered as well. The films of Emile de Antonio are largely about sociopolitical concerns, and this is well supported by the use of the televised image as a storytelling device. In a 1971 interview, de Antonio spoke of his impetus for creating the film:

> The Army-McCarthy hearings were a peak in American political theater. And there were lessons derived from it . . . . You get something like the Army-McCarthy hearings on television—in all its body, all of it—and something is revealed about the nature of our governmental structure, our society, where the real power is . . . because the whole thing about American politics is that it's a game, a game whereby you hide what's really happening from the American people while its happening. And that's part of what the film is all about, to show that game.
>
> (Weiner, 1971: p. 9).

This concept continued to propel de Antonio's work throughout the 1960s and 1970s.

Among de Antonio's best-known works is 1968's *In the Year of the Pig*, a film comprised of found footage from many diverse sources designed to illustrate the high-level confusion of the Vietnam War. De Antonio skillfully organized images to raise difficult questions about the nature of U.S. involvement in the war. Composed of his own interviews and new footage—combined with material gleaned from a detailed study of footage shot by the National Liberation Front, the Democratic Republic of Vietnam, the French Army, the American Broadcasting Company, and the British Broadcasting Company—*In the Year of the Pig* examines a complex issue from many angles. At the time of the 1971 *Film Quarterly* interview, de Antonio spoke of the impact of the news media and the war that was still underway.

> There is nothing as bad that's happened concerning the war as the networks' coverage of it, because it seems as if they're covering the war whereas in fact, they're not. The networks have made the American people, in a final way, comfortable with the war—because it appears between commercials, every day; it's become part of our quotidian existence, like armpit commercials. There's never the question asked, "Why are we doing this? What is this war about?" It's never suggested by anything that occurs on television that we should even be interested in that type of question. Television is a way of avoiding coming to terms with the fact that we're in this war.
>
> (Weiner, 1971: p. 7).

It is intriguing that this statement has continued relevance today.

Perhaps the most unique of de Antonio's films is *Painters Painting* (1972), in that it is unlike any of his other work. This exploration of several artists' thoughts and concerns in their working environments is still compelling today for its direct approach to the artists and their processes. His first film in 35mm, this work sought to create a synthesis of form and content as it used this collage style of filmmaking to look at several artists who worked in collage painting. De Antonio stated:

> This is a film about the System of the art world in the words of the people in that world: [Willem] de Kooning, [Robert] Motherwell, Jasper Johns, Andy Warhol, Robert Rauschenberg, Frank Stella, Barney Newman . . . and so on. Most of these are people I've known and who are friends of mine, but the film also includes the collectors, the manipulators, and the museum people and how an art market is created.
>
> (Weiner, 1971: p. 14).

The film is entertaining and insightful, like other de Antonio works, but its political inquiry is less overt than in the rest of his catalog.

Emile de Antonio remains an important figure in documentary filmmaking. In recent memory, his works have taken on a renewed sense of social poignancy and verve. As documentary film has become more mass produced and widely screened throughout the world, the significance of de Antonio is heightened.

TAMMY A. KINSEY

See also **In the Year of the Pig**

Biography

Born 1919. Studied History at Harvard University. Figure in New York Art scene. Began making films at age 40. Pioneered use of found television footage as documentary filmmaking tool. Died 1989.

Selected Films

1964 *That's Where the Action Is*
1965 *Rush to Judgment*
1968 *In the Year of the Pig*
1969 *America Is Hard to See*
1970 *Millhouse: A White Comedy*
1976 *Underground*
1989 *Mr. Hoover and I*

Further Reading

Kellner, Douglas, and Dan Streible (eds.), *Emile de Antonio: A Reader*, Minneapolis: University of Minnesota Press, 2000.
Lewis, Randolph, *Emile de Antonio: Radical Filmmaker in Cold War America*, Madison: University of Wisconsin Press, 2000.
Weiner, Bernard, "Radical Scavenging: An Interview with Emile de Antonio," *Film Quarterly*, XXV, no. 1, Fall 1971.

APTED, MICHAEL

Michael Apted has been involved in documentary filmmaking since the early 1960s. He has long been known for his patient, probing interviews and the simple truths revealed through them. Apted is perhaps best known for his *Up* series, a remarkable continuation of a project he worked on as a researcher in 1963. Directed by Paul Almond for Grenada TV, this film (*Seven Up*) was the start of what is now clearly an idea that is uniquely Apted. Fourteen British boys and girls were interviewed for this work, and the thoughts and hopes of seven-year-olds were revealed. Apted endeavored to continue this notion in 1970, when he interviewed the same set of youngsters (now 14 years old) in his *Seven Plus Seven*. At seven-year intervals, Apted has interviewed these same people, producing *21 Up* (1977), *28 Up* (1985), *35 Up* (1991), *42: Forty Two Up* (1998), and now production has begun on *49 Up*. This is unlike any other cinematic endeavor on record, and although a few of the original fourteen have dropped out of the project, those who remain have become very close to Apted and to each other. This careful study of human life, its simplicity, joys and sorrows, is indeed an epic documentary project.

Amid the years of this ongoing cinematic task, Apted has worked as a director for both independent and Hollywood features as well as continuing his documentary work. In 1985, he released *Bring on the Night*, a document of musician Sting and his tour experience, both backstage and in concert.

Apted's interest in political and social issues is evident in much of his work. His 1992 documentary, *Incident at Oglala,* explores the controversial case of two murdered FBI agents on the reservation at Pine Ridge, South Dakota, and the incarceration of Native American Leonard Peltier for these crimes. The film painstakingly investigates witnesses' accounts of the events of July 1975, showing testimonials from the legal proceedings, surveying evidence, and interviewing various players. Apted ultimately provides a study not only of the events themselves but also of the way people respond to the pressures of accusation, the role race plays in such a case, and the notion of justice itself. Apted's 1994 film, *Moving the Mountain,* continues with this political framework as it explores the Tienanmen Square student demonstrations of June 1989 in Beijing, China. The 1997 project, *Inspirations,* is not overtly political, yet it investigates ideas themselves in a very critical manner, a kind of creative activism at play in the film. Apted interviewed artists about the specifics of their process in art-making, with attention paid to the exercise of problem solving. Musician David Bowie, pop art painter Roy Lichtenstein, glass artist Dale Chihuly, dancer Edouard Locke, actress Louise LeCavalier, architect Tadao Ando, and ceramicist and poet Nora Noranjo-Morse answer questions regarding the nature of their creativity and the origins of their ideas. In an interview with Pamela Klaffke, Apted explained his views on filmmaking and art:

> You have to have a vision. That was why I was so interested in having an architect [in the film]. I felt a real sense of camaraderie with him because I felt both of our jobs are very public jobs, very collaborative, very man-management, very political jobs. It's a form of art, but not what I would call pure art of the blank page, the oil, the clay, the glass or whatever. It is a sort of art, but a wider view of art being a film director than being a composer, poet, painter or sculptor—because there are so many hands on your work.

> (Klaffke, 1998)

Apted continues this tack of social and political observation in his new serial documentary, *Married in America.* A production of A&E Television Networks, this 2002 work represents the second time Apted has used the notion of returning to a subject as a method of storytelling. *Married in America* explores the lives of nine diverse couples, including racially mixed pairs, those who were previously married or of different religions, and a lesbian couple. All of these couples live in or near Los Angeles, New York, or Birmingham, Alabama. Surely this regional specificity will allow for closer examination of the social issues at hand in these places and the things they create in these relationships. Apted intends to visit the couples every two years, whether they remain together or not, to see what has transpired in their lives. Of interest to him is the question of "family values" rhetoric in a society filled with divorce and single-parent households. Do age and class differences, past relationships, and family pressures complicate these unions in similar ways? (Chocano, 2002). The institution of marriage itself is examined here. Are there things that make a marriage work in today's world? Can the success of a union be predicted from the interactions between the people involved? Are the struggles of the early years always beneath the surface as the relationship continues? Apted is intrigued by these simple human dramas that shape society's attitudes.

TAMMY A. KINSEY

Biography

Born February 10, 1941, in Aylesbury, Buckinghamshire, England. Worked as a researcher for Grenada TV. Member of the Director's Guild of America since 1978. Received the International Documentary Association (IDA) Award for *28 Up* in 1985. Vancouver International Film Festival Best Documentary Feature Award, 1994, for *Moving the Mountain.* In 1998, *42: Forty-Two Up* received the Flaherty Documentary Award. Awarded the Doubletake Documentary Film Festival's Career Award in 1998. International Documentary Association's Career Achievement Award, 1999. Special Jury Award, Florida Film Festival, 2000, for *Me and Issac Newton.* Elected President of the Director's Guild of America, June 29, 2003.

Selected Filmography

1963 7 Up
1970 *7+7 (14 Up)*
1977 *21 Up*
1985 *28 Up*
1985 *Bring On the Night*
1991 *35 Up*
1992 *Incident at Oglala*
1994 *Moving the Mountain*
1997 *Inspirations*
1998 *42: Forty-Two Up*
2002 *Married in America* (TV)

Further Reading

Chocano, Carina, "Who Wants to Marry a Regular Person?" www.salon.com/ent/tv/diary/2002/06/15/married/print.html.

Klaffke, Pamela, "Up and Away with Michael Apted," *Moviemaker,* April 1998.

Robinson, Julie, "Michael Apted's *7 Up* Series," *DGA Magazine,* 27, no. 3, September 2002.

ARCAND, DENYS

Denys Arcand made his first film, *A l'est d'Eaton (East of Eaton's)*, 1959, with Stéphane Venne when he was 18 years old. A few years later, while studying history at the Université de Montréal, he co-directed *Seul ou avec d'autres (Alone or with Others,* 1962) with Stéphane Venne and Denis Héroux. *Seul ou avec d'autres* was a docudrama on the life of university students. Although Arcand did not intend to pursue a career as a filmmaker at that time, he applied for a summer job at the National Film Board of Canada (NFB) and was hired to research and write a screenplay for a documentary on the founder of Québec city, Samuel de Champlain. He was eventually hired to direct the short film *Champlain* (1964) and two other shorts on the history of New France, *Les Montréalistes/Ville-Marie* (1965) and *La route de l'ouest (The Westward Road,* 1965). After working on a few generic shorts in the late 1960s, such as *Volleyball* (1966), he made his first feature-length documentary, *On est au coton (Cotton Mill, Treadmill,* 1970), an examination of the textile industry in Québec. The film was deemed subversive by NFB commissionaire Sydney Newman, and banned from distribution until 1976.

The controversy surrounding *On est au coton* brought attention to Arcand, and he was given the opportunity to direct three fiction films in the private sector: *La maudite galette (The Damed Dough,* 1971), *Réjeanne Padovani* (1973), and *Gina* (1975). The latter offers an intriguing commentary on the then-censored *On est au coton* by presenting a fictionalized account of the shooting of the documentary.

Before leaving the NFB to work in the private sector, Arcand had shot a film on the provincial electoral campaign of 1970. Released in 1972, *Québec: Duplessis et après . . . (Québec: Duplessis and After . . .)* argues that the right-wing ideology of Maurice Duplessis, who dominated the Québec political scene from 1936 to his death in 1959, was still present in the political discourse of 1970, even in the supposedly left-wing platform of the separatist Parti Québécois. With this film, Arcand managed to attract criticism from both sides of the political spectrum. He returned to the NFB in the late 1970s to make his last documentary, *Le confort et l'indifférence (Comfort and Indifference,* 1981), on the failure of the 1980 referendum on Québec's independence (60 percent voted against Québec's sovereignty). Arguing that pro-sovereignty Premier René Lévesque (in power from 1976 to 1985) misread the population's seeming enthusiasm for separation from Canada, Arcand was reproached by nationalists for his claim that residents of Québec were more interested in personal gratification than social and political issues.

Since the 1980s, Arcand has worked exclusively in fiction. *Le déclin de l'empire américain (Decline of the American Empire,* 1986) and *Jésus de Montréal (Jesus of Montreal,* 1989) enjoyed tremendous success both in Canada and abroad.

From *Champlain* to his latest fiction film, *Stardom* (2000), Arcand has consistently adopted a dialogic approach to his material, always articulating at least two discourses simultaneously as a means of "problematizing" any simplistic reading of his subject matter. For instance, although *On est au coton* carries out a Marxist examination of working conditions in textile mills, it also undermines Marxist teleology by demonstrating the proletariat's inability to improve its circumstances. Similarly, in *Le confort et l'indifférence,* he exposes the weaknesses of both the separatist project and the federalist status quo. Arcand rarely provides solutions in his films, but never fails to make his audience think.

ANDRÉ LOISELLE

Biography

Born 1941. Studied history at the Université de Montréal. Directed several documentaries before turning exclusively to narrative/fictional film, 1980s.

Selected Filmography (Documentaries)

1964 *Champlain*, 28 min. (director, screenwriter)
1965 *Les montréalsites/Ville-Marie* 27 min. (director, screenwriter)
1965 *La route de l'ouest / The Westward Road*, 28 min. (director, screenwriter)
1965 *Montréal un jour d'été / Montréal on a Summer Day*, 12 min. (director, editor)
1966 *Volleyball*, 13 min. (director, editor)
1967 *Parcs atlantiques / Atlantic Parks*, 17 min. (director, editor)

1970 *On est au coton / Cotton Mill, Threadmill,* 159 min. (director)
1972 *Québec: Duplessis et après . . . / Québec: Duplessis and After . . .,* 115 min. (director, editor)
1976 *La lutte des travailleurs d'hôpitaux / The Struggle of Hospital Workers,* 28 min. (director)
1981 *Le confort et l'indifférence / Comfort and Indifference,* 109 mins. (director)

Further Reading

Coulombe, Michel, *Denys Arcand: la vraie nature du cinéaste,* Montréal: Boréal, 1993.
Loiselle, André, and Brian McIlroy (eds.), *Auteur/Provacateur: The Films of Denys Arcand,* Trowbridge, England: Flicks Books, 1995.

ARK, THE

(UK, Dineen, 1993)

The Ark of the title refers to the Regent's Park Zoo in London. Shot over the course of a year, Molly Dineen's four-part series won a BAFTA for its portrayal of the zoo as it struggled to find both financial security and a resolution to the often conflicting demands of being both a center of scientific research and a popular visitor attraction.

As producer, photographer, and director, Dineen is central to all aspects of the film. As in her previous work, Dineen uses a minimal contextualizing voice-over and develops an informal, dialogic relationship with her subjects. Dineen's direct interjections are also fairly minimal and used only where necessary to draw out further revelations. These are often interspersed with long observational sequences that reveal the workings of the zoo, and interactions between the staff and between keepers and animals. However, Dineen's presence is clearly announced. The "performance," both in terms of her own interventions and direction, as well as her subjects' response to her and the camera, provides the dynamic on which she builds her narratives (Bruzzi, 2000). By creating such clearly authored films, Dineen makes transparent the constructed nature of documentary filmmaking, and, to a certain extent, avoids the more extravagant claims for objectivity that normally accompany observational approaches. Rather than an attempt to disguise her presence, the films are a record of the developing and fairly informal relationship between Dineen and her subjects.

Episode one, *Survival of the Fittest,* establishes the basic financial crisis facing the zoo. The second episode, *Natural Selection,* illustrates the logistical problems facing the zoo after a round of layoffs, and the next phase of cost cutting—the reduction and dispersal of the animal collection. *The Political Animal* covers the complex negotiations surrounding the arrival of two giant pandas and establishes the growing struggle over the future of the zoo, underscored by the open challenge to management by a dissident group of keepers and the Fellows of the Royal Zoological Society. The last episode, *Tooth and Claw,* shows the final confrontation between the reform group and management, which leads to the departure of David Jones, the zoo's director.

The role and fate of public and cultural institutions in the face of neo-liberal economic theory was a central theme in the political discourse of the 1980s and 1990s. *The Ark* creates an intriguing picture of the internal workings of a venerable and seemingly unshakeable organization under threat in the shifting economic sands of the period. However, the wider issue of the place of zoos in relation to contemporary cultural mores and environmental concerns go unexamined in *The Ark.* Dineen's focus here, as in her other work, is primarily on character. As she states, "Through focusing on the human drama and trying to tell a story through character . . ., you can portray more of life's transparent complexities and contradictions" (MacDonald and Cousins, 1998: p. 365). In the crisis that overtakes the zoo, Dineen's sympathy appears to lie with the keepers, due mainly to their clear dedication to their work and attachment to the animals. Yet, they are presented either as relatively passive in their acceptance of layoffs, or—in the case of those who organize to oust management—inappropriately conspiratorial. The dedication of the keepers is most dramatically revealed in the twenty-four-hour battle to save a sick koala bear. This emergency is contrasted with the ruthless politicking of senior management and the reform group of keepers and Fellows. However, David Jones, the zoo's director, who oversaw the cuts to the staff and collection, becomes a figure who, in turn, is treated with increasing sympathy as his own job is threatened. The eventual death of the koala is tellingly juxtaposed with news of Jones's redundancy.

Dineen's expressed determination to treat all sides with equanimity and to avoid stereotyping makes her appear uncomfortable at times with the very real conflicts made manifest as the crisis develops. Her frequent return in the final episode to seek the views of the world-weary, apolitical Senior Keeper of Birds, David Robinson, is perhaps indicative of the need to find expression for her own neutral stance to the situation (Bruzzi, 2000). Much of Dineen's work, such as *Home from the Hill* (BBC2, 1985) and *In the Company of Men* (BBC2, 1995), is overtly constructed around her relationship with male characters. This is also apparent in *The Ark*. Although the female staff members are approached, these interactions tend to be relatively formal in tone and lack the more familiar, even flirtatious, manner of her dealings with some of the central male figures. Her sympathetic treatment of Jones is perhaps symptomatic of the "glorifying and exonerating of masculinity" (Bruzzi, 2000: p. 169), which, it could be argued, is an underlying tendency in much of her earlier work. The final

shots show the zoo's disused Bear Mountain, portrayed as a desolate wasteland. Shot in this way, this highly symbolic indicator of the zoo's well-being appears to reflect Dineen's own uncertainty about the situation, after the status quo has been disrupted by Jones's dismissal.

If Dineen's approach consciously glosses over the details and wider implications of the zoo's crisis, her ability to develop close relationships with her subjects, and to entreat them to speak openly about themselves before the camera, allows for a revealing glimpse of the zoo to be communicated. *The Ark* is also memorable for the finely observed relationships between the keepers and their animals, providing moments of real affection and humor.

DAVID CHAPMAN

See also **Dineen, Molly; Docusoap**

The Ark (UK, RTO Pictures for BBC2, 1993, 4 × 59 mins.). Photographed, produced, and directed by Molly Dineen. Executive producer, Edward Mirzoeff. Associate producer, Margaret Young. Sound by Phil Streather. Editing by Edwards Roberts with Heather Morley. Graphics by Christine Büttner. Music by John Keane.

Further Reading

Billen, Andrew, "Where's Molly," *Observer Review*, December 10, 1995, p. 9.
Bruzzi, Stella, *New Documentary: A Critical Introduction*, London: Routledge, 2000.
Lawson, Mark, "High Flyer on the Wall," *The Guardian*, October 10, 1995, pp. 10–11.
MacDonald, Kevin, and Cousins, Mark, *Imagining Reality*, London: Faber & Faber, 1998.

ASCENT OF MAN, THE

(UK, 1973)

The Ascent of Man (1973), the BBC-TV's critically acclaimed major television documentary series of 13 × 50 minute parts, is a television history of scientific ideas from prehistory to the late twentieth century. Its central organizing metaphor is the optimism of the "long childhood" of the growth of

human intelligence. The BBC saw the series as the scientific counterpart of *Civilisation,* its impressive series on Western art and architecture. *The Ascent of Man* was written and narrated to camera by the late Dr. Jacob Bronowski, a scientific humanist whose aim throughout was to portray science as a historically contextualized human achievement and progress, made possible by evolving human biology and intelligence, and not as a dry, abstract, and de-personalised array of scientific theories and facts. For example, in Part 5, "The Music of the Spheres," Bronowski humanizes mathematics: "Calculation was an endless delight to Moorish scholars. They loved problems." Similarly, in Part 6, "The Starry Messenger," he observes: "There are good Renaissance reasons—emotional, rather than intellectual—that made [Copernicus] choose the golden sun" as the centre of the universe. Late in life, Bronowski wrote: "All that I have written . . . turns on the same centre: the uniqueness of man that grows out of his struggle (and his gift) to understand both nature and himself" (O'Conner and Robertson, 2003).

Although remembered mainly as a scientist and mathematician, Bronowski was also an accomplished writer and poet. His first book, *The Poet's Defence* (1939), examined the relationship between scientific and poetic or human truth. Bronowski's integration of biology and physics is the central motif of *The Ascent of Man*. In the final chapter of the book of *The Ascent of Man* series, Bronowski states that he moved from physics to biology when it occurred to him that "justice is part of the biological equipment of man," that we are "ethical creatures" and that "knowledge is not a loose-leaf notebook of facts." In his *Science and Human Values* (1956, revised 1965), Bronowski addressed the two-culture debate between science and humanism. He believed that through science the human mind has always sought to find unity in the chaos of nature. Bronowski's instinct for presenting his ideas as strong, interesting narratives is central to his desire to make abstract and normally difficult notions lucid, and to facilitate narrativity, he organised the vast amount of content thematically. Sir David Attenborough, Director of Programmes for the BBC when the series was made, commented, "Bronowski was nothing short of inspired . . . [He] understood that one of the secrets of programme-making is great story telling."

Permeating Bronowski's script is his rejection of the subject-object dualism that characterised scientific rationality up to the nineteenth century and that was discarded in the twentieth century with the revolution in philosophy toward a relational reality: In *The Ascent of Man* he states, "Physics becomes . . . the greatest collective work of art of the twentieth century." In episode 11, "Knowledge or Certainty," Bronowski prioritises humanity over scientific preoccupation in an unforgettable sequence where, as he wades into the ashes pond at Auschwitz death camp, he says to the camera, "We have to cure ourselves of the itch for absolute knowledge and power. We have to close the distance between the push-button order and the human act. We have to touch people." He then reaches into the water and pulls up a handful of mud in a sequence of stop motion shots. The effect, in context, is a sudden, emotionally charged move from cognition to emotion. Another example from Part 11 is when Bronowski states to the camera, "There is no absolute knowledge. And those who claim it, whether scientists or dogmatists, open the door to tragedy. All information is imperfect. We have to treat it with humility. That is the human condition; and that is what quantum physics says. I mean that quite literally." His statement is followed by actual images of what the world would look like if seen successively through each band of the electromagnetic spectrum, not only from infrared to ultraviolet but also through the radio waves of radar, X-rays, and the electron microscope. He concludes that, in seeking the ultimate image of reality, there is no ideal wavelength: "Even the hardest electrons do not give a hard outline. The perfect image is still as remote as the distant stars."

The Ascent of Man, Dr. Jacob Bronowski, writer-narrator, 1973. PBS 13-part series.
[*Courtesy of the Everett Collection*]

Responses to the series also reflect the old tension between Education and Media Studies over assumptions that television is so constrained that it can say nothing that is not intrinsically superficial. This is part of the continuing contest for cultural authority between conceptual knowledge derivable from the printed word and the kind of knowledge of actuality derivable from pictures. Prior to making *The Ascent of Man,* Bronowski had shown considerable ability in both writing and broadcasting for television and radio and he believed that the written word had advantages over the audiovisual medium in the amount of detail of data that can be presented. But as both poet and scientist, Bronowski was interested in successfully reconciling abstraction and actuality: Previously in BBC-TV's *Insight* he had won a reputation for being able to express abstract and difficult ideas in science (e.g., entropy), mathematics (e.g., probability), human intelligence, and philosophy. He similarly approached *The Ascent of Man* with a strong sense of the need for television to acquit itself as a medium capable of effectively representing abstract ideas. The title of the series is ironic: The work of male scientists abounds but the contribution of women to the history and philosophy of science is lacking.

Critically, *The Ascent of Man* is still regarded as a *tour de force* among television documentaries. Dunkley of the *Financial Times* wrote that it was the "most colossal concept I have ever come across in television," and the *Daily Telegraph* described its form as "splendid." Another observed that *The Ascent of Man* is a series "looked up to by every producer of factual, educational programmes" and that it is made "in a style much copied since." *The Ascent of Man* is number 65 in the British Film Institute's list of the top "TV 100" and number 7 on its list of the "Top 20" in the "Factual Category." The series continues to be broadcast—for example, in June 2004 on UKTV cable network.

BRUCE HORSFIELD

Further Reading

The Ascent of Man, BBC-TV, London, 1973.

Bronowski, Jacob, *The Ascent of Man*, Boston: Little, Brown, 1974.

O'Connor, J. J., and Robertson, E. F., *Jacob Bronowski*, School of Mathematics and Statistics, University of St Andrews, Scotland, 2003. www.history.mcs.st-andrews.Ac.uk/mathematicians/bronowski.html.

"The BFI Top 100: *Ascent of Man*." http://www.bfi.org.uk/features/tv/100/list/prog.php3?is=65.

"The BFI Top 100: Top 20 in the Factual Category." http://www.bfi.org.uk/features/tv/100/list/genre.php3?gid=4.

ASSOCIATION INTERNATIONALE DES DOCUMENTARISTES

"The documentary film is in a sorry state, and I think it would be a good idea to do something about it." With these words, Danish filmmaker Jrgen Roos turned to his Italian colleague, Gian Vittorio Baldi, head of the Istituto del Documentario Italiano (IDI), in March 1963. According to Roos, the remedy was a global organization of documentary filmmakers. Later that year, Baldi met his Belgian colleague, Henri Storck at the Festival dei Populi in Florence. Both reached a similar conclusion and decided to set up an international organization. In October 1964 the Association Internationale des Documentaristes (AID) was launched at the Mannheim Film Festival. The AID was registered in Belgium, for purely practical reasons, as it was the only country where an international association could be set up by Royal Decree, without going through complex procedures. John Grierson was elected president; Joris Ivens, Georges Rouquier, and Richard Leacock were named vice-presidents; and Storck was named treasurer. The secretariat was in Rome, at Baldi's IDI office.

Roos and Baldi believed that the AID should avoid the most glaring mistakes made by the World Union of Documentary (1947–1950). Therefore, no effort was made to define the genre, as such undertaking would, it was believed, only cause divisions. Members joined on an individual basis, paying an annual fee of $10. Jean Rouch, Mario Ruspoli, Don Pennebaker, Edgar Anstey, Erwin Leiser, Bert Haanstra, Albert Maysles, Pierre Perrault, and Luc de Heusch were among the first to join. They represented the widest possible variety in styles and approaches with regard to documentary filmmaking. When East European filmmakers reported that they were not permitted to join on an individual basis, efforts were made to find some form of accommodation, but the AID leadership persistently refused the membership of national organizations from the Socialist countries. Given that such organizations often had up to 1,000 or more members, they would inevitably have dominated the AID, a consequence that the AID's leaders, remembering the fate of the WUD, wished to avoid. Still, Karl Gass (German Democratic Republic, or East Germany) and Roman Karmen (Soviet Union) managed to actively participate by traveling to the festivals where the AID met. Marianne Szemes (Hungary) circumvented the problem by setting up an AID section in her country. Her interesting proposal, inspired by Cesare Zavattini and his Cinegiornali Liberi, to have members exchange "letters" shot on 16mm film stock, failed to materialize.

At the start, the AID's presence was largely restricted to the growing number of film festivals. In Leipzig, Mannheim, Oberhausen, Tours, and Florence, AID members met and held heated debates about the merits of cinéma vérité, the social role of the cinema, and other issues. In February 1968, the first and only Annual General Meeting (AGM) took place in Algiers. AID members were flown in by charter plane from Rome, assured of luxury accommodations and taken on excursions to exotic places. But Baldi, who had put this package together with the support of the Algerian government, came under fire for using AID funds to meet his personal ends. Furthermore, the meeting was overshadowed by heavy-handed attempts by the Algerian government to prevent its own filmmakers from speaking out freely.

After the AGM, Baldi was forced to resign from his position as secretary. Rouquier was his successor (with Basil Wright taking over the presidency from Grierson), but it was only after Marion Michelle took over administrative affairs that the AID regained its sense of purpose. Originally a photographer, Michelle had been Ivens's assistant and secretary of the International Federation of Film Archives. Her Paris apartment became the new center of the AID. From 1971 to 1972, three issues of *AID News*, a cross between a newsletter and a serious journal, were published. Rouquier, who had started his profes-

sional career as a typographer, was a great help in this regard. Among the numerous contributors were Grierson, Wright, Haanstra, Storck, Hurwitz, Ivens, and other members. The academic Jean-Claude Batz discussed the implications of the introduction of the videocassette, while critic Gideon Bachman raised serious questions on the issue of television and truth.

By 1972, the AID had more than 130 members. Michelle's role was taken over by the Zürich-based documentarist Erwin Leiser and Moritz and Erika de Hadeln. This couple (i.e., Moritz and Erika de Hadeln) had founded the Nyon Film Festival, the location of which in neutral Switzerland seemed ideal for meetings between East and West. There were plans for an international centre to distribute the films made by AID members. Moreover, the Staatliches Filmarchiv der DDR offered to build up a documentary film archive. Although the AID leadership admitted that the archive in East Berlin had possibly the best storage facilities in the world, they were wary of the political strings attached to the offer. Neither the distribution center nor the documentary archive ever materialized. Instead, a meeting on the ethics, aesthetics, and dramaturgy of the documentary was organized in conjunction with the Nyon Film Festival in October 1974. For five days filmmakers and critics discussed a range of issues related to the topic of the meeting, using films that were screened at the festival as examples. It turned out to be the last big event held under the auspices of the AID. In the second half of the 1970s, the association slowly came to an end. Many members continued to meet each other informally at the increasing number of film festivals, while some put their energy in building national networks, such as AG Dok in Germany. In May 1999, the AID was officially disbanded.

BERT HOGENKAMP

See also **Baldi, Gian Vittorio; Roos, Jørgen**

Further Reading

AID News, 3 issues, 1971–1972.

Hogenkamp, Bert, "Definitions and Divisions: The International Documentary Film Movement from 1946 to 1964," in *International Documentary Filmfestival Amsterdam 1999 Catalogue*, Amsterdam: IDFA, 1999, pp.160–165.

van Lier, Miryam, "Better to Have a Big Useless Noise than None at All. The Association Internationale des Documentaristes, 1964–1999, in *International Documentary Filmfestival Amsterdam 1999 catalogue*, Amsterdam: IDFA, 1999, pp.166–170.

AUBERVILLIERS

(France, Lotar, 1945)

Aubervilliers was made early in the post-World War II period by the director Eli Lotar. The French provisional government under Charles de Gaulle had some communist representatives, and the Fourth Republic, the Marshall Plan, and the prosperity and baby boom of the late 1940s and 1950s were yet to come. In the film, the narrator asserts that the ruins of Aubervilliers, a suburb of Paris, "are not the brand new ruins of the war," but rather "ancient, commonplace ruins, the mere ruins of workers' misery."

Appearing ten years after Anstey and Elton's *Housing Problems, Aubervilliers* embraces the documentary forms of its time. Shot with no

Aubervilliers, 1945.
[*Still courtesy of the British Film Institute*]

synchronous sound, it relies on commentary and music to maintain its discursive function. The narrative is driven by both the commentary and a song performed by Germaine Montero, both written by Jacques Prévert. The essentially denunciative intention intertwines with nostalgia, irony, humanism, and optimism. This approach recalls the feature films of French poetic realism. Lotar had previously worked as a cameraperson with Jean Renoir (*Une Partie de Campagne*), Pierre Prévert (*L'Affaire est dans le Sac*), Luis Buñuel (*Las Hurdes*), and Joris Ivens (*Zuiderzee*).

In a firm demonstration, sustained by striking and often shocking images, the film rises up in protest before misery, siding with workers and paying tribute to their strength and dignity. The commentary, as well as the song, salute repeatedly the "good children of Aubervilliers, good children of proletarians, good children of misery, good children of the whole world." At the end, the voice-over states, "It is once again the simple, rude hand of the worker that will shake up this stiff and depressed world, this world that badly needs to change, that will finally change some day."

The documentary strategy employed by *Aubervilliers* is threefold. An unconcealed camera presents shots and scenes that depict the general mood of the time. Short sequences are obviously reenacted, such as one of a girl walking to a water fountain. More specifically, persons working at home are filmed frontally, as if posing for a photographer, in a collaborative relationship. Their words, failing to be recorded, are reformulated off screen.

Aubervilliers is the major work of a minor filmmaker.

JEAN-LUC LIOULT

See also *Housing Problems*; Ivens, Joris

Aubervilliers (France, Lotar, 1945, 24 min.). Directed by Eli Lotar. Co-directed by Jacques Prévert and Joseph Kosma. Narrated by Jacques Prévert. Filmed in Aubervilliers, France.

Further Reading

Collas, Gérald, "D'*Aubervilliers* (1945) à *La Courneuve* (1967), Correspondances," *Images Documentaires* 20, 1995, pp. 23–32.

AUSTRALIA

From the very birth of cinema, successive Australian governments had observed and developed strategies to explore and use the possibilities of film as a means of national projection. Before 1912, the Commonwealth Government contracted private production companies to film official events and produce short nonfiction films for theatrical release. Following the appointment of an official cinematographer in 1912, the Cinema and Photographic Branch was established on a temporary basis with the brief "to film anything of interest."

On 27 May 1913, the Department of External Affairs sent a letter to cinematographer Bert Ives: "Sir: in confirmation of my telegrams of yesterday's date I have the honour to inform you that the Minister has approved of your appointment as cinematographer and photographer in this department at the rate of pounds five per week." Ives was now the official cameraman to the nation (he

remained in the position until 1939), with the more specific brief to make films promoting Australia abroad and to record major events.

The new department developed along predictable lines. During the 1920s and 1930s, the Melbourne Cinema Division increased its staff and produced newsreels and short features, much as the Empire Marketing Board under John Grierson would a decade later in Britain. Wheat, beef, and tobacco were featured in a series, "Know Your Country," using a simplistic flat-on film style and using the mantra of Australia—"the vast and rich land."

From 1915 to 1930, approximately one reel of film per week was produced by the Branch for theatrical release. During the 1930s, sound films were released less regularly. There are several of these in the National Film and Sound Archive Collection, including *This Is Australia*, *Mineral Wealth,* and *Australian Sugar*. Such films were typically overburdened with long-winded commentaries that were still the official mode of address until the war years when there was something to be portentous about. The stereotypes of the nation thus projected were directly in line with the views of national character advanced by historians such as C.E.W. Bean and film studios (Efftee and Cinesound) producing epic and pastoral features or rural comedies like *Dad and Dave* (1932).

Documentary features were also intermittently produced, notably featuring the location cinematography of pioneering documentary maker Captain Frank Hurley. Hurley was celebrated for his sweeping romantic nature still photography and film work in the heroic style of colonial painters like John Glover. Hurley established an early international fame with his Antarctic films *Home of the Blizzard* (1913) and *In the Grip of the Polar Pack-Ice* (1917), which contained much sensationalisation of "cannibal attacks" but was a huge touring success in England and the United States as well as later tropical adventures documented in *Pearls and Savages* (1921).

The now-developed tradition of filming in exotic or dangerous locations would, sixty years later, be a feature of the political documentaries of Gil Scrine and David Bradley (*Chile Hasta Cuendo*, *Frontline* qv). During World War II, it saw the rise of a generation of war correspondents. Damien Parer won the Best Documentary Oscar in 1942 for his coverage of Pacific action in World War II in *Kokoda Front Line* (Cinesound Review, 1942). Following an invitation by the Australian government, John Grierson visited Australia in 1940 to report on the setting up of a more responsive and creative film production arm of government along the lines of the Crown Film Unit.

Grierson strongly recommended the nontheatrical use of 16mm film for general purposes. The Commonwealth Government established the ANFB (Australian National Film Board) in 1945 with the principal task of overseeing the production and distribution of documentary films and the importation of overseas documentaries. The National Library, in collaboration with the state libraries, became the national distributor of 16mm films for nontheatrical, educational use.

Instead of being set up as an independent statutory authority along the lines of the Canadian National Film Board, the ANFB in Australia soon came under the direct control of the Department of Information. In 1946, Stanley Hawes was appointed to the new position of Producer-in-Chief, a position he held until his retirement in 1970. Hawes was effectively a Grierson appointment, having worked with the GPO Film Unit in London and later with Grierson in Ottawa before accepting the new post in Australia.

The key films produced by the Film Division in this period were *Native Earth* (John Heyer, 1946), *Journey of a Nation* (John Heyer, 1947), *School in the Mail-Box* (Stanley Hawes, 1947), *Born in the Sun* (John Heyer, 1947), *The Cane Cutters* (Hugh McInnes, 1948), *The Valley Is Ours* (John E. Seyer, 1948), *Goldtown* (R. Maslyn Williams, 1949), *Mike and Stefani* (R. Maslyn Williams, 1951), and *Outback Patrol* (Lee Robinson, 1952). All of the films of this period were very much in the GPO Film Unit mold, but featured mobile and fluid camera work (influenced by the successful Cinesound and Movietone Newsreels) and a keen sense of a plastic landscape molded by heat and time to very different forms and vistas than the familiar European models. Cities might look much alike the world over but the documentary filmmakers of this period were concerned, in line with nationalist literary movements, to express the difference of the Australian landscape and its unique challenges. Thus, *School in a Mail-Box* (1947) dealt with the unique outback correspondence school systems developed to serve far-flung rural communities and the oeuvre of the filmmakers taken as a collective expressed a coherent vision of Australia as a country where highly urbanised cities clung to the rim of a harsh and unrelenting (the favourite adjectives of voice-over) inland.

The outstanding filmmaker of this period was to be John Heyer, whose best work was with the ANFB and whose most iconic and successful work was *Back of Beyond* (Shell, 1954), a lyrical film about the overland delivery run of the mail and provisions truck driver, shot entirely on location often in the most difficult circumstances—a decision rewarded with some of the finest location cinematography of the period and an outstanding film dealing with a vanished outback world that still has resonance today.

The aims and styles of the ANFB production slate changed little throughout the 1950s and 1960s, The 1964 film, *From the Tropics to the Snow,* however, dealt in a self-reflexive way with the efforts of a team of ANFB producers to showcase Australia's tourist attraction. It provided a humorous insight into the production system and it introduced many of the key figures of the postwar period. The film is now considered an essential research aid for any film historian rather than a great piece of documentary work, indicating an institution more interested in self-perpetuation than breaking new ground—or the rules.

Public Broadcasting and Documentary Practice

The national broadcaster ABC (Australian Broadcasting Commission to 1983, the Australian Broadcasting Corporation thereafter) provided both the training and the showcase for more innovative documentary practice from the introduction of television in 1956.

The tradition of Australia's Public Broadcaster as major producer of documentaries, inherited from the BBC in the early 1960s, continues today in diminished form. In the 1960s, outstanding documentary filmmakers like director Bill Fitzwater (*Boom Radio*, 1967) and Geoff Barnes (until recently head of Documentary at the ABC) all shot their early films with the national broadcaster. Oscar-winning cinematographers Dean Semmler (*Dances with Wolves*) and John Seale (*The English Patient*) both trained as news and documentary cameramen) at the ABC.

The best work of salaried ABC directors and crew was often to be seen in cinema-verite documentary series such as *Chequerboard* (1968–1972). Other series that used documentary techniques and often tackled major subjects were *A Big Country* (1968 and continuing) and *Four Corners* (1961 and continuing), based on the BBC Panorama series, which on occasion continues with its one-hour format to produce and break major investigative stories, beginning with a controversial feature documentary on the Returned Services League (RSL) in 1963 and continuing to disturb the status quo to this day. As a documentary forum, *Four Corners* has consistently produced programmes that have effected more social and political change than any comparable series in the media history of the nation.

Outside the Public Broadcasters: Independent Documentary and Dramatised Documentary

Today, the market and creative development systems are now dominated by a near monopoly on larger budget film funding by the (Australian) Film Finance Corporation. Some documentaries continue to be produced by both the ABC and the multicultural broadcaster, SBS, under various banners (*The View from Here*, ABC) through the late 1990s, and some fine documentaries are still being produced in-house—notably and most regularly, the short weekly documentary series *Australian Story* (1996 and continuing).

Former ABC producers such as Jenny Brockie continue to contribute personal evocations of the Australian (mainly suburban) zeitgeist with series like *Our Street* (2000–2001). Here, personal style and involvement painted a striking series of portraits of Australia in cinema verite style, focusing on lives as far apart as those of the middle class in the larger coastal cities to the wilder eccentricities of hot and coastal Darwin.

The most influential free-to-air filmmakers of the period work outside the main channels as freelancers and include the writer Ian David, whose research and obsession led to the making of two dramatised documentaries of great influence, politically as well as aesthetically. The first was *Police State* (Chris Noonan, 1989), which mixed transcripts and newsclips to project a detailed and powerful vision of Queensland as a police state under the long surviving rightist government of Joh Bjelke-Petersen. David writes dramatised documentary films that stylistically and thematically have much in common with Errol Morris's *Thin Blue Line* (1988) in their handling of suppressed materials and silenced witnesses. *Blue Murder* (Michael Jenkins, 1995) moved from a collagist approach to a more dramatised and character-driven style, documenting corruption within the New South Wales police force that had major legal repercussions and was partly responsible for the establishment of a Royal Commission. Few writers, however, have been as influential as David, and his writer-director (auteurist) mode of work remains the norm as well as the most likely to be funded under the rubric of "director's vision" obsessively employed by all the major bodies (both Federal and State).

SBS and its independent production arm, SBSi, have also become key players in factual film production from experimental and arts programming to documentaries commissioned to reflect the multicultural remit of the channel. Arguably the most successful and important initiatives from SBS came with a season of documentaries on aboriginal dispossession (*Unfinished Business*, 2000) from which grew the outstanding films *Stolen Generations* by Tom Zubrycki and Sally Browning and *Cry From the Heart* (Jeni Kendall). Both films examined the disastrous effects of the policies of forced removal of aboriginal children that had been the subject of a national inquiry (published as *Bringing Them Home*, released in 1997. These and similar films on Aboriginality and cultural identity have been produced and screened by SBS at a steady rate and seem set to continue as a core activity for the broadcaster as long as it survives under its current charter.

The Independent Sector Up to the Present

The most consistently interesting and provocative documentary makers of the last two decades have been those filmmakers who engaged with the margins of political and social themes.

David Bradbury's documentary ouevre has proved paradigmatic of many Australian filmmakers' fascination with international political trouble spots and the exotic. Works echoed the much earlier work of Frank Hurley and Damien Parer and the more recent outstanding work of front-line war zone cinematographers like Neil Davis, who was himself the subject of a film by Bradbury.

"Keep the camera rolling, no matter what" was Neil Davis's motto, and in 1985 he literally filmed his own death. Bradbury's powerful tribute, *Frontline*, was an account of the Vietnam War as seen through the camera of Neil Davis and is a fine recor, full of astonishing action footage of a life lived on the edge—Davis's own death and legend echoing Damien Parer's death while filming in a war zone forty years before. The more political films of Bradbury include *Public Enemy Number One* (1980), an examination of controversial Australian journalist Wilfred Burchett who chose to report from the "other side" in the Vietnam War and whose unorthodox views and activities caused him to be labeled a traitor by many. Burchett was the first Western journalist to report on the devastating aftereffects of the atomic bomb dropped on Hiroshima.

Nicaragua—No Pasaran (Bradbury, 1984) tracks from 1978 the postrevolutionary Sandinista movement and the past, present, and future of this small Central American nation—another strongly personal portrait of a brutal military dictatorship made during a three-month visit to Chile. The footage reveals a country torn with civil strife and political unrest; military intimidation of the population, and indiscriminate arrests, murder, torture, and disappearances. Bradbury's personal involvement in his subjects and his sharp sense of irony are nowhere more apparent than in the opening scenes showing a wealthy right-wing couple in their Santiago mansion pontificating uninterrupted on the excellence of Augusto Pinochet's attitude to and actions against dissenters (especially young students). Bradbury often narrates his own work, diary style, and his work overall has a spare quality that makes overt political comment unnecessary. *South of the Border* (1988) examines how the political and economic struggle in Central America is expressed through the music of the people south of the U.S. border. Recently, Bradbury has turned to more local Australian themes with films such as *State of Shock* (1989), which deals with a notorious court case involving the dispossessed semi-tribal aborigines.

Tom Zubrycki is widely respected as one of Australia's leading documentary filmmakers. He has worked consistently over the last decades as director of a series of films with strong social and political themes. *Waterloo* (1981), *Kemira: A Diary of a Strike* (1984), and *Friends and Enemies* (1987) were all shot in an offhand style. The subjects were allowed free expressive rein and thus remained valuable documents of Australian union and class struggle in confrontations in what were primarily heavy industry and inner-urban settings. *Lord of the Bush* (1989), *Amongst Equals* (1990), *Homelands* (1993), and *Billal* (1996) continued Zubrycki's role as diarist of social upheaval and issues-based filmmaking. Later he was to become equally influential as a producer of equally edgy films ranging from the migrant experience, as relived through the filmmaker's return to a war-shattered former Yugoslavia in *Exile in Sarajevo* (1997) (International Emmy 1998) as well as more quirky local subjects like *Dr Jazz* (1998), and social documents such as *Whiteys Like Us* (1999) and *Stolen Generations* (2000).

Arguably Zubrycki's own most "international" film was also his most internationally successful: *The Diplomat* (2000) follows East Timor's freedom fighter and Nobel Peace Prize winner José Ramos Horta in the final tumultuous year of his campaign to secure independence for his country. This feature-length film takes up Ramos Horta's story in the final dramatic stages of his long journey—the fall of Indonesia's President Suharto, the referendum to determine East Timor's future, the overwhelming vote for independence, the devastating carnage that ensued, the intervention of United Nations peacekeepers, and Ramos Horta's final triumphant return to his homeland.

Dennis O'Rourke, the most internationally recognised of recent Australian independent documentary filmmakers, for example, began his career with two films dealing with the early days of Papua New Guinea (Niugini) independence: *Yumi Yet* (1976) and *Ileksen* (1978), featuring striking handheld cinematography by Dick Marks. The films are distinguished by unusual access to key figures of power, such as the first Prime Minister of Niugini, Michael Somare.

O'Rourke had now attracted international funding as well as critical acclaim. His next film, *Yap... How Did You Know We'd Like TV?* (1980), dealt with the total corruption of local Solomon Islands' culture by a wholesale bombardment of American daily television (flown in daily from Los Angeles). The film revealed a sardonic streak in O'Rourke's later projects that became a recognisable trait in all his work as he has moved into edgier territories with *The Shark Callers Of Kontu* (1982), *Couldn't Be Fairer* (1984), and the fine *Half Life: A Parable for the Nuclear Age* (1985), which established O'Rourke as a world filmmaker whose filmmaking and sociological interests were now outrunning the Pacific Rim.

Nevertheless, O'Rourke returned to Niugini with *Cannibal Tours* (1988), a witty examination of European tourists juxtaposed with the "authentic" lives of the Niuginians held up for their entertainment.

With (again government funded) *The Good Woman of Bangkok* (1991) O'Rourke became the centre of an international controversy as the film documented his relationship with a Thai prostitute, Aoi. The resulting outcries circled the globe through every means, both at academic conferences and at professional associations, and raised issues of gender, sexism, third-world politique, and exploitation.

O'Rourke's work continues to provoke and attract audiences and his film *Cunnamulla* (2000) played to a wide art house audience in Australia and has garnered interest and acclaim internationally. Although it deals for the first time with O'Rourke's own very personal "'backyard"—the people who live in the fast-failing outback town of Cunnamulla—the film, with all the irony and quiet savagery, is O'Rourke's best work.

Bob Connolly was another filmmaker to have developed his skills at the ABC (1964–1978), first as a foreign correspondent and later as a documentary filmmaker. He and Robin Anderson (as cameraman-director and sound recorder, respectively) worked from a base of strict social observation and deep research, using on location a remarkable degree of ability to relax and literally live with their filmic subjects. Anderson also had worked at the ABC, as a researcher, and both he and Connolly left to begin work as independent filmmakers with the masterful interweaving of themes of colonialism and kinship with *First Contact* (1983). The film was an anthropological study of the impact of the pioneering Leahy brothers in New Guinea Highlands in the 1930s, leading to a consideration of both the cultural impact of their visit and the effects produced on Old Joe Leahy's scarcely acknowledged son, Joe, the child of a liaison with a tribal woman. This subject and associated themes developed further in three years of filming that produced *Joe Leahy's Neighbours* (1989) and the richly ironic and ultimately tragicomic *Black Harvest* (1992). These films, like the earlier parts of the trilogy, won many international and local awards and enjoyed successful cinema releases, setting a pattern that has now become quite common for at least two or three major documentaries a year—creating an broad audience where none had really existed outside the academy since the 1950s. Anderson and Connolly have become the exemplars of the nonpurist anthropological style that has helped raise both public appreciation and, in association with independent cinema owners, much broader cinema screenings and good box office returns for most of their films in the commercial film market. Their success has also interacted with that of other equally accessible filmmakers' works, notably those of Dennis O'Rourke, in being able to guarantee good audiences by strength of reputation alone.

Rats in the Ranks (1996) was also the product of Connolly and Anderson's ability to win the trust of their subjects. This film, also running for a long season in cinemas before becoming a best-selling video, deals with the machinations and power struggles in an inner-city municipal council led by a Machiavellian mayor who will do anything to stay in power. The extraordinary access to all parties to the back-room death struggles leading up to an internal party schism and the next election are as powerful and revealing as Pennebaker and Hegedus' *War Room* (1992) (which, along with *Rats in the Ranks*, makes a perfect Australian political primer).

Equally successful and also the result of nearly a year of filming is *Facing the Music* (2001), another multiple award winner that also penetrated the independent cinema market, indicating that Connolly and Anderson now had a steady following and a "brand name" among audiences. Shot inside Sydney University's Music Department and focusing on the travails of Department Head Professor Anne Boyd (herself also a noted Australian composer), this film actually treads deeper waters of unconscious irony than even the filmmakers may have realised. Their portrait of a threatened university department reveals a group of apparently self-serving academics—and, in one shocking scene, a young woman composer is both verbally and artistically assaulted by a teacher. However, the positioning of the film seems to be on the side of the "threatened" teachers. What are perceived by the filmmakers as the strengths of the focus of the film, the professor and the role of the Music Department, are never interrogated.

The subsequent selling of the film by the filmmakers as unproblematic suggests that Australian documentary or its audiences are not necessarily possessed of a wide range of analytical or comparative tools. If shot and screened in Europe, for example, this film might well have been pitched as a satire on academic self-absorption and the dysfunctional approach taken by so many teachers working in "creative" departments to their very raison d'etre, the hapless students. For these reasons, of course, *Facing the Music* is the most tantalising and intriguing work yet from Australia's leading cinema verité team.

Few documentaries have dealt in detail with the supposed Australian national obsessions of sport and drink. Remarkably, only one major documentary has penetrated the mystique of a sporting club, but Michael Cordell's *The Year of the Dogs* (1997) manages to sum up an Australian ambivalence to sporting heroes with cinema vérité filming and a laconic and undercutting editorial style. As with the work of Connolly and Anderson and Dennis O'Rourke's later projects, *Year of the Dogs* proved a success at cinemas. Audiences were composed in roughly equal parts of sports enthusiasts and those in search of the more complex pleasures of the well-made cinema vérité film in a society where subjects are often surprisingly candid and articulate about their obsessions.

Although the supposed wry self-deprecating defining characteristics of Australians are not always in evidence in documentary (feature films have appropriated that territory), two film have become small national treasures by stressing the darker aspects of living in contemporary Australia: David Caesar's *Bodywork* (1989) and Mark Lewis's *Cane Toads* (1987).

Bodywork is a cool and subtle gaze at the undertaking profession and Australian attitudes to death and what follows, shot in a Candide-like (wide angles) shooting style. The international success of the film is in part due to Caesar's great directorial control over the carefully composed "look" of the film. Caesar uses the interviewees as dramatis personae and often interviews two or more at a time to increase the sardonic effect. This documentary, still very influential as a model for film students of the full possibilities of the care-

fully constructed documentary, led Caesar directly into a career as a maker of sharp and satirical feature films.

Cane Toads, too, was a success and won numerous awards. It took a bleak view of the disastrous attempts of overly optimistic scientists to solve ecological problems. The film is aobout the introduction in the 1930s of the Bufo Marinus (Cane Toad) to Queensland (in semi-tropical northern Australia) to control small insects annoying the crops. Toads multiply and then assume a horrific and unending advance from the northern Australia slowly throughout the nation. Bleak, yet very funny, *Cane Toads* remains influential and indicates a road down which Australian documentary may profitably stray.

JONATHAN DAWSON

See also Cane Toads; Good Woman of Bangkok; Heyer, John; O'Rourke, Dennis; Zubrycki, Tom

Further Reading

Bean, C. E. W., *The Story of Anzac*, Sydney: Angus & Robertson, 1921.

Berry, C., H. Hamilton, and L. Jayamanne (eds.), *The Filmmaker and the Prostitute*, Sydney: Power Institute, 1997.

Bertrand, Ina, *Government and Film in Australia*, Sydney: Currency Press, 1981.

Bringing Them Home: The Report of the National Inquiry into the Separation of Aboriginal and Torres Strait Islander Children from their Families, Canberra: Commonwealth of Australia, 1997.

Creed, B., et al. (eds.), *Don't Shoot Darling: Women's Independent Filmmaking in Australia*, Sydney: Greenhouse, 1987.

Cunningham, Stuart, and Graeme Turner, *The Media in Australia: Industries, Audiences*, Sydney: Allen and Unwin, 1993.

Dawson, Jonathan, and Bruce Molloy, *Queensland Images*, Brisbane: University of Queensland Press, 1990.

Dimond, Peter, *Writing Documentary Script and Narration*, Sydney: Australian Film and Television School, 1980.

FitzSimons, Trish, Pat Laughren, and Dugald Williams, "Towards a Contemporary History of Australian Documentary," *Metro*, 123 (2000), pp. 62–73.

Hartley, John, *Popular Reality: Journalism, Modernity, Popular Culture*, London: Arnold, 1996.

Inglis, Ken, *This Is the ABC*, Melbourne: Melbourne University Press, 1983.

Lansell, Ross, and Peter Beilby, *The Documentary Film in Australia*, Melbourne: Cinema Papers, 1982.

Moran, Albert, *The Projection of Australia*, Sydney: Currency, 1991.

Moran, Albert, and Tom O'Regan (eds.), *Australian Film Reader*, Sydney: Currency Press, 1985.

The Big Picture: Documentary Filmmaking in Australia, Papers from the Second Australian Documentary Conference, Clayton Monash University, 1991.

Turner, Graeme, *National Fictions*, Sydney: Allen and Unwin, 1986.

AUSTRIA

The Origins: 1895 to 1918

In the summer of 1895, a moving pictures machine was installed for the first time in Prater, an amusement quarter that continues to exist in Vienna today. Five machines were placed in a "Kinetoscope Hall," where documentary pictures from American Thomas Alva Edison and his assistants were exhibited (Fritz, 1980). The Viennese Prater was one of the first sites of the Habsburg monarchy Austria–Hungary, where moving pictures were projected; also, Prater was a popular film location during the beginnings of film history. On March 26, 1896, Eugene Dupont, collaborator of the firm Lumiere, organized the first public performance in Austria: Documentary films about Vienna were shown in the building located at Kaertnerstrasse 45 (later in the contiguous building number 39). The work of Charles Moisson, principal operator of Lumiere, was presented there. In the exhibition programme were the films *Feuerwehr-Centrale am Hof, Kaertnerstrasse Le Ring,* and *Freudenau, Sattelraum nach dem Pisek-Rennen.* Pictures of Prater—such as *Der Volksprater, Der Prater,* and *Die Hauptalle (Main Avenue)*—were among the scenes that Alexander Promio and his assistant and interpreter Alexander Werschinger were shooting in Vienna on behalf of Lumiere in mid-April 1896. These pictures belong to the earliest examples of Austrian cinematography. The company Pathe Freres's produced in 1908 two documentary films: *Blumenkorso in Mai (Flower Parade in May)* and *In der Prater Hauptallee (In Prater's Main Avenue)* (Buettner/Dewald, 2002: p. 22).

Pioneer documentary films, which have been referred in this way only since 1926, joined images together without tying them into a story. Different film types, such as newsreels, scientific films, and educational and cultural films, were later developed from this technique. At the beginning, the camera viewer played the role of a passive observer; afterwards, the camera viewer was converted into a tourist or researcher (Büettner and Dewald, 2003). The camera reflected the world exactly like it was: The Viennese places filmed between 1896 and 1910

by Lumiere, Pathe, and other directors staged representation rooms for the Viennese bourgeoisie. The Opera House, the "Ring," the "Trabrennplatz," and the "Burgmusik" staged theatrical rooms in the film *Wien um 1908 (Vienna around 1908)* (director: Pathe Freres) within the frame of related patterns between time and behavior. The early documentary film showed principally the large city and the bulk as admiring spectacles in themselves. In this sense, in the film presented in 1896 by Lumiere (Kaerntnerstrasse 45) *Verkehr bei dem Cinematographen (Traffic by the Cinematographer)*, the spectators convert themselves into their own performers. "Open to the public" is an understood political institutional kind of openness that serves only to create a specific audience (around 1900, only 4 percent of the inhabitants were elective). The early (documentary) film created a carefully selected image of the city and therefore did not show only a sensory real picture in which the spectacle is based. At the turn of the century these early film pioneers were followed by other filmmakers who produced "scientific films." As examples we can cite the ethnologist Rudolf Poech and the Viennese teacher Alto Arche. The first attempts took place from 1904 to 1908. The beginnings of the "racial research" in Austria are associated with the ethnographic film pioneer, the Viennese doctor, and the anthropologist Rudolf Poech (1870–1921). The central themes of Poech's first film about the so-called *Buschmaenner der Kalahari (Kalahari Bushmen)*, which was produced between 1908 and 1909, were technical aspects of specific works, such as culling and trampling on grass and bulbs, fabricating ropes, and/or sparking off a fire. The external characteristics of the people created by Poech's camera categorized him as a specific "people classificator."

In 1909, the first Austrian full-length documentary film was shown as an independent film in Viennese movie theaters: *Die Kaisermanoever in Maehren (The King's Maneuver in Moravia).* The film *Se, Majestaet Kaiser Franz Josef I auf der Gemsjagd (Majesty Kaiser Franz Josef I at the Gem Hunt)* was shown in the Viennese Prater in the cinematographic exhibition "International Hunt Exhibition Vienna 1910" (Pathe Freres,

August 1909). Besides feature films, film pioneers such as the couple Kolm (*Der Faschingzug in Ober-St. Veit, Der Trauerzug Sr. Exzellenz des Buergermeisters Dr. Karl Jueger*) [(*The Carnival Train at Ober St. Veit, The Funeral Procession Sr. Exzellenz of Mayor Dr. Karl Jueger*), 1910], regularly produced documentary films. In 1910, Graf Alexander "Sascha" Kolowrat—he later founded the *Sascha Film*—also began with the production of documentary films (*Die Gewinnung des Erzes am steirischen Erzberg in Eisenerz*) (*Ore Extraction at the Ore Mountain in the Iron Ore, 1912*). Hans Theyer shot cultural films about glassblowers, painters, and carpenters; his works lead to the creation of the "Central Office for Scientific and Educational Cinematography."

This function of the documentary film had also been used to give pictures another conscious meaning, which was deliberately created, particularly during war time. In August 1914, the war department commissioned film producers *Sascha-Filmfabrik, Wiener Kunstfilmindustrie-Gesellschaft,* and *Oesterreichisch-ungarische Kinoindustrie-Gesellschaft,* the production of war film propaganda based on war archives. The first serial of the *Kriegs-Journal* (*War Journal*) produced by *Wiener Kunstfilm* appeared in September. At the end of 1914, *Sascha-Film* in cooperation with *Philipp und Pressburger* and the *Oesterreichisch-Ungarischen Kinoindustrie-Gesellschaft* presented a war newsreel titled *Oesterreichischer Kino-Wochenbericht vom noerdlichen und suedlichen Kriegsschauplatz* (*Austrian Weekly Report from Northern and Southern War Theater*). Until 1918, field cinema was limited to showing the world of upstate images. Front-line experiences could not find a visual expression any more.

In 1918, *UFA* started the production of documentaries in Berlin with a popular scientific content. This concept was imitated in Austria by Kurt Koefinger in his tourist films of the 1920s and later in the controlled propaganda documentary films of the *Wien-Film* (1938–1945). The newsreels had combined characteristics of newscast and chronicle documentaries in its theme mixture of politics, sports, and culture, which actually were sometimes presented in Newsreel-Cinemas (since 1936 as nonstop cinemas in Vienna and also in Linz, Salzburg, and Innsbruck). The Viennese documentary film was presented as a "war journal" for the first time in 1914, followed in 1930 to 1933 by *Sascha-Messter-Wochenschau* (*The Newsreel of Sascha Messter*), an international newsreel production based on the Austrian "Selenophon" technique (*Selenophon* together with *Gustav-Mayer-Film* produced a newsreel from 1930 to 1932) and from 1934 to 1938 by *Oesterreich in Bild und Ton* (*Austria in Vision and Sound*).

Austro-Fascism / Third Reich: 1933–1945

In 1927, cameraman Rudi Mayer shot a three-piece documentation about the burning of the palace of justice in Vienna. The 10-minute documentary titled *Die Schreckenstage in Wien* (*The Horror Time in Vienna*) shows objectiveness: The destruction of a national institution is in the foreground, and the film compares the national values (order, security) with the crowd's bestiality (disorder, chaos).

On a traumatically staged world picture, the burning of the palace of justice represents a sign of imminent danger of civil war and collapse of the government's power and control. Since the historic event of 1927, the documentary practices and stylistics were invaded by Austro-Fascism propaganda concepts, which eventually became the rigorous standardized type of newsreels and documentary films (Achenbach and Moser, 2002). Since then, documentary films had to be systematically concerned on increasing the credibility and authenticity of the government's image. Just three weeks after the parliaments release, the Dollfuss-Regime deliberated on a central organization for film propaganda. One of the most important productions of this propaganda machinery was the Austro-Fascistic newsreel *Oesterreich in Bild und Ton (OEBUT)* (*Austria in Vision and Sound*). It was created by the initiative of the federal chancellor Engelbert Dollfuss and produced between June 1933 and March 1938 by the *Vaterlaendischen Tonfilmgesellschaft* of the enterprise *Selenophon Licht- und Tonfilm Ltd.* OEBUT worked principally on the establishment of the authoritarian regime's legitimacy. To spread catholic values, reinforce the Austrian identity, and counteract the annexation to the German Reich were among the principal objectives of OEBUT.

Beginning in November 1934, all movie theaters had to show in their preliminary programs a "cultural movie." These were sometimes art and nature documentaries but very often they were also propaganda movies about racial doctrine, political parties, and military matters. The newsreel became the most important propaganda instrument during war time and its screening became mandatory every night at every showing of a movie. The center point of these educational and advertising short films was always Austria—its cultural, scientific, and political autonomy, together with its tradition and historical legacy.

Marshall Plan Movie and "Documentary Films": 1945–1965

During the first two decades of the postwar period, documentary productions were characterized principally by the creation of cultural and propaganda films that were produced either for the Wiener ECA-Mission (Economic Cooperation Administration, the local office for the distribution and translation of the European Recovery Program [ERP], better known as the Marshall plan) or for important cultural performances (screen adaptation of operas and theater plays).

The *Oesterreichische Produktivitaetszentrum* (OEPZ) *(Austrian Center for Productivity)*, founded in spring of 1950, is a direct outcome of the American reconstruction program. The OEPZ's section "film office" was established in 1951 by the initiative of the U.S. administration in line with the "technical assistance" to effectively disseminate the pedagogy of the "productive managing and working" among the Austrian population. The "Marshall Films," distributed by the OEPZ, promulgated a capitalistic Europe befriended with America (Reichert, 2000: p. 83).

The Information Officer of the European film unit commissioned diverse documentary filmmakers to produce regional documentary films aimed at building consensus on specific local and regional needs. Austrian Georg Tressler, film officer of the ECA-Mission, was one of the most relevant documentary film producers of that time (Buchschwenter, 2003). The films *Gute Ernte (Good Crop,* 1950), *Hansl und die 200,000 Kuechen (Hansl and the 200,000 Kitchens,* 1952), *Traudls neuer Gemuesegarten (Traudls new Vegetable Garden,* 1952), *Ertagreicher Kartoffelanbau (Fruitful Potato Cultivation,* 1952, exhibited in the Documentary Film Festival in Venice), *Wie die Jungen Sungen (How the Boys Sung,* 1954), and *Rund um die Milchwirtschaft (Around the Dairy Farming,* 1954) followed the same objectives as the Marshall plan films from Tressler. These films focused on educating the public about techniques of effective management, promoting the identification with the concept "productivity improvement," and propagating the extension of the U.S. economic aid to broader population spheres.

An antique pedagogical film type of the so-called cultural films dominated until the 1960s. This type of film is still produced today, mainly for government-commissioned TV productions, such as tourism promotional films and Austrian historical reportages. These films were dependent on subsidies because they were not commercially viable.

About 680 cultural films were produced during the period from 1945 to 1961. Most of them fell more into line with the style of the National Socialist (NS) cultural films than with the artistic evolution of the international documentary films. Tourism promotion was the principal motivation for regional and federal supporters. In this sense, Hans Pebahl produced the popular documentary film *Und neues Leben blueht aus den Ruinen (And New Life Blooms of the Ruins)* in 1953. In this film, like in other postwar films, the reconstruction of the old cultural monuments was overvalued. This overvaluation was based on a restorative cultural meaning, which simultaneously devalued the contemporary culture. In award-winning films such as *Wege in die Zukunft (Roads to the Future,* 1959, director: Erich Pochlatko) and *Die andere Seite (The Other Side,* 1958, director: Bruno Loetsch), a pathetic voice-over commented nice pictures that ritualized the NS suppression.

In 1955, prizes for documentary films were awarded for the first time. The films were divided into two categories: The first category was comprised of those films that were a baring representation of existing subjects; the second category consisted of the documentary films that went beyond the central theme, looking for a creative, imaginary, or artistic interpretation (Reichert, 2000: p. 84). Most of the movie theaters had to close at the beginning of the 1960s because of their low demand caused by the introduction of the television's "culture for the masses." Also, the documentary films experienced a decline in the market. Due to the overvaluation of civic education based on the projection of cultural images, the National Funding Policy for Documentary Productions was dedicated exclusively to the screen adaptation (in studio) of diverse performances presented in the Viennese Burg Theater between 1955 and 1965.

The New Documentary Film

At the end of the 1960s and the beginning of the 1970s there was little structure for the production and commercialization of independent documentary films in Austria. Since the 1970s a tendency to produce films called "New Documentary Films" was identified, but they have had only a marginal importance in the film evolution. Most of these films were produced in personal studios of individuals who financed the productions with their own money produced from work in another job field (Bluemlinger, 1986). In this way Michael Pilz, who worked for three years on his five-hour film essay, *Himmel un Erde (Sky and Earth,* 1979–1982), and lived one year of that time with the miners whom he filmed, could perform a project of this kind only as an independent producer. The controversial film *Bonjour Capitaliste* (1982) from Werner Grusch, which deals with the colonizing of white tourists in Black Africa, was also financed with private resources.

The Film Advisory Board of the Board of Education, founded in the 1970s, could implement a policy for the promotion of documentary films only until the creation of the *Oesterreichischen Filmfoerderungsfonds (Austrian Film Promotion Fund;* OEFF). The cultural film thereby faded into the background. In the early 1970s, Ferry Radax, who was involved with documentary film production since the 1950s, created some outstanding artist portrayals. After a great effort, he achieved the outstanding formal depiction of the painter *Hundertwasser* (1965), for which he was awarded with the Austrian State Prize [other films: *Konrad Bayer,* 1969; *Thomas Bernhard,* 1970; *Ludwig Wittgenstein,* 1975; and *Japan oder die Suche nach dem verlorenen Reis (Japan or the Search for the Lost Rice,* 1981/1982)].

At the end of the 1970s, the Filmladen (film store) and the Medienwerkstatt (medium workshop) were founded and a longer-term structure for independent documentary film and video work could be finally be created. Ruth Beckermann was cofounder of the rental-business "film store," which was founded in 1977 with the appropriate structure for commercialization and public distribution of documentary films beyond the Austrian television. During the beginning of the rental-business "film stores," a serial of so-called "Flugblattfilme" (flight sheet films) about sociopolitical and work-political themes came into existence. In this sense, the film from Josek Aichholzer and Ruth Beckermann, *Auf amol a Streik (On Amol a Strike,* 1978), expounded the problems of a more than three-week strike in Semperit in Traiskirchen. The film was presented on numerous union meetings and was enthusiastically accepted. The fight for the former Viennese slaughterhouse Sankt Marx was documented in 1977 by "Video Group Arena" in the film *Arena besetzt (Arena Occupied).* The same year began the collective work *Wier kommen wieder (We Come Back)* from *Syndikat der Filschaffenden* about the Austrian movement against atomic power plants. From many *Medienwerkstatt (Media Workshop)* productions emerged important experimental and sociopolitical video work. From 1983 to 1984, Niki List filmed—without any public financial support—on 16mm/SW *Mama Lustig,* a sociocritical

documentary about the daily life of a disabled young person, which caused a sensation all along Austria because of its wiggled scenes.

The films from Margarethe Heinrichs called "solidarity films" were devoted to the real production conditions in the revolutionary Latin American countries, unlike the ethnographic-oriented films about Black Africa from director Grusch. The 16mm film *Traum des Sandino (Sandino's Dream,* 1981) and the television reportage *No Pasaran (They Won't Get Through,* 1984), both subsidized by the government, describe without any formal experiments the alphabetization campaign in Nicaragua and the exploitation conditions in the so-called third world. The development of new documentary films has a connection with sociopolitical tendencies—essentially in the "Neue Linken" environment. They were involved with daily life, the world of workers, and emancipated projects. The primordial objective for the film organization for documentary productions was that the values of socially and politically segregated people, which were already faded out by the mass media, became visible.

Historical Archaeology into the Present Context

In the 1980s, the infrastructure of political groups (Peace Movement, Third World, Anti-Nuclear Power, Anti-Racism) and the search for opposing ideas gradually extinguished. Since then, a new trend in content and form emerged: an orientation toward contemporary issues, but also toward ordinary life and subjective themes. Since the early 1980s, the Austrian film has practiced historical archaeology, which was so meaningful that this film category revived and the past started to open up for the present (Beckermann and Blüemlinger, 1996). *"Wien Retour—Franz West 1924–34"* (1983) is the first Austrian documentary film to deal with contemporary history. The film *Erzschmerz (Ore Pain,* 1983), produced by Bernhard Frankfurter on behalf of ORF, tried for the first time to expose the long repressing time of fascism through some miners' experiences.

Axel Corti, motivated by the taboos of the historical development during the NS-Time, produced films such as *Die Verweigerung (The Refusal,* 1971), *Der Fall Jaegerstaetter (Fighter's Fall,* 1972), and *An uns glaubt Gott nicht mehr (God Does Not Believe in Us Any More,* 1985) with documentary film elements. Some techniques were the lighted blade, which provides the spectator with information about date and place; newsreel material insertions, which gave the film a realistic note; and the use of black and white, which provided a more authentic reference. This mixture of fiction and reality may serve to remind the audience that that time was real and it did exist not only in films. In the 1980s, other documentary producers besides the remarkable precursor Corti, such as Josef Aichholzer, Ruth Beckermann, Karin Berger, Karin Brandauer, Eduard Erne, Bernhard Frankfurter, Andreas Gruber, Johanna Heer, Margareta Heinrich, Egon Humer, Wilma Kiener, Dieter Matzka, and Werner Schmiedel, undertook a memorial documentary work that the Austrian feature film was not capable of accomplishing because of melodramatic fictionalization. In 1997, Ruth Beckermann received the prize of the Bibliotheques at the Festival Cinema du Reel in Paris for the documentary film *Jenseits des Krieges (Beyond War,* 1996), which became very popular in the so-called Armed Forces Exhibition.

In the film produced by the multimedia performer Andre Heller and the documentary producer Othmar Schmiederer, *Im toten Winkel (On the Dead Angle,* 2002), the 81-year-old Traudl Junge narrates the time when she was working as private secretary of Adolf Hitler. In February, in the Berlin Film Festival 2002, "On the Dead Angle" was presented with great acceptance of the media and distinguished with the "Audience Prize."

In the 1980s, the "oral history" projects, which relied on the presence of speaking-time-witnesses and on the authenticity of the in-the-camera-speaking effect, became more popular within the documentary field. Angela Summereder used a radically different semidocumentary technique for relating a historical court case. The male discourse about jurisdiction was staged in the film *Zechmeister (Carousing Master,* 1981). The film does not reconstruct a "case" per se, but does recreate the history of a patriarchal law dominated by male representatives. The film *Zur Lage (To the Circumstance,* 2002), filmed by four directors (Barbara Albert, Michael Glawogger, Ulrich Seidl, and Michael Sturminger), is an ethnological study about the conservative and reactionary thinking that emerged in Austria after the change of government.

The Globalization of Documentaries

Numerous documentary productions of the last decade led filmmakers out of the country: *Megacities* (1998) from Michael Glawogger was the most successful Austrian documentary of the 1990s. Glawogger links his observations to portrayals of individual inhabitants in this film, which was shot in four "mega cities": Bombay, New York, Mexico City, and Moscow. *Megacities* is a documentary film that presents wigged images and refuses any statement that relates the social condition of individual persons with complex structures.

One of the most successful contemporary documentaries is *Hundstage (Dog Days,* 2002) produced in Austria by Ulrich Seidl. *Dog Days* consists of five independent stories of Viennese suburbs that had been arranged and interwoven together. It is a feature film that cleverly makes use of the documentary style of reality TV. *Dog Days* was awarded in the Vienna Film Festival with the "Grand Prize of the Jury." Ulrich Seidl became famous because of his provocative documentaries in which he had exposed the unpleasant side of the Austrian soul. In his second film, *Der Ball (The Prom,* 1982), he staged the preparation of a high school's prom and thereby exposes the class conceit, smugness, narrow-mindedness, and prudish behavior of a town. In *Good News* (1990), he documents the living conditions of foreign newspaper salesmen. *Die letzten Maenner (The Last Men,* 1994) is a TV drama about men who have no self-confidence who look in a catalog for a Thai woman for themselves. In *Tierische Liebe (Animal Love,* 1995) Seidl senses the intimate relations of Austrian domestic-animal owners with their pets, and *Models* (1999)—a documentary film with wiggled scenes—tells of the daily degradation of a photo model's life.

In the last decade, films from Nikolaus Geyrhalter have found a significant cinema audience. The film *Pripyat* (1999), awarded with numerous international prizes, narrates the survival in the dead man's zone at the former atomic power plant Tschernobyl, evacuated in 1986. *Elsewhere* (2000), Geyrhalter's Opus Magnum, is a time protocol of the year 2000. Twelve 20-minute episodes, one for every month of year 2000, filmed at a remote, supposedly untouched, place of the globe, raises the consciousness that there could not be a single place on earth that is really unaffected by the tragedy. "Phantom rides" is the name that was given to those films (roller coaster travels, railway journeys) that created a subjective experience by installing the camera onto a moving object. Martin Bruch created in his film *Handbikemovie* (2003) a phantom ride of special kind: the audience sits to a certain extent on the tricycle handbikes, on which the film producer, diseased of multiple sclerosis, moves himself.

It can be concluded that the sensibility for symbolic images and the interest on different political cultures were developed during the second half of the 1970s, when the "newer" documentary film, which displaced the antiquated "cultural film" of the 1950s and 1960s, make his appearance. Since the 1980s, contra-cultural references to established cultures and societies have been gradually expanded. During the last decade, a clear rejection to subjective-essayistic documentary productions was developed. In this sense, in the era of medium format reality TV, the Austrian documentary film production was characterized by the need of visualizing "reality."

RAMON REICHERT

Further Reading

Achenbach, Michael, and Karin Moser (eds.), *Österreich in Bild und Ton. Die Filmwochenschau des austrofaschistischen Ständestaates*, Wien: Filmarchiv Austria, 2002.
Aichholzer, Josef (ed.), *Dokumentarfilmschaffen in Österreich*, Wien: Filmladen, 1986.
Beckermann, Ruth, and Christa Blümlinger, *Ohne Untertitel: Fragmente einer Geschichte des österreichischen Kinos*, Wien: Sonderzahl, 1996.
Blümlinger, Christa, *Verdrängte Bilder in Österreich. Möglichkeiten des Dokumentarfilms in der II. Republik*, Salzburg: Univ. Diss., 1986.
Buchschwenter, Robert (ed.), *Georg Tressler: Zwischen Auftrag und Autor*, Wien: Filmarchiv, 2003.
Büttner, Elisabeth, and Christian Dewald, *Das tägliche Brennen, Eine Geschichte des österreichischen Films von 1945 bis zur Gegenwart*, Salzburg: Residenz, 2002.
Fritz, Walter, *Dokumentarfilme aus Österreich 1909–1914*, Wien: Filmarchiv, 1980.
Reichert, Ramón, "Die Popularisierung der Produktivität: Die Filme des Österreichischen Produktivitätszentrums 1950–1987: Ein Beitrag zur Diskussion um den Film als historische Quelle," in Österreichische Akademie der Wissenschaften (ed.), *Relation 2* (7/2000), pp. 69–128.

AUTOBIOGRAPHY AND DOCUMENTARY

From its beginnings, the documentary enterprise has been largely understood and practiced as a means of knowing the material, social world. From the earliest days of filmmaking, when the Lumière brothers sent cameramen worldwide, documentary has been associated with ethnography and empire. So, too, has documentary been considered a means of providing visible evidence of social injustice, and a powerful tool of national propaganda. Although the Lumière records of family domesticity made routine life public, few families had access to moving picture technology in the early twentieth century, and far more rare was any means of public distribution or exhibition of "home movies." As the century progressed, documentary's links to journalism, social science, and government deepened and, consequently, exploration of personal subjectivity was considered anathema to the documentary enterprise. Thus, curiosity about private or psychological worlds (outside of narrative film) found expression in experimental or avant-garde filmmaking.

As 16mm independent filmmaking developed in the late 1940s and into the 1950s in the United States, émigrés Maya Deren and Jonas Mekas and American Stan Brakhage merged formal experimentation and subjectivity in a cinema of personal revelation. The individual—and often idiosyncratic—filmmaker became subject matter. Her or his inner life—revealed by dreams, released by ritual, and universalized by myth—became the site of interest (Dyer, 1990). These independently produced films, exhibited publicly but narrowly, marked an important shift from traditional documentary impulses to create a hybrid cinema that combined documentation with creative interpretation (for example, Mekas's diaries and Brakhage's films of lovemaking and his children's births and growth). This experimental urge to explore subjectivity continues as a potent influence for contemporary film and video artists. Simultaneously, in the postwar years, making home movies, as a hobby, became an economic and technical possibility for many middle-class families (Zimmerman, 1995). Using amateur gauges and shown only in domestic environments, home movies of the 1950s and beyond would become important aesthetic and topical influences as well as rich archival sources for autobiographical documentaries made by professional filmmakers.

A conflation of technical and social changes—the introduction of lightweight, relatively inexpensive 16mm equipment; a distrust of all things official; the burgeoning Women's Movement; and a heightened interest in the political dimensions of personal life in the late 1960s and early 1970s—led to a surge in autobiographical filmmaking, especially in the United States. One strain of autobiography employed direct cinema methods to create motion picture diaries that emphasized the immediacy, intensity, and unpredictability of experience—the mantra of direct cinema—but with one crucial difference: The typical self-effacement of the direct cinema practitioner was replaced by a focus on the filmmaker whose life became the film's subject. Thus, a potent configuration that was neither pure direct cinema nor journalistic cinema vérité was shaped from two dominant documentary styles of the period. Jim McBride's seminal, darkly comic *David Holzman's Diary* (1967) simultaneously introduced and satirized the form in a pseudo-documentary that has become a template for the possibilities and excesses of autobiographical documentary (and included in the [U.S.] National Film Registry). Callow, self-absorbed, by turns bullying and insecure, Holzman (as played by L. M. Kit Carson) is the quintessential film student who lives for filming and, consequently, has nothing in his life worth filming. He violates his girlfriend's privacy and bores his friends, but, amazingly, he did not destroy a willingness in other filmmakers to continue the format. Both the diary form and McBride's entanglements in sexual politics were embraced earnestly in Edward Pincus's multiyear exploration of open marriage and family life in *Diaries* (1971–1976), and comically in Ross McElwee's nervous journey to the American South in *Sherman's March: A Meditation on the Possibilities of Romantic Love in the South during an Era of Nuclear Weapon Proliferation* (1986). Pincus was drawn to autobiographical production (as many others have been) through interest in philosophy, phenomenology, and politics. His diary films have been influential in their exploration of the concept of "presence"; in their investigation of the interactive consequences of filming; and in their recognition of subjectivity as the great problem of film (Lane, 2002).

However, the diary form—shooting everyday events for a sustained period of time and the construction of a subsequent narrative in chronological order—has not been the dominant autobiographical documentary style. More commonly, autodocumentaries combine observational footage with interviews and archival materials to create life stories situated historically, often organized achronologically, usually with a voice-over narration by the filmmaker, and frequently bound by the parameters of family life. By the mid-1970s, the proliferation of film schools and the inauguration of feminist production and exhibition networks increased opportunities for women filmmakers. This situation produced a concomitant increase in autobiographical productions that centered on the complexities of intergenerational relationships among women. Joyce Chopra's *Joyce at 34* (1973), Amalie R. Rothschild's *Nana, Mom and Me* (1974), Michelle Citron's (partially) faux autobiographical *Daughter Rite* (1978), and Chantal Ackerman's *News from Home* (1991) all interrogate the complex, tenuous bonds between mothers and daughters, which were undergoing special strain during a historical moment when many Western women were resisting the values and expectations that had driven their mothers' lives.

Feminist critics have noted that patterns of openness and dialogic engagement characterize women's autobiographical production (Lesage, 1999). Intensified by the Lacanian turn in feminist film theory, autodocumentaries made by both women and men (who were often either part of academe or strongly influenced by it) demonstrated a heightened interest in the consequences of patriarchy and frequently saw childhood trauma as a defining autobiographical moment. Unsatisfactory relationships with fathers saturate autodocumentary. Maxi Cohen's *Joe and Maxi* (1978), Abraham Ravett's *Everything's for You* (1989), Su Friedrich's *Sink or Swim* (1990), and Marco Williams's *In Search of Our Fathers* (1992) are but a cluster from a far larger pool of films that confront the primal father-child bond and its lasting effects on the adult child.

Ethical issues of consent, an abiding problem in all documentary production, are repositioned, rather than avoided, in autobiographical productions that center on often volatile and fragile family relations (Katz and Katz, 1988). Some autodocumentaries, such as Alan Berliner's *Nobody's Business* (1996), are built around a family member's resistance to participation in the construction of a family portrait. In contrast to Oscar Berliner's pugnacious contempt for his son's project (albeit a disdain that never erases the old man's affection for his son), many autodocumentaries include a minor complaint, or a slight hesitation, or a look of discomfort that is fleetingly included amid a general appearance of cooperation, leaving the viewer puzzled as to how strident off-camera resistance or edited objections from family members might have been.

Incentives toward self-inscription were numerous in the 1980s. Memoirs flooded the book market, confessional talk shows filled the airwaves, and autobiography seemed ubiquitous. A new expression, identity politics, gained currency. Some of the spurs toward self-representation were long in coming and well deserved. Widespread and sustained critiques challenged the assumptions and presumptions of traditional ethnographic work and fostered the growth of a documentary subgenre newly labeled autoethnography, in which members of (often maligned or ignored) cultures and subcultures took control of the politics of representation to produce work that investigated the cultural through the personal, and vice-versa. Individuals whose identities were partially constituted through membership in groups that had been disenfranchised by earlier documentary work—people of color, gays and lesbians, members of the working class, the chronically or terminally ill and their families—embraced autoethnography. Productions that joined the specificity of personal history with broader cultural concerns resulted in a vibrant, oxymoronic form: the collective autobiography. These collective autobiographies, or autoethnographies, were bolstered by targeted federal support in many nations in the West and made available to large audiences through new venues for exhibition (for example, the *P.O.V.* series on U.S. public television and specialized film and video festivals, such as gay and lesbian festivals, worldwide). Rea Tajiri (*History and Memory: For Akiko and Takashige,* 1991), Marlon Riggs (*Tongues Untied,* 1989), Tony Bubba (*Lighting over Braddock,* 1988), Derek Jarman (*The Last of England,* 1987; *The Garden,* 1990; and *Blue,* 1993), Deborah Hoffman (*Complaints of a Dutiful Daughter,* 1994) and scores of other producer/directors created provocative work that situated the individual within a decidedly cultural (and often historical) context.

By the mid-1980s, some documentary critics and producers considered reflexivity not only a stylistic choice, but an ethical imperative. Although all autobiographical production is by definition reflexive (that is, self-conscious), if not reflective (regarding its processes of construction) (Ruby, 1988), a strain of autobiographical documentary is particularly focused on its own construction process. Such is the case with *Silverlake Life: The View from Here* (1993), the poignant journal Tom

Joslin made of his life, and death, which a former student and friend completed after both Joslin and his partner died of AIDS. Autodocumentaries structured as personal accounts of the difficulties a filmmaker faces in completing a project range tonally to work that is wry, intensely engaged with political struggle, and deeply sorrowful (for example, Jill Godmilow's *Far From Poland* [1987] and Elia Suleiman's *Chronicle of a Disappearance* [*Segell Ikhifa,* 1997]) to pieces that are light and comical (such as Renos Haralambidi's *No Budget Story,* 1997).

In the last decades of the twentieth century, both literary and cinematic autobiography was greatly influenced by western European postmodern theory. Many film and videomakers working in autobiographical registers challenged the concept of the unified self as autodocumentary became a means, and a method, for recognizing the construction of identity and for confronting the paradox of reality fiction at the core of all documentary production.

As confidence in realism diminished (arguably more for filmmakers than for their audiences), a performative turn permeated many types of documentary production, blurring boundaries between fiction and nonfiction. A growing number of producers of autodocumentary visualized their dreams, nightmares, and fantasies through nonrealist techniques such as animation, stylized performance, and theatrical set design, continuing to pursue goals established a half century earlier by experimental artists. Camille Billops and James Hatch's *Finding Christa* (1991) and Kidlat Tahimik's *Why Is Yellow the Middle of the Rainbow* (1981–1993) turn to expressive means to explore subjectivity, while still retaining many traditional documentary features. Tracey Moffat's stylized *Night Cries: A Rural Tragedy,* (1989), although informed by the filmmaker's autobiography, crosses an increasingly indeterminate line between performative autodocumentary and experimental psychodrama.

Autodocumentaries that explore the director's sexuality or gender identity frequently approach documentation of sexual activity through striking experimental methods that feature imagery of the filmmaker's body (and often the body of his or her partner[s]) as physical presence(s), but also attempt to visualize the phenomenology of erotic life. Carolee Schneemann's *Fuses* (1964–1967) remains a memorable example of this tendency that is continued in Barbara Hammer's *Women I Love* (1976) and Mindy Farber's *The Man Within Me* (1995).

Perennial documentary concerns of authenticity and credibility are both diffused and intensified with autodocumentaries. Since subjects are usually not public figures, there are few reference points outside the autodocumentary text; trust between filmmaker and spectator is (relatively) automatic (until or unless disrupted). The fiction of *David Holzman's Diary* demonstrates how easily that trust can be exploited and violated. Counterfeit images in autodocumentaries are sometimes announced mid-film, as when Ruth Ozeki Lounsbury notifies viewers of *Halving the Bones* (1995) that she has "faked" archival family footage. Far more often reenactments or misappropriations are acknowledged in ending credits, as in Marlon Fuentes's *Bontoc Eulogy* (1995), which begs questions of authenticity in the tension between historical specificity (about Fuentes's actual grandfather) and cultural truth (about the display and mistreatment of Filipino men as World Fair exhibits).

By the beginning of the twenty-first century, production of autodocumentaries had proliferated worldwide, partly through the accessibility of increasingly inexpensive equipment and the global possibilities of Internet distribution systems. Imaginative young artists like Sadie Benning proved that even the most low-tech equipment (the short-lived pixel vision camera) could, in the right hands, be used to produce compelling, original (and in Benning's case, influential) autodocumentary. Easily operated equipment makes the production of video diaries feasible for amateurs. As digital production and distribution technologies expand, so, too, will the number and the variety of autobiographical documentaries.

CAROLYN ANDERSON

See also **Ackerman, Chantal; Berliner, Alan; Brakhage, Stan; Deren, Maya; Domestic Documentary; *Finding Christa*; Godmilow, Jill; Guzzetti, Alfred; *History and Memory*; Interviews; McElwee, Ross; Mocumentary; Moffatt,Tracey; *Nana, Mom, and Me*; Pincus, Edward; Reflexivity; Riggs, Marlon; Video Diaries**

Further Reading

Citron, Michelle, *Home Movies and Other Necessary Fictions*, Minneapolis: University of Minnesota Press, 1999.

Dyer, Richard, *Now You See It: Studies on Gay and Lesbian Film*, London: Routledge, 1990.

Eakin, Paul John, *Touching the World: Reference in Autobiography*, Princeton, NJ: Princeton University Press, 1992.

Freeman, Mark, *Rewriting the Self: History, Memory, Narrative*, New York: Routledge, 1993.

Katz, John Stuart, and Judith Milstein Katz, "Ethics and the Perception of Ethics in Autobiographical Film," in *Image Ethics: The Moral Rights of Subjects in Photographs, Film and Television*, edited by Larry Gross, John Stuart Katz, and Jay Ruby, New York: Oxford University Press, 1988.

Kuhn, Annette, *Family Secrets: Acts of Memory and Imagination*, London: Verso, 1995.

Lane, Jim, *The Autobiographical Documentary in America*, Madison: University of Wisconsin Press, 2002.

Olney, James (ed.), *Autobiography: Essays Theoretical and Critical*, Princeton, NJ: Princeton University Press, 1980.

Rabinowitz, Laura, *Points of Resistance: Women, Power, and Politics in the New York Avant-Garde Cinema, 1943–1971*, Urbana: University of Illinois Press, 1991.

Renov, Michael, "The Subject in History: The New Autobiography in Film and Video," *Afterimage* 17, no. 1, Summer 1989, pp. 4–7.

Ruby, Jay, "The Image Mirrored: Reflexivity and the Documentary Film," in *New Challenges for Documentary*, edited by Alan Rosenthal, Berkeley: University of California Press, 1988.

Ruoff, Jeffrey, "Home Movies of the Avant-Garde: Jonas Mekas and the New York Art World," *Cinema Journal* 30, no. 3, Spring 1991, pp. 6–28.

Russell, Catherine, *Experimental Ethnography: The Work of Film in the Age of Video*, Durham: Duke University Press, 1999.

Zimmerman, Patricia, *Reel Families: A Social History of Amateur Film*, Bloomington: Indiana University Press, 1995.

Avant-garde film. *See* **Modernism: Avant-garde and Experimental Early Silent European Documentary**

B

BACK OF BEYOND, THE

(John Heyer, 1954)

One of the most successful documentary films ever made in Australia, *The Back of Beyond,* was also one of the most significant productions of the Shell Film Unit during the 1950s. A dramatized documentary in the tradition of *Night Mail* and *Fires Were Started*, it won critical acclaim at international film festivals and was the most widely seen Australian film of the era, due to extensive nontheatrical distribution at home and overseas.

The Back of Beyond was produced, written, and directed by Tasmanian-born John Heyer, who had left the Australian National Film Board in 1948 to lead the newly formed Australian Shell Film Unit. Given a brief to make a "prestige" documentary that would capture the essence of the country, he undertook an extended three-month trip into the Outback, traveling through the Central Australian desert before returning to Sydney to prepare a detailed shooting script with the assistance of his wife, Janet, and writer Roland Robinson. Narration and dialogues were written in collaboration with the poet and playwright Douglas Stewart.

The Back of Beyond follows mailman Tom Kruse along the 300 miles of the Birdsville Track between Marree, South Australia, and Birdsville, in southwest Queensland. His two-week journey in a 1936 Leyland truck takes him across hazardous terrain to deliver the post and supplies to remote outposts, crossing sand dunes, flooded creeks, and featureless plains. Dramatized scenes with locals playing themselves alternate with fictional reenactments, such as the story of two girls losing their way in the desert following the death of their mother on an isolated farm. The narration alternates between the commentary, spoken by Kevin Brennan and a chorus of voices—the mailman, women chatting on two-way radio, and an aboriginal man reflecting on the abandoned Lutheran mission where he grew up—and the Birdsville policeman's laconic diary entry. The poetic, multilayered quality of the sound track is matched by the music of John Kay and complemented by the strong picture composition of cinematographer Ross Wood.

The Outback, the ostensible subject of *The Back of Beyond*, is seen in both a realistic and romanticized light. Beyond the obvious themes of

The Back of Beyond, 1954.
[*Still courtesy of the British Film Institute*]

communication (the mail run) and the battle against the elements, the film touches on some of the complexities of Australian identity, including not only indigenous people but also characters such as one of the very last Afghan camel-drivers in Marree. Heyer has a touch for comedy, a feel for evocative locations, and an eye for surreal details and recurring leitmotifs. Although some elements, such as the dubbed dialogues, might now seem somewhat wooden, the achievement of the film is the subtle interweaving of disparate story elements into a satisfying whole. Regarded as a minor classic of the genre, it was awarded the Grand Prix at the 1954 Venice Film Festival before being screened across Australia in theatrettes, town halls, schools, and traveling vans.

JOHN BURGAN

Back of Beyond (Australia, Shell Film Unit, 1954, 66 mins.). Distributed by National Film and Sound Archive, Australia. Produced and directed by John Heyer. Script by John Heyer, Janet Heyer and Roland Robinson. Cinematography by Ross Wood. Music by Sydney John Kay. Editing by John Heyer. Sound by Mervyn Murphy and John Heath. Commentary and dialogues by Douglas Stewart and John Heyer. Narrated by Kevin Brennan. Cast: Tom Kruse, William Buttler, Jack the Dogger, Old Joe the Rainmaker, the Oldfields of Ettadina, Bejah, Malcolm Arkaringa, the people of the Birdsville Track. Filmed on the Birdsville Track between Marree, South Australia, and Birdsville, Queensland.

See also **Documentary Film: Australia; Heyer, John**

Further Reading

Else, Eric, *The Back of Beyond: A Compilation by Eric Else for Use in Studying John Heyer's Film of Inland Australia*, London: Longman, 1968.

Pike, Andrew, and Ross Cooper, *Australian Film 1900–1977*, Melbourne: Oxford University Press, 1980.

BALÁZS, BÉLA

Béla Balázs—a European intellectual who wore the hats of poet, librettist, critic, scenarist, teacher, and filmmaker—is best known as a film theorist and one of the most important early champions of the art of film. Hungarian by birth, Balázs also lived and worked in Austria and the former Soviet Union. At times he faced opposition, having been castigated for his supposedly idealistic and bourgeois artistic principles in Stalinist Russia and persecuted for unclear reasons in his home country after World War II (Zsuffa, 1987, p. 324). His reputation today as a formalist classical film theorist is secure, although overshadowed by the monumental figures of Sergei Eisenstein and André Bazin. With certain key exceptions, many of Balázs' claims, though no doubt innovative in their historical context, are accepted as common knowledge today in introductions to the art and techniques of film. Balázs' work on the documentary, however, is insightful and prescient, prefiguring many contemporary debates about the subject.

Balázs' first books of film theory—*Der sichtbare Mensch* (*The Visible Man,* 1924) and *Der Geist des Films* (*The Spirit of the Film,* 1930)—were originally published in German and have not been translated into English. In 1947, he completed *Filmkultúra,* later translated into English and published as *Theory of Film: Character and Growth of a New Art.* This book, which incorporates segments of the earlier two works, introduced Balázs to the English-speaking world. Like other classical film theorists, Balázs took it upon himself to promote the art of film and direct it in ways he thought properly cinematic. The prescriptive elements of Balázs' more moderate theory, however, seem temperate when compared with those of Kracauer and Bazin, in part because Balázs had both formalist and realist tendencies.

Since it developed in an industrial, mechanical age, the first impulse of the art of film, Balázs writes, will be to provide "photographic theater"; film must resist such tendencies and develop its own language, "a totally different film language" (p. 31), rooted in cinematography (variations in scale, distance, angle, perspective, and focus) and montage, including the representation of scenes as constructed from discrete shots. Balázs embraced an expression theory of film (similar to the later auteur theory), by which a film is seen as the expression of the intentions and/or personality of the filmmaker. Cinematography and montage are the cinematic tools of the filmmaker, and her or his chief means of expression. Much of *Theory of Film* is devoted to a description of the uses of various filmic techniques for such expression.

Balázs also thought that the art of film would allow for a new human sensibility, new perceptive and cognitive skills, and changes in visual culture. This occurs mainly because film encourages a unique form of "identification." Balázs promotes what might be called the "Invisible Observer Hypothesis," which holds that the film transports the spectator into "the film picture itself." In part this melds the spectator's eye and consciousness "with the characters in the film," and the spectator's "eyes are in the camera and become identical with the gaze of the characters." In this, Balázs writes, "the film manifests its absolute artistic novelty" (p. 48). Today some would argue that such views of identification are inaccurate and lead to an underestimation of the independent agency of the spectator. Nonetheless, Balázs' description of identification anticipates that of Christian Metz (on primary and secondary identification) and other apparatus theorists.

Although Balázs is regarded as a formalist for his theory of filmic expression, he also strongly believed in the power of the cinema to reveal reality, thereby altering human perception. Like the later media theorists Marshall McLuhan and Harold Adams Innis, Balázs argued that changes in communications media would lead to altered human consciousness. Balázs held that film, as the dominant popular medium of the century, would have an effect as great as that of the printing press centuries earlier. He championed the close-up as generating "a tender human attitude in the contemplation of hidden things, a delicate solicitude, a gentle bending over the intimacies of life-in-the-miniature, a warm sensibility" (p. 56). In a passage taken from his earlier *Der sichtbare Mensch,* Balázs writes that due to its ability to reveal microphysiognomy (faces and gestures in minute detail), film can communicate emotion more incisively than any other medium. This language of gestures and faces, which he calls "the aboriginal mother-tongue of the human race" (p. 42), not only projects but also creates emotion in the spectator (p. 44).

Balázs' discussion of the nonfiction film shows the problems of categorization so common to treatments of the topic. He discusses the nonfiction film in relation to an odd lot of subcategories: the travel film, the instructional film "with a hero," "epics of labor," "news films," nature films, and so on. All are species of "films of reality," and so can be treated as various kinds of documentary. Balázs' expressionism extends to the documentary in his contention that every film, even one that depicts reality, has an intention, and is consciously or unconsciously an expression of the filmmaker. Thus, Balázs rejects from the outset the idea that the documentary is or can be a mere imitation or recording of visible reality, or a wholly objective account of factual reality. Whether a documentary should be seen as expressing a filmmaker's intention is no doubt a contentious claim; in any case, Balázs clearly sees that the documentary is a rhetorical construct. His observation that the travel film is "a curious transitional art form . . . which lies between a mere recording of reality and the interpreting intentions of a film director" (p. 162) could be applied to many types of documentary film.

For Balázs, the art of the travel film lies not in "invention" but in "discovery" (p. 160). Out of "the immense jungle of experienced reality the artist must find what is most characteristic, most interesting, most plastic and expressive and brings out most vividly" her or his "ideological intention," whether that intention be conscious or unconscious. A travel film never functions as a mere objective record of a journey. Whoever undertakes a journey with the idea of writing or making a film about it must "already have a preconception of his experiences" (p. 162). But a key point for Balázs is the contention that the absence of objectivity does not compromise the ethical requirement that the truth be told (or shown). Indeed, for Balázs, interpretation of reality and the revelation of the truth are not mutually exclusive but dependent. He writes, "Out of the empirical fog of reality the truth—that is, the law and meaning of reality—may emerge through the interpretation of a seeing and experiencing maker" who uses "every means of expression available to the art of the film" (p. 162). Thus, the documentary is a created, rhetorical construct by which the filmmaker interprets the world, and ideally reveals something true about it and in the process about himself or herself.

Balázs' suspicion of objectivity in nonfiction films is most visible in his treatment of the "news film," or newsreel. Newsreels, he writes, seem to be "an innocent form of pictorial reporting," but are in fact "the most dangerous instruments of propaganda," designed to further the interests of the "power groups who pay for them" (p. 165). Their rhetoric implies that they are "objective and authentic photographic records," when in fact they "lie" (p. 165). Newsreels would be instructive and interesting only if we were to view two such films in succession, made by mutually hostile interests. We would then see "no similarity at all, although they purport to show the same things" (p. 165). For Balázs, the individual shot is "mere reality," and it is only montage that gives film propositional value, and the possibility of making true and false claims. Those who make the newsreels have an "immense responsibility," for the convincing power of film lies in the fact that the spectator accepts the moving photograph "as fact, a presentation of conclusive proof," and by implication tends to underestimate the power of shot choice and montage in making meaning (p. 166). Here, Balázs presages many current discussions of documentary, in their concern with the rhetoric of authenticity and objectivity, together with the seductive power of the photographic image, the evidential status of which many spectators are prone to overestimate. This also seemingly contradicts, however, his earlier discussions of the means by which individual shots, due to framing, angle, and so on, are expressive of ideas and attitudes and are not mere recordings or "mere reality."

Balázs is enthusiastic about the work of Dziga Vertov, in part because the films of the *Ciné-Eye*, as Balázs describes them, do not pretend to objectivity. In these films the filmmaker uses the close-up to "peep with his camera at the little events of our workaday lives" (p. 164). These shots are entirely subjective, and the films have no "hero," except the unifying personality of the filmmaker, whose "subjective feeling" determines the choice of material, and becomes the "constructive principle on which the film is built" (p. 165). Such films "will form the most significant, the richest, the most filmic art form of that lyrical film-poetry which is yet to be born" (p. 165).

The relationship of the documentary to reality gives the documentary its peculiar character. In reference to the war film, Balázs writes that representing reality through film is unique in that during the film's production, the events being filmed are still in the making. The filmmaker "does not dip into his memory and recall what has happened—he is present at the happening itself and participates in it" (pp. 170–171). It is this "tangible being-present," Balázs writes, "that gives the documentary the peculiar tension no other art can produce" (p. 171), a tension that is perhaps maximized in representations of extreme events such as war or natural disaster.

Theory of Film was published in 1950, so it is not surprising that this relationship to reality of which

Balázs speaks does not preclude the legitimacy of staging. The staging of events for the camera, common to the films of Flaherty, Humphrey Jennings, the Grierson school, and many others, apparently did not seem to be inherently deceptive or manipulative for either audiences or critics until the rise of cinéma verité some years later. Of Merian Cooper and Ernest Schoedsack's *Chang* (1927), for example, Balázs writes that the film contains not a single "invented" scene, but that "every scene is directed" (p. 163). Balázs recognizes that the film makes heavy use of staged scenes and acting on the part of its participants, but he does not find this to compromise its documentary authenticity, arguing that "reality is shown more convincingly by such acting" (p. 163).

Balázs' anthropocentrism surfaces when he clearly favors documentary films "with a hero," by which he means a central human figure around whom the drama or information coheres. The example he gives is Robert Flaherty's *Nanook of the North* (1922), in which Nanook is often the locus of action. It is this central figure, he writes, "who gives meaning and functional life to that reality" depicted in the film, making the representation more vivid, more interesting, and "often more true" (p. 163). The realities of nature, he writes, "are given their deepest meaning for man if presented as a social experience" (p. 163). Even the experience of solitude, he says, fundamentally depends on one's experience of its opposite.

In his writing about problems of objectivity, the microphysiognomy of the close-up, the subjectivity of documentary filmmaking, and the relationship of the documentary to reality and the resulting influence on the spectator, Balázs prefigured many of the debates about the documentary that continue to this day. His theory deserves more attention than it has so far received.

CARL R. PLANTINGA

Biography

Born Szeged, Hungary, August 4, 1884, as Herbert Bauer. Composed the libretti for two works by Bartók, 1911 and 1914 to 1916. Forced into exile in 1919 for communist activity. Worked as scenarist and director in Austria and Germany, from 1919 to 1932. Wrote the scenario for Pabst's *Dreigroschenoper* (*Threepenny Opera,* 1931) among other films, and co-directed (with Leni Riefenstahl) *Das blaue Licht* (*The Blue Light,* 1932). After Hilter's rise to power, he left for Russia, where he lived from 1933 to 1945, teaching at the State Film Institute in Moscow. Returned to Hungary in 1945. Taught film art in various Eastern European countries. Died in Prague, Czechoslovakia, May 17, 1949.

Selected Works

Der Geist des Films, Halle/Saale: Verlag Wilhelm Knapp, 1930.
Der sichtbare Mensch, oder die Kultur des Films, Vienna and Leipzig: Deutsch-Österreiche Verlag, 1924.
Theory of the Film: Character and Growth of a New Art, trans. Edith Bone, originally published 1952, New York: Dover Publications, 1970.

Further Reading

Andrew, J. Dudley, *The Major Film Theories: An Introduction,* London: Oxford University Press, 1976.
Koch, Gertrud, "Béla Balázs: The Physiognomy of Things," trans. Miriam Hansen, *New German Critique,* 40, winter 1987, 167–177.
Zsuffa, Joseph, *Béla Balázs, the Man and the Artist,* Berkeley: University of California Press, 1987.

BALCON, MICHAEL

Michael Balcon was an eminent British film producer from the 1920s through the 1960s. He made a significant contribution to a viable national film industry and, especially at Ealing Studios, oversaw a body of films that projected an influential image of national character and identity.

After World War I, Balcon entered film distribution with his boyhood friend Victor Saville, but he quickly moved on to production in the industrial film sector, completing two titles in 1921 for the Anglo-American Oil Company: *Liquid Sunshine* and *The Story of Oil.* At a decidedly unpropitious time for British film production, Balcon and Saville, in partnership with director Graham Cutts, entered into commercial feature production, making a success of the risky *Woman to Woman* (1923), featuring the American star Betty Compson. Within a short time Balcon had formed the production company Gainsborough Pictures and was producing at Islington Studios.

Balcon established himself as a leading producer relatively quickly, working successfully with star Ivor Novello, and raising the young Alfred Hitchcock to director, most notably on the critical hit *The Lodger* (1926). Balcon contributed greatly to the revival of the British film industry as studio head at Gaumont-British (G-B), which he joined in 1931, and commenced with a commercial program of comedies, thrillers, and historical romances. Balcon's support of Robert Flaherty's romantic documentary *Man of Aran* (1934) was quite out of character and, though referred to at the time as "Balcon's Folly," the film was a modest commercial success. In contrast to his G-B years, he experienced a far more frustrating period as head of production of MGM British, where he served from 1936 to 1938 and completed only a single film, *A Yank at Oxford* (1937). Balcon's most celebrated period began in 1938 when he was appointed head of production at the small Ealing Studios. For two decades he oversaw a modest program of commercial features that made a distinguished contribution to the national wartime cinema and further served Balcon's declared postwar aim of national projection through film. This was achieved in heroic reconstructions such as *Scott of the Antarctic* (1948), literary adaptations such as *Nicholas Nickleby* (1947), and more subtly in the acclaimed Ealing comedies. Production ceased at the company in 1958 and Balcon assumed the role of Elder Statesman to the British cinema industry, serving in a variety of advisory and producer roles to the film and television sectors.

Factual cinema was of minor interest to Michael Balcon, but his conception of a distinctive and viable national cinema was tied to an aesthetic of realism where documentary style informed dramatic fiction. For him, native simplicity and sincerity were the hallmarks of an authentic British cinema, and while only fleetingly in evidence in the Gainsborough and Gaumont periods, as in the candid treatment of workers' leisure in *Hindle Wakes* (1931), they become the ethos of production at Ealing. Here, filmmaking was documentary in approach, and often tied to narratives that did not shy from social issues, tentatively emerging in the boxing drama *There Ain't No Justice* (1939) and the depression tale *The Proud Valley* (1940).

The studio's recruitment of Alberto Cavalcanti and Harry Watt from the documentary movement intensified the trend toward realism and veracity. Actual events underpinned *The Foreman Went to France* (1942) and *San Demetrio London* (1943), while Watt's lean and sparse *Nine Men* (1943), characteristically using some nonprofessional actors among its carefully articulated regional types, was

a sober alternative to wartime flag-waving propaganda. Location shooting became a common approach at Ealing and contributed greatly to the films' respectable surface. The POW drama *The Captive Heart* (1946) was partly shot in a recently liberated camp in Germany; London streets and landmarks were an integral element to the thrillers *The Blue Lamp* (1950) and *Pool of London* (1951) as well as to the melodrama *It Always Rains on Sunday* (1947); and the cycle of Empire films, notably Watt's *The Overlanders* (1946) and *Where No Vultures Fly* (1951), provided some authentic locales. Even the celebrated comedies were construed to play within actual settings: *Hue and Cry* (1947) and *Passport to Pimlico* (1949) made effective use of London's postwar landscape, while Alexander Mackendrick took the crew on demanding location jaunts for his Celtic tales *Whiskey Galore!* (1949) and *The Maggie* (1954). The penultimate Ealing film, Seth Holt's *Nowhere to Go* (1958), maintained the tradition of superficial realism and was one of the first features to be influenced by the Free Cinema documentary movement.

After Ealing, Balcon's creative influence was limited, but as chairman of both Bryanston and the British Film Institute Experimental Film Fund, he was involved with the new generation of Free Cinema filmmakers, kitchen-sink realists, and such maverick talents as Ken Russell, Peter Watkins, and Kevin Brownlow, who forged very individual paths in documentary.

ALAN BURTON

See also Cavalcanti, Alberto; Flaherty, Robert; *Man of Aran*; Watt, Harry

Biography

Born in Birmingham in 1896. Educated at George Dixon's Grammar School, worked briefly in the jewelry trade and completed his war work at the Dunlop Rubber Company. Entered the field of film sales after the war, but quickly transferred to film production, forming the Gainsborough Company with Victor Saville in 1924. Later head of production at Gaumont-British from 1931 to 1936; MGM (British) from 1936 to 1938; and Ealing Studios from 1938 to 1958. Knighted in 1948. Founding member of Bryanston Films, Chairman of British Lion from 1964 to 1968 and the British Film Institute's Experimental Film Fund from 1951 to 1972, and a director of Border Television. He retired in 1972 and died at Hartfield, Sussex, on October 16, 1977.

Further Reading

Balcon, Michael, *Michael Balcon Presents . . . A Lifetime of Films*, London: Huthinson, 1969.
Barr, Charles, *Ealing Studios*, London/Newton Abbot: Cameron Tayleur with David and Charles, 1977.

Barsam, Richard, *The Vision of Robert Flaherty*, Bloomington, IN: IUP, 1988.
Michael Balcon: The Pursuit of British Cinema, New York: The Museum of Modern Art, 1984.

Moat, Janet, "The Aileen and Michael Balcon Special Collection: An Introduction to British Cinema History, 1929–1960," *Historical Journal of Film, Radio and Television*, 16, no. 4, October 1996.

BALDI GIAN VITTORIO

See Adolescents, The

BANG CARLSEN, JON

Best known for his radical approach to the staging of documentaries, Jon Bang Carlsen has played a prominent role on the Danish film scene since about 1980, and remains one of Denmark's most innovative documentarists, with a number of feature films behind him as well.

Bang Carlsen's documentaries often focus on the daily lives and rituals of people whom viewers would consider either ordinary or marginal. Often living outside his native Denmark, Carlsen is drawn to other cultures and landscapes, and a number of his documentaries were shot in other countries—in the United States (*Hotel of the Stars* [1981] and *Phoenix Bird* [1986]), Germany (*Ich bin auch ein Berliner* [1990]*)*, Ireland (*It's Now or Never* [1996], *My Irish Diary* [1996], and *How to Invent Reality* [1997]), and South Africa (*Addicted to Solitude* [1999], *My African Diary* [2000], and *Portrait of God* [2001]). Each of his films forcefully evokes a sense of place as an integral part of its storytelling, and Carlsen often uses long takes, dwelling on faces and settings as part of a highly controlled visual style.

Carlsen's unconventional views on the staging of documentaries date from the very start of his career and were given their fullest expression in his film-essay *How to Invent Reality* in which he outlines his method and explains its underlying logic. Casting as his actors people who essentially play themselves on screen, but speak the lines he has written for them to say, Carlsen deliberately blurs the boundaries between documentary and fiction, uninhibitedly transforming the data other documentarists might prefer to record unchanged. He argues: "I don't want to be a hostage to life's coincidences in my work. I allow myself to rearrange reality in order to express the inner life of my characters" (*How to Invent Reality*, 1997). But these transformations are not gratuitous: The lines of dialogue he writes are tailor-made to suit the people speaking them, so that their words come across as natural and unrehearsed expressions of their own experience. And at the same time, this staging of reality is an act whereby the filmmaker becomes a part of—and illuminates—what he films. As Carlsen puts it, "My films are not the truth. They are how I sense the world. Nothing more" (*How to Invent Reality*, 1997).

In some cases, the viewer is entirely unaware of the degree to which the action has been staged and the dialogue written by the director. This is true, for example, of *Before the Guests Arrive* (1986), in which a woman who runs a small seaside hotel and her one employee are shown preparing the place for the approaching season. The viewer has every reason to believe that the two women are spontaneously expressing their own thoughts during their dialogue. On the other hand, with *It's Now or Never,* about an aging Irish bachelor who is searching for a bride, the observant viewer will notice the rapidly changing camera positions and realize that the action must have been carefully orchestrated as a series of shots, just as if the film were a work of pure fiction.

In Jon Bang Carlsen's own words:

> Whether you work with fiction or documentaries, you're telling stories because that is the only way we can approach the world: to fantasize about this mutual stage of ours as it reinvents itself in the sphere between the actual physical world and the way your soul reflects it back onto the world. For me documentaries are no more real than fiction films and fiction films no more invented than documentaries.
>
> (p.o.v. article, 2003)

His most recent works depart somewhat from the staged documentaries in that his interviewees do in fact tell their own stories—for example, inmates in a South African prison describe how they imagine God in *Portrait of God* (2001). But the director is just as present here as in his earlier works, in that he tells of his own life in a voice-over, speaking in the first person:

> When I was a boy I often lay for hours staring up into the summer sky for a hole into heaven or a lazy angel daydreaming on a cloud who'd forgotten old God's strict orders never to be seen by us people from down on this earth.
>
> In middle age my search for God had taken me all the way to southern Africa, but his trail was as fleeting as the banks of mist that rolled in from the Atlantic to mist up my windowpane as I tried to create a portrait of a person, who might only be a rumour.

In one way or another in all of Jon Bang Carlsen's work, the subjective experience of the filmmaker is deliberately made a central part of the film, and the director's own doubts and ongoing, tentative explorations are as much the subject of the documentary as are the people whose stories unfold before the camera.

RICHARD RASKIN

Biography

Born September 28, 1950, in Vedbæk, Denmark. Worked in theater, then entered the National Film School of Denmark, from which he graduated in 1976. Published books of essays and poetry and has lectured extensively at film schools and universities throughout Europe. Won numerous national and international awards for his films. Lives in both Denmark and Ireland with his wife and four children.

Selected Films

1979 *A Rich Man*
1981 *Hotel of the Stars*
1984 *The Phoenix Bird*
1986 *Before the Guests Arrive*
1990 *Ich bin auch ein Berliner*
1996 *It's Now or Never*
1997 *How to Invent Reality*
1999 *Addicted to Solitude*
2001 *Portrait of God*
2002 *Zuma the Puma*
2004 *Confessions of an Old Teddy*
    forthcoming *Landscapes and Remembrances*

Further Reading

Carlsen, Jon Bang, "How to Invent Reality: Extracts from a Forthcoming Book," *p.o.v.— A Danish Journal of Film Studies*, 16, December 2003, 96–98. http://imv.au.dk/publikationer/pov/Issue_16/section_1/artc10A.html.

Carlsen, Jon Bang, *Locations: Essays*, Copenhagen: Tiderne Skifter, 2002. [In Danish, soon to be available in English translation.]

Hjorth, Mette and Ib Bondebjerg (eds.), *The Danish Directors: Dialogues on a Contemporary National Cinema*, Bristol: Intellect Books, 2001, 195–207.

Madsen, Mette, "Art versus McBurger Dramaturgy: An Interview with Jon Bang Carlsen," *p.o.v.—A Danish Journal of Film Studies*, 12, December 2001, 7–18. http://imv.au.dk/publikationer/pov/Issue_12/section_1/artc1A.html.

Nielsen, Allan Berg, "A Modern, Humanist Profession of Faith," *Film*, November 2001, 19. http://www.dfi.dk/sitemod/moduler/index_english.asp?pid = 8170.

BARCLAY, BARRY

Barry Barclay established his unique place in the history of New Zealand culture during 1973 to 1974, when a six-part documentary series called *Tangata Whenua* aired on New Zealand television. Since then he has enhanced his significance with completion of the first feature film directed by a Maori male (*Ngati*, 1987), a book on issues associated with indigenous representation (*Our Own Image*, 1990), social activism (resulting in increased New Zealand on-air funding for Maori-produced and targeted film material for local broadcast television), and *The Feathers of Peace* (2000), a mixture of documentary and drama that carries local history studies into controversial terrain.

What unites Barclay's filmmaking, writing, and activism is his respect for community and his advocacy for the integrity of indigenous communities. Early in his career he began working for John O'Shea's Pacific Films, a breeding ground for filmmakers inclined toward an independent point of view. Along with the trade films and television commercials that were Pacific Films' primary source of income, Barclay made documentaries and feature films with O'Shea's backing from the 1970s until *Te Rua* (1991), when the director and the producer had a falling out. With the appearance of *The Feathers of Peace*, Barclay's public profile has again increased; out of the limelight, he has also been involved in further efforts supporting Maori training and filmmaking.

Despite funding and policy obstacles, Barclay has creatively developed filming strategies designed to accommodate cultural sensitivities. Chief among these has been a set of practices designed to make documentary subjects feel comfortable throughout the filming process, from the extensive use of lenses to keep cameras as far as possible away from subjects while they are speaking, to the synching of sound and image via the clapperboard at the end, rather than the beginning, of takes. He also argues that the Western medium can accommodate indigenous narrative strategies. Taking *Ngati* as an example, he speaks of its emphasis on the community rather than the individual, with a narrative structure that avoids single heroic figures in favor of group interaction. From *Te Rua*, he cites moments involving Maori oral practice and traditions that would be clear to an audience familiar with them, but which could not be read in the same way by most non-Maori audiences. In the docudrama *The Feathers of Peace*, using text from legal testimony of the day as well as other historical documents, he gives nineteenth-century characters the opportunity to speak, following the example of marae practice.

For Barclay, the heart of a movie is its metaphor; until he has his metaphor, he says, the film cannot be made. Simultaneous with making the *Tangata Whenua* series, Barclay was a member of Nga Tamatoa, a group of young Maori organized around undermining social institutions that prevented *Tino Rangatiratanga* (self-determination) at every level. Although Barclay is modest about the extent of his involvement in a left-wing group that critiqued the television establishment that allowed Barclay to make his films, Barclay agreed with Nga Tamatoa's ideological premises. He was among the earliest members of Te Manu Aute, a group that, like Nga Tamatoa, focused on media control.

Our Own Image, the most important published statement of his philosophy so far, is in part a gift to Native Americans and First Peoples, made after Barclay attended a film festival of indigenous people's work. Among Barclay's most interesting points in this short book is the distinction between "talking in" and "talking out." The latter could refer to an indigenous group trying to speak to a dominant culture, but "talking in" refers to the opportunity for a group within the nondominant culture to speak in its own terms rather than in those of the dominant culture, without regard for whether the dominant culture understands (*Our Own Image*, Barclay, 1991, p. 75).

Not a speaker of Maori himself, Barclay has said that he thinks "a Maori filmmaker is someone Maori who identifies as Maori and is proud to use the camera as a Maori for Maori purposes, at least some of the time," adding that "it's good fun to do other things as well" (Read, 2000–2001, p. 3). To be Maori is to have a strong awareness of the spiritual; to be a filmmaker is to be aware of film's "access to . . . visceral communal icons" (Read, 2000–2001, p. 4).

As Barclay moved away from television toward feature filmmaking, he also turned away from lobbying for political change. In the late 1990s, however, Barclay returned to political activism in a spectacular way. He picketed one of Aotearoa, New Zealand's funding bodies, camping out on the median in the boulevard in front of their office building. His private campaign gained widespread public attention. Barclay himself benefited through funding for *The Feathers of Peace*. At least one Maori filmmaker acknowledges Barclay as a force behind funding and other policy changes that have increased opportunities for Maori filmmaking, along with exhibition possibilities encompassing mainstream audiences.

Throughout his career, Barclay has mentored other filmmakers, particularly young Maori who have trained with him. Along with Merata Mita, he has called for and tutored in workshops to train Maori as well as internships and apprenticeships. Like Mita, he and his work have been well received in Hawaii, and he has used his speaking opportunities there to discuss indigenous filmmaking as he conceives of it. For example, in 2001, he gave a keynote address in which he developed his concept of "indigenous cinema," or "fourth cinema." Unlike "Hollywood, arthouse, and Third World cinema" (Read, 2000–2001, p. 1), fourth cinema should be committed to using its viscerally persuasive powers to raise consciousness of ethical issues, particularly through giving indigenous peoples their own voice (Turner, 2002, p. 11).

Barclay has developed and articulated his philosophy regarding the representation of indigenous groups through his own films, in interviews and talks, and in his own published work. He has influenced archival protocol, government funding, and public opinion through his work and action. Barclay's oeuvre is at least as well appreciated overseas as it is in his home country, where he has often raised issues others wish to forget.

HARRIET MARGOLIS

See also **Activist Filmmaking; Aesthetics and Documentary Film: Rhetoric and Documentary; Anthropology and Ethnography: Critical Overview on, and Documentary; Documentary Drama: Australasia/ New Zealand; Documentary Film: New Zealand/ Oceania; Documentary Film and Globalization; Human Rights and Documentary Film; Interviews; Media Theory and Documentary: Social Responsibility; Race: Critical Overview of, and Documentary; Reconstruction; Sound; Spoken Commentary (Voice of God)**

Biography

Born (1944) in the Wairarapa, an agrarian area near Wellington, New Zealand, of Ngati Apa, Scottish, and French descent. Trained in Australia to be a Roman Catholic priest (1960–1967). After making the *Tangata Whenua* series lived and worked in Sri Lanka, England, France, and the Netherlands, before returning to Aotearoa, New Zealand, and making *Ngati*. Media Peace Award, 2000. "First Legacy Appreciation Award," Hawaii Film Festival, 2001.

Further Reading

Barclay, Barry, "Alistair in the Dreaming: A Personal Reflection on Maori Image Sovereignty," in *A Century of Film in New Zealand: Papers from the Conference "Cinema, Film & Society"* [sic], edited by Margo Fry, Wellington: Stout Research Centre (Victoria University of Wellington), 1998, 13–16.

Barclay, Barry, "Amongst Landscapes," *Film in Aotearoa New Zealand*, edited by Jonathan Dennis and Jan Bieringa, Wellington: Victoria University Press, 1992, 116–129.

Barclay, Barry, *Our Own Image*, Auckland: Longman Paul, 1990.

Barclay, Barry, "A Way of Talking," *Te Ao Marama*, edited by Jonathan Dennis and Sergio Toffetti, Turin: Le Nuove Muse, 1989, 117–120.

Blythe, Martin, *Naming the Other: Images of the Maori in New Zealand Film and Television*, Metuchen, NJ: Scarecrow, 1994.

Dalzell, Julie, "The Independents of Our Film Industry," *Designscape*, 70, June 1975, 23–26.

Fox, Derek Tini, "Honouring the Treaty: Indigenous Television in Aotearoa," *Channels of Resistance: Global Television and Local Empowerment*, edited by T. Dowmunt, London: BFI, 1993, 126–137.

King, Michael, *Being Pakeha: An Encounter with New Zealand and the Maori Renaissance*, Auckland: Hodder and Stoughton, 1985.

May, Sue, "No More White-Wash," *On Film*, February 1984, 13–15.

Quennell, Megan, "Te Manu Aute," *Illusions*, 5, 1987, 4–5.

Read, Lynette, "Interview," *Illusions*, 31, 2000–2001, 2–6.

Turner, Stephen, "Cinema of Justice: *The Feathers of Peace*," *Illusions*, 33, 2002, 11.

BARNOUW, ERIK

Erik Barnouw was a Netherlands-born, American-raised media scholar and historian. He was also a creator of media, working in many capacities and over a long period of time in the production of both commercial and educational material. With his broad and varied background, Barnouw was able to consistently combine and reconcile the needs and tendencies of production and research, activity and reflection, private and public. As a member of the faculty of Columbia University, Barnouw was instrumental in establishing media studies as an academic discipline. He was also central in disseminating the insights of the academy beyond its boundaries, both through his own extensive, accessible publications, as well as by establishing and serving as the first head of the U.S. Library of Congress's media division.

Barnouw's life and work address documentary film at a number of important and instructive points. His most obvious contribution is the book

Documentary (1974, revised 1983 and 1993), a seminal history of the form, which continues to serve as its ideal introduction. The book was undertaken in part as a response to two prevailing perspectives—essential to a proper rendering of the documentary landscape, but tending to obscure the full view because of their very predominance. These were Western bias (as in Rotha), and an anecdotal or editorial approach to both events and their implication (Jacobs, 1971; Rosenthal, 1971). In preparing his work, Barnouw's approach was to situate the subjective—the practitioners' accounts and the perspectives of power—within a broader context, applying historical methodology and theoretical awareness to the telling of the tale.

Documentary remains exemplary for its combination of clarity and complexity, and for the accessible way it sets forth the multifarious and often contradictory events and issues relating to the nonfiction film. It also manages a more difficult and more affecting reconciliation, which is that it balances scholarly rigor with real generosity. For Barnouw, the documentary, at a basic conceptual and historical level, seeks not only social justice but also, to use the term in a particular sense, charity. With this conviction, Barnouw tempered clear and vigorous criticism with a sympathy that takes into account both inadequacy and accomplishment, good desires along with disappointments.

Barnouw's sympathetic attitude is partly rooted in his experience as a practitioner, and the fact that his production activities (advertising, radio scripts, instructional and educational material, government propaganda, documentary films) far predated his work as a media scholar and historian. A career broadcaster responsible for the definitive history of American broadcasting, and the first president of the International Film (Flaherty) Seminars who became the champion of his documentary associates, Barnouw demonstrated how direct connection with, and descent from the subjects of, study need not compromise that study.

That Barnouw could meld intimacy with effective scholarship had much to do with his disposition, and also with the circumstances in which it operated. Many of film history's most notable artist/scholars (Eisenstein, Vertov/Delluc, Dulac/Grierson) worked in revolutionary or critically unstable contexts, where the avant garde had (at least briefly) official approval, or where experimentation could be fostered. This ground was conducive to the cultivation of firebrands, of temporarily autonomous auteurs with ideas that they wished to emphasize over other alternatives, and the means to carry out those ideas. Here was the kind of

partisanship—occasionally even the self-absorption and distortion—that historians are supposed to temper or even counter.

Although Barnouw's most celebrated and significant documentary production is the magisterial *Hiroshima-Nagasaki 1945* (1970), made in collaboration with Akira Iwasaki, the majority of his production work, at least in the first decades of his career, did not reach or even attempt such heights. At first, and for a long time, Barnouw worked as a foot soldier in hierarchical, infrastructural, and/or entrepreneurial settings that did not value or even allow revolutionary innovation. In these settings, Barnouw developed the historian's virtues of patience and perspective. Knowing what it was not only to act, but also to be acted upon, Barnouw managed something that has proved to be very difficult for artists/scholars. He observed and participated in history, developing from the experience an insider's authority while still maintaining the long-range view. Barnouw avoided the temptations of theoretical advocacy. Instead, he pursued a course both more objective and more kindly, laying out theoretical alternatives, and the historical factors that gave rise to, that limited, and that justified them.

Erik Barnouw's critical openness leads to a final point, which is that he made a great contribution to documentary culture by exceeding—or more accurately by extending—the boundaries often imposed upon it. As a survey of the publications reveals, his historical and critical work ranged very widely. He spoke authoritatively about social activity and a number of the arts, as well as of the various media through which their effects were disseminated. In this he accomplished a kind of scholarly horizontal integration, to which he added an unusual, essential, vertical element.

Barnouw was interested in and illuminated the ancestry of current forms and conditions. With his interdisciplinary and chronological range, and his synchronic and diachronic reach, he could expose and clarify connections between diverse times and places. Some of this must be ascribed to the beneficent influence of Barnouw's father, Adriaan, a distinguished linguist, translator, anthologist, scholar, and teacher whose work concentrated primarily on his native Netherlands. Through Adriaan, Erik early understood, among other things, how the documentary idea could be manifest in the didacticism of a medieval morality play, in Dutch and Flemish genre painting, or in the development of vernacular poetry. The result was real, unstrained coherence, notwithstanding apparent great gulfs in time and discipline and geography.

As a communications scholar, Erik Barnouw labored extensively in a public and popular field, and in its diversity he consistently came back to consider the nonfiction film and the documentary idea. He believed in documentary's leavening powers, and he showed that documentary research and production cannot be separated from educational impulse, nor from citizenly activity and activism. For Barnouw, the documentary was not simply an object of study or an abstraction. Rather, it was a call to citizenship, encouraging and enabling journalists, filmmakers, broadcasters, academics, teachers, and students to extend personal lines into public discourse, and private interest into positive public action.

DEAN DUNCAN

See also **Grierson, John; Rotha, Paul; Vertov, Dziga**

Biography

Born in the Netherlands in 1908. Over the course of his life, worked in advertising, television, and journalism. Also a songwriter, a filmmaker, and a film preservationist. Served on the boards of many media organizations. Joined the faculty of Columbia University in 1946. Organized the Film Division in the School of the Arts. Served as department chair until 1968. Won a Peabody Award for the documentary radio series entitled "Words At War," 1944. Named chairman of the Writers' Guild of America, 1957. Retired in 1973; named professor emeritus of dramatic arts. Died in Vermont, July 19, 2001.

Selected Works

Barnouw, Erik, *A History of Broadcasting in the United States*, New York: Oxford University Press, 1966–1970.
Barnouw, Erik, *Documentary: A History of the Non-Fiction Film*, New York: Oxford University Press, 1974 (revised, 1983, 1993).
Barnouw, Erik, *Tube of Plenty: The Evolution of American Television*, New York: Oxford University Press, 1975 (revised 1982, 1990).
Barnouw, Erik (ed.), *International Encyclopedia of Communications*, Philadelphia: University of Pennsylvania, 1989.
Barnouw, Erik, *Media Marathon: A Twentieth Century Memoir*, Durham: Duke University Press, 1996.
Barnouw, Erik, *Media Lost and Found*, New York: Fordham University Press, 2001.
Barnouw, Erik, and Krishnaswamy, Subrahmanyam, *Indian Film*, New York: Oxford University Press, 1963 (revised, 1980).

Further Reading

Barnouw, Adriaan, *Coming After: An Anthology of Poetry from the Low Countries*, New Brunswick: Rutgers University Press, 1948.
Barnouw, Adriaan, *Monthly Letters: On the Culture and History of the Netherlands*, Assen: Van Gorcum, 1969.
Jacobs, Lewis, *The Documentary Tradition: From Nanook to Woodstock*, New York: Hopkinson and Blake, 1971.
Rosenthal, Alan, *The New Documentary in Action: A Casebook in Filmmaking*, Berkeley: University of California Press, 1971.
Rotha, Paul, *Documentary Film*, London: Faber and Faber, 1952 (revised 1963, 1968).
Zimmerman, Patricia R., and Ruth Bradley, "A Festschrift in Honor of Erik Barnouw," *Wide Angle*, 20, no. 2, April 1988, University of Ohio.

BASIC TRAINING

(US, Wiseman, 1971)

The first of three films about the United States Armed Forces made by American documentary filmmaker Frederick Wiseman, *Basic Training* documents the standard eight-week training for new army inductees and enlistees at Fort Polk, Kentucky, before being shipped out to Vietnam. The processes of institutional indoctrination and maintenance of power, primary aspects of institutional functioning explored in Wiseman's other films, are emphasized in the film's vision of the military machine. As commanding officer Lt. Hoffman puts it bluntly in his welcoming speech to the men early in the film, "The best way to go through basic training is to do what you're told, as you're told, and there'll be no problems."

In the brief montage sequence that opens the film, the new inductees are immediately stripped of their individuality. The opening shot is of the men arriving on a bus, from which they walk unhurriedly to the barracks, dressed in a variety of civilian clothes. In the second shot, they are assigned bunks by number; in the third shot, they are measured for uniforms, the tailor calling out measurements. Next come three shots of men having their hair cut short, all the same, a recurrent Wiseman image signifying loss of individuality and absorption into an institutional system. Then there is one quick shot each of fingerprinting, ID photos being taken, and one man, in answer to an interview question, giving his social security number, his identity now only a statistic. At the end of this opening sequence, the men are in uniform, a striking contrast to their varied appearance just a few moments before.

The music in the film further emphasizes the loss of individuality within the larger group. The function of music is established early on in *Basic Training*, when the commanding officer and his entourage smartly march into a room to welcome the trainees accompanied by the musical fanfare of "The Caissons Go Rolling Along." The entire film is punctuated with shots of the men drilling, keeping time to marching tunes. In these shots the camera frequently tilts down to isolate in close-up the legs and feet of the men, showing that no one is allowed to march to the beat of a different drum.

When Lieutenant Hoffman tells a black private that "the Army's not just one man, it's millions of people," and that he must work with the group, he echoes the social message of virtually every classic Hollywood war movie, but with a crucial difference, for while the classic war films depict the compromise of individualism as a noble sacrifice necessary for the war effort, Wiseman views the military as unacceptably dehumanizing. In one particularly striking shot in *Basic Training*, the soldiers march in the foreground as if "beneath" a large American flag waving

Basic Training, 1971.
[*Still courtesy of the British Film Institute*]

in the background. Here, Wiseman finds a visual expression of the extent to which the individual is subject to the state—a point ominously reiterated in the image of the soldiers entering a transport plane shot from a position within or under it, the dark, jagged edges of the plane's bay doors suggesting a giant maw about to consume the men.

Basic Training also offers a disturbing view of masculinity in its suggestion that violence is innate in men and easily nurtured by the process of basic military training. The men readily cheer each other on ("Get him from behind," "Hit him in the head") as they fight in pairs. Even after the whistle blows, signaling that the combatants should stop, we see one pair continue on, their potential for violence now fully aroused. In the tooth-brushing scene, several of the men are shown, in effect, foaming at the mouth, and in the scenes of bayonet practice, the men seem reduced to animals, "grunts" abandoning language for screams of violence. Several scenes make the connection between firearms and the phallus. On the firing range, a demonstrator fires his weapon from his crotch, accompanied by a crude joke from the instructing sergeant; and one trainee is visited by his family, who concentrates their attention and conversation on his rifle, "fetishizing" it and investing it with unmistakable phallic implications.

Much screen time is devoted to the hapless Private Hickman, a trainee who has trouble with everything from executing the to-the-rear-march to making his bed. Attempting to learn something as simple as reversing his direction while marching, behind him we see the other men drilling with increasing uniformity and competence. Just as they tend to march in the opposite direction from Hickman within the frame, so the lack of ability by this one individual in the foreground sets him up as a foil to the many in the background, all of whom are quickly becoming professional soldiers. (Their growing proficiency also provides Wiseman with a visual way of "marking time" in the film.)

For Wiseman, Hickman is emblematic of the misfit literally out of step with society, scorned by his comrades as a result. The weakest link, he is threatened with a "blanket party," a military hazing ritual in which a blanket is thrown over the victim before he is beaten, thus rendering him unable to name his attackers. Hickman's response, we discover, is to attempt to overdose on drugs. Finally, Hickman evolves from a comic figure to a tragic one, for he represents that spark of human imperfection that is all but ruthlessly eliminated as the men become trained soldiers.

BARRY KEITH GRANT

See also **Wiseman, Frederick**

Basic Training (USA, 1971, 89 mins.). Distributed by Zipporah Films. Produced, edited, and directed by Frederick Wiseman. Cinematography by William Brayne. Sound recorded by Frederick Wiseman.

Further Reading

Atkins, Thomas R. (ed.), *Frederick Wiseman*. New York: Monarch Press, 1976.

Benson, Thomas W., and Caroline Anderson, *Reality Fictions: The Films of Frederick Wiseman*. Carbondale: Southern Illinois University Press, 1989.

Grant, Barry Keith, *Voyages of Discovery: The Cinema of Frederick Wiseman*, Urbana and Chicago: University of Illinois Press, 1992.

Mamber, Stephen, *Cinema Verite in America: Studies in Uncontrolled Documentary*, Cambridge, MA: MIT Press, 1974.

Nichols, Bill, *Ideology and the Image*, Bloomington: Indiana University Press, 1981.

BASSE, WILFRIED

Wilfried Basse's oeuvre bridged the gap between German avant-garde filmmaking of the Weimar Republic and the conventional educational filmmaking propagated during the Nazi period. When he started out in 1929, he counted prominent avant-garde artists such as Kurt Schwitters and other members of the Kestner-Society as his friends. He dissociated himself from the Bauhaus aesthetic.

Basse's main filmic interest was people in their everyday surroundings, whom he observed from a short distance. His first film, *Baumelutenzeit in Werder* (1929), about a crude spring fair near Berlin, was noted for the satirical tone it employed with regard to human foibles and inadequacies. The film garnered comparisons to George Grosz and Heinrich Zille for Basse.

Basse used a small handheld camera that allowed for great immediacy and intimacy in shooting. This was illustrated by *Market in Berlin* (1929), which depicts the hustle and bustle of a Berlin peasants' market. The film's style was praised by many reviewers; others, Siegfried Kracauer among them, criticized it for its lack of an overt political message. The same could not be said of *Das Rote Sprachrohr* (1931), a portrait of a communist agitprop company. Inspired by Russian formalism, this film was Basse's experiment with a specified screenplay and indoor shooting with studio lighting.

Basse's primary work was *Deutschland—zwischen gestern und heute* (1932–1934), which demonstrated how historical developments determine the present. While Basse was editing the film, the Nazis came into power. Reviewers criticized the lack of Nazi ideology in the film, while audiences seemed to avoid the film exactly because they expected Nazi propaganda. Nevertheless, it was awarded a gold medal at the Venice Film Festival in 1935.

Suspected of communist sympathies, Basse and his production company faced numerous obstacles. For the rest of his career, he worked with the Reichsanstalt für den Unterrichtsfilm (RfdU, Reich Institute for Educational Films), for which he shot nearly forty films. Since these films were not publicly shown, they were not censored. In fact, the RdfU worked independently, free of Nazi control. During this time, Basse's films focused on topics relating to handicrafts and sports. In 1940, he was commissioned to make a film about genetic diseases—*Erbkrank—Erbgesund*—Basse's only overt concession to the Nazi regime.

ULI JUNG

Biography

Born on August 17, 1899, the son of a banker. After several failed attempts at various professions, turned to filmmaking, due to the influence of the films of Hans Cürlis. Formed his own production company in 1929. The Nazis' takeover brought about political difficulties, which led him to the Reichsanstalt für den Unterrichtsfilm, for which he was one of the most prolific contributors. Assigned to oversee the slow-motion photography for Leni Riefenstahl's film, *Olympia,* 1936. Died June 6, 1946.

Films

1929 *Baumblütenzeit in Werder*
1929 *Market in Berlin*

1929 *Wochenmarkt auf dem Wittenbergplatz*
1930 *Der wirtschaftliche Baubetrieb*
1931 *Mit Optik 1,4 – Kamerastudien von Wilfried Basse*
1931 *Das Rote Sprachrohr*
1930–1932 *Abbruch und Aufbau (1930–32)*
1932–1934 *Deutschland—zwischen gestern und heute*
1934–1934 *Glückliche Heimat*
1934–1935 *Bunter Alltag*
1935 *Der Böttcher baut einen Zober*
1935 *Der Kohlenmeiler*
1936 *Roggenernte*
1936 *Hausbau*
1936 *Dachschiefer*
1936 *Der Schuhmacher / Wie ein Schuh entsteht*
1936 *Tabakbau in der Uckermark*
1936 *Handweberei*
1936 *Wie ein Ziegelstein entsteht*
1936 *Wie ein Pflasterstein entsteht*
1936 *Ein Brief wird befördert*
1936 *Braunkohle-Tagebau*
1936 *Ein Kohlenschleppzug auf dem Mittelrhein*
1936–1940 *Erbkrank–Erbgesund*
1937 *Kugelstoßen*
1937 *Schwälmer Bäuerin am Spinnrad*
1937 *Perspektivisches Sehen*
1937 *Städtische Feuerwehr*
1937 *Dämmen einer Schornsteingruppe*
1937 *Kurzstreckenlauf*

1937 *Weitsprung*
1937 *Schwimmen*
1937–1940 *Vom Korn zum Brot*
1938 *Junge Löwen im Zoologischen Garten*
1938 *Junge Paviane im Zoologischen Garten*
1938 *Junge Bären im Zoologischen Garten*
1938 *Das Anlernen junger Pferde zum Zuge*
1938 *Schwäbische Kunde*
1939 *Ein Tag auf einer fränkischen Dorfstraße*
1939 *Deutschland–gastliches Land*
1939 *D-Zug fertig zur Fahrt*
1939–1940 *Der Jockey*

Further Reading

Frank Avril, *Avantgardisten des deutschen Film: II. Wilfried Basse*. In: *Der deutsche Film Nr. 8*, February 1937.

Wilfried Basse – Notizen zu einem fast vergessenen Klassiker des deutschen Dokumentarfilms. In: Kraft Wetzel, Peter A. Hagemann, Liebe, Tod und Technik: *Kino des Phantastischen, 1933–1945*. Berlin, 1977, 75–97.

Rolf Freier, *Linksbürgerliche Filmaktivitäten am Beispiel Ella Bergmann-Michels und Wilfried Basses*. In: Rolf Freier, Der eingeschränkte Blick und die Fenster zur Welt: *Zur politischen Ästhetik visueller Medien*. Marburg, 1984, 96–111.

BATAILLE DU RAIL, LA

(France, Clément, 1946)

La Bataille du Rail (*The Battle of the Rails*) began as *Résistance Fer*, a short film relating the contribution of the *cheminots*, the French railway workers, to the struggle against German occupation. This documentary, among a series of projects commissioned in 1945 to celebrate the *Résistance* by the *Comité de Libération du Cinéma Français*, made such a strong impression on the producers that they asked the director, René Clément, to turn it into a feature-length film. Professional and amateur actors were hired, stories of resistance in the railways were collated by the writer, Colette Audry, and German prisoners of war were brought in. *La Bataille du Rail* was released in 1946 and gained instant acclaim as the most moving account of the *Résistance*.

La Bataille du Rail is a rather disjointed film, half-documentary and half-fiction, where its transformation from a *court-métrage* to a ninety-minute full-length feature is quite apparent. It is rather chaotic in its loose structure and confusing in its script. The odd juxtaposition of a fiction to a documentary is nevertheless what makes *La Bataille du Rail* so special. As a docudrama, it acquires unique qualities of being a detailed and dramatic account of the plight of railway men trying desperately to put all sorts of obstacles to prevent the movement of trains through sabotage, diversion, and cooperation with the *Maquis*, the armed resistance to German occupation.

The film spans over the four years of the war, and can be divided into two sections. The first part

La Bataille du Rail, 1946.
[*Still courtesy of the British Film Institute*]

is a documentary using actors; it explains the resistance to German occupation in the railways during these years, in particular its effect on the movement of trains between the occupied zone in the north and the "free zone" in the south of France. The considerable risks taken by the workers of the SNCF, the nationalized French railways, are described in detail, almost in a didactic manner: the sabotage of the rolling stock, the meticulous deception of the German army officers, and the ensuing reprisals narrated with an acute sense of patriotic duty and drama.

The second part of the film is set in the aftermath of D-Day and describes the attempts by the *cheminots,* allied with the *Maquis,* to stop a heavily armored train taking German reinforcements to the front line, ending with its dramatic derailment. The film becomes much closer to a work of fiction than a documentary. It finishes with scenes of triumph, greeting the arrival of the first train in a liberated France, ultimate symbol of a nation freed by the sacrifice of its railway workers.

La Bataille du Rail received the award for best film at the 1946 Cannes festival, and René Clément received the award for best director. It is still considered the first film that managed to capture the spirit of the *Résistance,* the heroism of a nation, and the dangers involved in resisting German occupation. Undoubtedly, the circumstances of its release explain its success, among a public desperately looking for the film that would capture the emotional intensity of such

acts of bravery. It is also a fine and rare example of French neorealism, not unlike the Italian postwar films, in its unique blend of reality and fiction and in its attempts to reach humanity in the most inhumane circumstances of war against an occupying army.

René Clément envisages acts of resistance in the SNCF as a patriotic epic and relies quite heavily on the "feel good" factor that prevailed after the war, hence its considerable success. The film does not, however, demonize German occupation—there is even some sympathy for the German soldiers relaxing on the side of the tracks where their military convoy is stranded, a sharp contrast with the violence unleashed in the attack that follows.

La Bataille du Rail portrays a collective struggle, where there is no hero, where the fight for survival from both sides is described with a sense of the unavoidable. It ignores the real divisions that existed during these years among the French population. There is also little reference to the involvement of allied troops or of the Gaullist *resistance.* Patriotism is mixed with socialist undertones: These acts of bravery are those of the *cheminots,* who symbolize the working class as the driving force in resisting German occupation.

The style of Clément is a cold assessment as well as a tense account of resistance by railway workers: There is some of Eisenstein's sense of drama in the languishing whistling of a steam engine during the summary execution of *cheminots* suspected of sabotage, and in the accordion rolling down the side of the track after the spectacular derailment of the German convoy. The photography of Henri Alekan contributes greatly to the dramatic effect of the film, and *La Bataille du Rail* will establish him as one of the greatest photographers in black and white for the cinema. He had already collaborated to the *Beauty of the Beast* of Jean Cocteau and worked with Wim Wenders in 1983 on *The State of Things* and on *Wings of Desire* in 1987.

La Bataille du Rail transformed the career of René Clément from that of a minor documentary filmmaker to one of the prominent directors of his generation. Born in 1913, he made short documentary films during the 1930s and 1940s, in particular *Ceux du Rail* in 1942, which gave him an insight into the railway industry that would be useful when filming *La Bataille du Rail.* Until the late 1950s, Clément confirmed his stature as a world-class director, receiving an Oscar for *Au-delà des Grilles* in 1948 and *Jeux Interdits* in 1952.

Clément belongs to the generation of directors left behind by the desire for change demanded by *La Nouvelle Vague,* who criticized his filming technique for its lack of subjectivity and its detachment from reality. His last noticeable success, *Plein Soleil,* released in 1960, inaugurated a slow decline in a career that had been prolific and successful, until his last film, *Jeune fille libre le soir,* which came out in 1975, the year before his death. *La Bataille du Rail* remains the film for which he is best known.

YVAN TARDY

La Bataille du Rail (*The Battle of the Rails*) (85 min.). Distributed by L.C.J. Editions et Productions, 2002. Produced by La Coopérative générale du cinéma Français, 1946. Directed by René Clément. Script by René Clément. Photography by Henri Alekan. Music by Yves Baudrier. Dialogues by Colette Audry. Filmed in black and white. Played by Jean Clarieux (Lampin), Jean Daurand (*Cheminot*), Jacques Desagneaux (Athos), François Joux (*Cheminot*), Latour (*Cheminot*), Tony Laurent (Camargue), and French railway workers.

Further Reading

Barrot, Jean-Pierre, *L'Ecran Francais*, 27 February 1946.

Bertin-Maghit, J.-P., "*La Bataille du rail: de l'authenticite a la chanson de geste,*" in *Re ue d'histoire Moderne et Contemporaine*, 33, April-June 1986, 280–300.

O'Shaughnessy, Martin, "*Bataille du rail:* Unconventional form, conventional image?" In *The Liberation of France*, edited by R. and N. Wood, Berg, 1995.

Totaro, Donate, "*La Bataille due rail,*" *Hors Champ*, September 1997.

BATTLE FOR OUR SOVIET UKRAINE, THE

(USSR, Dovzhenko, 1942–1943)

The Battle for Our Soviet Ukraine (Bitva za nashu Sovetskuiu Ukrainu) is an account of the German Army Group South's invasion of the Ukraine and its repulsion in the Great Patriotic War. Produced for the Central and Ukrainian Newsreel Studios, the film was begun in early May 1943, completed on October 6, and released on October 25, 1943. Often attributed to Alexander Dovzhenko, the nominal directors were his wife, Julia Solntseva, and Jacob Ovdeyenko. However, although credited only as "supervisor," bucolic sections link to Dovzhenko's earlier feature films, particularly *Earth.* The contrast between these lyrical scenes showing, in an idealized manner, what life was like before the invasion, and the starkness of the war footage, gives the images of destruction much of their impact.

Dovzhenko, with a number of other documentarists, remained in Moscow when the bulk of film production, along with much of industry that stood in the path of the invading forces, was evacuated to the east. He also spent time in liberated areas of the Ukraine, so he saw firsthand more of the effects of war than many of his colleagues. The authenticity that Dovzhenko's team managed to convey is remarkable. The film is put together with a freedom from the bureaucratic interference that filmmakers working on fiction production experienced, allowing Dovzhenko greater latitude than if he had gone to Alma Ata with the others.

Dovzhenko's feelings about the invasion are summed up in a letter to his wife dated June 4, 1942 (Marshall, 1983, p. 152), in which he wrote that although Hitler would be defeated, the Ukraine had been ruined. Despite this pessimism, he and his team made another documentary, *Victory in Right-Bank Ukraine and the Expulsion of the German Aggressors from the Boundaries of the Ukrainian Soviet Earth* (released in May 1945), which contained material on reconstruction. Of the two films, *Battle for Our Soviet Ukraine* is more harrowing, with many shots of dead bodies, including children, and the devastation in the reconquered areas is brought vividly home.

This graphic depiction of despoliation and despair runs contrary to Graham Roberts's (1999,

p. 136) characterization of wartime Soviet documentary as "a mirror image of reality," projecting confidence in a time of tragedy. Dovzhenko's diary indicates that before its release he was skeptical about the film's likely official reception, as it ran counter to the positive portrayals depicted in the bulk of Soviet films. He feared that it might be banned altogether, or marred "by cutting the difficult and unheroic scenes." His more subtle conception of the complexity of war—"the grandiose woe of retreat and the incomplete joy of advance" (Dovzhenko, 1973, p. 91)—was at odds with the simplistic official ideology.

The original title was *Ukraine in Battle*, but the addition of the word *Soviet* served to lessen the nationalistic interpretation by stressing the common struggle of all the Soviet peoples. The political message was that the Ukraine was still part of the Soviet Union. The sensitivity of the nationalism issue can be gauged by the fact that, while working on *The Battle for Our Soviet Ukraine*, Dovzhenko also wrote the script for *Ukraine in Flames* (not to be confused with *The Battle for Our Soviet Ukraine*'s U.S. release title). It had a similar theme to *The Battle for Our Soviet Ukraine*, but its perceived nationalism blocked its realization and blighted Dovzhenko's career.

Many contemporary reviewers claimed that there were twenty-four camera operators, although in fact twenty-nine are credited on *The Battle for Our Soviet Ukraine* and twenty-five on *Victory in Right-Bank Ukraine*. Both films feature footage taken by German forces (that was later captured), providing a more rounded depiction of the conflict. There was enough material to allow adherence to the 180-degree rule, with Germans usually attacking from left to right and the Soviet forces from right to left. Interspersed are speeches from party and army leaders, including Nikita Kruschev, head of the Ukrainian Communist Party, and direct-to-camera witness accounts from ordinary people with harrowing stories to tell. Considering the disparate origins of its elements, *The Battle for Our Soviet Ukraine* displays a remarkable coherence. Jay Leyda (1983, p. 377) proclaimed it "an inspiration to every artist who works in the documentary film."

Dovzhenko was dismayed by the indifferent reception the film received in the United States when it was released there in the spring of 1944. He noted in his diary entry for April 8, 1944: "She [the United States] didn't even want to look at the blood she is buying with her canned bacon" (1973, p. 105). This was a sentiment that echoed his government's demand for the opening of a second front, and the feeling that the Soviet Union was being asked to make enormous sacrifices while its allies stood by.

Critical opinion in the United States was indeed lukewarm. While acknowledging the unvarnished presentation and the effectiveness of the battle sequences, many of the reviews were carping, with negative comments on the clarity of the photography, the quality of the translated commentary, and the tendency of the pictures of devastation to have a certain sameness. These blasé assessments of the film's lack of technical polish ignored the far from ideal circumstances of production.

The British *Kinematograph Weekly*, by contrast, while noting the "family resemblance" of films depicting the effects of occupation, could still concede that *The Battle for Our Soviet Ukraine* was "a vivid indictment of German brutality," and highlight its depiction of suffering and the realism of the battle sequences. Similarly, *Monthly Film Bulletin* considered that, of the many documentaries originating from the Soviet front, few had "been so vivid or poignant as this." The difference in tone perhaps reflected the relative complacency of a country that had not experienced invasion, compared to one whose civilian population had itself suffered from direct attacks, and thus could therefore empathize with the misery of those subjected directly to the German war machine.

TOM RUFFLES

See also **Documentary Film: Russia/Soviet Union**

Further Reading

"The Battle for the Ukraine," *Kinematograph Weekly*, 16 March 1944, p. 33.

"The Battle for the Ukraine," *Monthly Film Bulletin*, 11, no. 125, 31 May 1944, p. 61.

Dovzhenko, Alexander, *The Poet as Filmmaker: Selected Writings*, Cambridge, MA: MIT Press, 1973.

Kenez, Peter, *Cinema and Soviet Society: From the Revolution to the Death of Stalin*, London: I.B. Tauris, 2001.

Leyda, Jay, *Kino: A History of the Russian and Soviet Film* (3rd ed.), London: George Allen and Unwin, 1983.

Marshall, Herbert, *Masters of the Soviet Cinema: Crippled Creative Biographies*, London: Routledge and Kegan Paul, 1983.

Roberts, Graham, *Forward Soviet: History and Non-Fiction Film in the USSR*, London: I.B. Taruis, 1999.

"Ukraine in Flames," *Motion Picture Critics' Reviews*, 22 January 1945, pp. 419–421. (A compilation of reviews from New York newspapers published in April 1944.)

"Ukraine in Flames," *Motion Picture Herald*, 15 April 1944, p. 1845.

BATTLE OF ALGIERS, THE

See **Near/ Middle East**

BATTLE OF CHILE, THE

(Cuba, Guzman, 1975–1977)

Patricio Guzman's *The Battle of Chile* marks the end of a brief but intense period of revolutionary filmmaking in his native country. In the late 1960s and early 1970s, Chilean feature and documentary filmmakers joined together in support of Popular Unity, a coalition of left-wing parties, producing work that protested the endemic poverty in their country. Guzman's film covers the political upheaval of 1973 from the election of Salvador Allende in February to the coup in September that overthrew the political changes effected by the Popular Unity and forced Guzman and his colleagues to work in exile.

The Battle of Chile is composed of three parts, "The Bourgeois Insurrection" (1975), "The Coup d'état" (1977), and "Popular Power" (1979). Part One covers the election of Allende and the ensuing middle-class revolt. Part Two covers popular demonstrations in support and opposition to Allende. It also treats strategic debates within the left. Part Three focuses on later mass organization efforts. The film opens with some of the last footage shot by Guzman and his crew: Allende is killed in the bombing of the La Moneda Palace and the Popular Unity party is effectively overthrown by the military coup supported by the middle class. With the denouement established at the outset, *The Battle of Chile* is set up to be studied more than experienced as a surprising narrative. Guzman intended the film, while polemical, to be more analytic than propagandistic: "From the very beginning, our idea was to make an analytical film, not an agitational one" (Burton, 1986, p. 51). After this opening shot, the film moves back to February, when the crew began filming, shortly before the narrow election of Allende.

Led by cinematographer Jorge Müller Silva, *The Battle of Chile* was shot with a team of handheld cameras by Guzmán and his team of collaborators, called El Equipo Tercer Año (The Third Year Group). The group participated in extended technical and theoretical discussions before filming began, defining five "fronts of struggle" to focus the project. (See *Cine-tracts,* No. 9 (Vol. 3, No. 1), 1980, pp. 46–49.) This allowed the cameramen to focus on capturing certain events effectively rather than worry over which events to record or neglect. By Guzmán's account, the more polished shots of the film were the result of his collaboration with

The Battle of Chile, 1975–1977.
[*Still courtesy of the British Institute*]

Müller, where he would survey ongoing events while relaying specific filming strategies to Müller: "Since I tried to anticipate for him what was about to happen, I could tell him to pan, to lower the camera, to raise it, instructing him to make certain movements that are much more readily identified with fictional than with documentary filmmaking" (Burton, 1986, p. 57).

Even with this preplanning and improvised direction, the nature of the subject meant that the group had a limited amount of control over what they were able to film or, in some cases, found themselves filming. The filmmakers often capture planned events, such as governmental meetings, protests, and funerals, but as frequently tape unexpected developments.

Distinct scenes are often bridged by voice-over commentary, but the majority of analysis is provided by interviewed subjects. This one camera, one soundman style of filmmaking is most commonly known as direct or observational cinema. Here, the cameramen aim more to record as much of what unfolds before them than to produce polished shots. The editors of *The Battle of Chile* seem to have selected which scenes to include based on their impact or historical significance much more than their technical perfection. Shots with a shaky axis or blurring pans are often left in the film. In one scene, amidst unrest in the streets, the camera sweeps past the marquee of a movie theater. It announces that *Violent City*, starring Charles Bronson, is showing in Metrocolor. This brief reference to mainstream feature filmmaking reminds the spectator of the rhetorical, stylistic, and substantive differences between the type of cinema exemplified by *The Battle of Chile* versus this American feature. Moving past the marquee, the camera reveals an urban landscape lit with fire, running crowds, and the sounds of an ambulance. The fact that *Violent City* is showing in a truly riven, violent city jolts the spectator into recognition that, though certainly not shot in 35mm or Metrocolor, *The Battle of Chile* is a real document not to be conflated with Hollywood filmmaking. A more insistent reminder of this comes later.

In the most famous scene of the film, which closes Part One and opens Part Two, Argentine cameraman Leonardo Henricksen is shot and killed by a Chilean Army officer during the aborted coup in June. Here, the camera focuses on an officer who looks directly at the camera and fires; the image loses its balance and turns black.

Although the observational method of filmmaking employed in *The Battle of Chile* frequently produces objective shots that don't explicity support nor oppose Allende, the left-wing political interest that was the impetus behind the project is more forcefully present in certain scenes, sometimes even in the shooting style. While the filmmakers begin by covering both sides of the electorate prior to Allende's election, often interviewing families at home in addition to mass demonstrations, afterwards the filmmakers appear more frequently and more intimately with Allende's sympathizers. Guzman and his colleagues frequently film amidst leftist demonstrations, interviewing participants in the middle of crowds. They also travel with and interview workers on truck beds en route to union meetings. The right wing is shown in more formal settings or, if on the streets, from a greater distance. At a meeting of the American Institute for Free Trade Unionism (a group funded indirectly by the CIA that encourages managers in the transportation sector to oppose Allende's policies), an unidentified speaker is shot in a low-angle close-up. His face monstrously fills the screen, with deep black nostrils flaring and a gaping mouth. Words that may already displease the viewer are colored even more insidiously by this stylistic choice.

In an interview, Guzman states that the film was made to support Popular Unity, but none of its constitutive parties, mostly notably the Communists and Socialists, in particular. This was typical of Chilean documentary in this period, which was galvanized by a manifesto by Miguel Littín, another filmmaker and head of Chile Films, the national film production company. Littín called for the development of a leftist cinema that would valorize the workers and labor leaders who fought for Allende's reforms. Although Guzman follows the principles that Littín outlines, *The Battle of Chile* was made without the help of Chile Films, which was too unstable to support the project.

The Battle of Chile, while shot by Chileans, received a great deal of international support in terms of production. French documentary filmmaker Chris Marker provided the film stock with which the picture was shot. After shooting was complete, fearing the destruction of his footage, Guzman smuggled his film to Cuba following Allende's assassination. *The Battle of Chile* was edited in Cuba at the Cuban Institute of Film Art and Industry (ICAIC). With the help of solidarity campaigns, the film was distributed around the world and became the most prominent testament of the coup. Guzman and other Chilean filmmakers went on to produce a startling amount of work in exile (176 films, 56 of which were features between 1973 and 1983), becoming the most successful Latin American "cinema of exile" in this period.

JESSE SCHLOTTERBECK

See also **Guzman, Patricio**

The Battle of Chile / La Batalla de Chile (Chile, El Equipo Tercer Año / ICAIC, 1975–1979, 315 min.). Directed by Patricio Guzman. Produced by Chris Marker. Cinematography by Jorge Müller Silva. Film editing by Pedro Chaskel.

Further Reading

Burton, Julianne (ed.), "Patricio Guzman: Chile, Politics and the Documentary in People's Chile," in *Cinema and Social Change in Latin America: Conversations with Filmmakers*, edited by Burton, Austin, TX: University of Texas Press, 1986.

Gupta, Udayan, and *FLQ* Staff, "An Interview with Patricio Guzman, director of *The Battle of Chile*," *Film Library Quarterly*, 11, no. 4, 1978, 16–20.

King, John, *Magical Reels: A History of Cinema in Latin America*, New York: Verso, 2000.

Lopez, Ana M., "*The Battle of Chile*: Documentary, Political Process, and Representation," in *The Social Documentary in Latin America*, edited by Julianne Burton, Pittsburgh, PA: University of Pittsburgh Press, 1990, 267–288.

Martin, Michael T. (ed.), *New Latin American Cinema*, Detroit: Wayne State University Press, 1997.

Pick, Zuzana M., "Chile: The Cinema of Resistance, 1973–1979," "Interview with Patricio Guzman: *La Batalla de Chile*," "Letter from Guzman to Chris Marker," "Reflections Previous to the Filming of *The Battle of Chile*," "*The Battle of Chile*: A Schematic Shooting Script," Part of a Special Section on Chilean Cinema, *Cine-tracts*, No. 9, vol.. 3, no. 1, 1980, 18–49.

Schumann, Peter B., *Historia del cine latinoamericano*, Buenos Aires: Editorial Legasa, 1987.

BATTLE OF CHINA, THE

(US, Capra, 1944)

Sixth in the "Why We Fight" series produced by the U.S. Army during World War II, *The Battle of China* builds on *The Nazis Strike* (1943), *Divide and Conquer* (1943), and *The Battle of Russia* (1944) through collaboration among Hollywood's top hands. Frank Capra, one of America's premier theatrical filmmakers, directed the film, stamping it with his recognizable personal style. Anatole Litvak, another influential Hollywood figure co-directed and oversaw production, without credit in both cases. Julius Epstein handled writing, William Hornbeck edited, Dimitri Tiomkin composed original music, and Anthony Veiller narrated. All worked together on the earlier documentaries.

Lacking Germany's propaganda machinery, Japan offered meager film footage for Capra to exploit for propaganda purposes. While some scenes in *The Battle of China* originated in Japan, Capra turned to stock Hollywood theatrical footage to help offset the deficit. The film states, "Certain non-combat stock scenes were used from historical pictures," but never identifies theatrical footage. Where documentary film ends and Hollywood stock begins is deliberately indistinct.

The Battle of China appropriates and makes use of several stock patriotic symbols and images. Visual and auditory cues, such as the "V for Victory" symbol superimposed on a ringing Liberty Bell, solicit predictable audience response. A rousing bugle call summons the troops, over an image of a road sign pointing to Tokyo. Thematic elements emphasize similarities, real and imaginary, between China and the United States. Confucius represents the Golden Rule and Sun Yat Sen becomes China's George Washington. While General Chiang Kai-Shek marches, Patton-like, across the screen, Madame Chiang addresses Congress. "China's war is our war" is the resounding theme.

The Battle of China permits neither balance nor misinterpretation. The Chinese, with "indestructible spirit," proceed on their "Homeric journey to freedom," while their "courage never faltered." Through simplistic graphics, Chinese military disasters become "trading space for time," while "feverish," or "blood-crazed" Japanese soldiers "outdid themselves in barbarism," perpetrating a "nightmare of cruelty." The "oldest and youngest of the world's great nations," filmgoers are assured, fight "side-by-side," "civilization against barbarism," "good against evil." In the process, this film demonstrates effective propaganda. In 2000, *The Battle of China* won the National Film Registry award of the National Film Preservation Board.

MICHAEL S. CASEY

See also **Battle of Russia; Capra, Frank; Litvak, Anatole; War: WWII**

The Battle of China (USA, Army Signal Corps, 1944, 65 min., black and white). Produced by War Department. Directed by Frank Capra and Anatole Litvak (un-credited). Music composed by Dimitri Tiomkin (un-credited), performed by Army Air Force Orchestra. Editing by William W. Hornbeck (un-credited). Narration by Anthony Veiller.

Further Reading

Capra, Frank. *The Name Above the Title: An Autobiography*, New York: Da Capo Press, 1997.
Capra, Frank (ed.), *The Men Who Made the Movies*, Chicago: Ivan R. Dee, 2001.
Jeavons, Clyde. *A Pictorial History of War Films*, Seacaucus, NJ: Citadel Press, 1974.

BATTLE OF MIDWAY, THE

(US, Ford, 1942)

The first U.S. combat documentary to receive wide commercial distribution during World War II, *The Battle of Midway,* was a project largely without precedent. As might be expected of a work sanctioned by the U.S. Navy and President Franklin Roosevelt, the film commemorates the heroism of American forces in battle and illustrates the vital link between home front and war front at an early stage of U.S. involvement in the war. But director John Ford, who was on leave from Hollywood as head of the Field Photographic branch of the Office of the Coordinator of Information (later the OSS), also experiments with formal elements and incorporates themes of importance to his work as a fiction filmmaker. In this regard, *The Battle of Midway* seems no less deeply personal a work for the political calculations that shaped its making.

Ford had previously supervised the production of training films for new recruits and reconnaissance films for the high command. But the three-day battle at the Pacific Ocean atoll of Midway, 1,100 miles northwest of Pearl Harbor, in early June 1942 provided Ford with an opportunity to extend his wartime work in a new direction. Accepting an assignment to photograph the defense of the U.S. Naval Air Station at Midway, Ford navigated the shoals of military, governmental, and studio bureaucracies to retain control over the footage, shifting postproduction from Washington to Los Angeles on the Twentieth Century Fox lot. Speculations about the distribution of Ford's new documentary was a topic of much comment in the Hollywood trade press in late summer, leading up to the release of *The Battle of Midway* by the War Activities Committee and Fox in September. Seven first-run houses in New York ran the film, as did six in Los Angeles; eventually 500 prints were circulated nationwide. The following March, *The Battle of Midway* was among four films named Best Documentary by the Academy of Motion Picture Arts and Sciences.

Remarkably, *The Battle of Midway* devotes little of its eighteen minutes to explaining the wider causes and significance of the battle, a turning point in the Pacific campaign. We learn nothing about the arrangement of naval and air forces on the eve of battle or the tactical maneuvering on either side, including the crucial decoding of cables that alerted U.S. officials to a feint of Japanese forces toward the Aleutians and the pending Midway air attack. Instead, the film offers a series of impressions of the Midway outpost and its occupants before, during, and after the battle, emphasizing the natural beauty and serenity of the islands and surrounding waters, the ominous stillness of an evening watch as silhouetted soldiers stand guard before a setting sun, the perceptual disorientation and confusion produced by the bombing and strafing of the islands, and the

Battle of Midway, 1942.
[*Courtesy of the Everett Collection*]

resilience and determination of the American marines tested by the attack.

Ford's account of the battle, moreover, does not shy away from images of destruction—billowing black smoke against a cobalt sky; gutted buildings; twisted metal, wreckage, and rubble; the injured and the dead—and a concluding account of burial-at-sea functions as elegiac counterpoint to a more aggressively martial coda in which victory is asserted and the costs to the enemy enumerated. Alfred Newman's musical score, incorporating familiar military and national anthems and hymns, is crucial to the overall rhythmic effects. In this regard, *The Battle of Midway* seems less journalistic than musical in design, indebted, as Tag Gallagher has suggested, to nineteenth-century battle compositions, with different musical markers signaling striking shifts in tone.

Contemporaneous reviewers found *The Battle of Midway*'s combat footage—shot in 16mm Technicolor by Ford and Jack MacKenzie, his 20-year-old first mate, from their post on Midway's Eastern Island—particularly compelling. (Additional air and sea photography was provided by Kenneth M. Pier, who accompanied pilots off the *U.S.S. Hornet*, and brief footage of an "Ohio family" at home was supplied by cinematographer Gregg Toland.) The footage was assembled by editor Robert Parrish in two extended battle passages marked by free-hand camerawork and expressively disjointed cutting, with the descent of planes and multiple explosions interspersed with the reactions of marines returning anti-aircraft fire. At times, the image track seems to slip its sprockets, as a visible frame line optically registers the force of the concussion, and a sense of geography is lost amid the smoke and floating debris. Early in the assault, Ford was knocked unconscious by one such explosion and received a flesh wound, for which he was awarded the Purple Heart. Reports of this, circulated by the press, only served to enhance the perceived authenticity of the film as photographic document.

Ford's experiments with vocal commentary proved of greater controversy. Soliciting scripts from screenwriter Dudley Nichols and MGM executive James Kevin McGuinness, based on personal notes, Ford supervised the reading of the commentary by four actors—Donald Crisp, Irving Pichel, Henry Fonda, and James Darwell—the last two of whom were currently at work on *The Ox Bow Incident* on the Fox lot. Above and beyond conventional scene-setting, the commentary dramatizes, and works to bridge, the gap between depicted events and their presentation to the viewer, a function most conspicuously evident when Darwell, speaking as if an American mother watching the Midway footage, expresses urgent concern for the well-being of the young pilots far from home.

Some critics at the time found the commentary overly intrusive or sentimental; Darwell's dialogue, in particular, was thought an unwarranted Hollywood touch. Ford, however, who claimed to have wanted to make the film for "the mothers of America," never expressed regret about these choices, and Parrish recalls that audiences at Radio City Music Hall were audibly moved by it. Certainly the selection of this particular quartet of voices was not gratuitous; Fonda and Darwell evoke the poignant leave-taking scene from Ford's film version of *The Grapes of Wrath* (1940); Crisp and Pichel likewise use Ford's adaptation of *How Green Was My Valley* (1941), with its wistful memorial view of a Welsh mining family. Strands of "Red River Valley," lifted from the sound track to *The Grapes of Wrath* for the evening watch in *The Battle of Midway*, reinforce these associations. Trading in heightened emotion, certain moments on the sound track thus demonstrate possible points of intersection between combat narratives and domestic melo-drama, genres then sharing the screen of movie houses. They also serve a wider project of re-imagining community ties between home front and battle front under the pressure of a global war.

CHARLES WOLFE

Battle of Midway, The (US, United States Navy, 1942, 18 mins.). Distributed by Reel Media International, Twentieth Century Fox Film Corp., and the War Activities Committee. Directed by John Ford. Written by John Ford Dudley Nichols and James Kevin McGuiness (as James K. McGuiness). Produced by John Ford. Original music by Alfred Newman. Cinematography by John Ford, Jack MacKenzie, and Kenneth M. Pier. Edited by John Ford and Robert Parrish.

Further Reading

Doherty, Thomas, *Projections of War: Hollywood, American Culture and World War II*, New York: Columbia University Press, 1993.

Ford, Dan, *Pappy: The Life of John Ford*, New York: DaCapo, 1998.

Gallagher, Tag, "John Ford: Midway, The War Documentaries," *Film Comment* (September–October 1975), 40–46.

Gallagher, Tag, *John Ford: The Man and His Films*, Berkeley: University of California Press, 1986.

McBride, Joseph, *Searching for John Ford: A Life*, New York: St. Martin's Press, 2001.

William T. Murphy, "John Ford and the Wartime Documentary," *Films & History*, February 1976.

Parrish, Robert, *Growing Up in Hollywood*, New York: Harcourt Brace Janovich, 1976.

Wolfe, Charles, "Historicizing the 'Voice of God': The Place of Vocal Narration in Classical Documentary," *Film History*, 9, no. 2, 1997, 149–167.

BATTLE OF RUSSIA, THE

(US, Litvak, 1944)

The Battle of Russia was the fifth installment in the group of American World War II propaganda films known as the *Why We Fight* series. The films in the series, a total of seven, fall into two major groups: those that provided historical background for the events in Europe and Asia (*Prelude to War* [1943], *The Nazis Strike* [1943], *Divide and Conquer* [1943], and *War Comes to America* [1945]), and those that detailed specific campaigns of the war and the respective allies involved in those campaigns. *The Battle of Russia*, along with *The Battle of Britain* (1943) and *The Battle of China* (1944), form the latter group. *The Battle of Russia*, like the other films in this subgroup, was intended to educate the audience about a nation and ally to which most Americans were traditionally adverse. The resulting film is one of the only pro-Soviet films ever produced by the U.S. government.

Although most of the credit for the *Why We Fight* series has traditionally, and justifiably, been given to Frank Capra, these films were collaborative projects, and thus it is important to recognize all of those involved in the production of *The Battle of Russia*. Capra received producer credit for the film, and by all accounts worked closely and intensively with director Anatole Litvak to give the film its shape and orientation. Eric Knight, who headed a team of seven screenwriters, is largely responsible for the film's verbose scripted narration, which was spoken by Walter Huston. The score for the film was done by Hollywood veteran Dmitri Tomkin and drew heavily on Tchaikovsky as well as traditional Russian folk songs and ballads. Although collaboration was obviously important to the genesis of *The Battle of Russia*, it is important to reiterate the important role that Litvak and Capra played in combining the elements of the film into a cohesive whole. As a compilation film, *The Battle of Russia*'s footage is derived from various sources, including newsreels, amateur filming, and fiction films. From these disparate sources Litvak and Capra, along with veteran editor Walter Hornbeck, created a cogent report on the Russian people and their battle against Hitler's army.

The film itself consists of two parts, the first dealing with a history of the Russian people up to and including the peak of the Nazi invasions of Russia (December 1941). The second part of the film begins with winter falling on the Nazi invaders and goes on to detail the heroic Russian counterattack launched during that winter, which not only

Why We Fight 5 (Battle of Russia), documentary by Frank Capra and Anatole Litvak, 1943.
[*Courtesy of the Everett Collection*]

drove the Germans back, but also, as the film's narrator pointedly reminds us, "shattered the myth of Nazi invincibility," and thus boosted the Allied hopes for an eventual defeat of Hitler and his forces. To illustrate all of this, the second part focuses especially on two decisive battles, those at Leningrad and those at Stalingrad.

Formally, *The Battle of Russia* is the epitome of the compilation film. Shots and sounds are recontextualized in such a way as to present the images as supportive of the film's argument, without a questioning of the image itself; thus, viewers take footage from *Alexander Nevsky* (Eisenstein, 1938) as representation of historical fact. This phenomenon is achieved in *The Battle of Russia* not only through skillful montage but also through the employment of a unifying voice-over that dominates the film's soundtrack. Thomas Bohn points out that voice-over narration is present in 75 percent of the film, well above contemporary theoretical protocol, which called for no more than two-thirds of the visual track to be accompanied by narration. Nonetheless, the narration in *The Battle of Russia* is not excessive. The material presented was both complex and obscure to the film's audience, and at no point does the film's propagandistic tone break down into obvious repetition. Besides the prominent narration, the film's informative mode demanded an abundance of animated effects to illustrate tactical concepts such as "wedge and trap" and "defense in depth," as well as troop movements and other military maneuvers.

Thematically, the film falls in line with the messages presented throughout the *Why We Fight* series: Germany's invasion of Russia represents an encroachment of the "slave world" into the "free world" of Russia, with a fascist army threatening a

Why We Fight 5 (Battle of Russia), documentary by Frank Capra and Anatole Litvak, 1943.
[*Courtesy of the Everett Collection*]

peace-loving, pious, and proud people. The depravity of the Germans is reiterated throughout the film with constant reminders that German soldiers were literally raping and pillaging their way through the Russian countryside. But, as the film's most famous line, "Generals may win campaigns, but people win wars," indicates, the film is concerned with showing how the spirit of a people can defeat even the mightiest army. The film's concluding shots, showing the Russian army along with the armies of all of the Allies marching off to presumable victory, underscore the idea that the United States and Russia are "in this together," and thus point to the film's true goal, that of propagandizing unity with the heretofore (and afterwards as well) adversarial Russians.

The success of the film in achieving this goal is illustrated by the film's popularity, which extended beyond the military audience for which it was initially intended. *The Battle of Russia* was the second of the *Why We Fight* films to receive an Academy Award nomination for Best Documentary feature. The film was also popular abroad, with Stalin ordering hundreds of prints to be shown in Russian theaters. But like all propaganda films, *The Battle of Russia* served its historical purpose and was quickly dated as an artifact of government policy. The necessary propagandistic elisions that the film presents (not mentioning the word *communist* once, the avoidance of any mention of the Stalin-Hitler nonaggression pact, and the praise for the piety of an officially atheist state), made the film unsuitable for post-war policies. The film was too good at sympathetically portraying Stalin and Russia, and was withdrawn from circulation during the Cold War, making it one of the most ironically effective propaganda pieces in documentary history.

CHRISTOPHER MEIR

See also **The Battle of China; Capra, Frank; Litvak, Anatole**

The Battle of Russia (US, 1944, 80 min.). Distributed by Twentieth Century Fox Film Corporation, Questar Pictures, and the War Activities Committee of the Motion Pictures Industry. Produced by Frank Capra. Directed by Frank Capra and Anatole Litvak. Written by Julius J. Epstein, Philip G. Epstein, Rober Heller, Anatole Litvak, and Anthony Veiller. Film editing by William Hornbeck. Original music by Dimitri Tiomkin. Non-original music by Pyotr Ilyich Tchaikovsky. Commentary by Walter Huston.

Further Reading

Barsam, Richard, "Why We Fight," in *Frank Capra: The Man and His Films*, edited by Richard Glatzer and John Raeburn, Ann Arbor: University of Michigan Press, 1975, 149–154.

Bohn, Thomas, *An Historical and Descriptive Analysis of the "Why We Fight" Series*. New York: Arno Press, 1977.

Culbert, David, *Film and Propaganda in America: A Documentary History Vols. II–IV*, New York: Greenwood Press, 1990.

Maland, Charles J. *Frank Capra*. Boston: Twayne Publishers, 1980.

Rollins, Peter C., "Frank Capra's *Why We Fight* Series and Our American Dream," *Journal of American Culture*, 19, no. 4, 1996, 81–86.

BATTLE OF SAN PIETRO, THE

(US, Huston, 1945)

The Battle of San Pietro, a documentary about one battle in Italy in the Allied campaign in World War II, is the most critically acclaimed wartime documentary ever produced under the auspices of the U.S. War Department. The film makes use of maps, charts, and voice-over narration to provide an account of this battle. The more lasting contribution of *The Battle of San Pietro*, however, emerges from its meditation on the experience of the infantryman, and its larger insights into the destructiveness of war and the resilience of the human spirit.

The Battle of San Pietro bears the unmistakable stamp of its director, writer, and voice-over narrator, the Hollywood filmmaker John Huston. Before the war, Huston had been primarily known as a screenwriter, but his talents as a director were proven after the release of *The Maltese Falcon* (1941). Along with Frank Capra, William Wyler, John

Ford, and others, Huston was one of several prominent filmmakers enlisted in the American war effort. Huston made three war documentaries for the U.S. Army Pictorial Service: *Report from the Aleutians* (1943), *The Battle of San Pietro*, and *Let There Be Light* (1945). The latter film, about veterans under treatment for various mental problems resulting from combat, was suppressed by the War Department until 1980 (Simmon, 2000, p. 58).

Huston was sent to Italy in 1943 to document the triumphant entry of American forces into Rome, but the ground offensive met stiff resistance from the Germans and slowed to a halt north of Naples. Huston was reassigned to make a film "that would explain to American audiences why U.S. forces in Italy were no longer advancing" (Huston, 1980, p. 109). American forces had moved into position at the foot of the Liri Valley, through which meandered the main road to Rome. The German defenses had taken position in and around the little village of San Pietro, and were about to offer some deadly resistance to Allied advances.

The film begins with a two-minute introduction by General Mark Clark, who led the U.S. Fifth Army into the Liri Valley, explaining that San Pietro was key to the region and that in light of the importance of the objective, casualties were "not excessive." It is widely assumed that Clark's introductory words were designed and tacked on by the War Department to counter the film's implication that casualties *were* excessive. According to William Nolan, however, Huston wrote the opening narration for Clark, thinking that Clark would have it reworked for his own purposes. Huston was surprised when Clark used the speech unaltered: "Now, there was this four-star general repeating, word for word, the strategy of the campaign as I saw it . . . and me just a dogface in it! I guess he didn't know any more about what was going on than I did" (Nolan, 1965, p. 51).

In part the film chronicles the progress of, and military strategy employed in, Allied attempts to take San Pietro and the surrounding hills. The film's finest points are to be found elsewhere, however. Huston's film unit, with its 35mm handheld Eyemo newsreel cameras (Haskew, 2000, p. 82), was attached to the 143rd Infantry Regiment of the 36th Texas Infantry Division. *The Battle of San Pietro* manages to convey the men's experience through footage that captures the violence of battle, including numerous close-ups of men's faces, shots of the many casualties as they lie on the battlefield or are wrapped in shrouds, and narrated accounts of the extreme danger of the infantry attacks. The 143rd Regiment alone required 1,100 replacements after the Battle of San Pietro (Hus-

ton, 1985, p. 115). Huston has said that he made the film to express admiration for the courage and fortitude of the common foot soldier.

Where Frank Capra's wartime documentaries are highly propagandistic, Huston was unable or unwilling to hide his strong misgivings about the war. *The Battle of San Pietro* archly and subtly demonstrates the war's effect on the townspeople, on the town, on San Pietro's artistic and cultural treasures, and on nature itself. It does so in part through what has been called "one of the most memorable voice-over narrations in film—both in script and delivery" (Simmon, 2000, p. 59). After shots of the broken town of San Pietro, we see a pock-marked statue of St. Peter as well as the ruined church of St. Peter's, its dome missing to reveal the sky above. In voice-over, Huston intones something apparently taken from a tourist guidebook: "Patron Saint, Peter, point of interest, St. Peter's, 1438, note interesting treatment of chancel." Toward the film's end, Huston sums up with shots of men digging graves and slow pans across the faces of the survivors:

> The lives lost were precious lives—to their country, to their loved ones, and to the men themselves . . . many among these you see alive here have since joined the ranks of their brothers at arms, who fell at San Pietro. For ahead lay San Battore, and the Rapido River, and Cassino, and beyond Cassino more rivers, and more mountains, and more towns, more San Pietros, greater or lesser, a thousand more.

Toward the film's end, we see a montage of images of children emerging from the rubble, some smiling, some obviously frightened but too curious to remain in hiding. James Agee objected to the "emotional sales pressure" of the music of the Mormon Tabernacle Choir here. Nonetheless, he called the scene "radiant with illimitable suggestions of meaning and mystery" and "the first great passage of war poetry that has got on the screen" (Agee, 1945). We see shots of the people of the village returning to their daily routines, carrying water, plowing, and sowing seeds. Huston's narration tells us that although the prime military aim had been to defeat the enemy, the people looked upon the Americans as their deliverers. We see a religious procession, and the voice-over narration ends the film: "And the people pray to their patron saint to intercede with God on behalf of those who came to deliver them . . . and passed on to the North with the passing battle."

Upon finishing the film, Huston showed it to a group of officers, who pronounced the film "antiwar" and decided to withhold distribution. Huston told the officers that if he ever made a picture that *was* pro-war, he "hoped someone would take me out and shoot me" (Huston, 1980, p. 120). *The Battle of San Pietro* presented the battle not as a strategic victory, but as a small battle in a costly and continuing campaign. General George C. Marshall later asked to see the film, and later pronounced that all army trainees should see it to become better prepared for the shock of battle. Huston was promoted to major. *The Battle of San Pietro* was released in 1945, however, after the Allied victory, and having been cut from five to three reels. Although it did not fulfill its original military objective, it remains one of the most humane and artful war documentaries ever made. As James Agee wrote in 1945, "it is in every way as good a war film as I have seen; in some ways it is the best."

CARL R. PLANTINGA

See also **Huston, John**

The Battle of San Pietro (US, John Huston, 1945, 33 min.). Produced by the U.S. Army Pictorial Service. Directed, written, and narrated by John Huston. Cinematography by Jules Buck, John Huston, and other Signal Corps cameramen. Music by Dmitri Tiomkin, performed by the Army Air Force Orchestra, the Mormon Tabernacle Choir, and St. Brendan's Boys Choir.

Further Reading

Agee, James, "Review of *San Pietro*," *The Nation*, 160, May 1945, 608.
Haskew, Michael E., "San Pietro: Capturing the Face of War," *Military History* 17, December 2000, 50–59.
Huston, John, *John Huston: An Open Book*, New York: Alfred A. Knopf, 1980.
Nolan, William F., *John Huston: King Rebel*, Los Angeles: Sherbourne Press, 1965.
Simmon, Scott, "The Battle of San Pietro," in *Treasures from the American Film Archives*, National Film Preservation Foundation, 2000, 58–61.

BATTLE OF THE SOMME

(UK, Urban, 1916)

Of the various documentaries made under official auspices during WWI, *The Battle of the Somme* has rightly assumed a key place. It broke all box office records, as thousands were turned away in the first week despite its having opened simultaneously at over thirty London cinemas. More than one theatre was exhibiting it to 10,000 people a day, and the Finsbury Park Cinema attracted over 50,000 people in that first week. Thereafter, 100 prints were distributed around the provinces, and within two months hiring fees had been scaled down from £40 a week to £8 for three nights, bringing it within reach of the smallest cinemas. *Bioscope* complained of unfair competition when music halls hired it instead of limiting themselves to shorts. But it drew many into the cinema for the first time. Still more important, it provided a huge stimulus for the idea of a British film archive. Langford Reed noted that in 1913 both Copenha-

gen's Royal Library and the Louvre had established film sections, similar archives existing in the Vatican, Madrid, and New York. Meanwhile, the British Museum resisted because film was combustible and impermanent. But the press considered it unthinkable that *Somme* prints should not be preserved for posterity.

The film covers the first phase of the Somme offensive, which was to last about four months, with an advance of some thousand yards at the expense of more than half a million British casualties. This opening phase, and the huge preparations that had been necessary, generated footage enough for a feature-length propaganda film, although disjointedness betrays its opportunist origins. Both the Germans and French produced their own Somme films, the former, claimed by *The Times* to be technically superb. It focused on the devastation wrought on French towns by Allied guns, and

German care for enemy wounded. The two German attacks were obvious fakes. The film allegedly "followed the British model as closely as possible," and certainly the French version did so. This began with preparations: "long files of marching soldiers and vast stores of ammunition," then trenches "full of soldiers ready to leap out," the attack, and numerous Germans surrendering.

French troops, who had bled too freely at Verdun to be able to make their expected contribution on the Somme, have little place in the British film. But there is an image of enduring French peasant women, toiling within view of a military camp that proclaims the ever-present hazards of war. The film is especially distinguished by the amount of attention given to casualties. Topicals, no longer free from censorship, were shorn of "realistic horrors of war" by either civil censor or service departments, leaving *Cinema*'s reviewer unprepared for the Somme film's images of "war, rich with death." These same images continue to shape people's understanding of the war, because the "over the top" sequence has been used repeatedly as television producers' shorthand. Indeed, it was passed off, in the official compilation *America Goes Over* (1927), as U.S. Signal Corps filming of the Doughboys' "Jump-off" at St Mihiel in September 1918. A contemporary letter to the *Nation* quoted the *Manchester Guardian*: "Two years ago the public exhibition of horrors like this would have been condemned as an indecency." Its writer, wondering what could have happened in the course of those two years, resented the soldiers' sufferings being turned into an entertainment. Others, notably the Dean of Durham in a letter to *The Times*, protested "against an entertainment which wounds the heart and violates the very sanctities of bereavement." But the *Daily News* gloated that the provinces were devouring it "with an eagerness which must be not a little disturbing to the Dean of Durham"; and bereaved *Times* readers found his objections "squeamish and sentimental."

John Raphael, *Era*'s Paris correspondent, focuses on those "over the top" scenes, the core of the film since without them people would have been unconvinced by the remainder. Apparently an officer friend gave him an eyewitness account of their filming, when the cameraman "was actually crouching in that foremost trench, protected by nothing but a few sandbags, and operating through a hole." These scenes were almost certainly staged, though his remarks may result from confusion rather than a desire to tell a good story or offset rumors of faking. Faked or not, they worked powerfully on many people. "My God, they're dead," cried one woman; at another cinema "two men fainted, but not a single

woman." Elsewhere "a woman felt faint, but after a sip of water outside insisted on returning to the theatre and seeing the film through." On the whole, audiences seem to have been awe-stricken at feeling themselves witness to youthful vitality extinguished by unseen forces; but one evening-gowned flapper complained: "It is rather too sad. They ought to cut out the gruesome bits."

That "gruesome bits" were included at all was doubtless due to the need to make some acknowledgment of the appalling casualty lists, and of public resentment that official films had revealed so little. Thus, this film purports to let people in on war's grim secrets while still keeping them from the truth. Malins knew how mild it was. Even so, he had feared "that some of the dead scenes" might offend. Graves's "certain cure for lust of blood" had to be avoided if the film was not to provoke demand for an end to the carnage. At the same time thrills were needed to draw the public; the trick was to offer glimpses of war's grimness before sending them home, cheered with the prospect of victory. Malins discovered that editing involved "discretion, diplomacy and tact" with so many interests to be served and "so much ... at stake." The central ploy was to translate death to willing and glorious sacrifice. This was the rhetoric used in Lloyd George's statement that accompanied the film, canny enough to infect responses from some of the bereaved: "I never understood their sacrifice until I had seen this film." It was blazoned on countless happily smiling faces of men marching up the line, earnest in their belief in what they were doing. The authorities, far more skilled in mass psychology than in handling world affairs, understood that people *wanted* to be persuaded: It was so much easier to cope with loss if the bereaved could believe in the cause and its leaders. But the justness of a cause is not sufficient to maintain people's commitment to it; they must believe that it will prevail. Raphael was one among many who found the film worked wonderfully in this respect. Although he had never doubted final victory, the film made him feel safer and more confident than ever: "Look at the German prisoners as they pass on the film and you can see that Germany knows that she is fighting a losing fight." To his selective eye, personal shabbiness proclaims their loss of morale, whereas there is not "a dirty or unshaven man" among the British (the German film showed Germans brushing their uniforms). British citizens smile while Germans cringe, and the "poor fellow whose own leg is badly smashed, giving up the corner he has found to rest it in to a fainting German prisoner," typifies the chivalry of troops assured of their own superiority.

Another resource for victory on display was British hardware—guns of many calibers being shown in action. Here is the neat evasion used in TV coverage of the Gulf War. Audiences marvel at the technology, losing sight of end results: people blown to pieces or shredded by shrapnel. But there was also targeting of the many munition workers seeking relief in the cinema. Pre-battle sequences include great stacks of shells that not only acknowledge the logistics of conflict but also the hard work being done at home to sustain the army in the field. This is both a pat on the back and an exhortation to continued effort. The aim is to balance humanity with technology. As "Blanche" says in the *Bystander*, the horror of modern war is that people become cogs in a destructive machine. Naturally, it is the Hun who has robbed war of its romance, and a main objective of the struggle is to reeducate him. This shows on screen when "a German prisoner, sitting dazed among his enemies, is offered a cigarette by a British soldier. In a moment, as someone put it, 'his face is beautifully lit—lit with the sudden glory of the truth that men are men, and in their humanity triumphant over any process that would make them less than men.'"

There were complaints that the film was sometimes screened in incongruous company, even farce; but it was often slotted at short notice into existing programs. Whatever the circumstances, it is clear that the film was never viewed passively, although there is evidence that audiences had generally lost their old demonstrativeness. People shouted excitedly when they recognized someone on screen. At the Maida Vale Palace one interruption came from "a wounded Gordon [who] saw himself being medically attended at Minden Post." There were also more formal commentaries: Lieutenant F. R. Holmes, later to accompany one of the cinemotors touring the country, lectured at the Scala in "a breezy, pleasant, chatty manner." At Norwich and elsewhere parties of wounded were taken to see the film, and many of them would have had no trouble in filling out the gaps left by editorial reticence. One wounded soldier in a Shaftesbury Avenue cinema broke down when he saw the "the dead Devons lying on the battlefield, with the battery of artillery moving forward. He sobbed like a child and a nurse led him out of the theatre." *Cinema*'s reviewer noted how dozens of wheels passed the bodies without any desecrating them. But perhaps the wounded soldier was an artilleryman, who knew that gun teams could hardly avoid sprawled bodies as they careered along corduroy tracks. Besides, the fastidiousness of men and horses (who prefer not to trample on bloodied corpses) succumbs to the terrors of shellfire.

There are various other moments when front-line experience would have taken viewers behind the film's glib narrative. Even scenes of soldiers' ablutions, reassuring to mothers with soldier-sons still young enough to forget to wash behind their ears, would remind the trench soldier of the scarcity of clean water up the line. And if he had been in any large attack, he would probably imagine General de Lisle's pep talk on the eve of battle not in the clichéd terms recorded by Malins, but more like Brigadier-General Tuxford's distortions about German war on the wounded, which had fighting mad troops screaming "Remember the *Llandovery Castle!*"

Some deconstruction of the film's narrative has been undertaken by Smithers, who points to a dozen questionable episodes. Most striking is the July 1 mine explosion at Hawthorn Redoubt, which is followed by a shot of what purports to be the resulting crater. It probably represents the aftermath of a July 5 explosion, and its later repetition smacks of editorial carelessness. What was probably editorial calculation was the inclusion of that moment of irritation as "one of the English 'Tommies' gives a German prisoner a dig in the ribs." The American trade paper *Variety*, seeing the film as a potential "gold mine," proposed the omission of this moment of "actual feeling" and some rearrangement. American audiences demanded a stronger narrative, and Charles Urban, handling British official documentaries in America, achieved this by splicing in sections of *Britain Prepared* and shots of an American Field Ambulance (interest was apt to lapse without an American presence). Titles were rewritten, "eliminating what we should call British patriotism," and the resultant seven-episode serial proved highly successful with American audiences. It was shown in 16,000 theatres in 12,000 towns from coast to coast, and by the end of 1917 some 65,000,000 people had paid to see it.

GORDON WILLIAMS

See also **War: WWI**

The Battle of the Somme (UK, British Topical Committee for War Films sponsored by War Office, 1916, 79 min.). Produced by William Jury. Cinematography by J. B. McDowell and Geoffrey Malins. Edited by Charles Urban and Geoffrey Malins. Filmed in France.

Further Reading

Badsey, Stephen "*Battle of the Somme*, British War-Propaganda," *Historical Journal of Film, Radio and Television*, 3, 1983, 99–115.

Brownlow, Kevin, *The War, the West and the Wilderness*, London: Secker and Warburg, 1979.

Culbert, David, "The Imperial War Museum: World War I Film Catalogue and 'The Battle of the Somme' (video)," *Historical Journal of Film, Radio and Television.* 15, 1995, 575–80.

Hiley, Nicholas, "The British Cinema Auditorium," *Film and the First World War*, edited by Karel Dibbets and Bert Hogenkamp, Amsterdam: Amsterdam University Press, 1995, 160–170.

Reeves, Nicholas, "Cinema, Spectatorship and Propaganda: *Battle of the Somme* (1916) and Its Contemporary Audience," *Historical Journal of Film, Radio and Television*, 17, 1997, 5–29.

Reeves, Nicholas, *Official British Film Propaganda During the First World War*, London: Croom Helm, 1986.

Rother, Rainer, "'Bei unseren Helden an der Somme' (1917): The Creation of a 'Social Event,'" *Historical Journal of Film, Radio and Television*, 15, 1995, 525–542.

Smither, Roger (ed.), *The Battles of the Somme and Ancre*, London: Imperial War Museum/DD Video, 1993.

Smither, Roger, "'A Wonderful Idea of the Fighting'; The Question of Fakes in *The Battle of the Somme*," *Historical Journal of Film, Radio and Television*, 13, 1993, 149–168.

BAZIN, ANDRÉ

André Bazin, the influential post-World War II French film critic, played a pivotal role in the development of French film culture in the 1950s and 1960s. He is also considered (along with Sergei Eisenstein) to be one of the two most important classical film theorists, and an insightful and poetic champion of realism in film. As co-founder and editor of *Cahiers du Cinéma*, for years Europe's most influential film journal, as spiritual leader of the French *Nouvelle Vague* (New Wave), and in his theoretical writings and support of the *politique des auteurs*, Bazin had a marked impact on filmmaking in France and elsewhere. Through his writing he also promoted various film movements, in particular Italian neorealism, and did much to elevate the critical reputations of directors such as Jean Renoir, Orson Welles, Robert Flaherty, and Charlie Chaplin.

Bazin was an insightful realist film theorist. Although his theory of realism is problematic in some regards, it built the foundation for debates that continue to this day. His strengths lay in his criticism more than in his systematic thought. He tended to make theoretical points in the context of writing on specific filmmakers, films, or genres; and, as his chief English-language biographer points out, summarizing Bazin's thought is "extremely difficult" (Andrew, 1976, 136). Bazin is a writer of grace and beauty, however, and an expert with the insightful turn of phrase and the suggestive metaphor. Not least among his qualities was an ability to transmit his enthusiasm for film to his associates and his readers. As Jean Renoir writes, "it is for his influence on his contemporaries that I hold him so deep in my affections. He made us feel that our trade was a noble one much in the same way that the saints of old persuaded the slave of the value of his humanity" (Bazin, 1967, vi).

Bazin did not explicate a theory of documentary, but he valued documentaries and wrote about them often. He accepted the documentary film as an artistic equal to fiction film and, in his criticism, did not draw a sharp distinction between fiction and nonfiction. Yet Bazin's theory of cinema has special import for the documentary, because he argued that film has a unique and powerful capacity to "reproduce" the phenomenal world with an authenticity and psychological power hitherto unseen. For that reason, it is useful to concentrate here on the notion of realism as Bazin developed it.

Like the other classical theorists, Bazin approached the cinema from the perspective of medium specificity theory, introduced by Gotthold Lessing in his *Laocoön* in the eighteenth century, and upheld by various critics and theorists since then. The theory holds that each art form has its own special subject matter and/or unique function that it performs especially well, and that for a work of a particular art form to reach its potential, it needed to exploit that subject matter or perform that function.

The formalist classical theorists assumed that like all art, film needed to be expressive. Formalists saw the dependency on motion photography in film to be a liability. Hence, they favored various formative techniques as a means to make the cinema *art*, more than the mere recording of visible reality. Conversely, the realist theorists— among whom Bazin and Siegfried Kracauer were the leading figures—claimed that the uniqueness of film stems from its roots in photography and the concomitant realism that it brings. For a film to reach its potential, filmmakers need to respect the realist nature of the medium. Kracauer did not favor any particular technique over another in achieving realism, but Bazin is famous for promoting the use of long take and deep focus as properly cinematic uses of the medium. For Bazin, the essence of the cinema could be found in its most important function, to "reproduce" phenomenal reality. As J. Dudley Andrew writes, Bazin saw the cinema as "a 'sesame' to universes unknown; cinema as a new sense, reliable like our natural sense, giving us knowledge of empirical reality otherwise unavailable" (Andrew, 1976, 145). Grounded on this conception of the essential function of the cinema, Bazin made judgments about the aesthetic success and failure of particular films, and about cinematic and uncinematic uses of the medium.

This kind of medium specificity theory has come under attack for its overly prescriptive tendency, and for focusing on the supposed *nature* of the medium at the expense of *uses* of the medium (Carroll, 1988, 258–263). Even if one rejects the claim that realist uses of the medium are especially cinematic, however, few would deny that the nature of cinematic realism is a central issue of film theory, and that Bazin's thoughts on the matter have been more influential than those of any other theorist. Bazin's contention that film is essentially a realist medium, and that its inception and development stemmed from the human need to record and preserve the world around us, accounts for a central difference between Bazin and the formalist theorists, namely, that Bazin welcomed sound and the sound film. Sound brings the film representation closer to phenomenal reality, and its coming alarmed the formalists and heartened the realists. For Bazin, sound brings film one step closer to "total cinema," the complete reproduction of the world. As Bazin writes in "The Myth of Total Cinema," the purpose that motivated the inventors of film was "a recreation of the world in its own image, an image unburdened by the freedom of interpretation of the artist or the irreversibility of time"(Bazin, 1967, 21). Like the "asymptote," the cinema will always reach out to, but never achieve, ultimate realism.

Bazin's theory of realism had both physical/temporal and psychological components. That is, Bazin thought that the film could reproduce or imitate some of the spatial and temporal characteristics of the phenomenal world and could also provide for the spectator a *sense* of authenticity and realism. For Bazin, the two are inseparable. Spatial realism is essential, a realism "without which moving pictures do not constitute cinema" (Bazin, 1967, p. 212). Cinematic representation ought to give the spectator a sense of the location of objects and the spatial layout of a scene. Bazin also favored temporal realism, an attempt to preserve a sense of the temporal experience of lived reality. He gives the example of Robert Flaherty showing Nanook hunting a seal in *Nanook of the North* (1922). Bazin lauds the director for preserving the actual length of the waiting period as Nanook hunts; "the length of the hunt is the very substance of the image, its true object . . ."(Bazin, 1967, p. 27). Bazin writes that the motion picture "embalms time," but this is not embalming an instant, like an insect preserved in amber. Instead, duration is taken into account, and change itself is "mummified."

Bazin thought that filmic representations could and should resemble phenomenal reality both spatially and temporally. Yet the most interesting elements of his realism went beyond this claim. For Bazin, what makes the moving photograph powerful and expressive extend beyond resemblance to its roots in "mechanical reproduction" (Bazin, 1967, p. 12), in the fact that to a degree the production of the photograph escapes the subjectivity of the filmmaker. This provides the photograph with a special relationship to the scene before the camera and a special power to affect the spectator. Photography carries with it a credibility because it transfers something of reality "from the thing to its reproduction" (Bazin, 1967, p. 14). In this way the moving photography affects us almost like a phenomenon of nature, like a "flower" or a "snowflake." Bazin also writes of the photograph as a decal, a fingerprint, or like the ruins of an ancient building. In each case, the photographic sign bears a special relationship to its referent that lends it not only credibility but expressive power.

Although Bazin did not use these terms, one way to get at the relationship between the moving image and the real is to use philosopher Charles Sanders Peirce's trichotomy, by which he categorized signs according to the way they relate to their referents: icon, index, and symbol. Where the icon *resembles* its referent, and the symbol relates to its referent solely by *convention*, the index is connected with its referent by *causality* or *proximity* (like a fingerprint), typically bearing a strong physical connection with that to which it refers. In these terms, then, the film scene is both an icon and an index, as it (under specifiable conditions) can resemble its referent spatially and temporally, and has an indexical bond with it by virtue of the mechanical reproduction that created the photograph.

That Bazin had reverence for that indexical relationship between image and reality can be scene in his discussion of the Thor Hyerdahl documentary, *Kon Tiki* (1950). The film was made when Hyerdahl and his associates attempted to prove that the Polynesian Islands might have been populated by sea migrations from Peru. The voyage of the Kon Tiki proved that a primitive boat could make the voyage. The footage of the journey was obviously made by amateurs and is imperfect in many ways. For Bazin, however, this serves to minimize artifice and to strengthen the indexical bond. He writes that the film is imperfect, but marvelous, because "the making of it is so totally identified with the action it so imperfectly unfolds; because it itself is an aspect of the adventure"(Bazin, 1967: 161). At one point, a whale appears and threatens the boat, but the cinematographer fails to capture the whale for the most part. Nonetheless, Bazin writes, the footage is powerful because it captures the sense of danger. It conveys that danger in large part is due to the indexical bond between the moving photograph and scene before the camera. Bazin refers to this indexicality when he compares *Kon Tiki* to "those moss-covered stones that, surviving, allow us to reconstruct buildings and statues that no longer exist." It is the cinematic image, the "objective image," that gives memory "its eternal substance" (Bazin, 1967: 160, 163).

Bazin thinks that the roots of the moving image in mechanical reproduction give the moving image its psychological force. This consists in part of the sense of credibility and authenticity it imparts to the spectator, but also in the sense that reality itself is literally re-presented. (Bazin's ideas here prefigure those of philosophers Kendall Walton and Stanley Cavell, both of whom discuss viewing photographs as a kind of seeing.) Bazin sometimes writes, however, as though the realism he promotes is more a psychological attitude than a relationship between film and reality, seemingly cashing in his ontology for a subjective psychology. He writes, for example, "If the film is to fulfill itself aesthetically we need to believe in the reality of what is happening while knowing it to be tricked" (Bazin, 1967: 48). Elsewhere he remarks that "realism in art can only be achieved in artifice," and that the necessity of making artistic choices necessarily entails a choice "between one kind of reality and another"(Bazin, 1971: 26, 29). One should take these remarks as evidence that Bazin understood that audiences were not naïve in granting authenticity to a filmic image, and that realism in film is always a matter of degree and not an absolute. And although it would be unfair to deny the problematic nature of Bazin's theory, it does seem most accurate to insist that Bazin's realism is both psychological *and* ontological.

Bazin is famous for his promotion of the long take and deep focus at the expense of montage. Bazin tended to favor any technique that would preserve for the spectator a sense of the unity and ambiguity of reality. He championed Italian neorealism for "never making reality the servant of some *a priori* point of view" (Bazin, 1971: 64), claiming that the films of neorealism have "an exceptionally documentary quality" and that even when they represent fictional events, the films "are first and foremost reconstituted reportage" (Bazin, 1971: 20). Bazin favored the use of gaps and ellipses in narrative for the mental activity they demand of the spectator. Of the films of Rossellini, Bazin writes that the "mind has to leap from one event to the other as one leaps from stone to stone in crossing a river. It may happen that one's foot hesitates between two rocks, or that one misses one's footing and slips. The mind does likewise" (Bazin, 1971: 35).

Montage works against realism, Bazin argued, because it creates "a sense or meaning not proper to the images themselves but derived exclusively from their juxtaposition" (Bazin, 1967: 25), and in so doing carves up prereflective reality according to the purposes of the filmmaker. Thus Bazin favored directors like Renoir or Flaherty, who put their faith in reality rather than in the plastics of film technique. Bazin often singled out director Robert Flaherty for praise, and Flaherty's refusal to use montage at certain key points also generates approval. The film shows Nanook struggling with a seal. Bazin writes, "it is inconceivable that the famous seal hunt scene in *Nanook* should not show us hunter, hole, and seal all in the same shot. It is simply a question of respect for the spatial unity of an event at the moment when to split it up would change it from something real into something imaginary" (Bazin, 1967: 50).

Just as Bazin argued against montage, he promoted the long take and deep focus. He took great care in describing the use of deep focus in the Italian neorealist films, or the use of long takes and camera movement in the films of Jean Renoir, for example.

Bazin's biographer, Dudley Andrew, suggests several motivations and influences for Bazin. Andrew foregrounds the importance of philosopher Henri Bergson in Bazin's intellectual development. Bergson wrote about modes of apprehending the world, distrusting the powers of analysis, and emphasizing the importance of reflection, including suprarational modes such as art, faith, and sexuality. Bergson's heritage can easily be seen in later French phenomenology, and as Andrew writes, "Bergson gave Bazin a deep feeling for the integral unity of a universe in flux" (Andrew, 1978: 21). Bazin also had a deep reverence for, and interest in, nature and kept assorted animals around his home throughout his life. Other influences include the journal *Esprit* and the Christian activism of the *Esprit* study group, and also Malraux, Sartre, and the existentialist ethos of France at the time.

Taken to an extreme, Bazin's theory would seem to champion films that merely record, visually and aurally, phenomenal reality, while respecting the temporal unity of such reality. Perhaps a slow and continuous 360-degree pan for the length of the film would be the best way not to add anything to prereflective reality, allowing the spectator freedom to interpret the ambiguous world free of the subjectivity of the filmmaker. Such a film, however, would be unacceptably dull for must of us. The interpretive and creative work of the filmmaker(s) is what is missing from such a film; yet this is precisely the element that Bazin seems to want to preclude. Bazin certainly understands that all films require such creative input, but his theory demands that subjectivity be put at the service of objective reality without sufficiently describing how this might be accomplished. Perhaps it is an impossible demand.

Reality is obviously complex, with many levels. We can believe, as Bazin argues, that film can "reproduce" or represent phenomenal reality, that is, the world as it is seen, heard, and experienced temporally. But certainly there is a deeper sense in which a realistic film would provide explanations for phenomena, would insightfully draw out relationships, implications, psychologies, ideas, and other nonphenomenal elements of reality. Two things need to be said here. First, film images that provide a veridical record of phenomenal reality do not necessarily get at reality in this deeper sense, as the case of the 360-degree pan illustrates. Second, films that "respect" phenomenal reality through the use of deep focus or long takes may nonetheless mislead us about reality in that deeper sense.

The "rhetoric of authenticity" in a documentary, derived in part from that indexical bond between image and scene that Bazin celebrated, can often be misleading. Reality does not speak for itself, and no film technique or set of techniques that merely "reproduces" reality guarantees truth or accuracy. Although filmic images and sounds may sometimes provide evidence for a perspective or a claim, and may give us a richness of information unavailable in other media, it is ultimately the creative work of the filmmaker that enables a documentary to become informative, compelling, and illuminating.

André Bazin introduced these problems with an eloquence that has ensured his work a central place in the history of film theory.

CARL R. PLANTINGA

Biography

Born April 18, 1918 in Angers, France. Studied to become a teacher at La Rochelle, Versailles, and finally, the École Normale Supérieure in St. Cloud, where he passed his exams in 1938. Called into the army in 1939. Quit the teaching profession in 1942. In 1944, began to establish ciné-clubs throughout France and Europe and to write extensively on film for various newspapers, magazines, and journals. Revived *La Revue du Cinéma* in 1947. Became Francois Truffaut's foster father in 1949. With Jacque Doniol-Valcroze, founded *Cahiers du Cinéma* in 1951. Died November 11, 1958 in Paris.

Further Reading

Andrew, Dudley, J., *The Major Film Theories: An Introduction*, London: Oxford University Press, 1976.

Andrew, Dudley, J., *André Bazin*, New York: Oxford University Press, 1978.

Bazin, André, *What Is Cinema?*, vols. I and II, trans. Hugh Gray, Berkeley: University of California Press, 1967, 1971.

Bazin, André, *Jean Renoir*, editor, Francois Truffaut, originally published 1973, trans. William H. Simon, New York: Da Capo Press, 1992.

Bazin, André, *Orson Welles*, trans. J. Rosenbaum, New York: Harper and Row, 1978.

Bazin, André, *Bazin at Work: Major Essays and Reviews from the Forties and Fifties*, editor Bert Cardullo, trans. Alain Piette, New York: Routledge, 1996.

Carroll, Noël, *Philosophical Problems of Classical Film Theory*, Princeton: Princeton University Press, 1988.

Graham, Peter, editor, *The French New Wave*, Garden City, NY: Doubleday, 1968.

BBC: THE VOICE OF BRITAIN

(UK, Legg, 1934–1935)

BBC: The Voice of Britain was the first General Post Office Film Unit film to use synchronized sound. It featured appearances by H. G. Wells, J.B. Priestley, G. K. Chesterton, George Bernard Shaw, and even a brief showing by the young film-maker Humphrey Jennings (as a witch in Macbeth).

As early as 1932, the Empire Marketing Board was approached by the BBC to produce a film advertising and celebrating the new national broadcaster. "They informed the EMB that, after an examination of the field, they were satisfied that Mr Grierson and his EMB Film Unit were best qualified to make the particular type of film they desired" (Post Office memorandum to the Select Committee, undated 1932, in Rotha, 1973; p. 128).

In many ways *BBC: The Voice of Britain* was the first film internationally to make clear the power of any major broadcasting institution, as well as spelling out the reithian ideals that informed her public face. The irony of yet another government body making such a project is invisible in the film itself. Nevertheless, the film gives some clues as to why Legg, in his subsequent career, was to be so favoured by large institutional backers including, after the war, that ultimate global player, the United Nations. Grierson biographer, Forsyth Hardy, commented: "The GPO film is admittedly diverse, but not only is there a plan behind the diversity but an individual approach is established and maintained. The film dramatises its material but humanises it as well" (Hardy in *Cinema Quarterly*, vol. 3, no. 4, 1935).

The plan of the film is a straightforward, now classic, one for the "behind the scenes" film ever since: the film diary of a day's broadcasting activity at the British Broadcasting Corporation, itself less than ten years old at the time of the shoot.

The set-up of the film is equally normative. The popular cinematic trope of the sleeping (British) countryside is used to convey a land whose natural voice the BBC had, in the mind of the literary and intellectual world, rapidly become. An early morning service conducted by the Reverend Dick Sheppard is the first of the BBC programmes (that day) to "gently wake the land." This lyrical and elegiac mode, later often referred to as the "ecclesiastical," using musical and poetic thematics and images quite unselfconsciously, was to be more fully worked out in later films such as *Coal Face* (1935) and *Night Mail* (1936). In these films the word of poet W. H. Auden and the music of Benjamin Britten were woven into the visual montage in what has become the paradigm of early British public documentary (the GPO and the Crown Film Unit) style and the bedrock of the BBC's own characteristic (and schooled) Documentary House Style for the next fifty or more years.

Paul Rotha saw no particular signs of personal style in the film, however. Writing of a group of films made in the mid-1930s he wrote: "None of them had any individual characteristics of direction. Any of these three directors (Evelyn Spice, Stuart Legg, and Edgar Anstey) could have made any of the three films" (Of *BBC: Voice of Britain*).

Apparently there were many periods of funding crisis in the making of the film. This might have been expected in Elton's first (public) filmmaking intersection with the perpetually beleaguered world

BBC: The Voice of Britain, 1934–35.
[*Still courtesy of the British Film Institute*]

BBC: The Voice of Britain, 1934–1935.
[*Still courtesy of the British Film Institute*]

of public broadcasting. Elizabeth Sussex reported that according to World Film News, in May 1936, the actual cost of the shoot through to the final release print was between £7,000 and £8,000.

JONATHAN DAWSON

See also **General Post Office Film Unit; Legg, Stuart**

BBC: The Voice of Britain (UK, GPO Film Unit, Legg, 1934–1935) 56 min, black and white. Directed, scripted, and edited by Stuart Legg.

Further Reading

Barnouw, Erik, *Documentary: A History of the Non-Fiction Film*, Oxford: Oxford University Press, 1977.
Hardy, Forsyth, *Grierson on Documentary*, London: Collins (rev. ed.), 1966.
Rotha, Paul, *Documentary Film*, London: Faber, 1933, rev. 1952.
Rotha, Paul, *Documentary Diary*, New York: Hill and Wang, 1973.
Sussex, Elizabeth, *The Rise and Fall of British Documentary*, London: Faber and Faber, 1976.

BEDDINGTON, JACK

Jack Beddington was a corporate professional specialising in publicity and public relations. In this role in the 1930s, he bestowed patronage to young artists in the fields of painting and cinema and raised the standard and taste in publicity films. In particular, he supported the talents emerging at the documentary film movement, dispensing commissions to filmmakers and providing employment at the Shell film unit. In 1940, he was appointed to head the Films Division of the Ministry of Information, where he improved the effectiveness of film propaganda and greatly raised the profile of documentary in wartime cinema.

As head of publicity at Shell, Beddington became interested in modern forms of public relations. As a cultured man, he aimed to pursue this work with taste and dignity. He therefore commissioned many promising young artists, such as Graham Sutherland and McKnight Kauffer, to work on promotions and advertising. In 1933, Imperial Airways hired Paul Rotha, on Beddington's recommendation, for the documentary film *Contact*. Such commissions helped develop an independent sector for documentary in Britain, alongside the "official" units at the Empire Marketing Board and subsequently the General Post Office. Again, Beddington was instrumental in this when he commissioned John Grierson to write a report on film publicity and from this sprang the Shell film unit in 1934, headed initially, on Grierson's recommendation, by Edgar Anstey. After some "teething" troubles, the Shell unit settled into a close relationship with the documentary film movement, which was reflected in its celebrated detached approach to public relations rather than a narrow corporate publicity, made a significant contribution to wartime propaganda, and continued with popular, acclaimed technical films for many years.

The Films Division of the Ministry of Information made an inauspicious start to the war. Its first head, Sir Joseph Ball, was a tactless appointment, as he was closely associated with the Conservative Party and its political film machinery. Furthermore, he cultivated the populism of the commercial cinema and the newsreels, and he offended the progressive educated classes through the rejection of the leftist documentary movement in the scheme for cinema propaganda. His abrupt replacement by Kenneth Clark, in December 1939, was an improvement, as the new incumbent was artistically and intellectually acceptable to the critics, and he fostered a new spirit of openness; but he was largely ignorant of film propaganda and lasted only three months. Finally, a successful appointment was made with Jack Beddington, who held the post until the Ministry was wound up in 1946. Beddington benefited from some administrative and policy improvements put in place by the new Minister, John Reith, who developed a clearer direction for film propaganda and found a significant place for the documentary filmmakers in the new scheme. Eventually, Beddington won the confidence of the cinema trade and the Films Division earned an enviable reputation for wartime propaganda.

Beddington was instrumental in arranging, with the Cinematograph Exhibitors' Association, the screening of "official" five-minute films in each programme, an important early victory in his relations with the trade. In the long term, his achievement was to bring the documentarists into wartime film propaganda while at the same time maintaining effective links with the commercial producers and newsreels. This balancing act could be precarious, and the documentarists were as quick to make criticism as the commercial interests of Wardour Street. He was greatly helped in this task of reconciliation by Sidney Bernstein, both a cinema entrepreneur *and* a friend of minority film culture, who acted as honorary advisor to the Films Division.

The Films Division managed varied responsibilities ranging across news film, guidance of commercial filmmakers in terms of war-related themes, liaison with the official film units attached to the services, and stewardship of the MOI's Crown Film Unit. It is now widely recognised that Britain's wartime achievements with film propaganda was exceptional. Much of the important work derived from Beddington's tenure at the Films Division: effective programmes of theatrical and nontheatrical distribution of propaganda films, adroit handling of Treasury officials seeking restraints on the filmmakers, and the smooth cross-fertilisation of policy and practice through the Ideas Committee, an informal gathering of Ministry officials and filmmakers that promoted awareness on both sides. Such methods ensured "precisely the line that the Ministry wished it to follow in mobilising support for the war effort and in constructing the essential wartime ideology of popular national unity" (Aldgate and Richards, 1986: 10). After the war, Beddington returned quietly to business and seemingly had little direct contact with film.

ALAN BURTON

See also **Crown Film Unit; Ministry of Information; Shell**

Biography

Born John Louis Beddington January 30, 1893. Educated at Wellington College and Balliol College, Oxford. 1914–1919, served with the King's Own Yorkshire Light Infantry. 1919–1927, employed in China by the Shell Petroleum Co. Invalided home in 1928, he was appointed publicity manager, then assistant general manager at the London office of Shell-Mex and B.P. Ltd. 1940–1946, served as Director of Films Division, MOI. Awarded the CBE in 1943. After the war, he joined the board of Colman, Prentis and Varley as Deputy Chairman. Honorary Fellow of the Society of Industrial Artists and the Royal College of Arts. Died April 13, 1959.

Further Reading

Aldgate, A., and J. Richards, *Britain Can Take It. The British Cinema in the Second World War*, Oxford: Blackwell, 1986.

Arts Enquiry, The. The Factual Film, London: PEP, 1947.

Chapman, James, *The British at War. Cinema, State and Propaganda, 1939–1945*, London: IB Tauris, 1998.

Legg, Stuart, "Shell Film Unit: Twenty-One Years," in *Sight and Sound*, April/June, 1954.

Sussex, Elizabeth, *The Rise and Fall of British Documentary. The Story of the Film Movement Founded by John Grierson*, Berkeley: University of California, 1975.

Rotha, Paul, *Documentary Diary. An Informal History of the British Documentary Film, 1928–1939*, London: Secker & Warburg, 1973.

Swann, Paul, *The British Documentary Film Movement 1926–1946*, Cambridge: CUP, 1989.

Thorpe, Frances, and Nicholas Pronay, *British Official Films in the Second World War*, Oxford: Clio Press, 1980.

BENELUX

See **Newsreel Series: Benelux**

BENOIT-LÉVY, JEAN

Jean Benoit-Lévy was a filmmaker, screenwriter, and one of the most important producers of French educational and scientific films before World War II. Deprived of his professional position by the anti-Jewish statutes promulgated by the Vichy government in 1940, he sought refuge in the United States in 1941. There, by refocusing and redefining his contribution to educational films, he became a teacher, an author, and an executive officer for the United Nations. He continued his dedication to the importance of film in mass education.

His vision of film is based on his strong family values and the late nineteenth-century's scientific outlook, imbued with positivism. He began his career as assistant filmmaker just before World War I, a time when Europeans were adjusting to the political, social, and educational challenges of mass society. Benoit-Lévy was introduced to the promising new technology by his uncle, Edmond Benoit-Lévy, a lawyer and pioneer of French cinema. The family shared a commitment to the republican ideals of equality, rationality, modern teaching, social reform, and progress.

Benoit-Lévy perceived film as both an art and formidable educational tool. His films testify to his preoccupation with applied scientific knowledge—particularly in medicine, hygiene, and engineering—to improve the living conditions of ordinary people, especially children. He believed that everyone had the right to live a healthy and rewarding life. His films on professional training and craftsmanship are tributes to technical skills and beauty.

He was well acquainted with the small group of talented avant-garde filmmakers of the late 1920s who connected formal research and social documentary. In 1945–1946, Jean Benoit-Lévy would consult this group, which included John Grierson, Alberto Cavalcanti, Paul Rotha, and others, when he reflected on the role and the orientation of future film production for the United Nations Film Board.

In his work during the 1920s and 1930s, Benoit-Lévy's position was reformist, opposed to the revolutionary and authoritarian solutions that flourished during his lifetime. He was attached to traditional values, a strong work ethic, and individual freedom. Nevertheless, he believed that state intervention was necessary to ensure adequate ongoing funding for educational film production, as well as to create a centralized institution dedicated to documentary film exchanges. Furthermore, he was convinced that France had an international cultural influence in this field that should be maintained and strengthened. He was well known in France, a person of stature among the cultural elite of the interwar period, and well acquainted with government officials. The war completely disrupted his personal and professional life. The deprivation he suffered and his exile contributed to his being almost forgotten.

Benoit-Lévy made more than 300 films, many commissioned by institutions and ministries. As an educational film expert, he wrote articles and reports. His proposal to further the use of film in the school system was ambitious: the development of a new pedagogy (*pédagogie cinégraphique*) that would involve a connection between filmmaker, teacher, and student. Moreover, different kinds of educational and social films were required, because learning was not restricted to the classroom. In accord with several documentary filmmakers of his time, Benoit-Lévy believed film audiences should be educated to appreciate different genres. His friend, Germaine Dulac, called this *éducation cinégraphique*. His films were shown in both nontheatrical and theatrical networks. For the latter, he used the category "films *éducatifs spectaculaires*" that included such films as *Pasteur* (1922).

He referred to *films de vie* (films of life) to describe more precisely what documentary films should be. Films of life were "documents of life"; they not only express human activities but "transfer life itself to the screen." They had a profound social function. During the interwar period, he focused on educational and scientific films but also made eleven feature films. For many of those, he worked with Marie Epstein as a writer-director team. The most well known, *La Maternelle* (1933) and *La Mort du Cygne* (*Ballerina*, 1937), follow his film of life (documentary) approach. The truth and reality of social issues could be addressed through a free creative process.

In 1941, Benoit-Lévy and his family came to New York with the help of the Rockefeller Foundation. Unwilling to compromise his vision of film to participate in the American commercial film industry, he taught film studies at the New School for Social Research alongside many refugee scholars. It was during his teaching tenure that he wrote *Les Grandes Missions du Cinéma*, published in 1945. Film was an autonomous art with its own laws, technique, and means of expression. He believed that logic and visual and intellectual clarity were indispensable to filmmaking. The aesthetics and the editing—beauty and drama—contributed to the *idée-force*, the main idea, that must always be immediately accessible.

He was also convinced that cinema had a social and civic mission. This idea was not new, but it was forcefully repeated as the war was ending and social concern predominated. Then Benoit-Lévy insisted on freedom more than in his prewar writings. Film was a most powerful medium for the diffusion of human thought. After World War II, the discourse was about film bringing people closer together to learn, to discover, and to understand the world.

SUZANNE LANGLOIS

Biography

Born in Paris in 1888, to a middle-class family originally from Alsace. Trained at the Laboratoires Pathé and Gaumont, then began his career as an assistant in 1910. In 1922, founded his company, the *Édition française cinématographique*, dedicated to producing educational films. In 1945, named Director of the Film and Visual Information Division of the United Nations Department of Public Information. Appointed director of the United Nations Film Board in January 1947. Left the U.N. in 1949 but maintained a lifetime commitment to the ideals of international cooperation and mass education. In 1958, the International Council for Film and Television (ICFT) was founded under the patronage of UNESCO, and he was elected its first delegate general. Died in Paris in 1959.

Selected Films

1915 *Les Vainqueurs de la Marne*: director
1920 *Le travail du potier*: director
1922 *Pasteur*: producer (Jean Epstein, director)
1925–1930 *L'École départementale primaire et professionnelle de Vitry-sur-Seine*: director, producer
1933 *La Maternelle*: co-director, co-writer, producer
1935 *La haute fréquence médicale*: director, writer, producer
1935 *Le Maroc terre de contrastes*: director, producer
1937 *La Mort du cygne/Ballerina*: co-director, co-writer
1948 *La Charte des peuples/The People's Charter*: director
1955 *Ballets de France*: director

Further Reading

Andrew, Dudley, *Mists of Regret. Culture and Sensibility in Classic French Film*, Princeton: Princeton University Press, 1995.

Benoit-Lévy, Jean, *L'Instruction visuelle aux États-Unis*, Paris: Éditions du Cinéopse, 1936.

Benoit-Lévy, Jean, *Les Grandes Missions du Cinéma*, Montréal: Parizeau, 1945 [*The Art of the Motion Picture*, New York: Coward-McCann, 1946].

Borde, Raymond, and Charles Perrin, *Les Offices du cinéma éducateur et la survivance du muet 1925–1940*, Lyon: Presses universitaires de Lyon, 1992.

Dictionnaire du cinéma français des années vingt, edited by François Albera and Jean A. Gili, in *1895 Revue de l'Association française de recherche sur l'histoire du cinéma*, 33, June 2001.

Eck, Hélène, "Notes et documents sur l'œuvre et les activités pédagogiques de Jean Benoit-Lévy de 1922 à 1934," *Revue internationale d'histoire du cinéma*, May 28, 1978, microfiche, 91 p.

Gauthier, Guy, *Le Documentaire. Un autre cinéma*, Paris: Nathan/VUEF, 2003.

Vignaux, Valérie, "Jean Benoit-Lévy, l'ignorance est une maladie contagieuse," in *Sur les pas de Marey*, edited by Thierry Lefebvre, Jacques Malthête and Laurent Mannoni, Paris: L'Harmattan, 2004.

BERLIN: THE SYMPHONY OF A GREAT CITY

(Germany, Ruttmann, 1927)

One of the internationally best known and most influential German documentaries of the 1920s was Walter Ruttmann's *Berlin. Die Sinfonie der Grosstadt* (1927, *Berlin: The Symphony of a Great City*). With Alberto Cavalcantis famous *Rien que les heures* (1926) on Paris, the film started the tradition of the city-films of that period. Walter Ruttmann and his two co-authors, Karl Freund and Carl Meyer, planned to show Berlin in a course of one day from sunrise to around midnight. The last two wanted to report simply on the daily life in the metropole, but Ruttmann prefered to create a visual symphony with his material. His tool was the montage of formal symbols and abstract structure, which was obviously influenced by his abstract animation films before. The form and movement became more important than the content. "During editing it became clear, how difficult it was to visualize the symphonic curve, I had before my eyes. Many of the most beautifull shots couldn't be used, because not a nice picture-book should be created, but something like a construction of a complex machine, which only can run, when even the smallest parts fit into each other with exact precision" as Ruttmann stated in an article shortly after the premiere on September 23, 1927.

Ruttmann suceeded, as the first images demonstrate, when waves of water change into graphic structures. These abstract images then dissolve to a train crossing; a fast-moving train comes, which is heading in the direction of Berlin. The landscape is rushing in front of the window. The rhythmic montage with details again builds up a close intensity. So the spectator already reaches Berlin with high expectations. What will happen next? After this hectic start, a calm moment follows. At five o'clock in the morning, life on the streets wakes slowly. The last night revellers go home exhausted, and the first workers start to rush to the factories. Now the streets and subway fill up. The machines start to run. The montage develops a growing speed, and Ruttmann sometimes experiments with ironic comparisons, for example, when a close-up of the walking feet of the laborers is followed by the feet of cows on their way to the slaughterhouse, which is then followed by marching soldiers. The second act shows pupils on the way to the school; the employees go to the offices; a group is riding in the park. The shops are opening, city life is awakening. An important element of the film is the traffic of cars, railways, trams, subway, and even airplanes, which symbolizes the rhythm of the modern metropole. The lunch break at noon follows the different classes with their specific meals and behavior. Even the animals in the zoo get something to chew. After a short nap, life goes on. A suicide of a woman attracts sightseers. When work is over, leisure time with different kinds of sports begins. The last part shows nightlife of the roaring twenties with theater, cabaret, varieté, dance, and drinking. Berlin is illuminated by neon light. The traffic is still running heavily. The film ends with fireworks. The next day is waiting.

In *Berlin. Die Sinfonie der Grosstadt* the metropole is the main actor. The people often appear in a

Berlin: The Symphony of a Great City, 1927.
[*Still courtesy of the British Film Institute*]

group, or they are anonymous elements and only part of a mass. There are no individuals to identify with, and Ruttmann shows different classes without preference. He often contrasts the rich and the poor, but he also shows the wealthy middle class or the simple workers. The film was therefore criticized by many, from Siegfried Kracauser to Jerzy Toeplitz to Klaus Wildenhahn. They claimed that the film showed only the surface and that Ruttmann did not analyze the society deeply enough. They also claimed that he did not take a political position. These criticisms miss the point. Ruttmann was interested mostly not in a sociological study, but in creating a special symphony of Berlin. "The strict rhythmic style of editing indicates that Berlin doesn't wait or pause for anything, and that the rythm of the city, of which the activities of the masses function as a part, is the very essence of the city itself" (Chapman, 1979: 39). Ruttmann aimed to show this as well as the modernity of Berlin. The broad range of impressions and images in their formalistic structure of editing become a dynamic flow and spectators were attracted by that rhythm, which shows typical life without any heroes. The Hungarian film theorist, Béla Balázs, experienced *Berlin* as "optical music." It was also discussed as an example of an "absolute film," where the structure and visual impression is more important than the story. The avant-garde worked on this new form of abstract film, and Ruttmann had been one of the leading persons of that group since 1922. The concept of new realism was best represented in this film, which became the model for many documentaries. Sequences of his Berlin film are still used in historical television programs to symbolize city life in the Weimar Republic. Ruttmann's symphony shows the city in a new way and was one of the first documentaries in the 1920s in Germany that attained the status of a classic.

The film was often adapted afterwards and quoted in many other films. Between 1936 and 1943, Leo de Laforgue shot another Berlin film. The theatrical release was in 1950 under the title *Symphonie einer Weltstadt (Berlin wie es war)* (1950, Symphony of the Metropole [Berlin as it was]), and it showed Berlin before the destruction resulting from World War II and tried to imitate Ruttmann, but he was not successful. The most recent adaption was Thomas Schadt's *Berlin: Sinfonie einer Grosstadt* (2002, Berlin: Symphony of a City). He was inspired by Ruttmann's classic film. The 2002 film is shot in black and white and follows a day in modern Berlin. But the new film also reflects the history of the metropole in the last century and thus develops its own quality. The film is accompanied by modern, abstract music, which gives the film a rhythm of its own. That proved the actuality, which Ruttmann's *Berlin* film still has.

KAY HOFFMANN

Berlin. Die Sinfonie der Grosstadt (*Berlin: The Symphony of a Great City*) (Germany, Deutsche Vereins-Film, 1927, 65 min). Directed by Walter Ruttmann. Writen by Karl Freund, Carl Mayer, and Walter Ruttmann. Original music by Timothy Brock and Edmund Meisel. Cinematography by Robert Baberske, Karl Freund, Reimar Kuntze, and László Schäffer. Edited by Walter Ruttmann. Art direction by Erich Kettelhut.

Further Reading

Chapman, Jay, "Two Aspects of the City: Cavalcanti and Ruttmann," in *The Documentary Tradition*, 2nd edition, edited by Lewis Jacobs, New York, London: Norton & Company 1979.

Goergen, Jeanpaul, *Walter Ruttmann. Eine Dokumentation*, Berlin: Freunde der Kinemathek, 1989.

Möbius, Hanno, and Vogt, Guntram, *Drehort Stadt. Das Thema "Großstadt" im deutschen Film*, Marburg: Hitzeroth, 1990.

Prümm, Karl, *Symphonie contra Rhythmus. Widersprüche und Ambivalenzen in Walter Ruttmanns Berlin-Film*, in *Geschichte des dokumentarischen Films in Deutschland, Bd. 2 Weimarer Republik (1918–1933)*, edited by Klaus Kreimeier, Antje Ehmann, and Jeanpaul Goergen, Stuttgart: Reclam, 2005.

Ruttmann, Walter, "Lichtbild-Bühne, 8.10.1927," quoted in *Berlin. Aussen und Innen*, edited by Berg-Ganschow, Uta, Berlin: Stiftung Deutsche Kinemathek, 1984.

Schadt, Thomas, *Berlin: Sinfonie einer Großstadt*, Berlin: Nicolai, 2002.

Toeplitz, Jerzy, *Geschichte des Films, Bd. 1 1895–1928*, Berlin: Henschel, 1979.

BERLINER, ALAN

Alan Berliner has been delving into the intricacies of family life in his documentary film work for many years. His style is at once one of meticulous research and down-to-earth story-swapping as he skillfully blends the personal and the universal. While Berliner's early work was essentially avant-garde or experimental in form and content, he gravitated toward documentary filmmaking largely out of a love for genealogy, family collections of home movies, and an interest in discovering his place in the world through an investigation of his own heritage. This is reflected in the various subjects he has taken for his work, both in form and content.

Berliner's early work explored notions of the avant-garde as well as documentary. Short films made between 1975–1985 are compiled from found footage and use scraps to create new narrative tales. His move into the style of his later, better known work came in 1987 with *Family Album*. Again, this film used found footage, but the 'bricolage' here (as Berliner calls it) was culled from estate sales. This led to a film reminiscent of Edward Steichen's *Family of Man* photographic project of the 1950s. Berliner constructed this experimental work from personal home movies from the 1920s through the 1950s, moving from birth to death in its progression. Footage celebrating new babies, graduations, birthdays and weddings are juxtaposed with images of life's more sorrowful passages. The film was screened at over twenty major festivals, including the 33rd Robert Flaherty Film Seminar (1987), the Sundance Film Festival (1988), and the Munich International Film Festival (1987). The work was featured in the 1987 Whitney Museum of American Art Biennial Exhibition.

Berliner's next work was *Intimate Stranger*. The 1991 film takes as its subject Berliner's maternal grandfather, Joseph Cassuto, a Palestinian Jew who worked as a merchant for the Japanese in the cotton industry in Egypt in the years prior to World War II. His break from his family during the war and the reunion in New York following it give a context for this study of a man admired in his professional life yet unpopular in his own family. Cassuto was unhappy in the United States and ultimately left his wife and children for most of the year to live in his beloved Japan to pursue business interests. Berliner finds means of constructing an elaborate portrait of his grandfather in a way that gives credence to the man's two distinct lives. The multifaceted approach to the discovery of this man's humanity brings dynamism to this complex investigation. This film was accepted into nearly forty international festivals upon its release, including the Margaret Mead Film Festival, Sundance, and Cinéma du Réel in Paris (where it garnered a Special Jury Award in 1992). Berliner was honored with the Distinguished Achievement Award from the International Documentary Association in 1993.

Following a pattern of increasingly personal approaches to his particular style of exploring family and history, Berliner revealed *Nobody's Business* in 1996. This film investigates his father, Oscar Berliner, a self-professed "ordinary guy." Berliner's reclusive father is initially in no way interested in being a willing participant in his son's investigation. The film is delightful in its depiction of the conflict between the two men, one endeavoring to learn more about his father's life, the other deeply concerned with his own privacy and seclusion. *Nobody's Business* takes its title from Oscar's relentless insistence that no one needs to know anything about him. It is not their business, it is not interesting, and he is not interested in making these things known to anyone. Slowly, though, the events of his life are discovered, as Berliner presses his father for clues and explanations. He shows his father old photographs and asks personal questions about their contexts. Stock footage is also employed, most notably the repetition of an image of boxers sparring, seen whenever the discussion between father and son becomes heated. Berliner's research took him to the massive archive run by the Church of Jesus Christ of Latter Day Saints in Salt Lake City, and he shows the magnitude of this genealogical project alongside the microcosm of records relating to his father. This work was an enormous success in its ability to unite the personal tale of one man with the universal story of all of mankind.

The film was shown as the first installment in the tenth season of PBS' *POV* series, where it created a massive level of viewer response. This prompted the combined efforts of several agencies, including the National Archives, to encourage people to explore their own genealogies. The film was screened in over fifty festivals, including a place in the "Frames of Reference" show at the Guggenheim Museum. It won an Emmy in 1998 from the Academy of Motion Picture Arts and Sciences, and received major awards from several international festivals.

The 2001 release of *The Sweetest Sound*, Berliner's film exploring the meaning of our names, takes him to Holocaust Memorials, the Vietnam Wall, the NAMES project, AIDS quilt, and other great repositories of memory. He finds that he shares a name with many other Alan Berliners in the world, including another filmmaker, Belgian Alain Berliner. He deals with the concept of "Same Name Syndrome," visiting the Jim Smith Society and the National Linda Convention, before finally deciding to invite the Alan Berliners of the world over to his house for dinner. The study again shows the exquisite communion shared by all humans, even in the face of so much difference. Again a large success, this film was screened by over fifty festivals throughout the world and in such venues as the Hirshhorn Museum in Washington, DC. Berliner won the Storyteller Award at the Taos Talking Picture Film Festival in 2001, and has had retrospectives of his work at the Museum of Modern Art as well as the International Center for Photography in New York City. He continues to explore documentary forms, and is also very active as an installation artist working with found sound and audio environments.

TAMMY A. KINSEY

Biography

Born New York, NY, 1963. Attended SUNY—Binghamton and the University of Oklahoma. Early film work explored notions of the avant-garde and documentary. Film *Family Album* featured in 1987 Whitney Museum of American Art Bienniel. Recipient of grants from National Endowment for the Arts, New York State Council for the Arts, New York Foundation for the Arts, Rockefeller Foundation Fellowship. Guggenheim Foundation Fellowship. Distinguished Achievement Award from the International Documentary Association, 1993, for *Intimate Stranger*. Berlin International Film Festival, Caligari Film Award, 1997. Nyon Visions du Réel, Switzerland, Grand Prix Award, 1997. Retrospective show at the International Center for Photography, New York. Storyteller Award, Taos Talking Picture Film Festival, 2001. *Family Album*, *Intimate Stranger*, and *Nobody's Business* all screened on PBS series *POV*. Artist-in-residence at Walker Center for Art, Minneapolis, Minnesota.

Selected Films

1986 *Family Album*
1991 *Intimate Stranger*
1996 *Nobody's Business*
2001 *The Sweetest Sound*

Further Reading

Albert, Mitch, "A Family Affair: The Films of Alan Berliner. When is Personal Documentary Nobody's Business?" *The Independent Film and Video Monthly*, 20, 1997.

Cuevas, Efren, and Carlos Muguiro, ed., *The Man Without the Movie Camera: The Cinema of Alan Berliner*, Ediciones Internacionales Universitarias, 2002.

MacDonald, Scott, *A Critical Cinema 4: Interviews with Independent Filmmakers*, University of California Press, 2004.

BERUF: NEONAZI

(Germany, Bonengel, 1993)

Beruf: Neonazi (*Profession: Neo-nazi*) sparked a controversy at its release in June 1993 leading to its temporary ban in several regions of Germany. Later it served as evidence in the trial of the main protagonist, who was convicted on grounds of comments he made in the documentary, pre-eminently those in which he denied that the Holocaust took place. In Germany, the "Auschwitz-lie" is a crime that has been punishable in law since 1985 and 1994 (Long, 2002). The intense reaction to the film also has to be seen against the backdrop of growing right-wing violence in Germany during the early 1990s.

The post-verité documentary was criticized for its sympathetic treatment of the hero, Ewald Althans, whose neo-nazi views, it was argued, the film presented without taking a stance against them. Althans was not merely a private person, a social actor, observed by the documentary, but an experienced agitator. *Beruf: Neonazi* made the limitations of observational documentary apparent and raised questions as to whether observation is an appropriate method to "expose" a political per-

former, or whether it merely provides a neo-nazi demagogue with a platform. The director, Winfried Bonengel, argued that only observation could penetrate the slick veneer of Althans, who would unmask himself involuntarily in moments in which his expressions manifested his doubts. Challenging Althans verbally would not lead anywhere, because he was such a rhetorically articulate operator who would dismiss any opposition as merely defensive. Instead of countering his views in a direct verbal debate, the film, Bonengel claimed, visually parodied the convictions of its protagonist through low camera angles that depicted his poses as pompous, like an exaggeration of the elevated angles in Leni Riefenstahl's *Triumph of the Will* (1935). The director and the cameraman saw Althans as "a robot with a tiny little ball for a head" (Niroumand, *Die Tageszeitung*, 18.11.1993). The film's critics, on the other hand, contested the claim that the images provided a parody or critique and found that the camera's positioning merely depicts Althans as superior and enhances his appeal. The cameraman had no choice other than to make images from a low angle, it was suggested, because he was short and his subject was tall (Donner, *Frankfurter Allgemeine Zeitung*, 1993).

In the documentary's most controversial scene—the one which ultimately led to Althans' conviction—he talks a visibly shocked young American into the ground with his rhetoric that no one could have been gassed in Auschwitz. Instead, Althans manages to label him as rude and leaves the debate as a victor. Whether the close-up of his face when he is not speaking arrests it in a telescopic prison, as the cameraman Johann Feindt argued (Niroumand, *Die Tageszeitung,* 18.11.1993) and reveals a "rare loss of composure" (Bathrick, 1996—or not, is down to interpretation. In fact, that none of the other Auschwitz visitors objects strongly to Althans' provocations might also be due to the fact that they were intimidated because he was accompanied by a film team rather than by his rhetorical skills. After this scene, the camera, arguably, takes Althans' side when it shows him walking away, and not the young tourist, whose political views the filmmaker and most of the film's audience share: Bonengel "shows Althans from behind as with upright stride he moves away from the camera toward the exit. Like a cowboy who has just brushed off the dust from his pants or like a gladiator leaving the arena" (*Frankfurter Rundschau* 19.11.1995).

The director's argument against using direct verbal challenge does not preclude an expository commentary. Bonengel rejected authoritative voice-over, because it would be patronising and block an allegedly less educated audience from judging for themselves. The dangers of the attraction of fascism needed be experienced in order to be properly rejected, and not be contained by a pedagogic narration, one newspaper agreed (Niroumand, *Die Tageszeitung*, 18.11.1993). Similarly, the German Studies scholar David Bathrick finds that the reception in Germany expressed "an immense fear of any visual ambiguity" rooted in a "legitimating notion of antifascism, that comes to function so successfully in the service of *Bilderverbot* (censoring of images)" (Bathrick, 1996).

Beruf: Neonazi was also criticized for showing a right-wing extremist who was attractive, eloquent, and young (born 1966) rather than repellent, repetitive, and old as were the usual exponents of National Socialism in Germany at the time. These were much easier to dismiss. The "Nazi-Yuppie" constituted an unwelcome reminder that beauty does not preclude fascism and earned the documentary the reproach of glamorizing fascism. Althans himself proclaimed elsewhere: "I am a National Socialist and I am socially acceptable. And National Socialism is then only dangerous, when it becomes socially acceptable" (from Eckerle, Hohmann, "Sein Kampf, mein Sieg" in *Münchner*, 1992, cited in Long, 2002: 4). However, in another of the paradoxes that make out *Beruf: Neonazi*'s history of reception, Althans was regarded as dangerous only by the media and the courts, which in turn boosted his visibility. This was in contrast to his much lower standing in the Holocaust-denial movement itself, especially after he was outed as gay. The 'revisionist international' did not want another closeted gay leader after the neo-nazi Michael Kühnen had died of AIDS in prison (Long, 2002: 76).

At the end of November 1993, the Hessian state parliament banned *Beruf: Neonazi* and confiscated copies because the film did not counter the neo-nazist statements with its own commentary, and it rather seduced young viewers to Althans' positions. The Frankfurt court ruled that the documentary "circulated national socialist propaganda without providing commentary, incited the masses, insulted and disparaged the memory of the dead, and maintained that Auschwitz was a lie." ("Die Deutschen sind noch nicht reif dafür" in *Berliner Zeitung* 11.12.1993, cited in Bathrick, 1996). Rallies were held against screenings of the film, it was demanded that the director pay back the film's grant money, and the distributors withdrew. At the end of December 1993, by contrast, the public prosecutor's office in Berlin pronounced that *Beruf: Neonazi* could be screened in that region, since it was a "critical and realistic representation of actual neo-nazi activities" and "maintains distance to its protagonist . . . through artistic means, through the presentation of counter-positions and externally through the choice of its title." (*Frankfurter Allgemeine Zeitung,* 24.12.93).

In a typical succession of contradictory moves for the sake of generating publicity, the German magazine *Der Spiegel* initially attacked the film as neo-nazi propaganda paid for by tax money in November 1993 (*Der Spiegel*, 15.11.1993). Three months later, however, *Spiegel-TV* wanted to broadcast the whole film, but was forced to drop this on account of the strong protest of prominent German public figures (*Frankfurter Rundschau,* 18.2.1994.) Instead, it screened a discursive programme with the title "Show It, Don't Censor It" about the film including interviews with the director and the protagonist, and a 30-minute excerpt of the 83-minute film (Bathrick, 1996). Bonengel objected to a broadcasting of his film. While he defended a screening in the cinemas, arguing that the public space of the movie theatre would foster a debate among an audience, a broadcast to individuals at home would diminish their ability to be critically distanced and make the solitary viewer more susceptible to Althans' views. Had the film not originated in Germany—or had it indeed had been neo-nazi propaganda rather than a production by a serious filmmaker—it would probably not have evoked such a heated debate.

In September 1994, the same State Court of Berlin that previously had allowed the screening of *Beruf: Neonazi* arraigned Althans on grounds of his utterances in the film, which again effected a temporary ban of the documentary. Ironically, the screening of the film resulted in a court case against its main protagonist, which eventually resulted in his conviction after he previously had been acquitted due to lack of evidence for his right-wing activism. The former documentary subject represented himself in the trial, claiming that he had merely re-enacted his previous neo-nazi persona for the documentary. He further maintained that with his statement in the documentary "What is going on here is a massive hoax," he meant the film itself and not the gas chambers of Auschwitz, in which he stood at the time. In a sense, Althans claimed to have taken the same position toward his own comments as the filmmaker did: he "only wanted to make a neutral statement, as to what an orthodox neo-nazi would be." (*Associated Press*, 13.6.1995). He furthermore argued that he played up to the image of a neo-nazi, because he did not want to alienate anyone. While conducting his own defense, Althans was sometimes moved to tears by his own depictions of his life, bearing witness to the director's suggestion that his subject

became the victim of his own narcissism. The film team was enlisted in court as witnesses that their subject was authentic in the documentary. The cameraman testified that Althans' behavior in the documentary was genuine; that is, he was not acting when making his right-wing comments (*Associated Press*, 13.6.1995). The courts accepted his utterances as evidence, and in 1994 and 1995 Althans was sentenced to three and one-half years altogether, six months longer than asked for by the prosecution, for denial of the Holocaust, glorification of Nazism, defaming the memory of the dead, and incitement to hatred.

SILKE PANSE

Further Reading

Bathrick, David, "Anti-Neonazism as Cinematic Practice: Winfried Bonegel's Documentary Film *Beruf Neonazi*" in *New German Critique*, 67, 1996, 33–46.

Davidson, John E., "'In der Führer's Face': Undermining Reflections in and on *Beruf: Neonazi*" in *Arachne: An Interdisciplinary Journal of the Humanities*, 3, 1996, 67–96.

Donner, Wolf, "Draufhalten is nicht genug," in *Frankfurter Allgemeine Zeitung*, 27, 1993, 11.

Long, Anthony, "Forgetting the Führer: the Recent History of the Holocaust Denial Movement in Germany," *Australian Journal of Politics and History*, 48, 2002, 72–84.

Niroumand, Mariam, "Vorsicht Bissiger Hund" and "Nimm die Sonnenbrille ab. Zwischen Golem und Robocop: Gespräch mit Johann Feindt, dem Kameramann von *Beruf Neonazi*" in *Die Tageszeitung*, 18, 1993, 12.

Wienert, Klaus, "Proteste kippen Filmausstrahlung. *Spiegel-TV* sendet *Beruf: Neonazi* nur in Auschnitten" in *Frankfurter Rundschau*, 18, 1994.

BEVERIDGE, JAMES

For five decades, James Beveridge was known widely in the documentary community as a producer, director, presenter, administrator, and educator. His career was strongly influenced by his mentor, John Grierson, with whom he maintained a close friendship. In 1939, Beveridge was the first Canadian to be hired by Grierson at the nascent National Film Board. He was trained on

the job at the wartime Board, serving as Executive Producer for a number of production units as well as working on many films as writer, director, producer, editor, host, and narrator. After Grierson's departure from the NFB in 1945, Beveridge became the Secretary of Production. Beveridge began a long association with India in the early 1950s, helping to shape the postwar Indian documentary through his work as Head of Production of the Burmah Shell Film Unit and his co-founding of the Pune Film and Television Institute (India) and Jamia Millia Islamia Institute Mass Communications Research Centre. Beveridge was also founding Director of the North Carolina State Film Board. Like Grierson, Beveridge was a television presenter of documentary films, hosting the series *Let's Face It* on CBC television, co-hosting *Four Religions with Arnold Toynbee & James Beveridge,* and later serving as the daily critic on Canada's private network, CTV. His work as an educator included a visiting professorship at New York University and the founding of Canada's largest university-based film program at York University in Toronto.

The more than 150 films Beveridge produced and directed can be divided into two categories. Most are shot in the voice-over style of the classic Griersonian documentary and focused on the specific social issues that concerned the agencies with which he worked. Beveridge attacked these projects with a high degree of social commitment. *Inside Fighting Russia* challenged the limits of the official commitment to Canada's wartime ally. Beveridge's series, *Minority Report,* produced at the North Carolina State Film Board, was a rare (perhaps only) example of a southern U.S. state examining its own racial policy at the height of the civil rights movement. But Beveridge also had a passion for exploring the work of musicians and other artists. He was a regular contributor to the PBS *Creative Persons* series. *Glenn Gould—Off the Record*, the film he edited at the NFB in 1959, was among the first attempts to use the new *cinema verité* style to document an artist at work. That same style shaped the films he produced and directed on Indian artists: *Satyajit Ray* and *Bismillah Khan*, a series, *Musicians of North India* and *A Himalayan Tapestry* (for which he won the President of India's Gold Medal Award for best documentary). It is also apparent in his documentary *Hands*, about the national living treasures of Japan. His wrap-around multi-screen film for EXPO '67's *Man In Control* theme pavilion tested his lifelong versatility and creativity with a third approach to documentary.

SETH FELDMAN

See also **National Film Board of Canada**

Biography

Born in Vancouver, British Columbia, in 1917. Graduated from the University of British Columbia in 1938 and began work at the nascent National Film Board the following year. Met John Grierson in England in 1939. Served as the NFB's Production Secretary (head of production) from 1945 to 1951 when he was transferred to the NFB's London distribution office. In 1954, moved to Bombay to become the Head of Production for the newly formed Burmah Shell Film Unit. With the closing of that unit in 1959, returned to the NFB. From 1959 to 1960 he was moderator on the Canadian Broadcasting Corporation programme "*Let's Face It.*" Seconded by the NFB to establish the North Carolina State Film Board where he produced fifteen films between 1962 and 1964. Returned to India in 1967 as consultant/Chief Officer of the Indian Films Division in Bombay and as adviser on the establishment of the Television Production Wing for the Pune Film and Television Institute. Served as a consultant for the Canadian International Development Agency and UNESCO, on the development of rural television programming strategies. Returning to Canada in 1970, became the founding chair of the Department of Film and Video at York University in Toronto. In India again from 1982 to 1987, founded and directed the Jamia Millia Islamia Insititute Mass Communications Research Centre in Delhi. Received the Academy of Canadian Film and Television's Lifetime Achievement Award in April. 1991. Died the following year in Toronto.

Selected Films

1941 *Peace River*: producer, director
1942 *Inside Fighting Russia*: producer, director
1957 *A Himalayan Tapestry*: producer, director (President of India's Gold Medal Award for best documentary).
1959 *Glenn Gould—Off the Record*: editor
1961 *Four Religions with Arnold Toynbee & James Beveridge*: producer, moderator
1964 *The Minority Report* series: *Vote and the Choice is Yours, A Knocking at the Gate, Goodbye to Carolina*: Executive Producer
1967 *The Creative Person* series *(PBS)—Wealthy Fisher, Satyajit Ray, Bismillah Khan*: producer, director
1970 *Music of North India* series—*Amjad Ali Khan, Bhimsen Joshi, Pandit Jasraj, Vijay Raghav Rao*: producer, director
1974 *The Dalai Lama*: producer, director
1975 *Hands*: producer (Winner, Grand Prize, International Craft Festival, NYC)

Further Reading

Beveridge, James A., *John Grierson: Film Master*, New York: MacMillan Publishing, 1978.
———, *Scriptwriting for Short Films*, Paris: UNESCO, 1969.
Bidd, Donald. *The NFB Film Guide: The productions of the National Film Board of Canada from 1939–1989*, Montreal: National Film Board of Canada, 1991.
Ellis, Jack C., *John Grierson: Life, Contributions, Influence*, Southern Illinois University Press, 2000.
Evans, Gary, *John Grierson and the National Film Board of Canada: The Politics of Wartime Propaganda, 1939–1945*, Toronto: University of Toronto Press, 1984.
Hardy, Forsyth, *John Grierson: A Documentary Biography*, London: Faber and Faber, 1979.

McInnes, Graham, *One Man's Documentary; A Memoir of the Early Years of the National Film Board.* Edited with an introduction by Gene Walz, University of Manitoba Press, 2004.

McKay, Marjorie, *History of the National Film Board of Canada*, Montreal: National Film Board of Canada (internal publication), 1989.

Rotha, Paul, *The Film Till Now: A Survey of Cinema*, London: Spring Books, 1967.

BIRRI, FERNANDO

Fernando Birri has been dubbed the "godfather," "father," and "pope" of the pan-continental film movement known as the New Latin American Cinema. Birri was one of the first filmmakers to document underdevelopment, poverty, and other social problems in what Michael Chanan calls a critical realist style. In his 1962 manifesto entitled "For a Nationalist, Realist, Critical and Popular Cinema" Birri explains:

[It [New Latin American Cinema] was born because . . . a generation of filmmakers was growing up who wanted to provide a reply to some of the problems of the moment. . . . They were questions that came from an historical necessity, a necessity in the history of our peoples . . . a place denied us for so many years, a place which . . . as the title of the beautiful Nicaraguan film has it, is a place of bread and dignity. These ideas, I believe, explain something of the tension out of which the New Latin American Cinema was created and motivated.]

(Birri, in Barnard, 79)

Birri was formally trained at the Centro Sperimentale in Rome during the 1950s by some of the great masters of Italian neorealist cinema. It was there that Birri learned to film ordinary people living their everyday lives, and to valorize a "culture of the people," or popular culture. His aim was to create a popular cinema that elevated the folkloric elements in Argentine popular culture and to initiate a cinema that would raise peoples' consciousness about the disparities of wealth and degrees of human suffering in Argentina as well as Latin America as a whole. As John King observed, Birri made the attempt to adopt and transform neorealism in the context of Latin America, to break with the distribution and exhibition circuits of commercial cinema, and incorporate new working class and peasant audiences into more democratic cultural practices (King 85).

Birri's philosophy initially stemmed from the tenets of liberation theology, a movement that gained prominence in Latin America in the 1960s, as well as from Brazilian educator Paulo Freire, in his work on "the pedagogy of the oppressed." More specifically, Birri drew from Freire's idea of *concientización* (conscientization) and a philosophy of praxis (Chanan, 38). From these ideas Birri made films such as *Tire dié* (1958, Toss Me a Dime) and *Los inundados* (1961, Flooded Out). The latter film features a family from Santa Fe whose home is destroyed every time the flood season hits the region. Despite the dramatic content, the film is a picaresque comedy, using actors from the popular theatre, and non-actors. The sound track is by folk singers from the provinces as well as by famous *payadores* (gaucho troubadours). Without losing the human side of the characters, the film avoids converting the family and others into stereotypes of victims, but at the same time, the film's storyline is replete with satirical jabs at political figures, the government, bureaucracy, and even poor people in the area (Ruffinelli,1).

Birri called his films and others comprising the New Latin American Cinema "a poetics of the transformation of reality." He goes on to explain that "it generates a creative energy which throughout cinema aspires to modify the reality upon which it is projected." The ultimate objective for Birri was "to have no abyss between life and the screen." (Birri, in Barnard, 81).

Birri's documentaries from the late 1950s and early 1960s were considered revolutionary in their time because they varied so drastically from the mainstream films produced within the prevailing studio system based in Buenos Aries. Birri was reacting to what he deemed "an accomplice cinema" in veiling the brutal social realities affecting the majority of people in Argentina.

He worked in the province of Santa Fe in the hopes of democratizing film production to areas often considered the "periphery" of the nation. However, after his films were completed, he faced problems with official censors because the films did not present "a pretty picture" of social conditions in Argentina. In 1962, when *Los inundados* played in film festivals, the censors under the centrist Frondizi government responded by attempting to seize all copies in circulation. When it won prizes at the Venice film festival and Karlovy Vary (Czech Republic) that year, the official censor and other critics were offended and accused Birri of poor technical ability and low production values. Birri, in defending the film, said the technical imperfections were the result of the non-professional means he had been forced to work with, and that he preferred "the contents to the technique, to make sense imperfectly than to have a senseless perfection" (Birri, in Gamucio Dagron, 87).

After the military coup of 1963, Birri left the country definitively and fled to Italy. There he worked on a series of experimental and documentary films under the aegis of the Laboratory of Film Poetics. During this period he filmed political documentaries, such as *Mi hijo el Che* (1985, My Son Che), and a 3-hour experimental film (ORG, 1986) directed under the pseudonym Fermaghorg. His philosophy of life and filmmaking shifted from a less militant, realist outlook to one stressing more eclectic and hedonistic tendencies. In his manifesto poem, "For a Cosmic Cinema, Raving and Lumpen: The First Cosmunist (Cosmic Communist) Manifesto," he expresses the need for a "revolution in language" that included "a montage of attractions," "a sensorial experience," involving what he deems a "sensual hedonistic erotic communism" (Birri in Barnard, 83).

In 1986, he helped found the International School of Film and Television in San Antonio de los Baños in Cuba and worked as its director until 1991. During this period he directed a magical realist film, *Un señor muy viejo con alas enormes* (*The Old Man with Enormous Wings*), based on a short story written by Colombian novelist Gabriel García Marquez. Birri has continued to make a diverse range of films about Latin American topics, the latest a critically acclaimed film project that is an adaptation of Uruguayan cultural critic Eduardo Galleano's *Century of Wind* (1999), a transcontinental mosaic of Latin American history in the twentieth century.

TAMARA L. FALICOV

See also **Tire dié**

Biography

Born in Santa Fe, Argentina, in 1925. Studied at the Centro Sperimentale di Cinematografia de Roma, 1950–1953. Returned to Argentina and founded the Film Institute of the National University of the Litoral in Santa Fe, 1956. Founded the "Laboratory of Cinema Poetics" in the Film Department at the University of the Andes in Venezuela, 1982. Worked as Director of the School of the Three Worlds, San Antonio de los Baños, Cuba, 1986–1991. Received a lifetime achievement award at the International Documentary Film Festival of Leipzig, 1997. Founded the Birri Foundation, dedicated to funding young artists and fostering media education, 1999.

Selected Films

1958 *Tire dié* (Toss Me a Dime)
1959 *Buenos días, Buenos Aires*
1961 *Los inundados* (Flooded Out)
1963 *Pampa gringa*
1985 *Mi hijo el Che* (My Son Che)
1986 *ORG*
1988 *Un señor muy viejo con alas enormes* (An Old Man with Enormous Wings)
1999 *El siglo del viento* (A Century of Wind)

Further Reading

Barnard, Tim, *Argentine Cinema*, Toronto: Nightwood Editions, 1986.

———. "Los inundados" (Flooded Out), in *South American Cinema: A Critical Filmography, 1915–1994*, edited by Tim Barnard and Peter Rist, University of Texas Press, 1996, 39–41.

———. *La escuela documental de Santa Fe*, Santa Fe: Editorial Documento del Instituto de Cinematografía de la U.N.L, 1964.

———. "For a Nationalist, Realist, Critical, and Popular Cinema," in *Argentine Cinema*, edited by Tim Barnard, Toronto: Nightwood Editions, 1986, 79–82.

———. "For a Cosmic Cinema, Raving and Lumpen: The First Cosmunist (Cosmic Communist) Manifesto," in *Argentine Cinema*, edited by Tim Barnard, Toronto: Nightwood Editions, 1986, 82–83.

———. *Pionero y peregrino*, Buenos Aires: Editorial Contrapunto, 1987.

Burton, Julianne, *Cinema and Social Change: Conversations with Filmmakers*, Austin: University of Texas Press, 1986.

Burton, Julianne, *The Social Documentary in Latin America*, Pittsburgh: University of Pittsburgh Press, 1990.

Chanan, Michael, "Rediscovering Documentary: Cultural Context and Intentionality," in *The Social Documentary in Latin America*, edited by Julianne Burton, Pittsburgh: University of Pittsburgh Press, 1990, 31–84.

Gamucio Dagron, Alfonso, "Argentina: A Huge Case of Censorship," in. *Argentine Cinema*, edited by Tim Barnard, Toronto: Nightwood Editions, 1986, 84–98.

King, John, *Magical Reels: A History of Cinema in Latin America*, London: Verso, 1990 (reprint in 2000).

Pick, Zuzana, *The New Latin American Cinema: A Continental Project*, Austin: University of Texas Press, 1993.

Ruffinelli, Jorge, "Fernando Birri y Leonardo Favio: La Construccion de lo Popular," unpublished paper, 2000.

Sendros, Paraná, *Fernando Birri*, Buenos Aires: Centro Editor de America Latina con el Instituto Nacional de Cinematografia, 1994.

BIRTLES, FRANCIS

Adventurer Francis Birtles started his career with a solo cycle ride from Perth to Melbourne in 1905. By the end of his life, he had cycled several times across and around Australia, had been the first person to drive a car from London to Melbourne (1928), had set records for other car journeys across the continent, and had traveled extensively over the routes of early explorers. He always carried a camera, creating illustrations for books and journal articles, including images of life in outback towns or on remote station properties, encounters with native peoples, and confrontations with the natural world (including wild animals, flooded rivers, duststorms, and bushfires).

The Gaumont company was sufficiently impressed to send cameraman Richard Primmer along with Birtles on his 1911 ride from Sydney to Darwin, out of which came the film *Across Australia* (1912). In 1914, Frank Hurley accompanied Birtles on a trip to the Gulf country, commissioned by Australasian Films. Hurley returned to Sydney to join the Shackleton Antarctic expedition, but completed the film (*Into Australia's Unknown,* 1915). After that, Birtles did his own cinematography, producing *Across Australia on the Track of Burke and Wills* (1915), *Through Australian Wilds: Across the Track of Ross Smith* (1919), and *Australia's Lonely Lands* (1924). For him the film was always a by-product of the adventure, and he seemed unaware that he had pioneered a new genre—the expeditionary film (or outback adventure film). Other examples of the genre included Hurley's *Pearls and Savages* (1921), and William Jackson's *In New Guinea Wilds* (1920). A new flowering occurred in the 1960s, and included Keith Adam's *Northern Safari* (1966), Malcolm Douglas's *Across the Top* (1969), and numerous films by the Leyland brothers (starting with *Wheels Across the Wilderness* (1969). Currently, the genre lives on in television series such as *Outback Adventures with Troy Dann* and *Bush Tucker Man*.

By the late 1920s, documentary films were not quite so lucrative, and— following the example of Frank Hurley and J. E. Ward (*Australia's Own* 1919)—Birtles turned briefly to narrative fiction. He still set his films in the outback, but now weaved a story around the familiar images of indigenous life and the natural world. *Coorab in the Island of Ghosts* (1929, directed by Francis Birtles and Torrance McLaren) was ahead of its time in employing no white cast at all, but by current standards is uncomfortably paternalistic. It is the only one of Birtles' films to survive, and is held in ScreenSound Australia (the National Collection of Film and Sound).

INA BERTRAND

See also **Documentary Film: Australia; Hurley, Frank**

Biography

Born Fitzroy, Victoria, Australia, November 7, 1881. Served in the merchant navy from age 15, then in South African army and police from 1899. Returned to Australia 1905, began a career of outback traveling, taking still photographs and cinematograph films. Joined the board of Austral Photoplays Ltd, surveyed the overland telegraph route from Adelaide to Darwin (1920–1921), and discovered a payable gold mine (1934). Died July 1, 1941 in Sydney.

Further Reading

Bertrand, Ina, "Francis Birtles—Cyclist, Explorer, Kodaker," *Cinema Papers*, January 1974, 30–35.

Birtles, Francis, *Lonely Lands: Through the Heart of Australia*, Sydney: NSW Bookstall Co., 1909.

———. *Battle Fronts of Outback*, Sydney: Angus & Robertson, 1935.

Birtles, Terry G., "Francis Birtles," *Australian Dictionary of Biography*, vol.7, 1881–1941, 297–298.

BITOMSKY, HARMUT

In his essay, "The Documentary World," the German documentary filmmaker, Hartmut Bitomsky, advanced the idea of the documentary film image as ready-made. Like the artist, the filmmaker takes an object out of its original environment into a new context (Bitomsky, 2003: 206). Taking this idea further, it is not only that he treats images as objects but that his images are also of objects: the Autobahn, the beetle, the B-52 bomber. Arguing against the current focus in documentary film on the depiction of lives as individual or bizarre cases, Bitomsky is interested in the socioeconomic and planned effects of these functional objects of transport and war (Bitomsky, 2003: p. 275). Tellingly Bitomsky did the voice-over narration on the experimental documentary *Four Corners* (1997) by James Benning, another filmmaker who prefers the filming of streets, machinery, and landscape to that of individuals. (Benning also did the sound on *B-52*.)

The "object" of Bitomsky's films, however, is not a closed entity. For Bitomsky, the dialogue with the images is imperative. The images are not merely "objective" material untouched by the viewing process. *Playback* (1995), for example, follows the articulated thoughts of workshop participants at the Amsterdam Film museum, as they closely analyze early silent film footage. In *Playback* the filmmaker narrates: "There are not new films and old films, there are only films one has seen and films one has not seen." It is the relation between both the visible, on the one hand, and the imagination of the filmmaker and the viewer, on the other, that produces a new entity. His documentaries do not merely depict an empirical, visible surface, but they *make* it visible (Bitomsky, 1972). Bitomsky is interested in not only creating original images but in producing new images through the viewer's interaction with existing ones. His films examine the processes of production and trace the path of its material in the way they are made, as well as in what they depict. *Der VW-Komplex* begins the way *B-52* ends, with the dismantling of its object on a scrapheap. The discarded machinery makes for new images, though. Bitomsky's "recycling" of images is economic.

In many of his documentaries, Bitomsky finds "reality" in photos and footage stored in archives. In his examination of cinema through the medium's own means, the fragment retains its quality in itself and is not subsumed under a new whole. Bitomsky's "interest starts after reality and event has already been formed into story'" (Pirschat, 1992: 5). The fragment can be a part of a machine or a section of a moving image. Exposing the found footage as fragments that are not integrated allows the viewer to examine their construction without being drawn in. In Bitomsky's films, the viewer is always made aware of the viewing process. This is achieved by making the image itself into an object by, for example, framing it. Bitomsky follows Levi-Strauss's dictum that to understand images better, one must resist experiencing them, and this is realized by making them smaller (Bitomsky in *Süddeutsche Zeitung*, 1992). In *Die UFA*, for example, the camera films several monitors at the same time, each showing different footage. Another way Bitomsky distances the viewer is to show photographs instead of moving images with the hand of the filmmaker moving his material and turning the pages of books full of images, rather than having the image fill the whole of the screen. This gives viewers the space to detach themselves from the image, but it also depicts the filmmaker as a manual worker given that the still images are propelled forward by manual labor.

Work has an aesthetics and aesthetics are work. Both impact on one another. At the beginning of *Reichsautobahn* the filmmaker narrates: "The Autobahn is the biggest German edifice. At its inauguration Hitler said: 'We'll make sure that the work does not become separated from those who built it.'" Bitomsky argues that it was the aestheticisation of the Autobahn—it it was made for sight—which which was a means for work placement, rather than its functionality. His documentaries reflect the reciprocal influencing of ideology, industry, and images, as well as the interlacing of the civilian and the military and of culture and war (Bitomsky, TAZ 2002). Bitomsky's interest in the functional aspects of the aesthetic is consonant with Brecht, who wrote that "less than ever does a simple reproduction of reality tell us anything about reality. A photograph of Krupps or the AEG yields hardly anything about those industries. True reality has taken refuge in the functional" (Brecht, 1967: 161). The subject matter of his documentaries often is industrial and technological (roads, cars, fighter planes) and, as such, decidedly masculine. The image engineer Bitomsky, however, is interested in the unplanned malfunctions of these grand designs of modern technology: the disintegration of the pompous, totalitarian plans of Hitler's Autobahn in *Reichsautobahn,* or the many accidents in the power weapons of the Cold War in *B-52.* In *Die UFA,* another example, Bitomsky points out that the Nazi propaganda minister Joseph Goebbels had to prohibit the anti-communist propaganda films they initially had commissioned. Even though the Nazis used communist footage against the Soviet's original intent, this inspired people to see the original films. This does not happen with Bitomsky's documentaries using found footage, however, as they examine and work through the originals and do not just reject them. In Germany, showing Nazi propaganda footage within a film has to be indexed by commentary, subtitles, or inter-titles. The German film scholar Klaus Kreimeier argued that announcing the Nazi footage as propaganda precludes any experience of the images as anything other than propaganda (Kreimeier, 1992: 16). In contrast to television reports or other German documentary filmmakers such as Erwin Leiser and Joachim C. Fest, who use Nazi footage as evidence, Bitomsky's documentaries do not use the markers of authenticity such as speech in sync-sound technology as proof. Rather, his films show Hitler before he talks and then paraphrase the content. Moreover, unlike for instance Emile De Antonio's narration in his compilation films, Bitomsky's is not merely contrapunctual against the original footage of, for example, Nazi images. Instead, Bitomsky carves out their inherent contradictions. Even though Bitomsky's documentaries address the concrete consequences of an ideology, they are not directly political. His films delineate the conflicts between the concepts of ideology and the causes and effects

of industry not only in terms of his subject matter but also with respect to the film industry, which his documentaries are in the least possible way part of.

Since 1974, Bitomsky has published, edited, and contributed to the influential German film journal, *Filmkritik* (1957–1985), amongst others with his friend the documentary filmmaker Harun Farocki. With his fellow Anglo-American and French film semioticians at the time, the documentary filmmaker shared an enthusiasm for American fiction film such as those by Samuel Fuller or John Ford. The latter features *Das Kino von John Ford* (1979) in Bitomsky's portrait. Although his earlier reviews in *Filmkritik* and his book *Die Röte des Rots von Technicolor* (1972) were influenced by semiotics, they are written like an instruction manual. Bitomsky approached semiotics like the Volkswagen in *Der VW-Komplex.* His style of writing is similar to that of his film narrations: profound and—untypical for analytic texts in German—constructed in short sentences. Bitomsky does not only analyze found images in his documentaries, but unusual for a documentary filmmaker, he has published texts about his films. The visual "quoting" of found images in Bitomsky's films can perhaps be seen as a continuation of his frequent citing of texts in his early film reviews. In writing about the reception of his documentaries that already reflect production processes of other objects of modernity, Bitomsky constructs a circular trajectory in which he engages in a similar process with his writing about his films as he does in his filming about found images and objects.

Before Bitomsky left Germany, his documentaries could broadly be divided into two groups: films that reflect on their medium such as the videofilms about the cinema *Das Kino und der Tod* (1988), *Kino Flächen Bunker* (1991), and *Das Kino und der Wind und die Photographie* (1991), and films about images of Germany such as *Deutschlandbilder* (1983), *Reichsautobahn* (1986), and *Der VW-Komplex* (1989) (Pirschat, 1992). *Die UFA* (1993), about the national-socialist image politics with respect to the German cinema studios, combined both. With *B-52* (2001), invented by the Germans in the World War II and further developed by the Americans for the Cold War, the focus has shifted to his chosen home country. Hartmut Bitomsky has produced more than forty documentaries.

SILKE PANSE

BITOMSKY, HARMUT

Biography

Born in Bremen, Germany, 1942. Read German literary studies, theatre studies, and journalism at the Free University Berlin, 1962–1966. Changed to the then-new German Film and Television Academy Berlin, 1966–1968. Expelled for political activism during the student revolts. Worked for the West German Television (WDR) from 1973. Published, edited, and wrote for the film journal *Filmkritik*, 1974–1985. Visiting Lecturer at the Academy for Film and Television in Munich, the Free University Berlin and the German Film and Television Academy Berlin after 1975. Dean of the School of Film and Video at the California Institute of the Arts in Los Angeles, 1993–2002. Still teaches there. Fellow of the Rockefeller Foundation.

Selected Films

1970 *Die Teilung aller Tage*
1971 *Eine Sache, die sich versteht*
1976 *Humphrey Jennings. Bericht über einen englischen Filmemacher*
1976 *Das Kino von John Ford*
1980–1981 *Highway 40 West – Reise in Amerika*
1983 *Deutschlandbilder* (with Heiner Mühlenbrock)
1985–1986 *Reichsautobahn*
1988 *Das Kino und der Tod*
1988–1989 *Der VW-Komplex*
1991 *Kino Flächen Bunker*
1991 *Das Kino und der Wind und die Photographie*
1993 *Die UFA*
1995 *Playback*
1999–2001 *B-52*

Further Reading

Bitomsky, Hartmut, introduction, Béla Balázs *Der Geist des Films*, edited by Hartmut Bitomsky, Frankfurt/Main: Makol Verlag, 1972.

Bitomsky, Hartmut, *Die Röte des Rots von Technicolor. Kinorealität und Produktionswirklichkeit*, Neuwied und Darmstadt: Sammlung Luchterhand, 1972.

Bitomsky, Hartmut, in *Filmkritik* 1974–1985.

Bitmosky, Hartmut (ed), *André Bazin. Was ist Kino? Bausteine zur Theorie des Films*, introduction by Eric Rohmer, Cologne: DuMont Schauberg, 1975.

Bitomsky, Hartmut, in Peter Paul Kubitz, "Man muß die Dinge verkleinern, damit sie verstanden werden," *Süddeutsche Zeitung*, 10, 1992, 9.

Bitomsky, Hartmut, "Die Dokumentarische Welt" ["The Documentary World"], in *Hartmut Bitomsky. Kinowahrheit*, edited by Iilka Schaarschmidt, Berlin: *Verlag Vorwerk*, 2003, 8.

Brecht, Bertold, "Der Dreigroschenprozess, ein soziologisches Experiment," in *Gesammelte Werke in 20 Bänden*, Band 18, Frankfurt-am-Main: Suhrkamp Verlag, 1967.

Kreimeier, Klaus, "Deutschlandbilder: Ein imaginärer Indizienprozess," in *Die Wirklichkeit der Bilder. Der Filmemacher Hartmut Bitomsky*, edited by Jutta Pirschat, Essen: Edition Filmwerkstatt, 1992.

Pirschat, Jutta, "Die Wirklichkeit der Bilder," in *Die Wirklichkeit der Bilder. Der Filmemacher Hartmut Bitomsky*, edited by Jutta Pirschat, Essen: Edition Filmwerkstatt, 1992.

BLACK AUDIO FILM COLLECTIVE

The Black Audio Film Collective was formed by a group of British filmmakers and audiovisual technicians committed to independent filmmaking. The collective began as an informal grouping in 1982 and was soon established as a cooperative in 1983. It became a franchised workshop in 1986 under the workshop declaration, along with other London-based film and video workshops Sankofa, Ceddo, and Retake Film and Video Collective. Support for an independent filmmaking practice emerged from the election of a Labour administration in 1981 to control the Greater London Council (GLC). The combination of the Thatcher government and inner-city riots gave rise to a politics of difference and identity. The GLC increased funding for the arts and the priority given to representing the ethnic diversity of London. The Black Audio Film Collective emerged out of the context of a changing cultural politics and ailing British film production funded by a combination of The London Borough Grant Scheme, British Film Institute, Channel 4, The London Borough of Hackney, and the Calouste Gulbenkian Foundation. The problem of dependency on grants was not new to marginal filmmaking, but it did enable the collective to innovate and challenge dominant practice.

Black Audio's commitment to experimentalism and audiovisual form incorporated documentary film practice as a means of articulating the diasporic experience of the British nation and empire. The films of the collective interrogate and hybridize the cultural history and language of the documentary form by taking existing dominant cultural signs and radically recontextualizing them. This is demonstrated in the early work of the collective, a tape-slide show called *Expeditions: Signs of Empire and Images of Nationality* (1982).

One of the key reference points for Black Audio was the British documentary and modernist tradition of filmmaking. The production of the award-winning documentary, *Handsworth Songs* (1986), juxtaposed media coverage of the civil disorder in the Handsworth district of Birmingham in 1985 with a reflexive excavation of the documentary and newsreel archive that records the journey, arrival, and settlement of the Afro-Caribbean population into the mother country and the industrialised West Midlands. The contested critical reception of *Handsworth Songs* amongst not only black cultural critics underlined how the collective effectively countered both the expositional documentary realism that represented blacks in Britain and the politics of the monologic black subject.

The growth of the workshop sector in the 1980s was encouraged by the commitment of Channel 4 to British filmmaking and the decision to establish an Independent Film and Video department with Alan Fountain as senior commissioning editor. *The Eleventh Hour* became an "independent" and avant-garde slot where at eleven o'clock on Monday evenings Channel 4 would broadcast workshop productions and documentaries from outside the United Kingdom that resisted the "impartial" conventions of television documentary.

The Workshop Declaration was agreed on in 1982 between Channel 4, the Association of Cinematograph Television and Allied Technicians (ACTT), the British Film Institute, the Regional Arts Association, and the Independent Filmmakers Association. The nonprofit-making, and noncommercial workshops were run cooperatively and committed to an integrated and collective practice of production, exhibition, distribution, and development of audiences, research, education, and community work more generally. The Black Audio Film Collective was active outside London; it staged program at independent cinemas and toured the country with its tape-slide program *Expeditions*, gaining insights through discussions with audiences. The distribution of the black workshop sector went beyond regional and metropolitan art house cinemas and into social clubs, community centers, and cultural associations (Pines, 1988). Pressure exerted by the Independent Filmmakers Association led to an independent distribution group, The Other Cinema opening the Metro Cinema in London, where films such as Sankofa's *Passion of Remembrance* (1986) and Black Audio's *Handsworth Songs* gained the first West End runs of workshop films (Williamson, 1993).

After the Broadcasting Act of 1990, Channel 4 was responsible for selling its own advertising and consequently withdrew its backing for the workshops. The prior abolition of the GLC compounded the situation for the workshops. Black Audio Film Collective continued its commitment to an innovative filmmaking practice and secured commissions for the production of documentaries such as *Touch of the Tarbrush* (1991) for the BBC as part of a series about English identity; *Mysteries of July* (1991), a documentary for the Channel 4 series *Critical Eye* concerning deaths in police custody; and *Seven Songs for Malcolm X* (1993) *and The Mothership Connection* (1995), a documentary exploring the connection between pan-African culture and science fiction, with the latter documentaries circulating via the international film festival circuit.

Black Audio Film Collective forms part of the tradition of British Independent filmmaking maintained by similarly organized groups such as the London Film-makers' Co-operative founded in 1966 and the Independent Film-makers' Association formed ten years later. The presence of the Black Audio Film Collective and the workshops meant that a number of experiments took place involving filmmaking practice that questioned the critical agendas of British documentary, British cinema, and black culture and politics and also demonstrated that British documentary filmmaking was not solely confined to television.

IAN GOODE

See also **Handsworth Songs**

Further Reading

Mercer, Kobena, *Welcome to the Jungle*, London: Routledge, 1994.

Mercer, Kobena, editor, *Black Film/British Cinema*, London: ICA, 1988.

Pines, Jim, "Black Independent Film in Britain: Historical Overview," in *The Black and White Media Book*, edited by John Twitchin, Stoke-on-Trent: Trentham, 1988.

Williamson, Judith, "Handsworth Songs." 1993.

BLACK BOX BRD

(Germany, Veiel, 2001)

Germany's long and painful struggle to overcome the legacy of the Nazi regime reached a cataclysmic peak during the terrorist siege to which the Rote Armee Fraktion (RAF, Red Army Faction) subjected the nation and its government in the late 1960s and 1970s. The terrible violence during the fall of 1977 was portrayed by Rainer Werner Fassbinder, Volker Schlöndorf, and a team of other directors in their joint film *Deutschland im Herbst* (Germany in Autumn, 1978). The following decades saw a decrease in the number of terrorist assaults, but the attacks on representatives of industry and government continued into the 1990s and ended only when the RAF eventually announced its own dissolution on April 20, 1998.

In his much-acclaimed film, *Black Box BRD*, which won both a German and a European Film Award, Andres Veiel follows the lives of two people directly connected to this conflict, Alfred Herrhausen and Wolfgang Grams. In the film, they represent the two opposing sides, although both died a violent death. Herrhausen was senior manager of Deutsche Bank when he was killed by an RAF bomb on November 30, 1989 while driving to work in his car. Grams, a leader of the third generation of the RAF, had been living underground since 1984. He died on June 27, 1993 during an exchange of fire with police officers attempting to arrest him. Investigations into the exact circumstances of his death have failed to provide conclusive answers.

Veiel approaches his difficult topic in a manner that is personal, yet remains distant from a narrative point of view. At no point in his film does the filmmaker comment directly on the events portrayed. The film ends with a few lines of text that do not attempt to answer the many questions raised by the film, but simply provide specific historical data on Herrhausen's and Grams's deaths. The text states that it is "unclear" whether and to what extent Grams was involved in the attack on Herrhausen, causing hesitation on the part of the viewer who may be attempting to create a direct connection between the two stories.

The personal atmosphere of the film is a result of the many private memories shared by family members, as well as former friends and colleagues of the two main characters. These interviews are the main sources of information from which the film draws. In addition to these interviews, which make up the overwhelming majority of the film's running time, Veiel incorporates archival footage from private home movies that strengthen the personal tone of his biographical film. To provide the audience with some context, *Black Box BRD* also includes scenes from original news programs, thereby providing not only necessary historical information for a contemporary audience, but also a sense of the urgency and drama that surrounded the political conflicts during the decades when Germany was finally taking a closer look at its historical legacy.

It becomes increasingly apparent throughout *Black Box BRD* that the unconstrained idealism with which both segments of society were pursuing their political and societal goals still prevents many people, years and decades later, from analyzing the incidents with any degree of objectivity. The issues that initially stirred the student demonstrations, and then escalated into the RAF's terrorism might have been overcome had those issues been dealt with appropriately during the conflict. One of the great and sad ironies of Herrhausen's murder is that it occurred at a time when he was already starting to steer Deutsche Bank away from the hard-line capitalist ideology of the postwar boom years. After a meeting with Mexico's president, he proposed to the bank's board that they take greater account of the social consequences of their operations. Although his intentions alienated many of his senior colleagues, Herrhausen's plans might have found much support in the public debate about the social role and responsibilities of corporations.

Black Box BRD is aptly named after a technological device, the workings of which most of its users do not comprehend. The film is structured like a mosaic or puzzle and thus also presents itself as a mysterious object. Its manifold pieces, mostly brief segments smoothly cut from longer interviews, resist the temptation of presenting a conclusive or linear narrative. The film moves back and forth between the lives of its two main subjects, following their biographies in more or less chronological order. Beyond the interviews, Veiel filmed very little additional material: staged footage of the fateful auto convoy, neighborhoods, Deutsche Bank, and prison buildings. Veiel clearly refused to follow the current trend of producing a docudrama, in which historical and archival material is edited in a way that it becomes almost indistinguishable from reenacted scenes. The additional (fictitious) footage that Veiel included is helpful, however, as it often provides subtle clues whenever the film's narrative moves from one of its main characters to the other. Because there is no voice-over narrator in *Black Box BRD*, these transitions perform a crucial function. In general, however, the film's almost detached relationship to its topic is noticeable. The camera remains mostly immobile, and sound is natural, with only the theme song occasionally providing some distraction from the tense statements of the people on the screen.

As did his earlier film about German youth in the 1970s, *Die Überlebenden* [The survivors, 1996], Veiel's *Black Box BRD* refuses to judge the two people it portrays so intimately. It presents them as complex individuals who have, on occasion, questioned their own ideologies and principles. As a rule, the interviewees are not questioned while on camera. The film instead presents testimonials, memories, and the lasting pain deriving from the search for answers by the friends and relatives of Herrhausen and Grams, who represent all those who did not survive the dark terrorist phase of Germany's postwar history. *Black Box BRD* is not afraid of silence, as when family members are overcome by emotion and unable to continue. Yet, the film's very existence provides an outspoken and powerful reminder that the absence of clear answers does not have to mean that the past can be forgotten, thereby providing a valuable counterweight to cultural and political amnesia.

GERD BAYER

See also **Veiel, Andres**

Black Box BRD (Germany, 2001, X Verleih/Zero Film, 102 min) Distributed by Warner Home Video. Produced by Thomas Kufus. Directed by Andres Veiel. Shooting script by Andres Veiel. Cinematography by Jörg Jeshel. Assistant direction by Andreas Teuchert. Music by Jan Tilman Schade. Editing by Katja Dringenberg. Sound direction by Paul Oberle.

Selected Films

1991–1992 *Winternachtstraum*: director, writer
1993 *Balagan*: director, writer
1995–1996 *Die Überlebenden*: director, writer
2001 *Black Box BRD*: director, writer
2003 *Die Spielwütigen*: director, writer

Further Reading

Becker, Jillian, *Hitler's Children: The Story of the Baader-Meinhof Terrorist Gang*, 3rd edition, London: Pickwick, 1989.

Varon, Jeremy, *Bringing the War Home: The Weather Underground, the Red Army Faction, and the Revolutionary Violence in the Sixties and Seventies*, Berkeley: University of California Press, 2004.

Veiel, Andres, *Black Box BRD: Alfred Herrhausen, die Deutsche Bank, die RAF und Wolfgang Grams*, Stuttgart: Deutsche Verlags-Anstalt, 2002.

BLANK, LES

An independent documentary filmmaker from the United States, Les Blank is considered a maverick for his lush films on food, regional music styles, and communities on the fringes of mainstream American society. The founder of Flower Films in El Cerrito, California, Blank has directed and/or produced approximately thirty-three documentary films since 1960. In addition, he has served as crew member on approximately seven other films, including additional photography on *Little Dieter*

Needs to Fly (1997, Werner Herzog) and uncredited second camera on *Easy Rider* (1969).

Les Blank studied in the Ph.D. film program at the University of Southern California and worked as a freelance industrial and commercial filmmaker in Los Angeles before directing his own independent documentary films. Blank initially financed these films by continuing to make promotional films for such companies as Holly Farms Poultry, Archway Cookies, and the National Wildlife Federation. His work has since been funded by such entities as the National Endowment for the Arts, the American Film Institute, The National Endowment for the Humanities, The Ford Foundation, The Guggenheim Foundation, PBS, and the British Broadcasting Corporation (BBC).

Major retrospectives of his work have been mounted worldwide, and feature articles have appeared in such publications as *Film Quarterly, The New York Times, The Los Angeles Times, Mother Jones, Rolling Stone,* and *The Village Voice.* Blank was awarded the American Film Institute's Maya Deren Award for outstanding lifetime achievement as an independent filmmaker in 1990, and his documentaries have been internationally recognized with awards, including The British Academy Award, the Grand Prize at the Melbourne Film Festival, The Special Jury Award at the Sundance Film Festival, the Grand Award at the Houston Film Festival, the Golden Jugo at the Chicago Film Festival, and the Best of Festival Award at the San Francisco Film Festival.

His documentary films are praised for the intimate and privileged glimpses they provide into artistic and culinary subcultures in the United States and are particularly recognized for capturing and visually/aurally preserving aspects of American culture that have now faded or disappeared altogether. He incorporates an organic and sensual shooting style that allows the viewer privileged views of artists, food lovers, and others who are committed to living life to the fullest. Possibly best characterized as artistic visual ethnographies, most of Blank's films invite the viewer to a better appreciation of common folk who have dedicated their lives to community around a common interest. These interests include garlic; late 1960s flower children; Serbian-American, Hawaiian, Afro-Cuban, Louisiana-French and Tejano music; bluegrass fiddling; German filmmaker Werner Herzog; women with gaps between their front teeth; beer; and Cajun and Creole cooking. Music is often an important cinematic element in his films, and close-up shots of steaming pots of sauce, pigs suckling, women dancing, people laughing and enjoying

whatever it is that gives them pleasure and their lives meaning, are delicately paced to weave a tapestry of experience for the audience. Often presented as tight vignettes or segments, Blank's films unfold to gradually allow the viewer more information on the subject and people at hand. The subject matter, often quirky and outside of mainstream American experiences, are engaging and gratifying to observe. Blank uses a delicate hand to unfold stories of commitment to craft and community, often intercutting snatches of informal conversations, relaxed interviews, imbedded and privileged observational footage, and occasional hand-lettered explanations and subtitles. As a filmmaker, Les Blank appears to be at ease in every situation he documents and with every person he engages. He allows them to demonstrate and discuss their cultural nuances with dedication and passion, rarely seeming sentimental or patronizing. His shooting and editorial styles are as earthy and dedicated as the subjects he explores, and his films are noted for their devotion to vision and independence.

C. MELINDA LEVIN

See also **Del Mero Corazón**

Biography

Born November 27, 1935, in Tampa, Florida. Received a B. A. in English literature and an M.F.A. in theatre from Tulane University. Studied in the Ph.D. film program at the University of Southern California. Awarded the American Film Institute's Maya Deren Award for outstanding lifetime achievement as an independent filmmaker in 1990.

Selected Films

Running Around Like a Chicken With Its Head Cut Off (1960)
Dizzie Gillespie (1965)
God Respects Us When We Work, But Loves Us When We Dance (1968)
The Sun's Gonna Shine (1969)
The Blues Accordin' to Lightnin' Hopkins (1969)
Chicken Real (1970)
A Well Spent Life (1971)
Spend It All (1971)
Dry Wood (1973)
Hot Pepper (1973)
Chulas Fronteras (1976)
Always for Pleasure (1978)
Del mero corazon (1979)
Werner Herzog Eats His Shoe (1980)
Garlic Is As Good As Ten Mothers (1980)
Burden of Dreams (1982)
Sprout Wings and Fly (1983)
In Heaven There Is No Beer? (1984)
Cigarette Blues (1985)

Huey Lewis and the News: Be-FORE! (1986)
Ziveli! Medicine for the Heart (1987)
Gap-Toothed Women (1987)
*Ry Cooder and the Moula Banda Rhythm Aces: Let's Have a
    Ball* (1988)
J'ai ete au bal (1989)
Yum, Yum, Yum! A Taste of Cajun and Creole Cooking
    (1990)
Christopher Tree (1991)

Julie: Old Time Tales of the Blue Ridge (1991)
Marc and Ann (1991)
Puamana (1991)
Sworn to the Drum: A Tribute to Francisco Aguabella
    (1995)
Maestro: King of the Cowboy Artists (1995)
My Old Fiddle: A Visit with Tommy Jarrell in the Blue Ridge
    (1995)

BLUE EYED

(Germany, Verhaag, 1996)

Blue Eyed was selected as one of the outstanding documentaries of 1996 by the Academy of Motion Pictures. The film is centered on Jane Elliot, who has committed herself to fighting prejudice, ignorance, and racism in society after the assassination of Martin Luther King in 1968. Elliot, a former teacher, offers a special training course, in which she divides people on the basis of two arbitrary physical properties: blue or brown eyes. She declares the latter to be better and more intelligent and grants them privileges that she denies to the blue-eyed, who are deemed to be inferior and less intelligent. When she started this workshop in her school, all the members of her family were aggressively attacked by their white fellow citizens and their restaurant had to close.

At the beginning of the experiment, the blue-eyed people are marked with a green collar around their necks. These seventeen candidates are sent to a small, overheated room with only three seats. They have to wait a long time for their appearance in the workshop and do not really know what will happen. The brown-eyed participants are encouraged to consider themselves special, and to treat the blue-eyed contemptuously. For the first time, many white people become acquainted with the feeling of belonging to a condemned group that can never win. They experience the feeling of being discriminated against, in the same way that society today discriminates against women, people of a different color, homosexuals, or the disabled.

The film documents this workshop with three observing cameras. They keep close to the protagonists, creating a sense of discomfort and tension for the viewer. There are only short breaks with typical images from America, beautiful shots that are accompanied by a jazz sound track, giving an impression of the atmosphere of the American middle class. The film was shot with a budget of $200,000, and the crew shot seventy hours of Digi-Beta material. The final film was than transferred to 35mm. The director, Bertram Verhaag, shows how the group dynamics work and why nobody among the blue-eyed can resist the mechanisms of suppression. The film shows the core of racism: power and its use against the weak or disenfranchised.

As film critic Thomas Klingenmaier wrote: "It won't help much to be prepared to face Jane Elliot. This elderly woman will tear down any shield. Even we, the spectators of *Blue Eyed*, can't get rid of this feeling of uneasiness, embarrassment, anxiety and utterly helpless hatred when she starts putting people down, humiliating them, deriding them, incapacitating them. No doubt about this: for three quarters of the time in this documentation Jane Elliot is the meanest, the lowest, the most detestable, the most hypocritical human being hell has ever spit back on earth. But she should be an example for all of us."

KAY HOFFMAN

Blue Eyed (Germany, 1996, 90 min) Directed by Bertram
    Verhaag, in cooperation with Jane Elliot. Produced by

Denkmalfilm Ltd., in co-production with: WDR, 3SAT, BR. Production Manager: Alon Gilk. Director of Photography: Waldemar Hauschild. Additional cameras: Hans-Albrecht Lusznat and Glenn Eddins. Camera Assistant: Christina Schultz. Editing by Uwe Klimmeck. Music by Wolfgang Neumann. Sound by Zoltan Ravasz, with Bopp King and Joe Thoennes.

Further Reading

Kleber, Reinhard, *Wenn er läuft, dann schlägt er ein*, in Filmecho/Filmwoche, 1997, 34.

Klingenmaier, Thomas, Blaue Augen, weiche Hirne, in: *Stuttgarter Zeitung*, 16,1997, 1.

Platthaus, Andreas, Blaue Augen, schwarze Hände, in *Frankfurter Allgemeine Zeitung*, 6, 1997, 6.

Weidinger, Birgit, Blauäugige sind blöd, in *Süddeutsche Zeitung* 29–30, 1997, 11.

Wolf, Fritz, Denn ich bin eine Weiße, in *Epd Medien*, 18.1.1997.

BOND, RALPH

Ralph Bond's talent as a filmmaker was limited, but his political activism and organisational abilities have clearly left a mark on British documentary. Having worked in the insurance business, Bond, a young Communist, started a career in politics in 1927 as the secretary of the National Left Wing Movement. In 1929, the new Communist political line favouring the development of an independent proletarian culture offered Bond the chance of organising the cinema side of it. Following the examples of Germany (Volksfilmverband) and France (Les Amis de Spartacus), he set out to establish a workers' film movement to give working-class audiences access to Soviet and other films of artistic and political merit. Like its "bourgeois" counterpart, the Film Society, and its political rival, the Masses Stage and Film Guild (controlled by the Independent Labour Party), the workers' film movement used the legal and organisational form of the private society to get around censorship measures. The London Workers' Film Society, the flagship of the UK-wide Federation of Workers' Film Societies (FOWFS), was the first to start its activities in November 1929. Writing in periodicals as far apart as the cinephile *Close-Up*, the CP controlled *Daily Worker* and the movement's own *Workers' Cinema*, Bond acted as a tireless propagandist for the cause.

As a manager of the Atlas Film Co. that imported films from Germany and the Soviet Union for FOWFS member-societies, he also embarked on an ambitious production program.

With limited means, Atlas produced three issues of the newsreel *Workers' Topical News* (1930–1931), a compilation film *Glimpses of Modern Russia* (1930) and a twenty-minute film to support the Workers Charter Campaign, entitled *1931 The Charter Film*. By the end of that year, however, the supply of new Soviet films dried up as a result of the coming of sound, and Atlas was on the verge of bankruptcy. Bond was happy to accept an invitation by John Grierson, who had occasionally helped out Atlas, to join his Empire Marketing Board (EMB) Film Unit.

Working as production and studio manager at the EMB Film Unit, Bond earned the respect of his colleagues for his knowledge of Marxism, which in the eyes of many in the documentary movement offered the only viable political alternative to the crisis-ridden capitalist system. Bond, on the other hand, completely endorsed the social realism of the documentary movement, "the drama of the doorstep" as he coined it later, and respected Grierson as "a man of extraordinary talent." Bond had the chance to direct a few documentaries at the General Post Office (GPO) Film Unit, successor to the EMB Film Unit, and then moved on to Strand Films. In *Today we Live* (1937) he was able to show his views on the plight of the unemployed. Commissioned by the National Council for Social Service, the film was co-directed by John Grierson's sister, Ruby. Her location was a seemingly picturesque Cotswold village, but Bond chose the bleak coal mining village of Pentre in South Wales. This visit resulted among others in the archetypical depression years sequence of unemployed miners looking for coal on the Tylorstown slagheap, shot by Bond's assistant, Donald Alexander. From 1938, Bond was given the chance to make a series of short films demonstrating the virtues of cooperation, as part of a "five-year plan" of the big London Co-operative Societies. The first, *Advance, Democracy!* (1938) was directed by Bond himself, with a musical score by Benjamin Britten. It showed how a London crane driver and his wife, a staunch member of the Women's Co-operative Guild, start taking an interest in the political situation and join the May Day demonstration. Like most of his colleagues, Bond was busy making documentaries for the Ministry of Information during the war.

A committed trade unionist (he was an active member of the Association of Cinematograph and Allied Technicians [ACT] from 1935 onwards, serving as vice-president from 1942 to 1974), Bond welcomed the fact that at the end of the war, some unions were finally showing an interest in having their own film. For the Amalgamated Engineering Union (AEU), he directed *Unity Is Strength* (1945), and he acted as producer for *A Power in the Land* (1946), commissioned by the Electrical Trades Union. In 1950, the ACT started its own production company, ACT Films Ltd., with Bond serving as its general manager. With the financial support of the National Film Finance Corporation ACT Films managed in the 1950s and 1960s to produce more than a dozen feature films, thus helping film technicians who were out of work with temporary employment. But to Bond's personal regret it was not until 1970 that a trade union—once more the AEU—would commission ACT Films to make a film. Bond, by now retired as general manager from ACT Films, acted as production controller for what was a rather disappointing documentary directed by Robert Kitts, *We Are the Engineers*.

As a delegate of the ACT (from 1958 ACTT, when an extra T for Television was added), Bond attended the annual Trades Union Congress (TUC) without fail. In 1960, he successfully moved a resolution that called for "a greater participation by the Trade Union movement in all cultural activities." It prompted playwright Arnold Wesker to establish Centre 42 (referring to the number of the resolution), which, for lack of financial support, did not become the success that Bond had envisaged. Likewise the recommendations of a TUC Working Party on the Arts (1975–1976), of

which Bond was a prominent member, failed to make an impact.

In the 1970s, Bond became Documentary Course Director and Lecturer at the London International Film School, enabling him to pass on his experiences to a younger generation. Bond witnessed the reemergence of a left-wing film culture in Britain in the same decade with a certain detachment, always willing to share his recollections, but unrelenting when it came down to what he considered basic trade union principles.

BERT HOGENKAMP

Biography

Born in London, December 5, 1906. Educated at the Tottenham Grammar School. Secretary of the National Left Wing Movement, 1927–1929. Manager of Atlas Film Co., 1929–1931. Joined the EMB Film Unit in 1931. Joined Strand Films in 1936 and Realist Film Unit 1938. Member of the Association of Cinematograph and Allied Technicians 1935, elected to the ACT Executive Committee in 1936, vice-president of the ACT 1942–1974. Founding member of the World Union of Documentary, Brussels 1947. Founding director of ACT Films Ltd., 1950. Director of Bond Films, 1951–ca. 1954. Moved Resolution 42 at the 1960 Trades Union Congress. Documentary Course Director and Lecturer at the London International Film School. Died in Torbay, May 29, 1989.

Selected Films

1930–1931 *Workers' Topical News* Nos.1-3: director
1931 *1931 The Charter Film*: director
1937 *To-day We Live*: director (with Ruby Grierson)
1938 *Advance, Democracy!*: director
1939 *People with a Purpose*: director
1940 *Neighbours under Fire*: director
1945 *Unity is Strength*: director
1945 *Today and Tomorrow*: producer
1946 *A Power in the Land*: producer
1970 *We are the Engineers*: production controller

Further Reading

Bond, Ralph, "Cinema in the Thirties: Documentary Film and the Labour Movement," in *Culture and Crisis in Britain in the Thirties*, edited by Jon Clark et al., London: Lawrence and Wishart, 1979.
Hogenkamp, Bert, *Deadly Parallels. Film and the Left in Britain, 1929-1939*, London: Lawrence and Wishart, 1986.
Hogenkamp, Bert, "To-day We Live: The Making of a Documentary in a Welsh Mining Valley," in *Llafur. Journal of Welsh Labour History*, 5, 1, 1988, 45–52.
Hogenkamp, Bert, *Film, Television and the Left in Britain, 1950–1970*, London: Lawrence and Wishart, 2000.
MacPherson, Don, editor, *Traditions of Independence. British Cinema in the Thirties*, London: BFI, 1980.
Orbanz, Eva, *Journey to a Legend and Back*, Berlin: Edition Volker Spiess, 1977.

BOSNIA AND HERSEGOVINA

See **Bosnian Documentary Movement; Yugoslavia: Death of a Nation; Yugoslavia (former)**

BOSNIAN DOCUMENTARY MOVEMENT

Given its history as a part of the former Yugoslavia, the Republic of Bosnia and Herzegovina never had a chance to gather the means necessary for film production in its own capital of Sarajevo. Laboratory and postproduction work was generally done in Belgrade or Zagreb. In general, it was not uncommon for filmmakers to go without equipment as basic as the 35-mm film camera. That may explain why local filmmakers focused primarily on making documentary films predominantly on 16-mm film.

Bosnian documentary film production began in the 1950s in the newly formed Studio Film, a department of the larger parent company, Bosna Film. The field developed fully only during the 1960s, however, when Sutjeska Film was established. Soon, pioneers of filmmaking in Bosnia—including Zika Ristic, Toma Janic, Hajrudin Krvavac, Suad Mrkonjic, Nikola Djurdjevic, Midhat Mutapcic, Gojko Sipovac, Bakir Tanovic, Mehmed Fehimovic, Vefik Hadzismajlovic, Vlatko Filipovic, Petar Ljubojev, Milutin Kosovac, Bato Cengic, and Mirza Idrizovic—were making the films that would ensure their reputations. Although they had different preferences regarding subjects and stylistic expression, the unifying element for most of these documentaries was the ability of the filmmakers to penetrate the essence of film language and concentrate on the power of visuals. One more important attribute of Bosnian documentary-makers was an awareness of social issues, resulting in critical and often satirical documentaries.

The appellation "Sarajevo's Documentary Film School" was used by film critics and theoreticians during the 1970s to mark the specifics of Bosnian production, characterized by this unique approach. The work of the filmmakers of this school was often lyrical, with little verbal communication, and marked by a minimalist style. Some directors created conspicuous miniature studies and film essays on the tensions between tradition and modernity, the struggles of rural dwellers, city workers, poverty, and social injustice. Most of the films were less than fifteen minutes long and were screened on a regular basis as trailers in cinema theatres.

Vlatko Filipovic, who later focused exclusively on making fictional films, made *Hop Jan (1967)*, an eleven-minute masterpiece on the stone cutters of Herzegovina, celebrating the human devotion to work and the struggle with nature. The powerful synergy of image and sound, edited in a significantly rhythmical pace, makes this film ecstatic and memorable.

Vefik Hadzismajlovic's documentary, *In the Inn* (*U kafani*, 1969), is virtually silent but portrays the mentality of the Bosnian people eloquently, their rhythm of life conflicting with the hectic pace of the city. Hadzismajlovics made approximately twenty documentaries, displaying an ability to accurately render the psychology of children who had to struggle either to go to school (*Walking school children* [*Djaci pjesaci*, 1966]) or to earn a living (*Charcoal children* [*Ugljari*, 1973]; *Dreamers* [*Sanjari*, 1971]) without disrupting the integrity of their emotional world. One of his most powerful films is *Two Laws* (*Dva zakona*, 1969) about the conflict between the law on education and the unwritten law of traditional Bosnian village life, which dictates that daughters stay at home.

From 1945 to 1992, when Yugoslavia split into five independent states, film production was owned and financed by the government. There was considerable censorship by the state. Bosnian filmmakers learned to be critical of official practices and decrees in an indirect manner, so as to avoid the risk of seeing their film censored or forbidden. They practiced the so-called "language of flowers," by which criticism is conveyed in a hidden and discreet manner. The documentaries generally focused on humankind's struggle to survive, or on the misery caused by poverty or injustice in the socialist system. Examples of these films include *The Barge-Steerers of the Drina* (*Splavari na Drini*, Zike Ristica 1951), *The Stolen Land* (*Oteta zemlja*, Hajrudin Krvavac, 1954), *In the Leeward of Time* (*U zavjetrini vremena*, Vlatko Filipovic, 1961), and *Potters* (*Cancari*, Midhat Mutapcic, 1967).

Petar Ljubojev, who was for several years the head of Sutjeska Film, developed a unique style of bitter humor for approaching and discussing serious social issues in works such as *Black Gardens* (*Crne baste*, 1972) and *Ismet Kozica's Mission* (*Misija Ismeta Kozice*, 1977).

Bakir Tanovic gained recognition early in his career with his somber portrayal of heavy labor in the underground pipes (*Kesonci*, 1965). His films (as well as the films of many other Bosnian documentary directors) have been awarded with the highest prizes at European festivals in Leipzig, Oberhausen, and Krakow, and some have been screened at Cannes.

During the 1980s, Sarajevo became a notable center of documentary production, as a younger generation arrived on the scene. Zlatko Lavanic won the Grand Prix at Krakow with his first film, *One Day of Rajko Maksim* (*Jedan dan Rajka Maksima*, 1976), and became one of the most promising Bosnian directors. This film, as well as other future works of his, deals with loneliness. The peasant Rajko Maksim is a goose shepherd with a life full of long, lonely, days. Lavanic's film is a nostalgic ode to the lives of people faced with few choices and prospects, who make do with what they have. He died during the last war in Bosnia (1992–1995).

Until 1992, women directors in Bosnia were extremely rare. Vesna Ljubic remains the only woman who has directed fiction feature films, in addition to her docu-drama work such as *The Illu-*

sionist (*Iluzionisti*, 1991), which centers on the dreams and hopes of a poor family man. Another female documentary filmmaker, Mirjana Zoranovic, devoted her entire opus to individuals, mainly working women, who struggle in patriarchal society (*Ana*, 1984; *Marija*, 1988).

In the 1990s, new young directors appeared with a fresh approach. They were mostly schooled either at the Prague Film School (FAMU), or in Belgrade or Zagreb, as Sarajevo did not have a film academy at the time. An example of one such director is Sahin Sisic, who was awarded the Golden FIPA award at Cannes for his impressive documentary *Margina 88*. Sisic has developed his own cinematic style, reminiscent of the Black Wave Movement in Yugoslavian film of the 1960s and 1970s.

The war in Bosnia (1992–1995) raised an unforeseen obstacle in terms of documentary production and brought to an end the style of documentary filmmaking nourished in Sarajevo since the 1950s. Films, made mostly on video, became diaries of filmmakers who stayed in the besieged city during the four years of war. Sahin Sisic's *Planet Sarajevo* (*Planeta Sarajevo*, 1994–1995) and Vesna Ljubic's *Ecce homo* (1994) are examples of the rare documentaries done on negative and distinguish themselves from the common diary format and style with a moving mixture of sadness and horror. With no words, using only images and sophisticated sound, these two films reflect on the phenomenon of dying in the city, deprived of food, water, and freedom.

The majority of films produced during the war were done so under the auspices of Sarajevo's Group of Authors, or SAGA. This company, whose films were presented at Cannes, received, in 1995, the European Academy Felix award, which honors the achievements of filmmakers from across Europe. Their films prove that, even in times of war, filmmakers instinctively act as creators and register their everyday misery in an inspiring way. Ademir Kenovic, Nedzad Begovic, Mirza Idrizovic, Srdjan Vuletic Zlatko Lavanic, Mirjana Zoranovic, Vuk Janic, Pjer and Nino Zalica, Haris Prolic, and others made some of the most remarkable films on human endurance, as well as the human ability to do evil.

I Burnt Legs (*Palio sam noge*, 1992–1993) by Srdjan Vuletic is a testimony marked by a clear, confessional style. The author observes his emotional alterations, as well as the changes in the destroyed city.

Bosnian filmmakers used all possible means to make documentaries during the war. The end result was approximately fifty works that became available worldwide. After the war, documentary film-making was still beset by numerous problems. Money was not available to filmmakers, nor was there a supportive infrastructure of arts organizations. After 2001, however, the government began overseeing cinema production, and independent film companies were formed.

RADA SESIC

See also **Yugoslavia (former)**

BOSSAK, JERZY

Jerzy Bossak, a teacher, filmmaker, and journalist, was one of the most important and influential figures in post-World War II Polish cinema. He has often been called, in fact, the "father" of Polish documentary filmmaking. He was instrumental in organizing the film company, Start, a company founded on the following philosophy of cinematography: filmmaking should be as free as possible from commercial constraints and corporate demands, and filmmakers should understand their work not only as art, but as useful art. This pragmatic notion of usefulness went hand-in-hand with the notion of action; Bossak argued that film, documentary film in particular, should work to raise its viewers' social consciousness and inspire them to act, to make changes in their society. Such thinking was at the center of Bossak's philosophy of documentary filmmaking. He was critical of the film industry before the war, observing that, "In prewar Poland there were no good films, not just because there was no difference between the maker of films and the maker of artificial jewelry, but also because we did not know how to make films and look at them. . . . Today we have to create conditions in which Polish film can flourish" (Haltof, 2002). Bossak's company, Start, was successful in altering the industry and in many ways instituting his fresh philosophy of cinematography.

Bossak's theory of documentary filmmaking is derived in part from the Aristotelian approach to persuasion, which involves the three rhetorical appeals of logos (logical argument, an appeal to reason), pathos (pathetic argument, an appeal to the emotions), and ethos (the way in which writers, or director, situate their characters and present their work). Bossak felt that, for the most part, English and American documentary film focused far too much (or even entirely) on logical or reasoned presentations, on attempting to present just the "facts." Together with logical appeals, Bossak also played to his audiences' "heart strings," or to their emotions, in an attempt to move them to action; both reasoned persuasion and emotional appeal, he espoused, were necessary. Also necessary in this equation was the way in which the filmmaker presented, organized, and interpreted the material. The "authors" of any film presented themselves through the film by the way in which the chosen material was arranged. That is, the way in which logical and emotional footage were arranged by the filmmaker (the way the filmmaker set out his ethos) went a long way to whether an audience might be persuaded to act.

Underlying much of Bossak's work was an interest not only in war but in the tenuous relationship that existed between the government and the general population. He attempted to break away from the typical nationalistic propaganda films that both dominated the industry and disseminated what Bossak saw as untrue messages operating to pacify the masses. *Warszawa 1956*, by many accounts one of his best films, is a good example of his attempt to critique the government. Completed in 1956, this film juxtaposes modern, towering, clean government buildings with the run-down, filthy tenement buildings that the masses were forced to live in. *Warszawa 1956* was one of the first films of the "Black Series" of documentary film, a term attributed to the cinematography of Kazimierz Karabasz, which depicted the stark, everyday harsh realities of living under a socialist state. As part of such a cinematic approach, Bossak chose to focus on single, simple events, or on specific people and their individual realities to try and extract some fundamental, universal truths that apply to all humans. Such an inductive move—moving from a specific premise (or focus) to a more general conclusion—can be seen in many of his films, particularly *Deluge* (award winning film from 1947 depicting the catastrophic flooding of the Wistula river) and *Requiem for 500,000* (award winning film from 1963 depicting a montage of German propaganda footage from the Warsaw ghetto).

In working from specific events to more universal conclusions, Bossak's films often took on an epic aura; in fact, Bossak saw himself in some regard as an epic historian. It was this epic element of his filmmaking, however, that drew some criticism of his work. Several critics noted that the political and human issues he attempted to address were so large that the specific person or place from which he started often got lost (in asserting such a claim, critics have pointed, for instance, to Bossak's film *273 Degrees Below Zero*). In the same vein, others have argued that the overarching conclusions he attempted to reach necessarily dictated that he oversimplify the issues at hand. Such criticism notwithstanding, however, Jerzy Bossak remains one of the most respected and influential filmmakers in the history of Polish cinematography.

JOE WAGNER

See also **Poland**

Biography

Born in Rostow in 1910. Studied law and philosophy at Warsaw University. Worked as a film critic for several newspapers and was instrumental in forming the film companies Start and Kamera. Fought as an officer during World War II in the Soviet Union and returned to Poland to serve as the senior editor of Polish Film Chronicles and program director of Polish Film from 1944–1949. Served as the dean of the department of film directing in Lodz from 1956 to 1968, and then from 1987 to 1989. Received numerous awards for his filmmaking, including Cannes, and several lifetime achievement awards including one from the Ministry of Art and Culture in 1978. Died in Warsaw, 1989.

Selected Films

1944 *Majdenek: Cemetery of Europe*
1947 *Deluge*
1954 *Return to Old Town*
1956 *Warszawa 1956*
1963 *Requiem for 500000*
1967 *Document of War*
1985 *Impressario*

Further Reading

Avisar, Ilan, *Screening the Holocaust: Cinema's Images of the Unimaginable*, Bloomington: Indiana University Press, 1988.
Bren, Frank, *World Cinema 1: Poland*, London: Flicks Books, 1986.
Fuksiewicz, Jacek, *Film and Television in Poland*, Warsaw: Interpress, 1976.
Haltof, Marek, *Polish National Cinema*. New York: Berghahn Books, 2002.
———. "Film Theory in Poland Before World War II," *Canadian Slavonic Papers* 40, 1–2, 1998, 67–78.
Sobanski, Oskar, *Polish Feature Films: A Reference Guide 1945–1985*, West Cornwall, CT: Locust Hill P, 1987.
Whyte, Alistair, *New Cinema in Eastern Europe*, New York: Dutton, 1971.

BÖTTCHER, JÜRGEN

Jürgen Böttcher is a documentary film director from eastern Germany. Initially a painter, Böttcher turned to film, regarding it as a medium more in keeping with reality: "documentary film, the way I understand it, is one of the most magic forms of art, the invocation of the entire and indeed real" (Böttcher, 1989, p. 5). The influence of the painting background on the filmmaker is clear. In his films, Böttcher has repeatedly examined artists and their work. Moreover, he attempts to mimic the compositional methods and attributes of visual art in his films. He constructs precise and atmospheric settings, mostly in black and white, shot on 35-mm film. Böttcher belongs to "GDR's true avant-garde" (Roth, 1984), a paradox in a political system that did not tolerate subversive artistic expression.

From 1961 until its dissolution in 1991, Böttcher was a documentary director at the state's DEFA-Studio, shooting short films for the cinema program. His first film for DEFA, *Three of Many* (1961), is an homage to three friends, all workers and artists. Böttcher shows the young men in their spare time, painting or relaxing. In their shabby apartments, they do not act as exemplary representatives of their class. *Three of Many* was censored by the government and had its first public screening only in 1988, at the Edinburgh Film Festival.

With *Furnace Builders* (1962), on an ironworks factory, Böttcher found his subject. The primary focus of his work thereafter was the lives of the working class. *Furnace Builders* follows workers as they attempt to move a fifty-six-meter-high, 2000-ton furnace roughly eighteen miles. The film depicts the precise mechanics of the work and conveys a belief in the power of the workers to achieve their goal, while assiduously avoiding sentimentality.

In *Stars* (1963), which follows a group of women working in a Berlin lightbulb factory, Böttcher attempted for the first time to record synchronous dialogue. The filmmaker was unable to procure a low-noise camera for shooting the film, as none were in available in Berlin at the time. Therefore, the cameraman wrapped covers around the Arriflex to soften the sound it made while in operation. The words of the women themselves form the heart of the film, although they were impeded by both the poor sound technology and censorship.

Böttcher again focused on the plight of working women in *Washerwomen* (1972). The film follows apprentice washerwomen at a large laundry. Although their work is dull, Böttcher does not look at them condescendingly. Instead, he allows these young women to articulate their work and their lives, and they appear honest and confident.

Böttcher eventually pared down narration and dialogue in his films, protesting "the inflation of language." The highlight of this evolution is *Rangier* (1984), a lyrical black-and-white movie, shot in winter in the freight depot in Dresden. The switchers at the depot carry out their difficult and dangerous work, focused and silent. The low sounds of the ghostly rolling wagons, the screech of the shocks, the hollow loudspeaker announcements, and the few words the workers speak to one another make up the aural aspect of the film.

In *Georgia* (1987), Böttcher's first full-length feature motion picture, marks the first occasion on which he was allowed to direct in a foreign country. The film is a document of a trip through a land with an ancient culture and living traditions.

Böttcher directed *The Wall* (1990) in November and December of 1989 near the Brandenburg Gate. It documents without commentary, making use of long, silent shots, the activities of people at the Berlin Wall in the days after its opening. The director sees the Berlin Wall, the symbol of the German division, as a document on which history has written itself. Historical images of the Brandenburg Gate are projected on a huge, painted area, including scenes of Prussian military parades, Nazi torch processions, Hitler in an open car, soldiers of the Red Army raising the Soviet flag, men starving during wartime, and the construction of the wall.

Böttcher stopped making films for ten years, instead working as a visual artist. In 2001, he returned to filmmaking with *Konzert im Freien* (A Place in Berlin). In this experimental documentary, Böttcher examines the shifting meanings of the Marx-Engels-Forum in Berlin, a large monument of the East German era. He presents footage of the monument's construction he shot in the 1980s in new and unexpected ways.

BRITTA HARTMANN

Biography

Born July 8, 1931 in Frankenberg/Sachsen (Germany) and raised in the small village Strawahlde in Oberlausitz. Studied at the Academy of Formative Arts in Dresden (GDR), 1949–1953. From 1953 until 1955, self-employed artist and lecturer at the Volkshochschle. In 1965, took a directing course at the newly opened German College for Cinematic Art (today College for Film and Television "Konrad Wolf") in Potsdam-Babelsberg, which ended 1960. Worked from 1961 to 1991 as a director of documentaries for DEFA. In 1989, became a member of the Academy of Arts Berlin (West). After the reunification of the two German states in 1990 and the dissolution of DEFA in 1991, worked as an artist. Works were shown in exhibitions in Berlin, Paris, Salzburg, Toronto, Brussels, Toulouse, Chicago, and New York; and retrospectives of his films could be seen in Paris, Edinburgh, Frankfurt am Main, Munich, Berlin, Bologna, and Leipzig. Received the European Award for Films for *The Wall*. The Festival for Documentary and Animation Film from Leipzig awarded him the "Goldenen Taube" (*The Golden Pigeon*) in 2000. Lives in Berlin.

Selected Films

1960 *Notwendige Lehrjahre* [*Necessary Years of Apprenticeship*] (25 min., Diploma film): writer, director

1961/1988 *Drei von vielen* [*Three of Many*] (33 min., forbidden, staged 1988): writer, director

1962 *Im Pergamonmuseum* [*In the Pergamon Museum*] (19 min.): writer, director

1962 *Ofenbauer* [*Furnace Builders*] (15 min.): writer, director

1963 *Stars* (20 min.): writer, director

1964 *Barfuß und ohne Hut* [*Barefoot and without a Hat*] (26 min.): writer, director

1966/1990 *Jahrgang 45* [*Born in '45*] (94 min., fiction, forbidden. Made available and first performed 1990): co-writer, director

1967 *Der Sekretär* [*The Secretary*] (29 min.): writer, director

1968 *Ein Vertrauensmann* [*A Shop Stewart*] (19 min.): writer, director

1969 *Arbeiterfamilie* [*A Working-class Family*] (31 min.): writer, director

1970 *Dialog mit Lenin* [*Dialogue with Lenin*] (32 min.): writer, director

1971 *Song International* (45 min.): writer, director

1972 *Wäscherinnen* [*Washerwomen*] (23 min.): co-writer,
director
1974 *Erinnere dich mit Liebe und Haß* [*Remember with Love
and Hate*] (40 min.): co-writer, co-director
1977 *Ein Weimarfilm* [*A Weimar Film*] (69 min.): writer,
director
Im Lohmgrund [*In the Loamy Soil*] (27 min.): writer,
director
1978 *Martha* (56 min./abridged version 46 min.): writer,
director
1981 Experimental film-Triptychon: *Potters Stier, Venus
nach Giorgione, Frau am Klavichord*
[Experimental Film Triptych: *Potter's Bull, Venus
According to Giorgione, Woman at the Clavichord*] (16
min., 21 min., 17 min.): writer, director
1983 *Drei Lieder* [*Three Songs*] (28 min.): writer, director
1984 *Rangierer* [*Shunters*] (22 min.; reconstructed long
version, 2000 first performed: 45 min.): co-writer,
director
1985 *Kurzer Besuch bei Hermann Glöckner* [*Short Visit to
Hermann Glöckner*] (32 min.): writer, director
1986 *Die Küche* [*The Kitchen*] (42 min.): co-writer, director
1987 *In Georgien* [*In Georgia*] (107 min.): writer, director
1990 *Die Mauer* [*The Wall*] (99 min.): co-writer, director
2001 *Konzert im Freien* [*A Place in Berlin*] (88 min.): writer,
director

Further Reading

Böttcher, Jürgen, "Zu meinem Film *Stars*," in *Dokumentar-
isten der Welt in den Kämpfen unserer Zeit. Selbstzeugnisse aus zwei Jahrzehnten (1960–1981)*, edited by
Hermann Herlinghaus. Berlin (GDR): Henschelverlag
Kunst und Gesellschaft, 1982, 408–416.
———, "Die Wahrheit des Märchens ist unerhört gültig,"
in *Abenteuer Wirklichkeit. Dokumentarfilmer in Deutsch-
land*, edited by Akademie der Künste Berlin, Abteilung
Film- und Medienkunst und Aktuelle Presse ZDF/3sat.
Berlin, 1989, 5.
Brinckmann, Christine Noll, "Experimentalfilm, 1920–
1990" in *Geschichte des deutschen Films*, edited by Wolf-
gang Jacobsen, Anton Kaes and Hans Helmut Prinzler,
Stuttgart/Weimar: Metzler, 1993, 417–450.
Dokumentaristen der DEFA und ihre Filme, edited by Pro-
gress Film-Verleih. Berlin (GDR), o.J. [1979], 4–13.
"Filme von Jürgen Böttcher: *Die Küche* (1986), *Im Lohm-
grund* (1976), *Frau am Klavichord* (1980/81)," in *17.*

Internationales Forum des Jungen Films, Berlin 1987 [pro-
gramme notes and transcripts of interviews].
Filmmuseum Potsdam, editor, *Schwarzweiß und Farbe.
DEFA-Dokumentarfilme 1946–92.* Red. Günter Jordan
and Ralf Schenk. Berlin/Potsdam: Jovis/Filmmuseum
Potsdam, 1996.
Jordan, Günter, "Schatten vergangener Ahnen. Bilder aus
der Arbeitswelt: die 60er und 70er Jahre," in *Der geteilte
Himmel. Arbeit, Alltag und Geschichte im ost- und
westdeutschen Film*, Edited by Peter Zimmermann and
Gebhard Moldenhauer. Konstanz: UVK Medien, 2000,
103–131.
Kilborn, Richard, "The Documentary Work of Jürgen
Böttcher: A Retrospective," in *DEFA. East German
Cinema, 1946–1992*, Edited by Seán Allan and John Sand-
ford, New York/Oxford: Berghahn Books, 1999, 267–282.
Prinzler, Hans Helmut, "Babelsberger Elegie. Frank Beyer,
Jürgen Böttcher und Erika Richter im Gespräch mit
Hans Helmut Prinzler," in *Filmgeschichte*, Nr. 16, 17,
2002, 57–64.
Richter, Rolf, ". . . vom Leben der Arbeiter Bericht geben"
[Interview], in *Film und Fernsehen*, Nr. 11, November
1974, 20–27.
Roth, Wilhelm, "Jürgen Böttcher—Dokumentarfilmregis-
seur," in *Cinegraph. Lexikon zum deutschsprachigen
Film*, Edited by Hans-Michael Bock. München: Text
und Kritik, 1984ff, Lieferung, 17.
Schenk, Ralf, "Erinnere dich mit Liebe und Hass. Zum 70.
Geburtstag des Dokumentaristen Jürgen Böttcher," in
Film-Dienst 54,14, 2001, 8–11.
Strawalde (Jürgen Böttcher)—Maler und Filmregisseur.
Berlin: Berliner Festspiele, 1990.
Voss, Gabriele, editor, *Dokumentarisch arbeiten. Jürgen
Böttcher [. . .] im Gespräch mit Christoph Hübner*. Berlin:
Vorwerk 8, 1996, 10–27.
*Wenn die Begegnung das Ereignis ist . . . Filme von Jürgen
Böttcher*, [Programmheft zur Retrospektive des Bundes-
archiv-Filmarchivs während des 43. Internationalen
Leipziger Festivals für Dokumentar- und Animations-
film], edited by Bundesarchiv-Filmarchiv Berlin, 2000.
Wetzel, Kraft, "Jürgen Böttcher: Eine Karriere im Arbeiter-
und Bauern-Staat," in *Abenteuer Wirklichkeit. Doku-
mentarfilmer in Deutschland*, edited by Akademie der
Künste Berlin, Abteilung Film- und Medienkunst und
Aktuelle Presse ZDF/3sat. Berlin, 1989, 6–18.
Wetzel, Kraft (Red.), *Jürgen Böttcher. Films/Filme. 1957–
2001* [German/English]. Berlin: Nirwana Edition, 2000.

BOULTING, JOHN AND ROY

The Boulting brothers were one of the great partnerships in British film. As independent producer-
directors, they made a substantial contribution to
the national cinema between the 1930s and 1970s,
principally with intelligently made commercial feature films. They came to prominence with the wartime *Pastor Hall* (1940), a thought-provoking and
controversial drama about Nazi persecution. Their
work in documentary was largely confined to the
wartime period, and they participated in a number

of important and ambitious productions of the service film units.

Before enlistment, the Boultings produced *Dawn Guard* (1941) for the Ministry of Information, a propaganda short of immense significance. It features two members of the Home Guard on sentry duty discussing peace aims and reconstruction, cut against contrasting images of slums and new house building, dole queues and busy factories, and playgrounds swarming with jolly children. The film stands out as the first cinematic expression of "New Jerusalemism" and the desire for a better postwar world and was an early indication of the filmmakers' social views.

For a brief period, the brothers served conventionally in the armed forces, Roy as a trooper in the Royal Armoured Corps, and John as a flight mechanic in the RAF. Eventually, Roy was redirected to the Army Film and Photographic Unit (AFPU), eventually reaching Captain, and John to the RAF Film Unit, in time becoming a flight lieutenant. The service film units had been established early in the war to produce record and training films but gradually progressed to more substantial documentaries suitable for commercial release. This was the only sustained period when the brothers worked apart, and in fact they were each given a special period of leave to make the propaganda feature *Thunder Rock* (1942). With its pronounced interventionist theme, it was deemed an important film to help develop the Anglo-American entente.

Roy was the more prolific of the brothers. With the AFPU based at Pinewood, he contributed to a number of shorts such as *Via Persia* (1942), *Minefield!* (1944), and *REME* (1944). Of much greater consequence was his involvement in the trilogy of Victory documentaries, feature-length records of significant Allied campaigns. These began with *Desert Victory* (1943), which dealt with the war in the Western Desert and the British breakthrough at El Alamein. The film was compiled from footage shot by service cameramen and augmented by some material staged at Pinewood. Major David MacDonald was in charge of production, but the creative work of editing and direction was the responsibility of Roy Boulting. The production enjoyed support at the highest levels of government, where it was deemed crucial to publicize Britain's first significant success in the field. Released in February 1943, it won great praise and popular acclaim. In America it was surprisingly granted an Academy Award as "the Most Distinctive Documentary of 1943" and was generally held up as among the best achievements of wartime documentary. The film's distinctive imagery and treatment of the Desert campaign clearly influenced later reconstructions, notably *The Way Ahead* (1944), *Sea of Sand* (1958), and *The Desert Fox* (1951), with the latter film relying heavily on documentary footage taken uncredited from *Desert Victory*.

Tunisian Victory (1944) and *Burma Victory* (1945) were similar campaign records, this time detailing the Anglo-American liberations of North Africa and Southeast Asia, respectively. The Tunisian film eventually emerged as a co-production between the AFPU and the official American filmmaker Frank Capra, who assumed dominance over the production. The collaboration was troubled by tension and rivalry, and *Tunisian Victory* has fared the least well with critics. The final Victory film was much more securely in the hands of the AFPU and Roy Boulting, as the British and Americans had wisely decided on separate documentaries covering the theatre of operations. The war in Southeast Asia was somewhat secondary to events in Europe, and hence *Burma Victory* was an important document to publicize and memorialize the conflict. The film effectively brings out the hardships and unpleasantness of the experience, with troops enduring rain, mud, exhaustion, dysentery, and malaria, as well as confronting a fanatical enemy. Each of the Victory films relied heavily on the striking images secured by combat cameramen. They brought an immediacy to war never previously experienced by a cinema-going public, and this has been their considerable legacy. Acclaimed American documentaries of the later war years, such as John Ford's *The Battle of Midway* (1944), were clearly in their debt.

The RAF Film Unit had been established in 1942 and was also based at Pinewood, meaning that the twins could remain in close contact. John similarly contributed to the routine training and informational films of the unit, such as the short *Between Friends* (1943). Throughout 1944 however, he was engaged as director on the RAF's principal film production of the war years, *Journey Together* (1945), a realistic but scripted depiction of pilot trainees. A small role was played by Hollywood star Edward G. Robinson, with the principal British characters being played by the up-and-coming actors Richard Attenborough and Jack Watling. *Journey Together* used much location shooting, including scenes in the United States, and the film propagandized British-American collaboration. The film was a significant example of the wartime trend in British documentary that blended fictional and factual styles. Each of the Victory films had incorporated small but significant staged scenes shot at Pinewood under the guidance of Roy, and John substantially developed this approach into what was essentially a feature-length treatment. John has declared that he was after a "straightforward public entertainment," and in this sense *Journey Together* was more in line with developments in realism taking place at commercial studios like Ealing, with such productions as *Nine Men* (1943), rather than the more austere experiments in documentary fiction being conducted at the Crown Film Unit, especially in the celebrated *Western Approaches* (1944).

ALAN BURTON

See also **Burma Victory; Desert Victory**

Biography

Born identical twins at Bray, Berkshire, England, November 21, 1913. Educated at Reading School, where they formed one of the first film societies in a public school. John joined a small film distribution company in 1933; Roy gained some film experience in Canada. Early in 1937, John volunteered for the Republican forces in the Spanish Civil War. Later in November 1937, the twins formed Charter Films and produced modest films for quota distribution. During World War II, Roy served with the Army Film and Photographic Unit and John with the RAF Film Unit. For three decades after the war, the Boultings were important independent producer-directors in British commercial films. John died on June 17, 1985 in Sunningdale, Berkshire and Roy at his Oxfordshire home November 5, 2001.

Further Reading

Burton, A., O'Sullivan, T., and Wells, P., editors, *The Family Way. The Boulting Brothers and British Film Culture*, Trowbridge: Flicks Books, 2000.

Chapman, James, *The British At War. Cinema, State and Propaganda, 1939–1945*, London: I. B. Tauris, 1998.

Coultass, Clive, *Images for Battle. British Film and the Second World War, 1939–1945*, London, AUP, 1989.

BOWLING FOR COLUMBINE

See **Moore, Michael**

BRAKHAGE, STAN

Stan Brakhage, one of the most influential American avant-garde filmmakers of the twentieth century, is not strictly considered a documentary filmmaker. However, his "lyrical" films, often shot from a first-person perspective, are part of an American artistic culture interested in documenting individual perception and defamiliarizing everyday life (Sitney, 1974). For Brakhage, perception is radically subjective; reality is comprehensible only through the implied point of view of the camera. Documentary, then, has an anti-traditional or anti-normative purpose. Instead of using conventional narratives or assuming objectivity, it should take nothing for granted, showing the world as it is experienced from a specific place.

Brakhage's position as an artist who rejects conventional forms to depict his own view of reality comes out of a long tradition of American individualism and rejection of tradition (Elder, 1998). During the postwar era, existentialist philosophers and abstract expressionist painters also rejected traditional notions of self and tradition, believing that fixed definitions were forms of commodification. For them (and for Brakhage) the only way of relating to the world was through action. The rapid cuts in early films such as *Cat's Cradle* (1959) and *Mothlight* (1963) were influenced by Sergei Eisenstein's theories of montage as a tool that documented reality while it created ideas. In *Cat's Cradle*, for example, the rapid movement between shots of a cat's head, a man and a woman, and the flowers on their bedspread and wallpaper blur the line between man and animal, nature and artifice. The quick cutting also prevents the films from fetishizing the images they present, focusing instead on the movement of vision and ideas.

The dynamic quality and shifting perspective seen in these films are central to his early documentaries. Brakhage was the cameraman for two early documentaries shot under the direction of American surrealist Joseph Cornell. The first film on which they collaborated, *The Wonder Ring* (1955), was a documentary of Manhattan's last elevated train, shot just before the city closed it down. Rather than an objective presentation of the El's history, Brakhage offers a silent and mobile first-person depiction of a typical ride on the train. The film starts with squares of light falling through the El tracks to the pavement below and an ascent to the El platform that repeats the abstract rectangular patterns. Throughout the film, the city flows past, occasionally focusing on a picturesque sight in a dialectic that echoes the train's stopping and going. People are on the train with our stand-in viewer, but they are mostly seen reflected in windows, glimpsed through the door into the next car, or framed off-center. The focus of this film is vision itself, as epitomized by the film's last shot. The focus on what's seen through a train window becomes more and more blurry until the focus is on the dusty and scratched glass itself.

The idea of defamiliarization is important to early twentieth-century avant-garde artists like Marcel Duchamp and Phillip Glass who took everyday objects and sounds out of context to transform them into art and music. Like *The Wonder Ring*, most of Brakhage's films contain many close-ups that defamiliarize the objects being shown in order to explore how vision makes sense of the world when it is not mediated by language or convention. Language was social and, he believed, eliminated the personal perceptions of the world; Brakhage felt that the raw experience of the physical unmediated by structure is only authentic way to know the world. In his early manifesto, *Metaphors on Vision*, he asks his readers to "Imagine . . . an eye which does not respond to the name of everything but which must know each object encountered in life through an adventure of perception. How many colors are there in a field of grass to the crawling baby unaware of 'Green'?" (Brakhage, 1960).

The final, and perhaps most important, influence on Stan Brakhage is Gertrude Stein. Stein shares this use naïve perspective of reality as a means of redefining it; her book *Tender Buttons* repeats simple words and phrases from daily life in various permutations that do not have conventional linguistic meaning but instead offer a combination of sound and intuitive sense. Brakhage uses repetition in a similar way in his films, both to imbue the images with new meaning in each context and to rid them of their conventional metaphorical associations. In *Window Water Baby Moving* (1962), his first film depicting his wife's pregnancy and childbirth, Brakhage repeats shots of his wife's pregnant stomach as seen in the film's first scene, where she sits in the bathtub kissing and embracing him. When this scene repeats in the middle of a sequence graphically depicting her giving birth, it serves both as a flashback to more peaceful times and an assertion that both states of being depict the body as sexual and natural.

Brakhage's interest in the body is another way he attempted to document the prelinguistic experience of reality. The struggles of humanity against the natural world are most evident in his quasi-mythic epic film cycle called *Dog Man Star*, but he also attempted to connect the mythic with documenting everyday physical reality in his work. One grant proposal described a project he wished to pursue, which he called a "dailiness film"; through this film, he wished to document his and his family's daily life as it allegorically represented principles of creation in the natural world:

> our coming to life in the morning would also be visualized as the creation of the world; that sun which streaks our room with light still being the explosive source of life, drying our eyes (or rather the photography through rippled glass) as we emerge from the waters of sleep. The very sheets we push away from us in arising would photographically relate to the thaw of the glaciers. (Brakhage, 1960)

With the films of his wife's birth and this unproduced mythical documentary, Brakhage moved beyond depiction of the subjective and into universal realities. In his lyrical and mythical work, Brakhage uses the documentary form to alter people's perceptions of reality by defamiliarizing either sight itself or the context in which the sight makes sense. Later films take this even further, moving into the abstraction of hand-painted colors and swirls of light.

SUNNY STALTER

Biography

Born in Kansas City, Missouri, January 14, 1933. Attended Dartmouth College in 1951, dropped out, and attended the Institute of Fine Arts in San Francisco in 1953. Met Joseph Cornell in 1955 and shot several films with him. Married Jane Collom in 1957 and had five children with her. Taught at the School of the Art Institute of Chicago in the 1970s, later at the University of Colorado, Boulder. Received American Film Institute award for independent film and video in 1986. Divorced Jane Collum in 1987. Married Marilyn Jull in 1989 and had two children with her. Died March 9, 2003.

Selected Filmography

1955 *The Wonder Ring*: cinematographer
1955 *Centuries of June*: cinematographer
1959 *Cat's Cradle*: director
1962 *Window Water Baby Moving*: director
1963 *Mothlight*: director
1968 *Lovemaking*: director

Further Reading

Barrett, Gerald R, *Stan Brakhage: A Guide to References and Resources*, Boston: G.K. Hall, 1983.
Brakhage, Stan, *Essential Brakhage: Selected Writings on Filmmaking*, edited by Bruce R. McPherson, Kingston, NY: Documentext/McPherson, 2001.
——, *Metaphors on Vision*, edited by P. Adams Sitney, Film Culture, 1976.
Elder, R. Bruce, *The Films of Stan Brakhage in the American Tradition of Ezra Pound, Gertrude Stein, and Charles Olson*, Waterloo, Ontario: Wilfrid Laurier University Press, 1998.
Keller, Marjorie, *The Untutored Eye: Childhood in the Films of Cocteau, Cornell, and Brakhage*, Rutherford, NJ: Fairleigh Dickinson University Press, 1986.
Sitney, P. Adams, *Visionary Film: The American Avant-Garde*, New York: Oxford University Press, 1974.

BRAULT, MICHEL

Although Michel Brault has directed a number of important documentaries, his first passion was photography, and it is as a cinematographer rather than as a film director per se that he has had the most influence on Québec cinema. His achievements as director of photography greatly influenced the look of both documentary and narrative cinema in Québec in the 1960s and 1970s, as he shot some of the most significant works of the period, from his own and Pierre Perrault's *Pour la suite du monde* (1963), Claude Jutra's *A tout prendre* (1963), *Mon oncle Antoine* (1971), and *Kamouraska* (1973) to Anne Claire Poirier's *Mourir à tue-tête* (1979) and Francis Mankiewicz's *Le temps d'une chasse* (1972) and *Les bons débarras* (1980). His contribution to the imaging of "la Nation québécoise" on screen has been crucial.

In 1957–1958, he worked on the "Candid Eye" series, developed by the Anglophone filmmakers of the National Film Board of Canada's (NFB's) renowned Unit B, which used recently developed lighter film equipment to capture people in everyday situations with spontaneity and free from judgmental commentary. After shooting the milestone "Candid Eye" film *The Days Before Christmas* (1958, Terence Macartney-Filgate, Stanley Jackson and Wolf Koenig), Brault co-directed with Gilles Groulx *Les raquetteurs* (1958, *The Snowshoers*), about a congress of snowshoeing clubs in Sherbrooke (Québec). Both in its form and its content, this film marked a turning point in Québec documentary. Unlike the "Candid Eye" films, which sought to observe everyday activities from a distance, *Les raquetteurs* attempted to show the event from within. The film's innovative visual style resulted from Brault's use of a handheld camera equipped with a wide-angle lens to shoot the subjects from up close. He walked among the "snowshoers" and their entourage, capturing with immediacy their conversations and interactions.

On the eve of the Quiet Revolution (the period of liberalization and modernization that began in 1960 and saw the emergence of Québec's separatist movement), *Les raquetteurs* was hailed as a sort of manifesto for *cinéma direct*, a home-grown film practice that could depict real people and their everyday concerns. Brault has always insisted that *Les raquetteurs* itself is not actually an instance of *cinéma direct*, but it did trigger the movement, as subsequent NFB documentaries tried to reproduce its style and nationalist purpose in, for example, *La lutte/Wrestling* (1961, Brault, Marcel Carrière, Claude Fournier, and Claude Jutra) and *Québec-USA ou l'invasion pacifique/Visit to a Foreign Country* (1962, Brault, Jutra). *Les raquetteurs* also had an impact beyond the frontiers of Québec. A screening at the Flaherty Seminar in 1959 inspired Jean Rouch to develop his conception of *cinema verité* and led him to invite Brault to film *Chronique d'un été/Chronicle of a Summer* (1961) and *La Punition/Punishment* (1963) in France.

While Brault and Groulx's *Les raquetteurs* announced the emergence of *cinéma direct*, Brault's first feature-length documentary, *Pour la suite du monde/For the Continuation of the World* (1963), which he co-directed with Pierre Perrault, marked the culmination of the movement. In this film, Brault and Perrault follow the habitants of a small island in the St. Lawrence River, Île-aux-Coudres, as they attempted to revive the traditional hunt of the beluga whale. Acclaimed both in Canada and abroad, especially in France, *Pour la suite du monde* owes its success to two fundamental aspects of direct cinema. First, Brault's cinematography, which is equally sensitive to the beauty of the island's landscape as to the weathered faces of old fishermen and the bewildered expressions of the young people who have no knowledge of the practice that their parents are trying to rediscover, and second, a profound respect for the subjects, based on a trusting relationship established before filming.

Brault transposed this documentary practice to fiction, first in *Entre la mer et l'eau douce/Drifting Upstream* (1967), a fictionalized depiction of the life and career of the film's main actor, Claude Gauthier (the title of this film actually comes from a quote in *Pour la suite du monde* taken from Jacques Cartier's diaries) and later, in *Les ordres/The Orders* (1974), on the effects of the War Measures Act decreed during the hostage crisis of October 1970. Brault interviewed dozens of innocent people incarcerated as a result of the sweeping powers that the Act gave the police and created fictional characters to reenact the humiliating experiences of those imprisoned. Brault's ability to put the techniques of direct cinema at the service of narrative film earned him the best director's award at the Cannes Film Festival in 1975. He remains the only Canadian cineaste to have received this honor.

From 1974 to 1980, Brault produced and directed, with André Gladu, an ambitious series of documentaries entitled *Le son des français d'Amérique* devoted to the various manifestations of francophone cultures throughout North America. He had already examined the question of French Canadian culture outside Québec in *L'Acadie, l'Acadie?!?/Acadia/Acadia?!?* (1971) co-directed with Pierre Perrault and *Éloge du chiac* (1969, Praise "chiac"). He also directed a series of documentaries on René Lévesque (three shorts in 1969, 1972, and 1976), a docudrama on domestic violence, *L'Emprise* (1988, with Suzanne Guy), and a portrait of a little-known Québec painter, *Ozéas Leduc ... comme l'espace et le temps* (1996, Ozéas Leduc ... like space and time). Since the 1980s, he has made a handful of fiction features, the best of which is *Les Noces de papier/Paper Wedding* (1989) with Geneviève Bujold. His most recent fiction is *Quand je serai parti ... vous vivrez encore* (1999), a historical epic on the rebellion of French Canadian patriots against British forces in 1837–1938.

ANDRÉ LOISELLE

Biography

Born in 1928. Began making amateur films in the late 1940s with Claude Jutra. Directed a short film, *Matin*; worked briefly at the National Film Board of Canada, 1950. Assistant director on *La petite Aurore l'enfant martyre,* the most commercially successful French Canadian feature film of the 1950s, 1950–1951. Worked on a number of short films for the Canadian Broadcasting Corporation (CBC) television series, "Petites médisances," 1953. Began his career as a filmmaker in earnest after the NFB moved from Ottawa (Ontario) to Montréal (Québec), 1956.

Selected Films (Main Documentaries)

L'Acadie l'Acadie?!?/Acadia, Acadia?!? 1971, 117 min: director of photography
Le Beau Plaisir/Beluga Days 1968, 14 min: director
Éloge du chiac [Praise "chiac"] 1969, 27 min: director of photography
Les Enfants du silence [Children of silence] 1962, 23 min: director of photography
Freedom to Move 1985, 23 min: director
La Lutte/Wrestling 1961, 27 min 45 s: director of photography
Pour la suite du monde/The Moontrap 1962, 105 min: director of photography
Québec-U.S.A. ou l'Invasion pacifique/Visit to a Foreign Country 1962, 27 min: director of photography
Les Raquetteurs [Snowshoers] 1958, 14 min: director of photography; editor
René Lévesque pour le vrai [René Lévesque for real] 1972, 27 min: director of photography
René Lévesque, un vrai chef [René Lévesque a true leader] 1976, 28 min: director of photography
René Lévesque vous parle: les 6 millards [René Lévesques speaks with you: 6 Billion.] 1969, 25 min: director of photography

"Le son des français d'Amérique" [The sound of French in America] 1974–1980. Series of 27 short films:
Le Temps perdu/The End of Summer 1964, 27 min: director of photography

Further Reading

Loiselle, André, "Michel Brault's *Les Ordres*: Documenting the Reality of Experience and the Fiction of History," in *Canada's Best Features: Critical Essays on Fifteen Great Canadian Films*, edited by Gene Walz, Amsterdam and New York: Rodopi, 2002.

Marsolais, Gilles, *Michel Brault*, Montréal: Conseil québécois pour la diffusion du cinéma, 1972.

Special issue on Michel Brault, *Copie Zéro* 5. Montréal: Cinémathèque québécoise, 1980.

BRAZIL

Documentary film production stretches back to the origins of film in Brazil. In 1986, film first arrived in Brazil, brought by European immigrants. Early documentary films from this time focus on the natural landscape, as well as habits and traditions of the different regions of Brazil. These remained the primary focus of early Brazilian documentary. Afonso Segreto and Pascoal Segreto dominated the production of Brazilian documentary through its first decade.

Early ethnographic documentaries exposed urban Brazilian to images of an immense and unknown country, while emphasizing national integration and an idealized image of an Indian still savage. Major Luiz Thomas Reis made several films for the Comissão de Linhas Telegráficas e Estratégicas do Mato Grosso ao Amazonas (Commission of Telegraphic and Strategic Lines of Mato Grosso to Amazonas), known as Comissão Rondon (Rondon Comission). His *Rituais e Festas Bororó* [1917, Bororo's rituals and parties] was considered by film critics as an early example of skillful film editing, while also being an important early anthropological film.

The classics of the silent period include Rudolf Rex Lustig and Adalberto Kemeny's *São Paulo, A Sinfonia da Metrópole* [1929, São Paulo, the Symphony of the Metropolis], which portrays the continuing urbanization of the city; and *Lampião, Rei do Cangaço* [1936, Lampião, King of the Cangaço], directed by Benjamim Abrahão. This film is a study of the Lampião group, in the Northeastern interior.

In 1936, the federal government created the Instituto Nacional do Cinema Educativo (National institute of Educational Movies, INCE), with the goal of bringing intellectually stimulating works to the working classes. For thirty years the direction of INCE was the responsibility of film director Humberto Mauro, who completed 354 short educational films in the period. Despite the official and didactic nature of the produced material, the INCE was able to stamp a personal aesthetics to most of their work. Approximately fifty directors have their films financed by the INCE.

In the 1960s, the prevalent theme of an exoticized forest and rural milieu gave way to a focus on national underdevelopment and social inequality, advancing aesthetic subjects of the *cinema novo* (new cinema) movement. Paulo César Saraceni and Mário Carneiro directed *Arraial do cabo* [1959, Village of the Cable], and Linduarte Noronha directed *Aruanda* [1960, Aruanda], two films that display the influence of this trend. Brazilian documentaries increasingly focused on issues relating to culture, economy, and popular religiosity, but without the overtly educational and didactic tone of INCE films.

In 1962, the Swedish director Arne Sucksdorff held a film seminar in Rio de Janeiro. As a result, the techniques of *cinema verité* films spread throughout Brazil. Leon Hirszman's *Maioria Absoluta* [1964, Absolute Majority]; Paulo César Saraceni's *Integração Racial* [1964, Racial Integration] and Arnaldo Jabor's *O Circo* [1965, The Circus] are films influenced by this trend early on.

Brazilian documentary was also influenced by the work of Chilean filmmakers. In São Paulo a group formed by Vladimir Herzog, João Batista de Andrade, Maurice Capovilla, Sérgio Muniz, and Renato Tapajós maintained contact with Argentina's documentary filmmakers, through Fernando Birri, an initiate in practice of the *cinema verité*.

Between 1964 and 1965, the producer Thomas Farkas produced four documentaries: Geraldo Sarno's *Viramundo* [1965, Viramundo], Paulo Gil Soares's *Memória do Cangaço* [1965, Memory of Cangaço], Manuel Horácio Gimenez's *Nossa Escola de Samba* [1965, Our Samba School], and Maurice Capovilla's *Subterrâneos do Futebol* [1965, Undergrounds of Soccer]. These filmmakers formed the Caravana Farkas, and they collectively documented popular culture. The group produced nineteen documentaries of short films between 1969 and 1971 under the series title *A Condição Brasileira* [The Brazilian Condition], all influenced by *cinema verité*.

From the 1960s, Brazilian film was censored by the military dictatorship in power. Eduardo Coutinho's *Cabra Marcado para Morrer* [1964–1984, Guy Marked to Die]; João Batista de Andrade's *Liberdade de Imprensa* [1966, Press Freedom of Press], and Vladimir Carvalho's *País de São Saruê* [1970, São Sarue's Country] were all censored.

In 1972, the public television station of São Paulo began airing *A Hora da Notícia* [Hour of the News] to show the real Brazil, as opposed to the official, sanitized images propagated by the military government. Film director João Batista de Andrade was called on to create small-scale documentaries directly in the streets. After a period of political persecution, the show was cancelled in 1974. Batista de Andrade was invited by Paulo Gil Soares to assume management of the team of special reporters for TV Globo of São Paulo. Eduardo Coutinho, Maurice Capovilla, Hermano Penna, and Walter Lima Jr were a part of the group. Thus the Globo Repórter was born.

Composed of a series of ten documentaries called *Globo Shell Especial* [Shells's Globe Special Shell], the *Globo Repórter* was enthusiastically supported by the film directors and displayed accomplished cinematographic and authorial style. A few films in particular stand out from the series: João Batista de Andrade's *Wilsinho Galiléia* [1978, Wilsinho Galiléia], Eduardo Coutinho's *Teodorico, o imperador do sertão* [1978, Teodorico, the emperor of the interior], and Maurice Capovilla's *O Último Dia de Lampião* [1975, The Last Day of Lampião]. Although the nation was taking steps toward democracy at the time, the program suffered several occasions of forced internal censorship.

The boundary between fiction and documentary was explored in 1975 by Jorge Bodansky and Orlando Senna in *Iracema, uma transa amazônica* [Iracema, an Amazonian Affair]. Bodansky contin-

ued as a documentary filmmaker for German television, in partnership with Wolf Gauer.

A number of filmmakers who have focused on documentary film stand out: Vladimir Carvalho of *Conterrâneos velhos de Guerra* [1990, Old Fellow citizens of War], Sylvio Back, *Revolução de 30* [1980, Revolution of 30], Sílvio Tendler, director of. *Os anos JK, uma trajetória política* [1976–1980, The years JK, a political path], which was a popular success, and Eduardo Coutinho, who eventually focused on making films in video that were later enlarged for 35-mm film, such as *Santo Forte* [1999, Strong Saint].

In the 1980s, two Brazilian documentary filmmakers in particular stood out. Sérgio Bianchi's *Mato Eles* [1982, Bush them?] and Jorge Furtado's *Ilha das Flores* [1989, Island of the flowers] are both marked by an innovative narrative style and resonant visual references.

The Associação Brasileira de Vídeo Popular (Brazilian Association of Popular Video, ABVP) was founded in the early 1980s. Its aim was to popularize a cohesive production model for filmmakers across the country, while encouraging popular participation in documentary filmmaking. One of the founders of the ABVP, Luiz Fernando Santoro, was also the first member of the Comitê de Cineastas da América Latina (Committee of Film Directors of Latin America), which emphasized the value of works done on video, as much of the recent history of Latin America had been documented in this format.

The Centro de Trabalho Indigenista (Center of Indigenist Work, CIT) encourages debate and discussion of the documentary use of video, while also encouraging reflection on the identity of indigenous people and their place in the contemporary world.

In the mid-1990s, television became increasingly involved in the production and screening of documentary film. Several film directors made works for television. Nelson Pereira directed *Casa Grande e Senzala* [2000, Big House and Slave quarter], a film in four episodes on the work of the anthropologist Gilberto Freire.

Documentary film assumed a central place in Brazilian media in the late 1990s. Paulo Sacramento's *O Prisioneiro da Grade de Ferro* [2003, The Prisoner of the Grating of Iron], made inside the prison of Carandiru, was filmed in digital video with the assistance of the prisoners. Brazilian video documentaries continue to push the boundaries of documentary film, questioning the relationship between the documentary and the reality it purports to represent.

GUSTAVO SORANZ

See also **Coutinho, Eduardo**

Further Reading

Andrade, Joaquim Batista de, *João Batista de Andrade por ele mesmo!*, Revista de estudos avançados da USP n.o. 16, São Paulo: Edusp, 2002.
————. *O povo fala*, São Paulo: Senac, 2002.
Bernardet, Jean-Claude. *Cineastas e imagens do povo*, São Paulo: Brasiliense, 1985.
————. *Cinema brasileiro: propostas para uma história*, Rio de Janeiro: Paz e Terra, 1979.
————. *Brasil em tempo de cinema: ensaios sobre o cinema brasileiro*, Rio de Janeiro: Paz e Terra, 1978.
Carvalho, Vladimir, *O país de São Saruê*, Brasília / Distrito Federal: Ed. Universidade de Brasília, 1986.
France, Claudine de, Do Filme Etnográfico à Antropologia Fílmica, Campinas: Ed. Unicamp, 2000.
Gomes, Paulo Emilio Salles, *Cinema: trajetória no subdesenvolvimento*, São Paulo: Paz e Terra, 2001.
Lins, Consuelo, *O Documentário de Eduardo Coutinho- televisão, cinema e vídeo*, São Pualo: Jorge Zahar, 2004.
Ramos, Fernão and Miranda, Luiz Felipe, Enciclopédia do cinema brasileiro, São Paulo: Senac, 2000.
Santoro, Luiz Fernando, *A imagem nas mãos: o vídeo popular no Brasil*, São Paulo: Summus, 1989.
Teixeira, Francisco Elinaldo (Org.), *Documentário no Brasil: tradição e transformação*, São Paulo: Summus, 2004.
Xavier, Ismail, *O cinema brasileiro moderno*, São Paulo: Paz e Terra, 2001.

BRIDGE, THE

(Holland, Ivens, 1928)

De Brug (*The Bridge*) can be considered as the first notable work of Joris Ivens's film career, although initially it was for him nothing else more than an experiment and a film study. As manager of the Amsterdam branch of father's photo business, Ivens's career was already determined for him. However, this did not stop him from using the available equipment for some film experiments and other projects. By 1927, Ivens had become increasingly involved in film. As one of the co-founders of the Dutch Film League, he participated in the projection and discussion of artistic films. He thoroughly analyzed films such as Pudowkin's *The Mother* and Eisenstein's *Potemkin*, and he himself was experimenting with camera work and editing. *De Brug* was for Ivens nothing more than a study in movement, made by an amateur in order to learn about camera movements, composition and editing. Upon its first projection at a Film League screening, however, the film was received with much acclaim, and it put Dutch film on the map of European avant-garde filmmaking.

While he was working on some films for Leiden University, Ivens took long lunch breaks to go to Rotterdam to film the lift bridge. He used a simple handheld Kinamo camera, normally used by amateur filmmakers. The use of this handheld camera allows the transformation of the huge static steel object into a dynamic filmed sequence.

The structure of *De Brug* is simple, composed entirely of the opening and closing of a rail road lift bridge. Though technically imperfect, the careful construction of the film, the composition of the images, the camera movements and the editing still encourage the consideration of this film is considered as an avant-garde masterpiece. The film starts with two long shots of the bridge, to show its place and function. Spanning the water, it allows trains to cross the river and ships to pass underneath. Next there is a beautiful sequence of shots and camera movements that depict the massive steel bridge, emphasizing its vertical, horizontal, and diagonal lines and the shadows it casts on the water and the pillars. Ivens shows the interplay between these lines by carefully composing the images and following them with camera movements.

The static structure of the bridge is contrasted with the speed and dynamics of the approaching train, which has to stop when the signal is urging it to halt. With the train slowly coming to a standstill the bridge slowly begins to move. Ivens repeats the

The Bridge, 1927.
[*Still courtesy of the British Film Institute*]

first sequence, but now with many parts of the bridge in movement: the big wheels turning round, the contrasting movements of the bridge going upwards and the counterweights going down, the ships passing slowly underneath and the train impatiently waiting and steaming. Ivens carefully composes the vertical, horizontal and diagonal lines and plays with the movements within the frame. He adds to the dynamics of this moment with several camera movements, before the scene reassembles itself, and we see a closed bridge and trains crossing the river. The result is an almost abstract composition of lines and movements. The bridge is no longer operative, but is now an industrial monument in Rotterdam.

KEES BAKKER

See also **Ivens, Joris**

De Brug/The Bridge (the Netherlands, CAPI Amsterdam, 1928, silent, 11 min). Produced, directed, and edited by Joris Ivens. Cinematography by Joris Ivens.

Further Reading

Bakker, Kees, editor, *Joris Ivens and the Documentary Context*, Amsterdam: Amsterdam University Press, 1999.
Delmar, Rosalind, *Joris Ivens, 50 Years of Film-making*, London: British Film Institute, 1979.
Ivens, Joris, *The Camera and I*, Berlin: Seven Seas Books, 1969.
Ivens, Joris and Destanque, Robert, *Joris Ivens ou la mémoire d'un regard*, Paris: Éditions BFB, 1982.
Schoots, Hans, *Dangerous Life. A Biography of Joris Ivens*, Amsterdam: Amsterdam University Press, 2000.
Waugh, Thomas, *Joris Ivens and the Evolution of the Radical Documentary 1926–1946*, New York: Columbia University, 1981.

BRITISH FILM INSTITUTE

The British Film Institute (BFI) attempts to foster the public's cultural engagement with cinema in the United Kingdom. Historically, it has had a close relationship with documentary production and exhibition. Established in 1933 after the Commission of Educational and Cultural Films was formed during a conference organized by the British Institute for Adult Education, the BFI's remit was to investigate and report on the use of film in education. It was also intended to develop a public appreciation of film, with a view to establishing a permanent agency to achieve these objectives.

The Commission's report, "The Film in National Life," contained recommendations for the creation of an independent film institute funded by public money. The original tasks of the BFI were to encourage public appreciation of film, to undertake research, to maintain a national archive of films, and to undertake the certification of films as cultural or educational on behalf of the government.

The BFI is currently holder of the largest film archive in the world. It is a world leader in film restoration and preservation. The BFI operates the internationally renowned National Film Theatre and London Film Festival, the BFI IMAX Cinema, and the world's largest film library and educational resource. In addition, the BFI also distributes films on video and DVD, manages and operates educational programmes, and maintains a publishing department that produces *Sight and Sound* (formerly the *Monthly Film Bulletin*).

The BFI has had an innovative role in documentary preservation in the United Kingdom. Initially, the National Film Library (NFL) was created in 1935, under its pioneering curator Ernest Lindgren. The NFL subsequently became the National Film Archive, then the National Film and Television Archive, which it remains today. Under Lindgren, the BFI became one of the pioneers of the international film archiving movement. The general bias of most of these pioneering film archives was heavily toward preservation of narrative feature film.

At the time that the BFI was developing as a national institution, however, documentary was seen as key to Britain's contribution to film as an art form. Consequently, the NFL was unusual among these early film archives in ensuring that it preserved and recorded documentary and other nonfiction films because of their value as historical evidence, as well as any aesthetic value they might possess.

The preservation and archiving of documentary material have since become more widespread in moving image heritage institutions in the United Kingdom, but its relatively early application by the BFI has contributed to its becoming the holder of one of the largest archives of documentary and nonfiction production in the world. It currently holds approximately 100,000 cinema and non-broadcast productions that can broadly be classified as nonfiction. The BFI is an important resource for the study of the development of film as a documentary and communications medium, particularly in the context of the UK's indigenous production.

Consequently, much of the UK's rich heritage of filmmaking by a number of documentary producers, including the General Post Office, Shell, and British Transport Film, is extensively represented in the BFI collection. The strength and diversity of the Archive's documentary holdings were further increased by the decision to actively collect television shows, today mostly via an extensive program of off-air recording. Inevitably many of the BFI's more than 500,000 archived television programs fall into the documentary category.

The BFI's former role as a financer of independent documentary is complex. Although the BFI was, at its inception, a multi-functional film organization, its primary direct involvement in film production dates to 1951, with its creation of the Experimental Film Fund (EFF). The EEF was created as part of the Festival of Britain celebrations, which also led to the setting up of the National Film Theatre.

The EFF engaged both in co-production with other organizations and in financial support of new filmmakers and industry professionals engaged in independent production outside their normal professional commissions. The main emphasis was on short films, ranging from fiction through documentary to highly experimental.

The EEF's contribution to documentary was wide-ranging. A key example was Paul Dickson's classic docudrama *David* (1951), which was sponsored by the Festival of Britain's Welsh Committee, and for which the BFI provided essential financial support.

In 1966, the EFF developed into the BFI Production Board, which throughout the 1970s continued to fund a variety of films, including documentary work. Much of this work tended toward the formally experimental within a documentary framework or toward the use of documentary as a political and campaigning tool. During this period many film workshops and collectives such as Cinema Action, Liberation Films, and The Newsreel Collective received BFI funding, but the level of the BFI's funding of new film work and the transparency of its criteria for its funding were frequently the subject of fierce controversy among independent filmmakers.

The BFI now consists of three main departments: Culture and Education, Development and Communication, and Planning and Resources. In 2000, the BFI's production activities ceased when the BFI Production Board moved to the newly formed UK Film Council, which has continued to fund documentary and forms of production. In 2003, the award-winning film director Anthony Minghella was appointed as the new Chair of the BFI and Amanda Nevill was appointed

Director. The BFI continues to be at the fore-front of documentary preservation and archiving and remains an important and valuable cultural institution.

KIRSTY FAIRCLOUGH

Further Reading

BFI Film and Television Handbook, London: British Film Institute, 2004.
Houston, P, editor, *Keepers of the Frame: Film Archives*, London: British Film Institute, 1994.

BRITISH INSTRUCTIONAL FILMS

Formed by H. Bruce Woolfe in 1919, British Instructional Films garnered a reputation for producing a wide variety of films. Their first productions were war reconstructions and could be regarded as early examples of documentary, with their combination of animation, maps, models, actuality footage, and reenactments. In the late 1920s, the company diversified their output with comedies and dramas, but the backbone of British Instructional was the factual film, particularly the *Secrets of Nature* series, which ran for more than 10 years.

Bruce Woolfe entered the film business as a provincial exhibitor in 1910. In August 1919, he and H. M. Howard registered British Instructional with £3000 capital. They rented an army hut from Ideal Films at the old Neptune Studios at Boreham Wood in Elstree and began making their first film, *The Battle of Jutland* (1921), about Admiral Beatty's victory over the German navy in World War I. Using animated models and maps, as well as live action sequences, *The Battle of Jutland* did well enough, critically and commercially, to fund a second film, *Armageddon* (1923). Tracing General Allenby's campaign in Palestine, *Armageddon* was made with the assistance of British Lion producer, A. V. Bramble, and the War Office. It received a Royal premiere and was a commercial and critical success. These new types of film (the composite actuality/animated feature film) became known as "patriotics."

In 1923, Woolfe took over a small studio in Surbiton previously owned by Stoll Picture Productions, which, in 1924, bought British Instructional. Bruce Woolf remained in control of the company and continued to make WWI reconstruction films, including *Ypres* (1925) and *Mons* (1926). The "patriotic" was *The Battles of the Coronel and Falkland Islands* (1927), which proved to be as popular with cinema audiences as had the earlier films. It was reissued in 1932 with an added soundtrack and a new title, *The Deeds Men Do* (1932). Film historian Paul Rotha later commented that these films were early examples of the documentary style.

Around the same time as *Armageddon* was being made in 1922, British Instructional began making the *Secrets of Nature* series. Intended for screening in the cinema, each film lasted eight to ten minutes and examined an aspect of natural history in Britain. The first series was released in 1922 and featured the life of the cuckoo, the evolution of the caddis fly, birds tending their young, a peek at a spider's lair, and the skills of different insects. Four more series were released in 1922, followed by another nineteen until 1933, when the series ended. More than one hundred films were made investigating the lives of insects, birds, flowers, and plants, as well as several about the weather and another half a dozen showcasing creatures at the zoo. By the end of 1925, the importance of the *Secrets of Nature* films was such that British Instructional created an Educational Department, headed by Mary Field, to oversee their production. The series really came into its own when the cameraman Percy Smith was recruited in 1926. His microcinematography of insects, underwater photography, and stop-frame animation of plants are visible in the most well known of the *Secrets of Nature* films. In his book *The Film Till Now* (1930), Paul Rotha referred to the series as "the sheet anchor of the British film industry."

In 1926, the company made their first foray in to drama with the feature-length *Nelson* (1926) and *Palaver* (1926). The latter film was shot and written in Nigeria by the actuality cameraman, Geoffrey Barkas, and is interesting in that it foreshadowed the use of nonprofessionals and local people as actors within a strand of the documentary movement of the 1930s. The film observed the attempts a British district officer to "peaceably" colonize the indigenous population of an isolated region in the British Empire. Intended as an entertainment film, *Palaver* did not do very well at the box office, and Barkas returned to actuality filming. The next year Stoll, who owned British Instructional, sold the company to the producer E.A. Bundy, but Bruce Woolf remained in the new post of Managing Director.

In May 1927, the new company, British Instructional Films (Proprietors), was registered, and, in 1928, construction began on a new studio at Welwyn. By the beginning of 1929, it was recognized that the arrival of sound was imminent, so a small sound studio was also built. The new company began making exclusively fiction films, apart from films in the *Secrets of Nature* series and some nontheatrical shorts. Most of these films were features for the quota, introduced as a result of the 1927 Cinematograph Films Act to protect British production against the increasing domination by American films in the British market. Although many of these quota films were derided by the industry, some of the best technicians in the business were given their start at British Instructional. Anthony Asquith made his first film, *Shooting Stars* (1928), there; Arthur Woods began his film career in their art department; Stuart Legg directed his first film *Cambridge* (1931) with the assistance of British Instructional funding before joining Grierson at the Empire Marketing Board; and Paul Rotha made his cinematic debut, as well as one of the first commer-

cially sponsored films, *Contact* (1933), with Woolfe as producer. The fledgling documentary movement was also loosely connected to British Instructional via its distributor, New Era, who co-produced several of the early documentaries including John Grierson's *Drifters* (1929).

When British Instructional was taken over by the commercial feature company British International Pictures in 1930, Pathé took over the distribution of the extensive back catalogue of British Instructional educational and factual films. Woolfe continued to make films for the nature series under the British Instructional banner until both he and Field left in 1933, and the company ceased production of the nature films. After a short spell with his new company, British Independent Pictures, Woolfe joined Mary Field at Gaumont-British Instructional, where they continued to make nature films using the new series title, *Secrets of Life*.

SARAH EASEN

See also **Field, Mary; Pathé;** *Secrets of Nature*

Further Reading

"British Instructional," in *Kinematograph Weekly*, February 1, 1924, 32.

Field, Mary, "Secrets 1919–1940," in *Documentary News Letter*, January 1941, 3–5.

Field, Mary, and Percy Smith, *Secrets of Nature*, London: The Scientific Book Club, 1939.

Low, Rachael, *The History of the British Film 1918–1929*, London: Allen and Unwin, 1971.

———, *The History of the British Film 1929–1939: Documentary and Educational Films of the 1930s*, London: Allen and Unwin, 1979.

BRONX MORNING, A

(US, Leyda, 1931)

A Bronx Morning was photographer-turned-filmmaker Jay Leyda's first film and the only solo effort in his filmmaking practice. Leyda is best known for his translations of Sergei Eisenstein's film theories, and for his own books in film analysis and history ranging from Soviet and

Chinese cinema to the compilation documentary. But Leyda's actual work in film is an essential part of his wide-ranging career as an artist-scholar, and this eleven-minute experimental documentary is significant on several fronts. It is, first, a highly creative and accomplished film that explores many tropes of film style and renders a memorable impression of New York City early in the Depression years. Among those who admired the film in its day were no less than Eisenstein and Dziga Vertov: This was the film that gained Leyda admission to the Moscow Film School in 1933, and both Soviet artists were pleased to claim that they saw their influence upon Leyda. (Surely the numerous shots of the baby carriage in one sequence show Leyda referencing the Odessa Steps massacre in *Potemkin*.) Thus, this film enabled to some degree Leyda's seminal years studying and working in Moscow and all the later books and translations of Eisenstein and others that Leyda brought to English-language readers, filmmakers, and cinema studies in general. In some sense, then, this effort also matters because it indirectly had a huge impact on generations of scholarship and production. Third,

A Bronx Morning in more recent years has proved to be a key film in the historiographic re-evaluation of American avant-garde cinema. For years a great variety of film made in the 1920s and 1930s was understudied and undervalued. Now, however, the days are gone when Maya Deren's undeniable landmark *Meshes of the Afternoon* (1943) was somehow seen as giving birth singlehandedly to experimental film in the U.S. Finally, Leyda's film makes an interesting and significant contribution to the city symphony, a documentary subgenre more often studied in the light of a handful of earlier European classics. Indeed, city films such as this one point to a time when distinctions between documentary and the avant-garde had not become fully established (Uricchio, 1995).

An impressionistic portrait of New York's northernmost borough in the early days of the

A Bronx Morning, 1931.
[*Still courtesy of the British Film Institute*]

Great Depression, *A Bronx Morning* does not follow the chronological "day in the life" structure of many city symphonies of the period. Rather, the film has a sense of formal play that heralds a new filmmaker, a student emulating but not merely copying his teachers. One finds awnings and sacks used as wipes; a graphic match from two pumpkins to the O's in the "LOOK" on a sandwich-board man's placard; and even an example of the Kuleshov effect, when shots of cats are followed by ones of birds scattering, as if in fear of the felines. The use of the "LOOK" is but one of many highly reflexive tropes active in the film, starting with its disorienting opening as the camera rides along an elevated train. The train enables not only a vivid and self-conscious tracking shot, but also an interplay with light and dark patches evocative of the filmstrip itself, and also later reflected images in the train windows and distancing created by grating in the foreground. Leyda's work in still photography and his apprenticeship with Ralph Steiner appear too, in the film's fascination with objects and the care with composition, photographically centripetal yet cinematically centrifugal, as the film transcends traditional, premodernist ideas of framing. Even the focus upon feet hints at the still photographer traipsing about to set up his next shot (Lugowski, 1999).

Historians have aptly linked the film with Ruttmann (Uricchio, 1995) and have also read the film as a tribute to Eugene Atget, one of Leyda's favorite photographers. (Horak, 1993). Images of objects in deserted streets, before they are filled with pedestrians and cars, delay anything resembling an establishing shot until 25 shots into the film, and have a surrealistic touch like Atget. Leyda himself, though, admitted a far wider range of influence, from art cinema and documentary he saw when he moved to New York, to many films (Cavalcanti's *Rien que les heures*, Man Ray's *L'etoile de mer*, Dudley Murphy and Fernand Leger's *Ballet Mecanique*) he had only seen via stills in camera magazines he collected as a youth in Ohio.

In later years, Leyda tended to downplay his first film, complaining that it was too "formalistic" and not sufficiently political. And yet, critics have argued that the city symphony, in moving experimental film away from abstraction and frequently either documenting the plight of the poor, or criticizing urban institutions, was actually a politicized, experimental play with realism. One certainly finds such commentary in Leyda's sardonic use of three intertitles. "The Bronx does

business ..." is followed by shots of businesses that have lost their leases. A second title, "And the Bronx lives ...", while followed by shots of tenements that denotatively represent living quarters, nonetheless heralds a series of shots devoid of any people, as if to highlight the difficulties of living in such crowded, impoverished conditions. Finally, the third title, "... on the street" continues the ongoing trope of irony, as we see garbage trucks and a possibly homeless woman's legs sprawled on the pavement. This shot of the legs is but part of a larger fragmentation of the body seen throughout the film, combined with decentered framings and a prominent use of empty spaces. Horak (1993) notes that the film displays an essentially "feminine perspective" in its world of children, pets and cleaning, unlike those city symphonies that emphasize men at work. Others have argued that a gender politics is in play here, that the absence of agency speaks to the "crisis in masculinity" brought about by the socioeconomic conditions of the Depression (Lugowski, 1999). However read, the film has belatedly come into its own for film scholars and cultural historians.

DAVID M. LUGOWSKI

See also **Leyda, Jay**

A Bronx Morning (USA, 1931–32, 11 minutes, silent), directed, photographed, and edited by Jay Leyda.

Further Reading

Horak, Jan-Christopher, "Avant-Garde Film," in Tino Balio, *Grand Design: Hollywood as a Modern Business Enterprise, 1930–1939*, New York: Charles Scribner's Sons, 1993.

Kirstein, Lincoln, "Experimental Films," *Arts Weekly*, vol. 1, March 25, 1932, pp. 52, 62.

Leyda, Jay, "A Note on *A Bronx Morning*," Lausanne, Switzerland: FIAF Symposium, 1979, in clippings file on Jay Leyda, Museum of Modern Art, New York.

Lugowski, David M. *Queering the (New) Deal: Lesbian, Gay and Queer Representation in U.S. Cinema of the Great Depression, 1929–1941*, Ph.D. dissertation, NYU, 1999.

Uricchio, William, "The City Viewed: The Films of Leyda, Browning and Weinberg," in *Lovers of Cinema: The First American Avant-Garde, 1919–1945*, Jan-Christopher Horak, ed., Madison: University of Wisconsin Press, 1995, pp. 287–314.

Wolfe, Charles, "Straight Shots and Crooked Plots: Social Documentary and the Avant-Garde in the 1930s," in *Lovers of Cinema: The First American Avant-Garde, 1919-1945*, Jan-Christopher Horak, ed., Madison: University of Wisconsin Press, 1995, pp. 234–266.

BRUNEI

See **Southeast Asia**

BUMMING IN BEIJING

(China, Wenguang, 1990)

The 1980s was a period in contemporary Chinese history when artistic ideals often came into conflict with official political reality. With intensive economic reform and a flood of new ideas from abroad, all kinds of art forms, including music, drama, film, and painting, flourished and attempted to experiment in a spirit of rebellion against authority. From the late 1980s, independent documentary filmmaking also became increasingly significant within the history of Chinese documentary filmmaking. One such film, Wu Wenguang's *Bumming in Beijing (Liu Lang Beijing)*, opened up a new chapter in Chinese contemporary documentary film history as an independent film made entirely outside the official system. This film did not follow the traditional approach of focusing on mainstream subjects, as did most newsreel, propaganda, travelogs, and the most common forms of television documentary. *Bumming in Beijing* was the first documentary film in China to be shot in a fly-on-the-wall style and looking at China's underclass and marginalized peoples. Using techniques such as nonsynchronised and synchronised sound, long takes, held camera shots, and interviews, the film departed from the official style, which relied heavily on narrative voice-over to support the subject so as to make the right kind of propaganda statement.

Alongside the other early independent documentary filmmakers and their films of the late 1980s, such as Duan Jinchuan and Zhang Yuan's *The Square*, and Kang Jianning's *Yin Yang*, Wu Wenguang is regarded as one of the pioneers of the New Documentary Movement. This term was coined by author Lu Xinyu, who, in defining the term *New Documentary Movement*, referred to a "the solicitude for the human spirit, attention to the rock bottom of society, and a bottom-up perspective." In late 1988, Wu Wenguang, as the first independent documentary filmmaker working outside of China's film system, started shooting *Bumming in Beijing*. Wu "felt a strong urge to record this rapidly changing China and this group of artists, because I sensed it would be changed or even disappear very soon."

Bumming in Beijing focuses on a group of young artists who come to Beijing to explore their dreams and hopes for the development of their art. Through a direct cinema approach, and interactive interviews, the film expands on the lives of the artists as they struggle to match their ideals with reality. In 1991, *Bumming in Beijing* gained international attention when it was first premiered at the Hong Kong International Film Festival. Later, Wu Wenguang was invited to show his film at Japan's Shanxing Film Festival. With financial support from the Japanese NHK, Wu Wenguang then started shooting the sequel to *Bumming in Beijing*, *Everywhere Is Home*, a film that follows the five artists of *Bumming in Beijing* to the different countries where they finally choose different directions in which to pursue their lives. The five artists are no longer bumming, but the new challenges they face still pose unanswered questions in *Everywhere Is Home*.

WEIMIN ZHANG

Bumming in Beijing—the Last Dreamer (China, 1990, 69 mins). Directed and edited by Wu Wenguang. Cinematography by Lu Wangping.

Further Reading

Reynaud, Berenic, "Sense of Cinema," in *Documenting China: The Contemporary Documentary Movement in China*, edited by Lu Xinyu, Beijing: SDX Joint Publishing Company, 2003 (in Chinese).
Yingjin, Jhang, "New Cinemas," *Journal of Contemporary Film*, 2, 2, September 2004, 119–136.

BUÑUEL, LUIS

See Land Without Bread

BURCH, NOËL

Although Noël Burch was schooled as a filmmaker in France in the early 1950s, his career as a director did not become fully realized until much later in life. From the time he graduated from L'IDHEC (translated roughly as the Institute for the High Cinematographic Studies) now known as la FEMIS (the National Film School of France) until the mid-1980s, Burch gained recognition as a film theorist, teacher, and critic, engaging in landmark studies of formal film analysis, Japanese cinema, and early, silent cinema.

Throughout his life, Burch was never far from the camera. In the 1950s, he assisted directors Preston Sturges and Michel Fano. Soon afterward, while becoming a respected film critic and theorist, Burch honed his filmmaking skills by making several short films. These included *Et Sur Cette Pierre ...* (1963), *Noviciat* (1964), *Tout Est Ecrit* (1970), *Correction, Please* or *How We Got Into Pictures* (1979), *The Year of the Bodyguard* (1981), *The Impersonation* (1983), and *Not Distant Observers* (1985). As Burch himself admits, however, before 1986, he "was not really going anywhere" as a filmmaker.

In 1986, he made a series of six documentaries for England's Channel Four Television, titled together, *What Do Those Old Films Mean?* As his subject, Burch chose an often neglected period of film history: early cinema. In each of the six segments, Burch investigated how cinema developed after the turn of the century in a different part of the world. The six volumes are divided as follows: Volume One examines English cinema from 1900 to 1912, Volume Two examines French cinema from 1904 to 1912, Volume Three examines American cinema from 1902 to 1914, Volume Four examines Soviet cinema from 192 to 1930, Volume Five examines Danish cinema from 1910 to 1912, and Volume Six examines German cinema from 1926 to 1932.

That Burch chose to highlight the cinematic art in those particular countries during those specific time frames comes as no surprise. In his first book, *Theory of Film Practice* (1967), Burch had analyzed the work of key filmmakers who fit into those parameters, extolling, for example, the editing technique of Soviet filmmaker, Sergei Eisenstein, and the structure of the gags in the films of American slapstick performer Buster Keaton.

As a self-proclaimed communist and expatriate, strongly influenced by the radicalism of the student movement in France in May 1968, it is not surprising that Burch was deeply critical of U.S. politics. This criticism, along with his ongoing dedication to cinema, became the basis for Burch's most acclaimed documentary, *Red Hollywood* (1995). Although Burch had explored the subject of American dissidents in his 1994 film, *Voyage Sentimental*, he and co-director Thom Anderson's investigation into the blacklisted filmmakers of 1950s Hollywood brought him greater recognition as a documentarian than any of his previous films. *Red Hollywood* examines the forgotten works of several blacklisted filmmakers who fled to France rather than struggle within the U.S. film industry. Burch and Andersons' subjects included Dalton Trumbo, Michael Wilson, John Berry, and Jules Dassin. Using fifty-three clips from their films, *Red Hollywood* explores the ways in which these political leftists were able to infuse communist ideas into their work. The documentary received a great deal of praise from critics in the United States.

Early in his career as a film theorist, Burch defined himself as a formalist, calling attention to a film's *mise en scène* over its narrative in his writing and teaching. Burch analogized cinema to music, arguing in *Theory of Film Practice* that film form could be conceived of in terms of "atonal" formal elements, in which no single element consistently dominates. In that sense, in any given film, narrative is just another element, not inherently more important than sound, editing structure, or a different aesthetic component. Burch demonstrates his thesis using a wide range of films and filmmakers, including Fritz Lang's *M* and Jacques Tati's *Play Time*.

Burch opposes what he calls mainstream cinema's Institutional Mode of Production (IMP), which uses invisible editing, framing, and *mise en scène* to call the spectator's attention to the narrative, rather than the aesthetics of the film. Burch holds that the rise of the IMP in the early days of the medium was linked to the film industry's economic interest in attracting a bourgeois demographic. Toward that end, the industry wanted to create films the audience could identify with psychologically, films that created the effect of reality. Burch preferred modernist and avant-garde films that stressed formal properties such as off-screen space and spatial framing. He praised the films of Antonioni and Resnais, in particular, for their elaborate orchestration and use of off-screen space.

In his seminal book on Japanese cinema, *To the Distant Observer*, Burch argues that Japanese film is inherently critical of the Hollywood realist cinema of the 1930s and 1940s. Burch points to the directors Ozu Yasujiro and Mizoguchi Kenji as two stylistically different filmmakers, whose works both illustrate the difference between the realism of Hollywood and modernism of Japanese cinema. Whereas Hollywood privileges a continuous, coherent, character-driven narrative above other formal elements in film, Japanese cinema uses long shots, frontality, and, in the case of Ozu, a narrative in which nothing seems to be happening. For Burch, this is a deliberate and intentional stylistic indifference to the codified mode of filmmaking manufactured by Hollywood.

Although Burch has continued teaching, writing, and theorizing about film, publishing several books during the 1990s and beyond, *Theory of Film Practice* and *To the Distant Observer* remain his most influential and ground-breaking achievements. His attention to film form and overall concern for the medium became the subjects of his filmmaking ventures. His most successful documentaries, *What Do Those Old Films Mean?* and *Red Hollywood* both encourage a reevaluation of film outside the narrative-driven conventions of American cinema. As both a scholar and a filmmaker, Burch continues to be a powerful influence on the field of film studies.

STARR MARCELLO

Biography

Born in San Francisco, 1932. Emigrated to France for film school in 1951. Graduated from L'IDEC (presently called La Femis) in 1954. Worked as an assistant to Preston Sturges and Michel Fano in the 1950s. Began teaching and making short films in the 1960s. Joined the Communist Party. Published *Theory of Film Practice* in 1967, and participated in the radical student movement in Paris in May 1968. Moved to Japan in the mid-1970s to study Japanese film. Published *To the Distant Observer* in 1979. Returned to Europe and agreed in 1986 to direct the six-part series on early cinema, *What Do Those Old Films Mean?* For England's Channel Four Television. Published his third book, *Life to Those Shadows* in 1990. Continued writing on film theory and practice. Directed the critically acclaimed *Red Hollywood* with Thom Anderson in 1995.

Further Reading

Bordwell, David, "The Musical Analogy," in *Yale French Studies*, 60, Cinema/Sound 1980, 141–156.

Burch, Noël, *Theory of Film Practice*, trans. by Helen R. Lane, New York: Praeger Publishers, 1973.

———, *To the Distant Observer: Form and Meaning in the Japanese Cinema*, edited by Annette Michaelson, Berkeley: University of California Press, 1979.

———, *Life to Those Shadows*, translated and edited by Ben Brewster, Berkeley: University of California Press, 1990.

————, *In and Out of Sync: The Awakening of a Cine-Dreamer*, translated and edited by Ben Brewster, London: Scolar Press, 1991.

Burch, Noël and Geneviève Sellier, *La drôle de guerre des sexes du cinéma français : 1930–1956*, Paris: Nathan, 1996.

————, *Loin de Paris, cinémas et sociétés : textes et contexts*, edited by Laurence Allard, Paris: Harmattan, 2001.

Elsaesser, Thomas and Adam Barker, editors, *Early Cinema: Space, Frame, Narrative*, London: BFI Publishing, 1990.

Rosen, Philip, editor, *Narrative, Apparatus, Ideology: A Film Theory Reader*, New York: Columbia University Press, 1986.

BURDEN OF DREAMS

(Germany, Blank, 1982)

Regarded as one of the finest films ever made about movie-making, *Burden of Dreams* is also the most widely seen work by prolific documentarian Les Blank. In October 1979 and again in April–June 1981, director Werner Herzog brought in Blank and Maureen Gosling to document the production of his feature *Fitzcarraldo* (1982), being shot in Peru. Herzog eventually completed his quixotic jungle venture, but Blank's portrait of the director running amok in the Amazon emerged as the superior film. *Burden of Dreams* combines a "making-of" chronicle with Les Blank's characteristic humor, keen eye for detail, and ethnographic sensitivity, creating a compelling portrait of the notoriously eccentric German filmmaker.

Burden of Dreams begins with a sequence both beautiful and cheeky. To the sounds of a Vivaldi chorale, aerial shots display the Peruvian Amazon. Unlike Hitler's arrival through the clouds in *Triumph of the Will* (1935), Herzog's shaky landing in a small plane signals his lack of command over this place. Blank then cuts to the director sitting in a small boat, explaining his film's "Sisyphus-like story," which he based on a historical character. Fitzcarraldo, an Irish rubber merchant, dreams of bringing Enrico Caruso to sing at a new opera house in the Amazon. To finance his venture, he accesses untapped rubber trees by transporting a steamship over a mountainous isthmus. As we learn, although the actual Carlos Fitzcarrald disassembled his boat, Herzog insists on having his hauled in one piece, even though it is ten times heavier. Blank builds his documentary's narrative around this literal and metaphorical feat.

The film next takes us back to November 1979, when shooting commenced. A narrator's detached voice condenses the production history throughout, emphasizing the complicated negotiations between the European crew and the divergent groups of people living in these remote parts of the Amazon. We see Aguaruna Indians working at the *Fitzcarraldo* encampment while one explains the political tensions and violence that force the production to flee. Cut to the city of Iquitos, Peru, where shooting resumed in January 1981, only to be suspended when star Jason Robards fell ill. We see outtakes of Robards with co-star Mick Jagger, as Herzog relates: "If I abandon this project, I would be a man without dreams." In April, actor Klaus Kinski arrives to take the title role, as he had for Herzog's earlier tale of madness, *Aguirre, der Zorn Gottes /*

Burden of Dreams, 1982.
[*Still courtesy of the British Film Institute*]

Aguirre, the Wrath of God (1972), also filmed in the rain forests of Peru.

The remainder of *Burden of Dreams* chronicles three months of shooting from a second camp, 1,500 miles to the south of Iquitos. Blank records moments of danger and the tedium of numerous delays. An understated voice-over narrator relates that, in fact, the crew must work with three ships, all representing Fitzcarraldo's one. In addition to the 300-ton steamer to be forced over a hill, a similar vessel stays in Iquitos for principal photography, and a third goes down a river for shooting on the "Rapids of Death." Alternating with verité sequences of the production are interviews with Herzog, which become articulate but mad monologues on the "curse" on his production, the "authentic natives" in his cast, and the "collective murder" and "obscenity of all this jungle." Blank concludes with a qualified fulfillment of the director's quest. We hear that, after several hazardous attempts, Herzog wins "a painful victory" by getting his ship to the mountaintop with bulldozers. This climax, however, falls between despondent soliloquies. First, asked by Blank what he will do after the movie has wrapped, Herzog grimaces as he jokes that he "shouldn't make movies anymore." Even if *Fitzcarraldo* gets done, he says, "Nobody on this earth will convince me to be happy about all that." Finally, Blank concludes his portrait of the artist on a note of bittersweet redemption, with Herzog saying: "I make films because . . . it is my duty. Because this might be the inner chronicle of what we are, and we have to articulate ourselves."

As a commissioned documentary, *Burden of Dreams* gives Werner Herzog the first and last word, but the film far from lionizes him. With characteristic aplomb, Les Blank reveals the beauty of the Amazon and the people who live in this place that Herzog finds both irresistible and horrible. His portrait is sympathetic to Herzog's artistry but revelatory of its cruel excesses. We see, for example, the filmmaker playing football with local Indians, only to find that when the Machiguengas engage in their traditional sport of arrow catching, he urges them to shoot harder, and at one another's heads. Blank intercuts this with footage of Herzog first explaining that a hostile tribe has attacked three of his camp members, then smiling as he says he will give his son the gruesome arrow that went through a man's throat.

Burden of Dreams was only one of several documentaries of the time that centered on the German filmmaker's eccentricities and droll lunacy. Erwin Keusch's *Was ich bin, sind meine Filme/I Am My Films* (1979) shows the director during the making of *Stroszek* (1977). It reveal a less assured cineaste, but one who declares that films are more important than life itself, hence Herzog's predilection for dangerous locales and outlandish actions. Shortly before embarking on *Fitzcarraldo*, he also participated in *Werner Herzog Eats His Shoe* (1980), Blank's whimsical short about his comrade's appearance at the premiere of Errol Morris's *Gates of Heaven* (1978). Herzog had encouraged the fledgling filmmaker to make this peculiar nonfiction feature about pet cemeteries, claiming he would eat his shoe if Morris succeeded. In filming the literal cooking of leather boots at Chez Panisse, Blank not only paved the way for his 1980 film *Garlic Is as Good as Ten Mothers* (in which Herzog briefly appears), he also established the character rendered full-scale in *Burden of Dreams*—Herzog, the cinema-obsessed extremist who wants to save the world from banality by pursuing cinematic visions.

Although movies routinely commission documentaries about their making, Blank's work began a subgenre about troubled productions, often with their own directors going half mad in isolated locations. Most notably, *Hearts of Darkness* (1991) chronicles Francis Ford Coppola's tribulations in directing *Apocalypse Now* (1979). The former, incidentally, includes footage shot by Les Blank, who Coppola hired to film the *Apocalypse* wrap party. Mika Kaurismäki's *Tigrero: A Film That Was Never Made* (1994) records Sam Fuller's return to the Brazilian locales of a movie he abandoned forty years prior. And Terry Gilliam's failure to complete *The Man Who Killed Don Quixote* is recorded in *Lost in La Mancha* (2002). Arguably, the subgenre evolved beyond parody with a twisted homage to *Burden of Dreams*. In Zak Penn's presumed mockumentary, *Incident at Loch Ness* (2004), a crew sets out to film a documentary about Werner Herzog, who is himself directing a documentary about the Loch Ness monster.

Whatever the strengths of these kindred films, only *Burden of Dreams* goes beyond its commission. Rather than simply presenting a portrait of a filmmaker lost in an alien environment, Blank also respectfully documents the people who live in the place that Herzog can only see as "unfinished" and "prehistorical." As in his many films celebrating American subcultures, Blank delights in presenting people via their music and food. Although we see Klaus Kinski disgusted by the fermented masato that the Campas Indians offer to Fitzcarraldo, Blank counters with a long sequence documenting the communal process of making this staple food and ritual drink, even recording a zesty Campas song about the subject. After giving Herzog the last word, he tellingly gives Peruvians the final image. *Burden of Dreams* ends with the visiting German filmmaker having his portrait taken by an itinerant photographer, who frames the black-and-white photo in a heart, trimmed with drawings of flowers, vines, and songbirds, an artful domestication of the jungle to which Herzog could only surrender.

DAN STREIBLE

See also **Blank, Les; Herzog, Werner**

Burden of Dreams (USA/Germany, Flower Films, 1982, 94 min.) Produced, directed and photographed by Les Blank. Editing and sound recording by Maureen Gosling. Written by Michael Goodwin. Narrated by Candace Laughlin. Interpreting, interviewing, and camera assistance by Bruce "Pacho" Lane. Cast: Werner Herzog, Klaus Kinski, Claudia Cardinale, Jason Robards, Mick Jagger, Huerequeque Bohorquez, José Lewgoy, Walter Saxer, Thomas Mauch, Paul Hittscher, Evaristo Nunkuag Ikanan, Nelson de Rio Cenepa, Carmen Correa, Elia de Rio Ene, Alfredo de Rio. Tambo, Miguel Angel Fuentes, Laplace Martins, David Pérez Espinosa, Angela Reina, Jorge Vignati, Father Mariano Gagnon. Music: Vivaldi's "Dixit Dominus," performed by Vienna Kam-

merchor; "Uchpagallo," "Mi Selva Obscura," "Madrugador," performed by Corazón de la Selva; "Vamos a Belén," performed by Los Solteritos; "M'Appari," "Demeure, Chaste e Puro," "Pagliacci," "Chi mi Frena in tal Moment," recordings of Enrico Caruso; chorale music by Popul Vuh. Filmed in Peru. Robert Flaherty Documentary Award (1983), British Academy of Film and Television Arts. Alternate version: U.S. broadcast, for the series "Non-Fiction Television" (PBS, 58 min.)

Further Reading

Blank, Les and James Bogan, editors, *Burden of Dreams: Screenplay, Journals, Reviews, Photographs*, Berkeley: North Atlantic Books, 1984.

Corliss, Richard, "*Burden of Dreams*," in *Time*, October 25, 1982, 77–78.

Durgnat, Raymond, "*Burden of Dreams*," in *Films*, November 1982, 29–30.

Goodwin, Michael, "Herzog the God of Wrath," in *American Film*, June 1982, 36–51, 72–73.

Margolis, Janet, "Burden of Dreams," in *Cineaste* 12, 4, 1983, 54.

Rouyer, Philippe and Sophie Bordes, "Jubilation de la caméra: sur le cinéma de Les Blank," in *Positif*, March 1988, 19–25.

BURMA VICTORY

(UK, Boulting, 1945)

Burma Victory was the final film in a wartime series of documentaries dealing with significant Allied campaigns. The previous "victory" films, *Desert Victory* (1943) and *Tunisian Victory* (1944), had addressed the war in North Africa, whereas *Burma Victory* was an account of the arduous fighting in Southeast Asia. The feature-length documentaries were compiled from footage taken by the service film units and *Tunisian Victory* and *The True Glory* (1945), about the liberation of northern Europe, were notable, if troubled, collaborations between the British and Americans. The films were widely screened, both theatrically and nontheatrically, and were considered principal achievements in the war documentary.

Britain's main contribution to the war in the East was the struggle to recover Burma. It was a long, hard-fought, and unpleasant campaign, yet it was secondary to the events in Europe. The Fourteenth Army that operated there was awarded the epithet of "the forgotten army" and its commander, Admiral Lord Mountbatten, aimed to get the recognition the Allied forces were due. One way to achieve this goal was an ambitious campaign film such as *Tunisian Victory*, and early in 1944 he was encouraging London and Washington into a further Anglo-American documentary film. In the event, and very much a consequence of the previous difficulties of co-production, it was decided in May 1945 to make separate British and American records of the Burma campaign.

Burma Victory begins with a series of bleak images depicting the hostility of the terrain and the ravages attendant on the monsoon. After early setbacks at the hands of the Japanese, a firmer resolve is brought to the Fourteenth Army by its new commander Mountbatten, who is seen addressing groups of servicemen and demanding no further retreats. The Allied campaign of 1944–1945, including the successful defense of Imphal and Kohima, the system of supply by air operated by the Americans, the daring behind the enemy lines mission of the "chindits," Stilwell's Chinese Expeditionary Force advancing from the northwest, the crossing of the Chindwin and Irrawaddy rivers, the long, hard-fought march to Mandalay, and the relief of Rangoon, is presented through a combination of combat and documentary footage, reenactments, models, and diagrams. The war ends with the Japanese surrender in September 1945, after the dropping of atomic bombs on Nagasaki and Hiroshima.

David MacDonald of the Army Film and Photographic Unit (AFPU) had arrived in the region late in 1944 to commence work on a film. He was able to draw on and coordinate the activities of the Southeast Asia Command (SEAC) Film Unit, which was led by Derek Knight. After his work on the previous "victory" films, Roy Boulting was again assigned to direct and edit the project, and everyone was required to work fast as the war was concluding. *Burma Victory* understandably bears much similarity to its predecessors. In a few respects, though, it develops techniques introduced in the earlier titles and gives them a new prominence. Boulting had staged a small but vitally effective scene in *Desert Victory* to provide some dramatic impact to the commencement of the Battle of El Alamein. Here, he opens the film with a studio-staged scene featuring two British Tommies in a tent, one of whom is reading aloud from a guidebook to Burma. Dispirited of its idea-

Burma Victory, 1945 Documentary by British Army Film Unit.
[*Courtesy of the Everett Collection*]

lized vision, he tosses the book into the previously concealed rain and mud outside, now brought into view with a panning shot. A further, more developed, reenactment occurs in the middle of the film. It is a nighttime scene and Boulting effectively uses sound, performance, and lighting to evoke the eerie atmosphere of the jungle. These scenes were shot at Pinewood Studios, the home base of the AFPU. Although examples of the wartime trend in blending fiction and documentary, such reenactments are of a quite different order to those being developed within the documentary film movement at the Crown Film Unit, such as Pat Jackson's work on *Western Approaches* (1944). Boulting was primarily a commercial filmmaker and intended such scenes to help dramatize the material and make the film more palatable at the box office. In a similar vein, the film makes use of the narrative device of a diarist, thus individualizing and humanizing the events depicted.

Burma Victory also includes restaged briefings of the Allied commanders. These scenes would have been shot on location by the SEAC Film Unit and, although extremely stilted, perform the vital democratic function of information and explanation. The "victory" documentaries have been credited with promoting the ideals of a people's war, and access to the military leaders and strategists is seen as a fulfillment of this. The notions of a democratic leadership and citizen army, strongly present in *Desert Victory*, are further stamped into the *Burma* film. On reflection, however, these qualities are compromised by Britain's imperial role in the region, the aristocratic credentials of the Supreme Commander, and the over-prominence of the British Tommy in the film. After all, the brunt of the action was borne by Empire troops, especially the highly tenacious Indians who were fighting to keep the Japanese out of their homeland.

Burma Victory differed from its two predecessors in one important respect. They had carefully established the connection between the war front and the home front—that the former relied on the material produced by the latter. This was a central articulation of people's war ideology. The geographic remoteness and sideshow status of the Southeast Asia theatre seemingly precluded such a presentation, and, besides, virtually all of the heavy equipment on view—tanks, planes, bulldozers—was of American origin. Perhaps a growing rivalry at that stage in the war prompted the British filmmakers to leave unmentioned such factors. In addition, the British were still smarting from Hollywood's astonishingly insensitive treatment of the war in the region, *Objective Burma* (1945), which depicted Errol Flynn and a few American troops dispatching the Japanese single handedly.

Despite the intense effort, the film was not complete until October 1945. It attracted excellent reviews and was praised in the *Monthly Film Bulletin* as a "masterly survey of a vast and complex campaign, presented with vivid realism." It clearly went some way in providing recognition to the struggle in the East, and was the last great documentary to emerge from the wartime service film units.

ALAN BURTON

See also **Boulting, John and Roy;** *Desert Victory;* *Tunisian Victory*

Burma Victory (UK, British Army Film Unit, 1945, 62 min) In Charge of Production, Lieut.-Col David MacDonald. Director and Supervising Editor, Capt. Roy Boulting.

Commentary written by Capt. Frank Harvey, Capt. Roy Boulting. Commentary spoken by David King-Wood, Ivan Brandt, Norman Claridge. Music by Alan Rawsthorne.

Further Reading

Chapman, James, *The British at War. Cinema, State and Propaganda, 1939–1945*, London: I.B. Tauris, 1998.
Coultass, Clive, *Images for Battle. British Film and the Second World War, 1939–1945*, London: AUP, 1989.
Jarvie, Ian, "The Burma Campaign on Film: 'Objective Burma' (1945), 'The Stilwell Road' (1945) and 'Burma Victory' (1945)," in *Historical Journal of Film, Radio and Television*, 8, 1, 1988, 55–73.
Paris, Michael, "Filming the People's War: *The Dawn Guard, Desert Victory, Tunisian Victory* and *Burma Victory*," in *The Family Way. The Boulting Brothers and British Film Culture*, edited by Burton, A., O'Sullivan, T. and Wells, P., Trowbridge: Flicks Books, 2000.

BURNS, KEN

Ken Burns is the documentary phenomenon of the last decade of the twentieth century. From *The Civil War* (1990) through *Jazz* (2001), Burns has produced and directed nine documentaries with a total running time of more than sixty hours for the Public Broadcasting System (PBS) in the United States. More than 70 million viewers have seen *The Civil War* and more than 50 million *Baseball* (1994). Budgets for the Burns projects range from more than $3 million for *The Civil War* to $14 million for *Jazz*. (The sales of *The Civil War* on video had exceeded a million copies by 1993.) Public schools and libraries across America present this documentary to children and make it readily available to the public. *The Civil War* can stand with *The Birth of a Nation* (1915) and *Gone With the Wind* (1939) as landmarks in the politics of historical representation and of popular culture in twentieth-century America. Burns himself is a media celebrity, featured widely on television, radio, and in the press. (He was invited to the White House by both George H. Bush and Bill Clinton). Few would contest Gary Edgerton's observation that this documentary filmmaker is "arguably the most recognizable and influential historian of his generation." With the financial backing of PBS and the General Motors Corpora-

tion, and an experienced team of collaborators, at mid-career Burns appears likely to continue production at a remarkable pace.

Burns's project is to grapple with the national identity by exploring American history. His belief that the Civil War, baseball, and jazz are central to our culture motivated his grand documentary trilogy. So too, his conviction that individuals shape our historical destiny underlies his parallel series of American profiles. His respect for American institutions and his biographies of "great" men and women testify to an allegiance to traditional values; yet his projects regularly portray reformers and even revolutionary figures, such as Frank Lloyd Wright, Susan B. Anthony, and Thomas Jefferson. Burns claims that America's racial heritage is the thread connecting all his work. (African Americans are obviously central to *The Civil War* and *Jazz*, and the prominence given the Negro leagues and Jackie Robinson's integration of the sport in *Baseball* offers more compelling evidence of the centrality of race to the Burns understanding of the United States.) A liberal, progressive sensibility guides the Burns exploration of what it means to be an American, and a fundamental allegiance to the national heritage unites the work.

157

The Ken Burns style helps to account for his enormous productivity. His historical documentaries have a fixed vocabulary of elements that offer flexibility within a well-established formula. Central to the method is the animation of still materials: photographs, paintings, periodicals. With editing, moving camera, or zooming lens, Burns constructs a scene out of a single image. He wants his viewer to inhabit the picture as he brings it to life. The volume of this material can be enormous. *The Civil War* is reported to have used 16,000 photographs. In counterpoint, the filmmaker takes filmed footage, unpopulated landscapes, or empty buildings associated with an era and uses a stable, balanced composition to invest the image with stillness, allowing the shot to evoke a frozen past. A range of archival moving pictures fills out his compilation. Of course, the animation of still images in documentary goes back to *Michelangelo* (1940) and was used with eloquence by Alain Resnais in his documentaries from the 1950s. Burns himself acknowledges the influence of films such as *City of Gold* (1957) and *The Real West* (1961). The Burns visual style is derivative, but in his best work, outstanding.

The images from the past are further brought to life with the accompanying soundtracks. Various characters (such as Elijah Hunt Rhodes, Mary Chestnut, or Frederick Douglas among many others from *The Civil War*) constitute a "chorus of voices" whose letters, diaries, speeches, and so forth are read by a distinguished actor, cultivating a highly personalized vocal delivery as the basis for each characterization. The documentaries establish and return to the cast of historical characters, allowing them to assume the intimacy and depth of figures from fiction. At their best, this chorus establishes contending characters animating dramatic conflict, as well as a sense of the variable forces propelling change. The soundtrack further evokes the past with folk tunes, period music, or other sounds associated with the era. These voices from the past are integrated with a general narrator and contemporary authorities (such as Gary Giddens, Gerald Early, or Wynton Marsalis in *Jazz*), who offer commentary and analysis culled from interviews. However, the authorities speak directly to the camera and address the viewer in the absence of any prompting or presence from the filmmaker. Rather than appearing as interviewees, these on-camera storytellers appear to be speaking directly to the viewer.

Finally, Burns segments his episodes into short sections of approximately ten to fifteen minutes, each one introduced by a simple title framed in black. The sections allow for a shift in subject or emphasis from a narrative description to an affecting personal tale, a flash forward or backward in time, or a montage of contending opinions. Episodes typically begin with an evocative introduction setting the tone before the general subject of the installment is announced with the credits.

In 1981, Burns's first film, *The Brooklyn Bridge*, appeared to have a fresh and engaging approach to the historical documentary. By the turn of the century, his style had become so widely imitated that television programming on the *History* or the *Discovery* Channel seems to have transformed it into an institutional practice. A challenge facing Burns at this point in his career is to develop his style, lest his work become undistinguishable from a movement he is largely responsible for inspiring.

The historical documentaries of Ken Burns have excited a new interest in history among the general public. Historians have greeted the phenomenon with mixed feelings. Though gratified by the attention, scholars are concerned because the films glide past controversy over evidence, method and interpretation that characterizes the discipline of history. Nonetheless, Ken Burns's documentaries address serious questions about what it means to be an American and explore a range of answers for an audience that is eager for more.

LEGER GRINDON

Biography

Born July 29, 1953 in Brooklyn, New York to Robert Kyle Burns, an anthropologist, and Lyla Smith (Tupper) Burns. Grew up in Newark, Delaware, and Ann Arbor, Michigan, where his father held positions as a university professor. Graduated from Hampshire College in 1975, majoring in film studies and design under the direction of Jerome Liebling and Elaine Mayes. Founded Florentine Films in 1975 with former classmates Buddy Squires and Roger Sherman. Beginning with *The Brooklyn Bridge* (1981) through *Horatio's Drive: America's First Road Trip* (2003), has worked as the producer and director, and frequently cinematographer and co-writer, on seventeen documentaries focusing on various aspects of American history and culture. Many of these works are multiple episode programs running between ten and twenty hours, most notably *The Civil War* (1990), *Baseball* (1994), and *Jazz* (2001). Has co-authored five illustrated books that have accompanied his documentaries. Recipient of many awards including the Television Critics Association Awards (1991,1995, 2001), Peabody Awards (1990,1999, 2000), Emmy Awards (1991, 1994), and the Erik Barnouw Prize.

Selected Films

1981 *Brooklyn Bridge*
1985 *The Statue of Liberty*

1990 *Lindbergh*
1990 *The Civil War*
1991 *Empire of the Air: The Men Who Made Radio*
1994 *Baseball*
1996 *The West*
1997 *Lewis & Clark: The Journey of the Corps of Discovery*
1998 *Frank Lloyd Wright*
1999 *Not for Ourselves Alone: The Story of Elizabeth Cady Stanton & Susan B. Anthony*
2001 *Jazz*
2001 *Mark Twain*
2003 *Horatio's Drive: America's First Road Trip*

Further Reading

Blight, David W., "Homer with a Camera, Our 'Iliad' without the Aftermath: Ken Burns's Dialogue with Historians," in *Reviews in American History*, 25, 2, 1997, 351–359.

Burns, Ken "In Search of the Painful, Essential Images of War," in *New York Times*, 27, January 1991, sec. 2:1.

Cripps, Thomas, "Historical Truth: An Interview with Ken Burns," in *American Historical Review* 100, 3, 1995, 741–764.

Edgerton, Gary R., "Ken Burns—A Conversation with Public Television's Resident Historian," in *Journal of American Culture* 18, 1, 1995, 1–12.

Edgerton, Gary R., *Ken Burns's America*, New York: Palgrave, 2001.

Hackney, Sheldon. "A Conversation with Ken Burns on *Baseball*," in *Humanities* 15, 1994, 4–7, 48–53.

Henderson, Brian, "*The Civil War*: 'Did It Not Seem Real?,'" in *Film Quarterly* 44, 3, 1991, 2–14.

Lancioni, Judith, "The Rhetoric of the Frame: Revisioning Archival Photographs in *The Civil War*," in *Western Journal of Communication* 60, 1996, 397–414.

———. "Ken Burns: The Art of the Artifact," in *Prime Time, Prime Movers: From I Love Lucy to L.A Law—America's Greatest TV Shows and the People Who Created Them*, edited by David Marc and Robert J. Thompson, Boston: Little, Brown, 1992.

McPherson, Tara, "Both Kinds of Arms: Remembering *The Civil War*," in *Velvet Light Trap* 35 1995, 3–18.

Thelen, David, "The Movie Maker as Historian: Conversations with Ken Burns," in *Journal of American History* 81, 3, 1994, 1031–1050.

Tibbetts, John C., "The Incredible Stillness of Being: Motionless Pictures in the Films of Ken Burns," in *American Studies* 37, 1, 1996, 117–133.

Toplin, Robert B., editor, *Ken Burns's The Civil War: Historians Respond*. New York: Oxford, 1996.

C

CAMBODIA

See **Southeast Asia**

CAMERA NATURA

(Australia, Gibson, 1984)

Camera Natura uses an essay mode to deconstruct the discourses around the nonaboriginal imaging of the landscape. The film had its origins in director/writer Ross Gibson's writings, in particular his essays "Camera Natura: Landscape in Australian Feature Films" and "Geography and Gender," which appear in rewritten form in his book *South of the West* (1992). Gibson used images from films such as *The Sons of Matthew* (1949), *Gallipoli* (1981), *Picnic at Hanging Rock* (1975), and *Mad Max II* (1981) in *Camera Natura* to answer the question he set for himself in the initial article:

"What can the preoccupation [with the landscape] tell us about Australian culture, cinematic and general?" Gibson's essaying in this film involved the same elliptical image-voice relationship that is evident in the seminal role model for this mode: Chris Marker's *Sunless* (1983), except that *Camera Natura* exhibits a critical poesy informed by a postcolonial and deconstructionist examination of Australian film culture evident in several independent films of the early to mid-1980s. These include Helen Grace's *Serious Undertakings* (1983) and Tracey Moffatt's *Nice Coloured Girls* (1987).

Although *Camera Natura* involves a bricolage of images, voices, and sounds, it contained a distinct line of argument, which is that the dominance of landscape images in Australian feature films of the 1970s and early 1980s can be linked to a reemergent nationalism at the time, and the landscape was seen as a delimited, manageable source of "Australianness." In this respect, *Camera Natura* could be called an "essay in futility," bolstered by the inclusion of such images as the girls entering the rock from *Picnic at Hanging Rock*, footage of Donald Campbell's failed attempt at the world land speed record, and of Jack Thompson crashing his car from *Sunday Too Far Away* (1975). The idea of nonproductivity that these images denote implies that Australian film culture was exhausting itself and creating few future opportunities for itself.

Formally, *Camera Natura* is an adventurous departure from traditional documentary practices, including poetic and evocative voice-overs, drawing on the "personal" style associated with a lineage of writing that can be traced back to the writing of the sixteenth-century essayist Michel de Montaigne. The film is also partly a compilation film, drawing on a host of images and sounds from Australian feature films to reconfigure these images and sounds in relation to the contemporary Australian social imaginary. In this regard the critical aspect of *Camera Natura* is related to the kind of postcolonial critique operating in a host of Australian films, all of which are concerned with examining white settler culture's inherited discursive patterns.

DEANE WILLIAMS

Camera Natura (Australia, 1984, 32 min) Distributed by Ronin Films. Directed and written by Ross Gibson.

Camera Natura, 1982.
[*Still courtesy of the British Film Institute*]

Produced by John Cruthers. Cinematography by Ray Argall. Edited by Ian Allen. Sound by John Cruthers. Commentary by Vivienne Garrett, Alan Becher, Susan Dermody and Steve Bisley.

Further Reading

Gibson, Ross, *The Diminishing Paradise: Changing Literary Perceptions of Australia*, Sydney: Sirius-Angus and Robertson, 1984.

Gibson, Ross, *South of the West: Postcolonialism and the Narrative Construction of Australia*, Bloomington: Indiana University Press, 1992.

Martin, Adrian, and Tina Kaufman, "Bushed: An Interview with Ross Gibson," in *Filmnews*, 16, 1986, 9–10.

Williams, Deane, "From *Camera Natura* to *Dead to the World*," *Metro*, 86, 1991, 27–31.

Williams, Deane, *Mapping the Imaginary: Ross Gibson's Camera Natura*, Melbourne: Australian Film Institute/ Australian Teachers of Media, 1996.

CAMERA TECHNOLOGY

Since the emergence of documentary filmmaking as a distinct genre in the interwar period, two important features of documentary filmmaking have included a lower budget in comparison to feature films and a preference for location filmmaking. The first factor is important, as it often led documentary filmmakers to use less expensive film cameras, particularly 16mm cameras (though this was not the case with Grierson's documentary film movement). At this stage, however, 16mm was considered an "amateur" gauge and was therefore restricted to amateur documentary filmmakers, including left-wing filmmakers. The majority of documentary films were still shot on 35mm.

The preference for location filmmaking is also an important factor relating to camera technology, as it paved the way for one of the most dramatic periods of innovation in documentary filmmaking:

direct cinema. Location footage was often difficult to capture in a spontaneous manner, which necessitated extensive preplanning (and occasionally the use of studio reconstructions). In addition, sound cameras were so heavy that the ability to capture synchronised sound and cover movement at the same time was extremely difficult. Both of these aspects restricted documentary filmmakers' ability to capture life as it was lived, which was becoming an increasing concern.

In the late 1950s, a number of filmmakers in America, including Richard Leacock and the Maysles brothers, sought to transform documentary filmmaking through modifying camera technology so that real life could be captured in a far more spontaneous, immediate fashion. A series of camera modifications led to a stage where a lightweight camera was synchronised with a mobile sound unit, so that life could be captured "on the move." This led direct cinema filmmakers largely dropping narration from their films. In France, Andre Coutant made a similar breakthrough with his Éclair camera, which would eventually become the most favoured lightweight camera amongst documentary cameramen in the 1960s and 1970s (a prototype version of this camera was used on Rouch's *Chronique d'un ete* [1959]).

The technical modifications and aesthetic breakthroughs achieved in direct cinema largely took place with the support of television backing (with the help of Time, Inc. who made films for ABC). Although this particular mode of cinema came to be largely sidelined by television, the medium of television provided a new, dominant site for the production of documentaries and could provide this mode of filmmaking with a more secure financial backing. In Britain, direct cinema did not become a common fixture, but the use of 16mm lightweight cameras did create more mobile and exterior-based documentary productions.

Whilst video cameras were being used within documentary filming in the 1960s, they were rarely used for such purposes. During the 1970s and 1980s, video gradually superseded the use of 16mm film in the shooting of documentary. This was a cheaper alternative, but it did not lead to any comparable aesthetic breakthroughs. Brian Winston, for example, argues: "Video was introduced to documentary without much fanfare and has thus far had a less radical effect on production norms and aesthetics than did the move from older methods to 16mm synch" (Winston, 1995: 206). He contends that video has, however, heightened the

trends that 16mm set in place. Its cheapness compared to film means that much more footage can be shot and then edited down, which allowed for an extension of the "fly on the wall approach," in that the minutiae of everyday life could be captured in more detail. In addition, video cameras could shoot in much lower lighting conditions than film cameras, which meant that camera mobility could be extended into darkness with more ease. This had the added advantage of further reducing the number of film crew, which aided the ability to capture the spontaneous events of everyday life. Some filmmakers did not appreciate video cameras, however, bemoaning its image quality in comparison to film. Videotape was also seen to offer less flexibility within the editing department.

However, Winston fails to mention the new forms of documentary material that were being produced with low-tech camcorders, which were becoming increasingly used by amateurs during the 1980s. The large uptake of camcorders was reflected on broadcast television during the 1990s, which began to show homemade "diary" films, most famously in the United Kingdom with *Video Nation* (BBC, 1994–1999), a much more "subjective" approach to documentation than "fly on the wall" documentaries.

Another important development was the use of surveillance footage within television documentaries, such as closed camera TV (CCTV) footage. Such cameras were of course not designed for filmmaking, but the extraordinary amount of footage obtained by these cameras has led to a market in selling such footage, which can then be incorporated into documentaries. Crime programming, in particular, has benefited from the availability of such footage, with UK series such as *Police, Camera, Action* (ITV, 1994–) and *Crime Beat* (BBC, 1995–1999) proving popular with audiences. Subsequently, surveillance cameras have been incorporated more directly into programming formats, particularly within the genre known as "reality television," the most famous example undoubtedly being *Big Brother* (first shown in the Netherlands, 1999), which proved to be popular in a number of different countries. With CCTV footage, the "objectivity" of observation becomes extended by the absence of a camera director, as well as the possibility that those filmed are not aware of the camera's presence. In reality television, this "objectivity" is somewhat attenuated through the way in which the cameras are manipulated for creative/entertainment purposes, as well as the fact that the filmed subjects are aware of the presence of these cameras.

The emergence of digital technology has opened up documentary filmmaking to a whole new generation of filmmakers. The affordability of many digital cameras has led to their adoption amongst a range of practitioners, many of whom can gain control of such equipment because of its extreme lightness and increasing miniaturisation. This also enables for a more "personal" approach to filming, because filming crews can be reduced to the singular. Though a film made by a single person, without much film training, on a tiny digital camera, may not be sufficient for screening on broadcast television or on a conventional cinema screen, the opportunities offered by other digital developments within postproduction and exhibition potentially enable such films to be seen on a wider basis than previously. It is now possible for a single individual to edit his or her own work on a home computer and to get the film screened on the Internet, with many new websites emerging to screen new work. Thus digital cameras, in association with other technologies, have led to the production of a great number of documentaries by both personal and political filmmakers working outside of the conventional media structures.

JAMIE SEXTON

See also **Leacock, Richard; Maysles, Albert**

Further Reading

Coe, Brian, *The History of Movie Photography*, Westfield, NJ: Eastview Editions, 1981.

Corner, John, *The Art of Record: A Critical Introduction to Documentary*, Manchester: Manchester University Press, 1996.

Dovey, Jon, *Freakshow: First Person Media and Factual Television*, London: Pluto, 2000.

Fielding, Raymond (ed.), *A Technological History of Motion Pictures and Television*, Los Angeles: University of California Press, 1967.

MacGregor, Brent, with Roddy Simpson, "Towards Defining the Digital Documentary," in *From Grierson to the Docu-Soap: Breaking the Boundaries*, edited by John Izod, Richard Kilborn, and Matthew Hibberd, Luton: University of Luton Press, 2000.

Mamber, Stephen, *Cinéma Vérité in America: Studies in Uncontrolled Documentaries*, Cambridge, MA and London: MIT, 1974.

Salt, Barry, *Film Style and Technology: History and Analysis*, London: Starword, 1992.

Winston, Brian, *Claiming the Real: The Documentary Film Revisited*, London: BFI, 1995.

Winston, Brian, *Technologies of Seeing: Photography, Cinematography and Television*, London: BFI, 1996.

CANADA

If documentary is the "the creative treatment of actuality," as John Grierson said, then in the beginning there was a lot more actuality then creative treatment. However, the actuality was not Canadian and the pattern that prevailed throughout the twentieth century was established. Moving pictures shown in Canadian theatres were rarely Canadian.

Lumière Bros representatives, Messieurs Minier and Pupier, brought moving pictures to Canada with a cinematographe screening in Montreal on June 27, 1896, at 78 Boulevard St. Laurent. Among the early Lumiere films shown that night were a train arriving at a station, a cavalry charge, waves breaking against rocks at the seashore, a card game between Lumiere and friends in a garden, and a wall being torn down.

Three weeks later, on July 21, 1896, the rival Edison Vitascope was shown to an outdoor audience in Ottawa at the West End Park. Organized by Andrew and George Holland, the evening included live tricks on stage by pioneer exhibitor John C. Green, then known as Belsaz the Magician. The audience saw May Irwin, Canadian actress from Whitby, Ontario, kiss John Rice, as well as a train, a bathing scene at Atlantic City, four "coloured boys" eating watermelons, and LoLo Fuller's serpentine dance.

Itinerant cameramen, such as Felix Mesguich and W.K.L. Dickson, began arriving in 1897 to shoot "scenics" of the Canadian landscape. They usually headed for Niagara Falls, which was added time and again to the exotic sights seen by film viewers around the world. Robert Bonine went further afield to shoot footage of the Klondike Gold Rush.

James D. Freer, a Manitoba farmer and cinema hobbyist, is probably Canada's first filmmaker. He shot local scenes in 1897 and then was hired by the

Canadian Pacific Railway (CPR) to tour Britain, showing his films and promoting immigration to Canada's "golden west." The CPR ensured that winter scenes were not on the program. Thus began a long tradition of sponsored films by the CPR, which led to the creation of a production company, Associated Screen News. Massey-Harris, which made farm equipment, and other companies also began sponsoring films.

The Battle for Canadian Screens

Leo-Ernest Ouimet, who established Canada's first luxury movie theatre in Montreal in 1906, soon began showing his own newsreels. After World War I, he started the twice-weekly *British Canadian Pathe News* (1919–1922), which combined Canadian and British newsreel items. Though popular, it could not compete with better funded and distributed American newsreels.

In fact, led by Adolph Zukor's Paramount, the major American companies were vertically integrating into exhibition, distribution, and production by the end of the war. This "Hollywood studio system" left little room for an independent film industry in the United States or Canada. By 1922, the Allen's, the largest Canadian exhibitor and one of the largest theatre chains in the world, went bankrupt competing against Famous Players, Paramount's Canadian theatre chain.

Private Canadian producers, such as Ouimet or Ernest Shipman, whose most successful film was the feature drama *Back to God's Country* (1919), could no longer access the first-run Canadian theatre screens if they were outside the Hollywood system. They had to leave Canada and move to Los Angeles or New York if they wanted their films seen in Canada, or anywhere else.

The Canadian public did not seem concerned that their movie theatres showed mostly American films until the United States entered World War I. Then Canadians were outraged by patriotic war movies awash in American flags that ignored the sacrifices of the French, British, and Canadians on the Western Front. Led by the Ontario Government, and soon followed by the federal government, public production bureaus were established to make Canadian nonfiction films.

State production of films in Canada began in 1917 with the establishment of the Ontario Government Motion Picture Bureau (1917–1934). The Ontario Bureau produced educational films, often on agricultural subjects, until it was closed down during the Depression. It was soon followed by the Canadian Government Motion Picture Bureau,

which was absorbed by the National Film Board during World War II (see later). Thus, the National Film Board and its predecessors is probably the oldest continuously operating public film producer in the world (1918–).

Besides direct production through the public sector, the Canadian Government Motion Picture Bureau, and the Ontario Bureau to the NFB, the most important impetus to the production of Canadian nonfiction films was the Ontario "talking newsreel" quota. This provincial screen-time quota was established in 1930 and continued until the end of theatrical newsreels in the 1950s. It required that each newsreel had to have 40 percent "British Empire" content, including 25 percent Canadian content. This created a theatrical market for Canadian newsreel items. Some private newsreel producers, such as Associated Screen News, then expanded into related documentary production.

Later, with the arrival of television, similar measures were tried, and Canadian programming was assured through the production of the public broadcaster and Canadian content quotas for all broadcasters.

Documentary Explorers

Explorers increasingly used film to record their work and help raise funds for their explorations. From 1913 to 1916, George H. Wilkins filmed Canadian explorer Vilhjalmur Stefanssons's expedition in the Arctic. Richard S. Finnie shot many films about the North and directed the first Canadian feature documentary for the Canadian Government Motion Picture Bureau, *In the Shadow of the Pole* (1928), which recorded Canada's 1928 Arctic expedition.

Explorers like Robert Flaherty in northern Quebec, or Varick Frissell in Labrador, used film to document their work. Then, following the lead of Edward Curtis, they began to record the life of the people they knew and respected before their way of life was gone.

American photographer Edward S. Curtis had begun a lifelong project to record the American Indians before they disappeared. In 1914, he extended this work to create a "documentary drama" using Kwakiutl natives of British Columbia as actors. His film, *In the Land of the War Canoes* (1914), however, is more fiction than nonfiction, more drama than documentary.

Varick Frissell was an American who had been drawn to the work of the Grenfell Mission in northern Newfoundland and went on to explore the interior of Labrador. By 1930, Frissell had raised enough money to produce a feature based on his own experiences in the seal hunt. At the insistence of the distributor, Paramount Pictures, *The Viking* (1931) had a romantic story and drama sequences directed by George Melford. Frissell directed the incredible documentary sequences in the film. These cost him his life when his ship blew up while he was filming.

Robert Flaherty, another American who grew up in Canadian mining camps and had spent most of his life in Canada, explored and prospected along Hudson's Bay for the Canadian Northern Railway. His employer, Sir William Mackenzie, encouraged Flaherty to record the life of the Inuit on film. In 1913, Flaherty began taking camera gear on his prospecting trips. His first film on Inuit life caught fire while being edited in Toronto. Undeterred, Flaherty returned to Hudson's Bay with the support of France's Revillon Freres fur traders. His second film was also produced with the help of Inuit, from developing film to suggesting ideas to shoot. *Nanook of the North* (1922) was about survival in the Arctic, and its dramatic footage was real, or seemed real. It was a hit around the world.

Robert Flaherty created a new film form by successfully marrying nonfiction, or apparent nonfiction, with a narrative story line. Flaherty wanted a film showing the Inuit before their use of firearms, so his work is not an accurate record of the period. Yet *Nanook* seems true in its whole if not its parts, and it is usually considered the first Canadian documentary and indeed the first documentary ever made. Flaherty's work was an inspiration to a young John Grierson who developed a close, and often contentious, relationship with Flaherty.

Associated Screen News

The most important early Canadian production company was Associated Screen News (ASN), which was organized in 1920 in Montreal by the Canadian Pacific Railway. Ben Norrish moved from the public sector to run this company until it was sold in the 1950s. ASN produced sponsored films, newsreel segments, and theatrical shorts. It also depended on release print laboratory work from Hollywood companies.

A series of monthly nonfiction theatrical shorts called *Canadian Cameos* (1932–1954) was produced by Gordon Sparling for ASN. One of the best of these is *Rhapsody in Two Languages* (1934), which Sparling directed in the "city symphony" style with imaginative special effects. It is about a day in the life of Montreal and is one of the first Canadian

sound films to have an original music score (by Howard Fogg).

Sparling directed *Royal Banners Over Ottawa* (1939), a record of the Royal visit to Canada's capitol. This is the first Canadian documentary shot in colour. Sparling also ran the Army Film and Photo Unit during the war and, after ASN's production department was closed down in 1957, he joined the National Film Board.

Crawley Films

The Canadian Film Awards was organized in 1949 and was Canada's first competitive film festival. Its first "Film of the Year Award" went to a short documentary on Indian masks titled *The Loon's Necklace* (1948) by F.R. (Budge) Crawley and his wife Judith. Budge Crawley produced *Newfoundland Scene* (1952), which also won the Canadian Film Awards' "Film of the Year." Budge and Judy Crawley set up their film company in Ottawa during the war, but it came to national attention after winning these awards. Crawley Films grew, depending primarily on sponsored production, and became the largest private film production house in Canada from the 1950s to the 1970s. Toward the end of his career, Budge Crawley risked his company by making feature films, and Crawley films had to be sold for its debt in 1982. (See *Janis* and *The Man Who Skied Down Everest*.)

Canadian Government Motion Picture Bureau

In response to requests for films on Canada's resources and industry, the Canadian Government established a film production unit in 1918 under Ben Norrish, who moved on to ASN. This Publicity and Exhibits Bureau produced a successful series of theatrical shorts, *Seeing Canada* (1919–1939), to encourage tourism and foreign investment.

Under Raymond Peck, the Publicity and Exhibits Bureau was renamed the Canadian Government Motion Picture Bureau in 1923. The Bureau's most ambitious project was the feature documentary *Lest We Forget* (1935), produced and directed by Frank Badgley, who was also head of the Bureau. This film was a compilation documentary using newsreels, graphics, and reenacted scenes to tell the story of Canada's involvement in World War I.

NFB and John Grierson

Under the leadership of John Grierson, the work of the British Documentary Movement in the

1930s impressed Ross McLean, a member of the Canadian High Commission in London. By contrast, the films of the Canadian Government Motion Picture Bureau seemed dull and uninspired. Ross McLean believed that Grierson could do something about that.

In 1938, the Canadian Government invited Grierson to report on the work of the Bureau, and how it might be improved. Grierson quickly wrote a report that recommended a new organization be established to centralize all government film production. The National Film Board of Canada (NFB) was established in Ottawa in 1939 under its first Government Film Commissioner and CEO, John Grierson (1939–1945). The Canadian Government Motion Picture Bureau was absorbed by the NFB in 1941.

The war provided a propaganda focus for the NFB, which quickly grew under Grierson's energetic leadership. Grierson invited veteran documentary filmmakers, such as Boris Kaufman and Joris Ivens, to work at the Ottawa offices of the Board, which were located in an old sawmill. Members of the British Documentary Movement, such as Stanley Hawes, Stuart Legg, Raymond Spottiswoode, and Norman McLaren, arrived to teach documentary and animation to their young staff.

Canadians hired by Grierson included Tom Daly, Sydney Newman, Louis Applebaum, Jim McKay, Vincent Paquette, Margaret Ann Adamson, George Dunning, Lorne Greene, Donald Buchanan, Grant McLean, Jim Beveridge, Jane Marsh Beveridge, Julian Roffman, Evelyn Spice Cherry, Lawrence Cherry, Guy Glover, and many more. At war's end the NFB had a staff of more than 700 employees.

The Case of Charlie Gordon (1939), directed by Stuart Legg, was the first film distributed by the NFB. The NFB went on to produce hundreds of films during the war but was best known for its two theatrical series of one- or two-reel shorts. The *Canada Carries On* (1940–1959) series was produced by Stuart Legg and began with the release of his *Atlantic Patrol* (1940).

The World in Action (1942–1945) series took a more international slant and began with a re-release of *Warclouds in the Pacific* (1941) by Stuart Legg. It warned of a possible Japanese attack on the American Pacific fleet. As a result of this timely film, the NFB got a contract to show this series in 6,000 American theatres. This series was also produced by Stuart Legg with the assistance of Tom Daly, using a great deal of compilation footage from all the combatants.

Other important titles included *Inside Fighting Russia* (1942), *Our Northern Neighbour* (1943), *The War for Men's Minds* (1943), and *Balkan Powder Keg* (1944).

The NFB won the first Oscar for documentary in 1941 with Legg's *Churchill's Island* (1941). It showed English resolve to resist an anticipated German invasion, and was narrated by Lorne Greene, who became known as "the voice of doom."

The Canadian Army Film and Photo Unit was created in 1943 to provide newsreel footage shot by Army cameramen. It included ASN's Gordon Sparling and future Canadian Film Development Corporation head Michael Spencer. However, Grierson was unsuccessful in his attempt to incorporate this unit into the NFB's operations.

The *Canada Carries On* theatrical series continued until 1959, as did the *Eye Witness/Coup d'oeil* (1947–1959) series, which replaced the *World in Action* series. But Grierson often said that there are more seats in community halls than in theatres.

In 1942, Donald Buchanan, co-founder of the National Film Society in 1935, was hired by the NFB to organize nontheatrical film circuits. Itinerant NFB projectionists took films to rural, industrial, and union audiences. In 1943, the Volunteer Projection Service was established to encourage film distribution to urban community groups not covered by the industrial or trade union circuits. More than 600 libraries distributed NFB films under contract by the end of the war. After the war, the film circuits continued as Film Councils, which numbered nearly 500 in 1955.

John Grierson resigned as Government Film Commissioner in November 1945, and was replaced by his deputy Ross McLean (1945–1950). Now at the peak of his influence, Grierson became one of the first victims of the Cold War red scare. Cipher clerk Igor Gouzenko defected from the Soviet Embassy in Ottawa with documents proving the Soviets ran a spy ring in Canada during the war. One ambivalent reference to Grierson cast suspicion on him. As the red scare deepened, the staff of the NFB came under growing suspicion. The new Film Commissioner Arthur Irwin (1950–1953) let some staff go to satisfy the Board's political critics.

NFB's Unit B

After World War II, NFB filmmakers wanted their work identified with screen credits that Grierson had discouraged to avoid undermining anonymous "public service" values. When the NFB was reorganized into four production units in 1948, the "ungriersonian" idea that "public service" filmmakers should be recognized as artists took hold and screen credits were initiated.

Unit B was responsible for scientific, cultural, and animated films. Under executive producer Tom Daly, Unit B became known for its groundbreaking work that won numerous awards and gave the NFB an international reputation for quality and innovation. The core of Unit B included Roman Kroitor, Wolf Koenig, Terry Macartney-Filgate, Stanley Jackson, Colin Low, Bob Verrall, Bill Greaves, Don Owen, Gerald Potterton, Arthur Lipsett, as well as the veteran animator Norman McLaren.

Neighbours (1952), a live-action pixilation film by the NFB's Norman McLaren, won the Oscar for Best Documentary Short. This was a surprise because his film is not a documentary, but rather an animated drama. It also has a strong anti-war message, which one would not expect the American Academy to appreciate since it was at that time fighting the Cold War and losing soldiers in Korea.

One of the first films directed by Colin Low, and shot by Wolf Koenig, was *Corral* (1954), about a cowboy breaking a wild horse on a ranch in Alberta. Breaking with traditional griersonian voice-over narration, Eldon Rathburn's guitar score is the only sound in the film. Another important NFB production was *Paul Tomkowicz: Street-railway Switchman* (1954), directed by Roman Kroitor. It is a melancholy "film noir" short about an immigrant who keeps the trolleys running through Winnipeg's severe winter.

American ex-patriot Bill Greaves joined Unit B as an editor. When he directed the NFB documentary *Putting It Straight* (1957), he became Canada's first black filmmaker. Encouraged by the Civil Rights movement, Greaves returned to New York and continued his film career.

Using an animation stand modified by Roman Kroitor, Wolf Koenig and Colin Low successfully combined historical photos and new footage in *City of Gold* (1957). A new kind of photo-documentary, their evocative film about the Klondike Gold Rush was narrated by Yukon native Pierre Berton.

NFB and Cinema Verité

The NFB was a key innovator in the worldwide race to produce location synch-sound films better known as cinema verité or "direct cinema." The Board's staff worked on many technical innovations to make its 16mm synch-sound production equipment much lighter and more portable. The key to the NFB's early handheld shooting was the "Sprocketape" portable magnetic sound recorder invented by Ches Beachell in 1955.

Influenced by the work of French photographer Henri Cartier-Bresson, Unit B experimented with cinema verité sequences in the *Candid Eye* (1958–1959) TV series. *Days Before Christmas* (1958) directed by Terry Macartney-Filgate, Stanley Jackson, and Wolf Koenig is a pastiche of events preceding 1957's Christmas in Montreal, and includes some of the first handheld synch-sound location shooting. Terry Macartney-Filgate's *The Back-breaking Leaf* (1959), about migrant tobacco workers in Ontario, used more extensive synch-sound location shooting.

The *Candid Eye* films, together with NFB French-language productions such as Michel Brault and Gilles Groulx's *Les Raquetteurs* (1958), as well as the work of Robert Drew Associates in New York, Jean Rouch in Paris, and the Free Cinema filmmakers in England, began the cinema verité documentary movement.

Perhaps the most important cinema verité film made at this time was *Lonely Boy* (1961) directed by Wolf Koenig and Roman Kroitor and shot by Koenig. It is a portrait of Canadian teenage pop singer Paul Anka. This film experiments with sound as well as image and "reflexively" puts the filmmakers into the story.

Although not a Unit B alumnus, ex-journalist Don Brittain becomes one of the NFB's foremost documentary filmmakers with a cinema verité portrait of Canada's greatest living poet in *Ladies and Gentleman . . . Mr. Leonard Cohen* (1965), co-directed with Don Owen. Brittain then co-directed and wrote *Memorandum* (1965) with cinematographer John Spotton. This film blends archival and cinema verité footage to create a moving testament to the Holocaust. Later in his career, Brittain increasingly turned to drama documentary and TV drama in a series of CBC-NFB co-productions.

NFB's Labyrinth

The Montreal World's Fair, Expo 67, was a showcase for film experimentation and prestige multiscreen or large screen projects. Two notable Canadian contributions were antecedents of IMAX. One was *A Place to Stand* (1967) by

Chris Chapman, a multi-image short projected in 70mm on a large screen at the Ontario Pavilion. The other was the NFB's most ambitious project, its *Labyrinth* pavilion for Expo 67, created by Hugh O'Connor, Roman Kroitor, and Colin Low. They invented a cruciform, multi-image screen as well as a display on two screens at a ninety-degree angle from each other. The $4.5 million pavilion was a stunning success with more than 1.3 million visitors.

Kroitor, Graeme Ferguson, and Robert Kerr formed the Multiscreen Corporation to bring the new IMAX format to the Osaka World's Fair. Their first IMAX film was *Tiger Child* (1970), directed by Don Brittain. Graeme Ferguson directed *North of Superior* (1971), which opened the first dedicated IMAX theatre, the Cinesphere in Toronto. IMAX films are also projected in 360-degree dome theatres called OMNIMAX. The first 3-D IMAX film, *Transitions* (1986), by Colin Low and Tony Ianzelo, was produced by the NFB for Vancouver's Expo 86. (See also *Titanica*.)

NFB's Challenge for Change

The Things I Cannot Change (1966), directed by Tanya Ballantyne, shot by Paul Leach, and produced by John Kemeny, is a cinema verité film about a poor Montreal family. Unfortunately, the family was ridiculed after the film was broadcast, and they decided to leave their neighbourhood. However, the film was a critical success and sparked the groundbreaking *Challenge for Change* (1967–1980) program of social action filmmaking developed by John Kemeny, Colin Low, and George C. Stoney.

A French counterpart, *Société nouvelle*, was established under producer Léonard Forest. *Challenge for Change/Société nouvelle* experimented with half-inch video technology as early as 1967. *VTR St-Jacques* (1969) by Bonnie Sherr Klein and Dorothy Henaut was produced entirely on videotape. Despite the occasional controversy, this innovative program produced about 140 films, which encouraged communication between the disenfranchised and the decision makers. It was renewed until 1980.

NFB and Aboriginal Production

Challenge for Change changed the way the NFB, and perhaps the country, looked at native issues when it brought together natives from across the country to learning filmmaking skills. The most significant result was *The Ballad of Crowfoot*

(1968) by Willie Dunn, a compilation documentary of photos and old footage about the white man's broken promises. The sound track is a bitter ballad written and sung by Dunn.

Other important *Challenge for Change* films on native issues include *You Are on Indian Land* (1969) by Mort Ransen, which showed natives demonstrating at a Mohawk reserve on the St. Lawrence River. *Cree Hunters of Mistassini* (1974) by Boyce Richardson and Tony Ianzelo follows Cree families at a winter camp and shows the ecological principles that guide their way of life.

The best known aboriginal filmmaker in Canada is the NFB's Alanis Obomsawin. Her work has documented social and political problems, often providing historical context. Obomsawin made *Kanehsatake: 270 Years of Resistance* (1993) and *Rocks at Whiskey Trench* (2000) about the confrontation between natives and the military at a Mohawk reserve near Montreal.

NFB's Studio D

In 1974, *Challenge for Change* producer Kathleen Shannon (*Working Mothers* series, 1974) succeeded in setting up a feminist production studio to "make films by, for, and about women." *Studio D* was known for innovative nontheatrical distribution and controversial films. It also won more Oscars than any other NFB studio, often for content more than filmmaking style. Oscar winners are *I'll Find A Way* (1977) by Beverly Shaffer, who interviewed a child with spina bifida; *If You Love This Planet* (1983) by Terre Nash, an antinuclear war speech by Dr. Helen Caldicott; and *Flamenco at 5:15* (1984) by Cynthia Scott, which gives an impressionistic view of a flamenco class at the National Ballet School of Canada.

Among the studio's more controversial and popular films were *Not a Love Story: A Film About Pornography* (1981) by Bonnie Sherr Klein and Dorothy Henaut, and *Forbidden Love: The Unashamed Stories of Lesbian Lives* (1993) by Margaret Pettigrew, Aerlyn Weissman, and Lynne Fernie about the portrayal of the lesbian subculture of the 1950s and 1960s. Studio D was closed down as the NFB faced growing financial pressures in the mid-1990s.

NFB Decentralization

The NFB moved its headquarters from the Ottawa sawmill to a new building in Montreal. This move had a large impact on the use of

French at the Board, and the balance of relations between the linguistic groups. Guy Roberge (1957–1966), former Liberal member of the Quebec National Assembly, replaced Albert Trueman (1953–1957) as Government Film Commissioner and CEO of the NFB. He was the first francophone Film Commissioner and, arguably, his tenure marked the creative peak of the Board.

The NFB set up an autonomous French Production unit under Fernand Dansereau in 1962. In 1964, Pierre Juneau was appointed director of French Production and Grant McLean headed English Production. McLean dismantled the producer-run unit system in favour of the "pool" system, which gave greater autonomy to directors through a program committee, and decentralized program planning.

The 1965 Sheppard Report, commissioned by the Government from filmmaker Gordon Sheppard, recommended that the NFB should "gradually cease to staff-produce most of its films and instead have the majority of them made by private Canadian producers and freelancers on contract." Partly in response to the Sheppard Report, the NFB took the first steps toward regionalization of English production by setting up an office in Vancouver under Peter Jones in 1965. Eventually, most English production was produced by regional offices from Vancouver to Halifax. Over time, regionalization and privatization had a radical impact on the NFB and Canadian filmmaking.

"Make or Buy?"

The Canadian Government had responded to the problems of a small and linguistically fragmented market by establishing public-sector production organizations such as the NFB and CBC. The private sector producers then complained about the resources going to the public sector and successfully lobbied to have public-funding schemes created to finance private or independent production such as the Canadian Film Development Corporation in 1967 (now Telefilm Canada) or the Canadian Broadcast Program Development Fund in 1983 (now the Canadian Television Fund).

This production funding was aimed at independent producers but also supported private commercial broadcasters. As a result, direct funding for vertically integrated public producers or broadcasters, such as the NFB and CBC, has declined. The government has shifted its emphasis from "make" in the public sector to "buy" in the private sector. Now it is often difficult to tell whether a documentary is an "NFB film," a "CBC film," or "independent."

Decline of the NFB

NFB budgets declined beginning in 1968 when the federal government announced austerity measures that reduced NFB revenues. In addition, the filmmakers and technicians organized a union and negotiated a collective agreement that increased the Board's costs. Hugo McPherson, the new Film Commissioner (1967–1970), was forced to fire recently hired staff. Caught between ongoing financial cuts and filmmaker discontent, McPherson resigned in 1970.

French and English tensions increased during the tenure of Sydney Newman (1970–1975). He was a unilingual NFB wartime producer who had worked extensively in British television drama. Despite the appointment of francophone producer Andre Lamy as his deputy, Newman had ongoing problems with Quebec nationalist filmmakers. Andre Lamy (1975–1979) succeeded Newman as Film Commissioner.

In 1980, the Federal Cultural Policy Review Committee was created and chaired by Louis Applebaum and Jacques Hebert. Its "Applebert" report suggested that the NFB had outlived its usefulness, and all of its production should be in the private sector. The report recommended that the NFB should be scaled back to a research and training facility. NFB head James Domville (1979–1984) forcefully rejected this recommendation, but the report influenced government policy.

In 1984, Minister of Communications, Francis Fox, released his "National Film and Video Policy," which significantly reduced the responsibilities and size of the NFB. The Board lost control of government-sponsored films, the still photo unit, film certification, and most of its foreign offices.

The new Film Commissioner, Francois Macerola (1984–1988), was forced to initiate more cutbacks, and he then faced a major controversy. The docudrama *The Kid Who Couldn't Miss* (1982) by Paul Cowan claimed that Canada's most famous World War I flying ace, Billy Bishop, had lied about the number of enemy planes he shot down. Veterans' groups were outraged, though they could not disprove the thesis of the film. A Senate subcommittee requested that the NFB withdraw the film, but Film Commissioner Francois Macerola refused. A compromise was reached and a credit was added to the film that it was interpretive and dramatic in nature.

After Macerola, Joan Pennefather (1989–1994) became the first woman to head the NFB and celebrated its fiftieth anniversary in 1989. Sandra MacDonald (1995–2001) replaced her and faced the most severe of many funding cutbacks in 1995 and 1996. MacDonald cut 180 jobs, closed the Board's film laboratory, and rented out the soundstage. Jacques Bensimon became Film Commissioner in 2001. In constant dollars, the current budget of the NFB is about 25 percent of its budget in 1966, and nearly all of its productions now require some outside financing and are made by freelance filmmakers.

Canadian Broadcasting Corporation

In 1952 Canadian Broadcasting Corporation Chair and CEO Davidson Dunton launched Canadian television in Toronto and Montreal. The American television networks wanted the CBC to become their affiliate and launched a program boycott that lasted three months. Dunton overcame the boycott, and the CBC won the battle for control of television in Canada. TV soon became the primary distribution outlet for documentaries.

CBC Public Affairs Series

The line between CBC documentaries and public affairs programs has not always been clear. The development of CBC public affairs programs began with *Tabloid* (1953–1963) and *Close-Up* (1957–1963), which were produced by Ross McLean (no relation to the NFB's Ross McLean) and his protégées, Douglas Leiterman and Patrick Watson.

Leiterman and Watson, influenced by the cinema verité movement and the British program, *This Was the Week That Was* (1962–1963), developed the hugely popular and controversial *This Hour Has Seven Days* (1964–1966). This program was cancelled by the CBC in a clash between senior management and the producers over control of the program's content and its increasingly dramatic, even theatrical, approach to journalism.

Douglas Leiterman and Patrick Watson left Canada after the program was cancelled and worked for some years in New York. There Leiterman was involved in the development of CBS's *60 Minutes* public affairs series, while Patrick Watson hosted WNET's public affairs program *The Fifty-First State*. He later produced the series *The Struggle for Democracy* (1989–1990) with Ted

Remerowski, Nancy Button, and Michael Levine, which was broadcast by CBC.

Following *Seven Days*, the flagship CBC public affairs series has been *the fifth estate* (1974–). Its best known documentary was *Just Another Missing Kid* (1982) by Ian Parker and John Zaritsky, which won the 1983 Oscar. *The Trouble with Evan* (1994) by Neil Docherty recorded a troubled young boy's home life using cameras attached to ceilings in his family's apartment. There was no camera crew for much of the film.

The CBC moved the twenty-two-minute national news from 11 to 10 PM and added a public affairs segment called *The Journal* (1982–1992) for the balance of the hour. This new program was produced by Mark Starowicz and proved a popular success.

The longest running public affairs series has been the science program, *The Nature of Things* (1961–), first produced by James Murray. It is currently produced by Michael Allder, hosted by David Suzuki, and called *The Nature of Things with David Suzuki* (1980–). This program has been a powerful voice, and Suzuki a popular advocate for environmental issues.

CBC Documentary Series

As early as 1953, the CBC established a film unit in Vancouver under Stan Fox. It became a training ground for Allan King, Ron Kelly, Daryl Duke, Gene Lawrence, Arla Saare, and many others. Memorable among these early CBC documentaries was *Skid Row* (1956) by Allan King.

The *Document* (1962–1969) series was also produced by Douglas Leiterman and Patrick Watson and later Richard Nielsen. It often ran cinema verité documentaries. Among the most powerful were *The Seven Hundred Million* (1964) by Patrick Watson about China; *Summer in Mississippi* (1964) by Beryl Fox about the Civil Rights movement in the U.S. South, and *Mills of the Gods: Vietnam* (1965) directed by Beryl Fox, shot by Erik Durschmeid, and edited by Don Haig. This was one of the earliest films critical of the Vietnam War and is considered by some to be the best Canadian documentary of all time.

After the demise of *Document*, the centre of documentary gravity in the CBC moved from Toronto to Ottawa. Cameron Graham produced a number of important series such as *The Tenth Decade* (1971) about Canada from 1957 to 1967; *First Person Singular* (1973 and 1975), with Munroe Scott, the memoirs of former Prime Minister Lester Pearson; *The Days Before Yesterday* (1973), with Brian Nolan, Scott, and Ed Reid, about Canadian history in the first half of the twentieth century; and *The Canadian Establishment* (1980–1981) with Marrin Canell, Ted Remerowski, and Peter Pearson and based on Peter C. Newman's book. James Murray produced the extremely popular *The National Dream* (1974) narrated by Pierre Berton and based on his history of the Canadian Pacific Railway.

Besides *The Journal*, Mark Starowicz produced an hour-long anthology documentary series called *Witness* (1982–2003). This was the major venue for one-off prime time documentaries on the English network and included documentaries from Canada and around the world.

The most ambitious documentary series the CBC ever attempted was the international coproduction *Canada: A People's History* (2000). This seventeen-part series included dramatic sequences in both languages was the brainchild of Mark Starowicz. It became a popular event attracting as many as 2.3 million English-speaking viewers.

Controversial CBC Documentaries

As a public broadcaster, controversial subjects often generate a great deal of criticism for the CBC. Therefore, management has sometimes been hesitant to broadcast a documentary it feared would cause controversy. More recently, the nature of the criticism, and the CBC's reaction to it, has changed.

The CBC refused to broadcast *Mr. Pearson* (1964) by Dick Ballentine and shot by Donn Pennebaker. This cinema verité portrait showed the Prime Minister in a sometimes unflattering light and was not broadcast until 1969 after Alphonse Ouimet had stepped down as president of the CBC.

The cinema verité classic *Warrendale* (1967), by Allan King, is about a controversial home for disturbed kids. It was never broadcast by the CBC because the children in the film used profanity. King then made the cinema verité *A Married Couple* (1969), shot by Richard Leiterman, about a disintegrating marriage. Gradually, he moved into dramatic films.

Perhaps the most influential CBC documentary was *Air of Death* (1967) by Larry Gosnell. This film raised questions about air pollution in a small Ontario town and helped start the environmental movement in Canada. It was attacked by the Ontario government and the industries in question. The federal regulator (CRTC) held a major hearing in 1969 to review the criticisms. The CBC stood by the program and said that a democratic society needed to see minority, or controversial, opinions. The CRTC agreed.

The Valour and the Horror (1992) was a brilliant series of three feature documentaries with dramatic segments. The series was a CBC, NFB, and Galafilm coproduction directed by Brian McKenna with Terrence McKenna and produced by Arnie Gelbart, Andre Lamy, Darce Fardy, Adam Symansky, and D'Arcy O'Connor. Particularly controversial was the episode *Death by Moonlight* (1992), which maintained that the bombing campaign against Germany was deliberately planned by Air Marshall Athur Harris to maximize civilian casualties. Veterans' organizations were outraged, though they couldn't dispute the facts cited, and Senator Jack Marshall investigated. The CBC seemed to indicate that it would be more careful in the future, especially with dramatic reenactments in documentaries. Together with the NFB's *The Kid Who Couldn't Miss*, it would seem that revisionist military history is the most sensitive subject on Canadian television.

Theatrical Feature Documentaries

The subjects of Canadian feature documentaries have evolved over the decades, from royal visits, wildlife, and shipwrecks to more controversial subjects. As the economics of the industry changed, feature documentaries also moved from NFB productions to NFB co-productions and independent films.

Theatrical dramas have also been influenced by Canadian documentary style, particularly in the 1960s and 1970s. Examples include the NFB's *Nobody Waved Goodbye* (1964) by Don Owen and the independent *Goin' Down the Road* (1970) by Don Shebib.

The NFB's *The Royal Journey* (1951), directed by David Bairstow, Gudrun Parker, and Roger Blais, recorded the visit of Princess Elizabeth and Prince Philip to Canada and the United States. It was shot in the new Eastman color negative stock. In three months, more than two million saw *The Royal Journey* in theatres, and it becomes Canada's most successful theatrical documentary feature.

Naturalist Bill Mason's NFB feature documentary about raising wolves, *Cry of the Wild* (1972), became a surprise hit, opening in 500 American theatres. It grossed $4.5 million in North America.

Budge Crawley had built the largest private film company in Canada on sponsored films, but he always had larger ambitions and wanted to produced features. *Janis* (1974), produced by Crawley and directed by Howard Alk and Seaton Findlay, is a compilation documentary on the life of singer Janis Joplin before her untimely death in 1970. *The Man Who Skied Down Everest* (1975) was produced and directed by Crawley from footage he acquired of Japanese skier Yuichiro Miura attempting to ski down Everest. It won the Oscar for best feature documentary.

Peter Wintonick and Mark Achbar co-produced with the NFB a magnum opus on Noam Chomsky titled *Manufacturing Consent: Noam Chomsky and the Media* (1992). This film found clever visual metaphors to demonstrate Chomsky's ideas about the media, as well as his life as a public intellectual. Despite its length and subject, it has grossed about $1 million in theatres worldwide.

Titanica (1992) was produced by Stephen Low and Pietro Serapiglia and directed by Stephen Low. It is a feature IMAX documentary about the exploration of the wreck of the Titanic. It has been one of the highest-grossing Canadian films.

Independent filmmaker Ron Mann has explored a range of marginal cultures through his feature documentaries. These include *Poetry in Motion* (1982), *Comic Book Confidential* (1988), and *Grass* (2000), which is about marijuana.

A Place Called Chiapas (1999) by Vancouver filmmaker Nettie Wild, is produced with Kirk Tougas and Betsy Carson It is a cinema verité look at the Zapatista uprising in Mexico that takes a strong political position.

Another independent Vancouver production, *The Corporation* (2003), directed by Mark Achbar and Jennifer Abbott, written by Joel Bakan, and produced by Bart Simpson, takes a critical look at capitalism by psychoanalyzing the corporation. It has grossed nearly $5 million in theatres worldwide.

At present, the audience for theatrical feature-length documentaries has never been greater or more interested in seeing a uncompromising point of view, as *The Corporation* and Michael Moore's *Fahrenheit 9/11* have shown.

Television Explosion: The Best of Times and the Worst of Times

Between 1952 and the arrival of commercial television in 1960, the CBC was the only television outlet for documentaries. As a public broadcaster, it accepted its responsibility to broadcast public affairs and documentaries. In general, the commercial channels were not interested in documentaries and preferred scheduling dramas, usually from the United States, which could attract larger audiences.

In 1970, the first provincial educational channel was set up in Ontario, *TVOntario*, and this was followed by a similar educational channel in Quebec in 1974, *Télé-Québec*. These, and other provincial channels that followed, increased the market for documentaries, but they could not pay as much as national broadcasters.

Three fundamental changes occurred in the broadcasting landscape in the 1980s and 1990s that increased the demand for, and supply of, Canadian documentaries. First, in 1983, the federal government set up the *Canadian Broadcast Program Development Fund* (now called the *Canadian Television Fund*) with $35 million to support independent television production. Some of this money, as well as tax benefits, was available for documentaries. The creation of these funds shifted the balance of financial power from public broadcasters and the NFB, which faced ongoing cutbacks, to commercial broadcasters. This trend to private broadcasters also increased the industrialization of documentary production and commercialization of subjects, including "reality TV." Second, in 1984, the federal broadcast regulator (CRTC), began licensing "specialty channels," which were distributed by satellite and cable. In 1987, the CBC's second channel, *Newsworld*, was licensed, along with *Vision TV*, a multi-faith channel. These were followed by other specialty channels that depended heavily on documentaries such as *Discovery Channel* (1994), *Bravo* (1994), and the *History Channel* (1996). In 2000, the NFB and CBC became minority partners with a private broadcaster in *The Documentary Channel*, a specialty digital cable network. Although these channels increased the demand for documentaries, this market fragmentation lowered the average fees paid to documentary producers. Third, documentary production was revolutionized by videotape and digital technology. These technological changes reduced the cost of production compared to film. Yet the supply of new funding, through a complicated network of tax credits and production funds, could not keep pace with demand created by a cascade of new specialty channels. As a result of these technological and market changes, the average budget for Canadian documentaries fell rapidly in the last 10 years while audiences for documentaries increased, both on television and in theatres.

Faced with deteriorating budgets and working conditions, independent documentary filmmakers started an organization in Toronto in 1983 to lobby on their behalf. Called the Canadian Independent Film Caucus (CIFC), it created *POV* magazine in 1991 and the *Hot Docs* film festival in 1993. The CIFC expanded nationally in 1995 and changed its name in 2003 to the *Documentary Organization of Canada.*

KIRWAN COX

See also **National Film Board of Canada**

Further Reading

Bidd, Donald F., *The NFB Film Guide: The Productions of the National Film Board of Canada from 1939 to 1989*, Ottawa: NFB, 1991.

Evans, Gary, *John Grierson and the National Film Board: The Politics of Wartime Propaganda*, Toronto: University of Toronto Press, 1984.

Evans, Gary, *In the National Interest: A Chronicle of the National Film Board of Canada from 1949 to 1989*, Toronto: University of Toronto Press, 1991.

Leach, Jim, *Candid Eyes: Essays on Canadian Documentaries*, edited by Jeanette Sloniowski, Toronto: University of Toronto Press, 2003.

Morris, Peter, *Embattled Shadows: A History of Canadian Cinema 1895–1939*, Montreal: McGill-Queen's University Press, 1978.

Steven, Peter, *Brink of Reality: New Canadian Documentary Film and Video*, Toronto: Between the Lines Press, 1993.

Véronneau, Pierre, *Self Portrait: Essays on the Canadian and Quebec Cinemas*, edited by Piers Handling, Ottawa: Canadian Film Institute, 1980.

Wise, Wyndam, *Take One's Essential Guide to Canadian Film*, Toronto: University of Toronto Press, 2001.

CANADA CARRIES ON

(1940–1951)

Canada Carries On is the title given to the first major program of films undertaken by the National Film Board of Canada (NFB). The brainchild of NFB founder and Commissioner John Grierson and his chief lieutenant, Stuart Legg, it was initiated immediately after Canada's entry into World War II and continued long afterward. Sixty-two films were made for the series during the war, and 136 after the war. The wartime phase of the series is its most significant.

Grierson put Legg in charge of the series. Legg directed, edited, and wrote the early entries, and throughout the war the series reflected Legg's approach to filmmaking. The films' style was inspired by the American *March of Time* series. They were compilation films, made from a combination of original footage, Allied combat footage, captured enemy footage, and other material that poured into the Film Board's vaults during the war. The first film in the series, *Atlantic Patrol* (1940), used some original footage but mostly stock footage from the Canadian Navy. The next two films, *Letter from Aldershot* (1940) and *The Home Front* (1940), used mostly original footage but some stock material. Whatever the particular mix of footage, the films were fast-paced and ranged from ten to twenty-two minutes long. They contained no or little dialogue and were narrated somewhat bombastically by Lorne Greene. Structurally they aimed to capture the audience's full attention early on, then rise in intensity, leading to a climactic ending. They were essentially filmed lectures, but the rich variety of footage, deft editing, solid writing, and other production values, such as original music, rendered them highly watchable.

The original aim of the series was to build and sustain Canadian morale by dramatizing Canada's war effort. Although the series emphasized Canada, however, it portrayed Canada's war efforts in relation to the world, and a few of the films had little or no Canadian content. The films displayed an intellectual boldness that often led to controversy for the NFB. When they were criticized for acknowledging the military strength of the Axis powers, Grierson countered that to deny the strength of the enemy would undermine the films' credibility. Occasionally, the perceived ideology of the films upset politicians and government officials.

Churchill's Island (1941), about the defense of Britain, made use of British material and footage from captured Germans. It presents the Germans as a ferocious enemy, but the British as determined and able to repel them. It was regarded at the time as innovative in its treatment of its subject a whole, and it won a special Academy Award in 1942. *Geopolitik: Hitler's Plan for Empire* (1942) also shows Germany as a formidable enemy while exemplifying the broader view that Grierson and Legg wanted the series to project, and it probably stands up even today as reliable history. *The Gates of Italy* (1943) was alleged to be soft on fascism because it lauds Italian culture and history and treats the Italian people warmly, praising them for honesty and lamenting their suffering. The film quotes contemptuous remarks about Hitler by Mussolini, but it also portrays Mussolini as a fool. Other films provoked charges of communist sympathies.

The analytical caliber of the series, as well as its creative energy, was exemplified in *War Clouds in the Pacific* (1941). Compiled from stock footage, the film predicted, against prevailing expert opinion, a Japanese attack on North America. Ten days after the film's release in late November, the Japanese attacked Pearl Harbor. Suddenly the film was in demand in the United States. The NFB released the film there under a new series title, *World in Action*, which became a free-standing series in its own right for the duration of the war. The new series closely resembled *Canada Carries On*, the main difference being that while the original series emphasized Canada in relation to the world, the new series emphasized the world in relation to Canada; however, it is sometimes difficult to tell from the film itself to which series it belonged.

Legg took over *World in Action*, and *Canada Carries On* was turned over to Canadian filmmakers Sydney Newman and Guy Glover. They employed a range of Canadian directors, put more Canadian content into the films, and loosened them up stylistically. Lorne Greene was dropped as the narrator. Postsynchronized sound effects began to be used, as in *Ordeal by Ice* (1945). After the war, the series continued, but grew increasingly parochial and dull. By the late 1950s, it had become somewhat eclectic. Some outstanding films, such as *Corral* (1954), although not initiated by the series, were appropriated for it and distributed under its title, as were various animation films such as *The Romance of Transportation in Canada* (1953).

D.B. JONES

See also **Beveridge, James;** *Churchill's Island;* **Compilation; Daly, Tom; Grierson, John; Legg, Stuart;** *March of Time;* **National Film Board of Canada; War: WWII;** *World in Action*

Further Reading

Beveridge, James, *John Grierson: Film Master*, London: Macmillan, 1979.
Ellis, Jack, "John Grierson's Relation with British Documentary During World War Two," in *John Grierson and the NFB*, The John Grierson McGill University Project, ECW Press, 1984.
Evans, Gary, *John Grierson and the National Film Board*, Toronto: University of Toronto Press, 1986.
Fielding, Raymond, *The March of Time, 1935–1951*, New York: Oxford University Press, 1978.
Jones, D.B., *Movies and Memoranda*, Ottawa: Deneau, 1982.
Jones, D.B., *The Best Butler in the Business: Tom Daly of the National Film Board of Canada*, Toronto: University of Toronto Press, 1996.
Leyda, Jay, *Films Beget Films: A Study of the Compilation Film*, London: George Allen & Unwin, 1964.
Nelson, Joyce, *The Colonized Eye: Rethinking the Grierson Legend*, Toronto: Between the Lines, 1988.
Rotha, Paul, *Documentary Film* (3rd ed.), London: Faber & Faber, 1952.

CANADA, FRENCH

The history of documentary film practice in French Canada is closely related to the history of the National Film Board of Canada (NFB). Although the NFB, from its inception in 1939 to the mid-1950s, focused almost exclusively on English-language productions, the relocation of its headquarters from Ottawa (Ontario) to Montréal (Québec) in 1956 had a profound impact on francophone documentary filmmaking. In fact, the move to Montréal could be seen as marking the beginning of the documentary in Québec. Undoubtedly, the period immediately after the 1956 move represents something of a "golden age" in the history of French language cinema in Canada. However, a documentary practice in Québec can be traced back to at least the 1930s, and the foundations laid during the early years of the sound film had a lasting influence on the documentaries made by the NFB's *équipe française* starting in the late 1950s.

The three most important figures of the "pre-NFB" era in French Canada are Maurice Proulx (1902–1988), Paul Provencher (1902–1981), and Albert Tessier (1895–1976), all of whom made their first documentaries in the 1930s. The former, a priest educated at Université Laval and Cornell University, is primarily associated with the conservative Union National government of Maurice Duplessis (Premier of Québec from 1936 to 1959 with a brief interruption during World War II). Proulx was often commissioned by governmental agencies to make films on agricultural, religious, and touristic topics. His most famous work *En pays neufs/In New Lands* (1937), the first feature-length sound documentary made in Canada, glorifies the life and work of settlers in the developing Abitibi region of northwest Québec. Although the voice-over commentary comes across as little more than a conservative propagandist lecture on the virtues of rural traditions and Catholic faith, the images of Abitibi evoke a strong sense of place and belonging that influenced later filmmakers. Bernard Devlin's (1923–1983) *Les brûlés/The Promised Land* (1958), one of the first significant films made by the NFB after the move to Montréal, was directly inspired by *En pays neufs* in its depiction of settlers in Abitibi; and in the mid-1970s, Pierre Perrault (1927–1999), one of the central figures of the francophone documentary after 1960, borrowed images from Proulx's film for his *Le retour à la terre/Back to the Land* (1976) about the failure of the Abitibi developments of the 1930s.

Other NFB films by Perrault also bear witness to the influence of the ethnographic tradition established by Paul Provencher in the 1930s. A forestry expert by trade, Provencher spent thirty-five years making films on nature and Native people. His *Les Montagnais/The Montagnais* (1935) and *Les scènes montagnaises/Montagnais scenes* (1936) were perhaps the first attempts by a French Canadian filmmaker to produce authentic documents on the customs and rituals of Amerindians. Perrault's *Le goût de la farine/The Taste of Flour* (1977), with Bernard Gosselin (b. 1934) and *Le pays de la terre sans arbre ou le Mouchouânipi/The Land without trees or Mouchouanipi* (1980), Arthur Lamothe's (b. 1928) series of documentaries "Chronique des Indiens du Nord-Est du Québec"/"Chronicle of North-Eastern Quebec Indians," (1973–1983), as well as the films of Native cineaste Alanis Obomsawin (b. 1932) follow in the footsteps of Provencher, whom Jean-Claude Labrecque (b. 1938) nicknamed *Le dernier coureur des bois* in his 1979 film portrait of the documentary pioneer.

Albert Tessier shared Provencher's interest in nature and the relationship between people and their natural environment. But Tessier's interest was less ethnographic than poetic. Tessier wanted to celebrate the beauty of his country to arouse in his audience an emotional connection to the ancestral land, the *terroir*. Many of his films, such as *Hommage à notre paysannerie/A Tribute to Our Peasantry* (1938), show images of simple Québec folk, working on the farm or sharing a meal. Tessier was a priest like Proulx, but his documentary practice was quite different. He was never commissioned to make films and was less didactic than his contemporary, preferring the panegyric to the lecture. He made amateur films that he distributed himself. The visual style of his work is perhaps best described as rustic. He never used a tripod, artificial lighting, or preconceived scenarios and always preferred spontaneity to classical aesthetics. As such, he has been recognized by Québec film historians such as Yves Lever (*Histoire générale du cinéma au Québec*), as the precursor of *cinéma direct*, the most important documentary movement to occur after the move of the NFB to Montréal. Perhaps not surprisingly, some shots from Tessier's early films bear an uncanny resemblance to images from landmark works of *cinéma direct*, such as Perrault and Michel Brault's (b.1928) *Pour la suite du monde/The Moontrap* (1963). Tessier's films of the 1930s and 1940s had shown with candor a way of life that was prevalent in Québec until the end of World War II but that had become obsolete by the 1960s. In *Pour la suite du monde*, Brault and Perrault sought both to recapture this disappearing tradition—here the tradition of beluga-whale hunting formerly practiced by the inhabitants of Île-aux-Coudres—and to reproduce the qualities of spontaneity, intimacy, and respectfulness that Tessier had displayed twenty-five years earlier.

Michel Brault was among the new generation of francophone filmmakers who joined the NFB in 1956, and he quickly emerged as the leading cinematographer of *cinéma direct*. In 1957–1958, Brault worked on the "Candid Eye" series developed by the Anglophone filmmakers of the NFB's renowned Unit B, who used recently-developed lighter film equipment to capture people in everyday situations with spontaneity and free from judgmental commentary. After shooting the milestone "Candid eye" film *The Days before Christmas* (1958, Terence Macartney-Filgate [b.1924], Stanley Jackson [1914–1981], and Wolf Koenig [b.1927]), Brault co-directed with Gilles Groulx (1931–1994) *Les raquetteurs/The Snowshoers* (1958), about a congress of snowshoeing clubs in Sherbrooke (Québec).

In both its form and its content, this film marked a turning point in Québec documentary. Unlike the "Candid Eye" films, which sought to observe everyday activities from a distance, *Les raquetteurs* attempted to show the event from within. The film's innovative visual style resulted from Brault's use of a handheld camera equipped with a wide-angle lens to shoot the subjects from up close. He walked amongst the snowshoers and their entourage, capturing with immediacy their conversations and interactions. Breaking with the griersonian rules of expository documentary, replacing rhetorical narrative and authoritative composition with a sense of picaresque spontaneity, Brault and Groulx made a film that endeavored to evince the customs and rituals of French Canadians as a gesture of national affirmation.

On the eve of the Quiet Revolution—the period of liberalization and modernization that followed the fall of the Duplessis regime in 1960 and marked the beginning of Québec's separatist movement—*Les raquetteurs* was hailed as a sort of manifesto for a home-grown film practice that could show real people (*vrai monde*) and contribute to their emancipation. Until the 1980s, the nationalist aspirations introduced by Groulx and Brault would remain the unofficial mandate of most French-speaking filmmakers working at the NFB. Immediately after *Les raquetteurs,* numerous NFB documentaries tried to reproduce, to various degrees, its style and nationalist purpose. *La lutte/Wrestling* (1961, Brault, Marcel Carrière [b.1935], Claude Fournier [b.1931], and Claude Jutra [1930–1986]), *Golden Gloves* (1961, Groulx), and *Québec-USA ou l'invasion pacifique/Visit to a Foreign Country* (1962, Brault, Jutra) are but a few examples of films that took as their subject matter the mundane but important communal practices of French Canadians to assert, more or less explicitly, the distinct culture of Québec. *Les raquetteurs* also had an impact beyond the frontiers of Québec. A screening at the Flaherty Seminar in 1959 inspired Jean Rouch to develop his conception of *cinéma vérité* and led him to invite Brault to film *Chronique d'un été/Chronicle of a Summer* (1961) in France. For the first time in the history of Québec cinema, French Canadian filmmakers were at the vanguard of an international movement that included such significant filmmakers as Rouch, D. A. Pennebaker, Richard Leacock, Robert Drew, and the Maysles brothers.

The year 1963 marked the culmination of *cinéma direct.* First, the term itself was officially adopted at the MIPE TV (*marché international des programmes et équipements*) in Lyon to clarify the confusion surrounding the term *cinéma vérité.* Furthermore, the NFB's first feature-length *cinéma-direct* documen-tary, *Pour la suite du monde,* was released and presented at the Cannes Film Festival. With this film, Perrault became one of the few Québec filmmakers to find a place within the high-brow discourse of French film theory through the work of writers such as Gilles Deleuze and Jean-Louis Comolli. Finally *cinéma direct* took a turn towards fiction with Claude Jutra's new-wave inspired feature, *À tout prendre/Take It All* (1963), one of the few productions of the early 1960s made outside the NFB. Jutra used techniques of direct cinema to tell the convoluted love story of a young French Canadian bourgeois repressing his homosexuality and his girlfriend who claims to be from Haiti. The next year, Groulx made *Le chat dans le sac/The Cat in the Bag* (1964), an even more explicit hybrid of direct cinema and fiction. Groulx actually used funds allocated by the NFB for the production of a short documentary on how young people spend their time during the winter to make his feature-length drama on the nationalist awaking of a Québécois intellectual and the disintegration of his relationship with an English-speaking Jewish woman. These two films are often acknowledged as marking the beginning of modern Québec fiction cinema. Starting in the mid-1960s, many cinéastes left documentary practice and followed Groulx's and Jutra's lead to produce fictions that adopted *cinéma direct*'s visual style. To this day, much of Québec's narrative cinema still exhibits a degree of documentary realism.

Those who continued to make documentaries used direct-cinema techniques to create increasingly political films, thus shedding any claim to objectivity that earlier productions might have harbored. Furthermore, the observatory mode of direct cinema started being replaced by a more interactive and self-reflexive approach, with the filmmakers' involvement with their subjects becoming more explicitly acknowledged. Tanya Ballantyne's (b.1944) English-language *The Things I Cannot Change* (1966) is worth mentioning here as a precursor for two important developments. On the one hand, this film about a poverty-stricken family in Montréal did not only observe but *denounced* the unbearable conditions in which these people live. Such proactive use of documentary eventually became the official mandate of the NFB's program "Société nouvelle"/"Challenge for change," established in 1969 to foster social improvement. This program, which lasted until 1979, sponsored film and video productions in French and English Canada that dealt with everything from the disenfranchisement of immigrants and terminal illness to child abuse and the struggle of French-speaking Acadians in the largely anglophone Maritime provinces east of

Québec. The "Société nouvelle" films often encouraged the full participation of the public, even at the level of production.

On the other hand, as the first feature-length documentary directed by a woman in Canada, *The Things I Cannot Change* paved the way for the emergence of a feminist voice at the NFB. A year after Ballantyne's film, Anne Claire Poirier (b. 1932) directed the feature *De mère en fille/Mother-to-Be* (1967), which dealt with the issue of pregnancy and maternity and is generally recognized as the first French Canadian feminist documentary. Poirier consolidated her position as the leading figure of feminist cinema in Québec by producing the six-film series "En tant que femme, sponsored by "Société nouvelle" from 1972 to 1975, which laid solid foundations upon which a woman's cinema could grow in French Canada. Poirier's most famous film is *Mourir à tue-tête/Scream from Silence* (1979), a powerful and controversial docudrama on the tragic effects of rape.

Controversy often accompanied the more politically radical documentaries of the late 1960s and 1970s. Some films, such as Jacques Leduc's (b. 1941) *Cap d'espoir/Cape Hope* (1969), Denys Arcand's (b. 1941) *On est au coton/Cotton Mill, Tread Mill* (1970) and Groulx's *24 heures ou plus . . .* ([24 hours or more . . .] 1973) were literally banned from circulation for a few years by NFB commissionaire Sydney Newman because of their putative Marxist critique of Canadian society. In fact, Arcand's defeatist perspective on the textile workers' struggle in *On est au coton* undermines any Marxist agenda the film might have had. But it doubtlessly remains a caustic condemnation of capitalism in Québec. Arcand was equally caustic in his documentary on Québec politics, *Québec: Duplessis et après . . . /Quebec: Duplessis and After . . .* (1972), which argues that the right-wing ideology of Maurice Duplessis was still present in the post-Quiet Revolution 1970s, even in the supposedly left-wing platform of the separatist Parti Québécois. With this film, Arcand managed to attract criticism from both sides of the political spectrum. Arcand's *Le confort et l'indifférence/Comfort and Indifference* (1981) was also controversial in its commentary on the failure of the 1980 referendum on Québec's independence (60 percent voted against Québec's sovereignty). Arguing that sovereignist Premier René Lévesque (in power from 1976 to 1985) misread the population's seeming enthusiasm for separation, Arcand was reproached by nationalists for his claim that Quebeckers were more interested in personal gratification than social and political issues, a point he reasserted in his fiction film *Le déclin de l'empire américain/Decline of the American Empire* (1986). In

1992, Jacques Godbout (b. 1933) came to a similar acknowledgment of political apathy in his documentary *Le mouton noir/The Black Sheep* on the 1990 failure of the Meech Lake Accord, which proposed to grant special status to Québec in the Canadian federation.

Whether Arcand's analysis of the failure of the first referendum is accurate remains debatable. But the 1980s and 1990s were certainly characterized by a pull away from Québec politics on the part of documentarians and an increased interest either in private questions or international issues. In a number of documentaries, individual experiences became more important than the collective condition of the people of Québec. Jean Beaudry (b. 1947), François Bouvier (b. 1948), and Marcel Simard's (b. 1945) *Une classe sans école/A Class without a school* (1980) on high school dropouts; Guy Simoneau (b. 1953) and Suzanne Guy's (b. 1956) *On n'est pas des anges/We're No Angels* (1981), on the sexual life of handicapped people; and Michel Audy's (b. 1957) *Crever à 20 ans/Dead at 20* (1984) on male prostitution, and Gilles Blais's (b. 1941) *Les adeptes/The Followers* (1981), on the initiation of three young people in the Krishna religious sect, are early signs of this shift toward the personal experience of marginalized characters. Bernard Emond's (b. 1951) *Ceux qui ont le pas léger meurent sans laisser de trace/Those with a Light Step go without a Trace* (1992), about an anonymous man in an urban wasteland, and Andrée Cazabon's *Enfer et contre tous/No Quick Fix* (2000), which documents the struggle of drug addicts and their parents, are more recent examples of this interest in individuals on the margins of society. Marginalised celebrities, if such an oxymoron can be used, also became the focus of several films, such as in Jacques Leduc's *Albédo/Albedo* (1982) about a little-known photographer, in Serge Giguère's (b. 1946) *Oscar Thiffault* (1987) about a folk singer, and *Le roi du drum/King of Drums* (1991) about an eccentric jazz musician, as well as in Pierre Falardeau (b. 1946) and Manon Leriche's *Le steak/The Steak* (1992) about an aging professional boxer. Introspection started to appear in several films, as in Marilú Mallet's (1944) *Journal inachevé/Unfinished Diary* (1982) a film diary, Michka Saäl's *L'arbre qui dort rêve à ses racines/A Sleeping Tree Dreams of Its Roots* (1992) about the personal experiences of cultural displacement, Esther Valiquette's *Le singe bleu/The Measure of Your Passage* (1992) about the personal journey of a woman diagnosed with AIDS, and Anne Claire Poirier's *Tu as crié LET ME GO/You Screamed: LET ME GO* (1997), a moving reflection on the violent death of the filmmaker's daughter in a drug-related dispute. These films often have little in common with the *cinéma-direct* tradition. *Le singe bleu*, for instance, is much closer to experimental film aesthetics than to *Les raquetteurs.*

At the opposite end of the spectrum, but equally far from the nationalist politics of pre-1980 productions, documentaries on international or global issues have emerged in large numbers during the last twenty years. Although the NFB has long produced films on international subjects, including Jutra's *Niger, jeune république/The Niger—Young Republic* (1961) and Louis Portugais's (1932–1982) *Alger 1962— chronique d'un conflit/Algeria 1962— Chronicle of a Conflict* (1962), such topics became increasingly common after 1980. Films such as Diane Beaudry's (b.1946) *L'autre muraille/The Great Wall of Tradition* (1986) about the condition of Chinese women, Laurette Deschamps's (b.1936) *La fin d'un long silence/No longer Silent* (1986) about women in India, and Louise Carré's (b.1936) *Mon coeur est témoin . . . au pays des femmes des mondes musulmans/My Heart Is My Witness* (1996) have extended feminist discourses far beyond the frontiers of Canada. Recently, political documentaries have also focused their criticism on the broken promises of free-trade agreements and the threat of globalization on marginal cultures. From Godbout's *Un monologue Nord-Sud/A North-South Monologue* (1982) to Magnus Isacsson's (b.1948) *Le nouvel habit de l'empereur/The Emperor's New Clothes* (1995) and *Vue du sommet/ View from the Summit* (2001), a large portion of *engagé* documentaries are now used as symbolic weapons in the struggle against globalization.

There are obviously a few relatively recent documentaries that still deal with specifically French Canadian questions. These films, however, often adopt the disillusioned perspective of Jean-François Mercier's *Disparaître/*Vanishing (1989), a veritable requiem for French Canadian culture. Georges Payrastre's *Parlons franc/Frankly Speaking* (1992), Stéphane Drolet's *Référendum— prise 2/take 2/Referendum—Take 2/Prise 2* (1996), and Marie-Claire Dugas's *L'Eternité? ou la disparition d'une culture/Eternity? Or the Disappearance of a Culture* (2000) all express strong doubts regarding the ability of francophone cultures to survive in an overwhelmingly English-speaking North America.

ANDRÉ LOISELLE

See also **Arcand, Denys; Brault, Michel; National Film Board of Canada; Perrault, Pierre**

Further Reading

Coulombe, Michel and Marcel Jean, *Le dictionnaire du cinéma québécois*, Montréal: Boréal, 1999.

Evans, Gary, *In the National Interest: A Chronicle of the National Film Board of Canada from 1949 to 1989*, Toronto: University of Toronto Press, 1991.

Lever, Yves, *Histoire générale du cinéma au Québec*, Montréal: Boréal, 1995.

Marshall, Bill, *Québec National Cinema*, Montréal and Kingston: McGill-Queen's University Press, 2001.

Marsolais, Gilles, *L'aventure du cinéma direct revisitée*, Laval: Les 400 coups, 1997.

Véronneau, Pierre (ed.), *Les cinémas canadiens*, Montréal: Cinémathèque québécoise; Paris: Pierre Lhermier Editeur, 1978.

CANADIAN BROADCASTING CORPORATION

Although overshadowed by Canada's National Film Board, at least in terms of the academic attention it has received, the Canadian Broadcasting Corporation has been one of Canada's major documentary producers and programmers for almost seventy years. The Corporation began making radio documentaries in the early 1930s, mostly factual dramatizations and continuing series, and its

output was formidable, amounting to several hundred hours a year by 1948 and covering most areas of the country in a form that was more popular (in ratings terms) and, arguably, just as innovative as Canadian documentary films.

Television documentaries were an even more ambitious project at the CBC, designed to record the entire range of times and spaces of the nation.

Verité observational features, produced by film-makers such as Allan King, focused on the hitherto hidden dimensions of day-to-day life, while investigative reports, by producers like Cam Graham and Norman Dapoe, examined public affairs issues and personalities of the day. At the same time, docudramas and cultural essays, by directors like Terrence and Brian McKenna and Vincent Tovell, tackled the larger events and trends of national life. At its height, in the 1950s, 1960s, and 1970s, the Corporation was supporting six departments and employing hundreds of producers to create these programs. Documentary emerged as perhaps the country's defining public service broadcasting genre, the realism and formal diversity of which stood in marked contrast to the supposedly homogenous fantasy fare being produced by its neighbour to the south.

The CBC remains an important, though somewhat diminished, producer and commissioner of programs of this type. In recent years, the Corporation has focused on in-house mega-projects like the (2000) series *Canada: A People's History*, while making incremental efforts to relax its restrictive point-of-view policies and commission independent productions. Finally, the Corporation has worked to transnationalize its lineup, airing imported programs while showcasing its own productions on a number of foreign satellite services.

But the golden age of public service documentary production is over in Canada. The growth sector in documentary production is clearly the specialty channels, many of which are active in low budget markets. And although the CBC remains one of Canada's preeminent documentary institutions, it is by no means the lone player in the field.

DAVID HOGARTH

See also **National Film Board of Canada**

Further Reading

Hogarth, David, "The Other documentary tradition: early radio documentaries in Canada," in *Historical Journal of Film, Radio and Television*, 21, 123–135.

Hogarth, David, *Documentary Television in Canada: From National Public Service to Global Marketplace*. Montreal: McGill-Queen's University Press, 2002.

Houle, Michel. *Documentary Production in Quebec and Canada*, 1991/2–1998/9, www-ridm.qc.ca, 2000.

CANADIAN MOTION PICTURE BUREAU

When British documentary production began at the Empire Marketing Board (EMB) in the late 1920s, the most substantial government film enterprise in the British empire was Canada's Motion Picture Bureau (MPB). A pioneer organization, it had been established in 1917 under the Department of Trade and Commerce. In the 1920s, the MPB produced travel and other promotional films, which were said to be lively, visually pleasing, and unpretentious. It developed a highly effective network of outlets for distribution of these films, and claimed to reach an audience of 25 million in North America each year.

In 1928 the head of the MPB, Captain Frank Badgley, visited England and the EMB. In 1931 the EMB sent its film officer, John Grierson, to visit Canada. At the MPB, Grierson was impressed primarily by the equipment and organization, rather than the films produced there. Grierson returned with seventeen new films for the growing nontheatrical library at the EMB and 15,000 feet of positive film as editing material for the unit. Grierson seems to have gotten the idea of emphasizing nontheatrical from the MPB. This trip would provide the foundation for a later trip and for the establishment of the National Film Board of Canada, with Grierson as film commissioner (the executive officer).

By the mid-1930s, however, the MPB was no longer expanding and developing. Its personnel, mostly World War I veterans, were firmly locked into civil service positions. The Depression had so depleted the budget that no sound recording equipment was purchased until 1934. When the Film Board was established, Grierson wrote its regulations. Realizing the delicacy of the situation of an existing government film entity, he envisioned that the Bureau would continue the government production of films, while the Board would initiate ideas for films, as well as for their promotion and distribution. But with Canada's entry into World War II alongside Britain, the need for films to support the war effort called for a rapid expansion of personnel and production, and the Bureau had to try to meet the demands being made of it with limited equipment and personnel.

Problems of equipment, time, and personnel were overcome in part by assigning productions to the few existing outside firms, such as Associated Screen News of Montreal and the newly formed Crawley Films. But Grierson was beginning to see that the real impediment to the Board's development was the administrative anomaly by which it set policy but did not itself produce films. Inevitably, friction had grown between the enterprising, ambitious new people hired by the Board, and the members of the original Motion Picture Bureau, who wanted to retain the status quo and who resented the ways films were now being made. Standing in Grierson's path most directly was the Bureau's director, Captain Frank Badgley.

Grierson had tried to maintain an amiable relationship with Badgley and was reluctant to take the step he now believed to be necessary. At the December 1940 meeting of the Board, Grierson gave his resignation. He stated as his grounds the unmet need for more money and more flexibility in hiring filmmakers so as to remove them further from strict civil service categories and full supervision by the film commissioner of the Motion Picture Bureau. He was resigning, he said, so that he could speak on these two matters crucial to the future of creative government filmmaking without it being charged that he was simply trying to increase his personal power in the government.

The resignation was not accepted; the press urged that Grierson be retained, and evidently that was the Prime Minister's desire as well. The stalemate lasted six months, Grierson holding his ground, until the government eventually capitulated under the mounting pressure. In June 1941, by Order of Council, the Film Board absorbed the Motion Picture Bureau, and Grierson moved his office into its former premises. It was thus that the NFB became responsible not only for planning and advising on all government films but also for making them or having them made by outside producers. Captain Badgley, offered the directorship of the Stills Division of the Motion Picture Bureau, rejected that offer and secured a transfer to the Department of National Revenue. Two months later the Stills Division was also transferred to the NFB by another Order in Council.

JACK C. ELLIS

See also **John Grierson, National Film Board of Canada**

Further Reading

Backhouse, Charles, *Canadian Government Motion Picture Bureau 1917-1941*, Ottawa: Canadian Film Institute, 1974.

Ellis, Jack C., *John Grierson: Life, Contributions, Influence*, Carbondale: Southern Illinois University Press, 2000.

Hardy, Forsyth, *John Grierson: A Documentary Biography*, London: Faber and Faber, 1979.

Jones, D. B., *Movies and Memoranda: An Interpretive History of the National Film Board of Canada*, Ottawa: Canadian Film Institute and Deneau Publishers, 1981.

McKay, Marjorie, *History of the National Film Board of Canada*, Montreal: National Film Board, 1964.

CANE TOADS: AN UNNATURAL HISTORY

(Australia, Lewis, 1988)

Cane Toads: An Unnatural History was Mark Lewis's first "feature" documentary, and probably the most commercially successful Australian documentary film ever released. It has been screened at film festivals and has enjoyed significant worldwide television and video sales. From its inception as a television documentary, *Cane Toads* was pitched at a commercial audience, with all the attendant marketing considerations taken into account (Stott, 103).

The *Bufo marinus*, introduced to Queensland from Hawaii to combat pests attacking the sugar cane crop, is a real threat to the environment of northern Australia. With the release of Lewis's film, the cane toad also entered the Australian and international imagination as fictional kitsch symbol, emblematic of everything from colonization and regional identity to environmental neglect and tourism. Former journalist Lewis worked closely with Glenys Rowe, a publicist with Film Australia, in a collaborative venture that emphasized the marketing potential of such a film. They flew in Betty, a live cane toad, to accompany Lewis on a day-time variety show. They sent one hundred stuffed cane toads to journalists who were to attend the media previews and had T–shirts, badges, and radio advertisements, replete with cane toad noises, produced to facilitate publicity (Stott, 104).

Like the films of Errol Morris, *Cane Toads* uses the rhetorical devices of a range of fiction and nonfiction films to render a multiperspective account of this environmental and social phenomenon. In this regard, Lewis is as interested in the broader cane toad "culture" that can be ascertained only through interviews with so-called expert interviewees and the rendering of this (un)natural being as it stands within the cultural world. While the film constantly oscillates between a topic that is a serious and major threat to the environment and rhetoric that fictionalizes and diminishes any such threat, *Cane Toads* successfully enlarges the issues at hand to appeal to a wide range of audiences.

Self-conscious in its form, *Cane Toads* teeters on the brink of "mockumentary" without the hollowness of topic that is featured in the likes of *This Is Spinal Tap*, melding formal satire with savage social critique in the manner of films such as *Roger and Me* and *The Thin Blue Line*. Because of its scope, the film has been used in environmental studies, Australian history, documentary film theory and criticism, biology, and cultural studies, successfully negotiating the borders these disciplines have attempted to erect for themselves. In keeping with the multidisciplinary applications of the film, *Cane Toads* exists in a space between independent film and commercial, mainstream television documentary and therefore extends both the griersonian traditions of social imperative and those of commercial entertainment (McMurchy, 1994: 198).

DEANE WILLIAMS

See also **Morris, Errol; *Roger and Me*; *The Thin Blue Line***

Cane Toads—An Unnatural History, Monica and Her Pet Cane Toad, 1988.
[*Courtesy of the Everett Collection*]

Cane Toads: An Unnatural History *(Australia, 48 min). Distributed by Film Australia. Written and directed by Mark Lewis. Executive producer: Tristram Miall. Camera: Jim Frazier, Wayne Taylor. Editor: Lindsay Frazer. Sound: Rodnet Simmons. Sound Mix: George Hart. Music Mix: Michael Stavrou. Original Music: Martin Armiger, Tim Finn, Don Spencer and Allan Caswell. Graphics: David Johnson. Voice-overs: Stephanie Lewis, Paul Johnstone. Production Manager: Ian Adkins.*

Further Reading

Gibson, Ross, "A Marriage Made in Heaven," in *Filmnews (Australia)*, February, 1988, 7.

McMurchy, Megan, "The Documentary," in *Australian Cinema*, edited by Scott Murray, Sydney: Allen and Unwin/Australian Film Commission, 1994.

Moran, Albert, "Multiculturalism, Ecology and the Invasion of the Body Snatchers," *Queensland Images in Film and Television*, edited by Jonathan Dawson and Bruce Molloy, Brisbane: University of Queensland Press, 1990.

Stott, Jennifer, "Case Study: Cane Toads," in *Taking Care of Business: A Practical Guide to Independent Film and Video Production*, edited by John Cruthers, Australian Film, Television and Radio School/Australian Film Commission, 1990.

CANUDO, RICCIOTTO

An Italian expatriate who settled in Paris in 1901 and a friend of artists such as Apollinaire and Gabriele D'Annunzio, Marcel L'Herbier, and Jean Cocteau, Ricciotto Canudo was a multitalented intellectual. He was a poet and a novelist; a prolific critic of art, literature, music, and cinema; a theorist; a trendsetter; and a vivacious cultural mover. Canudo is, with Boleslaw Matuszewski, one of the first intellectuals to acknowledge the artistic quality of the cinema and to attempt a definition of the specificity of its language. He is particularly well known for having coined the fortunate expression "seventh art" (and, as some claim, *photogénie*) and for his pioneering vision of cinema as the total art that presents characteristics of all the other arts, and that merges the arts of "space" (architecture, painting, sculpture) and those of "time" (music, dance, poetry), synthesizing and superseding them (Canudo, 1995: 161–164).

Canudo is probably the first theorist to have pointed to the necessity of distinguishing between types of films and to have attempted a classification of the genres—a classification in which he gave particular relevance to the documentary (Canudo, 1995: 334–335). It is opportune to read his contribution on two levels: against the backdrop of the theorization on modernist documentary filmmaking in France in the 1920s and against the backdrop of Canudo's own theoretical framework, which is split between the idea of a "pure cinema," the ultimate purpose of which is the representation of inner life through the creation of a high aesthetic and poetic emotion, and the conception of cinema as the perfect expression of the dynamism, speed, and scientism of modern life.

French modernist documentary filmmaking, which produced films such as Alberto Cavalcanti's *Rien que les heures* (1926)/*Nothing but the Hours* and Jean Vigo's *À propos de Nice* (1930)/*On Nice*, was influenced by poetic impressionism and by naturalism. These influences are evident in the use of terminology and in the ideas that informed the articles and reviews of critics of the time, such as Hubert Revol and André Sauvage. Canudo was no exception; he saw the documentary as particularly suited for representing nature. Its mission was to show the relationship of humans with their envir-

onment (Canudo, 1995: 303–305). "Such a mission clearly draws on the French naturalist and realist tradition, and illustrates the extent to which these documentaries constituted a bridge between impressionist modernism and naturalist pictorialism" (Aitken, 73).

In particular, Canudo's conception of the documentary is partly "poetic" and partly "historical." He defined the documentary as both the true art film (Canudo, 1995: 222) and—abhorring the melodramatic style of costume dramas at that time—as the true historical film (Canudo, 1995: 183). In a review of W.G. Barker's *London by Night* (1913), Canudo noticed that the best documentaries are able to reconcile the "commercial instinct of the cinema with a vast and exact expression of life" (Canudo, 1995: 259). He repeatedly praised the documentary for its ability to elicit emotion and even attain the tragic. Rather than being confined to the lower status of intermission filler, as was the practice in Canudo's time, the documentary must inspire "*new* dramas" (Canudo, 1995: 222, 237). In an article about some documentaries of the early 1920s, including Flaherty's *Nanook of the North* (1922), he praised them for having reached a level of expression far superior to that of contemporary fiction films: "more moving, more 'direct' than all the most pathetic plot complications that the poets have ever imagined" (Canudo, 1979: 20). He singled out the "prodigious" *Nanook*, in which he admired the depiction of the struggle between humans and the elements, and which he compared to Aeschylus's tragedies, but then extended his praise to all travel and mountaineering documentaries: "The voyages around the world, the 'documentaries' of the well-known lakes and famous sites, . . . have acquired a personality and are loved by all audiences. They attain the dimension of tragedies" (Canudo, 1995: 222). Canudo's idea of the tragic quality of documentaries reflects his belief that these should "transcend the limitations of the photographic reportage and transfigure the contingency of the observed phenomenon, communicating to the spectator universal meanings" (Boschi, 1998: 149), as is true for *Nanook*, in which "the Everyday Tragedy of polar man spreads out into the emotion of the entire world" (Canudo, 1979: 20), as well as for the minor *A l'assaut du mont Everest* (1922), which shows "the tragedy of the struggling man, only armed of the weapon of his courage, against the formidable power of nature" (Canudo, 1995: 222).

With the documentary format, Canudo distinguished the biographical film, the war documentary, the propaganda film, and the scientific film. A biographical film (or "retrospective documentary," as he also called it) that has been reviewed by Canudo is Jean Epstein's *Pasteur* (1922), which for the author showed how this type of film is, once again, "a drama of the struggle of man against the hostility of evil" (Canudo, 1995: 216). War documentaries are particularly valued by the author and are seen as being in-between contemporary epic and novel journalism, with the camera operator depicted as the heroic witness of the human tragedy of the war (Canudo, 1995: 229–231). The propaganda film, instead, a sort of biased subgenre of the war documentary, is for the author the cinematographic equivalent of the newspaper article. The cinema is destined to replace the printed newspaper with a product that will be suitable for "unintelligent and utterly illiterate people" (Canudo, 1995: 229). In line with the "fascination with the science film [that] since the mid-1920s French avant-garde film circles had developed" (Barnard, 2000: 14), as well as with his own conception of the cinema as educational art, Canudo also pointed to the importance of the use of film in popularizing great discoveries and scientific advancements (Canudo, 1995: 167–168), as well as in the diffusion of visual knowledge of other peoples (Canudo, 1995: 325).

LAURA RASCAROLI

See also **Cavalcanti, Alberto; Documentary Film: France; Flaherty, Robert; Modernism: Critical Overview of, and Documentary Film;** *Nanook of the North*; *Rien que les heures*; **Sauvage, André; Vigo, Jean**

Biography

Born in Gioia del Colle, Bari (Italy), January 2, 1877. Moved to Florence to study oriental languages, 1898, and then to Rome, 1899. Wrote for magazines under the pseudonym of Kàrola Olga Edina. Published his first volumes of poetry, 1898. Moved to Paris, 1901. Founded the journal *Montjoie!*, 1913. Fought with the French army in World War I. Published the manifesto of a movement called Art Cérébriste, 1914. Founded *Le Gazette de sept arts*, 1920. Founded the world's first film club, the Club des amis du septieme art, 1920. Died in Paris, November 10, 1923.

Further Reading

Aitken, Ian, *European Film Theory and Cinema. A Critical Introduction*, Edinburgh: Edinburgh University Press, 2001.

Barnard, Timothy, "From Impressionism to Communism: Léon Moussinac's Technics of the Cinema, 1921–1933," in *Framework*, 42, (Summer), 2000, www.frameworkonline.com/42tb.htm.

Boschi, Alberto, *Teorie del cinema. Il periodo classico 1915–1945*, Rome: Carocci, 1988.

Canudo, Ricciotto, *L'Usine aux images*, Paris: Séguier, 1995.

Canudo, Ricciotto, "Another View of Nanook," translated by Harold J. Salemson, in *The Documentary Tradition*, edited by Lewis Jacobs, New York: W.W. Norton & Company, 1979.

Dotoli, Giovanni, *Riccio o Canudo ou le cinéma comme art*, Bari-Paris: Schena and Didier Érudition, 1999.

CAPRA, FRANK

Initially known for his Hollywood features, Frank Capra became recognized as a documentary filmmaker through his famous *Why We Fight* series, which he made between 1942 and 1945. Capra also produced and directed a series of military informational films entitled *Know Your Ally/Know Your Enemy* during the war, but these motion pictures were not as critically acclaimed. His wartime documentaries differed substantially from those made by other Hollywood directors in the military at this time. Filmmakers John Ford, William Wellman, and John Huston shot their footage in actual combat zones, thereby capturing the immediacy of the war, but Frank Capra's films were produced from behind the lines. The *Why We Fight* pictures were compilation documentaries that used "found footage" to inform new soldiers as to why they were being asked to fight.

Frank Capra was commissioned as a major in the U.S. Army Signal Corps in 1942, where General George Marshall assigned him the task of making informational films for the war effort. Never having made documentaries, Capra educated himself on the subject by looking at propaganda films produced by the enemy. He was particularly affected by Leni Riefenstahl's classic Nazi propaganda film, *Triumph of the Will* (1934). Capra was both impressed with how Riefenstahl artfully conveyed her message through film and appalled at the way she used the medium to promote Adolph Hitler and the Nazi party.

Although Frank Capra had no qualms about attacking Riefenstahl's dogma, he was concerned about his method for rebuttal. Unlike Riefenstahl, Capra did not have the unlimited resources of his government to produce propaganda. He also felt challenged by the fact that while the enemy could tell lies, his documentaries had a moral obligation to uphold the truths of a free society.

Capra justified becoming a propagandist by taking a position similar to that of John Grierson. He envisioned himself as an educator who was using propaganda to teach. Instead of staging expensive sequences for the camera, Capra became a spin doctor who reedited found footage taken from enemy propaganda films to promote his own ideological views. The seven *Why We Fight* films were presented as a series of history lessons in which Capra contrasted the negative philosophy and behavior of the Axis powers with the positive alternative of the Allies. Originally intended to be used solely as instructional films for raw recruits, these documentaries were so effective in delivering their message that they were shown to civilian audiences in the United States and to millions of viewers overseas.

Although Frank Capra claimed to have had qualms about making propaganda films during World War II, he is considered one of the most ideological Hollywood directors of the 1930s and 1940s. *Mr. Deeds Goes to Town* (1936), *Mr. Smith Goes to Washington* (1939), *Meet John Doe* (1941), and *It's A Wonderful Life* (1946) are particularly overt in expressing Capra's populist philosophy. Starring either Gary Cooper or James Stewart, these films feature a heroic "common man" whose deeply rooted values challenge the corruption fostered by dishonest government officials and big business interests. This type of message film fell out of favor after the war. By the 1970s, Capra's most famous pictures were criticized for being overly sentimental and labeled "Capracorn." Despite Capra's condemnation of Adolph Hitler in the *Why We Fight* series, some detractors even accused his films of being fascist.

Other critics have suggested that Capra's populist motion pictures are not so easily pigeonholed. His most famous work clearly champions a heroic common man, but the existence of corrupt government officials and angry mobs in his movies can also be interpreted as revealing a darker and less idealistic side to this director's view of humanity. Frank Capra clearly believed that the individual hero can prove a moral point. How much more the Capra hero is capable of doing relative to combating corruption, controlling a mob, or formulating governmental policy is questionable given the information provided in his films.

Capra went into semiretirement when his postwar Hollywood movies failed to be popular at the box office. The government was now torn between involving Capra in various projects and questioning his loyalty. The depiction of corrupt American politicians in Capra's 1948 feature *State of the Union,* for example, was viewed as a controversial theme during this period of McCarthyism, and questions about Frank Capra's politics affected his career. Capra was able to exercise some creative expression using the film medium by returning to the documentary. He wrote, produced, and directed a series of educational documentaries for Bell Systems entitled *Our Mr. Sun* (1955), *Hemo the Magnificent* (1957), *The Strange Case of Cosmic Rays* (1957), and *The Unchained Goddess* (1958).

Frank Capra pursued the role of being an educator in the 1970s by visiting universities and speaking to film students. During this time the American television producer Bill Moyers hosted a PBS broadcast for which Capra was invited to compare his philosophy of documentary filmmaking with that of the young filmmaker Barbara Kopple, who was receiving recognition for her feature *Harlan County, USA* (1976). In a taped review made after their conversation, Moyers noted that Capra had felt compelled to use this occasion to claim that his production of the *Why We Fight* series was justified because of Hitler's misuse of power. Moyers saw Capra's defense of the series as an indication that the filmmaker was uncomfortable with having made propaganda, justifiable though it may have been. If Bill Moyers's interpretation is true, Frank Capra, like some of his critics, was still finding it difficult to reconcile ideological contradictions in his work decades after it was produced.

FRANK SCHEIDE

See also **Grierson, John;** *Harlan County, USA;* *Triumph of the Will; Why We Fight*

Biography

Born Bisaquino, Sicily, May 18, 1897. Emigrated with his family to the United States in May 1903, and settled in Los Angeles. Attended Throop College of Technology (Caltech) in 1915, where he discovered poetry and began writing. Enlisted in the army in 1917 when the United States entered World War I, discharged in 1918 after he contracted Spanish influenza, graduated from Throop College with a bachelors degree that same year. Involved in various aspects of filmmaking, 1919–1924. Achieved success as a gag writer for Mack Sennett in 1924 when he worked on a series of short comedies with Harry Langdon. Followed Langdon to First National in 1925 and directed the comedian's feature length picture, *The Strong Man*, in 1926. Employed as a director at Columbia in 1927, a very modest studio at the time. Popularity of his films between 1927 and 1941 transformed Columbia into a major studio. President of Academy of Motion Picture Arts and Sciences from 1935 to 1941. Commissioned as a major in U.S. Army Signal Corps in 1942, and produced the *Why We Fight* series, 1942–1945. Formed Liberty Films in 1946, which proved unsuccessful, and career went into decline. Recipient of the Distinguished Service Medal and American Film Institute Lifetime Achievement Award. Winner of three Best Director Oscars. Died September 3, 1991, in La Quinta, California.

Selected Films

1915 *Our Wonderful Schools* (Wagner): uncredited editor
1943 *Prelude to War*: uncredited co-director, uncredited co-producer
1943 *The Battle of Russia*: co-director, producer
1943 *The Nazis Strike*: co-director, producer
1943 *Divide and Conquer*: co-director, uncredited producer
1943 *The Battle of Britain*: co-director, producer
1944 *Tunisian Victory*: co-director, producer
1944 *The Battle of China*: co-director
1944 *The Negro Soldier* (Heisler): producer
1944 *Attack! Battle of New Britain*: producer
1945 *San Pietro* (Huston): uncredited co-supervising producer
1945 *Two Down and One to Go*: director, producer
1945 *War Comes to America*: co-director, producer
1945 *Your Job in Germany:* director
1945 *Know Your Enemy: Japan*: co-director, producer, cowriter
1956 *Our Mr. Sun*: co-director, producer, writer
1957 *Hemo the Magnificent*: co-director, co-producer, writer
1957 *The Strange Case of the Cosmic Rays*: co-director, co-producer, writer
1958 *The Unchained Goddess*: co-director, co-producer
1964 *Rendezvous in Space*: director

Further Reading

Capra, Frank, *The Name Above the Title*, New York: Macmillan, 1971.
Carney, Raymond, *American Vision: The Films of Frank Capra*, Cambridge: Cambridge University Press, 1986.
Gehring, Wes D., *Populism and the Capra Legacy*, Westport, CT: Greenwood Press, 1995.
Maland, Charles J., *Frank Capra*, New York: Twayne Publishers, 1995.
McBride, Joseph, *Frank Capra: The Catastrophe of Success*, London: Faber, 1992.
Poague, Leland, *Another Frank Capra*, Cambridge: Cambridge University Press, 1995.

CARRIBEAN

See **West Indies and Carribean**

CATHY COME HOME

(UK, Loach, 1966)

Cathy Come Home (1966) has become a classic landmark of British television drama and is undoubtedly the best-known program made within the *Wednesday Play* slot (BBC, 1964–1970). The program is famous for bringing the subject of homelessness to the attention of the general public in a sympathetic manner, which led to the establishment of the homeless charity, Shelter. Much of the force of this drama is due to the way in which the program incorporated many documentary techniques, which at the time was perceived to be unique.

Although *Cathy Come Home* is an original combination of documentary and drama, it should be seen in the context of a turn toward greater realism and location shooting within television drama. Until 1965, television drama was mostly studio-bound, but in that year Ken Loach and Tony Garnett demanded the use of more filmed material within their play *Up the Junction* (1965). To get a more realistic feel, they shot with portable, lightweight, 16mm equipment, which was being used increasingly within documentary. Loach and Garnett wanted to get away from the theatrical binds on television drama, and in doing so they brought the drama closer to the documentary in style and tone. This is a technique that they extended in *Cathy Come Home*.

The play covers the story of Cathy, who runs away from home and meets and eventually marries Reg. After Reg has an accident that prevents him from working, they are continually forced from their accommodation, moving into a series of temporary homes (including a caravan that is burned down, resulting in the death of two of Cathy's children). The authorities continually separate the two and, after Reg drifts away, Cathy is left homeless on the streets after her children are taken away from her.

Although the drama documentary was an established form in the 1950s, this was a form that reconstructed documentary incidences within a studio, a form related to the technological limitations of the period. In contrast, *Cathy Come Home* is a drama that used documentary elements to strengthen the credibility and impact of the drama. Although Jeremy Sandford, who wrote *Cathy*, did base the script on a radio documentary, it was written very much in the form of a drama.

Nevertheless, documentary elements informed the program in three major ways. The first documentary influence was seen in the use of handheld, 16mm cameras, similar to the equipment being used in documentaries, which produced a sense of movement and immediacy. An operator with a lightweight 16mm camera could follow protagonists down streets and into buildings, and we often see Cathy and Reg walking down streets and talking while the camera moves with them. This gave the

Cathy Come Home, 1966.
[*Still courtesy of the British Film Institute*]

program a degree of environmental authenticity compared to the mainly interior sets of studio dramas. In addition, the camera shakes in some of the scenes in which it follows the protagonists on the move, providing a stylistic denotation of realism established through the shaky shots obtained in documentaries such as *World in Action* (which was a major influence on Loach and Garnett).

The second major documentary influence is seen in the use of voice-over statistics that punctuate the play at various moments. Cathy, who speaks about her experiences in the past tense, provides the main narrative orientation on the sound track. At times, though, such as when Cathy and Reg are having difficulties with finding housing, an anonymous voice-over provides facts and figures relating to homelessness and other housing information. This intrusion is not connected to the narrative in any integral manner; rather, it is a documentary intrusion into the narrative that helps place the story in a wider social context.

The third major influence of documentary can be found in the observational sequences that occur and break up the narrative thrust. Occasionally, there are shots of an environment that Cathy is placed within, which are documentary-like shots detailing surroundings. In conjunction with such observational camera work, subjective voices of other people are placed on the sound track. The most prominent example of such an audiovisual mode occurs when Cathy is living with Reg's mother in a crowded tenement. After a shot of Cathy and Reg conversing in their flat, a montage of life around the building follows, showing people walking up and down stairs and children playing outside. A montage of voices on the sound track accompanies these shots, in which other residents express their views on what it is like to live in the tenement. This sequence is extremely reminiscent of the style that Denis Mitchell used in some of his documentaries such as *Morning in the Streets* (1959).

These three infusions of documentary stylistics, combined with the extensive factual research that Sandford included in the script, has led to *Cathy Come Home* being termed a "docudrama." The prominent and (for the time) unusual extent to which documentary elements pervaded the narrative gave the program a different feeling for the audience. Rather than being based around a small number of scenes in which character interactions develop, *Cathy* is fragmentary in structure. It uses edits to break up scenes with haste, so that many events are squeezed into a limited time frame.

Documentary techniques in *Cathy Come Home* are mainly used to broaden the canvas of personal drama by emphasizing social context, stressing the social forces that affect personal destiny. Near the beginning of the film, in which Cathy first meets Reg, the tone of the scenes is romantic and idealistic, an impression enforced by the use of romantic pop songs and of shots of the couple walking through the trees in the sun. This mode of filmmaking is, like Cathy's life, disrupted by the intrusion of external social forces. The program is thus marked by a need to "open out" both the focus on individuals and the spatial constrictions that characterized television drama.

Cathy Come Home marked a point in which documentary techniques began to play a crucial part in the evolution of television drama. A number of directors and technicians (such as Jack Gold, Charles Stewart, and Chris Menges) worked in both documentary and drama, and there was a certain degree of fluidity between the two genres in the late 1960s and early 1970s. This trend continues to feed into contemporary television, in which docudramas are still produced (such as Jimmy McGovern's *Hillsborough* [Granada, 1996]). *Cathy Come Home* still appears original and fresh, however, for the way in which it merged documentary and dramatic techniques in a particularly unique manner.

JAMIE SEXTON

See also **Documentary Drama; Loach, Ken**

Cathy Come Home (UK, 1966, 75 min) Aired November 16, 1966 on BBC1. Produced by Tony Garnett. Directed by Ken Loach. Script by Jeremy Sandford and Ken Loach. Production design by Sally Hulk. Music by Paul Jones. Edited by Ray Watts. Sound direction by Malcolm Campbell.

Further Reading

Banham, Martin, "Jeremy Sandford," in *British Television Drama*, edited by George Brandt, Cambridge: Cambridge University Press, 1981.

Caughie, John, *Television Drama: Realism, Modernism and British Culture*, Oxford: Oxford University Press, 2000.

Corner, John, *The Art of Record: A Critical Introduction to Documentary*, Manchester: Manchester University Press, 1996.

Fuller, Graham (ed.), *Loach on Loach*, London: Faber and Faber, 1998.

Goodwin, Andrew, Paul Kerr, and Ian Macdonald (eds.) *Drama Documentary*, London: BFI, 1983.

Hogenkamp, Bert, *Film, Television and the Left in Britain 1950-1970*, London: Lawrence and Wishart, 2000.

Leigh, Jacob, *Ken Loach: Art in the Service of People*, London: Wallflower, 2002.

MacMurraugh-Kavanagh, M.K., "'Drama' into 'News': Strategies of Intervention in 'The Wednesday Play,'" *Screen*, 38, 3, Autumn, 1997.

Paget, Derek, *True stories?: Documentary Drama on Radio, Screen and Stage*, Manchester: Manchester University Press, 1990.

Petley, Julian, "Factual Fictions and Fictional Fallacies: Ken Loach's Documentary Dramas," in George McKnight (ed.), *Agent of Challenge and Defiance: The Films of Ken Loach*, Trowbridge: Flicks, 1997.

Sandford, Jeremy, *Cathy Come Home*, London: Pan, 1967.

Shubik, Irene, *Play for Today: The Evolution of Television Drama*, revised edition, Manchester: Manchester University Press, 2000.

CAVALCANTI, ALBERTO

Alberto de Almeida Cavalcanti was born in Rio de Janeiro on February 6, 1897. His father, Manoel, was originally of Italian extraction, while his mother came from the north of Brazil. It was his mother, Doña Aña, who was to have the greater influence on Alberto and, when he left for England in 1934, he lived with his mother until her death in 1945. In 1923, Alberto began work in Paris for the impressionist film director Marcel L'Herbier, as a set designer and assistant producer, but his first significant nondirectorial involvement in filmmaking came as an editor, with his participation in *Voyage au Congo* (1927), a documentary directed by Marc Allégret, with the participation of the novelist André Gide. Between 1926 and 1934, when he left France for England, Cavalcanti directed a number of films, but the most important of these were *Rien que les heures* and *En Rade*. Both films exhibit the influence of the French avant-garde cinema of the 1920s. *Rien*, in particular, can be described as a work of high-modernism, although Cavalcanti was to make few other films in this mode during his career.

The coming of the sound film in 1927 had a terminal impact on the French cinematic avant-garde, whose aesthetic was based on the silent film. As opportunities for filmmaking dried up and to support his family (his father had died in 1922, and Alberto was forced to support his mother, his brother, and a maid), Alberto accepted employment in the Paris studios of Paramount Studios. He had wanted to work in sound film since 1927, but, between 1928 and 1930, ended up working on a number of undistinguished, commercial sound film projects, The exceptions here were his more experimental short sound films: *La P'tite Lilie* and *Little Red Riding Hood*. Between 1930 and 1931, Cavalcanti made a number of sound films for Paramount, but his involvement was mainly that of making foreign language remakes of popular Hollywood films. Between 1930 and 1934, Cavalcanti continued to be involved in a number of undistinguished projects, and this led him to eventually take up an offer of employment to work for John Grierson's documentary film movement in England. When he left France, in 1934, the major influences on him were French realism and cinematic impressionism, and a tendency toward popular melodrama. However, life in England was to be very different from France.

By 1934, then, Cavalcanti's filmmaking remained grounded in the French realist tradition, and also exhibited a use of modernist features, melodramatic and sentimental formats, and comic, musical or folkloric elements. This complex and uneven set of stylistic characteristics did not add up to a systematic or coherent aesthetic

Line from Tschierva Hut, 1937.
[*Still courtesy of the British Film Institute*]

position, although had Cavalcanti not been thrown off course by his involvement in the commercial film industry, it might well have eventually done so. Cavalcanti left France in 1934 because he had become increasingly frustrated by the lack of opportunity available to him within the French film industry. It is debatable, however, whether this was the right thing to do. Had he remained, he may well have emerged as one of the most important French directors of the 1930s, and one can imagine that his style may have evolved into something like that of Jean Vigo, the filmmaker whom he most admired, and to whom he devoted his *Filme e Realidade* (1952).

In England Cavalcanti made decisive contributions to both the British documentary film movement and Ealing Studios. However, his approach to filmmaking at both organisations was often at odds with those who employed him. Consequently, although Cavalcanti made some important films between 1934 and 1946, he was often unable to make the sorts of films that he would, ideally, have liked to make. In fact, it was only with *For Them that Trespass* (1949), and after a gap of some twenty years, that he was able to return to the French poetic realist tradition, which he was most at home in. However, even that film was the product of compromise, and it was not really until *O Canto do Mar* that he was able to effect a full return to poetic realism. Unfortunately, however, what some Brazilian critics described as the "unjustified gloom and futility" of the film was not what the film industry and film critics in Brazil wanted either.

Cavalcanti's contribution to the documentary film was made in England, both at the GPO Film Unit, and at Ealing Studios. At the GPO, Cavalcanti brought a command of filmmaking technique to the young filmmakers employed by John Grierson. In particular he brought expertise in the creative treatment of sound to a production unit that had only just acquired sound facilities. The first fruits of his involvement came with one of the most important documentaries to be produced during the 1930s. Basil Wright's *Song of Ceylon* (1934) is particularly impressive in its use of impressionistic, nonsynchronous sound technique, a technique that was brought into the documentary film movement by Cavalcanti. The same use of modernist technique can be found in Cavalcanti's first directed film for the documentary film movement, *Pett and Pott* (1934). However, this surrealist fantasy was at odds with the intentions of John Grierson, and the film was criticised elsewhere within the movement, for example by Paul Rotha.

The problem over *Pett and Pott* was to illustrate a more general problem. Cavalcanti and Grierson were very different people, with very different sensibilities. Grierson was a dogmatic, obsessive Scot; Cavalcanti was an expressive, cultured man—and a homosexual. Grierson's distrust of Cavalcanti resulted in the latter directing few films between 1934 and 1936. However, he did make important contributions to a number of the GPO Film Movement's most important films over this period, most notably, *Coal Face* (1935) and *Night Mail* (1936). These two films, with their use of music by Benjamin Britten and poetry by W.H. Auden, also exhibit Cavalcanti's knowledge of the creative use of sound and modernist technique.

Grierson left the GPO Film Unit in 1936, after which Cavalcanti was promoted to production leader. He remained in charge of the Unit until 1940, when it became integrated into the war effort as the Crown Film Unit. Between 1936 and 1940, Cavalcanti's major involvement was again as a producer. In particular, he formed a close relationship over this period with Humphrey Jennings. Jennings' *Spare Time* (1939) again exhibits Cavalcanti's concern for indeterminate, evocative forms of filmmaking and for associative editing. The section in the film showing a Welsh male choir is a remarkably affecting piece of filmmaking. Another important documentary in which Cavalcanti played a major role was *Men of the Lightship* (1940). Cavalcanti's influence is apparent here in the pictorial quality of some of the images and in one edited sequence which employs the kind of subjective camerawork characteristic of the French impressionist movement of the 1920s and which Cavalcanti first employed in *Rien que les heures* and *En Rade*.

In 1940, Cavalcanti left the GPO Film Unit, shortly to become the Crown Film Unit, to work for Michael Balcon at Ealing Studios. Cavalcanti really wanted to get back to the feature film, and this was the major influence on his move; however, during his first year at Ealing, he continued to make documentaries. The most important of these films were *Yellow Ceasar*, a parodic send-up of Mussolini, in which Cavalcanti again uses the forms of caricature he used in some of his French films, and *Pett and Pott*. But Cavalcanti soon switched to feature film direction and production, and he brought to Ealing films a complicating sensibility, which often elevated the films out of the mundane. This is apparent, for example, in the highly caricatured *The Big Blockade*, and in the montage edited sequences of *The Foreman Went to France*. A concern for forms of documentary realism is also apparent in *Champagne Charlie* and in Cavalcanti's first post-Ealing film: *They Made Me a Fugitive*. They same concern for documentary realism also surfaces in Cavalcanti's Brazilian films, particularly *Caiçara, O Canto do Mar, Terra é sempre Terra*, and *Volta Redonda*, a documentary about steel-making in Brazil. During the 1950s, Cavalcanti also made a documentary in East Germany with Joris Ivens. *Die Windrose* was made as part of East Germany's attempt to build a cultural reputation for itself. Made to celebrate International Woman's Day, the film does not particularly display Cavalcanti's influence, and is now little known. Later, in the 1960s, Cavalcanti made *Thus Spoke Theodore Herzl*, a film made in Israel, celebrating the Israeli leader. The fact that Cavalcanti could make such a film, however, after making the pro-communist *Die Windrose*, and his 1955 adaptation of Brecht's *Herr Puntila und sein Knecht Matti*, speaks volumes for Cavalcanti's lack of political nous. His involvement with East Germany, for example, was to lead Michael Balcon, at Ealing Studios, to blacklist Cavalcanti from any future work at Ealing.

One final documentary which must be mentioned here was Cavalcanti's 1942 film, *Film and Reality*, a compilation documentary which attempted to put together the high points of achievement in the documentary film up to that date. In his film Cavalcanti emphasised the aesthetic achievement of the documentary. However, this had the effect of enraging Grierson and his associates, who believed that the prime purpose of the documentary film should be a social one. The fuss over *Film and Reality* was to rumble on for a long time, and it significantly affected Cavalcanti's relationship with Grierson. The film is not remarkable in itself, and the controversy it engendered says much more about the sorts of conflicts that Cavalcanti tended to get involved in with all his employers than about the film itself.

Cavalcanti's most important films can be divided into three groups. First are those which attempt to subvert dominant mores or positions. This group includes the avant-garde *Rien que les heures*, and, in England, the films *Pett and Pott, Went the Day Well?*, and *Dead of Night*. However, although these films are important, they do not fully represent Cavalcanti's core filmmaking concerns. The second major group of films consists of transitional films such as *Champagne Charlie, They Made Me a Fugitive*, and *One Eyed Simon*. Although these films also critique dominant mores, they are also more positive in approach to their subjects. This shift from critique to a more affirmative approach, for example, differentiates a film such as *Champagne Charlie* from one like *Went the Day Well?* Finally,

there are those films which come closest to realising and embodying Cavalcanti's core aspirations for his own filmmaking. These include *En Rade, For Them That Trespass*, and *O Canto do Mar*. These films are all made within the French poetic realist tradition.

Cavalcanti's major contribution to film culture was made in England, not as a director but as a producer, and his production work at both the GPO Film Unit and Ealing Studios had a considerable impact on two of the most important institutions within British film culture. In fact, Cavalcanti was not really a documentary filmmaker, and he made few documentaries after leaving the documentary film movement. In France, in the 1920s, he was also mainly active within the feature film industry, and even *Rien que les heures* is better described as an avant-garde modernist film, than a documentary. Within the domain of documentary, however, his greatest achievements came in England, with the GPO Film Unit, where he was able to inject a poetic sensibility into films such as *Song of Ceylon, Coal Face, Night Mail*, and *Spare Time*.

IAN AITKEN

See also **Coal Face; Line to Tcherva Hut; Night Mail; Rien que les heures; Song of Ceylon; We Live in Two Worlds**

Biography

Alberto de Almeida Cavalcanti. Born Rio de Janeiro, February 6, 1897. Son of Manoel and Doña Aña de Almeida Cavalcanti. Educated in Brazil, France, and Switzerland. Directed more than fifty films between 1926 and 1976, and produced many more. Died, Paris, 1982.

Selected Films

1926 *Rien que les heures*
1927 *En Rade*
1927 *La P'tite Lilie*
1931 *Au Pays du scalp*
1934 *Pett and Pott*
1934 *The Song of Ceylon*
1934 *The Voice of Britain*
1935 *Coal Face*
1936 *Night Mail*
1936 *Line to Tcherva Hut*
1937 *We Live in Two Worlds*
1938 *North Sea*
1939 *Spare Time*
1939 *The First Days*
1940 *Men of the Lightship*
1941 *Yellow Ceasar*
1942 *The Big Blockade*
1942 *The Foreman Went to France*
1942 *Film and Reality*
1944 *Champagne Charlie*
1945 *Dead of Night*
1947 *They Made Me a Fugitive*

1949 *For Them That Trespass*
1952 *Volta Redonda*
1953 *O Canto do Mar*
1955 *Herr Puntila und sein Knech Matti*
1956 *Die Windrose*
1967 *Thus Spoke Theodore Herzl*
1976 *Un Homem e o Cinema*

Further Reading

Abel, Richard, *French Cinema: The First Wave, 1915-1929*, Princeton, NJ: Princeton University Press, 1984.

Aitken, Ian, *Alberto Cavalcanti, Realism, Surealism and National Cinemas*, London: Flicks Books, 2001.

Aitken, Ian, *The Documentary Film Movement, An Anthology*, Edinburgh: Edinburgh University Press, 1998.

Aitken, Ian, *Film and Reform*, London: Routledge, 1990.

Audra, Mário, *Cinematográfica Maristela: Memórias d um produtor*, São Paulo: Silver Hawk, 1997.

Cavalcanti, Alberto, *Filme e Realidade*, Rio de Janeiro: Editora Artenova, in collaboration with Empresa Brasiliera de Filmes—Embrafilme, 1977.

Danischewsky, Monja, *White Russian—Red Face*, London: Victor Gollancz, 1966.

Ghali, Noureddine, *L'Avant-Garde Cinématographique en France dans les Anées Vingt*, Paris: Editions Paris Experimental, 1995.

Ivens, Joris, *The Camera and I*, Berlin: Seven Seas Publishers, 1969.

Low, Rachel, *The History of the British Film 1929–1939: Documentary and Educational Films of the 1930s*, London: George Allen & Unwin, 1979.

Orbanz, Eva, *Journey to a Legend and Back: The British Realistic Film*, Berlin: Volker Speiss, 1977.

Pellizari, Lorenzo and Claudio M. Valentinetti (eds.), *Alberto Cavalcanti*, Locarno: Éditions du Festival international du films de Locarno, 1988.

Sussex, Elizabeth, "Cavalcanti in England," in *Sight and Sound* 44, 4, Autumn, 1975.

———, *The Rise and Fall of British Documentary: The Story of the Film Movement Founded by John Grierson*, Berkeley: University of California Press, 1975.

Swann, Paul, *The British Documentary Film Movement, 1926–1946*, Cambridge: Cambridge University Press, 1989.

Watt, Harry, *Don't Look at the Camera*, London: Paul Elek, 1974.

CENTRAL OFFICE OF INFORMATION

Beginning in February 1946, a Films Committee made plans for the British Central Office of Information (COI), the peacetime equivalent of the wartime Ministry of Information (MOI). Chairman of the committee was Bernard C. Sendall, who had succeeded Jack Beddington as head of the MOI Films Division. On April 1, 1946, the COI officially took over the film-sponsoring activities of the MOI. Unlike its predecessor, however, the COI Films Division was not provided in its terms of reference with any power of initiation, nor did the COI have ministerial status, as had the MOI. Instead, it was controlled by a committee composed of the public relations officers of the ministries of the British government. An annual sum was set aside to cover its expenses, but it did not administer even that money itself. Each item of expenditure had to be submitted to, and authorized by, the Treasury. Much of MOI's administrative personnel carried over into the COI, including Sendall as chief film controlling officer.

The transition from war to peace was understandably difficult, considering the nature and size of the problems faced. Though Crown Film Unit, part of the MOI, had made the finest of the wartime documentaries, 90 percent of the output from MOI Films Division had been produced on contract by independent units. In fact, during the war all units were working completely on government contract (there was no other sponsorship available), and many small new units were formed on the basis of the vast government demand. The continuation of government-commissioned production under the COI was therefore crucial to the entire field.

If doing little for the uncertainties, some of the frustrations of documentary-making in the immediate postwar years were released through increasingly bitter attacks on the Central Office of Information Films Division. Because of its pivotal position in the British film situation and size, it was an obvious target. Six months after its creation, the COI was weathering persistent criticism.

Regardless of the alleged difficulties, the COI was the largest source of sponsorship in Britain, supervising the production of about 107 films in 1947. During that calendar year, fifteen films were sold to theatrical distributors, the highest figure achieved in any one year by the government information services. More important, the COI nontheatrical component included the Central Film Library in London and twelve regional offices. In all, more than 80,000 16mm prints had been mailed in 1947. A total of 144 projection vans provided shows in factories, institutes, and clubs, which had no projectors of their own. It was estimated that during 1947, the mobile units played to an audience of nearly 5 million, who attended some 45,000 showings.

In February 1948, John Grierson, prewar leader of the documentary movement, returned to Britain (from UNESCO) to take over the job of controller of government film activities. Part of his responsibility was to coordinate the work of the Crown Film Unit and the COI Films Division. As Crown was in direct succession from the Empire Marketing Board and General Post Office units, it was in a sense a return to the work Grierson had begun twenty years before. (The Colonial Film Unit, founded in October 1939, was also under the COI.) Crown, which had been under the MOI, had achieved considerable postwar autonomy through a charter, putting it on an equal level with the COI. Both organizations reported to the Controller of the Treasury. One of Grierson's early moves was to reduce Crown's autonomy and put it under COI administration.

Altogether, as Grierson liked to point out, the Central Office of Information was the biggest producer of short films in the world. However, it produced few films of significant value or lasting quality. Heading the list would probably be *Waverly Steps*, *Daybreak in Udi*, and *The Undefeated*.

Waverly Steps (1948) was made by Greenpark Productions for the Scottish Home Department and directed by John Eldridge. A "city symphony," in the tradition founded in the 1920s by Cavalcanti in Paris and Ruttmann in Berlin, it attempted to give the "feel" of Edinburgh by tracing a dozen minor human incidents over twenty-four hours. Lovely and moody, it even contains some of the ambiguity of thought appropriate for works of art and rarely consciously permitted by orthodox documentarians.

At the time, *Daybreak in Udi* (1949) was generally considered the most successful of the COI releases. Made for the British Colonial Office by Crown, with the cooperation of the Nigerian government, it was produced by John Taylor and Max Anderson and directed by Terry Bishop. William Alwyn composed the score, which was performed by the London Philharmonic. The script, by Montagu Slater, recounted the building of a maternity hospital by native Nigerians and a British district officer. Short-feature in length and form, using indigenous nonactors, it won a number of international prizes, including an Oscar. Today, however, *Daybreak in Udi* looks strangely patronizing and naive. It is almost hard to believe the British made it in their own self-interest, but in 1949 the course of African national aspirations had yet to be run.

Finally, *The Undefeated* (1950), from World Wide Pictures, was produced by James Carr and directed by Paul Dickson for the Ministry of Pensions. It chronicles the bravery and endurance of a former glider pilot, who lost both his legs and the power of speech in the battle of Arnhem, as he struggled to become a useful and active member of society once again. Somewhat sentimental, perhaps, it was nonetheless regarded as highly effective when released, the performance of the amputee being singled out for special praise. The British Film Academy named it Best Documentary of the Year.

During Grierson's two-year tenure at the COI, there was a general reduction of funds, general in the sense that it was aimed at COI as a whole in the name of economy and the usual and general lack of enthusiasm for information services: overall expenditures were cut almost 25 percent. Although Grierson was keeping his forces and funds comparatively intact, government film production, which had increased from the 211 reels of the year prior to his arrival to 257 during his first year, fell to 167 during his second—the lowest figure recorded in the history of the Ministry of Information and the Central Office of Information up to that time.

Given the proud tradition of British government documentary filmmaking, it was small comfort to know that it was suffering as part of a general trend. Affected by prevailing conditions as it was, there were unique factors connected to the central government operation which Grierson was unable to fix. Two months after he left COI, the Colonial Film Unit was transferred to the Colonial Office. Exactly one year after Grierson's departure, Crown Film Unit was disbanded under a newly elected Conservative government. Given the centrality of the EMB-GPO-Crown succession to the development of documentary theory and practice, its elimination could hardly be compensated for by the postwar burgeoning of independent commercial units.

JACK ELLIS

See also **Crown Film Unit; Grierson, John; Taylor, John, MOI**

CEYLON TEA PROPAGANDA BOARD

Formed in 1932, the Ceylon Tea Propaganda Board is best known as the sponsor of the British documentary *Song of Ceylon* (1934). Although the Ceylon Tea Propaganda Board and England's General Post Office (GPO) film unit worked together on similar projects throughout the 1930s, this film was by far the most impressive of their collaborations. It is also the only one of their combined efforts that is still widely discussed and taught in film schools today.

Films produced with a government/commercial partnership would come to exemplify the tension between the propagandistic foundations and the artistic aims of documentary legend John Grierson's Empire Marketing Board (EMB)/GPO film unit. This film unit, and the larger British government departments that directed it, was charged with using film to better the British citizen. The idea was that an empowered and educated populace would be more able to participate in the joys of English culture and citizenship. Pushing heightened trade with the colonies was another, though less discussed, motive for the EMB to begin making films. Several critically important documentaries emerged from the film unit under Grierson, including *Drifters* (1929), *Housing Problems* (1935), and *Night Mail* (1936).

Song of Ceylon was begun under the direction of the British EMB and completed as a GPO product when the EMB film unit folded and was absorbed by the GPO. The GPO connection is vital to understanding the importance of the Ceylon Tea Propaganda Board. Assessing the process by which the Ceylon Tea Propaganda Board came to be involved in filmmaking provides an excellent means to understanding the documentary situation in Britain in the 1930s.

Initially a government public relations worker, Sir Stephen Tallents was central to the evolution of the thriving British documentary movement of the era in both his methodology and his actions. Under Tallents, the EMB hired John Grierson, began feature filmmaking, and started using commercial sponsors. As the British government and public began to scrutinize the EMB before its eventual dissolution, Tallents moved from EMB secretary to GPO public relations manager and brought the film unit with him in 1933. When Tallents left the EMB, his former public relations staff members scattered across the United Kingdom. One of them, Gervas Huxley, began working for the Ceylon Tea Propaganda Board. After this move, the Ceylon Tea Propaganda Board began sponsoring films as part of its public relations efforts. The sponsorship seeds planted under Sir Stephen Tallents blossomed, and the commercial promotion of product grew to be inexorably tied to the aesthetic goals of the British filmmakers of the period. Though Grierson worked to ensure that a film's aesthetic or social message was not compromised for the commercial sponsor, the aforementioned tension between a film's financial backing and its social agenda was apparent in each project, sometimes blatantly.

The forty-minute film, *Song of Ceylon*, was produced by Grierson and directed, filmed, and edited by Basil Wright. Though announced in its credits as being sponsored by the Ceylon Tea Propaganda Board, the film does not present the tea industry directly until its second half. Divided into four sections, the film's first two parts, "The Buddha" and "The Virgin Land," focus primarily on the people of the region and their daily rituals and beliefs.

The style is lyrical and the shooting abstract. There is no clear story line, nor a clear connection to Ceylonese tea or the film's sponsor. The style seems to tow the line between adoration and patronization of the British colonized Ceylonese people. For example, the visual treatment of cultural practice is elated, but the opening titling reads "Honor and Service of the Devil." In the lengthy third section, "The Voices of Commerce," the tea trade audibly enters the film on the sound track along with other intrusive Western industries as the section's title takes on a literal meaning, with men's voices and commercial sounds overlapping in a near Eisensteinian mode. Again, the role of the sponsor is seemingly contradictory, as the message of the third section seems to be the infringement of industry on the beauty of an ancient culture. The tea trade formally enters the film in the last section, "The Apparel of a God," with shots of the gears of the Ceylon tea industry in action: workers, ships, cargo, etc. working together to push the process along. Ceremonial dance and dress are also included in the film's final section. The people remain beautiful and their culture predominantly the focus, but with the introduction of industry one can finally understand how the film could possibly be pitched as positive public relations for the Ceylon Tea Propaganda Board. As previously discussed, however, the relationship between the sponsor and the message of the work remains unclear, undoubtedly by Grierson's design.

What did the Ceylon Tea Propaganda Board have to gain from the film? *Song of Ceylon* won critical accolades with the London Film Society and performed relatively well with audiences at theatrical showings. The film brought acclaim to the British documentary movement, though not necessarily to the GPO or the Ceylon Tea Propaganda Board. This is probably due to the confusing role of the sponsor in the film. The reverent and beautiful first half of the film shows a love and near idolization of the Ceylonese and their culture. This could perhaps reflect well on the Ceylon Tea Propaganda Board if there was not such a blurred line between respect and the orientalization of the Ceylonese tradition by these Western filmmakers. The antiquity of the Ceylonese way of life is contrasted in the first half with the rude intrusion of commerce in the second half. Intercutting between shots, such as a train alternated with an elephant, or coconuts and a steamer, could be seen to represent clashes of East/West or traditional/modern commerce, such that the message and sponsorship of the film is conflicted. One is unsure how the tea trade benefits the culture in the long run, though one is sure of the beauty of the film.

Song of Ceylon was one of a handful of "prestige" films produced by the GPO. The films were distinguished by their quality, budget, and length (longer that their usual fare), and all were made for organizations separate from the GPO, like the Ceylon Tea Propaganda Board. Through such partnerships, the GPO was able to gain a positive reputation for England's documentary filmmaking abilities and their overall cultural interest and social agenda. These relationships, with the Ceylon Tea Propaganda Board and other like organizations, provided the resources necessary to accomplish the feats that John Grierson, Sir Stephan Tallents, and their contemporaries envisioned.

JUSTINE NAGAN

See also **Empire Marketing Board Film Unit; General Post Office Film Unit; Grierson, John; *Song of Ceylon*; Tallents, Stephen; Wright, Basil**

Further Reading

Aitken, Ian, *Film and Reform: John Grierson and the Documentary Film Movement*, London and New York: Routledge, 1992.

Barnouw, Erik, *Documentary: A History of the Non-Fiction Film* (2nd rev. ed.), New York, Oxford: Oxford University Press, 1993.

Ellis, Jack C, *John Grierson: A Guide to References and Resources*, Boston: G.K. Hall, 1986.

Lovell, Alan and Jim Hiller, *Studies in Documentary*, New York: The Viking Press, 1972.

MacDougall, David and Lucien Taylor, *Transcultural Cinema*, Princeton: Princeton University Press, 1998.

Morris, Peter, "Re-Thinking Grierson: The Ideology of John Grierson," *Dialogue: Canadian and Quebec Cinema* 3, 1987, 21–56.

Swann, Paul, *The British Documentary Movement 1926-1946*, Cambridge and New York: Cambridge University Press, 1989.

CHAIR, THE

(US, Shuker, 1963)

One of the most important films produced in the 1960s by Drew Associates, and certainly the most widely known of "The Living Camera" series, *The Chair* remains grounded in many of the stylistic conventions of cinema verité while telling a compelling and tense narrative. Originally titled *Paul*, following the practice of naming the films in a series after the main subject of each film (it was the last produced in the series), the film has since been referred to as *The Chair*, that central, inanimate object that plays so crucial a role in the documentary. Filmed in July 1962, *The Chair* recounts a crisis in Chicago, that in five days Paul Crump is sentenced to die in Cook County Jail's electric chair for a murder he committed nine years ago. His lawyers, the young Donald Page Moore and the experienced Louis Nizer, must convince the Illinois State Parole Board that their client has been rehabilitated (a line of argumentation that in the United States had yet to be successful in the overturning of a death sentence), and that Governor Kerner should commute Crump's sentence.

As with the more than forty films produced by Drew Associates in the 1960s, *The Chair* is really a collaborative effort between Executive Producer Robert Drew; his chief filmmaker Gregory Shuker; the two additional filmmakers, Richard Leacock and D. A. Pennebaker; and his team of correspondents: Shuker, Drew, John MacDonald, and Sam Adams. Drew assigned the ideas of the film and oversaw production, the filmmakers photographed and planned the shoots, and the correspondents often acted as soundmen and journalists. The role each associate played often changed from film to film. Having first worked with Drew Associates as a correspondent in *On the Pole* (1960), Shuker was soon assigned the role of filmmaker. *The Chair* and *Crisis: Behind a Presidential Commitment* (1963) are his two most realized accomplishments with Drew Associates.

As with *Crisis*, *The Chair* involves just that, a crisis. In *The Chair*, the resolution of the crisis

The Chair, 1963.
[*Still courtesy of the British Film Institute*]

may end with a man being executed. Shuker and his filmmakers were able to achieve a dramatic unity within the film by initially introducing us to the principal characters, Crump being the first. At the start of the film, narrator James Lipscomb states gravely, "It's Sunday, less than five days before the condemned man, Paul Crump, is scheduled to die in the chair." The phrase "the chair" is repeated several times in the opening few minutes, and the direness in which Lipscomb repeats it only heightens the urgency of the crisis situation.

One of the more significant scenes of *The Chair* that builds on this crisis involves the introduction of Warden Jack Johnson. In charge of executions at the jail, Johnson is seen, ironically enough, as the man who will execute Crump (he is Crump's best friend, and the convict asked the Warden to perform the execution) and also as one of many who will testify on Crump's behalf. Through a series of following shots, we journey with the Warden from his office down endless hallways lit with eerie florescent lighting. We hear the sound of Johnson's echoing footsteps, down a dark elevator, through the bowels of the jail that are lit by a single window (producing wide cast and attached shadows), into the chapel, and then finally into the sealed room that houses the chair. The handheld camera continues to follow Johnson as he circles the chair and then pans from the chair to the Warden's sullen face, and then back to the chair to end the scene. The long takes in this scene show the effectiveness at hiding the presence of the camera so as to allow the true emotions of the Warden, especially in his office, to be brought forth.

Some believe that the stylistic differences between the two camera crews (Pennebaker and Shuker; Leacock and Drew) coupled with the sudden alternation between one filmed subject and another, with little regard for temporality, created an oversimplified crisis situation that resembled a fictional story rather than a realistic one. Thus, at times *The Chair* appears to drift away from the stylistic and creative precepts of cinema verité, namely that of filming real people in real and uncontrolled situations. Nizer, and particularly Moore, often resemble characters from a play or a novel; they are teeming with emotions, and one could argue they are overacting. Some of Moore's performances, particularly his phone conversation filmed in a very long take with Church officials who will make a statement on Crump's behalf in which the lawyer weeps openly (later in the scene, they decide not to release their statement), do not appear genuine. Yet in another apparent disregard for filming in the cinema verité style, portions of the film were shot well after Crump's sentence had been commuted. Jean-Luc Godard who, with his fellow directors from the French New Wave influenced the cinema verité movement, was highly critical of *The Chair*, calling it a melodrama full of stereotypical images and simplified, one-dimensional characters.

Members of Drew Associates admit that there are problems with the film. Pennebaker believes that the real story was too complex. Drew, who made the final edit, acknowledges his error in simplifying the story in exchange for hype and suspense. Yet, despite these apparent drawbacks, the film succeeds in placing a human face on a condemned man. Although Paul Crump does not appear as often in *The Chair* as other title characters in "The Living Camera Series," most notably the exceptionally strong film *David* (1961), Crump's brief time on camera, as well as his brevity and humility of speech (as opposed to Moore's), allows him to be viewed sympathetically. While

Crump's sentence is commuted by Governor Kerner (he will serve 199 years with no parole), the final shot, that of the doors of Crump's dim cell being shut and his cell backlit by a small window, creating high contrast between light and dark, underscores Crump's future as one of confinement and isolation.

ALEXANDER L. KAUFMAN

See also **Drew Associates, Pennebaker, DA; Shuker, Gregory**

The Chair (USA, Drew Associates, 1963, 58 min). Distributor (since 1980): Drew Associates in Brooklyn, New York. Executive Producer: Robert Drew. Co-producers: Time-Life Broadcast and Drew Associates. Filmmaker: Gregory Shuker. Additional filmmakers: Richard Leacock and D. A. Pennebaker. Correspondents: Gregory Shuker, Robert Drew, John MacDonald, and Sam Adams. Editing by Ellen Huxley, Joyce Chopra, Patricia Powell, and Richard Leacock. Assistants: Gary Youngman, Sylvia Gilmour and Nicholas Proferes. Narration by James Lipscomb. Filmed in Chicago and Springfield, Illinois. Winner of the Special Jury Prize at the 1962 Cannes Film Festival; Invited Participant at the 1963 New York Film Festival.

CHALLENGE FOR CHANGE/SOCIÉTÉ NOUVELLE

The National Film Board (NFB) of Canada's Challenge for Change and its Francophone component, Société Nouvelle, were designed to use documentary filmmaking to address social, cultural, and economic disenfranchisement in Canadian society. Between 1967 and 1980, the initiative produced approximately 150 films in the areas of community organization, native issues, labor, welfare and poverty, and women's issues. The most conventional were mass audience social documentaries, typified by their prototype film, Tanya Ballantyne's *The Things I Cannot Change.* The program produced films such as the series on the American community organizer, Saul Alinsky, meant to train social activists.

Most emblematic of Challenge for Change/Société Nouvelle were the films and videotapes gener-

ated by the disenfranchised themselves. The first example produced were Colin Low's twenty-eight films shot in the remote Newfoundland fishing community of Fogo Island. The Fogo residents, threatened with the failure of their fishery and a forced relocation, spoke uninterrupted, directly to the camera and were given the opportunity to edit the footage before its release.

Portable videotape recorders and community access cable television facilitated the use of the Fogo model as a tool for community organization. Challenge for Change/Société Nouvelle sponsored individual community video projects (and the documentation of those projects in films such as *VTR St. Jacques, VTR Rosedale*), as well as the establishment of ongoing community video centers.

Challenge for Change/Société Nouvelle generated considerable discussion as to the role of the documentary filmmaker. Was it not disingenuous in an institution like the NFB, known for its documentary *auteurs*, to now claim a complete disinterest in style? Was it possible? John Grierson, while offering an equivocal approval of Challenge for Change, found that "the old unsatisfactory note of faraway liberal concern for humanity-in-general creeps in, in spite of these real excursions into the local realities" (Grierson, 134).

A second critique of Challenge for Change/Société Nouvelle was the mandate itself. As Jones points out: "A film could criticize practices, policies or situations that tended to bar certain groups from equitable participation in the mainstream of Canadian life . . . But films which criticized something fundamental about society were not encouraged and rarely permitted" (Jones, 1981: 171). Even when focusing on the needs of their constituencies, the seven Federal ministries cosponsoring the program could be put off by issues hostile to their own agendas. Indian Affairs, for example, attempted to block production of *Cree Hunters of the Mistassini*, a film that countered the Trudeau government's refusal to negotiate land claim treaties with native bands.

By the late 1970s, all but two of the sponsoring federal ministries had left the program, making its collapse inevitable. The legacy of Challenge for Change/Société Nouvelle, however, remains in its raising of fundamental issues of public sponsorship of political filmmaking, the role of the documentary filmmaker in such work, and the uses of video and other ostensibly democratizing media. The program also served as a training ground, most notably for the women who were to become the founders of the National Film Board of Canada's women's unit, Studio D.

SETH FELDMAN

See also **Canada; Grierson, John; Low, Colin; National Film of Canada**

Selected Films

1966 *The Things I Cannot Change*: Tanya Ballantyne, director
1967 *Fogo Island Films*: Colin Low, director
1967 *Encounter with Saul Alinsky, Pts I and II*: Peter Pearson, director
1968 *Saul Alinsky Went to War*: Peter Pearson and Donald Brittain, directors
1968 *Challenge for Change*: Bill Reid, director
1969 *Up Against the System:* Terrence Macartney-Filgate, director
1969 *You Are on Indian Land*: Mort Ransen, director
1969 *VTR St. Jacques*: Bonnie Sherr Klein, director
1974 *Cree Hunters of the Mistassini*: Boyce Richardson, Tony Ianzelo, directors
1974 *VTR Rosedale*: Len Chatwin, director
1974 *Luckily I Need Little Sleep*: Kathleen Shannon, director
1974 *Urba 2000 series*: Michel Régnier, director
1980 *Unemployment: Voices from the Line*: Pierre Lasry, director

Further Reading

Fourteen issues of *Challenge for Change Newletter* (a.k.a. *Challenge for Change/Société Nouvelle Newsletter* and *Access: Challenge for Change/Société Nouvelle*) were published by the National Film Board of Canada between Spring, 1968 and Spring, 1975.

Bodolai, Joe, and Harry Isobel, "Decentralization of the Means of Visual Production," *Artscanada*, 30, 4, October, 1973, 66–72.

Burnett, Ron, "Video: the Politics of Culture and Community" in *Resolutions: Contemporary Video Practices*, Minneapolis: University of Minnesota Press, 1966, 282–303.

———, "Video/Film: From Communication to Community," in *Video, the Changing World*, edited by Alain Ambrosi and Nancy Thede, Montreal: Black Rose Books, 1991.

Cox, Kirwan. "Vidéographe," *Cinema Canada*, 4, October-November, 1972, 16–19.

Dansereau, Fernand, "Saint-Jérôme: The Experience of a Filmmaker as Social Animator," in *Canadian Film Reader*, edited by Seth Feldman and Joyce Nelson, Toronto: Peter Martin Associates, 1977, 128–131.

Friedlander, Madeline S, "Challenge for Change: An American View," *Film Library Quarterly*, 2, 4, Fall, 1969, 48–52.

Grierson, John, "Memo to Michelle About Decentralizing the Means of Production," in *Canadian Film Reader*, edited by Seth Feldman and Joyce Nelson, Toronto: Peter Martin Associates, 1977, 132–136.

Hénaut, Dorothy Todd, "Film as an Instrument for Social Change," *Artscanada*, 26, 1, February, 1969, 34–35.

———, "Implicating People in the Process of Change: Canada's New King of Film Making," *Film Library Quarterly*, 2, 4, Fall, 1969, 44–47.

———, "Films for Social Change: The Hammer and the Mirror," in *Studies in Canadian Communication*, edited by Gertrude J. Robinson and Donald Theall, Montreal: McGill University Press, 1975, 175–188.

———, "The Challenge for Change/Société Nouvelle Experience," in *Video, the Changing World*, edited by Alain Ambrosi and Nancy Thede, Montreal: Black Rose Books, 1991, 48–53.

Jones, D.B., *Movies and Memoranda: An Interpretative History of the National Film Board of Canada*, Ottawa: Canadian Film Institute, 1981, 157–175.

Kurchak, Marie, "What Challenge? What Change?" in *Canadian Film Reader*, edited by Seth Feldman and Joyce Nelson, Toronto: Peter Martin Associates, 1977, 120–128.

Low, Colin, "Grierson and Challenge for Change," in *John Grierson and the NFB*, Toronto: ECW Press, 1981, 103.

Mackenzie, Scott, "Société nouvelle: The Challenge for Change in the Alternative Public Sphere," *Canadian Journal of Film Studies*, 5, no. 2, Fall, 1996, 67–83.

Marchessult, Janine. "Amateur Video and the Challenge for Change," in *Mirror Machine: Video and Identity*, Toronto: YYZ Books, 1995, 13–25.

———, "Reflections on the Dispossessed: Video and the 'Challenge for Change' Experiment," *Screen*, 36, 2, Summer, 1995, 131–146.

Summers, Bob, "Challenge for Change," *Cineaste*, 3, 4, Spring, 1970, 16–18.

Watson, Patrick, "Challenge for Change," in *Canadian Film Reader*, Edited by Seth Feldman and Joyce Nelson, Toronto: Peter Martin Associates, 1977, 112–119.

Weisner, Peter K. "Media for the People: The Canadian Experiments with Film and Video in Community Development," *American Review of Canadian Studies*, 22, 1, Spring, 1992, 65–99.

CHAN, EVANS

Although best known as a transnational fiction filmmaker based in New York City and Hong Kong, Evans Chan has a considerable body of documentary work to his credit. Before making his debut feature, *To Liv(e)*, in 1990, Chan had spent the preponderance of his professional life as a journalist and media arts commentator in Asia and within the Chinese-language press in America. His interest in political affairs, current events, social trends, and the broad spectrum of personalities that make up the contemporary arts scene from Hong Kong to New York underpins all of his films—both fiction and nonfiction. Influenced by Bertolt Brecht's epic theater and Jean-Luc Godard's counter-cinema, Chan breaks the illusion of a seamless fiction in his dramatic features by including interviews with political figures, snippets of stage performances, and documentary inserts of life on the street. Like Godard and Marker, Chan works within the tradition of the film essayist. He uses fiction and nonfiction, as Georg Lukacs says of the essay form, as a "springboard" (Lukacs, 1974: 16) to engage the critical events of the day with the commitment of an activist.

The shockwaves that went through the global Chinese community after June 4, 1989 can be felt throughout Chan's entire oeuvre; and the impact the events in Beijing in 1989 had on Hong Kong in 1997 and Macau in 1999, when those two colonies returned to Chinese rule, plays a major role in Chan's film dramas as well as his documentary work. To date, Chan has made four feature-length documentaries: *Journey to Beijing* (1998), *Adeus Macau* (1999), *The Life and Times of Wu Zhong-Xian* (2003, based on the play *The Life and Times of Ng Chung Yin*), and *Sorceress of the New Piano* (2004).

Journey to Beijing and *Adeus Macau*

These two documentaries constitute a filmic diptych with the umbrella title of "China Decolonized." The pair of documentaries deals with the transfer of sovereignty of Hong Kong in 1997 and Macau in 1999 to China. Whilst neither film adopts an alarmist or negative perspective on the respective handovers, each expresses the aspiration for the retention of unique local characteristics, some of which represent the inevitable legacy of a long period of colonial influence. The thorny issue of political self-determination is raised in both films, and Chan's documentary approach is to allow his subjects to speak for themselves, unencumbered by intrusive voice-over.

Journey to Beijing, which brought Chan's documentary making to international critical attention at festivals in 1998, follows the trail of an assorted, Canterbury Tales-like group of Hong Kong "pilgrims" on a charity walkathon from Hong Kong to Beijing under the auspices of Sowers' Action Group, which collects funds through sponsorship and other activities to develop schooling facilities in poorer regions of

China. At the literal level the film charts the progress of the unlikely band of walkers toward their destination, with their arrival timed to coincide with the handover of Hong Kong, thus ensuring maximum publicity. At the metaphorical and symbolic level, however, the journey is presented as a microcosm of the complex process of reunification and mutual understanding.

Although Chan does not use a "walk" as a metaphor for Macau's return to Chinese sovereignty in 1999, he does look broadly at the cultural landscape of Macau, the response of artists and intellectuals to the transfer of power, the distinct Portuguese colonial history of Macau, and some of the misunderstandings and failed hopes that accompanied the handover there. The film unfolds through a series of interviews and visual observations of the cityscape of Macau, including the handover ceremony and demonstrations/street theater by artists critical of the event. Law Kar, who was born in Macau and who has been involved in Hong Kong film culture through the Hong Kong Film Festival and Hong Kong Film Archive for many years, talks about making an experimental film in Macau during the late 1960s, when riots inspired by China's Cultural Revolution spilled across the border: "We felt compelled to express our disorientation—dangling between the ruthless rioters and the repressive imperialists. Setting the film in Macau seemed safer, more disarming . . ." Although not as long or elaborate as *Journey to Beijing*, *Adeus Macau* may, indeed, be a more "disarming" view of the end of European colonialism in the Pearl River Delta.

The Life and Times of Wu Zhong-Xian and *Sorceress of the New Piano*

In *Sorceress of the New Piano*, Evans Chan's camera literally gets inside the piano with Tan, actively engaging her as a creative force during her performances and bringing to the screen the excitement of seeing how musical experimentation opens new avenues for aesthetic expression. As in many of his other documentary and fiction films, Chan highlights the role women artists and intellectuals play in the international avant-garde. Just as Tan opens up this world to new audiences by playing Beatles' tunes on toy pianos, Chan's film brings Tan's music to those who have never considered the importance of Asians, Asian Americans, and women within the musical avant-garde.

The 2002 film adaptation, *The Life and Times of Wu Zhong Zian*, is based on a play by Asian People's Theatre Festival Society about the Hong Kong-born democracy activist, Ng Chung Ying, who is strongly associated with Hong Kong's emergent political awareness in the 1970s. Chan's film title reflects the film's appeal to a broader audience in using the mandarin Chinese version of his name. Chan assisted actor and director, Mok Chiu Yiu (who also appears in *Adeus Macau*) in the New York English stage adaptation. His decision to base the film version primarily, but not exclusively, on a filmed performance of the piece at Club 64 in Hong Kong's Lan Kwai Fong, testifies to his keen understanding and empathy with the aims of the original dramatic project.

Chan does an effective job of giving a film audience a clearer idea of the egregious character of Ng than would be possible in a purely filmed recording of the live performance. His blend of the respective media works well in giving a rounded portrait of Ng's passionately committed but inevitably frustrated idealism. To understand the derivation of popular activism in Hong Kong in the response to the Tiananmen massacre, and more recently the July 1 demonstrations against planned anti-subversion legislation emanating from Beijing, Ng Chung Ying's role and legacy are of crucial significance. The documentary is compelling for its typically dialectical quest for a balanced, if at times ironic and bitter, truth instead of mere hagiography.

Lukacs observes about the essay, "the value-determining thing about it is not the verdict . . . but the process of judging" (p. 18). Chan's film essays are very much about this process of judging, thereby opening up transnational conversations about contemporary Hong Kong, Chinese, and global politics through his documentaries.

MICHAEL INGHAM AND GINA MARCHETTI

Biography

Evans Yiu Shing Chan was born in China and raised in Hong Kong. Staff film critic for *The Hong Kong Standard*, 1981 to 1984. Founded his production company, 1990. Has lived in both New York and Hong Kong since 1984.

Selected Films

1998 *Journey to Beijing*
1999 *Adeus Macau*

2003 *The Life and Times of Wu Zhong-Xian*
2004 *Sorceress of the New Piano*

Further Reading

Georg Lukacs, "On the Nature and Form of the Essay," *Soul and Form*, translated by Anna Bostock, London: Merlin Press, 1974, p. 16.

CHANG

(US, Cooper and Schoedsack, 1927)

In part because of its considerable craftsmanship, Merian Cooper and Ernest Schoedsack's *Chang* is a vivid record of its time and setting, or at least an engineered perception of the time and setting in question. If its commercial motivations and narrative contrivances ultimately reduce its strictly documentary value and status, then it remains of great interest and importance in the history of both the documentary and the commercial fiction film.

Grass (1925) and *Chang*, which Cooper and Schoedsack referred to as their "natural dramas," were created at a time when the parameters and ethics of the documentary form were being debated and established. Robert Flaherty's early work in this period, in both its exemplary and problematical aspects, would have the most influence on this defining process.

Chang was shot and set in Siam (modern-day Thailand). It tells the story of a family of Lao tribesmen homesteading on the outskirts of a Siamese settlement, trying to eke out a living in the harsh jungle environment. The plot of the film was substantially formed in Cooper's head before he ever reached Siam, and its central aim was to entertain while taking advantage of a novel and exotic setting. On-set preparations were devoted to embodying the producers' preconceptions.

The filming of *Chang* was marked by an atmosphere of improvisation and openness, even of collaboration, in keeping with Cooper and Schoedsack's production method. As a result, the film's primarily fictional representations are embellished with documentary details. The film provides a brief but vivid representation of the fictional family's domestic arrangements and agricultural practices, for example. There were also incidents (such as when the mother elephant pulls the house down in the process of rescuing her baby) that occurred spontaneously during preparation for filming and were subsequently reenacted for the camera. The details of the film's many hunting sequences, such as the traps and dummies used, reflect authentic processes and methods.

Chang has been criticized for its perceived insensitivities and cultural missteps. At times, Cooper and Schoedsack subjected their actors (including children) to dangerous situations for the sake of the narrative. A modern may also be struck by the amount of violence against animals in the film. It is clear that a number of beasts were rather indiscriminately harmed during the picture's production.

Although *Chang* was well received at the time of its release, even contemporary reviews took consistent exception to the film's alternatively stilted and facetious titles: "The very last grain of rice is husked, O very small daughter," says the noble native, and "Give him hell, boys!" says the ribald-talking gibbon.

Chang reflects and implicitly supports the subservience and oppression that characterize colonial relations. Such attitudes are evident in the treatment of animals during the filming and in the film. The animals, who are domesticated and often killed, might be seen as having a metonymic relation to the Siamese themselves. Nevertheless, it is necessary to remember that *Chang* is a product of its time, and that much of common

Chang, 1927.
[*Still courtesy of the British Film Institute*]

intercultural practices we now take for granted cannot fairly be expected of its producers. The film, for good and ill, reflects the enthusiasms and insensitivities of its time. The influence and continued presence of these incomplete, essential sensibilities should not be underestimated.

It is clear that Cooper and Schoedsack were motivated by more than just commercial or financial considerations. They encountered numerous technical challenges during the production of the film, and their recollections suggest that much of their motivation and satisfaction stemmed from finding successful solutions to these difficulties. The problems they faced included determining how to trap wild cats without killing them, inciting a tiger to attack, filming said attack without endangering the cameraman, protecting film stock from mildew, and incorporating the wide-screen magnascope process.

As they would again later with *King Kong*, Cooper and Schoedsack demonstrated remarkable ingenuity and aplomb in solving each of these problems. As was the case with Robert Flaherty and Werner Herzog, the adventures encountered during production were at least as important as the adventures portrayed in the

production. With few exceptions, the serious, groundbreaking, critically validated documentary film would not follow in *Chang's* manic steps. Nevertheless it has many descendants, and its good-natured absurdity and superb sleights of hand are echoed in a great many diverse places. The influence of *Chang* is present in Jean Painlev's surreal scientific films. They prefigure, as Kevin Brownlow has observed, Walt Disney's *True Life Adventures* and in some ways the films of Arne Sucksdorff as well. Its influence is discernible in any number of large format nature films that couch cinematic spectacle in appreciation of the natural.

Contemporary audiences seem to have taken *Chang* at face value for the most part. *Chang* is emblematic of a great deal of commercial cinema; although there is much in it to criticize, we may finally find it difficult, and too delightful, to dismiss.

DEAN DUNCAN

See also **Flaherty, Robert;** *Grass;* **Sucksdorff, Arne**

Chang (US, Paramount Famous Lasky Corp., 69 min). Presented by Adolph Zukor and Jesse Lasky. Produced by Merian Cooper and Ernest Schoedsack. Direction by Merian Cooper and Ernest Schoedsack. Intertitles by Achmed Abdullah (with uncredited work by Schoedsack and Cooper). Cinematography by Ernest Schoedsack. Editing by Merian Cooper and Ernest Schoedsack. Starring Kru and Chantui as the pioneers, Nah and Ladah as their children.

Further Reading

Behlmer, Rudy, "The Adventures of Merian Cooper," in *Register to the Merian C. Cooper Papers*, edited by James V. D'Arc, Provo, Department of Special Collections/College of Fine Arts and Communications, 2000.

Behlmer, Rudy, "Merian C. Cooper," in *Films in Review*, 17, 1, January 1966, 17–35.

Brownlow, Kevin, *The War, the West, and the Wilderness*, New York: Alfred A. Knopf, 1979.

Cooper, Merian C., *Grass*, New York: Putnam, 1925.

———, "Mr. Crooked," in *Asia Magazine*, 27, 6, June 1927, 477–481, 504–516.

———, "The Warfare of the Jungle Folk: Campaigning Against Tigers, Elephants, and Other Wild Animals in Northern Siam," in *National Geographic*, 53, 2, February, 1928, 233–268.

Mould, D.H. and G. Veeder, "The Photographer-Adventurers: Forgotten Heroes of the Silent Screen," in *Journal of Popular Film and Television*, Washington, DC, 16, 3, Fall, 1988.

Turner, George, editor, *The Cinema of Adventure, Romance and Terror*, Hollywood: The ASC Press, 1989.

CHELSEA GIRLS

(US, Warhol, 1966)

The Warhol film, *Chelsea Girls*, comprises twelve reels designed to be shown side by side as a double screen projection. Each of the reels contains a single discrete episode in the individual lives of the people who resided at the Chelsea Hotel in New York City. The reels themselves are each thirty-three minutes long, and the action was shot sequentially and in real time. The idea of watching film in real time is further complicated here by Warhol, as the viewer must divide his or her attentions between the two different reels as they are projected. The film comes with a set of instructions for the coordination of the sound information on the reels as well. These elaborate notes indicate the rise and fall of the volume on each projector at various places in the film. This means that at times the audio information is in conflict, with both sound and image, as the auditory construction of the film is indeed distinct from that of the image. Indeed some projectionists then (as today) find the film to be more interesting when shown in permutations other than those proscribed by the standardized set of screening instructions. The "actors" seen in this film are those well known in and around the Factory scene in the mid-1960s. The film is a strange mixture of narrative fiction, documented reality, and further formal experimentation in the inherent voyeurism of the camera. In his book *POPism*, Andy Warhol writes, "If anybody wants to know what those summer days of '66 were like in New York with us, all I can say is go see *Chelsea Girls*. I've never seen it without feeling in the pit of my stomach that I was right back there all over again. It may have looked like a horror show—'cubicles in hell'—to some outside people, but to us it was more like a comfort—after all, we were a group of people who understood each other's problems."

It is interesting to note that this was the first Warhol film that saw much commercial success. There was a seven-month run of the film on the Lower East Side at the time of its release. (Waugh,

1996: 67). *Chelsea Girls* was sympathetically reviewed by several mainstream publications, but one Chicago reviewer called it "3½ hours of homosexual garbage disposal" (Waugh, 1996: 68). Of course, bad reviews may have brought audiences out as much as favorable ones, especially among the art scene of the 1960s. Colin McCabe writes in *Who Is Andy Warhol?* that *Chelsea Girls* "caricatures the look of documentary movies . . . Deliberately bad cinematography, sloppy zooming, and scratched up prints" (102). The scratches seen in reel 2 are inherent to the work itself, but what is called poor camerawork here may well be seen as an aesthetic approach to filmmaking that was ahead of its time. The zooming noted here is an effect used in a film with very little camera movement.

This film is best appreciated as an unflinching look at the time, place, and subculture it explores. One may say that this work is scripted and therefore lacks the purity of a documentary or the clarity of Direct Cinema that Warhol's work so cleanly references. But *Chelsea Girls* is a powerful document of this strange collection of Warhol superstars in the

The Chelsea Girls, 1966.
[*Still courtesy of the British Film Institute*]

act of creating a performance. These people are playing out their lives as creatures within Warhol's world at this time, enacting scenes in their own rooms and interacting with their peers as they dance, laugh, argue, shoot up, dress up, improvise, perform scripted actions, and respond to their own worlds with real emotion. Jonas Mekas, creator of Anthology Film Archives and editor of *Film Culture* (the hip film journal of the avant-garde), wrote about *Chelsea Girls* at the time of its release. "And one of the most amazing things about this film is that the people in it are not really actors, or if they are acting, their acting becomes unimportant, it becomes part of their personalities, and there they are, totally real, with their transformed, intensified selves." (Wolf, 1997: 128). [Original text appeared in "Andy Warhol: 'the Chelsea Girls,'" *Village Voice*, 24 November 1966, 29. First published in "Movie Journal" *Village Voice* 29 September 1966.]

As a film, it is both extremely flawed and sublime in its temporal capture of the mood of this pivotal time and scene. It is also a grand experiment in both the voyeurism of the viewer and the filmmaker. Warhol insisted that the camera run continuously for each reel, so there are no cuts called when the characters become confused or wish to have something removed. There is a certain sadistic structural approach here that shows many levels of odd relations between subject and viewer.

TAMMY A. KINSEY

Chelsea Girls, Directed by Andy Warhol. Produced by Andy Warhol. Cinematography by Andy Warhol. Written by Andy Warhol and Ron Tavel. 204 min, 16mm, color and b&w. Featuring Brigid Berlin (Polk), Christian Aaron "Ar" Boulogne, Ronnie Cutrone, Angelina "Pepper" Davis, Eric Emerson, Patrick Flemming, Ed Hood, International Velvet (Susan Bottomly), Gerard Melanga, Marie Menken, Mario Montez, Nico, Ondine (Bob Olivio), Rona Page, Ingrid Superstar, Mary Woronov, and others. Music by The Velvet Underground in Reel 8, the 70-minute portion of the film known as "The Gerard Melanga Story" (or "Marie Menken"), as well as in Reel 12, "Nico Crying" (sound is not heard in this reel until the final ten minutes, as the sound instructions for the film have the Reel 11 dialogue on at this point).

Further Reading

Koch, Stephen, *Stargazer*, New York: Marion Boyars, 1973

O'Pray, Michael (ed.), *Andy Warhol: Film Factory*, London: British Film Institute, 1989.

Warhol, Andy and Pat Hackett, *POPism: The Warhol 60's*, New York: Harper & Row, 1980.

Waugh, Thomas, "Cockteaser" in *Pop Out Queer Warhol*, edited by Jennifer Doyle, Jonathan Flatley, and José Esteban Muñoz, Durham and London: Duke University Press, 1996.

Wolf, Reva, *Andy Warhol, Poetry, and Gossip in the 1960s*, Chicago and London: University of Chicago Press, 1997.

CHICANO TRADITION

The representation in film and television of Mexican Americans and their cultural heritage has long been of interest to scholars, in part because of the Los Angeles area's function as the primary setting for the formation of a self-labeled Chicano culture, and further because of Hollywood's geographical centrality in Aztlán, the mythological homeland of the Aztec people that occupied roughly the same territory as the United States Southwest. Beyond the map, the overlap of documentary film and the history of Chicano traditions and activism is polyvalent. The Chicano Movement (1965–1975) can be understood as a series of protests, conferences, and other events that coincided with the Civil Rights Movement and the anti-war marches of the same time and helped to consolidate and give voice to a politically active community of Mexican Americans, who would label themselves "Chicanos." One key event in the Movement, in March 1968, occurred when four Los Angeles Unified School District high schools organized student walkouts and demanded the reform of both the school conditions and the curriculum, the latter to incorporate more positive and in-depth portrayals of Mexican-American heritage and history. Most of the documentary films produced to date that can be categorized as *Chicano* either respond in some way to this demand for education and visibility or document the Movement itself. The most common themes in Chicano documentary filmmaking include reflections on national identities and their geopolitical limits, biographies of community leaders, explorations of Mexican-American traditions in daily life, and the political issues surrounding immigration, migration, and acculturation, such as labor, education, and citizenship.

The difficulty in clearly outlining a group of filmmakers who could be identified as "Chicano documentary filmmakers" is that most of the key participants do not limit their work, thematically or stylistically, to the two defining categories. Many Chicanos who make films have received recognition for work in both fiction and documentary, which quite often varies between short-, medium-, and feature-length formats. As film scholar Chon Noriega has thoroughly elaborated in his research, the existence of a cohesive body of Chicano feature-length fiction films is inseparable from its roots in documentary television and news footage, especially in its connection to the political activism of the Chicano Movement.

One film that is considered a cornerstone of both the political movement and its filmic representation is *Requiem-29* (1971), made collaboratively by students of UCLA's Ethno-Communications Program along with teaching assistant David Garcia. The program, founded in 1969, offered the opportunity for formal audiovisual media training to a handful of racial minorities, many of whom would later become the influential voices of Chicano media productions. The film includes footage of a central event in the antiwar protest of 1970 called the Chicano Moratorium on the Vietnam War, a protest that ended in police interventions, riots, and the death of *Los Angeles Times* journalist Rubén Salazar, a major voice of the Movement. Police involvement in Salazar's death had been under investigation and hearings were broadcast on local television. *Requiem-29* was made as a documentary rebut to the implication in the television broadcast that the Chicano activists incited the violence that led to Salazar's death, and it uses an overtly emotional history of the events leading up to the tragedy to speak to the manipulative power of the seemingly objective news coverage.

Just a year earlier than the formation of the UCLA program, a government-funded program, The New Communicators, was formed, giving young minorities a chance to train on University of Southern California graduate film productions. Although the program itself was short-lived, it allowed Jesús Salvador Treviño, one of Chicano film and television's most prolific figures to date to immerge from the program with a Konica Super-8 and begin filming his experiences during the Movement. Within New Communicators

group, Treviño wrote and filmed the docudrama, *¡Ya Basta!* (1969)/*Enough Already!,* using nonprofessional actors to depict the unhealthy conditions of the public education system. He helped to initiate the Chicano media coverage of the Movement by filming the high school walkouts of 1968, the hearings that attempted to bar walkout leader Sal Castro from his teaching position, as well as the sit-ins in protest of his expulsion, and the trials of thirteen walkout leaders—known as the L.A Thirteen—accused of conspiring against the city and the school district. The footage was incorporated into his next film, *La Raza Nueva* (1969)/*The New People.* Footage and themes from both films were used in Treviño's early television documentaries, *La Raza Unida* (1972) and *Yo Soy Chicano (1972)/I am Chicano.* The latter film helps to establish an important subgenre, one that mixes images of historic leaders and events, from the pre-Columbian era to through the Mexican Revolution, including interviews with recent leaders, such as political activist Dolores Huerta and poet Rodolfo "Corky" Gonzalez. The film creates a series of diachronic, bi-national political parallels. Chon Noriega has pointed out that because these early films by Treviño were made to circulate within an audience of activists, many already familiar with the events firsthand, the narrative form implies a tacitly agreed-upon, politically unanimous reading of the images, rather than the unbiased, informative tone of his later work in television documentaries. Trevino's Chicano-hosted television talk-show *Acción Chicano* was an important site of production and broadcast for his and other filmmakers' documentation of the changing times. The low cost of the talk-show format allowed Treviño to reallocate budget funds to produce documentary film footage that could be aired on his television show and then circulated independently for its cinematic value in the form of documentary shorts. The show also helped several television stations to begin to acknowledge and address a local Chicano audience.

Many films made in the same period use the aforementioned style of mixing footage, images, interviews, and inspirational art and literature to create a film collage that falls on the categorical border between documentary and experimental film and presents a poetic take on historical reality. Teatro Campesino director Luis Valdez is often credited with creating the first Chicano film by inserting a reading of Corky Gonzlaez's famous epic poem, "I am Joaquín," over a series of historical and contemporary images of the mestizo struggle. The director recruited the efforts of the United Farm Workers' photographer, George Ballis, to produce the film, embalming a more ephemeral, precursory production that involved reading the poem while projecting a series of Ballis's slides. Whereas many still applaud the film's innovative style and rousing tone, Valdez's *I am Joaquín* initiated a critical dialectic with other films of the movement. Sylvia Morales's *Chicana* (1979) responds to the male-centered mythology of the Chicano imaginary, particularly as it is played out in the historical citations of Gonzalez's poem, Valdez's film, and the warrior trope that pervades the La Raza's ideology. Morales and fellow Chicana filmmaker Susan Racho, both founding participants in the UCLA program, were faced with the task of seeking racial solidarity with their group while denouncing a certain sexism implicit in much of their colleagues' rhetoric. In *Chicana*, Morales incorporates live-action shots that portray female participation in both public activism and daily domestic struggles and a uses polyphonous feminine voice-over to counter the univocality of her predecessors. The film's working title, *Bread and Roses,* is an allusion to James Oppenheim's poem about child labor, moving the reference to political struggle beyond the Chicano-centered discourse.

In a break from the work of the past two decades, Chicano film in the 1980s saw a shift from the need to ground current events in distant historical myths to an interest in Chicano histories from earlier in the century, in periods that could be considered harbingers of the Movement. One example is *The Lemon Grove Incident* (1985), written and produced by Paul Espinosa. The title recounts a historical moment comparable in scope to *Brown v. the Board of Education*, albeit less publicized and fourteen years earlier. Combining dramatized scenes and historical documentation, the film tells how families in Lemon Grove, California, reacted to a 1930 school board's attempt to segregate Mexican and Anglo students. Also written and produced by Espinosa, *Ballad of an Unsung Hero* (1983) retells the life story of Pedro J. Gonzalez, a pioneer of Spanish-language radio who was framed and imprisoned on rape charges in 1934. Both films recognize the early mobilization effort in the Mexican-American community of the Great Depression as a necessary forerunner to political transformation in decades to come.

Aside from film, other visual mediums have seen significant innovation in the realm of Chicano artistic and political expression. Through diligent collaborations in exhibitions strategies, film has work symbiotically with other arts to bring Chicano visions to the attention of a nation of spectators. A category in itself of Chicano documentary films are those that explore the role of artistic expression and cultural production in the history of the Chicano Movement. Mario Barrera's *Chicano Park* (1989) recalls a century-long roller coaster of development and displacement in one of San Diego, California's Chicano communities, as well as the way the muralists and other artists fought to preserve a piece of their heritage.

Lourdes Portillo: Crossing Every Border

The work of filmmaker Lourdes Portillo is of particular importance to the notion of Chicano documentary film precisely because of how her work has redefined the category itself and reshaped its audience's expectations. Born in Chihuahua, Mexico, Portillo began her documentary career in her early twenties, studied at the San Francisco Art Institute in the late 1970s, and has spent much of her time since as a major figure in California's film-arts community. One of her contributions to the ideological progress of Chicano cinema came in 1990, when she challenged the dominance of male perspectives within the exhibition of Chicano film and video. The same year that the Chicano Art: Resistance and Affirmation (CARA) film series opened with program sparse in female authorship, Portillo organized the *Cruzando Fronteras/Across the Border* conference for Latin America women film and video artists in Tijuana, Mexico. Her work in telling stories from throughout Latin American and the Caribbean demonstrates a commitment to a community broader than just U.S. Latinos. Her involvement with the organizers of the International Festival of New Latin American Cinema in Havana, Cuba, reveals a geographical and political alignment with Latin America's revolutionary cinemas, a trait common to many of her Chicano colleagues.

Portillo's work is deeply introspective and self-reflexive in its examination of the artist's self and her medium, while, almost paradoxically, pushing outward to explore beyond the thematic limitations of the more officially engaged Chicano films. In the process of investigating Mexican and Latin American heritage, she comments on the social expectations within both the sphere of mass communication and in the broader realms of social interaction. Her earliest work on in the documentary format, co-directed with Argentine-born Susana Muñoz, is the Academy-award nominated *Las Madres / The Mother of the Plaza de Mayo* (1986). It focuses on the work of the mothers of disappeared and tortured victims in Argentina's Dirty War and details the history of the group's outspoken resistance to dictatorial oppression. Critically acclaimed throughout the world, *Las Madres* marked the self-labeled Chicana director's entrance into a transnational sphere of activism through film. *La ofrenda / The Days of the Dead* (1988) appears on paper to be a retreat into a more conservative filmmaking style, recounting the Mexican tradition of honoring deceased loved ones on the Day of the Dead and showing how the holiday has been adapted in Chicano cultural practice. Half of the footage is taken from Mexican festivities, the other half from the United States, with a clear contrast between the traditional Mexican style steeped in religious practice and a flashier counterpart in Chicano culture, morphed by both consumerism and artistic experimentation. But when the altars of the latter reveal tributes to AIDS victims, the film becomes not simply an observation of the tradition of remembering the dead, but a critique of the varying taboos and social expectations of mourning in both cultures. The film plays with voice-over and festive costume to deconstruct essentialist cultural boundaries, such as those within gender, religious orthodoxy, and the rules of expression in public versus private domains. It reflects ironically on a temporal notion of ancestry and heritage as it looks at the future deviations of a tradition that concerns itself with those who lived before us and the recuperation of their image in the present.

One of Portillo's most discussed works, *El diablo nunca duerme / The Devil Never Sleeps* (1994), is also a more literal border-crossing between U.S. and Mexican cultures, but its stylistic experimentalism challenges existing documentary depictions of the Chicano identity quest. Portillo narrates her own journey into Mexico to visit her relatives and investigate the mysterious death of her uncle, Tío Oscar. The contradictions in her findings offer a reflection on a culturally distinct definition of *truth*, an exposure into the public realm of traditionally unspeakable topics, and an allegorical reading of contemporary Mexican politics' abuse of deception. The theme of betrayal threads throughout the film, from parodying the melodramatic conflicts of the Mexican

telenovela, to her family's criticism of both her investigation of family secrets and her choice to live in the United States. The interviews with family members, the use of the *telenovela*, and the playful animation of family photographs pointedly mocks the trope of family portraiture and overturns the notion of a unified Mexican family that was approaching stereotypical status in Chicano self-representation.

Portillo's most recent work includes *Corpus: A Home Movie for Selena* (1999), an homage to the late Tejana music star and the eternal adoration of her fans, as well as *Señorita Extraviada / Missing Young Woman* (2002), which investigates the social causes surrounding the alarming rise in unsolved murders and sexual assaults on young women in the Mexican border town of Ciudad Juarez since the early 1990s. *Señorita Extraviada* offers a portrait of both the victims and their families in the struggle for justice and closure.

Global Coalitions and Bi-Cultural Influences

Chicano documentary filmmaking has co-evolved with the United States' public broadcast system since the inception of both in the late 1960s. To a certain extent, its interaction with public television organizations such as the Public Broadcasting Service and the Corporation for Public Broadcasting has born a recognizable bi-national, bi-cultural, and bilingual constituency of Mexican-American viewers, while also expanding audience spectrum to incorporate other U.S. Latino groups. For example, Treviño's *Acción Chicano* joined forces with the New York-based, Puerto Rican-hosted public-affairs program *Realidades* to exchange resources. To consolidate costs, *Acción Chicano's* host station, Los Angeles's KCET, proposed further exchange among public television stations serving large Chicano audiences, creating the Latino Consortium in 1973. While the *Acción Chicano-Realidades* program collaboration offered both training grounds and broader exhibition for up-and-coming Chicano and Latino filmmakers, the Latino Consortium's executive directors would also establish names for themselves in the field, as with Sylvia Morales and Rick Tejada-Flores. Tejada-Flores's award-winning feature, *Fight in the Fields: Cesar Chavez and the Farmworkers Struggles* (co-directed with Ray Telles, 1996), is among the recent documentaries that have brought Chicano stories to more diverse film-festival, theatrical-release, and public-television audiences.

The manifestos written by the filmmakers of the late 1960s and early 1970s, who defined the continentally unifying New Latin American Cinema movement with such topics as "Imperfect Cinema" and "Third Cinema," were models for the articulation of similar and even overlapping, but necessarily separate, stance for Chicano filmmakers of the same era. For example, Francisco X. Camplis's 1975 publication, "Towards the Development of a Raza Cinema," takes its inspiration from Argentina's Octavio Getino and Fernando Solanas anti-imperialist proclamation "Towards a Third Cinema" and their film *La hora de los hornos (1969) / The Hour of the Furnaces.* The manifesto also acknowledges the tactics of Latin American contemporaries such as Bolivia's Jorge Sanjinés and Brazil's Glauber Rocha. Camplis proposes that a "Raza Cinema" would embrace the work of other oppressed peoples within the United States and throughout the world in its active political resistance. However, citing Treviño's *Yo Soy Chicano* as a valuable prototype, it asks that Chicanos and Latinos evaluate these ideological positions in terms of their own circumstances, and further, take charge of their own representations in the U.S. media, as the job is too often left to filmmakers who are unfamiliar with the nuances of their cultural issues. An even more polemical take on the latter issue is Santa Barbara-based Cine-Aztlán's "Ya Basta Con Yankee Imperialist Documentaries," published the previous year. It calls for Chicanos to use their documentary-making skills as arms against the male-centered, Anglo perspectives in broadcast television's monopolistic control of Chicano representations, and to replace the projection of appeasement and middle-class assimilation with one of liberation, class-struggle, and revolution. Numerous publications by Treviño over the course of his career illustrate another articulate, if didactic, voice that used written texts to analyze the course of the audiovisual medium.

It is important to recognize the role of Chicano scholars, specifically film historians, in preserving, promoting, and articulating a body of cinematic work that can be considered Chicano, as well as in maintaining a supportive dialogue with the filmmakers themselves. Chon Noriega's continues to investigate the history of this ever-evolving movement, both as a unique, nationally specific immergence of a minority culture's self-expression and within a broader international context of Mexican cultural production and Spanish-language media. Rosa Linda Fregoso's work investigates how Chicana filmmakers, such as Portillo, Morales, and Racho, have complicated the dominant notions of Chicano identity. Both Fregoso and Noriega served as advisors on *The Bronze Screen* (1999), a feature documentary written and co-produced by Racho and Nancy de los Santos about the history of Hollywood's love-hate relationship with Latino identity, both in front of and behind the camera.

MISHA MACLAIRD

See also **Hour of the Furnaces, The**; **Portillo, Lourdes**

Selected Films

1969 *La hora de los hornos / The Hour of the Furnaces,* Getino, Octavio and Fernando Solanas.
1969 *La Raza Nueva / The New People,* Treviño, Jesús Salvador
1969 *¡Ya Basta! / Enough Already!,* Treviño, Jesús Salvador
1972 *La Raza Unida,* Treviño, Jesús Salvador
1972 *Yo Soy Chicano / I am Chicano,* Treviño, Jesús Salvador
1979 *Chicana,* Morales, Sylvia
1983 *Ballad of an Unsung Hero,* Espinosa, Paul
1985 *The Lemon Grove Incident,* Espinosa, Paul
1986 *Las Madres: The Mother of the Plaza de Mayo,* Portillo, Lourdes and Susana Muñoz
1988 *La ofrenda: The Days of the Dead,* Portillo, Lourdes
1989 *Chicano Park,* Barrera, Mario
1994 *The Devil Never Sleeps / El diablo nunca duerme,* Portillo, Lourdes
1996 *Fight in the Fields: Cesar Chavez and the Farmworkers Struggles,* Tejada-Flores, Rick and Ray Telles.
1999 *The Bronze Screen,* Racho, Susan and Nancy de los Santos
1999 *Corpus: A Home Movie for Selena,* Portillo, Lourdes
2002 *Señorita Extraviada / Missing Young Woman,* Portillo, Lourdes

Further Reading

Fregoso, Rosa Linda (ed.), *Lourdes Portillo: The Devil Never Sleeps and Other Films.* Austin, TX: University of Texas Press, 2001.
Noriega, Chon (ed.), *Chicanos and Film: Representation and Resistance.* Minneapolis: University of Minnesota Press, 1992.
——, *Shot in America: Television, the State, and the Rise of Chicano Cinema.* Minneapolis: University of Minnesota Press, 2000.
——, and Jesús Salvador, Treviño. *Eyewitness: A Filmmaker's Memoir of the Chicano Movement.* Houston: Arte Público Press, 2001.

CHILDREN AT SCHOOL

(UK, Wright, 1937)

The National Film Archive summarizes the content of *Children at School* with the following: "Deals with the physical conditions of schools in which many children are educated." The accompanying shot list is as follows:

> Democratic education compared with that in a dictatorship; the organization of education in England—nursery, infant, junior, senior and secondary schools progressing to technical schools and universities. Scenes from life in the progressive schools follow. Nursery schools: free activity, air and sunlight, meal times and rest periods; training in hygiene and social habits; a trained nurse supervises the children's health. Infant schools; teaching of a sense of rhythm, reading by acting, confidence through verbal expression, creative play, provision of mid-morning milk. Reading aloud; regular supervision of health by school doctor—parents' help encouraged. Post primary schools: encouragement of freedom, self-reliance. School scenes show gymnastics, woodwork, geography, chemistry, etc; the use of films in teaching. Provision of nutritious meals.
>
> In contrast there are many "blacklist" schools, insanitary, unsafe, out of date. Great difficulties experienced by teachers in out of date buildings not yet scheduled for destruction—inadequate light, overcrowded classes, outside noises.
>
> Mr. Fred Mander, Secretary of the N.U.T. [National Union of Teachers], campaigns for better working conditions. We see a meeting of the Council for the 10 year plan for children at which Lady Astor speaks. Student teachers discuss large classes. A meeting of headmaster and staff of his school. The question remains "Can democracies afford to fall behind?"

Children at School was the first production arranged through Film Centre, which had been established in 1937. Realist Film Unit had been established in the same year by Basil Wright, after his departure from the General Post Office Film Unit. The commentator, Wilson Harris, was editor of the *Spectator*, which published a good deal of writing on the documentary film. It is a continuation of the series sponsored by the gas industry, which had included *Housing Problems* (1935) and *Enough to Eat?* (1936). Through reportage and argument, these films called public attention to pressing problems faced by the nation, insisted that they needed to be solved, and suggested their causes and possible solutions. By making use of stock shots and newsreel footage plus interviews, they were given coherence and rhetorical effectiveness through editing and voice-over commentary. Heavily influenced by the American *The March of Time* series, they represent the beginnings of what would become standard format for subsequent television documentaries.

Though competent in technique and hard-hitting as exposé, in its impersonality *Children at School* might have been directed by any number of documentarians. It represents Wright's deep and genuine social concern arrived at intellectually rather than the emotional core of his being out of which his most personal and best work came. The journalistic style of this film and the lyricism of *The Song of Ceylon* is frequently contrasted.

JACK C. ELLIS

See also **Enough to Eat?; Grierson, John; Housing Problems; Song of Ceylon; Wright, Basil**

Children at School, 1937.
[*Still courtesy of the British Film Institute*]

Children at School (UK, Realist Film Unit for the British Commercial Gas Association, 1937, 24 min) Distributed by Film Centre and then Technique Distributors. Produced by John Grierson. Directed by Basil Wright. Cinematography by A. E. (Adrian) Jeakins and Erik Wilbur. Assistant direction by Patrick Moyna. Commentary read by H. Wilson Harris.

CHILE

See **Underground/ Activist Documentary: Chile**

CHINA!

(US, Greene, 1965)

A socially and politically important film when first released, *China!* remains a striking and powerful document of Felix Greene's desire to show the West, for the first time, just how vibrant and progressive life was for the majority of Chinese since the Communist Revolution. The film is not as complete as some of Greene's other documentaries on China, such as *One Man's China* (1972), or as focused, as in *Freedom Railway* (1974). But *China!* can be seen as an early representation of Greene's guerrilla filmmaking style, which is more fully realized in *Inside North Vietnam* (1973), and of his artistic skill of using color, montage, sound, and a highly controlled narrative structure so as to inform, but also persuade, the viewer that the West has been misinformed as to the quality of life in Communist China.

In 1963, Greene did not set out to make a documentary when he visited China. His goal was to study the nation so as to gather material for another book. After filming for four months and traveling 15,000 miles, Greene and his photographer Hsu Chih-Chiang had more than twelve hours of film. The resulting film was produced and written by Felix Greene and edited by John Jeremy. Greene recorded the music, mostly of Chinese songs played on traditional instruments. Narrator Alexander Scourby's minimal contribution of informative voice-overs allows the viewer to focus on the images and the actions of the people. However, the U.S. Justice Department attempted to prevent the exhibition of *China!* on the grounds that, since the film stock was exposed in China, bringing the film into the United States would make it an import that would require a special license that they would not grant. Senator Fulbright intervened on Greene's behalf and convinced Secretary of State Rusk and members of the White House that the film should be released. This controversy did not hurt, for *China!* proved to be a success, earning favorable reviews from the *New York Times*, running for sixteen weeks at Carnegie Hall Cinema, and shown in 165 American cities.

China! is organized in two distinct sections. The first, a prologue narrated by Greene, serves as a preview of representative images to come (of

China!, 1965.
[*Still courtesy of the British Film Institute*]

schoolchildren, or parades, for example) while also establishing the central theme of the film—that Greene's own perceptions of China, and therefore possibly our own, have been incorrect. As Greene comments in the prologue, "I know very well how personal feelings and evaluations can influence any kind of reporting, whether it's in newspapers or on film. So you will see China as I saw it." There are two montage sequences in *China!*, and both exhibit a distinct stylistic difference from the rest of the film. The first comes soon after Greene's statement. Here, a series of quick shots of life in China, the first being a dramatic point of view parachute drop, followed by parades, workers, dancers, and other archetypal images that are repeated throughout *China!*, are cut together to the rhythm of the song "Socialism is Good," sung by the Shanghai Workers' Cultural Palace. It is a sequence and song that, despite Greene's previous statement regarding the inclusion of one's own beliefs in a movie, lies at the heart of the film's argument that the Marxist Revolution helped bring China from a destitute nation rife with poverty, disease, and class warfare to a civilization that was ready to enter into the modern world and succeed.

The prologue sets the argument in place, but it is with the remainder of the film that Greene attempts to support his ideological convictions. Communist China is first contextualized by Greene in a series of archival images of the 1931 Japanese invasion and the subsequent civil war between the factions of Mao Tse-tung and Chiang Kai-shek. The final black-and-white newsreel shot, that of an infant wailing in the arms of its mother while their village lies in ruin, fades, and suddenly we are witness to a sea of red flags at the annual celebration of the Revolution.

This use of graphic discontinuity serves to bring the audience into modern China; it is a country that is alive with striking colors—the orange molten metal used to make trucks, the green rice fields, the white snow in the northern regions. This sudden graphic transition also supports the film's sense of historical progression, that through surviving the horrors of the first half of the twentieth century, China has established a system of government that treats all citizens as integral persons who will help bring about positive moral and industrial change.

The citizens of Shanghai are better off because of the sweeping economic and social reforms that transformed the city from a criminal and moral cesspool into a leading economic and sober example of socialism at work. This may be one of the more serious drawbacks of Greene's film; at times it borders on propaganda. Although there were areas of China that were off-limits to Greene and Chih-Chiang, Greene did not attempt to broach the subject of human rights abuses in the nation, or of the countless millions who were executed in political purges. Instead, there are short segments on different aspects of Chinese life: school, entertainment, manufacturing, family, art, farming, advancements in medicine, life in a typical rural village, and the building of a causeway from the mainland to the island of Amoy. Each segment follows the same general style of framing: a series of extreme long shots to introduce the topic, of terraced farming, for example, followed by a series of medium and close-up shots of the people at work. Life in *China!* does not seem very different from life in the Western world, and although that may be Greene's implicit belief in this far-left-leaning film, the unanswered questions regarding the past and current state of human rights in China remain highly problematic.

ALEXANDER L. KAUFMAN

See also **Greene, Felix**

China! (USA, 1965, 60 min). Distributor (since 1984): Contemporary Films, Great Britain. Produced by Felix Greene. Written by Felix Greene. Associate producer: L. M. Cole. Photography: Felix Greene and Hsu Chih-Chiang. Edited by John Jeremy. Sound edited by Walter Storey. Music recorded in China by Felix Greene. Music by The Peking Symphony Orchestra, conducted by Li The-Lun, piano by Yin Cheng-Tsung. Opening chorus "Socialism Is Good" sung by members of the Shanghai Workers' Cultural Palace. Narration by Alexander Scourby. Filmed throughout China, including Shanghai, Peking, the Sinkiang region, Inner Mongolia, Kweichow Province, and Amoy. Winner of the first prize at the Melbourne International Film Festival and received the Award of Merit at the Edinburgh Film Festival.

CHRONIQUE D'UN ÉTÉ

(France, Rouch and Marin, 1960)

From its opening sequence, *Chronique d'un été/ Chronicle of a Summer* self-consciously proclaimed its novelty: "this film was not played by actors, but lived by men and women who have given a few moments of their lives to a new experiment in cinema verité." The film has since been celebrated as a turning point in the history of documentary film.

A joint project of sociologist Edgar Morin and filmmaker Jean Rouch, *Chronique d'un été* was conceived as a query into how Parisians lived their lives. Taking advantage of a newly portable synch-sound technology that made it possible to film people speaking spontaneously, the filmmakers took to the street, stopping Parisians with the question: "Are you happy?" The film gradually comes to focus on a handful of characters: a worker, two immigrants, and a concentration camp survivor. Following them through the summer of 1960, the film achieved an unforgettable portrait of its times and breached a new way of filmmaking—cinema verité. Despite the confusion generated by this term, *Chronique d'un été* did not make simplistic claims to truthfulness. A self-reflexive film if ever there was one, it articulated the question of what truth means in the cinema, with unprecedented force and sophistication.

This experiment certainly did not arise in a void. The name *cinema verité,* a translation of the Russian *kino pravda*, was meant to honour a predecessor, Dziga Vertov, who had done away with actors and gone out into the city in an attempt "to catch life unawares" in the 1920s. Another often-mentioned predecessor was Robert Flaherty's *Nanook of the North*. The last scenes of *Chronique d'un été* directly mirrored Flaherty's practice of showing the film subjects rough cuts and recording their reactions.

The experiment was also deeply rooted in its own times. For those documentary filmmakers who were becoming weary of "showing life in its Sunday best" (Morin, 1985: 4), the new portable synch-sound equipment opened the way to unprecedented explorations of the everyday. In its attempt to go beyond "the official and the ritualised," the *cinema verité* introduced by *Chronique d'un été* shared many affinities with its American contemporary, direct cinema (Rothman, 1997: 87).

The classic distinction between cinema verité and kindred experiments like direct cinema is that "cinema verité provokes and participates, whereas direct cinema observes" (Rothman, 1997: 87). In Erik Barnouw's memorable formulation, the filmmaker acts as a "catalyst" for the action of its subjects (Barnow, 1993: 253). Rouch insisted that "he did not film reality as it was but reality as it was provoked in the act of filmmaking. It is this new reality, which would not exist apart from the making of the film, that the filming 'documents' revealing a new truth, a cinema truth" (Rothman, 1997: 87). Insofar as his subjects were concerned, Rouch did not try to play down or disguise the presence of the camera. Assuming "the disjunction caused by the very presence of the camera," he expected "that people will act, will lie, will be uncomfortable," and regarded "this manifestation of this side of themselves as the most profound revelation that anything a 'candid' camera or 'living cinema' could reveal" (Eaton, 1979: 51). In other words, cinema verité is based on the premise

Chronique d'un été, 1960.
[*Still courtesy of the British Film Institute*]

that the masks that people choose for themselves, and the way they wear them on screen, can be more telling than a soul-baring confession.

The truth that cinema verité hopes to reveal is thus akin to "psychoanalytic truth, that is, precisely that which is hidden or repressed comes to the surface in these roles" that people play in front of the camera (Morin, 1985: 5). From the very beginning, Morin envisioned replacing the interviews and dialogue of traditional documentary film with a "psychodrama carried out collectively among authors and characters" (Morin, 1985: 6). He believed that this intersection between psychoanalysis and film was "one of the richest and least exploited universes of cinematographic expression" (Morin, 1985: 6). The response of the characters to this psychoanalytic side of the cinema verité experiment varied widely. These differences are polemically articulated in the last scene of the film, as the participants openly discuss their impressions of the rough cut. They are largely divided into two camps that reproach each other for having been either "too real," or "not real enough." This polemic crystallizes around the two women protagonists, Marceline and Marilou. Marilou argues that "to have a tiny spark of truth the character has to be . . . alone and on the verge of a nervous breakdown" (Feld, 1985: 68). This is, of course, exactly how she is throughout the film, baring her soul in tete-à-tete with Morin. In her confession she attempts to communicate her extreme alienation from the world and from herself. Her success in communicating her alienation, that is, her inability to communicate to Morin and, through the camera, to the world would have de facto cured her alienation. But this talking cinema cure fails and Marilou falls helplessly, desperately silent in front of the camera in a gesture that Rothman interprets as an on-stage suicide (Rothman, 1997: 77–78). Unable to express and thus vanquish her alienation, Marilou is condemned to poignantly reenact it in front of the camera.

While Marilou's confessions are considered by some of the characters/viewers to be the most moving part of the film, other characters openly attack them as "indecent and exhibitionistic." The starkest critic is Marceline, who opposes Marilou's confessional mode with a careful direction of her own stage persona. Marceline revisits her most intimate and traumatic memories in front of the camera— memories of her time in the concentration camps, her relationship to her father who was also deported, and to the family she had left behind. But Marceline insists that the heartrending scene of her walking alone through a deserted Paris and reminiscing about her past was a thoroughly controlled and crafted performance that she had care-

fully planned in advance. What we see in the film, Marceline claims, is just one of many possible "characters of Marceline" that she created for the medium of film (Morin and Rouch, 1985: 77). Marceline's self-creation testifies to her sophisticated understanding of film as a specific medium with certain expressive possibilities and limitations. (Marceline also notes that during her performance she consciously thought of *Hiroshima Mon Amour* and also of Michelangelo Antonioni's films). Marceline's insistence on her acting is also a reminder of the existence of a part of her that is not on display in the film, a part of her that is not public and not accessible through this particular medium. While exposing a most vulnerable part of herself, Marceline also lays claim to her ability to control that exposure, not only by acting but also by directing her performance. (Thus her displeasure when the directors of the film override her self-direction and manipulate her character [Morin and Rouch, 1985: 77]). Of all the characters, Marceline appears most aware of the politics and power dynamics of the film, and most invested in controlling her own representation.

The debate between Marceline and Marilou's modes of self-presentation throws new light on the initial psychoanalytic ambitions of the film. In the course of the filming, it is clear that Morin's idea of a communal psychodrama openly played between actors and authors remains utopian. The direction of the psychoanalytic exploration is marked by strong power dynamics. There is no psychoanalyzing of the directors by the characters. And among the characters, it is the women who are the choice subjects of analysis. Marceline accepts the premise of the game, that is, that the roles that one plays in front of the camera may reveal a deep part of oneself, but she is intent on carefully directing what gets revealed. In carefully constructing a persona or mask that expresses her, she guards herself against those privileged moments in *cinema verité* where the director and spectator see, through the cracks and slippages of hasty masks, parts of the character that she is unaware of or would rather repress. Unlike Marilou, who has little control over her persona and helplessly lays herself bare in front of the camera, Marceline usurps the position of power that the *cinema verité* director, spectator, and the psychoanalyst traditionally share.

If *Chronique d'un été* uses a psychoanalytic lens to approach some of its characters, its overall scope is much wider. In Edgar Morin's words, the film was conceived as an ethnographic study "in the strong sense of the term: it studie[d] humanity" (Morin, 1985: 6). The film was to participate in forging a new direction in ethnographic filmmaking "by emphasizing kinship rather than exotic foreignness" (Morin, 1985: 5). Having made his name directing ethnographic films in Africa, Rouch intended to turn his ethnographic lens toward "his own tribe." One of the most interesting aspects of this ethnographic project is contributed by Laundry, a student from Cote d'Ivoire. The film's casting of Laundry in the role of "African explorer of a France on vacation" (Morin, 1985: 13) attempts to reverse the traditional ethnographic relationship between white observer and colonized subject. Laundry catalyzes some of the most revelatory discussions of the film, revealing a rich spectrum of contemporary French attitudes towards colonization, race, and racism. At the same time, this casting of Laundry in the role of explorer is limiting. The film is interested in Laundry in as much as he can shed light on French society, and less in him as a new member of that society. For example, as Laundry remarked, in the discussion on interracial marriage, the film gave airtime only to the white women's attitudes toward marrying blacks, while excluding his and other black students' ideas about marrying whites.

Chronique d'un été's ethnographic project was planned as a survey of contemporary France taken "at three levels: the level of private life, internal and subjective; the level of work and social relations; and finally the level of present history, dominated by the war in Algeria" (Morin, 1985: 10). The two directors disagreed, however, on the method of bringing this project into being. Rouch was interested in organizing the film chronologically and focusing it tightly on just a few characters (Morin, 1985: 24). Morin wished for a less individualized, "mosaic-like montage of sequences" sustained by the question "How do you live?" (Morin, 1985: 24). As a result, the film often vacillates between these two main approaches, sometimes further divided by the diverging approaches of the characters. Nowhere is this more evident than in the representation of the worker's plight in contemporary France. The film starts by formally interviewing a group of workers who sharply express their dissatisfaction with the conditions of their work. Then, in one of its most innovative moves, the film focuses on one worker, Angelou, following him from the moment his eyes open in the morning throughout his workday and leisure hours to bedtime. This sequence suggestively shows the alienation that the workers had openly articulated in the previous scenes. Once again changing registers, the camera descends into the factory where it films people at work. This factory scene briefly flirts with another movie genre, what a worker calls "a film about work in the twentieth century," a film that Angelou wishes would record life in the factory, with an emphasis on relationships among workers, unions, and management (Morin and Rouch, 1985: 76–77). This oscillation between different cinematic registers is representative of the experimental, searching quality of the film. At times this experimentation might threaten the unity of the film, but it also allows for a plurality of approaches to the worker's problem to coexist.

As Edgar Morin modestly put it: "The film is a hybrid, and this hybridness is as much the cause of its infirmity as of its interrogative virtue" (Morin, 1985: 26). *Chronique d'un été* relinquished the authority of the traditional voice-over and instead allowed its subjects to speak spontaneously. As the debate between Marceline and Marilou shows, the ensuing dialogue was not always free of tension or of problematic power dynamics. Furthermore, allowing a plurality of voices to be heard assumed the risk of creating a cacophony. And still, this imperfect plurality is one of the path-breaking achievements of the film. It gave the film its experimental novelty and complexity, which has made *Chronique d'un été* an inspiration for the upcoming documentary and Nouvelle Vague cinema.

CRISTINA VATULESCU

See also **Morin, Edgar; Rouch, Jean**

Chronique d'un été / Chronicle of a Summer (France, 1961, 90 min.) Directed by Jean Rouch and Edgar Morin. Production: Argos Film (Anatole Dauman and Philippe Lifchitz). Production Director: André Heinrich. Production Secretary: Annette Blamont. Photography by Roger Morillère, Raoul Coutard, Jean-Jacques Tarbés, Michel Brault. Assistants: Claude Beausoleil and Louis Bocher. Lighting by Moineau and Crétaux. Sound by Guy Rophé, Michel Fano, Barthélémy. Editing by Jean Ravel, Nina Baratier, Françoise Colin. Filmed in Paris and Saint Tropez.

Further Reading

Barnouw, Erik, "Catalyst," in *Documentary: A History of the Non-Fiction Film*, New York: Oxford University Press, 1993.

Dornfeld, Barry, "Chronicle of a Summer and the Editing of Cinema Vérité," in *Visual Anthropology*, 2, 1989, 3–4.

Eaton, Mick, *Anthropology — Reality — Cinema: The Films of Jean Rouch*, London: British Film Institute, 1979.

Feld, Steven (ed.) *Chronicle of a Summer*, special issue in *Studies in Visual Communication*, 1, 1985, 38–71 (an abridged translation of Jean Rouch and Edgar Morin, *Chronique d'un été*).

——, "Themes in the Cinema of Jean Rouch," in *Visual Anthropology* 2, 1989, 223–247.

Freyer, Ellen, "Chronicle of a Summer—Ten Years After," in *The Documentary Tradition*, edited by Lewis Jacobs, New York: W. W. Norton, 1979.

Gauthier, Guy, "Jean Rouch, gourou nouvelle vague," in *CinémAction*, 104, 2002, 70–75.

Georgakas, Dan Uayan Gupta and Judi Janda, "Politics of Visual Anthropology, an Interview with Jean Rouch," *Cineaste* 8, 4, 1978, 22.

Morin, Edgar, "Chronicle of a Film," in *Studies in Visual Communication*, 1, 1985, 4–29.

Morin, Edgar, and Jean Rouch, "The Point of View of the "Characters," in *Studies in Visual Communication*, 1, 1985, 71–78.

Rothman, William, "Eternal Verités," in *Beyond Document: Essays on Non-Fiction Film*, Edited by Charles Warren, Hanover: Wesleyan University Press, 1996.

Rothman, William, "Chronicle of a Summer," in *Documentary Film Classics*, Cambridge: Cambridge University Press, 1997.

Rouch, Jean, "The Cinema of the Future?" in *Studies in Visual Communication*, 1, 1985, 30–38.

Rouch, Jean, and Enrico Fulchignoni, "Conversation Between Jean Rouch and Professor Enrico Fulchignoni, in *Visual Anthropology*, 2, 1989, 265–301.

Rouch, Jean, and Edgar Morin, *Chronique d'un été*, Paris: Interspectacles, Domaine Cinéma 1, 1962.

Stroller, Paul, *The Cinematic Griot: The Ethnography of Jean Rouch*, Chicago: University of Chicago Press, 1992.

Wintonick, Peter, and National Film Board of Canada, *Cinema Verité: Defining the Moment*, Montreal: The Board, 1999.

CHULAS FRONTERAS

(US, Blank, 1976)

Les Blank's *Chulas Fronteras* holds a prominent place in this documentary director's notable body of work, many of the films dealing with the folk music of communities on the fringes of mainstream America or with the specific delights of particular foods. It is a loving ode to the *conjunto* music of the Texas-Mexico frontier. (A *conjunto* is a small group including an accordion, a twelve-string guitar, a bass, and drums.) The solid research was provided by producer and writer Chris Strachwitz, founder of Arhoolie Records. When *Chulas Fronteras* was made (in 1976), the music was little known outside the Chicano world, but Blank's film contributed to its wider dissemination and was to inspire later, enthusiastically appreciative documentary treatments. The title means "Beautiful Borderlands" and it suggests the considerable strengths but also the limits of *Chulas Fronteras*. It is above all a presentation and celebration through music of a simplified, occasionally sentimentalized version of Tex-Mex life (in general outside the big cities) and only "a selective" exploration of the more complex experience, emotions, and society behind the music.

The Rio Grande (for Mexicans the Rio Bravo) passes behind the credits as water and a blue curve on the map along with a song of yearning for the Mexico left behind. The beauty of Texas-Mexican women is sung and soon after, the camera roams through a barbecue and later, in the kitchen of singer Lydia Mendoza, another mouth-watering abundance of food as she and other women prepare tamales. We hear Mendoza's rendition of *Mal Hombre*, about a woman enchanted and deceived in her youth by an unfaithful man. The song plus the food (and other songs about women performed by male *conjunto* singers) add up to a traditional depiction of the role of the woman in an essentially conservative and seemingly static society. There is no presentation of the extended impact of machismo or of possibly more independent roles for women in a society of immigrants. Even for its time, the film tends toward a nostalgic vision rooted in the past. And it also ignores the darker, more stoically tragic side of the northern Mexican sensibility in general. There are no songs (common in *norteño* music) about the defense of honor or a man's reckless or heroic embracing of death.

CHULAS FRONTERAS

The social dilemma of the Mexican immigrant (or illegal "wetback") of the time does appear strongly, taking up the middle third of the film. Blank uses a mixture of expressively cut footage from the present, moments of interview and photos of workers (and some of their oppressors), many from decades earlier. The photos are seen through an orange-tinted filter as we hear a *corrido* (ballad) sung about a strike in the melon fields, with the footage full of oranges and carrots and the laborers who pick them. A story of anti-Mexican prejudice and an organizing song for Cesar Chavez's Farmworkers Union led up to the high point of the sequence, the blessing of the vehicles, suddenly without music, as a priest sprinkles rows of cars and trucks with holy water and blesses them in Spanish. The camera panning across vehicles and faces, together with the rare absence of music, turns the blessing of the vehicles into the most solemn moment of *Chulas Fronteras*. Most of these vehicles will carry Mexican farm laborers northward in search of more crops, often with adolescents taken out of school to help feed the families.

The extended cadenza on social issues ends with a fairly long interview sequence, at least for this film, which skims along elegantly and boisterously to the swift, dance-beat of the *conjuntos*. A tractor driver working near the border comments on the need for schooling, for youngsters to have the time to learn how to better themselves, and on the hardships of the wandering life, which he has earlier described as the pattern of his own childhood, a constant moving from state to state and crop to crop through a long year of harvesting. More securely employed as he is now, he is grateful that he need not travel "north."

This sense of enforced travel, a necessary but difficult roaming away from home, is the primary serious underpinning of *Chulas Fronteras*, like a bass note below all the visible and audible vocals and accordions and guitars. It marks the present-day Mexican Diaspora, too, with its much greater numbers and its dispersion across the entire United States into numerous different lines of hard work. But it is still a Diaspora that retains close links to its spatial origins—practical (in the importance of the money sent back home) and emotional (in the will to return). From this angle, the tone of the film still rings true about important aspects of the Chicano and emigrant Mexican experience.

Chulas Fronteras, 1976.
[*Still courtesy of the British Film Institute*]

The concluding movement, as it should be, is all musicians and music, with one performer, El Flaco ("Skinny") Jiménez, embodying continuity in time. He performs, he teaches the accordion to his young son, and we also see his father playing the same instrument and telling us he learned from his father, who was "one of the best accordionists of his time" and whom we know only through a photo. Then quickly, with a sound cut to another voice repeating the word *padre*, another photo of a musician father appears and another description of musical skill passed down as inheritance, to yet another accordionist, Eugenio Abrego of the group *Los Alegres de Terán*. The elegant sequence deserves its critical placement, because the rapid runs of the accordions dominate the instrumental sound of the film while, for most of the many songs, clever lyrics soar with a sense of music as pure pleasure. And it is from the beautifully recorded music and the inventive images mirroring its notes—from animals skittering at a zoo to dancers to farm laborers to a bouncing, swaying lowrider automobile—that *Chulas Fronteras* derives its verve and its lasting value.

MIRA BINFORD

See also **Blank, Les**

Chulas Fronteras (U.S.A., 1976, 58 min.) Production Company, Brazos Films. Language: English and subtitled Spanish. In color. Directed by Les Blank. Conceived, produced, and sound-recorded by Chris Strachwitz. Cinematography by Les Blank. Film Editing by Les Blank. Assistant editing by Maureen Gosling. Assistant Camera and Interpreter: Pacho Lane. Consultant: Guillermo Hernández. Performers: Lydia Mendoza, Flaco Jiménez, Narciso Martínez, Los Alegres de Terán, Rumel Fuentes, Don Santiago Jiménez, Los Pingüinos Del Norte, Ramiro Cavazos (Canción Mixteca), and others. Filmed in Texas and Mexico.

Further Reading

Acosta, Belinda, "Roots of Tex-Mex Music," *Austin Chronicle*, May 20, 2003.
Goodwin, M. A., "Tex-Mex Masterpiece," *Village Voice*, January 3, 1977.
Scruggs, T. M., "Chulas Fronteras, Del Mero Corazon," *Journal of the Society for Ethnomusicology*, 43, 3, Fall 1999, 572.
Wald, Elijah, "Various Roots of Tex-Mex Music," *Sing Out! The Folk Song Magazine.*, Winter, 2004.

CHURCHILL'S ISLAND

(Canada, Legg, 1941)

Churchill's Island is primarily remembered as the first film of the National Film Board of Canada to win an Academy Award (best documentary, 1941). But it is not so much its acceptance by the commercial mainstream, as its departure from that mainstream's conventions and institutional presuppositions, that makes the film historically significant and of some continuing interest. *Churchill's Island* marks the visible beginning of a Canadian film alternative to industrial Hollywood and an extension and elaboration of the documentary idea to new national circumstances and possibilities.

In the early years of its existence, the Board's founder and first commissioner, John Grierson, discovered that much of his time was occupied by administrative and political duties. As a result, much of the responsibility for day-to-day producing and mentoring fell to Stuart Legg, a Grierson recruit from the days of the Empire Marketing Board. Legg was particularly noted for his subtle grasp of public, political, and—as he would increasingly demonstrate—geopolitical issues. As head of production, he would explore these topics through the Board's flagship wartime series, *Canada Carries On* (of which *Churchill's Island* was an early entry) and *The World in Action*.

The March of Time was an acknowledged influence on the Canadian series. Legg was impressed by the quality of its reporting, its concision, and its cinematic craft; however, Legg and his collaborators began immediately to move beyond the entertaining reportage so often characteristic of the existing newsreels. Propaganda played a role in this decision. The United States was still officially neutral with regard to the European conflict, and so the Board series had a great gap to fill in informing and motivating its domestic audiences.

Churchill's Island is a vivid response to this challenge. The film, which recounts the details of Britain's defense of itself against the Nazis, is completely compiled from the Board's extensive stock library. Future Board stalwart Tom Daly was largely responsible for maintaining this library. His seemingly complete recall of its holdings would make him increasingly central to the compilation films that would make up a good portion of the Board's early output. Daly has ascribed much of their motivational success to Legg's principle of "waves," which was that sequences were to rise to a climax and then diminish, before the next sequence came along and increased the intensity. The emotional results are still clear in *Churchill's Island*, in which the high stakes, the national peril, and the national opportunity are quite palpable.

Although there were motivational (and manipulative) imperatives, Legg also intended to move his films toward the depth and breadth of the best investigative journalism. In *Churchill's Island* this deepening process is visibly well underway. There is a conceptual, and even dialectical, element to the film that was emblematic of the innovations and elaborations that Legg and his newsreel collaborators would develop throughout the war period. In addition to emotional appeal, there is a constant illumination of causal chains, a setting forth of the tactical and strategic elements of the conflict.

Legg introduces us to the main participants and the key processes, ensuring not only sympathetic identification, but also understanding. The exposition discusses varying threats of invasion, the defensive responses thereto, and the courage of Britain's army. These three elements recur through what are essentially the film's three acts. The first gives an account of the Blitz, during which Legg takes a characteristic retrospective turn, reviewing the causes and conditions of the German action to that point, ensuring that the audience member remains historically oriented. Next we witness the Royal Air Force's defense of Britain's skies, and, from the Nazi perspective, the German blockade that was devised in response. During this second act, there is a clear discussion of the tactics of the U-boats and a frank admission of the great cost of their activities. There is also a clear message, quite common in this period (cf. *London Can Take It, Foreign Correspondent*), to the neutral United States. With the rising toll of sinkings, the ever more bold encroachments toward North American soil, it is intimated that no one is safe, and no one can remain neutral.

In keeping with Grierson's instruction that these films be "truthful, but not defeatist," the warnings give way to an expression of gratitude for help rendered, and confidence for the future. The U-boats are on the run, and even as the third act outlines, and then just slightly glosses over, the possibilities of and preparations against a possible land invasion, the film moves toward a stirring climax. As the last wave crashes we hear narrator Lorne Greene's mighty challenge to the Nazis to "come if you dare!" This justifiably famous conclusion remains extraordinarily powerful.

Churchill's Island was a great success. Along with the practically prophetic *War Clouds in the Pacific* (November 1941), it facilitated the remarkable access that Board newsreels would have not only to Canadian audiences but to screens in the United States as well. Although that access would continue, the tone of the newsreels would be altered. Wartime propaganda under Legg would further shift from the emotional and the partisan—however justifiable such approaches may have been at the time—to a more global, humanitarian approach. In this endeavor, Legg's sensibilities coincided with one of Grierson's most important convictions, which was that wartime films were also a preparation for peacetime, and that an awareness and anticipation of the needs of peacetime were essential to their successful execution. The Board's activities strongly prefigured the international role that Canada, and Canada's documentary films, would assume in the decades after the war.

DEAN DUNCAN

See also **Canada Carries On; Grierson, John; Legg, Stuart;** *The March of Time*; **National Film Board of Canada;** *World in Action*

Churchill's Island (Canada, National Film Board, 21 min). Produced, directed, and edited by Stuart Legg. Commentary by Stuart Legg. Narration by Lorne Greene. Music by Lucio Agostini. Sound by Walter Darling. Research by Tom Daly.

Further Reading

Aitken, Ian, *Film and Reform*, London: Routledge, 1990.
Aitken, Ian, *The Documentary Film Movement: An Anthology*, Edinburgh: Edinburgh University Press, 1998.

Ellis, Jack C., *John Grierson*, Carbondale: Southern Illinois University Press, 2000.

Evans, Gary, *In the National Interest: A Chronicle of the National Film Board of Canada from 1949 to 1989*, Toronto: University of Toronto Press, 1991.

Evans, Gary, John Grierson, and the National Film Board, Toronto: University of Toronto Press, 1986.

Grierson, John, *Grierson on Documentary*, edited by Forsyth Hardy, London: Collins, 1946, New York: Harcourt Brace, 1947; revised edition, London: Faber, 1966, New York: Praeger, 1971; abridged edition, Faber, 1979.

Hardy, Forsyth, *John Grierson: A Documentary Biography*, London: Faber, 1979.

James, C. Rodney, *Film as a National Art: The NFB of Canada and the Film Board Idea*, New York: Arno Press, 1977.

Jones, D. B., *The Best Butler in the Business: Tom Daly of the National Film Board of Canada*, Toronto: University of Toronto Press, 1996.

Rotha, Paul, *Documentary Diary*, London: Secker and Warburg, and New York: Hill and Wang, 1973.

Sussex, Elizabeth, *The Rise and Fall of British Documentary*, Berkeley: University of California Press, 1975.

CINEMA ACTION

Cinema Action was founded in 1968 by Gustav Lamche (known as Schlacke) and Ann Geddes (formerly Lamche). They were soon joined by Eduardo Geddes. Cinema Action was a London-based collective of socialist filmmakers initially producing campaign films (political films determined as either propagandist or agitational). Over the next twenty-five years many other filmmakers worked with them, some as part of the group, some only loosely associated with it. Heavily influenced by the events in Paris in 1968, where they had been living until they left for England that year, and wanting to spread its message to the working class in Britain, they imported a French film about the riots. Borrowing a truck and a mobile projector, they took the film into the Ford car plant in Dagenham, England, to show the workers. At first only a few workers turned up to watch, but after a few screenings, they were playing to packed rooms.

After this success, the group took the film to other workplaces. This led Cinema Action to make its own campaigning films and then travel around the country, showing them to audiences throughout England. The group operated as a collective without a formal structure or wages, and individuals were not credited on the films, which were made with donations from trade unions and collections from workers. Approximately twenty prominent trade unionists worked closely with Cinema Action, and it had ties with most political groups on the left in Britain, as well as with the independent filmmakers move-ment, particularly the Independent Filmmakers Association. Later, Cinema Action received funding from the British Film Institute and other grant-giving bodies.

Dave Douglass, a miner and National Union of Mineworkers activist describes how:

> The people who were making the films were presenting them. It was a very exciting thing. They'd put films on in factory canteens, in bus depots, in dock areas, in shipyard assembly areas, in locations where there were masses of workers. The UCS film (*The UCS Struggle/UCS1*) was shown at Plessey's during the occupation there. It's very evocative when you've got films thrown as a huge projection against a big factory wall showing images of workers in struggle!

> (Dave Douglas interviewed by Margaret, Dickenson *Rogue Reels*, 1999, p. 273)

Between 1968 and 1972, the collective produced several simple, functional, campaign films. The main elements of these campaigning films were:

> Images of working class mass campaigning action, demonstrations, rallies or pickets;
> Interviews with working class militants and activists shown directly to camera or as voice-over;
> Speeches by militants and leaders to working class audiences;
> Statements, texts and graphics prepared for the film by activists;
> Footage of the location where the struggle was taking place;
> Music, usually protest songs.

The films often ended with text calling for militant action or a request for donations. They displayed a clear allegiance to the working class (see *Fighting the Bill*). There was also an absence of commentary, which, while making them distinct from the type of commentary then employed by the BBC (the privileged voice, which presents itself as a "natural" emanation outside the text), also marked the virtual effacement of any notation of the speaking source. This absence of discourse was underlined by the group's relationship with trade unionists. Trade unionists advised on subjects, organised people to be interviewed, and arranged access to locations.

Editorial control of the film was often handed over to trade unionists entirely. The Shop Stewards Committee of the Upper Clyde Shipyard occupation had editorial control of the UCS film; they ensured that key arguments over the way the occupation was going were removed from the film. Such decisions relegated most of the films to the role of cheerleader, rather than that of a challenging and provocative work.

Fighting the Bill (1970) is typical of the films made in that period. Speakers at demonstrations and meetings call for action against the Industrial Relations Bill, which sought to curtail the power of the trades unions, particularly the growing strength of the shop stewards movement. Meanwhile images of banks, the stock exchange, and workers in factories underline the points they are making. The film ends with a clear call for action through strikes, but there is no analysis or inclusion of the need for political leadership or for a political programme.

Although aimed at working class audiences, Cinema Action did show their films at international film festivals, and their films won several awards. *The Miners Film* (1974–1975), probably their most influential film for other campaigning filmmakers at the time, won the International Film Critics' award at Oberhausen and the Jury award for documentary at the Moscow Film Festival. This film documents the industrial action taken by miners in the winter of 1973–1974, which was instrumental in bringing down the Conservative government.

So That You Can Live (1981) marked a radical departure from these films. Shot over five years, it shows the impact on one family in South Wales of local mine and factory closures. It describes the inscription of history through landscape and cityscape, over which the camera is constantly slowly panning, as well as through photographs, texts, and books. These are montaged with scenes of family life and social life in the village. Texts written by Raymond Williams are read by the daughter of the family. The filmmakers' presence is specifically represented through the interviewer's voice and the daughter's observation of how she first encountered them. It was the start of a more reflexive style of political filmmaking, although by this point in time, Cinema Action was beginning to break up.

The importance of Cinema Action is that it revived the tradition of making and screening campaign films, a tradition that had languished for more than thirty years. Following their example, other groups of campaigning socialist filmmakers appeared, most notably the Berwick Street Collective (later Lusia films), Amber Films, and later Black Audio.

In the late 1980s, Cinema Action made two low-budget feature films, *Rocinante* (1986) and *Bearskin: An Urban Fairytale* (1989). It continued as a facility for independent filmmakers until 1993 when the collective disbanded.

JILL DANIELS

Selected Films

1969 *Not a Penny on the Rent* (Cinema Action)
1969/70 *Squatters* (Cinema Action)
1970 *Fighting the Bill* (Cinema Action)
1973 *People of Ireland* (Cinema Action)
1973 *Arise Ye Workers* (Cinema Action)
1973 *Launch* (Amber Films)
1974/5 *The Miners Film* (Cinema Action)
1975 *Bowes Line* (Amber Films)
1975 *The Nightcleaners* (Berwick Street Film Collective)
1977 *Class Struggle: Film from the Clyde* (Cinema Action)
1981 *So That You Can Live* (Cinema Action)
1987 *T. Dan Smith* (Amber Films)

Further Reading

Chanan, Michael, *So That You Can Live (For Shirley), Rogue Reels, Oppositional Film in Britain 1945-90*, edited by Margaret Dickinson, 1945 BFI Publishing, 1999.

Delmar, Rosalind, "The Miners Film," *Monthly Film Bulletin*, June 1975, 142.

Dickinson, Margaret, *Rogue Reels, Oppositional Film in Britain, 1945-90*, BFI Publishing, 1999.

Glyn, David and Paul Marris, "Seven Years of Cinema Action," *Afterimage* 6, Special Issue: Perspectives on English Independent Cinema, 1976.

Green, John, "The Function of Film in the Working Class Struggle," *Marxism Today*, February 1973, 54.

King, Noel, "How Welsh Are My Eyes? So That You Can Live, Textual Analysis and Political Cinema," *Undercut*, 10/11, Winter, 1983.

Szczelkun, Stefan, *Exploding Cinema 1992–1999, Culture and Democracy*, Ph.D. Thesis, RCA 2002, Chapter 2: Film Provenances of Exploding Cinema, 2.03 British Counter Culture and Film 1960s and 70s.

CINÉMA DU RÉEL

The *Cinéma du Réel* festival of documentary film has taken place in Paris every year since 1979. It was officially born the year after the inauguration of the Pompidou Centre, Paris's main institution for modern and contemporary art, and has run over a period of eight days during the first three weeks of March each year since, with the exception of 1981 and 1982, when it began in early April and at the end of February, respectively. The festival, whose secondary title is "international festival of ethnographic and sociological film," is the brainchild and celebrated progeny of the Bibliothèque Publique d'Information (BPI)/Public Information Libary, the library and mediatheque housed by the Pompidou Centre and given an impressive refit and extension in time for the 2000 millennium celebrations after being relocated nearby for two years. Although it is not a lending library, the BPI usually fulfills the important function of serving Paris's large student population, many general readers and viewers, and a significant number of researchers and journalists able to take advantage of its range of free facilities.

The competitions of the "Réel" festival, as it is commonly known, are open to French and international documentaries made during the calendar year preceding each annual event. Initially just two in number, the "Grand Prix" and the "Prix du Cinéma du Réel," prizes have multiplied over the years to reach a total of seven, not including the Pierre and Yolande Perrault grant awarded to the most promising young filmmaker by the selection committee. In 1979, the festival was organised simply into international and French sections with correspondingly appointed juries, but with the addition of more prizes (the Prix des Bibliothèques in 1984, the Prix du Patrimoine in 1988, the Prix Louis Marcarolles in 1991, awarded by the Ministry of Foreign Affairs from among the French-produced films, and the Prix de la Scam in 1994), the number of juries has also grown. In 1994, the Jury des Bibliothèques became the Jury des Bibliothèques et du Patrimoine, and a new prize offered in 1992 by PROCIREP, the association of French television producers, subsequently merged with the Grand Prix to increase the reward on offer. The festival's international jury has often included major names from the world of cinema, the visual arts, and literature, such as Jean Rouch (also a long-serving member of the organising committee and coordinator of several days of screenings of ethnographic films at Paris's Musée de l'Homme/Museum of Mankind directly after the "Réel"), Edgar Morin, Freddy Buache, Laura Betti, Idrissa Ouedraogo, Chantal Akerman, Abbas Kiarostami, Malik Chibane, Annie Ernaux, and Edith Scob.

The year 1984 saw the foundation of the Association of the Friends of the *Cinéma du Réel*, which has subsequently played a central part in strengthening relations with the festival's correspondents abroad, encouraging meetings and exchanges during the festival, and assisting in the distribution of the films shown. The structure of the event itself has varied less over the years than its size and scope, and is generally organised into a limited number of special screenings of films that are not new, the International Competition, the French Competition (simply called the Panorama of French production until 1997), and a major themed section whose aim is to discover and promote the world's underrepresented documentary schools and traditions. In 1983, this was Hong Kong, in 1987 Brazil, and in 1989 the USSR. Since 1990, countries and regions chosen have included India, Australia, Latin America, Africa (multiple countries), the Baltic states, Japan, Iran, and Algeria. Two exceptions to the internationalist theming of what is often the largest section of the festival occurred in 1995, when the centenary of cinema made "100 years of the Real: Experimenting with Limits" more appropriate, and for the millennium in 2000, when the chosen theme was love. France's pride in internationalism (as well as in its own culture) is also reflected in the consistently high number of countries and combinations of co-producing countries that participate—an average of twenty-nine in the decade from 1994 to 2003, with a maximum of forty-four in 1996 when the special international focus was "Africa, Africas." The total number of films screened has risen from approximately 60 in the early years to an average of 112 in the ten years up to 2003.

Diversifying the conditions of circulation of the films it features and thereby maximising the festival's audience has always been built into the goals of the *Cinéma du Réel*, an objective first significantly advanced by an agreement made between the BPI and the Médiathèque des Trois Mondes (a French organisation distributing to associations, sociocultural groups, schools, and universities) in 1983. Librarians from France's many municipal library/mediatheques regularly attend the festival and arrange distribution of selected films to their locality, and parts of the festival have been screened in the United States, Japan, and Greece, as well as the more regular destinations of Belgium and Germany. Partnerships with television got off to a rough start in the mid-1980s, but the French subscription channel Canal Plus has purchased films from the festival on a regular basis since its inception in 1984, a role also adopted later by La SEPT.

The *Cinéma du Réel* has always styled itself as somewhat removed from fashionable trends and dedicated to keeping alive the cultural dimension of creative work in documentary. At times this has equated to a moral mission. Dominique Wallon, the Director of France's Centre National de la Cinématographie, wrote in the 1994 catalogue that "filming what's real" "is a matter of rigour and moral standards" increasingly ignored by television, whose increasing tendency to the sensational and the sordid (one could argue that reality television has proved him right) ignores the "acute sense of responsibility," the "full respect of human dignity" and the commitment to his time and to humankind shown by the documentarist. In sum, the *Cinéma du Réel* is certainly the most important screening and viewing opportunity for new documentary films in France, where it is only rivalled by Marseille's *Fictions de réel* and the *Etats généraux du film documentaire de Lussas*, both founded in 1989. It must also rank high in a global listing of comparable events.

KATHERINE INCE

Further Reading

Scant information about the *Cinéma du Réel* is available in books, even in French. By far the best source is the event's annual catalogues, all the critical material in which is given in English translation, as well as in French. The catalogues are available on open access shelves in the Bibliothèque Publique d'Information. The festival's web pages, reached by following links from http://www.bpi.fr, list its sponsors and partners, and give an introduction to its history, organisation, and the rules of its competitions.

CINEMA NOVO

The documentary films that were made in Brazil during the 1960s are closely related to the horizon of Brazilian Cinema Novo. Its leading figure, Glauber Rocha, has an extensive documentary filmography. The most important Rocha documentaries include *Amazonas, Amazonas* (1965); *Maranhão 66* (1966); the feature *História do Brasil/History of Brazil*, made in Cuba in 1972/74; *Di* (1977), his documentary masterpiece about the Brazilian painter Di Cavalcanti; the mid-length *Jorjamado no Cinema/Jorjamado at the Cinema* (1977); and *As Armas e o Povo/Weapons and the People* about Portugal's revolution of 1974.

Paulo César Saraceni was the first filmmaker of the Cinema Novo generation to venture into the documentary, back in 1959, with his pioneering *Arraial do Cabo,* a film about a colony of fishermen located about twenty-five kilometers from the city of Cabo Frio, in Rio de Janeiro state. One of the strong reference points for the formation of the Cinema Novo style was the cycle of documentaries that burst out of the faraway northeastern state of Paraíba in 1959. The principal figures were Vladimir Carvalho, Rucker Vieira, João Ramiro, and Linduarte Noronha. The first film of this cycle, Linduarte Noronha's *Aruanda*, made a powerful impact when it was first shown in São Paulo in 1960, with its vibrant images depicting the people from sertão, Brazil's lost northeastern interior.

The definitive meeting of the Cinema Novo generation with documentary filmmaking happened through the ideas and techniques of cinema verité, capturing the intense rhythm and pulse of the world. In Brazil and Latin America, the verité style had the singularity of showing an image until then missing: the image of the poor masses from the cities and the countryside. In this sense, one important landmark was the seminar on documentary film organized by UNESCO and the governmental Ministry of Foreign Relations (Itamaraty) in 1962, which brought the Swedish documentary filmmaker Arne Sucksdorff to Brazil (later Sucksdorff would live here for many years). The Cinema Novo director Joaquim Pedro de Andrade was another source for the introduction of the new documentary in Brazil. In 1961 he received a grant from the Rockefeller Foundation to visit New York, where he maintained close contact with Albert and David Maysles during the first half of 1962. His enthusiasm for the new documentary inspired the producer Luiz Carlos Barreto to invite him to direct *Garrincha, Alegria do Povo/Garrincha, Joy of the People* during the second half of that year. Eduardo Escorel was in charge of the sound for this film about the well-known Brazilian soccer player.

Maioria Absoluta/Absolute Majority, directed by Leon Hirszman, is the first documentary to fully explore the potential of the new Nagra sound recorder, which was operated by the young Arnaldo Jabor. The theme of *Maioria Absoluta/Absolute Majority* is illiteracy. It was filmed in the states of Rio de Janeiro, Pernambuco, and Paraíba just before the military coup of March 1964. This film marks the first time in Brazilian cinema that we hear the true voice of the people in all its particular flow and with its own rhythm, vocabulary, and accent. Paulo César Saraceni's *Integração Racial/Racial Integration* was also filmed in the second half of 1963. It was completed in the beginning of 1964 and features a style similar to that of Maioria *Absoluta/ Absolute Majority*. There is

no internal structure other than the theme of race, followed through random interviews. The film uses direct sound, handheld camera and an analytical voice-over that talks about social injustice. In *Opinião Pública/Public Opinion* (1967), Arnaldo Jabor extended this method to explicitly make a portrait of the Brazilian middle class. In this film, consecutive long takes of casual conversations and interviews defiantly explode the parameters of film composition.

In São Paulo, during the 1960s, another important group of documentary filmmakers worked with the new documentary style. Thomas Farkas was a producer (and also a great photographer) who functioned as a catalyst, putting the new ideas into practice. Between September 1964 and March 1965, Farkas dived into the adventure of producing four mid-length films about Brazilian popular culture. Paulo Gil Soares, a filmmaker who had been a contemporary of the young Glauber Rocha in the city of Salvador, was invited to direct *Memória do Cangaço/Memories of the Cangaço*. In *Viramundo/Migrants*, Geraldo Sarno joins the São Paulo documentary group, bringing along his experience with the reality of the poor Brazilian northeast. Maurice Capovilla directed *Subterrâneos do Futebo/The Soccer Underground*. There were also contacts with Fernando Birri's Santa Fé documentary group, and Manuel Horácio Gimenez, an Argentine, came to direct *Nossa Escola de Samba/Our Samba School*. Farkas was the sole producer of the four films and also served as the photographer. The films were later assembled into a feature-length film that was released under the title of *Brasil Verdade* (in a free translation, *Brazil Verité*). After this experience, Farkas produced a series of nineteen shorts documentaries jointly titled *A Condição Brasileira/The Brazilian Condition* (1969–1971).

Although the major Cinema Novo directors made documentaries later in their careers (for example, David Neves, Eduardo Escorel, and Joaquim Pedro de Andrade), Leon Hirszman is the one with the most systematic documentary filmography and strong authorial work. His 1969 short, *Nelson Cavaquinho*, is about Rio's famous samba singer and composer. The film offers us a privileged moment, presenting a stylistically mature director who is at ease as he moves his camera through the slums of Rio. In 1975, in a more classical narrative style, Hirzsman made *Cantos de Trabalho/Work Songs*, three short films about the traditional songs that manual laborers sing while they work. In March 1979, the first workers' strike in Brazil since 1964 broke out, and Leon Hirtzsman filmed *ABC da Greve/The ABC of the Strike* (long length, completed posthumously), about the workers of the automobile industry in São Paulo. *Imagens do Inconsciente/Images from the Unconscious* is the huge project of the last part of Hirtzsman's life. Between 1983 and 1985, he dedicated himself to the making of three feature-length films about drawings, paintings, and sculptures created by psychotics, through art activities pursued in the mental hospital of the Jungian psychiatrist Nise da Silveira (Centro Psiquiátrico Pedro II). Each of the three features that composes *Imagens do Insconsciente* portrays the life and artwork of one artist-patient. The sophistication of his style and the singularity of his projects place Hirzsman among Brazil's most significant documentary filmmakers. However, the success of his fiction films sometimes overshadows this fact.

FERNÃO PESSOA RAMOS

Selected Filmography

1959 *Arraial do Cabo*: Paulo César Saraceni and Mario Carneiro

1959 *O Mestre de Apipucos e o Poeta do Castelo/The Master of Apipucos and the Poet of Castelo*: Joaquim Pedro de Andrade

1959 *Aruanda*: Linduarte Noronha

1962 *Garrincha, a Alegria do Povo/Garrincha, Joy of the People*: Joaquim Pedro de Andrade

1964 *Maioria Absoluta/Absolute Majority*: Leon Hirszman

1964 *Integração Racial/ Racial Integration*: Paulo César Saraceni

1965 *O Circo/The Circus*: Arnaldo Jabor

1965 *Cinema Novo (Imporvisiert und Zielbewusst)*: Joaquim Pedro de Andrade

1965 *Viramundo/ Migrants*: Geraldo Sarno

1965 *Memória do Cangaço/Memories of the Cangaço*: Paulo Gil Soares

1965 *Nossa Escola de Samba/Our Samba* School: Manuel Horácio Gimenez

1965 *Subterrâneos do Futebol/The Soccer Underground*: Maurice Capovilla

1965 *Amazonas, Amazonas*: Glauber Rocha

1966 *Maranhão 66*: Glauber Rocha

1966 *Bethania Bem de Perto/Bethania Close Up*: Eduardo Escorel and Julio Bressane

1967 *Opinião Pública/ Public Opinion*: Arnaldo Jabor

1967 *Brasília, Contradições de uma Cidade Nova/ Brasilia, The Contradictions of a New City*: Joaquim Pedro de Andrade

1968 *Mauro, Humberto*: David Neves

1968 *Vinicius de Moraes*: David Neves

1969 *Nelson Cavaquinho*: Leon Hirzsman

1970 *O Tempo e o Som/ Time and Sound*: Walter Lima Jr.

1970 *Visão de Juazeiro/Juazeiro's Vision*: Eduardo Escorel

1972–1974 *História do Brasil/The History of Brazil*: Glauber Rocha

1972–1997 *Bahia de Todos os Sambas/Bahia of All Sambas*: Paulo Cesar Saraceni/Leon Hirzsman (posthumously)

1974 *As Armas e o Povo/Weapons and the People*: Glauber Rocha

1974–1976 *O Fazendeiro do Ar/ The Farmer of the Air*: David Neves

1974–1976 *Em Tempo de Nava/ Nava's Time*: David Nevers

1974–1976 *O Habitante de Pasárgada/ The Inhabitants of Pasárgada*: David Neves

1975–1977 *Cantos de Trabalho: Mutirão/Work Songs: Working Together*: Leon Hirszman

1975–1977 *Cantos de Trabalho: Cacau/Work Songs: Cocoa*: Leon Hirzsman

1975–1977 *Cantos de Trabalho: Cana-de-Açucar/Work Songs: Sugar Cane*: Leon Hirzsman

1975–1979 *ABC da Greve/The ABC of the Strike*: Leon Hirzsman (posthumously)

1976–1977 *Partido Alto/Samba Improvisations*: Leon Hirzsman

1977 *Di-* Glauber Rocha

1977 *Jorjamado no Cinema/Jorge Amado at the Cinema*: Glauber Rocha

1978 *O Aleijadinho*: Joaquim Pedro de Andrade

1978 *Cantos do Trabalho: Cacau/Work Songs: Cocoa*: Leon Hirzsman

1978 *Cantos do Trabalho: Cana-de-Açucar/Work Songs: Sugar Cane*: Leon Hirzsman

1983/1985 *Imagens do Insconsciente* (I, II e III)/*Images from the Unconscious*: Leon Hirszman

Further Reading

Bernardet, Jean-Claude, *Cineastas e Imagens do Povo*, São Paulo: Brasiliense, 1985.

Bernardet, Jean-Claude, *Le Documentaire*, in *Le Cinéma Brésilien*, edited by Paulo Antonio Paranaguá, Paris: Centre Georges Pompidou, 1987.

Burton, Julianne, *The Social Documentary in Latin America*. Pittsburgh: University of Pittsburgh Press, 1990.

Marinho, José, *Dos Homens e das Pedras—o ciclo do cinema documentário paraibano (1959–1979)*, Rio de Janeiro, Eduff, 1998.

Marsolais, Gilles,. *L,'Aventure du Cinéma Direct Revisitée*, Québec: Les 400 Coups, 1997.

Neves, David, *A Descoberta da Espontaneidade—breve histórico do Cinema Direto no Brasil*, in *Cinema Moderno Cinema Novo*, edited by Flavio Moreira Costa, Rio de Janeiro: José Álvaro Editor, 1966.

Ramos, Fernão Pessoa. *A Cicatriz da Tomada—ética, documentário e imagem-intensa* in *Teoria Contemporânea do Cinema*, vol. II, Edited by Fernão Pessoa Ramos, São Paulo: SENAC, 2005.

Ramos, Fernão Pessoa, *Cinema Verdade no Brasil*, in Teixeira, Francisco Elinaldo (org) *Documentário no Brasil—tradição e transformação*. São Paulo: Summus, 2004.

Salem, Helena, *Leon Hirszman—o navegador das estrelas*, Rio de Janeiro: Rocco, 1997.

Stam, Robert and Randal Johnson, *Brazilian Cinema*. New York: Columbia University Press, 1982.

CINEMA VERITÉ

See **Morin, Edgar; Pennebaker, DA: Rouch, Jean**

CINEMAGAZINE

The cinemagazine was a periodically released film series (known also as screen magazines), which, in its popular cinema form, covered light topics such as travel, sport, hobbies, personalities, animals, and fashion. Cinemagazines were a staple of cinemas around the world, flourishing in particular in the United States and Great Britain, where they were a common feature of cinema programs for decades.

The true cinemagazine form, however, ranged more widely that this. There were news cinemagazines, industrial cinemagazines, and cinemagazines sponsored by government organizations used for the dissemination of information and national propaganda. Neglected by historians of film, only recently has the cinemagazine begun to attract some critical attention, and a general understanding of the genre has started to emerge.

Britain in particular was the home of the cinemagazine. The first film series that was recognizably in the cinemagazine format was the *Kinemacolor Fashion Gazette*, issued by Charles Urban in 1913; however, the first true cinemagazine was *Pathé Pictorial*, first issued in 1918 as an adjunct to the *Pathé Gazette* newsreel. Pathé became cinemagazine specialists, introducing a cinemagazine for women, *Eve's Film Review* (1921–1933), and *Pathetone Weekly* (1931–1941). Other newsreel companies followed suit in the 1920s, with *Gaumont Graphic* introducing *Gaumont Mirror* (1926–1931) and *British Screen News* producing *British Screen Tatler* (1928–1931). The Ideal

Film Company issued *Ideal Cinemagazine* (1926–1933, then *Gaumont-British Magazine* from 1934), the series that introduced the term. *Ideal Cinemagazine* was produced by Andrew Buchanan, who became the leading advocate of the form, seeing it as an educational genre ideally suited to bringing light, palatable information to the cinema audience. In the United States, Charles Urban was instrumental in establishing the form with his *Charles Urban Movie Chats* (1919–1922) and *Kineto Review* (1921–1923) series.

Although the cinemagazine was generally dismissed as being among the lightest of cinema fare, there were others who shared Buchanan's belief in the form. John Grierson admired them, detecting in them an extension of the popular lecture format, while warning that they "describe, and even expose, but in any aesthetic sense, only rarely reveal." Grierson was referring to American series such as the *Fitzpatrick Traveltalks* (1931–1950) produced by James A. Fitzpatrick (a Charles Urban protégé) and Grantland Rice's *Sportlights*. Other American series in the same vein included the long-running *Pete Smith's Specialities* (1936–1955), *John Nesbitt's Passing Parade* (1938–1949), and *Screen Snapshots* (1920–1958), all of them popular in their day, though with a flippant humor that is badly dated.

The popular cinemagazine, with its frivolous view on life leavened with a touch of sly subversiveness, bowed out by the end of the 1960s. *Pathé Pictorial* closed in 1969, after fifty-one years of publication. But the cinemagazine flourished in other forms. The need for a film series that could show how things were beyond the immediate concerns of the newsreel first emerged during World War I, with Cherry Kearton's *The Whirlpool of War* (1914–1915). The most significant news cinemagazine was *The March of Time* (1935–1951), the dynamic series produced by Louis de Rochemont for Time-Life, which revealed the background stories behind the news in a dramatic and multifaceted fashion. In Britain, the Rank Organization produced its own version, *This Modern Age* (1946–1951), and Pathé revealed a more serious tone with its *The Wealth of the World* (1948–1951) on the industrial development of natural resources. The news cinemagazine recognized that the news was not all scoops and headlines, and that it could follow stories in greater depth, revealing trends and granting the cinema audience greater intelligence than some would have allowed it to have.

The sort of background look at industry that *The Wealth of the World* demonstrated was taken up by industrial concerns themselves. In Britain, Shell produced *Oil Review* (1950–1952), the gas industry produced *Mr. Therm's Review* (1955–1956), the steel industry produced *Ingot Pictorial* (1949–1958), while the mining industry produced the long-running *Mining Review* (1947–1982). Such cinemagazines seldom made it into conventional cinemas (*Mining Review* was shown in public cinemas close to mining communities), but they reached targeted audiences through the nontheatrical circuit. These films delivered carefully constructed images of benevolent, forward-thinking industrial concerns for the benefit of investors, schools, societies and clubs, other businesses, and their own workers.

The cinemagazine form was most effectively used as a tool of government. In Britain, the Central Office of Information (COI, successor to the wartime Ministry of Information) produced a number of film series that were targeted as audiences at home, the Commonwealth and America. Such cinemagazines were viewed by the COI as a means to project positive images of Britain, to encourage international trade, and simply to provide information to British audiences. *Britain Can Make It* (1945–1947) championed innovation in British manufacturing, *Colonial Cinemagazine* (1947–1957) gathered stories from around the Common-

wealth, and *This is Britain* (1946–1951) and *This Week in Britain* (1960–1978) exported images of British life that stressed both tradition and modernity. Other COI series (some of which in latter years were intended for television) include *Transatlantic Teleview* (1956–1957), which featured interviews with British politicians and economists for American consumption; *Calendar* (1963–1967), which provided general background stories; and *Living Tomorrow* (1971–1978), which focused on scientific innovation.

The cinemagazine was a wide-ranging and varied genre, the precise parameters of which have yet to be defined. Often it is difficult to determine where newsreels ended and cinemagazines began, especially for British newsreels of the 1960s and 1970s (given the example of *Gaumont-British News,* which in 1959 was turned into a cinemagazine, *Look at Life*). Another unclear boundary is that between the cinemagazine and the documentary film series, such as the British *Worker and Warfront* (1942–1945) or the American *Why We Fight* (1943–1944).

The cinemagazine was an amalgam of many styles, from the documentary to the newsreel to the travelog. What is clear is that the magazine film series of the twentieth century, be they interest-led, information-led, industrial, or propagandist, need to be recognized collectively as a significant and influential part of moving image history. Rich in content, rich in the ways that such content was delivered to audiences, rich simply in their variety of form, the cinemagazines must now receive the critical attention that they deserve.

LUKE MCKERNAN

See also Central Office of Information; Grierson, John; Newsreel Series: UK; Pathé; Urban, Charles

Further Reading

Buchanan, Andrew, *The Film in Education*, London: Phoenix House, 1951.

Fielding, Raymond, *The March of Time, 1935–1951*, New York: Oxford University Press, 1978.

Hammerton, Jenny, *For Ladies Only? Eve's Film Review: Pathe Cinemagazine 1921–1933*, Hastings: The Projection Box, 2001.

Hardy, Forsyth (ed.), *Grierson on Documentary*, London: Collins, 1946.

Maltin, Leonard, *The Great Movie Shorts*, New York: Bonanza Books, 1972.

CITY, THE

(US, Steiner, 1939)

A brief history of the American city and a call for better civic planning, made at the behest of the American Institute of Planners, *The City* was one of the most celebrated and widely viewed documentary films of the 1930s and 1940s in the United States. The production benefited from financial backing from the Carnegie Corporation, which awarded $50,000 to the project, and from close collaboration among a group of gifted artists brought together to make the film. *The City* also had the advantage of a well-publicized debut at the New York World's Fair in May 1939, where it was screened in the Science and Education Pavillion four times daily for the next eighteen months, aptly placed among an array of fairground exhibitions devoted to the theme of "The World of Tomorrow." Subsequent distribution through various channels boosted *The City*'s reputation further, although not always in ways that were in keeping with the sponsor's intentions.

Key figures in the making of *The City* included director-photographers Ralph Steiner and Willard Van Dyke, who formed American Documentary Films in 1938 to handle sponsored films of this kind; associate producer Henwar Rodakiewicz, who assisted at various points with the writing, directing, and editing; and composer Aaron Copland, who participated during the editing stage to create an integrated score, his first for film. Pare Lorentz, mentor to both Steiner and Van Dyke, contributed an outline that shaped the film's tone and structure. Urban critic Lewis Mumford wrote the narration, which was spoken by Morris Charnovsky of the Group Theater. The assembled talent alone ensured that critical attention would be given to this particular documentary.

For the American Institute of Planners, *The City* was intended to promote not simply the idea of thoughtful planning but a specific development project: "garden" or "green" cities, suburban centers built into the countryside, ringed by trees and hillsides and equipped with efficiently designed modern housing and hospitable spaces for work and play. In the past,

the planners argued, unregulated industrial development had fractured community relations and led to incalculable environmental and human waste. "Green" cities were the remedy. Inhabitants of these planned communities would regain the sociability and breathing space of the nineteenth-century village, while also enjoying the advantages of modern engineering, a combination made possible by the emergence of what Mumford labeled a "neo-technic" age.

The assignment presented to the filmmakers thus involved a problem-solving narrative and images of nature and industry common to many American social documentaries of the previous decade, including those of Lorentz. In its finished form, *The City* organizes this material into five loosely bracketed sequences: a New England village idyll; an industrial city marked by smoke, slag heaps, and decay; a modern metropolis where the work day is automated and congested; a weekend traffic jam on a suburban highway; and a "green" community of the kind the planners sought to promote.

Stylistic differences underscore social distinctions among the five segments. Compositions in the New England section, for example, favor horizontal framing, leisurely and lateral movement, and a balanced arrangement of people and structures, whereas the modern metropolis is defined through spatial constriction, sharp angles, and diagonal lines. Commentary, gentle and poetic in the village sequence, becomes clipped and sardonic in the industrial section that follows. Copland's innovative score establishes motifs for each section while also linking passages, as when a melodic line accompanying scenes of the New England village is recast in an elegiac key during bleaker parts of the industrial and metropolis segments, or a series of dissonant brass chords at the beginning of the industrial segment are converted into a harmonious closing at the film's end. Select stylistic devices exemplify the power of technological change, as when smokestacks multiply through superimpositions, or editing rhythms accelerate in coordination with the pace and mechanized movement of metropolitan life. A picture of the "green" town—composited from footage of working prototypes filmed in Maryland, New Jersey, Wisconsin, and Ohio—includes aerial views of buildings set amid foliage and curved streets and roadways that thread their way to and through the community in patterns that are seemingly organic yet dynamic, conforming to topographical features. In this fashion, *The City* itself constituted a form of spatial planning and design.

Yet if such strategies lent emotive or expressive force to the planners' arguments, the filmmakers also clashed with the sponsors over key details, leading to telling compromises on both sides. The automated movement, rapid cutting, and sprightly music of parts of the metropolis sequence, for example, had a humorous, playful aspect that the sponsors believed undercut their sober critique. Steiner prevailed on this point, and the passage was singled out for discussion by critics, pro and con. Moreover, a contentious off-screen debate among a quartet of voices, scripted for the final segment by Rodakiewicz, was vetoed outright by the sponsors, who also demanded the filmmakers extend the ending and spell out the advantages of the "green" community in detail.

The City also circulated in ways that emphasized values that fell outside, and even ran counter to, the sponsor's promotional aims. The teaming of the film on a double bill with the French film *La Principessa Tarakanovz* [*Betrayal*] at New York's Little Carnegie Theater in the fall of 1939, and the inclusion of *The City* in major documentary retrospectives mounted by the Museum of Modern Art (MoMA) in the winter

The City, 1939.
[*Still courtesy of the British Film Institute*]

of 1939–1940 and again in 1946, foregrounded the aesthetic accomplishment of the film over the planners' argument. (MoMA's curator, Iris Barry, in 1946 declared the *The City* a "three-quarter masterpiece on town-planning," alluding to the aesthetic weakness of the sponsor-imposed ending.) Nontheatrical distributors, including MoMA, also circulated 16mm prints to educational groups, where the historical claims of the film were more closely scrutinized. The American Association for Adult Education, for example, published a movie study guide for community groups that asked discussants to assess the political adequacy of *The City*'s history of urban development, opening up the topic to the kind of controversy that the planning association wanted the filmmakers to avoid. During the 1940s, excerpted passages from *The City* also were recycled in montage sequences of urban life in a variety of different films, including *War Comes to America* (1945), a U.S. Army documentary; *Humoresque* (1947), a Warner Bros. urban melodrama; and *Mr. Blandings Builds His Dream House* (1948), an RKO urban-suburban comedy. From this angle, the durability of *The City* seems in part a function of the varied kinds of attention it attracted and a stylistic virtuosity that permitted individual sequences to take on an identity apart from the whole.

CHARLES WOLFE

The City (US, American Documentary Films, Inc., 1939, 43 min) Distributed by Civic Films. Directed by Ralph Steiner and Willard Van Dyke. Written by Pare Lorentz and Lewis Mumford. Cinematography by Ralph Steiner and Willard Van Dyke.

Further Reading

Alexander, William, *Film on the Left: American Documentary Film from 1931 to 1942*, Princeton: Princeton University Press, 1981.

Barry, Iris, "Challenge of the Documentary Film," in the *New York Times*, January 6, 1946, SM9.

Gillette, Howard, Jr., "Film as Artifact: *The City* (1939)," in *American Studies*, Fall, 1977, 71–85.

Griffith, Richard, "Films at the Fair," *Films* 1, 1, 1939, 61–75.

Keil, Charlie, "American Documentary Finds Its Voice: Persuasion and Expression in *The Plow That Broke the Plains* and *The City*," in *Documenting the Documentary: Close Readings of Documentary Film and Video*, edited by Barry Keith Grant and Jeannette Sloniowski, Detroit: Wayne State University Press, 1998.

Mumford, Lewis, *The Culture of Cities*, New York: Harcourt, Brace & World, 1938.

Rodakiewicz, Henwar, "Treatment of Sound in *The City*," in *The Movies as a Medium*, edited by Lewis Jacobs, New York: Farrar, Straus and Giroux, 1970.

Wolfe, Charles, "The Poetics and Politics of Nonfiction: Documentary Film," in *Grand Design: Hollywood as a Modern Business*, edited by Tino Balio, New York: Charles Scribners Sons, 1993.

CITY OF GOLD

(Canada, Koenig and Low, 1957)

The National Film Board of Canada's *City of Gold* (1957) is one of the most celebrated short films ever produced and is one of the most decorated. Its numerous international awards, as well as its influence on the historical documentary and on noted contemporary filmmakers, testify to its merit and innovation.

City of Gold relates the history of the 1898 Klondike Gold Rush. The origins of the film lie in the

1949 discovery of several hundred Klondike era photographs in Dawson City, of the Yukon Territories. These images, preserved on 8 × 10 glass plate negatives, had been stored and forgotten in a sod roof cabin and were found only by chance just before its demolition. They were largely the work of A.E. Hegg, an American photojournalist and entrepreneur, who captured the ferment of the Gold Rush with extraordinary vividness.

Paying With Gold Dust. Fall 1899.

City of Gold, 1957.
[*Still courtesy of the British Film Institute*]

In ensuing years, through numerous means, these remarkable images attained wide circulation. In 1955 board director and animator Colin Low saw them at Ottawa's National Archive. He had been working on a Gold Rush project and quickly saw that these photographs might provide his film's centre. The challenge for Low and his collaborators was determining how to render this windfall of static imagery in some kind of dynamic cinematic fashion.

The solution came in the form of a mechanism devised by Roman Kroitor and Brian Salt, which enabled Low and co-director Wolf Koenig to plot and execute the most minute camera movements with complete precision and to explore their fixed images with unprecedented flexibility and fluidity. It is for this innovation that *City of*

Gold is most cited today, but the film would probably remain a mere technical footnote were it not for the material that the technology served and the sensibilities that informed the arrangement and presentation.

City of Gold was a collaboration. In its production there was a democratization of roles and relationships and a neutralization of film elements, resulting in an impressively integrated work of art and information. These characteristics and qualities were strongly associated with the board's legendary Unit B, of which *City of Gold* is perhaps the most well-known product. In the ideal Unit B production, the ego of individualism was subordinated to the needs and values of the creative community and, as behooved a publicly funded institution, of the

230

larger community the creators served. The idea and actuality of Unit B at the Film Board was not without contradiction and controversy. Nevertheless, with this film and with many others besides, the ideal and the real seem to have been substantially correlated.

City of Gold is notable for being very well made. There is a telling tension between the stasis of present-day Dawson, as illustrated by the film's live action prologue and epilogue, and the dynamism of the still photographs that preserve the vivid past. The contrast is emphasized by the exquisite transitions between the two periods. Much of the credit for this seamless assembly goes to editor, and Unit B head, Tom Daly.

Daly pointed out that the edges of the photographs were never shown, leaving audiences with the illusion of extended off-screen spaces. This quality had been integral to realist filmmaking for some time, but what was remarkable was how that space operated in a photographed context. As Erik Barnouw observed, it was not only space that was expanded in *City of Gold,* but time as well. The vividness of the images and the superb coordination of their rendering opened up the documentary film to times and events that predated it.

Some of the credit for this must also go to Eldon Rathburn's superb score. The immediacy of the historical is also aided by the film's narration, cowritten and delivered by Pierre Berton, a Dawson native who was on the brink of becoming Canada's most prolific and popular historian. The voice that he presents combines the scholar's rigor with the citizen's affection and commitment. This combination communicates a concrete sense of past realities, as well as a clear sense of their relevance to the present.

Low and Koenig's film appeared at an important juncture in the development of the North, and the Canadian identity. Dire notions of the inhospitable and the impossible had long pervaded northern representations. Inevitably these pictures had affected the perceptions and self-concept of the nation as a whole; however, competing voices had also spoken for the necessity, even the inevitability, of successful community in this savage environment. In the light of more recent events (the Leduc oil strike of 1947, the subsequent establishment of the Canadian pipeline system, the dissemination of native cultural ideas and aspirations), this idea

had assumed even greater importance. For the sake of the region's own economic and social development, there was a need for a more nuanced, more optimistic view of the region.

City of Gold filled a number of present needs, and it continues to resonate in more contemporary contexts. In parallel to the organization that produced it, the film recalls how individual pursuit within a strong community led to great prosperity in the midst of environmental and geographical obstacles. It presents a model for peaceful relations between Americans and Canadians, in which the values of both sides are defended and combined to greatest mutual advantage. It affirms the importance of history's obscure, for whom difficulties are assured, but whose flexibility and decency in the face of inevitable frustration presents a worthy model for living, and for representing life.

DEAN DUNCAN

See also **Daly, Tom; Koenig, Wolf; Low, Colin; National Film Board of Canada**

City of Gold (Canada, National Film Board, Unity B, 22 min). Produced by Tom Daly. Directed by Wolf Koenig and Colin Low. Commentary by Pierre Berton and Stanley Jackson. Narration by Pierre Berton. Location camera by Wolf Koenig and Colin Low. Animation camera by Douglas Roberts. Music by Eldon Rathburn. Editing by Tom Daly. Sound by George Croll. Filmed in Dawson City, Yukon Territories.

Further Reading

Berton, Pierre, *The Mysterious North*, Toronto: McLelland & Stewart, 1954.

Berton, Pierre, *Klondike*, Toronto: McLelland & Stuart, 1958.

Evans, Gary, *In the National Interest: A Chronicle of the National Film Board of Canada from 1949 to 1989*, Toronto: University of Toronto Press.

Grey Owl, *Tales of an Empty Cabin*, Toronto: Key Porter Books, 1998.

Houston, James, *Confessions of an Igloo Dweller*, Toronto: McLelland & Stewart, 1995.

James, C. Rodney, *Film as a National Art: NFB of Canada and the Film Board Idea*, New York: Arno Press, 1977.

Jones, D. B., *Movie and Memoranda: An Interpretive History of the National Film Board of Canada*, Ottawa: Canadian Film Institute, 1981.

Jones, D. B., *The Best Butler in the Business: Tom Daly of the National Film Board of Canada*, Toronto: University of Toronto Press, 1996.

London, Jack, *Klondike Tales*, New York: Modern Library, 2001.

Service, Robert, *The Shooting of Dan McGrew and Other Poems*, New York: Dover, 1993.

CLAIR, RENÉ

René Clair was a French filmmaker whose films spanned forty years and represented a wide variety of genres, from experimental shorts to musicals to Hollywood studio dramas. His contribution to theories of documentary film was chiefly as a writer who championed the power of the film image as a nonnarrative form of communication, the importance of film rhythm and movement, and the independence of film as an art form. Condensing the thinking of several different French avant-garde intellectual traditions in the late 1910s and 1920s with his practical experience in the French studio system, Clair valued films whenever their fantastic or documentary powers circumvented, or offered alternatives to, traditional fictional narratives. As a practitioner of documentary and documentary-influenced film, he was interested in conveying the realities of the city (in his case, Paris) through on-location shooting. He was not a believer in the absolute truth conveyed by the image itself. His experiences with Dada, the iconoclastic post-World War I art movement, led in part to his films playing with an image's absolute truth through contrapuntal sound or camera work. In theory and in practice, Clair always foregrounded the process of filmmaking as it created reality rather than simply reproducing it on film; in addition, he always emphasized the power of film in general (and documentary film in particular) as a visceral experience with its own unconscious communicative power unrelated to that of other arts.

Clair first participated in the film industry as a newspaper writer and actor. His writing entered into the "great debates" in French film magazines during the 1920s, where film critics and practitioners argued over the purpose and direction cinema should take (Abel, 1988). Poetic documentaries—epitomized by *Nanook of the North* (1923)—flourished in this period, and Clair used these documentaries as examples of what film could achieve as an independent art form. In his opinion, the documentary was the only genre that could communicate its message in a wholly new way because it was the only one not parasitically dependent on earlier art forms. While the French *films d'art* of the 1920s seemed dependent on theater and literature as models, Clair believed that the documentary made it possible to communicate ideas, emotions, and intellectual arguments purely through the visual experience. In an essay on the Abel Gance film *La roue*, he rejects the literary and theatrical aspirations of the "cinema of ideas" in favor of a cinema that creates ideas in the mind of the viewer through image and movement alone:

> Oh, if M. Abel Gance would only give up making locomotives say yes and no, lending a railroad engineer the thoughts of antiquity, and quoting his favorite authors! If he were willing to create a pure *documentary*, since he knows how to give life to a machine part, a hand, a branch, a wisp of smoke! If only he were willing to contribute in that way to the creation of the Film that can barely be glimpsed today! Oh, if he were willing to give up literature and place his trust in the cinema!"

(quoted in Abel, 1988)

Here, Abel Gance is made to stand in for all filmmakers who lazily use conventions for earlier art forms instead of using film to communicate in a new way. Gance's films are both metaphorical and descriptive, but Clair believed that "pure documentary" could show instead of telling. Through lighting, shot framing, and the like film invested an object with meaning and life that could be interpreted or intuited by the viewer on an unconscious level. This idea is similar to that of other theorists of "photogenie," a belief that the skill of an auteur and the power of film as a medium could articulate previously unseen truths about objects, faces, and places (such as the "life" Gance imbues in hands, branches, and smoke). This understanding of the image is similar to that expressed in cinematic impressionism, a French movement that used pure and often not referential film images to convey a subjective, poetic emotion. Clair's ideas about the power of the documentary image are not purely impressionist, however, as they focus on the power of the image and the film as both subjective and objective, fantastic and realistic, expressive and iconoclastic.

Cinematic impressionism was an important influence, but Clair's understanding of the power of documentary film belongs to a larger tradition of European modernism. This movement held, among other things, that old narrative forms could no longer adequately communicate the realities of the newly mechanized world (particularly after World War I), and instead it turned to forms that worked through fragmentation, collage, juxtaposition, and unconscious association. For Clair, this meant that "pure cinema" untainted by commercial concerns could never truly exist, but the filmmaker could create fragments of purely visual story that communicated emotion unconsciously and helped the audience arrive at a new understanding of reality. Clair is best known as a filmmaker shaped by Dada and surrealism, and those art movements shared with cinematic impressionism a belief in the dreamlike power of images. Clair also took from Dada in particular a sense of film's power, through montage, to thwart conventional understanding. He believed that the logical culmination of the poetic documentaries of the 1920s would be a chain of images held together by "no definable link but united by a secret harmony" (Clair, 1972) like that which unified his seemingly nonsensical Dadaist film, *Entr'Acte*. Clair thought that a film whose sense was structural rather than narrative would hold a viewer's attention in the same way that a symphony does. And although Clair was initially opposed to sound film (chiefly because he thought it would return film to the status of theater), he later believed it had the same power to shock through juxtaposition with the image. His musicals in the 1930s and his later writing used sound to counterpoint, ironize, or call into question the unmediated reality the image presents, a technique important to many documentarians, and to those who use found footage in particular.

As an actor in Louis Feuillade's troupe, Clair was exposed to an important early French film tradition, one that had the most concrete influence on his experiences as a documentary filmmaker. This movement, described by critics as "pictorialist naturalism" was influenced by the theories of nineteenth- and twentieth-century writer Emile Zola, whose novels of lower-class life explored the effect environment has on character (Aitken, 2001). In practice, this meant that the films used on-location shooting and nonprofessional actors in an attempt to represent objective, unmediated, and unaestheticized reality. Even in his serials like *Les Vampires*, a fantastic crime thriller that the surrealists loved for its bizarre plots and imagery, Feuillade still shot on-location to document the reality of Paris at night, a reality that he believed could not be realized on a constructed set.

Clair shot on location for *La Tour/The Tower* (1928), his only documentary, as well as the street scenes in his science fiction film, *Paris qui dort (1925)/The Crazy Ray*. These films emphasize film's rhythmic qualities and the emotional and intellectual resonance of an image's movement and duration. For Clair, movement was the most important and effective technique for unconsciously conveying the film's meaning to the viewer: "I don't mean the movement recorded in the shot itself, but the movement of the shots in relation to one another. Movement, the primary base of cinematic lyricism, whose mysterious rules become clearer every day" (Dale, 1986). He used this concept to think about the basic elements of montage, such as shot length, action, and the visual field, in a musical way, taking into account the feelings of shock and connection that arise from each shot's place in the larger composition.

Through both his on-location shooting and his musical techniques of composition in *La Tour* and *Paris Qui Dort*, Clair can be understood as part of a larger tradition of European modernist documentary films of the 1920s and 1930s, and in particular the "city symphony films" such as *Rien que les Heures/Nothing but the Hours* (1926), *Chelovek s kinoapparatom/Man with a Movie Camera* (1929), and *Berlin: die Symphonie der Grossstadt/Berlin, Symphony of a Great City* (1929). Neither of Clair's films aspires to the kind of epic totality in its presentation of the rhythms of urban life seen in those films. The city scenes in *Paris Qui Dort* are part of a larger narrative and *La Tour* is about one landmark rather than Paris as a whole. Clair does share with Vertov the interest in paralleling the rhythms of city life with those of film itself, in particular by calling attention to materiality and construction of the film. In *Paris Qui Dort*, a mad scientist uses a ray to stop all motion in Paris, and the few residents who are not immobilized ransack the city, eating in fine restaurants and stealing from stores. Because of the scientist's actions, documentary footage of Paris pauses, fast forwards, and rewinds, showing the city while calling attention to how the city gets shown. Here, Clair is using film techniques such as stop-motion to undercut the intrinsic, unquestioned reality of the city in the same way he later uses sound to undercut the intrinsic truth of the image.

La Tour uses rhythm and movement to redefine the viewer's understanding of the most clichéd of Paris landmarks, the Eiffel Tower. This film is an articulation of all Clair's theories of the poetic documentary, as it unites film's ability to show the world in a fantastic or impossible way and its ability to communicate the concrete details of reality. Clair starts the film with a conventional postcard view of the Eiffel Tower, then splits this whole image into rapidly changing impressions of different pieces of the tower coming together and moving apart. This section's composition owes much to Cubist painting, particularly its method of presenting disparate views of an object as a way of both emphasizing the subjective nature of perception and presenting a more complete picture than a "whole" view of the Eiffel Tower would give. Clair transcends the techniques of the canvas, however, by constantly showing these different fragments in motion. As with *Paris Qui Dort*, Clair uses techniques such as fast motion and superimposition as a way of defamiliarizing a familiar place and calling into question precisely how we perceive it. Clair is somewhat interested in the tower's history. He shows a picture of Georges Eiffel and some blueprints and then mimics the construction of the Tower through matching dissolves of still images. The film then returns to the subject of perception through a first-person focus on the experience of ascending to the top of the tower; once the top has been reached, a shot multiplies this experience, looking down on a lower platform where a man looks down on even lower spectators. Throughout the film, shots where the camera moves upward mimic the structure of the tower and the first-person experience of moving to the top. After a rapid descent, the film ends with the same establishing shot of the Eiffel Tower, invested with new meaning through the firsthand experience of it.

The interplay of poetic fantasy and prosaic reality is important both to Clair's entire filmography and to the genre of poetic documentary that was shaped during his most productive and influential period as a writer in the 1920s. Clair's experience working on a variety of film projects, from the most independent and experimental to studio-funded adaptations of classic French plays, led to a more balanced view on the possibilities of documentary film than other film theorists and practitioners of the period. He agreed that film should attempt to communicate through visual effects, but this never descended into a purely subjective vision of the cinema. Perhaps his most important contribution to documentary film was the idea that images and their movement on screen, no matter how fantastic, could always intervene into reality and alter the audience's perception of it.

SUNNY STALTER

See also **Man with a Movie Camera**; **Rien que les Heures**

Biography

Born René Chomette, November 11, 1898. In ambulance corps on the frontlines during WWI, 1917–1918. Wrote newspaper articles and appeared in films, 1919–1922. Worked as an assistant director, 1922. Involved with Paris Dada/surrealist group throughout the 1920s. First novel, *Adams,* published in 1926. Made films in Paris in the early 1930s, London in the late 1930s, and the United States during World War II. Returned to Paris after World War II. Directed stage and radio plays throughout the 1950s. Elected to the Academie Francaise in 1960. Died in 1981.

Selected Films (all as director)

1924: *Entr'acte*
1925: *Paris qui dort/The Crazy Ray*
1928: *La Tour/The Tower*

Further Reading

Abel, Richard, *French Film Theory and Criticism: A History / Anthology 1907–1939*, vol. 1, Princeton, NJ: Princeton University Press, 1988.

Aitken, Ian, *European Film Theory and Cinema: A Critical Introduction*, Edinburgh: Edinburgh University Press, 2001.

Amengual, Barthelemy, *René Clair*, Paris: Seghers, 1969.

Clair, René, *Cinema, Yesterday and Today*, translated by Stanley Applebaum, edited by R.C. Dale, New York: Dover Publications, 1972.

Dale, R.C., *The Films of René Clair*, Metuchen, NJ: Scarecrow Press, 1986.

De La Roche, Catherine, *René Clair, an Index*, London: British Film Institute, 1958.

Mcgerr, Celia, *The Films of René Clair*, Boston: Twayne Publishers, 1980.

CLOSE-UP

(Iran, Kiarostami, 1990)

Like certain films of Buñuel, Chris Marker, and others, *Close-Up* puts into question what it is we are prepared to call reality, or documented reality, on film. Despite all its words and reasoning, its modernity and sophistication, *Close-Up* brings us at last to the issue of faith. What is to be feared in faith? What can faith bring?

Without title, credits, or any announcement, the film begins with a fifteen-minute sequence in which a journalist travels with two policemen in a taxi to a Tehran residential district to arrest an impostor. He has been taking advantage of a well-off family, pretending to be the famous film director Mohsen Makhmalbaf. The sequence feels like fiction, a careful staging with precise timing of lines and the camera set up where the car's dashboard or windshield would be. But once the arrest is made, the film's title and credits appear, informing us of a "screenplay" by Kiarostami "based on true events," and listing the names of the persons of the film, who "appear as themselves." The titles are superimposed over the image of a press printing newspapers, which suggests that the film understands its status as something like that of a newspaper, hardly a transparent medium, yet a medium of mass communication to which one turns for information and, presumably, truthful and accurate information.

The film proceeds to present four scenes that, to all appearances, are directly filmed, first-encounter interviews with individuals involved in the story. The first interview, with policemen outside the jail where the arrested man is being held, gives Kiarostami his first information about the arrest. Therefore the opening sequence, showing the arrest at the time it happened, is certifiably a reenactment, as Kiarostami did not know about the arrest at the time it occurred and thus could not have been present at the actual event.

The film moves on to an interview with the victimized family, the Ahankhahs, in their well-appointed home. They address Kiarostami by name, bringing him more explicitly into the film. The interview seems a first encounter simply because the family so frankly expresses its concern not to be depicted as credulous in what appears now to be a film project in which they have agreed to participate. The family makes clear its interest in film. The unemployed son, Mehrdad, writes screenplays as an escape from bourgeois boredom and disappointment. Interest in film drew the family in with the impostor, and it now draws them in with Kiarostami.

Next, in a prison interview, we meet the impostor, one Hossein Sabzian, the figure on whom the whole film hinges. Here we actually see Kiarostami for the first and only time, although only from the back. It is the filmmaker pressing forward to confront his subject, the source that generates the film. Kiarostami's cameraman frames the prison office where the

Close-Up, 1990.
[*Still courtesy of the British Film Institute*]

interview takes place, staying, presumably as required by prison rules, on the near side of a glass partition with columns, beyond which sit Kiarostami and Sabzian. A lens is used gradually to penetrate the barrier and come close to Sabzian's face as he speaks. The situation here illustrates documentary's perennial task and desire, to overcome barriers, to look closely, to let its attention be drawn by what is interesting. Here that interest is the face of this complex, emotional working-class man possessed, he tells us, by cinema, and drawn by this possession into committing his crime. "Make a film about my suffering," he entreats.

Kiarostami speaks with a court official and then the judge who presides over Sabzian's trial, securing permission to film the trial and getting the court date moved forward. Film's power to intervene in the justice system is impressive, and, at the end of the interview, two of the filmmakers pass in silhouette across the foreground, spectral figures, suggestive of angels. The judge, a small man with large eyes, dressed as a cleric, wants to participate in the film.

A filmmaker's chalkboard announces the trial scene, which will take up the lengthy middle portion of *Close-Up*, at once a crucial public event and a film. The first words are the judge's "In the name of God," picking up on the suggestion of angels, reiterating the issue of faith, and opening the dimensions of film's power and source wider than the film has done so far.

If this is God's court, it is very much a film director's court, or film's court. The episode appears to be shot on videotape or some lower grade of material than the rest of *Close-Up*, perhaps out of necessity in the courtroom setting, or perhaps to set this material apart formally. Are we watching the actual trial or a reenactment, perhaps with changes? Does it matter if we trust Kiarostami? Here Sabzian and the Ahankhahs are allowed to explain fully their motives and actions in all that has transpired.

Kiarostami asks questions and guides the proceedings to a degree, directing them. He explains to Sabzian that he will use a "close-up lens" to allow Sabzian to express himself fully. Pans across the room reveal Kiarostami's lighting man, making it clear that the filmmakers suggestively put Sabzian's face half in strong light, half in deep shadow. The long trial scene involves two flashback reenactment scenes, suggesting that what is being talked about builds a pressure that requires staged scenes to make things clear, to let things be fully what they are. There is argument about whether Sabzian is still performing, now as a repentant, which raises the question of whether performance can be avoided. Sabzian says that he speaks from the heart and quotes Tolstoy to the effect that the sincere sharing of feeling is art. *Close-Up* is at once sincere and artful, if we accept it. At the judge's behest, the Ahankhah family forgives Sabzian.

Close-Up concludes with a sequence in which, seen at a distance, Mohsen Makhmalbaf appears on the street and meets a weeping Sabzian, and the two ride across Tehran on Makhmalbaf's motorbike to call on the Ahankhahs and offer them flowers. Kiarostami and crew follow in another vehicle, filming. Makhmalbaf's lapel microphone appears to fail, and Kiarostami and an associate appear to make on-the-spot comments about the progress of the scene, such as "we can't retake this." From its opening (that first journey across town to the Ahankhahs), *Close-Up* has established a pattern of confinement breaking out into the open. The trial scene breaks out into flashbacks. The whole film seems a preparation to break out into the highly mobile final sequence, a complicated artistic trick or a case of film doing all it can to keep up with events not under its control. The film ends on a freeze frame of Sabzian's face, his head bowed in repentance, tears having flowed, a subtle smile starting to take over.

CHARLES WARREN

See also **Kiarostami, Abbas**

Close-Up (Nama-y Nazdik, Iran, 1990, 90 min) Produced by A.R.Zarin. Directed and edited by Abbas Kiarostami. Screenplay by A. Kiarostami based on a true story, with the persons concerned appearing as themselves. Photographed by A.R. Zarindast. Filmed in Tehran.

Further Reading

Dabashi, Hamid, *Close Up: Iranian Cinema, Past, Present and Future*, London and New York: Verso, 2001.

Perez, Gilberto, *The Material Ghost: Films and Their Medium*, Baltimore and London: Johns Hopkins University Press, 1998.

Mehrnaz Saeed-Vafa and Jonathan Rosenbaum, *Abbas Kiarostami*, University of Illinois Press, 2003.

COAL FACE

(UK, Cavalcanti, 1935)

The National Film Archive summarizes the content of the film *Coal Face* as the following: "The work of the British miner and its importance." The shot list is as follows:

> Shots of pitheads. Overhead transporters dump slag onto slagheaps. Mechanized washing and grading of coal at a pithead. The location and size of the main coalfields are indicated on a map of Britain. Miners walk along a shaft to the *Coal Face* for the night shift. Horses pulling wagons. A miner working at the face. A Davey safety lamp in operation. A naked flame lamp in a gasless Scottish pit. Miners working at the face. A sandwich break. An electric coal cutter in operation. Coal is shovelled into trucks which are hauled off—commentary gives statistics of accidents in the mine. The winding machinery brings the men to the surface in the morning. They check out. The miners make their way home, rows of terraced houses owned by the company. Pithead chimneys. A tree. A miner walks under a line of washing. Slagheaps. Tree blowing in the wind. Ruined building. Trees and sky. A railway marshalling yard. A train moves off with coal. Shunting coal wagons—a signalman operates points. Horse-drawn coal carts distribute coal locally. Commentary gives statistics of coal used by the major industries: the electricity industry—shots of pylons, worker in a power station; railways: coal is loaded into a tender, the locomotive moves off; express trains. Shipping: dockers loading coal into a ship. A mechanical grab hoists a load of coal and empties it. Industrial landscapes. Pitheads. Miner walking along a street. Pithead at evening.

Coal Face was presented at the [London] Film Society as an experiment in sound. The commentary provides factual information—data, processes, by-products—overpoetic images of coal mines. The commentator's voice is unconventional and non-professional sounding (even the maps are abstract at first). The music is modern, cacophonous, discordant piano with percussion are prominent. As miners walk into the mine, choral speech and drumbeat begin. The choruses are of male and female voices, separate and combined. The commentator is objective, the chorus subjective. We hear snatches of miners' talk, individual men's voices, whistling, choir in a kind of keen. The poem sung by the female voices on the return of the miners to the surface was written for the film by W. H. Auden:

> O lurcher loving collier black as night,
> Follow your love across the smokeless hill.
> Your lamp is out and all your cages still.
> Course for her heart and do not miss
> And Kate fly not so fast,
> For Sunday soon is past,
> And Monday comes when none may kiss.
> Be marble to his soot and to his black be white.

Coal Face continued the formal experimentation with sound in relation to sight so strongly evident in *The Song of Ceylon* (1934), though this time as an exalted tribute to the lives of British miners. It was the editing of sound in relation to image that was the strongest and most original line of formal invention in the British documentary of the 1930s (and on into the 1940s). It is generally agreed that Cavalcanti, much more than Grierson, was responsible for that rich and innovative use of sound, ahead of anything being attempted in feature fiction filmmaking at the time. Of course it was Grierson who brought Cavalcanti, with his background in the avant-garde and work in early sound features, from France to the General Post Office Film

Coal Face, 1935.
[*Still courtesy of the British Film Institute*]

Unit for that purpose. (Though it was also suggested, given the youthfulness of the GPO Unit filmmakers, that Grierson may have invited Cavalcanti to have someone his age to talk with.) In any case, the films they worked on together maintain their interest as artistic experiments. *Coal Face* won a medal of honor at the International Film Festival in Brussels in 1935.

Cavalcanti, while assisting on most of the GPO Unit's production, had films for which he was mainly responsible. *Coal Face* was the second and perhaps most important of these. (*Pett and Pott*, 1934, the first.) It was, wrote Roger Manvell, "an oratorio of mining." He added that "oratorios are not popular with film-goers. The visuals were good but not exceptional," in Manvell's opinion. "What mattered was the sound" (*Film* [Harmondsworth, Middlesex: Penguin, 1946], p. 362). Part of the problem may well have been that the recording quality of this sound track is substandard. Because of government regulations, the GPO Film Unit was at first required to purchase British sound equipment (Visatone-Marconi) for its Blackheath Studio. RCA equipment was purchased later.

In addition to Grierson and Cavalcanti the poet W. H. Auden and the composer Benjamin Britten were part of the film crew. They worked together and separately on subsequent documentaries (most notably *Night Mail*, 1936). In 1935 Britten would have been twenty-three years old and at the begin-

ning of his career. Edgar Anstey suggested that *Coal Face* anticipated Britten's later operatic work, in *Peter Grimes*, for example ("The Sound-Track in British Documentary," n.d., typescript, 13 pp.). It also anticipated and may even have been a source of inspiration for Willard Van Dyke's *Valley Town* (US, 1940), with its daring use of sung soliloquy. But the mixing of stylized song and actuality footage was not actively pursued in documentary.

Even in *Coal Face*, along with the experimentation and poetry, the drabness and hardship of the miners' lives, including their resilience, courage, and dignity, are made prominent. Although the last images we see are of an individual miner walking against a background of mining village and pithead at evening, the commentary ends with the assertion that: "Coal mining is the basic industry of Britain."

JACK C. ELLIS

See also **Cavalcanti, Alberto; Grierson, John; General Post Office Film Unit**

Coal Face (UK, GPO Film Unit, 1935, 11 min) Distributed by Associated British Film Distributors. Produced by John Grierson. Direction and script by Alberto Cavalcanti. Commentary by W. H. Auden and Montagu Slater. Music by Benjamin Britten. Sound supervision by Cavalcanti, Stuart Legg, Benjamin Britten. Sound recording by E. A. Pawley. Editing by William Coldstream.

COLUMBIA BROADCASTING SYSTEM

During the 1950s, the Columbia Broadcasting System (CBS) pioneered the news documentary with *See It Now*, whose co-producers, Edward R. Murrow and Fred Friendly, set the standard for advocacy journalism and demonstrated television's power as a new documentary medium of vast social impact. *See It Now* triggered a series of evolutions in form and content across all three networks. These changes propelled the television documentary into a golden era of relevance and popularity that did not wane until the late 1960s.

See It Now debuted Sunday November 18, 1951 with "Christmas in Korea," a landmark in television documentary for its sustained use of the camera as a

narrative tool to establish time and place. CBS promoted the weekly series as "the ultimate sight-and-sound development of the Murrow-Friendly documentary ideas," and a television news magazine containing biographies, international stories, in-depth interviews, feature stories, and breaking news (Merron, 1988). A generous budget enabled *See It Now* to deploy up to five camera crews across the globe; a single production could exceed $100,000 and only 5 percent of the film shot was used. CBS also granted Murrow and Friendly an unprecedented degree of editorial freedom, as evidenced in the two *See It Now* documentaries that are among the most significant and controversial in American television.

The first documentary, "The Case Against Milo Radulovich, A0589839" (1953), reported the story of an Air Force lieutenant who was discharged as a "security risk" based on anonymous charges that his father and sister read subversive material. The documentary revealed the denunciation's specious basis: Radulovich's father and sister read a Serbian newspaper. Five weeks after the broadcast, the Secretary of the Air Force vindicated Radulovich.

The second documentary, "Report on Senator McCarthy" (1954), achieved milestone status for Murrow's courageous exposure of the Senator's bullying scare tactics and wild, unsubstantiated denunciations. A production innovation, the cross-cut interview, cutting lengthy interviews into staccato bursts to present a point of view, heightened the film's emotional impact.

In 1958, despite the prestige it brought the network, CBS cancelled *See It Now*. Controversial subjects, presented in an adversarial fashion, had provoked strong complaints of editorial bias and repelled sponsors. Also quiz shows, such as *The $64,000 Question*, had proven more lucrative to profit-minded executives.

CBS chairman William Paley was still committed to Murrow and Friendly and the documentary idea, and in 1959, with essentially the same staff, *See It Now* metamorphosed into *CBS Reports*, an hour-long documentary program. One year later, *CBS Reports* aired one of the greatest works of television documentary art, "Harvest of Shame," produced by David Lowe and narrated by Murrow.

Broadcast the day after Thanksgiving, "Harvest of Shame" exposed the plight of America's migrant workers, "the humans who harvest the food for the best-fed people in the world." Images of squalor and social misery never before seen on television were masterfully integrated with the story line. Footage of men penned in an overflowing flatbed truck for the chance to earn seventy cents a day accompanied Murrow's voice-over: "This scene is not taking place in the Congo. It has nothing to do with Johannesburg or Capetown. It is not Nyasaland or Nigeria. This is Florida. These are citizens of the United States, 1960." Murrow's editorial stance brought charges of bias and distortion.

In addition to the news documentary, CBS also nurtured several notable programs that suggested new avenues for the television documentary. The earliest was *The Search* (1954), created by Irving Gitlin (creator of another cultural-educational documentary, *Wide Wide World*, for the rival NBC in 1956). *The Search* documented innovative university research and scholarship.

NBC's *Victory at Sea* (1952–1953), twenty-six half-hour programs detailing the U.S. Navy's role in World War II, established the power of the compilation documentary. Producer Henry Salomon complied 60,000 feet of film from more than 60 million feet. In 1956, CBS answered with its own compilation documentary, *Air Power*, produced by Perry Wolff, whose crew fashioned twenty-six stories from more than 300 million feet of film. Narrated by Walter Cronkite, the program conveyed its story of American victory in the sky through the historical compilation of milestones in aviation, from the Wright Brothers to the F-104.

In 1957, producer Burton Benjamin continued work in the compilation genre with *The Twentieth Century*, a regularly scheduled documentary program (26 annually) that ran until 1964. *The Twentieth Century* expanded the genre's range with an innovation borrowed from radio, the eyewitness. Jack Warner, for example, recounted the first talkie, and Pearl Buck, devastation in China. By the early 1960s, each network had exploited the compilation form: ABC documented Winston Churchill's *The Valiant Years* and NBC documented the twentieth century's great social upheavals in *Project XX*.

By the late 1960s, however, the audience for the single subject television documentary had declined precipitously. Low ratings and red ink killed *CBS Reports*, NBC's *White Paper*, and ABC's *Close-Up*. Ever since the adversarial *See It Now* broadcasts, documentary producers had felt an unrelenting corporate pressure to avoid controversy and adopt a neutral stance toward their subjects. The television documentary had become the voice of the corporation. Seeking to counter this malaise, in 1968 CBS producer Don Hewitt launched *60 Minutes*, a weekly documentary news magazine consisting of three, fourteen-minute subjects. *60 Minutes*, a descendant of *See It Now* (Hewitt and many on the *60 Minutes* staff worked on *See It Now*), has lasted more than thirty-five years and become the most profitable program in television history.

Thus, in truncated, prime time form, the idea of *See It Now* and the news documentary of the 1950s survives. More than form and technique, *See It Now's* legacy has to do with honesty, courage, and social justice. At the height of the red scare and blacklists the documentary series took on McCarthyism. In giving shape and content to a new medium, old radio hands Murrow and Friendly fulfilled John Grierson's documentary idea of bringing current events to the screen "in any fashion which strikes the imagination and makes observation richer than it was."

TONY OSBORNE

See also **Murrow, Edward R.**

Further Reading

Barnouw, Eric, *Documentary: A History of Non-Fiction Film*, New York: Oxford University Press, 1974.

Barsam, Richard, *Nonfiction Film: A Critical History*, Bloomington: Indiana University Press, 1992.

Benjamin, Burton, "The Documentary Heritage," in *The Documentary Tradition*, edited by Lewis Jacobs, New York: W.W. Norton and Company, Inc., 1979.

Bluem, William, A., *Documentary in American Television*, New York: Hastings House, 1965.

Campbell, Richard, *60 Minutes and the News: A Mythology for Middle America*, Urbana: University of Illinois Press, 1991.

Edwards, Bob, *Edward Murrow and the Birth of Broadcast Journalism*, Hoboken, NJ: John Wiley & Sons, Inc., 2004.

Friendly, Fred, W., "The McCarthy Broadcast," in *New Challenges for Documentary*, edited by Alan Rosenthal, Berkeley: University of California Press, 1988.

Hammond, Charles Montgomery, Jr., *The Image Decade: Television Documentary: 1965–1975*, New York: Hastings House, 1981.

Merron, Jeff, "Murrow on TV: See It Now Person to Person, and the Making of a Masscult Personality," in *Journalism Monographs*, 106, 1988, 1–35.

Persico, Joseph, E., *Edward R. Murrow: An American Original*, New York: McGraw-Hill, 1988.

Sperber, Ann, M., *Murrow, His Life and Times*, New York: Freundlich Books, 1986.

COMIZI D'AMORE

(Italy, Pasolini, 1964)

Pier Paolo Pasolini made some documentaries, in addition to his fictional films: the "notepads" or *appunti*, a film about sewer workers, and *The Walls of Sana'a,* a documentary in the shape of a call to UNESCO. *Comizi d'Amore* (*Assembly of Love* or *Love Meetings*), however, is the sole example of an interactive-reflexive documentary, not only within Pasolini's works but also in the Italian cinematography of the time. As Alberto Moravia points out in the film itself, *cinema verité* did not catch on in the homeland of neorealism.

Comizi d'Amore consists of a sociopolitical, broad-scale, Italian discourse on sex and love. The shooting period extended from August to November 1963, in such various locations as Naples, Palermo, Cefalù, Viareggio, Florence, the countryside of Emilia-Romagna, Bologna, Milan, the Lido of Venice, Catanzaro, the beaches of Rome's coastline and Calabria, Tuscany, Bagheria, Rome, and eventually Pasolini's own home garden. Pasolini paid attention not only to demarcation lines (men versus women, rich versus poor, young versus old, North versus South, rural versus urban) but also to the way various societal groups intersect with one another. The reflection in progress thus acquires a provocative relevance.

In his bittersweet consciousness, Pasolini conceived of the argument as a fight against monsters and had considered inscribing titles "against images of dreadful animals, spiders, microbes, amoebas, monsters, snakes devouring one another." In concrete terms, the film is built on a two-part basis: first, people from "the very audience of the film" and second, "those who know," "persons of culture."

Comizi d'Amore, 1964.
[*Still courtesy of the British Film Institute*]

Some humor and irony nonetheless interferes in the investigation. Irony is at the center of the device when Pasolini, a homosexual man, registers with solemnity some terribly homophobic lectures that turn into knowing understatement with Cesare Ungaretti. Off-screen asides underline some rather insincere accounts. Occasional self-censorship is displayed in large characters. A few pop songs add their significantly inane lyrics. The filmmaker is not deluding himself about the validity of the enquiry, serious as it is. He appears to be conscious of the unsaid (which he makes apparent especially near the end) and of the remaining gaps (which he defines with a shift in perspective as "the void left by the bourgeoisie").

The conclusion is twofold again. On the one hand, Pasolini points out that "in the Italy of the economic miracle we expected another miracle," which had not occurred. On the other hand, as "an element of conclusion and catharsis," he wishes for a (fictitious) new married couple, Tonino and Graziella: "may to your love be added the consciousness of your love."

JEAN-LUC LIOULT

Comizi d'Amore (Italy, Pasolini, 1964) Distributed by Titanus Distribuzione S.p.a. Produced by Alfredo Bini. Directed and written by Pier Paolo Pasolini. Cinematography by Mario Bernardo and Tonino Delli Colli. Assistant direction by Vincenzo Cerami. Editing by Nino Baragli.

Further Reading

Betti, Laura, and Michele Gulinucci, (eds.), *Pier Paolo Pasolini, Le Regole di un'illusione—i film, il cinema*, Roma: Fondo Pier Paolo Pasolini, 1991.
Biette, Jean-Claude, "Pasolini, souvenirs d'un enragé," in *Cahiers du Cinéma* 496, 1995.

COMMONWEALTH FILM UNIT

The Commonwealth Film Unit (CFU) was the de facto name given to the Australian government film production body between about 1956 and 1973, when its name was changed to Film Australia. The organization had a long ancestry going back to at least 1911, when a government photographer and filmmaker had been appointed by the federal government for the purpose of making information films. These films tended to focus on such subjects as the products of Australia's primary industries and were intended both to promote agriculture and migration in the United Kingdom. After the end of World War II, the government decided to act on the advice of John Grierson and reestablish the film body on a larger scale with a twin brief—to produce films both for particular government departments and agencies and for more general, national interest.

Known informally as the Film Division, an arm of the News and Information Bureau of the Department of the Interior, the body found itself referred to as the Commonwealth Film Unit from 1956 onward. The chief presence at the Unit in these years, Stanley Hawes, had learned his craft and its supporting ideology at the British Post Office film division in the 1930s. Hawes followed Grierson to the Canadian National Film Board toward the end of that decade and later came to Australia to help set up and run the newly expanded film production instrument.

Under Hawes's leadership over the next two decades, the CFU was responsible for the making of more than 400 information films, most of them consisting of a single reel but with one or two running to feature length. The most notable of the latter was *The Queen in Australia* (1954), which was, undoubtedly, its most prestigious (and among its most dullest) films. Overall, this period of Australian history was marked by postwar affluence and consensus, which was articulated and expressed in many films of this period. The pillars of this affluence were, variously, those of material development social and physical improvement, a consensual populace, a suburban society, and renewed and expanding consumption.

The preferred mode of film at the Unit, at least until the mid-1960s, was that of the classical documentary style. Such an approach bespoke not just the legacy of Grierson's role in establishing the expanded film production effort but was also suited to a consensualist view of Australian society. The most important feature of these films was undoubtedly the use of an expository voice, "the voice of God." Always confident and authoritative, the speaker is invariably male, neither obviously young nor old, nonethnic, and apparently classless in accent. In other words, as a means of affirming and maintaining its authority, this voice is impersonal, objective, acting on behalf of the general interest, and able where necessary to conjure up voices as well as images in support of its exposition. Thus, for example, in the film *The Earth Reveals,* the film calls up both images of the new mining technologies now in operation and a controlled cacophony of voices of miners and others at work in these fields.

The consensus implied by these films was beginning to erode by the early 1960s; this change was paralleled by shifts in the style of film emerging from the CFU. The obvious driving force for this change in the preferred mode of filmmaking lay not in any ideological determination to reflect the new, emerging mood and tone of the society. Rather, it came about in part because of the advent of new filmmaking technologies and the desire on the part of the Unit to remain contemporary in this arena. Thus the use of color became increasingly common, and toward the end of the 1950s, films such as *Paper Run* were made in a CinemaScope format.

It was the advent of new sound equipment and film techniques, however, that fractured the style of the classical documentary's reign at the CFU. Meantime, the CFU itself was changing. In 1962, it moved to more spacious premises specially designed to meet its needs. Its budgets rose sharply over the next dozen years, and the political/bureaucratic attacks that had dogged it now fell away. New, younger staff members were recruited, and the Unit briefly won a reputation as Australia's de facto national film school.

The paradigmatic film of this phase was *From the Tropics to the Snow* (1964), a highly reflexive film about the CFU itself and the impossible and irreconcilable claims of people and place involved in making a film about Australia. Paralleling the social shifts in Australian society toward a more pluralist outlook, the film used its more flexible sound resources to create and hold together the competing claims of both tropics and snow and everything in between. This was not the only impressive work to emerge at this time, however, and mention should also be made of two anthropological series pertaining to indigenous peoples. *People of the Western Desert and Towards Baruya Manhood* were completed in the late 1960s. Other notable works include a trilogy dealing with social outsiders who were also remarkable visionaries: *The Man Who Can't Stop* (1973), *Mr. Symbol Man* (1974), and *God Knows Why But It Works* (1975). The change of name to Film Australia in 1973 was prophetic of other changes in Australia itself and in the film organization. The oil crisis of 1973–1974 heralded the disruption of the postwar consensus and the commencement of a neoliberalism that would shortly begin to affect staff levels and budgets at the unit.

ALBERT MORAN

Further Reading

Bertrand, Ina, and Diane Collins, *Government and Film in Australia*, Sydney: Currency Press, 1982.

Lansell, Ross, *The Documentary Film in Australia,* Melbourne: Thomas Nelson, 1984.

Moran, Albert, *Projecting Australia: Government Film Making Since 1945*, Sydney: Currency Press, 1991.

COMOLLI, JEAN-LOUIS

Jean-Louis Comolli is best known internationally for his writings in *Cahiers du cinéma* from 1962 to 1978. He was editor-in-chief of the journal from June 1965, a role he shared from October 1968 with Jean Narboni, with whom he co-authored many articles, including the influential "Cinema/Ideology/Criticism." In October 1968, Jean-Luc Godard withdrew from *Cahiers* to found the Dziga Vertov collective, and exactly one year later "Cinema/Ideology/Criticism" marked the onset of the journal's most intensely Marxist, historical materialist and then Maoist phase. Comolli has continued to write extensively about cinema and the media since his time at *Cahiers*, as the publication of a collection of his articles from 1988 to 2003 early in 2004 indicates. But he has also worked actively as a filmmaker and particularly as a documentarist since the late 1970s, after a first documentary made in 1968. He teaches at the Paris film school FEMIS, at Paris VIII, and in Barcelona, and writes for the French reviews *Trafic*, *Images documentaires*, and *Jazz Magazine*.

The *politique des auteurs* was officially buried by *Cahiers du cinéma* in its November 1965 issue, and quickly replaced by the so-called New Cinema, supported by Comolli's editorial line. The films of Godard, Jacques Rivette, Howard Hawks, and John Ford were ardently praised, and Comolli lambasted the bourgeois morality of the cinema of Claude Lelouch. After the Langlois affair and *Cahiers'* involvement in the 1968 Estates General of the Cinema (Harvey, 1978), the publication of "Cinema/Ideology/Criticism" and the hardening of the journal's editorial policy into Althusserian-influenced materialism caused a three-month suspension in publication. Traditional tensions between *Cahiers* and *Positif* opened up again as *Cahiers* drew closer to *Tel Quel* and *Cinéthique* after François Truffaut's withdrawal from its editorial committee. In June 1971, Comolli launched his six-part series of articles "Technique and Ideology," the last installment of which appeared in November 1972.

Cinema/Ideology/Criticism starts from the assumption that all films seen in the West are produced, distributed, and exhibited by the capitalist economy and the dominant ideology and establishes seven types of relationship a film may have with this economy and ideology according to its type of passive determination by or active, reflective, critical operation on them. Films "imbued through and through" with the dominant ideology (Comolli and Narboni, 1977: 5) and produced in response to audience demand, itself an economic, ideological, and political category, constitute the largest group, (a). Films in categories (b) and (d) have explicitly political content, but category (b) films actively use this content to attack the ideological system in which they are embedded, whereas (d) films "unquestioningly adopt its language and imagery" (Ibid.: 6). Group (c) films do not work with explicitly political signifieds, but "in some way" politicise their content by means of "the criticism practised on it through its form" (Ibid.). Comolli and Narboni specify that category (b) and (c) films "constitute the essential in the cinema and should be the chief subject of the magazine" [*Cahiers*]. Films in group (e) are apparently representative of the ideology they are subject to, but in

them a distortion or rupture occurs between the film project and the final product, so that the ideology is exposed and turned against itself by the cinematic framework, and becomes subordinate to the text, presented by the film but not operational. Categories (f) and (g) apply to "live cinema" (*cinéma direct*) films, but despite usually having sociopolitical subject matter, films in (f) "do not challenge the cinema's traditional, ideologically-conditioned method of 'depiction'" (Ibid.: 7–8); they are still subject to the illusion that the truth of reality can be offered up, whereas group (g), a smaller proportion of *cinéma direct* films, do at least tackle representation as a problem, and produce meaning "by giving an active role to the concrete stuff" of the film (Ibid.: 8). Comolli and Narboni conclude by declaring that *Cahiers'* programme—in their view the only viable future direction for film criticism—will be the elaboration and application of a dialectical materialist critical theory of the cinema.

As Christopher Williams (Williams, 1973) sets out, Comolli's "Technique and Ideology" attempts to address the problematic of articulating semiology into a discourse about science, ideology, technique, and history. Placing film and cinema in the ideological domain, Comolli argues with the emphasis often placed on neutrality and scientificity in accounts of film technology. One example is the set of codes of perspective film adopted from Renaissance painting; another is the pressure early cinema inherited from photography to "confirm the impressions of the human eye" (Ibid.: 2), a prime instance of the ideological character of realism and naturalism passing unnoticed. Comolli argues with the formalism of Bazin's and Mitry's writings on deep focus, and to propose replacing "the Bazinian chain of forms and styles.[...] with the study of film signifiers" (Ibid.: 3). A constant emphasis of the six parts of "Technique and Ideology" is the demand for a materialist theory and history of the cinema that uses semiotics and takes proper account of economic and ideological factors.

Turning to Comolli's work as a filmmaker, the five fiction films he has directed are vastly outnumbered by his documentaries, which range from a nostalgic look at the French custom of the *bal musette* [accordeon dance] to a loving account of a weekend in the kitchens of chef Alain Ducasse at Monte Carlo's *Hôtel de Paris*. But politics has been his dominant subject, and particularly politics in Marseilles, in a series of four films covering the city's political life from 1986 into the 1990s, *Marseille de père en fils* (1989), *La Campagne de*

Provence (1992), *Marseille en mars* (1993), and *Marseille contre Marseille* (1995). The quartet was a collaboration with editor Anne Baudry and Michel Samson, a *Libération* journalist who conducts the interviews in the films. Samson's body is a focal point for Comolli's camera, and in recent interviews for *Cahiers du cinéma*, Comolli has spoken of attempting to film a physical and human dimension of political speech and exchange overlooked, fragmented or atomised by today's globalised media coverage. Comolli has worked extensively for French television, output that includes an acclaimed film about the aftermath of the desecration of Jewish graves at Carpentras in southern France in 1990, *Jeu de rôles à Carpentras* (1998).

Biography

Born July 30, 1941, in Phillippeville, Algeria. Editor-in-Chief of *Cahiers du cinéma* from June 1965, a role he shared from October 1968 with Jean Narboni, with whom he coauthored many articles, including the influential "Cinema/Ideology/Criticism." Has continued to write extensively about cinema and the media since his time at *Cahiers*, as the publication of a collection of his articles from 1988 to 2003 early in 2004 indicates. Has also worked actively as a filmmaker and particularly as a documentarist since the late 1970s, after a first documentary made in 1968. Teaches at the Paris film school FEMIS, at Paris VIII, and in Barcelona, and writes for the French reviews *Trafic*, *Images documentaires*, and *Jazz Magazine*.

KATHERINE INCE

Selected Films

1968 *Les Deux Marseillaises*: director
1976 *La Cecilia*: director
1981 *L'Ombre rouge*: director
1981 *On ne va pas se quitter comme ça*: director
1988 *Tous pour un!*: director
1989 *Marseille de père en fils*: director
1992 *Une semaine en cuisine*: director
1992 *La Campagne de Provence*: director
1993 *Marseille en mars*: director
1995 *Marseille contre Marseille*: director
1998 *Jeu de rôles à Carpentras*: director

Further Reading

Browne, Nick, (ed.), *Cahiers du Cinéma 1969–72: The Politics of Representation*, London: Routledge, 1990.

Comolli, Jean-Louis, and Jeam Narboni, "Cinema/Ideology/Criticism," translated by Susan Bennett, in *Screen Reader 1: Cinema/Ideology/Politics*, London: The Society for Education in Film and Television, 1977. [Also reprinted in *Cahiers du Cinéma 1969–72: The Politics of Representation*, edited by Nick Browne, London: Routledge, 1990, and in *Contemporary Film Theory*, edited and introduced by Anthony Easthope, Harlow, Essex: Longman, 1993].

Comolli, Jean-Louis, "Historical Fiction—A Body Too Much," translated by Ben Brewster in *Screen* 19, 2, 1978, 41–54.

Comolli, Jean-Louis, "Technique and Ideology: Camera, Perspective, Depth of Field," translated by Diana Matias in *Cahiers du Cinéma 1969–72: The Politics of Representation*, edited by Nick Browne, London: Routledge, 1990.

Harvey, Sylvia, *May '68 and Film Culture*, London: British Film Institute, 1978.

Rodowick, D., *The Crisis of Political Modernism: Criticism and Ideology in Contemporary Film Theory*, Urbana: University of Illinois Press, 1988.

Williams, Christopher, "Ideas about film technology and the history of the cinema, with reference to Comolli's texts on technology (*Cahiers du cinéma*)," pamphlet of paper for British Film Institute Educational Advisory Service/Society for Education in Film and Television seminar, 26 April 1973.

Williams, Christopher, *Realism and the Cinema: A Reader*, London and Henley: Routledge & Kegan Paul in association with the British Film Institute, 1980.

COMPILATION

There has been a long and distinguished tradition, beginning with the pioneering efforts of Esfir Shub in her 1927 films *Fall of the Romanov Dynasty* and *The Great Road*, of the use of archival material by filmmakers to make found footage documentaries of the type that Jay Leyda first termed *compilation* in his 1964 seminal work *Films Beget Films: A Study of the Compilation Film*.

Ledya defines the compilation film as work that "*begins* on the cutting table . . . with already existing film shots," and one that is an "*idea*, for most of the films made in this form are not content to be mere records or documents." He also notes that the "aim" of "correct compilation" is to use "[a]ny means by which the spectator is compelled to look at familiar shots as if he [or she] had not seen them before, or by which the spectator's mind is made more alert to the broader meaning of old materials."

Distinguishing among three forms of found footage films (compilation, appropriation, and collage), William C. Wees further defines and discusses the compilation film in *Recycled Images: The Art and Politics of Found Footage Films*. He describes three "principal characteristics" that can be found "with varying degrees of subtlety and sophistication" in "virtually all" compilation films: "(1) shots taken from earlier films that have no necessary relationship to each other; (2) a concept (theme, argument, story) that motivates the selection and order in which they appear; and (3) a verbal accompaniment (voice-over or text on the screen or both) that yokes the shots to the concepts ... [and] guide[s] viewers ... and tell[s] them how they should think about it." In addition, Wees notes that "the effect of all found footage films . . . [,] whether they preserve the footage in its original form or present it in new and different ways, [is to] invite us to recognize it *as* found footage, *as* recycled images, and due to that self-referentiality, they encourage a more analytical reading . . . than the footage originally received."

Wees points out that although compilation films "may reinterpret images taken from film and television archives, they do not challenge the representational nature of the images themselves . . . [because] they still operate on the assumption that there is a direct correspondence between images and their profilmic sources in the real world." In addition, he notes that such films "do not treat the compilation process itself as problematic . . . [,]" that is, while "[t]heir montage may make spectators 'more alert to the broader meaning of old material,' they do not, as a rule, make them more attentive to montage as a composition and (more or less explicit) argument." Ledya also points out, "[T]he manipulation of actuality . . . usually tries to hide itself so that the spectator sees only 'reality'—that is, the especially *arranged* reality that suits the filmmaker's purpose."

There is a great number and large variety of found footage films in existence. While there is no strict rule regarding the percentage of found footage a film must contain to be considered a bona fide found footage film, Wees maintains that such a film should include a "fair amount of original footage" and "emphasi[ze] found footage." In addition, while there is no set standard to distinguish between a film that has found footage and one that is a found footage film, Wees argues that a found footage film should be based "*as a whole*" on found footage, and "highlight this fact and make it one of the film's principal points of interest."

SUZANNE EISENHUT

Selected Films

1927 *Fall of the Romanov Dynasty*: Esfir Shub
1927 *The Great Road*: Esfir Shub
1928 *October* (*Ten Days That Shook the World*): Eisenstein, S.M.
1929 *Conquest*: Basil Wright
1929 *Die Melodie der Welt*: Walter Ruttmann
1929 *Man with a Movie Camera*: Dziga Vertov
1930 *L'Histoire du soldat inconnu*: Henri Storck
1933 *Adventures of the Newsreel Cameraman*: Truman Talley
1936 *Madrid*: Luis Bunuel
1937 *Le Cinema au Service de l'Histoire*: Germaine Dulac
1938 *Twenty Years of Liberty*: Jiri Weiss
1939 *Rose Hobart*: Joseph Cronell
1940 *The Panzer Ballet*: Charles Ridley
1941–1945 *The World In Action*: Stuart Legg (series)
1943–1944 *Why We Fight*: Frank Capra (series)
1955 *Nuit et Brouillard*: Alain Resnais
1958 *A Movie*: Bruce Conner
1959 *Science Friction*: Stan Venderbeek
1960 *Description d'un Combat*: Chris Marker
1961 *Allons enfants pour l'Algerie*: Karl Gass
1961 *Rabindranath Tagore*: Satyajit Ray
1962 *Stalin*: Lino del Fra and Cecilia Mangini
1963 *Waehle das Leben*: Erwin Leiser
1967 *Fluxes*: Arthur Lipsett
1969 *Our Lady of the Sphere*: Larry Jordan
1969 *Year of the Pig*: Emile De Antonio
1970 *Dangling Participle*: Standish Lawder
1970 *Hart of London*: Jack Chambers
1972 *La Dialectique peut-elle casser des briques?*: Rene Vienet
1973 *Society of the Spectacle*: Guy Debord
1974 *Spare Parts*: Peter Lipskis
1978 *The Doctor's Dream*: Ken Jacobs
1981 *Murder Psalm*: Stan Brakhage
1982 *The Atomic Café*: Jayne Loader, Kevin Rafferty, and Pierce Rafferty
1983 *Decodings*: Michael Wallin
1985–1996 *Peggy and Fred in Hell: The First Cycle*: Leslie Thornton
1986 *Rocket Kit Kongo Kit*: Craig Baldwin
1987 *Man in the Mirror*: Michael Jackson
1989 *Futility*: Greta Snider
1990 *Home Stories*: Matthias Muller
1990 *Short of Breath*: Jay Rosenblatt
1993 *The Death Train*: Bill Morrison
1993 *In Memory*: Abraham Ravett
1995 *Imaginary Laughter*: Keith Sanborn
1996 *The Shanghaied Text*: Ken Kobland
1997 *Maelstrom: A Family Chronicle*: Péter Forgács
1998 *L'Arrivée*: Peter Tscherkassky
1998 *Pomegranate Tree*: Garine Torossian

2000 *The Fourth Watch*: Janie Geiser
2001 *Hallowed*: Kerry Laitala
2001 *She Puppet*: Peggy Ahwesh
2002 *"Views from the Avant-Garde": Where the Girls Are*: Abigail Child

Further Reading

Arthur, Paul, "The Status of Found Footage," in *Spectator* 20.1 (1999–2000): 57–69.

Barnouw, Erik, *Documentary: A History of the Non-Fiction Film* (2nd rev. paperback ed.), New York: Oxford University Press, 1993.

Beauvais, Yann, "Inside Out-Takes," in *Desmontaje: Film, Video/Apropiacion Reciclaje* (Valencia: Institut Valenci dí Art Modern, 1993): 170–182.

———, *Found Footage*, Paris: Galerie nationale du Jeu de Paume, 1995 (in French).

Katz, Joel, "From Archive to Archiveology," *Cinematographe* 4, 1991, 96–104.

Leyda, Jay, *Films Beget Films: A Study of the Compilation Film*, New York: Hill and Wang, 1964.

MacKenzie, Scott, "Flowers in the Dustbin: Termite Culture and Detritus Cinema," *Cineaction* 47, 1998, 24–29.

Peterson, James, *Dreams of Chaos, Visions of Order: Understanding the American Avant-Garde Cinema*, Detroit, MI: Wayne State University Press, 1994, 126–177.

Russell, Catherine, *Experimental Ethnography: The Work of Film in the Age of Video*, Durham, NC: Duke University Press, 1999,: 238–272.

Sandusky, Sharon, "The Archeology of Redemption: Toward Archival Film," *Millennium Film Journal* 26, 1992, 2–24.

Sjoberg, Patrik, *The World in Pieces: A Study of Compilation Film*, Stockholm: Aura forlag, 2001

Wees, William C., *Recycled Images: The Art and Politics of Found Footage Films*, New York: Anthology Film Archives, 1993.

———, "Old Images, New Meanings: Recontextualizing Archival Footage of Nazism and the Holocaust," in *Spectator*, 20, 1, 2000, 70–76.

———, "The Ambiguous Aura of Hollywood Stars in Avant-Garde Found Footage Films," in *Cinema Journal* 41, 2, 2002, 3–18.

COMPUTER IMAGING

Computer imaging allows for the documentation and observation of phenomena that would otherwise not be visible to the unaided human eye, because they are too large, too small, too fast, too distant, or involve frequencies of light beyond the visible spectrum. Coupled with other instruments that read and provide data taken from the subject of study, the computer compiles and integrates the data, producing images from it that can be seen and analyzed.

Computer imaging extends the capabilities of traditional technologies such as telescopes, microscopes, radar, and high-speed photography. For example, it aids astronomers in the visualization of large objects such as galactic clusters and the distribution of matter over millions of light years and allows distant planets to be viewed more closely through computer imaging systems like those found on board the *Voyager* or *Magellan* spacecraft. Whereas high-speed photography is limited by the exposure time needed to fix an image photochemically, scientists using computers and lasers to record molecular reactions now work with femtosecond photography (a femtosecond is a quadrillionth of a second), and in particle physics, banks of sensors record and replay complex high-speed collisions in accelerators. Likewise, computer imaging is used to view structures far smaller than any optical microscope could ever see, or, in the case of medical imaging, inside solid materials that are otherwise opaque. To do so, computer-controlled sensors record light waves or energies that fall outside the spectrum of visible light (infrared, ultraviolet, radio waves, sound waves, and so on) and transduce them into the visible portion of the spectrum, creating visual imagery from recorded data. In this sense, many computer imaging techniques are analogous to photography and can be considered an extension of it.

Examples of this kind of imaging include general radiography (computer imaging involving X-rays), computerized axial tomography scans, positron emission tomography scans, and magnetic resonance imaging, which all use radio waves to generate their imagery. For three-dimensional medical imaging, a series of image slices are made at varying depths, and these slices are then used to reconstruct a three-dimensional model that the computer can display on screen, using different tones or colors to represent different intensities. Ultrasound works in a similar fashion, using sound waves below the range of human hearing.

Other types of energies can also be used. Nuclear medicine, which images the functioning of organs, records emissions given off by radio-pharmaceuticals circulating inside a patient's body. For the viewing of objects smaller than the wavelengths of visible light, beams of electrons are used instead of light waves in scanning electron microscopes and transmission electron microscopes. And since the 1980s, scanning-tunneling microscopes and atomic force microscopes measure tiny changes in electromagnetic force to image areas so small that individual atoms can be resolved.

By transducing light from outside the visible spectrum and other energies, computer imaging greatly extends the range of what can be visually documented, even though its subject matter lies beyond the range of human visibility and in the realm of instrumental realism.

MARK J.P. WOLF

See also **Computer Simulation; Indexicality; Subjunctive Documentary**

Further Reading

Binnig, Gerd, and Heinrich Rohrer, "The Scanning Tunneling Microscope," in *Scientific American*, 253, 1985, 40–46.

Breuker, Horst, Hans Drevermann, Christoph Grab, Alphonse A. Rademakers, and Howard Stone, "Tracking and Imaging Elementary Particles," *Scientific American*, 265, 1991, 58–63.

Ihde, Don, *Instrumental Realism: The Interface between Philosophy of Science and Philosophy of Technology*, Bloomington and Indianapolis: Indiana University Press, 1991.

Wolf, Mark J. P., "Subjunctive Documentary: Computer Imaging and Simulation," in *Collecting Visible Evidence*, edited by Michael Renov and Jane Gaines, Minneapolis: University of Minnesota Press, 1999.

Zewail, Ahmed H., "The Birth of Molecules," in *Scientific American*, 263, 1990, 76–82.

COMPUTER SIMULATION

Computer simulation involves the creation or re-creation of events based on initial conditions, data, and laws by which the data are manipulated. These simulations often attempt to reproduce objects and events that have occurred or could occur in the physical world. Uses for computer simulation include the study of molecular and chemical reactions, flight simulations used for pilot training, architectural walkthroughs, product design and testing, reconstructions of crimes and airplane crashes, and the visualization of mathematical constructs such as fractals and hypercubes. It can also be used to illustrate the hypothetical, for example, to show how relativistic distortions would appear to an extremely high-speed traveler.

The basis of computer simulations is mathematical reconstruction, in which simplified versions of the objects and events being studied are created in the computer's memory and manipulated according to rules and laws that control behavior (an example would be rules simulating the laws of physics and their effects on three-dimensional objects). As more data gathered in the physical world are used, the simulation's indexical linkages to real-world referents is strengthened; likewise, detailed and precise rules simulating physical behavior deduced from real-world events make it possible to simulate behavior realistically. The accuracy of the models and laws used to model objects and behaviors determines the documentary value of a simulation and the extent to which it can be said to represent a real object or process. Because the object or events simulated may be hypothetical or involve speculation, computer simulation could be considered a form of subjunctive documentary, documenting possibilities or probabilities instead of actualities.

Computer simulations are often considered real enough to be relied on as the bases of decisions, predictions, and scientific theories. Courts of law have admitted computer simulations as substantive evidence with independent probative value (that is, they may be used as evidence or proof).

Computational biochemists give simulations a status similar to physical experimentation, and computer simulation is routinely used in the training of pilots, doctors, and the military.

Because events in a computer simulation can be shown from any angle or point of view, they appear to have a kind of objectivity not available in traditional media such as film and video, with their limited points of view. Biases, speculations, and assumptions are present in computer simulations through the selection and abstraction of the data used and the ways in which data are animated by the laws and rules controlling the simulation. The epistemological problems of computer simulation can shed new light on the speculative nature of documentary film and video, when they are viewed as "simulations" of events. Unlike film and video, however, computer simulations are relied on in medicine, science, industry, law, and other institutions in which human lives may depend on decisions that are based on computer simulations. By concretizing speculations and extrapolations through visualization, computer simulation creates new ways in which an image can be linked to an actual object or event and makes that link as flexible and selective as the user wishes to program it.

MARK J.P. WOLF

See also **Computer Imaging; Indexicality; Subjunctive Documentary**

Further Reading

Bylinsky, Gene, and Alicia Hills Moore, "The Payoff from 3D Computing," *Fortune*, 128, 1993, 32–40.
Odum, Howard, and Elizabeth Odum, *Modeling for all Scales: An Introduction to System Simulation*, London; San Diego, California; and Burlington, Massachusetts: Academic Press, 2000.
Thaller, Bernd, *Visual Quantum Mechanics: Selected Topics with Computer-Generated Animations of Quantum-Mechanical Phenomena*, New York: Telos Press, 2000.
Wolf, Mark J. P., "Subjunctive Documentary: Computer Imaging and Simulation" in *Collecting Visible Evidence*, edited by Michael Renov and Jane Gaines, Minneapolis: University of Minnesota Press, 1999.

CONTACT

(UK, Rotha, 1933)

Contact was Paul Rotha's directorial debut. It was released when the British documentary film movement was being critically hailed within intellectual circles. Rotha had already established himself as a film critic with his large history/theory of the cinema, *The Film Till Now* (1929), and had then gone on to briefly work for John Grierson at the Empire Marketing Board (EMB) film unit. Although clashes with Grierson led to Rotha leaving the EMB film unit, *Contact* can be placed firmly within the more aesthetic school of filmmaking at the EMB and subsequently at the General Postal Office film unit (a school that also includes, most significantly, *Drifters*).

Contact was made to advertise Imperial Railways at a time when the company was facing stiff competition from new air companies, after its civic aviation monopoly came to an end in 1930. The film was originally shot by British Instructional Film (BIF) cameraman Horace Wheddon, who was replaced by another BIF employee, Frank Goodliffe, as a result of illness mid-way through shooting. During the making of the film, Rotha and crew traveled 35,000 miles around the world to shoot footage in different countries. As the camera could not be mounted on the airplane used because of insurance restrictions, aerial shots were obtained by shooting through a small sliding window in the cockpit.

The film dramatizes the evolution of transport and also constructs air travel as something to marvel at, aestheticizing the flight of the aircraft. It can roughly be divided into two parts, the first much shorter than the second. The first part looks at the

Contact, 1932–33.
[*Still courtesy of the British Film Institute*]

evolution of travel and the background of air flight; the second concentrates on aerial vision. The film begins with a fast montage of different transportation vehicles from a variety of angles. Titles then announce that the plane is the next wonder of transport and a montage of airplanes and views from the plane follow briefly. We then see workers involved in constructing the airplane and people boarding a plane. The film then enters a more relaxed, leisurely mode, as the plane in mid-air is contrasted with the many images that can be seen from the plane: deserts, seas, mountains, and famous landmarks from places such as Nairobi, Athens, and Cairo. The second part of the film settles into a romantic, picturesque view of distant lands. It provides a kind of symphony of air travel, an impression bolstered by its musical score by Clarence Reybould, who mostly adapted music by Mozart, Rossini, and Tchaikovsky.

Contact can be considered alongside the early travel films that were a staple of cinema's first decade. Early travel films used transportation (especially trains) to provide mobile views of distant, exotic lands for audiences who would not have been able to experience such views first hand. Many early railroad films also provided covert advertising, as did *Contact*. *Contact* is, in one sense at least, an updating of these early travel films, with the plane now replacing the wonders of the railway. At the time the film was made, only a small fraction of economically advantaged people could afford to travel by air, so *Contact* provided a simulated virtual reality of an aerial journey.

The film also tackles a theme that was prevalent within the more modernist films of the documentary film movement: the dialectic between nature and industry. Both *Drifters* (1929) and *Song of Ceylon* (1933–1934), in different ways, portray links between nature, humankind, and technology. In both of these films, industrial progress is largely seen in a positive light (despite elements of criticism), and a benign process of evolution is posited in which industry develops in a manner that also respects and preserves nature. Likewise, *Contact* extols the wonders of industrial progress in creating new modes of transport and, at the same time, admires at the wonders of nature. Technology and nature are thus seen as interdependent in this film: technological progress has enabled new ways of perceiving natural beauty.

Contact is ultimately less successful than both *Drifters* and *Song of Ceylon*, as it does not attain the level of formal sophistication of either of those films. It begins interestingly, but its dominant mode of aerial views, although beautifully photographed, is rather repetitive and uninspired. It feels, for the most part, like a straightforward travelog, which was exactly the type of filmmaking that both Grierson and Rotha attacked. They thought that travelogs were nothing more than an agglomeration of pretty pictures, lacking both aesthetically and sociologically. Aesthetically, they were not structured in an imaginative or "artistic" manner; sociologically, they did not reveal anything about the structure of the modern world.

The beginning of *Contact* does, to an extent, integrate Rotha's aesthetic and sociological agenda. The film uses highly stylized montage, with images and titles interwoven at a rhythmic pace, displaying a modernist approach to filmic organization. The evolutionary sketch of technological progress, although promotional, builds a sense of industrial purpose. The film also shows a number of materials needed to construct an airplane and shows workers involved in construction, thus moving beyond the superficial details of the flight to the complex assemblage involved in its constitution.

Yet the main pictorial sequences of the film dominate *Contact,* and these are more one-dimensional than the earlier scenes. The industrial interconnections at the beginning of the film become overshadowed by a more romantic portrayal of travel cinematography. The film does share with *Drifters* and *Song of Ceylon* an evolutionary purview that nevertheless stresses the importance of nature, but it also tends to provide a somewhat more ruthless, simplistic view of progress in comparison to those two films. Rotha does not quite manage to negotiate the rather complicated mixture of aesthetic expression, sociological investigation, and promotional message in a successful manner. Instead, the promotional origins of the film become all too evident.

JAMIE SEXTON

See also **Drifters**; **Rotha, Paul;** *Song of Ceylon*

Contact (UK, 1933, 42 min) Produced by British Instructional Films and Imperial Airways. Directed by Paul Rotha. Camera work by Frank Goodliffe. Sponsored by British Petroleum and Shell-Mex

Further Reading

Aitken, Ian (ed.), *The Documentary Film Movement: An Anthology*, Edinburgh: Edinburgh University Press, 1998.

Aldcroft, Derek H., *British Transport Since 1914: An Economic History*, Newton Abbot: John Sherratt & Sons, 1975.

Kirby, Lynne, *Parallel Tracks: The Railroad and Silent Cinema*, Exeter: Exeter University Press, 1997.

Musser, Charles, "The Travel Genre in 1903–1904: Moving Towards a Fictional Narrative," in *Early Cinema: Space, Frame, Narrative*, edited by Thomas Elsaesser and Adam Barker, London: BFI, 1990.

Petrie, Duncan, and Robert Kruger (eds.), *A Paul Rotha Reader*, Exeter: University of Exeter Press, 1999.

Rotha, Paul, *Documentary Diary*, London: Secker and Warburg, 1973.

———, *Documentary Film*, London: Faber and Faber, 1952; originally published 1935.

———, *The Film Till Now*, London: Vision Press, 1963; originally published 1930.

Sussex, Elizabeth, *The Rise and Fall of the British Documentary Movement*, Berkeley: University of California Press, 1978.

Swann, Paul, *The British Documentary Film Movement 1926–1946*, Cambridge: Cambridge University Press, 1989.

COOPER, MERIAN C.

Merian C. Cooper—best known in cinema history for his role as co-producer, cowriter, and codirector of the 1933 classic film *King Kong*—began his filmmaking career in documentaries. In partnership with Ernest B. Schoedsack, Cooper made expeditionary documentaries such as *Grass* (1925) and *Chang* (1927). These films (especially *Chang*) are part travelog, part adventure tale. Even *King Kong* was originally conceived as a semidocumentary project to be shot on location and feature a real gorilla enlarged through trick photography. As has often been pointed out by critics, the fictional filmmaker Carl Denham, the adventurous protagonist of *King Kong* who is willing to travel far and risk his own life as well as the lives of others for the most exciting film possible, could very well stand in for Cooper himself. Like Denham, Cooper was a natural showman intent on thrilling his audience through cinema's ability to place the spectator in the midst of the action.

Cooper and Schoedsack's first completed documentary together, in close collaboration with foreign journalist Marguerite Harrison, was entitled *Grass: A Nation's Battle for Life*. The team traveled to the Persian Gulf to chronicle with two cameras the forty-eight-day annual migration of a nomadic Iranian tribe called the Bakhtiari over hundreds of miles in search of suitable grazing land. The film follows in the documentary tradition established by Robert Flaherty's classic film about the North American Inuits, *Nanook of the North* (1922). Cooper originally intended to screen *Grass* on the college lecture circuit. However, a Paramount executive named Jesse Lasky, who had distributed *Nanook*, saw the film by chance at a private dinner and later obtained *Grass* for theatrical distribution. Intertitles were inserted into the action to provide the film with some kind of conventional structure for mainstream audiences. In its final form, *Grass* begins with scenes of Harrison interacting with the tribespeople. Then the tribe embarks on its quest in a huge caravan, a scene evocative for American audiences of mythic pioneer migration westward. (Lest the point is missed, the film's inter-titles frequently refer to covered wagons.) The tens of thousands of Bakhitiari, including their hundreds of thousands of cattle and goats, journey through an impressive range of hazardous terrain, including desert and mountain and raging water, to reach the grasslands. Frequently, against this epic backdrop, the film foregrounds the chief of the tribe and his son, perhaps in an effort to provide a narrative focus for audience identification among the mass of humanity. As a Hollywood feature film, *Grass* proved exciting in its visual spectacle of the Bakhtiari mass migration. Also, the film was exotic enough in subject matter to appeal to the American imagination, yet close enough to American pioneer myths to seem familiar to domestic audiences. Most important for the future direction of Cooper's career, the film was profitable. Cooper and Schoedsack promptly began planning other films.

The pair's next film was *Chang: A Drama of the Wilderness*. In some ways, *Chang* anticipates the contemporary craze for "reality programming" in combining elements of live action shot in Siam (Thailand today) into a preconceived storyline for maximum dramatic effect. The result is a hybrid film that is fictional but partially constructed from spontaneous, real-life events. Cooper and Schoedsack captured the wild animals that appear in the film and shot the action sequences themselves, including the famous shot where a tiger leaps up a tree toward the camera. After fourteen months of often hazardous location shooting, Cooper and Schoedsack returned to the United States to complete postproduction at Paramount. The completed film centers on a Siamese family. The central characters are played by local people, not professional Hollywood actors. The patriarch of the family is Kru (Cooper and Schoedsack's interpreter in real life). His wife is Chantui, their son is Nah, and their daughter is Landah. They have livestock and a pet white gibbon. The family attempts to establish a rice-farming homestead in the jungle while threatened by tigers, leopards, snakes, elephants (the "chang" of the title), and about every other menace the filmmakers could coerce into action for the cameras. The plot is set in motion by predators' attacks on the family's animals. Kru successfully fights back by organizing his pioneer neighbors into hunting parties. The jungle's threat to domesticity escalates, however, when a rampaging "chang" herd destroys Kru's home and a nearby village. Kru has to organize another hunting party that eventually captures the elephants. The primal natural force represented by the elephants is finally conquered when the elephants are domesticated to work for Kru. Victorious, Kru and his family rebuild their home. Continuing his usual flair for showmanship at the film's New York premiere, Cooper had installed a special projector lens (or "magnascope") that enlarged the screen to three times its normal size during the film's intense action scenes, such as an elephant charge that levels a village. In addition to garnering favorable critical reviews, *Chang* was nominated for an Academy Award for Unique and Artistic Production on the occasion of the first Academy Awards ceremony in 1929—the only year this award was presented.

Cooper's work in the documentary and semidocumentary genre paved the way for his next and greatest success. While in Africa with Schoedsack to shoot location footage for the fictional film *Four Feathers*, Cooper photographed many apes and began thinking of a story about a giant gorilla captured and taken to the urban jungle of Manhattan. In Cooper's scenario, the gorilla would escape and eventually climb to the top of the Empire State Building before being killed by fighter planes. The publication of a friend's book about the fearsome monitor lizards or "dragons" of Komodo Island inspired Cooper to incorporate a fight scene between the giant gorilla and the giant lizard into his proposed film. Cooper then took the name for "gorilla" from the language of an East Indies tribe and entitled his proposed film *Kong*, or as it came to be known, *King Kong*. The film production ultimately eschewed location shooting and live animal photography for the special-effects work of animator Willis O'Brien, but Cooper applied all of the lessons he had learned from *Grass* and *Chang* to *King Kong*. The phenomenal success of *King Kong*, starring *Four Feathers* veteran Fay Wray as the giant gorilla's "love interest," enshrined Cooper as one of the industry's legends. Over the years, he was twice a studio vice-president and a producer. After more military service during World War II, he formed a production company named Argosy Film Pictures with famous director John Ford in 1941. He served as producer for many classic films, including *Rio Grande* in 1950, *The Quiet Man* in 1952, and *The Searchers* in 1956. For all of his contributions, Cooper was given a special Academy Award in 1952. He died in 1973.

PHILIP L. SIMPSON

See also **Chang; Grass**

Biography

Born in Jackonsville, Florida, on October 24, 1893. Attended the United States Naval Academy in Annapolis, Maryland, 1911–1915. Resigning from Annapolis, became a military aviator who saw combat in France in 1918, was a prisoner of war on two separate occasions, and aided the Polish in their struggle against the newly formed Communist government of Russia. In Poland, met a combat photographer, Ernest B. Schoedsack, who would later become his business partner. During the 1920s, gave up military flying, worked as a reporter for the *New York Times* and the *New York Daily News*, published an anonymous autobiography entitled *Things Men Die For*, and sought adventure as a traveler on a world cruise led by explorer Edward A. Salisbury. Served as producer for many classic films, including *Rio Grande* in 1950, *The Quiet Man* in 1952, and *The Searchers* in 1956. Honored with a special Academy Award in 1952. Died in 1973.

Selected Films

1925 *Grass*: director
1927 *Chang*: director

Further Reading

Brownlow, Kevin, *The War, the West, and the Wilderness*, New York: Alfred A. Knopf, 1978.

Cooper, Merian C., *Grass*, New York: G.P. Putnam's and Sons, 1925.
Goldner, Orville, and George E. Turner, *The Making of King Kong*, Cranbury, NJ: A.S. Barnes and Company, 1975.
Steinbrunner, Chris, and Burt Goldblatt, *Cinema of the Fantastic*, New York: Galahad Books, 1972.
Vertlieb, Steve, "The Man Who Saved King Kong," in *The Girl in the Hairy Paw: King Kong as Myth, Movie, and Monster*, edited by Ronald Gottesman and Harry Geduld, New York: Avon Books, 1976.

CORPORATION FOR PUBLIC BROADCASTING

The Corporation for Public Broadcasting (CPB) is a private, nonprofit corporation created by the Public Broadcasting Act, which was passed by Congress in 1967. The catalyst for this legislation was the report, *Public Television: A Program for Action*, by the Carnegie Commission on Educational Television, which made recommendations for the coordination of the Educational Television (ETV) stations that operated as a loosely affiliated consortium of primarily university and college-owned broadcasters in the 1950s and 1960s. The Commission recommended the establishment of an independent foundation that would promote national noncommercial broadcasting in the United States by supporting the building of noncommercial stations and organizing the local stations into a nationwide public broadcasting network of program exchange (Carnegie Commission, 78). President Lyndon B. Johnson, perceiving educational broadcasting as a priority and aid to his administration's "Great Society," encouraged the writing of the legislation and signed it into law on November 7, 1967 (Jarvik, 1998: 22). Among the mandates the CPB was charged with were to "facilitate the full development of public telecommunications in which programs of high quality, diversity, creativity, excellence, and innovation, which are obtained from diverse sources, will be made available to public telecommunications entities, with strict adherence to objectivity and balance in all programs or series of programs of a controversial nature" (CPB, "Terms and Conditions," 2002).

Although funded in part by Congressional appropriations, the CPB is not a government agency and is not subject to governmental oversight or accountability. The CPB is the largest single source of funding for public telecommunications (radio, television, and online) and the major regulatory body of public broadcasting in the United States whose main activity is to provide fiscal support to FCC-licensed Public Radio and Television stations in the United States. The bulk of this funding goes toward the production of television and radio programs, but a portion of it also supports the technological updating of these stations' broadcast abilities (such as digital television broadcasting facilities). It should be noted that the CPB neither produces nor distributes public telecommunications products, but rather provides funding to producers via grants to independent producers and Public Broadcasting Service (PBS) and National Public Radio (NPR) member stations. The majority of CPB-funded radio and television programs are distributed through the PBS, created by the CPB in 1969 to produce and distribute CPB-funded television programs and NPR, which the CPB created in 1970 to produced and distribute CPB-funded radio.

The funding sources of CPB have always included appropriations from the federal government, but the percentage of its revenue coming from the federal government has changed since its creation. In 1967, 50 percent of CPB's funding came from the federal government, with the Carnegie and Ford Foundations and NET providing the additional funding. Fundraising and membership drives began in the early 1970s in response to the national financial crisis and a desire to avoid the political influence of the Nixon White House. This resulted in the CPB's funding shifting from appropriations to donations and sponsorships. By 2004, 14.9 percent of its funding was granted by Congress and membership contributions from "viewers like you," obtained primarily through fundraising drives and "pledge weeks" accounted for 25 percent of its operating costs. Other funds come from tax-free donations from private sources such as corporations, foundations, and local and state governments and colleges.

The CPB is administered by a nine-member Board of Directors whose members are appointed to six-year terms by the President and confirmed by the Senate (Public Broadcasting Act). To maintain neutrality, no more than five members of the board may be members of the same political party. A President, hired by the Board, and a Chairman and Vice Chairman, selected by the Board from its own members, form an executive committee and serve at the pleasure of the Board (Public Broadcasting Act). The CPB submits a comprehensive report of its activities to Congress each spring, which includes a financial accounting and listing of grantees and programs the CPB has aided over the last year.

Throughout its history, the CPB has had to respond to critics regarding its programming choices, as well as threats to its federal appropriations. The Nixon administration presented the fledgling CPB with the first of many challenges to its autonomy and existence. While recommending an additional $5 million appropriation in 1969, the funding came with a condition: "Government funding of CPB should not be used for the creation of anti-administration programming or for the support of program producing organizations which used other funds to create anti-Administration programs" (Jarvik, 1998: 24). Ultimately, Nixon vetoed a 1972 authorization bill for the CPB appropriation, and through the lobbying efforts of the public and local stations owners, the veto was overridden and the CPB appropriation provided. Nonetheless, this spurred the CPB to become much more proactive in its solicitation of funding

from sources other than the government, and, in 1972, the CPB formalized underwriting guidelines for corporate funding of programs and series (Ouellette, 2002: 96).

The Reagan administration's opposition to "big government" threatened the CPB's survival in the 1980s. As the appropriations began to decline, the CPB responded by allowing corporate underwriters to create and broadcast "noncommercial 'commercials'" before and after the shows they had sponsored (Day, 1995: 274). The late 1980s found the CPB under attack for programming choices because of "cultural elitism," which resulted in a new "commitment to cultural diversity." This period also saw the CPB commit to becoming a leader in children's programming (Day, 1995: 305). The rise of cable and satellite television, VHS, DVD, and DVR ownership, as well as satellite TV systems have all affected public television viewership in recent years. At the same time, the Communications Act of 1996, which mandated digital transmission for all broadcast stations by 2006, has provided public broadcasting stations with an opportunity to increase the number of broadcast channels they offer, and to begin to narrowcast in ways that compete with the vast number of specialized channels available through cable systems.

The unique structure of the CPB and its collaboration with PBS to provide educational television to the United States has resulted in a vast amount of nonfiction and documentary material being broadcast to the American Public. *Nova*, the longest-running documentary series in American began broadcasting in 1974. *Nature*, *Frontline*, and *P.O.V.* have offered opportunities for independent documentarians to have their work broadcast to a wide audience, and Ken and Ric Burns's documentaries, *The Civil War*, *Jazz*, *Baseball*, and *New York: A Documentary Film*, have garnered critical and public acclaim, further raising the profile of both Public Broadcasting and documentary film in the United States.

M. J. ROBINSON

Further Reading

Carnegie Commission on Educational Television, *Public Television: A Program for Action*, New York: Harper & Row, 1967.

Carnegie Commission on the Future of Public Broadcasting, *A Public Trust*, New York: Bantam, 1979.

Corporation for Public Broadcasting, "Terms and Conditions for Television, Radio and Other Media Production Grants," November 2002.

Day, James, *The Vanishing Vision: The Inside Story of Public Television*, Berkeley, CA: University of California Press, 1995.

Horowitz, David, and Laurence Jarvik, (eds.), *Public Broadcasting and the Public Trust*, Los Angeles: Second Thoughts Books, 1995.

Jarvik, Laurence, *PBS: Behind the Screen*, Rocklin, CA: Prima, 1998.

Ledbetter, James, *Made Possible By ... The Death of Public Broadcasting in the United States*, London: Verso, 1997.

Ouelette, Laurie, *Viewers Like You?: How Public TV Failed the People*, New York: Columbia University Press, 2002.

"Public Broadcasting Act of 1967," 47 USC Sec. 396.

Stewart, David, *The PBS Companion: A History of Public Television*, New York: TV Books, 1999.

Twentieth Century Fund, *Quality Time?: The Report of the Twentieth Century Fund Task Force on Public Television*, New York: The Twentieth Century Fund, 1993.

COUSTEAU, JACQUES-YVES

Jacques-Yves Cousteau, a prolific author, environmental activist, explorer, inventor, and filmmaker, has long been regarded as a respected pioneer of the documentary film genre for his innovative efforts to record the undersea environment. Cousteau is often considered to be the creator of the underwater documentary, not only because of his novel approach to documentary filmmaking but also because he was, along with French engineer Emile Gagnan, the cocreator of the first underwater diving apparatus, the aqualung, or scuba (McGill, 2000). Cousteau's underwater breathing invention, coupled with his creation of a waterproof enclosure for movie cameras, made it possible for divers, scientists, and film crews to explore and document the undersea world as they never could before (Kempke, 2002). By using these new inventions, Cousteau, who had previous experience producing, directing, and acting in feature films, began to make his unprecedented documentaries about the sea, its vegetation, animal inhabitants, and sunken vessels. For many members of the audience, Cousteau's documentaries heralded the actual viewing of entities and environs that once could be conjured only in the imagination.

Although Cousteau had made several short documentaries in the 1940s during the German occupation of France, it was his feature-length documentary films and television programs that gained him worldwide recognition. Cousteau's film *Le Monde du silence* (1956)/*The Silent World*, his first feature-length documentary film, which was co-directed by Louis Malle, won the Grand Prize at the Cannes Film Festival in 1956 (McGill, 2000). A 1956 review of *The Silent World* in the *New York Times* lauded the film for its ability to leave the audience not only in awe but also wishing to participate in the deep-sea dives themselves, owing to the unique way the film contrasted the images of undersea explorers with the ocean creatures being investigated (Crowther, 1971).

After the success of *The Silent World*, Cousteau continued to make feature-length documentaries for the cinema chronicling marine life and its environs, including *Histoire d'un poisson rouge* (1959)/ *The Golden Fish* and *Le Monde sans soleil* (1964)/ *World Without Sun*.

In the late 1960s and the 1970s, Cousteau's documentaries began to reach audiences differently. Instead of feature-length films for the cinema, Cousteau's documentaries became the subject of several critically acclaimed television series and specials, including his most famous, *The Undersea World of Jacques Cousteau*, which ran from 1968 to 1976. Each episode of *The Undersea World of Jacques Cousteau* was the result of a minor feat of filmmaking and would not have been possible without an extraordinary amount of editing. Extra footage was a requirement for Cousteau's documentaries, because undersea creatures are not often cooperative with the filmmakers, and because of the temperamental nature of the ocean itself. For approximately fifty-one minutes of air time, 1,750 feet of picture edit was necessary, and it often took the production staff more than ten weeks to prepare (Shaheen, 1987). In addition to the remarkable images, another factor that made the series well received among critics and viewers alike was its innovative narration. With co-narration responsibilities divided between Cousteau and Rod Serling (widely recognized for his work on the television series *The Twilight Zone*), the audience was presented with two very distinct tones of voice and narration styles, which helped to ward off monotony (Shaheen, 1987).

Perhaps the most enlightening element of these later documentaries, however, was the intensification of Cousteau's environmental activism, which ultimately became his greatest passion when his undersea explorations revealed to him the destruction the sea and its inhabitants were enduring at the hands of humankind. As a consequence of his environmental concerns, Cousteau founded several nonprofit organizations to help spread awareness about the endangered ecology, including the most famous one, which is still in existence, the aptly named Cousteau Society (McGill, 2000).

In a June 1985 interview in the Cousteau Society's membership publication, the *Calypso Log,* Cousteau mused about the significance of film in his own personal life. Cousteau asserted that he considered the cinema so "important" because it encompasses other forms of art, including literature and music. Cousteau also declared that because cinema is an art form that uses the element of time, film is akin to "a flower, [created] to bloom and die." Apparently, for Cousteau, the ephemeral nature of film is preferable to art forms that are "here for eternity" and represent a "challenge to death"; thus, for Cousteau, film was ostensibly analogous to humanity itself, a living and breathing entity (*Calypso Log,* 1985).

TRUDI VAN DYKE

*See also **Silent World, The***

Biography

Born in St. Andre-de-Cubzac, France, on June 11, 1910. After high school, served in the French navy. Also a prolific author and staunch environmentalist. Died of heart failure June 25, 1997 in Paris.

Selected Films

1956 *Le Monde du silence/The Silent World*: director, writer, cinematographer
1959 *Histoire d'un poisson rouge/The Golden Fish*: producer
1964 *Le Monde sans soleil/World Without Sun*: producer, director
1968–1976 *The Undersea World of Jacques Cousteau*: executive producer, actor

Further Reading

Crowther, Bosley, "Cousteau's *The Silent World*," in *The Documentary Tradition: From Nanook to Woodstock*, edited by Lewis Jacobs, New York: Hopkinson and Blake Publishers, 1971.
"Jacques Cousteau: Interview," in *Calypso Log*, 1985, n.p.
Kempcke K., "Jacques Cousteau," in *St. James Encyclopedia of Popular Culture*, 2002 Gale Group, http://articles.findarticles.com/p/articles/mi_g1epc/is_bio/ai_2419200261.
McGill, Sara Ann, "Jacques Cousteau," in *History Remembers Scientists of the 20th Century*, 2000.
Shaheen, Jack G., "The Documentary of Art: 'The Undersea World of Jacques Cousteau,'" in *Journal of Popular Culture*, 21, 1, 1987, 93–101.

COUTINHO, EDUARDO

Coutinho played an important role in the first generation of Brazil's Cinema Novo. He began his career in 1962 as the production manager of the feature-length fiction *Cinco Vezes Favela/Five Times Shantytown,* produced by the National Student Union (União Nacional dos Estudantes, UNE). In the same year, he filmed the travels of the so-called UNE-on-the-Move. UNE's idea was to make a documentary about the cities that the student union leaders were visiting in 1962 and 1963. They filmed in Manaus, Paraíba, Maranhão, Belo Horizonte, and other places, but the

material was never assembled into a documentary. Through UNE-on-the-Move, Coutinho met Elizabeth Teixeira, the widow of João Pedro Teixeira, a peasant leader who was murdered in 1962. When he returned to Rio de Janeiro, Coutinho made a new proposal to the UNE through their cultural centers (CPCs). He wanted to make a film about the life of João Pedro Teixeira in which the same peasants who had experienced the tragedy would participate as actors. In February 1964, Coutinho began to film the never-to-be-completed first version of *Cabra Marcado*

Para Morrer/Marked for Death, a docudrama that reconstructs the life of João Pedro Teixeira. It was filmed at the Galiléia Plantation in the city of Vitória de Santo Antão of Pernambuco state, and Elizabeth Teixeira played the role of herself as a widow. The film was interrupted by the military coup of March 31, 1964, and the production team was dispersed. Elizabeth Teixeira changed her name and spent seventeen years hiding in the interior of the northeastern state of Rio Grande do Norte.

Coutinho returned to Rio and developed a career in fiction films as a screenwriter and director. He encountered documentary film during the second half of the 1970s when he began to work for Globo Repórter, a program of Rede Globo, Brazil's major television broadcaster. He directed several editions of the program, some in a true *verité* documentary style. The remake of the unfinished *Cabra Marcado Para Morrer* (also known as *Twenty Years Later)* marks the beginning of Coutinho's authorial career. Based on his experience in television, Coutinho incorporated the flexible techniques of the new documentary, including a nervous moving camera, direct sound, and the intense use of interviews. Coutinho began to see the possibility of a second version of *Cabra* in 1979, when amnesty was decreed and it became possible for him to safely contact Elizabeth Teixeira. The idea for this documentary was to search for the same peasants who had participated, as actors, in the docudrama that had been interrupted in 1964 and to film their daily life in 1981. Coutinho had secretly kept the negatives of the first *Cabra* for twenty years, and he used them in his new film. The main part of the documentary was filmed in March 1981, in the state of Rio Grande do Norte, interviewing the same peasants of 1964. Back in Rio de Janeiro, during 1982 and 1983, Coutinho finished filming interviews with Elizabeth's sons and daughters, with whom she had lost contact for twenty years. The film was released in 1984, generating a strong response from the public and the media. By portraying the fragmentation of Elizabeth Teixeira's family, *Twenty Years Later* presented a portrait of a country that, after a twenty-year military dictatorship, was also finding itself.

In 1986 Coutinho directed *Santa Marta—2 Semanas no Morro/Santa Marta—Two Weeks in a Slum* at the Santa Marta *favela* (Brazilian hillside slum) in the middle of Rio's wealthy and chic southern region. The film was produced by the Superior Institute of Religious Studies (ISER, a nongovernmental institution) and is the first documentary work Coutinho made in a Rio's *favela*. Coutinho's career as a documentary filmmaker became more firmly established in the 1990s. In 1992, he rediscovered the strongest stylistic vein of his work in a *verité* form documentary, *Boca do Lixo/The Scavengers.* It was filmed in video and takes place in a large garbage dump in the city of São Gonçalo, close to Rio de Janeiro. Through interviews, marked by Coutinho's active participation, the film manages to discover unique characters with strong and impressive personalities. This search for "types" can be defined as the core of Coutinho's style, based on interviews or testimonies that his subjects deliver directly to the camera. During the 1990s, the interview scenes of Coutinho's documentaries became more and more static, resembling a series of identity card photos with intense facial expressions.

It is through this kind of minimalist method that Coutinho affirmed his distinctive style throughout the 1990s and even today. In 1998–1999, he filmed *Santo Forte/The Mighty Spirit,* which depicts the everyday religiosity of the people of Vila Parque da Cidade *favelas,* in Rio de Janeiro. The narrative portrays the common people of Brazil by using religious experience and trance as motifs. *Santo Forte* is a landmark of Coutinho's work, where his style takes the shape we will find in his three next feature-length documentaries (*Babilônia 2000, Edifício Master/Master a Building in Copacabana,* and *Peões/Workers*). *Babilônia 2000* was made during the celebration of the new millennium in the hillside of Babilônia, where the *favelas* Chapéu Mangueira and Babilônia are located, with an extraordinary view of Rio de Janeiro's most famous beaches. Most of the documentary was shot on December 31, 1999.

After his "trilogy" about *favelas* (*Santa Marta; Santo Forte; Babilônia 2000*), Coutinho continued to use this characteristic "portrait" style but switched social classes and filmed in a typical petit bourgeois building in the Copacabana beach neighborhood. Through Coutinho's static interview method, *Master, a Building in Copacabana,* reveals astonishing personalities living in the small apartment rooms. Coutinho's most recent film, *Peões/Workers* (2004), is a project made together with João Salles, a new figure in Brazilian contemporary documentary. They planned to make two feature-length films together (*Peões/Workers* directed by Coutinho and *Entreatos/Entr'acts* by Salles) about the life of the poor northeastern migrant who became Brazil's current president. Loyal to his distinctive method, Coutinho went to the factories and the neighborhood where Lula used to work and live and interviewed the anonymous metallurgical workers who once met him. Through a series of personal testimonies, *Peões* unveils the diverse personalities and life stories of Brazilian industrial workers.

FERNÃO PESSOA RAMOS

See also **Cinema Novo**

Biography

Born in São Paulo, 1933, and lives and works in Rio de Janeiro. Studied at the IDHEC (Institut de Hautes Études Cinematographiques) before starting his career as the production manager of *5 Vezes Favela (Five Times Favela)*. Films the unfinished *Cabra Marcado para Morrer (Marked to Die)* in 1954, which would later be transformed in *20 Years Later* (1981–1984). During the 1960s and 1970s, worked with fiction films, mostly as screenwriter (*Garota de Ipanema/The Girl from Ipanema* (1967), *Dona Flor e Seus Dois Maridos/Dona Flor and Her Two Husbands* (1976); *Lição de Amor/A Lesson in Love* (1975); *A Falecida/ The Death* (1963); and also as director of one episode from *ABC do Amor* (*The ABC of Love*, 1966), *O Pacto (The Agreement)* and the features *O Homem que Comprou o Mundo* (*The Man Who Bought the World, 1968)* and *Faustão* (1970). In 1970s, films for television, in Globo Networks, making programs to the Globo Reporter series. In 1980s, starts an authorial career, working exclusively in documentary. Last four features, (*Santo Forte/The Mighty Spirit*, 1999; *Babilônia, 2000*; *Edifício Master/Master, a Building in Copacabana*, 2002; and *Peões/Workers*, 2004) have been showed widely in cinemas.

Selected Filmography (as director)

1964 *Cabra Marcado Para Morrer/Marked to Death* (unfinished)
1976 *Seis Dias de Ouricuri/Six Days of Ouricuri* (TV–Globo Reporter)
1977 *O Pistoleiro da Serra Talhada/The Pistoleer of the Carved Mountains* (TV–Globo Reporter)
1978 *Theodorico, o Imperador do Sertão/ Theodorico—The Emperor of the Backlands* (TV–Globo Reporter)
1979 *Exu, uma Tragédia Sertaneja/Exu, a Tragedy in the Back Country* (TV–Globo Reporter)
1980 *Portinari, o Menino de Brodósqui/ Portinari, Brodosqui's Little Boy* (TV–Globo Reporter)
1981–1984 *Cabra Marcado Para Morrer/Twenty Years Later* (feature)
1987 *Santa Marta: Duas Semanas no Morro/Santa Marta: Two Weeks in the Hillside Slums* (mid-length)
1989 *Volta Redonda, Memorial da Greve/Volta Redonda: Memorial of a Strike* (mid-length, co-direction with Sérgio Goldenberg)
1989 *O Jogo da Dívida/The Debt Game* (mid-length)
1991 *O Fio da Memória/The Strand of Memory* (feature)
1992 *Boca do Lixo/The Scavengers* (mid-length)
1994 *Mulheres no Front/Women in the Front* (mid-length)
1999 *Santo Forte/The Mighty Spirit* (feature)
2000 *Babilônia 2000* (feature)
2002 *Edifício Master/Master, a Building in Copacabana* (feature)
2004 *Peões/Workers* (feature)

Further Reading

Bernardet, Jean-Claude, *Vitória Sobre a Lata de Lixo da História*, in *Cineastas e Imagens do Povo*, edited by Jean-Claude Bernardet, São Paulo: Companhia das Letras, 2003.

Bernardet, Jean-Claude, *Le Documentaire*, in *Le Cinema Brésilien*, edited by Paulo Antonio Paranaguá, Paris: Centre Georges Pompidou, 1987.

Lins, Consuelo, *O Documentário de Eduardo Coutinho: televisão, cinema e vídeo*, Rio de Janeiro: Zahar, 2004.

Mattos, Carlos Alberto, *Eduardo Coutinho: O Homem que Caiu na Real*, Portugal: Festival de Cinema Luso-Brasileiro de Santa Maria da Feira, 2004.

Ramos, Fernão, and Luis Felipe Miranda (eds.), *Enciclopédia do Cinema Brasileiro*, São Paulo: Senac, 2000.

Schwarz, Roberto, *O Fio da Meada*, in *Que Horas São?* Edited by Roberto Schwarz, São Paulo: Companhia das Letras, 1987.

Xavier, Ismail, *Indagações em Torno de Eduardo Coutinho*, in *Cinemais*, 36, 2003, 221–236.

CRAIGIE, JILL

Although frequently referred to as the first female film director in Britain, several directors preceded Jill Craigie in the silent period. Nonetheless, Craigie's contribution to British film culture is important. Her directorial career was relatively brief, spanning seven years, but two of her films stand out because of their innovative approach to documentary filmmaking and because of Craigie's feminist and socialist political beliefs.

Craigie entered the film industry in 1937 as an actress but made only one film. When war broke out she began writing short documentary scripts for the British Council, as well as cowriting the script for the Two Cities production *The Flemish Farm* (1943) with her then husband, Jeffrey Dell. This inspired her to direct her first short film, *Out of Chaos* (1944), a documentary about how to appreciate modern art, using the work of British war artists as examples.

After the war, Craigie's interest in the postwar reconstruction of Britain's bomb-damaged cities and, in particular, the need to consult with the citizens living there, led to the making of *The Way We Live* (1946), a drama-documentary outlining plans for the rebuilding of Plymouth. The socialist leanings of the film did not deter the conservative J. Arthur Rank from backing the film, and it was funded by the Rank subsidiary, Two Cities Film, which distributed *Out of Chaos*. *The Way We Live* combines an orthodox documentary style of straight visual exposition with a dramatic narrative featuring a cast drawn almost entirely from the local community. Seen predominantly from the female characters' viewpoint, the plight of a bombed-out family living in temporary accommodation provides the framework for a social and political examination of town planning procedures. During the making of this film Craigie met her third husband, the Labour MP Michael Foot.

Craigie next directed a short documentary for UNESCO about efforts to improve the living conditions of children displaced by two world wars. She followed this with *Blue Scar* (1949), which, like *The Way We Live*, blurred the boundaries between fiction and documentary. Set in a South Wales mining village, *Blue Scar* is a feature-length drama-documentary about poverty and conflict in a South Wales mining village, partly scripted by the villagers themselves. Made by Outlook Films, the production company Crai-

gie formed with William MacQuitty in 1948, the film also featured several cast members drawn from the local population. She then directed a documentary short for Outlook, *To Be a Woman* (1951), arguing the case for equal pay for women.

Frustrated by the feature industry's obstructive attitude to women directors, Craigie gave up directing and returned to scriptwriting before retiring from the film business. Her political fervor did not diminish with age, however, and in 1994, appalled by what was happening in wartorn Yugoslavia, she financed and directed a documentary about the ravaged city and people of Dubrovnik. *Two Hours from London* (1994) was shown on BBC television in 1995 and was her final film.

Sarah Easen

Biography

Born in London, March 7, 1914. Educated at various boarding schools in Britain and Europe. Journalist on teen magazine, *Betty's Paper*, 1932. Journalist and writer, 1933–1937. Actress, 1937. Documentary scriptwriter, British Council 1940–1942. Scriptwriter and director, Two Cities Film 1943–1946. Director, Crown Film Unit. 1948. Director, Outlook Films 1948–1951. Scriptwriter, Group Film Productions, 1952–1953. Scriptwriter, Rank Film Productions, 1957. Director, independent production, 1994. Died in London, December 13, 1999.

Films

1944 *Out of Chaos*: director, writer.
1946 *The Way We Live*: director, producer, writer
1948 *Children of the Ruins*: director
1949 *Blue Scar*: director, writer
1951 *To Be a Woman*: director, producer, writer
1994 *Two Hours from London*: director, co-producer

Further Reading

Haggith, Toby, *Castles in the Air: British Films and the Reconstruction of the Built Environment 1939–1951*, London: I B Tauris, 2003.

CROATIA

See **Yugoslavia (former)**

CROWN FILM UNIT

The onset of World War II established new priorities for the documentary film industry in Britain. With the Nazis beginning their destructive inroads northward, the General Post Office Film Unit underwent a name change to the Crown Film Unit in 1939 and became a part of the Ministry of Information. The unit embarked without template or guidebook on the sole purpose of providing audiences with insights into the humanity and machinery of war.

The arduous task involved using the medium of film to bolster a nation's spirit in times of extreme sacrifice. The war had brought, and would continue to bring, death and economic hardship. Mothers would continue to lose sons; wives would continue to lose husbands; children would continue to lose fathers. Rations and sacrifice would become patriotic terms, and the documentary film would serve as a tool to encourage civilians in their sacrifices at home and in their sacrifices of loved ones serving and dying on the battlefield. Under the leadership of Ian Dalrymple, the Crown Film Unit built on the achievements of past documentarists and released features currently considered to be the classics of British war cinema.

The first cinematic response of the newly organized film unit was titled *The First Days* (1939). The encroaching Nazi threat left Britain no alternative to signing a declaration of war. The film depicts concerned royal subjects gathered in front of radios listening for some hint of their collective destiny. The audience sees that London's historic beauty has been marred by the presence of war: sandbags by the millions piled strategically to reinforce buildings, tanks rolling slowly into the shadows of trees, gunners, searchlights, and sirens, all suddenly vital parts of the landscape. Within the madness of war, however, director Humphrey Jennings offers audiences a glimpse into human behavior under extraordinary stress. This film captures the thematic heart of the Crown Film Unit: to observe the British mood in crisis and to chronicle the everydayness, the unspectacular moments of human determination to carry on amidst chaos. Women shopped, but in stores with broken front windows. People slept, but in bunkers beneath the street.

The Crown Film Unit went on to produce various short works including *Words for Battle* (1941) and *Listen to Britain* (1942) before creating *Desert Victory* (1943), a sixty-two-minute production representing one of the finest examples of wartime documentary. Never before had filmmakers so thoroughly documented the horrors or the drama of war. Viewers underwent a nightmarish journey as troops battled and eventually drove the Germans from North Africa, thereby gaining one of the first decisive military victories for the Allies. The film won the 1943 Academy Award for Best Documentary Feature, but at a price. The unit suffered great personal losses in creating this film. Four cameramen lost their lives, six more were wounded, and the Germans captured another seven demonstrating the level of courage and commitment of these men to the documentary and its ability inform the world.

The 1944 release of *Western Approaches*, like *Desert Victory*, captured for viewers some of the most treacherous weather and battle conditions ever seen on film. Using active naval servicemen, the documentary revealed the hazards merchant seamen suffered on their Atlantic convoys to bring vital supplies back to war-torn Britain. Viewers watched the great risk being undertaken so as to avoid disruption to the fundamental needs of an Empire under siege. Through the guidance of the Crown Film Unit, the horrors of battle again became the dignity of a nation.

The Crown Film unit also undertook the production of docudramas. In the 1943 release, *Fires Were Started*, the film unit used fictional characters played by actual firemen and real scenes interspersed into staged action. This lengthy project hails as a lasting monument in British wartime cinema. Under the devastating blows of the Nazi air blitz, members of the Auxiliary Fire Service set about the enormous task of squelching the flames brought on by the nightly holocaust. Surrounded by death and disaster, the unit produced a film that stepped away from the hate-the-enemy themes filling newsreels and presented the crisis as if observers to some horrific natural disaster.

CROWN FILM UNIT

The eighty-minute film records the movements of seven firemen and a new recruit over a fictional twenty-four-hour period that turns the ordinary into the heroic. Jennings's refusal to accept dehumanization as a by-product of war mirrored the drive of the Crown Film Unit to capture and evoke the tremendous strength found within the people of the British state. Using the medium of documentary, whether by dramatization or actual footage, the film unit was repeatedly able in film after film, one reel or several, to affirm human dignity despite the extremes of war.

After the Allied victory of World War II, the Crown Film Unit produced postwar propaganda including *A Defeated People* in 1946. The unit enjoyed continued success and industry accolades, winning the Oscar for Best Documentary Feature in 1949 for *Daybreak in Udi* and the Short Film Oscar for *Royal Scotland* in 1952. The documentary film movement as a whole receded and the Crown Film Unit ceased operations in 1952. The Crown Film Unit played a vital role not only in supporting a nation through the hells of war but in capturing for future generations the spirit of a nation determined to emerge from foreign assault with dignity and honor.

CHRISTINE MARIE HILGER

See also **Dalrymple, Ian;** *Desert Victory;* *Fires Were Started;* **General Post Office Film Unit; Jennings, Humphrey;** *Listen to Britain*

Further Reading

Aitken, Ian, *European Film Theory and Cinema: A Critical Introduction*, Edinburgh: Edinburgh University Press, 2001.
Barnouw, Erik, *Documentary: A History of the Non-Fiction Film*, New York: Oxford University Press, 1993.
Barta, Tony, *Screening the Past: Film and the Representation of History*, Westport, CT: Praeger, 1998.
Low, Rachael, *The History of the British Film 1929–1939: Documentary and Educational Films of the 1930s*, London: George Allen and Unwin, 1979.
Sussex, Elizabeth, *The Rise and Fall of British Documentary*, Berkley: University of California Press, 1975.

CUBA, SI!

(France, Marker, 1961)

Of the many filmmakers drawn to Cuba by the Revolution of 1959, it was Chris Marker who made what Cubans regarded as the best documentary on the Revolution at the time. According to Marker, in his preface to the published version of the script, the film was shot rapidly in January 1961, "during the first alert period (you know, at the time when the majority of French papers were hooting over Fidel's paranoia in imagining himself threatened with invasion)," and it "aims at communicating, if not the experience, at least the vibrations, the rhythm of a revolution that will one day perhaps be held to be the decisive moment of a whole era of contemporary history (Marker, 1961)."

Marker's sense of solidarity is announced by the title, one half of the slogan that was one of the Revolution's mottos: ¡Cuba Si! ¡Yanqui No! Marker's method is interrogative, inclusive, and visually ironic. Filming the crowds in the streets or at a baseball match (baseball and tourist posters remind the viewer that the United States is less than an hour away by plane), he picks out faces who look at the camera directly and unaggressively, as people enjoying their new-found right to take full possession of public space. The effect is to ask the viewer to consider before judging. These scenes give way to newsreel of the guerrillas in the mountains, with shots of Fidel Castro, Che Guevara, and Camilo Cienfuegos, through which the events and motivations of the Revolution are recounted, including the hostile responses of the U.S. administration. The interpellation of shots of a printing press and an open-air film projection speak of the necessary supplement to guerrilla struggle and victory: the battle of the media at home and abroad. The headline of a Miami newspaper reads "Fidel Hurls New Barbs at US." A moment later, we hear shots of execution by a firing squad followed by crowds at a boxing match, and then a French newspaper headline appears that reads, "The State Department accuses Fidel Castro of having betrayed the Cuban Revolution."

Marker eschews the conventional solidarity film and instead uses montage to raise the question of how the events he chronicles are to be represented. Hence, the comparison he makes between Fidel and Robin Hood. As the commentary puts it: "Perhaps he is Robin Hood . . . Only in this century taking from the rich to give to the poor does not necessarily mean attacking stage-coaches. And when Robin Hood has read Marx, when, up in the mountains he is preparing the laws and reforms of the future republic, some parts of the world realize painfully that they too are one Robin Hood late" There is a song about revolutionary decrees on Agrarian Reform and Rent, and the commentary concludes, "So legends die. The myth of Robin Hood is shattered. In its place a Revolution."

The film was banned in France for three reasons according to the Minister of Information: it was not a documentary but "an apologia for the Castro regime"; no film "which is ideological propaganda can be authorized if only

because of the risks this type of production entails for public order"; and the Cuban press frequently attacks the administrations of Martinique and Guadeloupe, and it therefore "does not seem suitable to offer a cinematographic hearing to Cuba's leaders" (1962). Marker got round the ban by providing a new commentary full of the touristic clichés of a travelog, which enabled him to get an export visa, then sending the film to Belgium with the original commentary restored.

If the ban tells us of French government nervousness about its Caribbean territories in the year that Paris finally acceded to Algerian independence, it is doubtless Fidel Castro's analysis of democracy, which he gives in an interview in the film, that the government wished to keep as inaccessible to the public as possible. For sixty years, he says, Cuba had to put up with the farce of a pseudo-democracy, and

> the French ought to be the first to understand: the French have an election almost every year: municipal. . . national. . . for a president, for an MP . . . perhaps no other country in the world has had more elections than France in the last six decades. And even so the French are not content . . . they can perfectly understand that political factions [and] electoralism have not solved a single one of France's fundamental problems.

In sum, *Cuba Si!* is a political travelog that never collapses into mere rhetoric. If Marker now regards it as more a pamphlet than a film, edited in a hurry as an urgent response to events (Marker, 2003), it exemplifies, nevertheless, something of what the Argentinian filmmakers, Fernando Solanas and Octavio Getino, would define at the end of the same decade as one of the aims of what they called "third cinema," the political film feared and rejected by the political mainstream.

MICHAEL CHANAN

See also **Marker, Chris**

Cuba, si! (France, Marker, 1961, 50 min). Directed and written by Chris Marker. Cinematography by Chris Marker.

Further Reading

Marker, Chris, Cuba Si!,' in *L'avant scène du cinéma*, 6, 1961.
———, Cuba Si!, Censor No!' translated by Garry Broughton, *Movie* 3, 1962, 15–21.
———, Personal communication, 2003.

Cuba, si!, 1961.
[*Still courtesy of the British Film Institute*]

CULLODEN

(UK, Watkins, 1964)

"They have created a desert and have called it peace." The last lines of voice-over in Watkins's 1964 television documentary are heard while the last full-scale battle fought on British soil from 1746 to the contemporary world of Vietnam is being shown. The Battle of Culloden was fought between the trade-oriented colonial army of the English king and the last of the feudal hierarchy of the Scottish Highlands, under the leadership of Bonnie Prince Charlie. In Watkins's account, Charles Stewart, far from the heroic figure of legend, was not just an effete and selfish leader prepared to sacrifice his supporters in a vainglorious battle. He was also a European aristocrat without the least understanding of the men he led onto the moor at Culloden, vastly rich in the midst of squalor, unable even to understand the Gaelic they spoke. As he flees the battlefield, the voice-over tells us, a clan chief screamed after him: "Run, you cowardly Italian." Italian was almost the only blood that did not run in his veins.

On the British side, the professional army paid its generals 25,000 pounds a year and its foot soldiers sixpence a day. Watkins has a razor-sharp eye for the blind iniquity of an historical event in which there were no "good guys," only the self-serving dying dream of an absolute monarchy against a rising tide of constitutional capitalism. Between these sides, Watkins's cameras linger on faces of the downtrodden crofters and their subtenants. The heat of battle is caught in rapid camera movement and fast editing, but its build-up and aftermath, depicting cold limbs and hungry eyes and moments of random suffering, are filmed in slower shots.

What makes the film still vibrant is not so much its passion, although that is still effecting and is still a hallmark of Watkins's work. It is rather its skillful use of lightweight 16mm equipment to imitate in a historical drama the techniques developed for contemporary news footage that makes the film still relevant and interesting. Likewise, the use of location sound recording technologies to interview characters on the field replicates the voices of electronic news gathering. During the battle, commentary is provided with the gusto of a sports reporter from an on-screen character, biographer of the Duke of Cumberland, who led the British forces.

Watkins had developed his reportage style of drama-documentary in the award-winning amateur short *Forgotten Faces.* To some extent, that amateur period haunts all his later work, with its ethos of participation in storytelling, and in the empathy of ordinary people for others divided from them by time or circumstance. Watkins pitched a "sort of *World In Action*" style, a reference to the groundbreaking documentary, to the BBC's Head of Documentaries, Huw Weldon. To some extent the BBC's reaction to the surprising popularity and critical success of ITV's *Armchair Theatre* seemed to offer a way of making entertaining television that would still serve the corporation's brief of education and information, while also improving its paternalistic and old-fashioned image as compared to its then new rival service. The production was relatively inexpensive, with small numbers of Inverness locals playing the thousands involved in judiciously selected vignettes from the battle, with judicious use of smoke and editing to multiply their effect on screen. Budgetary constraints in this instance moved in the same direction that Watkins

Culloden, 1964.
[*Still courtesy of the British Film Institute*]

was moving ideologically. It encouraged an aesthetic that firmly situated the role of the media between event and audience, by inviting the participants in history to speak for themselves, and in so doing to reveal the structures of meaning—clan revenge, group loyalty, fear, and force—that brought them to the fight.

The freshness of the unfamiliar faces that fill the screen and of the halting dialogue spoken to the camera by a number of the amateur cast stand as much against the slickness of normal television as it did against the prettification of history at the hands of English and Scottish myth-makers. Likewise the grain of history is preserved in the rawness of the location sound recording even when, for example, in a scene shot in the prisons in Inverness, the chatter of the camera is quite audible as prisoners give their testimony. Those voices and experiences, lost otherwise in dusty archives of court martials and prison logs, gain in intensity from their direct address to camera, their "un-actorly" delivery, and the shifting pitch of voices raised against canon fire or lowered in moments of quiet.

Diffused daylight under rain before the battle, or ragged firelight in its aftermath, along with slightly jerky reframing and photographic rather than dramatic framing adds further to this application of television's metaphysics of liveness to the documentary genre. Working in the opposite direction, however, at least to more recent tastes, the otherwise ubiquitous voice-over may seem overdone. Like John Pilger today, the young Watkins seems not to trust his audience with his subjects. Yet at the same time, the voice-over has several novel features, notably a turn of phrase repeated in *The War Game*: "This is grapeshot, and this is what it does." The dispassionate delivery works to distance the brutality of the image, rather than to naturalize

it, and likewise leaves to the viewer the possibility of arguing with the overall project of the film. The present tense and the use of the word "this" both imitate actuality TV and distance it, as what we see is clearly reconstruction and stunt work.

It is perhaps in this way that the film gained its reputation. It is not merely that the highland clearances provide an historical parallel for the U.S. Army's "pacification" program in Vietnam, but that the world's first television war might be met with an account of what television coverage of warfare might be like if, unlike the coverage of Vietnam, it allowed itself access to both sides in the conflict and was ready to see that there are as many conflicts within armies as there are between them.

SEAN CUBITT

See also **Watkins, Peter**

Culloden. (UK, BBC, 1964, 69 min). Produced by Peter Watkins. Directed by Peter Watkins. Script by Peter Watkins. Cinematography by Dick Bush. Film Editing by Michael Bradsell. Production Design by Anne Davey, Colin MacLeod and Brendon Woods. Sound by John Gatland and Lou Hanks.

Further Reading

Cook, John R., and Patrick Murphy, "After the Bomb Dropped: The Cinema Half-Life of The War Game," *Journal of Popular British Cinema 3*, 2000, 129–132.

Gomez, Joseph, *Peter Watkins*, Boston: Twayne Publishers, 1979.

Kilborn, Richard, and John Izod, *An Introduction to Television Documentary: Confronting Reality*, Manchester: Manchester University Press, 1997.

Murphy, Robert, *Sixties British Cinema*, London: BFI, 1992.

Walker, Alexander, *Hollywood, England*, London: Harrap, 1986.

CÜRLIS, HANS

Perhaps one of the most overlooked directors in Germany is Hans Cürlis, who continuously produced cultural and educational films from 1919 to 1964. His more than 400 films (some even say 500 films) consisted mainly of portraits of artists, as well as conventional cultural films on regional

landscapes and traditions. He is the most important pioneer of the subgenre of films on art. Cürlis developed his own individual style in this field, for example, in his cycle *Schaffende Hände/ Creative Hands*, where he concentrated on the hands of artists to visualize how creative

thoughts and ideas were transferred into the work of art.

From early on, Cürlis put sculptures on a rotating table, which was slowly turned to give the viewer the opportunity to see the artwork from different perspectives. This idea also brought movement to the objects, which was documented by the moving images. This method was heavily criticized by art historians in the 1920s but set a standard of how to visualize sculptures.

Cürlis developed mastery in working with light and shadow to find the perfect way to present the artwork to his spectators. His main interest was producing educational and scientific films for schools, and in doing so he had pedagogic goals to establish film as a teaching tool.

Before 1926, he also produced political propaganda films, which attacked the conditions of peace that the allied victors of World War I had placed on the German Reich, as well as polemic films against the danger of Bolshevism. These films had nationalistic and reactionary tendencies, which resulted in political conflicts and his dismissal at the Ministry of Foreign Affairs in 1921. However, his institute for cultural studies, which he had founded in 1919, was still supported by official sources later on. Besides these political films he produced films with geographical and artistic content.

From 1922 on, he created his cycle *Schaffende Hände/Creative Hands*, in which he portrayed the most important artists of the Weimar Republic, including George Grosz, Max Liebermann, Lovis Corinth, Wassiliy Kandinski, Käthe Kollwitz, Max Pechstein, and Heinrich Zille, who all lived in Berlin. These films are extraordinary documents on the production of art at the beginning of the twentieth century with its broad range of styles and methods.

Cürlis's films had a lasting influence on films on art that were produced afterwards. With his films, he wanted to bring art and the creative process closer to the general public, and he wanted to document these artists for future generations. During the Third Reich, he concentrated on producing inconspicuous educational films, but he also produced portraits of the most important Nazi artists, namely Josef Thorak and Arnold Breker, who Cürlis visited in their studios where they were working on gigantic sculptures for the representation of the fascist regime.

Between 1946 and 1948, Cürlis worked for the DEFA, producing art films as well as cultural films exactly like before. From 1948 on, he taught history of art and journalism at the newly founded Free University in West Berlin, and he produced his films in the western part of Berlin. He often reshot films on artists he had already portrayed in the 1920s, thus giving the audience the possibility of following the development of these artists.

KAY HOFFMANN

Biography

Born in Niederdorf (Kreis Geldern), Germany, February 16, 1889, the son of a vicar. Grew up in Essen. Studied art history in Munich and Berlin and finished his Ph.D. on Albrecht Dürer in 1914. From 1918 to 1921 worked as an advisor for film and photography for the Ministry of Foreign Affairs. In 1919 founded his own institute for cultural studies (Institute für Kulturforschung) and used film as a medium of enlightment. In the 1920s became head of the association of the producers for educational and "Kulturfilm" until 1933. During the Third Reich concentrated on educational films. Worked for the DEFA, 1946–1948. In 1947, again became head of the association of producers of educational films (Bund Deutscher Lehrfilmhersteller). Taught at the Free University in West Berlin from 1948 to 1962. Died in Berlin, 1982.

Selected Films

1919 *Altdeutsche Madonnen/Old German Madonnas*: director

1920 *Kohlennot und "Friedensvertrag"/Need for coal and the "Peace Contract"*: director

1921 *Besatzungskosten und Kinderelend in Deutschland/Costs of Occupation and Misery of the Children in Germany*: director

1922 *Lovis Corinth*: director

1923 *Gefilmte Künstlerhände/Hands of Artists on Film*: director

1923 *George Grosz*: director

1924 *Max Slevogt in seinem Atelier/Max Slevogt in His Studio*: director

1925 *Heinrich Zille auf dem Balkon seiner Wohnung/Heinrich Zille on the Balcony of His Home*: director

1926 *Weltgeschichte als Kolonialgeschichte/World History as Colonial History*: director

1926 *Max Liebermann in seinem Atelier/Max Liebermann in His Studio*: director

1926 *MOPP (Max Opppenheimer)*: director

1927 *Max Pechstein*: director

1927 *Wassily Kandinsky in der Galerie Nierendorf/Wassily Kandinsky at the Galerie Nierendorf*: director

1932 *Der Rhein, Deutschlands Strom/The Rhine, Germany's River*: director

1933 *Von deutschen Domen/On German Cathedrals*: director

1935 *Herstellung eines Bauernstuhls/Manufacture of a Farmer's Chair*: director

1936 *Mädel im Landjahr/Girls in the Countryside*: director

1938 *Schöpferische Stunde—Josef Thorak/Creative Hour—Josef Thorak*: director

1943 *Josef Thorak Werkstatt und Werk/Josef Thorak Workshop and Oevre*: director

1944 *Arno Breker:* director
1945 *Fleckfieber droht!/Threat of Spotted Fever!:* director
1946 *Vitamine an der Strasse/Vitamins beside the Street:* director
1947 *Junges Leben/Young Life:* director
1947 *Formende Hände/Creative Hands:* director
1952 *Zeichnungen Dürers und seiner Zeitgenossen/Drawings by Dürer and his Contemporaries:* director
1952 *Drei Meister schneiden in Holz/Three Masters Cut in Wood:* director
1954 *Der Welfenschatz—ein Schatz für die Welt/The Guelf Treasury—a Treasure for the World:* director
1956 *Max Pechstein—ein Meister des Expressionismus/Max Pechstein—a Master of Expressionism:* director
1957 *Albrecht Dürer:* director

1957 *Schaffende Hände—Corinth, Liebermann, Slevogt/ Creative Hands—Corinth, Liebermann, Slevogt:* director
1958 *George Grosz—Berlin 1958;* director
1964 *André Masson beim Zeichnen/*André Masson at Drawing: director

Further Reading

Cürlis, Hans, *Zehn Jahre Institut für Kulturforschung*, Berlin, 1929.
Cürlis, Hans, Kunstwerk-vom Film entdeckt, in *Der Deutsche Film*, 6, 1939, 118–120.
Ziegler, Reiner, *Kunst und Architektur im Kulturfilm 1919–1945*, Konstanz, 2003.

CZECH REPUBLIC/SLOVAKIA

The evolution of documentary film in both the Czech Republic and Slovakia can be traced back to the 1900s, when the two separate states were intermingled into one; Czechoslovakia. After its formation into an independent republic in 1918, Czechoslovakia faced grave economic insecurity. Although Czechoslovak documentaries were gaining popularity thanks to their emphasis on patriotism, producers struggled to compete with foreign imports in order to realize success. Until the early 1920s, technical standards were hampered by the lack of properly equipped studios. In 1921, the A-B company was converted into a film studio and technical standards began to ameliorate. In 1933, the A-B Company built the Barrandov Film Studios in Prague. Being the heart of the majority of prewar and postwar developments, the establishment of these film studios led to an increase in domestic film production. Czechoslovak films gained early international success in the late 1940s, when the Venice Grand Prix was awarded to Karel Stekly's locally produced film *Sirena/The Stroke* (1947). As Czechoslovak films continued winning film prizes and Oscars, critics around the world became more and more familiar with Czechoslovak cinema.

After World War II, a newly established democracy in Czechoslovakia lasted less than three years before a new communist rule was established in 1948. With the communist rule came the nationalization of the film industry, which led producers to focus their films on politically significant themes (Hames, 1985: 37). During this time, all documentary films were expected to portray reality and its revolutionary transition as accurately as possible. Jiri Weiss's film *Uloupena Hranice/The Stolen Frontier* (1947) is one such film in which Munich and the crisis in the Sudetenland is depicted. This film was an immediate success because the Munich problem was a massive ordeal that especially affected those growing up in Weiss's generation. In making *Uloupena Hranice*, Weiss takes advantage of his experience with British documentaries, in which amateur actors and nonprofessionals are videotaped with the use of a hidden camera.

Similarly, Otakar Vavra makes use of the expectation of shorts to capture reality and the transition that individuals were undergoing in Czechoslovakia. Vavra's film *Nema Barikada/Silent Barricade* (1948) documents the Prague uprising against the Nazis before the arrival of the Red army. His film, although extremely nationalistic, manages to document the struggle of the Czechoslovak people in a time of war.

After World War II, "The Theory of Lack of Conflict." emerged. This theory introduced the concept of positive heroes, also known as protagonists, triumphing over negative characters, also known as antagonists. This theory quickly became the foundation for films and gave rise to a standardized plot in which a happy ending was inevitable. Producers would continue documenting reality, while illustrating conflicts between heroes and villains, but ensuring that their films would always end in the expected, optimistic light.

The years 1947 and 1948 marked the beginning of the Cold War. Despite the war, the radical youth went on believing that the revolution went hand in hand with art and expression.

During the 1950s, Czechoslovak shorts mainly served to illustrate socialist realist dogma and historical events. In 1956, with the denunciation of Stalinism, Czechoslovakia experienced a scene of cultural "thaw" followed by reaction (Hames, 1985: 44).

In the 1960s, there were two main types of documentary films. As Anton Navratil, Czech historian of documentary film put it: "Ways of Lie, Ways of Truth." "The ways of lie" were those films produced using an ideological filter that supported what the communist authorities preached, regardless of how much this would distort reality. The filmmakers exploring "the ways of truth" were those who produced short films that were highly creative, and risky. Living in a communist nation, it was difficult to openly express one's opinions. Producers of truth documentaries went out on a limb many times and found ways to express concepts and opinions that would otherwise be impossible to state verbally and openly. This approach gave audiences a glimpse into what communism really was, without the authority's filter of distortion and propaganda.

In 1956, once "de-Stalinization" was under way, an enormous hunger developed for the flourishing of ideas, the sphere of culture, and the need for freedom of expression. By the 1960s, a new film movement emerged, also known as the Czechoslovak New Wave. By 1963, the First Wave of the Czechoslovak New Wave, was underway. The First Wave is defined as "that group of directors who prepared the way for the developments of the 1960s through thematic or formal breaks with the conventions of Socialist Realism" (Hames, 1985: 35).

Czechoslovakia's film movement, also referred to as The Czechoslovak New Wave, can be traced back to the years after World War II. During this movement, film producers looked for ways to portray society in a new light by "combining criticism of the status quo with the rejection of traditional narrative" (Hames, 1985: 92). Filmmakers desired the ability to portray society in a nonstereotyped fashion, without the integration of propaganda, or communist standards and expectations. The focus of shorts revolved around the everyday life, of the everyday individual, less emphasis on protagonists and antagonists, and more on just the average individual going about daily life. The need to have to end the film with a happy ending diminished, as filmmakers continued ensuring that their films would record and expose everyday reality.

Milos Forman, a scriptwriter and director, is one of many who has produced a number of films that follow the trend of recording and exposing the every day. This standard procedure, known as the realist/documentary tradition, reflects an Italian neorealism and cinema verité approach. Both approaches strongly influenced the Czechoslovak film industry. The use of the two approaches helped audiences and filmmakers deal with social reality and its connection with the individual. Film producers relied on these techniques to tie together the world of the subjective with that of the objective. Cinema verité can best be described as "the act of filming real people in uncontrolled situations. Uncontrolled means that the filmmaker does not function as a director nor, for that matter, as a screenwriter . . . no one is told what to say or how to act" (Hames, 1985: 120).

Most scholars, when referring to the Czechoslovak New Wave, are aware that the majority of the films produced during this time, were concerned with both the individual and society. For example in two of Forman's films, *Cerny Petr/Black Peter* (1963) and *Lasky Jedne Plavovlasky/Loves of a Blonde* (1965), Both take on a boy-meets-girl theme, which is deemed acceptable by socialist realist cinema audiences. By integrating elements of cinema verité and classical film comedy into their work, Forman carefully describes the life of two young children and the society in which they live. The importance of personal life is juxtaposed next to the struggle of everyday life. The result in both films is one of the most profound analyses of Czechoslovak society yet to be illustrated.

Because short films would often stimulate one's mind, individuals turned to them as a means to stimulate change in reality. Documentaries represented a factor of real life; in fact, they changed real life. As the presence of creative ideas increased in documentaries, ideas on economics, politics, literature, and the arts also increased. It was not long before all these ideas led to the development of the Czechoslovak Reform Movement, which led to the fall of the Novotny regime. In 1968, Alexander Dubcek, the first secretary of Communist Czechoslovakia, implemented a variety of democratic, political, and economic reforms known as the Prague Spring. A Socialist democracy was underway in Czechoslovakia. The Soviet Union, alarmed at

what appeared to be the collapse of communism in Czechoslovakia, invaded the republic in August 1968 in hopes of crushing the Prague Spring. The invasion was successful in abolishing any continuation of democratic reforms, and Czechoslovakia was forced into "normalization" back into a communist state. For the brief period that the Czechoslovaks had a taste of a western-style democracy, the level of filmmaking surpassed any level known before. As Pryl argues "these remarkable achievements were not merely works born during the spell of freedom . . . they were quite conscious demonstrations of a refusal to give in" (Hames, 1985: 257).

Although the republic had again been taken over by a communist authority, the government did not actually reorganize the film industry until the latter part of 1969. Many films were forced to cease production, one of which Helge's *Jak Se U Nas Pece Chleba/How Bread Is Made* (1969). By 1973, a number of films that were perceived as segregating society, as oppose to strengthening it, were banned, including Forman's *Hori, Ma Panenko/The Fireman's Ball* (1967).

In the 1970s, rather than producing films based on aesthetic value, conviction, ideas, and risks, the majority of filmmakers centered their work around the theme of the world wars and Czechoslovakia's struggle. One of the most popular films produced during this time was Vladmir Cech's *Klic/The Key* (1971), a film illustrating the life of a communist official during World War II. "The unifying characteristic of nearly all the films made in the seventies was a lack of ideas at the script level—a fear of ideological nonconformity that resulted in films being about almost nothing at all" (Hames, 1985: 261). Kachyna's *Laska*/Love (1973), Hubacek's *Znamost Sestry Aleny/Sister Alena's Boy* (1973), and Jires' *Lide Z Metra/People of the Metro* (1974) are three of the many films that fell into the standard category of 1970s empty films.

As a result of the declining economy and the reorganization of the film industry between 1968 and 1970, many of Czechoslovakia's best-known film directors immigrated to different parts of the world to continue producing successful films. Forman and Passer took their talents to North America; Stanislav Barabas and Jan Nemec moved to West Germany. The majority of film producers who did choose to stay in Czechoslovakia faced unemployment.

The mid-1970s marked the return of a number of skilled and talented directors and actors who were eager to rejuvenate the Czechoslovak film industry.

The number of films produced slowly improved. Although there is not much room to deviate from the status quo and the communist authority beliefs, scholars are optimistic that with the continuance of this "thaw," brought about by the post-1969 regime, film achievements may again parallel those brought about during the New Wave. Scholars are hopeful that as political pressure lifts, a critical and aesthetic diversity will surface, as it did amidst the New Wave.

On March 11, 1985, Mikhail Gorbachev was made the general secretary of the Communist party of the Soviet Union. Gorbachev introduced Perestroika (restructuring) and Glasnost (openness) to the communist regime, and these two practices posed unexpected challenges to the status quo.

By the 1990s, the years after the time known as the Velvet Revolution, voices in favor of Slovakia's independence grew stronger. Finally, the prime ministers of both republics were left with no choice but to divide the country into two parts. On January 1, 1993, Czechoslovakia was broken up into Slovakia and The Czech Republic.

Today, many look at Czech cinema as being on the verge of experiencing a New Wave in the film industry, just as Czechoslovakia did in the 1960s. Since 1993, Czech films have been winning countless prizes and awards. In 1997, Jan Sverak's short *Kolya/Kolja* (1996) won an Oscar, and many have cited this event as marking the beginning of a resurgence of the film industry in the Czech Republic. With a number of Czech films, such as Petr Zelenka's *Knoflikari/Buttoners* (1997), gaining praise all across the world, it is no wonder that the Czech film industry is so admired. As Hames states, "Since 1993 no fewer than 30 directors have made feature debuts, most of them graduates of the documentary and screenwriting departments of the Prague Film School . . ." (Hames, 1985: 32).

The majority of Czech documentaries that are produced today juxtapose every day life with the politics prevalent in society. Czech shorts depict individuals' means of adapting, conforming, and changing according not only to their surroundings but to historical experiences as well. Filmmakers are careful to integrate the critical, the personal, and the historical into their documentary masterpieces. One of the many documentaries produced during the 1990s that hit the box office top ten lists was Jan Hrebejk's *Pelisky/Cosy Dens*, (1999). This short illustrates family relations during the Prague Spring. By taking on their own personal approach to filmmaking, Czech directors are producing critically acclaimed masterpieces.

By contrast, since its 1993 separation from the Czech Republic, Slovakia's film industry has been struggling to survive. Having only produced two or three movies per year on average, the Slovak film industry is far behind compared to its neighbors. The lack of technical progress and financial security is the biggest impediment of both the quantitative and qualitative growth of Slovak cinema. The majority of filmmaking equipment has to be imported, while a great deal of production is being completed abroad (Karpaty, 2002: 1). Because of the underdeveloped film industry, many Slovak film producers are immigrating to neighboring countries.

Although Slovakia still faces great challenges before realizing a healthy film industry, critics comment that the industry has improved greatly since 1998, when Mikulá Dzurinda became head of the government. New means of support are being established to make the gaining of funds for film production a lot easier. Initiatives such as the founding of The European Community's Media Plus Program and the establishment of an advisory Media Desk office are helping to ensure that the Slovak film industry will see vast improvement in the coming years.

Despite all the social, political, and economic changes of the past, documentary film in both the Czech Republic and Slovakia has survived and continues to evolve and develop in both regions. Shorts are realizing higher levels of success in the Czech Republic than in Slovakia, but scholars are convinced that, in time, Slovakia will catch up to its neighbor, just as the two regions' documentary film industries once paralleled each other's success.

SAPNA GUPTA

Further Reading

Broz, Jaroslav, *The Path of Fame of the Czechoslovak Film*, Prague: Edmunds Inc, 1967.

Dwyer, Ruth, and Graham Petrie (eds.), *Before the Wall Came Down*, Lanham: University Press of America, 1990.

Forbes, Jill, and Sarah Street, *European Cinema: An Introduction*, New York: Palgrave, 2000.

Hames, Peter, *The Czechoslovak New Wave*, Los Angeles: University of California Press, 1985.

Hames, Peter, "Czechs on the Rebound," in *Sight and Sound*, 10, 7, 2000, 32–34.

Karpaty, Miroslav, "Slovak Cinema Shows Signs of Life," in *The Slovak Spectator*, 8, 47, December 9–15, 2002 http://www.slovakspectator.sk/clanok-11301.html.

Liehm, J Antonin, *Closely Watched Films: The Czechoslovak Experience*, New York: International Arts and Sciences Press Inc, 1974.

Zalman, Jan, *Films and Filmmakers in Czechoslovakia*, Prague: Orbis, 1968.

D

DALRYMPLE, IAN

Given his feature film background, Ian Dalrymple was not the most obvious choice to lead the GPO (General Post Office) Film Unit in August 1940. Aspects of his character and previous experience, however, suited him for this role. Dalrymple's modest demeanor, liberal sympathies, and intellectual leanings made him more compatible with the documentary filmmakers at the Unit · than many commercial industry figures would have been. He began his career at Brunel and Montagu Ltd., a firm specializing in reediting fiction and nonfiction films (Perkins and Stollery, 2004). In certain respects this firm was seen as an informal "film university" similar to John Grierson's documentary unit at the EMB (Empire Marketing Board). The editing team at Brunel and Montagu Ltd. prepared foreign art films exhibited by the (London) Film Society. The Society's screenings were also a major influence on early British documentary.

In the 1930s Dalrymple worked as a senior editor, writer, and producer at leading British studios Gaumont-British and London Films, but the unusual joint "production personnel" credits he received on certain projects suggest an openness to team work similar to that prevalent within the British documentary movement (Barr, 1997). *The Good Companions* (1933) and *South Riding* (1938), two films Dalrymple worked on with director Victor Saville, inclined toward documentary values inasmuch as they addressed social issues, advocated consensus, and incorporated location shooting. Dalrymple had also been involved in the Gaumont-British newsreel compilation film, *The Prince of Wales* (1933), and co-directed *Modern Orphans of the Storm* (1937) with documentarist Basil Wright.

The last major project Dalrymple was associated with prior to his appointment as head of the GPO Film Unit was the hastily constructed *The Lion Has Wings* (Michael Powell, Brian Desmond Hurst, Adrian Brunel, 1939). This propaganda film, designed to highlight the Royal Air Force's preparedness for war, combined dramatized sequences with newsreel and documentary footage (Short, 1997). Although criticized in some quarters for its assumption that an upper-middle-class officer and his wife (Ralph Richardson and Merle Oberon) could speak for Britain as a whole, *The Lion Has Wings* anticipated the merging of fictional and documentary strategies characteristic of certain strands of British wartime film production. During this period Dalrymple became interested in the broader issue of how film could serve the war effort. He submitted a paper to the MOI (Ministry of Information) outlining his thoughts on the subject, and produced two shorts for the Ministry's "five-minute film" scheme (Dalrymple, 1982).

After an initial period of uncertainty, the MOI Films Division began to establish a more coherent sense of direction around the time Dalrymple was appointed. Jack Beddington, appointed Director of Films Division in April 1940, was sympathetic to documentary and supported Dalrymple throughout his tenure. Harold Boxall's report on the GPO Film Unit, delivered in November 1940, acknowledged the unit could make a distinctive contribution to wartime propaganda. This report initiated a streamlining of the unit's operations and an eventual move to the well-equipped Pinewood studios in early 1942 (Swann, 1989; Chapman, 1998). A change of name was recommended. Dalrymple's suggestion that it should be called the Crown Film Unit was implemented at the end of 1940.

Dalrymple gained the confidence of the documentary filmmakers working with him by fighting for relatively generous budgets, acting as a buffer between them and the Films Division, and striving to improve their pay (Barr, 1989). He even argued, unsuccessfully, for an annual block grant to maximise the filmmakers' autonomy (Chapman, 1998). Most Crown filmmakers thrived under Dalrymple, and he proved adept at developing younger talent—not only directors but also other production staff (Drazin, 1998). Established star director Harry Watt found Dalrymple aloof and left in 1942, but Pat Jackson was more typical in appreciating the balance Dalrymple offered between discreet guidance and creative freedom (Watt, 1974; Jackson, 1999). Dalrymple fought hard to make those projects he believed in possible. He negotiated strenuously with the Admiralty and underlined to Jack Beddington the propaganda value and box-office potential of *Western Approaches* (Pat Jackson, 1944). This Technicolor film about merchant seamen was Crown's most expensive production (Aldgate and Richards, 1994).

Under Dalrymple, Crown produced a large volume of routine short films. At the more prestigious end of the spectrum there was a marked tendency toward the production of reconstructed narrative documentaries. This trend had been developed at the GPO Film Unit in the late 1930s with films such as *North Sea* (Harry Watt, 1938) and *Men of the Lighthouse* (David Macdonald, 1940). Dalrymple's regime saw this emphasis on narrative and characterisation extended in films such as *Target for Tonight* (Harry Watt, 1941), *Fires Were Started* (Humphrey Jennings, 1943), *Close Quarters* (Jack Lee, 1943), as well as *Western Approaches*. Some of these documentaries of ordinary heroism performed very well at the box office, despite the absence of heterosexual romance and stars. At the same time, Dalrymple also supported the more obviously experimental documentaries *Words for Battle* (Humphrey Jennings, 1941) and *Listen to Britain* (Humphrey Jennings and Stewart McAllister, 1942).

Dalrymple's departure from Crown in May 1943 seems to have been prompted by several factors. He pleaded exhaustion and the fact that he was earning much less than in the features sector of the industry. The new Board of Management set up early in 1943 seemed unnecessary to him. He also believed, contrary to MOI policy, that following the publication of the Beveridge Report postwar reconstruction should become one of the themes explicitly addressed by the Crown Film Unit (Sussex, 1975). After his resignation, Dalrymple retained an involvement with official documentary production by helping the Army Film Unit during the final years of the war. His postwar production company, Wessex Films, attempted to incorporate a documentary ethos into some of its projects, such as *Once a Jolly Swagman* (Jack Lee, 1948). Dalrymple remained close to fellow Cambridge graduate Humphrey Jennings, with Wessex producing the last two documentaries he directed.

Dalrymple's achievements at the Crown Film Unit did not go unchallenged. Some representatives of the feature film industry argued that prestige films produced by the Unit encroached on their territory and amounted to state-subsidized competition. From another direction, some commentators belonging to the documentary film movement outside Crown argued that the Unit ignored wartime social problems and strayed from the proper path of truly educative documentary (Swann, 1989). What is indisputable is that Dalrymple presided over and deserves much of the credit for the most vigorous phase of the Crown Film Unit's existence.

MARTIN STOLLERY

See also **Crown Film Unit; GPO Film Unit; MOI**

Biography

Born Johannesburg, South Africa, August 26, 1903. Studied at Cambridge University and edited the literary journal *Granta*. Joined Brunel and Montagu Ltd. in the 1920s. Worked as a senior film editor, writer, and producer at Gainsborough, Gaumont-British, and

London Films during the 1930s. Associate producer of *The Lion Has Wings* (1939). Led the Crown (initially GPO) Film Unit between August 1940 and May 1943. Established Wessex Films, which supported projects directed by some former Crown personnel, including Jack Lee and Humphrey Jennings. Formed a company to make a documentary series, *The Changing Face of Europe*, under the Marshall Plan. Produced and wrote some notable postwar British feature films, including *The Wooden Horse* (Jack Lee, 1950) and *The Admirable Crichton* (Lewis Gilbert, 1957). Published occasional essays on topics including his experience as a film editor, working with Alexander Korda, and leading the Crown Film Unit. Died April 28, 1989.

Further Reading

Aldgate, Tony, and Jeffrey Richards, *Britain Can Take It*, Edinburgh University Press, 1994.

Barr, Charles, "Desperate Yearnings: Victor Saville and Gainsborough," in *Gainsborough Pictures*, edited by Pam Cook, London: Cassell, 1997, 47–59.

Barr, Charles, "War Record," in *Sight and Sound*, 58, no. 4, autumn 1989, 260–265.

Chapman, James, *The British at War : Cinema, State, and Propaganda 1939–1945*, London, I. B. Tauris, 1998.

Dalrymple, Ian, "The Crown Film Unit, 1940–43," in *Propaganda, Politics and Film, 1918–45*, edited by Nicholas Pronayand D. W. Spring, London, Macmillan, 1982, 209–220.

Drazin, Charles, *The Finest Years: British Cinema of the 1940s*, London, André Deutsch, 1998.

Jackson, Pat, *A Retake Please! Night Mail to Western Approaches*, Liverpool: Liverpool University Press, 1999.

Perkins, Roy, and Martin Stollery, *The British Film Editor*, London: BFI, 2004.

Short, K. R. M., *Screening the Propaganda of British Air Power*, Trowbridge: Flicks Books, 1997.

Sussex, Elizabeth, *The Rise and Fall of British Documentary*, Berkeley: UCP, 1975.

Swann, Paul, *The British Documentary Film Movement 1926–1946*, Cambridge: CUP, 1989.

Watt, Harry, *Don't Look at the Camera*, London: Elek, 1974.

DALY, TOM

Tom Daly's entire 45-year career in film was spent with one organization, the National Film Board of Canada. He was known as both a meticulous and effective editor and a brilliant, responsive teacher. He could establish a connection between a decision whether to cut an extra frame off the end of a shot to a grand philosophical principle. Daly was involved in some of the key developments in Film Board documentary.

During the war, Daly (who arrived at the Film Board with no knowledge of film) apprenticed to Stuart Legg on the two wartime newsreel series, *Canada Carries On* and *The World in Action*. From Legg, he learned how to see potential in almost any piece of film, given an appropriate context for it. He also developed, under Legg, a meticulous approach to the craft of editing, as well as a sense of film structure.

After the war, Daly made two compilation films of note, *Guilty Men* (1945), about the Nuremberg trials, and *Hungry Minds* (1948), about UNESCO relief efforts in war-shattered European countries. In the mid-1950s, he presided over Unit B's burst of documentary innovation. Working closely with key filmmakers Colin Low, Roman

Kroitor, Wolf Koenig, and Stanley Jackson, among others, he produced and in some cases edited Unit B's classic *Corral* (1954), *Paul Tomkowicz: Street-Railway Switchman* (1954), *City of Gold* (1957), *Universe* (1960), *Circle of the Sun* (1961), the Candid Eye series (1958–61), and *Lonely Boy* (1961). He and members of his unit also spearheaded the Film Board's exhibit for EXPO '67, *Labyrinthe*.

In the 1960s and 1970s, Daly encouraged young filmmakers and gave many of them their first significant opportunity. He produced films for Michael Rubbo, Tony Ianzelo, Donald Winkler, Derek May, and Paul Cowan, among others. His last two major Film Board projects were Malca Gillson's documentary about palliative care, *The Last Days of Living* (1980), which he produced, and Colin Low's *Standing Alone* (1982), which he produced and edited.

Although revered by many, Daly had his critics at the Film Board. Managers considered him a weak administrator, because he allowed projects to go over budget, exceeded deadlines, and broke various production rules. He also encouraged some filmmakers who proved untalented. But the very best of the films he produced needed the extra time or extra budget; they would have been unremarkable without them. Although not every filmmaker he mentored became successful, most of them—some of whom management had given up on—became accomplished and recognized.

D. B. JONES

See also **Brault, Michel; *Canada Carries On*; *Churchill's Island*; *City of Gold*; Koenig, Wolf; Kroitor, Roman; Legg, Stuart; *Lonely Boy*; Low, Colin; National Film Board of Canada; *Sad Song of Yellow Skin*; Unit B; *Waiting for Fidel*; *World in Action***

Biography

Born in Toronto, Canada, April, 18, 1918. Graduated from the University of Toronto, where he studied classics, in 1940. Joined National Film Board of Canada in September 1940. Retired from the NFB in May 1984.

Selected Films

1945 *Guilty Men*: producer, director, editor
1946 *Hungry Minds*: producer, director, editor
1954 *Corral* (Low): producer, editor; *Paul Tomkowicz: Street-Railway Switchman* (Kroitor): producer
1957 *City of Gold* (Koenig, Low): producer, editor
1958-61 *Candid Eye* (series): executive producer
1960 *Universe* (Kroitor, Low): producer, editor
1961 *Circle of the Sun* (Low): producer, editor; *Lonely Boy* (Koenig, Kroitor): producer
1974 *Sananguagat: Inuit Masterworks* (May): producer; *Waiting for Fidel* (Rubbo): producer
1976 *Blackwood* (Ianzelo): producer; *Coaches* (Cowan), producer
1980 *Last Days of Living* (Gillson): producer
1982 *F.R. Scott: Rhyme and Reason* (Winkler): producer; *Standing Alone* (Low): producer, editor

Further Reading

Cartier-Bresson, Henri, *The Decisive Moment*, New York: Simon and Schuster, 1952.
Daly, Tom, "The Growth of a Craft: My Debt to Legg and Grierson," in *John Grierson and the NFB*, The John Grierson McGill University Project, ECW Press, 1984.
Elder, Bruce, "On the Candid Eye Movement," in *The Canadian Film Reader*, edited by Seth Feldman, Toronto: Peter Martin, 1977.
Harcourt, Peter, "The Innocent Eye," in *Sight and Sound*, winter, 1964–66, 19–23.
Jones, D. B., *Movies and Memoranda*, Ottawa: Deneau, 1982.
———, *The Best Butler in the Business: Tom Daly of the National Film Board of Canada*, Toronto, University of Toronto Press, 1996.
Páquet, André (ed), *How to Make or Not to Make a Canadian Film*, Montreal: La Cinémathéque Canadienne, 1967.

DAVIS, PETER

Director, producer, writer, and cinematographer Peter Davis challenged political and public institutions with his documentary television and film works in the 1970s, courting controversy in the process. He began working on documentaries for CBS television in 1965. Davis served as an associate producer and writer for *Hunger in America* (1968), which won a Writer's Guild Award. For *CBS Reports* he served as a writer and producer of both *Heritage of Slavery* (1968) and *The Battle of East St. Louis* (1968).

This training prepared Davis well for taking on U.S. politics and institutions during the social unrest of the Vietnam War. In *The Selling of the Pentagon* (1971), writer and producer Davis explores how the public relations arm of the Department of Defense manipulated public opinion about the war through propaganda. The film questions how the department spent large amounts of tax money by scrutinizing its films, speakers' bureau, and corporate contracts. The film also looks at how the Pentagon controlled news about the military; daily briefings did present information, but the newsmedia could not verify the information, given much of its status as classified.

The Selling of the Pentagon aired on February 23, 1971. Its controversial subject matter led to a House Special Subcommittee investigation into the film's production. The subcommittee subpoenaed outtakes and other production-related materials, but CBS refused to turn them over, citing the First Amendment. Congress eventually threw out its own subpoena, resulting in a win for CBS. *The Selling of the Pentagon* went on to win an Emmy award.

Davis took a leave of absence from CBS in 1972 to pursue his next project, *Hearts and Minds* (1974). He wanted to explore three questions about the Vietnam War and its impact: "Why did we go to Vietnam? What precisely did we do there? And, what did doing this do, in turn, to all of us?" (Berman, 1975). Davis interviews U.S. political leaders, U.S. military members, Vietnamese leaders, and Vietnamese civilians. Following the direct cinema tradition, Davis remains offscreen. In an interview with famed economist Walt Rostow, Davis, offscreen, asks, "Why do they [the Vietnamese] need us?" Stuttering in surprise, Rostow first replies, "Because they were subject to, uh, military attack from the outside," and after more stuttering, he asks, "Are you really asking me this goddamn silly question?" Unlike other documentaries about the Vietnam War, *Hearts and Minds* features interviews with Vietnamese individuals. Vu Duc Vinh lost both his son and his daughter in a bombing mission. He demands to know, "What have I done to Nixon so that he comes here to bomb my country?" Another unidentified Vietnamese person observes, "Look, they're focusing on us now. First, they bomb as much as they please, then they film." *Hearts and Minds* also incorporates archival footage, including some now-famous images that capture the horror of the Vietnam War. At age 9, Kim Phuc was immortalized in a famous photograph as she ran away from her bombed village, her clothes burned off her body from a napalm blast. Another famous archival piece shows a Vietnamese prisoner shot in the head by a passing military officer. All of these elements combine to create a hard-hitting look at an unpopular war.

Hearts and Minds, like *The Selling of the Pentagon*, generated controversy. Rostow filed an injunction against the film, claiming his reputation was compromised, and the lawsuit provided Columbia Pictures with an excuse for withholding the film from distribution for six months. A California court dismissed the case in January 1975, but Columbia's monetary problems became another obstacle to distribution, until Warner Brothers eventually distributed the film. *Hearts and Minds* won the Oscar for Best Documentary Feature.

The next major project for Davis was *Middletown* (1982), a documentary series about life in Muncie, Indiana. He served as executive producer for the six-episode series, which included *The Campaign*, *The Big Game*, *Community of Praise*, *Family Business*, *Second Time Around*, and *Seventeen*. The series again followed the direct cinema style Davis preferred, and it aired March 24 to April 21, 1982. As with *The Selling of the Pentagon* and *Hearts and Minds*, the series was controversial, especially the episode titled *Seventeen*. An examination of the life of a high school student, the episode includes scenes of pot smoking, interracial dating, drinking, and teen pregnancy. Excessive swearing punctuates the dialogue in the episode. *Seventeen* was never broadcast, partially because of its subject matter and foul language. Because of the episode, sponsor Xerox also withdrew its funding in late January 1982, leaving Davis to scramble for additional funds. Some groups began to campaign for certain cuts, but preferring to leave *Seventeen* intact, he pulled it from the air.

Davis continues exploration of sociopolitical subjects through writing. He is the author of several books, including *Hometown* (1982), *Where Is Nicaragua?* (1987), and *If You Came This Way: A Journey through the Lives of the Underclass* (1995). He currently contributes articles to *The Nation*.

HEATHER McINTOSH

See also **Hearts and Minds; Selling of the Pentagon, The**

Biography

Born in 1937 in Los Angeles to a family of screenwriters. Father, Frank Davis, and mother, Tess Slesinger, did script work on such films as *A Tree Grows in Brooklyn* (Elia Kazan, 1945), *The Train* (John Frankenheimer, 1964), and *The Good Earth* (Sidney Franklin, 1937). In 1957, graduated *magna cum laude* with an English degree from Harvard University. After college, worked as an editorial assistant for the *New York Times*. Drafted by the army in 1959, and during his time in the service he worked as a public relations officer. Following discharge, returned to New York to work as an interviewer, researcher, and writer for Sextant Productions. Worked for WNET-TV. Did film work for WNBC-TV. Currently writes for *The Nation*.

Selected Films

1971 *The Selling of the Pentagon*: director
1974 *Hearts and Minds*: director
1982 *Middletown*: producer

Further Reading

Berman, Bruce, "The Making of *Hearts and Minds*: An Interview with Director Peter Davis," in *Filmmakers Newsletter*, 8, April 1975, 20–24.
Davis, Peter, *Hometown*, New York: Simon and Schuster, 1982.

———, *If You Came This Way: A Journey through the Lives of the Underclass*, New York: John Wiley & Sons, 1995.

———, *Where Is Nicaragua?* New York: Simon and Schuster, 1987.

Handleman, Janet, "The Selling of the Pentagon," in *The Documentary Tradition*, edited by Lewis Jacobs, New York: W. W. Norton, 1979, 518–520.

Hoover, Dwight W. *Middletown: The Making of a Documentary Film Series*. Philadelphia: Harwood, 1992.

Vander Hill, Warren, "The Middletown Film Project: Reflections of an 'Academic Humanist,'" in *Journal of Popular Film and Television*, 10.2, summer 1982, 48–65.

DEAD BIRDS

(US, Gardner, 1963)

Dead Birds is a landmark film by Robert Gardner, about both ritual warfare and cultural conceptions of humanity, as refracted through symbolism of mortality, among the Dugum Dani of Irian Jaya, Indonesia (formerly Netherlands New Guinea). *Dead Birds* marks an extraordinary achievement in both nonfiction filmmaking and in collaborative anthropological research. It is the result of the three-year 1961–1963 Harvard-Peabody New Guinea Expedition. Under the auspices of the Harvard Film Study Center, the Expedition's members included the initiator and filmmaker Robert Gardner; anthropologist Karl Heider as assistant cinematographer; anthropologist Jan Broekhuijse as interpreter; Michael Rockefeller as sound recordist and still photographer; and naturalist and writer Peter Matthiessen.

Although the Dani had already encountered the Western world and industrial modernity before the Harvard-Peabody expedition arrived, many were still using stone axes and conducting warfare with spears and bows and arrows. Gardner has written that his

> job was made much easier because no on knew what I was doing. My camera was no more or less interesting or threatening than my belt buckle or sunglasses. It was part of the strange costume which I always wore and that it made a noise was a matter of complete indifference. I might have been holding a large insect which occasionally murmured as I put it to my eye. Such innocence worked, of course, to my advantage, and I kept as strictly as

possible to the rule that no photographs be shown to anyone.

> ("On the Making of *Dead Birds*," in Karl Heider's *The Dani of West Irian: An Ethnographic Companion to the film* Dead Birds, 1972, pp. 2–34).

This interest in nonacted behavior, unprovoked by the presence of a camera, continues to characterize the core of ethnographic filmmaking today, unlike mainstream documentary, which has become in recent decades increasingly performative and, in certain respects, fictional.

Gardner has explained that the intention of the Expedition was "to make a comprehensive study of a single community of Neolithic warrior farmers . . . [and to] document verbally and visually the whole social and cultural fabric of this community" (Gardner and Heider, 1968, p. xv). Thus, in addition to the feature-length *Dead Birds*, Matthiessen published the ecological essay *Under the Mountain Wall: A Chronicle of Two Seasons in Stone Age New Guinea* (1962), Heider completed his Ph.D. dissertation, *The Dugum Dani* (1970), Broekhuijse authored *De Wiligiman-Dani* (1967), and Gardner and Heider together composed the remarkable photographic essay, *Gardens of War: Life and Death in the New Guinea Stone Age* (1968). With affinities to both the Griaule-Leiris Mission Dakar-Djibouti of 1931–1933 and the Marshall family expedition of 1952–1953, this collaborative Harvard-Peabody Expedition has been essentially without sequel in both the social sciences and the visual arts. Although the aspiration to complete a "comprehensive" verbal and visual documentation of the "whole social and cultural fabric" of the Dani might be thought to imply a yearning after a totalizing holism that has since been abandoned by anthropology, the multi-disciplinary, multi-authored, multi-media, and multi-genre nature of the Expedition and its publications in certain regards prefigured experimental, reflexive anthropology by almost half a century. In Heider's words in *The Dani of West Irian* (1972), a study guide designed to complement the film, the intention was to produce a multitude of image-based and textual materials "from different points of view, and give somewhat different pictures of the Dugum Dani . . . which has important implications for anthropological methodology" (pp. 2–3).

The film is perhaps best known for its extraordinary sequences of actual, unstaged warfare between different Dani alliances. These were produced, it must be remembered, during the Vietnam War, at a time when the ethics of U.S. military involvement in Southeast Asia were on the minds of filmmakers and spectators alike. Although the battle scenes in *Dead Birds* would later be criticized for their synthetic nature—they were composed of shots taken from various battles in various locations—they were no less astonishing for that. As anthropologist Margaret Mead wrote, invoking the contrast between a filmic depiction of people's actual, lived experience, and interview testimony commenting on that experience, "There is a great difference between hearing from the lips of people to whom warfare had been forbidden what war was once like . . . and on the other hand, having a visual record of how such warriors really confront each other across a traditional battlefield" (Gardner and Heider, 1968, p. viii). Moreover, any cut between shots necessarily entails a rupture in time and/or space, and for the most part written ethnography is also synthetic in similar ways to film. *Dead Birds* was also notable for its innovations with technical limitations of the time, especially with the recording of location sound. Produced on the eve of portable synchronous equipment, much of the audio in *Dead Birds*, and even some (unsubtitled) dialogue, was postsynchronized in the editing studio.

Dead Birds follows a classic narrative structure, akin to those of fiction films. It reveals social patterns through the actions of two main characters: Weyak, a warrior, and Pua, a child swineherd who functions as a surrogate son of Weyak. Both stand apart from their peers. Weyak is characterized as

unusually vigilant, and also responsible. Pua, on the other hand, is slower, frailer, and weaker than his friends. As the film progresses, various tensions and contrasts are developed within the narrative. There is the large-scale conflict of Weyak and Pua's alliance against a neighboring one. There are the visual and thematic contrasts between the labor of women and the labor of men. There are the pitfalls little Pua encounters as he struggles to take care of his pigs. There is the larger symbolic contest that humans wage, however vainly, with death. Indeed, the film's climax comes when Wejakhe, a young tribe member, is found dying by the Aikhe River. The film's denouement occurs after his funeral, as Weyak and the others ponder their roles in the boy's death and contemplate revenge, and in turn the audience is implicitly prompted to reflect on its own mortality.

Significantly, much of Gardner's work draws from symbolism and world mythology. *Dead Birds* is no exception. The very title, *Dead Birds*, is a translation of the Dani term for weapons and other ornaments captured during warfare (Gardner, 1972, "On the Making of Dead Birds" in *The Dani of West Irian*, pp. 2–35). The image of birds as a symbol for war, death, and mortality is prevalent throughout the film. Bird plumage is the desired battle attire, as the otherwise almost unclothed Dani adorn themselves with feathered headdresses. After Wejakhe is killed, Pua finds and eats a small dead bird, bedecking himself with its feathers "like a warrior." The recurring, ominous image portending Wejakhe's fate is one of ducks swimming on the Aikhe River. These birds, we are told early on, are avoided at all costs because of the debilitating magic they contain. They ascend with piercing squawks as the narrator announces Wejakhe's death. It is later revealed to be the very place where Wejakhe ("wrong path") is killed.

In addition to presenting its disparate images of battles as a pastiche of a single battle, *Dead Birds* has been criticized on various counts. The apparently affectless narration, voiced in the third-person passive by Robert Gardner himself, has been taken to task for its omniscience of its characters' actions and thoughts, at times resulting in a literal one-to-one correspondence between picture and sound track. However, anthropologist Karl Heider has contended that the thoughts and sensations attributed to individual Dani in the film are, to his mind, entirely credible. Moreover, as with that in John Marshall's *The Hunters*, it is also possible to understand the narration as an experimental exercise in mythopoetic representation, obliquely evoking the inner lives of its subjects through narratively constructed poetic symbolism, rather than as purporting to convey a comprehensive, objective account of their thought processes *in toto*.

Additionally, the film has been criticized in contemporary classrooms for its inattention to the lives of Dani women. Although the bulk of women's activities are shown in a subordinate light to those of men, this criticism is not entirely correct. We are introduced to Weyak's wife, Lakha, and follow her and other women as they process salt (even if the salt-making is intercut, as parallel action, with the more visually arresting scenes from the battlefield). Later in the film, after Wejakhe's death, women and girls figure prominently—as funeral mourners and as instruments of religious sacrifice. Indeed, one of the most unsparing sequences of the film shows tiny girls whose fingers have been partially chopped off by the Dani in order to placate the ghosts of the deceased. For all its containment within the symbolic logic of the film, the realism and violence of this sequence in many ways resists metalinguistic translation, making it both "cruel," in Antonin Artaud's sense, and "obtuse," in Roland Barthes's sense.

Finally, some anthropologists have taken Gardner to task for being a universalist, with insufficient interest in and knowledge of the cultural particularities of the subjects he has chosen for his films. However, this line of criticism is arguably more revealing about the trajectory of late twentieth-century cultural anthropology, with its increasing and arguably disproportionate attention to cultural difference in the face of widespread global homogenization, than it is a shortcoming of the films themselves. As Gardner himself has spoken of *Dead Birds*:

> I seized the opportunity of speaking to certain fundamental issues in human life. The Dani were then less important to me than those issues . . . . I saw the Dani people, feathered and fluttering men and women, as enjoying the fate of all men and women. They dressed their lives with plumage, but faced as certain death as the rest of us drabber souls. The film attempts to say something about how we all, as humans, meet our animal fate.
>
> ("On the Making of Dead Birds" in *The Dani of West Irian* (1972), pp. 2-34–2-35).

In 1989, Gardner returned to the Baliem Valley to work on a sequel film, called *Roads End*. While there he located both Pua and Weyak, who were working in the tourist industry. Although a video cassette copy of *Dead Birds* had made its way to the local Protestant Mission, it had not been seen by its subjects. Gardner consequently arranged (and documented on film) a screening of *Dead Birds* for them. Afterwards, Gardner wrote,

> It was not long before I realized that it hardly mattered what they saw that day. Their pleasure was not in the shape but in the content of what they watched. The film could have begun in the middle or gone backwards or forwards or have been composed of any of the thousands of scene that had been left out when I edited the film so scrupulously more than twenty-five years ago.

(Gardner, 1993, p. 65)

ILISA BARBASH

See also **Gardner, Robert**

Dead Birds (USA, Harvard Film Study Center, 1964, 85 mins.). Produced by the Film Study Center of the Peabody Museum with help from the former Netherlands Guinea Government and the National Science Foundation. Direction, photography, editing, writing by Robert Gardner. Sound recording by Michael C. Rockefeller. Sound editing by Jarius Lincoln and Joyce Chopra. Photographic assistant, Karl G. Heider. Titles by Peter Chermayeff. Advisors, Jan Broekhuisje and Peter Matthiessen. Filmed in Irian Jaya, Indonesia.

Further Reading

Barbash, Ilisa, "Out of Words: The Aesthesodic Cine-Eye of Robert Gardner: An Exegesis and Interview," *Visual Anthropology*, 14, no. 4, 2001.

Cooper, Thomas W., *Natural Rhythms: The Indigenous World of Robert Gardner*, New York: Anthology Film Archives, 1995.

Gardner, Robert, "The Impulse to Preserve," in *Beyond Document: Essays on Non-Fiction Film*, edited by Charles Warren, Hanover, NH: University Press of New England, 1996.

———, "On the Making of *Dead Birds*" in *The Dani of West Irian: An Ethnographic Companion to the Film* Dead Birds, edited by Karl Heider, Warner Modular Publications, Module 2, 1972.

Gardner, Robert, and Karl G. Heider, *Gardens of War: Life and Death in the New Guinea Stone Age*, New York: Random House, 1968.

Heider, Karl G., *Ethnographic Film*, Austin: University of Texas Press, 1976.

———, *The Dani of West Irian: An Ethnographic Companion to the Film* Dead Birds, Warner Modular Publications, Module 2, 1972.

———, *The Dugum Dani: A Papuan Culture in the Highlands of West New Guinea*, New York: Wenner-Gren Foundation for Anthropological Research, Incorporated, 1970.

Mattheissen, Peter, *Under the Mountain Wall: A Chronicle of Two Seasons in the Stone Age*, New York: The Viking Press, 1962.

Mead, Margaret, "Introduction," from *Gardens of War: Life and Death in the New Guinea Stone Age*, New York: Random House, 1968.

Ruby, Jay, *Picturing Culture*, Chicago: University of Chicago Press, 2000.

DEATH OF A PRINCESS

(UK, Thomas, 1980)

Death of a Princess was one of the most controversial documentary dramas ever screened on British television. Filmed in the style of the investigative documentary for which British television had achieved a justified reputation in the postwar period, it depicts a journalist's attempt to discover the truth behind the public executions of a member of the Saudi royal family and her lover. London's *Daily Express* had reported the incident in 1977, using the account of a British contract construction worker who had witnessed and taken photographs of the executions. Antony Thomas, a South African–born documentary filmmaker, researched this story of royal adultery and its punishment under Islamic law in both the UK and the Middle East between July and November 1978. He was struck by the stark contrasts in interpretation among the various Western and Arab witnesses and authorities he met.

The film caused a diplomatic furor before and after its screening in 1980. Between April (just before the film was transmitted) and July, diplomatic relations between Saudi Arabia and Britain were directly affected. The Saudis at one point asked ATV to withdraw the film; at another time, they demanded cuts to be made. King Khalid's planned State Visit to Britain was then cancelled, and finally Lord Carrington, the British Foreign Minister, felt constrained to offer what amounted to an apology. Only then could relations be normalised and lucrative contracts for British industry restored. In the United States, too, there was pressure on the PBS network from both government and programme sponsors (Mobil Oil) to withdraw the film. It was, however, transmitted in the UK, Europe, Australasia, and the United States.

The controversial subject caused additional questions to be asked about the form and function of the film. Writer/producer Thomas chose to dramatise his own real quest for truth about this historical incident via a fiction structured like a documentary. He did this, he claimed, because he was especially concerned about protecting his Arab sources. He also felt that the very excess evident in the opinions and prejudices the incident generated meant that fictional analogy held out greater possibilities than pure documentary. Thomas's intention was to interrogate the difficulty of establishing truth through the documentary form in a fraught situation where cultures were clashing. Ironically, he succeeded in making the East/West situation even more fraught, as well as raising questions about the legitimacy of the documentary drama. *Death of a Princess* was accused of blurring the boundaries between fiction and nonfiction, and it intensified the debate about what was permissible in mixing modes on broadcast television.

The film illustrates the truth of the proposition that it is never the form of a documentary drama

Death of a Princess, 1980 Documentary by Anthony Thomas on the Execution of a Saudi Princess and Her Lover.
[*Courtesy of the Everett Collection*]

that causes controversy in the wider political world beyond media representation. Thomas's angle on the comprehension gap between Western and Middle Eastern societies was certainly sophisticated; the film's self-conscious attempt to meditate on the wider ramifications of the act of representation makes it into one of the first "meta-documentary dramas." The film's main protagonist, standing for Thomas himself, is journalist Christopher Ryder (played by Paul Freeman). Identification with this character situates the audience in the subject position of "seeker after truth." Ryder takes a literal and metaphorical "journey to the East" as a kind of cultural explorer (clearly evident in a central sequence of the film in which shots of religious chanting and calls to prayer are juxtaposed with his difficulties in making headway with Saudi officials).

In Ryder's gathering bafflement can be discerned a critique of the documentary claim of authenticity as well as a measurement of the East/West divide. By 1980, documentary no longer had an unproblematical claim on truth—its essentially constructed nature being increasingly seen by academics as based on a questionable belief in the representational power of the camera and the quasi-legal authority of the witness. In the narrative structure of *Death of a Princess* can also be seen the fictional template of an international thriller. This genre-hybridizing tendency was to become a major feature of late twentieth-century British and American docudrama.

Death of a Princess, 1980 Documentary by Anthony Thomas on the Execution of a Saudi Princess and Her Lover.
[*Courtesy of the Everett Collection*]

The form, then, was more conscious, more knowing, in 1980 than it ever had been before, but it did not protect this film from blatantly aberrant readings in the public sphere. Its co-producer, Martin McKeand, once remarked that it became a film about which everybody had an opinion—even if they had not actually seen it. The controversy was primarily generated by the sensitive nature of U.S./European relations with the Middle East at this point in history. Formal experimentation was no guarantee against the film becoming a media event, and part of a wider "moral panic." The film's fascination for a Western audience was increased by the portrait it offered of a sexually active Arab woman making choices in a quasi-Western way. (Allegedly, Saudi princesses regularly procured men for casual sex.) Ten years after the beginning of the women's movement, this aspect played provocatively to Western audiences, going against the stereotype of the submissive Arab woman hidden behind a veil. The punishment suffered by the Arab princess was all the more shocking when seen from this angle. Thus, not only was the Saudi government infuriated but also postcolonial cultural commentators such as Edward Said (in his *Covering Islam*, 1981) felt that the film shamelessly used the Arab as "Other" and was more interested in debating Western social and political issues than in understanding Middle Eastern culture and values.

The documentary drama achieves a kind of formal maturity in films like *Death of a Princess*, even more so than in the other "foreign policy" films of the same era. Many of these dealt with the struggle toward political liberalization in Iron Curtain satellite states (e.g., Granada's 1980 *Invasion*). Because they had a European cultural and political focus, and human rights credentials, these films were seen as campaigning against the worst abuses of a discredited political system. *Death of a Princess*, by contrast, mobilised a much more complex set of issues. Issues of form, function, and reception have continued to reverberate around the documentary drama.

DEREK PAGET

See also **Thomas, Antony**

Death of a Princess (tx. 09/04/80 120 mins.). Co-production UK (ATV), USA (WGBH, Boston), Netherlands (Telepictures), Australia (Seven Network), New Zealand (Eastern Media). Produced by Antony Thomas and Martin McKeand. Directed by Antony Thomas. Scripted by Antony Thomas and Sala Jaheen.

DECEMBER 7

(US, Ford/Toland, 1942)

December 7 deals with the surprise attack on U.S. military installations in Hawaii by the Japanese in 1941. Two versions exist. The first, an 83-minute docudrama, was never released to the public. The other, comprising 34 minutes of footage drawn entirely from this original, was exhibited widely, winning an Oscar for Best Short Subject in 1943. Footage from *December 7* has since been used extensively in World War II documentaries—yet almost all of it is bogus, having been created in a Hollywood studio. Through constant repetition, its spurious images have become the accepted record of the "Day of Infamy."

The U.S. government, in consultation with John Ford, chose Gregg Toland (photographer of *Citizen Kane*) to direct. In Hawaii Toland discovered that less than six minutes of indifferent quality footage of the actual raids existed. On his return to Hollywood, he proceeded to restage events using miniatures, rear screen, and matte projection. U.S. aircraft were painted with Japanese insignia and military personnel were pressed into service as extras. The dramatic leads were played by Walter Huston, Charles Davenport, and Dana Andrews.

A weary Uncle Sam (Huston) is convalescing in Hawaii on December 6 after a year of international crises that have sorely tried his endurance. His conscience (Davenport), whose geniality masks a racism no less chilling for being charmingly delivered, materialises to cast doubt on America's trust in the loyalty of the 157,000 Japanese Americans on the islands. A series of vignettes would seem to prove a proliferation of spies exists. Also bemoaned is the ostrich-like behaviour of Washington's politicians faced with evidence of Japanese militarism in the Far East. Following the simulated raids and massive reconstruction effort, the film concludes in Arlington National Cemetery with a ghostly sailor (Andrews) insisting to a skeptical fellow-phantom from the Great War that the United States will not return to its isolationist shell when this conflict ends.

Official reaction was almost unanimously negative. The major flaw was seen as the picture's fence-sitting equivocation. Effective screen propaganda must be factually selective, allowing no room for doubt or compassion. Those aims are not achieved by providing a forum for reasoned debate. Given *December 7*'s intended audience, the need was for a work that would elicit a negative response to all things Japanese as well as pride in the accomplishments of those who had literally salvaged much from the débâcle that was Pearl Harbor. The print remained locked away until 1943, when Ford suggested the government could obtain some recompense for its $80,000 investment. The result was the abbreviated version, shorn of all but the attacks and reconstruction footage.

December 7 in either format is not a negligible achievement. It provides an excitement and immediacy few World War Two documentaries surpass. Continued recourse to its images by filmmakers over the past half-century bears testimony to its lasting impact and, specifically, to the visual and dramatic flair of Gregg Toland, its discredited director.

JAMES SKINNER

December 7 (USA, Field Photographic Unit, 1942-43, 83 & 34 mins.). Produced by John Ford. Directed by Gregg Toland and John Ford. Shooting script by Sam Engel. Edited by Robert Parrish. Music by Alfred Newman.

Further Reading/Viewing

Eye of the Eagle: December 7. Documentary hosted by Richard Schickel. Britannica Learning Materials, Cambridge, Ontario, Canada. VHS format.

Gallagher, Tag, *John Ford: The Man and His Films*, Berkeley: University of California Press, 1986.

Koppes, Clayton R., and Gregory D. Black, *Hollywood Goes to War: How Politics and Profits Shaped World War II Movies*, New York, NY: The Free Press, 1987.

Murphy, William T., "John Ford and the Wartime Documentary," in *Film and History* 4, February 1986.

Rollins, Peter C. (ed.), *Hollywood as Historian: American Film in a Cultural Context*, Lexington: University of Kentucky Press, 1983.

Skinner, James M., "December 7: Filmic Myth Masquerading as Historical Fact" in *Journal of Military History*, 55, no. 4, October 1991, pp. 507–516.

DECONSTRUCTION, DOCUMENTARY FILM AND

Deconstruction is a critical practice founded by French-Algerian philosopher Jacques Derrida (1930–2004) who, along with a group of literary scholars in the United States including Paul de Man (1919–1983), Geoffrey Hartman, and J. Hillis Miller, came to be seen as members of a movement in the 1960s and 1970s. The term, first used by German philosopher Martin Heidegger (1889–1976), refers to a mode of analysis that focuses on the logical foundation or structure of a work and exposes the very idea of structure as essentially unstable. As the name implies, deconstruction is an investigation of structures and their relation to forms, discourses, and representations.

For Derrida, deconstruction initiates a mode of reading: It recognizes that in the structural foundation of any work resides a set of uninterrogated assumptions that interfere with the completion of a work. Following Nietzsche, Derrida identifies these premises as "Western meta-physics," a system of fixed ideas that generate unexamined axioms of truth and untruth, reality and fantasy, meaning and nonsense, subjectivity and otherness, and so on. The deconstruction of Western meta-physics seeks to discover the transcendental core of each work and expose the logical contradiction it produces. In a deconstructive reading, each work is divided from itself, but is also revealed to have always sustained this self-division: Deconstruction is thus less a dismantling than a displacement of each work from itself. At the foundation of every work lies a multiplicity of competing works, filled with displacements, deferrals, and traces of other works.

Deconstruction is also a sensibility, a phenomenal orientation that leads one to look not only at the surfaces and themes of a specific work but also at the relationship between expressed ideas and the rhetorical structures that facilitate them. Derrida's writings form a veritable archive of theses, reflections, and speculations on visuality and sound, as well as on perception, sensuality, and fantastic experience as such. In spite of the attempts to describe it as such, deconstruction is neither a technique nor an application forced on works from the outside. In this sense, the conflicted relationship between deconstruction and a certain practice of journalism yields significant consequences for the subject of documentary.

In place of systems and repeatable methods, each deconstructive reading is always closely allied with the work it engages, and is built around the specific contours of that work. Deconstruction is a kind of graft: The language and idiom of each deconstructive reading is drawn from the work under investigation, and comes to resemble the work as a mimetic extension of it. As such, no deconstructive reading can ever be repeated; one set of protocols can never be transferred from one work to another. Each reading generates a new but finite language. As Derrida often noted, most texts are prone to an autodeconstruction; to a moment of self-disclosure achieved by pursuing a particular logic and rhetorical economy to its end. Deconstruction never destroys or dismantles a work, but rather exposes it; deconstruction reveals a work that is at odds with itself, fraught with ambiguities and unresolved conflicts—in a literal sense, a work beside itself or a para-work.

Earlier deconstructive criticism of the 1960s and 1970s addressed philosophical and literary works, but since then, deconstruction has engaged other genres of writing as well as a wide spectrum of media. It has traveled across the arts, humanities, and social sciences; into the fields of architecture, art, film, law, politics, and sexuality, among many others; and has been taken up by activists, artists, scholars, and students around the world. Derrida himself resisted the term *deconstruction* and its application to his work for much of his career, but relented and began to use the term—although almost always in a qualified manner—when he realized it had gained a currency apart from him. Deconstruction provides new perspectives for the visual arts in particular, especially for the set of discursive and formal practices that constitute documentary film and video.

The relationship between deconstruction and documentary film, video, and television is particularly instructive since the idea of documentary has been bound, like deconstruction, by a set of familiar but also contested assertions vis-à-vis the documentation and representation of actuality, reality, and, ultimately, truth as such. Regarding the question of truth, deconstruction and documentary can be said to move—in a superficial register—in opposing directions. The overstatements that have characterized deconstruction and documentary film and video would appear to be antithetical: Documentary insists on reality, whereas deconstruction denies its existence. Documentary establishes and renders an order of truth, whereas deconstruction abolishes truth and refuses its representability. (The assertion that Derrida denies reality and truth is a fabrication repeated frequently by careless and sometimes malicious journalists who tend to cite each other rather than primary sources. Derrida insists on the necessity and value of truth and reality, and perhaps most importantly, justice. He challenges without apology, however, those claims made in the name of truth and reality that come at the expense of excluded figures, typically minorities and women, but more broadly the voiceless, including prisoners, animals, and others condemned to suffer in the name of truth and justice. The most progressive aspects of documentary theory and practice closely resemble the deeply ethical and experimental nature of Derrida's work.) The absolute nature of each claim regarding deconstruction and documentary is disproved by a body of works, texts, and documents that question both the impossibility of any unequivocal representation of truth and, at the same time, the impossibility of abandoning the pursuit of truth and justice.

The most radical forms of documentary film and video have unrelentingly disturbed the assertion of self-evident truths. Can a historical event be truly recounted in a documentary? What does it mean to portray another individual or culture? Can the singularity of life—one's own or another's—be authentically rendered in a film or video? What are the limitations as well as the possibilities of representing the unrepresentable? The most creative and innovative documentaries have posed questions that disrupt the very projects at hand without abandoning the possibility of the project, the possibility of arriving in another, entirely unintended realm of discovery. Like deconstruction, documentary practice supplements the inherent brevity and speed of journalism. The idea of documentary—pursued to its limit, to the critical intersection of reality and its representation—is deconstruction. More than any other medium and more than any other genre of film and television, documentary film and video illuminates the activities of a deconstructive inquiry that posits, points to, frames, renders, and then questions its own rhetoric and the viability of its own attempts at representation.

Derrida was himself the subject of two documentary films, Safaa Fathy's *D'ailleurs, Derrida* (*Derrida's Elsewhere*, 1999) and Amy Ziering Kofman and Kirby Dick's *Derrida* (2002). In each quasi-biography, Derrida produces a meta-commentary on the nature of biography and autobiography, challenging the configuration of the apparatus, alluding to the unnatural conditions of a film biography, and underscoring the impossibility of achieving an authentic biography in any medium. Other documentaries that can be seen as forms of deconstruction include Jean Rouch and Edgar Morin's *cinéma verité* work, *Chronique d'un été* (*Chronicle of a Summer*, 1961), which generates a *mise-en-abîme,* or film within a film by persistently questioning its own mode of production. Claude Lanzmann's *Shoah* (1985) seeks to distinguish between the documentation and representation of the unrepresentable genocide of Jews during World War II by eschewing images and affect and insisting instead on detailed testimony, witness accounts, and interviews with both survivors and participants. It seeks to generate a picture without pictures. Trinh T. Minh-ha has sought in an important body of work to travel along the borders that separate documentary from fiction, subjectivity from its outside, and oneself from the many others that inhabit the world. Many more filmmakers and video artists have taken up deconstructive themes, inadvertently or not, before and after the fact, rendering the practice of deconstruction autonomous and diverse. Sadie Benning, Stan Brakhage, Emile de Antonio, Haroun Farocki, Peter Forgacs, Su Friedrich, Errol Morris, Hara Kazuo, Frederick Wiseman, Walid Raad, Marlon Riggs, Jay Rosenblatt, Rea Tajiri, and Caveh Zahedi, to name only a few, have made films and videos that defer a total revelation by insisting on the impossibility of unqualified knowledge. Jane Gaines, Bill Nichols, Michael Renov, B. Ruby Rich, Trinh T. Minh-ha, and Brian Winston are among the many critics and theorists who have deployed forms of deconstruction to illuminate the complex forces that inscribe race and identity, actuality and truth, and violence and politics in a myriad of documentary works. In the hands of critical documentarians and theorists, documentary comes to resemble deconstruction, a method of critique and observation that yields profound insights and produces rigorous work, while challenging the complacency of final truths and fixed realities.

AKIRA MIZUTA LIPPIT

See also **Brakhage, Stan; Chronique d'un été; de Antonio, Emile; Forgacs, Peter; Morris, Errol; Nichols, Bill; Riggs, Marlon; Shoah; Trinh T. Minh-ha; Wiseman, Frederick**

DEL MERO CORAZÓN

(US, Blank, 1979)

According to its collaborators, director Les Blank's *Del mero corazón: Love Songs of the Southwest* (1980) was an attempt to preserve some of the cutting-room leftovers from their previous venture into the world of Tejano and Norteña music, *Chulas fronteras* (1975) / *Beautiful Borders*. In the process of making the first film, the scope of the subject matter grew from an investigation of a regional music tradition into a poetic commentary on the lifestyles and hardships of the musicians and the communities that support them. Producer and sound recorder Chris Strachwitz worried that despite the cinematic accomplishment of *Chulas*, many of the songs that initially sparked his interested in the subject—the heart-wrenching love ballads—were not given enough depth. A DVD released by Strachwitz's Arhoolie Records in 2003 puts both films together, with an abundance of commentary and outtakes from the entire project.

Watching the films in chronological order, *Del mero corazón's* stylistic and thematic inspiration can be seen in two of *Chula's* most poignant moments: In an interview the legendary Lydia Mendoza explains that with every song she performs, she experiences emotionally what the lyrics detail; later, the camera fixates on a taut barbed wire, pulls its focus to a spiny cactus paddle, continues to the plant's bursting yellow blossoms, all while the lead vocalist of Los Alegres de Teran bittersweetly contemplates long-distance love. The latter sequence illustrates the overlay of lyrical poetry and symbolically relevant images that serves as the staple of *Del mero corazón's* montage structure. The result is an audiovisual poem stripped of narrative interpretation, which allows the viewer—like Mendoza—to live rather than listen to each song on the soundtrack.

The film's opening sequence shows a hand chopping *chiles*, barbecue festivities, several close-ups of flames and glowing embers, and a crimson crepuscular sky. As each shot burns red, the lyrics of Ricardo Mejía and Rubén Valdez's "Seis pies abajo" ("Six Feet Under") weeps of unrequited love and bleeding hearts. At same time, the boun-

cing accordion and rhythmic clapping align the mood with the general revelry of the banquet, pointing out that tragic lyrics and celebratory music are not mutually exclusive in the culture under scrutiny.

The film's primary concern is a consistent matching of visual, musical, and emotional passions in a variety of settings. In nearly all of the 12 sequences, a unique musical track is performed, while the visuals build a bricolage of voyage and place icons, from trains and 18-wheeler trucks, to the landscape they traverse and the towns and truck stops they approach. Spliced together five years after *Chulas* was released, *Corazón* makes a point to "travel" beyond its predecessor's border theme. The footage is taken primarily from filming done in San Antonio, Texas, and Monterrey, Nuevo León; it also includes performances in California, showing that the Tejano music's audience is geographically

Del Mero Corazón, 1979.
[*Still courtesy of the British Film Institute*]

broader than its name implies. Much like *Chulas,* it brings the political issues of migratory work and travel (in particular with regard to the toll distance takes on romantic relationships) into a film that at first glance simply celebrates the southwestern traditions of music and dance, food, and beer. One fictitious heroine's story pervades various lyrics in both films with Homeric tribulations, as Zenaida's laments are interpreted in corridos by Los Madrugadores and later by Andrés Berlanga.

In two sequences late in the film, the interview and performances of accordionist Chavela Ortiz break up the masculine voices and gazes, bring an inspirational air of political evolution to this musical field heavy with history and tradition. Ortiz tells of her beginnings performing with her mother and sister, but that neither chose to continue due to the pressure and resentment shown by many male colleagues, romantic partners, and audience members. Ortiz persisted and succeeded despite the same struggle until her untimely death after the production of the film (mentioned by the filmmakers in the 2003 DVD commentary). This documentation of her music and insight augments *Del mero corazón's* value as a cultural-historical artifact.

Rich in color, the film uses fuchsia stucco buildings and aqua wedding attire to underscore the musical excitement. Hand-painted graphics on the façades of Mexican and Texan businesses, along with California murals, show how the vibrant rural landscape infuses artistic and artisan sensibilities. The desire to capture the chromatic intensity can be seen carried over into editor Maureen Gosling's later directorial work, *Blossoms of Fire* (2000), about the matriarchal Zapotec culture of Mexico. Gosling considers this project with Blank and Strachwitz to have informed much of her later work on Latin American cultures. At other points in the film, the colorful exteriors are left behind in order to show the true home of the music: inside the bars, cantinas, and dance halls. Les Blank films an energetic performance by Leo Garza's *conjunto,* with shots from a shadowy stage behind the two vocalists. The camerawork creates the aura of their sweat-drenched profiles with the moisture reflecting a makeshift lighting set-up attached to the rafters of an otherwise dark locale. The film ends by studying the details of a Chicano Power mural in California while the ballad "Las Nubes" / "The Clouds," updated to a 1970s sound and style with electronic keyboards and infusion of English call-outs, is performed by Little Joe y la familia. The vocalist contemplates a life journey of political struggle, and much as in *Chulas,* the theme of love is pushed beyond romance, to cultural pride, passion, and self-empowerment.

The few small segments of narration in the film, read by María Antonia Contreras, are recent. Historical lyrical texts chosen by professor of Hispanic literature professor Guillermo Hernández to underscore the Mexican American culture's extensive tradition of emotive expression through lyrical verse. The film is seamlessly subtitled for both Spanish- and English-speaking audiences, thanks to a government grant awarded to the filmmakers shortly after the production of Blank's *Burden of Dreams* (1982), allowing several of the director's films to be screened throughout Latin America.

MISHA MACLAIRD

See also **Chulas fronteras**

Del Mero Corazón (US, Blank, 1979, 29 mins.). Directed and written by Les Blank. Produced by Les Blank and Chris Strachwitz. Edited by Maureen Gosling.

DENKMAL-FILM

DENKmal-Film started as an ambitious collective guided by idealistic principles: to work collectively on all projects, shared ownership and control of all production equipment, free choice of topics drawn from political-social issues, intended to give the underprivileged a voice.

The collective began in 1976 with three members: Bertram Verhaag, Claus Strigel, and Walter Harrich, who left DENKmal-Film in 1983. The name they had chosen has two meanings in German. The first is "memorial," and the other is "think one time."

From the beginning, DENKmal-Film wanted to avoid the boring monotony of educational film. They wanted their films to be popular and raise curiosity. Although Bertram Verhaag and Claus Strigel no longer produce all their films together, having developed their own distinctive style, they have worked together on 75 documentaries, 9 feature-length documentaries, and 5 fiction films.

Many of the films of the collective depict the struggle of the individual for his or her rights, or the individual's daily struggle. In *Der Mensch an sich . . . /There Is No Consideration . . .* (1980) the filmmakers followed for three years a group of senior citizens who tried to stop their homes from being destroyed to make way for the construction of luxury bungalows. One of DENKmal-Film's main topics was ecological issues in general and especially the fight against nuclear power. *Spaltprozesse/Nuclear Split* (1987) depicts the nuclear energy policies linked with the planned construction of a reprocessing plant in Wackersdorf. The whole region fought successfully against this plant. The film won over a dozen festival prizes, including the Silver Dove at the International Leipzig Documentary Festival 1987.

Restrisiko/Residual Risk (1989) presents the arrogance of powerful people who ignore the justified fears and objections of citizens and scientists. In *Das achte Gebot/The Eighth Commandment* (1991) the filmmakers offer evidence to support the belief that the use of nuclear energy could only be made acceptable through the constant and repeated deception of the majority of the population. *Sonnengeflecht/ Solar Plexus* (1995) presents a sturdy solar boiler that is easy to build and extremely efficient. In *Tote Ernte/Killing Seeds* (2001), a Canadian farmer fights against a multinational agrochemical corporation that sued him for patent violation. That is contrasted with a protest movement in Germany against genetically modified corn. *Die grüne Wolke/The Last Man Alive* (2001) was a huge feature film production and a nine-part television series based on the novel of A. S. Neills.

Another crucial topic for DENKmal-Film is the conditions faced by people in modern German society, and how they handle their psychological and social problems. An interesting trilogy was on the individual's relation to the trappings of modern life, including the television, the computer, and the car, clearly depicting people's dependence on them. All three films are made in a very essayistic style. *Blue Eyed* (1996), which brought Bertram Verhaag international fame, documents the seminars of Jane Elliot. The blue-eyed participants are confronted with pseudo-scientific explanations of their inferiority, culturally biased IQ tests, and discrimination.

Although their thematic range is broad, most DENKmal-made films address issues of power and control, and have an emotional style. The renunciation of any commentary is perhaps the most striking stylistic trait common to DENKmal-made films.

DENKmal-Film bought an Avid nonlinear editing system in 1991, and they continue to explore the new aesthetic possibilities of digital editing for the documentary genre.

KAY HOFFMANN

Selected Films

1978 *Klaufieber [Thief Feaver]:* director, producer (Strigel)

1980 *Der Mensch an sich wird nicht in Betracht gezogen / There Is No Consideration Given to the People:* director, producer (Verhaag, Strigel)

1986 *Kinder brauchen Zombies / Children Need Zombies:* director, producer (Strigel)

1987 *Spaltprozesse/ Nuclear Split:* director, producer (Verhaag, Strigel), author (Verhaag)

1989 *Tatort Familie / Crime Scene Family:* director, producer (Strigel)

1989 *Restrisiko oder die Arroganz der Macht / Residual Risk or the Arrogance of Power:* director, producer (Verhaag, Strigel), author (Verhaag)

1991 *Das achte Gebot/ The Eighth Commandment:* director, producer (Verhaag, Strigel), author (Jutty Sartory, Verhaag)

1991 *Mama Pappa Auto / Mum, Dad, Car:* director, producer (Strigel, Verhaag), author (Strigel)

1992 *Angst — Tor zur Freiheit / Fear—Gate to Freedom:* director, author, producer (Verhaag)

1993 *Bleiben Sie dran! / Stay Tuned:* director, producer (Strigel, Verhaag), author (Strigel)

1995 *Sonnengeflecht / Solar Plexus:* director, producer (Verhaag)

1996 *Beziehungskiste / The Great Love Affair:* director, author, producer (Strigel)

1996 *Blue Eyed:* director, author, producer (Verhaag)

1997 *Grenzgänger / The Cross-Over Artist:* director, author (Verhaag), producer (Strigel)

2000 *Der Agrar-Rebell / The Agro Rebel:* director, producer (Verhaag)

2000 *Die grüne Wolke / The Last Man Alive:* director (Strigel), author (Strigel, Martin Östreicher), producer (Verhaag)

2001 *Los Alamos / The Secret and the Sacred:* producer (Strigel)

2001 *Tote Ernte / Killing Seeds:* director (Kai Krüger, Verhaag), producer (Verhaag)

2002 *Planet Hasenbergl:* director, producer (Strigel)

2002 *86000 Sekunden—Irgendwann ein Tag in Amerika / 86,000 Seconds—Sometimes Someday in America:* director, producer (Verhaag)

Further Reading

Koch, Luitgard, "Lichtgestalten im Fernsehalltag," in *Natur*, 11/1995, 98–100.

Matschek-Labitzke, Birgit, "Claus Strigel / Bertram Verhaag. Bayerische Spaltprozesse," in *Dokumentarisches Fernsehen*, edited by Cornelia Bolesch, Munic, Leipzig: List, 1990, 101–104.

Rasper, Martin, "Vier Fäuste für ein Filmprojekt," in *Cut*, 12/1997 + 1/1998.

Vahabzadeh, Susan, "Fiktion wird Wirklichkeit. Wie Claus Strigel den Roman 'Die grüne Wolke' verfilmte," in *Süddeutsche Zeitung*, 2/2001.

DEPARDON, RAYMOND

Raymond Depardon began his professional life as a photographic journalist. Having worked for press agencies and co-founded the agency Gamma in 1966, his subsequent move into filmmaking in 1969—with his first film *Ian Pallach*—owes a great deal to his initial training. Although the trajectory of his career has gradually taken him away from the more journalistic reportage style of the earlier work, his filming and his photography remain inextricably linked. Known mainly for his documentaries, Depardon also explores the border between fact and fiction, straying into the latter domain almost entirely in some films (e.g., *Empty Quarter*) and revisiting documentary subjects to test the limits of fictional representation in others (e.g., *Tchad (2) et (3)* and *La Captive du désert*). From the outset, he has traveled the world to work in settings as varied as Prague, Yemen, Chad, India, and New York, to name but a few, but returning periodically yet repeatedly to film French-based subjects in Parisian and, most recently, rural settings.

Depardon became interested in filmmaking at a time when the direct cinema of Leacock, Pennebaker, and the Maysles brothers was prominent. When he eventually began making his own films, they turned out to be more influenced by this U.S. tradition than by that of the French *cinéma vérité* of Rouch. Depardon's filming is not participatory in the Rouchian sense in that he does not intervene or communicate with his subjects, nor does he explicitly interrogate his own relationship to them. Although the filmed subjects of his documentaries may acknowledge the presence of the camera, neither Depardon nor any of his assistants stages this encounter in order to turn the camera on the observer(s).

This activity is saved for his more autobiographical, self-reflective works. Another crucial connection to the direct cinema tradition is via the work of Wiseman. Like Wiseman in the United States, Depardon has filmed institutions crucial to the French establishment, notably in the three films *Faits divers*, *Urgences*, and *Délits flagrants*, all set in Paris, which deal respectively with law and order, psychiatric health care, and justice. In contrast to the filming of Wiseman, however, Depardon films the institutions concerned in order to focus on the people who allow them to function and not on a critique of the institutions in themselves.

Although infinitely varied in approach to his subjects and adopting a correspondingly appropriate style, Depardon's films have traits that recall the influence of still photography in his work. The photograph features literally in *Les Années Déclic,* as does discussion of the profession of photographer in. *Reporters* and in his section of the collaboratively made *Contacts*. Yet, even when there is no place afforded to the photographic still, Depardon's filming is characterized by a patient, motionless focus that is reminiscent of this other medium. This is particularly apparent in the Parisian-based *Urgences* and *Délits flagrants*, for example, where the psychiatric emergencies of the Hôtel Dieu and the interviews of offenders at the Palais de Justice are stationary encounters. Even within the films that deploy this fixed framing technique most frequently, the camera becomes more mobile when necessary. However, when he uses the long static shot, Depardon does not steer the viewer's gaze to certain aspects of a given scene but keeps a steady focus on the space of the encounter, allowing people to enter or leave it without following them.

Depardon waits for his subjects to come into the space of his enclosure rather than moving into theirs, even though he is conscious of being located in the space of the other as soon as he begins filming. He keeps his distance, an ethical one in some respects, but he is fully aware that approaching any of his subjects with a camera is a form of violence. He comments specifically on the violence of the filming encounter when making *San Clemente*—set in the Italian asylum. His contribution to *Contacts* focuses on the photographer as a professional voyeur, distance here becoming ultimately more damaging than respectful. Continuing from his desire not to disturb the scene he is filming, this does not, however, prevent him from focusing on himself in other ways. Indeed, consideration of the filming self becomes an important ethical concern. The presence of what he terms "le regard mixte" or "la caméra mixte" in the fiction *Empty Quarter* is an attempt to negotiate a point of view for the camera that is somewhere between the gaze of the filmmaker and that of the fictive male subject of the film. Without turning the camera on himself in *Contacts*, he sees himself being totally implicated in the pain he views such that the greatest violence is done toward the filming self. The most complete turn toward the filming self, however, has been in the more autobiographical mode of *Les Années Déclic*.

Numéros zéro and *Reporters* focus on linked aspects to his profession but *Les Années Déclic*, in contrast, features photographs that tell the tale of his life up until that point while featuring extracts from some of the films he had made thus far. One film in particular, *50.81 pour cent*, was still banned by Giscard d'Estaing at the time, since he did not like its portrayal of his electoral campaign (the film is now distributed as *1974: Une partie de campagne*). *Les Années Déclic* is a film with a difference, since Depardon sits in front of a projector with the light shining in his eyes, looking down at the still images that he then comments on. These images are brought to life occasionally by the films they relate to. He dedicated this quasi-autobiography to his parents. He makes touching reference to his father, who died when Depardon was on location making another film; his mother died during the making of this particular film. Rather than having gone round the world, he states that he should perhaps have spent more time getting to know his father whom he loved a great deal.

Although this is now impossible, the return to film a French rural community in his most recent work (*Profils paysans: l'approche*—chapter one in an evolving series) seems in some way to represent the displacement of this desire to return home.

SARAH COOPER

See also **Leacock, Richard; Maysles, Albert; Pennebaker, D. A.**

Biography

Born in Villefranche-sur-Saône, July 6, 1942, into a farming family. Left home for Paris in 1958 to work alongside Louis Foucherand, his first contact with the profession of photographic journalist. Became attached to the Dalmas agency, via Foucherand, in 1959. Left for the Sahara at the request of Louis Dalmas, then subsequently to Algeria for his first trip to Africa, 1960. Employed on return by Dalmas, part of a team of photographers who worked with papers such as *Samedi-Soir, France-Dimanche*. Called to military service in March 1962, Dalmas agency insisted that he be photographer for *Bled 5-5*, the journal for the armed forces and is subsequently transferred to Paris. Co-founded the Gamma agency with Hubert Henrotte and Gilles Caron, 1966. A special report on Chile earned him and two other Gamma photographers a Robert Capa Gold Medal Award. In 1977 he received a Pulitzer Prize for his work in Chad. Among his prestigious film accolades to date, he was awarded the Prix Georges Sadoul for *Numéros zéro* and Césars for best documentary for *Reporters, Délits flagrants* and for the documentary short, *New York, N.Y.*

Selected Films

1969 *Ian Pallach*
1974 *50.81 pour cent*
1975–76 *Tchad (2) et (3)*
1977 *Numéros zéro*
1980 *Reporters*; (date of filming) *San Clemente*
1983 *Faits divers*
1984–85 *Empty Quarter*; *Les Années Déclic*
1986 *New York, N.Y.*
1987 *Urgences*
1989 *La Captive du désert*
1990 *Contacts*
1994 *Délits flagrants*
1996 *Afriques: comment a va avec la douleur?*
2001 *Profils paysans: l'approche*

Further Reading

Confrontations avec Raymond Depardon, Daniel Humair, Emir Kusturica, Artazvad Pelechica, Claude Regy, Alain Rocca, Martin Scorsese, Paris: Femis, 1993.
Depardon, Raymond, *Tchad*, Paris: Gamma, 1978.
———, *Correspondance new-yorkaise*, Paris: Libération/ Éditions de l'Étoile, 1983.

————, *San Clemente*, Paris: Centre National de la Photographie, 1984.

————, *Errance*, Paris: Seuil, 2000.

Depardon, Raymond, and Frédéric Sabouraud, *Depardon/ Cinéma*, Paris: Cahiers du cinéma, 1993.

Gauthier, Guy, *Le Documentaire, un autre cinéma*, Paris: Nathan, 1995.

Guerrin, Michel, *Raymond Depardon*, Paris: Centre National de la Photographie, 1999.

DEREN, MAYA

Maya Deren (nee Eleanora Derenkowsky), one of the most prolific advocates for experimental and independent film practice in the United States, helped establish a paradigm (based on a unified front of institutional patronage and collective social action by art cinema's practitioners) for the funding, circulation, and presentation of avant-garde films. Her labours as both a filmmaker and proponent of "non-industrial" film work were a result of her interest in sustaining a countersystem to that of the distribution circuit of America's popular commercial cinema, and include a range of activities that enriched the fields of independent film manufacturing, distribution, exhibition, and promotion following World War II.

Although Deren's contributions to the language of indigenous art cinema in the United States have been characterized by some critics and historians within formalist categories and as autoethnography, the broad language of her work, including the corpus of critical texts she produced in order to frame her films' reception, suggests otherwise. Her awareness and concern with the acts of historical classification and collective modes of interpretation were as much a part of the working methodology of her artistic practice (thus eluding or making complex the subsequent linear categorization of her work) as the construction and circulation of the art-object she produced.

During World War II, the state of experimental or avant-garde film production in the United States was limited by a lack of material resources and exhibition venues. Further restricting potential attempts at filmic experimentation or production outside of the commercial center of film manufacturing in Los Angeles was the high cost of 35mm film production, with its large and cumbersome equipment, and the lack of funding bodies engaged to support non-industrial film work.

The conclusion of the war helped to rectify these conditions as new and used portable 16mm equipment and a surplus of 16mm stock produced by Eastman Kodak for use by the U.S. military prompted a consumer market to be developed in order to expend the surplus film resources that were now available domestically. In New York, the end of the war brought with it a great number of import films that were available for commercial use and an art house exhibition circuit that quickly expanded in order to serve this market.

During this period, Deren had completed work on her first film, *Meshes in the Afternoon* (1943), in collaboration with her husband, filmmaker Alexander Hammid, in Los Angeles. By 1946, she had her first opportunity to screen her films "outside of the law of industrial production" in a rented theatre in Greenwich Village. It was her first few initial experiences with self-distribution and production that exposed Deren to the difficulties of operating outside of the commercial mainstream. However, through her ability to sustain a market for her work from the support of screenings held at educational institutions, museums, and film societies, a viable model for alternative praxis was developed. This model was held together primarily through Deren's own advocacy, taking the form of public lecture presentations, numerous published articles, and seeking the support of organizations offering fellowship support or financing for the plastic arts, which led to her being awarded the first Guggenheim Fellowship granted for "creative work in the field of motion pictures" in 1946. By 1954, unable to have obtained consistent financial backing, Deren focused her efforts into establishing the Creative Film Foundation (CFF), a nonprofit organization that was to offer grants for the "development of motion pictures as a creative fine art form." She expanded the CFF's activities in 1956 with the Creative Film Awards that promoted the work of a select group of experimental filmmakers. Although limited funds would end up being distributed through the CFF, the organization helped aid the dissemination of avant-garde film work in the United States and provided a formal platform for the broad dissemination of experimental filmic praxis.

In 1946, Deren was invited to collect her writing on film by Alicat Press publisher Oscar Baradinsky. For Deren, this was an opportunity to make available for the first time the range of her theories on film and film art in one concise volume that could then subsequently be made available through her distribution company, Maya Deren Films, and aid her in the management of her financial difficulties. This text, published as *Anagram of Ideas on Art, Form and Film* (1946), is an exploration of numerous topics, including an analysis on the field of documentary film and documentary realism. In *Anagram*, Deren posits that the "real value" of the documentary mode is found in its ability to make material an "otherwise obscure or remote reality," but cautions that its status as art must result not from its pursuit of narrative or poetic realism but by its particular affinity to film form. She criticizes the successes of documentaries produced during the 1930s and 1940s as misguided, and asserts that the integrity, or by her own term "validity," that these films found was a false celebration of the medium's capabilities. Of the documentaries that she praises in *Anagram* for producing an "art reality ... independent of the reality by which it was inspired" she includes *Song of Ceylon* (1934) and the early work of Dziga Vertov (aka Denis Arkadyevich Kaufman).

A year after the publication of *Anagram*, Deren had the opportunity to perform within the field of documentary through ethnographic field work while in Haiti, where she began to film secular dance and voudoun possession rituals with the financial backing of her 1946 Guggenheim Fellowship. By 1953, having made multiple trips to Haiti in order to gather footage for her voudoun project, Deren was still in pursuit of financing, but had been able to publish the monograph, *Divine Horsemen: The Living Gods of Haiti*, an observational analysis and history of Haitian voudoun culture. Although she was never able to complete work on her documentary film project, she continued to look for financing until her death in the early 1960s. In 1977, Deren's Haitian footage and audio recordings were collected and edited together by Teiji Ito, her third husband, and Cherel Winett Ito and released under the same title as her monograph.

JOSHUA AMBERG

See also **Divine Horsemen**

Biography

Born in Kiev, Ukraine, 20 April 1917. In 1922 arrived with parents at Ellis Island in the United States. Attended the League of Nations' International School in Geneva, Switzerland, 1930–1933. Received B.A. degree from New York University in 1936. Participated in activities with the socialist movement and the Young Peoples Socialist League, 1934–1937. From 1938–1942, worked as a freelance secretary and editorial assistant, including a period in which Deren had a position with the Dunham Dance Company during 1941–1942. Earned a master's degree in English Literature from Smith College in 1939. Married filmmaker Alexander Hammid in 1942. Production of *Meshes in the Afternoon* in 1943. In 1945, began to self-distribute and promote films, arrange speaking engagements, and publish written work about film. In 1946, received Guggenheim Fellowship and published *Anagram of Ideas on Art, Form and Film*. Awarded the "Grand Prix International for 16mm Film, Experimental Class" at Cannes for *Meshes in the Afternoon*, 1947. From 1947 to 1955, toured the Caribbean and studied secular and ritualistic dance and culture focusing on Haitian Voudoun. In 1954 founded the Creative Film Foundation and in 1956 established the Creative Film Awards. Married composer Teiji Ito in 1960. Died 13 October 1961 in New York.

Selected Films

1934 *Song of Ceylon* (Basil Wright)
1943 *Meshes of the Afternoon*: Director, Writer
1944 *Witch's Cradle*: Director
1944 *At Land*: Director
1945 *A Study in Choreography for Camera*: Director
1946 *Ritual in Transfigured Time*: Director
1948 *Meditation on Violence*: Director, Writer
1958 *The Very Eye of Night*: Director, Writer
1977 *Divine Horsemen: The Living Gods of Haiti* (Teiji Ito and Cherel Winett Ito)

Further Reading

Clark, Veve A., Millicent Hodson, and Catrina Neiman, *The Legend of Maya Deren: A Documentary Biography and Collected Works: Volume One, Part One—Signatures (1917–1942)*, New York: Anthology Film Archives, 1984.
———, *The Legend of Maya Deren: A Documentary Biography and Collected Works: Volume One, Part Two—Chambers (1942–1947)*, New York: Anthology Film Archives, 1988.
Deren, Maya, *An Anagram of Ideas on Art, Form and Film*. Yonkers: Alicat Book Shop Press, 1946.

Deren, Maya, *Divine Horsemen: The Living Gods of Haiti*. New York: Thames and Hudson, 1953.

Jackson, Renata, *The Modernist Poetics and Experimental Film Practice of Maya Deren (1917–1961)*, Lewiston: Edwin Mellen Press, 2002.

Maya Deren and the American Avant-garde, edited by Bill Nichols, Berkeley: University of California Press, 2001.

Rabinovitz, Lauren, "Maya Deren and an American Avant-garde Cinema," *Points of Resistance: Women, Power & Politics in the New York Avant-garde, 1943–71* (2nd ed.), Chicago: University of Illinois Press, 2003, 49–91.

DESERT VICTORY

(UK, Boulting, Macdonald, 1943)

Desert Victory is a documentary record of the British Eighth Army's campaign in North Africa against German and Italian forces under the command of Field Marshall Erwin Rommel. It consists almost entirely of footage shot by combat cameramen, including some captured German film. In this kind of filmmaking, two creative problems are uppermost for the filmmakers working with miles of actuality material: first, to give clarity to the mass of confusing, technical detail, and second, to give it dramatic form.

In *Desert Victory*, the first problem was solved by the use of animated maps to establish the overall patterns and movement of the campaign, and by a carefully planned narration. As for the second, all of the nonartistic material with the randomness and irregularity of history inherent in it was given a beginning, middle, and end—like the chronicle plays of Shakespeare. (*Henry V* gives considerable attention to an English army at war on foreign soil, and Laurence Olivier's film version of it [1944] fitted into the patriotic spirit of the time.) To organize these events so they would appear both clear and dramatic, the filmmakers contrived an alternation of cause and effect. To personalize the mass action and to gain empathy, a number of close-ups of individual soldiers are inserted. (Some of them were obviously recreated; for those, actuality footage was augmented with brief scenes shot at Pinewood Studios.) Generals Alexander, Montgomery, and Wavell, and Prime Minister Churchill are introduced as well. In addition, the irrelevancies of the sponsor's requirements—to show each branch of the armed forces, the civilian workers, the presence of U.S. aid, and so on—were fitted into the whole without warping it out of shape.

Desert Victory starts at the lowest point of the campaign, in the summer of 1942. The British, who had retreated across the Sahara, pursued by the seemingly invincible Afrika Korps, are halted just sixty miles from Alexandria, deep inside Egypt. Then, in October, there is the fierce battle at El Alamein, with the British emerging victorious. From there the film follows the triumphant 1,300-mile pursuit of the German and Italian armies to the final victory at Tripoli.

In comparison with the British indoctrinational semi-documentaries (*Target for Tonight*, 1941; *Fires Were Started*, 1943; *Western Approaches* [*The Raider* in the United States], 1944), which tended to make the violence of war part of a job of work to be done, *Desert Victory* is singularly bloodthirsty. Perhaps these filmmakers weren't inclined to conceal their elation over this first major British victory following the battering Britain had received in the previous desert fighting and from the air blitz of England itself.

Desert Victory was an enormous critical and popular success. Apparently its sincerity and feeling of authenticity were most responsible for this. In Britain it became the most successful of all official films at the box office up to that point. *The* [London] *Times* wrote of it that it was not

Desert Victory, 1943. The British 8th Army Routs Rommel in Africa.
[*Courtesy of the Everett Collection*]

only a valuable document but that it also succeeded in being good "cinema" as well (March 4,
1943). In the United States two respected
reviewers (tough-minded realists) praised it
highly. Manny Farber wrote that it was a pleasure and an excitement: "It is a real documentary, not a newsreel assembly. . . . This is the
first time a movie has been the original source
for the clearest account of an event. The filmmakers of the British government were obviously
as well prepared . . . as was the Eighth Army
under Montgomery" (*New Republic*, April 12,
1943). James Agee thought that "*Desert Victory*
is the first completely admirable combat film,
and if only film makers and their bosses can
learn the simple lessons it so vigorously teaches,
its service to the immediate future and to history
will be incalculably great" (*The Nation*, May 1,
1943). It received an Academy Award as the
year's most distinctive achievement in documentary features.

Its success prompted a series of large-scale
feature-length "victory" films. *Tunisian Victory*
(1944), a British-American co-production, also
directed by Roy Boulting, carried the North
African story from the U.S. landings in November 1942 to the annihilation of the German
forces at Cape Bon. *Burma Victory* (1945),
also directed by Boulting, may have been prompted in part by a Hollywood feature, *Objective
Burma* (1945, directed by Raoul Walsh), which
annoyed the British. In it Errol Flynn, as a
U.S. paratrooper, pretty much single-handedly
mops up the Japanese enemy. *The True Glory*
(1945), the final film in the series, was produced
jointly by the British Ministry of Information and the U.S. Office of War Information.
It was co-directed by Englishman Carol Reed
and American Garson Kanin, fiction film directors of considerable distinction. It covers the
period from the preparation for the D-Day
landings in Normandy, through the fall of Berlin, to the establishing of contact between the
Western Allies and Soviet troops at the Elbe
River. *Desert Victory* may also have been a
model for the highly successful and influential American television series *Victory at Sea*
(1952–1953).

JACK C. ELLIS

See also **Boulting, Roy**; *Fires Were Started*; *Tunisian Victory*

Desert Victory (UK, Army Film and Photographic Unit
and the Royal Air Force Film Production Unit,

1943, 60 mins.). Distributed by Ministry of Information. Produced by David Macdonald. Directed by Roy Boulting; assistant direction by Patrick M. Jenkins. Cinematography by British Service Film Units.

Music by William Alwyn. Editing by Richard Best and Frank Clarke. Screenplay and commentary spoken by James Lansdal Hodson.

DIARY FOR TIMOTHY, A

(UK, Jennings, 1945)

The last of Humphrey Jennings's artime documentaries, *A Diary for Timothy,* looks to the end of war with a disturbing, perhaps disturbed, ambivalence. Following his attempt to integrate documentary materials with rather conventional, heavily fictionalized narrative structures in *Fires Were Started* and two subsequent short films (*The Deserted Village* and *The True Story of Lilli Marlene*), Jennings returned in *A Diary for Timothy* to what Jim Hillier has called the "distinctively associative and non-narrative style" of such earlier short films as *Listen to Britain* (Hillier, 1972). The result was arguably the most aesthetically accomplished of Jennings's films, with regard to both the graphic quality and compression of its individual images (photographed by Fred Gamage) and the sophistication and complexity of its montage. At the same time, Jennings's own ideological uncertainties as to the significance, for Britain, of the imminent end of World War II are embodied in the film's formal irresolution, the impression it conveys of a filmmaker straining against both the Griersonian model of documentary and his own aesthetic of synthesis. It is precisely this sense of strain that gives *A Diary for Timothy* a poignancy and tension missing from Jennings's earlier films, and that makes it a more interesting work than either its partisans or its antagonists have allowed.

Jennings began work on *A Diary for Timothy* in the summer of 1944 and began location work in the autumn; filming continued into the following spring, and the war was over by the time the film was released. Although it documents some setbacks for the Allied side

(notably the Arnhem campaign of late 1944), the whole film is shaped by the certainty of the war's end, and all its images of sacrifice, loss, and mortality are set in relation to the filmmaker's—and the viewer's—confidence in a happy ending (one of the narrative conventions Jennings both adopts and worries over). The voice-over commentary was written by E. M. Forster, but clearly he worked to Jennings's design; indeed, some phrases from Jennings's working notes turn up more or less intact in the final version. While the film was certainly affected by the unfolding of public, historical events, the essential structure was in place early on in the filming.

A Diary for Timothy presents itself as an account, addressed to the protagonist, Timothy

A Diary for Timothy, Frederick Allen, Dame Myra Hess, 1945 British Documentary.
[*Courtesy of the Everett Collection*]

James Jenkins, of the first six months of his life. Jennings weaves together scenes from the child's life (homecoming, baptism, first Christmas) with episodes from the lives of four other "typical" characters: Goronwy, the Welsh coal miner; Alan, the gentleman farmer; Bill, the London engine driver; and Peter Roper (the only one of these characters with a surname), an injured fighter pilot recovering in a hospital. Intercut with these continually interrupted and deliberately inconclusive narrative strands are scenes of landmines being cleared from the British coastline (as fears of invasion recede); children playing amidst the wreckage of bomb sites; people standing in line for coal on the street; Myra Hess performing Beethoven at an afternoon concert; John Gielgud playing Hamlet; rescue workers looking for survivors of a V-2 attack; a woman unable to sleep in an underground shelter; young people at a dance hall; and, running through the whole film, within and around all these other strands, scenes of people listening to the radio for news of the war. The familiar voices of the radio newsreaders connect the listeners in their separate rooms, but what we *see* is the separation; the montage isolates what it joins.

Jennings's scenario in *A Diary for Timothy*, with its simple stock characters identified by their work, has certain qualities reminiscent of a children's story. This makes sense in a film addressed to an infant, but that device itself may have the effect, as Andrew Britton contends, of infantilizing the spectator. There is some truth to this observation, although it oversimplifies the multiple levels on which the film actually addresses its audience, and its multiplicity of voices. Jennings constructs representative rather than individualized characters in order to convey a sense of social totality: a Griersonian strategy, but adapted by Jennings to more critical and less obvious ends. Here, the sense of totality is a product of total war. "You were part of the war, even before you were born," the commentary runs. "Everyone was in it; it was everywhere; not only on the battlefields but in the valleys, where Goronwy, the coal miner, carries his own weapons to his own battlefront." Such language might be taken to affirm a patriotic sense of connectedness and common purpose, but equally it articulates a feeling of inescapability, of history as nightmare—and not only in wartime, as the film's recurrent references to the unchangingly terrible conditions in the mines make clear.

A Diary for Timothy celebrates the Allied advances of early 1945, but it also pushes its audience to think more critically about war and its "sides." In a 1948 essay, Jennings named a "propensity for endless aggressive war" as one of the defining traits of the English, and wrote that "some of the English achievements in the late war, notably the burning of Hamburg, make the blood run cold." So, in a late sequence in the film, when we see a series of shots of London being rebuilt while on the soundtrack a radio announcer describes massive Allied bombing raids on Berlin, the juxtaposition should complicate our response to the good news from the front, as should a later sequence intercutting images of bombing with Timothy crying in his small white cot. Timothy's comfortable whiteness is contrasted throughout the film with the hellish darkness in which Goronwy works, and it is Goronwy's voice we hear in a sequence just after the Berlin air raids: "I was sitting thinking about the past: the last war, the unemployed, broken homes, scattered families. And then I thought, has all this really got to happen again?" The apprehension that runs through *A Diary for Timothy* as to what comes after the war's end is not rooted in a hollow nostalgia for "the war as golden age" (Britton, 1989), but in a disenchanted historical memory of the economic and social conditions—not just "there," but "here"—that brought the war into being.

HAL GLADFELDER

See also **Fires Were Started**; Grierson, John; Jennings, Humphrey; *Listen to Britain*

A Diary for Timothy (UK, Crown Film Unit, 1945, 38 mins.). Produced by Basil Wright. Written and directed by Humphrey Jennings. Commentary by E. M. Forster, read by Michael Redgrave. Cinematography by Fred Gamage. Edited by Jenny Hutt and Alan Osbiston. Music by Richard Adinsell. Sound by Ken Cameron and Jock May.

Further Reading

Aitken, Ian, *The Documentary Film Movement: An Anthology*, Edinburgh: Edinburgh University Press, 1998.

Anderson, Lindsay, "Only Connect: Some Aspects of the Work of Humphrey Jennings," in *Nonfiction Film Theory and Criticism*, edited by Richard Meran Barsam, New York: Dutton, 1976, 263–270.

Britton, Andrew, "Their Finest Hour: Humphrey Jennings and the British Imperial Myth of World War II," in *CineAction!* 18 (1989), 37–44.

Drazin, Charles, *The Finest Years: British Cinema of the 1940s*, London: André Deutsch, 1998.

Hillier, Jim, "Humphrey Jennings," in *Studies in Documentary*, edited by Alan Lovell and Jim Hillier, New York: Viking, 1972, 62–132.

Jennings, Humphrey, "The English," and working notes for *A Diary for Timothy*, in *The Humphrey Jennings Film Reader*, edited by Kevin Jackson, Manchester: Carcanet, 1993.

DIGITAL VIDEO

Digital video differs from analog video in the way that it stores the video signal on tape. Whereas analog video formats record the video signal as a continuous waveform, digital video quantizes and digitizes the video signal, storing it as a series of discrete binary units (ones and zeroes) that encode color, brightness, sound, and timing information. Digital video is compatible with computer equipment, with transfers typically made through the IEEE 1394 connector, called Fire-Wire by Apple and i.Link by Sony. Once the video is transferred into the computer, it can be stored and edited there (with a great number of video effects that can be applied) and finally be output back to tape. Other advantages of digital video over analog video include a sharper and clearer picture, better sound, less susceptibility to radio interference, and virtually no generational loss when transfers or copies are made (due to the binary ones and zeroes being copied exactly). Many digital video cameras can also take still images and work with established image formats.

Professional grades of digital video are often used by the film, television, and special effects industries because of their high chrominance bandwidth and excellence in chroma-keying. D1 and D2 are composite video in a 19mm cassette, whereas D3 and D5 use a half-inch tape. Other formats, ranging from professional to consumer grade, include Digital Betacam, Digital8, Digital-S, DV, DVC, DVCAM (Sony), and DVCPRO (Panasonic).

A particularly strong consumer-grade digital video is the Mini-DV format, which has become a standard since its introduction in 1995. A Mini-DV tape is 6.35mm wide, 65 meters long, and holds an hour of video, which is 11 gigabytes of data. The sound quality is as good as a CD, with 12-bit and 16-bit encoding. The cassette itself is $66 \times 48 \times$ 12.2mm, only a fraction of the size of a VHS tape (which measures $188 \times 104 \times 25$mm). The compactness of Mini-DV tape is made possible by a high recording density (about 6.7 times that of VHS) and data compression done in real time as the camera runs. Some Mini-DV tapes even have small, 4-kilobyte chips imbedded in them known as "memory in cassette" (MIC). The chip can store such information as a contents list, times and dates of recordings, and camera settings used. Mini-DV cassettes are manufactured by Fuji, JVC, Maxell, Panasonic, RCA, Sony, and TDK.

Another consumer format is Digital8, which uses the same 8mm cassettes as Hi-8 analog video. Digital8 is cheaper than Mini-DV, but the equipment is larger and heavier, and because of the digital encoding, only 40 minutes of digital video can be recorded on a 60-minute tape.

Digital video is well suited to documentary filmmaking due to its compactness, ease of use, high quality of image and sound, and archival qualities, including digital storage, computer compatibility, and a virtual lack of generational loss when copies are made. With the shift to computers and digital technology, digital video appears to be the medium that will replace 16mm filmmaking.

MARK J. P. WOLF

Further Reading

Jack, Keith, *Video Demystified* (3rd ed.), Eagle Rock, VA: LLH Technology Publishing, 2001.

Newton, Dale, and John Gaspard, *Digital Filmmaking 101: An Essential Guide to Producing Low-Budget Movies*, Studio City, CA: Michael Weise Productions, 2001.

Collier, Maxie D., *The IFILM Digital Video Filmmaker's Handbook 2001*, Los Angeles: Lone Eagle Publishing, 2001.

DIGITIZATION

The term *digitization* refers to a method of using computers to convert visual and audio information into an electrical signal alternating between binary numbers composed only of two digits: 1 and 0. Whereas an analog signal is continuously variable, a digital signal is a series of fixed, discreet pulses. The primary virtues of digital signals are that they are not subject to distortion or degradation when processed or reproduced; they can be stored in memory, allowing for random access to any portion of the information; and there are no limits to the ways in which video and audio inputs may be manipulated with computer software. These advantages have encouraged the use of computer processing at every stage of media production and distribution to the extent that image makers generally believe that digital signals will eventually replace analog signals created on film and videotape.

The distinction between digital and analog signals has been a major point of contention for documentary theorists, who claim that digitization subverts the ontological status of the photographic image. For example, in his groundbreaking book, *Representing Reality*, Bill Nichols maintains that digital sampling destroys documentary's authenticity and credibility, which depend on an indexical bond between analog photographic technologies and the subjects, or referents, they photograph. That is, analog technologies record the light reflected from physical objects directly onto a photosensitive substrate (celluloid or electromagnetic tape), guaranteeing that the photographed objects did indeed exist in the past. Therefore, the profilmic event, or that which occurred in front of the camera, is believed to be identical to the actual event that could be witnessed in the historical world, regardless of the camera's presence. Other than being recorded, photographic referents have undergone no manipulation by the image maker, thus preserving a relation to the real perceived as immediate and transparent. As such, referents serve as a form of historical evidence, the basis for documentary's claims for truth and objectivity.

Documentary theory has generally incorporated André Bazin's influential assertion that photography had surpassed all previous forms of mimetic representation precisely because its technologies automatically copy an image of the referent's existence without the need for human interpretation or manipulation. Digitization, however, mediates between image and referent by translating profilmic representations into a complex series of mathematical logarithms before reconverting them into visual and audio signals. The digital image, therefore, may be seen to refer not to the object photographed, but to the computer's memory banks and software applications—in essence requiring an intervention between the originating object and its reproduction, which exists as a signal rather than as a stored image. Regarding the photographic image as ontologically uncoded, defenders of analog technologies compare digitization to plastic arts such as animation or painting, which are governed by a set of coded, conventional transpositions. This opposition between analog copy and digital code in turn has generated a series of critical polarities distinguishing analogical from digital representations, the latter typically regarded as models, simulations, or fictions—in short, icons rather than indexes.

The power bestowed on analog photography as the more sanctioned technology for documentary production stems in part from the influence of the Direct Cinema movement of the 1950s and 1960s, which limited documentary filmmakers to subjects existing in the present moment and required their presence on the scene of the event as it occurred. As witnesses to the profilmic event's contemporaneous existence, practitioners of direct cinema were motivated to represent the world in which they lived, both on location and at the time of shooting. The indexical bond of analog photographic technologies supported their project by aligning presence, existence, evidence, and history with indexicality.

The question remains, however, if indexicality is a requisite criterion defining documentary as an ontological category. Revisionist documentary theorists such as Michael Renov and John Tagg have demonstrated, respectively, that the markers of nonfictional authenticity have been historically variable, and that their authority is defined less by ontological disposition than by institutional discourses collapsing truth claims into the technological substrate producing them. Martin Lister has demonstrated that digital images are better understood not as radically different from analog images, and that most of the controversial issues digitization raises were also raised by celluloid photography when invented in the nineteenth century.

If documentary theory and practice should categorically be confined to analogical reproduction, then perhaps the term *documentary* should be redefined as a subset of a broader nonfictional media practice, rather than synonymous with it. As an epistemological category, "nonfiction" encompasses discourses about historical events lying outside the possibility of their photographic representation. Historical epochs prior to the invention of photography, extinct species such as the dinosaur, and scientific speculations about global warming lack existing referents available to light rays, and thus escape indexical photographic signification. If incapable of being "documented," these subjects are, nevertheless, suitable subjects for documentary treatment, in that they are concerned with what could be or what might have been, if not presently what is.

Mark J. P. Wolf has referred to the nonfictional treatment of conditional subject matter as "subjunctive documentaries," which use digitization to translate abstract concepts and entities invisible to both the human eye and the camera lens into visible analogues. Subjunctive documentaries trade in the indexical bond for its extrapolation and speculation to produce new knowledge that would otherwise be unattainable within the stricter definitions of documentary sanctioned only by analog technologies. For example, virtual architectural walkthroughs, experiments with chaos theory, and cosmological maps may be simulated, rendered from any angle, and replayed repeatedly for further analysis.

Subjunctive documentaries are less concerned with recording data to prove existence as evidence; instead, they analyze objects, events, systems, and concepts to speculate about the past, illustrate the hypothetical, and predict the future. Shifting from the perceptual to the conceptual, digitization documents probabilities and possibilities rather than actualities. As digital simulations include larger and more comprehensive data sets, their indexical link to their object of study grows stronger, until their iconic status is thought to sufficiently represent a truth about the historical world.

JAMES M. MORAN

See also **Indexicality**

Further Reading

Bazin, André, "The Ontology of the Photographic Image," in *What Is Cinema?* vol. I, edited and translated by Hugh Gray, Berkeley: University of California Press, 1967, 9–16.

Lister, Martin (ed.), *The Photographic Image in Digital Culture*, New York, Routledge, 1995.

Moran, James M., "A Bone of Contention: Documenting the Prehistoric Subject," in *Collecting Visible Evidence*, edited by Jane M. Gaines and Michael Renov, Minneapolis: University of Minnesota Press, 1999, 255–273.

Nichols, Bill, *Representing Reality*, Bloomington: Indiana University Press, 1991.

Renov, Michael (ed.), *Theorizing Documentary*, New York: Routledge, 1993.

Tagg, John, *The Burden of Representation: Essays on Photographs and Histories*, Amherst: The University of Massachusetts Press, 1988.

Wolf, Mark J. P., "Subjunctive Documentary: Computer Imaging and Simulation," in *Collecting Visible Evidence*, edited by Jane M. Gaines and Michael Renov, Minneapolis: University of Minnesota Press, 1999, 274–291.

DINDO, RICHARD

Richard Dindo is the best-known documentary filmmaker to emerge from Switzerland, and one of the country's most prolific. Active since the early 1970s, he has made over twenty documentaries and one fiction film. Within Switzerland, Dindo's reputation is based primarily on his rereadings of key episodes of twentieth-century Swiss history. Several of his films—such as the 1975 *The Execution of the Traitor Ernst S.*, on Swiss collaboration with the Nazis, and *Dani,*

Michi, Renato & Max (1987), on police brutality against the youth movement—raised controversy when they were first released but are now considered definitive accounts of the period in question. *Grüninger's Case* (1998) took a critical look at Swiss refugee policy during the Second World War through the case of a police chief who was dismissed in disgrace for helping Jewish refugees to enter the country at a time when the borders were officially closed to Jews.

Internationally, Dindo is known mainly for his critical biographies of literary as well as artistic and political figures, such as Arthur Rimbaud, Jean Genet, Max Frisch, Charlotte Salomon, and Che Guevara. In nearly every case, Dindo has based his film on documents and/or art works created by the protagonists themselves, and the films are thus often filmic adaptations of their subjects' own autobiographical accounts.

Throughout his career, Dindo has continually returned to a handful of major themes: the process of artistic creation; the potentially political role of the artist in society; oppositional social movements and the often-tragic outcome for their participants; and the way in which accounts of such movements and individuals have been suppressed or distorted by official history. In his 2003 *Ni olvido ni perdón* (*Neither Forget Nor Forgive*) Dindo combines all these themes in his analysis of the 1968 student movement in Mexico, which was brutally crushed by the government but continues to live on in the films, plays, monuments, and songs created to try to come to terms with the tragedy.

Dindo's body of work is distinctive not only in the consistency of his themes and choice of subjects but also in his signature filmmaking approach, which has remained remarkably constant over the years. Dindo has often referred to himself as "a documentarist of the past," more interested in rereading past events than in chronicling the present as it unfolds. In most cases his protagonists are long dead, forming a central absence around which the films are structured. Dindo's aim is to reconstruct past events so that they may be re-examined by contemporary viewers. In doing so he makes little use of standard methods such as archival footage or docudrama. Instead, he relies on a range of other devices that suggest fragmentary links with past events, rather than directly reproducing them.

A main element in Dindo's films is always testimony, both written and spoken, whether in the form of his protagonists' autobiographical writings or the memories of surviving witnesses. Letters, photos, paintings, excerpts from fiction films, old newspaper coverage, and other historical materials are also cited for their ability to partially recall the past. A recurring motif in nearly every Dindo film is the return to the location of a key event, where the very absence of any traces testifies to the difficulty of bridging the gap between then and now. To emphasize this juxtaposition of past and the present, Dindo will often contrast a writer's description of a place with newly shot views of the location. In other cases, eyewitnesses visit the scene of the events they are describing and may comment on what is missing in the present time.

If Dindo does use staging, it is usually partial or indirect: introducing a catalyst into a situation but not determining its outcome. The return to a historical location may provoke an eyewitness reaction, but the reaction itself is clearly unrehearsed. In some cases Dindo has had actors follow the path of his dead subjects, retracing their steps as described in their writings. Only rarely has he used actors to literally restage scenes from a protagonist's life. In his *Arthur Rimbaud, a Biography* (1990) Dindo explicitly addresses the boundary between documentary and fiction by having actors playing Rimbaud's friends and having relatives read authentic texts from the poet's life, such as diaries and letters, in the original locations. And in his 1983 portrait of actor and film director Max Haufler, he films scenes from a project Haufler himself was unable to shoot, with Haufler's actress daughter playing the role her father had intended for himself (*Max Haufler, "The Mute"*).

In talking about his work (see for instance the chapter-length interview in Hübner, 1996), Dindo has often expressed a fundamental mistrust in the ability of the film image alone to adequately represent a documentary situation. For Dindo, the true power of documentary film as an analytical tool resides in the juxtaposition of, or the dialectical relationship between, image and text. Thus, an idyllic landscape gains new significance when we are told by a witness that the film's hero died there, and a scene read out loud from a protagonist's diary becomes truly moving when it is accompanied by contemporary footage of the place it describes.

Moving the spectator and inspiring the viewer's imagination—these play a fundamental part in Dindo's declared documentary goal of restoring contact with his absent protagonists. Dindo has cited Marcel Proust's *In Search of Lost Time* novel cycle as his biggest artistic influence. In Dindo's own attempt to temporarily conjure up an otherwise irrecoverable past, he depends on the viewer's willingness to take an active role. In his 2000 essay, "Ich erzähle die Erzählung des anderen" (which can be loosely translated as "I Am the Teller of

Others' Stories") Dindo writes: "My viewers must also perform the work of memory by participating in the construction of the film they watch it, shot by shot and sentence by sentence." Through the artifice of his films' construction, Dindo invites the viewer to engage in authentic dialogue with historical figures and events.

MARCY GOLDBERG

See also **Switzerland**

Biography

Born in Zurich on June 5, 1944, as the grandson of Italian immigrants, left school at age fifteen, working at a series of odd jobs and traveling widely before moving to Paris in 1966. The encounter with French culture—literary and cinematic—would have a lasting influence on his work. As a self-taught filmmaker with no formal training, considers the hundreds of books and films he encountered in those years as his filmic education. In 1970, returned to Switzerland to make his first film, and has divided his time between Zurich and Paris ever since. Has made over twenty documentaries and one fiction film, *El Suizo* (*A Love in Spain*, 1985).

Selected films

1972 *Naive Maler in der Ostschweiz/Naive Painters in Eastern Switzerland*
1973 *Die Schweizer im Spanischen Bürgerkrie /The Swiss in the Spanish Civil War*
1975 *Die Erschiessung des Landesverräters Ernst S./The Execution of the Traitor Ernst S.* (with Niklaus Meienberg)
1977 *Hans Staub, Fotoreporter/Hans Staub, Photojournalist*
1981 *Max Frisch, Journal I–III*
1983 *Max Haufler, "Der Stumme"/Max Haufler, "The Mute"*
1987 *Dani, Michi, Renato & Max*
1990 *Arthur Rimbaud, une biographie/Arthur Rimbaud, a Biography*
1992 *Charlotte, "Leben oder Theater?"/Charlotte, "Life or Theatre?"*
1994 *Ernesto "Che" Guevara, le journal de Bolivie/Ernesto "Che" Guevara, the Bolivian Diary*
1998 *Grüningers Fall/Grüninger's Case*
2000 *Genet à Chatila/Genet in Chatila*
2002 *La Maladie de la mémoire/The Illness of Memory*
2003 *Aragon, le roman de Matisse/Aragon, the Novel of Matisse*
2003 *Ni olvido, ni perdón/Neither Forget Nor Forgive*
2005 *Wer war Kafka?/Who Was Kafkar?*

Further Reading

A booklet on Richard Dindo and his entire filmography is available in English or German from the Swiss Films foundation, www.swissfilms.ch.
Dindo, Richard, "Ich erzähle die Erzählung des andern," *Neue Zürcher Zeitung*, 14 January 2000, p. F11.
Goldberg, Marcy, "Hier ist es geschehen: Dindos Landschaften der Erinnerung," *CINEMA* 47, Zurich: Chronos Verlag, 2002, pp. 84–94.
———, "Performances of the Act of Remembering," in *The Image and the* Witness (forthcoming, 2005) edited by Frances Guerin and Roger Hallas (eds.).
Hübner, Christoph, "Richard Dindo: Alles ist Erinnerung," chapter in his *Dokumentarisch Arbeiten*, Berlin: Verlag Vorwerk 8, 1996.
Lachat, Pierre, Marcy Goldberg, and Richard Dindo, "Werkschau Richard Dindo," *Filmbulletin* 4.03, pp. 41–51.
Perret, Jean, "The Archives of Richard Dindo," in *DOX Documentary Magazine*, winter 1994, pp. 30–32.

DINEEN, MOLLY

See Ark, The; **United Kingdom**

DINNER PARTY, THE

(UK, Watson, 1997)

While not his most well-known work, Paul Watson's *The Dinner Party* (1997) exemplifies the British filmmaker's "fly on the wall" documentary style, his socially introspective slant and biting tone. Watson's methodology and cinematic aim are prevalent as the camera turns a critical and often satirical eye on society to reveal all of the quirks, warts and banalities of everyday people in a particular class or social situation.

Like the majority of his other works, the film was created for and broadcast on television allowing it to reach a expansive spectrum of society in their own homes.

Paul Watson has made a career of creating powerful and award winning documentaries for television entities including the BBC, ITV, Granada and Channel 4. Watson's earlier works, the groundbreaking *The Family* (1974), *The Fishing Party* (1985) and *Sylvania Waters* (1993) were striking in their then innovative portraits of working and middle class British and Australian life on camera.

The Dinner Party focuses on a wealthy group of British Conservatives gathered for dinner preceding the Labour Party's election victory. The film's release caused great controversy due to both the dramatic interactions unfolding in the work on-screen and the resulting accusations by the dinner party guests off-screen. The bold bigoted views, largely centering around race and sexual orientation, expressed by the participants in the film predictably shocked many viewers. These same film participants then maintained that Watson distorted their conversations and attitudes following the public outcry. The discussion about truth and representation in the media that developed brought the film to light again, and served to both re-establish Watson as a progressive and non-orthodox documentary filmmaker and fit *The Dinner Party* sturdily into his socially critical "docusoap" oeuvre.

Paul Watson, known for his years at the BBC, as Governor of the Bournemouth Film and Television School in England and then at Granada TV, is part of a 'new generation' of British documentary directors. While earlier British documentary works were renowned for their concern with greater societal issues, the films of Watson and his contemporaries present a more focused, personal view of the world. Watson's first major foray into this style that gained critical and audience attention was *The Family* (1974) for the BBC. This film became part of a genre of so-called "docusoaps," a grouping that Watson credited with founding, but tries to separate himself from as they developed into reality television trends. These controversial films use the power of the documentary form to entertain instead of educate. They also often feature a biased narrator and seemingly bizarre individual everyday lives rather than large societal issues that effect a collective. *The Dinner Party* fits into the later part of the docusoaps' reign with British audiences as popular interest began to wane toward the end of the century. Watson tries to distance his career from this heading and maintains his films' serious intent over entertainment.

However, it cannot be overlooked that the primary themes in his body of work, over 300 films total, resound with the style and popularity of the docusoap genre. It is significant that *The Dinner Party*, made nearly 25 years following Watson's initial success with *The Family*, employs similar cinematic styles to corresponding rhetorical aims.

JUSTINE NAGAN

See also **Docusoap**

The Dinner Party (UK, 1997) Produced and directed by Paul Watson.

Further Reading

Bruzzi, Stella New Documentary: A Critical Introduction, London and New York: Routledge, 2000
Ogle, Tina "Lord of the fly-on-the-walls" The Observer 01.27.02

DISTRIBUTION AND EXHIBITION

In the summer of 1988 the Independent Feature Film Market showed a rough version of a documentary entitled *A Humorous Look at How General Motors Destroyed Flint, Michigan*. An investor expressed interest, contacted the journalist-turned-filmmaker, encouraged the production team as it shaped the film, and negotiated a deal with Time Warner to distribute, coordinate publicity, and handle exhibitions. Eighteen months later, moviegoers from Fort Lauderdale to Berlin had seen *Roger & Me* (1989), the retitled, vastly influential film by Michael Moore, on approximately 300 screens (Pierson, 1995, pp. 137–176).

Roger & Me's transition from film festival favorite to widely distributed movie is not unique: Documentarians enter their almost-finished films into festivals domestically and abroad; buyers, producers, studio heads, media representatives, and distribution agents view the films, then enter into a bidding war to secure the rights to distribute those deemed worthy to various exhibition outlets, including movie theaters, schools and libraries, cable or network television, websites, home video suppliers, and nontheatrical venues, such as correctional institutions, airline in-flight entertainment, and health-care facilities. Potential distributors closely monitor both a film's presence at the best-known festivals (Cannes, Sundance, New York Film Festival, Hot Docs) and any awards garnered therein (Audience Award, Best Director, Best Documentary, Jury Prize). After choosing a work, these executives essentially buy it, thereby receiving the legal privilege not only to influence any last-minute edits and exhibit the film but also to benefit financially from these exhibitions. Generally, theatrical venues earn between 10 and 50 percent of profits from showings; the distribution company and the filmmakers split the remainder, based on terms outlined in the distribution agreement. Films also earn money even after leaving theaters, through home entertainment sales or rentals: After acquiring the rights, the Criterion Collection re-released *Nanook of the North* (Flaherty, 1922), *Night and Fog* (Resnais, 1955), *Gimme Shelter* (Maysles, Maysles, and Zwerwin, 1970), simultaneously preserving these—and other—prints and exposing them to new viewers.

Self-distribution remains an option for documentarians, although the strong economic link between studios, distribution companies, and commercial theaters sometimes makes this prohibitively difficult. Self-distributors usually four-wall, or rent out a theater in which to show the film, which allows them to pocket most of the ticket sales. Other distribution or production companies specifically target smaller, artier venues for exhibition, in part to circumvent the aforementioned corporate triumvirate. Technological advancement in satellite transmission of digital video, as well as the burgeoning use of fiber-optic cables, are eliminating the necessity of making multiple prints of a film (a single copy of which traditionally would be given to a single theater to "run," or show), thus lessening the costs of distribution and allowing for film runs at less conventional locations. Finally, several foundations, including the Soros Documentary Fund, provide grants to aspiring or first-time filmmakers, who frequently have trouble financing the postproduction process and getting distribution deals, due to the film industry's tendency to view newcomers as risky monetary propositions.

In return for their investment, distributors promise to promote the film by hiring publicists, creating press packets, advertising, scheduling interviews, arranging for contests or marketing tie-ins, producing special features to include on DVDs, and paying for producers, directors, and actors to attend promotional junkets. Sometimes this agreement leads to unintended consequences, as when Miramax decided to market Errol Morris's *The Thin Blue Line* (1988) as a nonfiction movie, rather than a documentary—a decision that helped eliminate the possibility of a Best Documentary Academy Award. Under cloudy circumstances, Disney backed out of its contract to distribute Moore's *Fahrenheit 9/11* (2004); Lions Gate, IFC Films, and the Fellowship Adventure Group then stepped in—and the film has since become history's highest-grossing documentary, as of August 2004.

Before committing to a film, distributors attempt to estimate the documentary's potential audience—both in theaters and in video sales or rentals—and thus its potential earning power. *Winged Migration* (Perrin, 2001) opened in one U.S. theater but earned approximately $34,000 in its first weekend; it eventually played on 200 theaters, grossing more than $11 million. Once attached to a distributor, a documentary might debut in the major markets first, including Los Angeles and New York, then show in other theaters throughout the United States and internationally, after it has developed sufficient "buzz"—positive feedback from the press or grassroots word-of-mouth. Many filmmakers also choose to host exhibitions in locations central to their work: Moore screened *Roger & Me* in his hometown of Flint, Michigan, and *Fahrenheit 9/11* in President George W. Bush's adopted hometown of Crawford, Texas.

While theatrical release and home entertainment systems remain the most common exhibition outlets, other venues have become increasingly important. Distribution agents regularly license films to libraries and educational institutions as a way of broadening the viewer base or exposing patrons to topical issues. *Control Room* (Noujaim, 2004), for instance, screened at the Museum of Television and Radio in conjunction with a panel discussion featuring notable journalists, members of the military press corps, and the film's director about issues highlighted in the documentary. Recognizing that many documentaries seek social change but sometimes miss their target audiences, in 2004 the National Video Resources and the American Library Association's Public Programs Office launched the Human Rights Video Project, which presents documentaries and other materials to libraries in order to raise awareness.

Some documentarians generate films almost exclusively for nontheatrical outlets; this group includes Ken Burns, who usually showcases his work on the Public Broadcasting Service (PBS). Similarly, television networks now possess documentary production and programming divisions: HBO produced Spike Lee's *4 Little Girls* (1997), as well as the video release of Barbara Kopple's *American Dream* (1990), and its America Undercover series sponsors darker slice-of-life features; Cinemax Reel Life selects independently created films, including Steve James's *Stevie* (2003), to premiere each month; and Spike TV, a division of MTV, announced plans in 2004 to solicit and debut documentaries aimed exclusively at men, including a BBC–produced film based on the lives of amateur body builders. In an unprecedented— and undisclosed—deal, NBC Universal purchased *Deadline* (Johnson and Chevigny, 2004) at Sundance to debut on *Dateline NBC* in summer 2004.

The Internet provides another progressively more viable means of exhibiting, as web-based contests, including those hosted by the Toronto Online Film Festival, gain prestige. Currently the Center for Independent Documentary plans to utilize streaming video technology to offer films through its website, documentaries.org, and recently the D-Word, an online community of documentarians, hosted a collaborative collection of documentaries about the art of documentary filmmaking online at d-word.com, self-referentially heralding the future of documentary distribution and exhibition.

JESSICA ALLEN

See also **Burns Ken; Kopple, Barbara; Moore, Michael; Morris, Errol;** *Roger & Me*; *Thin Blue Line, The*.

Selected Films

1922 *Nanook of the North* (Flaherty)
1955 *Night and Fog* (Resnais)
1970 *Gimme Shelter* (Maysles, Maysles, and Zwerin)
1988 *The Thin Blue Line* (Morris)
1989 *Roger & Me* (Moore)
1990 *American Dream* (Kopple)
1997 *4 Little Girls* (Lee)
2001 *Winged Migration* (Perrin)
2003 *Stevie* (James)
2004 *Control Room* (Noujaim)
2004 *Deadline* (Johnson and Chevigny)
2004 *Fahrenheit 9/11* (Moore)

Further Reading

Ascher, Steven, and Edward Pincus, *The Filmmaker's Handbook: A Comprehensive Guide for the Digital Age* (rev. ed.), New York: Plume, 1999

Barnouw, Eric, *Documentary: A History of the Non-Fiction Film* (2nd ed.), New York: OxfordUniversity Press, 1993

Kindem, Gordon, and Robert Musburger, *Introduction to Media Production: From Analog to Digital* (2nd ed.), Boston: Focal Press, 2001

LoBrutto, Vincent, *The Encyclopedia of American Independent Filmmaking,*. Westport, CT: Greenwood Press, 2002

Pierson, John, *Spike, Mike, Slackers & Dykes: A Guided Tour Across a Decade of American Independent Cinema*, New York: Hyperion, 1995

Simonelli, Rocco, *Shoot Me: Independent Filmmaking from Creative Concept to Rousing Release*, New York: Allworth Press, 2002

DIVIDED WORLD, A

(Sweden, Sucksdorff, 1948)

While not the most acclaimed of Arne Sucksdorff's shorts at the time of its premiere, *En kluven varld* (*A Divided World*) stands now as one of his best-known films and one of his masterworks. The film's "story" is simple and, unlike a number of Sucksdorff's other nature shorts, has no voice-over narration. After opening shots of water and the dark Swedish forest in winter, we see a church and graveyard as the music of Bach's "Fantasia," continuing from the credits, swells. A white weasel stops munching its food and hides in the snow from a wolf. The wolf eats the rest of what the weasel had started. We next see a white rabbit eating from the branches of a tree. Similarly spooked, it dashes across the snow. A pair of flashing eyes indicate, however, that the wolf is near. The weasel and an owl watch and listen as the wolf captures and kills the rabbit. The owl then swoops down next to the wolf, successfully battling the larger animal and flying off with the rabbit. Later, however, we see the wolf licking at another piece of food. The film ends with shots of a house, separated from the forest by a modest fence.

Seemingly highly Darwinian, the film nonetheless posits that the world of humans is strongly divided from that of animals. One way to read Sucksdorff's film, in fact, is as a response to those who were inclined to anthropomorphize the motivations of the animals in his work. Early on, the reflections of trees bent over the water appear on its surface, separated from the actual trees, giving the film's first signifiers of division. We see shots of a graveyard, a repository for when people die. But when animals die, they receive no burial, but rather are eaten by their predators or by scavengers. That said, there is no sense of judgment in the framing, camera movement, or editing; this very lack is also part of what gives the film its remarkable suspense. No reason is given for a world in which cute bunnies die, lucky weasels hide, and an owl can defeat a wolf. The film thus combines the almost childlike, observational innocence that is one of Sucksdorff's greatest strengths as a filmmaker with a maturity resigned to the harsh beauty of the ways of nature.

Sound plays a crucial role in the film. The opening sound of water bubbles calls attention to the precision and intensity of sounds that pierce the winter silence. The expressionistic use of sound

A Divided World, 1948.
[*Still courtesy of the British Film Institute*]

critics find in other Sucksdorff films is in evidence here, especially in the howling wind, highlighted in stunning shots of moonlight through trees, that seems to warn the animals of impending danger. Sound is especially important in telling Sucksdorff's highly arranged narrative. We only hear the rabbit's death as the camera dwells on what we read as the reactions of the weasel and the owl. Later, we see the owl land next to the wolf but are not privy to their battle for the rabbit. Only the weasel is seen as, with another use of somewhat amplified sound, the scuffle between the owl and the wolf takes place, ending with the surprising sound of the wolf's whimper. Thus, neither of the film's moments of violence is actually shown. Either Sucksdorff was unable to fully capture the battle, or it did not turn out as scripted, and what we see later is either a different owl or the same one carrying a different carcass. What is equally likely is that Sucksdorff was uninterested in the gore attendant upon the kill and the battle. Such scenes would have disrupted the austere beauty, or worse, they would have encouraged viewers to pass judgment on the animals. In Sucksdorff's vision, there are no villains. The sound proves that he does not exploit the savagery, but neither does he find it contemptible or unnecessary.

The use of Bach works on several levels. Given that it is heard most clearly during shots that show, or appear to be near, the world of humans, this music represents civilization, the separation from the world of animals. This latter world has its own music, one of rustling trees, burbling water, roaring winds, scampering animals, and of course the fierce, isolated cries of attack and the agonized death screams of the rabbit. At the same time, the music suggests the stylized nature of the entire enterprise, one well aware of the ominous tones in Bach's deep chords. For all the appeal of the animals, this film is no Disney Fantasia: Winsome animals kill, or they die painfully.

Critics have complained about the fakery in shots of the church and graveyard. But such criticism is essentially beside the point, for this fakery only emphasizes the larger theme of a divided world. The same might apply to those shots where the wolf's eyes flash and suddenly disappear. Since one continuous shot pans and tracks from the frightened rabbit to the lupine eyes, one might wonder whether Sucksdorff staged two flashes of light to suggest the moonlight momentarily capturing the animal's glassy eyes. An earlier flash of the wolf's eyes appears where one of the film's buildings appears in the distance; this, too, raises the question of staging in order to contrast the world of humans with that of animals. Elsewhere, concerns about staging arise simply because some shots seem too amazing to be "true." Was the wolf's tail that close to the hiding weasel, or did Sucksdorff place a fake tail near the hole and film the weasel's emergence? One might similarly wonder how he managed to track the owl flying off with the rabbit's carcass, or if it battled the wolf at all. It is in the framing and the editing that, while the observational strength of individual long takes gives the film its persuasiveness, Sucksdorff's film states its themes in an overtly essayistic manner.

The tendency of critics to read this film allegorically also stems from its structure of repetition and variation. When the wolf appears, the weasel responds by hiding, and it survives. When the rabbit senses the wolf, it runs, but is caught and killed. Finally, when the owl sees that the wolf has food, it attacks and successfully seizes the carcass. To hide, to flee, to confront—these choices, the film suggests, cover the range of options in the animal world. For all the timeless quality of this film, given that it was made just after WWII and the Holocaust, hiding, fleeing, and attacking must have summed up for many the choices that people made. The fence that separates the cozy cottage from the forest in the film's final shot, while demarcating a divided world, nonetheless appears jagged and rickety.

DAVID LUGOWSKI

See also **Sucksdorff, Arne.**

A Divided World/En kluven varld (Sweden, Svenska Filmindustri, 1948, 8.5 mins.). Direction, scenario, and cinematography by Arne Sucksdorff. Music: "Fantasia" by J. S. Bach, played by Erik Johnsson.

Further Reading

Cowie, Peter, *Swedish Cinema, from Ingeborg Holm to Fanny and Alexander*, Stockholm: Swedish Institute, 1985
———, *Scandinavian Cinema*, London: Tantivy Press, 1992
Hardy, Forsyth, *Scandinavian Film*, London: Falcon Press, 1952
Soila, Tytti, Astrid Soderbergh Widding, and Gunnar Iversen, *Nordic National Cinemas*, London and New York: Routledge, 1998
Wakeman, John (ed.), "Arne Sucksdorff" in *World Film Directors, Vol. One, 1890–1945*, New York: H. W. Wilson, 1987

DIVINE HORSEMEN

(US, Deren, 1977)

Maya Deren's *Divine Horsemen: The Living Gods of Haiti* is a visually rich, ethnographic study of the rituals of the Haitian religion of *voudoun* and its dance rituals. Unable to edit her own footage during her lifetime, Deren instead wrote a book with the same title, which, although she had no formal training in anthropology, became an authoritative work on Haitian voudoun—more commonly known by its colloquial name "voodoo"—for many decades to come.

Divine Horsemen is Deren's last film, and probably also her most mystical piece of work, not least due to its subject matter. Teiji Ito, who had composed the music for Deren's *Meshes of the Afternoon* and who became her third husband, produced the film after Deren's death, together with his later wife, Cherel, using Deren's 20,000 feet of film and her music recordings. The film had its first screening in 1978.

Having worked as an assistant to Katherine Dunham, a choreographer and anthropological researcher of Caribbean dance, Deren had seen Dunham's dance footage from the West Indies and was inspired to write essays on religious possession and dancing. In 1946, Deren received a grant of $3,000, the first given out by the Guggenheim Foundation for filmmaking. Deren had originally proposed a film that would contrast the ritual of children's games with ritual ceremonies of traditional societies in Bali and Haiti, but once in Haiti she changed her mind, feeling, according to her own account, "defeated in her original intentions" (Deren: 1953, 7). Over the period of four years, Deren took three trips to Haiti and spent a total of eighteen months on the island, mostly staying with a community outside Port-au-Prince.

Divine Horsemen, shot in black and white, is divided into two parts. The first part—consisting of seven of the film's eight chapters—explores Haitian religious dance ceremonies and the various gods for whom these are performed. The last chapter shows footage from carnival festivities in Port-au-Prince. The individual chapters begin with a black screen and the *vever*, the sacred symbol of the god, drawn with flour onto dust. The film follows the ceremonies in the order they are performed for the gods. Hence, the first chapter shows a dance for the loa *Legba*, the gatekeeper between the visible and mortal and the invisible and immortal world. There follow dance ceremonies for *Agwe*, the loa of wisdom, *Erzulie*, the goddess of love, *Ogoun*, the loa of might and power, *Ghede*, the loa of life and death, *Azacca*, the god of agriculture, and last, a presentation of the fast rhythmic music of the Kongo tribe.

Maya Deren was highly suspicious of an alleged scholarly detachment from the subject matter as a means to understand the "object," and instead regarded subjectivity as the characteristic approach of the artist (Deren: 1953, 8, 9). She particularly avoided learning anything about the dances and their meaning beforehand, in order to respond purely to the direct impacts they would have on her.

In recording the energetic dances, Deren's camera focuses on the individual and collective bodies of the dancers and, in particular, their arms and legs. The camera is unusually close to the action, at times immersed, and yet the dancers and bystanders hardly ever seem distracted by the camera. The fast music and the numerous close shots of moving limbs, rather than the focus on the faces of the dancers, pull the viewer into the action and by doing so almost make it difficult to treat the dancers as exotic objects. The result is the intimate perspective of a camera that is very close but never intrusive. Also, the recorded "possessions" —the visible manifestations of the gods—are not artificially dramatized or exoticized. Were it not for the voice-over the viewer might hardly notice them. Voudoun, "a religion of rare poetic vision and artistic expression" (Deren: 1953, 15), is depicted as a complex social ritual and a source of communal enjoyment and strength rather than as an unfathomable primitive cult.

Divine Horsemen is also a study in movement. Although Deren made only seven films, she is often considered the first dance filmmaker. Her interest is not so much in documenting facts as in representing the diverse aesthetic forms that reality takes, as is made clear in her use of slow motion and freeze-frames. They also reveal Deren's interest in these ceremonies as aesthetic, sensory experiences.

The impression of an immersed rather than a "prying and staring" (Deren: 1953, 7) spectator is further reinforced by the voice-over. Although Deren's other films usually do not use language, *Divine Horsemen* uses a male and a female voice-over to elaborate on the ceremonies. The voice-over narration is also used to move the film outside the purely aesthetic and visual spheres, as it links the religious dances of the *Petro* rites to the political history of Haiti, and to its successful fight for independence in 1804. The *Petro* loa incorporates "the rage against the evil fate which the African suffered, the brutality of his displacement and his enslavement" (Deren: 1953, 62), and eventually gives the slaves the moral force to pursue independence. Throughout, these descriptions—themselves excerpts from Deren's book—are given in the language of an insider who very benevolently explains the facts of this society to an outsider.

Although superficially the film does not have much resemblance to Deren's earlier films—partly because *Divine Horsemen* is her only documentary film—there are important themes that link the film with her broader work. Like the majority of her films, *Divine Horsemen* is concerned with dance and body movement as an aesthetic form of communication. The film also focuses on an aspect of a theme that is core to Deren's other work: transformation of identities. It seems that all these concerns amalgamate in *Divine Horsemen* in a way unforeseen by Deren herself. The inclusion of voudoun in her life stands as an experience that transformed her personally and as an artist. Deren herself read her inability to edit her material as a sign of the power of voudoun: "I had begun as an artist . . . I end by recording, as humbly and accurately as I can, the logics of a reality which had forced me to recognize its integrity, and to abandon my manipulations" (Deren, 1953, p. 6).

JACOBIA DAHM

See also **Deren, Maya**

Divine Horsemen: The Living Gods of Haiti, (USA, 1947–1951/1977, 52 min.). Directed by Maya Deren. Cinematography by Maya Deren. Sound recording by Maya Deren. Film editor: Cherel Ito. Sound editor: Teiji Ito. Narrators: John Genke and Joan Pape. Titles and animation: Yudel Kyler. The narration was adapted from Deren's book *Divine Horsemen. The Living Gods of Haiti* (1953).

Further Reading

Arnheim, Rudolf, "To Maya Deren," in *Film Culture Reader*, edited by P. Adams Sitney, New York: Praeger, 1970, 84–86.

Brakhage, Stan, *Film at Wit's End. Eight Avant-Garde Film-makers*, New York: McPherson & Company, 1989.

Clark, Veve Amasasa, Millicent Hodson, Catrina Neiman, and Francine Bailey, *The Legend of Maya Deren: A Documentary Biography and Collected Works*, Volume I, Part I: Signatures, Part II: Chambers (1942–47), New York: Anthology Film Archives, 1984 (I) and 1988 (II).

Deren, Maya, *Divine Horsemen: The Living Gods of Haiti*, Foreword by Joseph Campbell, London: Thames and Hudson, 1953.

Epple, George M., "Divine Horsemen: The Living Gods of Haiti," Film Review, *American Anthropologist*, 84, no. 4, December 1982, 979–980.

Nichols, Bill (ed.), *Maya Deren and the American Avant-Garde*, Berkeley: University of California Press, 2001.

O'Pray, Michael, *Avant-Garde Film. Forms, Themes and Passions*, London: Wallflower Press, 2003.

Rich B. Ruby, *Chick Flicks: Theories and Memories of the Feminist Film Movement*, Durham: Duke University Press, 1998.

Sitney, P. Adams, *Visionary Film. The American Avant-Garde*, Oxford: Oxford University Press, 1979.

Sullivan, Moira, "Maya Deren's Ethnographic Representation of Ritual and Myth in Haiti," in *Maya Deren and the American Avant-Garde*, edited by Bill Nichols, Berkeley: University of California Press, 2001, 207–234.

Warren, Charles (ed.), *Beyond Document. Essays on Nonfiction Film*, Hanover: University Press of New England, 1996.

Wilcken, Lois, "Divine Horsemen: The Living Gods of Haiti," Review of Film, Book, and Audio Recordings, *Ethnomusicology*, vol. 30, no. 2 (spring–summer 1986), 313–318.

DOCKERS

(UK, Anderson, 1999)

Dockers stands at the ambiguous intersection between feature and documentary film. It tells the story of a fictitious family's involvement in a historical event: the industrial dispute at Liverpool Docks from 1995 to 1998. But what is unique about the film is that it has been written, acted, produced, and televised, in part, by participants of the dispute, with the intention of documenting their experiences during this dispute.

In September 1995, Mersey Docks sacked 500 Liverpool dockers for refusing to cross the picket line raised by fellow dockers over a labor rights dispute. *Dockers* narrates the events of the strike from the dockers' point of view. It focuses in particular on the life of one family, the Waltons, in which both father and son are caught up in the strike. The story's starting point are the days immediately before the strike—the miserable working conditions on the dockside—and it continues up to the workers' defeat 28 months later, when 300 dockers were paid off with £28,000 ($50,000) each.

Dockers was written as a three-part television drama and televised in the summer of 1999. In

Dockers the fact-fiction boundary is an intricate one. The sacked dockers and their wives themselves—in workshops run by the Workers Educational Association (WEA)—wrote the screenplay and successively signed a contract for the screenplay to be televised. Moreover, even though the film uses professional actors in many key roles, some of the dockers who wrote the script also acted in the film, although they do not play themselves. Actors play alongside nonactors and together they reconstruct a dramatized version of reality. All this makes *Dockers* a drama that could be described as a "creative treatment of actuality" (Rotha, 1952, p. 70).

As is the nature of a television drama, *Dockers* focuses more on the individual and private repercussions of the strike than on the collective and political ones. It uses the development of these personal narratives to move from one dramatic sequence to the next. The drama of the film is heightened by a focus on two brothers, one who supports the strike, and dies as a result of the hardship of the strike, and the other, who, to support his family, turns "scab" and crosses the picket line, losing the friendship and support of all around him. The music—for the most part a highly dramatic refrain carried by multiple violins and intended to draw the audience emotionally in—complements the dramatic structure and adds to the tension of the story.

Dockers continues a long tradition of the representation of working class lives in British film. It works by juxtaposing the public and the private aspects of the conflict into a tightly woven tableau of interrelations, where the fight of the dockers and their families touches all spheres of life and all is political. Despite the focus on the personal experience of fictitious characters, the film follows a tight script, aimed at conveying as much historical information about the politics of the strike as possible. Alongside a representation of the daily struggles of the working class is a more bitter critique of the unions that failed the dockers—despite huge international support for their actions—and ultimately of the new left Labour government of Tony Blair.

JACOBIA DAHM

Dockers (UK, 1999, 90 min.). Directed by Bill Anderson. Script by Jimmy McGovern, Irvine Welsh, and the Dockers of the Writers' Workshop. Produced for Channel 4 by Parallax Pictures and The Initiative Factory. Cinematography by Cinders Forshaw. Edited by Kristina Hetherington. Music by Nick Bicât. Filmed in Liverpool, London, and Dublin.

Selected Films

1999 *Writing the Wrongs* (Planet Wild)

Further Reading

Bruzzi, Stella, *New Documentary: A Critical Introduction*, New York: Routledge, 2000.

Gibbons, Fiachra, "Union Leader Is Traitor in Strikers' Film." *The Guardian*, 2 July 1999, online source: http://www.guardian.co.uk/uk_news/story/0,,293276,00.html.

Lawson, Mark, "Work Experience," *The Guardian*, 5 July 1999, onlinesource: http://www.guardian.co.uk/tv_and_radio/story/0,290518,00.html.

Lay, Samantha, *British Social Realism: From Documentary to Brit Grit* (Short Cuts 15), London: Wallflower Press, 2002.

Rotha, Paul, *The Documentary Film* (2nd ed.) (originally published 1935), London: Faber and Faber, 1952.

Rowbotham, Sheila, and Huw Beynon (eds.), *Looking at Class: Film, Television and the Working Class in Britain*, London: Rivers Oram Press, 2001.

DOCUMENTARY DRAMA: CRITICAL OVERVIEW

Documentary drama has been one of the most problematic programme categories in UK television history. In their 1983 survey, Andrew Goodwin and Paul Kerr even claimed that it was "not a programme category" at all, but "a debate" (about terms, definitions, intentions, and methodologies). Distinctively televisual, the documentary drama is best described as a subgenre linked to the documentary and the drama programming so important to British television's historical remit to inform, instruct, and entertain. It has clear links to traditions of film and radio documentary on the one hand, and realist stage and film drama on the other. It has gathered a number of often confusing labels over the years, but there are enough significant distinguishing characteristics for these types of programmes to be labeled and to be recognisable to audiences. They are not regular features of television schedules, tending rather to be occasional ones related directly to events and issues in the public sphere. Tied as they often are to a news and current affairs agenda, this direct connection has sometimes resulted in controversy.

It is not surprising, then, that this subgenre has proved difficult to define, generating arguments about the balances that can or should be struck between forms often seen as antithetical. With documentary borrowing the privileged status of the "fact" itself, and acquiring the patina of the overtly "truthful" in the twentieth century, the documentary drama has caused broadcasting institutions increasingly to have recourse to "Producers' Guidelines" to police its making. Programme makers, real-world individuals depicted, audiences and commentators alike have been concerned that the overtly fictional structures of drama add an almost equal and opposite veneer of inherent "untruthfulness" to the treatment of a subject, contaminating the sober purity of documentary. The two terms *documentary drama* and *drama documentary* are the most common, but it is doubtful which is the more accurate. The terms have been routinely contracted ("docudrama," "dramadoc") and periodically sidelined in favour of neologisms (such as "faction," briefly fashionable in the 1980s). Corner (1996) and Paget (1998) contain discussions of some of the issues arising from the complex history of the naming of the mixed forms. The documentary drama appears to make a "both/and" claim, its documentary research base making a bid for the moral high ground of the documentary while its dramatic structure vies for the territory of the "make-believe" diversion, the entertainment. Because of this, it invites an "either/or" counterclaim. The suspicion that the status of factual information is compromised when set within a drama is likely to remain a constant in quotidian criticism (just as fidelity to the text will always remain an issue in popular discourse about the adaptation of novels into films).

A hybrid form from the outset, the documentary drama can so easily be deemed bogus and exploitative. Definition and discussion alike, then, have articulated doubts about:

1. The nature and status of factual material used in making the film.
2. The extent and reliability of the facts presented directly.
3. The modes of dramatic representation employed.
4. The resultant potential for misinforming and misleading audiences.

The overarching worry is an ethical one about the justification for and effects of "dramatic licence" on factual material. The fear that liberties are taken with, and gross simplifications made about, complex real-world issues by the very act of dramatization lurks especially behind much newspaper commentary on documentary drama. By the end of the twentieth century, a further worry developed about the effects on this already "suspect" form of the general tendency of a television ecology rapidly becoming globalized. The commercial interests of international capital were widely perceived to be transcending any national "public service" interests, however deeply enshrined it might be in charters. A sensational "tabloid tendency" was perceived to be driving television output toward melodramatic and

emotive treatments of issues. This was not just the case for drama and its subgenres; it began to be debated right across the "flow" of television, and included doubts about new current affairs and news formats too. Documentary drama moved increasingly toward Hollywood-inspired genre filmmaking toward the end of the twentieth century, a tendency exacerbated by 1990s co-productions between British and European broadcasters and U.S. companies such as Home Box Office. This development moved the documentary drama ever closer to the US "Movie of the Week" docudrama. More sophisticated audiences, too, became familiar with the idea that the boundary between fact and fiction is becoming dangerously blurred, even in the documentary proper, and the vogue for "reality television" increased the anxiety about this.

Whatever the doubts and suspicion generated, docudrama is unlikely to disappear from the schedules in a new century of globalized, digitized mass media production. Its principal advantage for production companies is that its real-world template offers a high level of pre-publicity (from the airing of events depicted in previous news and current affairs coverage). Although this can be a double-edged sword, it virtually guarantees that audiences will have some prior knowledge of a film's subject before viewing, and that screenwriters can use a ready-made story as a pitch/treatment template and to provide a narrative structure for scripting. These factors are such a potential advantage in the market place that Hollywood itself began to make docudramas more systematically in the last decade of the twentieth century.

Documentary drama was a feature of broadcast television from the earliest days. When the fledgling BBC television service went back on the air after the Second World War, the "story documentary" was a staple on the only available channel. At this time some level of fictionalization had to be accepted in order to counter-balance technical restrictions. The practical advantages to hard-pressed programme makers (and the relative willingness of their audience to trust them) ensured that definitions of the form were not seen as crucial, nor was much controversy evident, in this early period.

The first justifications for mixing documentary with drama came from writers and producers such as Robert Barr, Arthur Swinson, and Caryl Doncaster. In a 1951 memorandum to his BBC Head of Service, Robert Barr (clearly revealing his Griersonian heritage) claimed that documentary itself was about "the dramatization of facts, reconstruction of events"; he was happy for "any dramatic device" to be used in order for his programmes to make their point (see Paget 1998). Swinson (1955) made a distinction between the studio-based "story documentary" on the one hand, and the "built Outside Broadcast" on the other. In the former, actors presented live in the studio a scripted and rehearsed play that had been carefully researched; in the latter programme, equally live, real-life individuals devised and rehearsed illustrative dialogue polished by TV writers. They then performed scenarios based on their actual work in front of cameras in their actual workplaces. This tells us much about the negotiations of form necessary technically and the unproblematic conflation of the documentary and the drama forms that obtained at this time. The focus, as with the "human interest" journalism these programmes most resemble, was on the individual professional. Doncaster gave her definition of the story documentary as "a method of translating complex social problems into human terms" (see Rotha 1956). This human story as a conduit for information, so often sought by broadcasters and journalists alike, has remained a vital part of the documentary drama.

If the mixed form of television was not a controversial issue in the 1950s, a change occurred in the 1960s. Two factors heightened documentary drama's visibility to audiences and commentators alike: the influence of "Direct Cinema" documentary from the USA, and the rise of the self-consciously realistic, socially focused drama in Britain. Within the institution of British television, programmes now began to emerge from more than one department. The dramatized, story documentaries of the early 1950s were the responsibility of the old-style current affairs "Features" departments, whose personnel inherited their methodology from radio and journalism. But drama departments became eager to participate in the new realism, and their search for real-world material began to make an impact. For example, studio-based series such as *Emergency—Ward 10* (1957–67) and *Probation Officer* (1959–62) were categorised by ITV as "documentary dramas." They were really more akin to soap operas, but their makers claimed a basis in research to justify the categorization. More significantly, British television drama began to exhibit a pronounced documentary "look" based on the portable equipment and visceral camera techniques so much a feature of Direct Cinema. Television writers, too, increasingly used research to underscore social commentary, research often generated in other contexts. The groundbreaking 1966 film *Cathy Come Home*, for example, was written by Jeremy Sandford, a journalist who had spent a considerable time researching homelessness for press and radio. The

BBC's "Wednesday Play" and "Play for Today" strands (which between them ran from 1964 to 1984) often broadcasted teleplays that, like *Cathy*, had a documentary base. Examples include *Up the Junction* (1965), *In Two Minds* (1967), *Edna the Inebriate Woman* (1971), *The Cheviot, the Stag, and the Black, Black Oil* (1974), *Days of Hope* (1975), and *The Spongers* (1978)—all but two of these produced by Tony Garnett and directed by Ken Loach. In his 1966 reflection, 'The Merging of Drama and Documentary," Norman Swallow noted that the "personal documentary," as he called it, had "much in common with the more serious forms of television drama."

Meanwhile, departments with an informational remit continued to provide continuity with the pioneers of the story documentary. Their output tended to stake more of a documentary claim on the research base generated by staff engaged in producing news and current affairs. From the early 1970s, Granada Television's *World in Action* team made dramas regarded by their makers primarily as documentaries. Often citing problems of access and/or political sensitivity as their reason for making these films, they dramatized under license, as it were, and as a last resort. Leslie Woodhead, a prominent exponent of the form, observed in a 1981 lecture that his own motive for "taking up the dramadocumentary [sic] trade was simple, pragmatic, and . . . to some degree representative. . . . I came across an important story I wanted to tell but found there was no other way to tell it" (see Rosenthal 1999). Woodhead's drama documentaries for Granada (such as the 1980 *Invasion* and the 1981 *Strike*) set a standard both for critics and for other programme makers over the next twenty years. Nor were current affairs departments the only locus of production; BBC Science has a long record of incorporating drama in its largely explanatory and informational output. Roger Silverstone (see Corner 1986) has called attention to the generally dramatic and personal story-centered approach taken to explaining science in, for example, the *Horizon* series that began in 1964.

The ongoing debate about the form has been fuelled again and again by controversies. Besides *The War Game* in 1965 and *Cathy Come Home* in 1966, controversies followed the transmissions of *Days of Hope* in 1975, *Death of a Princess* in 1980, *Tumbledown* and *The Falklands Play* in 1987, *The Monocled Mutineer* in 1988, *Who Bombed Birmingham?* and *Shoot to Kill* in 1990, *Hillsborough* in 1996, and *No Child of Mine* in 1997. Usually, controversy rages around content issues, with the form itself dragged into public attention as a by-product. This was reversed in the case of Granada's 1992 *Hostages*, when some of the former Beirut captives depicted (notably the just released John McCarthy and Brian Keenan) actually objected to the form itself as a means of telling their story (see Paget 1998). Many films, however, have coincided with, and contributed to, ongoing public debate and even revived dormant issues. The 1993 murder in London of the black teenager Stephen Lawrence inspired two such teleplays in 1999: *The Murder of Stephen Lawrence* and *The Colour of Justice* (actually a televised version of a stage play), both based on the 1998 Macpherson Inquiry. In 2002, a fresh inquiry into the infamous 1972 "Bloody Sunday" incident in Northern Ireland provoked *Sunday* and *Bloody Sunday*. All these films coincided with investigations of the incidents they depicted, and contributed to a wider public debate on racism in the former case and peace in Northern Ireland in the latter.

Much of the academic debate about documentary drama and drama documentary goes back to an article in 1980 by John Caughie in the periodical *Screen* (anthologized in Goodwin and Kerr 1983). He drew a distinction between the naturalistic filming and acting techniques employed by Garnett and Loach in their *Days of Hope* series and the disruptive montage employed by John McGrath in *The Cheviot, the Stag, and the Black, Black Oil*. The former, a four-part mini-series written by Jim Allen, charted the pressures toward compromise experienced by the revolutionary elements of the British working class in the 1920s. The latter (based on a successful "fringe" theatre production that toured Scotland in 1973) utilised a wide range of both documentary and dramatic techniques and devices to explore Scotland's historic, and ongoing, exploitation by a colonial power—England. Caughie argued that naturalism was such a fatally compromised form (associated too much with consensual drama) that it lacked the politically "progressive" credentials of McGrath's triumphant merging of stage and TV dramatic and documentary procedures. Playwright David Edgar added another dimension to understanding of the form when he wrote an important essay in *The Stage and Television Today* in 1981. He stressed the persuasiveness of facts when harnessed to the rhetorical power of drama. His classic formulation was that "the factual basis of the story gives the action of the play its credibility" for an audience (see Edgar 1988).

The increased level of interest in the documentary drama evident in the 1980s, partly to do with its relatively high visibility, is evidenced in Goodwin and Kerr's 1983 *BFI Dossier 19: Drama-Documentary*, which reprinted the essays of Caughie, Edgar,

and others. The anthology examined the form's history and provenance, then documented the critical reception of contemporary work. Goodwin's 1986 *Teaching TV Drama-Documentary* summarised much of this, and examined the pedagogical implications of the form for the burgeoning field of academic Media Studies. Practitioners were also entering the debate in order to explain and justify their work. When the two worlds met, as when Leslie Woodhead's filming of *Strike* was observed for the journal *Sight and Sound* by Elizabeth Sussex in 1981, valuable insights into methodology resulted. This essay and others were anthologized by writer and filmmaker Alan Rosenthal in his 1988 *New Challenges for Documentary*. Rosenthal linked the growing theorization of documentary itself with the rise of the documentary drama. In two more recent interventions (1995, 1999), he has shed further light on current modes of and possibilities for production and edited another valuable anthology of essays tracing the subsequent path of critical thinking. *Why Docudrama?* (1999) does for the mixed form what *New Challenges* did for the whole conspectus of documentary.

It is notable that the mixed form has been of rather less interest to American critics (but see Lipkin 2002). One reason for this is that the American docudrama has routinely been seen as tabloid, and unworthy of comparison with the manifest seriousness of the documentary proper. The leading American theorist of the documentary, Bill Nichols, mentions the form once only in his influential 1991 *Representing Reality*, declaring it "an essentially fictional domain." In founding British work on documentary, Brian Winston (himself once a member of the *World in Action* team) contrastingly establishes the *ab initio* fictionalizing of the Grierson school (1995). He has also (2000) examined increasing cultural anxiety about documentary purity following a 1999 "fakery" scandal in British television (when Carlton TV's *The Connection* was found to have cheated in some aspects of its documentary claim).

The British "public interest" drama documentary, by contrast to American docudrama, has had plenty of academic attention. John Corner's 1986 collection titled *Documentary and the Mass Media* traced the linkage with radio features (in an essay by Paddy Scannell), and with the early TV story documentary (in an essay by Elaine Bell). By the 1990s, there was more extended consideration for the mixed form from academics. Description, commentary, analysis, and definition are particularly evident in Corner (1996) and in Derek Paget's book-length considerations of the form (1990, 1998). Corner not only interrogated the form's provenance but he also writes persuasively on the increasing influence of fiction film genres on the mixed form. Paget makes the performative connection between documentary film and European and American left-wing theatre practices of the interwar years, noting in particular the influence of their disruptive non-naturalistic acting and production strategies (1990). He has also suggested a radical difference between U.S. and British traditions of mixed form filmmaking. Using the distinction first made by Caughie (and reinforced by Corner), he contends that the American tradition valorizes drama, in part as a consequence of U.S. television's commercial history, whereas the British tradition retains traces of a public service imperative (1998). Although, historically, the British documentary drama has favoured Caughie's "documentary look," pressures in the wider ecology of the broadcasting industries mean that the American melodramatic "docudrama" began to preponderate over Granada-style "dramadoc" by the 1990s. Co-production deals have exacerbated this tendency, but a public interest dimension is still observable in many fusions of drama and documentary. Some commentators see the "documentary look" returning finally as farce in the "mock documentary"; Roscoe and Hight (2001) identify this form as part of the documentary drama tradition. They see in films such as *The Blair Witch Project* (1999) fictions made in a self-consciously documentary style that provocatively subvert the codes and conventions of the documentary film, thus further interrogating the documentary's truth claims.

DEREK PAGET

Further Reading

Caughie, John, "Progressive Television and Documentary drama," *Screen*, 21, no.3, 1980, 9–35.

Corner, John (ed.), *Documentary and the Mass Media*, London: Edward Arnold, 1986.

Corner, John, *The Art of Record: A Critical Introduction to Documentary*, Manchester: Manchester University Press, 1996.

Edgar, David, *The Second Time as Farce: Reflections on the Drama of Mean Times*, London: Lawrence and Wishart, 1988.

Goodwin, Andrew, and Paul Kerr, *BFI Dossier 19: Drama-documentary*, London: British Film Institute, 1983.

Goodwin, Andrew, *Teaching TV Drama-Documentary*, London: British Film Institute, 1986.

Lipkin, Steven N., *Real Emotional Logic: Film and Television Docudrama as Persuasive Practice*, Carbondale: Southern Illinois University Press, 2002.

Nichols, Bill, *Representing Reality: Issues and Concepts in Documentary*, Bloomington: Indiana University Press, 1991.

Paget, Derek, *True Stories?: Documentary Drama on Radio, Stage and Screen*, Manchester: Manchester University Press, 1990.

Paget, Derek, *No Other Way To Tell It: Dramadoc/docudrama on Television*, Manchester: Manchester University Press, 1998.

Roscoe, Jane, and Hight, Craig, *Faking It: Mock-documentary and the Subversion of Factuality*, Manchester: Manchester University Press, 2001.

Rosenthal, Alan (ed.), *New Challenges for Documentary*, Berkeley: University of California Press, 1988.

Rosenthal, Alan, *Writing Docudrama: Dramatizing Reality for Film and TV*, Boston: Focal Press, 1995.

Rosenthal, Alan (ed.), *Why Docudrama?: Fact-Fiction on Film and TV*, Carbondale: Southern Illinois University Press, 1999.

Rotha, Paul (ed.), *Television in the Making*, London: Focal Press, 1956.

Swinson, Arthur, *Writing for Television*, London: Adam and Charles Black, 1955.

Swallow, Norman, *Factual Television*, London: Focal Press, 1966.

Winston, Brian, *Claiming the Real: The Documentary Film Revisited*, London: British Film Institute, 1995.

Winston, Brian, *Lies, Damn Lies and Documentaries*, London: British Film Institute, 2000.

DOCUMENTARY FILM INITIATIVE

Since 1998, the Documentary Film Initiative (dokumentarfilminitiative, DFI) has acted as the successor of the European Documentary Institute (EDI), which was located in Mühlheim and founded in 1988. The EDI conceived the documentary film as an independant form of art that must be developed and defended—in the cinema and television. Because of financial cutbacks, the institute had to be closed after ten years of activities. The DFI works toward similar goals, but works with a smaller budget and with only a half-time position, financed by public funding. It supports documentary filmmakers in the state of Northrhine-Westfalia, and offers one large, annual conference a year, as well as smaller workshops and thematic film screenings. The intention is to train the public to watch and analyse high-quality documentaries. The DFI often cooperates with other local media initiatives, or the Haus des Dokumentarfilms Stuttgart. Because it is a small initiative, it can be extremely flexible in reacting to current developments on the documentary market and succeed in discussing new topics first. For example, the use of the Internet for factual production and research was already discussed in 1999, which resulted in a homepage (www.dokumentarfilminitiative.de/dokfilm-net) with links to interesting sources for production and distribution. A year later, the DVD as a new distribution medium was discussed.

Another crucial task of the DFI is to analyse the economic situation of documentary filmmakers in Germany. For example, in 2003 journalist Fritz Wolf published a study about the representation of documentary on German television. He came to the conclusion that nearly 1,500 factual programs were broadcast on all stations in October 2002, but many of them were reruns and they were also integrated in a very tight programme structure. Not surprisingly over 90 percent of the documentaries could be seen on public TV and only 12 percent have a length of at least 60 minutes and more. The classical documentary as a solitaire became the exception; most of the programmes are part of serials, multi-part-programmes, or sequences. The study also discusses changes in the formats and the status of the documentary form in German television today.

The DFI also publishes a series of books, in which volumes on documentary filmmakers such as Marcel Ophüls, Alexander Kluge, and Hartmut Bitomsky have been published, as well as books on documentary theory, or in-depth interviews with filmmakers on their work. Despite its small budget, the DFI plays an important role on the German documentary scene.

KAY HOFFMANN

See also **Haus des Dokumenterfilm Stuttgart**

Further Reading

Blümlinger, Christa (ed.), *Serge Daney. Augenzeugenberichte eines Cinephilen*, Berlin: Vorwerk 8, 2000.

Eue, Ralph, and Constantin Wulff (eds.), *Marcel Ophüls. Widerreden und andere Liebeserklärungen*, Berlin: Vorwerk 8, 1998.

Farocki, Harun, and Kaja Silverman, *Von Godard sprechen*, Berlin: Vorwerk 8, 2002.

Hohenberger, Eva (ed.), *Bilder des Wirklichen. Texte zur Theorie des Dokumentarfilms*, Berlin: Vorwerk 8, 2000.

Hohenberger, Eva, and Judith Keilbach (eds.), *Die Gegenwart der Vergangenheit. Dokumentarfilm, Fernsehen und Geschichte*, Berlin: Vorwerk 8, 2003.

Schaarschmidt, Ilka (ed.), *Hartmut Bitomsky. Kinowahrheit*, Berlin: Vorwerk 8, 2003.

Schulte, Christian (ed.), *Alexander Kluge. In Gefahr und größter Not bringt der Mittelweg den Tod*, Berlin: Vorwerk 8, 2001.

Voss, Gabriele (ed.), *Dokumentarisch Arbeiten*, Berlin: Vorwerk 8, 1998.

Voss, Gabriele (ed.), *Ins Offene—Dokumentarisch Arbeiten 2*, Berlin: Vorwerk 8, 2000.

Wolf, Fritz, *Alles Doku—oder was? Über die Ausdifferenzierung des Dokumentarischen im Fernsehen*, Düsseldorf: Landesanstalt für Medien Nordrhein-Westfalen, 2003.

DOCUMENTARY TECHNICIANS ALLIANCE

During World War Two, documentary cinema attained a prominent cultural position in Britain, and shortly after hostilities was assessed as the nation's "outstanding contribution to the film." In wartime, numerous filmmakers and technicians had been engaged on documentary commissions and with the coming of peace established or joined production companies in the greatly expanded sector. One distinctive new company was Documentary Technicians

Alliance Ltd (DATA), formed in 1944 as a co-operative co-partnership society by a group of creative technicians formerly with Paul Rotha Productions, including Donald Alexander, Jack Chambers, Wolf Suschitzky, and Budge Cooper. The idealism of DATA was evident in its self-declaration as "independent of monopoly and special interests," imbuing it with that sense of social responsibility characteristic of the period.

The Alliance operated from the same address in Soho Square that had once been the base of operations for the GPO Film Unit. During the last year of the war it won commissions from the Ministry of Information and made the uncertain transition into peacetime making documentaries for the Cotton Board and British Council, and then taking on numerous projects for various Ministries through the Central Office of Information: *Fair Rent* for the Scottish Office, *Here's Health* for the Ministry of Health, and *Probation Officer* for the Home Office. In particular, commissions were sought for "films dealing with matters of national interest and particularly matters concerned with reconstruction and other post-war problems." Of considerable significance for DATA was the award of the contract for *Mining Review* in 1948, a monthly film magazine for the recently nationalised coal industry. The films aimed "to foster a different outlook in the miner: to convince him that he was no longer a mere worker in an isolated mine, but an important member of a great industry of which he was part owner; to make him aware of the steps that were being taken to modernise the industry and to safeguard his health and welfare." The films were given many hundreds of nontheatrical showings each month for the National Coal Board, as well as theatrical screenings in some 300 cinemas in mining districts.

Following the general reduction of government film contracts from 1949, DATA assumed more work from industrial sponsors such as the British Iron and Steel Federation. It also began to generate a few speculative productions, such as *Britain at Work and Play* (1950), which was accepted for theatrical distribution. In 1952, DATA welcomed into membership the experienced documentary filmmaker J. B. Holmes, formerly at the Crown Film Unit. The Alliance was also ideally placed to pick up contracts from labour organisations. In 1949, it produced *Through a Needle's Eye*, a rare commission from a trade union, the National Union of Tailors and Garment Workers. While in the 1950s, it produced a number of documentaries for the cooperative movement, such as *It's Up To You!* (1954), promoting member democracy, and *Your Business* (1956), explaining the principles of common ownership. The Alliance was dissolved in the 1970s when documentary film commissions went into serious decline.

ALAN BURTON

See also **Alexander, Donald; Crown Film Unit, General Post Office Film Unit; Rotha, Paul**

Further Reading

The Arts Enquiry. The Factual Film, London: PEP, 1947.
"Behind the Screen," *The Co-operative Productive Review*, December 1951, 270–274.
Burton, Alan, *Film and the Co-operative Movement in Britain*, Manchester: MUP, 2004.
Hogenkamp, Bert, *Film, Television and the Left 1950-1970*, London: Lawrence and Wishart, 2000.
The Informational Film Yearbook 1947 and 1948, Edinburgh: Albyn Press, 1947.
They Make Your Films. No.1. DATA" in *Film Sponsor*, June 1950, 306–307.

DOCUSOAP

The growth of docusoap programming in the late 1990s was one of the most significant developments within British documentary television. A docusoap is an observational-style documentary series that returns to the same individuals in each programme and follows the progression of events in which they are involved. Of principal importance are the characters who are, ostensibly, ordinary members of the public engaged in everyday activities. There are also certain aspects of content and style commonly found: the use of a workplace location (usually one where staff regularly interact with the public); short, interwoven narrative segments; informal and audible interaction between the director and the subjects; a constant narration (which usually points out the obvious and/or creates drama where it is lacking in the visuals); and a cast of characters that often ncludes a potential "real-person-turned-celebrity."

By 1998, docusoaps were predominant in British peak-time schedules—particularly on the main terrestrial channels BBC1 and ITV—effectively replacing the sitcoms, game shows, and drama that had previously occupied this space. Series that established the potential for ratings success included *Children's Hospital* (BBC1, 1993–), *Driving School* (BBC1, 1997), and *Ibiza Uncovered* (Sky1/Channel 4, 1997–). Many new series were subsequently commissioned—notably by the BBC's documentary executive Stephen Lambert and by ITV's Head of Documentaries Grant Mansfield. Typically, programmes followed selected staff in holiday locations (as, for example, in *Hotel, The Cruise, Ibiza Uncovered*), in shops (*Superstore, The Shop*), and in medical centres (*Doctors, Vets in Practice*). The success of the British docusoap in terms of ratings, relatively low production costs, and widespread public discussion led broadcasters outside of the United Kingdom (in, for example, New Zealand, Australia, and the United States), to generate similar series of their own.

On British television, the sheer explosion of docusoap programming at the end of the 1990s led to a repetition of subjects as well as format. For example, Channel Four's series *Lagos Airport* followed on the heels of ITV's *Airline* (1998–) and the BBC's *Airport* (1996–), although the former did have the (less popular) distinction of being filmed overseas. Many series were produced in-house by the BBC and, to a lesser extent, by London Weekend Television; production company Lion TV was also dominant in this field.

Significant for audience appeal is the promise of seeing "behind the scenes" of an organization such as an airport that viewers are likely to have encountered themselves. Low-key dramas, such as a passenger's late arrival to board a plane or the security alert surrounding an abandoned suitcase, also form a central part of individual episodes. However, long-term viewer interest and the likelihood of a series being recommissioned rest largely on the appeal of regular characters (the larger-than-life woman who works at the check-in desk, the world-weary customs officer, and so forth).

Although many of the characters filmed are striking for their "ordinariness," those who make the most impact, and consequently become central to the series' image, are generally either charming and witty (Jeremy from *Airport*) or sarcastic and mean (Eileen from *Hotel*). These people are invariably flagged as "stars" in the opening titles, with shots of them in a characteristically humorous or confrontational mode.

Beyond the editing and the social actors involved, the tone of a docusoap is quite literally set by the choice of a narrator. Well-known actors (often from soap operas or sitcoms) have been used for many of them (soap opera actors Ross Kemp on *The Clampers* and Susan Tully on *Holiday Reps*, sitcom actor Leslie Joseph on *Health Farm*, for example). Consequently, the connection between docusoaps and entertainment programming is emphasized.

The epithet *soap* suggests that the narratives are largely concerned with the domestic and the melodramatic; its attachment to the term *documentary* also serves to mock the (assumed) journalistic pretensions of the documentary makers involved and, when first applied, asserted that here was a new hybrid phenomena: part documentary, part serial drama. The serialized format and the promotion of character familiarity are undoubtedly common links these programmes have with soap operas, as are their concern with talk and day-to-day life. Indeed, it can be argued that docusoaps have moved away from the macho, investigative style traditionally associated with documentaries, toward a more "feminine" approach, which brings relationships and emotions to the fore. However, the most direct antecedents of docusoaps are to be found within the British documentary television tradition.

Constituting a subgenre of British documentary programming, docusoap series perpetuate traditional documentary claims to reveal truths about the world around us by adopting a realist style and by presenting evidence on the strength of "being there" ("catching" events on camera). The emphasis remains on filming in public places rather than private areas such as the home, although places of work that are also sites of consumerism and leisure have been predominant. Furthermore, they persist in the Griersonian project of (largely middle class) filmmakers revealing (largely working class) people's lives to as wide an audience as possible (although docusoaps have, arguably, been more successful in reaching audiences than Grierson's films were, having had the benefit of peak-time broadcasting).

Although the term *docusoap* only recently came into usage in the late 1990s, documentary series that could now be classed as docusoaps date back to Paul Watson's observational series, *The Family* (BBC1, 1974). The telling of stories through the experiences of individual characters had already been established within observational documentary and a more economical variation of this format, combining verite footage with interviews and voice-over, had been adopted within British documentary television in the 1970s and 1980s. By the mid-1990s, the BBC's *Modern Times* and Channel 4's *Cutting Edge* strands consisted of a high proportion of single documentaries that sought to illustrate everyday British culture through such an approach, with an emphasis again on observational footage.

Where docusoaps differ most significantly from more traditional forms of British documentary programming is in their relationship with the audience. First, entertainment has become at least as important an element as "investigation" and docusoaps are watched by audience groups that were not previously engaged by documentaries. Second, the nature of the programme-viewer interaction has shifted, as docusoaps (in common with many other contemporary forms of programming) involve a knowing relationship between subject, producer, and audience. They are relatively intimate and, at the same time, exhibit a self-conscious level of performance; they are voyeuristic but also participatory. Furthermore, they focus on the pathos of everyday life and incorporate comedy and irony.

It was not merely the existing traditions and trends within British documentary programming that precipitated the growth of the docusoap subgenre, but also technical and organizational factors occurring within the British broadcasting industry.

A docusoap production tends to involve several crews (each simultaneously following different characters and providing material for the series producer to edit). The availability of digital cameras has enabled one- or two-person crews to shoot broadcast footage at minimal cost and aided the proliferation of a commodified production system that suits the serialized and segmentary nature of docusoaps.

Although a perceived crisis within current-affairs departments (notably the BBC's) in the late 1980s had urged the production of investigative documentaries by documentary departments, the new crisis during the late 1990s seemed to lie within drama and light entertainment. Sitcoms, game shows, and dramas were proving financially expensive in relation to their audience appeal and so a space in the peak-time schedules was opened up for docusoaps, which were relatively cheap and entertaining, as well as sharing certain characteristics with both drama serials and sitcoms (not to mention easy family viewing). The revitalization of drama and the resurgence of game shows (led by ITV at the end of the 1990s) brought about a significant drop in the number of docusoaps aired.

It would seem that documentary's ability to cross genres, to play with both fact and fiction, and to be both informative and entertaining has enabled it to step into the breach when other television genres are judged by broadcasters to be failing. In its docusoap form, British documentary programming gained a level of populism previously unseen, but critics and programme makers have been as likely to argue this is a problem as to welcome the genre's reinvigoration. Unsurprisingly, it was the differences, rather than the similarities, between docusoaps and other forms of television documentary that formed the basis of critics' interest and practitioners' concerns about them. The characteristics most commonly claimed to differentiate docusoap from documentary were, first, the promotion of characters and performance and, second, the failure to critically investigate social issues (due to the superficial nature of events filmed and the alleged promotion of the institutions in which they took place).

The docusoap's establishment in Britain as a major new television phenomenon in 1997/1998 (in spite of its continuation of trends already established in factual programming) was secured, not only by its prevalence in the schedules but also by the extent of its public discussion: from chatty features in the *Daily Mail* newspaper and on the daytime magazine programme *This Morning* (where the real-life stars of docusoaps, such as Maureen from *Driving School*, were guests), to a debate on the dumbing-down of television on the news programme *Newsnight*.

When documentary programmes that were labeled docusoaps first emerged, commentators claimed it was refreshing—democratizing even—to have documentary cameras trained on supposedly ordinary people. It was not long, however, before some of these ordinary people (for example, Jeremy Spake from *Airport* and Jane MacDonald from *The Cruise*) became celebrities themselves and with this development commentators became more cynical. Critics found the emotional and confessional displays distasteful, the level of performance dishonest, and the kinds of people chosen as subjects objectionable. Furthermore, the programme makers were accused of choosing certain types of participants for their docusoaps simply to maximize the entertainment value of their productions.

What followed criticisms of the docusoaps for being cast like sitcoms or soap operas was the argument that all the participants are performing for the cameras and that, consequently, the programmes are taken even further away from the truthful revelations documentaries were generally assumed to provide. It could be argued, however, that in foregrounding their constructed nature, docusoaps have usefully encouraged audiences to engage more critically with the genre as a whole (a development also encouraged by accusations in the press of stage-managed scenes in docusoaps such as the BBC's 1998 series *The Clampers*).

Although docusoaps have been criticized for failing to continue in the perceived traditions of documentary, they are still commonly perceived by critics, practitioners, and audiences as being a part of—or at least a descendent of—that genre. The most common criticism of the docusoap, emanating from both commentators and documentary makers, has been that it is both the cause and symptom of the documentary genre's decline in quality. The innovations in format and style that docusoaps entail have been seen as driven primarily by commercial concerns with ratings and advertisers, rather than by producers' creative experimentation. Consequently, the docusoap subgenre has served an illustrative purpose in debates about the quality and future of an increasingly competitive British television industry and, in particular, the purpose and viability of public service channels.

The negative legacies of docusoaps include an emphasis on ratings at minimal cost and a disrespectful attitude amongst certain practitioners toward their programme participants. However, their positive contributions to the documentary television genre are a demonstrable ability to engage a wide audience, a revitalization of broadcasters' interest in the genre, and a widening of the range of programme participants from the "victims" and "experts" previously prominent.

CAROLINE DOVER

Further Reading

Bruzzi, Stella, *New Documentary: A Critical Introduction*, London: Routledge, 2000.

Corner, John, "What Can We Say about 'Documentary'?" *Media, Culture & Society*, 22, 2000, 681–688.

Dover, Caroline, "British Documentary Television: Tradition, Change and 'Crisis' in a Practitioner Community," PhD thesis, Goldsmiths College (University of London), 2001.

Dovey, Jon, *Freakshow: First Person Media and Factual Television*, London: Pluto, 2000.

Hill, Annette, *Real TV*, London: Routledge, 2003.

Kilborn, Richard, "From Grierson to Docusoap," *Media Education Journal*, 26, 1999, 31–33.

Kilborn, Richard, "The Docu-Soap: A Critical Assessment," *From Grierson to Docu-Soap: Breaking the Boundaries*, edited by J. Izod & R. Kilborn with M. Hibberd, Luton: University of Luton Press, 2000.

Winston, Bria, *Lies, Damn Lies and Documentaries*, London: BFI, 2000.

DOGME95

Dogme95 films are fiction films, but both in production and aesthetically they contain many similarities with the documentary film, this being part of their power. They further the problematic debates surrounding documentary film concerning the eternal conflict between objectivity and subjectivity (Bruzzi 2000).

In Copenhagen in the spring of 1995, a collective of film directors founded Dogme95. Lars von Trier and Thomas Vinterberg drew up "the vow of chastity" rules on 13 March. According to the founders it was established due to the predictability and superficiality of movie making. As the Dogme95 manifesto contends, the expressed goal was to counter "certain tendencies" in cinema. "Dogme95 is a rescue action!" states the manifesto, attacking the new wave movement of the 1960s, where antibourgeois cinema became bourgeois with its focus on the auteur. According to the manifesto, the film of the individual will be false and decadent by definition, Dogme95 cinema being its antithesis. The decadent filmmaker seeks to fool the audience with illusions via which emotions can be communicated. This illusion is an illusion of pathos and of love, but for Dogme95, as with documentary film, the movie is not illusion (Kelly 2000). Dogme95 films counter the film of illusion by following a set of rules.

Despite their fictional content, some Dogme95 films appear to be documentaries in form because of the "the vow of chastity." Bearing in mind the apparent relationship between Dogme 95 films and documentary, the rules are:

1. Shooting must be done on location. Props and sets must not be brought in. (If a particular prop is necessary for the story, a location must be chosen where this prop is found.)
2. The sound must never be produced apart from the images, or vice versa. (Music must not be used unless it occurs where the scene is being shot.)
3. The camera must be hand-held. Any movement or immobility attainable in the hand is permitted. (The film must not take place where the camera is standing; shooting must take place where the film takes place.)
4. The film must be in colour. Special lighting is not acceptable. (If there is too little light for exposure, the scene will be cut or a single lamp will be attached to the camera.)
5. Optical work and filters are forbidden.
6. The film must not contain superficial action. (Murders, weapons, etc., must not occur.)
7. Temporal and geographical alienation are forbidden. (In other words,the film takes place here and now.)
8. Genre movies are not acceptable.
9. The film format must be Academy 35mm.
10. The director must not be credited.

Professional actors are allowed, but in cases such as the film *Festen*, where a famous actor is used (Hunnz Moritzen), the actor plays against type—for example, being the archetypal monster paedo-phile rather than the benign figure he is well known for. The director must refrain from personal taste and from creating a work, as the instant is to be regarded as more important than the whole. We see here the connection to documentary and live footage. The goal is to force the truth out of characters and settings in the moment.

Many claimed the marketing hype created by Dogme95 was not matched by originality, suggesting it was merely continuing previous movements such as *cinéma direct* and Italian neorealism, influenced by the work of the likes of Lindsay Anderson, Dziga Vertov, and Jean-Luc Godard (Hjort 2003). Dogme95 plays with elements of the observational documentary mode. Here, the aim is to keep authorial intervention to a minimum by adopting a more casual, observational style, following action rather than dictating it, to show events in what is claimed to be an unadulterated state, collapsing the boundary between subject and representation (Bruzzi 2000). The film format must be Academy 35mm, but this is concerned with distribution not production, with digital video and handheld cameras producing a verisimilitude similar to documentary. The Dogme doctrine is about moving away from movie making which is too easy, making filmmakers think harder about how they are going to achieve desired results, without resorting to supposedly synthetic or false means. A number of Dogme95 films, particularly *The Idiots*, which indeed at times appears to be a documentary, are genuinely startling and liberating.

Dogme filmmaking attempts to avoid artifice and by doing so actively reveals itself as a work of art but clearly there is a naivety in the notion that authenticity is obtainable. Dogme95 maintains the concept that cinema is reality or truth, and the dubious notion that there can be purity. Despite this, the economic constraints and the limitations of the rules did lead to innovations, producing many entertaining and profound films that broke the mould. A change occurred with the certification of Harmony Korine's *Julien Donkey-Boy*, the director declaring he had adhered to the Dogme95 manifesto, rather than the Dogme95 collective issuing certification. It was impossible to know whether the rules had been adhered to, filmmakers not knowing if they had rejected personal taste and genre (Hjort 2003). Dogme films were made in Korea, Argentina, Spain, the United States, France, Switzerland, Norway, Italy, and Denmark, four of the thirty-one receiving worldwide critical and commercial success. In a final press release in June 2002 the Secretariat explained that Dogme95 had grown into a genre formula and as a consequence they would cease interpreting how to make Dogme95 films, closing down the Secretariat. From originally confronting Hollywood hegemony and homogeneity, Dogme95 became a global package, brand, and marketing tool. As with any successful movement, in time Dogme95 become part of the establishment, rather than a challenge to it.

CHARLES LEE

Selected Films

1998 *Festen/The Celebration* (Thomas Vinterberg)
1998 *Idioternel/The Idiots* (Lars von Trier)
1998 *Mifunes Sidste Sang/Mifune* (Søren Kragh-Jacobsen)
1999 *The King is Alive* (Kristian Levring)
1999 *Lovers* (Jean-Marc Barr)
1999 *Julien Donkey-Boy* (Harmony Korine)
2000 *Fuckland* (Jose Luis Margues)
2000 *Chetzemoka's Curse* (Rick Schmid)
2000 *Italiensk for Begyndere/Italian for Beginners* (Lone Scherfig)
2000 *Camera* (Rich Martini)
2000 *Bad Actors* (Shaun Monson)
2000 *Når Nettene Bli'r Lange/Cabin Fever* (Mona J. Hoel)
2001 *Babylon* (Vladan Zdravkovic)
2001 *Diapason* (Antonio Domenici)
2001 *Amerikana* (James Merendino)
2001 *Joy Ride* (Martin Rengel)
2001 *Et Rigtigt Menneske/Truly Human* (Åke Sandgren)

2001 *Era Outra Vez/Once Upon Another Time* (Juan Pinzás)
2001 *Resin* (Vladimir Gyoski)
2001 *Security, Colorado* (Andrew Gillis)
2001 *Converging with Angels* (Michael Sorenson)
2001 *The Sparkle Room* (Alex McAulay)
2002 *Strass* (Vincent Lannoo)
2002 *En Kærlighedhistorie/Kira's Reason-A Love Story* (Ole Christian Madsen)
2002 *Elsker Dig For Evigt/Open Hearts* (Susanne Bier)
2002 *The Bread Basket* (Matthew Biancaniello)
2002 *Dias de Boda/Wedding Days* (Juan Pinzás)
2003 *El Desenlace/The Ending* (Juan Pinzás)

Further Reading

Bruzzi, Stella, *New Documentary. A Critical Introduction*, London: Routledge, 2000.

Hjort, Mette, and Scott Mackenzie (eds.), *Purity and Provocation: Dogme 95*, London: BFI, 2003.

Jerslev, Anne (ed.), *Realism and 'Reaility' in Film and Media*, Copenhagen: Museum Tusculanum Press/University of Copenhagen, 2002.

Kelly, Richard, *The Name of This Book Is Dogme 95*, London: Faber and Faber, 2000.

Roman, Shari (ed.), *Digital Babylon: Hollywood, Indiewood & Dogme 95*, California: Ifilms, 2001.

Stevenson, Jack, *Dogme Uncut: Lars von Trier, Thomas Vinterberg and the Gang That Took on Hollywood*, Santa Monica, CA: Santa Monica Press, 2003.

DON'T LOOK BACK

(US, Pennebaker, Leacock, 1965)

Donn Alan Pennebaker's *Don't Look Back* is the prototypical rock performance/tour movie, a genre that promises an all-access pass to the onstage, backstage, and offstage arenas of the life of a public figure. Reveling in direct cinema's ability to provide unprecedented access to its subject, *Don't Look Back* goes well beyond simply documenting Bob Dylan's 1965 concert tour of England by criticizing attempts by more traditional media to label the young singer-songwriter, by turns, a precocious teen idol, an anarchist, and a poet. Dylan's propensity for "playing" these roles for the camera while offstage raises the question of whether or not the singer-songwriter participates in this packaging process as he negotiates the swirl of

adulation generated by his breakneck accomplishments as an emerging young artist.

As a performance-based observational documentary, *Don't Look Back* depends on Bob Dylan's ease before the camera. The brash and opinionated young Dylan's effusive willingness to speak for himself during press conferences, onstage performances, and offstage critiques of news reports about him makes him the perfect subject for a documentary that celebrates direct cinema's superiority to older forms of journalistic reportage such as print and radio. However, *Don't Look Back* also revels in the paradox inherent in its ostensibly objective presentation of a subject with an established public persona.

A shot during which Pennebaker follows Dylan as he strolls from a dressing room, down a dark passageway, and out onto a brightly lit stage to deafening applause exemplifies direct cinema's greatest advantage over radio and print media: its ability "to go into a situation and simply film what you see there, what happens there, what goes on, and let everybody decide whether it tells them" about an event of public significance (Pennebaker 1971, 235). Incumbent in this goal is a journalistic philosophy of filmmaking that insists that objectivity can be achieved by simply documenting an event and allowing the audience to decide for itself its newsworthy implications. In foregrounding the role of the journalist, direct cinema afforded Pennebaker the ability to mount a critique of other more traditional newsgathering practices on the basis of a realist style that characterizes photography, television news, radio interviews, and newspaper reports as inferior because of their subjective dependence on an intermediary to select and organize facts and details into a story.

For this reason, Pennebaker resisted attempts by critics to elicit an admission that *Don't Look Back* also harbors a hidden agenda of organizing details into a subjective construction of "Bob Dylan." On one hand, the director described Dylan as a "guy acting out his life" and gleefully noted that someone had performed part of *Don't Look Back* onstage. On the other hand, Pennebaker insisted that "you couldn't fake it in a hundred years" and that "if there's any artistry in what I do, it is deciding who to turn this fearsome machine on" (1971, 241, 261).

Don't Look Back delights in revealing the constructed nature of press images and words. By allowing Dylan to speak for himself, the film launches both direct and indirect criticisms of

Don't Look Back, Bob Dylan, 1967, Sunglasses.
[*Courtesy of the Everett Collection*]

print journalism. During a seven-minute retort to a *Time* magazine reporter, Dylan notes the potential for human error in newsgathering ("You might hear the wrong words" and "You have to weed it out—I can't teach you to weed it out"); the impossibility of objectivity in print journalism ("There's no ideas in *Time* magazine, there's just these facts"); and print's implicit use of social and cultural guidelines to "frame" the meaning of a news event ("I mean, it's a certain class of people that take the magazine seriously"). To be sure, Dylan simultaneously effaces direct cinema's own subjectivity by defining the truth as "just a plain picture," evading in the process any recognition of documentary's construction of truth through its juxtaposition of strips of celluloid frames. For example, Pennebaker contrasts Dylan's assertion to a reporter that he doesn't compose music or write lyrics while on the road with a scene of the songwriter hunching over a typewriter in his hotel room. While it is impossible to tell if Dylan is composing a song, the indisputable evidence provided by Pennebaker's "picture logic" suggests that the interviewer who relies on Dylan's "word logic" is more likely to get it wrong (Hall 1998, 232).

In a similar condemnation of radio as a newsgathering technique, Pennebaker abruptly cuts short an interview that begins with a British Broadcasting Corporation reporter asking, "How did it all begin for you, Bob? How did you get started?" As Dylan organizes a reply, Pennebaker suddenly cuts to even earlier footage of the singer accompanying himself on acoustic guitar and singing before a group of black men, apparently farm workers, in a rural setting. The timing of the cut again implies that if a picture is worth a thousand words then radio simply cannot convey the truth as vividly as direct cinema. That the director chose to include the pre-interview segment at all is perhaps best understood on the basis of how it upholds the film's agenda of flaunting its own ostensible verisimilitude. That Pennebaker shows the radio interviewer submitting his four questions to his subject for prior approval suggests that the director is once again criticizing the false spontaneity of the interview and the contrived nature of Dylan's pre-formulated responses.

In *Don't Look Back*'s final scene, Pennebaker and his subject launch one last fusillade at the mainstream media. Responding to another printed attempt to label him, Dylan sighs, "Give the 'anarchist' a cigarette. A singer such as I. It probably took them a while to think of that name." While the comment on one level offers a conclusive critique of the press's propensity for packaging

Dylan, on another plane it stakes out direct cinema's position as a decidedly liberal rather than revolutionary reportage style. In the tradition of the press's role as provocateur of public discussion, *Don't Look Back* offers the deceptively simple claim that detached observation can yield objective truth while masking its own implicit—albeit inspired—construction of reality.

CHARLES LEE

See also **Pennebaker, D.A.**

Don't Look Back (USA, 60 mins.). Distributed by LPI. Produced by Albert Grossman and John Cort. Directed by Donn Alan Pennebaker. Cinematography by Howard Alk and Jones Alk. Editing by Donn Alan Pennebaker. Sound direction by Bob Van Dyke and Jones Alk.

Further Reading

Allen, Robert C., and Douglas Gomery, *Film History: Theory and Practice*, New York: Knopf, 1985.

Bernard, Jami, *Review of* Don't Look Back, *New York Post*, September 4, 1992, 92.

Gilliatt, Penelope, "The Current Cinema: Under Thirty," *New Yorker*, September 9, 1967, 109–116.

Hall, Jeanne, "'Don't You Ever Just Watch?': American Cinema Verite and Don't Look Back," *Documenting the Documentary: Close Readings of Documentary Film and Video*, edited by Barry Keith Grant and Jeannette Sloniowski, Detroit: Wayne State University Press, 1998.

Issari, Mohammad Ali, *Cinema Verite*, East Lansing, MI: Michigan State University Press, 1971.

Levin, G. Roy, "D.A. Pennebaker," *Documentary Explorations: 15 Interviews with Film-makers*, Garden City, NY: Doubleday, 1971.

Mamber, Stephen, *Cinema Verite in America: Studies in Uncontrolled Documentary*, Cambridge: MIT Press, 1974.

Maslin, Janet, "Bob Dylan," in *The Rolling Stone Illustrated History of Rock and Roll*, edited by Jim Miller, New York: Random House/Rolling Stone Press, 1980.

Rosenthal, Alan, *The New Documentary in Action: A Casebook in Film Making*, Berkeley: University of California Press, 1971.

DREW ASSOCIATES

In the late 1950s, *Life* magazine photojournalist and editor Robert Drew assembled a group of skilled young cameramen and correspondents and produced a body of impressive films that revolutionized documentary cinema in the United States. Those associated with Drew are among the most noted names in documentary: Richard Leacock, D. A. Pennebaker, Albert Maysles, Gregory Shuker, James Lipscomb, and Hope Ryden. Drew sought to do in film what *Life* did with photography: to capture important portraits of human beings, which told stories and revealed character.

Drew Associates is credited with introducing cinema verité or direct cinema to the United States. While Grierson saw documentary as the "creative treatment of actuality," the Drew filmmakers attempted to minimize their presence. For Drew, the Griersonian style produced "illustrated lectures" (Barsam, 1992). Drew believed that with the right equipment, film crews could present rather than explain, to see events happen as they happen, thereby allowing the audience to observe and draw their own conclusions. Because they received limited exposure on broadcast television, the films were not widely seen, but the methodology the Drew team pioneered would have considerable influence on documentary film over several decades.

In 1958 Drew persuaded his Time-Life employers to finance the further development of synch-sound filmmaking. Several experiments were seen in brief segments on network television, but the first substantial achievement with the new technology was a documentary of the Wisconsin Democratic primary between U.S. Senators Hubert Humphrey and John F. Kennedy. The resulting film, *Primary*, is a landmark of the direct cinema style, capturing the intensity of the campaign for the White House. At that time, documentaries had a limited presence on American film screens, and were more likely to be screened on television (as long as they were produced by one of the three networks). Drew believed—incorrectly, he claims today—that the FCC's requirements that broadcasters provide public interest programming as part of maintaining their license to broadcast would give the networks an incentive to sponsor such innovative documentary filmmaking. Time, Inc. owned a few local stations and broadcast *Primary*, but no network picked up the film. The second film Drew produced for Time-Life, *On the Pole*, was even more technically accomplished than *Primary*. Asked by Time-Life to make a film about the Indianapolis 500, Drew focused on the pole-position winner, Eddie Sachs. Details such as the shots of Sachs praying before the start, and Sachs's speech during the practice run ("I want to do *so* well") present a compelling portrait of a man dealing with enormous pressure. This becomes a major theme of these early Drew films, and indeed Drew himself stated that the filmmakers' interest is in observing people under pressure and how they respond to it, for it is in such moments that character is revealed (Bachman, 1966).

The "pressure situation" has been described by Stephen Mamber (1975) as the "crisis structure." Because the crews filmed events not knowing how they would be resolved, a dramatic question is frequently set up. Will the Alabama governor yield to the federal order to integrate the university (*Crisis*)? Who will win the primary? Will Eddie win the race? Critics have claimed that this focusing on people in crisis forfeits claims to "realism," since these events are by definition extraordinary. Although the selection of material illustrates Drew's interest in telling stories, how these individuals respond is more important than their success or failure. A related critique is that the camera's presence necessarily alters the events, or alters the behaviors of those being filmed. Even though the filmmakers never directed their subjects to perform and attempted to be as invisible as possible, several of the subjects clearly acknowledge the camera. This does not necessarily invalidate the entire cinema verité process, but it is also evident that many of the subjects chosen were individuals used to being in the public eye: the Kennedys, actress Jane Fonda, Indian Prime Minister Nehru, and others. The best moments in these films always seem to have some important dynamic between the subject and the camera, either when the subject "forgets" the camera (an exhausted Kennedy listening to campaign returns in *Primary*) or when the subject responds to the camera in a revelatory way (Jane Fonda trying to hold back her tears when reading a brutal review).

Drew Associates' technical achievements are considerable. In developing light, handheld, synchronous sound filmmaking equipment, the crews could take their cameras to places previously impossible in documentary film, and do so with a heightened level of realism (an early example of this is the famous long tracking shot Albert Maysles took following Kennedy entering an auditorium in *Primary*). In *Yanki, No!*, at a major meeting of the Organization of American States (OAS), the Cuban foreign minister angrily leaves, and only Leacock is able to follow him all the way to the man's hotel room, since he is not using a tripod. But the achievements are not only technical. The selection of interesting subjects, the ability to get the "right shot," editing that is at times obtrusive but generally effective, all indicate the photographic and journalistic skills of those working at Drew.

The challenge was to find an audience. CBS aired *On the Pole* as a sports special, and ABC contracted Time-Life to have Drew produce a series of films (called *Close-Up*), but conflicts between *Time* and ABC led to a termination of the contract. *Time* invested in twelve more films from Drew, but with no outlet for them, the films were seen in limited syndication in the U.S. (although they were being screened in Europe to much critical attention). The stories Drew wanted to tell were not what commercial American television wanted to show, since they did not bring in audiences. *Crisis* was the last film of the "original" Drew Unit; Leacock and Pennebaker formed their own company in 1963. However, Drew Associates' films throughout the mid-1960s and 1970s won Peabody Awards, foreign film festival awards, and Emmys. The company, still in existence, has produced a substantial body of work since the early experiments that made it famous. The *verité* style can be found in numerous fictional media (television's *Homicide*) and even though some contemporary documentary filmmakers have openly rejected *verité,* they still define their films in relation to it. The *verité* style has been imitated by numerous "reality" television programs, from *Cops* to *The Real World*, but few would argue that such programs contain the kind of journalistic detail one finds in the best Drew films.

TOM GROCHOWSKI

See also **Leacock, Richard; Maysles, Albert; Pennebaker, D. A.;** *Primary*

Selected Films

The early Drew Associates films were highly collaborative efforts; individual film entries will list specific credits. Robert Drew is frequently listed as producer or executive producer, and his role as final editor is analogous to the role he held at *Life*.

1960 *Primary*
1960 *On the Pole*
1960 *Yanki, No!*
1961 *The Children Were Watching*
1961 *Mooney vs. Fowle*
1962 *Nehru*
1962 *The Chair*

1962 *Jane*
1963 *Crisis: Behind a Presidential Commitment*
1965 *Letters From Vietnam*
1966 *Storm Signal*
1967 *On the Road with Duke Ellington*
1968 *Man Who Dances: Edward Villella*
1976 *Parade of the Tall Ships*
1979 *Images of Einstein*
1982 *Herself, Indira Gandhi*
1985 *The Transformation of Rajiv Gandhi*
1990 *Life and Death of a Dynasty*

Further Reading

Allen, Robert C., and Douglas Gomery, *Film History: Theory and Practice*, New York: McGraw Hill, 1995, 215–241.

Bachman, Gideon, "The Frontiers of Realist Cinema," in *Film: A Montage of Theories*, edited by Richard Dyer MacCann, Dutton, 1966.

Barnouw, Erik, *Documentary: A History of the Nonfiction Film*, New York: Oxford University Press, 1993.

Barsam Richard M., *Nonfiction Film: A Critical History*, Bloomington: Indiana University Press, 1992.

Bluem, William, *Documentary in American Television*, New York: Hastings House, 1965.

Breitrose, Henry, "On the Search for the Real Nitty-Gritty: Problems and Possibilities in Cinema-Verite," *Film Quarterly*, 17, no. 4, 1964, 36–40.

Drew, Robert, "An Independent with the Networks," in *New Challenges for Documentary*, edited by Alan Rosenthal, University of California Press, 1988.

Hall, Jeanne, "Realism as a Style in Cinema Verite: A Critical Analysis of *Primary*," *Cinema Journal*, 30, no. 4, 1991, 24–50.

Issari, M. Ali, and Doris A. Paul, *What Is Cinema Verite?*, London: Scarecrow Press, 1979.

Mamber, Stephen, *Cinema Verite in America: Studies in Uncontrolled Documentary*, Cambridge: MIT Press, 1975.

Marcorelles, Louis, "Nothing But the Truth," *Sight and Sound*, 32, no. 3, 1963, 114–117.

O'Connell, P. J., *Robert Drew and the Development of Cinema Verite in America*, Carbondale: Southern Illinois University Press, 1992.

DREW, ROBERT

Aided and inspired as much by the programming opportunities in the still-developing medium of television as by technological improvements that added to a filmmaker's mobility, Robert Drew shares a reputation with his collaborator Richard Leacock as the father of "direct cinema." Drew Associates, the company they founded in the 1950s, produced seminal films that shaped what would become known as *cinema verité* and offered a new, intimate way of looking at news events.

As a photographer for the weekly magazine *Life*, Drew became interested in moving documentary film away from the authoritarian model of John Grierson and others and toward the "candid" viewpoint offered by photojournalism. After a year's fellowship at Harvard exploring his theories, Drew made an unsuccessful effort to develop a news show for NBC, but the results were unaired. Convinced that television remained the best vehicle for the films he envisioned and inspired by the similarly minded Leacock, Drew obtained sponsorship from his former publisher, Time-Life, which owned a few television stations and was interested in developing programming for them. Drew and Leacock formed Drew Associates in 1957 and began to explore the methods that would eventually become the standard techniques of Direct Cinema: multiple camera crews using lightweight, portable equipment and synchronized sound recording, combined with an objective approach to the subject which allowed no outside, authoritative narrative voice molding the viewers' perceptions.

After three years of producing short films designed to coincide with stories in *Life*, Drew and his team filmed what is commonly regarded as the first important work to come from Drew Associates. For *Primary*, Drew and Leacock, aided by D. A. Pennebaker and Albert Maysles, among others, spent five days covering the simultaneous efforts of two U.S. Senators, John F. Kennedy and Hubert Humphrey, as they campaigned in the Wisconsin primary for the Democratic presidential nomination. With its close, intimate focus on the campaigners, the film caught not only the details of a political campaign but also the historical moment in which style and image came to dominate the political process; Kennedy and his glamorous wife mesmerize their audience through sheer movie-star charm, making Humphrey's earnest but old-fashioned baby-kissing and hand-shaking style seem quaintly archaic by comparison.

Drew's narrative approach to documentary can be summed up by the title of one his most recognized films, *Crisis: Behind a Presidential Commitment*. For the 1963 film showing the behind-the-scenes reaction from the White House as the first black students prepared their court-ordered integration of the University of Alabama, Drew benefited from his previous access to Kennedy, who understood the importance of the media. Crisis, however, is also the implicit subject of many of the Drew Associates films of that period, which tend to focus on a group or an individual as they face a major decision within a set period of time: A young heroin addict faces a week without drugs (*David*), Jane Fonda rehearses a short-lived Broadway play (*Jane*), attorneys try to have a death sentence overturned in the week before the scheduled execution (*The Chair*).

Working in a challenging period while U.S. media was changing rapidly, the Drew films set many of the standard operational methods for documentary filmmaking, but the interest and support of the television broadcasting companies proved to be unreliable. While Leacock, Pennabaker, the Maysles brothers, and other filmmakers who worked for Drew continued to develop his model of an intimate and immediate form of film journalism, they turned to theatrical distribution to counter the indifference and interference of network television.

ROBERT HUNT

Biography

Born Toledo, Ohio, US, February 15, 1924.

Selected Films

1960 *Primary*
1960 *Yanki No!*
1961 *Adventures on the New Frontier*
1961 *Football (Mooney vs. Fowle)*
1962 *The Chair*
1963 *Crisis: Behind a Presidential Commitment*
1966 *Storm Signal*
1974 *On the Road with Duke Ellington*

Further Reading

Mamber, Stephen, *Cinema Verite in America: Studies in Uncontrolled Documentary*, Cambridge: MIT Press, 1974.
Monaco, James, "American Documentary Since 1960," in *Cinema: A Critical Dictionary, Volume One*, edited by Richard Roud, New York: Viking Press, 1980.
Musser, Charles, "Extending the Boundaries: Cinema-Verite and the New Documentary" in *The Oxford History of World Cinema*, edited by Geoffrey Nowell-Smith, Oxford: Oxford University Press, 1996.

DRIFTERS

(UK, Grierson, 1929)

Drifters (1929) encapsulates many of the paradoxes of the British documentary film movement, both in itself and in terms of how it is perceived. Sandwiched ideologically and aesthetically between the cinema of Robert Flaherty and the agitprop of the Soviet Union, John Grierson's directorial debut was both the annunciation of a new type of cinema for the United Kingdom and an attestation of its potential failings. Nominally a record of the working lives of herring fishermen working off the coast of Britain, the film charts the activities of an industrial flotilla of fishing boats and the role of their crew in bringing "the harvest of the sea" to the market of the world. It is divided into four parts, beginning with the departure of the men, proceeding through their casting of their nets before bedding down for the night, reaching a climax with the retrieval of the loaded nets in anticipation of a storm, and concluding with the cargo being brought to port, where it is bartered and packaged for delivery to the market.

Drifters was made with the avowed aim of documenting the hithertofore largely unrepresented life of the British working class and exploring the role their labour played in the physical and psychic fabric of the age of steam and steel. Representation of this section of society to date had mostly consisted of comic burlesques in fiction films in which actual labour played no part. Grierson's determination to change this came both as part of a general move toward realism to counter the increasing illusionism proffered by fiction film and as part of a more specific attempt to "open, for Britain, a new vista of film reference" (Grierson, 1938) by establishing reality-based filmmaking as an instrument of propaganda and education. Inspired by the political ideals of Soviet cinema, Grierson envisioned factual film as a conduit via which the experience of life need not be bound by geography or economic circumstance, but could be expanded through cinematic interconnection that showed one section of society how the others actually lived and worked.

The film went into production in the summer of 1928 with the New Era Film Company, known mostly for promotional shorts. *Drifters* was originally to be one of four films produced by the Empire Marketing Board that year as part of a package of educational/promotional material. It is said that the selection of this subject was partly an attempt to curry favour with the Treasury, the Financial Secretary of which was among the country's leading authorities on the fishing industry. The film would eventually cost just short of £3000. It was shot silently, with Grierson serving as both director and editor, assisted by cinematographer Basil Emmott, then known as one of Britain's most accomplished cameramen. Grierson himself had almost no practical experience of filmmaking, although he had been observing and writing about it since the early 1920s. At the time, he wrote, "What I know of cinema I have learned partly from the Russians, partly from the American westerns, and partly from Flaherty" (Grierson, 1929).

Superficially, *Drifters* demonstrates the influence of Flaherty most plainly. Its photographic style and narrative structure follow patterns of observation and visual storytelling used by Flaherty on *Nanook of the North* (1922) and *Moana: A Romance of the South Seas* (1926). Although less explicit in its use of character, it concentrates on observing real people in a mixture of real and recreated environments in the course of routine tasks that supposedly make up their everyday lives. It collects the action into an overall "story," then segments this story into broad narrative movements that are illustrated with anecdotal and illustrative detail. Its opening scenes portray fishermen departing their village and use repeated images of waves crashing against the shore. The combination of imagery prefigures Flaherty's *Man of Aran* (1934), while its sentimental inter titles signal an attempt to distance the film from Flaherty by hesitantly suggesting that it will document a moment in which the traditions of the past are giving way to technological and industrial progress.

The film is fraught with formal tensions, as if, regardless of its polemical objectives, it is uncertain as to whether or not the exaltation of the labours of the working man within the industrial infrastructure is enough in itself to sustain an emotional connection with the audience. Grierson responds by taking a Flahertyesque turn to the poetic, although he avoids the excesses of romanticism because of the continued presence of technological imagery and because of the subject's stated direct connection with contemporary social reality.

Drifters departs from Flaherty and moves toward the Soviets in its attempts to integrate its observation of the rhythms of man and the sea with industrial imagery. It establishes a dialectical relationship between the surface and the underneath through a form of montage that, although less pronounced than that employed by Eisenstein, nonetheless betrays his influence. Grierson had garnered experience as an editor by working on the print of *Battleship Potemkin* (Eisenstein, 1925) being prepared for exhibition in the United Kingdom. According to Basil Wright (1976), "to work with him at the editing bench was a liberal education." As such it is in its editing that *Drifters* assumed a more radical aspect. Shots of boats forging their way through the waves are inter-cut with images of pistons and engines, the sight of a man shoveling coal into the furnace below decks informs our perception of the operations above where a sea captain barks silent orders at his crew. Emblemetic imagery of scavenging dogfish stealing herring from the nets at night and ragged seagulls pecking and squabbling over the catch while men in suits barter for the payload indicate ideological awareness.

The film is organised around a series of physical conflicts: between land and sea, sea and boats, men and boats, fish and men, men and nets, nets and fish. It illustrates these tensions with close observation of the energies involved, be they expended preparing the boats for launch, fueling and driving them at sea, letting out the nets, catching fish, or preparing them for market. It also uses conflict, or the expectation of conflict, to supply the climax: The fishermen suit up in rain gear and prepare to haul in the nets as the storm moves in. Although Flahertyesque in one sense, these contests are portrayed within an overall rhythmic structure that demonstrates some attempt to create imagistic and intellectual collision reminiscent of the work of the Soviets. The film is also, like Eisenstein's, driven by a sense of movement, not only in terms of the overall story, but within individual frames and sequences where images are rarely static. Almost every shot is filled with objects or elements in constant motion, and many are filmed from the deck of actual ships being tossed on the waves. The rise and fall of the horizon makes for an onomatopoeic

Drifters, 1929.
[*Still courtesy of the British Film Institute*]

representation of the experience of being on board one of the boats.Imagistic and ideological conflict coupled with a sense of visual and social movement are cornerstones of montage, yet the film still seems to lean more toward Flaherty than Eisenstein. There is an underlying sense that the rhythms of the fishermen's lives are congruent with those of the sea, not quite to the point of the neo-Rousseauianism of Flaherty's work, but still demonstrating what Ian Aitken terms a "pantheistic humanism" (Aitken, 1998) not too far from it. Meanwhile, the relationship between labour and production is not framed so much by an overarching dialectic of society or economy as by a simpler, more mechanical attempt to illustrate the process of production (fishing) in an informative, expositional, and educational way.

The film is of questionable value as a social document insofar as the term implies an engagement with society that extends beyond the specific instance of social reality which it represents. The section of the film that has come in for most criticism in this regard is the final one, which undertakes to contextualise the activities of the fishermen by suggesting that they are part of a larger economic and social infrastructure. A series of uncomfortable juxtapositions attempt to link imagery of the fish being prepared for shipping with white-collar commerce and trade. Images are quite literally blended together by superimposition, clumsily forcing connections between them in attempt to convince the audience of a breadth of social analysis that is simply not present. The film concludes with faintly elegiac inter-titles suggesting that what has been seen is merely the first link in a great chain of commerce and enterprise, but it does not in itself attempt to chart it.

Brian Winston, citing David Schrire, has referred to this as a "flight from social meaning" (1995), a deliberate avoidance of the issues raised by social representation by recourse to the poetic. Winston sees this failure as symptomatic of the British documentary film movement on the whole. The recourse to the poetic is, he argues, endemic to the methodology of Grierson's "creative treatment of actuality," which, as he says, "depends on an assumption of a particular naivete in the audience. Without such naivete, the audience could not believe that anything of the real would survive 'creative treatment.'" Harry Alan Potamkin, writing on the film's original release, went deeper into its structural weaknesses by observing that Grierson had failed to understand that true power of montage cinema was cumulative. Though Potamkin recognised the qualities that Grierson had brought to individual scenes, he noted that the scenes were separated from one another on a level of deeper meaning. This prevented the film on the whole from achieving results at the measure of the political aesthetics of the Soviets. "This was a film intended to show labor. If Mr. Grierson thought to extend it to inferences beyond the facts of toil, to the total economy of exploitation, his attempts at inter-reference between sea and market, fisher and broker, were certainly too inadequate" (Potamkin, 1979).

In spite of its flaws, *Drifters* had enormous impact. It was famously premiered at the London Film Society on 10 November 1929 in a double-bill with Grierson's edit of *Battleship Potemkin*, and drew largely favourable notices. Its portrayal of the working class was seen as a triumph for the common man, and Grierson's direction was singled out for praise by many contemporary commentators. Many observers saw the film as a preferable alternative to *Potemkin*. Its humanism was more easily subsumed into a socially democratic conception of state-sponsored cinema. The film subsequently received screenings at a number of commercial venues, and was also shown at the House of Commons by special request. A year after its release, *Drifters* had recouped its production costs. Its success cemented the Empire Marketing Board's commitment to documentary film as a component of its publicity and promotional activities. The EMB Film Unit was officially established in 1930, by which time Grierson had already begun to gather talented young amateur filmmakers of similar mind to himself to make more of the same. As Erik Barnouw observed, "After *Drifters*, they flocked to the Grierson banner" (1993).

HARVEY O'BRIEN

Drifters (UK, New Era Film Company, 1929, 49 mins.). Produced and distributed by The Empire Marketing Board. Directed, written, and edited by John Grierson. Photography by Basil Emmott.

Further Reading

Aitken, Ian, "Introduction," in *The Documentary Film Movement: An Anthology*, edited by Ian Aitken, Edinburgh: Edinburgh University Press, 1998.

Barnouw, Erik, *Documentary: A History of the Non-Fiction Film* (2nd ed.), New York: Oxford University Press, 1993.

Grierson, John, "*Drifters*," in *The Documentary Film Movement: An Anthology*, edited by Ian Aitken, Edinburgh: Edinburgh University Press, 1998.

Grierson, John, "The Course of Realism" in *Footnotes to the Film*, edited by Charles Davy, London: Readers' Union, 1938.

Potamkin, Harry Alan, "Grierson's *Drifters*," in *The Documentary Tradition* (2nd ed.) edited by Lewis Jacobs, New York: Norton, 1979.

Swann, Paul, *The British Documentary Film Movement, 1926–1946*, Cambridge: Cambridge University Press, 1989.

Winston, Brian, *Claiming the Real: The Documentary Film Revisited*, London: BFI, 1995.

Wright, Basil, *The Long View: An International History of Cinema*, Herts: Paladin, 1976.

DSCHOINT VENTSCHR

As one of the most innovative Swiss production companies, Dschoint Ventschr has developed a genuine style and is supporting many young talents and first-time filmmakers. Thus far, the company has produced over 30 documentaries and fiction films, often as international co-productions. They are concerned above all with themes of cross-cultural encounters, changing national identities, and unconventional interpretations of historic developments.

Roots of the company are the very active youth and video movement in Zurich in the 1980s. Dschoint Ventschr started 1986 as an artists' collective with the video production *Morlove*, which experimented with self-made electronic effects. In 1994 the company was restructured and Baghdad-born Samir and Werner "Swiss" Schweizer took over, working as producers as well as writer/directors of their own projects. It was one of the first companies to work with an Avid as a computerized editing tool. For *Babylon 2* (1993), about the second generation of emigrants in Switzerland, Samir developed a special aesthetics with different layers for the image.

Up to three images can be seen parallel and can be related to each other. With that new digital style, he broke from the linearity of traditional editing, but did so in a way that it is not confusing at all. He also plays with different languages, dialects, written information, and all kinds of moving images from newsreels and amateur footage to film and video. The film symbolizes the fragmentation and polyphony of today's society and chooses to be subjective. In general, their productions make innovative use of film language, constantly searching for new ways of seeing and making use of the potential of new media and new technologies. His recent film *Forget Baghdad* (2002) is a filmic reflection about the stereotypes of "the Jew" and "the Arab" through one hundred years of film, linked with the biographies of five extraordinary people: Iraqi-Jewish communists, who are often in the wrong place at a time.

Werner "Swiss" Schweizer concentrates more on historical themes, but also chooses new ways to present his stories. One of his first films was *Dynamit am Symplon* (1989, *Dynamite at Symplon*) and he got most international recognition for *Noel Field—der erfundene Spion* (1996) / *Noel Field—The Fictious Spy*, which won the prize as Best International Documentary at the Karlovy Vary Festival. In the 1950s American Noel Field, his wife, and his brother got in between the lines in Cold War Europe and were arrested in Hungary. But after his release in 1955, Field remained in the East. Schweizer's most recent production is *Von Werra* (2002), which tells the story of a Swiss individual who became a flight hero in the Third Reich.

Besides their own films, both are very active in production, especially with young filmmakers. That has earned the company the reputation of a "talent factory" within the independent filmmaking scene in Switzerland. In 1997 Samir and Schweizer received the film prize of the city of Zurich for this support. But Dschoint Ventschr is also active in international co-productions. For example, it co-produced Maximilian Schell's *Meine Schwester Maria* (2002)/*My Sister Maria,* Johannes Holzhausen's *Auf allen Meeren* (2002)/*Sailing the Seas,* and Harmut Bitomsky's *B 52* (2001).

KAY HOFFMANN

Biography

Samir was born 1955 in Baghdad, Iraq. He moved with his parents to Switzerland in the early 1960s. Following studies at the Schule für Gestaltung in Zurich, he began an apprenticeship as a typographer. After training as a cameraman, in 1984 he began making his own films and got a reputation for their innovative aesthetics. In the 1990s, he worked for German TV stations as a director of television series and films. In 1994, he took over Dschoint Ventschr Filmproduktion together with Werner Schweizer and has since primarily produced projects by young filmmakers in Switzerland. He also realized some video installations and a multimedia theatre piece.

Werner Schweizer was born 1955 in Lucerne, Switzerland. He studied sociology, journalism, and European literature. Since 1982 he has worked as a journalist and filmmaker. In 1994, he took over Dschoint Ventschr with Samir. Schweizer also participated in the EAVE producer program of the European media initiative.

Selected Films

1984 *Stummfilm* (Samir): director, writer
1986 *Morlove* (Samir): director
1988 *Filou* (Samir): director, writer
1989 *Dynamit am Symplon* (Schweizer): director, writer
1991 *immer & ewig* (Samir): director, writer
1993 *Babylon 2* (Samir): director, writer
1996 *Noel Field - der verschwundene Spion* (Schweizer): director
1997 *La eta knabino* (Samir): director, writer
1998 *Projecziuns tibetanas* (Samir): director, writer
1999 *ID-Swiss* (Samir, Schweizer): producer
2002 *Von Werra* (Schweizer): director
2002 *Forget Bagdad* (Samir): director, writer

DVORTSEVOY, SERGEI

Sergei Dvortsevoy is a filmmaker who makes existential portraits of people, families, or small communities, mainly by showing how these people live amid poverty. If one would be looking for illustrations of "observational documentary," one would find the best examples in the films of Sergei Dvortsevoy. Patience and observation are the keywords of his filmmaking—as well in his preparatory work, as in the filming itself, as in the editing. Dvortsevoy makes the spectator observe long takes that seem to be waiting for something to happen. And generally, something does happen. In *Paradise* (1995), for example, we are watching at one moment a small boy, sitting on the ground and eating. "Nothing special," one would say, but when after many minutes the child falls asleep, while eating, it illustrates the circumstances in which the nomadic shepherd family of the boy live.

We find a similar example in *Bread Day* (1996), when in a bakery, the camera continues to record, even when all the customers are gone, for long minutes, until the spectator sees—to great surprise—a goat enter the bakery. These examples are not the result of mere luck or chance, but of the thorough working method of Dvortsevoy, who integrates the people and small communities he films for months, in order to analyze how they live their lives and what things happen that may seem odd to the average spectator, but don't surprise the people that are being filmed; these events characterize them. His film style reflects this working method: The long period of observation and filming is translated into films that demand patience from the spectator. This imposed patience turns the spectator into an observer, making the viewer reflect on existential questions that do not seem to bother the protagonists of the films of Dvortsevoy, since, paradoxically, they are much too occupied by the continuous struggle for their daily needs. In this way the spectator becomes an active participant in the construction of the existential portraits of a family (a shepherd's family in *Paradise* and a family performing circus acts for a handful of people in *Highway*), of a community of elderly people in a winter-isolated village (*Bread Day*), or of a blind man whose self-made string shopping bags are refused by passersby, even though they are free of charge (*In the Dark*). *In the Dark* (2004) shows that Dvortsevoy is not dogmatic in his film style: The blind man lives with his cat, which is chasing the balls of string the man is using to make his bags. The cat, jumping around the apartment, throws over a stack of papers, leaving the man desperate. At this moment Dvortsevoy himself comes into the image to help the man pick up the papers. Instead of cutting or editing this moment out, the camera continues filming—the whole scene is part of the life of the man, and thus part of what the spectator has to observe. Dvortsevoy is not a dogmatic Direct Cinema artist; rather, he is one of the better observing filmmakers of recent years, who makes the spectator feel, observe, and understand for half an hour what he has observed for weeks or months.

KEES BAKKER

Biography

Born in Kazakhstan in 1962, Sergei Dvortsevoy studied initially aeronautics before he started his studies in film directing and scriptwriting in Moscow. Graduated in 1993 he has worked as freelance film director since then and won many international film prizes for his work.

Selected Films

1995 *Chastie*/Paradise
1998 *Bread Day*
1999 *Highway*
2004 *In the Dark*

DYKE, WILLARD VAN

Willard Van Dyke, originally a photographer, joined the world of film as one of three cinematographers on Pare Lorentz's *The River* (1937). Along with a number of writers, playwrights, filmmakers, and others prominent in the arts at the time, he became associated with the left-wing organization Nykino, which metamorphosed into Frontier Films in 1937. When Van Dyke and Ralph Steiner left Frontier Films on ideological grounds, a large-scale sponsored project left with them (creating tension among some of those involved in Frontier Films which was never assuaged).

The film became *The City* (1939), produced for the American Institute of Planners. It promotes the concept of planned greenbelt communities detached from urban centers. Co-directed and co-photographed by Steiner and Van Dyke, it was a notable success, and well received at the New York World's Fair of 1939.

Van Dyke followed *The City* with *Valley Town* (1940). Throughout his life he considered those two films his best. Sponsored by the Sloan Foundation, *Valley Town* concerns the problem of technological unemployment. Directed by Van Dyke, the cinematography was by Roger Barlow and Bob Churchill, and the editing by Irving Lerner; the score was composed by Mark Blitzstein.

A dark view of a depressed U.S. industrial community, *Valley Town* offers a partial solution to the bitter problem it examines. But, as with many American documentaries of this era, the hopeful ending seems tacked on to meet the sponsor's requirements without much conviction on the part of the film's makers. The impression that remains after viewing it is of an impersonal and vast economic system that serves few well.

Aesthetically and technically, *Valley Town* is remarkable in several ways. The extraordinary force and effectiveness of its images is striking. Its use of soliloquy, including some sung soliloquy, is daring.

Following the U.S. entry into World War II, Van Dyke (with Ben Maddow) made a film for the Coordinator of Inter-American Affairs, *The Bridge* (1944). It is about the economies of South America and the importance of air transport in connecting its countries with each other and with North America. For the Office of War Information he made *Pacific Northwest* (1944), which describes and interprets the Northwestern states, rarely settings for Hollywood entertainment (or other documentaries, for that matter).

After the war, Van Dyke made films for industrial sponsors, such as *American Frontier* (1953),

produced for the American Petroleum Institute. Although he retained some of the themes and style of his earlier work, a prevailing blandness replaced his originality and conviction. He also made a film about his former teacher, Edward Weston, for the United States Information Agency entitled *The Photographer* (1948). He made films for television when that possibility became available, including a number for *The Twentieth Century* series: "Ireland: The Tear and the Smile" (1961), "Sweden" (1961), and "So That Men Are Free" (1962). From 1965 to 1973 he was director of the film department of the Museum of Modern Art, where he distinguished himself in being particularly interested in and supportive of emerging and young experimental and documentary filmmakers. In his retirement, he returned to his first love, still photography.

JACK C. ELLIS

See also **River, The**

Biography

Born in Denver, December 5, 1906. Attended University of California, Berkeley. Photographer on government Works Progress Administration (WPA) Art Project in San Francisco, 1934; photographer for *Harper's Bazaar* magazine, 1935; cinematographer on *The River*, 1936–1937; co-directed first film (with Ralph Steiner), *The City*, 1939; producer for Office of War Information's Motion Picture Bureau, 1941–1945; made films for a variety of sponsors and for television, 1945–1965; director of film department, Museum of Modern Art (New York City), 1965–1973; vice-president, International Federation of Film Archives. Died January 23, 1986, in Jackson, Tennessee.

E

EAST GERMANY

See **German Democratic Republic**

EDITING TECHNIQUES

Motion picture editing (whether film or television) is basically the act of shortening and rearranging audiovisual material, and can include the addition of music, sound effects, graphics, animation, voice-over narration, and other elements as needed for the unfolding of the film story. In documentary, the editor often must review and make decisions about many hours of location footage including observational, interview, and archival material.

The goal when deciding on specific editorial techniques, styles, and forms is to effectively communicate to the viewer, and may include various additional goals including producing a specific psychological or emotional response, educating on a specific topic, introducing interesting characters and ideas, and examining and exploring history and social trends. The documentary film editor is an artist who helps endow the film with a richness and resonance that did not exist in the raw materials. By using rhythm and pacing; holding back information; allowing pauses; using music, dialogue, and other sounds; emphasizing the emotional character of an actor or subject; using a variety of shots; and cross-cutting between scenes and actions, the editor prods the documentary toward the psychological and intellectual domain that we have come to expect from great art and effective communication.

Early in the history of filmmaking, several filmmakers theorized this unique stage of the process, and attempted to explain both the rationales for various techniques and the power inherent in the editorial process. Various fields, including psychology, sociology, and media politics, have examined editorial forms for their power to persuade and tell stories. Editors use dozens of commonly understood and effective techniques to unfold a documentary story for the film screen, television, and web presentation. Following are selected examples:

180-degree rule—when on location, one mentally places an imaginary line between two people talking or based on the direction of the action. The camera is placed on one side of this imaginary line, and it can move anywhere within 180 degrees of this line to keep screen direction constant.

30-degree rule—if one is planning to edit together two shots of the same person or thing, the camera should be placed 30 degrees away in the second shot from its placement in the first shot to avoid a visual jump cut.

Continuity—the successful and unnoticeable continuation of a scene in terms of placement of objects, weather conditions, and camera placement.

Cross-cutting—interweaving two threads of the story line from different locations and often different time periods.

Cut—an instant change from one shot to another.

Cutaway shot—a shot of something within or around the environment where the action or conversation is occurring; used to avoid visual jump cuts or to compress time.

Establishing shot—often an exterior shot of the location in which the action will be occurring; incorporated to help the audience get their bearings and to understand where they are.

L-cut or split edit—an editing technique that manipulates aural space by letting the audio of one shot continue under the visuals of another shot.

Montage—shots assembled in rapid succession to communicate a particular image, mood, or idea.

Reaction shot—a shot that shows the reaction of one person to another person or situation.

Transitions—techniques from segueing from one visual and/or sound to another, including Dissolve, Fade, Graphic Match, and Time Lapse; used to psychologically move the audience from one point of the story to the next.

C. MELINDA LEVIN

EDITING TECHNOLOGY

For film and video to become so pervasive in such a short time, editing pioneers in the form practiced, endured trial and error, tried new technologies, established theoretical premises, and constantly evolved the art of editing.

Almost all documentaries are postproduced, going through some final stage during which the footage and other filmic elements are honed and manipulated. This postproduction phase has undergone radical technological change in the past one hundred-plus years, and while motion picture film can and is still sometimes hand cut and spliced, most documentaries originating on either film or videotape are now edited using digital technologies.

Perhaps the most important current term relative to editing technology is *nonlinear*. Nonlinear as it relates to motion pictures is simply the ability to easily change editorial decisions without starting over. Physically cutting and splicing motion picture film has always been a nonlinear process. By physically cutting film, the editor can splice with tape, view the combined images, remove the tape, rearrange the shots, resplice, and view again until the results are satisfactory.

With the advent of analog video editing equipment in the 1950s, editing became a linear process, with images and sound recorded from one medium directly onto another in the order decided on by the editor. Because this evolved form of analog videotape editing requires making copies from one tape to another, the editor lays one shot down, finds another and lays it down, locates a third and edits it, and so on. The editor sequentially lays down pieces of the desired shots and audio onto a new tape, thus working in a linear fashion.

In the late 1960s and early 1970s, various entities worked together to invent truly nonlinear video editing, by using magnetic platters and later digital storage devices for video. CBS, Memorex, MCA, Pioneer, Magnavox, and other companies were among the first to develop primitive nonlinear computer-based editing technologies. In the early 1980s, U.S. film director and producer George Lucas and his company, Lucasfilm, Ltd., designed a high-resolution graphics workstation along with sound and picture editing devices. The EditDroid was controlled by a computer, was nonlinear and had disk storage, and was relatively user-friendly.

In the intervening years, many companies and filmmakers pioneered technologies and techniques for using nonlinear, computer-based editing; today most films and television shows, whether originating on film or video, are postproduced using such devices. Such computer-based editing has caused a true paradigm shift all the way from big-budget international productions to beginning and student filmmakers. Whereas obviously large scale films use very high-end postproduction software, hardware, graphics, animation, and compositing, even novice filmmakers are now using impressive less expensive editing software packages installed in home computers and even laptops.

C. MELINDA LEVIN

EDUCATIONAL FILMS (UNITED STATES AND UNITED KINGDOM)

"Educational" is an umbrella term for any documentary that results in public awareness of facts, values, or issues and consists of such subgenres as instructional, academic, and social guidance. Educational films are commonly distinguished from instructional or historical films, as those are made explicitly for classroom viewing (see Instructional Film). Educational films were part of a progressive movement in education in the early twentieth century in both the United States and Great Britain. Proponents saw them as part of a greater vision involving a participatory teaching style. They were embraced by advocates as an art form and, even as a force for social change.

In the United Kingdom in the 1920s, the British Film Institute and the Central Information Bureau for Educational Films helped to expand the nontheatrical film field. The goal of these nontheatrical films was to impart information about the greater world, as well as how to conduct oneself in that world. Such goals corresponded to John Grierson's belief in civic education. Grierson considered "education" and "propaganda" to be interchangeable terms, both applicable to this pedagogical mission. Indeed, some of the films that ended up in the classroom started out as promotional industrial films.

Some of the most prolific producers of educational films in the United States during the early years of the movement included Eastman Kodak, Encyclopaedia Britannica, Coronet, and later, for television, PBS. The world of academia naturally got involved as well. In 1921, Yale University began production of the *Chronicles of America Photoplays*, becoming one of the first producers to attempt to cover an entire subject—in this case U.S. history—in a film series. After World War II colleges and universities played an increasing role in the production of educational films following the success of military and civilian training films.

Film Use in Education

The term "visual education" was first used in 1906. In 1910, a distinction between theatrical and nontheatrical films emerged, and by 1920 even clearer demarcations between educational and entertainment films developed. However, educational film struggled for years to legitimize itself in a culture suspicious of film's connection to entertainment. When first introduced, classroom films represented the union of the philosophy of progressive education and the technology of film. Early audiovisual educators, like some multimedia educators today, were radicals or revolutionaries in their time compared to their colleagues supporting print.

George H. Green, director of Visonor Educational Films, believed that film would free teachers from the chore of what he called cramming in the facts and allow them to concentrate on the "formation of character." American inventor Thomas Edison, an early advocate of film in classroom, predicted it would revolutionize the existing educational system. In 1911 he released a series of historical films about the American Revolution, becoming one of the first producers of films for classroom use.

The first real educational films were produced in the first decade of the twentieth century by British film pioneer Charles Urban on topics including the microscope, marine life, and the growth of butterflies. Edison and other producers quickly followed, making educational films in great numbers. In 1910, the *Catalogue of Educational Motion Pictures* was published by George Kleine, which included more than 1,000 films that could be used in schools. In the same year, the school system in Rochester, New York, was the first to adopt films for regular instructional use. In the same year Boston banned films in schools because of the risk of fire from use of film equipment.

In 1914, the Educational Motion Pictures Bureau, Inc. was formed. It was the first production company to issue syllabi to accompany its films. In 1917, the Chicago Public schools established the Chicago Bureau of Visual Instruction and the first educational film library in a city school system. Within five years, there were ten libraries nationally, including Atlanta's, founded in 1922. In the years after WW I, many city school districts established similar bureaus. In the United Kingdom, the idea of film in education was also in the air. The Cinema Commission of Enquiry, set up in 1917, produced investigations with favorable results, which were published in *The Cinema in Education* in 1925.

The earliest use of film in the classroom, although promising in the eyes of many experts, had no organizational support, causing slow adoption of film use in schools. In both the United States and the United Kingdom, teachers did not have access to films or equipment and did not know how to use the films properly in their teaching. A few considered the innovation a threat to their profession. Implementation of films slowed in the 1930s as a result of the U.S. Depression, which prevented government-funded educational film production, and producers directed their energy toward the more lucrative entertainment market. In addition, with the arrival of sound pictures, even more detractors decried films as more entertainment than education.

Despite these obstacles, production of films continued. In 1920, Yale University Press produced forty-seven reels of a historical program called *Chronicles of America*. In 1928, Eastman (Kodak) Teaching Pictures produced the first comprehensive series of silent educational films. In 1929, *Dynamic America,* the first educational sound film, was produced by Western Electric and Manufacturing Company. As equipment became more available in the 1920s, educational film industries and associations were established, and school boards and state departments of education became more open to the idea. In 1920, the National Academy of Visual Instruction was formed, which later consolidated with the Visual Instruction Association. And in 1923 the Department of Visual Instruction was created within the National Education Association.

In 1928, George Eastman furthered the cause of film as a valuable teaching tool. He produced instructional films specifically to show to 10,000 students in a dozen city school systems as a regular part of the curriculum. Evaluations showed that grades improved, students were more interested in their studies, and teachers enjoyed their work more. Indeed, city school districts, having more funds and staff, tended to be the first places to decide to use the technological innovation. Advocates worried, however, about rural areas or poor, overcrowded schools.

By 1931, twenty-five state departments of education had boards for film and media. Fortunately for advocates and the future of the educational film, studies in the late 1920s and early 1930s consistently showed that films motivated students. In 1932, a Carnegie Foundation study demonstrated that when films were used in combination with textbooks, students learned and showed a greater conceptual understanding. Early textbooks in the use of motion pictures furthered the influence of film, as did film-oriented college courses for teachers, which also appeared in the 1920s.

Other studies, from the 1930s and 1940s, showed that most teachers were slow or resistant to adopt films in their classrooms. Either they used films infrequently, or they failed to see how films fit into their curriculum. In the mid-1950s, more than forty years after the first uses of educational film, most teachers used film in their classroom only as an occasional enhancement to normal classroom instruction.

New problems replaced the equipment and introduction problems of the 1920s. Many films produced for education were of low quality and had little educational value, producers rarely involved teachers in the development process, many of the commercial companies producing films for the educational market had little understanding of the importance of tying content to curriculum, and there was little incentive for the commercial companies to produce for the education market rather than the box office. So as not to waste any commercial value, in fact, theatrical versions of the some of the films intended for educational use were prepared and offered for cinematic distribution, both 35mm and 16mm, sound and silent. Throughout 1935–1936, for example, school films with titles such as *The Frog*, *How Plants Feed*, and *Wood Ants* would turn up at Gaumont-British Distributors with new titles such as *He Would a-Wooing Go*, *Queer Diet*, and *Community Life*.

In the United Kingdom the situation was even less optimistic. The British Film Institute took a census in 1935 and found that of 32,000 schools and colleges in the United Kingdom, projectors were used in only 669 schools and 69 colleges. This was compared with 17,000 of 55,000 schools in Germany and 10,097 projectors in 82,297 schools in the United States.

As in the United States, most British school and educational authorities were hesitant to commit to the endeavor until they were sure of an adequate supply of effective films. Producers were also reluctant to embark on any such large-scale production until they were assured of a sufficient and continuing market. Thus a vicious circle ensued. Consequently, throughout the 1930s, tests and investigations were conducted to evaluate the teaching value of film. These activities led to the formation of advocacy groups. The Association of Scientific Workers, one of the first bodies to see the potential of film outside the cinema, set up a Scientific Films Committee in 1929.

The Commission on Educational and Cultural Films, another newly developed group, produced a 1932 report called *The Film in National Life*, which resulted in the establishment of the British Film Institute, headed by H. Bruce Woolf. The Commission reported mainly on science, geography, and recreational silent films. It concluded that the best available films were American ones such as those held in the Kodak library. British instructional films were not yet available on substandard stock.

The report found that teachers' attitudes had become much more favorable as they witnessed that the use of films helped students to assimilate, retain, and enjoy their history lessons. This was especially true in senior schools and in rural or poor urban areas. It was suggested that films would be best produced with cooperation between teacher, historian, and producer but, not surprisingly, were unlikely "to provide adequate financial returns to the producer."

Woolf created the *Secrets of Nature* short films series and made many other important educational films including the *Classroom Films* series that were used in schools during the 1940s and early 1950s. He reconstructed World War I battles in a series of compilation films, a type of documentary that bases an interpretation of history on factual news material. Late in 1937, a memo by Woolf, John Grierson, and another educational film pioneer, Mary Field, asserted that a company making educational films could survive financially only if it was able to show them theatrically, as well as in schools.

In a 1937 study in the United States commissioned by the Rockefeller Foundation, F. Dean McClusky analyzed the failure of educational film production companies. He found what many educators already knew firsthand—that there was a profound communication breakdown between educators and producers, that some teachers resisted technology out of fear that it would replace them, that there were too many poor quality films and too few successful ones, that there was little educational leadership to promote instructional film, and that the risk of fire was a strong deterrent to use.

Another report vindicated sound film in education. It was felt, however, that the films used were poor and that England was lagging behind other countries in beating the vicious circle of production and outlets. Nevertheless, by the 1940s, classroom use of films became a symbol of progressive teaching methods in both the United States and the United Kingdom, much as the computer did in the 1990s.

Academic Films

Of the more than 100,000 educational films made in North America between the early 1900s and the mid-1980s, many of the most effective were in the subject fields of art, history, social science, literature, and science. Such films are yet another subset of educational films known as "academic." They can be differentiated from those concerning health, safety, civics, and other nonacademic educational subject areas.

In the late 1950s, academic film companies were availed of millions of dollars in federal funds, as government and education officials hoped to get American students to academically surpass Soviet students. This represented the most financial backing from the government ever dispensed to makers of nonfeature films.

Social Guidance Films

Thousands of "mental hygiene" films were produced in the United States from 1946–1971 and were considered by some to be a uniquely American experiment. Conceived as tools of social engineering, they were created to shape the behavior of audiences, especially young people. They dealt with the perceived problem of beatniks, nonconformists, loners, bad attitudes, odd habits, sexual freedom, and cultural inertia. They preached clean thinking, good grooming, lawfulness, togetherness, sobriety, and safety. They demonstrated rebellious behavior as self-destructive and portrayed happy, clean-cut teens, thus promoting conformity. English classes even showed films about how correct penmanship helps people fit in. Social problems were woven into plots and the characters tried to solve them. A few ended without resolution to encourage debate. However, they were generally only about ten minutes long and many teachers did not use them properly.

Using the inexpensive medium of 16mm film, Coronet and then Encyclopedia Britannica were the two leading producers of mental hygiene films in the United States. Coronet founder David Smart thought the postwar 1940s needed educators to guide students through their youth by teaching values. Beginning in 1947, Coronet produced dozens of films with titles like *How Do You Know It's Love?*, *Improve Your Personality*, and *Good Table Manners*. Coronet produced more than 500 such films in the 1950s alone. Like many producers, they tried to determine what schools would be teaching the following year so that they could produce marketable films.

Mental hygiene classroom film production came and went with educational theory trends and the public's demands, changing as American teens changed. Dating, manners, and juvenile delinquent films were popular in the 1950s; atomic bomb survival was popular in 1951; antidrug films appeared in the early 1950s and again in the late 1960s. Highway safety films were the most perennial of all and are still shown today. The films also addressed the deeper political challenges of the day, promoting citizenship during the Cold War,

noninvolvement during the McCarthy era and the status quo during the Eisenhower administration. They were not successful in modifying teenagers' behavior, though they were more effective in the 1940s and 1950s, when young people wanted to fit in, and less so in the 1960s, when teenagers were more interested in nonconformity. They were idealistic and ultimately impractical. At their core was an attempt to teach viewers how to find a comfortable balance between the demands of the individual and society.

A few major studios also created classroom films. Examples were Disney's 1946 cartoon *The Story of Menstruation* and Warner's 1962 political scare film *Red Nightmare*. Other studios included McGraw-Hill, Caravel, Sound Masters, Knickerbocker, Hardcastle, Portafilms, Churchill-Wexler, Gateway, Charles Cahill and Assoc., Frith Films, Jerry Fairbanks Productions, John Sutherland Studios, and Crawley Productions in Canada. Independent filmmakers of mental hygiene films included Leo Trachtenberg, Dick Wayman, and Sid Davis.

Mental hygiene films were an accepted part of the American public school system by the 1950s and catalogued in special audiovisual libraries under categories such as Social Development, Courtship, and Leisure Time. In 1953, 5,000 new 16mm films were released; they had virtually disappeared by 1970. Early 1970s classrooms had vague "discussion" films providing even less substance than their mental hygiene predecessors did.

In the United Kingdom there was a large body of films that presented the basic rules of hygiene, with an emphasis on prevention. The Central Council for Health Education distributed the films of the many associations that made them and also organized exhibitions. The Health and Cleanliness Council in London had its own traveling cinema vans and sound and silent 35mm films dealing with the rules of personal cleanliness. They mainly taught by way of humorous stories and cartoons. Typical titles were *How to Tell*, which helped parents discuss sex with their children, and *Dirty Bertie*, which dealt with personal hygiene.

The British Social Hygiene Council was also concerned with sex education and the campaign against venereal disease. They also had medical films made with the help of the Ministry of Health for postgraduate and medical teaching. Examples include *The Diagnosis and Treatment of Gonorrhea in the Male*, *Any Evening After Work*, and *Social Hygiene for Women*. Production was taken over by Gaumont-British Instructional when it inherited the British Instructional Unit.

Educational Film Today

In the early twenty-first century, film is a fully accepted part of teaching in both British and American classrooms. Educational documentaries are of high quality and are still produced both by large companies and by individuals. They are shown on television, especially on public television and cable networks such as the History Channel, the Learning Channel, the Discovery Channel, and the British Broadcasting Corporation. Though some are made expressly for a young audience, most are intended for a general audience. Many educational films today are made specifically for video sale and cross over into the instructional category with titles such as *Have a Healthy Baby* and *Video Math Tutor Series*. Recognition for educational films are given by the National Educational Media Network's Apple Awards.

KATHLEEN COLLINS

See also   **Instructional Films (United States and United Kingdom);** *Secrets of Nature*

Further Reading

Barsam, Richard Meran, *Nonfiction Film: A Critical History*, New York: E.P. Dutton, 1973.

Cuban, Larry, *Teachers and Machines: The Classroom Use of Technology Since 1920*, New York: Teachers College Press, 1986.

Jacobs, Lewis, *The Documentary Tradition*, New York: W.W. Norton, 1979.

Saettler, Paul, *The Evolution of American Educational Technology*, Englewood, CA: Libraries Unlimited, Inc., 1990.

Smith, Ken, *Mental Hygiene: Classroom Films 1945–1970*, New York: Blast Books, 1999.

Stevens, John D., "Sex as Education: A Note on Pre-1930 Social Hygiene Films" in *Film & History*, 8, 1983, 84–87.

EIFFEL TOWER, THE

(France, Clair, 1928)

René Clair's short film *La Tour* (*The Eiffel Tower*), with a running time of fifteen minutes, is a paean to the French icon of modernity—the Eiffel Tower. The film is constructed as a cinematic postcard using rhythmical montage and editing as its poetic means of expression. Similar to the "city symphonies," many of which were being made at the same time, Clair's film straddles the margins between documentary and experimental film in its treatment of subject matter. Traveling up and down the monument, Clair's camera emphasizes the "iron lass" itself and the materials used to create it: the iron girders, the elevators, the cages. Clair constructs his film with sequences of varying lengths and speed, which make up a visual poem. As a hybrid genre it represents, as do many of Clair's short films, an attempt at "pure cinema," a film that was totally free of narrative restraints, and whose subject is realized completely through the creative use of the film medium.

The Eiffel Tower was made after René Clair had completed *Une Chapeau de paille d'Italie* (*The Italian Straw Hat*) in 1927. Clair had used the French landmark as an important setting in his film, *Paris qui dort* (1924), and felt that he had not used it enough because of the requirements of the scenario. The director wanted to make a film ("*une documentaire lyrique*") expressing his adoration of the Eiffel Tower. He discussed the idea with his production company, Albatros-Kamenka, who in turn provided him with a camera and film for the project. The short film was shot on location at the Eiffel Tower during the spring of 1928, and editing was completed in the autumn of 1928.

The Eiffel Tower begins with a postcard-like image of the tower standing against a cloud-filled sky. This pictorial stasis is soon broken by a rapid montage of images of portions of the tower. Clair then returns to the opening shot and fades out. The director then uses a series of short sequences, interconnected by dissolves, showing the history of the construction of the monument. Beginning with a portrait of Gustave Eiffel and architectural blueprints, the sequence progresses through the birth of the tower. The final shot of this sequence shows the completed tower with a title card that reads "1889." Clair then uses a slow tilt all the way up the tower that fades to black. The camera then enters the structure and begins an upward ascent to the various observation decks. Clair's camera movements progress upward from shot to shot, either by tilting the camera or "crane shots" taken from the tower elevator. At each level Clair pauses the camera to inspect the surroundings before progressing to another upward tilt to the next platform. When Clair's camera reaches the top, it briefly looks down to observe a man below looking down on the crowd below him. The camera then begins to descend much more quickly until it reaches ground level. Clair then returns to a close shot of the top of the tower. The end of the film returns to its opening postcard-like image of the Eiffel Tower amid a cloud-filled skyline.

The Eiffel Tower can be placed in the category of the "city symphony" in that it is concerned solely with a particular monument associated with the city of Paris. According to Richard M. Barsam, the city symphonies "present brief and realistic views of city life, united within a larger rhythmic structure—a symphony—by the recurrence of images, motifs, and themes that provide continuity and progression of ideas." Two of the most famous city symphonies, Alberto Cavalcanti's *Rien que les heures* (1926) and Walther Ruttmann's *Berlin, Symphony of a Great City* (1927), attempted to express the life of a city on film through rhythmic and associational editing. The synaesthetic montage portrait is a key element of these films. Clair uses tilts, pans, crane shots, fades, and dissolves to provide a rhythmic movement to a stationary object. Clair's technique was created in the editing room in an attempt to produce a purely cinematic portrait of the French monument. In this approach, he was probably influenced by the ideas of his brother, Henri Chomette (1896–1941) whose short film, *Cinq Minutes de Cinema Pur* (*Five Minutes of Pure Cinema*), was made in 1926. Chomette had been promoting the idea of "pure cinema" as an avant-garde form, even collaborating on a film with the artist Man Ray. *The Eiffel Tower*, in many ways is, because of its editing technique, a realization of "pure cinema" in that it lets the camera create an impressionistic viewpoint. When a friend suggested that his film should be accompanied by a Bach fugue, Clair made sure that was suggested to theatre musicians wherever the film was shown. The mathematical precision of the fugue is the perfect accompaniment to the rhythmical cadence of Clair's editing technique.

RONALD WILSON

See also **Clair, René**

The Eiffel Tower aka La Tour (France, Films Albatros-Kamenka, 1928, 15 mins) Produced by Films Albatros-Kamenka. Directed by René Clair. Assistant directing by Georges Lacombe. Cinematography by Georges Perinal and Nicolas Roudakoff. Editing by René Clair. Filmed in Paris at the Eiffel Tower. Released by Film Albatros on December 15, 1928.

Further Reading

Barsam, Richard M, *Non-Fiction Film: A Critical History*, Bloomington: Indiana University Press, 1992.

Dale, R.C., *The Films of René Clair*, Metuchen, NJ: Scarecrow Press, 1986.

Greene, Naomi, *René Clair: A Guide to References and Resources*, Boston: G. K. Hall, 1985.

Loyrette, Henri, *Gustave Eiffel*, New York: Rizzoli, 1985.

McGerr, Celia, *René Clair*, Boston: Twayne Publishers, 1980.

ELLIOT, WALTER

Walter Elliot, a British public official, is represented here because of his longtime friendship with John Grierson, leader of the British documentary movement, and his understanding and support of the documentary aspirations. Elliot had been at Glasgow University in the generation preceding Grierson (along with playwright James Bridie and other notables), and Grierson said that his class lived in their shadow. After graduation Elliot served in the Army during World War I, as a physician, becoming a major (promoted to colonel in World War II).

From 1918 on, he became Conservative MP and, in succession, Parliamentary Under Secretary of State for Scotland, Financial Secretary to the Treasury, and Minister of Agriculture and Fisheries. He also became chairman of the Empire Marketing Board's (EMB) Film Committee and, at a crucial meeting in Whitehall, on April 1928, was a key figure in moving the government toward a film program, which was resisted by the Treasury. Elliot knew and agreed with Grierson's arguments and, supported by L. S. Amery, Dominions Secretary, countered the Treasury objections. Out of that meeting came Grierson's *Drifters* and the British documentary film movement. Elliot was one of the influential persons who appeared from time to time to screen the EMB unit's work. One of its productions, *O'er Hill and Dale* (direction and cinematography by Basil Wright, 1933), was shot on Elliot's sheep farm in the Cheviot Hills.

When the EMB unit became the General Post Office (GPO) Film Unit in 1933, Elliot was appointed to the GPO Film Committee. After Grierson left the GPO in 1937 to help form Film Centre, its largest project was the "Films of Scotland" series produced in conjunction with the Empire Exhibition held in Glasgow in 1938. A Films of Scotland Committee had been formed by the Scottish Development Council in consultation with Elliot, then Secretary of State for Scotland.

Grierson's believed that Elliot was one of the Conservative Party leaders who had an interest in, and properly understood, the role and function of government information services. The Labour Party lacked that understanding, he felt, and when it came into power after the war, it undercut much that had been accomplished. When Grierson received an honorary LLD degree from Glasgow University in 1948, his old friend Walter Elliot was the Lord Rector.

Finally, when Grierson moved from the Central Office of Information to become co-head of the government-sponsored Group 3, which produced low-budget fiction features, Elliot supported him once again. The third release from Group 3, *You're Only Young Twice* (directed by documentarian Terry Bishop, 1952), was based on a James Bridie play with a Glasgow University setting. Its harsh treatment by many reviewers prompted Elliot to defend it in a letter to *The Times*. "Fundamentally about the funny side of the immense seriousness of youth," he wrote, "a documentary of the spirit."

JACK C. ELLIS

See also *Drifters*; **EMB Film Unit; General Post Office Film Unit; Grierson, John**

Biography

Born in 1888. Educated University of Glasgow; BSc 1910, DSc 1922. 1914–1918, Army doctor in World War I. From 1918 Member of Parliament. 1921–1923 and 1924–1929, Under Secretary of State for Scotland. 1931–1932, Financial Secretary to the Treasury. 1932–1936, Minister of Agriculture and Fisheries. 1936–1938, Secretary of State for Scotland. Died 1958.

ELTON, ARTHUR

The career of Arthur Elton is an exemplar of John Grierson's approach to appointing and developing young, traditionally trained university graduates into documentary filmmakers throughout the 1930s in Britain and thereafter in Canada and Australia. Stuart Legg, Humphrey Jennings, and Basil Wright were Elton's contemporaries at Cambridge. As an undergraduate in English Literature and Psychology, as well as *Granta's* film critic, Elton embodied the qualities sought by Grierson and joined the screen writing department at Gainsborough in 1927 under Michael Balcon.

While at Gainsborough, Elton was encouraged by Ian Dalrymple to script and shoot a documentary about London, a film never finished. When the studios burned down, Elton immediately applied for a job at the EMB (Empire Marketing Board) under Grierson. Of the remit of the EMB and its successor under Grierson, the General Post Office (GPO) Film Unit, Grierson was later to state in part: "When it came to making industry not ugly for people, but a matter of beauty, so that people would accept their industrial selves . . . who initiated the finding of beauty in industry? (Grierson in Hardy, 1966: 91).

Arthur Elton's earliest works with the GPO Film Unit exactly matched this ideal. In speaking of his young directors, Grierson also noted that: "In the three years that followed (the founding of the GPO Film Unit in 1930) we gathered and, in a sense, created Basil Wright, Arthur Elton . . . . Wright was the best lyrical director in the country, Elton the best industrial . . ."(Grierson in Hardy, 1966: 167).

Elton's *Aero-Engine* (1933, silent), however, is elegantly photographed in black and white and is an intricate and richly detailed observation of every step in the making of an aircraft engine. Narrative is subordinated to the internal visual rhythms of the industrial flow, and the film lies almost more in the tradition of films like *Berlin, Symphony of a City* (Ruttman, 1927) than in the realist propaganda mode so often espoused by Rotha and Grierson.

I was asked to make a film on British craftsmanship, particularly in the aeroplane industry, so I made *Aero-Engine*, which took me at once into engineering . . . I became fascinated with the processes and the people.

(Elton in Sussex, 1976: 32)

Elton's fascination with craft and manufacturing set this work apart from the more formal artistic experimentations of Ruttman or Richter. His eye was always on the actual work, the design flowing into the final metal stamping. He was, in that sense, close to a director of drama in following the action and then cutting in the editing suite to make the narrative clearer.

Elton's *Voice of the World* (1932) also revealed elements of stylistic experimentation. Paul Rotha was later to reflect that the film was the first documentary: "at any rate in Britain which used sound at all imaginatively" (Rotha, 1973: 162).

Just as with *Aero-Engine*, Elton had experimented with the formal flows of industrial process. When he came to make *Housing Problems*, Elton (with Edgar Anstey) tried out new ways of using the sound track in a documentary film. Directed for the British Commercial Gas Association by Elton and Edgar Anstey, the film used no omniscient narrator, but rather a linked series of slum dwellers on location (in freezing kitchens, hallways) talking directly to the camera and offering a sound montage on the failures of modern housing policy.

One of the narrators, a woman detailing heroic struggles with a rat, offers a direct way into the experience, for all the "amateur" delivery of her words. Arthur Elton had also used direct address or spontaneous and unrehearsed speech in an earlier GPO film, *Workers and Jobs* (1935), but *Housing Problems* used the more tentative experiments of the earlier film to more powerful effect—foreshadowing the effects of British television documentary makers of the 1960s (notably Loach and Watkins) and beyond. John Grierson was to comment:

Housing Problems is not so well made nor so brilliant in technical excitements but something speaks within it that touches the conscience. These other films "uplift," *Housing Problems* transforms and will not let you forget.

(Grierson in Hardy, 1966: 216)

As Production Chief of the Films Division of the Ministry of Information during the War, Elton presided over the making of some superb footage, but also continued the running battle forever run by filmmakers on matters of both budget and policy. Immediately after the war, Elton revealed a griersonian ability to be influential everywhere, from acting as Film Adviser to the Film Department in the British Zone of Germany to, later, on invitation, producing a group of films on "Social Denmark" to which many outstanding filmmakers including Carl Dreyer, contributed.

As he had in the GPO and Gas Association years, Elton became a leading filmmaker for Industrial sponsors, taking over the prewar Shell Film Unit from Edgar Anstey and acting as its "able guiding spirit" (Barnouw, 1977: 214) as he moved to widen the remit and scope of the unit's work after the war, producing films as ambitious and successful as *Louisiana Story* (Robert Flaherty, 1948) and, in Australia, *Back of Beyond* (John Heyer, 1954).

Elton's work at Shell cannot be judged in any traditional sense as advertising work; indeed the company policy excluded references to any Shell product or to the company itself in the film. In the 1950s, however, films like *Grand Prix* (1949) and *21st Monte Carlo Car Rally* (1951) were palpably "Shell products."

JONATHAN DAWSON

See also **Anstey, Edgar; Dalrymple, Ian; Grierson, John;** *Housing Problems***; Rotha, Paul**

Biography

Attended Cambridge University, studied English literature and psychology. Joined the screenwriting department at Gainsborough in 1927 under Michael Balcon. Made documentaries at Shell and Film Centre. Worked as a freelancer before his death on January 1, 1973.

Selected Films

1932 *Voice of the World*: director
1933 *Aero-Engine* (silent): director
1935 *Workers and Jobs*: director
1935 *Housing Problems: director*
1939 *The Obedient Flame* (McLaren): producer
1940 *Transfer of Skill* (Bell): producer
1948 *Louisiana Story* (Flaherty): producer
1954 *Back of Beyond* (Heyer): producer

Further Reading

Balcon, Michael, *A Lifetime of Films*, London: Hutchinson, 1969.

Barnouw, Erik, *Documentary: A History of the Non-Fiction Film*, Oxford: Oxford University Press, 1977.
Dawson, Jonathan "A Brief History of the Documentary: the 1930s" in *The Documentary Film in Australia*, edited by Ross Lansell and Peter Beilby, Melbourne: Cinema Papers, 1984.
Hardy, Forsyth, *Grierson on Documentary*, London: Collins (revised edition), 1966.
Rotha, Paul, *Documentary Film*, London: Faber, 1933 (revised 1952).
———, *Documentary Diary*, New York: Hill and Wang, 1973.
Sussex, Elizabeth, *The Rise and Fall of British Documentary*, London: Faber and Faber, 1976.

EMIGHOLZ, HEINZ

Heinz Emigholz is highly regarded as an experimental filmmaker, but his body of work owes much to the aesthetics of documentary film in combination with a variety of ideas derived from the tradition of early film theory. Coming from a background as a plastic artist, Emigholz early adopted the notion that not only the film stock, but also time itself, captured onto the emulsion of the film base, is a material of its own and therefore can be shaped by filmmakers in any way they want. The premise of this thinking was the conviction that in the age of recording technology, time had become such an abstract concept that the cinematic representation of time can be analyzed based on its technical and physical occurrence. As a consequence, Emigholz suggests any filmmaker should always take into account the constructiveness of the technically reproduced motion (in opposition to the real-life motion).

With his first experiments, the short film cycle *Schenec-Tady I–III* (1972–1975), *Arrowplane* (1973–1974), and *Tide* (1974), Emigholz examined the process of cinematic motion and also established some key issues for his later films: (1) the parameters of time, architecture/landscapes, and memory; (2) the interaction of time and space in the continuity of the moving image, and (3) the moving image as an "imaginary architecture within time" (Emigholz). The method used in these early experiments was rather simple: Emigholz dismantled the linear motion of pan shots of landscapes into their smallest units, frames of a 1/24th second, which he then "reanimated" according to a complicated mathematical scheme, comparable to a musical score. The results were complex visual compositions, "artificially generated with cinematic time and real-life motion" (Emigholz). With his long-time project *Photography and Beyond* (1999–), Emigholz later returned to the principal ideas of his early work; however, at that time he had developed a less theoretical form of representation of time and space that would manifest within the aesthetical framework of documentary film.

With his examination of the process of technically reproduced motion, Emigholz indirectly referred to Roland Barthes's notion that the "filmic image," removed from a chronological continuity, reveals a "third sense": a disruption of its immediate significance as part of a pictorial sequence. The nature of film, according to Barthes, lies beyond the film itself. Emigholz picked up Barthes's conception of the single frame, applying the idea of its outer-filmic reality onto the motion picture. He considered the technicity of the medium as the key to this "other," metaphysical reality; however, metaphysics was never his concern.

Emigholz's theories did not drift into areas of irrationality, although the common use of image/sound asynchronicity and experimental printing techniques indeed projected a ghostly aura onto his 1980s films.

Throughout the 1970s, Emigholz had pursued a personal project of long-term observations titled *Eine kleine Enzyklopädie des Alltags: Wohnen, Essen, Schlafen, Räume, Straßen, Verkehr* (*A Little Encyclopaedia of the Everyday: Living, Eating, Sleeping, Space, Streets, Traffic*), which would mark a link to his narrative films of the 1980s. Sequences of this project, randomly shot on 16mm footage, were included in his first feature film, *Normalsatz* (1982). *Normalsatz* was Emigholz's departure from a strictly formalist method toward a less-structured, narrative-based essay form. The fact that Emigholz for the first time introduced actors into one of his films was a deliberate step, as he stated, to free the experimental film from its stigma as being solely self-referential. Emigholz had always rejected the label "structuralist film" for his own work. At that time it seemed he had lost his interest in documentary film aesthetics, but Emigholz's 1980s *oeuvre* essentially refined the ideas of his earlier experiments and paved the ground for his later "film-photographic" work. The angular compositions of his cinematic space were traceable back to his formalist short films, the shooting locations reflected Emigholz's fascination with extravagant architectural designs and the direction expressed a formal reference to photography, a discipline that would gain new importance in his work in the late 1990s. Emigholz's disapproval of any authoritative narrative concept had finally resulted in a open form of narrative film that he, as in his formalist short films, considered rather as "text" than as the product of an author. His conviction, that the meaning of a cultural object is brought by the audience instead of residing in the object itself, refers again to Barthes and his concept of intertextuality. The form of a narrative feature film allowed Emigholz to work with "text" on a more literal level.

In the late 1990s Emigholz returned to a more formal approach with his still ongoing film cycle *Photografie und Jenseits* (*Photography and Beyond*). The project is conceived as a system of 25 freely combinable "modules," each documenting a cultural artefact, and structured into topical groups as buildings, sculptures, paintings, photos, or historical documents. According to Emigholz, *Photographie und Jenseits* is intended to recall the origins of cinema and its ability to depict space and objects in a "preconditioned" state. As a consequence of this premise Emigholz dismissed the idea of montage in order to present these artefacts in a deliberately "undramatic" way. It is his pivotal concern to document the spatial relations of these artefacts as realistically as possible. Every film is shot on 35mm stock to guarantee that the viewer's experience will not be affected by the technical limitations of electronic recording systems.

Goff in der Wüste (*Goff in the Desert*, 2003), the seventh film in the cycle, is the most elaborate example of Emigholz's "film-photographic" films so far. It documents twenty-six buildings by the American architect Bruce Goff, each in a series of long, motionless shots of exterior and interior parts of the architectural design. Emigholz's decision to suspend all editorial comments from the sound track reflects his conviction that every space can create a specific "awareness"—apart from its external dramatization and functionalization. As another consequence, Emigholz worked only with the diegetic sound to preserve the initial experience of Goff's architecture.

This concept of "immediate" representation within a technical-reproductive framework might seem an utterly naïve approach, but it really is the essence of a thoroughly evolved, interdisciplinary art theory that Emigholz has developed during the last twenty-five years. Emigholz's film theory, in the cycle *Photography and Beyond* applied on documentary film aesthetics, takes into account his own experience as an artist, as well as the "institutionalized" circumstances of the spectator-object relationship. He described his films as an empowering act against the "passive look." In his mission statement for *Photography and Beyond*, Emigholz called for a new reception of the arts: "Seeing as an expression, not an impression." By "reversing the process of seeing" (Emigholz), his films aspire to mediate between the viewer and his environment.

ANDREAS BUSCHE

Biography

Born 1948 near Bremen, Germany. Trained as a drawer, later studied at the University Hamburg. Since 1973, has been active in various artistic disciplines, working as an independent filmmaker, director of photography, plastic artist, actor, publisher, and producer. In 1974, started to work on an encyclopedic series of documentary films titled *Die Basis des Make Up*. Founded his own production company Pym Films, in 1978. In 1984, finished the short film *The Basis of Make-Up I*, which later was recognized by Emigholz as the starting point for his film cycle *Photographie und Jenseits*. In the same year, published a journal that accompanied the release of *The Basis of*

Make-Up I. His books *Krieg der Augen, Kreuz der Sinne* (1991), and *Seit Freud gesagt hat, der Künstler heile seine Neurosen selbst, heilen die Künstler ihre Neurosen selbst* (1993) served as a first introduction to Emigholz's theories of the "arts as science." Since 1993, Professor for Experimental Film Design at the Akademie der Künste in Berlin. In 1999, started to conceive his film cycle *Photographie und Jenseits*, which is still a work in progress. In 2003 he released the seventh part about the American architect Bruce Goff. Eighteen parts are still to come.

Selected Films

1972–75: *Schenec-Tady I–III*
1973–74: *Arrowplane*
1974: *Tide*
1982: *Normalsatz*
1999: *Photografie und Jenseits* (*Photography and Beyond*)
2003: *Goff in der Wüste* (*Goff in the Desert*)

Further Reading

Emigholz, Heinz, *Krieg der Augen, Kreuz der Sinne*, Kassel: Martin Schmitz Verlag, 1991.

Emigholz, Heinz, *Seit Freud gesagt hat, der Künstler heile seine Neurosen selbst, heilen die Künstler ihre Neurosen selbst*, Kassel: Martin Schmitz Verlag, 1991.

Emigholz, Heinz (editor), Normalsatz–Siebzehn Filme, Kassel: Martin Schmitz Verlag, 2003.

Emigholz, Heinz, *Das schwarze Schamquadrat*, Kassel: Martin Schmitz Verlag, 2003.

EMMER, LUCIANO

Luciano Emmer's cinematic carreer began in 1942 when his cinematic exploration of a religious fresco, *Racconto da un affresco* [Tale after a fresco], met with unexpected success. At the time most documentaries (see the entry on Italian documentaries) dealt with aspects of Italian economic and social life or advertised tourist attractions, whereas art, and especially painting, was ignored. Emmer realised this might be a profitable corner; he was soon recognised as a master of art film and directed twenty-four documentaries. A few were concerned with contemporary issues. Such was the case of *Matrimonio alla moda* [1951, Fashionable Marriage] in which he mocked, in a funny way, wedding rituals. Italians at that time had developed an infatuation for travelogues, and Emmer indulged in the fancy with *Paradiso terrestre* [Heaven on Earth], an odd patchwork of pictures taken in Africa, South America, India, and Pacific Islands in which traditional ceremonies, dances, and religious celebrations alternated with forests, landscapes, and animals.

Emmer's art films are especially notable. Some were conscientious, not very innovative monographs of *Piero della Francesca* (1949), *Goya* (1950), *Leonardo da Vinci* (1953), and *Picasso* (1954), which recounted, in chronological order, the career of famous painters. But Emmer could also be original and imaginative. *Guerrieri* [1942, Warriors], mixing up paintings of different epochs and styles, showed what is permanent in the representation of fighting people, whereas *Sulla via di Damasco* [1947, On Damasco Road] was an attempt to recreate, thanks to details borrowed from various paintings, the conversion of Saint Paul. A first *Paradiso terrestre* (1948) explored, in a creative manner, a painting by Bosch. This time, instead of presenting a biographical sketch, the commentary read like a poem and was accompanied by images that revealed small animals, flowers, corners of sky, and other particulars that people usually did not notice. *La leggenda di Sant'Orsola* [1948, The Legend of St Ursula] offered visual variations on a popular tale. *Il dramma di Cristo* [Christ's Drama] stuck to the Gospels, but instead of merely illustrating the story, Emmer used aspects of Giotto's frescos in the Arena Chapel of Padua to offer another less factual, more emotional account of the Passion.

Despite the fame his works had brought him and the many awards he had received, Emmer did not feel satisfied. He wanted to launch feature-length films that would document the main trend of Italian society by way of gripping stories and fictional characters. "What interests me," he said, "is peoples' humanity, their daily life with the sad and happy, the banal and terrible things likely to affect them." He attempted to put the formula into practice in *Una domenica d'agosto* [1950, A Sunday in August], a chronicle of a hot Sunday in a popular district of Rome. The film met with a positive response; many thought it might give neorealism a new start, but the four following movies looked banal while the fifth, *La ragazza in vetrina* [The Girl in the Window], a look at Italians emigrated in Belgium, was a failure. Emmer felt all the more disheartened that, being used to working in black and white, he was surprised by the advent of colour film. Abandoning the studios, he turned to advertisement and television. He directed three feature films and a few turistic documentaries on Siena and the Trentino for Italian television. His last shorts are opinions of his own—the first, *Bella di notte* [1997, Night Beauty], on his relationship to art works; the second, *L'acqua, il fuoco* [2003, The Water, the Fire], on the role of naturale elements in human life.

PIERRE SORLIN

Biography

Born in Milan January 18, 1918. After graduating with a degree in law, militated in Milan, with other young intellectuals, for the promotion of a new Italian cinema. In 1941, took part in the founding of a small production company, *Dolomiti Film,* intended to make documentaries. Directed eight feature-length films and documentaries, most of which were art films. Since 1962 has been working for advertisement and television.

Selected Films

1942 *Racconto da un affresco* [Tale after a fresco]: writer, director, producer

1942 *Guerrieri* [Warriors]: writer, director, producer

1947 *Sulla via di Damasco* [On Damasco Road]: writer, director, producer

1948 *Paradiso terrestre* [Heaven on Earth]: writer, director, producer

1948 *La leggenda di Sant'Orsola* [The Legend of St. Ursula]: writer, director, producer

1949 *Piero della Francesca*: writer, director, producer

1950 *Una domenica d'agosto* [A Sunday in August]: director

1950 *Goya*: writer, director, producer

1951 *Matrimonio alla moda* [Fashionable Marriage]: writer, director, producer

1953 *Leonardo da Vinci*: writer, director, producer

1954 *Picasso*: writer, director, producer

1957 *Paradiso terrestre* [Heaven on Earth]: writer, director, producer

1957 *Il dramma di Cristo* [Christ's Drama]: writer, director, producer

1960 *La ragazza in vetrina* [The Girl in the Window]: director

1997 *Bella di notte* [Night Beauty]: writer, director

2003 *L'acqua, il fuoco* [The Water, the Fire]: writer, director

Further Reading

Guglielmo Moneti, *Luciano Emmer*, Bari/Florence: La Nuova Italia, 1992.

EMPIRE MARKETING BOARD FILM UNIT

Initially organized to promote trade and act as a mortar for the British Empire in need of a sense of unity among its globally scattered parts, the Empire Marketing Board (EMB) began a campaign featuring exhibitions, posters, and print media. After a visit by John Grierson in early 1927, the EMB's chief, Sir Stephen Tallents, went to the Financial Secretary of the Treasury and secured 2,500 British pounds for Grierson to create a documentary film on the herring industry. Titled *Drifters*, the fifty-minute silent film premiered at the London Film Society near the end of 1929.

This first attempt at film by the EMB was well received by the London Film Society. By putting faces to the men who worked daily in the herring fisheries, Grierson was able to bring to life a segment of the British Empire not recognized in the film industry outside of comedic roles. The EMB took a revolutionary new look at these men and their role in British society, allowing them to emerge as heroes. The film's success among British audiences in theaters called for a staffing change at the EMB. Grierson took on the role of creative organizer. From two employees at the onset of 1930 to a staff of more than thirty only three years later, Grierson transformed the EMB into the Empire Marketing Board Film Unit (EMB Film Unit). His pool of recruits came largely without professional experience. For some, the London Film Society screenings provided the only exposure to the film industry; however, these recruits, like Grierson, shared the same socialistic inclinations to consolidate the status quo and the British Empire.

The working environment at the EMB Film Unit would seem harsh by current standards. Staff members had no time cards or other means to keep track of working hours. A forty-hour workweek with two consecutive days off did not exist. The EMB Film Unit operated more like a monastic organization where staff members were expected to put in whatever time was needed, when needed. The goal was not the success of the individual, but the success of the film unit. Life outside the EMB Film Unit seemed nonexistent. Staff members kept identities of girlfriends from Grierson, who himself allowed his marriage to Margaret Taylor to go undisclosed for eighteen months. The men of the EMB Film Unit each displayed a unique focus for the underlying cause they served for the British Empire. The long hours and personal sacrifices held deeper rewards in the films produced that brought a sense of unity to the Empire's citizenry. The EMB Film unit, however, was not without its recreation, albeit work related. Grierson and his staff were frequent patrons of the local pub for hours of drinking and film-oriented discussions.

Other early works of the EMB Film Unit were compilations of acquired footage taken from large stocks of film available from Canada and other various parts of the Empire. Films such as *Plums that Please* (1931), *Australian Wines* (1931), *Netting Millions* (1931), and many others were assembled from film "stock," but the Royal Film Society, enthralled by the novelty of documentary, offered a warm reception to anything produced by the emerging film unit.

During its short tenure, the EMB Film Unit produced powerful documentaries that enhanced and reemphasized the image and dignity of the worker. *Housing Problems* (1935) and *Coal Face* (1936) both presented issues from a worker's point of view. These films were prolabor pieces that tested the limits of government sponsorship. Using British music as a backdrop, *Coal Face* dramatically presents the brutal conditions coal miners faced in a Wales community. Likewise, *Housing Problems* presents poor, working-class people from the slums of London as they endure a slum clearance program to include the rebuilding of new homes. Tenants are seen as articulate and spirited to the surprise of many viewers. Both films remain true to the EMB Film Unit's talent for leaving a lasting imprint on the minds of viewers by transforming a common subject into a heroic image.

Along with *Drifters*, *Song of Ceylon* exemplified the best of the EMB Film Unit. Seen from the perspective of a lone traveler, the film demonstrates the clear role tea played as an imperial link in British-ruled Ceylon and throughout the Empire. The tea trade does not enter into the film until the third of four sections despite the sponsorship of the Ceylon Tea Propaganda Board. Instead, the first two sections focus on the heritage of the Ceylonese. Director, photographer, and editor Basil Wright projects his admiration for the Ceylonese through scenes depicting the exceptional beauty of the region. His portrayal of the people and their culture through the medium of documentary film brought worldwide recognition for the British documentary as an industry. The London Film Society received *Song of Ceylon* with enthusiasm and accolades, and the film went on to enjoy a successful run in theaters.

The foundation of British documentary film was fashioned during the short tenure of the EMB Film Unit. Although the EMB Film Unit was dissolved in 1934, the investment of time, energy, and talent by Grierson, Tallents, Wright, and others would serve as a legacy for the General Post Office (GPO) Film Unit to follow. The directors, photographers, and producers compiling the films created by the EMB Film Unit brought the essence of the documentary to audiences, which visually demonstrated the dignity on life outside the mainstream middle-class British experience.

CHRISTINE MARIE HILGER

See also **Anstey, Edgar**; *Coal Face*; **Drifters**; **Elton, Arthur**; **General Post Office Film Unit**; **Grierson, John**; *Housing Problems*; **Legg, Stuart**; *Song of Ceylon*; **Tallents, Stephen**; **Wright, Basil**

Further Reading

Aitken, Ian, *European Film Theory and Cinema: A Critical Introduction*, Edinburgh: Edinburgh University Press, 2001.

Barnouw, Erik, *Documentary: A History of the Non-Fiction Film,* New York: Oxford University Press, 1993.

Low, Rachael, *The History of the British Film 1929–1939: Documentary and Educational Films of the 1930s*, London: George Allen and Unwin, 1979.

ENOUGH TO EAT?

(UK, Anstey, 1937)

Enough to Eat? (The Nutrition Film) was one of the celebrated films of social enquiry produced within the British documentary film movement in the latter half of the 1930s and on which its reputation for social progressiveness rests. The films investigated contemporary social issues such as slum housing (*Housing Problems*, 1935), nutrition (*Enough to Eat?*), education (*Children at School*, 1937), and public health (*The Smoke Menace*, 1938) and

attracted unprecedented popular discussion. Arthur Elton's *Workers and Jobs*, made at the GPO Film Unit in 1935, influenced this group of films. This film had used location shooting in a Labour Exchange and direct sound recording to capture spontaneous, unscripted interviews with unemployed workers.

John Grierson had sought to widen the corporate sponsorship of documentary production, and

Enough to Eat?, 1936.
[*Still courtesy of the British Film Institute*]

an important success was the commission for a programme of five films from the British Commercial Gas Association in the mid-1930s. Arthur Elton and Edgar Anstey were responsible for the productions and, significantly, were allowed to collaborate on the choice of subject. *Enough to Eat?* was the second film in the series, following *Housing Problems* (1935), and the general approach to the series was more direct and expositional than the classic griersonian model that combined montage with social reportage. In the absence of a suitable independent documentary film production unit, Elton and Anstey simply hired the necessary studio facilities to realise the first two films. The latter titles in the series were produced by the Realist Film Unit, which had been formed in 1937 to handle exactly this kind of commission.

Enough to Eat? is an examination into the problem of malnutrition among the working classes in Britain. The eminent scientist Julian Huxley, who occasionally speaks to the camera while seated at a desk, provides a commentary. The recent research of Sir John Orr are described and illustrated, and the results of contrasting diets are presented across various animal groups and humans. In a notable example, well-built Christ's Hospital schoolboys are compared with ill-fed, working-class boys. The principles of good nutrition are explained, and, with the use of diagrams and graphs, the link between income and dietary deficiency is established. Three working-class mothers give direct-to-camera interviews about their difficulties (in the style of the pioneering *Housing Problems*). The methods used to deal with the problem are outlined: the provision of cheap milk in schools, free school dinners, the distribution of free meals, education in nutrition to poor mothers, and so forth. At intervals, authorities and experts give their views, including Dr M'Gonigle, Herbert Morrison (on the work of the London County Council), and Viscount Astor (on the work of the League of Nations).

In the interwar period, the general health of the nation was improving. Nevertheless, social investigators consistently revealed the persistence of poverty, which was condemning a significant proportion of the population to ill health. Knowledge of nutritional science was increasing and many medical conditions were being recognised as "deficiency diseases," the result being a greater emphasis on diet as an agent of improving health. The most influential study into nutrition was *Food, Health and Income* (1936), conducted by John Boyd Orr. According to his findings, one tenth of the population were chronically ill nourished; the fig-ure was higher for children at one fifth, and half the population had a deficient diet in some respect. The study was severely criticised in some quarters; however, other surveys, such as Dr. G. G. M'Gonigle's in the Northeast, confirmed the link between poor diet, ill–health, and low income.

In terms of theme and style, two aspects stand out in relation to *Enough to Eat?* The first concerns the role and influence of sponsorship in these documentaries of social enquiry, and the view that the filmmakers were essentially compromised in their critical intentions by the nature of corporate funding. This criticism has been strongly levelled against *Housing Problems*, and holds for the later *Kensal House* (1936) and *The Smoke Menace* (1937), where the Gas, Light and Coke Company clearly had a stake in slum clearance and house building. In matters of nutrition, though, there is no such obvious narrow self-interest, and the film seems to conform to the griersonian ideal of disinterested corporate sponsorship, where documentary filmmakers were left free to tackle important social questions of the day. In the broader sense, though, the sponsored documentaries were only part of a larger public relations strategy to improve the standing of the gas industry, especially in relation to the electricity industry and its clean, smart, and modern image.

Although the social purpose of the film was widely applauded, there was a more mixed response to its method of construction. For some reviewers there was a clutter of detail, a tendency for the film to drag through repetition, and a basic simplicity to the solutions offered. There was particular praise, however, for the interviews with the mothers as assessed by the reviewer at *Sight and Sound* as "straight-forward, undramatized, infinitely revealing and shocking." Also, a sequence comparing the fate of two rats fed on contrasting diets had a noticeable impact.

Enough to Eat? was the cause of considerable press debate on the issue of nutrition, and brought much attention onto the documentary film movement. Its style of presentation through diagrams and graphs, although attracting some criticism at the time, was ultimately influential and was developed with great finesse by Paul Rotha in his wartime documentaries such as *World of Plenty* (1943). More immediately, the film led Anstey to the *March of Time*, which appreciated this didactic approach, and where he was invited to reprise his work for the documentary news series.

ALAN BURTON

See also **Anstey, Edgar; Grierson, John**

ENOUGH TO EAT?

Enough to Eat? (UK, 1936, 23 mins) Produced and distributed by the Gas, Light and Coke Company. Directed by Edgar Anstey, assisted by Frank Sainsbury. Cinematography by Walter Blakeley and Arthur Fisher. Sound by Charles Poulton. Commentary by Julian S. Huxley.

Further Reading

Aitken, Ian, *Film and Reform*, London: Routledge, 1990.

The Arts Enquiry, The Factual Film, London: PEP, 1947.
Monthly Film Bulletin, November, 1936, 187–188.
Sight and Sound, Autumn, 1936, 88–89.
Stevenson, John, *British Society 1914–45*, Harmondsworth: Penguin, 1984.
Sussex, Elizabeth, *The Rise and Fall of British Documentary*, Berkeley: Cambridge University Press, 1975.
Swann, Paul, *The British Documentary Film Movement, 1926–1946*, Cambridge: Cambridge University Press, 1989.

ENTHUSIASM

(USSR, Vertov, 1930)

On completion, *Enthusiasm* (also known as *Symphony of the Donbasin*), Dziga Vertov's 1930 film on coal mining in the Don Basin region of the Soviet Union, was criticized for its unconventional use of sound and visual style. The film was produced a few years after Soviet cinema had gained recognition on an international scale. Produced when films with simple and didactic narratives were endorsed by the Soviet state, this documentary was charged as being too abstract and belonging to the much maligned art movement of Formalism. Made during the Five Year Plan, *Enthusiasm* is an important documentary, as it is an experiment on Vertov's theories of the Kino-Eye and the Radio-Ear. It is one of the first full production sound films in the Soviet Union and illustrates how Vertov tackled the issue of sound at its advent in the cinema.

Vertov was the main creative force in all stages of the film's production. He developed the script in two stages. Beginning in 1929, Vertov conceived of an idea for the film in terms of its sound components. One year later, he came up with a plan outlining the film's visual shots. It was at this time that he gave the film its two titles, *Enthusiasm* and *Symphony of the Donbasin*; Vertov preferred the former title. Vertov wanted the speech and natural sounds of the film to be recorded as clearly and precisely as its musical score composed by N. Timofeyev and D. Shostakovich. However, in 1929, sound systems by inventors such as A.F. Shorin and P.G. Tager were only beginning to be produced and tested. By being the first film to use an innovative sound system created by Shorin, *Enthusiasm* pioneers the practice of producing high-quality, on-location sound as a means to further his approach of Kino-Pravda or Cinema Truth. This documentary was thus able to use the natural sounds from the coal mines, rather than rely on simulating industrial soundscapes during postproduction.

Enthusiasm is a documentary celebrating the coal mine laborers of the Don Basin community as they work toward realizing the agricultural and industrial goals established in their country's Five Year Plan. The film is not structured in chronological order but rather sets up and contrasts a series of themes surrounding the lives of the Don Basin coal miners at work and play. The first section of the film is about Russia of time past and its reliance on the Tsar and religion. The spell of religion leaves the people disoriented and drunk with idleness. The film then shifts its attention to the destruction of the church and its icons to signify the society waking up. The next section of the film focuses on the motivated laborers of the coal mine as they help move their country toward greater industrialization. Numerous shots of the workers mining coal and producing steel celebrate the hard-working Soviet people of the present and future. The final section of the film focuses on the agricultural sector of labor as people work alongside machinery to tend to the harvest and reap its benefits. *Enthusiasm* is one of many first Soviet sound films of the early 1930s to deal with workers and their role in constructing the Cultural Revolution. Others include Abram Room's *The Five Year Plan (The Plan for Great Works)*, Alexander Macheret's *Deeds and People*, and Yuli Raizman's *The Earth Thirsts*. In this context Vertov's film can be seen as having a very clear political agenda. However, the means through which he used the new technology of sound distinguishes *Enthusiasm* from these other films.

Consistent with Vertov's theories concerning documentary film, *Enthusiasm* was made to demystify the process of making a sound film for the spectator. In this film Vertov combines his Kino-Eye with his Radio-Ear. Throughout the film sound and aural reality is not used as a supplement of visual reality, but rather helps to heighten the spectator's ability to register Kino-Pravda. Like the image of the cinematographer in Vertov's *Man with the Movie Camera* (1929), images of sound technicians and composers appear in *Enthusiasm*. This is illustrated at the beginning of the film with a shot of a woman actually dispatching radio sounds onto a radio-telegraph. After recording these natural and ambient sounds as they unfold, Vertov then experimented at the postproduction stage to create complex dynamics between the sound and image tracks. Such innovation is found in the seemingly infinite ways the film works to disorient the spectator's sense of the sound in relation to the cinematic space. Vertov reveals sonic and visual realities through a number of techniques, some of which are the alteration of the speed of the sounds and visuals (acceleration/deceleration), mismatching and rupture of natural sounds from its image, and use of fragmented as well as disjointed sound/visual collages alongside severe tonal and distortion contrasts. Vertov's desire for the spectator to be aware of the technology was reinforced during the film's exhibition. Vertov would often alter the level of

Enthusiasm, 1931.
[*Still courtesy of the British Film Institute*]

volume of the film at individual screenings. Such techniques are meant to make the spectator see and hear what the human eye and ear on its own cannot.

Vertov's approach to sound in *Enthusiasm* works in direct opposition to the often cited "Statement on Sound" by Eisenstein, Pudovkin, and Aleksandrov, which limits sound in cinema to strictly contrapunctal uses. In the journal *Kino-Front* Vertov states cinema should not be divided by categorizing films as talkies, noisies, or sound films; rather the distinction should rest on whether the film is a documentary or is staged. More specifically, the filmmaker should be concerned with whether sound was produced through real or artificial means. Made at a time when recording sound on-location was repudiated, Vertov used *Enthusiasm* as a means to disprove sound critic Ippolit Sokolov's widely accepted *caterwauling theory*, which claimed nature was photogenic but not sonogenic. Vertov did not believe that the future of sound cinema resided in artistic simulacra of natural sounds in sound proof studios. Such a process was not conducive to Vertov's emphasis on cinema as producing a new world unmediated and freed from the limitations of human perception.

In what Vertov refers to as his "symphony of noises," *Enthusiasm* allows the spectator to not only see but also hear the new world created and freed by cinema. Techniques inaugurated in this film, such as the use of on-location sound, revolutionized how documentary film movements such as direct cinema and cinema verité construct sound/ image relations. A restored version of *Enthusiasm* by Peter Kubelka offers filmmakers, scholars, and cinéphiles insight into Vertov's perception of visual and aural (cinematic) truth.

THERESA SCANDIFFIO

See also **Vertov, Dziga**

Enthusiasm (SU, VUFKU, 1930, 69 mins.) Produced by Nemirovskii. Directed by Dziga Vertov. Assistant Directed by Elizaveta Svilova. Scenario by Dziga Vertov. Photography by B. Tsteitlin and K. Kuyalev. Sound Director Petr Shtro. Sound Assistants N. Timarzev and K. Chybiosov. Composed by Timofeyev and Shostakovich. Additional Music by Dziga Vertov. Filmed in Don Basin region in the Soviet Union. Restored by Peter Kubelka.

Further Reading

Dickinson, Thorold, and Catherine de la Roche, *Soviet Cinema*. London: Falcon Press, 1948.

Eisenstein, S., V. I. Pudovkin, and G. V. Alexandrov, "A Statement on the Sound Film" in Eisenstein, Sergei *Film Form*. Ed. Jay Leya. New York: Harcourt, 1977.

Fischer, Lucy, "Enthusiasm: From Kino-Eye to Radio-Eye," in *Film Quarterly* 31, 1977–1978, 25–36.

Herring, Robert, Enthusiasm? in *Close Up* 9, 1932, 20–24.

Koster, Simon, "Dziga Vertoff," in *Experimental Cinema* 1, 1934, 27–28.

Leyda, Jay, *Kino: A History of Russian and Soviet Film*, New York: Macmillan, 1960.

Taylor, Richard, Editor and Translator, *The Film Factory: Russian and Soviet Cinema in Documents*, Coeditor Ian Christie, Cambridge: Harvard University Press, 1988.

Taylor, Richard, and Ian Christie, Editors, *Inside the Film Factory: New Approaches to Russian and Soviet Cinema*. New York: Routledge, 1991.

Vertov, Dziga, *Kino-Eye: The Writings of Dziga Vertov*, Annette Michelson, Editor, Translator Kevin O'Brien, Berkeley, CA: University of California Press, 1984.

EPSTEIN, JEAN

Ever since his debut in 1922, director, writer, and philosopher Jean Epstein produced a number of films and theoretical texts that are essential to an understanding of the evolution of the cinema, both from a technical and an aesthetic perspective. Epstein's filmography comprises numerous avant-garde films, documentaries, and semi-documentaries, which are the product and consequence of his conception of the cinema as a machine that is able to produce an objective and novel form of vision, distinct from the human gaze. In 1926, he broke his contract with Pathé and founded his own production company, Les Film Jean Epstein, with which he made films such as *La glace a trois faces* (1927) and *La chute de la Maison Rouge* (1928). In 1929, after the collapse of his production company, he began to dedicate writings and films to Brittany, to its locations, inhabitants, folklore and traditions, and in particular to the relationship between the fisherman and the sea, seen as an emblem of the struggle between life and death. Even in his commercial films he always tried to use nonprofessional actors and local inhabitants, thus revealing an anthropological attitude. He often accompanied his films with writings about the shooting locations or with actual documentaries that he made alongside the fiction films.

Especially in the first phase of his career, Epstein shared the avant-garde spirit of renovation, a position that makes him akin to theoreticians/filmmakers such as Vertov and Canudo. He took part in the discussions on the artistic value of the cinema, which characterised the intellectual debate in 1920s France. In *Le Cinématographe vu de l'Etna* (1926, an account of his experiences in Sicily during the shooting of the lost documentary on Mount Etna, *La Montagne infidèle*, 1923), taking inspiration from the writings of Delluc, Epstein presents his opinion on the notion of *photogénie*. Epstein defines *photogénie* as the opposite of literariness and immobility: the founding characteristic of the cinema, *photogénie* belongs to any mobile element of the world whose moral quality is increased by being reproduced cinematically. The close-up has the power to annul the distinction between subjectivity and objectivity. For Epstein, the camera lens first produces an objective gaze, originated by the mechanical apparatus; thus the world as it is represented on screen is independent of human consciousness. Subjectivity comes into play only subsequently. These ideas push him in the direction of a type of animism similar to that of his contemporary Ricciotto Canudo. The cinema for Epstein allows the uncovering of a universe in which each object is endowed with its own life. Epstein has full confidence in the technical possibilities of the cinema to empower human sight, freeing it from its physical and psychic impediments. In this light, the introduction of sound is useful for Epstein only if it allows an increment of our knowledge of the noises and sounds of the world. The cinema must also become a source of *phonogénie*. This idea urged him to experiment on the slow motion of sound in his last fiction film, *Le Tempestaire* (1947).

Epstein made his debut in 1922 with the semi-documentary *Pasteur*, which was commissioned to celebrate the centenary of the birth of the famous scientist, and which attracted the attention and praise of contemporary French documentarists and, in particular, of Canudo, who defined it as "the first biographical film." In 1924, the lost documentary *Photogénies* marks the end of the first phase of Epstein's career. Made for a specific occasion, the lecture "A New Avant-Garde," which Epstein read at the Théatre Raymond Duncan on April 11, 1924, *Photogénies* was afterward disassembled. It consisted of a series of sequences that were meant to represent the idea of *photogénie*.

In fiction features such as *La chute de la maison Usher* (1928) and *Mauprat* (1926), exterior settings are often the only object of the exploratory and documentary gaze of the camera, which produces panoramic views of castles, landscapes, and trees shaken by the wind. Superimpositions and mobility of the camera are the main characteristics of Epstein's style. In the same locations of the exteriors of *Mauprat* Epstein shot the lost documentary *Au pays de George Sand* (1926), dedicated to the valley of the Creuse, North of the Massif Céntral. With *Finnis Terrae* (1929), Epstein moves to Brittany and starts to shoot without actors and sets, somehow anticipating Italian Neorealism and cinema verité. He focuses on the inhabitants of the Ouessant Archipelago and theorizes for the first time a cinema in which the work of the director is to try to endow an existing reality with the characters of fiction. Epstein defined *Finnis Terrae* as "a psychological documentary, the portrayal of a brief drama in episodes that really took place, of authentic people and things" (Epstein 1974–1975). By portraying the truth of places and people, the cinema is the witness of a reality that the director reconstructs in dramatic form.

Epstein insists on his anthropological interests with the subsequent *Mor Vran (La mer des corbeaux)* (1930), a semi-documentary about the inhabitants of the Island of Seine, which tells the story of a shipwreck, making use of authentic characters and settings. The film opens with a map of the island—a prologue that is already a declaration of the scientific aim of the film and of its anthropological value. Epstein here analyses Brittany's traditions, myths, and folklore and produces an accurate documentation of life in the Ouessant Archipelago, in relation to the idea that the sea brings both life and death, and in light of the always impending danger of a storm (a danger of which Epstein was a direct witness, having escaped a shipwreck).

Epstein returned to Brittany in 1931, to the isle of Hoedik, to shoot *L'or des mers* (1932), once again using locals for actors. He chose to live in close contact with them, sharing their relationship with the sea. In an era in which the cinema withdrew to the studios, Epstein continued to shoot on location, often in extreme conditions. He returned to Brittany once again to make the film in the Breton language *Chanson d'Armor* (1934) and the short documentary *Une visite à l'Ouest-Eclair* (*La vie d'un grand journal*) (1934), particularly interesting for the focus on Brittany's modern aspects. He then shot two documentaries intended for the promotion of the region: *La Bretagne* (1937) and *La Bourgogne* (1937), both for the Exposition Internationale des Arts et Techniques in Paris.

STEFANO BASCHIERA

Biography

Born in Warsaw, 1897, left Poland as a child to study in Switzerland. Moved to France and studied medicine in Lyon, a scientific formation that will always influence his work. Interested in the arts, befriended Auguste Lumière. Established the avant-garde magazine *Le Promenoir*, 1920, which had contributors such as Auguste Lumière and Fernand Léger. Moved to Paris to work at the Editions de la Sirène and as an assistant to Louis Delluc for *Le Tonnerre*. Published *La Lyrosophie* and his first essay on the cinema, *Bonjour cinéma*, 1922. Made first film, *Pasteur*, 1922; established production company, Les Films Jean Epstein, 1926. Moved to Brittany, 1929. Professorship of Aesthetics at the Istitute des Hautes Etudes Cinématographiques, Paris (1945). Wrote his two major essays on the cinema *L'intelligence d'une machine* (1946) and *Le Cinéma du diable* (1947). Died 1953 after a long illness.

Selected Films

1922 *Pasteur*: director
1924 *Photogénies*: editor
1926 *Au pays de George Sand*: producer, director
1929 *Finis Terrae*: writer, director
1930 *Mor Vran (La mer des corbeaux)*: writer, director
1931 *Notre Dame de Paris*: director
1934 *Une visite à l'Ouest-Eclair (La vie d'un grand journal)*: director
1937 *La Bretagne*: director
1937 *La Bourgogne*: director
1948 *Le feux de la mer*: director

Further Reading

Aumont, Jacques, Editor, *Jean Epstein. Cinéaste, poète, philosophe*, Paris: Cinémathèque Franaise, 1998.
Canudo, Ricciotto, *L'Usine aux images* (1927), Paris: Séguier/Arte édition, 1995.
Deleuze, Gilles, *L'image- mouvement*, Paris: Les Editions de Minuit, 1983 (*Cinema 1: The Movement Image*, London: Athlone, 2002).
Epstein, Jean, *Ecrits sur le cinéma* (2 vol.), Paris: Seghers, 1974–1975.
Leprohon, Pierre, *Jean Epstein*, Paris: Seghers, 1964.
Vichi, Laura, *Jean Epstein*, Milano: Il Castoro, 2003.

ERTEL, DIETER

The concept of a new form of documentary in West-German television was much influenced by Dieter Ertel. Having gained his first experience in the production of newsreels and as writer at the weekly magazine *Der Spiegel*, he had learned how powerful words could be and how important it was to search for facts and information. Ertel participated actively in the discussions about a new style at the Süddeutscher Rundfunk (SDR) in Stuttgart in the 1950s. His film *Ein Großkampftag* [1957, Boxing Day] became the model for the documentary serial *Zeichen der Zeit* [Signs of Time], which was regularly produced until 1973. It brought a critical analysis of German society in a dynamic visual style and with ironic commentaries into private homes and was not appreciated by all viewers. But this style, referred to as "Stuttgarter Schule," was influential for documentary production in German television and was an alternative to the documentary films from Hamburg, which were more oriented to Anglo-American reportage style. Ertel was quite aware that a documentary could not be an objective representation of reality and grasped the opportunity to make subjective statements.

His concept was to produce films that do not just present finished results but instead try to motivate the viewers to make up their own minds. Ertel did not trust the official versions of a story, but tried to look behind the scenes and searched for other perspectives. Although today his commentaries seem to dominate his films, for him the image was more important. His style was influenced by Ed Murrow and Richard Leacock, and, together with his cameramen, he looked for specific details that could be edited in a visual rhythm and as ironic as his commentaries. He was more interested in specific qualities and developments of the times and less in the daily business of politics. Over time he produced "something like filmic behavioural research about humanness" (Netenjakob, 1968). One of his main topics was classical music and portraits of conductors, but his masterpieces are on sports; these films are self-reflexive commentaries on media and bourgeois conformism, in which growing commercialisation was criticized. Good examples are *Ein Großkampftag* about boxing fights and *Tortour de France (1960)*, where he followed the Tour de France and tried to show the machinery behind the event. A portrait of a rifle club and its yearly meeting (*Schützenfest*, 1961) provoked massive protest because he interviewed drunken riflemen, asking them what importance guns have for them or why they shoot again after the experience of WW II; he got very open answers. In *Der totale Urlaub* [1967, The Total Holiday] he visited a holiday camp on the south coast of England, in which the whole day was strictly organized. After becoming responsible for the documentary department of the SDR, Ertel did not make many films anymore and ran into conflicts with the station because he tried to retain a privileged position for documentary film. He then went on to become manager of various public stations in Germany. He is one of the founders of the Haus des Dokumentarfilms in Stuttgart.

KAY HOFFMANN

Biography

Born in Hamburg, Germany, February 2, 1927. Studied German and English literature at Hamburg University from 1947 to 1950. 1950–1953 trainee, and editor at the German newsreel (Neue Deutsche Wochenschau). 1954–1955, sports editor at the news magazine *Der Spiegel*. From October 1955 to 1968, editor in the documentary department of Süddeutscher Rundfunk (SDR). 1968–1973, head of the documentary department of SDR. 1974–1979, head of TV-programming at Radio Bremen. 1979–1981, head of program III (television movies, film, entertainment, and family) at Westdeutscher Rundfunk (WDR), Cologne. 1981–1989, head of programming at Südwestrundfunk (SWF) in Baden-Baden. 1991–1994, Chairman of the Documentary Film Center Stuttgart.

Selected Films

1957 *Ein Großkampftag:* director, writer
1958 *Der große Cannes-Cannes: Beobachtungen am Rande der Filmfestspiele:* director, writer
1959 *Neubauwunderlichkeiten:* director, writer
1960 *Tortur de Fance. Bericht über eine Radrundfahrt* director, writer (together with Hans Blickensdörfer)
1963 *Fernsehfieber: Bemerkungen über das Massenmedium und sein Publikum:* director, writer (together with Georg Friedel)
1967 *Der totale Urlaub: Beobachtungen in einem englischen Ferienparadies:* director, writer
1974 *Richard Wagner:* director, writer

Further Reading

Ertel, Dieter, "Rückblick auf meine Stuttgarter Jahr" in *Stuttgarter Zeitung*, 16, 1, 1974, 29.
Gmelin, Otto, *Philosophie des Fernsehens*, Pfullingen: Gmelin, 1967, 143–152.
Harms, Michael, "Dieter Ertel" in *SWF Journal*, 2, 1992, 12–13.
Hattendorf, Manfred, *Dokumentarfilm und Authentizität. Ästhetik und Pragmatik einer Gattung*, Konstanz: Ölschläger, 1994.
Hoffmann, Kay, *Zeichen der Zeit: Zur Geschichte der, "Stuttgarter Schule,"* Munich: TR-Verlagsunion, 1996.
Netenjakob, Egon, "Schöner Zwang zur Wirklichkeit. Die zeitkritische Sendereihe, Zeichen der Zeit' und Dieter Ertel" in *Funk-Korrespondenz*, 19, 1968, 1–5.
Steinmetz, Rüdiger/Spitra, Helmut (editors), *Dokumentarfilm als "Zeichen der Zeit." Vom Ansehen der Wirklichkeit im Fernsehen*, Munich: Ölschläger, 1989.

ESPOIR

See Man's Hope

ETERNITY

(Australia, Lawrence Johnston, 1994)

Eternity is significant as an Australian documentary that makes use of a nonrealist documentary aesthetic to create a portrait of a well-known and enigmatic character who holds a unique place in the national consciousness. Directed by Lawrence Johnston, *Eternity* traces the life and work of Arthur Stace. Known as "Mr. Eternity," Stace spent forty years of his life writing the word *Eternity* in chalk on Sydney's city streets. The narrative moves from Stace's struggle with alcoholism following his experiences as a stretcher bearer in WW I, through his conversion to Christianity in 1930 and his death in 1967. Motivated by his religious beliefs, an essentially illiterate Stace roamed the inner city and wrote *Eternity* an estimated 500,000 times in perfect copperplate on pavements around Sydney. Stace's identity, however, was not revealed until 1956, twenty years after the first inscription had appeared.

As a biography, *Eternity* is remarkable in the way that it not only charts the life of Stace but also attempts to situate him culturally and spatially. The narrative of Stace's life is constructed through a voice-of-God commentary and interviews with a number of people who knew him. These accounts offer an intimate access to specific formative events in this enigmatic character's life. The film also draws on interviews with cultural commentators such as writers, artists, broadcaster, and journalists. The differing perspectives provided by these personalities reinforce the enigma that Stace has become while also suggesting the ways in which he has influenced Sydney's artistic community and cultural psyche.

Eternity is a highly stylized documentary that uses modes of reflexivity not only to question the production of meaning but also to express the multiple personal and cultural dimensions that contribute to the symbolism that Lawrence believes Stace represents. Each of the interviews is shot against a colorful back-projected image, which include landscapes, flowers, and the word "eternity" itself. This is a device through which Lawrence offers added insight into the experience and character of the interviewee. This device complements the move away from realist representation that characterizes the images that dominate the rest of the film, which construct a collage of archival or found footage and black and white recreations of Stace and his wanderings. The Sydney cityscape features prominently in these images. The noir-like scenes evoke a sense of the historical city in which the haunting figure of Stace and the myth that surrounds him can be located. The music of Ross Edwards's "Symphony Da Pacem Domine" accentuates this ghostly quality.

Eternity stands as one of the most internationally renowned Australian documentaries of the decade. Not only did it win the prize for the best documentary at the 1995 Sydney Film Festival, but also the Golden Gate award at the San Francisco International Film Festival and the 1995 Los Angeles International Documentary Association Award for Best Documentary, among others.

BELINDA SMAILL

See also **Documentary Film: Australia**

Eternity (Australia, Vivid Pictures, 1994, 56 mins). Distributed by Ronin Films. Produced by Susan MacKinnon. Directed and written by Lawrence Johnston. Cinematography by Dion Beebe. Edited by Annette Davey. Sound by Liam Egan and Paul Finlay. Music composed by Ross Edwards.

Further Reading

Deacon, Kathy, "Eternity Directed by Lawrence Johnston/Is That All There Is Directed by Lindsay Anderson" in *The Village Voice* New York; May 16, 1995, 40: 20, 60.

Hughes, Peter, Andrew Lindsay, and John Slavin, "M99—Documentaries at the Melbourne and Sydney Film Festivals" in *Metro Magazine* 99, 1994, 55–61.

Levy, Emanuel, "Eternity Directed by Lawrence Johnston" in *Variety*, New York, October 3, 1994, 356, 10, 64.

ETHNOGRAPHIC DOCUMENTARY FILM

Anthropology and documentary cinema have long had an uneasy relationship, in part because of conflicts between the scholarly objectives of anthropology and the broader interests of filmmakers. Nevertheless, ethnographic film has emerged as an important form of documentary, and ethnographic filmmakers have played a key role in the way in which documentary cinema has evolved. Ethnographic filmmaking, which began as a way of documenting body movement and material culture, has gone on to develop a variety of strategies for representing human social experience: didactic, expository, narrative, observational, poetic, and self-reflexive.

The origins of ethnographic film coincide with the invention of cinema. In 1895 (the year of the Lumière brothers' first public film screening), Félix-Louis Regnault used the chronophotographic techniques pioneered by Eadweard Muybridge, Étienne Jules Marey, and Ottomar Anschütz to make human locomotion studies of Wolof, Diola, and Fulani villagers brought to Paris for the Exposition Ethnographique de l'Afrique Occidentale. In the same year Thomas Edison used his kinetoscope to film Sioux Ghost dances in his "Black Maria" studio in New Jersey. Ethnographers soon began using the new technology in the field, with Alfred Cort Haddon's expedition to the Torres Strait Islands in 1898 making records of dances and fire-making techniques. Haddon encouraged Walter Baldwin Spencer to film Aranda ceremonial dances in central Australia in 1901, the results of which were later exhibited to the public in Melbourne. The Austrian, Rudolf Pöch, filmed in New Guinea and Southwest Africa between 1904 and 1909 and, like Spencer, also made wax cylinder sound recordings in the field, some in rough synchrony with his films.

These early efforts were devoted to producing filmed records not unlike museum artifacts. They concentrated on technical skills and ritual activities, reflecting the ethnographic priorities of the day and the practical difficulties of filming most other subjects. Emerging as a new discipline in the nineteenth century, anthropology had been strongly influenced by social evolutionary theory. There was much interest in photography from 1850 onward in documenting the racial "types" and technologies of "primitive" societies, so as to place them on a scale of human progress from savagery to civilization. Ethnographic filmmaking began with similar objectives. Regnault dreamed of an ethnographic museum of films and sound recordings of human societies. Interest in ethnographic filmmaking and photography waned after World War I, however, as anthropologists turned their attention increasingly to social structure and belief systems, for which visual documentation was deemed less helpful.

The problematic relationship between visual representation and anthropology has continued to the present day, affecting the development of ethnographic film and the subdiscipline of visual anthropology. Mainstream anthropology has remained predominantly a discipline of written description and analysis. Among anthropologists favoring approaches derived from the natural sciences, film has been thought useful primarily for compiling visual data for later analysis (for example, in specialized fields such as proxemics, kinesics, and ethnomusicology). But for those who view anthropology as more closely allied to the humanities, film has offered a method of representing social experience significantly different in content from anthropological writing. This use of film, however, has yet to be widely accepted or used by anthropologists, except to provide illustrative material for teaching. The development of ethnographic film has remained largely in the hands of a few pioneering anthropologists and documentary filmmakers.

The making of ethnographic films, as distinct from film records, is widely held to have begun with Robert Flaherty's *Nanook of the North* (1922), a film that also marks the beginning of the modern documentary tradition. Flaherty's contribution to documentary was to turn nonfiction filmmaking into a narrative form, while his immediate contribution to ethnographic film was to examine another society through an intimate and informed portrayal of individuals belonging to it. Although Edward S. Curtis had produced *In the Land of the Head-Hunters* in 1914, a fictionalized love story set among the Kwakiutl of British Columbia, Flaherty focused on everyday activities of the Inuit and their ingenuity in coping with the arctic environment. Flaherty's approach anticipated that of later ethnographic filmmakers by involving Nanook in the creation of the film and by showing footage back to his subjects in the field. He attempted a similar approach in *Moana* (1926) and *Man of Aran* (1934), but neither achieved the spontaneity or cultural insight of *Nanook*.

In 1925, Merian C. Cooper and Ernest B. Schoedsack produced *Grass: A Nation's Battle for Life*, a vivid account of a Bakhtiari migration in Iran, followed in 1927 by a more commercial film shot in Thailand, *Chang: A Drama of the Wilderness*. Jean Epstein, departing from his avant-garde projects, produced *Finis Terrae* in 1929, a semi-documentary film that foreshadowed Flaherty's *Man of Aran* but took a more subjective approach to the experiences of his subjects, kelp-gatherers on islands off the Brittany Coast. In 1932, Luis Buñuel produced what many consider the consummate parody of the "educational" ethnographic film, his surreal *Las Hurdes* (*Land Without Bread*), a grotesque depiction of the life of impoverished Spanish villagers, overlaid by a mock-didactic commentary and music from Brahms' fourth symphony.

Another key film of the 1930s was Basil Wright's *Song of Ceylon* (1934), begun for the Ceylon Tea Marketing Board under John Grierson's supervision and completed with the General Post Office Film Unit. Strongly influenced by Soviet *montage*, Wright's film combined images and sounds in associative ways to create a poetic image of the island's life and culture, both as it might have been perceived by early Western travellers and as it was being affected by colonial trade and development. Although the film was not conceived in ethnographic terms, its stylistic originality and sympathetic portrayal of another culture was to prove influential for both documentary and ethnographic filmmaking. Apart from *Song of Ceylon*, Grierson's influence on ethnographic film was indirect. His own film, *Drifters* (1929), set the tone for many of the later films made under his guidance: celebrations of working people, generally satisfied with their lot, carefully scripted and enacted by the people themselves (for example, *Night Mail*, Harry

Watt and Basil Wright, 1936, *North Sea,* Watt, 1938). Although politically ambivalent, these films constitute a sociologically important portrait of British working-class life in the 1930s and early 1940s. Grierson's influence made possible the production of Flaherty's *Man of Aran* and, less directly, Humphrey Jennings' sensitive depictions of the war years, such as *Fires Were Started* (1943) and *Diary for Timothy* (1945). These in turn prepared the ground for the more freewheeling evocations of postwar Britain of the Free Cinema movement of the 1950s (for example, Karel Reisz and Tony Richardson's *Mamma Don't Allow*, 1956). Grierson later played an important part in establishing the National Film Board of Canada, which was to influence documentary and ethnographic filmmaking in the 1960s, not least with its groundbreaking *Challenge for Change* program under George Stoney.

Films such as Flaherty's and Wright's, which straddled the worlds of documentary, ethnography, avant-garde, and commercial cinema between the world wars, were paralleled by more exploitative travel films made in exotic locations, such as Osa and Martin Johnson's *Congorilla* (1929), expedition films such as the Citroën-sponsored *La Croisière Noire* (Léon Poirier, 1926), and by the continuing efforts of ethnographic fieldworkers to make film records of small-scale societies for research purposes. In North America, F.W. Hodge produced a series of detailed films about the Zuñi in 1923, and in 1930 the anthropologist Franz Boas filmed dances, games, and technological processes among the Kwakiutl, whom he had been studying since the 1890s. In Australia a procession of ethnographers, doctors, dentists, and amateur ethnologists, including William J. Jackson, Brooke Nicholls, T.D. Campbell, O.E. Stocker, H.K. Fry, Norman B. Tindale, and Charles P. Mountford, made films of aboriginal life and culture in remote areas, with an emphasis on material culture, "racial" characteristics, and ritual activities. During this period, European anthropology, imbued with the folkloric tradition, inspired Georges Rouquier, Karel Plicka, and many now forgotten filmmakers to produce films on village rituals and traditional crafts. Many of these films are gradually being rediscovered in museum archives, along with a miscellany of promotional, educational, and travel films depicting life in Dutch, French, British, and other European colonies.

Because the dominant emphasis of anthropology at this time was on the structural and symbolic aspects of culture (or in continental Europe on folk traditions), ethnographic filmmaking, as it was understood by most anthropologists, was largely about recording the external features of social life, which could then be elucidated by anthropological writing. By contrast, the project that Gregory Bateson and Margaret Mead launched in Bali in 1936 constituted a revolutionary step in visual anthropology, for it aimed to use visual means to explore culture as an interior state. It was also unprecedented in the extent to which it used visual media, producing some 28,000 photographs and 22,000 feet of 16mm motion picture film. Although Mead and Bateson differed in their theoretical outlook, the overall aim was to examine the influence of parent-child interaction on Balinese character development, later described in their book *Balinese Character* (1942). The Bali project established a new research model and significantly extended the potential range of visual anthropology, but despite (or perhaps even because of) its innovations, it produced no substantive changes in anthropological research methods. World War II intervened, and it was not until the 1950s that several films were produced from Bateson's footage with commentaries by Mead, including *A Balinese Family* (1952) and *Childhood Rivalry in Bali and New Guinea* (1953).

Partly as a result of their wartime experiences, some European fiction filmmakers reacted against the frequent triviality of prewar cinema with a more observational style and a greater concern for social issues. Neorealist directors such as Roberto Rossellini and Vittorio De Sica began exploring the life of ordinary city dwellers, combining some of the approaches of Italian documentary with performances by nonprofessional actors in such films as *Roma Citta Aperta* (Rossellini, 1945) and *Sciuscia* (De Sica, 1946). These films brought a new sociological realism to fiction films, anticipated before the war in such French films as Jean Renoir's *Nana* (1926), George Lacombe's *La Zone* (1928), and Epstein's *Finis Terrae*. In the postwar period there was also a half-nostalgic desire to return to the verities of preindustrial life. In Italy, Lucino Visconti told a story of poor Sicilian fishermen in *La Terra Trema* (1948), using local nonactors; and Georges Rouquier, who had made the short ethnographic documentaries *Vendanges* (1929) and *Le Tonnelier* (1942), reconstructed the life of a French farming family in his classic film *Farrebique* (1946), in which a family reenacts the events of their daily lives throughout the four seasons with hardly any reference to the outside world.

World War II introduced changes that were to lead to a new climate for documentary and ethnographic filmmaking. First introduced in 1923, 16mm cameras, projectors, and film became more widely available, and educational institutions increasingly used film for teaching, particularly in North America. Although the tradition of anthropological scientific documentation continued, it was soon to be challenged by new developments in documentary cinema and within anthropology itself.

Perhaps the most conspicuous example of the persisting scientific model was the *Encyclopaedia Cinematographica*, developed under the leadership of Gotthard Wolf from 1952 at the Institute für den Wissenschaftlichen Film in Göttingen, Germany. Beginning as a collection of earlier scientific films, its objective became the "systematic filmic documentation of movement" from all cultures, recalling the interest in locomotion of Regnault and others at the end of the nineteenth century. The first films of the program were biological, but attention soon shifted to recording "thematic units" of human activities, and rules were set down to describe how the films should be made. In a similar vein, E. Richard Sorenson proposed strict procedures for a research filming program based on the Standard Cross-Cultural Sample of preindustrial societies devised by George P. Murdock. At the University of California, Samuel Barrett directed a program in the early 1960s to film the traditional food-gathering and food-processing techniques of Native Americans. Reflecting a more theoretical framework, the Choreometrics Project of Alan Lomax at Columbia University, beginning in 1961, assembled a large collection of ethnographic films in an attempt to find regional and cultural patterns of body movement in dance and work practices throughout the world.

Jean Rouch, a student of the anthropologist Marcel Griaule, first trained as an engineer and built roads in west Africa during World War II. He began filming with a secondhand 16mm camera on a trip down the Niger in 1946 (*Au pays des mages noirs*, 1947), thus beginning his career in ethnographic cinema. Rouch was the first trained anthropologist to make an impact on both ethnographic and documentary film, and his influence on each has been profound. *Les Maîtres fous* (1953), a study of the Hauka cult in Ghana (then the Gold Coast), became a *cause célèbre* for its disturbing depiction of spirit possession among the initiates. Some viewers accused Rouch of perpetuating African exoticism, whereas others praised the honesty and power of the film, which included showing the cult members in their everyday jobs under a colonial regime. Jean-Luc Godard hailed Rouch as the initiator of the French *Nouvelle Vague* for his development of a new, more personal way of filming, using lightweight equipment. But Rouch's anthropological shift was a no less radical departure, away from recording external "facts" and toward the exploration of the subjective experience of persons in other cultures. Many of his films were improvised in close collaboration with his subjects. Rouch acknowledged Flaherty and Vertov as his "masters." He went on to make more than one hundred films in west Africa, including *Jaguar* (1964, filmed in 1954), a lively, semi-fictionalized narrative of labor migration (the subject of Rouch's Ph.D. thesis); *Moi un noir* (1957), on the daily activities and fantasy life of two young men recently arrived in the Treichville district of Abidjan in Côte d'Ivoire; and *La Pyramide humaine* (1959), an experimental study of race relations.

Rouch's approach to visual anthropology can be usefully compared to that of John Marshall in the United States. In the early 1950s, Marshall, the teenage son of a Boston industrialist, accompanied a series of family expeditions to the Kalahari Desert in southwest Africa, organized in association with Harvard University's Peabody Museum. His father gave him a 16mm camera and asked him to document the material culture of the Ju/'hoansi people, whom other members of the family were also studying. Beginning with food-gathering and hunting methods, Marshall soon turned his attention to filming the social interactions and emotional life of the Ju/'hoansi. Although he had only a non-synchronous sound recorder, he filmed many scenes involving spontaneous conversations, the sound for which was laboriously "scissor-synched" to the images some years later. Like Rouch, Marshall was primarily interested in the thoughts, feelings, and distinctive cultural outlook of his subjects, and he realized that this could only be communicated to an audience by using the creative resources of cinema. Like Rouch, he constructed with his camera an integrated sense of time, place, and individual personalities, to be fleshed out by the imagination of the viewer. Although he is best known for his narrative film *The Hunters* (1957), it is perhaps in shorter films such as *A Joking Relationship* (1966) and *An Argument about a Marriage* (1969) that these principles are best demonstrated. Marshall went on to collaborate with Frederick Wiseman on *Titicut Follies* (1967) and to produce what he called an "ethnography of the police" in the Pittsburgh Police series, including *Three Domestics* (1970). A biographical film, *N!ai, The Story of a !Kung Woman*, appeared in 1980, followed by a series of films of advocacy on behalf of the Ju/'hoansi, *A Kalahari Family* (2002).

Marshall's work spanned both ethnographic and documentary filmmaking, and his methods anticipated many of those that were to emerge in cinema verité and direct cinema in the 1960s. There were strong stylistic and intellectual ties, if not direct contacts, between Marshall and such documentary filmmakers as Wiseman, Albert and David Maysles, Richard Leacock, Donn Pennebaker, and Robert Drew in the United States, as well as filmmakers at the National Film Board of Canada, such as Terence McCartney-Filgate and Michel Brault. Many of the social documentaries they made were a form of ethnographic filmmaking in all but name, such as Wiseman's studies of public institutions (for example, *High School*, 1968, and *Hospital*, 1970) and Pierre Perrault's films of the Québecois community on the Île-aux-Coudres. There were also links between Canada and France. Michel Brault, who along with Leacock had been one of the first in North America to develop lightweight synchronous sound filming equipment, joined Rouch in Paris to work on his film *Chronique d'un été* (1961).

During this period new sources of educational funding in the United States acted as a stimulus to ethnographic filmmaking. From 1963 to 1968, Asen Balikci directed the Netsilik Eskimo film project as part of a new experimental school curriculum, *Man: A Course of Study*. The project showed several Inuit families recreating various aspects of their life before contact with Europeans. Robert Young, who with Michael Roemer had previously made a sensitive film on the life of Sicilian slum-dwellers (*Cortile Cascino*, 1962), used the new lightweight equipment to great effect in capturing moments of spontaneous interaction previously unseen in ethnographic film. Timothy Asch, who had collaborated with John Marshall in editing many of his Ju/'hoansi films, began a series of films with the anthropologist Napoleon Chagnon on Yanomami groups in southern Venezuela, including *The Feast* (1970). Modeled along the lines of the "sequence film" concept that Asch had pioneered with Marshall, many of the shorter films used synchronous sound and long camera takes to encapsulate events for teaching anthropology at the university level. These projects produced forty short films, such as *Magical Death* (1973), *A Father Washes His Children* (1974), and *The Ax Fight* (1975), an innovative examination of a single event from five different perspectives. Asch was later to make another important group of films with Patsy Asch in Indonesia, collaborating with various anthropologists, including *A Balinese Trance Seance* (1981) and *A Celebration of Origins* (1992).

Chronique d'un été, co-directed by Rouch and the sociologist Edgar Morin in the summer of 1960, was one of the most important documentary films of its time and influenced a generation of filmmakers. Posed as an experimental study of how several young Parisians lived their lives, it involved its subjects directly in the making of the film and broke many of the existing rules and conventions of documentary. Its inventiveness and eclecticism produced a stylistic and conceptual breakthrough in documentary, inspiring others to explore new structural possibilities. Rouch and Morin freely borrowed devices from fiction films and, in blurring the line between fiction and nonficton, mirrored the approach of such feature-film directors as Jean-Luc Godard and François Truffaut, who at this time were freely borrowing devices from documentary. Rouch continued making films in a variety of styles in Africa, including eight on the Sigui ritual cycle of the Dogon with Germaine Dieterlen from 1966 to 1973, and *Madame l'Eau* (1992). Among the French ethnographic filmmakers influenced by Rouch and the spirit of *cinéma vérité* were Jean-Paul Olivier de Sardan (*La Vieille et la pluie*, 1974), Colette Piault (*My Family and Me*, 1986), Marc Henri Piault (*Akazama*, 1986), and Éliane de Latour (*Contes et comptes de la cour*, 1993).

Two other ethnographic filmmakers who pursued highly personal styles were Robert Gardner in the United States and Jorge Preloran in Argentina. Gardner had helped establish the Film Study Center at Harvard University in the 1950s and assisted Marshall with the postproduction of *The Hunters*. His film *Dead Birds* (1963) on ritual warfare among the Dani highlanders of New Guinea, became one of the most widely viewed ethnographic films. The film used a spoken story line that bound together a series of related and unrelated events, but, more important, created the sense of a subjective perspective on them. In later films, such as *Rivers of Sand* (1975), Gardner attempted a more abstract interconnecting of scenes; and in *Forest of Bliss* (1985), a film about death in Benares that provoked much controversy among anthropologists, he orchestrated a complex flow of symbolic elements in an attempt to evoke a particular network of cultural associations. Although Gardner's work spans both poetic and ethnographic documentary, his contribution to visual anthropology has been to show that cultural systems are not necessarily best described from realist perspectives, and that more abstract or embodied approaches are often better able to preserve the ambiguous meanings that permeate social practices.

Relatively isolated, and with limited equipment, Jorge Preloran began making films about marginalized groups in his native Argentina in the early 1950s. Returning from America with university film training, he developed a distinctive form of filmed "ethnobiography," in which he made extensive sound recordings of his subjects describing their lives and then returned to film them with a spring-wind 16mm camera. Such films as *Imaginero—The Image Man* (1970) and *Zerda's Children* (1978) convey their subjects' life histories and daily existence with political awareness and a sensitive eye for physical details.

By the mid-1960s, increasing use of ethnographic films in teaching was leading to the greater institutionalization of visual anthropology, expressed in new university programs, conferences, publications, and ethnographic film festivals. In France, ethnographic film was actively supported by the Centre National de la Recherche Scientifique. In Britain, the Royal Anthropological Institute created a film collection for teaching under the supervision of anthropologist and filmmaker James Woodburn (*The Hadza*, 1966). In the United States, ethnographic film programs were established at Harvard University, the University of California at Los Angeles, and Temple University in Philadelphia, where Jay Ruby also established a journal and an influential series of conferences on visual anthropology. Among the graduates of the California program, David and Judith MacDougall began applying recent documentary approaches in 1968 to their ethnographic filmmaking among pastoralists in East Africa, producing such films as *Nawi* (1970), *To Live with Herds* (1972), and *The Wedding Camels* (1977). These used subtitles extensively to translate filmed conversations, as John Marshall and Timothy Asch had also done, giving greater access to the intellectual and emotional lives of their subjects.

The use of synchronous sound was accompanied by a new concern for epistemological and ethical issues. To what extent did film images constitute evidence of an event when, through selection and editing, they could so easily be manipulated? Could this be overcome by the more observational approach of Leacock and Wiseman, using longer takes that better preserved temporal, spacial, and social continuities? And yet, did not such an approach tend to objectify the subjects, perpetuating (especially in ethnographic films) the unequal power relations of the colonial era? Much as Rouch had advocated a "shared anthropology" (*anthropologie partegée*), filmmakers such as the MacDougalls called for a "participatory cinema" acknowledging the realities of the filmmaking encounter in the film, thus altering the perspective of the viewers and giving the subjects a greater role. They attempted to apply these principles to their filming in Africa and, later, in Australia and India (for example, *The House-Opening* (1980), *Photo Wallahs*, 1991, *Doon School Chronicles*, 2000, and *Diya*, 2001).

Ian Dunlop, who in the 1960s had made the People of the Australian Western Desert series in a classic 35mm documentary mode (including the widely shown *Desert People*, 1966), adopted 16mm and an observational style for his long-running study of the ritual activities and social struggles of the Yirrkala community in Arnhem Land (for example, *Djungguwan at Gurka'wuy*, 1989), and two extensive film projects with Maurice Godelier to document Baruya initiation rituals in Papua New Guinea. Roger Sandall, working with the anthropologist Nicolas Peterson, made an important series of films on aboriginal rituals in central Australia, using synchronous sound and a fluid camera style. Gary Kildea, working initially in Papua New Guinea, where he made *Trobriand Cricket: An Ingenious Response to Colonialism* (1976), then filmed in the Philippines, producing *Celso and Cora* (1983) and *Valencia Diary* (1992). The first, a portrait of a poor family in Manila, was notable for its sympathetic interaction with its subjects and also for dispensing with conventional editing by inserting grey spacing between the shots. Kim McKenzie's *Waiting for Harry* (1980) took a fresh approach to aboriginal ritual by devoting more time to the politics of organizing the ritual than to the ritual itself. Other prominent Australian ethnographic filmmakers included Curtis Levy (*Sons of Namatjira*, 1975) and the team of Bob Connolly and Robin Anderson, who further refined the narrative ethnographic film in their New Guinea trilogy, *First Contact* (1982), *Joe Leahy's Neighbours* (1988), and *Black Harvest* (1992).

In Britain, Colin Young, who had established the UCLA Ethnographic Film Program, designed a program in conjunction with the Royal Anthropological Institute to train young anthropologists in filmmaking at the National Film and Television School. Among the students was Paul Henley, who filmed at his fieldwork site in Venezuela and then went on to train a new generation of ethnographic filmmakers as director of the Granada Centre for Visual Anthropology at Manchester University. Meanwhile, other young anthropologists, such as Chris Curling and Melissa Llewelyn-Davies, were gaining a foothold in ethnographic filmmaking through television.

Television created new outlets for nonfiction filmmaking and gave it new stylistic features derived from journalism, including the extensive use of interviews. Along with the Drew Associates' early experiments in direct cinema, one of the forms to emerge from this was the ethnographic television series, most clearly exemplified by Granada Television's *Disappearing World* in Britain. This long-running project, which produced more than fifty programs, was based on collaborations between television directors and anthropologists. The arrangement was not always a happy one. Sometimes the aims of the two clashed, or the anthropologist felt insufficiently consulted, or the result was a didactic exercise; but in the most successful examples (*Last of the Cuiva*, 1971; *The Mursi*, 1974; and *The Kawelka: Ongka's Big Moka*, 1974), there was a genuine meeting of minds, creatively and anthropologically. Inspired by recent ethnographic films, the producer of the series, Brian Moser, fought to include subtitled dialogue in the programs, a move at first fiercely opposed by senior Granada executives. Confounding expectations, the series became highly popular and opened a new window on ethnographic filmmaking for the British public. Directors such as André Singer who had worked on the series subsequently created similar programs at the BBC, some of which gave the anthropologist a freer hand as director. Perhaps the most outstanding example was Melissa Llewelyn-Davies' series of films on the Maasai, including *The Women's Olamal* (1984) and *Diary of a Maasai Village* (1984). The first was a cinematically sophisticated and anthropologically rigorous study of the controversy surrounding the holding of a fertility ceremony. It not only revealed the deliberations of the Maasai women in detail but, in a restrained use of interviews, gave a sense of the close relationship between them and the anthropologist-director. A similar rapport and depth of cultural knowledge is evident in films on the Hamar people by the anthropologists Ivo Strecker and Jean Lydall, and later by Lydall in films for the BBC, such as *Our Way of Loving* (1994), and still later *Duka's Dilemma* (2001), made with her daughter, Kaira Strecker.

During this same period, a long-running television series, *Subarashii Sekai Ryoko* (*Our Wonderful World*), produced by Junichi Ushiyama of Nippon A-V Productions, introduced the Japanese public to many unfamiliar societies. Although anthropologists were not often directly involved, the directors and their small crews frequently spent months in the field, a procedure rare in British television. The result was films of considerable intimacy, in which individual personalities were allowed to emerge. Among the most resourceful of the NAV directors were Tadao Sugiyama and Yasuko Ichioka. Filmmakers associated with Chinese television have begun producing a new wave of innovative ethnographic films, such as *Fading Reindeer Bell* (Sun Zengtian, 1997) and Hao Yuejun's *The Village in the Cave* (1994), and *The Last Horse Caravan* (2000). Television has also contributed to ethnographic film through more sociologically orientated programs. Like Wiseman's films in the United States, which were broadcast on public television, the various documentary series made by Roger Graef in Britain (for example, *Police*, 1982) used a direct cinema camera style to explore police activities, schools, corporate management, and industrial disputes.

Since the mid-1990s, the superior image quality and low cost of digital video have created new opportunities for documentary filmmakers. Increasingly, anthropology students are making their own films, either within existing anthropology departments or in new visual anthropology programs such as those at the University of Tromsø in Norway and Yunnan University in China. Digital video has also created a resurgence of independent documentary filmmaking in developing countries, where film production was formerly monopolized by government film units and state television networks. In India, for example, filmmakers such as Rahul Roy, Saba Dewan, Amar Kunwar, Rakesh Sharma, and Shohini Ghosh are exploring a widening range of social, political, and cultural subjects, many with substantial ethnographic content.

In the debate over what constitutes an ethnographic film, one of the most inclusive definitions is any film that may be of interest ethnographically, either because of its subject matter or as a reflection of the culture of its maker. Putting the latter principle to the test in 1966, the Navaho film project of John Adair and Sol Worth sought to discover what might be revealed culturally if people who had never made films were trained to do so. Seven Navaho men and women were given basic instruction. The results (distributed as the *Navaho Film Themselves* series) were suggestive of culturally distinctive ways of seeing, but not conclusively so, partly because of differences in participants' previous exposure to films. A more frequent practice has been to analyze existing films as cultural documents. Several projects during World War II, including one by Gregory Bateson, relied on fiction films and newsreels as sources for studying German and Japanese cultural attitudes "at a distance."

Films emanating from various national cinema traditions have also occasionally become "ethnographic" when used to teach anthropology (for example, feature films by such directors as Yasujiro Ozu [Japan], Satyajit Ray [India], and Ousmane Sembène [Senegal]). Certain fiction films, because of their content, can reveal much about a particular society or group (for example, Vittorio de Seta's *Banditi a Orgosolo* [1961]), about Sardinian shepherds, and Perry Henzell's *The Harder They Come* (1973), about the musical subculture of Jamaica.

With globalization proceeding apace, almost no community is now so remote as to be cut off from the mass media. Ethnographic filmmakers must now assume that the first and keenest critics of their films will often be the people in them. Access to video cameras is also increasing, and people from almost every society are beginning to use them. This development has shifted the balance of ethnographic representation, allowing those who were once the objects of others' images to represent themselves. Local and indigenous media production and broadcasting have extended the concept of ethnographic film. Native Americans, Inuit groups, indigenous Australians, and others have begun to use film and video as a political tool, as a means of cultural reinforcement and as a way of offsetting a long heritage of derogatory and romantic stereotypes. Indigenous broadcasting organizations include CAAMA (Central Australian Aboriginal Media Association), the Inuit Broadcasting Corporation (Canada), and Sami Radio (Norway and Finland). In Brazil, the Kayapo have been making astute use of video for years, and such projects as *Video in the Villages*, organized by Vincente Carelli, is spreading this use to other groups. Anthropologists such as Terence Turner have been instrumental in these processes. Members of indigenous groups have emerged as important ethnographic filmmakers and creative artists, in some cases closely linked to their ancestral communities and in others not. Among those currently well known are the Hopi filmmaker Victor Masayesva (*Ritual Clowns*, 1988; *Imagining Indians*, 1992), the Inuit filmmaker Zacharias Kunuk (*Qaggig*, 1989; *Atanarjuat: The Fast Runner*, 2001), Maori filmmaker Merata Mita (*Bastion Point: Day 507*, 1980; *Hotere*, 2001), and the Australians Tracey Moffatt (*BeDevil*, 1993), Rachel Perkins (*Freedom Ride*, 1993), Ivan Sen (*Shifting Shelter*, 1996; *Vanish*, 1998), Darlene Johnson (*Stolen Generations*, 2000), and Erica Glynn (*Ngangkari Way*, 2002).

By the 1980s, the epistemological issues that had preoccupied filmmakers in the 1970s were being reflected in questions anthropologists were asking about the construction and authority of anthropological writing. Anthropology was also changing in other ways, with new interests in the embodied experience of individuals and the cultural construction of the emotions and senses. These shifts have set the stage intellectually for a closer rapport between ethnographic film and anthropology. As national and social boundaries become more permeable, visual culture and the visible worlds of social performance and material culture are reemerging as anthropological concerns. Young anthropologists are taking a renewed interest in the conceptual and expressive potential of visual media, including interactive multimedia. If in the past ethnographic filmmaking was often a marginal or radical anthropological practice, it is now in a position to add a significant new dimension to anthropological knowledge. Ultimately, documentary as well may benefit from anthropology's renewed interest in the visible.

DAVID MACDOUGALL

See also **Brault, Michel; Drew, Robert;** *Fires Were Started;* *Farrebique;* **Flaherty, Robert; Gardner, Robert; General Post Office Film Unit; Grierson, John; Jennings, Humphrey; Leacock, Richard;** *Man of Aran;* **Marshall, John; Maysles, Albert;** *Moana; Nanook of the North;* **National Film Board of Canada;** *Night Mail;* **Preloran, Jorge;** *Song of Ceylon;* **Wright, Basil**

Further Reading

Banks, Marcus, and Howard Morphy, editors, *Rethinking Visual Anthropology*, New Haven and London: Yale University Press, 1997.

Crawford, Peter Ian, and Jan Ketil Simonsen (editors), *Ethnographic Film Aesthetics and Narrative Traditions*, Aarhus: Intervention Press, 1992.

Crawford, Peter Ian, and David Turton, editors, *Film as Ethnography*, Manchester and New York: Manchester University Press, 1992.

Gardner, Robert, and Ákos Östör, *Making Forest of Bliss: Intention, Circumstance, and Chance in Nonfiction Film*, Cambridge, MA, and London: Harvard Film Archive, 2001.

Griffiths, Alison, *Wondrous Difference: Cinema, Anthropology, and Turn-of-the-Century Visual Culture*, New York: Columbia University Press, 2002.

Grimshaw, Anna, *The Ethnographer's Eye: Ways of Seeing in Modern Anthropology*, Cambridge: Cambridge University Press, 2001.

Heider, Karl G., *Ethnographic Film*, Austin: University of Texas Press, 1976.

Hockings, Paul, editor, *Principles of Visual Anthropology* (2nd ed.), Berlin and New York: Mouton de Gruyter, 1995.

Loizos, Peter, *Innovation in Ethnographic Film: From Innocence to Self-Consciousness, 1955[–]1985*, Manchester: Manchester University Press, 1993.

MacDougall, David, *Transcultural Cinema*, Princeton, NJ: Princeton University Press, 1998.

——, *The Corporeal Image: Film, Ethnography & the Senses*, Princeton, NJ: Princeton University Press, 2005.

Piault, Marc Henri, *Anthropologie et Cinéma: Passage à l'image, passage par l'image*, Paris: Éditions Nathan, 2000.

Ruby, Jay, *Picturing Culture: Explorations of Film & Anthropology*, Chicago: University of Chicago Press, 2000.

Stoller, Paul, *The Cinematic Griot: The Ethnography of Jean Rouch*, Chicago: Chicago University Press, 1992.

Worth, Sol, and John Adair, *Through Navajo Eyes*, Bloomington, IN: Indiana University Press, 1972.

ÊTRE ET AVOIR

(France, Philibert, 2002)

One of the most celebrated feature-length documentaries of 2002, Nicholas Philibert's *Être et Avoir*, can in some ways be seen as the polar opposite of the other big documentary of that year, Michael Moore's *Bowling for Columbine*. Where Moore opts for bombast, Philibert strives for gentle tranquility. Where Moore's "argument" about the state of the world he is examining utterly dominates his film, Philibert offers no "argument" at all.

Not interested in making documentaries that are "about" a subject, Philibert prefers to construct his films, as he says, "with" subjects and locations. *Être et Avoir* examines a one-room school in Auvergne in France, where the dozen students, who range from 4- to 10-years old, are all taught by one teacher, M. Georges Lopez. The film takes place over the course of six months, beginning in a blustery snowstorm and ending in the bright breezes of summer. Adopting an almost entirely observational approach (with the exception of the interview sequence with Monsieur Lopez, the teacher, in which he explains why he is a schoolteacher), the film negotiates an intermediate space between those observational films that present a world as if it had not been recorded on camera and those that foreground the existence of the mediating existence of the cinematographic apparatus. Thus, there are scenes in which the teacher and pupils appear completely at ease and nonchalant in front of the camera, and others in which they seem acutely aware of it.

Philibert has expressed his deep conviction—echoing Cesare Zavattini's call for films about the poetry of everyday life—in the cinematic potential of the quotidian aspects of life. Situating his camera in a milieux in which the everyday struggles of children are, for these young humans, monumental ones—mastering basics of numeracy and literacy, not to mention the vital lessons of sociability and communication—Philibert has found ideal locations and conditions for allowing the poetry of everyday life to expose itself on film. As well, selection of a small school, with so few pupils and of such wide-ranging ages, allows for heightened connection with the characters. This is possible because their number and diversity allow us to know them as individuals to a larger degree than would have been the case had we been situated in a more traditional classroom—one grade level with twenty to thirty students.

As much as the film relies on audiences' willingness and ability to pay careful attention to the children, the film is centred on the quiet authority of Monsieur Lopez, the teacher. His commanding presence is felt (again to contrast with Moore's bombastic performance in *Bowling for Columbine*) in his gentleness and his quiet. He is one of those figures who, because he speaks so softly, demands our (and the children's) attention because he forces us to lean into what he is saying. In his dealings with the wee ones, he is a model of firm patience; with the older children, of guidance and

Être et Avoir, 2002.
[*Still courtesy of the British Film Institute*]

certainty; and with the parents, of understanding and empathy.

While much of what we see takes place in the classroom, the film emphasizes that which surrounds it. We are treated not only to pretty natural images of the local seasons but also to the farms where some of the children live, a school outing to a library, bus rides, and, significantly, the decamping of instruction from the classroom to the school's playground, tables, chairs, and all, once the warm summer breezes start blowing. The metaphor represented by this venue change by the teacher Lopez, and its inclusion in the film by Philibert, is perfectly representative of the film's expansive aspirations.

Formally, the film makes some powerfully affective choices. The first sounds and images of the film, though they contain no children and no teacher, suggestively set the tone for what follows: a blustery snowstorm, with cattle being guided through the pasture followed by a cut to a high-angle shot of the classroom floor, where gradually, leisurely, one turtle, and then another, ambles into the frame. These juxtapositions of chaotic nature with measured control illuminate the central tensions at the heart of the film—those between the individual and society, between teacher and pupil, between humankind and nature.

As well, Phillipe Hersant's tender and calming score is used only for scenes outside the classroom; in the classroom we have only direct sound. The images of rural life that surround the village school, gorgeously photographed as the seasons turn, place the developmental milestones of the children in a natural order in which snowstorms, rainstorms, summer breezes, and dappling sunlight all converge in a sensation of the small universalities of the human experience. We were all once children and had to learn how to grow up and make our way in the world.

The title, which translates as *To Be and To Have*, refers on the surface to a conjugation exercise that normally comes early in a French-language education, that is, at a moment in language-learning where we find these schoolchildren. However, the film's expansion outward from the classroom, into the rural countryside that surrounds it and further still into the universal experiences of childhood, lends this title a much weightier significance. The film's reach, then, ultimately strives to consider questions of existence in this world (being) and acquiring the means as children to navigate through it (having).

Produced partly with the participation of various French state bodies, *Être et Avoir* was a modestly budgeted film that attracted huge audiences in France (becoming the highest-grossing documentary in that country's history), as well as attracting significant critical attention around the world, winning both prestigious prizes and large audiences. Named best documentary of the year by both the European Film Awards and the National Society of Film Critics in the United States, the film was also nominated for (or won) major film prizes in Britain, France, and Spain.

PETER URQUHART

EUROPEAN DOCUMENTARY INSTITUTE

See **Documentary Film Initiative**

EUROPEAN DOCUMENTARY NETWORK

Based in Copenhagen since its founding in September 1996, the European Documentary Network (EDN) is an independent pan-European association that works for the promotion of the documentary genre. The association has 720 members from fifty-one countries including all old and new EU countries. Thirty-five of these are associate members with no vote, including film institutes, film funds, and TV companies; 10 percent are members from outside. The yearly budget is approximately 600,000 Euros. Apart from continuous support from the Danish Film Institute (approximately

50,000 Euros), the funding comes from member fees, sales of the EDN TV Guide, the EU-funded projects, and several other national and international events organised by EDN.

EDN was established as a continuation of the work that had been done by the EU MEDIA office Documentary from 1990–1995. This office had the task to distribute loans for the development of international documentary projects. Around the Documentary office a small group of internationally orientated producers, directors, and commissioning editors had joined forces through its five years of existence. This group urged the two Danes involved in the Documentary office, producer, and director Ole John and National Film Board's Tue Steen Müller to promote a continuation of the office as an independent organisation. A set of by-laws was written, the Danish Ministry of Culture provided the organisation seed money for two years, and Tue Steen Müller was appointed director of the organization, together with Anita Reher, who transferred her expertise from the Documentary office to be manager of EDN. Swedish director and producer PeÅ Holmquist was the first elected chair of EDN.

EDN provides members with answers to all kind of questions and aid to the development of treatments. EDN staff also views finished films and advises filmmakers where to market their films internationally. The network's strength is that it profits from all its internationally skilled producers and commissioning editors to be tutors and experts in the twenty yearly arranged workshops. Among the most active have been the producers Paul Pauwels of Belgium, Stefano Tealdi of Italy, and Steve Seidenberg of the United Kingdom; the director Emma Davie of the United Kingdom; and the commissioning editors Hugues Le Paige of Belgium, Leena Pasanen of Finland, Rada Sesic of The Netherlands, and Sabine Bubeck and Kathrin Brinkmann of Germany.

The first big effort of EDN was launched with the support of the EU MEDIA Programme. The EDN project for the Development of Documentary in the South of Europe was set up to encourage the weak documentary culture in Southern Europe. This workshop was intended for film producers and filmmakers and included the showing of films, guidance to European funding possibilities, and the provision of basic information on international co-productions. The first workshop was organised in Granada, Spain in 1997, followed by one in St. Vincent, Italy. In 1998 the first workshops in Lisbon, Portugal and Athens, Greece were set up.

By autumn 2004, twenty-eight workshops were organised in these four countries. Later the workshop became a speciality of EDN. They lasted three to five days and included work on each project with professionals; at the end of each session, there was a final pitching session with financial commitments. "Docs in Thessaloniki" in Greece runs parallel to the international documentary festival in the same city. Another workshop, "Docs Barcelona," which is the biggest of the four workshops in terms of participation—and focuses on a different theme every year (for example, who has the final cut? documentaries and archives, creative use of music in documentaries).

Southern Europe has not been the only priority of EDN. The group also holds annual workshops in France, the Nordic countries, and the United Kingdom. It also collaborates with IDFA for the Forum in Amsterdam, with the Discovery Campus training programme and many others. All twenty-five EU countries (except Malta) have been "visited" by EDN.

Activities in Eastern Europe have been strong during the last few years. For the second consecutive year EDN, held the Ex Oriente workshop in Prague that is a training programme primarily targeted at the documentarists in Poland, The Czech Republic, Slovakia, and Bulgaria. EDN has held three workshops in Yugoslavia; three human rights festivals in Bulgaria; made visits to Croatia, Bosnia, and Macedonia; and held workshops in Ukraine and Belarus. At all these sessions the aim has been to connect the filmmakers from these countries to the Western support system so as to expose their films to a larger audience.

Special attention has been given to the Baltic countries. A Baltic Sea Forum has been organized during the last eight years. The first five took place on the island of Bornholm in Denmark associated to the Baltic Film & TV Festival. The last three have taken place in Riga Latvia and in Tallinn Estonia. With the initiator of the festival, Baltic Media Centre, EDN has taken financial responsibility with regard to the EU MEDIA Programme that after the Baltic countries entry to the EU support the event. Several producers now regularly do international business with the public broadcasters and are co-producing with Western producers.

Collaboration with the West and Eastern Europe is in some way the same. EDN aims to be the matchmaker between broadcaster/funder and producer by creating a dialogue over the border. Whereas the Western documentary culture today is a mixture of commerce and art, the Eastern documentary is still primarily considered art. The EDN "philosophy" is to keep the best in the glorious Eastern European documentary tradition and at the same time make the producers and directors aware of the market demands.

EDN is responsible for two publications. The *EDN TV Guide* is often called "the producer's Bible" because of the concrete information it provides regarding broadcasting slots and strands. *DOX* is for many *the* only international documentary magazine that combines practical information about the market with reviews, festival reports, cultural articles, debates, and so on. It is published six time per year. *DOX* recently celebrated its fifti-eth edition.

EDN has members outside Europe and the orga-nisation has been called on several times from over-seas. Workshops have been organised in Turkey, Brazil, Canada, South Africa, and Zimbabwe. Plans are being made to introduce END in India,

Argentina, and Tahiti. Thus far, EDN has not developed a strategy for membership non-EU coun-tries. There is a debate within the EDN between those who wish the organization to remain Eur-opean and those who wish to "go global." EDN accepts members from all over Europe who can profit from its services.

RADA SESIC

EVERY DAY EXCEPT CHRISTMAS

(UK, Anderson, 1957)

Every Day Except Christmas was shown in the third Free Cinema programme, "Look at Britain," at the National Film Theatre, London, in May 1957 (along with Alain Tanner and Claude Goret-ta's *Nice Time*, 1957, and two earlier short films, Anderson's own *Wakefield Express*, and Nigel McIsaac's *The Singing Street*, both made in 1952). Like other Free Cinema films, all victims of the distribution difficulties of documentaries since the advent of television, even the best of the Free Cinema documentaries are not as well known or respected as they should be outside (and to some extent even inside) Britain.

The structure of the film is relatively simple, beginning with the loading of mushrooms in Sussex for transportation to Covent Garden market in central London, following the van through its late night journey—through the suburbs to the strains of the national anthem, signalling the end of radio broadcasting for the day. At the market, work is just beginning and the film follows the night's activities—laying out the produce, taking an early morning break, returning to the market for the arrival of the buyers, and ending mid-morning as the market winds down.

Free Cinema was a product of its time—John Osborne's play *Look Back in Anger* (1956) and the stir and storm it caused in British theatre (which also engaged Anderson's talents), and the emergence of the New Left. Anderson's 1957 man-ifesto for Free Cinema argued that their aim was to "say something about our society today . . . to look

at Britain, with honesty and affection." *Every Day Except Christmas* and *We Are the Lambeth Boys*, the two "Look at Britain" films sponsored by Ford, are probably the best examples.

Anderson's manifesto's "if we are to interpret . . ." invokes Grierson's creative interpretation of actu-ality, and in many ways we should see *Every Day Except Christmas* in a direct line from 1930s (and World War II) British documentary. In a revealing interview comment many years later, Anderson accused his interviewers of being too taken with direct cinema and having a narrow

Every Day Except Christmas, 1957.
[*Still courtesy of the British Film Institute*]

view of documentary. In his film, he says, "even the bits that have natural sound are all composed . . . [direct cinema is] just an excuse for not being creative." Though several sequences seem to want to persuade us that we are hearing what we can see, more recall the finale of *Housing Problems*, with conversational voices, as well as other sounds, over image, created at the editing stage. Anderson observed in a later interview that institutions like the BBC would not "understand the creative effort or the poetic quality" of a film like *Every Day Except Christmas*. Certainly, the film uses sound and image in "creative ways" much like earlier documentaries. Anderson likes to contrast busy scenes with quiet, still ones, and jaunty with slow, lyrical music. One central, striking sequence, for example, juxtaposes the bustle of Albert's café with the deserted market alleys, a stray cat, slow panning, and tracking shots over the laid-out flowers, with, first, silence and then poetic music.

One of the films shown in the second Free Cinema programme (September 1956) was Georges Franju's *Le Sang des bêtes* (1949), and Anderson's creative methods are sometimes reminiscent of Franju's evocative use of music and camera (though without the characteristic Franju "bite"). In the Free Cinema manifesto, Anderson's "if we are to interpret . . ." is followed by "we must have an attitude, we must have values and beliefs," which he seems to see as distinguishing Free Cinema from the "social propaganda" aspect of 1930s documentary. What are the "values and beliefs" in *Every Day Except Christmas*?

Although Anderson is interested in the different kinds of activities in the market, this is not a conventionally "polemical" film, hence, perhaps, the omission (as Basil Wright pointed out) of those podding peas in the market's dark basement. Anderson is clearly more interested in communicating what he saw as the dignity and importance of ordinary people as they go about their work, and enjoys observing the faces and simple skills of working men (particularly in relation to flowers, not without some hints of homoeroticism—compare the openly gay character in the café). The film's credentials at the class level are sustained by the voice-over commentary, spoken by Alan Owen, a prolific working class radio and television (and later theatre) dramatist during the 1950s and 1960s, with more than a suggestion of working class Welsh, but with a soft lilt. As the commentary concludes, things change "but work will still be with us, one way or another, and we all depend on each other's work as well as our own, on Alice, and George, and Bill . . . and all the others who keep us going."

At the same time, as in the Humphrey Jennings films, which Anderson so admired, there is an attachment—akin, perhaps, to Flaherty's in *Industrial Britain*, but more personalised—to history and tradition, and the present threat to their survival. There is a real sense of regret and loss, for example, when the film talks about the disappearance of women flower porters ("Alice has been on the job for thirty-five years, and when she goes, that's the end of it") and the aged women flower sellers who come round as the market closes down. Of course, in fifteen years or so, the markets had been removed to the concrete wastes of Nine Elms in Vauxhall, where there was precious little poetry to be had.

JIM HILLIER

See also **Anderson, Lindsay; Franju, Georges; Grierson, John; Jennings, Humphrey;** *We Are the Lambeth Boys*

Every Day Except Christmas (UK, Graphic Films for the Ford Motor Company Ltd, 1957, 47 mins) (first film in series "Look at Britain"). Distributed by the British Film Institute. Produced by Leon Clore and Karel Reisz. Directed and scripted by Lindsay Anderson. Cinematography by Walter Lassally. Music by Daniel Paris. Editing and sound by John Fletcher. Commentary spoken by Alun Owen. Assistants Alex Jacobs, Brian Probyn, and Maurice Ammar. Filmed in London.

Further Reading

Anderson, Lindsay, "Free Cinema," *Universities and Left Review*, No. 2, Summer 1957, reprinted in Barsam, Richard Meran, editor, *Nonfiction Film Theory and Criticism*, New York: E.P. Dutton, 1976.

Ellis, Jack, *The Documentary Idea*, Englewood Cliffs, NJ and London: E.P. Dutton, 1989.

Graham, Alison, *Lindsay Anderson*, Boston: E.P. Dutton, 1981.

Hedling, Erik, *Lindsay Anderson: Maverick Film-Maker*, London and Washington: E.P. Dutton, 1998.

Higson, Andrew, "Britain's Outstanding Contribution to the Film: The Documentary-Realist Tradition," in Charles Barr, editor, *All Our Yesterdays: 90 Years of British Cinema*, London: E.P. Dutton, 1986.

Jacobs, Lewis, editor, *The Documentary Tradition*, New York: E.P. Dutton, 1974.

Lambert, Gavin, "Free Cinema," *Sight & Sound*, 25, Spring, 1956.

Levin, G. Roy, editor, *Documentary Explorations*, Garden City, NY: E.P. Dutton, 1971.

Lovell, Alan, and Jim Hillier, *Studies in Documentary*, London: E.P. Dutton, 1972.

Orbanz, Eva, Gisela Tuchtenhagen, and Klaus Wildenhahn, *Journey to a Legend and Back: The British Realistic Film*, Berlin: E.P. Dutton, 1977.

Silet, Charles L. P., *Lindsay Anderson: A Guide to References and Resources*, Boston: E.P. Dutton, 1978.

Sussex, Elizabeth, *Lindsay Anderson*, London: E.P. Dutton, 1969/New York: Praeger, 1970.

EXHIBITION

See **Distribution and Exhibition**

EXILE AND THE KINGDOM

(Australia, Frank Rijavec, 1993)

Exile and the Kingdom is a unique and comprehensive historical account of a group of aboriginal peoples from ancient times to the present. It continues a mode of collaborative or consultative filmmaking between indigenous and nonindigenous Australians that was initiated in the 1970s. Frank Rijavec directed *Exile and the Kingdom* and also co-wrote the film in conjunction with Roger Solomon of the Injibarndi and Ngarluma tribes. As an on-screen narrator, Solomon also plays a central role in the finished film.

Exile and the Kingdom focuses on an area in the north of Western Australia around the Fortescue River and the town of Roebourne. Elders of the Injibarndi, Ngarluma, Kurama, and Bandjima tribes of this area were involved with developing the different approaches that the film used. *Exile and the Kingdom* begins by outlining a number of the traditional ceremonies that have been integral to the Injibarndi and Ngarluma cultures of the area since times well before colonisation. Themes that are reiterated throughout the documentary are the importance of ancestral lands, and sacred sites in particular, and the codes of respect and discipline that compose aboriginal law. *Exile and the Kingdom* goes on to chart a history of colonisation that includes forced labor, the dispossession of lands, wars against colonists or "squatters," and an eventual massacre of aboriginal people. This history extends into the present, with an account of the detrimental impact of alcohol, the iron-ore mining boom of the 1960s and 1970s and the ghettoization of these tribes in government reserves. *Exile and the Kingdom* persuasively argues for the recognition of land rights and an emphasis on aboriginal law and spirituality as a means of restoring indigenous communities.

In addition to Solomon's narration, the film is structured around interviews with a diverse range of aboriginal people about the history of the area, their experiences, and tribal knowledge. Written accounts by British colonists are also recited in the earlier part of the film. *Exile and the Kingdom* is a feature-length documentary that is divided into two 55-minute parts to facilitate television screening. In contrast with another significant indigenous/nonindigenous collaborative documentary, *Two Laws* (1981), *Exile and the Kingdom* was produced for viewing by a mainstream Australian television audience.

The importance of this collaborative mode as a means of self-representation to a broader national audience can be understood in the context of a history of Australian cinema. For the past century a huge archive of film has been produced that situates aboriginal people as ethnographic subjects, or, to a lesser extent, melodramatic stereotypes. Projects in the 1970s, such as Martha Ansara's collaboration with Essie Coffey on the landmark documentary *My Survival as an Aboriginal* (1979), led the way for more indigenous people to take up a position on the other side of the camera in order to represent alternative aesthetic and political strategies. This collaborative documentary mode of which *Exile and the Kingdom* is a part has been carried on in the 1990s by indigenous directors working in a more autonomous way such as Rachel Perkins, Tracey Moffatt, Darlene Johnson, and Ivan Sen.

BELINDA SMAILL

See also **Documentary Film: Australia**

Exile and the Kingdom (Australia, Ngurin Aboriginal Corporation/Frank Rijavec/Noelene Harrison, 1993, 110 mins). Distributed by Film Australia. Produced by Frank Rijavec and Noelene Harrison. Directed by Frank Rijavec. Written by Frank Rijavec and Roger Solomon. Cinematography by Frank Rijavec and Peter Kordyl. Edited by Liz Goldfinch. Sound by Lawrie Silvestrin and Roslyn Silvestrin.

Further Reading

Bryson, Ian, Margaret Burns, and Marcia Langton, "Painting with Light: Australian Indigenous Cinema" in *The Oxford Companion to Aboriginal Art and Culture*, edited by Sylvia Kleinert and Margo Neale, Melbourne: Oxford University Press, 2000, 297–305.

Langton, Marcia, 'Well I heard it on the Radio and I saw it on the Television . . ." *An Essay for the Australian Film Commission on the politics and aesthetics of filmmaking by and about Aboriginal people and things*. Sydney: Australian Film Commission, 1993.

O'Regan, Tom, Australian National Cinema, London: Routledge, 1996.

EXPERIMENTAL FILM

See **Modernism: Avant-garde; Experimental Early Silent European Documentary**

F

FAHRENHEIT 9/11

See **Moore, Michael**

FALKLANDS WAR

More than twenty years after British troops reclaimed the Falkland Islands from a brief Argentinean occupation, it is still difficult to assess what "meanings" have been attached to the conflict. Certainly documentary films about the war have broadly attempted to reexamine the picture of the Falklands conflict solidified by Britain's popular media in 1982. In addition, perhaps more than might reasonably be expected of a war fought in the late twentieth century, these documentary films have had to belatedly address deficiencies in journalism during the conflict. Indeed, any survey of documentaries about the war must begin with the efforts of the small band of journalists who accompanied the British Task Force to the South Atlantic.

As Julian Barnes remarks, the Falklands may well have been "the worst reported war since the Crimean" (*The Guardian*, February 25, 2002). Some of the problems were logistical; the Falklands are a very long way from Fleet Street and Broadcast House. However, many commentators since 1982 have focused more on the role of the Thatcher government in managing the release of information to the British public. These scholarly accounts frequently point to the quick release of "good news" and the apparent delays that befell "bad news" as it crossed the Atlantic. Images of the war, most of which were still photographs rather than film footage, were also tightly controlled by Ministry of Defence officials. Given these wide-ranging limitations on original coverage, it is clear that the documentary tradition of the Falklands War did not properly begin in 1982.

Indeed, the most important documentary about the Falklands was broadcast in 1987, coinciding with the conflict's fifth anniversary. Peter Kominsky's film, *The Falklands War: The Untold Story*, was produced by Yorkshire Television and originally broadcast on Wednesday, April 1, 1987. By this time Thatcher's government had retained power on the back of victory in the South Atlantic, and although Britain had dramatically enlarged its military presence in the Falklands after the war, the smoke of battle had cleared. Was it now appropriate to begin rethinking representations of a war that many had already come to see ambiguously? The text of an advertisement for Kominsky's two hour film, printed in the daily national press the day the film was broadcast, certainly suggested it might be: "Five years after the war in the Falklands, many facts are still wrapped in red tape. . . Many of the key figures have remained silent. . . And no one has been to Argentina to tell the other side of the story . . . until now."

The film did indeed break ground with material exploring the experience of Argentinean soldiers, from rank-and-file to officers, creating a new, even-handed representation. As one critic put it, writing in *The Times* the day after the film was broadcast, *The Untold Story* "achieved a miracle of balance." In addition to airing Argentine voices, the film used interviews and imagery to convey the physical and emotional pain of the war. The same *Times* critic continued, "Among all the general bewilderment, it is left to those who lost limbs or relatives to speak with the greatest bravery and painfully to drag up the details that put this whole matter in its absurd context" (*The Times*, April 2, 1987). Kominsky's film, then, appears to be a defining moment in reassessing the Falklands conflict and was quickly followed by a number of other skeptical treatments of the war and its aftermath. Most notable among the films following *Untold Story* was Richard Eyre's BBC television drama *Tumbledown* (1988).

If this strand of filmmaking about the Falklands campaign is broadly revising the image of the war formulated during and directly after the battle, there are at least two other distinguishable "groups" of Falklands documentaries.

The first is what might be called the military-interest tradition. This begins (and achieves its zenith) in the year or two after the conflict. *Falklands Taskforce South*, made by the BBC in 1982, is one of the earliest documentaries and focuses particularly on the military expertise and technology supporting the campaign. *Battle for the Falklands* (1984) is a piece of filmmaking ideologically related to the patriotic efforts of *The Sun* and other tabloids. A late addition to this category is *The Sinking of the Belgrano* (ori-ginally broadcast in Britain on the National Geographic Channel, May 25, 2003). The documentary provides a new interpretation of one of the war's most controversial episodes, suggesting that British forces may have been tactically justified in the strike.

The second category includes films that are difficult to place in ideological terms. These include the BBC documentaries made about the scarred British soldier Simon Weston, badly burnt during the bombing of the *Sir Galahad*. Starting in 1983 with *Simon's War*, and almost certainly (according to the producers) concluding with *Simon's Heroes*, marking the twentieth anniversary of the war, these documentaries have been produced sporadically over two decades and follow Weston's psychological, emotional, and physical progress. The Simon documentaries, directed by Malcom Brinkworth, provided the British public with a sustained opportunity for reflection in individualized, human terms.

This complex, careful revision of 1982's jingoistic bombast has characterized the best of Falklands war documentary. It sometimes seems as though this project of clarification has been only partially successful; at the beginning of the twentieth century two modes dominate popular discourse on the Falklands. The "liberal" position, broadly assumed by opponents of the Thatcher government, is that the war is a bizarre, "pointless" episode in British history. The other, imbued with the spirit of original war coverage in *The Sun*, exists in curiously transmuted arenas, as these lines from an article on the 2004 England football team allude: "If you had to pick a game in England's recent history that meant most things to most people, it would probably be the 1-0 win over Argentina in the World Cup two summers ago. All rolled into one penalty kick, here was a chance of progressing to the next round, a poke in the eye for Diego Maradona's shameless handball 16 years earlier, [and] confirmation of supremacy over Argentina as borne out by the Falklands war" (*The Guardian*, May 22, 2004).

The small but powerful tradition of Falklands war documentary has more frequently associated itself with the former position, but as a body of work these films are valuable not only for questioning a war, but for revealing the ways in which documentary filmmaking can serve as a long-term counterbalance to the dizzy, sometimes lurid, tone of popular wartime journalism.

PAUL GLEED

Further Reading

Adams, Valerie, *The Media and the Falklands Campaign*, Basingstoke: Macmillan, 1986.

Aulich, James, *Framing the Falklands War: Nationhood, Culture, and Identity*, Milton Keynes and Philadelphia: Open University Press, 1992.

Broadbent, Lucinda, et al. *War and Peace News*, Milton Keynes and Philadelphia: Open University Press, 1985.

Harris, Robert, *Gotcha!: The Media, the Government, and the Falklands Crisis*, London: Faber and Faber, 1983.

Monaghan, David, *The Falklands War: Myth and Countermyth*, Basingstoke: Macmillan, 1998.

Paris, Michael, *Warrior Nation: Images of War in British Popular Culture*, London: Reaktion, 2000.

FALL OF THE ROMANOV DYNASTY, THE

(USSR, Shub, 1927)

Assembled in 1927, Esfir Shub's *The Fall of the Romanov Dynasty* was the first compilation documentary ever produced. The film was the first of three compilation films she made during 1927–1928 (*The Great Way*, 1927, and *Lev Tolstoy and the Russia of Nicholas II*, 1928, were the others) that introduced this new genre of documentary. Shub's creation of a documentary film out of newsreel material not only establishes her as a pioneer of compilation and radical documentary but also emphasizes her position as one of the most significant women filmmakers of the first half of the twentieth century.

After assisting Sergei Eisenstein on scripts and editing newsreels with Dziga Vertov from 1924–1925, Shub saw a new direction for her work. She wrote, "it is clear that work in newsreel must begin with artistic labor. Newsreel apart from this must begin with history, profoundly with the party chronicle of our epoch." At the end of 1926, she received a commission from Sovkino to make a historical film for the tenth anniversary of the Bolshevik Revolution.

Shub researched the film at the Museum of the Revolution in Leningrad, where for two months she pored over 60,000 meters of film. Her major difficulties were locating and organizing existing film material. Much of the footage had been taken out of the country, sold to foreign producers, or destroyed by terrible archive conditions. She persuaded the government to buy 2,000 feet of negative about the February Revolution (including famous shots of Lenin) from the United States. Eventually, however, she had to shoot 1,000 of the total 6,000 feet of the film. Her other major challenge was organizing footage with different styles, film formats, and emulsion qualities into a coherent artistic and ideological whole. In *The Fall of the Romanov Dynasty*, Shub aims to convey in essay style her own ideological attitude without distorting the filmic documents. Her innovative method and editing skill enabled these potential problems to become the film's strengths.

From 1912 to 1917, *The Fall of the Romanov Dynasty* is divided into four sections: prewar Russia, international preparation for the war, the war, and the Revolution. The first part presents images of a doomed regime, opening with the title "Tsarist Russia in the Years of the Black Reaction." The slow, even pace recalls the rural atmosphere, whereas the images of State Duma politicians casually conversing and wealthy landowners enjoying leisure time contrast sharply with shots of industrial workers and peasants laboring in the fields. Shub's use of titles and editing patterns functions ironically to juxtapose the two social and economic spheres. The first part concludes with images of the Romanovs and other Russian nobility parading above a crowd. Whereas this procession is initially contrasted with the marching of needy peasants to prison, the parade scenes also function in contradistinction to the forthcoming images of the Bolsheviks. While the images of the nobility emphasize a static quality and distance from the crowd, shots of the Revolution articulate dynamism and an organic connection with the people, one of the central themes of the film.

In the second section, Shub illustrates the Marxist argument that the war was between imperial powers and contends that, instead, Russia should be fighting imperialism itself. "Europe at the time" is illustrated by capitalists, banks, and gold and European leaders are visually matched with the tsar. In preparation for the war, new destructive technology is manufactured and military training becomes intense. Shub's attitude is made clear in the title "Tsarist Russia Marched in Step with the Other Imperialist Powers." Dramatic and violent combat footage of land and sea follows, in one stretch, uninterrupted by titles for seven minutes. The slow, even pacing of the beginning of the film has become more rapid, heightening the drama and tension. The section concludes with the most powerful intertitle in the film: "Killed, Wounded, and Maimed in the World War—35 Million People." The devastating impact of the war on Russians is made apparent and leads to the final section of the film.

The title "1917" opens the extensive coverage of the uprising in which Alexander Kerensky seizes power. Shub's attitude toward the subject is unambiguous. Kerensky is a member of the "bourgeoisie, striving to use the revolution for its own purposes." Kerensky and the Mensheviks are visually and thematically equated with the tsarists. Like Nicholas II, he is shown advocating war, and like the previous Duma, the Mensheviks are seen disengaged from the people. In contrast, Lenin is shown speaking to huge crowds while the mass demonstrations are edited together with pages of *Pravda* calling for "Peace, Land, and Bread," the Bolshevik party slogan. Shub's film concludes as it must—with images of Lenin greeting and shaking hands with members of the crowd.

The Fall of the Romanov Dynasty presents the inevitability and the energy of the Revolution. The dynamism of the Bolshevik Revolution and the Party's connection with the people contrasts sharply the pomp and circumstance of the tsarists

The Fall of the Romanov Dynasty, 1927.
[*Still courtesy of the British Film Institute*]

and their distance from the people. Shub's editing and titling skill is apparent. Her montage is intuitive and associative rather than metrical or mathematical (terms often used to describe Vertov's method). She bitingly juxtaposes images and, in an innovative way, uses slogans found on flags and signs as titles. Yet while Shub's cinematic essay may be highly agitational and propagandistic, she, like Vertov, is devoted to maintaining the ontological authenticity of the filmic documents. She writes: "authentic material is something that gives life to a documentary film, regardless of the fact that it might be composed of archival footage or shot by the filmmaker." Shub's goal was to achieve a delicate balance between commenting on events by means of a juxtaposition of images and preserving the authenticity of each image, a goal resonating today with many compilation documentarists. Her exceptional skill and innovative method are both formidable and instructive.

JOSHUA MALITSKY

The Fall of the Romanov Dynasty (The Soviet Union, Sovkino, 1927, 90 minutes, restored Gosfilmofund, USSR, 1991) Distributed by Kino Video. Directed and edited by Esfir Shub. In Russian with English subtitles.

Further Reading

Leyda, Jay, *Kino*, New York: Collier Books, 1960.

Petric, Vlada, "Vertov, Lenin and Perestroika: The Cinematic Transposition of Reality," in *Historical Journal of Film, Radio, and Television*, 15, 1, 1995, 3–17.

Petric, Vlada, "Esfir Shub: Film as Historical Discourse," in *"Show Us Life"*: *Towards a History and Aesthetics of the Committed Documentary*, edited by Thomas Waugh, Metuchen, NJ: Scarecrow Press, 1984, 21–46.

Roberts, Graham, *Forward Soviet: History and Non-Fiction Film in the USSR*. London: I.B. Tauris, 1999.

Taylor, Richard, *The Politics of Soviet Cinema 1917–1929*, Cambridge: Cambridge UP, 1979.

Taylor, Richard and Ian Christie, editors, *The Film Factory: Russian and Soviet Cinema in Documents 1896–1939*, Cambridge: Harvard UP, 1988.

FAMILY PORTRAIT

(UK, Jennings, 1951)

Family Portrait, Humphrey Jennings' final film, was made for the 1951 Festival of Britain. Film was an integral part of the Festival's celebration of Britain's achievements in the arts, industry, and science, so a cinema was built at the London South Bank Exhibition site for the screening of the specially commissioned Festival films. More than twenty films were made for exhibition at the Telekinema, but *Family Portrait* most reflects the Festival's aims of celebrating the past and heralding a bright new future. Unfortunately, these aims proved more of a limitation than an inspiration, resulting in one of Jennings' least imaginative films.

The film is constructed around the opening and closing shots of a photograph album featuring images of family holidays, a christening, and a picnic. It proceeds to showcase British artistic achievement (the plays of William Shakespeare), science (Charles Darwin and Britain's records of exploration), and

industry (Stephenson's Rocket and James Watt), echoing the displays of the Festival exhibitions. Jennings regards these "heroes" of British life with warmth and refers to them as "local lads who used their wits and had a good laugh, and then, like Shakespeare and Newton and Watt started something at home that went right around the globe." Ultimately this is a quietly patriotic film that acknowledges the contradictions of the British character: an admiration for invention versus a love of tradition, eccentricity versus practicality, domesticity versus pageantry, agriculture versus industry.

Family Portrait is a rather literal film. Although the sentiments expressed in the voice-over and through the narrative structure of the film are poetic, the visual execution of these sentiments is lacklustre. All too often the images are simply a literal translation of the narrator's words; for example, the evolution of British tradition, particularly

373

democracy, is discussed over bland images of the field at Runnymede, clichéd shots of the Houses of Parliament, and council committee meetings. The images are frequently overwhelmed by the richness of the narration.

Nevertheless, *Family Portrait* was well received by the critical press and Jennings's fellow documentarists. In retrospect, however, it is difficult to say just how much of this praise was a result of Jennings's accidental death at the end of 1950. Many of the film's contemporary notices read like eulogies. Edgar Anstey pronounced it the most important documentary film made since the war. *Monthly Film Bulletin* thought it perhaps the most polished in style of all Jennings's films and *Today's Cinema* recommended it "as a yardstick for contemporary documentary." Three years later, Lindsay Anderson noted that *Family Portrait* could stand beside Jennings's wartime films but that it lacked the passion. In a 1981 reevaluation, however, Anderson decided the film should be dismissed as "sentimental fiction." He berated Jennings for his "fantasy of the Empire" and his use of the past as a refuge" (Jennings, 1982). Although the film's patriotism is very much of its time and Jennings closes the film by recognising the impact of Britain's imperial past, he also realises that Britain's future will depend on wider global alliances.

SARAH EASEN

Family Portrait, 1951.
[*Still courtesy of the British Film Institute*]

See also **Jennings, Humphrey**

Family Portrait (UK, Wessex Film Productions, 1950, 24 min).

Executive produced by Ian Dalrymple. Written and directed by Humphrey Jennings. Assistant direction by Harley Usill. Unit management by R L M Davidson. Film edited by Stewart McAllister. Sound by Ken Cameron. Photography by Martin Curtis. Music directed and conducted by Muir Mathison. Music composed and arranged by John Greenwood. Commentary spoken by Michael Goodliffe.

FANCK, ARNOLD

Arnold Fanck's name is closely linked with the filmic image of the Alpine mountains. He is primarily known for his feature films, which he mostly shot on location in the Alps. In his documentary films he glorified the experience of sports and nature, notably in *4628 Meter hoch auf Skiern. Besteigung des Monte Rosa* (1913), *Im Kampf mit dem Berge* (1921), and the two-part *Das Wunder des Schneeschuhs* (1919–1920; 1922). Moreover, Fanck's production company took charge of other sports subjects such as jiu-jitsu, boxing, sailing, soccer, and rowing. Likewise exotic subjects became relevant in a number of travelogs, notably Tibet, Africa, and especially Asia. On the occasion of the shooting of his feature film, *Die Tochter des Samurai* (1938), Fanck produced six short documentaries that he shot in Japan, China, and Manchuria. These films dealt with the history, traditions, and culture of the Japanese people. They took on a political undertone, for example, when they legitimized, under the guise of a "Kulturfilm," the Japanese occupation of southern Manchuria in *Winterreise durch Südmandschurien* (1938). *Kaiserbauten in Fernost* (1938) deals with the Chinese wall with the same emphasis as does *Atlantik-Wall* (1944) with the German bulwark along the coast of the North Sea.

Fanck was often accused of a certain proximity to the aesthetics of fascist film art. Although he was never a grassroots Nazi, he must be considered a protagonist of the reactionary avant-garde, as he advocated an ideology of virile strength. Still, because his feature films signified a certain lethargy vis-à-vis nature (where heroism was called for), the Nazis neutralized Fanck in 1940 and banned him from feature filmmaking. Leni Riefenstahl assigned him a documentary film on the New Berlin, a project aborted after years of work. Fanck's late short documentaries do not carry his personal style.

ULI JUNG

See also **Riefenstahl, Leni**

Biography

Born on March 6, 1889 in Frankenthal, the son of an industrialist. A frail child who, after recovering from tuberculosis, turned to skiing and mountain climbing. After studying geology (he earned a Ph.D. in 1915), founded his own production company, Berg und Sportfilm GmbH Freiburg, which produced feature and documentary films made by Fanck and other directors. Fanck specialized in mountain films. *Der Berg des Schicksals* (1924) and *Der heilige Berg* (1926) marked his breakthrough. Together with Luis Trenker and Leni Riefenstahl, more or less single handedly created the genre of the German mountain film. His success afforded him bigger budgets but greater dependencies. While the location shots of his feature films were still superb, the shallow storylines of his features failed to convince audiences. *Der ewige Traum* (1934) was the last feature he could accomplish in Germany. (There followed two films shot in Japan and Chile.) Concentrated on documentaries regardless of their impersonal styles, from which he made his living until the end of WW II. Postwar efforts to resume work in the film industry faltered. Died on September 28, 1974 in Freiburg.

Selected Films (documentaries only):

4628 Meter hoch auf Skiern. Besteigung des Monte Rosa (D 1913) Up 4628 Meters on Skies. Climbing the Monte Rosa
Das Wunder des Schneeschuhs (D 1920/22) The Wonders of the Skis
Das Wolkenphänomen in Maloja (D 1924) Clouds over the Malaja Pass
Das weisse Stadion (CH 1928) The White Stadion
Höchstleistungen im Skilauf (D 1931–1935) *Record Achievements in Skiing*
Training zum Skifilmen (D 1931–1935) How to Film on Skis
Kaiserbauten in Fernost (D 1936–1938) Imperial Buildings in the Far East
Josef Thorak, Werkstatt und Werk (D 1943) Josef Thorak, Studio and Oeuvre
Arno Breker (D 1944)
Atlantik-Wall (D 1944) Atlantic Bulwark

Further Reading

Arnold Fanck. Special issue of *Filmhefte*, summer, 1976, no. 2.
Cosandey, Roland, "4628 Meter hoch auf Skiern: Mit Ski und Filmkamera 1913 auf dem Monte Rosa," in *Neue Zürcher Zeitung*, 22 September, 2000.
Fanck, Arnold, *Er führte Regie mit Gletschern, Stürmen und Lawinen: Ein Filmpionier erzählt*. Munich: Nymphenburger, 1973.
Horak, Jan-Christopher, editor, *Berge, Licht und Traum: Dr. Arnold Fanck und der deutsche Bergfilm*. Munich: Bruckmann, 1997.
Kiefer, Bernd, "Eroberer des Nutzlosen: Abenteuer und Abenteurer bei Arnold Fanck," in *Idole des deutschen Films*, Thomas Koebner, editor, Munich: edition text + kritik, 1997.
Kreimeier, Klaus, editor, *Fanck – Trenker – Riefenstahl: Der deutsche Bergfilm und seine Folgen*. Berlin/West: SDK, 1972.
Revisited: Der Fall Dr. Fanck – Die Entdeckung der Natur im deutschen Bergfilm. Special issue of *Film und Kritik*, no. 1, June, 1992.

FAR FROM VIETNAM

(France, Resnais and Others, 1967)

Far from Vietnam (Loin du Vietnam) is an anthology film made by a collective of French filmmakers "to assert in the exercise of their profession, their solidarity with the people of Vietnam in their resistance to aggression" (*Loin du Vietnam*, 1967). Like other protest films made during the war by Newsreel collectives and others, its purpose is clearly polemical, underpinned by Che Guevara's manifesto of 1960s radical politics: "one, two, many Vietnams" whereby social, national, and racial differences, likewise geographical distance, are bridged by a common cause. But, as its title suggests, while the film endorses the cause of solidarity with the Vietnamese fighting America, it tempers the easy identification and "romantic populism" (Renov, 1990) characteristic of many other antiwar films produced in the period through its reflexive formal strategies.

The film was produced by SLON (Société pour le Lancement des Oeuvres Nouvelles/Society for the Launching of New Works), a Marxist arts collective begun by Chris Marker in 1966 specifically for the film. (Later, Marker would revive SLON and the collective would continue production into the 1970s.) In 1967, Joris Ivens and Marcelline Loridan went to Vietnam to work on what would become *17e Parallèle/The 17th Parallel*. Marker persuaded them to participate in the collective, and they sent back from Hanoi footage showing daily life under bombardment. Others that joined Marker and Ivens included New Wave filmmakers Alain Resnais, Agnès Varda, Jean-Luc Godard, as well as American photographer William Klein. Marker edited *Far from Vietnam* which, like his previous film, *Lettre de Sebérie/Letter from Siberia* (1957), plays on conventions and viewer expectations of nonfiction film.

The film begins in a manner similar to other antiwar films of the period, as it compares the "rich man's war" to a "poor man's war," with images of high-tech warfare—the aircraft carrier, Kitty Hawk, loading bombs in the Gulf of Tonkin—contrasted to a bucolic image of rural Vietnam. But it quickly undermines the simplicity of that opposition. What appears at first to be an empty field waiting to be torn apart by bombs is not empty at all; it comes alive when concealed soldiers emerge, advance, and then recede into the land. A simple but powerful image of guerilla warfare, it

Far from Vietnam, 1967.
[*Still courtesy of the British Film Institute*]

consolidates metaphorically a point addressed in various ways throughout the film—the difficulty for Europeans and Americans to understand, to clearly see the war in Vietnam. It is a point made a few years later by Frances Fitzgerald in her analysis of the war, *Fire in the Lake*: "American soldiers had . . . walked over the political and economic design of the Vietnamese revolution. They had looked at it, but they could not see it, for it was doubly invisible: invisible within the ground and then again invisible within their own perspective as Americans" (Fitzgerald, 1972).

The segments that follow are strikingly varied in style and quality, including vérité images of demonstrations in France and the United States in "A Parade Is a Parade," footage of a musical comedy performance by a travelling North Vietnamese theatre group in "Johnson Cries," a monologue by a fictitious contemporary Parisian author in "Claude Ridder," distorted and manipulated television images in "Why We Fight," a collage of vérité images, advertisements, store window displays, American icons, and cartoons in "Vertigo." Surveying in this way the formal options available to the political filmmaker, the discursive range of this anthology film works to forestall any possibility of the war's authoritative representation.

The best known of these segments and the most succinct in its discussion of the problem of representing the war from a western perspective is Jean-Luc Godard's *Camera Eye*. Despite the allusion to Dziga Vertov, Godard's comments on the difficulty of conceptualising Vietnam for film qualify the accessibility of what Vertov called *kinopravda* (film truth) while maintaining its political necessity as a goal. The segment begins with a close-up of Godard addressing the camera to say what he might film in Vietnam were he a cameraman for a newsreel or television network. But he is neither of those things and is still in Paris, having been refused entrance by officials in Hanoi. Reframed to a medium shot we see that Godard is seated behind a Mitchell camera, which functions in the sequence as a technological metonym for Hollywood and the United States. He then speaks of the difficulty of conceptualising Vietnam for film, despite a shared struggle against the United States—his against cultural imperialism and theirs against military aggression. Godard concludes that there's really no understanding Vietnam until such time as "we can let Vietnam invade us . . . and find out what part it plays in our everyday lives." Such are the limits and ideals of political filmmaking, that only complete identification could close the gap between Godard and his subject. Moreover, he continues to observe that the breach between himself and the Vietnamese is the same one as that which exists between himself and the French working class, for whom he also makes films and with whom he also claims solidarity, even though they never see his films. These are the conditions of the making of protest films like *Far from Vietnam*, in which ultimately all he and other filmmakers can do is "listen and . . . relay all the screams that we possibly can."

Like Godard in *Camera Eye*, the SLON collective makes its political alliance with North Vietnam clear, but *Far from Vietnam* focuses overall on the difficulty of representing the war, the difficulty of responding adequately to it on film, and of claiming identification as a European or American filmmaker with the struggle of the Vietnamese. In this way, it is a film about the war in Vietnam but is also about the conditions of political and nonfiction filmmaking more generally.

AMANDA HOWELL

Loin du Viêt Nam/Far from Vietnam (FRN, SLON, 1967, 115 mins). Distributed by New Yorker Films (U.S.). Directed by Alain Resnais, William Klein, Joris Ivens, Agnès Varda, Claude Lelouch, Jean-Luc Godard. Principal collaborators: Michèle Ray, Roger Pic, K.S. Karol, Marceline Loridan, François Maspero, Chris Marker, Jacques Sternberg, Jean Lacouture, Willy Kurant, Jean Boffety, Kieu Tham, Denis Clairval, Ghislain Cloquet, Bernard Zitztermann, Alain Levent, and Théo Robichet.

Further Reading

Ellis, John, *The Documentary Idea, A Critical History of English-Language Documentary Film and Video*, Englewood Cliffs, NJ: Prentice-Hall, 1989.

"*Far from Vietnam*," *Variety*, 4 October 1967, 12.

Fitzgerald, Frances, *Fire in the Lake: The Vietnamese and the Americans in Vietnam*, New York: Vintage Books, 1972.

James, David E., "Film and the War: Representing Vietnam," in *Allegories of Cinema: American Film in the Sixties*, Princeton: Princeton University Press, 1989, 195–213.

"*Loin du Viet-Nam (Far from Vietnam)*," *Monthly Film Bulletin* 35, 409, 1968, 29.

Plantinga, Carl, *Rhetoric and Representation in Nonfiction Film*, Cambridge: Cambridge UP, 1997.

Renov, Michael, "Imaging the Other: Representations of Vietnam in Sixties Political Documentary," in *From Hanoi to Hollywood: The Vietnam War in American Film*, New Brunswick: Rutgers University Press, 1990, 255–268.

Sarris, Andrew, "The New York Film Festival (1967)," in *Confessions of a Cultist: On the Cinema 1955–1969*, New York: Simon and Schuster, 1970, 317–318.

FARREBIQUE

(France, Rouquier, 1946)

Indisputably a milestone in film history, *Farrebique* achieved great success from the outset. It is still considered as both a documentary, perhaps even as an ethnological documentary, and as a sensitive and lyrical poem.

Georges Rouquier, a film lover (although a linotypist by profession) had previously made only two shorts: *Les Vendanges* [The Grape-Harvest, 1929], under amateur conditions, and *Le Tonnelier* [The Cooper, 1942]. It was Etienne Lallier, the producer for *Le Tonnelier*, who suggested Rouquier direct a feature film dealing with peasant life over the four seasons. The idea had initially been formulated by the journalist and war correspondent Claude Blanchard. Rouquier had first planned to revisit the subject of the vine-growing world; however, Lallier disliked the idea of repetition. When the young filmmaker suggested the farm run by his own family in Aveyron, Lallier remained reluctant but was eventually won over when Rouquier took him on location.

The film was produced with help from the (Vichy) government. The preproduction stage ran from September 1943 to November 1944. Shooting then took an entire year, with the exception of a short period for viewing rushes in Paris in March 1945. The editing took an additional nine months.

The viewer is presented with a traditional peasant family in the Aveyron region, near the small town of Goutrens. The family consists of the grandfather, the head of the farm; the grandmother, a modest, self-effacing woman; their two sons (Rouquier's uncles); daughter-in-law, Berthe; and their grandchildren.

Farrebique, 1946 documentary by George Rouquier.
[*Courtesy of the Everett Collection*]

The older son, Roch, is presented as a stubborn, money-grabbing figure. The younger son, Henri, as yet unmarried, is presented as having more modern ideas and common sense. The two daughters have both left the farm to become nuns. Other characters include Aunt Marie, who runs a grocery shop in the village, and the neighbours, Fabre and his daughter, "La Fabrette."

There is no plot in the usual sense; it is mostly a chronicle of the calendar year on a farm. In autumn there is talk of repairing the old farmhouse and installing electric power. Berthe becomes pregnant again. Winter is dreary; in the dull light of a parrafin lamp the family continually discuss the need to come to an agreement with the neighbour about sharing the cost of installing electricity. As spring goes into bud, Berthe brings a new baby into the world, and Henri courts La Fabrette. An agreement is made with Fabre for the installation of electric power. Then comes summer and harvest time. The grandfather feels himself growing weaker with age. Henri is injured as he falls from a cart; the house will not be restored this year. At the end of summer, the grandfather plans the division of the estate. Roch will keep with the farm; the younger siblings argue about their share. After the grape harvest the grandfather dies.

As an epilogue, Henri and La Fabrette talk about marriage; the wedding could take place next spring but "what," she teasingly asks, "if spring never returns?" He has the last word: spring always comes round again.

The whole action is set out of historical time. According to Rouquier himself, "anything that could have made reference to the war, the present, or their misery, was deliberately banished from the subject matter." Daily farm life is thus located within the cycle of Nature, creating a pastoral poem of *déjà vu*, without idealisation. To some extent it also reflects the young Rouquier's souvenirs of life at the farm.

Postwar audiences did not fail to pick up on the recent memories of Vichy's *retour à la terre*. In fact Rouquier (who had not escaped military service as he had served as an artilleryman till the 1940 armistice) tried to reconstruct some kind of timeless truth. And yet, the tools and gestures, the machinery, the production process, and the environment are filmed with such clarity and precision that it gives the film an almost anthropological value.

Nonetheless *Farrebique* is entirely staged in accordance with the conventions of the documentary *mise en scène* method. The script was completely written before shooting and leaves nothing to chance. The aim was to create a sense of the real. Rouquier was an admirer of Robert Flaherty and devoted a film to Flaherty's work. Like Flaherty's films, *Farrebique* is made up of the real life of real people. The "actors" indeed recite, but their lines were constructed with their own words. Rouquier knew them very well and wrote the dialogue with this insight, on the opposite page of the shooting script. Recording synchronous sound on location and lighting the indoor "sets" created countless difficulties. Rouquier noted that "direct filmmaking was easier in the times of silent movies." He was keen to dismiss most off-screen narration, but allowed himself a commentary about spring, which was both lyrical and on one occasion ironic when young girls dreaming are compared with potatoes germinating.

Can *Farrebique* be considered a documentary at all? Many elements are not directly drawn from

FARREBIQUE, 1946 documentary by George Rouquier.
[*Courtesy of the Everett Collection*]

reality. Henri was in actual fact married; Fabre was a friend of the family and had no daughter. There was a third son, a war prisoner, who was freed during the process of shooting, but played no part in the film. There were no plans for the installation of electricity, the division of the estate was not on the family's agenda, and of course the grandfather was not dying. Furthermore, the fast-motion shots of plants growing were made in a studio in Paris and then carefully matched with field images.

Nevertheless, the filmmaking process was constantly adapted because of unforeseen events. For instance, shooting was already underway when Roch announced that a baby was expected in late spring. Rouquier therefore made some changes to the script. The story was supposed to end with the building of the new farmhouse, which was thwarted because of a lack of money; again the script was modified by inventing Henri's accident.

Farrebique carries the nostalgic charm of a particular form of ethnography, which displays changing without change—a resistance to history (Piault). Thirty-eight years later Rouquier directed a sequel, *Biquefarre*, which depicted in a less optimistic way the disappearance of the peasant world.

JEAN-LUC LIOULT

See also **Rouquier, Georges**

Farrebique (France, 1946, 90 min.). Distributed by RKO Radio Films. Produced by L'Ecran Français and Les films Etienne Lallier. Written and directed by Georges Rouquier. Cinematography by André A. Dantan, assisted by Marcel Fradétal and Jean-Jacques Rébuffat. Additional fast-motion cinematography by Daniel Sarrade, assisted by Maurice Delille. Sound by René Lécuyer, assisted by Janisse, Barthélémy, Girbal, Olivier and Salagnac. Music by Henri Sauguet, directed by Roger Desormières. Editing by Madeleine Gug, assisted by Renée Varlet. Commentary by Georges Rouquier. Filmed in Goutrens, Aveyron.

Further Reading

Auzel, Dominique, *Georges Rouquier, de Farrebique à Biquefarre*, Paris: Petite Bibliothèque des Cahiers du Cinéma, 2002 (Editions du Rouergue, 1993).
Gauthier, Guy, "À propos de Farrebique," in *Le documentaire, un autre cinéma*, Paris: Nathan Université, 1995.
Marsolais, Gilles, "Georges Rouquier," in *L'aventure du cinéma direct revisitée*, Laval: Les 400 coups, 1997.
Piault, Marc-Henri, "Changer sans changements: résister à l'histoire avec Georges Rouquier," in *Anthropologie et cinéma*, Paris: Nathan Cinéma, 2000.

FASCIST ITALY

Fascism in Italy took hold in 1922 when Benito Mussolini secured power for the Fascist Party and became its undisputed leader. Ambitious and charismatic, Mussolini set out to firmly secure his role while promoting the glory and power of the Italian State within the imagination of the Italian people. Filmmaking was an important tool of Mussolini and the Fascists, but Mussolini was not a totalitarian leader. Unlike Hitler and Stalin, who maintained total political control of all filmmaking and produced only propaganda films, Mussolini gave filmmakers a certain degree of autonomy, preferring to censor some material rather than dictate all of it. Mussolini's political advisor, Luigi Freddi, was entrusted with the task of overseeing filmmaking and generally modified films to meet censorship standards instead of banning them. Yet, Mussolini's role within films, often as a featured subject/actor, remained undisputed throughout the fascist period. Mussolini's appearance, demeanor, and expressiveness were well suited to the medium, and Mussolini knew how to best shape his image on film. The State was personified through *il Duce*, the name used to refer to Mussolini, and transmitted to the masses.

By the time Unione Cinematografica was created in 1919 to oversee the production of feature films, Italian filmmaking was already in a state of deep crisis, and the organization was able to do little to help. Years of poor planning, rising costs, and the dominance of the American film market left the once-lustrous Italian film industry with the difficult task of trying to reinvent itself. Film historians credit Italian film distributor Stefano Pittaluga with attempting to rescue the Italian film industry from collapse by gaining greater financial backing from leading Italian banks. Before his death in 1931, Pittaluga helped the film industry to devise and put into action a plan for providing the structures and resources filmmakers needed to produce successful films. Mussolini was not seeking state control of the cinema, but he could aid filmmakers in returning Italian film to a dominant role. While the Fascists clearly wanted to revive the feature-film industry, Mussolini also realized the importance of securing hold of the production of newsreels and informative documentaries. Although he did not wish to dictate the content of narrative films, Mussolini recognized the political potential in merging political aims with filmmaking in informative productions.

The creation of L'Unione Cinematografica Educativa (LUCE) in 1924 helped breed new interest in filmic images and brought cinema to more Italians. LUCE was created to oversee the production of newsreels and documentaries; however, this entity did much more. LUCE contributed to promoting fascist glory while providing information to the masses. This meant that LUCE assumed several roles. One was to inform and educate the public about key events in Italy and the world. Other roles were to generate propaganda about Mussolini and the Fascists and ensure that information distributed to the public presented the State and its ruler in only the most favorable light. Moreover, the films produced by LUCE helped nationalize the Italian language and culture and advance patriotism and civic pride.

Before the formation of LUCE, private production companies produced most documentaries, but the Ministry of Propaganda favored a more regulated vehicle for distribution. Because LUCE films were made through approved government channels, they soon dominated Italian cinema and were distributed to Italian schools, as well as cinema houses. The expansion of traveling cinemas, *cine mobili,* provided another distribution vehicle for LUCE films and made moving pictures more accessible to larger numbers of Italians, especially those in rural areas.

LUCE distributed its first newsreel in June 1927, and another forty-three followed that year. By 1940, LUCE had distributed more than 1600 newsreels. Although these films varied in length and content during the course of the Fascist regime, they often repeated certain major themes: the greatness of *il Duce*, Italian progress, the increase of industrial productivity, and Italy's key role in the international landscape. LUCE films portrayed violence and hardship as conditions found only in other countries while depicting Italy as a nation of strong families, hard workers, and a certain peaceful harmony. In the 1920s, many newsreels had a distinctively Roman character and featured events in the capital city. Later newsreels placed the spotlight on other parts of Italy and on Italian initiatives to better the nation. In any case, the majority of LUCE newsreels closed with Italian subject matter. LUCE produced an annual documentary that summarized all the key events of that year and stressed Italian victories and moments of greatness. Each documentary was named after the corresponding year of the new Fascist calendar (*Anno V, Anno VI, Anno VII*, etc.). Most of the footage was borrowed from the year's newsreels and reedited in documentary form.

Under the leadership of Luigi Freddi, LUCE's educational goals expanded. Freddi believed LUCE could educate the public about Italy, the Fascists, and Mussolini while reinforcing civic pride and contributing to Italian progress. Freddi viewed filmmaking as a vehicle for serving the public and providing a filmic guide to proper moral behavior. Documentaries produced by LUCE in the mid-1920s stressed early Fascist objectives such as Mussolini's so-called battles for the people, including the *Battaglia del grano,* battle for grain, and the continued preservation of the Italian forests as in the film *Foresta fonte di richezze*. These early documentaries upheld the values of peasant life while at the same time giving a nod to modernization and urbanization. Mussolini even appeared without a shirt and holding farm tools in some of these images, thus reinforcing his direct support of a way of life. Films featuring traditional life and customs promoted *strapaese,* our town. Many of these films featured beautiful landscapes within which rural Italians engaged in artisanal or agricultural work. By focusing on these people and locations, LUCE evoked images of Italy's long history and introduced urban Italians to fellow citizens who had made their country great. At the same time, rural Italians saw that their customs and traditions were valued by the State and that they were not forgotten by urban dwellers, especially the Romans.

Documentaries produced by LUCE in the late 1920s and early 1930s were mostly educational. They highlighted the beauty and history of Italy in films about the excavations of Roman ruins, the celebration of the *Palio* in Sienna, and the grandeur of beautiful locations such as Lake Garda. Again, the goal was to draw on Italy's glorious past and the breathtaking beauty of its natural landscapes, both sources of great pride for Italians. Travel films, also popular, gave many Italians their first glimpse of locations such as Hungary and India. These films helped satisfy curiosities and took Italians to locations they might not otherwise have visited. LUCE also began to increase its production of *stracitta,* our city, films that featured urban nightlife and new technologies. They helped dispel some of the myths rural Italians held about urban life. Technological films also reinforced the idea of Italy as both a strong industrial nation and an economic producer. Films about the production of everything from beer and rubber to automobiles and trains demonstrated Italy's industrial capacity. The first documentary sound film, produced in 1930 to record Italo Balbo's solo flight across the Atlantic, included narration and music that enabled filmmakers to add greater drama and emotion to their productions and to emphasize key aspects of the visual image. Finally, the historical film, *Primi anni del fascismo,* chronicled the first decade of fascism and the heroism and accomplishments of Mussolini.

By the outbreak of World War II, fascist documentaries and newsreels had taken a more decisive political stance, showcasing Italian armaments and predicting the inevitable defeat of the Italy's enemies. LUCE films also began to devote more time to Italian military victories, especially in North Africa. As the campaign in North Africa gained momentum, Mussolini created a special unit within LUCE to cover the region. This group produced eighteen documentaries, some of which mimicked feature films through their use of musical scores and carefully planned camera angles. In fact, many LUCE newsreels and documentaries became more sophisticated in terms of camera angles, editing, and story telling as filmmakers began looking to fresher ways to convey their messages. The compare-and-contrast motif appeared in many of these films and helped the Fascists to stress the Italians' similarities to their allies and to point out the great differences separating the Italians from their enemies. Although wartime events tended to be the dominant subjects of most LUCE productions, the organization began supporting the production of films about leisure-time activities and youth-oriented subjects in order to maintain Italy's image as a country at peace on the home front.

The percentage of Italian subjects in LUCE films increased dramatically during the Fascist period. In the late 1920s, about 50 percent of LUCE films featured Italian subjects. By the mid-1930s the portion increased to about 75 percent. In the late 1930s, more films were produced about Italy's allies than about Italy itself, but by the 1940s, Italian subjects dominated almost completely. In 1933, the fascists decreed that at least 30 percent of all feature films shown had to be produced by Italians and that all foreign films had to be dubbed into the Italian language. These rulings tended to reinforce the production of Italian-subject documentaries.

Documentary films under fascism influenced the course of feature filmmaking. Some important feature films such as *Treno popolare* and *Camicia nera* included documentary and newsreel film footage. Others achieved a documentary feel by shooting on location, using nonprofessional actors and addressing historical subjects. The showing of newsreels and documentaries in the cinema houses attracted many Italians to the big screen and helped generate an audience for feature-length films. Beginning in 1931, 10 percent of box-office proceeds were reinvested in Italian filmmaking. This meant that larger audiences directly supported the production of new films. Moreover, the vast distribution of Italian-produced and Italian-controlled films helped in the process of nationalizing the Italian language and promoting the idea of a more unified country.

In 1935, the *Ente Nazionale Industrie Cinematografiche* (ENIC) was created under financing through LUCE and further contributed to Fascist control of filmmaking. The ENIC purchased a large movie-house chain and began to more attentively regulate film distribution. As a result, fewer foreign films were shown in Italian movie theatres. Mussolini and the Fascists also encouraged the education of future filmmakers by establishing the still-operational *Centro sperimentale di cinematografica,* directed by Luigi Chiarini. Students could gain professional film training and have better access to approved career channels by attending the school.

The inauguration of *Cinecitta,* on April 21, 1937, further marked the expansion of state involvement in filmmaking, especially in the production of Italian feature-length narrative films. The opening date was chosen not by accident but because Rome was believed to have been founded on that day. Mussolini made frequent references to the ancient Romans and certainly wanted to transmit the idea of the great importance filmmaking had in his vision of the State. His message was made more explicit through placement in the studios of a photograph featuring Mussolini with a film camera and this caption: "Film is the most powerful weapon."

Mussolini's image in films chronicled his life from glory to humiliation and defilement. After Italy's occupation by the Allies in 1943 and the ensuing Resistance Movement, Mussolini's image began to change. The cameras that had once favored his energy and might now had a difficult time hiding the dictator's fatigue and worry. Leaders of the Resistance Movement wanted to destroy Mussolini and his image and so burned photos and demolished statues of the befallen leader. They also decided he should be executed upon capture. Mussolini was shot with his mistress, Claretta Petacci, after being taken near Lake Como. Their bodies were taken to Piazzale Loreto in Milan and put on display. Angry crowds spat and kicked at the lifeless leader while U.S. troops filmed the event. The tragic images of Mussolini's body being dragged through the streets remain powerfully ingrained in the minds of many, as do

Mussolini's grand speeches from his balcony in Piazza Venezia.

WENDY POJMANN

See also **Documentary Film: Italy**

Further Reading

Bondanella, Peter, *Italian Cinema: From Neorealism to the Present*, New York: Continuum, 2001.

Brunetta, Gian Piero, *Cent'anni di cinema italiano*, Bari: Editori Laterza, 1995.

Brunetta, Gian Piero, *Storia del cinema italiano: il cinema del regime 1929–1945*, Rome: Editori Riuniti, 2001.

Hay, James, *Popular Film Culture in Fascist Italy: The Passing of the Rex*, Bloomington: Indiana University Press, 1987.

Landy, Marcia, *Italian Film*, Cambridge, England: Cambridge University Press, 2000.

Reich, Jacqueline and Piero Garofalo, editors, *Re-Viewing Fascism: Italian Cinema, 1922–1943*, Bloomington: Indiana University Press, 2002.

FASCIST SPAIN

Generally speaking, Franco's regime is usually identified with fascism. This identification was motivated by political factors, more so particularly during the second half of the twentieth century. This is also reflected in documentaries about the political regime in Spain between 1939 and 1975. The political history, however, clearly distinguishes between both realities. The difference is marked by the effort that the regime put into politically mobilising the masses, which is characteristic for totalitarian regimes. This was not the case of Franco's dictatorship after 1945. Franco promoted quite the opposite: the demobilisation of the Spanish people in order to convince them that democracy had historically been a dangerous experience for the country. In short, after 1945, Franco's regime became a dictatorship with a highly military character that used repression to rule out any form of popular participation in politics. It did not grant any guarantees with respect to political and cultural expression and freedom of trade association. From 1965 onward, the repression diminished noticeably,

and a highly authoritarian regime became institutionalised. It assumed the semblance of a regime that, to the outside world, was similar to Western democratic governments.

This distinction between Franco's rule and fascism is confirmed by historical data. Fascism, as a political movement in Spain, existed before the Spanish civil war and Franco's subsequent victory. Franco's attempt to establish a totalitarian state includes the period between February 1, 1938, when Franco's first government was formed, and July 18, 1945, when the Falangists lost power to the Asociación Católica Nacional de Propagandistas (Propagandist National Catholic Association).

Several fascist movements existed during the Spanish Second Republic. The most important one was the Spanish Falange Party. The leader of the movement was José Antonio Primo de Rivera. The movement had hardly any political significance until the elections of February 1936, which were won by the Frente Popular (Popular Front). From April to May 1936, this victory led to an avalanche of thousands of new recruits into the ranks of the Falange, whose number even increased during the civil war. In the meantime, the leaders of the movement were imprisoned by the Republican authorities. This first phase of Falangist development, which took place entirely independent of Franco's aspirations, was the first failed attempt to establish a Fascist party and state in Spain.

The Spanish civil war was the result of a failed military coup, which was not associated with the Falangist character of the organisation, although its militants were enthusiastic adherents of the party. The appointment of Franco as the rebels' political and military leader two months later started a practical process of a central command structure. The forced unification of the political forces that supported the military coup of April 1937 (Falangists, Carlists, and conservative Monarchists) continued. In practice, the Falangists, especially the recent recruits, controlled the movement, which from then onward was known by the name Falange Española Tradicionalista (Traditionalist Spanish Falange). The appointment of Franco's first government, in February 1938, marked the start of the move toward a totalitarian state in Spain. This development was always met with resistance from bishops and the military leaders. World War II and the defeat of the Axis powers caused a shift in the foreign and domestic politics of the regime, which led to the dismissal of the protagonists in the construction of the Spanish totalitarian state.

Here we distinguish between two important periods. One corresponds to the production of documentaries during the phase in which attempts were made to establish a Fascist regime: from the establishment of the Spanish Falange until its withdrawal from the project in 1945. The second covers the period from 1945 to the present. The civil war is the focal point of reference in documentaries about fascism in Spain, regardless of the ideology they represent and the period in which they were made.

The first documentary film on fascism in Spain was made by Paramount News in 1935. It shows several declarations from José Antonio Primo de Rivera, founder of the Spanish Falange. Its duration is a scarce four minutes and the declarations are in Spanish, French, and English. Primo de Rivera takes references from Italian fascism to authority, unity, and the substitution of the struggle between the classes to the cooperation between them. He maintains, however, that these ideas will produce a specific Spanish political

movement that will differ in its accomplishment from the Italian model. Before 1936, attempts were made to make propaganda film reportages, with no success.

Throughout the civil war, there were no documentaries, on either side, that focused on explaining the Fascist character of the so-called *nacionales* (Nationalists). The topic did not hold any possibilities for use as propaganda. The Republicans took this for granted, and some of the film and reportage titles make this clear. Examples include the anarchist documentary series *Madrid tumba del fascio*, [Madrid, tomb of fascism] and the documentaries *Bajo las bombas Fascistas* [Under fascist shelling] (SIE Films, 1938), *Contra el Fascismo* [Against fascism] (1938), *La obra del Fascismo* [Work of fascism], *Bombardeos de Madrid* [Bombardments of Madrid] (Socorro Rojo Internacional/Worker's International Relief, 1936), and *Solidaridad del pueblo hacia las víctimas del Fascismo* [Popular solidarity for the victims of fascism] (SIE Films, 1936). This also occurred when the Republican propaganda declared that the freedom fight was simply a fight against fascism. *El Frente y la Retaguardia* [The Front and the Rearguard] (Joaquín Giner, 1937) presents an anti-authoritarian fashion of defeating fascism on the battle field through democratic decision making in the popular command.

Another way was to emphasize the military support that the European Fascist powers gave to Franco was to suggest that international fascism supported Spanish fascism. This is the central theme in the first part of *The Defence of Madrid* (Ivor Montagu, 1936) and *Testimony of Non-intervention* (1938). This theme is also present in the fourth part of *España 1936* [Spain 1936] (Jean Paul Le Chanois, 1937) and several others such as *Challenge to Fascism* (Hellen Biggar, 1938). Shortly before the end of the war, *L'Espagne Vivra* [Spain will live] (Films Populaires, 1939) was released in France, which presented the viewpoint that supporting the Spanish Republic was helping France against its worst enemy, Nazi Germany. This idea is included in the documentaries that were made for distribution abroad.

The Nationalists did not declare themselves openly Fascist, although the more radical section of the Falangists wished to do so. They avoided referring to the German and Italian military aid to maintain an image of nonintervention. Only at the end of the war did some documentaries show this militarism, when foreign troops returned to their respective countries. This fact supposes the acceptance of the political alliance with both countries. Before that event, German and Italian newsreels showed images of their collaboration. These countries distributed reportages and documentaries that dealt with the topic, more so toward the end of the war.

Along this same line is *Deutsche Freiwillige in Spanien* [German volunteers in Spain] (1939), which shows Nazi officials instructing Spanish soldiers and German air raids. The footage clearly presents the importance of this help in gaining the final victory. *Legión Cóndor* [Condor Legion] (*In Kampf Gegen den Weltfeind* [Fighting the archenemy], Karl Ritter, 1939), has the same approach. It shows the Spanish civil war as Franco's reaction against the Communist revolution. Germany intervened in favour of the Nationalists to "stop the Communist advance in Europe." Similarly, some Italian documentaries do not hide their support for the Nationalists, which was openly admitted by Mussolini in several speeches included in LUCE newsreels. Their distribution was for Italy only. Although fascism is not identified with Franco's regime, the parallels are obvious. *I Fidanzati della Morte* [Death's brides] (Romolo Marcelini, 1938) is an example of this identification.

The Nationalist documentaries and newsreels do not mention the word "fascism." They include, however, many references to the Spanish Falange, converted into the only political party after the decree of unification. They show images and commentaries about the Falangists making up the political and ideological state structure. However, references to the totalitarian character of the new state are scarce and incidental in Francoist documentaries and newsreels during the war. For example, a short propaganda reportage (*Franco en Salamanca* [Franco in Salamanca], 1937) made for distribution abroad has two versions. One is directed toward Nazi Germany in which Franco says: "A totalitarian state in Spain will harmonise the joint operation of all of the potential and energies of the country." In addition, the images show Franco next to Wilhem von Fäupel (the German ambassador) saluting with his arm raised high in a meeting of Falangists in Salamanca. This scene is easily associated with the political manifestations of the Nazis. The version for "the rest of the world" omits both the gesture and the spoken references to Spanish totalitarianism.

Similarly, the Falangist manifestations, which imitated the Fascist way of expression, are at any time presided by Franco, or another military authority, together with the party leaders, who look like part of the scene, rather than its protagonists. The images leave no doubts about who is in power—the military. Even in propaganda documentaries distributed abroad and prepared by the Falangists before the unification, this subordination of the party to the state, whose head is Franco and not the Spanish Falange, is made clear in their commentaries and images. An example of this characteristic can be found in *España Azul* [Blue Spain] (Joaquín Martínez Arboleya, 1937), which is a propaganda documentary directed toward Latin America and shows the Falangist military head quarters with its various departments, in Salamanca, the capital of Franco's Spain at that time. It draws clear parallels with the organisation of the state. However, the documentary ends with the image of Franco as the supreme head of state. In *Frente de Vizcaya y 18 de Julio* [Front of Biscay and July 18] (Sección cinematográfica de Falange Española Tradicionalista/Film Section of the Traditionalist Spanish Falange, 1937), after a roundup of the Nationalist successes in the Northern campaign, the documentary shows a civil and military ceremony with military and Falangist parades, presided by the military and party leaders. In short, in Nationalist Spain the military were in command, although the Falange made up the ideological nerve system of the new state. The Nationalist films do not identify the Falange with fascism; however, the ideological proximity with its allies is clear through their images. Obviously, no effort is made to distinguish among the regimes in Madrid, Rome, and Berlin.

The proximity of the regime to the Axis powers and Franco's collaboration with Germany increased until 1943. The documentary *La División Azul Española* [The Spanish Blue Division] (Víctor de la Serna and Joaquín Reig-Gozalbes, 1942) is an example of this period. The film shows the brotherhood of the international Fascist parties that come to the aid of Germany, in the Spanish case with the Blue Division, to fight Stalin's communism; however, the estrangement soon set in, first diplomatically and later ideologically, which culminates in 1945. After World War II ended, Franco's rule started to be criticised.

After the beginning of the Cold War, documentaries on Franco and fascism presented one of two perspectives. One perspective is that of Franco's enemies from the democratic, socialist, and communist political camps. The other perspective was that of the regime itself, which tried to counter the attacks and accusations. Normally, Franco would only refuse to distribute films that were contrary to the regime. On rare occasions, the regime would respond with a film of its own, but without ever broaching the fascist character of the regime. At the same time, it tried to distribute foreign films with an anti-Communist slant, almost exclusively emphasizing this side of the regime.

The first Communist, anti-Fascist film, was *Ispania* [Spain] (Esfir Shub, 1939). The beginning of the film makes it clear that it is dedicated "to the great Spanish nation that fought against Fascism for three years enduring the siege and the blows of the traitors." This film reviews the civil war from the official communist standpoint. Initially, its distribution was modest because of the German-Soviet pact signed in the same year that the film was made. In 1950, *Guernica* (Alain Resnais and Robert Hessen) was made. This documentary converted the bombardment of the town into a Fascist symbol of the war and the winning party, quite the contrary of Picasso's painting.

Later, *Mourir á Madrid* [To Die in Madrid] (Frédéric Rossif, 1962) denounced Franco's regime at that time as Fascist. The plot is based on the Spanish civil war. Franco inherited a regime that was helped to power with the aid of the Fascists who had lost World War II and lacked legitimacy. The release of the film coincided with an international campaign against the execution of a militant member of the opposition; this was a drawback for the regime's image abroad. The significance of this can be explained by the following two factors: the attempts of the Spanish government to avoid the distribution of the film, and the production of another documentary that came out as a reaction to the first one (*Morir en España* [To Die in Spain], Mariano Ozores 1965). Between both films, several other productions were released with a similar perspective as Rossif's film. *España 1936* [Spain 1936] (Octavio Cortázar, 1964), for example, had little distribution outside of Cuba and repeated the arguments mentioned previously.

The film *Grenada, Grenada, Grenada Moja* [My Granada] (Roman Karmen, 1967) was made with financial aid from the Soviet government. It shows the struggle of international fascism against Soviet solidarity, a confrontation that first took place during the Spanish civil war. The end of the film blends certain episodes of the civil war with the outbreak of World War II and shots of large columns of German prisoners at the Russian front. The Spanish regime would be the survivor of the various forms of fascism that were defeated during the wars. Although it does not directly condemn the Fascist character of the regime, the documentary *Caudillo* [The Leader] (Basilio Martín

Patino, 1977) presents a fierce critique, larded with irony, of Franco during the civil war and an assertion of the anarchist principles and its antifascism. In short, these documentaries are strongly charged with critique, which was obligatory in view of the political position of the producers and, at times, of the governments involved in the production.

None of the films were shown in Spain while Franco was alive. The governments under the regime preferred to keep these films from the public and were for the most part successful. Although several films were made as responses, the regime generally showed foreign productions that gave another view of the regime and Franco himself. One of these films was *Franco Profile* (Jeremy Murray-Brown, 1966), a biographical review of Franco and of the regime's political and economic development from 1939 through 1965. In Spain, the film was distributed by NO-DO. Another film is *Only the Brave Are Free* (Edith Bardley, 1968), which focuses on the war, but ends with a link to the postwar years of peace in which any reference to fascism is avoided and gives a positive view of the regime through the economic and social improvements shown in the film.

After Franco's death in 1975, the production of documentaries about fascism declined. Incidental allusions to fascism were still made when dealing with other topics, but they did not form part of the main idea of the documentaries. The large television series productions on the Spanish civil war increasingly treated the subject in a more descriptive fashion. Franco's rule was viewed as a movement and political regime. In the end, the establishment of democracy in Spain eliminated the arguments that were used in productions between 1940 and 1975 to condemn the regime politically and socially, because it broke with the continuity between the Spanish civil war, fascism, and Franco's rule. And from then, the civil war, and its consequence, that is, Franco's rule, is no longer relevant as a subject of condemnation.

JULIO MONTERO

See also **Documentary Film: Spain**

Further Reading

Álvarez, R., and Sala, R., *El cine en la zona nacional, 1936–1939* [Film in The Nationalist Zone, 1936–1939], Bilbao: Mensajero, 2000.

Amo, A. del, and Ibáñez Ferradas, M. L., *Catálogo general del cine de la Guerra Civil* [General Catalogue: Film of the Spanish Civil War], Madrid: Cátedra, 1996.

Crusells, M., *La Guerra Civil española: cine y propaganda* [The Spanish Civil War: Film and Progaganda], Barcelona: Ariel, 2000.

Montero, J., "El cine y la Guerra Civil en España" [Film and the Civil War in Spain] en Ripoll, F., editor, *Las mil caras de la comunicación* [The Thousand Faces of Communication], Madrid: Servicio de publicaciones. Universidad Complutense de Madrid, 2001.

Sala, R., *El cine en la España Republicana durante la Guerra Civil* [Film in the Republican Spain during the Civil War], Bilbao: Mensajero, 1993.

FECHNER, EBERHARD

Eberhard Fechner is one of the most significant directors and authors of quality German television. Surprisingly, after a career of twenty years as an actor and director of fiction in theatre and television, he shot to fame with his first, rather mundane documentary about the suicide of a nondescript elderly woman: *Nachrede auf Klara Heydebreck* (1969).

Fechner was an early transgressor of the opposition between documentary and fiction film on German television. His first television drama, *Selbstbedienung* (1967), used the story line of a real crime case and took the dialogues verbatim from interviews he had conducted with the real offenders. He used a similar approach for *Damenquartett* (1968–1969), *Frankfurter Gold* (1970–1971), and *Geheimagenten* (1971), sometimes—as in the exemplary British drama-documentary *Cathy Come Home* (1965)—appending statistics for truth value. Fechner described these films as narrative reports in the style of a fictitious story. *Aus nichtigem Anlass* (1973), by contrast, was also inspired by a true event, but featured an invented story presented in the style of a documentary, thus making this potentially deceptive endeavour a drama-documentary.

In Germany the general term used to describe the various forms of dramatised documentary, *Dokumentarspiel,* was not differentiated into drama-doc and docu-drama. Fechner advanced the *Dokumentarspiel* in several directions: "I have made documentaries from fictional sources and fiction from documentary sources." (Nagel and Klaus, 1984 [this author's translation]). His work grew out of a public service ethos from the era before private television and has more in common with British dramatised case studies for terrestrial television than with American documentary drama derived from action cinema (Paget,

1998). Unlike plot-point driven docu-drama, Fechner's films do not present an argument. However, whereas Anglo-American drama-doc and docu-drama conventionally reinforce truth claims and use reconstruction to bring out essential truths otherwise inaccessible through traditional documentary methods (Roscoe and Hight, 2001), Fechner's *Dokumentarspiele* resist totalisation and investigate rather than assert. As he examines a situation only after it has become history, the drama-doc prerogative—that an experience needs to be dramatised because it is inaccessible to direct record (Kilborn and Izod, 1997)—does not apply. Fechner was interested in a life in retrospect and in memory. His documentaries dealt with past events recent enough to have living witnesses. Thus interview documentary was the perfect form. He referred to the step from *Dokumentarspiel* to the latter as starting to film his research. Like many other "documentary" filmmakers, he did not accept this label (Fechner, 1977). The notion of "story telling" would rule out the concept of "documentary." He did not want his films to be categorised as documentaries, fiction films, or interview films, but as filmic narrations, regardless of their status as fiction or nonfiction. "My films are even less so documentaries, as I do not film events. In my films people sit in front of the camera and talk" (Netenjacob, 1989 [this author's translation]).

In his nine documentaries Fechner defined a style of editing interviews that has since been ascribed to his name in Germany. His customary editor, Brigitte Kirsche; his wife and directorial assistant, Jannet Gefken-Fechner; and his cameraman, Rudolf Körösi, were the team that helped him from his first film onward. "Fechner's method" alludes to a refined montage of talking heads in which the utterances lead the image. In a concise orchestration of phrases, sentences started by one speaker were finished by someone else filmed in another place at another time, thereby pointing out corroborations or contradictions. Some interviewees did not even know each other and lived worlds apart; the impression of a dialogue is Fechner's achievement. From all of his documentaries, Fechner used only 5 percent of his source material. He created artificial conversations between people who had never met or would never talk with each other, such as a former concentration camp guard and a former prisoner. One protagonist, for instance, would ask himself or herself a rhetorical question that then is apparently answered by the next interviewee. While the dialogues and the reactions were fictitious, the meaning constructed by the montage was not. This composition of utterances finds its most prevalent expression in the documentary on the by then defunct *a cappella* band Comedian Harmonists. The interviews with the six former members brought together again the voices that harmonized before their split through the Nationalsozialist regime.

Fechner's landmark project, *Der Prozess* (1976–1984), deals with the monstrous as an effect of the ordinary. It captures the integration of the unbelievable and horrific into the everyday and the disciplined. *Der Prozess* followed the longest trial in German juridical history investigating the responsibility of the guards in the concentration and extermination camp Lublin-Majdanek. In depicting the Majdanek trial, Fechner was influenced by Hannah Arendt's account of the 1961 Adolf Eichmann trial in *Eichmann in Jerusalem*. (A montage of the 350 hours of Israeli television footage of the court proceedings against the latter has since been edited by Eyal Sivan in *The Specialist* [1999].) It gave all parties a voice in its kaleidoscopic examination as to why banality and evil had become close allies in the context of German history. Thirty years after the fact, after fourteen years of investigation, and 25,000 pages of eighty-five legal files, seventeen suspects were finally tried. The trial took six years (1975–1981) and the filmmaker's work lasted eight years. From seventy interviews with witnesses, defendants, plaintiffs, judges, prosecutors, lawyers, and investigating officers on 230 hours of film, four and a half hours were distilled for television. The film project was as monstrous as the trial (Fechner, 1985).

Der Prozess showed that the perpetrators were not extraordinary. The combination of multiplicity of voices with the ordinary meant that there was no singular, heroic point of view. This lack of judg-ment made it for some as indigestible as the deeds on trial. Whereas Adorno would have welcomed this, the television executives controversially banished *Der Prozess* to the third, regional channels, whereas the first, national channels screened programmes such as the American fiction drama *Holocaust*, as it allowed for identification with the good guys (Kreimeier, 1984). Fechner's interest in the many and the ordinary, rather than the one and the extraordinary, applied to nonfiction as well as fiction. He explored history through the lives of an ordinary family like the Kempowskis in *Tadellöser und Wolff* (1974–1975), rather than through an extraordinary "star" like, say, Hitler. Even with respect to the once famous *Die Comedian Harmonists* (1976), their personal biographies after their career peaked appealed to him more than their status as celebrities.

In *Der Prozess* the defendants argued that they had become the representatives and as such the scapegoats for a whole nation in the trial. A judge explains that, on the contrary, the notion of collective guilt does not work for a juridical system, as this requires evidence of a singular deed. Here, indirectly also the function of the interviewee as a representative is at stake. The documentary subjects are not representing the truth. The position of the witness was neither reified as in trauma theory, nor psychologised as in psychoanalytical theory. Fechner maintained, that he was not interested in fiction, poetry, or truth, but rather in reality. He conceived himself as a realist showing the mechanisms and the parts of reality, only using "documentary as a means to arrive at partly very artificial products" (Fechner, 1977 [this author's translation]). His films focus on the protagonists' actions as historical subjects and elude being limited by the subjective perspective of a singular person or being reduced by the abstractions of history: "In the centre of each of my works has to be the person in their precisely fixed historical dimension. Only then the universal can be represented by the personal" (Fechner, 1977 [this author's translation]). He avoided illustrating the stories of his interviewees with filmed footage, believing that doing so would limit the imagination. He did, however, use photos as documents, as they historicize because they freeze time.

As it avoids binarisms and resists totalisation, *Der Prozess* is utterly democratic. Neither the filmmaker nor the interviewees assume the position of a meta-perspective and no voice-of-God reflects for the viewer. The sound montage substitutes the commentary; the off-narration is also assembled from statements of the interviewees, and these are mostly factual. Emotions are levelled out as well, and there are no "higher," expressively dramatic outbursts. Crying was edited out. Even his adaptations of autobiographical novels such as *Tadellöser and Wolf* (1974–1975) and *Ein Kapitel für sich* (1978–1979) were more narrations than dramas and saturated with dry throwaway remarks. Visually, too, there is no meta-perspective. Every subject in his documentaries was exposed to the same treatment by the camera regardless of whether they were victimisers or victims. There are no continuity shots and no long shots. The camera would only move over objects. The avoidance of camera and character movement enabled him to cut their statements in fast succession. For the impression of a dialogue to be believable, the eye lines of the interviewees were matched. The interviewees were filmed from one angle and position and all seated at the same distance to the camera. Their faces were filmed in decontextualising close-up. In *Klassenphoto* or *Comedian Harmonists* these are so narrow that the border of the face is cut off. The space around the face is eliminated. There is no life for the interviewees outside of their utterances wrote Fechner's biographer (Netenjacob, 1984). The depth of the image was sacrificed for the depth of the argumentative architecture. With the focus on talking heads Fechner's style of documentary was television-specific. As Hi-8 video images today are used to create a documentary impression, Fechner preferred the grainier 16mm to 35mm, which at the time was still common as a television format.

Without either a visual or semantic meta-perspective, *Der Prozess* is without a grand narrative. At the interface of justice and representation, *Der Prozess* matches Lyotard's definition of a postmodern narrative.Via the multiple foci Fechner's "filmic narrations" point away from the influence of discourse as a reason for the individual to partake in historical activity. Symptomatically, Fechner concluded, after having filmed *Der Prozess*, that the perpetrators committed their crimes not because of the influence of abstract ideology but because of small-minded personal motivations. Thus the form of the documentary appropriately mirrored its content and manifested Fechner's conviction that the ordinary is more important than the extraordinary.

SILKE PANSE

Biography

Born in Liegnitz, Silesia, October 21, 1926. Grew up in Berlin. Started business apprenticeship at the UFA, 1943. Was drafted and became prisoner of war, 1944–1945. Drama student at Schauspielschule Deutsches Theater Berlin, 1946–1948. Theatre actor in Berlin, Bremen, Hannover, Hamburg, 1947–1969. Film actor since 1953. Theatre director since 1960. Directorial assistant of Giorgio Strehler in Mailand, 1961–1963. Married Margot Krell, 1949, Ingrid Fechner, mid-1950s, and Jannet Gefken, 1967. P.E.N. membership, since 1977. Since 1984 member and later deputy head of Media Arts Department of the Academy of Fine Arts in Western Berlin. Died in Hamburg August 7, 1992.

Selected Films

1969 *Nachrede auf Klara Heydebreck*
1970 *Klassenphoto*
1974–1975 *Unter Denkmalschutz - Erinnerungen aus einem Frankfurter Bürgerhaus*
1975 *Lebensdaten*
1976 *Die Comedian Harmonists*
1976–1984 *Der Prozess*
1984 *Im Damenstift*
1987–1988 *La Paloma*
1990–1991 *Wolfskinder*

Further Reading

Emmelius, Simone, *Fechner's Methode. Studien zu seinen Gesprächsfilmen*, Mainz: Gardez! Verlag, 1996.
Fechner, Eberhard, "Über das 'Dokumentarische' in Fernseh-Spielfilmen," in *Akzente*, no.4, 8.1973, 310–320.
Fechner, Eberhard, "Dokumentarfilm und Wirklichkeit" in *Deutsche Volkszeitung*, 17, 20.4, 1977.
Fechner, Eberhard, "Das Fernsehspiel—Dichtung und Wahrheit" in *FILM-Korrespondenz*, 12, 13.12.1977.
———, "Familiengeschichte als Zeitgeschichte" in Hufen, Fritz and Jäschke, Th., editors, *Tadellöser & Wolff. Ein Kapitel für sich*, München: Wilhelm Goldmann Verlag, 1979.
———, "Über die Entstehung der NDR-Produktion *Der Prozess*" in *15. Internationales Forum des jungen Films Berlin*, Berlin: Internationales Forum des jungen Films/ Freunde der deutschen Kinemathek, 1985.
Kilborn, Richard, and Izod, John, *An Introduction to Television Documentary*, Manchester: Manchester University Press, 1997.
Kreimeier, Klaus, "Im Lapidaren das Abgründige. Eberhard Fechner's Film über den Majdanek-Prozeß" in *Frankfurter Rundschau*, 24, 1984, 11.
Nagel, Joseph, and Kirschner, Klaus, editors, *Eberhard Fechner. Die Filme, gesammelte Aufsätze und Materialien*, Erlangen: Erlanger Beiträge zur Medientheorie und – praxis, 1984.
Netenjacob, Egon, "*Die Normalität und ihr Bezugspunkt*," *Medium* 12, 1984, 38.
———, *Eberhard Fechner: Lebensläufe dieses Jahrhunderts im Film*, Weinheim, Berlin: Quadriga, 1989, 137.
Paget, Derek, *No Other Way To Tell It. Dramadoc/Docudrama on Television*, Manchester: Manchester University Press, 1998.
Readings, Bill, *Introducing Lyotard. Art and Politics*, London and New York: Routledge, 1991, 125.

Roscoe, Jane, and Hight, Craig, *Faking It*, Manchester: Manchester University Press, 2001.

Saur, Karl Otto, "Jeder Mensch hat eine Geschichte, die interessiert. Neue Massstäbe für Dokumentationen: Eberhard Fechner und seine Befragungs-und

Schneidetechnik" in *Süddeutsche Zeitung*, 28,1, 1987, 20.

Tabori, George, "Ein Schulterzucken, ein Lächeln und eine Hand, die zittert" in *Süddeutsche Zeitung* 20, 11, 1984.

FEMINISM: AFRICA

The term "African feminist documentary" is complicated. To begin with, feminism and filmmaking are both relatively new to Africa: African women did not start making films until the 1960s. And although women are currently engaged in filmmaking throughout the continent, not enough is known about filmmaking in every African country to make generalisations about a continental cinema. The absence of indigenous cinema industries prevents African cinema from achieving a sense of individual national identities; there is great diversity among African filmmakers, and it is important not to subsume them all under the same label. Like many non-Western practitioners, they argue that they are not making "African" films; they are artists, making films. Added to this is the question of how one defines Africa. Although countries such as Algeria have an established group of women documentary makers, relatively few critics include North Africa in their studies of the continent's filmmaking. Arguing that the influence of neighbouring Arab countries on North African filmmaking excludes it from consideration as "African" film, they prefer to limit their focus to the sub-Saharan diaspora.

There is further debate among academics as to whether filmmakers such as Sarah Maldoror (born in Guadeloupe, raised in France) or Trinh T. Minh Ha (Vietnam), both of whom have made feminist documentaries in Africa about African women, can be included in the category of African feminist filmmakers. This debate arises not out of a pedantic desire for clear-cut nationalistic divisions but from the important dichotomy between ethnographic representations of African women as "other" and their own representations of themselves. Trinh's film of Senagelese women, *Reassemblage* (1982), is extremely avant-garde, and while it serves as an important deconstruction of Western

conceptions of the African female, it is certainly very different from how African women choose to present themselves in film.

African women make far more documentary and television films than features, undoubtedly as a result of the financial demands of the latter, and so their activities have received relatively little attention on an international level in terms of distribution and criticism. What criticism of African feminist filmmaking there has been tends to privilege avant-garde or narrative formats over documentary. In recent writing on the subject, filmmaking that adopts a humanistic perspective, reflected in a realistic narrative or documentary filmic form is frequently critiqued: Kenneth Harrow, for example, argues that in these films "the symmetries of the Symbolic are not disrupted, nor is there the silence of another order, but the acceptance of the conventional patterns of meaning in the only challenge to patriarchy . . . is to do battle on their own terms."

Harrow argues instead in favour of a filmic style that refuses to rely uncritically on the codes of realism, a vision influenced by poststructuralism and the French feminist school and exemplified by Trinh's film. Realism is problematic for any feminist critique because "such a simple formula occludes the problematic issue of representation." To call into question representation is to acknowledge that the "neutral order" of the image is actually the order of the symbolic. And the symbolic is conventionally the ground for patriarchal structures (Harrow, 1997).

The fundamental problem with the preceding approach is, as bell hooks writes, that "Feminist film theory rooted in an ahistorical, psychoanalytic framework that privileges sexual difference actively suppresses recognition of race, re-enacting and mirroring the erasure of black sisterhood that happens in films" (hooks, 1992). Those critics who apply Western feminist theories to African film fail to allow for a different kind of feminism that takes race into account. By acting as such, Western feminism becomes the new patriarchy, its approaches akin to the earlier colonialist approaches toward black African culture.

It is only logical that feminist theories emerging from African discourses and experiences should be inherently African. Obioma Nnaemeka agrees with hooks that Western versions of feminism prove ineffectual within Africa because African women have a different set of values. Priorities such as motherhood, resilience (rather than resistance) to colonial oppression, woman-against-woman violence, and female power hierarchies, which other models of feminism decry, are central to African feminism. Nnameke allows that feminist scholarship is one of the most powerful critical and analytical tools with the possibility for fostering international social change, but claims that the frequent inappropriateness of its aims has allowed African feminism to create a new structure of analysis, one that omits the questionable and presumptuous conceptual frameworks that external feminist theories have imposed on African women's experiences (Nnaemeka, 1997).

Filmmaker Anne Munghai, in an interview with Sheila Petty, explains the African woman's perception of Western feminism thus:

> It is very difficult to say [that one is a feminist] because in my country when you say that you are a feminist you're saying that you want to be like a man. . . I do not believe I'm like a man. What I believe in I do not exactly call it feminism, and this is what comes out in my film. . . What I believe, and what I wanted to show in my film, is that although men, according to culture, are in charge, women have to have a say. I believe it is a human right for women to be able to talk, to be allowed to have a voice. That is what I am advocating in my film and that is what I believe in. Women must be given a voice.
> (Petty, 1996)

This liberating of the unheard voice lies at the heart of African feminist documentary making. The first full-length documentary (or at least docudrama) made by a native African woman, Safi Faye's 1975 *Kaddu beykat/Letter from My Village*, takes exactly such an approach. Although Faye is not concerned solely with women, her slow description of the daily goings-on in a Serer village, which demonstrates in the end that it is impossible for a young peasant to live in an area of groundnut monoculture, gives an insider's view. "You are going to spend a while with me in my home",

announces the commentary. "I've had some criticism from my parents. They say people who watch this are going to laugh at us because we're badly dressed, because we're always working." At the end, she thanks them: "The letter is from me. All the rest is from my farming parents."

And just as it is easier for locally born filmmakers to listen to their people and understand their roots, so it is easier for women to make films about women. As Togolese filmmaker Anne-Laure Folly States: "In African culture, it is more important to experience something than to express it outside yourself." It is for this reason that her documentaries on African women (*Femmes du Niger entre intégrisme et démocratice* [1993, Nigerian Women Between Integration and Democracy], *Femmes aux yeux ouverts* [1994, Women with Their Eyes Open], but also *Les Oubliées/The Forgotten Women*, 1996) find their ability to listen and their emotion. In *Femmes aux yeux ouverts*, Folly presents portraits of contemporary African women from four West African nations: Burkina Faso, Mali, Senegal, and Benin. *Les Oubliées*, made in Angola, focuses on the victims of a country at war. In talking about history and politics, Folly listens to the people, not to the leaders—the people, and particularly the women, who she shoots in close-up to read in their faces the marks of thirty years of war.

We can argue, then, that African feminism establishes its identity through its very being; the very existence of female voices is an act of self-assertion. This technique of exposition, rather than arbitration, finds its apotheosis in Flora M'mbugu-Schelling's *These Hands* (Mozambique, 1992), which provides images of women whose lives consist of pounding rocks for a living. It begins with silence, restraint, and a rhythm that combines labour and detailing. Without even knowing why the women are working, the audience is lulled into the patterns of the work, patterns of "determination and pedestrian persistence." Without being eroticised, glorified, or victimised, these women assume a position that the spectator respects, even admires, for their perseverance and group solidarity. At the end of the film we are informed that it takes a woman two months to produce a mound of gravel of sufficient size to earn her $12. *These Hands* is exemplary for its ability to permit the cinematic experience to unfold as an "other" form of film, free of the constraints of Western feminist dictates yet no less powerful for it (Harrow, 1999).

In recent years, however, a number of female documentarists have begun to follow a more

Western, agitprop model of filmmaking, similar to the American documentaries of the 1960s exemplified by JoAnn Elam's *Rape* or, more recently, Alice Walker and Pratibha Parmar's *Warrior Marks* (1982) These films, rather than simply revealing women's lives to the camera, argue for a change in them. Zara M. Yacoub's *Feminine Dilemma* (Chad, 1994) and Soraye Mire's *Fire Eyes: Female Circumcision* (Somalia, 1994) are amongst a growing number of films that deal with the topic of female circumcision. These films consist mainly of a series of interviews with religious leaders, women group representatives, health workers, everyday people, and the girls themselves and asks the questions: Why female circumcision? Should it be performed? And how? What are the consequences? It is worth noting that both Yacoub and Mire's films have seen a great deal more success outside Africa than less controversial films such as M'mbugu-Schelling's film. Mire's film was shown at the Sundance, Berlin, and New York African Film. Festivals, as well as the International Human Rights Watch Film Festival, and is a staple of Women's Studies courses throughout the United States and United Kingdom. Although the two films are a step beyond Walker and Parmar's in that they have dispensed with the outsider figure who assigns to herself the authority to impose a meaning on every signifier (a role played with zeal by Walker), it nonetheless seems that Western feminists are still more accepting of African feminism when it is subordinated by mainstream Western feminist criticism; in other words, when it imitates their own constructs.

The question of how we should approach the study of African feminist documentary is as yet unresolved. To refer to "third world feminist filmmakers" lays a burden of the demonstration of cultural difference that might constrain the individual into making a film lacking in universality. But to subsume this activity under the general heading of "women's cinema" flattens out the difference entirely. And even today there remain critically neglected areas in the study of African cinema that are in need of attention (almost nothing has been written on the subject of white African filmmakers, for example). A closer critical focus on individual countries and directors is needed to best understand the nuances of African feminist documentary. As Folly puts it: "The important thing is to know who is looking at what. The fact of being a black woman doesn't give me the culture of a black woman in general, once I'm outside a little area of my particular upbringing. Contrary to the staggeringly immodest assertions one sometimes hears, being African doesn't mean being culturally aware of the whole of Africa, but simply that one has a culture which comes from Africa!" (Barlet, 2000).

Feminists have much to learn from the documentaries created by the women of the African diaspora. In many ways the films made by these women point toward, and deal with, some huge gaps in Western feminism. African feminist filmmakers continue to subvert the notion of any singular histories, providing a basis on which cross-cultural understanding may be built, to locate issues of gender and race within a wider perspective and to offer an analysis of social change.

HELEN WHEATLEY

Selected Films

Feminine Dilemma (1994, director Zara M. Yacoub)
Femmes aux yeux ouverts (1994, director Anne-Laure Folly)
Femmes du Niger entre intégrisme et démocratice (1993, director Anne-Laure Folly)
Fire Eyes: Female Circumcision (1994, Soraye Mire)
Kaddu beykat /Letter from my Village (1975, director Safi Faye)
Les Oubliées (1996, director Anne-Laure Folly)
Reassemblage (1992, director Trinh T. Min-Ha)
These Hands (1992, Flora M'mbugu-Schelling)
Warrior Marks (1993, director Pratibha Parmar)

Further Reading

Barlet, Olivier, *African Cinemas: Decolonializing the Gaze*, London & New York: Zed Books, 1996, trans. Chris Turner, 2000.

Diawara, Manthia, *African Cinema: Politics and Culture*, Bloomington and Indianapolis: Indiana University Press, 1992.

Foster, Gwendolyn Audrey, *Women Filmmakers of the African/Asian Diaspora: Decolonising the Gaze, Locating Subjectivity*, Carbondale, IL: South Illinois University Press, 1997.

Gugler, Joseph, *African Film: Re-imagining a Continent*, Bloomington: Indiana University Press, 2003.

Harrow, Kenneth, *African Cinema: Post-Colonial and Feminist Readings*, Trenton, NJ: Africa World Press, 1999.

———, *Western Feminism and African Feminist Filmmaking*, Rodopi: B.V. Editions, 1997.

———, *With Open Eyes: Women and African Cinema*, Rodopi: B.V. Editions, 1997.

hooks, bell, *Black Looks: Race and Representation*, Boston: South End Press, 1992.

Kaplan, E. Ann, *Looking for the Other: Feminism, Film and the Imperial Gaze*, London: Routledge, 1997.

Mikell, Gwendolyn, *African Feminism: The Politics of Survival in Sub-Saharan Africa*, Philadelphia: University of Pennsylvania Press, 1997.

Nnaemeka, Obioma, "Sisterhood, Feminisms and Power: From Africa to the Diaspora," in *Society, Film and Politics: From Africa to the Diaspora*, edited by Obioma Nnaemeka, Trenton: Africa World Press, 1997.

Petty, Sheila, "How an African Woman Can Be: African Women Filmmakers Construct Women," *Discourse* 18, 1996, 3.

FEMINISM: CRITICAL OVERVIEW

Women participated in all of the major documentary movements of the twentieth century, but their participation was often limited to less visible and less valorized aspects of filmmaking such as research, sound recording, and postproduction. Before the 1970s, there were exemplary female documentary filmmakers, including Leni Riefenstal, Maya Deren, and Shirley Clarke; however, none of these women explicitly affiliated themselves with an organized women's movement. One possible candidate for feminist documentary foremother is the French filmmaker Agnes Varda, but although Varda made documentary films in the 1950s and 1960s (*L'Opera Mouffe* (The Rue Mouffetard Opera), 1958; *Loin de Vietnam* (Far from Vietnam), 1967; *Black Panthers*, 1968), her best-known feminist works are narratives that incorporate elements of documentary aesthetics.

Although organized feminist movements existed in the nineteenth and early twentieth centuries, the conditions for feminist documentary filmmaking did not coalesce until the early 1970s. The profusion of feminist documentary filmmaking in the 1970s was predicated on the convergence of new and existing cinematic and political institutions, as well as the development of more accessible technologies. In the United States and elsewhere, second wave feminism emerged in the context of the civil rights and anti-war movements of the early 1960s. By the late 1960s, women had begun to form affinity groups within the institutions of the civil rights movement and the anti-war New Left. One such organization was the documentary film collective Newsreel. Founded in New York in 1967, Newsreel was dedicated to the depiction of social conflicts and activism. Originally dominated by a nucleus of white male filmmakers, by 1969–1970, a process of restructuring, initiated in part by women's groups within Newsreel, resulted in a reexamination of the collective's priorities. By 1971, women in New York Newsreel and its affiliate, San Francisco Newsreel, had produced two documentaries devoted to women's issues, *Janie's Janie* (Geri Ashur) and *The Woman's Film* (Judy Smith).

Another cinematic institution that laid the groundwork for feminist documentary filmmaking was the Robert Flaherty Film Seminar. Founded in 1955 by Frances Hubbard Flaherty, Robert Flaherty's widow, the Flaherty Seminar has historically provided an innovative space for screening and discussion of documentary films. In 1970, the seminar screened two feminist documentaries, Amalie Rothschild's *Woo Who? May Wilson* (1969) and Madeline Anderson's *I Am Somebody* (1970). In the following year, the Flaherty screened two more feminist works, Jim Klein and Julia Reichert's *Growing Up Female: As Six Become One* (1971) and Amalie Rothschild's *The Center* (date unknown). After a heated discussion of the role of women's cinema, a group of seminar participants met to discuss the limited opportunities for the distribution and exhibition of women's films. Members of this group would eventually become the organizing committee for the First International Women's Film Festival in 1972. Filmmakers Klein, Reichert, and Rothschild would also go on to form New Day Films, a feminist film distribution company. Several feminist film production cooperatives emerged in the early 1970s as well, including the London Women's Film Co-op, the Sheffield Film Co-op, and Women Make Movies, which would evolve into the dominant distributor of feminist film and video. These alternative film institutions laid the groundwork for feminist documentary filmmakers to reach new audiences and to share information about funding and production.

Between 1971 and 1976, the United States, Canada, and the United Kingdom witnessed an unprecedented flurry of feminist documentary filmmaking activity. Contemporary commentators tended to make distinctions between films with an explicit left political analysis, such as the Newsreel films, and films that examined women's experiences from a more individual, bourgeois perspective, such as *Three Lives* (Kate Millet, 1971) and *Joyce at 34* (Joyce Chopra, 1974). Although this distinction is not entirely stable, it is possible to identify some of the major thematic concerns that animated this early body of work and that continued to be relevant in the decades that followed. Several films from this period focus on women and labor, including Barbara Kopple's award-winning *Harlan County, U.S.A.*

(1976) and Reichert and Klein's *Union Maids* (with Miles Mogulescu, 1976). Films such as Michelle Citron's *Parthenogenesis* (1975), Madeline Anderson's *Clementine Hunter, Artist* (1976), and Jill Godmilow's *Antonia: A Portrait of the Woman* (with Judy Collins, 1974) portray women artists, but also address broader issues related to women and professional identity. As their titles indicate, films such as *Self-Health* (San Francisco Women's Health Collective, 1974), *Healthcaring: From Our End of the Speculum* (Denise Bostrom and Jane Warrenbrand, 1977), and *Taking Our Bodies Back* (Lazarus, Wunderlich, and Fink, 1974) introduced the burgeoning women's health movement, which encouraged lay women to conduct their own research, question received medical authorities, make their own decisions, and even organize to provide basic care. The formation of self-help groups and cooperatives was fundamental to the movement's challenge to the hierarchical distribution of knowledge and expertise in the practice of medicine. Films devoted to women's health issues were particularly important in the development of strategies of collaborative filmmaking that reflected this critique at the level of filmmaking practice.

In addition to health care, feminist documentaries of the 1970s addressed other mainstream feminist issues, including abortion rights (*It Happens to Us*, Amalie Rothschild, 1971), rape (*Rape Culture*, Cambridge Documentary Films, 1978; *Rape*, JoAnn Elam, 1978), and mass media depictions of women (*Killing Us Softly*, Jean Kilbourne, 1979). In 1975 the National Film Board of Canada established Studio D, a women's filmmaking unit directed by producer Kathleen Shannon. In a feminist twist on the NFB's griersonian mandate, Canadian documentary filmmakers contributed films on a diverse array of women's social issues, including *Good Day Care: One Out of Ten* (Barbara H. Martineau and Lorna Rasmussen, 1978), *This Film Is About Rape* (Bonnie Kreps, 1978), and *Not a Love Story* (1981), Bonnie Klein's controversial examination of the pornography industry.

Feminist documentaries addressed the philosophical concerns of the movement on the level of form and practice, as well as content. Feminist filmmakers brought a commitment to validating women's voices and experiences and a critique of the very forms of cultural authority that the official documentaries of the postwar period, with their disembodied narrators and expert interviews, had often helped to construct. Given feminist critiques of the power dynamics embedded in relationships, feminist filmmakers were often sensitive to power dynamics between filmmaker, subject, and audience. As a response to some of these concerns, the movement quickly evolved a fairly consistent visual and narrative style that combined interviews and observational footage. By the early 1970s, politically engaged filmmakers had already become disillusioned with observational cinema's failure to provide social and historical context. Direct address interviews allowed a film's subjects to offer political analysis and, at least theoretically, opened up the possibility of a more interactive relationship among filmmaker, subject, and spectator. Moreover, interviews allowed filmmakers to address historical topics, and recovering women's histories was an important project of second wave feminism. Although "talking heads" were heavily identified with official documentaries, the sight of women talking authoritatively about their own experiences was still potentially radical. Canadian filmmaker Barbara Martineau (1984) argued that feminist documentaries used "talking heads as empowering devices, representing people who represent themselves, and thereby suggesting that we are all capable of representing ourselves, of interpreting and acting upon our own interpretations of reality." She continued: "By empowering ordinary people to speak as experts, they question a basic assumption of dominant ideology, that only those already in power, those who have a stake in defending the status quo, are entitled to speak as if they know something."

Among feminist theorists, however, the conventions of realism would become increasingly suspect as the decade progressed. In 1973, feminist film critic Claire Johnston published an article titled "Women's Cinema as Counter Cinema," in which she argued that "the 'truth' of our oppression cannot be 'captured' on celluloid with the 'innocence' of the camera: it has to be constructed/manufactured." Johnston's article heralded the ascendancy of French post-structuralism within feminist film criticism in the 1970s and 1980s. This new body of criticism was grounded in the assumption that subjectivity and gender difference are constructed in discourse and that cinema itself is a discursive system whose conventions tell us more about dominant ideologies than some pre-existing reality. More than twenty years later, filmmaker Alexandra Juhasz (1994) described the legacy of Johnston's article and others like it: "as a feminist scholar of media in the eighties and nineties, I have been instructed to believe that realism and identification—which are claimed to be axiomatic of talking heads, cinema verité, or realist documentary—are not sophisticated, or even legitimate, formal strategies."

In an attempt to forestall the wholesale dismissal of realist feminist documentaries, documentary theorist Julia Lesage suggested that all realisms were not created equal and that realist tactics could be used for various purposes and effects. In "The Politics and Aesthetics of Feminist Documentary" (1978), Lesage argued that early feminist documentaries emerged from feminist consciousness-raising groups and shared the same ethos and goals. According to Lesage, consciousness raising "was an act of naming previously unarticulated knowledge, of seeing that knowledge as political (i.e. as a way of beginning to change power relations), and of understanding that the power of this knowledge was that it was arrived at collectively." Like the consciousness-raising group, the best feminist documentaries situated personal experience and testimony in a context of collectivity and political analysis that offered viewers the tools to challenge dominant representations of gender relations. Feminist film critic E. Ann Kaplan also attempted to interrogate the monolithic depiction of documentary realism in feminist film theory. Kaplan, along with Lesage, was one of the few feminist film critics to engage extensively with the documentary tradition and feminist documentary filmmaking. In her 1982 reading of *Janie's Janie*, Kaplan called for a more nuanced feminist film theory, one that could allow for varied and strategic uses of realist conventions.

The uniformity of the critique has never been equal to the complexity of individual feminist documentaries. Even a film like *Growing Up Female*, which has often been criticized for its bourgeois individualism, is acutely attuned to the discursive construction of femininity. The film juxtaposes interviews with individual girls and women with images from advertising and popular romantic songs. Interviews with teachers and an advertising executive emphasize the production of femininity. The film is particularly acute in its reading of the "freedom" of countercultural femininity as a product that is sold to women, particularly middle class women, whose real opportunities are actually quite constrained. The film uses some of the conventions of direct cinema, including extreme close-ups as indicators of heightened emotion and emotional transparency. Yet the proximity of advertising images makes possible alternative readings of the fragmented female body. Likewise, the editing of popular love songs over verité footage orients the spectator toward analysis rather than passive observation.

The next twenty years provides an interesting case study of the relationship between feminist film theory and the production, distribution, and preservation of feminist film. As successive generations of feminist scholars were inculcated with a suspicion of realism, realist documentaries were eclipsed by experimental films that emphasized the construction of subjectivity, the materiality of film, the relationship between spectator and text, and the active construction of meaning. Avant-garde works by Sally Potter, Chantal Akerman, Yvonne Rainier, and Laura Mulvey dominated the feminist film criticism of this era. Many documentary filmmakers, including some who had participated in the early wave of feminist documentary filmmaking, began to make more experimental works that highlighted the production of meaning and troubled the boundaries between fiction and nonfiction. British filmmakers were among the first to incorporate theories about discourse and subjectivity into their work. *The Nightcleaners* (Berwick Street Film Collective, 1975), a film about labor organizing among female custodial workers in London, uses black leader between shots to isolate familiar images and force the spectator into a more active role in the construction of meaning. The film also uses disjunctions in sound and image to highlight contradictions in the construction of "woman" as a stable category for political alliances across classes. Another British film, *Song of the Shirt* (Susan Clayton, 1979), combines a variety of modes, including acted scenes, written texts, and still photographs, to simultaneously document nineteenth-century women textile workers and investigate the process of constructing history. In the United States, Michelle Citron's *Daughter Rite* (1978) combines home movies from her childhood with scripted sequences shot in an observational style. Citron slows down seemingly innocent filmic images of her childhood and repeats them to reveal a different story about the construction of feminine identity in the family.

The evolution of Jill Godmilow's work bears witness to the changing emphases in feminist representational politics. According to the narrator, Godmilow's *Far From Poland* (1984) began as a project "steeped in the documentary traditions of the left." Inspired by news of the Polish Solidarity movement, Godmilow put together a film crew and raised money to travel to Poland. When she and her crew were denied visas, Godmilow made an eclectic film that queried the efficacy of documentary filmmaking and Godmilow's own stake as an American leftist representing Poland. Godmilow eventually managed to obtain some smuggled documentary footage, but rather than allowing the audience to believe in the immediacy of her representation of Poland, the filmmaker framed many of her images by recording them off a television screen. A reenacted interview with activist Anna Walentynowicz complicates masculinist portrayals of the Solidarity movement. However, the film's feminism is not limited to its content. Godmilow explains that her attraction to Solidarity was to a movement in which ordinary people refused to bow to the authority of experts. In representing Poland, Godmilow refuses to constitute herself as an expert providing knowledge about a fully knowable subject. In including scripted representations of her own work process as it overlaps with her domestic and romantic life, Godmilow's film offers a figure of the artist as situated and specific, ambivalent and invested.

In her refusal of the position of the expert, Godmilow's work overlaps with that of another feminist filmmaker who began working in the 1980s, Trinh T. Minh-ha. In films such as *Reassemblage* (1982) and *Surname Viet Given Name Nam* (1989), Trinh articulated a third world feminist critique of documentary and ethnographic traditions that was echoed in her books and articles, most notably *Woman, Native, Other* (1989) and *When the Moon Waxes Red* (1991). In *When the Moon Waxes Red*, Trinh argued that the documentary tradition was founded on an opposition between self and other and a totalizing quest for knowledge that reiterated the power relations of colonial domination. Trinh argued for a more embodied, situated ethics of filmmaking, which was attuned to the dialogic creation of self and other and the stakes of representation for people on both sides of the camera. Trinh's films eschew narrative coherence and closure and frequently blur the lines between fiction and nonfiction. In *Surname Viet Given Name Nam*, for example, Trinh commissioned Vietnamese American women to perform ethnographic interviews from Mai Thu Van's 1983 book *Vietnam: Un Peuple, des Voix* (*Vietnam: One People, Many Voices*.) Filmed in highly stylized settings, the nonprofessional performances disrupt the naturalism of the text, as does the heavy use of titles. In a later part of the film, the performers introduce themselves and talk about their lives in settings of their own choosing. Rather than signifying authenticity, these later sequences encourage viewers to reexamine received ideas about self-expression and "giving voice" to subaltern subjects.

Trinh's critique of the documentary tradition shares some of the central concerns of the contemporary third world feminist critique of Western feminism's ethnocentrism and its monolithic construction of third world women. As a movement, third world feminism encompassed strategic alliances between third world nationals and black, Latina, Asian, and indigenous women in the West. Given the breadth and diversity of its constituents, third world feminism was never united by a single agenda, but third world feminists did share a general understanding that sexism and gender identity are always informed by race, class, sexuality, nationality, and legacies of imperialism. Some of the most important feminist documentaries of the late 1980s and early 1990s attempted to articulate the complexity of these intersections. Diasporic filmmakers were particularly well positioned to address these issues—both by virtue of their experiences and their access to cinematic institutions. Not surprisingly, this period witnessed an outpouring of work by Asian, Middle Eastern, and African diasporic filmmakers living in Australia, Canada, and Great Britain, including Pratibha Parmar (*Sari Red* and *Khush*, 1988 and 1991), Mona Hatoum (*Measures of Distance*, 1988), Laleen Jayamanne (*A Song of Ceylon*, 1985), and Ngozi Onwurah (*The Body Beautiful*, 1991).

Although reclaiming suppressed histories had always been an important project for feminist documentary filmmakers, the 1980s and 1990s witnessed the excavation of lives and histories that had been marginalized within mainstream feminism. Works by Michelle Parkerson, including *But Then, She's Betty Carter* (1980) and *Gotta Make This Journey: Sweet Honey in the Rock* (1983), called attention to the lives and work of African-American female artists. Ngozi Onwurah's *And Still I Rise* (1993) explored media representations of black women's sexuality. Sylvia Morales's *Chicana* (1979) used pre-Columbian and Mexican history to challenge dominant media representations of Chicanas. Rea Tajiri's *History and Memory* (1991) appropriated clips from Hollywood movies and U.S. propaganda films to re-create the history of Japanese-American internment during World War II and to fill the void created by her own mother's amnesia about the camps. Reflecting the global orientation of third world feminism, Lourdes Portillo's Academy Award nominated *Las Madres: The Mothers of the Plaza de Mayo* (with Susana Munoz, 1985) documented the activism of the mothers of the disappeared in Argentina, and Ana Maria Garcia's *La Operacion* (1985) investigated female sterilization as a government sanctioned form of birth control in Puerto Rico.

Although a few lesbian filmmakers had contributed lesbian-identified works in an earlier period, including *In the Best Interest of the Children* (Iris Films, 1977), in the 1980s and 1990s lesbian filmmakers turned to the task of documenting lesbian histories. These films include *Before Stonewall* (Robert Rosenberg, John Scagliotti, Greta Schiller, 1984), *Nitrate Kisses* (Barbara Hammer, 1992), *Forbidden Love* (Aerlyn Weissman and Lynne Fernie, 1992), *L Is for the Way You Look* (Jean Carlomusto, 1990), *Not Just Passing Through* (Jean Carlomusto, Dolores Perez, Catherine Saalfield, and Polly Thistlethwaite, 1994), and *Greetings from Out Here* (Ellen Spiro, 1993). Reconstructing histories that had been marginalized or even obliterated posed particular problems for documentary filmmakers. Whereas some filmmakers relied solely on interviews to supply historical information, others developed innovative techniques to mark lacunae in the historical record. In *Nitrate Kisses*, for example, Hammer edited fragments of sound interviews over repeated images of architectural ruins and an older lesbian couple making love, as if to emphasize both the transient and material nature of a history of private life.

Another historical development that changed the course of feminism and feminist documentary in the post-1970s era was a series of highly charged debates over feminism's relationship to sexuality. In the late 1970s, anti-pornography activism developed from political work on rape and domestic violence. Bonnie Klein's *Not A Love Story* (1981) recruited stripper and performance artist Lindalee Tracey to investigate the pornography industry. Relying heavily on interviews with American anti-porn activists, the film's narrative structure enacts Tracey's conversion to a feminist position. Not all feminists, however, agreed on feminism's proper relationship to pornography. Many feminists were concerned that anti-pornography activism was too easily co-opted by the right and that anti-pornography activists' tendency to conflate the representation of an act with the act itself could ultimately be extended to a broader argument for censorship. Critics of anti-pornography feminism argued that it created a dichotomous and essentialist view of male and female sexuality. The movement for a "sex-positive" feminism was committed to a greater diversity of female sexual expression. Lesbian feminists, who had, at times, occupied an uneasy place in second wave feminism, were prominent in the sex-positive movement, as well as in third world feminist movements. German filmmaker Monika Treut's 1992 documentary *Female Misbehavior*

might be considered a documentary manifesto for diversity of female sexual expression. Composed of four short films, it features sex-positive performance artist Annie Sprinkle, controversial feminist author Camille Paglia, an experimental segment on S/M bondage, and a portrait of female-to-male transsexual Max Valerio.

The career of British filmmaker Pratibha Parmar illustrates some of the institutional structures and aesthetic strategies that informed feminist documentary in the 1980s and 1990s. In the early 1980s, Parmar was a graduate student in the Cultural Studies program at the University of Birmingham, where she contributed to *The Empire Strikes Back: Race and Racism in 70s Britain*, the influential volume that challenged traditional thinking about race, ethnicity, and British identity. In this context, Parmar began to make documentaries that dealt with racism and homophobia at the intersections of gender, class, and nation. Films like *Sari Red* and *Khush* juxtaposed traditional tactics, such as interviews, with more poetic, abstract sequences. Parmar's films often feature staged tableaux or sequences of dance. Rather than using interviews to explain or interpret the images, Parmar allows the connections between the parts to remain open-ended, as if to prevent the illusion of definitive knowledge. In *Khush*, a film about gay men and lesbians in India and the Indian diaspora, Parmar stages the interviews in blatantly constructed environments that feature highly saturated colors, dramatic lighting, and works of art. The *mise-en-scène* calls attention to interviews as rhetorical tools for representation and self-representation. Although documentary interviews may have the potential to communicate immediacy and transparency, Parmar's interviewees emphasize the construction of identity in a context that is layered with racism, classism, sexism, and homophobia.

Parmar's career also demonstrates some of the continuing influence of the civil rights movements of the 1960s and 1970s on feminist documentary filmmaking. Parmar's connections with civil rights activists from the United States, including June Jordan, Alice Walker, and Angela Davis, have formed the basis for some of her projects, including *Warrior Marks* (1993) and *A Place of Rage* (1991). Television, particularly Britain's Channel Four, has been a source of funding and distribution for Parmar's work; and Parmar's *Righteous Babes* (1998), a film about women in rock music, evidences a more traditional television aesthetic, with a declarative, authoritative (albeit female) voice-over and interviews with critics such as Camille Paglia and Gloria Steinem.

In the opening moments of *Righteous Babes*, the narrator asserts that "feminism is still an urgent and vital force." The film articulates that the continued relevance of feminism has been a major concern for third wave feminists, the generation of feminists born after 1964. In defining itself, third wave feminism has tended to emphasize issues of sexuality and culture, embracing complex female icons like Madonna for their ability to reconcile explicit sexuality and personal and professional power. Julia Query and Vicky Funari's *Live Nude Girls Unite* (2000) highlights these differences in style and substance. The film follows dancers at a peep show in San Francisco as they fight for the right to unionize. As a dancer, union organizer, and feminist, director Query is committed to recuperating sex work as a site of agency and empowerment. The film stages a confrontation between Query and her mother, a second wave feminist and advocate for street prostitutes, as a conflict between feminist generations. Lourdes Portillo's later work also wrestles with the complex connections between gender, consumption, and desire, but in the context of the new global economy. Portillo's career overlaps with second wave feminism, but the evolution of her work also suggests some of the changing foci of feminist activism and filmmaking in the third wave era. While her 1985 film, *Las Madres: The Mothers of the Plaza de Mayo*, reflected a more traditional orientation for activist filmmaking, *Corpus: A Home Movie for Selena* (1999), which focused on fans of the murdered Tejana pop star, Selena Quintanilla, suggested something of feminists' evolving interest in cultural production and consumption as important sites for community, identity, and resistance. Portillo's work has been consistently international in scope, and her 2002 film, *Seniorita Extraviada: Missing Young Woman*, which investigated the unsolved murders of more than 370 young women in Juarez, Mexico, spoke to third wave feminism's transnational orientation and commitment to social justice broadly defined.

The career of feminist documentary filmmaker Allie Light spans conflicts and transformations in feminism and suggests the continued relevance, and even radicalism, of the themes and aesthetics of early feminist documentaries. In the 1990s, Light and her partner, Irving Saraf, created two documentaries about women and medical institutions, *Dialogues with Madwomen* (1993) and *Rachel's Daughters: The Search for the Causes of Breast Cancer* (1997). Both films rely heavily on interview testimony, but both films use interviews in ways that interrogate the construction of expertise in medicine *and* documentary. *Dialogues with Madwomen* focused on a diverse group of women's narratives

of mental illness and institutionalization. The collected interviews function like a consciousness-raising group; certain shared experiences make possible a political analysis of hierarchical doctor/patient relationships and the resulting marginalization of women's experiences. But whereas *Dialogues* relies heavily on testimony as a means of giving voice to women's experiences, the film also includes surreal staged images and reenactments that point to the limitations of realist representation. These staged sequences encourage viewer identification with emotional states that cannot be empirically observed or fully known through the language of testimony. Many of Light's investigative and aesthetic strategies, including her use of first-person narration, her frequent appearance within the frame, and the inclusion of her own story with those of the other women, call attention to the relationship between investigator and subject, knower and known. Although these representational choices recall Trinh's call for a more embodied documentary filmmaking that does not reinforce simplistic notions of self and other, their theoretical foundations can also be traced back to the early women's health movement. In fact, Light herself provides a living link; she was a member of the collective that created *Self-Health* in 1974.

Health and health care have continued to be compelling issues for feminist filmmakers. In the late 1980s and early 1990s, feminist documentary filmmakers Ellen Spiro (*DiAna's Hair Ego: AIDS Info Upfront*, 1990), Jean Carlomusto (*Doctors, Liars, and Women*, 1988), Barbara Hammer (*Snow Job*, 1986), Pratibha Parmar (*Reframing AIDS*, 1987), and many others used their medium to inform women about HIV/AIDS, to document AIDS activism, and to mourn the loss of friends and loved ones. Other films, such as *Dark Circle* (Chris Beaver, 1982), *A Healthy Baby Girl* (Judith Helfand, 1996), and *Rachel's Daughters*, have explored the thicket of technological developments, environmental hazards, corporate interests, and women's health. Given the complex dynamics of power and knowledge that characterize such issues, these projects have pushed filmmakers to explore the filmmaker-subject relationship and develop new modes of production. Whereas some have attempted to resolve these dilemmas by turning the camera on themselves, others have looked to feminist documentary's tradition of collective and collaborative filmmaking. In *Rachel's Daughters*, Light and Saraf recruited eight breast cancer survivors, asked them to generate questions about environmental causes of breast cancer, and filmed these eight women as they interviewed leading researchers and doctors. The personal experience of the breast cancer survivors disrupts the traditional relationship between experts and lay people. The survivors lay claim to a powerful form of knowledge of their own, and they frequently push the scientists to examine their own personal investment in breast cancer research, thereby exploding the notion of scientific research as disembodied and objective and upsetting the valuation of facts over experience. While Light and Saraf retained authorial credit, they did involve the participants in the process of setting the agenda and gave them veto power in the editing process. Their process is not completely collaborative and nonhierarchical, but Light and Saraf's work reflects an awareness of power relations between filmmaker and subject and a commitment to what the editors of *Feminism and Documentary* (1999) call "shared goal documentary practices," which may, ultimately, be feminism's most enduring contribution to the documentary tradition.

PAIGE SCHILT

Further Reading

Johnston, Claire, "Women's Cinema as Counter Cinema," in *Feminism and Film*, edited by E. Ann Kaplan. Oxford: Oxford University Press, 2000.

Juhasz, Alexandra, "'They said we were trying to show reality—all I want is to show my video': The Politics of the Realist Feminist Documentary." *Screen* 36, summer 1994, 2.

Kaplan, E. Ann, "Theories and Strategies of the Feminist Documentary," in *New Challenges for Documentary*, edited by Alan Rosenthal Berkeley, CA: University of California Press, 1988.

Lesage, Julia, "The Political Aesthetics of the Feminist Documentary Film," in *Issues in Feminist Film Criticism*, edited by Patricia Erens, Bloomington, IN: Indiana University Press, 1990.

Martineau, Barbara, "Talking about Our Lives and Experiences: Some Thoughts about Feminism, Documentary, and 'Talking Heads,'" in *Show Us Life: Toward a History and Aesthetics of the Committed Documentary*, edited by Thomas Waugh, Metuchen, NJ: Scarecrow Press, 1984.

McCormick, Ruth, "Women's Liberation Cinema," in *The Documentary Tradition*, edited by Lewis Jacobs, New York: W.W. Norton and Company, 1979.

Rich, B. Ruby, *Chick Flicks: Theories and Memories of the Feminist Film Movement*, Durham, NC: Duke University Press, 1998.

Rosenberg, Jan, *Women's Reflections: The Feminist Film Movement*, Ann Arbor, MI: UMI Research Press, 1983.

Trinh, T. Minh-ha, *When the Moon Waxes Red: Representation, Gender, and Cultural Politics*, London: Routledge, 1991.

Waldman, Diane, and Janet Walker, editors, *Feminism and Documentary*, Minneapolis: University of Minnesota Press, 1999.

FEMINISM: NORTH AMERICA

From its birth in the 1970s, North American feminist documentary has been concerned with the best way to represent women's oppression. From the 1970s, many second wave feminist filmmakers were drawn to documentary for economic, political, and social reasons and because documentaries were less expensive to produce than fiction. It was more accessible because it could be made by semi-amateurs. It was appealing ideologically as well, as it could best capture the "reality" of women's lives, a central theme in nonfiction feminist film.

Feminist filmmakers of the second wave were at the forefront of the documentary film movement, as it could document "ordinary life," so central to the feminist project of making the personal political. They entered the traditionally male domain of filmmaking and found a place for themselves; out of necessity and in an effort to expand their audience, feminist documentary filmmakers created institutions for production and distribution outside of mainstream mass media. Many of these institutions exist today as models of women-run businesses and nonhierarchal educational institutions that continue to support feminist documentary filmmakers, although the opportunities for feminist film have expanded enormously since the 1970s.

The prominence of documentary was also determined at a functional level within the women's movement. Issues that women felt were important to discuss often lent themselves to the documentary form, such as health care, history, autobiography, family life, and sexuality. The effort to tell the truth, so central to documentary, is interwoven into the feminist project, with its emphasis on exposing the truths of women's lives. This has been done by North American feminist documentary filmmakers working in video and 16mm, many of whom entered the field as assistants to male filmmakers.

Because women had been historically misrepresented by mass media, and because documentary film is important as a means of granting legitimacy, the effort to present the "real" has been a central preoccupation of feminist filmmakers. Documentary film also fits well into the social and political objectives of the movement, which were to debunk the myths promoted by mainstream media and to retell the stories of women's lives. Direct cinema, in particular, was a philosophy and technique of filmmaking that appealed to women, as it has the elements of nonobtrusiveness, objectivity, and equality that encouraged subjects to speak for themselves. Many feminists are deeply concerned with showing reality from a female perspective. Films are also used as consciousness-raising tools, as it is assumed that by watching the film, viewers will be transformed and their consciousness raised by finally knowing the truth. Indeed, consciousness-raising groups were not only a model of viewership but also a source of content. For instance, the documentary *Women's Film* (1971), by the San Francisco Newsreel Group, records a consciousness-raising group, as does *The Politics of Intimacy* (1972).

Feminist documentary film has used oppositional as opposed to traditional methods, in both theory and practice. In terms of production, the collaborative filmmaking process in which many women participate in many parts of the film has been set against the traditional griersonian form of documentary. The individual filmmaker is replaced by a collective vision. Similarly, the address of the film reflects an effort to debunk the authoritative eye of the filmmaker. The direct cinema's access to reality without the intervention of an organizing point of view was seen as a distortion of the truth.

The construction of truth from an early feminist documentary perspective, which was uncritical in its belief that the documentary conveys truth without distortion, was produced using a number of techniques including direct interviews with women, various kinds of photographic evidence such as snapshots and home films, and more traditional sources such as journals, oral history, and filmed conversations. Other conventions of North American feminist documentary include collaborative production, reflecting values of shared labor and rejection of individualism, a lack of a narrative authoritative voice, the conveying of women's shared experiences through multiple interviews,

and the use of natural lighting. Many of these films are defined primarily by their collaborative methodology. Films also could bring into focus the relation of women to political events. As such they challenged the exclusive reality that documentary constructs through supplementing and displacing the terms in which that reality was conceived. But simply making women present historical events failed to analyze the subsidiary role they actually sometimes played in relation to these events.

The thematic concerns of early feminist documentary mirrored those of the larger feminist movement including health care, economic equality, and oppression. The Canadian films, *Prison for Women* (Holly Dale and Janis Cole, 1981) and *Yes We Can* (Louise Giguère and Louise LeMay, 1981), cover issues relating to prison and women in the workforce, respectively. Other themes include childcare and balancing motherhood and a career in *Joyce at 34* (1972) and *The Emerging Woman* (Helen Solbert Ladd, 1974). Young women's socialization and institutionalized sexism are examined in *Growing Up Female* (Julia Reichert and Jim Klein, 1971) and *My American Girls: A Dominican Story* (Aaron Mathews, 2001). Female sexuality and teenage pregnancy are considered in *Looking for Love* (Tami Gold & C. Vogel, 1986). *Taking Our Bodies Back: The Women's Health Movement* (1974) documents the development of the women's health movement, shows how women learned self-help treatments for simple health problems, and tells how many women turned to women's health groups for advice. Ayoka Chenzira's *Hair Piece* (1985) shows an African-American perspective on beauty, as does the Canadian film *Black, Bold and Beautiful: Women's Hair* (Nadine Valcin, 1999). Indeed, racism is a central theme in feminist documentary films, including *And Still I Rise* (Ngozi Onwurah, 1993). Narrating the diaspora is also a theme of films by women of color including Salem Mekuria's award winning *Ye Wonz Maibel* (1997). Women's hobbies and sports are also legitimated through documentary as in Sally Price's 2003 film *Cow Girls*.

Other films take a more traditional approach to this content in order to gain legitimacy with mixed audiences. The powerful *La Operacion* (Anna M. Garcia) uses standard documentary techniques, including a voice-over to argue that since the 1930s, the American government's efforts to control Puerto Rico's population by sterilizing its women has served the business interests of American corporations located there. The beauty industry is addressed in the more polemic taped lecture format of the popular *Killing Us Softly* series (Margaret Lazarus) featuring professor Jean Kilbourne on the portrayal of women in advertising and the effects of advertising on women and their self-image. Not surprisingly, feminism itself has been an important topic reflected in a focus on women's history in *The Emerging Woman* (Helen Soldbert Ladd, 1974).

Correcting historical inaccuracy and marking women's contribution to labor history was an important use of these documentaries, which for the first time united the stories of multiple women to show the commonalties they faced and their unique struggles. This is reflected in the important early film *Union Maids* (Klein, Reichert, and Mogulescu, 1976), in which three women talk about their experiences as labor organizers in Chicago during the 1930s, as well as in *With Babies and Banners: Story of the Women's Emergency Brigade* (1978), which described the role of women in the General Motors sit-down strike, 1936–1937, especially the formation, success, and subsequent disbanding of the Women's Emergency Brigade. These films use direct interview cut with representations of the past events, oral history on film, and newsreel footage to validate the place in history of working class women. Similarly, the popular *Life and Times of Rosie the Riveter* (Connie Field, 1980) tells the story of working women during World War II. Sylvia Moreales's *Chicana* (1978) is the first film history of the Mexican American women's struggle.

As in many feminist documentaries, the women are the central authoritative voices. These films have been criticized for using sources of "truth" such as newsreel footage uncritically, thus contributing to the notion that truth is accessible and occasionally also produced by traditional sources. Concern with women workers continues as a central theme in feminist documentary and has included the struggle of women in the global marketplace including *The Global Assembly Line* (Lorraine Gray). Indeed, many women were involved in documentaries concerning American foreign policy in Central America including *Nicaragua: Report from the Front* (1984, Deborah Shaffer, Ana Maria Garcia, and Glenn Silber) and three other films directed by Deborah Shaffer, the Academy Award winner *Witness to War* (1984), *Fire from the Mountain* (1987), and *Dance of Hope* (1989) shot in Chile. Canadian Nettie Wile's 1988 *A Rustling of Leaves: Inside the Philippine Revolution* is another important contribution to social documentary. Barbara Kopple's feature documentaries, *Harlan County USA* (1976) and *American Dream* (1990), although not explicitly about women, focus on the daily life of working people shaped by economic struggle.

Controversy with regard to pornography has been an ongoing feature of the feminist documen-

tary film movement paralleling the concern within the feminist debates over censorship, control of female sexuality, and the role of pornography. *Rate It X* (Lucy Winer and Paula De Koenigsberg, 1986) chronicled the pornography industry in direct cinema style to show the "real people" behind it and the degrading conditions that women face, as did *Not a Love Story* (Bonnie Sherr Kline, 1981). Responses to these films, which show the dangers of the pornography industry, have included documentaries that show the pleasures of female sexuality. A range of sex-positive films, which are also used educationally, for pleasure, and for art, have also been produced. Early films that sought to construct a feminist sexuality in film included Carolee Scheneemann's early *Fuses* (1967), Barbara Hammer's *SuperDyke*, and Lizzie Borden's *Regrouping* (1976). *We Are Ourselves* (1976) features two lesbians discussing their relationship and their sexual orientation and features explicitly sexual sequences.

Another major trend in documentary filmmaking has questioned the ability of film to capture truth and rejected realist strategies and modes of address. This counter-cinema has been theorized by feminists early in the movement. In particular Clarie Johnston's "Notes on Women's Cinema" challenged the status of woman as the source of truth given the complex ways in which women have been defined by discourse, including language, art history, economics, and political structures. Film, then, cannot use the "master's tools," to paraphrase Audre Lorde's famous call for a feminist revision of realist practices to dismantle the male cinema apparatus, bound as it is in the social practices that inherently are opposed to women's liberation. This kind of film then would deconstruct the psychic structure of subjectivity suggested by Laura Mulvey's analysis of gendered subjectivity and specularity (that is, the "male gaze").

One way of intervening in the system of gazes that defines cinema from this perspective is to put into place a feminine cinematic writing that self-consciously introduced "women's way of seeing and knowing" a feminist ontology expressed in films such as Yvonne Rainer's *Lives of Performers* (1972) and *Daughter Rite* (Citron, 1978). These films challenge spectator–text relations by privileging a feminine voice. *Lives of Performers*, for instance, draws from documentary filmmaking genre, as the performers actually play themselves; however, the film refuses any narrative closure, blurring the boundaries between the real and the constructed, the documentary and the fictional film. The film draws attention to the presence of the director, in a kind of Brechtian distancing device, unlike the hidden directorial presence of direct cinema and the hidden apparatus of filmmaking that defines Hollywood filmmaking practices. Similarly, *Daughter Rite* is an autobiographical film that speaks in the first person and shares elements of traditional feminist documentary filmmaking, but also subverts the audience's expectations. In the film, she reedits the family film to reveal the conflict between mother and daughter, wresting the mother away from the power of the father, through the film. Mixed modes of address, a synthesis of two different mothers in the film, and the use of different kinds of footage and film stock blur the boundaries between truth and fiction. Taking on father-daughter relationships, Su Friderich's autobiographical 1990 documentary, *Sink or Swim*, reworks a traditional documentary format by combining images from family vacations, the circus, and Death Valley, interlaced with her voice-over, suggest an unreachable distance, culminating in her father's betrayal.

Women of color have challenged the ability of realism to reflect their reality, given the history of ethnographic anthropological films that featured the person of color as exotic other. This cannot be addressed simply by telling the truth some filmmakers have argued. Trinh T. Minh Ha's *Surname Viet Given Name Nam* is an important documentary that argues the impossibility to represent the "truth" in a documentary film. This extraordinary documentary plays with the viewer's racialized expectations and historical privilege in a groundbreaking way, as does her earlier film, *Reassemblage* (1982), which also reflects on documentary filmmaking and the ethnographic. Feminist documentary has taken new forms and has even reached more mainstream distribution through the expansion of women's network cable programming. These documentaries rely on traditional documentary techniques, including Meema Spadola's 1996 HBO film *Breasts: A Documentary*.

Lesbian filmmakers have produced both historical and critical documentaries. Among the most prolific is veteran Barbara Hammer who has produced many important documentaries including her trilogy of documentary film essays on lesbian and gay history, *Nitrate Kisses* (1992), *Tender Fictions* (1995), and *History Lessons* (2000), which have received numerous awards. Many lesbian documentaries have used the format to reveal hidden lives and debunk media mythology, such as the clever *Forbidden Love: The Unashamed Stories of Lesbian Lives* by Aerlyn Weissman and Lynne Fernie, which paints a portrait of lesbian sexuality in Canada during the 1950s and 1960s. The film is set against a fascinating backdrop of book covers from lesbian pulp novels, tabloid headlines, archival photographs, and film clips.

Many early filmmakers chose to work in 16mm. However, documentary filmmakers have produced an important body of work in the video format that provided a lighter, more portable camera, less expensive film, and expanded opportunities for distribution including the newly formed pubic access cable stations. Distribution was another concern for documentary filmmakers. In relation to the rise of activity in the 1970s, there was a burgeoning of feminist filmmaking activity in the 1970s that included the production of important documentaries, film festivals, and journals focusing on feminist film. The first big women's film festivals in North America were held in New York City in 1972 and Toronto in 1973 and later, the Chicago Film by Women festival and the second New York International Festival of Women's Film (1976). The magazine *Jump Cut*, co-edited by feminist filmmaker Julia Lesage, premiered in 1974. Women Make Movies continues to be a central distribution and production center for feminist documentary as does New Day Films and the Filmmaker's Library. In Canada, besides the National Film Board, which sponsors feminist documentary films, Video Femmes is a center that independently produces films and videos and has also acted as a distribution center in Quebec City since 1974, with an emphasis on Quebecoise women's lives. Cinefocus Canada and the National Film Board of Canada also distribute documentaries about Canadian and Native women's lives.

New York's Downtown Community Television Center, founded in 1972 by Jon Alpert and Keiko Tsuno, trained many early video activists spawned by the growing public access movement. Paper Tiger Television and Deep Dish TV produced feminist media and analysis such as Martha Rosler's *Born To Be Sold* (Paper Tiger Television, 1986), which discusses the social and economic implications of surrogate motherhood using excerpts and quotations from media reports and court records of the Mary Beth Whitehead/Baby M case. Similarly, *Joan Does Dynasty* (1986), *Always Love Your Man* (Cara DeVito, 1975), and *The Mom Tapes* (Illene Segalove, 1974–1978) are personal, homemade feminist documentaries. Other recent areas of video activism documentary have recorded and analyzed the AIDS crisis movement. (In New York, the female-driven acquired immune deficiency syndrome, AIDS, activist video collectives included Testing the Limits, DIVA TV, and the WAVE project.)

DANIELLE SCHWARTZ

See also Joyce at 34; Klein, James; Life and Times of Rosie the Riveter, The; Reichert, Julia; Trinh T. Minh Ha; Union Maids

Further Reading

Armitage, Kay, Kass Banning, Brenda Longfellow, and Janine Marchessault, editors, *Gendering the Nation: Canadian Women's Cinema*, Toronto: University of Toronto.

Banning, Kass, "The Canadian Feminist Hybrid Documentary," in *CineAction 26/27*, winter, 1992, 108–113.

Becker, Edith, Michelle Citron, Julia Lesage, and B. Ruby Rich, "Lesbians and Film" in *Out in Culture: Gay, Lesbian and Queer Essays on Popular Culture*, edited by Coreey K. Creekmur and Alexander Doty, Durham, NC: Duke University Press, 1995.

Gaines, Jane, "White Privilege and Looking Relations: Race and Gender in Feminist Film Theory," in *Multiple Voices in Feminist Film Criticism*, edited by Diane Carson, Linda Dittmar, and Janice R. Welsch, 176–190.

Gever, Martha, "The Feminism Factor: Video and Its Relationship to Feminism," in *Illuminating Video*, edited by Hall and Fifer, San Francisco: Aperture Press and Bay Area Video Coalition.

Gibson-Hudson, Gloria, "Aspects of Black Feminist Cultural Ideology in Films by Black Women Independent Artists," *Multiple Voices in Feminist Film Criticism*, edited by Diane Carson, Linda Dittmar, and Janice R. Welsch.

Johnston, Claire, "Women's Cinema as Counter Cinema," in *Notes on Women's Cinema*, edited by Claire Johnston, London: Screen Pamphlet 2, Society for Education in Film and Television, 1973.

Kaplan, E. Ann, "Theories and Strategies of the Feminist Documentary," *New Challenges for Documentary*, 78–102.

Kuhn, Annette, *Women's Pictures*, London: Routledge and Kegan Paul, 1982.

Mulvey, Laura, "Visual Pleasure and Narrative Cinema," *Screen*, 16, 3, fall, 1975, 6–18.

Larkin, Alile Sharon, "Black Women Filmmakers Defining Ourselves: Feminism in Our Own Voice," *Female Spectators*, edited by Diedre Pribram, London: Verso Press, 1988, 157–173.

Lesage, Julia, "Political Aesthetics of the Feminist Documentary Film," *Quarterly Review of Film Studies*, fall, 1978.

———, "Feminist Documentary: Aesthetics and Politics," in *Show Us Life: Toward a History and Aesthetics of the Committed Documentary*, edited by Thomas Waugh, Metuchen, NJ: Scarecrow, 1984.

———, "Women's Fragmented Consciousness in Feminist Experimental Autobiographical Video" *Feminism and Documentary*, edited by Diane Waldman and Janet Walker.

McGarry, Eileen, "Documentary, Realism and Women's Cinema," *Women and Film*, 2, 7, 1975.

Rabinowitz, *They Must Be Represented: The Politics of Documentary*, London: Verso, 1994.

Rich, B. Ruby, "ChickFlicks: Theories and Memories of the Feminist Film Movement," in *Feminism and Documentary*, edited by Diane Waldman and Janet Walker, Minneapolis: University of Minnesota Press, 1999.

Waugh, Tom, "Lesbian and Gay Documentary: Minority Self-Imagine Opposition Film Practice and Question of Image Ethics," in *Image Ethics: The Moral and Legal Rights of Subjects in Documentary Film and Television*, edited by Larry Gross, John Katz, and Jay Ruby, Philadelphia: Annenberg Communication Series, 1985.

Williams, Linda, and B. Ruby Rich, "The Right of Re-Vision: Michelle Citron's *Daughter Rite*," in *Movies and Methods*, II, 359–368.

FEMINISM: UNITED KINGDOM

Feminist documentaries that state their agenda openly have been made in the United Kingdom only since the late 1960s, but British women filmmakers have been using the camera from as early as the 1920s to look at familiar elements of daily life and to define them in a new way.

In the silent period, Mary Field, Evelyn Spice, and sisters Marion and Ruby Grierson took advantage of the camaraderie and pioneering spirit of the time by joining the British documentary movement, where they made opportunities for themselves and other women to enter the system of film production. Field is noted for her work on the *Secrets of Nature* series (1922–1933), including *The Mystery of Marriage* (1931), a comparison, for educational purposes, of the courtship and marriage rituals of humans, animals, and plants, and for her inauguration, in 1944, of the children's entertainment division of British Instructional Films; Spice (born in Canada, but working in the United Kingdom) for her 1937 short *Job in a Million*. The Grierson sisters are primarily known today as John Grierson's assistants, but Mary edited a number of films from his footage (in particular *King Log*), and Ruby is generally credited with the direction (although she is listed in the credits as "assistant") of what can be seen, in retrospect, as the first feminist documentary, *Housing Problems* (1935), in which a female slum dweller tells the story of her encounter with a rat. Although the woman's story is framed by a traditional, masculine use of visuals and overlaid with a strong upper-class male commentary interpreting these images, her individual spirit comes across strongly. It is a remarkable representation of an English woman telling her own story in her own words.

Both Marion and Ruby can be considered to have contributed to John's renowned "creative treatment of actuality," and their influence and impact on the movement may yet be critically underestimated. Although not strictly feminist filmmakers, in the sense that their works were in no way reflective of any ideological commitment to the women's liberation cause, their output is an achievement in itself, viewed in the context of the 1930s documentary movement—a conservative institution almost exclusively composed of white, middle-class male filmmakers (and led by Grierson, a man openly hostile to feminine ideas—(see Aitken, 1998). Paul Rotha has written of them as "women directors" who "handled their characters with greater sympathy than is found in other documentaries of the Grierson group" (Rotha, 1952, p. 150).

During World War II, women were among many filmmakers employed to make films for the Ministry of Information. Muriel Box, once a continuity girl, began directing short documentaries before moving onto feature films. So too did Stella Court-Treatt and Kay Mander. Although the works of these women rarely deal explicitly with gender issues, they frequently reflect issues of work and domesticity and are indicative of the growing role for women in British film at the time. In the postwar period, directors such as Jill Craigie started to make documentaries that made some effort to promote women's causes, of which *To Be A Woman* (1951) is arguably the most politically committed.

At the time of the British New Wave Movement, two women directors contributed to the Free Cinema programme, showing at the NFT between 1956 and 1959: Lorenza Mazzetti, an Italian based in the United Kingdom (*Together*, 1956, directed with Denis Horne), and Elizabeth Russell (*Food for a Blush*, 1955, directed with Nicholas Ferguson). While neither film can be definitively categorised as documentary, as they both include strong fictional elements, they are significant for two reasons. First, seen in sequence with the other films from the programme, they stand out in their difference to the male-directed films; each uses a more refined means

of expression (long takes, formal composition, slow editing rhythms) and so express a woman's view to serve as a much-needed counterpoint to the other films of the movement. Second, by using documentary elements and taking the working class of Britain as a backdrop to an examination of other themes, Mazzetti's film in particular used a trope that would be taken up, to great effect, by the next generation of female documentary makers.

It was not until the early 1970s that feminism and women's consciousness really began to influence the content of documentary films. Feminist academics, in particular Laura Mulvey and Claire Johnston, began to produce a formidable amount of scholarship, working in tandem with activists and artists and later directing their own films. Women began to engage in debates about their position in society and the ways women were represented in film, television, and advertising and to respond with works of their own. Women's filmmaking collectives, such as the London Women's Film Group, the Hackney Flashers Collective, or the Sheffield Film Co-op in the 1970s, which were motivated, at least in part, by an interest in the use of the moving image as a medium for addressing feminist concerns, played a vital role in the dialectic between theory and practice. Using film and television as a communication tool to meet and educate women, these groups began working within communities in regional locations, producing documentaries such as *Women of the Rhondda* (1972, director, Esther Ronay), which examines the role played by women during the gruelling Welsh Miners' Strikes of the 1920s and 1930s, and *The Nightcleaners* (1975, director, Claire Johnston).

Although they were predominantly comprised of middle-class, educated white women, the film collectives are often described as socialist feminist documentary groups, concerned not only with feminist causes but with wider sociopolitical concerns. Both of the aforementioned films are typical of the movement's work in that they involve the relationship between sexual oppression and class exploitation. In *The Nightcleaners,* the feminist intervention redefines what we mean by "the class struggle." The film avoids the trap of presenting the working class as an ideologically homogenous bloc and focuses on its internal contradictions, such as the woman who continues to do night work even though it will most likely kill her, not because she cannot afford childcare, but because she can't trust anyone else with her children. It is worth noting that the film was badly received by the women's liberation movement, who felt it was too theoretical, and not sufficiently agitational. Certainly the documentaries produced by British female filmmakers of the time were much less rhetorical than those of their U.S. and Canadian equivalents, as can be evidenced by comparing *The Nightcleaners* with a film such as Barbara Kopple's *Harlan County, USA*, which tackles a similar theme with much more emotional engagement.

The arrival in 1982 of Channel 4, with its remit to cater for "minority audiences," gave work to a greater number of women film and video directors. Although there was no specific remit to support women's work, both Channel 4 and BBC 2 commissioned a number of documentary series by women, including the weekly current affairs programmes *20/20 Vision* and *Broadside*, and the magazine show *Watch the Woman*. Through the BFI's education department and production fund there was some temporary support for British feminist films and funding for feminist distributors. During the 1990s, shifts in politics and a transformation of production and exhibition technologies allowed greater accessibility to the media, but the new market economy and a backlash against feminism contributed to a move away from overtly feminist practice. From this background arose a new breed of female documentary maker, exemplified by Molly Dineen, less concerned with gender issues and more with commercialism.

Dineen's early documentaries, made for BBC 2, focus on "human-interest" stories such as the rebuilding of a tube station (*Heart of the Angel,* 1989) and London Zoo (*The Ark, 1993*) and follow the daily lives of everyday people and institutions, subject matter not far removed from the films of the seventies collectives, albeit much less concerned with issues of gender. As Dineen's career developed, however, a significant shift in subject matter occurred, a change that becomes noticeable with *In the Company of Men* (1995). From the portrayal of everyday people, Dineen moved on to an elite army regiment, and from herein her work has taken a much more celebrity-focused turn. Her most recent films take as their subjects a pop star (*Geri,* 1999), a prime minister (*Tony Blair*, 1997), and a peer of the House of Lords (*The Lord's Tale,* 2002). As a subject for comparison with other "star" documentary makers such as Nick Broomfield or the American Michael Moore, Dineen's films are remarkable for their less aggressive, more mediatory approach to their subjects, which is often attributed to the fact that they are made by a woman, and she has certainly succeeded in forging a career in a field dominated by men. But Dineen is perhaps most noteworthy for her lack of feminist sentiment and her adoption of a more traditional, masculine film format, totally divorced from the overtly feminist documentaries of the 1970s.

A parallel movement in women's documentary better echoed the sociopolitical concerns of the 1970s film collectives. Moving beyond the twin themes of class and gender to examine race and other hierarchies, women directors from ethnic minorities, such as Gurinder Chadha and Pratibha Parmar, continued to film everyday people and events, rather than celebrities. In their films, gender is always an important subject, but it is never figured in isolation, always in relation to class, ethnicity, nationality, or sexuality. Both women aim to produce new ways of seeing, new readings of the past (and present), and new images of interracial-looking relations. Like the feminist collectives that preceded and inspired them, they seek to intervene in the imaginary, and to change how images are produced, rather than to present minorities "as they really are." Parmar has been particularly prolific in the documentary genre and her work has seen international success. Her work, whilst often poetic in tone, combining documentary with dramatised episodes, tends to use popular culture—art, dance, music—to take on issues such as racial violence (*Sari Red),* what it is to grow up an Asian in Britain (*The Colour of Britain, Brimful of Asia),* and women's self-image (*The Righteous Babes*—an interesting counterpoint to Dineen's *Geri*). Like Mulvey and Johnston before her, she not only makes films but has also produced a substantial body of writings on film, which complements and informs her filmic oeuvre.

In many ways the work of Parmar and Chadha, amongst others, can be seen as an extension of the feminist collectives' socialist doctrine. Both directors are, for example, particularly interested in the situation of working class members of society. Despite the obvious influence of the 1970s feminist movement on these two women, however, their films to a certain extent constitute an attack on the white, middle-class origins of the filmmakers and theorists involved. It is their belief that, in representing the elements of the self that are considered "other" by dominant systems of representation, an act of reclamation, empowerment, and self-definition occurs. Put more simply, their works are aimed at righting the popular misconception that "racism is what happens to Black men . . . sexism is what happens to White women" (Smith, 1999). Significantly, the emphasis within their works is on the mainstream accessibility of concepts such as feminism, a radical departure from the theoretical esotericism of their predecessors.

It is now widely accepted that all documentary is subjective, in which case, any documentary made by a woman is worthy of consideration when discussing "feminist documentary," as its very composition is a statement of the female way of looking. To look separately at the role of women in the field of documentary in Britain is to recognise that the experiences of women in these areas are somehow different to those of men, hence the importance of directors such as Spice and Dineen. The work by women in documentary production both reflects and informs the position of women within British society through connotative elements and visual cues, as well as more open statements. And today, despite the successes of Sally Potter, Lynne Ramsay, and now Gurinder Chadha with their fictional works, there are still relatively few British women directing feature films. In the areas of documentary and experimental film, however, women have directed a substantial body of work. This suggests that away from the constraints of the commercial film industry, greater opportunities still exist to explore the representation of women's lives and their subjective experience within Britain.

HELEN WHEATLEY

Selected Films

The Mystery of Marriage (1931, director Mary Field)
Job in a Million (1937, director Evelyn Spice)
Housing Problems (1935, director Edgar Anstey / Arthur Elton)
Women of the Rhondda (1972, director Esther Ronay)
The Nightcleaners (1975, director Claire Johnston)
To Be a Woman (1951, director Jill Craigie)
Together (1956, director Lorenza Mazzetti & Denis Horne)
Food for a Blush (1955, directors Elizabeth Russell & Nicholas Ferguson)
I'm British But... (1990, Gurinder Chadha)
What Do You Call an Indian Woman Who's Funny? (1990, Gurinder Chadha)
Sari Red (1998, Pratibha Parmar)
The Colour of Britain, (1994, Pratibha Parmar)
Brimful of Asia (1998, Pratibha Parmar)
The Righteous Babes (1998, Pratibha Parmar)
Heart of the Angel, (1989, director Molly Dineen,)
The Ark, (1993, director Molly Dineen)
In the Company of Men (1995, director Molly Dineen)
Geri, (1999, director Molly Dineen)
Tony Blair, (1997, director Molly Dineen)
The Lord's Tale, (2002, director Molly Dineen)

Further Reading

Humm, Maggie, *Feminism and Film*, Edinburgh: Edinburgh University Press, 1997.
Johnston, Claire, editor, *Notes on Women's Cinema*, London: Society for Education in Film and TV, 1973.
Juhasz, A., "They Said We Were Trying to Show Reality: All I Want to Show Is My Video: The Politics of the Realist Feminist Documentary," *Screen*, 35 (2), 1994.
Kaplan, E. Ann, *Feminism and Film*, Oxford: Oxford University Press, 1999.
———, *Women and Film: Both Sides of the Camera*, New York: Methuen, 1983.
Kuhn, Annette, *Women's Pictures*, London: Verso, 1994.
Leith, Jaqueline, Judith Pleiss, and Valerie Raoul, editors, *Women Filmmakers: Refocusing.*
Mayne, Judith, *The Woman at the Keyhole: Feminism and Women's Cinema*, Bloomington: Indiana University Press.
Mulvey, Laura, *Visual and Other Pleasures*, Bloomington and Indianapolis: Indianapolis University Press, 1989.
Parmar, Pratibha, Martha Gever, and John Greyson, *Queer Looks: Perspectives on Lesbian and Film Video*, Toronto: Between the Lines, 1993.
Rich, B. Ruby, *Chick Flicks: Theories and Memories: The Feminist Film Movement*, Durham & London: Duke University, 1998.
Rotha, Paul, *Documentary Film: The Use of the Film Medium to Interpret Creatively and in Social Terms the Life of the People as It Exists in Reality*, London: Faber, 1952.
Smith, Barbara, *The Truth That Never Hurts: Writings on Race, Gender and Freedom*, London: New Brunswick, 1999.
Waldman, Diane, and Janet Walker, editors, *Feminism and Documentary*, Minneapolis: University of Minnesota Press, 1999.
Waugh, Thomas, editor, *Show Us Life: Towards a History and Aesthetics of the Committed Documentary*, Metuchen, NJ & London: Scarecrow Press, 1985.
Wells, Paul. "The Documentary Form: Personal and Social 'Realities,'" in *An Introduction to Film Studies*, 2nd edition, Jill Nelmes, editor, London and New York: Routledge, 1999, 211–235.

FERNHOUT, JOHANNES HENDRIK

At the age of 15, John Fernhout started his career as assistant cameraman, and later cameraman, for Joris Ivens in 1928. He assisted Ivens in making *Rain* (1929) and was responsible for the photography of *New Earth* (1934), *The Spanish Earth* (1937), and *The 400 Million* (1939). He developed skills in photography and filmmaking and was also asked by Henri Storck to do the photography for, amongst other films, *Easter Island* (1935). After World War II Fernhout started working as an independent director, focusing mainly on postwar Holland and Europe. After World War II he more or less lost his political engagement in his films, focusing on educational productions. Fernhout was particularly appreciated for his skills filming landscapes and cloudy skies, and it was easy for people to make references to the famous Dutch painters, Fernhout being the son of a Dutch painter. In 1967, he made this link very explicit in his most well-known and best awarded (Golden Palm in Cannes) 70mm film, *Sky Over Holland*, which shows the parallels between Dutch paintings and the very particular Dutch skies. After moving to Jerusalem, Fernhout mainly made films in and about Israel, such as *The Tree of Life* (1971) and *Museum on the Hill* (1980). Toward the end of his life, Fernhout made three more films in the Netherlands: one about the different generations of painters in the Toorop family (*Three Generations*, 1983), and his last about the interplay between the preserved landscape of the Dutch National Park, De Hoge Veluwe, and the Kröller Muller Museum that is situated in that park. In his work Fernhout was often looking for the parallels between painting and filming, which is sometimes an explicit subject of his films, but more often an implicit quality of his filmmaking skills. Still, internationally he remains noted more for his collaborations with Ivens and Storck than for his own film work.

KEES BAKKER

Biography

Better known as John Ferno once his international career took shape. Born in 1913 as son of the philosopher Hendrik Fernhout and the painter Charley Toorop. Learned filmmaking as the 15-year-old assistant of Joris Ivens and started career first as cameraman before directing films himself. Married photographer Eva Besnyö in 1933 (divorced in 1945). Worked with Joris Ivens in 1930s and moved in 1939 to North America, where he worked for the National Film Board of Canada. Returned to the Netherlands in 1945 from where he made several educational films. From 1969 to 1980, worked mainly in Israel, where he died in 1987.

Selected Films

1965 *Fortress of Peace*
1967 *Sky Over Holland*
1971 *The Tree of Life*
1980 *Museum on the Hill*
1983 *Drie generaties/Three Generations*
1984 *Mijn generatie is zwart-wit/My Generation Is Black and White*
1985 *Het bewaarde landschap/The Preserved Landscape*

FERNO, JOHN

See **Fernhout, Johannes Hendrik**

FIELD, MARY

Surprisingly, for someone with such a prolific career in educational film, little has been written about Mary Field in histories of documentary film. No doubt this is because educational film in the 1930s existed on the fringes of the documentary movement, regarded by Grierson and his followers as little more than lecture films unlikely to make a contribution to the fuller art of documentary (Grierson, 1966). However, the natural history films made by Field and her colleagues are the forerunners of the popular wildlife television programmes of today and should not be dismissed because they did not fit Grierson's definition of documentary.

Field started her career as a teacher and historian. She was an authority on seventeenth-century fishing in the West Atlantic, and it was with this specialist knowledge that she entered the film industry. Visiting Bruce Woolfe's British Instructional studios in late 1925 to advise them on the historical accuracy of one of their films, she was offered a post as Education Manager. Within a year she had became a member of the production staff, learning editing, continuity, script writing, and direction while working on educational, documentary, and feature films. By 1927 she was directing for the famous pioneering biological and wildlife series, the *Secrets of Nature*, started by Bruce Woolfe in 1919. Working with the cinematographer Percy Smith, an expert in time lapse and macro-photography, Field helped create a series covering many aspects of the natural world including insects, plants, animals, and sea life. Compared with the sophisticated technology available to wildlife filmmakers today, the equipment used by Field and Smith was cumbersome and noisy; the lenses were so long and heavy that braces were used to fix them to the camera and tripod. This makes the results they achieved all the more remarkable. In 1929, Field became the *Secrets of Nature* series editor, as well as the director of more than fifty films for the series in the next four years. Other films directed during this period include the hygiene film *Deferred Payment* (1929) and the comedy feature *Strictly Business* (1932). She also edited the World War I drama, *Tell England* (1931).

When British Instructional was taken over in 1933, Field worked briefly for Woolfe's new company before joining Gaumont-British Films' recently formed educational unit, Gaumont-British Instructional. When Woolfe joined her, they continued to make nature films under a new moniker, *Secrets of Life*. Field also diversified her subject matter and began directing films for geography, history, language, physical education, and hygiene syllabi in schools. Invited on to the Board of Gaumont-British Instructional, Field exercised a decisive influence in both policy matters and in the making of the films themselves. She began experimenting with the use of animated diagrams for classroom films as is seen in two of her films, *The Expansion of Germany* (1936) and *Changes in the Franchise* (1937). She was also active in promoting the pedagogical use of film in the wider world and sat on various committees, notably the British Film Institute Panels. Her early years in teaching meant she understood the importance of tailoring educa-

tional films to the requirements of the classroom, and the knowledge she acquired from teachers on these committees was more often than not successfully translated to the screen.

During the war, along with other documentary and educational filmmakers, Field's skills were used in making government films for the war effort. Drawing on the images of the nature series she had edited and directed, Field humorously adapted the wildlife genre to the human and political concerns of rationing, agricultural production, and the use of pigeons as messengers by the army. These home-front propaganda films demonstrate a clarity of thought and assured direction that had become Field's hallmark in more than fifteen years of educational filmmaking.

In 1944, J. Arthur Rank set up the Children's Entertainment Division of the Rank Organisation to produce entertainment films for his Saturday morning Odeon and Gaumont Children's Cinema Clubs. With her background in the production of classroom films and an increasing interest in the need for children's entertainment films, Field was the logical choice to head the new division. Her initial attempts to provide stimulating entertainment for children were not well received by the industry or critics, and she was accused of not knowing what children wanted by a technician at the 1946 Association of Cinematograph Technicians' conference. Nevertheless, Field is a figure who stands out in an era when cinema was often attacked as a morally degenerative influence on children; her motivation was to broaden the experiences of children through entertaining but informative filmmaking, and this legacy remains with us today in public sector children's television programming such as *Blue Peter*. When financial cutbacks closed the Children's Entertainment Division, Field spent a year at the British Board of Film Classification before taking up the post of Executive Officer at the newly created Children's Film Foundation.

In 1954, Field was awarded an OBE for her work in educational and children's entertainment film. In 1955 she was made a fellow of both the Royal Photographic Society and the British Kinematograph Society. Two years later the British Film Academy awarded her the same status. Her final years were spent doing consultancy work for children's television programming, as well as founding an International Centre of Films for Children of which she became Honorary President until her death in 1968.

SARAH EASEN

See also **British Instructional Films**

Biography

Born in Wimbledon, London February 24, 1896. Graduated with an MA in history and became a teacher. Married Gerald Hankin in 1944. Fellow of the Royal Photographic Society, the British Kinematograph Society, and the British Film Academy; Order of the British Empire 1951. Education manager, British Instructional, 1926. Production assistant, continuity, editor, scriptwriter, director, British Instructional Films, 1927–1929. Director, producer, series editor: *Secrets of Nature*, British Instructional Films, 1929–1933. Production manager, British Independent Pictures, 1933. Series editor: *Secrets of Life*, director, producer, board member, Gaumont-British Instructional, 1934–1944. Chief Officer, Children's Entertainment Division of the Rank Organisation, 1944–1950. Examiner, British Board of Film Classification, 1950. Chief Executive Officer, Children's Film Foundation, 1951–1955. Chair/Honorary President, International Centre of Films for Children (Brussels) 1957–1968. Children's Programme Consultant, ATV/ABC Television, 1959–1963. Died in Worthing December 23, 1968.

Selected Filmography

1933 *Secrets of Nature* natural history series: series editor and director

1933–1942 *Secrets of Life* natural history series: series editor and director
1934 *Farming in Suffolk* series: director
1934–1939 *Farming in East Anglia* series: director
1935 *Face of Britain: This Was England*: director
1939 *They Made the Land*: director
1940 *Wisdom of the Wild*: director
1941 *Winged Messengers*: director
1943 *Development of an English Town*: director

Further Reading

Field, Mary, and Percy Smith, *Secrets of Nature*, London: The Scientific Book Club, 1939.
Field, Mary, *Good Company: The Story of the Children's Entertainment Film Movement in Great Britain, 1943–1950*, London: Longmans Green, 1952.
Grierson, John, *Grierson on Documentary*, edited by Forsyth Hardy, Revised edition, London: Faber, 1966.
Low, Rachael, *Documentary and Educational Films of the 1930s*, London: George Allen and Unwin, 1979.
MacNab, Geoffrey, *J. Arthur Rank and the British Film Industry*, London and New York: Routledge, 1993.
Thorpe, Frances, and Nicholas Pronay, with Clive Coultass, *British Official Films in the Second World War: A Descriptive Catalogue*, Oxford: Clio Press, 1980.

FILM AND PHOTO LEAGUE, THE

In the 1930s, a group of radical left filmmakers and photographers in the United States joined forces as the Film and Photo League. Deriving its mission from the economic crisis of the Great Depression, it aimed to document and to support the struggles of labor in the United States. In contrast to the frivolous short subjects and escapist features offered by Hollywood, the League's newsreels and documentaries strove to depict socially relevant events from a working-class perspective. Showing hunger marches, strikes, boycotts, evictions, and trials, these films rescued images that would have been lost otherwise.

The League did not function autonomously but was allied with other left-wing organizations of the era. It operated under the American chapter of the Workers International Relief (WIR), which was governed by the Communist International. Based in New York City, the Workers' Film and Photo League—called simply the Film and Photo League

(FPL) after 1933—emerged from The Workers' Camera League and The Labor Defender Photo Group in 1930. Initial membership included Lester Balog, Sam Brody, Tom Brandon, Robert Del Duca, Leo Hurwitz, Irving Lerner, and Leo Seltzer. At one time, Lewis Jacobs, David Platt, Jay Leyda, Ralph Steiner, and Harry Alan Potamkin belonged to the group.

League action took place on several fronts. Along with its own newsreels and features, the FPL distributed leftist films from Germany and the U.S.S.R. These comprised the programs shown in union halls, independent theaters, and in the weekly film series conducted at the New School for Social Research from 1933 to 1935. Members wrote criticism for periodicals such as *The Daily Worker, New Theater, Experimental Cinema*, and *Close Up*. In 1931 Potamkin published a thirteen-point program propounding a critical and practical agenda that included exposing the ideology of Hollywood film; promoting Soviet film as a model; combating censorship; boycotting racist, fascist, and anti-labor films; and training filmmakers. For the last purpose the Potamkin Film School was founded in 1934.

In filmmaking practice, the League sought an alternative to Hollywood cinema in both the message or content and the formal means used to deliver it. Influenced by Soviet filmmakers such as Dziga Vertov and Esther Schub, the League aspired to the practice of associative montage and occasionally effected powerful results. More often, however, the demands of making and distributing newsreels entailed aesthetic compromise. As Russell Campbell points out, once shot, raw footage was soon processed and printed, edited quickly, and screened immediately to exploit its timeliness. Only later would such material be synthesized into documentary form. If the League lacked Hollywood's resources, however, it also possessed certain advantages over the cumbersome studio mode of production. Armed with lightweight handheld 35mm cameras, League journalists could cover events the official press ignored or missed.

Newsreel production was especially vigorous during 1931 and 1932. These short items would eventually be edited into the series called *America Today*. The early documentaries focused on demonstrations such as the two national hunger marches (*National Hunger March* [1931], *Hunger 1932* [1933]), and the veterans' march for extended benefits (*Bonus March* [1932]). In 1934, Hurwitz drew on footage shot by Brandon and Jacobs to make *The Scottsboro Boys*. By this time, projects had grown ambitious, though budgets remained small. *Marine*, a.k.a. *Workers on the Waterfront* (Seltzer and Edward Kern, 1934) testified to the increasingly sophisticated handling of "pure" documentary. In contrast, *Taxi* (Naumburg and Guy, 1935), a six-reel feature dramatizing the New York City cab drivers' strike of 1934, broke new ground by mixing enacted scenes with newsreel footage and employing actual taxi drivers in the cast. Aside from New York, League branches in Chicago, Philadelphia, Detroit, and Los Angeles contributed raw footage and finished films.

Representatives from these affiliates attended a 1934 conference that resulted in the formation of a National Film and Photo League. This body assumed the task of coordinating production and distribution. The publication of *Filmfront*, the League's official organ, began that year, although it survived for only five issues. Ironically, just as national consolidation promised greater cooperation, factional differences threatened to divide the ranks.

Hard liners such as Sam Brody and Tom Brandon considered making films only one form of activism, which must cede privilege to boycotting movies or distributing leaflets when necessary. Less politically charged members complained that such strict ideology stifled creativity, discouraged experimentation, and interfered with film production. A rift developed between those emphasizing cinema's role as propaganda and those pressing for greater attention to craft. Still, political differences among members were slight; instead, fiercer battles were waged over the value of dramatization versus reportage and over Hurwitz's proposal to establish a select, permanent troupe dedicated to film production. These disagreements came to a head following the 1934 conference, when representatives reaffirmed newsreel production as the primary goal. Shortly after, a dissident group including Hurwitz, Steiner, Lerner, and Sidney Meyers left to form Nykino. This significant loss of talent, and other departures that followed, inflicted serious injury on the organization yet did not prove fatal. More severe were the worsening funding difficulties that had continually plagued the league. The Nazis had shut down the Berlin-based WIR, which had provided film stock and paid processing fees, and the Communist International officially dissolved the WIR in 1935. For a period, Del Duca, Julian Roffman, and Victor Kendal persisted; but, by 1937, film production had ceased. Severed from the cinema section, the still photographers of the New York Photo League carried on until anti-communist pressure forced it to close in the 1950s.

Despite antiquated equipment, amateur personnel, and scant finances, the Film and Photo League had established radical cinema in the United States. It left a considerable legacy, the successes of which should count to its credit; Pare Lorentz hired Hurwitz, Steiner, and Paul Strand to shoot *The Plow that Broke the Plains,* and FPL alumni were the force behind Nykino and its offspring Frontier Films. It is the latter's final release, *Native Land* (Hurwitz and Strand, 1942), that represents both climax and coda for radical cinema, as domestic injustice lost its urgency and attention turned toward the war effort in the 1940s.

THOMAS COHEN

*See also **Native Land**; **Plow that Broke the Plains, The***

Selected Films

1932 *Bonus March* (Lester Balog and Leo Seltzer)
1932 *The Ford Massacre* (Jack Awringer, Robert Del Duca, Joseph Hudyma, John Shard, Leo Seltzer)
1933 *Hunger 1932* (Del Duca, Seltzer, Hurwitz, and others)
1933 *America Today No. 1* (Newsreel)
1934 *Marine* (Edward Kern, Julian Roffman, Leo Seltzer)
1934 *Scottsboro Boys* (Hurwitz, with assistance from Thomas Brandon and Lewis Jacobs)
1935 *Taxi* (Nancy Naumburg and James Guy)

Further Reading

Alexander, William, *Film on the Left: American Documentary Film from 1931 to 1942*, Princeton: Princeton UP, 1981.
Barsam, Richard M., "American Nonfiction Film: 1930–1939" in *Nonfiction Film: A Critical History*, Bloomington: Indiana University Press, 1992.
Campbell, Russell, *Cinema Strikes Back: Radical Filmmaking in the United States 1930–1942*, Ann Arbor: UMI Research Press, 1982.
Horak, Jan-Christopher, editor, *Lovers of Cinema: The First American Avant-Garde 1919–1945*, Madison: University of Wisconsin Press, 1995.
Jacobs, Lewis, editor, *The Compound Cinema: The Film Writings of Harry Alan Potamkin*, New York: Teachers College Press, 1977.
Kepley, Vance Jr. "The Workers' International Relief and the Cinema of the Left, 1921–1935" in *Cinema Journal* 23, 1983, 7–23.
Wolfe, Charles, "The Poetics and Politics of Nonfiction: Documentary Film" in *Grand Design: Hollywood as a Modern Business Enterprise, 1930–1939*, edited by Tino Balio, Berkeley: University of California Press, 1993.

FILM AUSTRALIA

The Australian Commonwealth Film Unit changed its name in 1973 to Film Australia. The same year also saw the division relocated within the Australian federal bureaucracy, shifting from the Department of the Interior to the Department of the Media, and yet again in 1975 to the Australian Film Commission. In 1988, the organisation was established as a government company; Film Australia Pty Ltd. Denys Brown was head at the time of the name change and, in turn, he was succeeded by John Mabey (1980–1984), Robyn Hughes (1985–1989), Bruce Moir (1989–1997), and Sharon Connolly (since 1997). During this period, the organisation made almost 2000 films, the majority of which were commissioned by government departments and the others produced from within its own budget in the national interest.

In line with changing industrial trends in the commercial production industry, a reorganisation in the 1980s led to the downsizing of the permanent staff and a policy of contracting out production, including in the 1990s increasing use of new technology. As might be expected given the orientation of the information/documentary film in general, the period from 1973 to the present has, for the most part, seen a continuing emphasis on social issues. One of the dominant strains has been involvement with fringe groups in the society, those that have been marginalised, invisible, and without a voice in the recent past. Film subjects that fall into this category include migrants (*The Migrant Experience*), Aborigines (*On Sacred Ground*), underdeveloping country areas (*Cunnamulla*), and the disabled (*Annie's Coming Out*). The last film, released in 1984 was a fictional feature film that achieved mainstream theatrical release and was a highly prestigious film, winning many awards. It was far from being the only such prize-winning film, which also included *Leisure* (1977) and *Mabo: Life of an Island Man* (1997). Indeed, the former film, made by popular cartoonist and filmmaker, Bruce Petty, won an Oscar, the second film of the unit to win such an award. The division's films have always been aimed at an education market, but, in the Film Australia period, television has replaced commercial release in theatres as a major distribution point. This, in turn, has often forced the organisation to produce its material not in the form of one-off films but rather in terms of series such as the aforementioned 1984 *The Migrant Experience* and the multi-part *The Human Face* series. Meantime, Film Australia has also continued to be significant to the Australian film production industry in general in training directors, producers, and cinematographers who have gone on to illustrious careers in other parts of that industry. Turning to the films themselves, it is noteworthy that, despite continuities with the output of the late Commonwealth Film Unit period, the films produced since 1973 project a different view of Australia than those of earlier films.

Although the society is still pluralist, nevertheless there is frequently competition and conflict that is sometimes resolved and brought into equilibrium and sometimes not. Essentially, Australia has become a darker, more diverse, and anxious society. Thus, the environment has become a central image, and a large cycle of the division's recent films have stressed the complexity and fragility of that phenomenon and the capacities both to adapt and to fail to survive. The mock documentary *Cane Toads* (1983), a film that examines the disastrous environmental consequences of introducing this species into Australia, is representative of this outlook. Meantime, as part of this readjustment of viewpoint toward Australia, Film Australia's style and mode of filmmaking have also subtly readjusted in recent years. If we think of documentary as involving a dialectic between experience and argument, the need to affirm the validity of individual experience and the necessity to generalise,

then recent division films, including the *Striving* series, *All That Glitters, The Migrant Experience, The Human Jigsaw, Cane Toads*, and many others, have been marked by the return of an interviewed-based commentary.

Characteristically, these films work by accumulating a series of particular cases and experiences, thus offering, first, a dramatisation of experience, and, then, an interpretation of these experiences. Epistemologically, the case studies and experiences legitimate and validate the commentary as do other strategies including the on-screen presence of the commentator. Finally, too, we can note that at least part of the reason for this (qualified) return to authoritative commentary is that, since the mid-1970s, the unit has come to rely more and more on the sponsorship of its films by different government departments. Undoubtedly, this kind of film style fits well with the pedagogical needs of these agencies.

ALBERT MORAN

*See also **Cane Toads*; **Commonwealth Film Unit***

Further Reading

Lansell, Ross, *The Documentary Film in Australia*, Melbourne: Thomas Nelson, 1984.
Moran, Albert, *Projecting Australia: Government Documentary since 1945*, Sydney: Currency Press, 1991.

FILM CENTRE (UNITED KINGDOM)

For some time in Britain, it had been clear that, with the expansion of the documentary field, there was a definite need for a body to act as a consultative centre to the documentary movement as a whole. As early as 1934, an Association of EMB Directors had been established for internal advisory issues, and by 1935 the GPO film unit had received numerous requests to produce films for outside companies, for which, because of its government stature, it was forbidden to accommodate.

In response to these outside requests Associated Realist Film Producers (ARFP) was set up in December of that year to liase between documentary filmmakers and potential sponsors. Its twelve members were largely made up of GPO practitioners

including Edgar Anstey, Arthur Elton, and Stuart Legg. John Grierson was not a member of ARFP. He was, however, one of its consultants, and with minimal negotiation it was agreed that, in 1936, ARFP would take over the Shell Film Units output, with Arthur Elton tactfully placed at the helm.

During this period British documentary was widening its horizons in many directions, experimenting in terms of technique and subject matter and increasing output by the formation of new units such as Strand and Realist. Yet it still remained a close-knit group of people—basically the twelve members of ARFP and those who worked with one or more of them—and it still shared a common allegiance, varying only in degree to John Grierson.

Once the Shell operation had started, it was clear to all involved that something more formal and rigid was needed, something more definite than a loose association of filmmakers. John Grierson resigned from the GPO in June 1937, noting that the world was expanding and that international organisations were looking in the direction of the documentary. He had seen that there was a real need for an outside body that could guarantee to look after the interests of the sponsors, and, in 1938, he formed a new, independently financed outfit, called Film Centre, to meet that need.

Established at 34 Soho Square in London, the idea was that Film Centre itself should not produce films, but should advise and supervise on production, make arrangements for distribution, undertake scenario work, promote new territories for production, and, in general, guide the policy and purposes for most of the movement. Film Centre could act as a middleman between sponsor and the film production company. It could see that the production company did not swindle the sponsor and in turn guarantee that a production outfit would not be swindled by a sponsor. These were, of course, the exact services, goals, and values that ARFP had stood for. Film Centre had in fact emerged out of ARFP.

From the beginning, Film Centre had strong links with the Shell Company, despite Shell having its own film unit. Shell was very keen to avoid entirely in-house productions that would appear as ordinary pieces of Shell's public relations. So a curious arrangement came into being; while Shell had its film unit under its own roof, the planning of the films and the supervision of them was done from outside by Film Centre. A long-lasting arrangement, that, no doubt, helped give the Shell films their detached objectivity, in postwar years aided the longevity of Film Centre.

The first clients wanting films for their companies came from the already established links that had been made whilst at GPO. First Shell, then the Gas Council, the government, and Imperial Airways were all keen to have films made.

In 1939, Grierson, at the invitation of the Canadian government, moved to Canada to help establish the National Film Board, leaving Film Centre in the hands of his protégés; however, Grierson did remain on the board of directors for Film Centre until his death.

With war in full swing, the need for documentary as a means of information and propaganda became more apparent than ever before and, in the eyes of the Ministry of Information, 1940 saw Film Centre rise to equal stature to that of the newly formed Crown Film Unit. Both Anstey and Wright remained at Film Centre during most of the war, graduating from directors to producers through the desperate need to output the near one hundred Ministry of Agriculture titles required and the Ministry of Home Security titles that followed. In January 940, Film Centre also published its first issue of the *Documentary Newsletter*, an extremely influential in-house paper that helped the production units by steering government thought to the power of documentary. Film Centre became busier than ever, and the floors of 34 Soho Square were a hive of activity, not only producing the *Newsletter* and meeting the remit of the company but also housing the Scientific Film Association.

In February 1946, Film Centre, after preparing a report on the use of film within the company, took on a new client, British Overseas Airways Corporation. Out of this report began a long and happy relationship between Film Centre and BOAC. This and the work provided by Shell proved the mainstay of Film Centre's production activities.

With the war won, Arthur Elton, who had been head of production at the Ministry of Information throughout hostilities, returned to Film Centre to take the reins once more. In 1949 Edgar Anstey left Film Centre to go to British Transport Films (a unit that Film Centre had advised on when first approached by the then new British Transport Commission), and Sinclair Road, George Seager, and Brian Taylor joined the staff. In that same year, Film Centre moved farther along Oxford Street, to 167 Tottenham Court Road.

It became the responsibility of Sinclair Road to source clients potentially interested in films for their company, films that Film Centre could then handle on its behalf. This approach not only brought in large companies who wished to vest their entire film output with Film Centre but also attracted various one-off productions and clients such as Tube Investments, English Electric, and British Petroleum that all dabbled with the documentary film via Film Centre.

The beauty of Film Centre was the fact that many documentary production staff were freelance workers. Film Centre was perfectly geared up to deal with freelancers and acted as an employment agency for reputable crew, enabling a large company to take on freelance production staff in a way that avoids all the problems that freelancing brings to large outfits. The company directors, secretaries, office personnel, and telephonists were the only permanent staff; everybody else was employed on a picture-to-picture basis.

As the 1940s turned into the 1950s, Film Centre entered a boom period, and as space became cramped, the company took on additional premises, this time at 24 Conduit Street. The year 1951 brought another move, this time for the Shell Company. They were moving from the original headquarters on the Strand to a new purpose-built premises to be known as Shell Centre. During the move the company was turning its interest more toward overseas oil-related issues, having little time for internal PR departments, and Film Centre was asked to house the Shell Film Unit for the duration of the move. A gigantic floor at 133 Oxford Street was taken on to house the unit, and Film Centre had it fitted with a 35mm viewing theatre and facilities to accommodate the vast distribution library. Similarly, the AEI Film Unit was also housed within this floor, all under the Film Centre umbrella.

With 50 percent of output taken up with Shell, overseas operations became a large part of their activities during this boom period, as Shell had provided them with an international platform. Shell overseas film units were established in Iraq, Singapore, Venezuela, Kuwait, Iran, Tehran, Beirut, and Nigeria, to name but a few, and a close association with the Australian Commonwealth Film Unit was also formed. The idea was to spread the documentary word and train filmmakers locally to be able to make Shell films, thus allowing Film Centre to pull out once the training was complete. This operation of an unimaginable scale was handled entirely from Oxford Street, with all camera stock, laboratory processing, and checking being handled through London. This extremely busy period was of course hampered by the various time-zone differences, resulting in frustrated overseas representatives calling the office at all hours of the day and night.

Such was the success of the documentary at this time that, in 1955, Film Centre actually reprinted Stephen Tallent's book *The Projection of England*, which Grierson had used to such great effect in convincing the GPO of the value of documentary.

An additional site at 371 Euston Road was taken on to accommodate the Shell Photographic Unit (the back entrance to this building was at 37 Warren Street, and it was always referred to by staff as the Warren Street site). It was called Film Centre Photographic (FCP) studios and originally looked after purely Shell stills but was soon allowed to take on work outside Shell. The FCP studios also housed the print library and Shell stock-shot library and, with some small cutting rooms onsite, provided the BBC and other television companies with library footage.

Eventually, after many years of wondering why there were two very large empty rooms at Shell Centre, Shell finally caught on and reclaimed its unit in-house. In 1965, the AEI operation was also wound up and Film Centre vacated its Oxford Street premises. Stuart Legg retired in the same year and remained a silent director of the company, turning his hand to writing.

The birth of television had not really taken hold on the documentary movement, but by 1970, things had obviously changed a great deal. Work had begun to tail off through the latter part of the 1960s, as revolutions and uprisings overseas had meant the return of Film Centres British representatives. With the claiming back of the Shell Film Unit, the bulk of Shell films were now being handled in-house and BOAC films began to decline as a merger with BEA loomed.

By the early 1970s many film units had been long established, and all were perfectly capable of producing films without the help of Film Centre. Arthur Elton was keen to retire and the nucleus of people at Film Centre had declined such that there was not enough staff to continue.

Sir Arthur Elton died in 1973, deprived of the retirement he had long deserved. By 1975, the Press Association had moved in to take over FCP photographic, BP took back the material Film Centre had operated for them, and the independently running stock shot library (more than 70 million feet) was considered a non-core activity of the company remit. It was radically thinned out and absorbed into the stock-shot company, Index Film. Film Centre owed a lot to the efforts of Vi Bebb who, under the guidance of Arthur Elton, had kept the company running so smoothly for so many years. The last of the staff found work elsewhere; Vi found television work with Michael Oram. In 1976, Film Centre finally closed its doors.

STEVEN FOXON

See also **Anstey, Edgar; Elton, Arthur; Grierson, John; Legg, Stuart; Shell**

Selected Films

1940 *The Fourth Estate*, Realist Film Unit, director Paul Rotha, for *The Times Newspaper*

1948 *Transport: Wealth of the World*, Associated British Pathe, director Peter Bradford, for British Transport Films

1951 *Forward a Century* Basic Films, director J. B. Napier-Bell, for the Festival of Britain

1957 *Rivers of Time* Film Centre, director William Novik for Iraq Petrolium Company

1957 *Approaching the Speed of Sound* Shell Film Unit, director Peter De Normanville, for Shell

1965 *The Linesmen* A.E.I Film Unit, director Peter Griffiths, for A.E.I.

Further Reading

Gordon, Douglas, *Shell Films: The First Sixty Years*, London: Balding and Mansell, 1994.

Roth, Paul, *Documentary Diary*, London: Seker and Warburg, and New York: Hill and Wang, 1973.

Sussex, Elizabeth, *The Rise and Fall of British Documentary*, Berkeley: University of California Press, 1975.

FILM STOCK

The world's first and longest-existent moving image carrier was the combination of two technologies, as well as the culmination of a process of research and development that took place throughout the nineteenth century. Photosensitive emulsions, that is, chemical compounds capable of recording a permanent image through exposure to light, evolved gradually since Thomas Wedgwood first saturated a leather canvas with silver salts in the early 1800s. The first film base, a flexible and transparent solid that offers the mechanical tolerances necessary to enable the images to be exposed and projected in rapid succession, thereby creating the illusion of a moving image, was developed over a similar timescale. The first film stock in roughly the form we know it today was manufactured by George Eastman's Kodak company in New York in 1889.

The most widespread film format to be used during the twentieth century was standardised, effectively by market forces, over the following decade. It was 35mm wide and perforated along each side. Each frame occupied a space adjacent to four perforations, producing an aspect ratio (ratio of height to width) of approximately 1:1.33. It was soon discovered that a shooting and projection speed of 16 frames per second was necessary to reproduce the illusion of movement without flicker, though speeds were not standardised until the conversion to sound in the late 1920s.

As with all other areas of production, nonfiction filming took place almost exclusively on this format until the 1930s. A number of smaller gauges were introduced during the intervening period, intended mainly for amateur use. Three of these formats achieved widespread sales of stock and equipment: 9.5mm, introduced by Pathé in 1922; 16mm, introduced by Eastman Kodak in 1923; and 8mm, introduced by Eastman in 1932. Of these, 16mm would eventually make the transition to a professional medium; in the postwar period it was used extensively for documentary, experimental film, and television news.

The main developments in black-and-white film stock during the silent period were improvements to its speed, chromaticity, and grain structure. The speed at which the emulsion registers an image in response to exposure (as distinct from the speed at which it moves through a camera or projector) determines the extent to which shooting in natural light is possible and was therefore a significant factor in the production of documentary and other nonfiction genres. The earliest stocks had required bright, direct sunlight and the use of wide lens apertures in the absence of any artificial light. A number of developments in the late 1920s significantly increased the creative possibilities available to documentary makers working with film, notably the introduction of higher speed emulsions (stocks equivalent to EI50 in today's terms were in mainstream use by the end of the decade) and of panchromatic film. This was sensitive to the entire visible colour spectrum, as distinct from the orthochromatic stocks it replaced, which could only "see" red and green. The newsreel industry was one of the first widespread users of panchromatic stock.

Colour film systems had been the subject of research and development almost as long as film itself. Although they were used on a limited scale before the 1930s, the early methods all fell by the wayside as a result of a combination of flawed technology, cost, and compatibility with existing industrial practices. The earliest feature-length, nonfiction film to have been made using a method that attempted to capture and reproduce colour photographically was probably *Britain Prepared* (UK, 1915), a World War I recruitment propaganda film using the two-colour Kinemacolor process. The first successful three-colour (that is, able to reproduce the entire visible colour spectrum) systems to be mass-marketed were Dufaycolor, introduced in 1934, and Kodachrome, introduced in 1935. Both were reversal systems (which made mass-duplication difficult, expensive, and of poor quality) and therefore sold mainly for amateur use. The significant quantity and breadth of amateur colour film produced during the 1930s and 1940s have been the subject of significant interest from television documentary makers at the start of the twenty-first century, notably in Trans World International's "in colour" series, which has been broadcast worldwide. Despite one or two documentaries shot on Kodachrome and then printed using the Technicolor process (for example, *Western Approaches*, UK 1943, dir. Pat Jackson), however, colour was not used on any significant scale for nonfiction until the 1950s, when the arrival of dye coupler emulsions made colour film inexpensive and easy to duplicate.

The two principal developments in the immediate postwar period were the replacement of cellulose nitrate by cellulose triacetate as the standard base (the former was highly inflammable, which had been a significant obstacle to its use outside studios) and the growth of 16mm as a professional format, prompted mainly by the needs of television. A new generation of documentary makers represented by figures such as Lindsay Anderson, D.A. Pennebaker, and Frederick Wiseman embraced the portability of 16mm cameras and sound equipment, as well as the emergence of new, high-speed film stock to produce work that would have been logistically impossible in 35mm.

Although the speed, grain density, and (in the case of colour) tonal range of film stocks in all the remaining formats have continued to improve, the use of film as an origination medium by docu-

mentary makers has been in steady decline since the 1980s. Videotape technology has become cheaper and more versatile, and the predominant outlet for documentaries continues to be television, in which the superior image quality of film is considered less important. Eastman Kodak has discontinued the manufacture of a number of 16mm stocks since 2002 (most notably the Ektachrome reversal film, a mainstay of TV news origination in the 1970s and 1980s), and the film stock manufacturer Ilford went into liquidation on August 24, 2004. It seems likely, therefore, that by the end of the current decade (2010), the only remaining uses for film on any significant scale will be in the 35mm format for studio origination and archival preservation.

LEO ENTICKNAP

See also **Anderson, Lindsay; Pathé; Pennebaker, D.A.; Wiseman, Frederick**

Further Reading

Fielding, Raymond, editor, *A Technological History of Motion Pictures and Television*, Berkeley: University of California Press, 1967.

Fullerton, John, and Astrid Soderbergh-Wilding, editors, *Moving Images, from Edison to Web Cam*, Eastleigh: John Libbey Publishing, 2000.

Hercock R.J., and G.A. Jones, *Silver by the Ton: A History of Ilford Ltd., 1879–1979*, Maidenhead: McGraw Hill, 1979.

Kattelle, Alan, *Home Movies: A History of the American Industry, 1897–1979*, Nashua, NH: Transition Publishing, 2000.

Salt, Barry, *Film Style and Technology: History and Analysis*, 2nd edition, London: Starword, 1992.

Smither, Roger, and Catherine Surowiec, editors, *This Film Is Dangerous: A Celebration of Nitrate Film*, Brussels: FIAF, 2002.

FINDING CHRISTA

(US, Billops and Hatch, 1991)

Finding Christa is an autobiographical account of filmmaker Camille Billops's 1961 decision to put her then four-year-old daughter, Christa, up for adoption. The film formalizes its episodic narrative beneath a backdrop of both con-

ventional documentary aesthetics and lightly avant-garde subjectivity. The resulting film both challenges and conforms to its subject matter. *Finding Christa* successfully manages to question multiple ideologies while offering up far more questions than it answers, thereby challenging the viewer.

Finding Christa is the third in an ongoing series of collaborative projects from the husband and wife team of James Hatch and Camille Billops including *Suzanne Suzanne* (1982) and *Older Women and Love* (1987) and shared a 1992 Grand Jury prize at Sundance. The series of films are not expressly related, yet there are various thematic threads coupled with the use of similar formal techniques. Although the couple seems to share in the production roles of their films, Billops usually takes on a more visual role. The films relays a definite female authorial voice with even Hatch's screen role within *Finding Christa* that more of supporting player to the complex dynamics of Billops and daughter Christa Victoria. The mother and daughter are not only presented in conventional dramatic installments, but multiple artistic sequences as well. Many of the formative passages also become vehicles for the participants, including numerous musical installments from both Christa and her adopted mother, Margaret Liebig.

The premise of *Finding Christa,* as the title implies, takes the viewer to the reunion whereby mother and child in essence find each other again after a twenty-year separation. Although the film does manage to keep the reunion as its predominant dramaturgical device, the overall focus is often that of Billops's life, displayed through moments of autobiographical reflections. The film addresses not only the complexities of the relationship between the reunited mother and daughter, but other interfamily relationships as experienced by Billops in response to her 1961 decision. Through a series of interviews with sometimes critical family members and ongoing personal commentaries (some in the form of rebuttals to her family's testimonials), Billops attempts to explain, and come to terms with, the choice to put her child up for adoption. This comes across as not being so much for herself, or even as justification of the act, but what seems to be more a type of education into the decision for the interviewees and viewers. Billops seems as secure in her decision at the end of the film as she was in 1961; it is only those around her who perhaps have changed their minds.

The title of *Finding Christa* reveals the complexities of the film. Among other meanings, it refers to the mother finding a child she left behind, the child finding herself through the mother, the viewer finding the child, and even the artist once again finding the mother. All of the relationships in the film seem to exist in a harmony that is anything but harmonious. This point seems to be one of the underlying currents of the narrative's questions of reality and its versions of such views. None of her family's reflections of the 1961 episode seem to be sufficient to answer the question of why Billops did what she did; yet the film and Billops herself seem content with that question remaining unanswered, instead positing the response of why is it necessary for others to feel content with something she needed to do.

One of the films underscored revelations is found in Billops's old family home movies. Shot by her mother and father, the clips present a middle-class counterpoint to the usual iconographic imagery of 1950s and 1960s black America, as well as the same eras portrayal of the unwed mother. The film uses such footage to call all such ideologies into question including those of the middle class, for it is the breakdown of middle-class ideologies that is at the heart of *Finding Christa.* Just as the title questions its linguistic interpretations, the film questions those of the roles of mother, woman, child, and others in the eye of such. Such a breakdown is not one of destruction so much as of analysis, as the film is not one for answers, merely one that questions, which is one of the ways it engages the viewer.

The narrative structure in *Finding Christa* is separated into four episodes, each with its own introductory intertitle. Besides providing a means for directional switches of the narrative, they serve as effective ways to voice that of the films' subjects, while maintaining the films ongoing dialectical conflict. The first title is that of Christa's, yet the segment is about Billops. Billops voices the next two and they end with the ambiguity of the closing, "Almost Home," title. This final title, which in essence not only reflects both subjects' voices, but exerts a certain surface level (previously exhibited in the subjective visualizations) of reflexive humor, because the film is almost over. In some ways, it is this final title that gives the viewer the most insight, being that it is the first and only title not posed in question form, allowing it to stand as more of a statement. Yet it reminds the viewer of an ambiguity that runs much deeper, as it provides no resolution, instead suggesting that the subjects never quite did get home. What this title and the subsequent scenes that follow reveal is not only did they not reach home, but that the mere notion of such a possibility might reside only in the ideological implications the film sets itself up to question.

Multiple interpretations of this film are inevitable, especially of Billops herself. Her demeanor throughout the film regarding the adoption is one that some might even find troubling, but that is all part of the intrigue that the film invokes. There are no easy answers to the questions addressed within *Finding Christa*, but that is part of the message being delivered, that of diversity and the complexities involved with such diversity.

DINO EVERETT

Finding Christa (USA, Hatch-Billops Productions, 1991, 55 mins). Distributed by Third World Newsreel. Produced by Camille Billops and James Hatch. Directed by Camile Billops and James Hatch. Written by Camille Billops and James Hatch. Cinematography by Dion Hatch. Archival footage by Alma and Walter Dotson. Editing by Paula Heredia. Sound editing by Ray McCutcheon. Original music by Christa Victoria. Filmed in Oakland, New York.

Further Reading

Goffman, Erving. *The Presentation of Self in Everyday Life*. Woodstock, NY: The Overlook Press, 1973.

Haskell, Molly. *From Reverence to Rape*, 2nd edition, Chicago: University of Chicago Press, 1987.

Lane, Jim, "Black Autobiographical Documentary," *Jump Cut* 40, 1996, 38–46.

Lekatsas, Barbara, "Encounters: The Film Odyssey of Camille Billops," in *Black American Literature Forum*, 25, 2, 1991, 395–408.

May, Elaine Tyler, *Homeward Bound: American Families in the Cold War Era*, Basic Books, 1988.

Nichols, Bill, *Representing Reality: Issues and Concepts in Documentary*, Bloomington: Indiana University Press, 1991.

Smith, Valerie, "Telling Secrets: Narrative and Ideology in *Suzanne, Suzanne* by Camille Billups and James V. Hatch," *Multiple Voices in Feminist Film Criticism*, edited by Diane Carson, Linda Dittmar, and Janice Welsch, Minneapolis: University of Minnesota Press, 1994.

White, Hayden, *Narrative Discourse and Historical Representation*, Baltimore: John Hopkins University Press, 1987.

FIRES WERE STARTED

(UK, Jennings, 1943)

Fires Were Started (1943) is considered the preeminent film about Britain at war. It was made by the highly acclaimed film director, Humphrey Jennings. *Fires Were Started* uses powerfully poetic visuals to offer a dramatic reconstruction of events associated with the Blitz on London, while at the same time offering a high degree of emotional realism in characterisation. The film has had a powerful influence on succeeding generations of British filmmakers. Leading filmmakers Lindsay Anderson and Karl Reisz, prominent figures in the experimental British Free Cinema Movement (1955–1959), have singled out *Fires Were Started* as a unique film that had a significant influence on their approach to filmmaking. In an article on Jennings's work for *Sight and Sound* (April–June, 1954), Anderson refers to the poetic power of Jennings's film style and argued that, "In fact it might reasonably be contended that Humphrey Jennings is the only real poet the British Cinema has yet produced" (Jacobs, 1979, p. 236). Reisz acknowledged the influence of Jennings's work and cited *Fires Were Started* as, "the source film for Free Cinema" (Orbanz, 1977, p. 57).

Fires Were Started was one of several films made by Humphrey Jennings under the auspices of the GPO Unit and the Crown Film Unit. This collection of films addressed the various ways in which the British civilian population were involved and affected by the war. *London Can Take It* (1940) co-directed by Harry Watt, represented the effects of the Blitz. *Listen to Britain* (1942) portrayed in a positive way the mood of the nation through descriptive sound, with scenes of high-spirited female factory workers collectively singing popular songs as they made their contribution to Britain's war effort. *A Diary for Timothy* (1944–1945) was a more poignant film, and commented on the uncertain effects of five years of a world at war.

Fires Were Started was made in cooperation with the Home Office Ministry of Home Security and

417

Fires Were Started, 1943.
[*Still courtesy of the British Film Institute*]

the National Fire Service, and was part of a propaganda drive to maintain high morale within civil defence organisations and the civilian population that they served. Brian Winston, in his book *Fires Were Started* (1999), comments on the propagandist function of the film while acknowledging the acute observation and impressive formal qualities deployed in Jennings's poetic realist style. He argues that, "*Fires Were Started*, not (say) *Triumph des Willens,* is the real propaganda masterwork of the BFI list" (Winston, 1999: 38).

Ostensibly, *Fires Were Started* is in the genre of documentary drama, in the sense that it is a dramatic reenactment of the type of events that the fire service encountered. Its documentary authority, however, rests more with the way in which the film communicated accurate information about

how the fire service was coordinated during war time. A variety of scenes accurately represented the levels of organisation involved in civilian defence, the functions of the chain of command, and the ways in which information was communicated to best use available resources. It offered a reassuring account of the way in which the organisations that served and protected the civilian population operated in times of crisis.

The narrative of *Fires Were Started* recounts twenty-four hours in the lives of the firemen of the Auxiliary Fire Service, from the time they leave home for work, through the routines of their job and every day interaction with colleagues, to the telephone call that summons the firemen to fight a dangerous warehouse fire at the docks, which threatens to spread to a heavily laden munitions ship. The narrative culminates in the death of one of the firemen, a popular Cockney character called Jacko who is much valued by his colleagues. The film ends with scenes of Jacko's funeral intercut with shots of the ship sailing out of dock with its vital munitions cargo intact.

The film graphically depicted that, although there may be a high cost in human terms to maintain Britain's war effort, the men and women on the home front were fulfilling their duties with an unquestioning bravery. This aspect of the film, a representation of the national spirit of Britain during the war, is perhaps more solidly anchored in the director's earlier interests. Jennings's friend and contemporary at Cambridge, the poet Kathleen Raines, commented that, "What counted for Humphrey was the expression, by certain people, of the ever-growing spirit of man, in particular, of the spirit of England" (Jacobs, 1979, p. 239). As a young man Jennings had co-founded the Mass Observation movement in 1937. The Mass Observation movement recruited a team of observers and a panel of volunteer writers who focused on British public life, attending public gatherings such as sporting events, open-air meetings, and entertainment venues.

The power of Jennings's representation of the men and women of the fire service in *Fires Were Started* lies in the dramatic tension created by a constant foregrounding of the ordinariness of the firefighters, which is contrasted with the unpredictable and heroic acts that the task of fire fighting requires. Winston (1999) argued that Jennings used masterly sociological or "indirect" propaganda in the way he tapped into the mythic qualities that already circulated around the men and women of the fire service in London, who were acclaimed for their part in tackling blazing infernos and for rescuing many people from heavily bombed areas during the Blitz.

Although the basic narrative structure of *Fires Were Started* is unremarkable, the characterisation, as well as the visually exciting representation of dramatic firefights, have attracted much praise. Actual firemen from the Auxiliary Fire Service played the fictional characters in the film, and throughout the film Jennings maintains the sense that he is telling real people's stories. The film clearly underscores the essential ordinariness of the characters and their daily routines, in the everyday scenes of men saying goodbye to their families as they leave for work, to scenes of friendly banter with colleagues at the station house. These scenes, which foreground the unexceptional in life and the ordinariness of the characters, however, are later contrasted with visually dramatic scenes of a raging inferno at the warehouse, and acts of fire fighting that necessitate extraordinary human courage as the fire spreads toward the munitions ship moored in the dock. Nevertheless, in these latter highly dramatic scenes, Jennings refrained from representing the firefighters as infallible heroes and managed to retain a sense of authentic ordinariness in the characterisation of the firemen. The firemen are shown making mistakes and having to deal with unpredictable situations as they arise in an often imperfect manner. This sense of ordinary men being called on to deal with superhuman events enables the narrative to play in the space between the mythic and the real.

The film achieves a more powerful emotional address by avoiding the depiction of the firefighters in action as invincible heroes, and instead by striving for a more authentic representation of the firefighters as ordinary men who risk their lives, and in the case of Jacko, die in the service of others. Lindsay Anderson (1954) cogently argued, "In outline it is the simplest of pictures; in treatment it is of the greatest subtlety, richly poetic in feeling, intense with tenderness and admiration for the unassuming heroes whom it honours." Anderson (1954) further argued that it was an exceptional film that had managed to capture an essential truth about the nature of the men and women it represented: "No other British film made during the war, documentary or feature, achieved such a continuous and poignant truthfulness, or treated the subject of men at war with such a sense of its incidental glories and its essential tragedy" (Jacobs, 1979:241).

Jennings's film career was cut short, as he died at the age of forty-three in an accident on the Greek island of Poros, while researching locations for a film. *Fires Were Started* is arguably his greatest film legacy and continues to be considered a classic film of the period.

PAT A. COOK

See also **Anderson, Lindsay; *Diary for Timothy, A*; Jennings, Humphrey; *Listen to Britain*; *London Can Take It*; Reisz, Karl**

Fires Were Started. (UK, Crown Film Unit, 1943, 80 mins.) Produced by Ian Dalrymple. Directed by Humphrey Jennings. Written by Humphrey Jennings. Cinematography by C. Pennington-Richards. Original music by William Alwyn. Musical direction by Muir Mathieson. Editing by Stewart McAllister. Sound recording by Ken Cameron and Jock May. Production management by Dora Wright.

Further Reading

Anderson, Lyndsey, "Some Aspects of the Work of Humphrey Jennings," printed in *Sight and Sound (London)*, April–June 1954.

Jackson, Kevin, editor, *The Humphrey Jennings Film Reader*, Manchester: Carcanet Press, 1995.

Jacobs, Lewis, *The Documentary Tradition*, Toronto: George J. McLeod Ltd., 1979.

Lovell, Allan, and Jim Hillier, *Studies in Documentary*, London: Secker and Warburg, 1972.

Winston, Brian, *BFI Film Classics: "Fires were Started,"* London: BFI, 1999.

FIRST LOVE

(Poland, Kieślowski, 1974)

One in a loose series of Krzysztof Kieślowski documentaries concerning ordinary people and places made across the 1970s, *First Love (Pierwsza Miłość)* follows a young couple as they marry and, within months, become parents. Despite the odds stacked against Romek and Jadźka—she is pregnant at age 17, and both are ill-prepared for their impending responsibilities and disoriented by the bureaucracy they face in terms of setting up a family home—they are resolute and determined. With severity, and just the occasional glimpse of sympathy, authority figures intervene in their lives but fail to detract from the couple's shared, unarticulated sense of joy and trepidation as they journey from "first love" to adulthood and parenthood. Jadźka's façade only cracks after the wedding (an austere and functional ceremony that begins with the paying of a fee); she weeps silently as she receives advice and best wishes from her family. Such scenes, and Romek's fumbling phone call to his mother from the hospital announcing the birth of their daughter, suggest emotional pain equal to the pain of the actual birth, which is also recorded.

Kieślowski does not flinch in the face of these intimate and private scenes and yet, shortly afterward, was to declare himself a trespasser on forbidden territory. Not only were such events inappropriate to film, but the act of filming itself blocked that which Kieślowski seems to have perceived as a greater, phenomenological "truth." From a Bazinian perspective, reality ultimately refuses to yield up such a truth for the camera. Žižek posits the resultant shift from documentary to feature films—indicative of a structural failure of documentary realism in the face of the all-too-real, something only encountered at the very limits of experience—as central to his reading of Kieślowski: "a fidelity to the Real" is only possible via the mask of fiction (Žižek, 2001). Such a tension is detectable in *First Love*'s reconstructed scenes (Jadźka learning of her pregnancy, for example) and the lack of a methodological objective rigor. At one point, Kieślowski presents an actual and precise point-of-view shot (Jadźka absent-mindedly gazes through

First Love, 1974.
[*Still courtesy of the British Film Institute*]

the glass panes of a phone booth at mothers and their children outside). Such a shot is impossible within the conceptual framework of an observational documentary.

Thus, by the 1980s, Kieślowski had virtually abandoned the documentary. For contemporary viewers primarily familiar with Kieślowski as one of the most celebrated European *auteur*s of the late twentieth century, *First Love* engenders a kind of ahistorical *déjà vu*. The intimacy and obsessiveness with which Kieślowski frames the female "recalls" *Trois Couleurs: Bleu*, 1993/*Three Colours: Blue*; the series of events that irrevocably alter the course of a protagonist's life "recalls" *Przypadek*, 1981/*Blind Chance;* and the figure of the lone male, calling up to his partner in a high window "recalls" the moment that closes *Trois Couleurs: Blanc*, 1994/*Three Colours: White*. In such ways, Kieślowski mapped the real onto the fictional.

With none of the savvy of their aspirational reality television successors, Romek and Jadźka seem mostly oblivious to the documentary makers (a minimal crew, shooting in 16mm for thirty to forty days over the course of a year). Kieślowski favours long takes, allowing the characters to dictate the rhythm of the sequences. Nevertheless, a measure of direct manipulation is apparent; as well as one self-confessed "clear provocation" (Stok, 1993), in an engineered visit by a policeman. Kieślowski surrounds Romek and Jadźka with friends and family, creating the situation in which they would behave freely and naturally. This is achieved to the extent that the occasional glance at the camera by Kieślowski's subjects and the intrusion of the microphone into the frame serves to remind the viewer of the documentary nature of the film. Discreet jump cuts work in the same way, as do reestablishing shots from semi-hidden positions, denoting the essentially voyeuristic nature of the film.

Despite the seemingly dour subject matter, and with Kieślowski's taste for the oppressive Polish cityscape much in evidence, the aesthetic choices allows no pessimism. The colours are bright and vibrant and speak of the *joie de vivre* of the time and place; sunny overexposures for externals blur colour and form, joyously re-imagining the *Woodstock*-esque cast of adolescent supporting characters with a kind of saturated pictorialism. And, indeed, these characters are the benefactors of 1960s liberalism. Jadźka is met with acceptance rather than ostracism, support rather than disdain (with the sole exception of the board of school teachers, who downgrade her for lack of sexual morals). Such subject matter, only a decade before, made for some of the bleakest expressions of postwar European realism, particularly in British Northern Realism.

The defining and dominant characteristic of Kieślowski's method is his use of the tightly framed medium close-up, even with the (mostly) handheld camera. Even during the wedding ceremony and the birth, Kieślowski deftly holds the faces, rendering such events as steps on the emotional journey of the protagonists, catching fleeting and sometimes contradictory expressions as they sweep across their faces. This is the vantage point, intimates Kieślowski, from which the sociopolitical order must be examined. After all, if there is no hope for such a couple, and no sense in which their tribulations, however commonplace, can be understood to be both gracious and noble, then what hope is there for society? This could be read as a strategy of subversion in relation to the historical prerequisite of a socialist perspective (or "optimistic facts," as Kieślowski jokingly referred to it, [Stok, 1993]): Kieślowski relocates the idea of socialist perspective, from the clichés of Socialist Realism (abundant farms, happy toiling workers, youths bright-eyed with ideology) to the everyman hopes of a contemporary young couple.

BENJAMIN HALLIGAN

See also Kieślowski, Krzysztof

First Love (*Pierwsza Miłość*, Poland, 1974, 52 min.; a 30-minute "short film" cut was subsequently prepared). Produced for Polish Television. Directed by Krzysztof Kieślowski. Cinematography by Jacek Petrycki. Editing by Lidia Zonn. Sound by Magorzata Jaworska, and Michae Zarnecki. Filmed in Warsaw. Grand Prize, 1974 National Short Film Festival, Kraków. Special Jury Award, 1974 International Short Film Festival, Kraków.

Further Reading

Coates, Paul (ed.) *Lucid Dreams: The Films of Krzysztof Kieślowski*, London: Flicks Books, 1999.

Haltof, Marek, *The Cinema of Krzysztof Kieślowski: Variations on Destiny and Chance*, London and New York: Wallflower Press, 2004.

Insdorf, Annette, *Double Lives, Second Chances: The Cinema of Krzysztof Kieslowski*, New York: Talk Miramax Books, 1999.

Stok, Danusia, editor and translator, *Kieslowski on Kieslowski*, London and Boston: Faber and Faber, 1993.

Žižek, Slavoj, *The Fright of Real Tears: Krzysztof Kieślowski between Theory and Post-Theory*, London: British Film Institute, 2001.

FLAHERTY, ROBERT

Robert J. Flaherty is a legendary figure in film history and often called the "father" of American documentary, with a reputation that rests primarily on four feature-length works: *Nanook of the North* (1922), *Moana* (1926), *Man of Aran* (1934), and *Louisiana Story* (1948). *Nanook* was the first documentary feature to achieve mainstream box-office success and is still considered by many as an exemplary piece of ethnographic filmmaking. Yet in recent years, Flaherty's films—and the more general construction of what has come to be known as the Flaherty myth—have been intensely scrutinized by scholars and critics. The problems most frequently found in Flaherty's work lie in two primary areas. The first relates to the question of documentary authenticity and, more specifically, to Flaherty's common practice of staging scenes and reconstructing "primitive" life in his films. The second area of inquiry examines the extent to which Flaherty might have reproduced imperial hierarchies in his representations of racial and cultural difference. This latter issue becomes particularly difficult to ignore given the director's early career as an explorer, surveyor, and prospector in the Hudson Bay region for the industrialist and financier Sir William Mackenzie, whom Flaherty once referred to as "the Cecil Rhodes of Canada" (Rotha, 1983).

The story of Flaherty's early life as an explorer forms the backdrop to his career directing films in a mode that John Grierson and Paul Rotha would define as the naturalist tradition of documentary. Born in Michigan, Flaherty began by closely following the career path of his father, a mining engineer who often took his teenage son on prospecting expeditions to the remote regions of northern Ontario. The young Flaherty had little patience for academics, and a brief attempt to study mineralogy at the Michigan College of Mines, where he met his future wife and collaborator Frances Hubbard, ended in dismissal. In 1910, after returning to prospecting, Flaherty encountered Mackenzie, who engaged him to explore for iron ore along the sub-Arctic coast of Hudson Bay. In 1913, at Mackenzie's suggestion, Flaherty purchased a Bell and Howell camera, which he took with him on a major expedition to the Belcher Islands. One important innovation during these early attempts to film in the frozen north was Flaherty's decision to develop the negative on site and then screen the rushes to local Inuits, so that they could see the results of his efforts and work together with him "as partners" (Rotha, 1983). The practice led Flaherty to be seen as a pioneer of the collaborative feedback method, later adopted by Jean Rouch for such films as *Moi, un Noir* (1958) and *Chronique d'un Été* (1961). By 1916, after several journeys and numerous failed attempts at filming in extreme conditions, Flaherty compiled 70,000 feet of exposed negative. Editing it in Toronto, he accidentally, though some have thought intentionally, dropped a cigarette on the film and it instantly went up in flames. He was left with a single positive print (now lost), which is sometimes called the Harvard Print after his intention to screen it at the university.

The survival of the Harvard Print had at least two significant effects on Flaherty's development as a filmmaker. The first involved aesthetics and narrative: viewing it after the fire, he determined it to be an inferior piece of work, lacking dynamic visuals and a coherent storyline. The second was material, as he was able to screen the print in subsequent years in an effort to secure financing for his "Eskimo film." In the meantime he concentrated on writing and collaborating with Frances, and he edited the journals of his numerous northern journeys, released in 1924 as *My Eskimo Friends*. It was not until 1920 that another filming opportunity arose, when the French fur-trading firm Revillon Frères agreed to sponsor a trek north to their trading post in Cape Dufferin, Ungava. The relationship with Revillon Frères has since disturbed critics as it raises unsettling questions about the commercial and imperial forces behind the film. This is further compounded by the evident product placement of Revillon's furs in scenes at the trading post and inside Nanook's igloo (Rony, 1996). After sixteen months of shooting in difficult climatic conditions, followed by months of editing and securing a distributor, the film was released by Pathé in 1922. With a total production and post-production cost of $53,000, the film was a relative bargain for a feature, and it is estimated that it grossed $251,000 by September of the year of its release (Murphy, 1978).

Flaherty had tapped into a growing public demand for films that not only documented travel to foreign places but also highlighted and investigated racial and cultural difference, a collective desire already partially in evidence in the success of the shorter and less structured travelog films. *Nanook of the North*'s commercial success paved the way for a range of expeditionary films, such as Osa and Martin Johnson's *Simba: The King of the Beasts* (1928) and Cooper and Schoedsack's *Grass* (1925) and *Chang* (1927). Though still held in higher critical esteem than these expeditionary adventures, Flaherty's film was arguably similar in relying on staged sequences and skillful editing to produce a seamless illusion of documentary reality. This practice of staging certain sequences while also filming candid scenes and events, then cutting the footage together to form a coherent episodic narrative, was to become a Flaherty trademark, evident in most of his major films. The key to appreciating Flaherty's style lies not in seeking out the strands of documentary or ethnographic authenticity, but in recognizing his skill in bridging the gap between on-site improvisation and narrative continuity on the screen. This improvisational skill is in evidence in *Nanook* near the end of the seal hunting sequence, where Flaherty's slight pans and tilts capture the raging sled dogs with the same fullness and immediacy as the more carefully produced moments earlier in the film, such as the dramatically staged opening shot of the walrus hunt.

Flaherty's next film, *Moana*, was shot in western Samoa, where he lived and worked with Frances and their children for nearly two years. The Flahertys were determined to recreate *Nanook*'s heroic survival tale while relocating the story to a tropical climate. *Nanook* had defined the major themes that would dominate Flaherty's other work: the visual power of natural settings, the importance of familial bonds, nostalgia for ways of life presumed to be dead or dying, and the human struggle against nature. But Samoan life failed to produce the latter key dramatic element, and the film that resulted was arguably the first feature-length documentary to focus to such an extent on the details of everyday life. *Moana* is reputed to have inspired the first written use of the term "documentary" (Grierson, 1979), though the claim has more recently been disputed (Winston, 1988). Some of the film's most lasting contributions were aesthetic. Flaherty experimented with long focus lenses while in Samoa, finding that a greater distance between the camera and observed subjects helped to capture performances that appeared less controlled and self-conscious. He also rejected the standard use of orthochromatic film stock in favour of more sensitive panchromatic film, resulting in resonant images that helped to influence a shift in Hollywood practice. Perhaps even more than his other films, *Moana* reflects Flaherty's alignment with a modernist primitivism that arrived with the emergence of American cultural relativism, embodying Western longings for an untouched and timeless native world where one might escape from the routines of an increasingly industrialized and mechanized society.

To fund *Moana*, Flaherty had been offered a "blank check" by Jesse Lasky of Famous Players-Lasky. But the film's lackluster box-office receipts meant that his honeymoon period with Hollywood was effectively over. Flaherty had, in any case, already gained a reputation for faithfully working in exotic locations with native peoples just at a moment when Hollywood was pioneering the large-scale location shoot and banking on the popularity of expeditionary films. After two smaller projects, *The Potterymaker* (1925) and the Manhattan "city symphony," *Twenty-four Dollar Island* (1927), Flaherty entered into a difficult period during which he contributed to a number of mainstream projects. Having provided a poetic image of the South Pacific as a lost paradise in *Moana*, he was determined to make a film that would reveal the effects of colonial exploitation upon the region. In 1927, he went to Tahiti to co-direct the MGM adaptation of Frederick O'Brien's best-seller, *White Shadows in the South Seas*, but his slow and extravagant shooting methods fell afoul of the more commercial expectations of his co-director, W.S. Van Dyke. Another opportunity in the Pacific came in 1929, when his brother David helped to cement a partnership between Flaherty and the German expressionist director, F.W. Murnau. The film was completed as the South Seas fantasy *Tabu* (1931), though Flaherty was also to abandon this project; he contributed to the screenplay and to the photography until aesthetic and financial disagreements led him to sell his share in the film. This episode ended what is sometimes called the first American phase of his career (Murphy, 1978).

Many have argued that Flaherty's next phase, working for the head of the film unit of the Empire Marketing Board, John Grierson, marked a subtle shift in his directing style. Certainly his trust in his own visual instincts was in full force when he decided to spurn a preconceived script while shooting *Industrial Britain* for Grierson. The relationship between Grierson and Flaherty during this period suggests their differing approaches to the documentary form. Grierson insisted on a script, which Flaherty refused to produce; and, while Grierson admired Flaherty's powers of observation, he ultimately enlisted Basil Wright and Arthur Elton to finish the photography, while Grierson himself completed the editing (Murphy, 1978).

In many respects, *Man of Aran* widened the rift developing between Flaherty and the purveyors of the British social documentary movement. Sponsored by Gaumont, it marked a return to studio financing arrangements, which also meant that Flaherty was able to draw on the long-term filming methods, high shooting ratio, and eye for ethnographic detail he developed while making *Nanook* and *Moana*. But the finished product also brought to a head debates about Flaherty's escapism and his penchant for reconstructing worlds from bygone eras. Many critics saw Flaherty's "evasive documentary" as a product of romantic idealism and even fascism (an argument exacerbated when it won the Mussolini Cup at the Venice Film Festival) (Murphy, 1978). Returning to the dramatic "man against nature" theme of *Nanook*, sequences such as the shark-hunt episode elided the fact that such practices had ceased to exist for nearly a hundred years. Rotha would argue that the film failed to achieve the paramount objective of documentary practice: the careful examination and analysis of contemporary social problems. Grierson, however, defended Flaherty's unquestionable influence on a generation of filmmakers, noting his gift for natural observation and his highly personal style.

Critics continued to ask whether Flaherty's contributions to the documentary form were primarily aesthetic. He appeared unable or unwilling to address the political and social demands of the 1930s documentary film movement. But his next nonfiction project, *The Land*, went some distance toward lessening, if not completely suppressing, these doubts. After working for Alexander Korda on *Elephant Boy* in India, he returned to the United States to make *The Land* for Pare Lorentz, who had recently become head of the United States Film Service. *The Land* takes as its subject the use and abuse of land, but also dwells on the themes of journey and displacement, perhaps revealing Flaherty's own preoccupations more than it examines the social and political contexts of its subject, an impression somewhat underscored by Flaherty's voice-over narration. Still, according to Rotha and Wright, this was the one film in which Flaherty had faced up to contemporary sociological and technological problems (Murphy, 1978).

"Sometimes you have to lie," Flaherty once stated; "one often has to distort the thing to catch its true spirit" (Calder-Marshall, 1963). Flaherty's final documentary was the Standard Oil-financed *Louisiana Story*, which was clearly made in the spirit of this quote, for it is a highly stylized work that, at the same time, draws on the moods, rhythms, and ambience of its bayou setting in an effort to capture the essence of Cajun life. It followed another aborted effort working for a larger film unit during the war, Frank Capra's Army orientation unit. Like many of Flaherty's efforts, this ended in a falling out. *Louisiana Story* was generously financed and thus provided the more relaxed conditions under which Flaherty thrived. Working with the team of Richard Leacock on camera, Helen van Dongen as on-site editor, and Frances, Flaherty produced what many have considered his finest achievement.

As Richard Barsam suggests, *Louisiana Story* perhaps best illustrates the ways that Flaherty's films defy classification within traditional notions of the nonfiction genre, suggesting that Flaherty's work is best understood as that of a realist filmmaker (Orbanz, 1988). Flaherty tended to avoid densely critical or philosophical assessments of his work, but it can be said that those elements most often criticized in the films—narrative distortion, romantic escapism, and nostalgia—might have been the preconditions that made possible a distinctive documentary aesthetic, and they provide the grounds for reading Flaherty as a documentary auteur.

JEFFREY GEIGER

See also **Capra, Frank; EMB Film Unit; Grierson, John;** *Industrial Britain***; Leacock, Richard; Lorentz, Pare;** *Louisiana Story***;** *Man of Aran***;** *Moana***;** *Nanook of the North***; Rotha, Paul; Wright, Basil**

Biography

Born in Iron Mountain, Michigan, 16 February, 1884. Attended Michigan College of Mines. Worked as prospector and explorer for Canadian industrialist Sir William Mackenzie from 1910–1916. Released his first feature, *Nanook of the North*, in 1922. Lived in Safune, Western Samoa, 1923–1925, while making the Famous Players-Lasky financed *Moana*, released in 1926. Worked on *White Shadows in the South Seas* for Irving Thalberg and M.G.M. in 1927; worked with F.W. Murnau on *Tabu* in 1929. Worked for the Empire Marketing Board making *Industrial Britain*, 1931. Lived in Ireland while making *Man of Aran*, 1932–1933. Won best foreign film, Venice Film Festival and National Board of Review, 1934. Returned to the United States for *The Land*, 1939–1941, and worked for Frank Capra and the Army orientation film unit, 1942. Lived in Abbeville,

Louisiana, working on *Louisiana Story*, 1946–1947, released in 1948. Nominated for best writing Academy Award (with Frances Flaherty), 1949. Died in Brattleboro, Vermont, 23 July, 1951.

Selected Films

1922 *Nanook of the North*: producer, director, writer, photographer, editor
1925 *The Potterymaker*: director, photographer, writer
1926 *Moana* (*Moana: A Romance of the Golden Age*; *Moana: The Love Life of a South Sea Siren*): co-producer, director, photographer, writer, co-editor
1927 *The Twenty-Four Dollar Island*: director, photographer, writer
1933 *Industrial Britain*: co-director, co-photographer
1934 *Man of Aran*: director, photographer, writer
1942 *The Land*: director, co-photographer, writer, narrator
1948 *Louisiana Story*: producer, director, co-photographer, co-writer

Further Reading

Barsam, Richard Meran, editor, *Nonfiction Film Theory and Criticism*, New York: E.P. Dutton, 1976.

Calder-Marshall, Arthur, *The Innocent Eye: The Life of Robert J. Flaherty*, London: W.H. Allen and Co., 1963.

Danzker, Jo-Anne Birnie, editor, *Robert Flaherty Photographer/Filmmaker: The Inuit 1910–1922*, Vancouver: Vancouver Art Gallery, 1980.

Grierson, John, "Flaherty's Poetic Moana," in *The Documentary Tradition*, Edited by Lewis Jacobs, New York: W.W. Norton, 1979.

Griffith, Richard, *The World of Robert Flaherty*, Boston: Little, Brown, and Co., 1953.

Murphy, William T., *Robert Flaherty: A Guide to References and Resources*, Boston: G.K. Hall and Co., 1978.

Orbanz, Eva, editor, *Filming Robert Flaherty's* Louisiana Story*: The Helen van Dongen Diary*, New York: The Museum of Modern Art, 1988.

Rony, Fatimah Tobing, *The Third Eye: Race, Cinema, and the Ethnographic Spectacle*, Durham, NC: Duke University Press, 1996.

Rotha, Paul, *Robert J. Flaherty: A Biography*, edited by Jay Ruby, Philadelphia: University of Pennsylvania Press, 1983.

Winston, Brian, "Before Grierson, Before Flaherty: The Documentary Film in 1914," in *Sight and Sound* 57, Autumn, 1988, 277–279.

FOR LOVE OR MONEY

(Australia, McMurchy, 1983)

For Love or Money is a feature-length documentary that was produced over a five-year period, from 1979 to 1983, which endeavors to comprehensively document the working lives of Australian women since colonial times. The scope of the documentary is impressive as it ranges from the exploitation of convict women and aboriginal workers to the equal pay debates of the 1960s and 1970s.

The film was made collaboratively by Megan McMurchy, Margot Nash, Margot Oliver, and Jeni Thornley. Three of the filmmakers, McMurchy, Oliver, and Thornley, also produced a book that draws on and extends the central themes addressed by the film. *For Love or Money* is constructed around four sections that divide the documentary into distinct historical periods. These periods are represented through a collage of extracts from other texts such as still photographs, newspaper archives, newsreels, feature films, and documentaries. Interviews with women from diverse social backgrounds are also interspersed between this collage. *For Love or Money* had its genesis in the late 1970s, and the final product is concerned with the feminist issues that dominated the movement at that time. It addresses the under-representation of women's experience and their contribution to the world of work. *For Love or Money* endeavors to "make visible," or "recover" that which has been consistently ignored and undervalued (Moore, 1987).

The voice-over is also compiled from a variety of sources drawing on testimonials, quotations, and a voice-of-God narration that was scripted specifically for the film. The juxtapositions and bricolage of sound and images lends the documentary a poetic quality that marks the film as the product of a

For Love or Money, 1983.
[*Still courtesy of the British Film Institute*]

creative authorship rather than a transparent historical record. This approach values the first person, subjective address as a legitimate form of historical knowledge, and this element again locates the film in relation to the strategies of feminist theory that developed through the 1970s and into the 1980s. However, *For Love or Money* also embodies the shifts and contradictions in theory and politics that were increasingly debated at this time. While many aspects of the film seek a subjective retelling of history, it also draws on an authoritative address and an objective historiography to represent the "truth" of women's exploitation and experience. When the film was finally released, as a result of this inherent ambivalence, it was afforded a mixed reception (Curthoys and Dermody, 1987).

For Love or Money is not only a painstaking account of women and work throughout Australian history, but, because of what Curthoys and Dermody call an "asynchrony" of theoretical paradigms, it also bears all the traces of the intellectual shifts of the time. It preceded a number of films produced in the 1980s that went on to use traditional modes of documentary representation such as the use of archival material and interviews, while also attempting to subvert this convention in different ways. Notable examples include *Red Matildas* (1985), *Snakes and Ladders* (1987), and *A Singular Woman* (1985). This fusion of formal elements became a hallmark of feminist filmmaking in Australia at this time (Blonski and Freiberg, 1989).

BELINDA SMAILL

For Love or Money (Australia, Flashback Films, 1983, 109 min.). Distributed by Ronin Films and Women Make Movies. Produced and written by Megan McMurchy, Margot Oliver, and Jeni Thornley. Directed by Megan McMurchy and Jeni Thornley. Cinematography by Erika Addis. Edited by Margot Nash. Sound by Cliff Pugsley.

Further Reading

Blonski, Annette, and Freda Freiberg, "Double Trouble: Women's Films," in *The Australian Screen*, edited by Albert Moran and Tom O'Regan, Melbourne: Penguin Books, 1989.

Curthoys, Ann, and Susan Dermody, "*For Love or Money*: A Work of Loving" in *Don't Shoot Darling!: Women's*

Independent Filmmaking in Australia, edited by Annette Blonski, Barbara Creed, and Freda Freiberg, Melbourne: Greenhouse, 1987.

Dermody, Susan, "Not Necessarily a Lead Dress: Thinking Beyond 'Redress' in Women's Films" in *Signs of Independents: Ten Years of the Creative Development Fund*, edited by Megan McMurchy and Jennifer Stott, Sydney: Australian Film Commission, 1988.

McMurchy, Megan, Margot Oliver, and Jeni Thornley, *For Love or Money: A Pictorial History of Women and Work in Australia*, edited by Irina Dunn, Melbourne: Penguin Books, 1983.

Moore, Catriona, "'Woman': *For Love or Money* and *We Aim to Please*" in *Don't Shoot Darling!: Women's Independent Filmmaking in Australia*, edited by Annette Blonski, Barbara Creed, and Freda Freiberg, Melbourne: Greenhouse, 1987.

O'Regan, Tom, *Australian National Cinema*, London: Routledge, 1996.

FOREST OF BLISS

(US, Gardner, 1986)

Forest of Bliss is a poetic nonfiction film by Robert Gardner about death and regeneration. Set in Benares, India, the film is at once highly specific to its setting, on the ghats (stone steps leading directly into the water) of the Ganges River, and universal in its resonance. The film has been much lauded for its revitalization of the genre of the city symphony, and for the almost sublime beauty of its unsparing yet evidently reverent images. Its detractors have been primarily anthropologists, who have highlighted as the film's shortcoming precisely that quality most acclaimed by film critics and historians—its absence of verbal explication in any form. There is no voice-over narration, nor subtitling of speech, nor any direct-address interviews with the film's subjects. However, the film's largely nonverbal engagement with its subject displays a critical acumen and perceptual acuity rare in ethnographic film, which conveys respect at once for its subject (Benares and its inhabitants) and for its viewers, who trusted to navigate through the images without any voice-over direction *Forest of Bliss* resolutely refuses to condescend to the viewer after the fashion of the canonical ethnographic film, travelog, or liberal documentary. In retreating from language, Gardner is renouncing the dominant expository modality of documentary, and seeking instead to impart a more corporeal, intersubjective engagement with his subject, the willful ambiguity and open-endedness of which seeks to mirror that of human existence itself.

Forest of Bliss is also the apogée of Gardner's own oeuvre to date (which includes *Blunden Harbor* [1951], *Dead Birds* [1963], *The Nuer* [with Hilary Harris, 1971]*, Rivers of Sand* [1974], *Deep Hearts* [1981], *Ika Hands*, and *Passenger* [1998]), in that it is his most consummate experimentation with nonrealist montage. The film moves back and forth between a number of protonarrative strands (or "slight narratives," in Paul Rotha's memorable phrase), but tells no story and develops no character in any conventional sense. Although *Forest of Bliss* contains three distinct main characters, Gardner is concerned more with situating them within the larger ecology of Benares, than establishing them as individuals. This is an ecology of water, fire, marigolds, dogs, cows, boats, bamboo, sand, stone, and wood, all elements with a significance, use, and interrelatedness that we grasp only gradually through the course of the film. It is an ecology of life and death, of dirt and purification, of the sacred and the profane. Death, no less than life, is marked by a limitless series of rituals, both individual and collective. Yet at the same time, death is the local industry; Benares, as the holiest Hindu city, has for millennia been the pilgrimage site of a vast mortuary migration. If *Forest of Bliss* is about the ecology of Benares, it is also about the economy of death. The "slight narratives" of the film—the sorting of the golden marigolds, the assembling of the bamboo funerary litters, the

Forest of Bliss, 1986.
[*Still courtesy of the British Film Institute*]

transporting of the sand, the weighing of the fire-wood, the caring and cleansing of the recently departed, the baptizing of a new boat—all coalesce on the Burning Ground of the sacred ghats on the banks of the Ganges.

The film is driven by a sense of constant motion, conveyed as much by the elaborate, polyphonic sound track as the interwoven images. The city of Benares bustles and rings with the collective activities of individuals. Gardner's gaze is simultaneously wandering and unwavering, as countless people, animals, and objects ascend and descend the extensive and elaborate flights of stairs that attach the city to its river—and life to death. Whereas the city streets resound with near collisions of vehicles and cargo, beggars and dogs, cows and children, and pilgrims and priests, the chorus of the Ganges is one of amplified splashes, squeaking boat oars, and chirping birds. The business of death is conducted both inside and outside,

with each space evoking the other through sound. Early in the film a priest is making offerings in a sheltered altar. His solitude and concentration are emphasized by the sounds of his labored breathing. At the same time we hear a chorus of children's voices playing nearby; adult men talking, coughing, hammering; birds singing—all unseen, but present nonetheless. Almost all of the nonverbal or ambient sounds in the film seem amplified, while the few verbal communications appear—unlike the more guttural exclamations—to be muted somewhat. The effect is to reflect an intention on the part of the filmmaker to divert us from attending to the denotative meaning of what is being said, and to evoke in us instead a synaesthetic response to the full realm of connotations in all that we see and hear.

Forest of Bliss is arguably without parallel in nonfiction cinema in its exploration of the polyvalence of (aural and visual) imagery, almost unmediated by any verbal exegesis, diegetic or extra-diegetic, circumscribing their meaning. The one verbal element whose significance the film, as it unfolds, repeatedly invites us to ponder is the opening epigraph from Yeats, itself a translation from the Upanishads: "Everything in the world is eater or eaten, the seed is food and the fire is eater." In its refusal of conventional notions of linearity and realism, its experimentation with montage, and its polyphonic, non-narrative sound track, *Forest of Bliss* explores the reciprocal provocations of ethnographic and avant-garde filmmaking in a fashion that had largely been neglected since the work of Maya Deren, but in a manner altogether more sensuous. Although the film was initially disavowed by anthropologists, it is now recognized as having taken ethnographic film to unequalled aesthetic and sensory heights.

Since its original release on 16mm and 35mm film in 1986, *Forest of Bliss* has been released on DVD as an accompaniment to a detailed exegesis of the film by Robert Gardner and his co-producer, Ákos Östör, *Making Forest of Bliss: Intention, Circumstance, and Chance in the Non-Fiction Film* (Harvard University Press, 2001).

ILISA BARBASH

See also **Gardner, Robert**

Forest of Bliss. A film by Robert Gardner. Produced for the Film Study Center, Harvard University by Robert Gardner and Ákos Östör. Cinematography and editing by Robert Gardner. Sound recording by Ned Johnston. Sound editing by Michael Chalufour. Production associates Baidyanath Saraswati, Om Prakash Sharma, and R. L. Maurya. Post-production assistant Maria Sendra. Second camera by Ned Johnston.

Further Reading

Coover, Roderick, "Worldmaking, Metaphors and Montage in the Representation of Cultures: Cross-Cultural Filmmaking and the Poetics of Robert Gardner's *Forest of Bliss*," *Visual Anthropology*, 14, 4, 415–433.

Chopra, Radikha, "Robert Gardner's *Forest of Bliss*: A Review," *SVA Newsletter*, spring 1989, 2–3.

Eck, Diana, *Banaras, City of Light*, London: Routledge, 1983.

Östör, Ákos, "*Forest of Bliss*: Film and Anthropology," *East-West Film Journal* 8, 2, 70–104.

Östör, Ákos, and Robert Gardner, *Making Forest of Bliss: Intention, Circumstance, and Chance in the Non-Fiction Film*, Cambridge: Harvard University Press, 2001.

FORGÁCS, PÉTER

An independent media artist working in Budapest since the 1970s, Péter Forgács emerged in the 1990s as an important creative force in the shaping of documentary style. He revitalized the art of compilation filmmaking by incorporating poetic, stylistic touches more often found in the experimental sphere. As an archivist and researcher, Forgács helped bring attention to amateur films as documentary materials to be mobilized in revising the historiography of the twentieth century, particularly that of Europe in the 1930s and 1940s.

Much of Forgács's early work was not in documentary film per se, but in eclectic parts of the fine arts: video installation, theater, and musical performance. In 1988, after five years of archiving home movie collections, he received his first commission from Hungarian television. Establishing a specialization in the revivification of amateur films, he turned to work that was more obviously, though not conventionally, documentary. He classified several of his feature-length pieces as "video operas," for the ways in which they shape actuality footage into musical and rhythmic arrangements. The mesmeric scores of his musical collaborator, Tibor Szemzö, are key to holding the patchwork visuals together. Although Forgács clearly retains the influence of experimental art movements, he has created a body of work dedicated to historical narrative and individuals living within the sweep of historical forces.

Forgács is often characterized as a "found footage" filmmaker, but this is misleading in two ways. He tracks down small-gauge amateur films (8, Super 8, 9.5, and 16mm footage), but does not treat them as anonymous, mysterious "found" objects. Rather, he does research about the owners, makers, and subjects of these home movies and other amateur productions. His short *Wittgenstein Tractatus* (1992), a collage of unidentified imagery and philosophical aphorisms, is the exception to his usual method of scrupulously identifying and historicizing such films. Although Forgács uses small-gauge celluloid as source material, his own production is video based. His authorial signature is indebted to the postproduction tools available in digital video. Without overwhelming the film artifact, his work uses a full palette of layered embellishments: color graphics, freeze frames, slow motion, tinting, superimpositions, and stylized text.

Since 1988, Forgács has produced more than a dozen hour-long documentaries in his "Private Hungary" series. Beginning with *A Bartos család (The Bartos Family)*, these contemplative works examine the daily life of Europeans at the time of World War II by reanimating home movies. Because amateur cinematography was an expensive hobby, the films principally record the households of privileged and bourgeois families. In addition to the expected birthdays, weddings, and holiday scenes, there are often artful, constructed passages done by filmmakers who edited, directed, and titled their silent footage. In the most remarkable episodes, such as *Az örvény* (1996) (*Free Fall*), Forgács suggests a radical re-reading of the history of documentary. His film reveals the process by which sophisticated amateur cineastes, such György Petö, photographed private, domestic moments. In so doing they also created documents of the social spheres in which their lives were shaped.

Forgács sparingly uses conventional archival materials, such as newsreels, in these compilations. When he does, it is to situate "private" films in public space and history. The contrasts between the private view and "official" documentation are dramatic, but left open and contradictory. In *De Maalstroom* (1997) (*The Maelstrom*) home movies of the Jewish Peereboom family (taken in Holland, 1933–1942) take on a tragic irony that is heightened by the intercutting of films shot at home by a Nazi commissar, who oversaw their deportation to a concentration camp. At other times, amateur footage takes on a heroic, public dimension. In *Angelos' Film* (2000), we see footage of the Nazi occupation of Greece, which aristocrat Angelos Papanasstassiou clandestinely recorded with a hidden camera: swastikas hung on the Acropolis, public hangings, and other events never shot by the official newsreels.

The legacy of Forgács's work is in both these finished tapes and the Private Film and Photo Archive he established to save these alternate histories. The collection is housed at the Central European University and includes more than 500 hours of amateur films (1910–1985) from Hungary and elsewhere, as well as 300 hours of audio interviews with the filmmakers' families.

DAN STREIBLE

See also **Compilation; Found Footage**

Biography

Born in Hungary, September 10, 1950. Studied at Academy of Fine Arts, Budapest, 1971–1972, 1974–1977. Began work at Béla Balázs Film Studio, 1978. Collaboration with the minimalist music ensemble, Group 180, including composer Tibor Szemzö, from 1978 on. Established Private Film and Photo Archives Foundation, 1983. Researcher at Hungarian Sociological Institute of the Academy of Sciences, 1987. Documentary series "Conversations on Psychoanalysis," for Hungarian television, 1988–1993. Taught for University of California Berkeley's Central European studies program in Budapest, 1990–1991. Visiting artist, Arizona State University, 1993. Fellow at the Getty Research Institute, Los Angeles, 2000–2001.

Selected Films

2002 *Bibó breviarium/Istvan Bibo's Fragments*
2000 *Angelos' Film*
1998 *A dunai exodus/The Danube Exodus*
1997 *De Maalstroom/The Maelstrom: A Family Chronicle*
1997 *Class Lot*
1996 *Az örvény/Free Fall*
1995 *Miközben valahol/Meanwhile Somewhere*
1994 *Egy úrinő notesza/Notes of a Lady*
1992 *Bourgeois Dictionary*
1992 *Wittgenstein Tractatus*
1991 *Photographed by László Dudás*
1989 *Dusi és Jenô/Dusi and Jeno*
1988 *A Bartos család/The Bartos Family*

Further Reading

Bikacsy, G., "*Privat Magyarorszag* [Private Hungary]," in *New Hungarian Quarterly* winter, 1991, 159–161.
Boyle, Deirdre, "*Meanwhile Somewhere*: A Conversation with Péter Forgács," in *Millennium Film Journal* 37, 2001, 53–66.
Forgács, Péter, "Filmic Memories," in *Film Quarterly* 52.1, 1998, 60–61.
Portugues, Catherine, "Home Movies, Found Images, and 'Amateur Film' as a Witness to History: Péter Forgács's *Private Hungary*," in *The Moving Image* 1.2, 2001.
Waller, Marguerite R., "*Notes of a Lady* (Private Hungary 8)," in *American Historical Review* 99, 1994, 1252–1256.

FOUND FOOTAGE

Found footage is generally understood as already-shot film from another source used in a different context than was originally intended. An important raw material of much documentary filmmaking, found footage shifts the auteurist role in the creation of a film from the director to the editor. Films using found footage can include historical retrospectives, experimental collages, and propaganda films, among others. Because of its flexibility to take on different meaning in different contexts, found footage calls into question the intrinsic authority of the documentary and of the photographic image in general. In fact, the found footage film's genesis is in just such deceptive editing. In 1898, Francis Doublier used stock footage of the Nile and a Finnish tugboat to fill in the gaps constructing a narrative of the Dreyfus case in France.

Although there are various uses of found footage, the chief purposes can be broken down into three categories: informative, critical, and aesthetic. In the first case, the film footage is either topical (as in newsreels) or historical (as in biographies or retrospectives), and it is assumed to communicate something about the reality it portrays in a direct, first-hand way. When found footage is used critically, it is recontextualized in an ironic way, one where the footage communicates nearly the *opposite* message from what was initially intended; *Triumph of the Will* (1936), for example, was often recut by Allied forces to make Hitler look ridiculous. The aesthetic use of found footage tends to avoid political positions, because, in that case, the footage is valued less for its content than for its formal qualities as a series of moving images. William Wees designates these relationships to found footage, respectively, as realist, modernist, and postmodernist; however, strict temporal divisions ignore the reality of techniques, which vary more according to region, political affiliation, and availability of footage than by historical period.

Most found footage film is influenced in technique by modernist theories of montage. Found footage makes explicit Sergei Eisenstein's theory of montage as an act of uniting images that, when combined, create ideas in the mind of the viewer. When footage is from disparate sources, the only way to give it continuity is by creating thematic or intellectual connections (Eisenstein, 1957). One common strategy in using found footage is adding a new soundtrack that comments ironically on the images onscreen, using Eisenstein's "vertical montage" of sound and image at any given moment. In *Swinging the Lambeth Walk* (1940), for example, Len Lye sets the Nuremberg parade scene in *Triumph of the Will* (1936) to a popular British dance song, a move that undercuts the scene's seriousness and self-importance. This technique continues to be used in political documentaries today and can be clearly seen in those of Michael Moore, particularly *Fahrenheit 9/11* (2004).

The idea of the found object is also important to understanding the intentions behind the use of found footage in film. Central to Dada and surrealist thought was the belief that objects could be removed from their everyday context and designated "art." A urinal that Marcel Duchamp signed "R. Mutt," titled "Fountain," and submitted to the Salon of Independent Artists in 1917 is perhaps the best-known found object in art history. Found footage is often used in documentaries simply for the sake of displaying its strangeness as a cultural and aesthetic object. Industrial films and home movies of earlier eras are often shown uncut for this purpose. Another

strand of surrealist thought, shared by 1930s Marxist thinkers such as Walter Benjamin, valued found objects because they communicated unconscious truths about the culture to which they belonged. *The Atomic Café* (1982) uses 1950s American educational films about nuclear war as these types of found objects. Their now-comical warnings to "duck and cover" under school desks show the audience the absurd naïveté of the era and the results of nuclear paranoia.

Perhaps the main stylistic division evident in the varied uses of found footage is one of continuity. The popularity of the newsreel, the rise of communism, and the World Wars all generated found footage that was often used by people who wanted to make coherent political or historical statements. Filmmakers such as Esfir Schub, Frank Capra, and Henri Cartier-Bresson, whose *Le Retour* (1945) "almost seems one cameraman's work" did this in part by using found footage that fit into a coherent narrative, either through stylistic similarity or through similarity in content (Leyda, 1964). Later and more experimental filmmakers such as Debord and Baldwin work against the seamlessness of these kinds of films, often using footage of different quality, not matching cuts, or cutting between different subjects to give a sense of chaos. This visual discontinuity may be a result of the sheer volume of material the artists work from, but more important it calls into question the validity of presenting a continuous, coherent version of the truth. One of the main reasons for the recent popularity of found footage in documentaries is the sense of media saturation, of being bombarded by images and feeling the need to respond to them in some way. The Situationists, an avant-garde French group most active in the 1950s and 1960s, even coined a word for using media images against themselves "*détournement,*" meaning a turning away or detour from the image's initial purpose.

Because of its roots in the past, found footage is often used in films dealing with history and questioning the possibilities for conveying historical truth. Many film theorists discuss found footage as a means of exploring the limitations and possibilities of film archives as a means of reconstructing the past. For some critics, using found footage is a way of displaying our collective unconscious, the cultural fantasies and fears of a particular period. Sharon Sandusky, in particular, sees found footage as a way of reliving and recovering from historical trauma (Sandusky, 1993). However, most critics agree that the danger of found footage is in its very power to be taken out of context. Without historical understanding of where the images have come from, it is very easy for an audience to feel nostalgic or superior to the past being portrayed. Found footage, then, is important as a raw material for documentary film precisely because it fits whatever intentions the filmmaker has.

SUNNY STALTER

Selected Films

1927: *The Fall of the Romanov Dynasty*
1936: *Rose Hobart*
1940: *Swinging the Lambeth Walk*
1943-44: *Why We Fight*
1958: *A Movie*
1973: *La societé du spectacle/The Society of the Spectacle*
1982: *The Atomic Café*
1990: *Tribulation 99: Alien Anomalies Under Americ*
2004: *Fahrenheit 9/11*

Further Reading

Baldwin, Craig, *Tribulation 99: Alien Anomalies Under America*, New York: Ediciones La Calavera, 1991.

Eisenstein, S. M., *Film Form*, edited and translated by Jay Leyda, New York: Meridian Books, 1957.

Hausheer, Cecelia, and Christoph Settele, *Found Footage Film*, Luzern: VIPER, 1992.

Katz, Joel, "From Archive to Archiveology," in *Cinematograph*, 4, 1991, 93–103.

Leyda, Jay. *Films Beget Films*. New York: Hill and Wang, 1964.

Mackenzie, Scott. "Flowers in the Dustbin: Termite Culture and Detritus Cinema," in *CineAction*, 47, September, 1998, 24–29.

Sandusky, Sharon, "The Archaeology of Redemption: Toward Archival Film," in *Millenium Film Journal*, 26, 1993, 3–25.

Wees, William, *Recycled Images*, New York: Anthology Film Archives, 1993.

400 MILLION, THE

(Holland, Ivens, 1938)

The Dutch filmmaker Joris Ivens used his camera in his roles as both political activist and humanitarian filmmaker. Ivens is noted for having produced social and political documentaries that go beyond depictions of nature and scientific feats. He had a prolific career, directing his camera toward monumental events and helping assert the role motion pictures can play in the recording of history. *The 400 Million* reflects this commitment to historical documentation.

The film was shot over four months during the spring of 1938 and documents China's struggle against invading Japanese forces. Ivens admitted that his recent experience shooting a film during the Spanish Civil War (*The Spanish Earth*) taught him the difficulties of documenting military conflicts; however, the experience also bolstered his commitment to giving voice to the courageous efforts being made against fascism. Production of *The 400 Million* forced Ivens to negotiate his way around multiple obstacles placed in his way by Chiang Kai-shek's government, testing his nerve

and his commitment to the project. He was initially restricted by the Chinese military commanders from going to the forefront of the conflict, but as he has stated, he drew courage and strength from the spirit and confidence displayed by the Chinese soldiers that surrounded him, who unfailingly continued in their roles as soldiers. Ivens mirrored this commitment as a filmmaker, unwilling to let surveillance, curfews, or personality differences keep him from carrying out his goals in filming this important moment in history. During production, Ivens moved between guerilla units, Communist Party members, and the nationalist army (under Chiang Kai-shek), much to the dismay and suspicion of each faction. Even though they were fighting the common enemy of Japan, these groups held opposing sociopolitical views; however, Ivens's film depicts these factions as comrades united by a common cause.

After six weeks of frustrating delay, Ivens and his crew were finally allowed access to the frontlines of the war. Nonetheless, once they arrived, the general

The 400 Million, 1938.
[Still courtesy of the British Film Institute]

in command changed his mind and told them they could go no further. Angry and determined, Ivens declared that he and his crew came to China to film battles as they unfolded, informing the general that the crew was going to push on, with or without him. Ultimately, the general conceded to Ivens's demands. Such encounters continued to limit the crew's access to the battles. Ivens was constantly frustrated with such limitations, but at the same time was sensitive to the fact that military personnel struggled to comprehend why someone would risk his life on the battlefield for no visible reward. Ivens had hoped that the film would not only garner support for the Chinese struggle but also serve in the fight against fascism and totalitarian regimes in Europe.

Ivens's critical talent for composing sequences of visual poeticism and his skillful editing to create engrossing and rhythmic sequences elevate this film above typical newsreel footage and most other early twentieth century war documentaries. Such techni-

ques are used to elicit sympathy for the Chinese people. The rich visuals and montage are aurally linked to commentary spoken by actor Frederic March, shifting between a subjective voice (adopting the perspective and sentiment of Chinese soldiers and civilians) and that of an authoritative, though impassioned, observer. Although the visuals are dramatic, moving, and at times horrific, the footage lacks continuity; therefore, because of the restraints placed on Ivens and his crew, the film relies heavily on the spoken word both to carry the story forward and to evoke a sense of the subjectivity and nuances of life in a nation under siege. Even Ivens himself admitted the commentary was rather extensive. Considering the limitations that tormented Ivens and his crew, the heavy reliance on voiceover appears somewhat justified, if not consistent with most documentaries of that age. The soundtrack is artfully and illustratively textured, complementing the visuals with a quasi-polyvocal narration,

Chinese folk music, the raucous sounds of war, and excerpts (in Mandarin) from military officials and youth leaders, which are accompanied by their English translations and spoken by American actors.

The film begins with a jarring image sequence of the aftereffects of Japanese bombings in northeastern China, blatantly referring to the atrocities as acts of unprovoked military aggression. The next section characterizes China as a nation with a long history whose cultural contributions have benefited the world since the time of Marco Polo. China's link with the West is hinted at as a further narrative means to stir interest and concern from Europe and North America. This section concludes by reasserting the value and import of Chinese culture on an historical and humanitarian level, while emphasizing that although it is a nation of 400 million (one fifth of the world's population at that time), its people are united in defending their vast and diverse homeland. The film then shows a China on the road to modernization after deposing its emperor, its emerging civil infrastructure and transportation system, and the development of modern technology and industry. These efforts at modernization, as the film suggests, may have provoked Japan's aggression, which saw China as an immense landscape of untapped natural resources.

This provocation is addressed in the next section of the film, in which Japan's history of military aggression toward eastern Asia is recounted. It is also noted that the United States was still exporting iron and steel to Imperial Japan, placing the United States in a position of complacency, if not accountability, in regard to the atrocities afflicted on the Chinese people. Ivens's own political sentiments are apparent through the film's privileging of commoners and China's former

Red Army. In tribute to the hurriedly trained commoners of China, brave farmers are shown using guerilla war tactics, which were an invaluable component to China's defense strategy. Ivens suggests that the most heroic military efforts are those of the Eighth Route Army, a unit from China's former Red Army.

None of this detracts from Ivens's overall effort to create a film that emphasizes, at least temporarily, the unity of China's various political factions. One of the final sequences of the film circumvents intra-China political differences to recount and emphasize the importance of China obtaining even the smallest of victories against Japanese forces (the recapture of Tai'erzhuang, for example). The overriding message of this final sequence is that one small victory is not only the essential first step toward reestablishing a free and stable China, but one that will, ideally, help to elicit support from the West.

On completion of *The 400 Million*, Ivens donated his film camera to a representative of the Chinese Communist Party. Little did he know that his camera was to become the first motion picture camera owned by the Yan'an Film Group, preserved today at the Museum of Chinese Revolutionary History. Portions of Ivens's film were later used by American director Frank Capra as part of his World War II propaganda film series, *Why We Fight*.

KEVIN TAYLOR ANDERSON

See also **Ivens, Joris; *Why We Fight***

The 400 Million. United States, 52 min., b/w, sound, 35mm, 1939. Directed by Joris Ivens; story by Ivens and John Ferno; photography by Ferno and Robert Capa; music by Hanns Eisler; commentary spoken by Frederic March. The film is also known as *China in 1938*, released in 1939.

FRANCE

From the famous film show of December 1895 to 1940, documentaries were considered uninteresting productions that were fine for amateurs but not worth being shown in movie theatres. Such contempt is all the more surprising, as during this initial period, theoreticians and filmmakers defined, on paper and in actual practice, the four main traits that have caracterized the French documentary tradition up to the present: (1) the observation films aimed at recording what is significant in an object or a procedure, (2) the explanatory films intended not only to describe but also to comment, (3) the critical films that explored the unseen side of actions or events, and (4) the formal movies that question the nature and purpose of documentaries. The respective importance of these groups varied according to the main concerns of any period and to spectators' reactions. In a second epoch, roughly from 1940 to 1968, documentaries became fashionable. At a time when their country was in decline the French were anxious to get information about the world and about the new techniques coming from the United States. Film directors no longer looked down on "factual" films. In the last decades of the twentieth century, those involved in the film industry were obliged to work for television. There was a division between the channels that made instructive movies and a handful of independent filmmakers eager to experiment new formulas.

The Lumière brothers, authors of the first French movies, were manufacturers of cinematic equipment and raw film. Their "views" were aimed only at showing the quality of their products. However some of their operators, instead of merely recording ephemeral happenings, filmed relevant aspects of the current social life. The first French documentary was shot in July 1986 by an unknown operator who went to Carmaux, a then important coal mining area. He filmed the coke coming out of the oven and, more important, the women sorting and carrying big coal blocks. His was a typical observer's attitude. He adopted, in both cases, a unique position. His presence cannot be spotted; the workers, absorbed in their job, never look at the camera. Only a small minority of the more than 1,400 "views" shot for the Lumières are of such quality. The firm soon stopped production.

The Lumières had dispatched operators throughout the world to advertise their material. A wealthy financier, Albert Kahn, thought he could carry out the same operation to constitute a vast picture library, the *Planet's Archives*. Instructed to film the customs, living conditions, and resources of the countries they visited, the cameramen sent to Europe, the Middle East, Asia, and Africa from 1908 to 1931 brought back hundreds of documents that were roughly edited for people to consult them. Wars, Kahn believed, are caused by reciprocal ignorance; a better knowledge of "the other" would help the progress of universal peace. Few were interested. Later, in the 1960s, this prodigious collection became famous and was used extensively by television.

Documentaries did not appeal to French spectators during the first decades of the century. The 8,000 movies Pathé, the main producer, diffused before 1920 were comedies or melodramas. Made in studio, they did not cost much and Pathé did not want his crew to work outside. One of his directors, Alfred Machin, personally shot, during his holidays, the pictures edited in 1913 for Pathé's only feature-length (fifty-five minutes) documentary *Voyages et grandes chasses en Afrique* (*Journeys and Big Hunts in Africa*).

Documentaries developed cut off from commercial circuits, thanks to various forms of sponsoring. Instead of merely recording aspects of the world, they were meant to reveal and explain precise, well-defined processes. A minority of scientists understood early the importance of moving pictures. Subsidised by Pathé and then Albert Kahn, Dr. Jean Commandon made a series of instructional movies on the functioning of the human body and on chirurgical operations. Accurate, surgical and detailed, his films were too difficult for the common people. Another doctor, Jean Painlevé (1902–1989), was less demaning and won an excellent reputation; his *La chirurgie correctrice* (*Corrective Surgery,* 1926) or *L'étude du sang* (*The Study of Blood,* 1935) introduced the topic clearly, displayed long shots with much contrast, and commented extensively on every image. Sometimes Painlevé proved fanciful; he treated animals—*Les oursins* (*Sea Urchins,* 1925), *Les crevettes* (*Shrimps,* 1930)—like humans, attributing them intention and siding with them against their enemies. Backed by the authorities, he was able to reach a wide audience of pupils and students.

Having lost their foreign clients during the World War I, the French producers were obliged to turn toward the domestic market. The state and various public offices provided them with a new outlet. Gaumont launched a "Série enseignement" ("Educational Series") and Pathé a "Pathé revue," both constituted of shorts (ten to fifteen minutes) dealing with a highly specific topic such as the making and functioning of an engine, the strength of various types of sewing threads, and the best way of using a tool. More than one thousand of these items found in the Gaumont or Pathé archive have been restored and are now available for consultation at the Paris Bibliothèque Nationale. Less interested in cinema than the state, industrial firms financed few publicity films. The case of car factories is typical. The Ford Company produced more than five thousand cinematic documents from 1914 onward; Fiat and Volkswagen made an extensive use of films to advertise their vehicles. In

France Citroën was content with sponsoring prestige operations; a film crew followed long-distance trips shooting *La croisière noire* (*The Black Cruise,* 1926) and *La croisière jaune* (*The Yellow Cruise,* 1933) in praise of Citroën cars' reliability. Renault, the main French manufacturer, ordered only four pictures between the World Wars. The longest (fifty-seven minutes), *Automobiles de France,* shot by Pathé-Natan in 1934, is a good example of average publicity documentaries. A journalist calls Renault and asks to visit the factory. He is first informed about steel production and about the components of a car. He is then taken through the plant, with much emphasis on the building of the body work and on the assembly line. The director, Jean Loubignac, used clever tricks; for instance he made a reverse tracking-shot from the end to starting point of the the assembly line to compensate for its slowness and apparently doubled its speed. Not accurate enough for a specialist but too long and complicated for the lay spectator, this movie illustrates the imperfections of most French documentaries—not aimed at a large public they were often of poor quality.

Oddly enough it was amongst these films that the first and possibly most challenging documentary theory was developed. France boasts a wealth of film experts who have never held a camera. Such was not the case of Jean Epstein (1897–1953) director of a series of fiction films and documentaries and author of several books, notably *Bonjour cinéma* (*Good Morning Cinema,* 1921). By playing with time and space, Epstein contended, by jumping from one point to another and by accelerating or slowing down, that cinema drastically alters our relationship to the world and suggests that other connections are possible. Its aim is neither to become a mechanical eye used to observe things nor to comment, but rather to go beyond appearances. Documentaries must not inform; they have to disclose a yet unknown universe. Epstein was not a loner but rather the spokesman of a small group of intellectuals hastily labelled "avant-gardists," although no army followed them. Avant-gardists loathed informative movies and wanted cinema to break with the humdrum of daily activities. They were divided into two groups: the critics and the formalists.

The critics reacted against the smooth, alternately sentimental and comforting vision offered by fiction films. With *La Zone* (*The Slum Belt,* 1928), Georges Lacombe, leaving Paris's animated centre, explored the most derelict sectors of urban periphery. Banking on surprise and disorientation, he mapped out no itinerary and wrote practically no commentary. This "zone" was a non-city, a no-man's-land close by affluent districts but totally neglected. Refuting in advance Africa's pleasant aspect filmed by the Citroën crew, Marc Allégret (1900–1973), traveling with André Gide, evoked in *Voyage au Congo* (*Voyage to the Congo,* 1925) a country threatened by malnutrition and illness. While denouncing another form of destitution, the absolute poverty of Estramaduran country-people in *Las Hurdes,* also known as *Terre sans pain* (*Land without Bread,* shot in 1932, released in 1937), Luis Buñuel (1900–1983) took another course (for the production context see the entry on Spanish documentaries). After traveling to the village of Alberca, he lined up a series of appalling pictures: chidren and pigs wallowing in the only fountain, a little girl about to die, brain-damaged boys smiling at the camera, and men and women sleeping together in tiny dark sheds. In contrast to these images, Brahms's Fourth Symphony and a pompous, dry voice-over was meant to disturb the audience and make it apprehend the artificial character of documentaries shot by foreigners and projected to far-away, indifferent spectators. Jean Vigo's *A propos de Nice* (*On the Subject of Nice,* 1930) played also on oppositions between rich and poor, leisure and work, life and death. Swift motions, unpredictable views, and aburd transformations (a man turned into lobster) made up for the banality of the comparisons; the movie mocked simultaneously modish resorts and the pseudo-objectivity of documentaries.

Less satirical, other avant-gardistes were intent on exploring the potential of cinema. Alberto Cavalcanti's *Rien que les heures* (*Only the Hours,* 1926) brought into fashion the city symphonies, movies attempting to visually document the frantic agitation of a big metropolis. Cavalcanti (1897–1982) fancied a "typical" Parisian day: bizarre linkings, freezed pictures coming after accelerated motions, wipes hinted at an engulfing of time by the whimsical rythm of urban life. Many drew their inspiration from this model in European capitals, so Marcel Carné chose to invert it. His *Nogent, Eldorado du dimanche* (*Nogent, Sunday's Eldorado,* 1929) stretched the Sunday hours by accompanying in slow panning shots the idle city dwellers who had left the town centre to rest by a river. Far away, at the very end of Britany, Jean Epstein evoked nature's timelessness in *Finis Terrae* (1930). The same waves assaulted in vain the same rocks; the same sky lingered over an infinite heath.

Avant-garde films have been revalued by critics, but at the time they were as despised as any other documentary. Financing them was problematic; it was only thanks to their friends' help that Buñuel or Vigo were able to work. Businessmen did not believed in cinematic advertisement. Public offices gave money for didactic movies provided they were mere illustrated lessons. French documentaries seemed not to have a future.

The year 1940, the year of France's most mortifying defeat, was a watershed for documentaries. In October, the Vichy government imposed the screening of a short during any film show. Nazi Germany and Fascist Italy had made an extensive use of informative movies for propaganda; the Vichy authorities thought that imitating them would accelerate France's recovery. The Republic regulated these films and decided that only those with professional qualifications could work in studios. The result was twofold. Producers were no longer reluctant to finance documentaries likely to yield a profit. And the young who wanted to be qualified had no choice but to make shorts. In liberated France, the Americans organized free film shows to illustrate their way of life and later to push the Marshall Plan. French audiences realized that documentaries were not necessarily boring by-products.

There was a flourish of documentaries, from 400 during the German occupation to 4,000 between 1945 and 1955. There was a great deal of quota quickies and among the good ones many were factual films. The big firms—Renault, Esso-France, the Electricity Company—funded instructional movies adapted to the needs of their potential clients. Technically, their products were of excellent quality, with sharp pictures, perfect lighting, and a didactic voice-over. They were all aimed to show how progress, symbolized by cars, tractors, fertilizers, and electricity, could improve daily life. Ministerial bodies, especially the Foreign Office and the Ministry of Agriculture, subsidised a significant number of shorts, but their funds were limited, which resulted in an uncomfortable mixture of awkardness and pretentiousness. *Paysans d'hier et d'aujourd'hui* (*Countrymen of Yesterday and Today,* 1946) is a typical example. While encoutering modern farmers, backward countrymen suddenly understand their ignorance. The film unveils a touch of scorn; the backward men never clean their hands and marvel at the use of electricity.

In addition to professional life, much attention was devoted to cultural activities, tourism first but also sport, moutain climbing, theatre, and architecture. One tenth of the movies focused on animals, nature, and landscapes. The same percentage dealt with the colonial empire. Except for Indochina, nothing was said about nationalism; the commentary stressed the mutual interest of France and African countries and the necessity of assimilation. Consider *Kalla*, produced as late as 1955. A black student (in fact an actor) confronts his former life in Cameroon and his present life in Paris, but if the camera follows him he is not allowed to speak: It is a French voice-over that tells what he is supposed to think.

Until 1964, there was one television channel in France that transmitted five hours a day in black and white. The programmes were also influenced by cinema because what was not broadcast live from a studio was shot on film. The ascendancy of cinema is apparent in the choice of themes and stylistic practice. Elie Lotar's *Aubervilliers* (1945), a stern description of slum-life in the north of Paris and a series of documentaries made by Jean Dewever, *La crise du logement* (*The Housing Shortage,* 1995) and *Des logis et des hommes* (*On Abodes and Men,* 1956) revealed how archaic housing conditions were in suburbs and had a strong impact on public opinion. Television followed suit with a documentary series, *A la découverte des Français* (*In Search of the French,* 1957–1958); fourteen programmes explored various regions, visited families, and invited their members to talk. These documentaries were more detailed than Lotar's or Dewever's, but did not introduce data they had not already tackled. The most popular television series were *La vie des animaux* (*Animals' Life,* 1952–1976) and *Les Médicales* (*Concerned with Medicine,* 1956–1984). The former adopted a cinematic approach with extensive panning shots on beautiful landscapes, animals shot at long distance, and surprising jumps from a distant to a close framing. The latter was built like a serial, a fight between human beings and illness in which every item opened on a problem (how to cure it?) and closed on a happy ending. Television, in its initial decades, was unable to give new life to audiovisual expression; however, it offered jobs to young filmmakers and helped acquaint spectators to documentary films.

Hurriedly interviewing derelict families was not likely to introduce new approaches to the documentary formulas. Documentaries changed when filmmakers adopted other methods. Georges Rouquier (1909–1989) was a printer. Fond of films, he succeeded in convincing a producer that it would be a good idea to make a full-length picture about a rural family that had been living for a long time in an isolated farm in Aveyron. Rouquier settled in at the farm, watched carefully, and wrote a script. A small crew of technicians then joined him, and shooting began in the autumn of 1944. Filming took a whole year. The editing was rather painful and the film was not released until the spring of

1947. It is as stunning today as it was in its time. After the credits, the nine members of the family and their neighbours are introduced. An establishing sequence, the longest in the film, describes a day in autumn, the emphasis being put on the children who have to walk several miles to the village school, care for the animals, and make bread. During the winter, long evenings allow the grandfather to tell the story of the family and its farm. In the spring, the mother gave birth to a child and the female livestock bred; the farm is furnished with electricity. The summer, as the most important season, is divided into three parts. The first section shows haymaking. The portrayal of a typical Sunday introduces important topics such as the relationship of the family with the village, the church, the café, and collective entertainment. The summer ends with harvesting and threshing. In autumn we see glimpses of vintage and tree cutting, but another topic, the division of the property between the children, is dealt with at length.

Superficial though it is, this summary gives an idea of the richness of a picture that is both clever and subtle. In 1947, audiences approved. This was the real thing, more credible than the fanciful farms of fictions. The film still appeals to contemporary spectators. They see precisely how oxen are harnessed, how they draw the plough and learn to build a haystack. More important, the film gives them a glimpse of the lifestyle, based on sociability and fairness, that brought the agricultural workers together. The relationships between the members of the family, the family and the neighbours, and the family and the village are vividly portrayed. The conflicts underlying the common life of three generations under the same roof are not hidden but are subtly exposed throughout the movie.

Rouquier was an amateur who filmed to please himself not to captivate an audience. In contrast, Jean Rouch, born in 1917, was a trained ethnographer. Investigating black Africa's traditions, he used a camera to record local ceremonies. He settled in a village and filmed the villagers' actions and attitudes when they were unaware. Some Africans condemned his practice as typically colonialist; others said he had captured a trace of customs that were soon to disappear. Rouch's *Les maîtres fous* (*The Manic Priests,* 1955) gave rise to much controversy. Accompanying villagers who had moved into a town, the short showed how the rituals they attempted to maintain had been distorted by the contact with whites. *Moi un noir* (*I, a Black,* 1958) a feature-length documentary was discussed for other reasons. Rouch reconstituted several days in the life of three Africans in Abidjan (Ivory Coast). They were authentic workers but played their own character according to a screenplay written by the filmmaker. Moreover, the voice-over alternated between two commentaries, one by the director and the other by one of the Africans.

While breaking with the optimistic vision of mainstream colonial documentaries, Rouch denounced neither the anarchic urbanization of African towns nor the French authorities' responsibility. The tradition of critical documentaries was not lost at the time; but in a difficult period marked by the German occupation, the Cold War, decolonization, and the Algerian conflict, criticism became mostly political. Its main exponents, Alain Resnais and Frédéric Rossif, both born in 1922, had witnessed war, resistance, and the opening of the concentration camps. The memory of such dramas weighed heavily on their movies. Resnais's *Nuit et brouillard* (*Night and Fog,* 1955) and Rossif's *Le temps du ghetto* (*The Ghetto Time,* 1961) were shot while French public opinion tried to forget war horrors, and Rossif's *Mourir à Madrid* (*To Die in Madrid,* 1963) was shot during the worst period of the Algerian war. Resnais flashed back and forth between past and present; archival footage of the camps was interspersed with clips of postwar trials and pictures taken for the film. Rossif stuck to chronology. Both raised serious questions about moral responsibility and the possibility of other mass murders. *To Die in Madrid* was a lampoon against Franco shot against the background of de Gaulle's authoritarian rule. Instead of merely narrating the Spanish civil war, Rossif attempted to evoke the atmosphere of a domestic conflict and to document its everyday nature by stressing civilians' sufferings, their fear of aerial bombings, and their anxious wait of a predictable issue. The editing was extremely clever. Describing the defence of Madrid, the director emphasized the deep involvement of an entire population. He showed the men digging trenches, the children and women passing on stones, all social groups taking part in a common action, without leaders and without any military presence. Rossif had slanted his message to appeal to those who opposed Gaullism, but even those who blamed its bias found his account gripping.

There was something new in Resnais's and Rossif's movies. They were keen on editing their own images and underlined the importance of "montage," which is not a mere linking of pictures but an association of correlated images. In the second epoch of French documentaries, the difference between critical films and formal films, with regard to investigating the nature and function of the cinematic language, was less and less visible.

Resnais's *Les statues meurent aussi* (*Statues also Die,* 1951) wanted to make spectators think over their relationship with images but also to criticise the presence of African statues in French museums. The film opened with a pan shot of visitors looking at a museum showcase: "Are you sure that African objects do not observe you like strange animals?" Such mixing of upsetting queries was stronger in the works of Chris Marker (born in 1921). His *Lettre de Sibérie* (*Letter from Siberia,* 1957) invited viewers to become aware of the deceptive influence of commentaries by showing the same visual footage three separate times with three different sound tracks, one full of enthusiasm for the Soviet achievements, one strongly disapproving, and one purely factual. His *Le joli mai* (*The Pleasant May,* 1963) feigned to deal with happiness in a France emerging from the Algerian war. A few people gave their opinion about that idea as in any banal public opinion poll. But once the viewer is confronted with violent, appalling, or thought-provoking images and challenged by other interviews, such answers looked vague and irrelevant. Ingenious and amusing, the film brought to the fore a gap between individuals' simple desires of happiness and the larger problems surrounding them. At the same time it expressed doubts about the reliability of documentaries; the way of organising one's images can radically transform a message.

Marker's works were often given as examples of "cinéma vérité," "truth cinema." This strange expression did not mean that cinema must copy life. On the contrary, it signified that truth, being never directly accessible, must be transcribed to become apparent. Any cinematic operation—framing, moving the camera, editing—is a manipulation. It is the filmmaker's duty to make spectators apprehend the manipulations and understand that what they see is partial and biased. Cinéma vérité was no more than a slogan, but most directors mentioned in this section, without forming a group, let alone a school, were convinced that they had to introduce in their films an instability of meanings and forms. Audiences were sometimes disconcerted but never repelled. The success of documentaries in the 1950s and 1960s resulted, to a large extent, from their ability to raise challenging questions.

With the end of the state monopoly on television (1982), the number of networks increased dramatically. All channels needed factual films to include in their schedule, and some even specialised in the broadcasting of documentaries. The avaibility of light cameras gave political and professional organizations an incentive to produce and circulate their own documents. Industrial and financial corpora-

tions anxious to diversify their clientele sponsored informative movies. Filmmakers were offered several opportunities to make shorts, but these proposals, coming mostly from private companies, modified the conception and structure of documentaries. Television channels wanted the films to fit either cinema or television; they provided little money and instructed their technicians to work as fast as possible and to leave space for advertisements.

In the wake of the 1968 student revolt and factory occupations, films were considered weapons for the class struggle. Cooperatives such as Slon and Ciné-lutte and Dziga Vertov Group, developed a "counter-cinema" informed by revolutionary ideologies. A few contended that by giving the most destitute the power of speech, cinema would disclose the misery of the human condition under capitalism. Militant filmmakers went to factories to ask the workers to depict their problems and demands. One of the most famous "ciné-tract" ("cinematic pamphlet") was *La rentrée des usines Wonder* (*The reopening of the Wonder factories,* 1968). After a big strike a woman worker does not want to return to work. In front of the factory, her co-workers, the foreman, and unionists try to persuade her that the main objectives of the walk-out have been achieved. In only ten minutes and one take, this short summarizes the worker-management-union relationship in May-June 1968. The method looked so convincing that it was used by Jean-Luc Godard, already well known as a major exponent of the New Wave. In *Vent d'Est* (*Wind from the East,* 1970) and *Louison* (1976), Godard let an individual speak at length with few cuts and no editing.

A question soon arose: Is it possible for people urged to talk in front of a camera to avoid perpetuating stereotypes? The interviewees seemed to play their role to perfection and said what they were expected to say, making the film look like a fiction. Most directors prefered "cinema d'intervention," a cinema that is part of an event; it does not observe it from without but intervenes and takes part in it. Marker led the way by filming a strike at the Rhodiaceta factory in *A bientôt j'espère* (*See you soon, I hope,*1968). Among the numerous "intervention-films" that followed a few deserve mention. During the 1972 strike at the Penaroya factory in Lyons *Penaroya,* a short denouncing scandalous labour conditions had such an impact on public opinion that the management gave in, provided that the film was no longer distributed. Other movies made by workers under the direction of a professional popularized social conflicts in Besançon (*Puisqu'on vous dit que c'est possible*—*As you are told that it is possible,* 1974) and

Sochaux (*Le lion, sa cage et ses ailes—The Lion, Its Cage and Its Wings,* 1976). The economic crisis of the mid-1970s put an end to mass demonstrations and strikes. The last militant film, *Lorraine coeur d'acier* (*Lorraine Steel Heart,* 1981) showed how internal dissension ruined a radio station founded by steel workers. Critical films abandoned the subject of social unrest to focus on more general concerns such as politics, education, and health.

Documentaries played a crucial part in staining politicians' reputation. Seen in retrospect, the evolution is striking. Jean-Louis Comolli's *Les deux Marseillaises* (*The Two Marseillaises,* 1969) presented the June 1968 election in the light of an ideological confrontation between Gaullism and the left. Raymond Depardon *1974, En campagne avec Giscard* (*1974, On Campaign with Giscard*) disclosed the mechanisms of a presidential election but showed much respect for president Giscard. Relating the March 1986 election that marked the defeat of the left, Serge Moati's *Chroniques de mars* (*Chronicles of March,* 1987) proved extremely ironic. Spectators could only laugh at the outgoing socialist minister's joking unnaturally and singing the *Marseillaise* nervously. Claude Otzenberger's *La conquête de Clichy,* (*The Conquest of Clichy,* 1994) was so devastating that public television postponed its broadcasting for three years. In it a cynical manipulator manifested he had no belief and was only interested in winning a seat in an affluent constituency.

Political scepticism lead to historical revisionism regarding the most dramatic periods of the twentieth century, the German occupation and the Algerian war. The Gaullist myth that all France had supported the Resistance was shaken by Marcel Ophuls's *Le chagrin et la pitié* (*The Sorrow and the Pity, 1971*). Some believe that the film was censored. In fact, the commercial company that had produced it offered it to public television, which did not respond. It was first screened in movie theatres and broadcast in 1981. Previously historical films were compilations with a well-structured commentary. Mixing archival material and provocative interviews, Ophuls adopted a colloquial, dispassionate tone. Evoking, for instance, the German invasion, the film showed French and German audiences watching the May 1940 newsreels in 1970. The former were grief-stricken by images they had tried to forget; the latter were satisfied but embarrassed to manifest their contentment in front of the French. Confronted with traces of their past, individuals acknowledged that for most, the main preoccupation had been to survive, not to fight. "Official" Resistance, either Gaullist or communist, had shadowed other forms of struggle. Mosco's *Terroristes à la retraite* (*Retired Terrorists,* 1983) explained how foreigners working in France, who were forced to go underground, increased the bomb attacks against the Germans but were never given the label of "patriots."

The most impressive documentary about the war was a six-hour film, Claude Lanzman's *Shoah* (1985). In their works on the mass murder of Jews, Resnais and Rossif had used old pictures and testimonies. Lanzman objected that such documents, taken either by the Germans or by the Allies at the end of the war, could not re-create the reality of the death camps. In his view all that had survived was the memory of both victims and executioners. Most did not want to remember, but they would soon die and it was urgent to make them talk. Taking witnesses to the former camps, now empty, plaguing them with questions, the filmmaker provoked painful reactions. People, often on the verge of crying, related what they had endured or seen. Such remembrance was not triggered by an historical account of the Nazi policy; it was stimulated by impressions coming back from the past, a walk in the forest where the prisoners worked, a song heard in the camp, an object that belonged to a companion in suffering. It was not the representation of torture and death but the unbearable sorrow of those who had remained alive that obliged spectators to feel sorrow for the annihilation of European Jews.

Documentaries on the Algerian war underwent a similar evolution. Yves Courrière's *La guerre d'Algérie* (1972) was a chronological account of the main events illustrated by well-chosen archival pictures. Using testimonies of 50-year-old men mobilised during the conflict, Bertrand Tavernier's *La guerre sans nom* (*The Nameless War,* 1991) exposed the doubts of a generation involved in dangerous, often brutal, and eventually effectless operations. It was only in 2002 that Patrick Rotman's *L'ennemi intime* (*The Close Enemy*) confronted Algerians and Frenchmen; posed harrowing, contentious questions such as the recourse to torture in both camps; underlined the abdication of French authorities; and attempted to evaluate the impact of the war on both countries.

The Close Enemy was broadcast to celebrate the fortieth anniversary of Algerian independence. Documentaries in the last decades of the twentieth century were often shot on the occasion of important events or to meet some general concern. While Parliament was debating about abortion rights, Charles Belmont's *Histoire d'A* (*A's Story,* 1973), following an anonymous A, disclosed the complication and dangers of illegal abortion, thereby elaborating a real dialectic of responsibility between those involved in the enforcement of a prohibitive law. For more than a decade, feminism and birth control education became ubiquitous topics. Contrasting the lives and concerns of eight women, Coline Serreau's *Mais qu'est-ce qu'elles veulent?* (*What Do They Want?* 1978) summarized the changes occurring in women's lives. In *Alertez les bébés* (*Alert Babies,* 1978) and *Votre enfant m'intéresse* (*I Am Interested in You Child,* 1981), Jean-Michel Carré dealt with medical care in delivery and with primary education. Exploring the foods that make up a meal Luc Moulet's *Genèse d'un repas* (*Genesis of a Meal,* 1978) expanded on food hygiene and on the alterations that take place from the producer to the consumer.

Owing to the continuing economic crisis, new anxieties surfaced in the 1990s that affected mainstream documentaries. Immigration, unemployment, mixed blood, and fear of downward mobility appeared daily on television. Continuing a tradition already present in other eras, Denis Gheerbrandt explored Marseilles' periphery in *Et la vie* (*Life Also,* 1991), but instead of lingering on abandoned industrial areas and impoverished houses, he concentrated on faces. People's behaviour, their willingness or their reluctance to talk, revealed social attitudes and reactions to a depressing situation.

Filmmakers focused less on misery than on another deep preoccupation of the late twentieth century, police and policing. After spending two months in a police station where he had filmed overtly, without trying to conceal either his presence or his possible influence on questioning, Raymond Depardon produced *Délits flagrants* (*Caught Red-handed,* 1994). Ignoring the spoils, fights, or aggression that had caused the arrests, he attempted to recreate the nocturnal atmosphere of the station and to interpret the relationship, half-hostile, half-conniving, that developed between the police and the offenders. In the same way, Renaud Victor's *De jour comme de nuit* (*Day and Night,* 1991), the result of several months spent in the prison of Beaumettes in Marseilles, focused neither on the prisoners nor on their vision of punishment, but rather on the tricks they use to survive without prospects for the future.

Many documentaries released between 1980 and 2000 were mere series of talking heads. The best tried to go beyond appearances and to suggest something that was not said but that was conveyed only visually. Yet most filmmakers were anxious to find a fashionable, up-to-date topic likely to seduce a producer and then to attract a large audience.

Once screened or broadcast, their works were left for tomorrow's historians to re-edit them in historical programmes. What was almost totally lost was the formalist inheritance. Not surprisingly only well-known directors could find funds to shoot documentaries dealing with the cinematic language itself, not with modish objects or events. Wandering through Marseilles, René Allio contrived in *L'heure exquise* (*The Delightful Hour,* 1981) an unlikely but possible city where past and present mingle harmoniously. Strolling around Los Angeles, Agnès Varda photographed hundreds of advertisements. Her *Murs, murs* (*Walls, Walls,* 1981) was a curious, often disturbing succession of lines, shapes, and colours linked by visual similarities. Varda also closed the century with *Les glaneurs et la glaneuse* (*The Gleaners and the She-gleaner,* 2000). Gleaners were often represented in late nineteenth century paintings as emblems of rural France. Varda used the figure of the gleaner to denounce archaisms in contemporary France but also to mock the modern tendency to buy short-lived consumer goods. Change occurs so fast that no time has been left for gleaning.

Varda's film could be taken as a symbol of the fate of French documentaries. During the first decades of cinema, the public paid little attention to informative movies. They were considered mere documents to be picked up when necessary and then discarded; audiences used to "glean" them. The 1950s and 1960s were the heyday of cinema. Being interested in all sorts of pictures, spectators stopped despising documentaries. Instead of "gleaning" they began to take these works seriously. With the expansion of television at the end of the twentieth century, the supply of factual programmes boomed. Audiences looked daily at documentaries but seldom noticed them; the wealth of information made "gleaning" useless.

PIERRE SORLIN

See also **Cavalcanti, Alberto; *Land Without Bread*; Lanzman, Claude; Lumière Brothers; Ophuls, Marcel; *Rien que les heures*; Rouch, Jean; *Shoah; Sorrow and the Pity, The; Voyage au Congo***

Further Readings

Breton, Emile, and Luce Vigo, editors, *Filmer le réel. La production dcumentaire en France*, Paris: La Bande à Lumière, 1987.

Coleyn, Jean-Paul, *Le regard documentaire*, Paris: Centre Pompidou, 1993.

Epstein, Jean, *Ecrits sur le cinéma*, 2 volumes, Paris: Seghers, 1974–1975.

Gauthier, Guy, *Le documentaire. Un autre cinéma*, Paris: Nathan, 1995.

Huret, Marcel, *Ciné actualités. Histoire de la presse filmée, 1895–1980*, Paris: Henri Veyrier, 1984.

Jacquinot, Geneviève, *Image et pédagogie*, Paris: PUF, 1977.

Leblanc, Gérard, *Quand l'entreprise fait son cinéma*, Saint-Denis, PUV, 1983.

Lyant, Jean-Charles, and Roger Odin, editors, *Cinéma et réalités*, Saint Etienne: Cierec, 1984.

Meusy, Jean-Jacques, editor, *La science à l'écran*, Paris: Cerf, 1986.

Odin, Roger, editor, *L'âge d'or du documentaire*, 2 volumes, Paris: L'Harmattan, 1998.

Pessis, Georges, *Entreprise et cinéma*, Paris: La Documentation française, 1997.

Prédal, René, editor, *Le documentaire français*, Paris: Cerf, 1987.

Prédal, René, *Cinquante ans de cinéma français, 1945–1995*, Paris: Nathan, 1996.

Sicsic, Josette, *Quand l'automobile fait du cinéma*, Paris: Editions France-Empire, 1986.

FRANJU, GEORGES

In the films of Georges Franju, the line between documentary and fiction, never all that clear in any case, seems continually on the verge of dissolution. Although his career as a filmmaker is usually described as falling into two parts—"the early period of documentary shorts, and a subsequent period of fictional features" (Wood, 1991)—the continuities between these two periods are more significant than the differences, and Franju himself, in his films as well as in interviews and other writings, undermined any straightforward opposition between artifice and reality.

For Franju, cinematic artifice is a device for making realities visible that we have not seen, or refuse to see: slaughterhouses secreted away on the outskirts of cities (*Blood of the Beasts*), the desolation and pain hidden behind historical myths of national honor (*Hôtel des Invalides*), the invisible by-products of industrialization that destroy the workers (*Les Poussières*). These three are among the most clearly "documentary" of Franju's films and could even be said to belong to such familiar subgenres as the industrial short (*Blood, Poussières*) or travelog (*Hôtel*). But what is one to make of the "surrealist overture" (Vialle, 1968) of *Blood of the Beasts*, with its young lovers in the midst of an antique bazaar in a featureless wasteland, or the horror-film visual style and music of *Hôtel des Invalides*, or the ghostly shadow of the worker's hand seen through a white porcelain plate in *Les Poussières*, which allegorically figures the silicosis in his lungs? According to Franju, "we strove in our film [*Blood*] to give back to documentary reality its artificial appearance and to natural settings their look of stage sets" (Leblanc, 1992). More broadly, he argued that "Dreams, poetry, the fantastic must emerge from reality itself. Every film is a documentary, even the most poetic" (Durgnat, 1967). The claim is deliberately provocative, but Franju meant it literally. Of his own unquestionably fictional feature *Thérèse Desqueyroux*, adapted from the novel by François Mauriac, Franju asserted that "the film is a documentary about a character in a novel" (Brown, 1983).

Nevertheless, if he rejected any strict differentiation between documentary and fiction, Franju recognized that there was a practical distinction, and it is the short films of the first half of his career that have earned him a significant place in the history of documentary cinema, in part because they are unlike the works of anyone else. The distinctiveness of Franju's documentaries is rooted in the specifics of his own intellectual and aesthetic development, which was far removed from the worlds of the university, journalism, politics, or colonialism, whose preoccupations and professional discourses have determined many of the conventions of mainstream documentary film. Franju, born in 1912, belonged to that first generation of filmmakers whose sensibilities were shaped within and by the history of cinema itself, and although his own career as a director only began after World War II, in 1949, Franju's greatest affinities were with the work of an earlier generation: the surrealism of Buñuel, the expressionism of Lang and Murnau, and the Popular Front-influenced poetic realism of Carné and Renoir.

Franju, born in Brittany, had a conventional provincial-religious education, which fostered his anarchism, atheism, and anti-clericalism. After leaving school, he evidently came to Paris, for he later wrote that "at the age of fifteen, I educated myself in the Bois de Vincennes with the following readings: Fantômas, Freud, and the Marquis de Sade" (Buache, 1996). Fantômas was the "Master of Terror" whose exploits are narrated in a thirty-two volume serial by Souvestre and Allain. Franju later observed that "the enthralling power of the novels lies precisely in their sadistic invention, the teeming violence, the spectacularly extreme cruelty" (Milne, 1975). These qualities endeared Fantômas to the surrealists, and Franju explicitly evoked Fantômas in his last feature film, *L'Homme sans visage*. After military service in Algeria from 1928 to 1932, Franju returned to Paris to work as a theatre set decorator. During this period he met Henri Langlois, a fellow cinephile with whom he made an experimental short film, *Le Métro* (1934)—later disowned by Franju—and, more significantly, with whom he founded a film club (the Cercle du Cinéma, 1935), a film journal (*Cinématographe*, 1937), and, in 1937, a film archive, the Cinémathèque Française.

The Cinémathèque, of which Langlois remained director until his death in 1977, was among the first and most important film archives in the world, and Franju's founding role attests not only to his centrality to the emergence of film culture from the 1930s on but also to the formative role of older styles of filmmaking in his own aesthetic development. The clearest instance of this is his fourth short film, *Le Grand Méliès*, a semi-fictional or reconstructed documentary on the career of the filmmaker-magician-toyshop proprietor Georges Méliès, inventor of such fantastic story-films as *A Voyage to the Moon* (1902). Franju reconstructs Méliès's workshop, revisiting, in effect, the origins of fiction film itself, and particularly of that strain of the fantastic that runs through much of Franju's own work. What is the periscope in *Hôtel des Invalides*, for example, in which the museum visitor can impossibly "see" scenes of trench warfare from the First World War, if not a magic projector such as Méliès himself might have devised?

If *Le Grand Méliès* is Franju's tribute to early cinema; it is also an elegy for the individual Méliès, for "the vanished, pre-1914 world" (Durgnat, 1967), even, in a sense, for cinema itself. In 1937, Franju and Langlois had come up with an idea for a film, *Le Métro fantôme*, to be based on a

"fantastic and poetic" script by Jacques Prévert (screenwriter for Renoir and Carné, and later for Franju's *Mon chien*). They asked Méliès, who had been forced out of the movie business by bankruptcy twenty-five years earlier, to design the sets and special effects. Méliès declined, writing Franju that he found the story "funereal," but when Franju went to visit him some months later, he saw that Méliès had actually made sketches for sequences set in Père-Lachaise cemetery, and that he "was looking forward merrily to animating . . . the funerary monuments of the well-known dead" (Brumagne, 1977). But Méliès, who had been in poor health, soon grew worse, and died a few weeks later; Franju and Langlois actually called the doctor who attended Méliès during his last days.

This personal connection between the two filmmakers is not presented in *Le Grand Méliès*, but it seems to underlie the film's elegiac mood. Opening with a series of shots of the home where Franju had visited Méliès just before his death, Franju's documentary ends with Méliès's widow emerging from a Métro station to take a bouquet of violets to her husband's grave in Père-Lachaise. One does not need to recognize the personal associations (Franju's visits, the Métro, Père-Lachaise) to grasp that *Le Grand Méliès* is a film of mourning, but the private iconography of grief is characteristic of Franju, who in both his short and feature-length films—as such critics as Wood, Durgnat, Milne, and Leblanc have demonstrated—returns again and again, almost obsessively, to certain images or motifs: dead landscapes, November skies, doves, the Paris Métro, windows, and World War I. His films, for all their black humor and "elements of rage and protest" (Wood, 1991), are filled with a sense of irretrievable loss. What Durgnat has called the archaism and nostalgia of Franju's work is the opposite of sentimental, however; he does not invoke the past as a golden age but as a repository of images charged with emotion. World War I, for example, recurs in Franju's films from *Hôtel des Invalides* through the features *Judex* (1963) and *Thomas the Imposter* (1965), not because the years preceding it were necessarily happier but because for Franju, who had grown up in its wake, it stood, simply, as the clearest embodiment of all that's most terrible, in every period, about our civilization.

Similarly, Franju's affinity for the films of the 1920s and 1930s has little to do with critical evaluation or his own intentions as a filmmaker, but testifies to the indelibility of the impression they had made on him, being, as they were, the films of his movie-mad youth. In an essay on

"Realism and Surrealism," Franju wrote, "I've often been asked whose films—as far as my own tastes are concerned, not as to any influence they might have had on me—are the most poetic of all, and I named Buñuel; the most beautiful works of horror, and I named Murnau; the most visually expressive, and I named Lang" (Vialle, 1968). Franju's essay on "The Style of Fritz Lang," which appeared in the first issue of his and Langlois's *Cinématographe* in 1937, was arguably the first critical analysis of a director's whole body of work in terms of visual style and *mise-en-scène*, and anticipated auteur criticism by almost twenty years. But it is most important in terms of Franju's own career for what it reveals of his overriding interest in the image, rather than in narrative or ideas in the abstract. "I can retell the stories of movies that have bored me," Franju stated in an interview; "of those that have captivated me, I retain images without stories" (Brumagne, 1977).

Franju's own films are nothing like those of Lang, Murnau, Buñuel, or Méliès; what he developed through immersion in their work was a way of seeing, a sensitivity to the poetic density and concentration of certain images. These might be images constructed in a studio—Franju had watched Renoir and Carné at work during the filming of, respectively, *Rules of the Game* and *Daybreak*—but equally they could be documentary images. In the same essay in which he invoked Lang, Murnau, and Buñuel, Franju ended with a rhapsodic account of a medical documentary: Dr Thierry de Martel's *Trépanation pour une crise d'épilepsie*, which recorded a particularly gruesome procedure of brain surgery. "That was an authentic horror film," Franju later recalled; "twenty people were out flat, I've never seen anything so drastic. It was an atrocious film, but a beautiful and poetic one, because it was also realistic" (Durgnat, 1967). Franju would never go so far in his own work, even in showing, for instance, the slaughterhouses of *Blood of the Beasts*, not out of timidity, but to keep us just this side of being knocked "out flat," which would excuse us from seeing.

Not long after the founding of the Cinémathèque, Franju and Langlois went their separate ways. In 1938, Franju became executive secretary of the International Federation of Film Archives and, in 1945, secretary-general of the Institute of Scientific Cinematography, directed by Jean Painlevé. In 1946, with his wife, Dominique Johansen, Franju founded the Académie du Cinéma. This immersion in the films of others, especially from the domains of scientific, avant-garde, and early cinema, meant that Franju's aesthetic was fully formed before he wrote and directed his first film, *Blood of the Beasts*, in 1949. There was no period of apprenticeship, but also, as Robin Wood has noted, no real development in Franju's own approach, even when he shifted from documentaries to fiction, and from short films to features, in 1958 (Wood, 1973). In his many interviews, Franju never expressed any interest in films made after his debut, other than his own—a symptom not of self-regard or an old-fashioned aesthetic (he worked with such modernist writers as Jean Genet and Marguerite Duras) but of a need to preserve a certain creative isolation, and an indifference to both controversy and fashion.

The consistency of Franju's work results in part from some sustained collaborations with the assistant director Michel Worms, the composer Maurice Jarre, and the cinematographer Marcel Fradetal. Fradetal had worked on Carl Dreyer's *Vampyr* in 1932, and his elegantly composed medium and long shots, unhurried camera movements, and mastery of the full tonal range of greys available on black-and-white film gave Franju's works their singular atmosphere, what he himself called their "sense of baleful, ceremonial ritual" (Milne, 1975). There is an inexorable quality to the unfolding of Franju's films, and an apprehension of mortality, even when the subject matter seems banal: travelogues on Notre Dame or the Lorraine province, for example (*Notre-Dame, cathédrale de Paris*; *En passant par la Lorraine*), or an instructional film on the wearing of safety masks (*Les Poussières*). The films' mood of dread is linked to certain recurrent themes: hellish factories (the slaughterhouses of *Blood of the Beasts*, the steel mills of *En passant par la Lorraine*, the porcelain works of *Les Poussières*), dead faiths (Catholicism in *Notre-Dame*, military glory in *Hôtel des Invalides*), and the propensity for violence and cruelty barely concealed by the veneer of conventionality.

Franju's method in his documentaries is to strip objects of their familiar associations. As Durgnat writes, "he removes the ordinary to reveal the tragic." But such stripping away of the visible surface is itself a form of artifice, no less than the cinematic and theatrical illusionism Franju celebrates in his films on Méliès and the Théâtre Nationale Populaire (*Le T.N.P.*). The filmmaker does not just turn on the camera and wait for reality to appear; instead, as he told G. R. Levin, "you must re-create reality because reality runs away . . . you illuminate the subject, go beyond the subject—and that's documentary."

HAL GLADFELDER

*See also **Hôtel des Invalides, Le Sang des bêtes***

Biography

Born in Fougères, Brittany, France, April 12, 1912. Educated at religious school in Fougères. Military service in Algeria, 1928–1932. Worked as theatre set decorator, Paris, 1932–1933. Co-directed (with Henri Langlois) *Le Métro*, 1934; co-founded (with Langlois) the Cercle du Cinéma, 1935; co-founded (with Langlois) *Cinématographe* (journal) and the Cinémathèque Française (film archive), 1937. Executive secretary of the International Federation of Film Archives (FIAF), 1938–1945. Secretary-general of the Institute for Scientific Cinematography, 1945–1954. Co-founded (with Dominique Johansen) the Académie du Cinéma, 1946. Directed first documentary short film, 1949; directed first feature-length fiction film, 1958. Director for French TV, 1965–1976. Died November 5, 1987.

Selected films (documentaries only; Franju is director and writer of all films)

1949 *Le Sang des bêtes/Blood of the Beasts*
1950 *En passant par la Lorraine*
1951 *Hôtel des Invalides*
1952 *Le Grand Méliès*
1953 *Monsieur et Madame Curie*
1954 *Les Poussières*
1955 *A propos d'une rivière (Le Saumon Atlantique)*
1955 *Mon chien*
1956 *Le Théâtre National Populaire (Le T. N. P.)*
1956 *Sur le pont d'Avignon*
1957 *Notre-Dame, cathédrale de Paris*

Further Reading

Brown, Robert, "Georges Franju: Behind Closed Windows" [interview], *Sight and Sound*, 52/4, 1983, 266–271.
Brumagne, Marie-Magdeleine, *Georges Franju: impressions et aveux*, n. p., Editions L'Age d'Homme, 1977.
Buache, Freddy, *Georges Franju: poésie et vérité*, Paris: Cinémathèque Française, 1996.
Durgnat, Raymond, *Franju*, London: Studio Vista, 1967.
Leblanc, Gérard, *Georges Franju: une esthétique de la déstabilisation*, Paris: Maison de la Villette, 1992.
Leblanc, Gérard, Pierre Gaudin, and Françoise Morier, editors, *Georges Franju: cinéaste*, Paris: Maison de la Villette, 1992.
Levin, G. Roy, *Documentary Explorations*, New York: Doubleday and Co., 1971.
Martini, Andrea, editor *Georges Franju*, Milan: Il Castoro, 1999.
Milne, Tom, "Georges Franju: The Haunted Void" [interview], *Sight and Sound*, 44/2, 1975, 68–72.
Milne, Tom, "Georges Franju," in *Cinema: A Critical Dictionary*, edited by Richard Roud, New York: Viking, 1980: 387–393.
Vialle, Gabriel, *Georges Franju*, Paris: Editions Seghers, 1968.
Wood, Robin, "Terrible Buildings: The World of Georges Franju," *Film Comment*, 9/6, 1973, 43–46.
Wood, Robin, "Franju, Georges," in *International Dictionary of Films and Filmmakers*, vol. 2: *Directors*, 2nd edition, edited by Nicholas Thompson, Chicago: St James Press, 1991.

FRANK, HERZ

Herz Frank, one of the founders and leaders of the Riga school of poetic documentary cinema (1940–1999), played a pivotal role in the development of the New Latvian documentary filmmaking. Although the films of Frank and his Riga colleagues did not directly attack the totalitarian Soviet regime, the personal and poetic approach to existence, and the exaltation of the individual, which are present in all of his works, created the basis for a new way of thinking and seeing things.

The Riga school of poetic documentary cinema came together in the early 1960s, when a group of young and talented filmmakers—of which Frank was the oldest and most experienced—entered the Riga Film Studio wishing to create documentary film art, but not newsreels. After years of Stalinist repression, they intended to re-create the forgotten tradition of documentary filmmaking marked by Dziga Vertov, their model of political consciousness and formal innovation.

This conception of cinema was in keeping with the intellectual trends of the postwar era, in which both filmmakers and avant-garde artists in general renewed the idea of a personal cinema. Documentary film became a vehicle for the filmmaker's beliefs and feelings (Thompson and Bordwell, 1994).

Herz Frank first worked as a scriptwriter. He made *The White Bells* in 1961 with Uldis Braun, the first poetic documentary of the Riga school. Six years later, *235,000,000* (1967) was received with international acclaim. A poetic documentary on the fiftieth anniversary of the Soviet Revolution, as seen through the eyes of a Latvian film team, it is a kaleidoscope of faces and situations spanning the Soviet Union, marked by an associative editing and composition.

Frank's first film as director was *The Salt Bread* (1965), a twenty-minute black-and-white film about a group of fishermen. To make this film, Frank and his cameraman Visvaldis Frijars lived with the fishermen. Frank and his Riga colleagues believed that was the way a documentary should be produced. Herz Frank conceived of documentary as an artistic method of capturing the genuine nature of the filmed subject. Thus, the film should be produced in close cooperation with the subject, and there should be an absolute mutual loyalty between filmmaker and subject.

Ten Minutes Older (1978) is considered his masterpiece. Using the nonintrusive technique of direct cinema, in one shot, Frank and his cameraman, Juris Podnieks, focused on the face of a very young child watching a puppet show. We never see the puppet show, but we do hear it and are therefore aware of its narrative trajectory. We experience it in the face of the child as he experiences the emotions conveyed by the show, and becomes "ten minute older" (Barnouw, 1993).

The Trace of the Soul (1972), and *Forbidden Zone* (1975) both exemplify Frank's commitment to extensive research, and his belief in the ability of film to express deep emotions. The subjects of his documentaries are shown at crucial points in their lives, as in *The Last Judgment* (1987), in which the confession of a double murderer condemned to death draws attention to the social and moral corruption of society, but leads to a plea for the abolition of the death penalty.

Frank's films encourage discussion of the ethics of filmmaking, and of the presence of the camera during the most private and extreme moments of a human life. Yet it is a given that his films have always been emotionally disturbing and provoke the audience to think (Daira Åboliņa, 2000).

As he wrote when explaining one of his last works, *Flashback*, (2002), Frank as a documentary filmmaker has always been attracted to the inner life and the eternal human issues of love, birth, death, and destiny. In *Flashback*, the filmmaker applies his technique to himself, turning the camera back on himself in an examination of his life and work. The film also covers Frank's heart surgery.

VERÓNICA JORDANA

Biography

Born in Ludza, Latvia, January, 17, 1926. Graduated from the School of Law, Moscow in 1947. Worked as a journalist, lecturer, and advertisement designer in Vladimir from 1952 to 1954. Worked at the newspapers "Padomju Jaunatne" and "Rigas Balss" in Latvia from 1954. From 1959 worked at Riga Film Studios as a photographer, editor, documentary scriptwriter, and director. One of the founders of the Riga School of Poetic documentary. Directed more than thirty documentaries and has received many international awards, and works have been covered in more than 160 publications, including books, magazines, and newspapers worldwide. Also the author of "*The Chart of Ptolemy*" (Moscow, 1975), a book about poetic documentaries. Since 1993 has been living in Israel and in Latvia. A member of the Editorial Board of the magazine *Art of Cinema* (Moscow) until 1993. In 2002, elected member of the TV Academy of Eurasia. That same year, founded his own production company, Studio EFEF.

Selected Films

1961 *Baltie zvani/ The White Bells:* script
1964 *The salt bread:* director
1967 *235.000.000:* script
1975 *Aizliegtā zona /Forbidden Zone*
1978 *Ten minutes older:* script, director
1984 *Līdz būstamai robežai /To the Edge of Danger"*
1987 *Augstaka tiesa/The Last Judgment:* director
1989 *The Song of Songs:* script, director
2002 *Flashback:* script, director, director of photography
2004 *Aufenhalt Germania:* script, director, director of photography

Further Reading

Åboliņa, Daira, *Riga Film Studio*, 2000.
Barnouw, Eric, *Documentary: A History of the Non-Fiction Film*, Oxford: Oxford University Press, 1993.
Stites, Richard, *Russian Popular Culture: Entertainment and Society since 1900*, Cambridge Russian Paperbacks: Cambridge University Press, 1992.
Taylor, Richard, *The BFI Companion to Eastern European and Russian Cinema*, London: British Film Institute, 2000.
Thompson, Kristin, and Bordwell, David, *Film History: An Introduction*, New York: McGraw-Hill, 1994.

FRANTZ FANON: BLACK SKIN, WHITE MASK

(UK, Julien, 1996)

Isaac Julien's 1996 documentary, *Frantz Fanon: Black Skin, White Mask*, explores the life of West Indian psychoanalyst Frantz Fanon, a key theorist in the decolonization movement of the 1960s. The documentary investigates the significance, as well as the more problematic aspects of Fanon's writings and especially of his most influential book: *An Essay for the Dis-alienation of Blacks*, later called *Black Skin, White Mask*. Published in 1952, the book was a milestone insofar as it provided the first study of the psychological impact of racism on colonized and colonizer and of the more sexualized aspects of racism.

Frantz Fanon was born in 1925 in French-ruled Martinique. Brought up within an assimilationist environment, he fought for France in WWII and later studied medicine in France, specializing in psychiatry. In 1953 he was appointed head of the psychiatric department of the government hospital in Algeria, where he arrived to find the non-French patients kept in appalling conditions. Drawn into Algeria's struggle for independence and increasingly demoralized by his work with victims of both sides of the violence, Fanon eventually dedicated his time fully to the Algerian uprising against France. In 1960 he became ambassador to Ghana for the Algerian provisional government. In the following year, he published his second book, *The Wretched of the Earth*, which concludes with the necessity of armed struggle to break the ties of dependency between colonizer and colonized. Fanon died of leukemia in the United States in 1961.

One of the most significant features of Isaac Julien's documentary, *Frantz Fanon: Black Skin, White Mask*, is its remarkable mixture of fictional and nonfictional material. Julien draws as much on excerpts from fictional material, such as staged imagery, films, and dramatic recreations of Fanon's life, as he does on classic documentary material, such as interviews and contemporary and historical footage.

The opening scenes introduce the usage of fictional material. In the first shot, the camera passes through two wooden window shutters and out onto a yard and is accompanied by the beautiful singing of a female opera voice. The next scene shows the shadow of a man in a cell, and a male voice-over is heard nervously uttering words in Arabic. The subsequent frame discloses the frightened, sweating face of an imprisoned man. Suggestively staged scenes such as these help situate the documentary contextually, but they also set an unsettling tone, mixing anguish and reflection, that continues throughout the film.

Later, such scenes, explicitly fictional, as signaled by the lighting, staging, and camera angels, combine with so-called *tableau vivants*, painterly staged scenes, that depict Fanon's life. Remarkably, not a single still or moving image of the historical Fanon is used. Instead, largely as a result of the lack of historical film footage of Fanon, the film reconstructs scenes from Fanon's life. Some of these scenes center on the more problematical aspects of Fanon's thinking, such as his support of the Algerian woman's veil as a means to support the rebellion (an argument welcomed by the Algerian conservatives) and also his denial of the existence of homosexuality in Martinique. In one dramatic mixing of archival material and staged imagery, the images of French war photographer Marc Garanger are projected onto veiled Algerian women; in a similarly staged scene, we see Fanon in the foreground and two men kissing in the background who turn their heads to look at Fanon as if in challenge.

The film moves effortlessly, and at times indistinctively, between historical and fictional material. A brief scene from Gillo Pontecorvo's *La Battaglia di Algeri* (*The Battle of Algiers*) (1965) mixes black-and-white and color archival and contemporary footage of Martinique, Algeria, and the Algerian War of Independence to recreate the historical background of Fanon's work. The more conventional documentary material consists of interviews with Fanon's family and friends, contemporaries, and critics of Fanon, who describe his complexities and contradictions.

The collage style of *Black Skin, White Mask* continues on the level of language, sound, and music. The film features English, French, and Arabic, as well as different music genres—classical opera music, jazz tunes, and drums. This constant juxtapositioning of different elements produces a brechtian alienation effect, one likely to reinforce the audience's act of intellectual participation with the subject matter.

The British actor Colin Salmon, who plays Fanon, recites excerpts from Fanon's writings throughout the film. His highly stylized, demonstrative performance is accompanied by uncanny, high-contrast, chiaroscuro lighting from below, which gives Fanon an isolated position within the frame.

British filmmaker Isaac Julien, who was short-listed for the Turner Prize in 2001, has long been concerned with questions of race and gender and their importance within the politics of looking. He takes up these themes on multiple occasions in the film. In one scene, Julien reconstructs one of Fanon's epiphanies: his encounter with a little girl on the streets of Paris. The girl, seeing Fanon, exclaims: "*Look, a Negro! Look, a Negro! Look, a Negro! Mum, look at the Negro, I'm frightened!*" The scene, in the film recounted, not staged, by Colin Salmon, triggered in Fanon a close examination of his blackness and his self-image in which he recognized the workings of an unequal, colonial relationship: *Black Skin, White Mask.*

Throughout, this multilayered film does not simply eulogize Fanon but examines the complexity of the historical figure and of the themes he dealt with. Tensions between his thinking and his actions are emphasized throughout, and highlighted particularly through a series of candid interviews. Hence, Fanon's explanation for why black women fall in love with white men is implicitly critiqued in the interviews through references to Fanon's failure to examine the implications of his logic for his own decision to marry a white woman.

Frantz Fanon: Black Skin, White Mask responds to a recent rediscovery of Fanon's social and psychological theories by psychologists and critical thinkers. The skillful fusion of fictional with nonfictional material creates a stimulating and informative work of art full of intertextual references. Fanon becomes the ghostlike narrator of his own life and his urgent and direct addresses of the camera transport his ideas and their relevance directly into the present. In the final image of the film, the fictional Frantz Fanon looks straight into the camera, presenting an undeviating gaze that challenges the viewer to grapple with the themes that the historical Fanon raised more than a half century ago and that are still unresolved today.

JACOBIA DAHM

See also **Julien, Isaac**

Frantz Fanon: Black Skin, White Mask (UK, 1996, 73 min.). Directed by Isaac Julien, written by Isaac Julien and Mark Nash, produced by Mark Nash for BBC & the Arts Council of England in assistance with Illuminations. Assistant directors: Catrin Strong, Carwyn Jones. Cinematography by Nina Kellgren. Camera assistants: Lorraine Luke, Nick Wheeler. Gaffer: Ashly Palin, Key grip by Phil Murray. Makeup artist: Sharon Martin, production managers: Grischa Duncker, Craig Paull. Sound recordists: Michel Hildéral, Trevor Mathison, Olivier de Neste. Online editor: Gary Brown, Costume design: Annie Curtis-Jones. Art director: Mick Hurd, dubbing mixer: Katja Sehgal. Music composed by Paul Gladstone, Reid Tunde Jegede. Avid editor: Nick Thompson and Robert Hargreaves. Frantz Fanon played by Colin Salmon. Musicians: Lynette Eaton, Dominic Glover, Tracey McSween, C. Wellington, Paul Weymont, Seddik Zebiri. Archive research: Nicole Fernandez Ferrer. Consultants: David Bailry, Ilisa Barbach, Homi Bhabha, Steve Farrer, Dora Bouchoucha Fourati, Paul Gilroy, Lucien Taylor. Archive film: ECPA, INA, Pathe, Archive stills: Bureau du Patrimonie Martinique, Oliver Fanon, Loïs Hayor, Martinique. Photographs: John Riddy. Film extracts: *Battle of Algiers, Alegerie en Flamme, J'ai Huit Ans, Dr Pinel delivrant les alienes, Selpetriere 1795.* Extracts from Frantz Fanon's *Black Skin, White Mask, Studies in a Dying Colonialism, Toward the African Revolution, The Wretched of the Earth*, extracts from "*Force of Circumstance*" by Simone de Beavuoir.

Further Reading

Black British Cultural Studies: A Reader, edited by Houston A. Baker, Jr., Manthia Diawara, and Ruth H. Lindeborg, Chicago: University of Chicago Press, 1996.

Black Film. British Cinema, ICA Documents No. 7, Institute of Contemporary Arts: London, 1988.

Contemporary British and Irish Film Directors, edited by Yoram Allon, Del Cullen, and Hannah Patterson, *A Wallflower Critical Guide*, London: Wallflower Press, 2001.

Fanon. A Critical Reader, edited, with an introduction, and translations by Lewis R. Gordon, T. Denean Sharpley-Whiting, Renée T. White, London: Blackwell, 1996.

Fanon, Frantz, *The Wretched of the Earth* (translated from the French), preface by Jean-Paul Sartre, New York, Grove Press, 1963 (original: *Les damnés de la terre*, préface de Jean Paul Sartre, Paris: F. Maspero, 1961).

———, *Black Skin, White Masks* (translated from the French), New York: Grove Press, 1967 (original: *Peau noire, masques blancs*, Paris, Éditions du Seuil, 1952).

———, *Studies in a Dying Colonialism* (translated from the French), New York: Monthly Review Press, 1965 (original: *L'an cinq de la revolution algerienne*, Paris, 1959).

The Fact of Blackness: Frantz Fanon and Visual Representation, edited by Alan Read, Seattle and London: Bay Press and ICA, 1996.

The Fanon Reader, edited by Azzedine Haddour, London: Pluto, 2003.

Frantz Fanon: Critical Perspectives, edited by Anthony Alessandrini, London and New York: Routledge, 1999.

Julien, Isaac, "*Black Is, Black Ain't: Notes on De-essentializing Black Identities*," in *Black Popular Culture*, edited by Gina Dent, Dia Center for the Arts, *Discussions in Contemporary Culture No. 8*, Seattle: Bay Press, 1992.

———, *The Film Art of Isaac Julien*, New York: Bard College (Center for Curatorial Studies), 2000.

Memmi, Albert. "The Impossible Life of Frantz Fanon," *Massachusetts Review*, winter, 1973, 9–39.

Mercer, Kobena, *Isaac Julien*, with essays by Kobena Mercer and Chris Darke, London: Ellipsis, 2001.

Stam, Robert, "Fanon, Algeria, and the Cinema: The Politics of Idenification," in *Multiculturalism, Postcoloniality, and Transnational Media*, Edited by Ella Shohat and Robert Stam, New Brunswick, NJ and London: Rutgers University Press, 2003.

FREYER, ELLEN

Ellen Freyer, an independent producer of award-winning family films, has also produced and directed three documentary films that address social and political issues affecting women and children. *Girls' Sports: On the Right Track* (1975) and *Marathon Woman: Miki Gorman* (1980) concern changing attitudes and opportunities for women in sports, and *The Splendors of Terror* (2003) reveals the culture of hatred and violence that is being taught to children in the West Bank and Gaza.

Girls' Sports: On the Right Track dispels myths and explores new opportunities in girls' sports as a result of Title IX. The seventeen-minute educational film, which includes archival footage of track stars "Babe" Didricksen and Wilma Rudolph, provides a short history of track and field, and contrasts the limited experiences of Didricksen and Rudolph with the expanded opportunities available to three contemporary high school girls. *Marathon Woman: Miki Gorman*, which premiered at the Lincoln Center Film Festival in New York, is an award-winning twenty-minute film that profiles a champion Japanese/American marathon runner whose tiny size did not deter her ambition. The film was broadcast on PBS and distributed internationally. *The Splendors of Terror* is a fourteen-minute program that includes footage produced by the Palestinian Authority and broadcast on Palestinian television that has never been broadcast in the Unites States. It shows generations of Arab children being educated to hate and kill (even themselves) in order to murder Jews.

Freyer's fiction films, *The Whipping Boy* (1994), *The Secret Garden* (1995), *The Summer of the Monkeys* (1998), and *Anatole* (1998), have all been based on award-winning children's books. *The Whipping Boy*, winner of the National Education and Cable Ace awards, was based on the Newberry Award-winning children's novel by Sid Fleischman. Produced for the Disney Channel and starring George C. Scott, the film follows the adventures of an orphaned street urchin who supports himself and his sister as a "rat catcher" until he is suddenly kidnapped to become the "whipping boy" for a spoiled, rich prince. *The Secret Garden* is an animated musical version of Frances Hodgson Burnett's classic children's story. Produced for ABC and distributed by Paramount Home Video, the film stars the voices of Sir Derek Jacob, Honor Blackman, and Glynis Johns, and was a Humanitas Award finalist. *Summer of the Monkeys*, based on the novel by Wilson Rawls (the author of the children's classic *Where the Red Fern Grows*), is a coming-of-age drama. Set on the western plains in the 1880s, it follows the adventures of a young boy who dreams of getting enough money to buy his own horse. Produced in Canada and distributed by Walt Disney Home Video, the film, which stars Michael Ontkean and Wilford Brimley, won the National Education Award, the Best of Festival at the Children's Film at the Breckeridge Festival, the Crystal Heart Award at the Heartland Film Festival, and the Audience Award, Best Feature Drama, at the Marco Island Film Festival. *Anatole*, an animated series about the adventures of a French mouse who is a "cheese taster," his wife, and their three sets of twins, was based on the Caldecott-winning children's books written by Eve Titus and illustrated by Paul Galdone. The series was produced in Canada and was broadcast internationally and in the United States on CBS.

Before working as an independent producer, Freyer was a television production executive and part of the original PBS team that created *Wonderworks*, a weekly family movie series. Produced for a PBS consortium under the leadership of WQED Pittsburgh, *Wonderworks* was described by *TV Guide* as the "Best Family Drama Series," and by the TV Critics Association as the "Best Children's Programming." From 1984 to 1992, Freyer supervised development, initiated and packaged programs from domestic and foreign producers, and traveled in the United States and abroad to supervise various productions. Included among the fifty productions that won an aggregate of 125 awards, were the international co-productions of *The Little Princess* and *The Lion, the Witch, & the Wardrobe* (UK), both three-hour mini-series based on the classic children's books; *The Haunting* (NZ), based on the award-winning book by Margaret Mahey; and *Clowning Around* (AU), an original mini-series produced in Perth, Australia. The domestic productions Freyer developed and supervised were *Jacob Have I Loved*, starring Brigit Fonda; *Sweet 15*, starring Tony Plana, Jenny Gago, and Jerry Stiller; and *Necessary Parties*, starring Alan Arkin, Julie Hagerty, and Mark Paul Gosselaar. The most well-known and loved production Freyer supervised was the four-hour Canadian co-production of *Anne of Green Gables*. Directed by Kevin Sullivan and starring Megan Follows, Colleen Dewhurst, and Richard Farnesworth, the program won more than fifteen awards including the Peabody, Emmy, and Prix Jeunesse.

Freyer has written numerous articles and reviews about experimental, documentary, and children's films. She has been awarded grants from the National Endowment for the Humanities, the NYS Council on the Arts, the NY Foundation for the Arts, the Women's Fund-Joint Foundation Support, the Hoso Bunka Foundation (Japan), and Mitsubishi International.

Freyer's recent projects include films based on Karen Cushman's Newberry Award-winning young adult book *Catherine, Called Birdy*, and *Mrs. Piggle Wiggle*, based on Betty McDonald's classic children's book series that is in development at Fox's New Regency Productions.

SUZANNE EISENHUT

Biography

Born in Hollywood, California. Father, Lewis Jacobs, was a pioneer filmmaker, critic, and historian, and the author of the 1939 seminal work *The Rise of the American Film: A Critical History*. Education: Barnard College, B.A. (Art History), New York University, M.A. (Cinema Studies). Taught art at elementary and intermediate schools in New York City and Madison, Wisconsin, before receiving her masters degree; taught Cinema Studies at St. Peter's College (established St. Peter's College Film Society), Syracuse University, and Hunter College; freelance assistant editor, post-production supervisor, and segment producer for independent documentary and educational films; award-winning documentary filmmaker; PBS production executive and member of the original team that created *Wonderworks*; independent producer of children's and family entertainment. Guest speaker: American Library Association, Columbia University, Marymount College, Mt. Sinai Hospital, National Academy of Television Arts and Sciences, National Conference of Teachers of English, Nassau Community College, Production East Conference, Teacher's College, New York University, and New York Women in Film. Juror/Consultant: American Film Festival, ACE Awards, Emmy Awards, International Festival of Films by Women, New York Film Festival, San Sebastian Film Festival (Spain), Student Academy Awards, Notable American Women. Listed in *Who's Who of American Women* and *Who's Who in Entertainment*.

Selected Films

The Splendors of Terror (2003): producer/director
Anatole (1998) (TV): executive producer
Summer of the Monkeys (1998) (TV): executive producer
The Whipping Boy (1995) (TV): producer
The Secret Garden (1994) (TV): producer
Marathon Woman: Miki Gorman (1981): producer/director
Girls' Sports: On the Right Track (1976): producer/director
Fifty productions and co-productions for *Wonderworks* (1984–1992): coordinating producer, project manager

Selected Publications by Freyer

"Adapting Children's Literature to Film," *The Lion and the Unicorn*, Johns Hopkins University Press, 1987.
"Profile of Nell Cox, Feminist Filmmaker," *Feminist Art Journal*, 1977.
"Women's Experimental and Personal Film Festival," *Feminist Art Journal*, 1977.
"Three Women's Films at the Whitney," *Craft Horizons Magazine*, 1974.
"Formalist Cinema: Artistic Suicide in the Avant-Garde," *Velvet Light Trap*, University of Wisconsin, 1974.
"The New York Underground," *Craft Horizons Magazine*, 1973.
Chronicle of a Summer—Ten Years After, *The Documentary Tradition: From Nanook to Woodstock*, Lewis Jacobs, editor, New York: Hopkinson and Blake, 1971.

FUMIO, KAMEI

Kamei Fumio's innovative editing and composition and bluntly political postwar documentaries changed filmmaking in Japan from the 1930s into the 1960s. Acknowledged within his own country as the central figure in the history of Japanese documentary filmmaking, Kamei is less well known outside of Japan. His ability to press the boundaries of conventional form as a film editor led to a key part for him in creating the role of director within the wartime studio system at a time when the authorship of documentaries was being contested.

The two years Kamei spent immersed in Leningrad's film culture (1929–1931) in tandem with his initiation into the Japanese film world at a time of rising cultural nationalism and brutal colonial expansion proved a difficult mix that led to a year spent in prisons in 1941–1942 and the subsequent curtailment of his filmmaking activities until the end of the war. His first postwar filmmaking endeavor, a compilation film made together with Iwasaki Akira (a leading film critic and former head of Prokino, the Japan Proletariat Film League) called *Nihon no higeki* (1946)/*A Japanese Tragedy* was so critical of the wartime regime that American Occupation authorities, probably at the behest of Japan's then Prime Minister Yoshida Shigeru, would not allow its release. That film contains a controversial dissolve in which the Showa Emperor transforms from full military garb into a suit-and-tie-clad everyman. The suggestion in this sequence that the Emperor was actively behind Japan's wartime military malevolence was sacrosanct to conservative forces.

In the postwar period, Kamei has been associated with a persistent myth that casts him as Japan's only anti-war wartime filmmaker, but the truth is considerably more complex. Although Kamei's airing of discontent with the war may not make him an all-out resister, his wartime films do represent a boldly innovative negotiation with a severe if inconsistent censorship apparatus. Kamei virtually dissected wartime conventions in his 1939 film *Tatakau heitai*/*Fighting Soldiers* while simultaneously producing them. In 1938, while employed by Toho Film's Culture Film Section, Kamei agreed to edit footage of the Japanese march to

Shanghai that other Toho filmmakers thought was too bleak to pass muster with film world and military authorities. The result, *Shanghai* (1938), was a perfection of long form documentary that found box office success and also met with critical acclaim. His next film, *Peking* (1938), made charmingly lyrical use of both synchronized and non-synchronized sound. The film, rediscovered in 1997, includes an extended traveling shot down a vibrant market street matched to a masterful montage of the exoticized sounds of local commerce.

That same year, Kamei was sent to China for four months with cinematographer Miki Shigeru and a film crew to make the army-sponsored film, *Fighting Soldiers*, about the Japanese advance to Wuhan. In one regard *Fighting Soldiers* must be understood in the context of the writing of Hino Ashihei, the popular chronicler of the daily lives of ordinary Japanese soldiers in China in the late 1930s. Hino is the lead expositor of a documentary literature whose reportage style shares definite resonances with socialist realist literature from the previous decade. But when human-scale heroes whose toils were so captivating on the page were shown on the screen, and when the images projected were those of real fighting soldiers, it was too much for the military sponsors of the work to tolerate. The completed work was shelved by Toho and not seen publicly until after its rediscovery in 1975.

Fighting Soldiers has no narration. It is as easy to see what is so compelling about this film as it is to understand what the Army found so objectionable. An extreme close-up of the distraught face of a Chinese peasant whose house is in flames, a cavalry pack animal lingering and then toppling, having succumbed to some battlefield hazard, Japanese infantry shown by a roadside in such a state of exhausted slumber as to look like corpses—these images are stitched together in such a way that they recall the controlled montage theories of Pudovkin and convey very plausibly the sense of how unpleasant the "daily-ness" of war is for the people who fight it as well as those noncombatants who are victimized by it.

When he bent the framework for sponsored filmmaking in his three commissioned tourism films in

1940 and 1941, Kamei prefigured the creative interpretation of the limits of public relations filmmaking that was to take place at Iwanami Productions two and three decades later, an experience that would give rise to independent socially engaged filmmaking in the 1960s. *Fighting Soldiers* was cited two years later as an example of Kamei's proclivity to inculcate dialectical materialism into his films, a charge supposedly substantiated by time Kamei spent studying film and art in the Soviet Union and by his depictions of peasants in *Kobayashi Issa* (1941). That film, ostensibly a piece commissioned by local officials in Nagano Prefecture to promote tourism to the area, integrated the haiku of eighteenth century ascetic poet Kobayashi to create a historically contextualized and compelling caricature of the people, their struggle to eke out a livelihood in farming and sericulture. In the margins of the beautifully shot 35mm film are the wealthy tourists, who enjoy the rugged beauty of the harsh landscapes, and rich pilgrims, who are patronizing a large temple complex and then vying to become, like Yasukuni Shrine in Tokyo, a repository for the souls of Japan's war dead. Critics at the time described *Kobayashi Issa* as a cine-poem. The Ministry of Education refused to certify the film as a *bunka eiga,* or culture film, but the studio used this refusal to tease audiences into seeing a supposedly controversial film.

Throughout his filmmaking career, his willingness to break with convention in big and small ways would repeatedly place him at the center of one controversy after another. His wartime filmmaking has consistently drawn more attention than his two and one-half very active postwar decades. In fact, the political films made after 1945 have proven to be as influential on other filmmakers as his wartime films. Making *Sunagawa no hitobito: kichi hantai tosô no kiroku* [1955, *The People of Sunagawa: A Record of the Struggle Against the Military Base,*] *Sunagawa no hitobito: mugi shinazu* [1955, *The People of Sunagawa: Wheat Will Never Die,*] and *Ryuketsu no kiroku: Sunagawa* [1956, *Record of Blood: Sunagawa,*], a trilogy of protest films about the struggle to forestall the expansion of an American air base in post-occupation Japan, led Kamei and his crew to spend a great deal of time with their filmic subjects and ultimately to depict their struggle from the insider perspective of the protestors. This lesson was absorbed by Tsuchimoto Noriaki, Ogawa Shinsuke, and Hani Susumu, who would commit themselves to their own subjects in much the same way a few years later.

Another well-regarded filmmaker (and artist), Teshigahara Hiroshi worked on two of the Suna-

gawa films as well as several of Kamei's films about atomic bomb blast survivors. Indeed, Kamei was the leading filmmaker of record for the nascent anti-nuclear movement in Japan in the 1950s. Beginning with *Ikiteite yokkata* [1956, *Still Its Good to Live*], he made five films that documented the after-effects of radiation, demonstrated the limits of government support afforded those who had been exposed to radiation at Nagasaki and Hiroshima, and showed the organizing activities of victims and their supporters. He also was the first documentarian to take up the highly volatile issue of discrimination against Japan's so-called *buraku* peoples by making a film about one such community in Osaka in 1960.

Across his career, Kamei Fumio showed a capacity to find inspiration in and borrow from unlikely spheres. In the late 1930s, he successfully integrated montage theory into the process of making a war record film with *Fighting Soldiers*. In the postwar period, he was the first in Japan to attempt filmic forays into the then raging debates on *shutaisei* (subjectivity) in his Sunagawa films. These achievements earn him a claim on being among the world's least known but most accomplished documentary filmmakers.

JEFFREY ISAACS

Biography

Born on April 1, 1908 into a locally prominent Catholic family in Fukushima Prefecture, Japan. Left his studies in fine arts at Bunka Gakuin in Tokyo in 1928 to go to the Soviet Union the following year to study art. Soon began studying film as an auditor at what became in 1931 the Leningrad Institute of Cinema Engineers (LIKI) during which time he was influenced by Grigori Kozintsev, Sergei Yutkevich, and Fridrikh Ermler. Became ill with tuberculosis, prompting his sudden return to Japan in 1931. In 1933, entered Photo Chemical Laboratory (later P.C.L. and then in 1937, Toho.) At P.C.L. and Toho in the Culture Film Section, distinguished himself as an editor, scenario writer, and then director of documentaries. Arrested in October 1941 and charged with inculcating Komintern ideals into films, spent just under a year in detention and was released on probation in August of 1942. Was a leader in the Toho labor disputes in 1947–1948. Directed or co-directed five feature films from 1947 to 1953. Began producing independent documentaries in 1953 establishing Japan Document Film in 1955. Opened an antique shop in Shibuya and continued to make occasional PR films for corporate clients into the 1980s. Returned to engaged filmmaking with two ecologically concerned films in the 1980s. Died February 27, 1987 in Itabashi, Tokyo.

Selected Films

1937 *Dottô o kette* [*Through the Angry Waves*]: Composition and editing

1938 *Shanghai*: Composition and editing
1938 *Peking*: Composition and editing
1939 *Tatakau Heitai/Fighting Soldiers*: Director
1940 *Ina bushi* [*A Song of Ina*]: Director
1941 *Kobayashi Issa*: Director.
1945 Seiku [Security of the Skies]: Story
1946 *Nihon no higeki/A Japanese Tragedy*: Director
1953 *Kichi no kotachi* [*Children of the Base*]: Director
1955 *Sunagawa no hitobito: kichi hantai tosô no kiroku* [*The People of Sunagawa: A Record of the Struggle Against the Base*]: Director
1955 *Sunagawa no hitobito: mugi shinazu* [*The People of Sunagawa: Wheat Will Never Die*]: Director
1956 *Ikiteite yokkata* [*Still Its Good to Live*]: Director
1956 *Ryuketsu no kiroku: Sunagawa* [*Record of Blood: Sunagawa*]: Director
1957 *Sekai wa kyôfu suru: shi no hai no shôtai* [*The World Is Terrified: The True Nature of the "Ash of Death"*]: Director
1958 *Araumi ni ikiru: maguro gyomin no seitai* [*Living in Rough Seas: The Lives of Tuna Fishermen*): Director
1958 *Hato wa habataku* [*Fluttering Pigeons*]: Director
1959 *Hiroshima no koe* [*Voice of Hiroshima*]: Director.
1960 *Ningen mina kyodai: buraku sabetsu no kiroku* [*All People Are Brothers: A Record of Discrimination in the Buraku*]: Director.
1961 *Gunbi naki sekai o* [*Toward a World Without Armaments*]: Director.
1984 *Minna ikinakereba naranai: hito, mushi, tori, nôji minzoku-kan* [*All Must Live: People, Insects and Birds*]: Director.
1987 *Seibutsu mina tomodachi: tori, mushi, sakana no komori uta* [*All Living Things Are Friends: Lullabies of Birds, Insects, and Fish*]: Director.

Further Reading

Abé Mark Nornes, *Japanese Documentary Film: The Meiji Era Through Hiroshima*, Minneapolis: University of Minnesota Press, 2003.

"Documentarists of Japan, No. 6: Kamei Fumio," introduction by Makino Mamoru, trans. A. A. Gerow, *Documentary Box* No. 6, Tokyo: Yamagata International Documentary Film Festival Organizing Committee, March, 1995, http://www.city.yamagata.yamagata.jp/yidff/docbox/6/box6-2-e.html.

High, Peter B., *The Imperial Screen; Japanese Film Culture in the Fifteen Years' War, 1931–1945*, Madison: The University of Wisconsin Press, 2003.

Hirano, Kyoko, *Mr. Smith Goes to Tokyo: Japanese Cinema Under the American Occupation, 1945–1952*, Washington, DC: Smithsonian Institution Press, 1992.

Kamei Fumio, *Tatakau eiga; dokyumentarisuto no showa-shi* (Fighting Films: A Documentarist's History of the Showa Era,) Tokyo: Iwanami Shoten, 1989.

Tsuchimoto Noriaki, "Kamei Fumio: *Shanhai* kara *Tatakau Heitai* made," ("Kamei Fumio: From Shanghai to Fighting Soldiers,") in Kôza Nihon Eiga no. 5, (Seminar in Japanese Cinema no. 5,) ed. Imamura Shôhei, Satô Tadao, Shindô Kaneto, Tsurumi Shunsuke, and Yamada Yôji, Tokyo: Iwanami Shoten, 1987.

Tsuzuki Masaaki, *Tori ni natta ningen: hankotsu no eiga kantoku—Kamei Fumio no shôgai*, (*The Human That Became a Bird: The Life of Rebellious Film Director Kamei Fumio*,) Tokyo: Kôdansha, 1992.

Yasui Yoshio, editor, *Kamei Fumio Retrospective*, Tokyo and Osaka: Amagata International Documentary Film Festival Organizing Committee Tokyo Office and Planet Bibliotéque de Cinema, 2001.

G

GALAN, HECTOR

Hector Galan is a prolific independent filmmaker, notable for his insightful and comprehensive documentation of the Latino experience in America. He has produced and directed more than thirty documentaries, most under the banner of the Austin, Texas-based Galan Productions Inc. Galan founded the company in 1984, in large part to fill a void in media representation of Mexican-American culture, politics, and history. Since then, Galan has won numerous national and international awards for exploring such diverse topics as illegal immigration, race relations in the military, HIV/AIDS prevention, college athletics, and women in ranching culture. His productions appear regularly on national PBS television. He has produced or directed eleven episodes of the provocative "Frontline" series, as well as two programs for the acclaimed "The American Experience" series. Galan's seminal four-part series, *Chicano! History of the Mexican American Civil Rights Movement*, was screened at the White House for President Bill Clinton. In 1998, a retrospective of his work was shown at the Smithsonian.

Taken as a whole, Galan's substantial body of work represents a compelling and multifaceted visual record of the Latino experience in America.

Mexican-American himself, Galan must be noted as one in a growing number of indigenous filmmakers who are using media to recover and reappropriate images and ethnic identities across diverse mediascapes. Yet Galan is unique among indigenous filmmakers for two important reasons. His productions achieve a thoughtful, objective distance despite the intimacy he shares with his subjects. And national public television has offered his productions a relatively large, mainstream audience. This is a credit to Galan, whose task is particularly challenging, for his films are made both *for* and *about* his audiences, for insiders *and* outsiders. They intend to both salvage *and* incite, to reflect *and* to inform. And yet, in speaking to different audiences with different needs, Galan's films rarely presume too much or too little. Instead, they achieve a delicate balance that faithfully serves both audiences with equal effect.

Galan's style reflects his tendency to produce for public television. His work is understated, balanced, thoughtful, informative, and objective, even though much of it borders on the controversial or macabre. He regularly relies on archival footage, photography, and voice-over narration to complement original footage and interviews. When he has opted for verité, as in his acclaimed production on border shantytowns, *Las Colonias,* his films still retain an unlikely reticence and stoicism. This subtlety is intentional. It serves his overarching goal—"to bring stories to the public that were not being told"—and modest ambition—"that a television show isn't going to change the world, but it can give you a glimpse, an insider's glimpse, that is very important." These reticent, unyielding "glimpses" into forgotten Latino worlds have established Galan as an important documentarian and an invaluable advocate, historian, spokesperson, and ethnographer for the Mexican-American community en masse.

Many of Galan's productions have explored some of the most desperate places in contemporary American society. Examples include maximum security prisons, shantytowns, copper mines, the foster care system, illegal immigration, life on the Mexican-American border, racism, HIV/AIDS infection, and the agrarian industrial complex and drug addiction. Galan has called these productions studies of the "invisible," those communities whose worlds have been disenfranchised by political and cultural systems beyond their control and whose plight have been swept beneath the carpet of national attention. Frontline's *Shakedown in Santa Fe* is an excellent example. The documentary examines the conditions of a New Mexico maximum security penitentiary eight years after one of the most violent riots in American penal history. Twelve prison guards were beaten, stabbed, and raped, and dozens of inmates were tortured to death by their peers. Despite its wretched details and violent imagery, the documentary is delivered with a sobriety that lacks moral judgment or sentimentality. By developing complex characters, exploring the culture of prison life, initiating questions about the criminal justice system, and inviting abstract questioning regarding the nature of punishment and reconciliation, Galan creates a multidimensional production that engages its audience on a variety of levels.

Galan is as equally concerned with making visible the many attributes of Latino culture and history as with exposing the inequalities and injustice that have plagued so much of the Mexican-American population. Galan appears particularly enamored by Latino musical culture. *Los Lonely Boys, Accordion Dreams, I Love My Freedom, I Love My Texas, Songs of the Homeland,* and *The Tejano Music Awards Selena Tribute* document the production, distribution, and reception of contemporary Latino musical forms. Yet they also explore how tradition has shaped and affected current trends in artistic expression. This is not extraordin-

ary for Galan who regularly favors historicity in his work. *Accordion Dreams, Power, Politics and Latinos, La Mujer en el Rancho,* and *Vaquero: The Forgotten Cowboy* trace ideas or subjects over time. Two of Galan's most renowned productions, *The Hunt for Pancho Villa* and *Chicano! History of the Mexican-American Civil Rights Movement*, are historical reconstructions. Galan's magnum opus (when it comes to explicating Latino ethnic heritage) is the six-part series *Visiones: Latino Art and Culture*. It provides a definitive visual history of Latino artistic achievement and includes theater, music, dance, and visual art, as well as its relations to history, ethnic identity, and social change. The series premiered in the fall of 2004 and took four years to complete.

The films of Hector Galan shed light on forgotten worlds rich in culture and history and beset by human suffering and degradation. They explore the systems and mechanisms of oppression and refuse to deny the resiliency of cultural tradition and the fact of individual complexity. They are remarkably sober and lacking in self-consciousness, less innovative, and original as they are thorough and comprehensive. They successfully appeal to a variety of audiences as evidenced by their success on national PBS television. With Latino populations in the United States ballooning at unprecedented rates, Galan's body of work as a documentarian of the Latino experience in America will undoubtedly prove to be an important resource.

JASON PRICE

Biography

Born in San Angelo, Texas, September 12, 1953. Received his B.A. in Telecommunications in 1977 from Texas Tech University in Lubbock. In 1980, became a senior producer for the Southwest Center for Educational Television in Austin. Produced *Checking It Out*, a twenty-six-part PBS magazine series for Hispanic teenagers. In 1982, became a producer for Warner-Amex in Dallas. His work in Texas won him a job as a staff producer/writer/director for WGBH-TV in Boston, Massachusetts. Began to produce long-form documentaries for the PBS news and public affairs series *Frontline*. In 1984, founded his own production company, Galan Incorporated in Austin. The company specializes in long-form news, cultural and public affairs documentaries for national broadcast. It has won numerous national and international awards.

Selected Films

1988 *Shakedown in Santa Fe*: Producer, Director, Writer, Film Editor

1990 *New Harvest, Old Shame*: Producer, Director, Writer, Film Editor
1993 *The Hunt for Pancho Villa*: Producer, Director
1996 *Chicano! History of the Mexican-American Civil Rights Movement*: Series Producer
2004 *Visiones: Latino Art and Culture*: Series Co-Producer

Further Reading

Berg, Charles Ramreg, *Latino Images in Film: Stereotypes, Subversion and Resistance*, Austin: University of Texas Press, 2002.
Davila, Arlene M., *Latinos, Inc.: The Marketing and Making of a People*, Berkeley: University of California Press, 2001.
Flores, William V., *Hispanic Cultural Citizenship*, Boston: Beacon Press 1998.
Fox, Geoffery, *Hispanic Nation: Culture, Politics and the Construction of Identity*, Tucson: University of Arizona Press, 1997.
Noriega, Chan A., *Shot in America: Television, the State, and the Rise of Chicano Cinema*, Minneapolis: University of Minnesota Press, 2000.
Rodriquez, Clara, *Latin Looks: Images of Latinas and Latinos in the U.S. Media*, Boulder: Westview Press, 1997.
Ruiz, Vicki L., *From Out of the Shadows: Mexican Women in Twentieth Century America*, Oxford: Clarendon Press, 1999.
Suoro, Roberto, *Strangers Among Us: Latinos' Lives in a Changing America*, New York: Vintage, 1999.

GARDNER, ROBERT

The films of Robert Gardner represent the conjunction of science and art. Gardner has said he would choose a large measure of Tarkovsky in making up an ideal cinematic genetic inheritance for himself. We should remember that Tarkovsky argues strenuously in his manifesto, *Sculpting in Time*, for film as a means to knowledge. All the art and technique of film is to be brought to bear for the sake of understanding the world, as only film can understand it, and to convey understanding to audiences.

Trained as an anthropologist, Gardner has made his largest and best known films about Native Americans, New Guineans, and African peoples living very traditional ways of life, or about an India where people withdraw, as it seems, from the country's modernity to focus attention on and to live out traditional rituals or life processes. A smaller body of films looks at artists at work: painters Mark Tobey and Sean Scully, printmaker Michael Mazur, filmmaker Miklós Jancsó, all notably resembling the many craftsmen seen at work in the films about traditional cultures. In all these films, there is a deliberate shooting style that probes for meaning, alert to the symbolic and the coincidental, and a deliberate sound and image editing that draws attention to certain things, makes connections, and fashions small stories within the larger study. In most cases there is a reflective, even poetic, voice-over commentary. Gardner seeks understanding and calls on all of film's creative powers to engage with the world, to render complex experience, and to move viewers in more than rational ways.

At the beginning of his first film, *Blunden Harbour* (1951), made using footage shot by William Heick and Pierre Jaquemin, the camera moves on a boat across a forested bay on the coast of Vancouver Island. A voice-over relates the story of how the Kwakiutls original godlike chief came here to establish a home, "become a real man," and begin the way of life of these people we observe throughout the twenty-minute film. The film approaches its subject; the first few shots take us naturally from the water to the dwellings and workplaces of the people who live along its edge and draw food from it. But in the movement of the camera and in our awareness of its uncanny power to find out and to create, we sense something like the coming of the god. And in the beautiful black-and-white images of the water surface reflecting various light and the surrounding forest, we have a figure for the realm of imagination and the numinous, so important to these people's life and way of understanding themselves. In the water surface we have even a figure for the film screen and the power of the medium of film. Film converges with the larger imagination here. *Blunden Harbour* goes on from its opening to give many images of people at work, focusing, characteristically of Gardner, on hands and their activity, as if the hand needs discovery and attention, or matters more, or means more, than the face. Also characteristic of Gardner is the voice-over's reminder, midway through the film, of the fact of death, the great counterforce to all the life and work and use of imagination that we see. And the film draws to a close accumulating images and sounds of mask-making and then ceremonial dancing, as if, on the part of the filmmaker as well as the Kwakiutl themselves, to fight off oblivion.

After *Mark Tobey* (1952) and collaborative work with John Marshall on *The Hunters* (1957), Gardner made his best known and most discussed film, *Dead Birds* (1964). This contemplation of the warring Dani of central New Guinea stands as the first of four major feature-length studies of the human condition, followed by *Rivers of Sand* (1974) and *Deep Hearts* (1981), both shot in Africa, and then *Forest of Bliss* (1986), shot in India. These films function as a tetralogy of research and meditation, or a large-scale four-movement symphony, each film with its own mood and way of tapping into layers of subrational experience. *Ika Hands* (1988), about a vanishing priestly culture in the high mountains of Columbia, serves as a coda to all this.

Dead Birds is a film of grandeur, in color like all the subsequent Gardner films discussed here, with wide shots of the lush valley setting, large-scale battle sequences between enemy tribes, and a homeric alternation of direct war material with the civic and domestic life that backs up the war, proceeding always in war's shadow. Here Gardner focuses on the day-to-day concerns of a few individuals whom we get to know by name. The film presents the beauty of life, great expense of energy, romantic images of human endeavor fitting into the patterns of nature, while the voice-over speaks of the grim and absurd condition under which the Dani live, committed to immemorial war, dominated by ghosts. Overall the film is very *interested* in these people and is hopeful and excited about life, despite the consciousness of death and of the cultural traps people fashion for themselves. Gardner's fast, tense spoken commentary, providing names and much detailed information, seems just a partial view of a larger and richer life the film senses and registers, but knows it cannot encompass. Like *Blunden Harbour* this film ends with ongoing chant and dance, a lyrical outpouring that seems to transcend its cause and definition, in this case at first a grief ceremony for an assassinated child, which then turns into celebration on the news of the death of an enemy.

Rivers of Sand, about the Hamar of southwestern Ethiopa, is Gardner's darkest film, and more than *Dead Birds* it stresses its own fragmentariness. Various means are used: a sparse voice-over commentary, a Hamar woman's recurrent address to the camera, shots of diverse and sometimes baffling activities of the Hamar, symbolism such as the dry riverbeds these people live among and look to with hope, or the perpetual grinding of sorghum that mirrors the grinding of women's spirits. The film has the feel of making one kind of attempt after another to look into a life that cannot be comprehended, in part because it is a forbidding horror. These beautifully formed and beautifully dressed people live a life of male oppression, vanity, and ineffectiveness, and female hard labor, whippings, decorative scarring where we see the blood flow, and cutting out of teeth to please the male eye. It is a world of hunger and thirst, hunger above all on the part of men and women to be liberated, and not daring to think of taking the first step. Yet through all of this, people maintain a perverse merriment.

Gardner's handheld camera moves restlessly over distances with people and domestic animals, seeking meaning, as if seeking escape. The camera's quieter attention is drawn, as always, to the work of hands, of women at work at home, or men casting the "sandal oracle" to see how things will go with their ostrich hunt. The vistas are of dust and sand, the desolate background to these people's lives, or of an evening thunderstorm that seems to threaten destruction. With the film's editing, animals and their sounds, mostly cattle and goats, are made present, as if a chaotic animal nature is the energy feeding human life, or as if the animal world cries out at its mistreatment by humans (there is marked contrast with *The Nuer*, made collaboratively a few years earlier with Hilary Harris and George Breidenbach, where the cattle seem both loved and loving, and there is an ecstatic blurring of a gentle human nature with a gentle animal nature). The film's mood of social critique, focused in the conscious and explicit feminism of the woman who talks to the camera, resonates with much thinking worldwide in the later 1960s and the 1970s. But the sense of a disturbing mystery that cannot be fathomed is more like a Faulkner novel than a confident political analysis.

Working with experimental filmmaker Robert Fulton, Gardner made in *Deep Hearts*, his most lighthearted film, the scherzo of the sequence one might say. The subject is the annual male beauty contest of the nomadic Bororo Fulani of central Niger, in the southern Sahara (the same subject is taken up seven years later, after devastating changes in Bororo life, by Werner Herzog in *Herdsmen of the Sun*). The words *deep hearts* suggest an Iago-like concealment of feeling, and we learn that the Bororo, in fact, value a deep heart and the hiding of desire and envy behind a sunny exterior. Further, Gardner's spoken commentary, even sparser here than in *Rivers of Sand*, refers to the hard life of the Bororo outside these few days of festival in the brief rainy season, while the images and sounds of the film give us a world of joy and good humor, a facade, it might seem. The power of film seems to yield to, and to be taken over by, the preparation of make-up and coiffure and costumes, the lines of men dancing and singing for days, the spectators, the everyday chores of maintaining a camp for this special period. Slow motion, freeze frames, swish pans, and altered sound all help film and viewer to get into the spirit of this prolonged lyrical outpouring that sublimates who knows what harsh experience or compromised feeling. The film brings us right into a particular event, without much distance or perspective. And yet the film works virtually on an abstract level, making the point that a great gulf lies between festival and art on the one hand, and on the other the matter of life we know must be resting there, but that festival and art transmogrify or obscure. In this film we live for a time in the pure ecstatic world.

Deep Hearts is about men who dress and behave as women, with the aim that one of the men be chosen as exemplar by a woman, who may be acting at the behest of still other men. Central to the festival is a freeing of gender identity. And the camera itself enters a zone of gender ambiguity, just as it lets go of the perspectives of psychological and sociological analysis. Midway through the film Gardner's voice-over tells us the Bororo are worried about consumption by others' eyes, and this reference makes us think of the camera, because nothing else in the film evokes such worry; we do not see it in the interpersonal relations of the people on view. The issue of the camera is raised, and a few minutes later, still in the same sequence alternating views of performers and spectators, the camera identifies itself with a woman, in a striking prolonged shot where we see a watching woman in sharp focus in the foreground, and the performing men an out-of-focus blur in the background, their visibility, their existence, as if subject to the watching woman's whim. The camera in *Deep Hearts* lets go in many ways, and transforms the film's subject matter overall into a dreamlike experience, perhaps a woman's experience, for the sake of getting close to, of getting to know, a certain reality.

With a complete withdrawal of voice-over commentary and subtitled translation of people's words, *Forest of Bliss* becomes a pure encounter of film's aural and visual sensitivities within a complex world, in this case Benares, India, and its business of care for the dying and disposal of the dead. Gardner has worked in India several times, collaborating on films about the perpetuation of ancient rituals: *Altar of Fire* (1976), *Sons of Shiva* (1985), and others. With *Forest of Bliss*, old and specifically Indian customs surrounding death come into play. But the film opens itself to something larger, the involvement of human activity in the metamorphoses and cycles of water and earth, feeding and excrement, wood and fire, light and dark, noise and silence. The film yields itself up to what is to be seen and heard in Benares, and to the suggestions everything makes of analogy to something else, human beings to scavenging dogs, marigolds, or the spirit vaguely sensed in kites, sails, and air. The film yields itself up, but at the same time the camera is probing and active, and the editing very deliberate, every cut seeming to start a new sentence. Some sounds are heightened, just as the camera finds visual close-ups in a larger perspective. One lives in the hospices and temples of Benares, in the lanes, along the ghats, and out on the broad Ganges. At times human faces and feeling, or the amazing funeral pyres, take over all consciousness. Yet one is aware throughout of an artist fashioning a film.

Gardner has always, and especially with *Forest of Bliss*, met with criticism from anthropologists who do not want to let go of words and rational understanding, and who look to film as properly a transparent medium to furnish illustration or proof for what words can comprehend. Gardner's work is impelled by belief in film as an unaccountable powerful force, which, if negotiated by an artist, will lead into areas of understanding that words cannot anticipate or be adequate to. The proof for any viewer is in the particular film, *Forest of Bliss* or another, opening oneself to it, reflecting, being willing to think in a new way.

In *Ika Hands*, Gardner confronts his way of doing things, and a race of people and way of life so strange and elusive as almost to defy filming; it is the filmmaker's ultimate interesting, mattering, difficult subject. The film begins with the image of Gardner talking with anthropologist Gerardo Reichel-Dolmatoff, whose writings have led Gardner to want to film the Ika. Thus these people begin as an idea for him, something on paper and imagined. Reichel-Dolmatoff's voice comes back and back in the film, juxtaposed with what we see of the Ika and their high mountain world. Also, brief inter-titles occur to name or explain actions. All of this comes to seem only a partial help to comprehend what is larger than our faculties. The camera follows these aristocratic, long-haired, essentially pre-Colombian beings as they walk ridges, sing, meditate, and see visions; and we seem to be in another time dimension, or not on this earth. The many images of hands at work seem to want to ground the film, but there is a humanity or spirituality here widely distant from the hands, constantly seeming to take off and fly out of reach. The film takes us somewhere remarkable and makes us aware that we can never fully be there.

CHARLES WARREN

See also **Dead Birds**; **Forest of Bliss**

Biography

Born in Brookline, Massachusetts, November 5, 1925. Graduated from Harvard University in 1948. Taught history and made and produced films in the state of Washington and on Vancouver Island, 1949–1952. Studied anthropology at the graduate level at Harvard, 1952–1956. Established the Film Study Center at Harvard's Peabody Museum of Archaeology and Ethnology in 1956, which continues to the present as an independent entity at Harvard for research and film production. Led the Harvard research team to the Grand Valley of the Baliem in Netherlands, New Guinea, 1960–1961, out of which grew *Dead Birds* (1964), which won the Flaherty Award and the Florence Film Festival Grand Prize and established Gardner's international reputation. Helped found Harvard's Carpenter Center for the Visual Arts in 1962, an exhibition space and teaching facility for the creative arts. Taught filmmaking and film study in Harvard's Visual and Environmental Studies Department, 1962–1998. Inducted into the American Academy of Arts and Sciences,

1964. Co-authored *Gardens of War* with Karl Heider, 1969, about the Dani of West Irian, New Guinea. Hosted *Screening Room*, a Boston television series of interviews and screenings with documentary and experimental filmmakers, 1973–1980. Won the Florence Film Festival Grand Prize for *Forest of Bliss* in 1985. Given retrospectives at the Film Forum Freiburg in 1989, the Oesterreichisches Filmmuseum in 1991, the Whitney Museum of American Art in 1992, Anthology Film Archives in 1995, the Zürich Völkerkunde Museum in 1997, and the Beeld voor Beeld Amsterdam in 1998.

Further Reading

Barbash, Ilisa, "An Interview with Robert Gardner," in *Visual Anthropology*, 14, 4, 2001.

Cooper, Thomas, *Natural Rhythms: The Indigenous World of Robert Gardner*, New York: Anthology Film Archives, 1995.

Gardner, Robert, "The More Things Change . . .," in *Transition*, 58, 1992.

———. "The Impulse to Preserve," in *Beyond Document: Essays on Nonfiction Film*, edited by Charles Warren, Hanover, NH: Wesleyan University Press/University Press of New England, 1996.

Gardner, Robert, and Akos Östör, *Making Forest of Bliss: Intention, Circumstance, and Chance in Nonfiction Film*, Cambridge, MA: Harvard Film Archive/Harvard University Press, 2001.

Loizos, Peter, *Innovation in Ethnographic Film: From Innocence to Self-Consciousness, 1956–85*, Manchester: Manchester University Press and Chicago: University of Chicago Press, 1993.

Paz, Octavio, "The Feather and the Grindstone," in *Harvard Magazine*, October 1974, 44–53.

Weinberger, Eliot, "The Camera People," in *Beyond Document: Essays on Nonfiction Film*, edited by Charles Warren, Hanover, NH: Wesleyan University Press/University Press of New England, 1996.

GASS, KARL

"I prefer documentaries *that fight for a cause*. For me, documentary is a weapon" (Herrlinghaus, 1982: 407). This is the professional credo of Karl Gass, one of the most productive directors in the East-German DEFA (Deutschen Film Aktiengesellschaft). Even today, his films continue to provoke controversial discussions, long after the fall of the Berlin Wall.

Before Germany's reunification, Gass had a strong impact on East-German documentary production and film culture. Not only was his 121-film-oeuvre influential in the realm of film, he also played an important role himself by holding a variety of positions in professional associations and festivals, such as president or as jury member, and by mentoring and teaching at the film school. Furthermore, Gass maintained his membership and faith in the ruling communist-party while simultaneously creating a spirit of contradiction.

Gass began working for the DEFA shortly after the foundation of the GDR in 1949, where he remained, after a few detours, until 1990, when the studios were closed. His oeuvre is closely linked to his own biography and, in a certain way, this West German, who because of political reasons moved from Cologne to East Berlin in 1948, personifies the contradictions of a divided Germany in general and of the GDR in particular. On the one hand, Gass was known as a propagandist who cinematically justified the Wall with *Schaut auf diese Stadt* (1962)/*Look at This City*. On the other hand, Gass is also famous for having introduced methods of direct cinema and cinema verité to East-German documentary.

Gass's style and aesthetic approach was influenced by his journalistic background in radio, where he started his career as commentator and reporter. Working for the DEFA newsreel *Der Augenzeuge/The Eyewitness* was also important for his development. Here, he wrote commentaries and learned the technique of montage as well as how to deal with archival material. On his first film projects, he wrote commentary, and he later received a collective prize for *Der Weg nach oben* (1950)/*The Ascending Path*, the first DEFA full feature-length documentary celebrating the early GDR. For Gass, however, his cinematographic career started with *Turbine 1* (1953): This film shows the process of repairing a turbine. Even though the film emphasises industrial progress and working class heroes as characteristic of the times, and although the commentary contains some typical propaganda keywords, the filming method differs from the average production: A hand camera is used to follow the work very closely, and thus, dramaturgy is created through observation. Gass chose Joop Huisken, a disciple of Joris Ivens, as the director for the film, as well as a young cameraman to avoid the euphemistic and aseptic UFA-aesthetics still dominating East-German documentaries at that time. The spirit of *Turbine 1* can also be found in *Vom Alex zum Eismeer* (1954)/*From the Alex to the Ice-sea*, a reportage about the hard labour of fishermen in which Gass combines a pedagogical function with a humorous and self-ironic perspective. Gass's employment of young people was a characteristic element in his vision of documentary making in an attempt to discover new approaches and means of representation in his films.

An important subject for his work during the late 1950s was Western society, which he portrayed in several reportages: A characteristic strategy that Gass used to accuse the West of social injustice was the juxtaposition between beautiful landscapes, on the one hand, and Westerners in Greece or Italy who lived in extreme poverty to deconstruct tourist clichés, on the other. Gass's first internationally acclaimed film was *Allons enfants . . . pour l'Algérie* (1961), a heterogeneous, three-part film that is a portrayal of the Algerian struggle for independence and, at the same time, a polemic against the Western world. As Gass expressed in his credo, documentary was his weapon, and he used this weapon to actively fight on the Cold War front. In 1962, he finished a film about Berlin: *Schaut auf diese Stadt* justifies the Wall, or in the words of the commentary the "antifascist fortification," as a necessary means of protection from a nearby West-German aggression. In the film, Gass uses irony and satire to warrant the building of the Wall. He also combines popular music to mock Americanized Western culture with heavy propaganda, for example, when the East-German tanks leave the barracks with Beethoven's 5th symphony as background music. The historical facts concerning the Berlin conflict are not only so carefully selected that history is falsified, they are also presented in a confusing way by means of editing.

Although propaganda is one major part of Gass's oeuvre, another important aspect is his sensitive look into the daily lives of workers in the GDR. By his will to portray the people not as they should have been, but as they really were, he gave a much more realistic portrait of his fellow citizen with a nonpathetic representation of workers' daily lives. To achieve this, the DEFA offered opportunities that resulted in jealousy among Western filmmakers: Gass, for example, was able to spend several years preparing his film *Asse* (1966)/*Aces*, a portrait of a working brigade. To reassure critics about this long time project and its important costs—16,000 meters of film were used,—Gass simultaneously filmed *Feierabend* (1964)/*Afterwork* in a direct cinema style. Without commentary, this documentary shows how workers spend their free time at an oil site, and alcohol plays an important role in the film. Because the workers are portrayed as people who are far from the official ideal of the socialist hero, both *Feierabend* and *Asse* were perceived negatively by party officials.

To obtain realistic material for his films, Gass used several methods. He was one of the first filmmakers in the GDR to use synchronous sound. In addition, the film team on the *Asse* project, for example, followed the working brigade closely for a long time, so as to establish a relationship based on trust and confidence. Even if Gass himself claims that Dziga Vertov is his model for realism, Gass's approach made him, along with his

DEFA-colleague Jürgen Böttcher, the most important author of GDR-produced cinema verité.

Even for a faithful communist party member, these types of films were not easy to produce. In the 1970s, it became more difficult to create realistic portraits of every day people. At this point, Gass decided that the representation of the present should be left in the hands of younger filmmakers. He himself leaded an artistic working group that contained up to thirty-five people. One of the members, Harald Junge, has continued, even in 2004, the long-term observation project *Die Kinder von Golzow* (since 1961)/*The Children of Golzow* based on an idea by his mentor. Karl Gass himself turned to contemporary history by linking the importance of World War II history with the present in his films. *Zwei Tage im August—Rekonstruktion eines Verbrechens* (1982)/*Two Days in August—Reconstruction of a Crime*, for example, draws a parallel between Hiroshima and the declaration of Ronald Reagan to construct the neutron bomb. Gass's compilation films about history are characterized by gifted editing and montage and by his intelligent formal use of archival material. Moreover, his films are animated with an anti-capitalist, anti-imperialist, and anti-fascist tone that attempts to provide evidence for the continuing presence of Third Reich-elites and the Nazi spirit within the FRG and for his belief that capitalism leads to fascism. Dealing with history and the system-concurrence through a schematic ideological perspective, Gass factors out all incommoding elements. He never did consider, however, the many contradictions of the "instrumentalized antifascism," which were used by the GDR, and of which his films played a major role.

The documentary gaze of Karl Gass can be described by the contradiction between a sensitive seismograph concerning the reality of the GDR, and an example of Cold War Manichaeism concerning the presentation of the reality behind the Iron Curtain.

MATTHIAS STEINLE

Biography

Born in Mannheim, Germany, February 2, 1917. A-levels, work as an intern in commercial economics in Cologne, champion rower. Called up into the German Wehrmacht in 1940. After liberation as British POW, from 1946, financial editor at the radio station/broadcast NWDR in Cologne. Moved to Berlin in 1948, worked for the East-Berlin radio station "Berliner Rundfunk" as a commentator and reporter. Writer and director at the at the Weekly Newsreel and Documentary Studios of DEFA, 1951–1954. Artistic head of the DEFA Popular-science Films, 1954–1960. Co-founder of the Leipzig Documentary and Short Film Week 1955. In 1961, the artistic working group "Karl Gass" is founded, later renamed "Gruppe Effekt." Presented a TV quiz show, 1964–1973. Teacher at the documentary classes at the Potsdam-Babelsberg Film School, 1965–1968. Member of the Board of Directors for Verband der Film-und Fernsehschaffenden der DDR, 1972–1988, and other activities in corporations and festivals. Director at the DEFA Documentary Studios until 1990.

Selected Films

1950 *Der Weg nach oben/The Ascending Path* (Andrew Thorndike): co-director

1952 *Ami go home* (Ella Ensink): co-director

1953 *Turbine 1* (Joop Huisken): co-director, writer

1954 *Vom Alex zum Eismeer*: director, writer

1961 *Allons enfants . . . pour l'Algérie*: director, writer

1961 *Licht für Palermo*: director, writer

1962 *Schaut auf diese Stadt / Look at This City*: director, writer

1964 *Feierabend*: director, writer

1966 *Asse*: director, writer

1967 *Vorwärts die Zeit / Time Onward*: director, writer

1969 *Anno populi—im Jahr des Volkes 1949*: director, writer

1975 *Asse Anno 74*: director, writer

1979 *Der Leutnant von Ulm*: director, writer with Ferry Stützinger

1982 *Zwei Tage im August—Rekonstruktion eines Verbrechens*: director, writer

1985 *Das Jahr 1945 / The Year 1945*: director, writer

1988 *Eine deutsche Karriere—Rückblicke auf unser Jahrhundert / A German career*: director, writer

1990 *Nationalität: deutsch / German Nationality*: director, writer

Further Reading

Filmmuseum Potsdam (ed.), *Schwarzweiß und Farbe. DEFA-Dokumentarfilme 1946–92*, Potsdam: Jovis, 1996.

Gass, Karl, "Von der filmischen Hymne zur realistischen Dokumentation. Auf den Spuren des Bitterfelder Weges?" in *Deutschlandbilder Ost. Dokumentarfilme der DEFA von der Nachkriegszeit bis zur Wiedervereinigung*, edited by Peter Zimmermann, Konstanz: Ölschläger, 1995.

Heimann, Thomas, *DEFA, Künstler und SED-Kulturpolitik. Zum Verhältnis von Kulturpolitik und Filmproduktion in der SBZ/DDR 1945 bis 1959*, Berlin: Vistas, 1994.

Herlinghaus, Hermann (ed.), *Dokumentaristen der Welt in den Kämpfen unserer Zeit. Selbstzeugnisse aus 2 Jahrzehnten (1960–1981)*, Berlin: Henschelverlag, 1982.

Leyda, Jay, *Films Beget Films: A Study of the Compilation Film*, New York: Hill and Wang, 1964.

Lichtenstein, Manfred, Evelyn Hampicke, Marianne Kleinert (eds.), *Filmdokumentaristen der DDR: Karl Gass*, Berlin: Staatliches Filmarchiv der DDR, 1989.

Noelle, Annemarie, "Karl Gass, in *Filmdokumentaristen der DDR*, edited by Rolf Liebmann, Evelin Matschke, Friedrich Salow, Berlin: Henschelverlag, 1969.

Opgenoorth, Ernst, *Volksdemokratie im Kino. Propagandistische Selbstdarstellung der SED im DEFA-Dokumentarfilm 1946–1957*, Köln: Verlag Wissenschaft und Politik, 1984.

Pflaum, Hans-Günther and Hans Helmut Prinzler, *Film in der Bundesrepublik Deutschland. Der neue deutsche Film. Von den Anfängen bis zur Gegenwart. Mit einem Exkurs über das Kino der DDR*, Bonn: Inter Nations 1992.

Roth, Wilhelm, "Dokumentaristen. Wege zur Wirklichkeit," in *Film in der DDR*, edited by Peter W. Jansen and Wolfram Schütte, München and Wien: Hanser, 1980.

Rülicke-Weiler, Käthe, *Film- und Fernsehkunst der DDR. Traditionen—Beispiele—Tendenzen*, Berlin: Henschelverlag, 1979.

Steinle, Matthias, *Vom Feindbild zum Fremdbild. Die gegenseitige Darstellung von BRD und DDR im Dokumentarfilm*. Konstanz: UVK, 2003.

GAZDAG, GYULA

Gyula Gazdag, a Hungarian director of feature and documentary films, is a key figure in understanding the cinema between the post-1968 era and the collapse of communism in his country. A graduate of the famed Hungarian Academy of Drama, Film and Television, Gazdag worked for state-run film and television studios in the 1970s and 1980s, directing a series of documentaries and fiction films that critiqued, with wry irony, the politics of power in a totalitarian regime. His most relevant work of the 1970s was banned, until it began to circulate abroad in the mid-1980s as a result of international pressure.

His diploma documentary short *Hosszú futásodra mindig számíthatunk/The Long Distance Runner* (1968) is considered the earliest example of cinema verité in Hungary. Gazdag's approach to the genre is encapsulated in this penetrating vignette of a small town that honors a national athlete by naming a restaurant after him.

A válogatás/The Selection (1970), a short about a Communist youth chapter choosing a rock band to sponsor, and the remarkable feature-length *A határozat/The Resolution* (1972), co-directed with Judit Ember, are notable. The camera chillingly records the two closed-doors meetings that frame the film and the workers' assembly where the *apparatchik's* stratagem backfires. *The Resolution* casts an ironic look, conveyed without voice-over narration or the filmmakers' intervention, at the exercise of power, paternalism, and corruption. The film was banned for public screening until 1984.

The same open-ended observational approach is practiced in *A Bankett/The Banquet* (1982) and *Társasutazás/Package Tour* (1984). Both documentaries deal, in the present time and without archival footage, with Hungarian political history. The first one records the reunion of participants in the foundation of a short-lived Soviet republic in 1944. Ultimately, the documentary reveals the impossibility of reconstructing the historical truth for lack of documents. *The Banquet* was banned for several years. *Package Tour* is based, like many other Gazdag's documentaries, on a chance occurrence, in this case the trip to modern-day Auschwitz by a group of Hungarian-Jewish concentration camp survivors. The camera follows these elderly people at close range but unobtrusively. It captures eerily not only the traumatic experience of revisiting this site of destruction—the German-speaking guide is a direct throwback to the past—but also the unresolved issue of identity faced by many of the survivors' children.

Made for French television in 1991, *Chroniques Hongroises/Hungarian Chronicles* is an astute two-part investigation on the impact of the Soviet invasion of Hungary in 1956 and its aftermath. It counterpoints, without narrator or explanations, two sets of contrasting views. In the first episode, a worker who supported the failed uprising confronts one of the participants in the firing squad that failed to kill him thirty-five years previously. His recollection powerfully contrasted with the nostalgic reminiscence of the widow of a staunch Communist military man. In the second, an intellectual gives an in-depth assessment of life under Communism, while a former member of the secret police candidly explains the rationale for his line of work.

Film critic J. Hoberman places the Gazdag oeuvre, including his six fiction films, in the aesopian tradition of Central European cinema, which uses fables and metaphors to probe politics and history. He considers the Hungarian filmmaker the most consistently innovative and iconoclastic director since World War II.

MARÍA ELENA DE LAS CARRERAS-KUNTZ

Biography

Born in Budapest, Hungary, July 19, 1947. Graduated from the Hungarian Academy of Drama, Film and Television (Színház- és Filmmüvészeti Föiskola) with a degree in film and television directing in 1970. Several documentaries directed for film studios in Budapest were also banned, such as *A válogatás/The Selection* (1970), *A határozat/The Resolution* (1972), *Hosszú futásodra még mindig számíthatunk . . ./ The Long Distance Runner II* (1977), and *A bankett/The Banquet* (1979). Directed more than a dozen stage plays and operas since the mid-1970s. *A sípoló macskakö/The Whistling Cobblestone* (1971), and *Bástyasétány hetvennégy/Singing on the Treadmill* (1974) banned for their critique of everyday life under communism. The last two, *Hol volt, hol nem volt . . ./ A Hungarian Fairy Tale* (1987), and *Túsztörténet/Stand Off*, were critical successes in Hungary, and launched his career as a professor of cinema, primarily in the United States. Based in Los Angeles since 1989 as a professor in the Department of Film, Television and Digital Media of the University of California, Los Angeles. Also teaches at the Hungarian Academy of Drama, Film and Television since 1985. Frequently directs the Sundance Institute's labs for filmmakers. Awarded the Béla Balázs Award, 1987, Artist of Merit, 1989, and the Official Cross of the Hungarian Republic for artistic achievement, 1997.

Selected Films

DOCUMENTARIES FOR HUNGARIAN TELEVISION, BUDAPEST:

1973 *Boldog békeidök I–VIII/Good Old Times of Peace I–VIII:* director
1975 *Asszonyok a palóc nagycsaládban/Women in Traditional Paloc Families:* director
1975 *A bevonulás/The Invasion:* co-director

1976 *Szûkebb hazánk, a Naprendszer I–VI/Our Home the Universe I–VI:* director
1978 *Házigazda: Lakatos Menyhért/Portrait of a Gypsy Writer:* director
1978 *Az emberi test I–VIII/The Human Body I–VIII:* director
1979 *Mikor megszülettem . . ./When I Was Born . . .: director*
1980 *Kedd/A Balázs Béla Stúdio története/Tuesday/The History of the Béla Balázs Studio:* director

DOCUMENTARIES:

1968 *Hosszú futásodra mindig számíthatunk . . ./The Long Distance Runner short:* director, writer, editor
1970 *A válogatás/The Selection short:* writer, director, editor
1972 *A határozat/The Resolution:* co-writer, co-director, editor
1977 *Hosszú futásodra még mindig számíthatunk . . ./The Long Distance Runner:* director, writer
1979 *A bankett/The Banquet:* writer, director
1984 *Társasutazás/Package Tour:* director, writer
1991 *Chroniques Hongroises/Hungarian Chronicles I–II:* director, co-writer
1997 *A Poet on the Lower East Side: A Docu-Diary on Allen Ginsberg:* writer, director, producer, editor

Further Reading

Báron, György, "The Failure of Paternalism: A Portrait of the Filmmaker Gyula Gazdag," *Mozgó Világ,* 1981, in Hungarian.
Gazdag, Gyula, *Képes Könyv 1968–1979.* Hungary: Jelenkor, 1994, no English translation available.
———. "Initiation Stories," interview, *Sundance Film Festival Catalog,* 1999.
Hoberman, J., "Gyula Gazdag: Lost Illusions/Found Metaphors," in *Pacific Film Archive,* Berkeley: University of California, 1987.
———. "In the Soviet Orbit: Shelf Life," interview, *Film Comment,* May–June 1989.
Lázár, István, "Commuting Camera: On the Films of the Béla Balazs Studio," *Filmkultúra,* 1971, in Hungarian.
Reynaud, Bérenice, "The Unshowable," *Afterimage,* November 1986.

GENERAL POST OFFICE FILM UNIT

At the time the Empire Marketing Board was being terminated, its secretary, Stephen Tallents, was hired by the General Post Office (GPO) as its first Public Relations Officer. Tallents accepted the job on condition that he could bring the Empire Marketing Board (EMB) Film Unit and the Empire Film Library with him. The Empire Marketing Board ended officially in July 1933 (the film work was the only part of it to survive) and the GPO Film Unit came into being.

If the Empire Marketing Board had been the launching pad of British documentary, the GPO would serve as a substantial refueling station in newly expanded space. Though documentary was still a relatively small and uncertain impulse, members of the EMB unit already had made films, under Grierson's guidance, for several other government departments and a number of businesses and industries. But it was vital that the seminal government unit continue as clearinghouse for documentary theory, training school for documentary practice, and laboratory for increasing experimentation.

After the grandeurs of empire, however, the subject matter presented by the GPO seemed limiting to the point of discouragement. At the EMB, Tallents had used the catch-phrase "to bring the empire alive." The need now was, as he saw it, "to bring alive, to the eyes of the public and its own staff, an immense organisation." Although perhaps pushed a step backward regarding subject matter, on the technical and aesthetic side the unit was able to surge ahead. It acquired a new headquarters in Soho Square and its first studio in a ramshackle building at Blackheath, in southeast London. There they installed a sound recording system, which, Tallents conceded, would have been of much better quality if they had not had to consider "the parsimonies of government." In any case, the unit that had started with one young filmmaker (Grierson), who admittedly made its first silent film "without knowing one lens from another," was now not only trained but minimally equipped to take on all comers.

At the GPO, veterans of the EMB were first into the field. In fact, Stuart Legg had directed a series for the GPO during 1932–1933 while the unit was still at the Board. More notable was Legg and Alexander Shaw's *Cable Ship* (1933), made at the GPO. By using the voices of the workers themselves to describe their jobs, it may be said to have begun the experimentation with sound. *Legg's B.B.C.—The Voice of Britain*, started in 1934 and completed in 1935, was even more ambitious. It was awarded a medal of honor at the International Film Festival held during the Brussels Exhibition of 1935.

Under the City (1934), another of the early sound films, was directed by Shaw under Arthur Elton's guidance. The same team made *Airmail* in 1935. *Weather Forecast* (1934) was Evelyn Spice's most notable achievement. Around a well-defined central event—the prediction and eventual onset of a storm—she ingeniously arranged the accessory phenomena of meteorology, the telegraph, and the telephone. In this "symphonic" form, sounds associated with the gathering storm are used contrapuntally.

In 1934, Basil Wright completed what, along with *Granton Trawler* and *Night Mail*, is the loveliest and most enduring of all the EMB-GPO films: *The Song of Ceylon*, made by the GPO Film Unit for the Ceylon Tea Propaganda Board. Wright went on to co-direct with Harry Watt the second GPO masterwork, *Night Mail*, completed in 1936. Watt had earlier directed *6:30 Collection* (1934) with Edgar Anstey, a film about the GPO's West End sorting office. It was Anstey's, and possibly the unit's, first use of sound recording equipment on location.

At the GPO the cadre of EMB veterans was augmented in numbers and advanced in distinction. In 1934, one of the most important of these recruits, Alberto Cavalcanti, came to fill a position as principal teacher and inspirer alongside Grierson. A Brazilian working in Paris in the 1920s and early 1930s, Cavalcanti made a living from commercial features, first as set designer (e.g., *The Late Matthew Pascal* [1924]) and then as director (e.g., *Le Capitaine Fracasse* [1928]) and made a name as producer-director in the avant-garde (e.g., *Rien que les heures* [1926], and *En rade* [1927]). He was responsible for inspiring a great deal of the technical experimentation, particularly in the use of sound, which would mark the GPO films. While assisting on most of the unit's production, he also had films for which he was mainly responsible: *Pett and Pott* (1934), *Coal Face* (1935), and five films the GPO Film Unit produced with Pro Telephon, Zürich, in 1937. Hired as a "guest producer," he stayed on at the unit until 1940, when he joined Ealing Studios as director and producer of features.

Although he had joined the unit during the late days of the EMB, R. H. (Harry) Watt became a star at the GPO. He pioneered a kind of story-documentary, first at the GPO and then at the Crown Film Unit. From *Night Mail*'s suggestion of melodrama (Will the Hollywood "royal mail" arrive in time for the Postal Special?), characterization and mild humor among the men in the sorting-car, and an overall chronological (i.e., narrative) line, Watt moved on to *The Saving of Bill Blewitt* (1937). Here clearly was a new type of story film, set in a Cornish fishing village and using real fishers in their own characters. *North Sea* (1938), again with Watt directing and Cavalcanti producing, was more nearly a total success. It took story and characterization a step further, with a dialogue script written around and for a group of people working in the ship-to-shore radio service and the crew of a trawler experiencing difficulties in a gale off the east coast of Scotland. It would lead to Watt's *Target for Tonight* (1941), that remarkable prototype for the cycle of wartime feature-length semi-documentaries. He then followed Cavalcanti to Ealing and feature films.

Len Lye, hired in 1935, originated the animation technique of painting directly on film, which another Grierson protégé, Norman McLaren, continued to perfect later at the National Film Board of Canada. (McLaren, though he, too, began at the GPO, worked initially on live-action films rather than animation.) A New Zealander who had immigrated to London, Lye was a painter before becoming a filmmaker. Beginning in 1935 with *Colour Box*, he made a series of brief abstract delights including also *Kaleidoscope* (1935), *Rainbow Dance* (1936), and *Trade Tattoo* (1937).

Humphrey Jennings, whose great achievements would come during the years of World War II, joined the GPO unit in 1934. Before and while making films he was also a surrealist painter. *Spare Time* (1939) was his first significant film as a director. Raymond Spottiswoode, who had written *A Grammar of the Film*, published in 1935 when he was just out of Oxford, came on at the GPO in that year. Spottiswoode would continue to work with Grierson at the Film Board in Ottawa and at The World Today in New York City. Alexander Shaw had started work at the EMB and continued on at the GPO. He would have an important career as director and producer in the main English units, and especially as a sort of international missionary for documentary. Pat Jackson joined the unit in 1936. Before switching to features, he was in documentary for a good many years as an editor and then director. In 1937, he co-directed *Big Money* with Harry Watt. Produced by Cavalcanti, it was remarkable in making interesting the unlikely subject of the Accountant-General's Department of the Post Office.

Before joining the GPO, J. B. (Jack) Holmes had directed some important educational films for Gaumont-British Instructional. For the GPO, *The Islanders* (1939) was among his documentaries. His wife, Winifred Holmes, who was earlier interested in education, entered films by writing the commentary for *Cover to Cover*, directed by Alexander Shaw at Strand in 1936, and then worked in various capacities at the GPO. Ralph Bond had joined the EMB in 1931, working first as a unit production manager and then as director. At the GPO he produced and directed. Max Anderson joined the unit in 1936. He became a director and remained there until 1940, when he joined Realist Film Unit.

Grierson also recruited outside filmmakers and would-be filmmakers, most notably among musicians. Walter Leigh composed some noteworthy scores for documentaries; among his last was for GPO's *Squadron 992* (1940), produced by Cavalcanti and directed by Watt. Leigh was killed in action in North Africa. Benjamin Britten, at the beginning of his career, joined the staff of the GPO to score *Coal Face* (1935), *Night Mail* (1936), and many subsequent post office pictures. William Alwyn scored *Wings Over Empire* (1939) for the GPO.

As for the other arts, Grierson had his eye on the poets as well. W. H. Auden joined the unit as a script writer in 1935. He wrote the verse featured in *Coal Face* and *Night Mail* and worked on scripts at the GPO and private units on many other films. J. B. Priestley, the novelist, wrote much of the script for the GPO film on international communications, which eventually became *We Live in Two Worlds* (1937). And the artist William Coldstream was one of the workers at the GPO, his painter's eye and individual sense of humor evident in *The Fairy of the 'Phone* (1935), for example. John Skeaping, the sculptor, had also served since first building a set for *Drifters* (1929).

As for distribution, it was expanded far beyond the early efforts at the EMB, especially in the nontheatrical field; the distribution staff came almost to equal the production staff. The more outstanding films continued to be theatrically released. The nontheatrical campaign moved ahead on three fronts, two already established and one new.

The showings at the Imperial Institute and at exhibitions throughout the country continued. By 1935, three fourths of a million people a year, the great majority of them children, attended the daily showings of EMB and GPO films at the Imperial Institute. At the big trade exhibitions, theaters were installed for continuous screening of GPO films, and the same procedure was followed every winter in conjunction with special post office exhibitions organized in various cities throughout the country.

In addition, traveling projection vans began to criss-cross the countryside from 1935 on, tapping an outlying public of considerable size and enthusiasm, an intensive method that Grierson admitted he had borrowed from Germany and that would later be exploited on a large scale in Canada.

Finally, the policy of free-loan mail distribution of 16mm prints by the Empire Film Library continued unchanged, and the EMB films were steadily added to as the GPO films were released. In 1936–1937, an audience of an estimated one million persons saw these borrowed films. All told, through its several means of nontheatrical distribution and exhibition, the GPO reckoned its annual audience in Great Britain at 2 1/2 million persons by 1937–1938.

Grierson left the GPO in 1937 to help set up Film Centre, a promotional and consultative body designed principally to relate sponsors to producers. J. B. Holmes replaced him as director of productions, with Cavalcanti as chief producer, and Watt as principal director. Subsequently Cavalcanti would be in charge. With the outbreak of war, the GPO Film Unit made, on its own, *The First Days* (1939), showing London adapting to wartime conditions. Watt, Jennings, and Jackson collaborated on this film. In April 1940, the GPO Film Unit was converted into the Crown Film Unit within the Ministry of Information, serving all departments of government.

JACK C. ELLIS

See also **Anstey, Edgar;** *BBC: The Voice of Britain;* **Cavalcanti, Alberto;** *Coal Face;* *Granton Trawler;* **Grierson, John; Jennings, Humphrey; Legg, Stuart; Lye, Len;** *Night Mail;* *The Song of Ceylon;* **Tallents, Stephen; Watt, Harry; Wright, Basil**

Further Reading

Aitken, Ian, *Film and Reform: John Grierson and the Documentary Film Movement*, London: Routledge, 1990.

——— (ed.), *The Documentary Film Movement: An Anthology*, Edinburgh: Edinburgh University Press, 1998.

Arts Enquiry, *The Factual Film*, London: Oxford University Press, 1947.

Beveridge, James (ed.), *John Grierson: Film Master*, New York: Macmillan, 1978.

Ellis, Jack C., *John Grierson: Life, Contributions, Influence*, Carbondale: Southern Illinois University Press, 2000.

Hardy, Forsyth, *John Grierson: A Documentary Biography*, London: Faber and Faber, 1979.

Low, Rachel, *The History of the British Film 1929–1939: Documentary and Educational Films of the 1930s*, London: George Allen & Unwin, 1979.

Orbanz, Eva, *Journey to a Legend and Back: The British Realistic Film*, Berlin: Verlag Volker Spiess, 1977.

Rotha, Paul, *Documentary Diary: An Informal History of the British Documentary Film, 1928–1939*, New York: Hill and Wang, 1973.

Sussex, Elizabeth, *The Rise and Fall of British Documentary: The Story of the Film Movement Founded by John Grierson*, Berkeley: University of California Press, 1975.

Swann, Paul, *The British Documentary Film Movement, 1926–1946*, Cambridge: Cambridge University Press, 1989.

Watt, Harry, *Don't Look at the Camera*, London: Paul Elek, 1974.

GEORGIA O'KEEFFE

(US, Miller, 1977)

Produced by WNET/THIRTEEN for the series Women in Art, Perry Miller Adato's portrait of the artist as an older woman was timed to coincide with the publication of the Viking Press edition of Georgia O'Keeffe's prints, selected by her and her assistant Juan Hamilton. Together, the film and the book relaunched O'Keeffe's career, turning her into a feminist icon of endurance, feistiness, and creativity. In the film, O'Keeffe wanders her beloved New Mexico landscape dressed in her signature black chemise and long coat, her hair pulled severely off her face in a tight bun. She describes her life before coming to New Mexico, how she came to meet her husband Alfred Stieglitz, and how she became attached to the Southwest. Especially when she sits in her studio inspecting the negatives of the prints for the book, O'Keeffe's brief comments about her life and art resemble, almost verbatim, its text. Declaring simply, "I tried to paint what I saw . . . I can see shapes," she explains her recurrent organic forms, her simple lines and bold colors.

Using the extensive archive of photographs made of O'Keeffe primarily by Stieglitz (she was known as the most photographed woman in the world) and pictures made by members of his circle, close-up scrutiny of the paintings, interviews with O'Keeffe, as well as commentary by leading art curators and critics Barbara Rose and Daniel Catton Rich, the film breaks no new ground cinematically. Its sixty-minute PBS format is designed to bring high culture into the living rooms of middle-brow America by emphasizing a one-to-one correspondence between objects or places and the paintings of them. Moreover, coming at a moment when feminism had been mainstreamed, and every woman was searching for foremothers who rebelled and excelled, O'Keeffe's insistence throughout the film that "I've taken hold of anything I wanted" not only brought the artist and her art into every woman's home (a gesture repeated in the posters, calendars, and postcards hanging in college dormitories and gynecologist's offices), but offered an inspiring example of how to be a homey, independent, creative woman. O'Keeffe's ecstatic claims to landscape and space: "When I got to New Mexico, that was mine," provided viewers with a model of female desire to the territorial rights to one's vision, to ownership of one's desires. Later, she describes why she pursued her ten-year struggle to purchase her Abiquiu home from the Catholic Church: "I thought that door [subject of many of her paintings] was something I had to have."

Nothing in this film would suggest the strategic way O'Keeffe and Stieglitz crafted her career, or the fortuitous convergence of film and book, which seems serendipitous. However, O'Keeffe learned from Stieglitz how to market one's art and one's artistic self. Thus the picture of the spry, pixielike O'Keeffe who just happens to have been "lucky" masks a more complicated story of self-promotion. Barbara Rose comments that "when Stieglitz married O'Keeffe, he not only married a woman, he married America." This emphasis on O'Keeffe's American roots, from her birth in Sun Prairie, Wisconsin, to her early years in Texas and South Carolina, to the mistaken attribution of her name as "Virginia" rather than "Georgia" when Stieglitz hung her first show of charcoal drawings, to her final merger with the New Mexico landscape, is part of the original myth of O'Keeffe that this film and the book supposedly subverted through their candid revelations. In effect, the film is merely the most recent version of O'Keeffe's public persona when she was profiled in *Life* magazine in the 1930s and *Time* magazine in the 1940s. Early in the film, while telling about how her interest in bones led to her skull paintings, she mocks "the great American everything" that obsessed her generation of playwrights, poets, and novelists. The stark white cow skull, suspended amid a field of blue, needed something to complete it; she shrewdly added two red stripes as borders, her sardonic commentary on the New York City men's lack of knowledge about the vastness of the country she had actually traversed and inhabited.

It is rare that film captures the full depths of paintings: usually the color is off, the texture invisible, the scale deceptive. O'Keeffe's paintings look exceptionally good in this documentary. In part, as she comments to Juan Hamilton apropos the prints for the book: "It doesn't really matter if the color isn't absolutely right, if it feels right when you finish the print." But there is more to it. O'Keeffe's early training at the Art Institute of Chicago, barely glanced over except to say she was a gifted, prize-winning student there and at the Art Students League in New York, stressed magazine illustration and design. She was extremely aware, through her close working relationship with Stieglitz, of presentation. Her work reproduces well because of its monochromatic colors, its Dow-inspired properties to "fill up space in a beautiful way," its rigorous lines, its recurrent shapes. Both she and her work were supremely suited to television: Her wry, laconic affect, coupled with her determination to control the interview, disclosing only what she wants known, makes her an engaging,

Georgia O'Keeffe, 1977.
[*Still courtesy of the British Film Institute*]

enigmatic figure. She appears to undo the legend surrounding her as she produces a new one for a new generation of fans. Her paintings repeat imagery with variations, much as television series depend on familiarity with a difference. As Rich comments, for O'Keeffe, landscape and still life are essentially the same; they are exercises in the serial investigation of forms and color, not psychological examinations typical of portraiture.

In this, the "portrait of an artist," made for the PBS series was "Women in Art," is also more of a study in comforting repetitive shapes, colors and forms—returning to a few key paintings, such as the New Mexico cross, the yellow and red pelvis, the red poppy, and a few melodic lines for flute—rather than a revelatory inspection of the woman. Despite the series' claims to "interweave the artists' works and their lives," O'Keeffe manages to subvert the filmmaker's push to learn her inner workings. She remains as implacable as the "dark place" she visits on foot and on canvas. By appearing to reveal herself—she speaks always in the first person, claiming over and over an identity: "I was busy"—she weaves the myth of O'Keeffe that has

lasted for three decades. In this, O'Keeffe once again demonstrates her savvy understanding of the terms and procedures of the art market, disclosing only what she deems apt, undercutting any efforts by others to read themselves into her. As she remarks of the critics who read all sorts of sexual symbolism into her gigantic flowers: "They were speaking of themselves, not me."

PAULA RABINOWITZ

Georgia O'Keeffe (USA, WNET/THIRTEEN, 1977, 60 min). Produced by WNET/THIRTEEN for Women in Art. Produced and directed by Perry Miller Adato. Associate Producer, Catherine Tatge. Music by John Morris.

Further Reading

Cowart, Jack, and Juan Hamilton, with Sarah Greenough, *Georgia O'Keeffe: Art and Letters*, Washington, DC: National Gallery of Art, 1987.

Merrill, Christopher, and Ellen Bradbury (eds.), *From the Faraway Nearby: Georgia O'Keeffe as Icon*, Albuquerque: University of New Mexico Press, 1998.

O'Keeffe, Georgia, *Georgia O'Keeffe*, New York: The Viking Press, 1976.

GERMAN DEMOCRATIC REPUBLIC

On May 17, 1946, the Soviet Military Administration (SMAD) handed a license over to German filmmakers for the production of new films. With it, the German Film Inc. (DEFA, acronym for this name in German) was created as the first German film enterprise after World War II. Four months earlier, in mid-January 1946, on behalf of "DEFA in Formation," Kurt Maetzig had already begun shooting the newsreel *Der Augenzeuge/The Eye-Witness*. Its first edition consisted of ten copies that where released to Berlin cinemas on February 19. Two more sequels had appeared from March to July, before *The Eye-Witness* turned into the actual "newsreel" in August 1946. This periodic film program continued until December 1980 when it was suspended.

During the course of its existence, DEFA produced 5,200 documentaries and popular scientific films for the cinema, including *The Eye-Witness* and other periodic programs (for example, a monthly cultural newsreel and a monthly sports

newsreel). In 1975, the former DEFA Studio for Newsreel and Documentary Films Berlin and DEFA Studio for Popular-Scientific Films Potsdam-Babelsberg merged and became DEFA Studio for Documentary Films. Here were produced hundreds of commissioned films for the GDR's (German Democratic Republic) television until the end of the GDR. As in the case of feature films, DEFA almost had a monopoly in the production of documentary films in the GDR. Documentary productions from students of the German University for Cinematographic Art (later the University for Film and Television) Potsdam-Babelsberg, soon followed to the screen.

Besides the newsreel *The Eye-Witness*, the first original DEFA documentary film was also created in 1946. On behalf of KPD (acronym for Kommunistische Partei Deutschlands [German Communist Party]), Director Kurt Maetzig filmed the documentary *Einheit SPD-KPD/SPD-KPD*

Unity (premiere: May 1, 1946), which to a large extent was an objective reportage about the unity of the two German labor parties, KPD and SPD, in the Soviet zone. The films *Berlin Im Aufbau/ Building Up Berlin* (director: Kurt Maetzig), *Postdam Baut Auf/Postdam Builds Up* (director: Joop Huisken), *Dresden* (director: Richard Groschopp), and *Halle/Hall* (Director: Red Braun) appeared in the same year, showing the same objectivity and redeemed pathos. They chose the new beginning as the central theme, and at the same time they referred to the root of the destruction: German militarism and imperialism. Likewise in 1946, Richard Brandt directed the film *Todeslager Sachsenhausen (Death Camp in Saxony)* about a concentration camp at the gates of Berlin.

The SED, other political parties, the Soviet Military Administration, the Metal Industrial Union, the Union of the Persecuted by the Nazi Regime (VVN by the acronym for its name in German), and the Red Cross were among the early clients of DEFA's documentary films. Enterprises and authorities commissioned cinematographic documents. DEFA developed self-help reportages and productions about injured war homecomings, industrial safety, energy savings, and women's rights.

In 1948–1949, after a time of relative freedom, the DEFA documentary films suffered from stronger political oppression. The cinema produced in the GDR, which was created in October 1949, had the main objective of convincing society to switch to socialism, thereby creating "new individuals." At the beginning of 1950, SED's leaders took the decision of tying DEFA documentary film production closely to the party. Since then, the SED guided and controlled the ideology. The SED demanded vehemently and exclusively the "political documentary film" that supported his objectives. Besides short films, movie theaters presented feature-length film productions, whose main objective was to provide a chronicle of successes: *Immer Bereit/Always Ready* (1950) directed by Kurt Maetzig and Feodor Pappe, a reportage about the Free German Youth (FDJ is its acronym for the name in German) meeting in Germany, and DEFA's first color documentary film, *Der Weg Nach Oben (The Way Upward)* (1950) and *Wilhelm Pieck—Das Leben Unser Praesidenten/Our President's Life* (1952) by director Andrew Thorndike. These films present neither doubts about the course of things nor questionable nuances of the social development in Soviet occupation zones and the GDR. They modeled German history and its current situation exclusively after the official propaganda format. The SED made

sure that tickets were distributed throughout enterprises, schools, and institutions and that hundreds of thousands of spectators got the impression that attending the film shows was a compulsory activity. The documentary film had become a political tool.

It was not until the mid-1950s, after Stalin's death and the institution of a "new course," that the studio production became more polymorphic. Joop Huisken reverted to filming simple humans instead of "heroes" in the film *Turbine I* (1953) in which he observed a specific working process in an electrical power station. His assistant, Karl Gass, and other directors dabbled with the production of film feuilletons *Im Paradise Der Ruderer/In Sculler's Paradise* (1953), *Vom Alex Zum Eismeer/ From Alex to the Polar Sea* (1954). Max Jaap produced feature-length films about the life of several artists such as *Ludwig van Beethoven* (1954) and *Friedrich Schiller* (1956). Hugo Hermann, a native Austrian, let children and workers talk directly into the camera about their hopes, desires, and concerns in *Traeumt Fuer Morgen/ Dream for Tomorrow* (1956) and *Stahl Und Menschen/Steel and People* (1957).

The commitment of the Netherlands director Joris Ivens, who produced on behalf of DEFA the international full-length film *Lied Der Stroeme/ Song of Streams* (1954) and *Die Windrose/The Wind Rose* (1957) among others, brought a new impulse to the world of documentary films. Andrew and Annelie Thorndike were dedicated to producing international material. They produced several compilation films based on international archive material, which highlighted the course of German history during the twentieth century, the emergence of the two world wars and the career of former Nazis in the Federal Republic. For the creation of the film *Du Und Mancher Kamerad/ You and Some Comrades* (1956), the Thorndikes had to sift through more than six million meter film, and the film's final version cites approximately 700 different films and newsreels. *Der Fall Harzmann Und Andere/The Harzmann's Case and Other* (1957) is a critic of former Nazi judges taking total control of the West German law system; *Urlaub Auf Sylt/Vacation on Sylt* (1957) is based on the biography of former SS officer Reinefahrt, who was involved in the abatement of the Warsaw rebellion in 1944 and afterwards became mayor of Sylt; *Unternehmen Teutonenschwert/Enterprise Teutonenschwert* (1958) described the role of a NATO's (North Atlantic Treaty Organization) General named Speidel in World War II and Speidel's career after 1945. The impressive assembly of these films sometimes helped to obscure the fact that the Thorndikes were not always moving on safe ground. They usually showed irrefutable facts but also suggested that simple presumptions were the truth and constantly affirmed that the West German state and its political leaders, Adenauer and Schuhmacher, were as bellicose as fascists.

On August 13, 1962, one year after the construction of the Wall, DEFA brought to the big screen the film *Schaut Auf Diese Stadt/Look into This City* (director: Karl Gass), which marked the end of the documentary film productions of the 1950s. On the one hand this film displays abhorrence to Western development, but on the other hand it provides certainty about the historical superiority of the GDR and the socialist system. Gass merely depicted West Berlin as a simple concentration area of war mongers, old Nazis, saboteurs, and agents, like a "stake in the flesh of the GDR." *Look into This City* soon became an enthusiastic "high song" of the GDR and its new borders; in this film there was no room for the tears and sorrow that the Wall brought to people on one or the other side of the razor wire.

The separation of the GDR raised DEFA's documentary film producers and co-workers hope of finally being able to deal with themselves more openly and critical, without any Western influence. A young generation of directors educated at the Babelsberg University for Cinematographic Art and interested in their own country's life and reality, started working at DEFA's studio. Karl Gass became the *spiritus rector* of many of this young people mainly after the presentation of his film *Feierabend/Closing Time* (1946), a spectacular survey that critically analyzes workers and shows them drinking and celebrating for the first time. Gass, who was temporal director of the documentary film class at the university and since 1961 has been head of its own artistic working group for documentary film at DEFA, encouraged Winfried Junge to produce a film series about children from the village of Golzow, which lies on the GDR frontier with Poland. In *Wenn Ich Erst Zur Schule Geh . . ./When I Will Go To School . . .* (1961) Junge narrates about a first school day; in *Nach Einem Jahr/After a Year* (1962), he takes a balanced look after one year; in *Elf Jahre Alt/Eleven Year Old* (1966) he shows a group representation in which the children talk about their experiences and dreams. Up to the end of the GDR, Junge produced five more "Golzow films," which, according to the original plan, should have reflected the growing up of the "first communist generation" until the year 2000.

The films actually emancipated themselves from this theoretical image and showed instead historical time-related and social insights. As a result of this perspective change, Junge could continue with the production of the Golzow series even after the end of the GDR and the end of DEFA. Thus far, the longest full-length international documentary series comprises almost twenty films from which the compilation of *Lebenlaeufe/Life Runs* (1980) and *Drehbuch: Die Zeiten/Screenplay: The Times* (1992) most attracted the attention of an international audience. In *Screenplay: The Times* Junge meditates on the special conditions for making films in the GDR and on censorship and self-censorship.

Like Junge, other important directors of his generation were also interested in contributing to the democratization of the community of the GDR by showing the life conditions and hopes of people, in this way touching people's sensitivity. Outstanding films were shot from the mid-1960s by Juergen Böttcher, Gitta Nickel, Richard Cohn-Vossen, Karlheinz Mund, Kurt Tetzlaff, and Volker Koepp. The French cinema verité and particularly the film of Chris Maker *Le Joli Mai* (1964), which had been awarded on the Documentary Film Week in Leipzig, became of enormous importance to these film producers. Juergen Böttcher was mainly tied to productions such as *Barfuss Und Ohne Hut/Barefoot and Without a Hat* (1965), about young people spending their summer vacations in the Baltic Sea, *Der Sekretaer/The Secretary* (1967) about an unorthodox party secretary, and *Waescherinnen/Laundresses* (1972). In 1978 he produced the film *Martha*, a subtle portrayal of a 68-year-old Berlin "rubble woman," who removes stones to pay the rent, lives a modest life, and is not interested in politics. This type of "heroine" had hardly been seen in the GDR's documentary film until that time.

Gitta Nickel produced *Heuwetter/Hay Weather* (1972), which narrates a one-decade period at an agricultural production cooperative. The film begins with unpublished images from 1963, which deal with several issues such as sloppiness, alcohol addiction, and irresponsibility, until the village chronicle reaches the present time. Thereby is the social development confirmed and fractionated by a countrywoman's personal memories. Volker Koepp let young women talk directly into the camera in *Maedchen In Wittstock/Girls in Wittstock* (1975), his first film about female personnel in a new knitwear factory. Reflections about work, free time, and dreams integrate themselves into a picture that shows the lack of democracy in a "large

471

socialist enterprise." This Wittstock enterprise became a cinematographic research object for Koepp more or less in the same way as village Golzow had been for Winfried Junge. Until 1996, he returned to *Wittstock* again and again, always following the life path of three women, observing the transformation of the place and its inhabitants in the free-market economy. Koepps's films are considered the best DEFA productions: the peace and tenderness of the expression, the confidence acquired through closeness, the sensitivity for landscape motifs, which also often represent the spiritual condition. The quality of the best DEFA documentary films was principally the result of the exceptional DEFA cameramen: Christian Lehmann, Thomas Plenert, Wolfgang Dietzel, and Hans Eberhard Leupold, among others, who always worked masterful and sensitively.

Walter Heynowski and Gerhard Scheumann gained a privileged position in the documentary film business of East Germany. Between 1969 and 1982, they managed their still existing "Studio H&S," which was financed by the State but was officially independent of DEFA. The studio was considered as an independent artistic workshop in the spirit of Dsiga Wertows and provided principally "anti-imperialistic enlightenment." Many H&S films, principally those in which the central theme is the war and peace cycles in Vietnam, the putsch in Chile, or the genocide in Kampuchea, attracted international attention during the 1970s and early 1980s. Retrospectives from Heynowsky and Scheumann were presented in more than forty cities all over the world.

Both directors owned their own studio principally as a result of the film *The Lachende Mann/The Laughing Man* (1966), for which they brought a West German major in front of the camera, who narrated his life as a mercenary in Africa. Under the influence of alcohol and unaware of the filmmaker's identity and the purposes of the film, the anti-hero frankly chatted about his war adventures. For H&S, this meant the exposure of the system in which they grew up: "West German imperialism." As a result of this film, as well as others such as *Piloten In Pijama/Pilots in Pajama* (1968) about U.S. pilots killed in Vietnam, Heynowski and Scheumann were considered political star directors, who enjoyed financial and material success. To fight against the worldwide class conflict, they shot a film cycle about Chile, which began in 1974 with *Der Krieg Der Mumien/The War of the Mummies* and continued with analytical work such as *Ich War, Ich Bin, Ich Werde Sein/I Was, I Am, I Will Be* (1974) and *Der Weisse Putsch/The White Putsch* (1975), as well as some sharply pointed short films. In their films H&S analyzed the mechanisms that led to the fall of Salvador Allende's government and outlined the roll of the Chilean bourgeoisie and the military. However, the films omitted, to a large extent, any objections against the left movement.

For the production of *Die Teufelsinsel/The Devil's Island* (1976), *Der Erst Reis Danach/The First Rice Thereafter* (1977), and others, H&S returned to Vietnam immediately after the end of war to search for crime traces, resistance, and a new life. They analyzed in the feature-length documentary films *Kampuchea—Sterben Und Auferstehen/Kampuchea—Dying and Resurrecting* (1980) and *Die Angkar/The Angkar* (1981) the terror regime of Pol Pot and the consequences for Kampuchea. However, neither director was interested in the GDR's contemporary life; Heynowski and Scheumann returned to their country only until they started the production of *Die Dritte Haut/The Third Skin* (1989), a beautifully colored homage to Erich Honecker's housing policy.

The denaturalization of the political songwriter Wolf Biermanns by the SED leaders began in autumn 1976, and this event, together with the government's attempt to discipline the GDR's artists, also left deep marks on the documentary film studio. One of the most important directors, Richard Cohn-Vossen, who produced the fascinating biography of composer *Paul Dessau* (1976) among other films and critically questioned the practice of socialistic democracy in films like *Monika* (1975) and *Abgeordnete In Rostock/Deputy in Rostock* (1976), left the GDR and migrated to the Federal Republic of Germany. His colleagues Juergen Böttcher, Werner Kohlert, and Heinz Brinkmann, who protested against Biermanns's denaturalization, experienced massive political pressure. During the 1980s, DEFA documentary producers as a whole showed the reality of the GDR in a more critical way and staged productions that displayed taboo subjects (often despite the resistance of the State), which were financed by DEFA.

The film *Erinnerung An Eine Landschaft—Fuer Manuela/Memory of a Landscape—for Manuela* (1983) by Kurt Tetzlaff, a full-length survey about a village in central Germany that had to succumb to the opening of a brown-coal mining, *Jugendwerkhof/Industrial School* (1982) by Roland Steiner about subjugated young people, *Abhaengig/Dependent* (1983) and *Rueckfaellig/Recidivist* (1988) by Eduard Schreiber about alcohol addicts, *Berlin—Auguststrasse/Berlin—August Street* (1981) by Guenter Jordan about young people in an East site of Berlin, as well as some films from Karlheinz Mund, Gunther Scholz, and Konrad Weiss about mentally and physically disabled persons are among the most outstanding films of the last decade of the GDR.

The documentary films from Juergen Böttcher, *Rangierer/Shunting* (1984) and *Die Kueche/The Kitchen* (1987), which show intense black-and-white pictures, reflected the end time mood: symbols of hard work in an imaginary room, in which shadowy movements seemed to be produced, but no real motive is given. Jochen Krausser approached the country's condition in a grotesque way: *Leuchtkraft Der Ziege—Eine Naturerscheinung/The Goat's Luminance—A Natural Phenomenon* (1988) was the first surrealistic contribution of DEFA's documentary film studio. The rock report *Fluestern & Schreien/Whispering and Shouting* (1989, directors: Dieter Schumann and Jochen Wisotzki) showed for the first time parts of the GDR's subversive music scene and put a piece of counterculture on the public cultural map. . . . *Und Freitag In Die Gruene Hoelle (. . . And Friday in the Green Hell)* (1989, director: Ernst Cantzler) portrayed football fans and rowdies in East Berlin, *Unsere Kinder/Our Children* (1988, Roland Steiner) brought punks, old gits, skinheads, and young neo-Nazis in front of the camera. In *Unsere Alten Tage/Our Old Times* (1989), Petra Tschoertner illustrated the treatment given to the elderly in the GDR, which was not always humane. All these productions are valiant films and the same can be said about Karl Gass's historic precise compilation *Das Jahr 45/Year 45* (1985), about existential confusion in the history of the German people.

Helke Misselwitz had great success with a production that covered a complex description of the GDR's condition and the mood of its inhabitants at the end of the 1980s. She undertook a cinematographic journey across the country for the production of the documentary *Winter Ade/Goodbye Winter* (1987), and she outlined experiences of women of different ages and diverse social positions. *Goodbye Winter* became the most significant and emotional film at the end of the GDR.

The film diary *Leipzig Im Herbst/Leipzig in Fall* from Andreas Voigt and Gerd Kroske, a reportage about demonstrators and policemen, oppositionists and functionaries, opened DEFA's last chapter. After the collapse of the prevailing state party and the fall of the Wall, there was no longer the need to say or show the facts between lines or images. Movies such as *Imbiss Spezial/Special Snack* (1990, director: Thomas Heise), *Kehraus/Last Dance* (1990: director: Gerd Kroske), *Sperrmuel/*

Bulk Waste (1990, director: Helke Misselwitz), *Wind Sei Stark/Wind Is Strong* (1990, director: Jochen Krausser), *Im Durchgang/On the Pathway* (1990, director: Kurt Tetzlaff), *Letztes Jahr Titanic/Last Year Titanic* (1991, director: Andreas Voigt), *Eisenzeit/Iron Age* (1991, director: Thomas Heise), and *Kein Abschied—Nur Fort/No Goodbye—Only Begone* (1991, director: Joachim Tschirner, Lew Hohmann) described the mood of the GDR citizens as agony and optimism and described the new difficulties that came from German unification. Heinz Brinkmann and Jochen Wisotzki produced the film *Komm In Den Garten/Come to the Garden* (1990) about three friends in the Berlin municipality Prenzlauer Berg, which was in fact homage to outsiders, who DEFA had considered before as "cinematic unworthy." In the film *Oestliche Landschaft/Eastern Landscape* (1990), which was completely filmed at a garbage place, Eduard Schreiber pleaded viewers not to sacrifice one's own roots exclusively for a new reality.

Directors and authors also worked on the history of the GDR and the history of the real socialism besides the contemporary reportages and essays. In the film *Walter Janka—Aufstehen Und Wiedersetzen/—To Rise And Resist* (1990), Karlheinz Mund depicted a publisher who had been under political arrest for many years. In *Christina Wolf—Zeitschleifen/Time Warps* (1991), Mund became known to the East German writer, who had become a positive role model for many countrymen due to her disturbed critical attitude towards politics. Konrad Herrmann revealed the biography of the GDR's first minister of culture and former expressionist poet Johannes R. Becher in *Die Angst Und Die Macht/Fear and Power* (1991). Director Sybille Schoenemann, who was arrested in the mid-1980s because of "subversive activities" and deported to the West, showed in her autobiographical film *Verriegelte Zeit/Barred Times* (1991) the role that DEFA's assistants had in the GDR political system. She outlined her own spying, arrest, and denaturalization experience.

Juergen Böttcher performed a special farewell to the GDR. His film *Die Mauer/The Wall* (1990), developed between paintings and film scenes, silently showed the slow disappearance of the Berlin Wall through long contemplative settings. One can see and hear, for example, bird swarms concentrated over the still desert city center, the closed underground station at Postdamer Platz, or the multicolored Graffitis, people and propaganda noise, sounds of excavators, fireworks of New Year's Eve 1989–1990, and wood crosses for the frontier's sacrifice. The director projected additional historical film passages onto the wall: from Emperor Wilhelm's ride through the Brandenburg gate, completely lit by Nazi torches, a picture of a policeman who jumped to the West in 1961, until the day of the fall of the Wall.

On July 1, 1990, the day of the monetary union between GDR and FRG and of the introduction of the D-Mark as the unique legal currency, the DEFA documentary film studio was transformed into a limited corporation and was put on sale by the privatization agency. To comply with the privatization conditions, the studio fired most of its employees until mid-1991. Nearly all were directors, cameramen, and dramaturges. The rest of DEFA, mostly service providers, were in charge of the TV programs production, made technology available, and assisted in co-productions. The quality of the DEFA documentary films survived the new productions of the East German directors. Even though many former directors, authors, and cameramen retired, lost their jobs, or changed professions, the work of Volker Koepp, Thomas Heise, Eduard Schreiber, Peter Voigt, Andreas Voigt, Jochen Krausser, Heinz Brinkmann, and Winfried Junge are still associated with the most exhilarating German documentaries.

Juergen Böttcher, the internationally best known DEFA's director, returned to the screen in 2001. In his film *Konzert Im Freien/Konzert Outdoors*, he assembled new pictures with old, nonpublic DEFA material about the construction of the Marx Engels Forum in East Berlin, which was conceived as a monument and parkway. The outcome of this work was an essay about hopes and errors, utopias and tragedies of the twentieth century.

RALF SCHENK

See also **Böttcher, Jürgen; Heynowski, Walter and Gerhard Scheumann**

Further Reading

Jordan, Günther, and Ralf Schenk (eds.), *Schwarzweiß und Farbe. DEFA-Dokumentarfilme 1946–92*, Berlin: Jovis Verlag, 1996, 1st ed., 2000, 2nd ed.

Kersten, Heinz, *Das Filmwesen in der Sowjetischen Besatzungszone Deutschlands*, Bonn/Berlin: Bundesministerium für Gesamtdeutsche Fragen, 1963.

Liebmann, Rolf, Evelyn Matschke, and Friedrich Salow (eds.), *Filmdokumentaristen der DDR*, Berlin (DDR): Henschelverlag, 1969.

Moldenhauer, Gebhard, and Volker Steinkopff (eds.), *Einblicke in die Lebenswirklichkeit der DDR durch dokumentare Filme der DEFA*, Oldenburg: Bibliotheks- und Informationssystem der Universität Oldenburg, 2001.

Mückenberger, Christiane and Günter Jordan, "*Sie sehen selbst, Sie hören selbst . . .,*" Die DEFA von ihren Anfängen bis 1949, Marburg: Hitzeroth, 1994.

Opgenoorth, Ernst, *Volksdemokratie im Kino*. Propagandistische Selbstdarstellung der SED im DEFA-Dokumentarfilm 1946–1957, Köln: Verlag Wissenschaft und Politik, 1984.

Pflaum, Hans Günther, and Hans Helmut Prinzler, *Film in der Bundesrepublik Deutschland*, München/Wien: Carl Hanser Verlag, 1992 (2nd ed.) Pusch, Steffi, *Exemplarisch DDR-Geschichte leben*. Ostberliner Dokumentarfilme 1989/90, Frankfurt/Main: Peter Lang Europäischer Verlag der Wissenschaften, 2000.

Roth, Wilhelm, *Der Dokumentarfilm seit 1960*, München/Luzern: Verlag C. J. Bucher, 1982.

Zimmermann, Peter (ed.), *Deutschlandbilder Ost*. Dokumentarfilme der DEFA von der Nachkriegszeit bis zur Wiedervereinigung, Konstanz: UVK-Medien/Verlag Ölschläger, 1995.

Zimmermann, Peter, and Gebhard, Moldenhauer (ed.), *Der geteilte Himmel*. Arbeit, Alltag und Geschichte im ost- und westdeutschen Film, Konstanz: UVK-Medien, 2000.

GERMANY

The production of nonfiction films in Germany is comparable to other European or North American countries. From 1895 on, short local views of cities and small towns were often shot by foreign film companies, such as Lumière, Pathé, Gaumont, and Raleigh & Robert, which worked on an international level. The content of the images is quite universal in this early period and follows a similar aesthetic direction. Besides views of marketplaces, streets, and important buildings in a particular city, the official visits of emperors, kings, dukes, and czars became regular subjects for films, as did military parades and festive processions. The German emperor, Wilhelm II, was open to the new medium and thus became one of the early movie stars. Natural disasters and sports were attractive subjects, along with exotic places and folkloristic traditions.

In November 1911, the first German newsreel, *Der Tag im Film*, was produced by Express Films in Freiburg. Oskar Messter, one of the most important German pioneers of film technology, had shot nonfiction films from 1897 on. He founded his Messter-Woche newsreel in October 1914, shortly after the beginning of World War I. With the *Eiko-Woche* it became the most important newsreel during the war. During World War I the important role of film for propaganda became clear, so around 1916 the state, the military, and heavy industry became interested in bringing film production companies under their control. On December 18, 1917, the Universum-Film AG (Ufa) was founded by the merger of the three most successful film production companies (Nordisk, Messter, and PAGU) and with the German state as the most influential shareholder.

In June 1918, the Ufa also opened a cultural department, which first produced educational films and *Kulturfilme*, the German term for documentaries in that period. This department was intended to produce and distribute scientific, educational, and entertaining films that which would be edifying and serve the educational system. One main activity was to produce medical training films and in the first five years, approximately 135 of these films were produced for a medical film archive. In 1920, the department visited universities to promote the concept of using film for educational purposes and to get suggestions for new topics. The idea was to produce films for the huge market of universities and especially the 60,000 schools. Some cities started or supported noncommercial film activities to create an alternative to the commercial, sensational fiction film.

But the Ufa discovered that there was no market in the educational field, because universities and schools had no budgets for film, and the costs for projectors and film rentals were quite high. The Ufa changed its strategy and started to produce ten- to twenty-minute-long cultural films that were screened with the newsreels before the feature film. Most of these films were given good ratings for their high quality, and created a tax reduction for the whole screening. Every year, a few long nonfiction films were also produced. Examples are Arnold Fanck's *Das Wunder des Schneeschuhs/The Wonder of the Snowshoe* (1920–1922) on skiing, *Der Rhein in Vergangenheit und Gegenwart/The Rhine River in Past and Present* (1922), and Wilhelm Prager's *Wege zu Kraft und Schönheit/Ways to Strength and Beauty* (1925) on modern body culture and sports. The *Kulturfilmbuch* (book on cultural film), published by Edgar

Beyfuss und Alexander Kossowsky in 1924, helped make the public aware of the broad spectrum of film production. It is a comprehensive study on the practical and theoretical state-of-the-art of nonfiction film in Germany and the subgenres that had already been developed (e.g., films on art, cities, biology, animals, geography, medicine, industry, promotion, animation, sports). The German Kulturfilm used and tested new technologies such as cameras, lenses, and film emulsions and experimented with new effects, such as slow motion, stop motion, fast motion, and dissolves. It gained an international reputation and the films were exported to various countries. In Russia the term *Kulturfilm* was even taken over. Besides the Ufa, there were many other production companies such as Deulig, Nationalfilm, Emelka, and Dafu that concentrated on nonfiction films. Some directors also founded their own production companies. Hans Cürlis and his *Kulturinstitut* produced portraits of artists from the 1920s to the 1960s; such continuity despite all the political changes is more typical than an exception.

In the second half of the 1920s, avant-garde directors such as Walter Ruttmann, Wilfried Basse, and Hans Richter produced the first so-called documentaries including *Berlin. Die Sinfornie der Grosstadt/Berlin. Symphony of a City* (1927), *Markt in Berlin/Street Markets in Berlin* (1929), and *Deutschland—zwischen gestern und heute/Germany Yesterday and Today* (1933). They were cross-section or montage films, which were influenced by the international avant-garde movement, especially French films and the Russian montage of Vertov and Eisenstein. In the second half of the 1920s, the filmmakers knew each other and exchanged and discussed their films. Associations were founded to present new styles and modern films in the United Kingdom, the Netherlands, France, the United States, and other countries. There was an active international exchange and it is hard to discuss these films as specifically national cinematography. In 1929, there was a meeting of the film avant-garde at La Sarraz castle in Switzerland. Now the rhythm of the montage, the modern aesthetic of extreme camera positions and unconventional use of sound and music developed a new style, which became very influential.

In 1933, the National Socialists took power and started to control film production through the Ministry of Enlightenment and Propaganda of Joseph Goebbels. Internationally best known are the films of Leni Riefenstahl, although she directed only seven films, as well as some propaganda films from that period. Between 1933 and 1945, approximately 12,000 nonfiction films, mainly industrial films and commercials, approximately 1,000 educational films, a few thousand cultural films, and 850 longer films of more than 1,000 m long (36 min.). There is a strong continuity in the style of nonfiction films and the people involved in making them, and few directors and producers were forbidden to work after 1933. Even former communist filmmakers, such as Carl Junghans, were able to make films such as *Jugend der Welt*/Youth of the World (1936) on the Winter Olympics in Garmisch-Partenkirchen. The visual style with the dominance of perfect images and modern montage was declared to be the new German camera style by official Nazi papers. The films of Leni Riefenstahl on the NSDAP party rallies in 1933 and 1934 and her two films on the Olympic Games were declared models for the new documentary. After 1945, the nonfiction production of the period was viewed as pure propaganda and nobody was interested in the films. Only recently have there been attempts to analyse these films again and to differentiate them more closely. Comparable to the fictional film production in Nazi Germany, where only approximately 15 percent of the films were regarded as propagandistic, in the nonfiction production the majority cannot seriously be discussed as propaganda. Of course, the NS propaganda films became famous and have been analyzed in detail. Central examples are Riefenstahl's *Triumph des Willens Triumph of the Will* (1935), Fritz Hippler's *Feldzug in Polen/Campaign in Poland* (1940) or his demagogic *Der ewige Jude/The Eternal Jew* (1940), Hans Bertram's *Feuertaufe/Baptism of Fire* (1940), and *Sieg im Westen/Victory in the West* (1941) by Svend Noldan and Fritz Brunch.

But these famous NS propaganda films were not the average nonfiction production. Of course, the state wanted to be presented in the best possible way, and in cultural films you will also find aesthetic styles very typical for the Nazi period; for example, the Swastica flag is omnipresent. But the flag was also part of the German reality at that time and cannot be discussed only as a symptom of propagandistic purpose. The nonfiction production covers the same broad range of subgenres described for the Weimar Republic period and reflects a high technical standard. Often the films tested new possibilities of microphotography and macrophotography and even x-ray films with sound were produced. Directors Walter Ruttmann, Martin Rikli, Ulrich K. T. Schulz, Svend Noldan, Willy Zielke, and others tried to break aesthetic limits and to push modern visual styles. Typical of this attempt is a mixture of real sequences, staged scenes, animation, effects and text, which now would be called hybrid forms. This form also has to do with the technical conditions. Generally the cameras were heavy and needed a tripod, and there were only a few minutes in the magazine. The speed of the film material was not very high, so it was only possible to shoot by sun or with artificial light. Therefore the shots had to be planned extremely carefully.

The four previously existing German sound newsreels (Ufa, Deulig, Tobis, and Fox) were merged into *Die Deutsche Wochenschau* during World War II. Newsreel screenings were obligatory for all 5,492 theaters in Germany from 1938 on. The number of prints was increased from about 400 in 1939 to 2,400 in 1943. So it was only during the war that newsreels were screened close to their production date, which was very professional. Special propaganda companies were formed, which were integrated in the military structure and which made it possible to shoot realistic images from the front lines. The silent shots were selected centrally in Berlin and combined with sound, an aggressive commentary, and a dynamic music score. "Nazi newsreel music makes the motor nerves vibrate; it works directly upon the bodily feelings," as Siegfried Kracauer analyzed as early as 1943. The Ministry of Propaganda viewed the newsreels as a perfect tool to influence the German public. But they worked well only in times of victory; from 1943 on they lost their credibility. Images from Nazi newsreels are regularly used in historical TV programs on the Third Reich; thus they still contribute to the image that we have of that time.

The years after 1945 are again characterized by continuity. Most of the people involved in the production of nonfiction film in the Third Reich were able to work again after the end of the war. Members of the propaganda companies became pioneers of German postwar television and of the various newsreels in East and West Germany. The film *Michelangelo. Das Leben eines Titanen* (1940) by Curt Oertel was reedited by Robert Flaherty for the American version as *The Titan. The Story of Michelangelo* (1950) and won an Academy Award as Best Feature Documentary in 1951. In East Germany the DEFA studio was founded in 1946 with a special documentary department. They developed their own style and regularly shot in 35mm black-and-white film. In West Germany, mostly small production companies continued to shoot the whole spectrum of nonfiction films.

Bernhard Grizmek was successful in the theaters with *Kein Platz für wilde Tiere/No Place for Wild Animals* (1956), on African wildlife, which also won a Golden Bear at the Berlin International Film Festival. Hans Domnick was also popular with *Traumstrassen der Welt/Dream Roads of the World* (1958), a travel through North and South America from Alaska to Chile.

In the 1950s, television was established in Germany, and it became the primary source for financing documentary films. Peter von Zahn established a more reportage-like style for the NWDR in Hamburg; in 1959, Klaus Wildenhahn started at the NDR and developed a special style of an observing camera, not disturbing reality too much. In the Southwest, the SDR founded a documentary department, which became known as the Stuttgart School. Its films were intended to be something different from the Nazi newsreels and the more pedagogic Kulturfilm tradition. They produced very critical and ironic commentaries on West German society, which were masterpieces of montage. In the 1960s directors such as Dieter Ertel, Wilhelm Bittdorf, and Roman Brodmann were highly influenced by the direct cinema movement. During the student protest movement, political documentaries were shot at the film school in Berlin, which was founded in 1966, and at the film school in Ulm, which was headed by Alexander Kluge und Edgar Reitz, and at the new film school in Munich. Most of the young directors then developed an interest in daily life in Germany and wanted to shoot films on political issues such as ecology, the socially underprivileged, or minorities including handicapped people. The declared goal of the video movement, which was very active in the 1970s, was to give such groups a voice, as well as to change society with the help of documentaries. Political content became more important than aesthetic quality and the documentaries got the reputation of being boring. In 1980, the German Documentary Association (AG Dok) was created at the Duisburg Festival. With more than 700 members, it has now developed into the most important pressure group for documentary filmmakers.

The documentary changed fundamentally in the 1990s, experiencing a renaissance in theatrical release and on TV. From 1990 on, the documentary film in Germany has developed a whole range of different styles and narrational forms and has abandoned the notion that a documentary has to be educational and boring. Often the films present subjective positions or follow a more essayistic style. The multiplicity is of course only one reason for the attraction of the genre. Also important are technical developments such as digital DV and HD cameras or digital editing, as well as because the commercial TV market, which was not introduced in Germany until 1984, is pushing new popular formats like docusoap, docudrama, or even reality TV. To be successful, a director has to develop a personal style and has to decide what she or he is willing to deliver to which system. Electronic editing as well as computer graphics and animation have an aesthetic influence and the digitization of production and postproduction enables a director to get exactly the images he or she wants. Questions of narration and storytelling become more relevant for documentaries. Sometimes these changes raise ethical questions about how far a documentary filmmaker can and should go, but these discussions have made the documentary so vivid and extraordinarily interesting and have furthered its new popularity.

KAY HOFFMANN

See also **Basse, Wilfried; Brodmann, Roman; Ertel, Dieter; Fanck, Arnold; Hitler and National Socialist Party; Junghans, Carl; Kluge, Alexander; Messter, Oskar; Riefenstahl, Leni; Rikli, Martin; Zielke, Willy**

Further Reading

Bartels, Ulrike, *Die Wochenschau im Dritten Reich*, Frankfurt: Peter Lang 2004.

Beyfuss, Edgar, and Kossowsky, Alexander, *Das Kulturfilmbuch*, Berlin: Chryselius & Schulz 1924.

Bolesch, Cornelia (ed.), *Dokumentarisches Fernsehen: Ein Werkstattbericht in 48 Portraits*, Munich, Leipzig: List 1990.

Drewniak, Boguslaw, *Der deutsche Film 1938–1945*, Düsseldorf: Droste 1987.

Hoffmann, Hilmar, *"Und die Fahne führt uns in die Ewigkeit." Propaganda im NS-Film*, Frankfurt: Fischer 1988.

Hoffmann, Kay, *Zeichen der Zeit: Zur Geschichte der "Stuttgarter Schule,"* Munich: TR-Verlagsunion, 1996.

———. "Propagandistic Problems of German Newsreels in World War II, in *Historical Journal of Film, Radio and Television*, 24, 1, 2004, 133–142.

Jacobs, Lewis, *The Documentary Tradition* (2nd ed.), New York, London: Norton 1979.

Jung, Uli; and Martin Loiperdinger (eds.), *Geschichte des dokumentarischen Films in Deutschland. Band 1: Kaiserreich (1895–1918)*, Stuttgart: Reclam, 2005.

Kalbus, Oskar, *Pioniere des Kulturfilms*, Karlsruhe: Neue Verlags-Gesellschaft, 1956.

Keitz, Ursula von, and Kay Hoffmann (eds.), *Die Einübung des dokumentarischen Blicks*, Marburg: Schüren 2001.

Kessler, Frank, Sabine Lenk, and Martin Loiperdinger (eds.), *KINtop Band 1: Früher Film in Deutschland*, Frankfurt: Stroemfeld, 1992.

——— (eds.), *KINtop Band 4: Anfänge des dokumentarischen Films*, Frankfurt: Stroemfeld, 1995.

Kreimeier, Klaus, Antje Ehmann, Jeanpaul Goergen (eds.), *Geschichte des dokumentarischen Films in Deutschland. Band 2: Weimarer Republik (1918–1933)*, Stuttgart: Reclam, 2005.

Roth, Wilhelm, *Der Dokumentarfilm seit 1960*, Munich, Lucerne: Bucher 1982.

Segeberg, Harro (ed.), *Mediale Mobildmachung I. Das Dritte Reich und der Film*, Munich: Wilhelm Fink, 2004.

Ziegler, Reiner, *Kunst und Architektur im Kulturfilm 1919–1945*, Konstanz: UVK, 2003.

Zimmermann, Peter, *Geschichte von Dokumentarfilm und Reportage von der Adenauer-Ära bis zur Gegenwart,* in Ludes, Peter, Heidemarie Schuhmacher, and Peter Zimmermann (eds.), *Geschichte des Fernsehens in der Bundesrepublik Deutschland Band 3: Informations- und Dokumentarsendungen*, Munich: Wilhelm Fink Verlag, 1994.

Zimmermann, Peter, and Kay Hoffmann (eds.), *Triumph der Bilder. Kultur- und Dokumentarfilme vor 1945 im internationalen Vergleich*, Konstanz: UVK, 2003.

——— (eds.), *Geschichte des dokumentarischen Films in Deutschland. Band 3: "Drittes Reich (1933–1945),"* Stuttgart: Reclam 2005.

GERTRUDE STEIN: WHEN THIS YOU SEE, REMEMBER ME

(US, Miller Adato, 1971)

Perry Miller Adato's *Gertrude Stein: When This You See, Remember Me* was initially conceived as a documentary about the Paris art scene of the 1920s and 1930s, the working title of which was *Paris, the Luminous Years.* When the concept was rejected by various networks as being too broad in scope, Miller Adato decided to focus on one person whose life, she believed, symbolised and encompassed the period, and to tell the story of the age through that person. True to Miller Adato's original idea, France, as it progresses from the early twentieth century through two world wars, is the film's leitmotif. One senses throughout Miller Adato's film the profound truth of Stein's observation that, "It was not what France gave you, but what it did not take away that was important."

There is much evidence of Miller-Adato's original, broader focus in the finished film. The film includes numerous talking head style interviews, with such notables as Virgil Thomson, Jaques Lipschitz, Sherwood Anderson, Janet Flanner, Daniel-Henri Kahnweiler, Pierre Balmain, and Bennett Cerf. Different people knew Stein at different times in her life: Kahnweiler knew both Stein and Picasso and touches on the early 1904 period; Janet Flanner knew her in the 1920s, and Virgil Thomson in the 1920s and 1930s. An interview with a Mrs. Bradley, wife of Stein's literary agent and acquaintance of Hemingway and Alice B. Toklas, discusses the later years of Stein's time in Paris, and a Mrs. Chapman, who brought Stein to America, covers the American period, along with Stein's publisher Bennett Cerf. In addition to these interviews are animation stills, film footage, segments of plays by Stein, and a great number of photographs and transparencies of paintings. Approximately 1,000 photographs and 70 transparencies were reduced to 400 and 50, respectively, for the final edit. The film is remarkably fast-paced for a documentary, incorporating a vast amount of material into ninety minutes, and features twice as many cuts as a standard Hollywood feature film.

In editing the phases of Stein's life, Alan Pesetsky does admirable work, for despite the diverse material on which Miller Adato draws, there is little sense of fragmentation. And Miller Adato counterbalances her reconstruction of the times with a tight focus on Stein herself. It is as if we see the entire period through Stein's eyes. The director works in a style consistent with Gertrude Stein's own artistic perception: the rhythm of repetition and the equalizing of elements. Repetition is a particularly important quality to the film just as it was to Stein herself, as anyone familiar with her famous rose poem could confirm. One beautiful sequence takes a single, realistic image

Gertrude Stein (right), with her biographer and companion, Alice B. Toklas and their pet dog, Basket, walking down a street of the village in the mountains of southeastern France in which they've lived in self-imposed isolation since the Nazi occupation.
[*Courtesy of the Everett Collection*]

shot a twenty-nine-second zoom, beginning with a long shot and ending with a close-up of the house. The timing and positioning of this shot accurately recreates the description of the incident in the book.

Miller Adato not only reflects Stein's work through the form of her film, but also incorporates actual segments of Stein's various literary pieces into the film. These include a sequence from Al Carmine's musical *In Circles*, based on Stein's play of the same name, which serves as evidence that Stein could still inspire something as contemporary as Carmine's work, and excerpts from *Four Saints in Three Acts*, which she and Virgil Thomson collaborated on. And there is no narration, per se, for the spoken text, outside of the interviews with her friends and colleagues and quotes from people who knew her well, is composed entirely of Stein's writings. *The Autobiography of Alice B. Toklas*, Stein's own biographical work, is the most heavily referenced work, but there are segments and quotations from *Tender Buttons, Lucy Church Amiably*, and *The Making of Americans* amongst other works.

The film presents us with an intimate portrait of Gertrude's day-to-day life and in particular her relationship with Alice B. Toklas. Some remember Alice's exquisitely tasty cakes; others recall that in their household Gertrude never bothered to do any chores, while Alice managed things deftly and

and gradually multiplies it. A prism lens was used to fragment, multiply, and distort the shapes of the photographed images to visualise the Cubist tendencies pioneered by Braque and Picasso and reflected in Gertrude's abstract writings. A Picasso drawing of Leo Stein is animated to show him walking rapidly first in one direction, then in the other, to portray the shifting paths of his involvements.

The camera also makes use of zooms, pans, and dissolves to keep the images constantly moving and to create dynamic visual equivalencies to the sensitive narration culled from the writings by or about Gertrude Stein. Visualising Stein's "A Valentine to Sherwood Anderson," for example, the camera dissolves from an old-fashioned valentine, resplendent with hearts, angels, and flowers, to a picture of Anderson nestled in its centre. And to bring to life the section of *The Autobiography of Alice B. Toklas*, which describes how Alice and Gertrude found the house they would live in, Miller Adato and her crew went to Bilignin and

Gertrude Stein with her companion and biographer, Alice B. Toklas and their dog, Basket, in front of her home in France.
[*Courtesy of the Everett Collection*]

479

smoothly. Gertrude, the woman, is contrasted with Stein, the writer, thinker, art collector, and genius, so as to bring a touch of humanity to what might otherwise be a documentary overwhelmingly populated with historical, literary, and artistic figures about whom so much is written and filmed that they cease to have any real meaning for us. Within Miller Adato's film, Stein's life and career incorporates the story of Paris in the early twentieth century as the director intended, but Gertrude never ceases to be the focus of the film as both artist and as a person. As the director herself puts it, *Gertrude Stein: When This You See, Remember Me* is basically, "the story of a woman and an artist who happened to live in the right place at the right time."

Gertrude Stein: When This You See, Remember Me received two Emmy nominations. The film has been shown numerous times on American TV, and has become WNET's most widely shown film in 16mm distribution to museums, universities, libraries, adult groups, and for film festivals.

HELEN WHEATLEY

See also **Miller Adato, Perry**

Gertrude Stein: When This You See, Remember Me (U.S., WNET, 1970, 89 min.). Distributed by Contemporary/McGraw-Hill. Produced by Perry Miller Adato, Mariana Norris, and Alan Pesetsky. Directed by Perry Miller Adato. Shooting Script by Mariana Norris. Cinematography by Francis Lee. Additional cinematography by Bert Gerard. Editing by Alan Pesetsky and Aveva Slesin. Voice-over by Barbara Chason (Gertrude), Betty Henritze (Alice), and William Redfield (male voices).

Selected Films

1970 *Gertrude Stein: When This You See, Remember Me*: director, Miller Adato
1987 *Waiting for the Moon*: director, Jill Godmilov
2003 *Hubby Wifey*: director, Todd Hughes

Further Reading

Gerard, Lillian, "When This You See, Remember Me—Review," *Film Library Quarterly* 5, 1, 1971–1972, 54–57.
Rogers, William Garland, *When This You See, Remember Me: Gertrude Stein in Person*, London: Greenwood Press, 1948.
Schutzer, Anne, "Interview with Perry Miller Adato," in *Filmmakers' Newsletter*, 5, 5, 1972, 20–25.

GIMME SHELTER

(US, Maysles, 1970)

Gimme Shelter depicts the intersection of 1960s rock music, the counterculture movement, and the cinema verité documentary. The film began as an agreement between the Rolling Stones and filmmakers Albert Maysles, David Maysles, and Charlotte Zwerin to document the band's 1969 Madison Square Garden concert in New York City. Following their instincts and using their own finances, the filmmakers traveled with the tour for about five days, and in the process they turned what began as a standard assignment into a landmark contribution to American documentary cinema.

In balancing the tensions between representing personality and representing social issues, *Gimme Shelter* functions structurally on two concurrent levels. On one level it features cinema verité concert film conventions: behind-the-scenes telephone calls and negotiations, press conferences, stage and equipment setup, the band's travel, and the fans' arrival. It also includes footage of the New York City performance and of the free concert at Altamont Speedway in California. In another technique, members of the Rolling Stones join the filmmakers in the editing room, reviewing footage and commenting on it.

This technique offers an additional form of commentary otherwise unavailable to the filmmakers, who practiced a purer variety of what Albert Maysles called "direct cinema." They eschewed both narration and formal interview segments; the press conference footage provides the closest substitute. But by following both song performances and other instances with the bandmates' reactions, the film offers a more intimate form of insight. During "Wild Horses," the camera cuts to band members' solemn faces. Charlie Watts, the drummer, looks directly into the camera that zooms in and frames him in close-up, breaking its fly-on-the-wall invisibility. He almost challenges the camera's presence before turning away and ignoring it.

The events at the Altamont Speedway provide the notoriety for which *Gimme Shelter* is well known. Approximately 300,000 fans attended the free concert, dubbed "Woodstock West" in the spirit of the several peace-and-love rock festivals also held in 1969. Comparisons to Woodstock occurred, but peace was not the dominant atmosphere in the crowd that day. Instead, a certain restlessness prevailed, and performers such as The Flying Burrito Brothers and Jefferson Airplane dealt with fans rushing the stage, climbing scaffolding, and fighting among themselves. The Hell's Angels were hired to provide security and crowd control, but their sense of maintaining order involved fighting back, a tactic that at one point led to Jefferson Airplane singer Marty Balin being knocked unconscious when he attempted to intervene in a dispute. By the time the Rolling Stones took the stage behind an escort of Harley Davidson motorcycles parting the masses, tensions were running high and the crowd was agitated.

The film's structure and cinematography highlight just how deep those tensions ran and just how keenly the Angels' presence was felt. Concert footage from Madison Square Garden focuses primarily on Mick Jagger's stage presence. As he sings "Jumpin' Jack Flash," "Satisfaction," and other songs, Jagger prances and struts freely around the stage, and shots of the audience show adoring fans gazing back and mouthing the words along with him. At Altamont the tone changes

Gimme Shelter, Mick Jagger, 1970, performing onstage. [*Courtesy of the Everett Collection*]

completely. The band constantly stops its performance so Jagger can issue pleas to the audience to settle down. The Hell's Angels dominate the scene. One shot frames Jagger singing on the left, while one Angel stares straight at the camera on the right. Another shot situates the scene from behind the band, with Jagger closest, a wall of Angels (and their logo jackets) between Jagger and the crowd, and then the obscured crowd behind them. The Angels also bodily remove anyone who sets foot on the stage.

A shot on the commotion in the crowd reveals another scuffle, and it shows a girl in a crocheted dress moving out of the way, a man in a green suit running past her, and a group of Angels crowding around someone. The distance and poor lighting make it difficult to discern what actually is happening. When Jagger in the studio asks, "Can you roll back on that, David?," the scene cuts back to the editing room, and David Maysles rewinds the tape and plays it again in slow motion. A question about a gun is raised, and Maysles freezes the shot that shows a gun's outline against the girl's dress. At this point the events become clearer, but other than, "It's so horrible," the film offers no commentary on them. Subsequent wrap-up scenes provide more explanation but little closure for the concert. A bystander explains how he saw events, explaining that the Hell's Angels saw the gun, took it away from a man, and then began to beat and stab him. The man, 18-year-old Meredith Hunter, dies from his injuries, and the Stones are airlifted out of the fray. The Stones exit the studio, and the fans leave.

Many American cinema verité films use a crisis structure, wherein the crisis, or emotional high point, becomes the organizational system (see Mamber, 1974). In *Gimme Shelter* the filmmakers document a potential moment with Hunter's murder, but they face a choice in focusing either on the crisis situation or on the personalities of the Rolling Stones. Earlier Maysles films such as *Salesman* (particularly in the case of Bible salesman Paul Brennan) center almost exclusively on character, and members of the Stones certainly offer much material with which to work. But the murder brings to light the question of the filmmaker's social obligation in representing it. *Gimme Shelter* also raises the question of the murder's exploitation as a form of publicity for the Rolling Stones. The film did, after all, begin as a promotional film of a concert, but whether the band should be held responsible for the incidents that occurred is a debatable issue. In the end Maysles and Zwerin leave the issue open to interpretation.

Gimme Shelter: Hells Angels beating an audience member at Altamont, 1970.
[*Courtesy of the Everett Collection*]

In direct cinema tradition, they offer no excuses or conclusions.

HEATHER MCINTOSH

See also **Maysles, Albert; Salesman**

Gimme Shelter (U.S., Maysles, 1970, 91 min) Distributed by Twentieth Century Fox and the Criterion Collection.

Directed by Albert Maysles, David Maysles, and Charlotte Zwerin. Produced by Richard Schneider. Cinematography by Ron Dorfman, George Lucas, Albert Maysles, and David Maysles. Editing by Joanna Burke, Ellen Giffard, and Kent McKinney. Sound by Walter Murch and Susumu Tokunow. Original music by Mick Jagger, Keith Richards, and the Rolling Stones.

Further Reading

"The Criterion Collection: *Gimme Shelter*," http://www. criterionco.com/asp/release.asp?id = 99.

Kael, Pauline, "*Gimme Shelter*," in *Imagining Reality: The Faber Book of Documentary*, edited by Kevin Macdonald and Mark Cousins, London: Faber and Faber, 1996.

Mamber, Stephen, "Cinema Verite and Social Concerns," *Film Comment* 9, 1973, 8–15.

———. *Cinema Verite in America: Studies in Uncontrolled Documentary*, Cambridge: The MIT Press, 1974.

Maysles, Albert, David Maysles, and Charlotte Zwerin, "A Response to Pauline Kael," in *Imagining Reality: The Faber Book of Documentary*, edited by Kevin Macdonald and Mark Cousins, London: Faber and Faber, 1996.

Maysles Films, Inc., http://www.mayslesfilms.com.

GLASS

(Holland, Haanstra, 1958)

Dutch film director Bert Haanstra was born May 31, 1916 in Holten, Overijssel, Netherlands, and died October 23, 1997 in Hilversum, Noord-Holland, Netherlands. He started his career in painting and photography, and eventually moved into documentary film directing in 1949.

Glass/Glas, produced in 1958, is one of the best-known films from Bern Haanstra's body of work, which includes forty-one documentary and fiction films produced between 1948 and 1988. Haanstra is considered one of the most original documentary film directors from Holland and won dozens of international awards for his films, including the Grand Prix at the Cannes Film Festival for *Mirror of Holland*, and the 1959 Academy Award and approximately twenty other awards for *Glass*.

Glass is a lyrical, process documentary that examines the simple act of manufacturing glass bottles and the people who craft them. Taking place entirely in a glassmaking plant in the Netherlands, the camera observes the equipment and raw materials coming together. The film weaves a story of machine-made glass versus handmade glass and makes superb use of various filmic elements, including color, sound, camera and subject movement, musical score, and editing.

Glass is often shown in filmmaking/cinematography classes as a classic example of proper exposure and color representation, complex shooting in terms of location lighting sources, and wide variety of camera angles and distances. The editing is poetic and finely paced, with wide shots, close-ups and extreme close-up shots weaving seamlessly together in a vivid representation of human beings, machine, and raw material. Although this topic may seem somewhat pedestrian, it is the lack of guiding voice-over narration that thrusts this film out of the realm of simple "how to" or "educational" documentary into the domain of a truly artistic visual essay that is part film ethnography and part nostalgic, sensitive vision of a dying artform.

C. MELINDA LEVIN

Glass (Holland, 1958, 11 min.). Directed by Bert Haanstra.

GLOBALIZATION AND DOCUMENTARY FILM

Critics are by no means agreed that such a thing as *documentary globalization* exists, or what it might entail. If by the term we mean the emergence of a sort of factual meta-market offering one sort of audiovisual product without regard for source of origin, documentary is almost certainly preglobal. To begin with, we should note that documentary, strictly defined, tends to fare best in countries with a strong public service broadcasting or film-making tradition, that is, in areas that have partly withstood the influence of global market culture. Second, commercial markets themselves seem to be stubbornly local, with studies in Europe and Asia suggesting that audiences prefer domestic documentaries where they are available, which they often are. At the same time, documentaries seem to be increasingly concerned with domestic content and local issues, with programs tackling international topics actually falling by more than 40 percent in the mid-1990s according to a study of British terrestrial television, and anecdotal evidence suggesting similar trends more recently in New Zealand and Spain. Even CNN, the world's self-styled global newscaster, reserves less than one-fourth of its documentary schedule for non-American programs. If anything, documentary markets seem to be more insular than ever, calling the whole idea of documentary globalization into question.

Nonetheless, a closer look suggests the genre has become more global in several key respects. Funding has become more transnational, for instance, with documentaries more frequently co-produced than any other type of programming, a trend that may well continue given a decline in public service supports and domestic license fees. Moreover, one recent cross-country survey indicates that less than one-fourth of documentary budgets are raised with no foreign investment whatsoever (though domestic funding tends to predominate). Even public service producer groups like Europe's Eurodoc acknowledge that domestic funding for quality documentaries is nearly nonexistent.

Documentary distribution systems are also increasingly global, often operating beyond national or even regional borders. Documentary films, for instance, can be seen at more than 2,500 festivals worldwide, allowing for at least an occasional meeting of producers and productions from around the world. Documentary programs are sold in what Rofekamp calls a "two-tier market" of national and transnational specialty sectors, mutually dependent and both vital to producers.

Documentary texts have also been globalized to some extent. Many are designed for a domestic audience but then "reversioned" to boost their foreign appeal. Others adhere to transnational formats that are adapted for home territories. The docusoap, for instance, can be seen as a global phenomenon, originating in Europe, North America, and Brazil and spreading to the rest of the world in the 1990s. Even public service documentaries have been globalized, with many depicting diasporic cultures, and others tackling local people and places in culturally specific ways that might appeal to overseas buyers.

It should be remembered that globalization is not a zero-sum game that proceeds only at the expense of local or national documentary cultures. Many transnational organizations make extensive efforts to commission local programs, or at least customize services, once markets have "matured" (Brown 2001: 18). Others cooperate with national public service broadcasters to create local and trans-local programs, the recent multi-million dollar co-venture between the world's largest documentary producers, Discovery Networks International and the British Broadcasting Corporation, being a case in point.

At the same time, globalization does not benefit every local culture or market equally. One recent survey suggests that only 1 percent of world market value is accounted for by Africa and the Middle East, compared with 40 percent for Europe alone (Vista Advisers for RAI 2002: 39). Overall, documentary globalization is perhaps best seen as process of flows—financial, conceptual, and technological—within what Castells calls an "uneven geography (Castells, 2000).

DAVID HOGARTH

Further Reading

Brown, Kimberley. "Discovery Hosts Open Day for UK Producers," in *RealScreen*, 1, 2001, p. 18.

Castells, Manuel, *The Rise of the Network Society*, (2nd ed.), Oxford: Blackwell, 2000.

Christie, Brendan, "By the Numbers: Factual Price Guide," in *RealScreen*, March 1, 2001, 38.

Cleasby, Adrian, *What in the World Is Going On? British Television and Global Affairs*. London: Third World and Environment Broadcasting Project, 1995.

Del Valle, David, "Upfront," *RealScreen*, September 1999, 6.

———, "Doc Opportunities Rise as Spanish Broadcasters Develop Taste for Infotainment," *RealScreen*, January 1, 2000, 60.

Hazan, Jenny, "The EBU," *RealScreen*, October 1, 2001, 14.

Kilborn, Richard, "How Real Can You Get? Recent developments in Reality Television." *European Journal of Communication*, 9, 1994, 421–439.

Kuzmyk, Jenn, "Hot Docs Welcomes the World," *Playback*, May 23, 1999, 23.

Rayman, Susan, "Financing Docs in France," *RealScreen* June 1, 2000, 46.

———, "Accessing Japan," *RealScreen*, December 1, 2000, 38.

Rofekamp, Jan, cited in Robert M. Goodman. "Is Content King?" *The Independent*, November 2000, 38.

Roscoe, Jane, "Australian Documentary: Safe in the Hands of the Next Generation," *Dox*, 36, August 2001, 7.

Vista Advisers for RAI, *The Documentary Market Worldwide*, Rome: Vista Advisers, 2001.

Zeller, Susan, "Reflecting on Features," *RealScreen*, September 1, 2001, 50.

GODARD, JEAN-LUC

Operation Béton/Operation Concrete (1954) is Godard's first film and his only documentary proper in his fifty-year career. The construction of the Grande Dixence dam, shot ambitiously in 35mm, is in fact his only conventional film, with only the odd nod to Russian cinema and a seeming fascination with machinery and structure testifying to his future preoccupations as a filmmaker. Although his most famous feature films, made in the early to mid-1960s are works of fiction, all featured documentary elements (*À Bout de Souffle/Breathless*) (1960) famously filming its actors on the streets of Paris during Eisenhower's visit and Godard always maintained that they were never fictional works in the standard sense: "reportage is interesting only when placed in a fictional context, but fiction is interesting only if it is validated by a documentary context." From the outset Godard considered himself as a creator of film-essays, finding audiovisual means (with particular attention given to montage) to extend his work as a *Cahiers du Cinéma* critic.

As the dozen or so features he made between *À Bout de Souffle* and *Deux ou Trois Choses Que Je Sais D'Elle/Two or Three Things I Know About Her* (1966) became progressively more political in terms of content, Godard began to seek new formal means to film his essays politically. *Caméra Oeil/Camera Eye* (1967), his contribution to the collective film *Loin du Vietnam/Far from Vietnam* (1967) proved a major step toward the unmistakable shape his essays would later take and provide the experimental groundwork he would continue to build on right up to the great masterpieces of the 1980s and 1990s. *Caméra Oeil*, a film about filming Vietnam far from the war, features Godard himself with his camera (the first of his films in which authorial intervention becomes a structuring element), the machinic nature of the camera pegged to images of the war machine. The fifteen-minute essay contains archive footage, shots from the films of other filmmakers as well as from his own work, and material specially shot for the film, thereby proving a trial run for most of the elements by which his later essays will come to be defined.

Godard's finest commentator, Alain Bergala, points out how the Fernand Braudel's distinction between *histoire événementielle*, the chronicling of events as they happen, and attention to the slower development of events over time (*la longue durée*) can be profitably applied to the changes Godard's essay film has undergone in the last thirty-five years.

The political films Godard made in the decade after *Caméra Oeil*, either alone, as part of the Dziga Vertov Group, or with Anne-Marie Mieville, are concerned with the short term and with topical events and are addressed to the present and to an audience of the already or soon-to-be-converted. These works, which have acquired a reputation for tediousness in the extreme, are not simply Maoist tracts but explorations of the medium as alternately oppressive and liberating, of desire and the gaze, of workers' and women's exploitation and of the (im)possibility of any form of representation or semiotic activity ever communicating with the "real," in short products of the post-1968 climate of disappointment and a generalised phobia of all forms of power. But Godard's return to fiction in the 1980s (with *Sauve Qui Peut [La Vie]/Slow Motion* [1979]) is accompanied by a major shift in the preoccupations of his essay work. Politics (in the sense of active militancy) is superseded by history as the focus moves to *la longue durée* as the devastating history of the twentieth century is tied to Godard's personal take on the death of cinema, not to mention his middle-aged preoccupation with the landscape of his childhood around Lac Leman. At this point it is the dead who become the primary addressees of this cinema of anamnesis seeking "to defend the dead against the living." The title of the Amnesty International film to which Godard contributed *Contre L' Oubli/Against Forgetting* (1991) could be said to exemplify this turn in Godard's work.

Godard had begun to experiment with video during his militant period but quickly discovered the aesthetic possibilities of the new medium. Beginning with *France/Tour/Détour/Deux/Enfants/France/Tour/Detour/Two/Children* (1978), the essays begin to display a range of techniques such as superimposition, rapid flashing, staccato slow motion, images that seem to be born from other images, and the electronic and computerized treatment of colour—in short, those formal features that have become a trademark of Godard's video works, elements retained from his militant experiments and often also incorporated into the feature films he continues to make.

But it is with his true masterwork *Histoire(s) du Cinéma/History/ies of Cinema* (1988–1998) that his mastery of video technologies is stretched to breaking point by the vast subject-matter: no less than the history of the twentieth century conceived as a series of parallel histories: of war and the concentration camps, of cinema, of literature, philosophy, and music. In eight episodes varying in length from twenty-six fifty-one minutes, *Histoire(s) du Cinéma* offers an extended montage of images and sounds full of startling and often very moving juxtapositions guided by the idea borrowed from Pierre Reverdy: "The image is a pure creation of the mind, it cannot be born from a comparison, but comes from the bringing together of two distant realities [. . .] An image is not powerful because it is brutal and fantastic, but because the association of ideas is distant and true." This might appear to give Godard carte blanche to bring together arbitrarily any images he pleases, but what is incredible in *Histoire(s)* is that the effect of Godard's image/sound clusters need bear no obvious relation to his conscious intentions, and therefore accusations of hermeticism or solipsism completely miss the mark. For example (and I choose one that has deliberately courted controversy), an image of Elizabeth Taylor cradling Montgomery Clift in her arms in George Stevens' *A Place in the Sun* (1951) finds an overwhelming poignancy (one completely independent of the individual images themselves) when superimposed on images of a pile of concentration camp corpses, as well as being autonomous of Godard's explanation. It refers to the fact that George Stevens had previously filmed the camps, and this is precisely why his close-up of Taylor could "radiate a kind of shadowed happiness." The effect is not one of tragedy plus sentiment (since the camp images of necessity need no embellishing in order to devastate us) but a new type of hybrid affect, of emotion *plus* thought, and patently a result of the very incongruity of these "distant realities." We can see that in fact the juxtaposition of images here (as so often in *Histoires*) involves the images in a process of mutual interpretation, but, in this case, the viewer need not know about Stevens's experience at the camps to feel the multilayered mystery of their coexistence.

The extraordinary novelty of Godard's essay films has yet to be widely appreciated, especially in the English-speaking world. His most recent features, *Eloge de L'Amour/In Praise of Love* (2001) and *Notre Musique/Our Music* (2004) have continued to develop further those formal elements discovered by him in the essays, for example, the second part of the former film being shot on DV and its colour treated to resemble Fauvist painting. Fictional essays or documentary fictions? As Godard said on the release of *Eloge de L'Amour*: "They say my film is a documentary but I don't even know the meaning of the word documentary."

FERGUS DALY

Biography

Born in Paris, December 3, 1930, to Protestant parents, his father was a doctor, his mother from a wealthy banking family. Studied anthropology briefly before devoting himself first to film criticism and from 1954 to filmmaking. Contributed to *Cahiers du Cinéma* on and off for many years before and during the development of his filmmaking career from the first shorts (beginning with *Operation Béton* [Operation Concrete] in 1954) to the success of his first feature *A Bout de Souffle/Breathless* (1960). Twenty-odd features and shorts later Godard turned his back on auteurist filmmaking and dissolved his identity in the work of the Dziga Vertov Group, which produced a series of politically militant films between 1969 and 1972. Following a serious motorcycle accident in 1972 Godard with Anne-Marie Mieville moved to Grenoble where they set up a small independent studio experiment with film/video relations before leaving France altogether in 1976 to settle in Switzerland. Godard returned to the commercial cinema in 1979 with *Sauve Qui Peut (la vie)/Slow Motion*. In 1988 he undertook a major video project *Histoire(s) du Cinéma/History/ies of Cinema* completed in 1998. Continues to alternate between feature films and essay films largely shot on video.

Selected Films

1954 *Operation Béton*
1966 *Deux ou Trois Choses Que Je Sais D'Elle*
1967 *Caméra-Oeil*
1972 *Letter to Jane* (as part of Dziga Vertov collective)
1975 *Numéro Deux* (with A-M Mieville)
1978 *France/Tour/Détour/Deux/Enfants* (with Mieville)
1982 *Scénario du Film Passion*
1988–1998 *Histoire(s) du Cinéma*
1991 *Contre L'Oubli* (with Mieville)
1994 *JLG/JLG: Autoportrait de Décembre*

Further Reading

Art Press (Special Journal Issue) *Le Siecle de Jean-Luc Godard*, November 1998.

Bergala, Alain (ed.), *Jean-Luc Godard par Jean-Luc Godard* (2 vols), Paris: Cahiers du Cinéma, 1998.

Bergala, Alain, *Nul Mieux que Godard*, Paris: Cahiers du Cinéma, 1999.

Godard, Jean-Luc, *Histoire(s) du Cinéma* (4 Vols.), Paris: Gallimard-Gaumont, 1998.

Temple, Michael, and James S. Williams, *The Cinema Alone: Essays on the Work of Jean-Luc Godard 1985–2000*, Amsterdam: U.P., 2000.

GODMILOW, JILL

Jill Godmilow's films straddle the boundaries between narrative and documentary; often deploying reenactment and thematizing performance. They are at once theoretically informed and visually engrossing. Beginning in 1973, her collaboration with Judy Collins on *Antonia: A Portrait of the Woman* brought to light the life story of an amazing, but relatively unknown, creative woman; the tale told a typical story of a lone woman struggling to make it in a sexist profession. What distinguished *Antonia* from many feminist films of the era was the emphasis on performance as a visual metaphor for lived experience, a theme continued in her film *Nevelson in Process*.

But it was *Far from Poland* (1984) that cemented her reputation as a theoretical practitioner of documentary. Invoking virtually all the postmodern debates about realism and the reality effect, about gender and romance, about ideology and truth, about politics and representation, about socialism and democracy circulating within the cultural left during the mid-1980s, it calls attention to theoretical developments in film studies' deconstructive concerns with the apparatus, narrative, and image by foregrounding the constructedness of (among other things) "location" shooting. "On location" has always signified access to the real, to the true scene, against the stagy atmosphere of the studio; yet locations themselves are carefully chosen to stage meanings. When Poland became unavailable to Godmilow, location's essentialist truth was called into question, as were virtually all the shibboleths of 1960s New Left politics under Ronald Reagan's regime. The film is a stunning achievement: at once offering detailed information on the Gdansk Strike and Solidarity, as well as undercutting its form of transmission—documentary—and all done with a wry, disarming sense of humor.

Working with reenacted texts performed by actors such as Ruth Maleczech, Godmilow evolved a form of feminist "speculative fiction" to tell the story of Gertrude Stein and Alice B. Toklas in the feature-length 1987 bioflick *Waiting for the Moon* produced for PBS's "American Playhouse," which won First Prize at the Sundance Film Festival. A crucial element of *Far from Poland* was the staged interviews of the striking crane operator Anna Walentynowicz and government censor K62. During these long segments, the camera reveals an intense identification between actors and their roles to the point of noting that Maleczech, who plays Anna, is crying when she concludes her life story. The concentration on performing extends as well to the interludes between Jill and Mark, directed by Maleczech as mini-soap operas. In *Waiting for the Moon*, the camera lingers over the faces and gestures of Linda Bassett (as Stein) and Linda Hunt (as Alice) in a series of brief sequences staged to foreground the verbal exchanges between these two difficult women. The repartee and the sets where they occur—a room, a car, a garden, a hillside—are designed to mimic steinian poetics as they repeat with a difference the same scene visually and linguistically. These awkward moments highlight the subtleties of performing for the camera, as the tiniest facial tic magnifies mood and emotion.

Roy Cohn/Jack Smith (1994), the film interpretation of Ron Vawter's theater performance, displays another aspect of her deconstructive documentary technique. The sheer tour-de-force performance by Vawter is matched by the uncanny way Godmilow reassembles a piece of theater into a film. Translating stage to celluloid, Godmilow queers the record by daringly cutting up the two performance pieces about two notorious gay men, one very out, the other very closeted, who both died of AIDS in 1989. This montage is then intercut them with video footage from rehearsals and of

Vawter, himself HIV positive, his body covered with lesions, making up in the dressing room. In challenging the sacred unity of the performance, she also mixes media, emphasizing the differences between film and video. The film dwells in the careful collaboration between Godmilow and Vawter—the way Godmilow's editing adds a third term, Vawter himself—to the dyad Roy/Jack to enrich our understanding of performance as a process of impersonation and identification even when the figure(s) are radically other than the self.

This theoretical interest in the place of the body and identity—gendered, sexual, ethnic, and political—in performance and of the tense relationship between filmic and theatrical performing animates the project Godmilow developed in collaboration with Mabou Mines' *Lear '87 Archive* (2001). Working again with Vawter and Maleczech, the six-hour DVD condensed archive of workshops to develop a fully gender-reversed production of Shakespeare's *King Lear* celebrates the labor of the actor and of the theater company. Recording the workshop process of the experimental and radical group through close, sometimes repetitive, dissections of how movements, intonations, and gestures are calculated to evoke emotions and thus create meanings for the viewer, the two (sometimes three) different video cameras also stress the differential meanings incurred through camera position, lighting, and format. Her continuing interest in the process of reenactment led to her 1998 remake of Harun Farocki's 1969 *Inextinguishable Fire*. *What Farocki Taught* contains a perfect replica of his black-and-white German documentary, itself made with actors reconstructing documents from Dow Chemical Company, as well as Farocki's self-inflicted cigarette burn demonstrating how Dow researched and tested Napalm B for use in Vietnam, in color and in English. This deconstructive work explores documentary technologies to represent history as/through representation. In restaging the already staged piece of documentary history that has never been shown in the United States, Godmilow engages debates about film preservation, cultural memory, and the historical archive. Once again, her political engagement with the form demands that she both trumpet anti-war sentiments and analyze how war itself is synonymous with the fabric of American life, including life as an oppositional filmmaker or her audience.

Nothing simply happens in Godmilow's work; just as history becomes a staged event and actors perform other lives with their bodies, viewers are required to produce meaning through the holes left by the filmmaker. This collaboration demonstrates an extraordinary commitment to furthering awareness of our culture's investments in the visual regime. Her films ask about the conditions of their own possibility. Documentary filmmakers may seek to change the world, but their efforts are premised on technologies and desires—machinery and voyeurism—that perpetuate it. Insisting that theatricality and presence are central to the documentary project, Godmilow traverses borders between liveness and projection, truth and memory; she claims responsibility.

PAULA RABINOWITZ

Biography

Born in Philadelphia in 1943 to a Jewish dentist and a Jewish truant officer. Studied Russian literature at the University of Wisconsin, Madison; never took a film course because there weren't any back then. Made her first film, *La Nueva Vida*, a feature-length romp, in Spanish, with her Puerto Rican boyfriend in 1968, and then her first documentary, *Tales*, in 1971 with an all-women crew in New York City. Recipient of two Rockefeller Fellowships and a Guggenheim Fellowship, as well as grants from the National Endowment for the Arts. Work has been featured at numerous film festivals and museums around the world, including the 2000 Whitney Museum of American Art Biennial Exhibition. Film *Antonia* was nominated for an Academy Award and received the Independent New York Film Critics Award for Best Documentary. Professor of Film, Theater and Television at Notre Dame University. Lives in New York.

Selected Films

1971 *Tales*
1973 *Antonia: A Portrait of the Woman Nevelson in Process*
The Popovich Brothers of South Chicago
The Odyssey Tapes
1984 *Far from Poland*
1987 *Waiting for the Moon*
1994 *Roy Cohn/Jack Smith*
1998 *What Farocki Taught*
The Loft Tapes

Further Reading

Godmilow, Jill, in conversation with Ann-Louise Shapiro "How Real Is the Reality in Documentary Films?" in *History And Theory*, 36, 4, 1997.
———. "What's Wrong with the Liberal Documentary?" in *Peace Review*, March, 1999.
Miller, Lynn C., "[Un]documenting History: An Interview with Filmmaker Jill Godmilow," in *Text Perfromance Quarterly*, 7, 3, 1997.
Rabinowitz, Paula, *They Must Be Represented: The Politics of Documentary*, London: Verso, 1994.

GOLD, JACK

Jack Gold was a director of both screen and stage works, having made twelve feature films, more than forty films for television, and hundreds of short films for television. He worked in radio as a trainee studio manager, moving to television in 1955 as a trainee assistant film editor for the BBC. He eventually became the film editor on school programmes and topical interview-based investigative documentaries and news reports such as *Tonight*. He found directing work on the latter, producing from three to five short items a week working mainly with reporters. He left the BBC in 1964 and became a freelance documentary filmmaker, directing television dramas such as *The Lump* (1967), a Tony Garnett production, and his first fiction film, *The Bofors Gun* (1968).

Gold had a notable ability to construct a story with a filmic approach, exploiting and showing locations, and interweaving pertinent commentary and music to create film stories, while exploiting the major technological revolution that transformed the documentary—the development of the 16mm camera and the transistorised sound recorder. This made him very much part of the British Realist Tradition that followed Free Cinema.

Journalistic techniques developed during his directing of reportage programmes and documentary essays between 1960 and 1964 for *Tonight* permeated into the documentaries he made, enabling him to analyse and comment on subjects in observational documentary, while using different forms of counterpoint to enforce his point of view.

His documentaries found another layer of illumination and revelation beyond observation, merging varied aspects to present another synthesis.

Gold explored different documentary techniques including reportage, impressionistic tendencies, analytical verité and drama-documentary. Feeling he was in the hands of his subjects and wanting to have more control in filmmaking, he moved into drama, having already had some experience with the style with *The Visit* (1959). In recreating real situations in drama, Gold used his experiences from documentary filmmaking regarding technology, location, and subject behaviour. He had experience of reconstruction with drama-documentaries such as *Ninety Days* (1966) a reconstruction using the protagonist as subject. Before that experience, he had used actors in other reconstructions.

His documentary films were often impressionistic, for example, *Wall Street* (1966), *Famine* (1967), and *The Schlemiel, the Schlemozzel, and the Doppess* (1990). They often had neither shape nor structure initially—that coming later in the cutting room—and the resulting film was always more than observational as Gold looked for ways to shape or comment on his subject using counterpoint, with a mix of different footage or between picture and sound.

In others, however, he organised and orchestrated his shoots to be shot in a way that meant he attained detailed coverage of a situation scripted and controlled rather than shaped in the cutting room. His move to the single drama resulted in features strong in character and storytelling with a naturalistic base.

ALISTAIR WARDILL

Biography

Born in London, June 28, 1930. Graduated from the University of North London (London Polytechnic), reading economics, in 1950, and University College London, reading law, in 1953, where he worked on amateur films for the College Film Society. In 1954, joined BBC Radio Department as trainee studio manager, where he worked on variety shows. Moved to British Television in 1955, first editing then directing factual programmes including current affairs programme *Tonight*. Moved to feature filmmaking forging a career that has spanned three decades. Has taught at the London International Film School, the Royal College of Art, and the National Film and Television School. Currently affiliated with Screen South, and the Directors Guild, chairing the status committee. Alongside filmmaking Gold has directed stage plays including *Council of Love* (1972), *The Devil's Disciple* (1976), *Tribute to Lili Lamont* (1978), and *Crossing Jerusalem* (2003). Recipient of the following awards (selected): BAFTA: Best Documentary: *Death in the Morning*, 1964. Best Drama: *Stocker's Copper*, 1973. Lew Grade/Radio Times award: *Goodnight Mr Tom*, 1998. Lew Grade/Radio Times award: *The Remorseful Day*, 1987. Evening News Best Film Award: *Aces High*, 1976. Evening News Best Comedy Award: *The National Health,* 1973. International: Emmy: *The Naked Civil Servant*, 1975. Prix Italia, Barcelona, Chicago, San Remo; *The Naked Civil Servant*, 1975. Peabody Award: *Catholics*, 1973. Christopher Award: *Little Lord Fauntleroy*, 1980. Christopher Award: *She Stood Alone*, 1991. Golden Globe: *Escape from Sobibor*, 1987. ACE Award: *Murrow*, 1986. ACE Award: *Sakharov*, 1984. Martin Luther King Award: *The Sailor's Return*, 1978.

Selected Films

1959 *Happy as Can Be*. BBC: Director
1959 *The Visit*. BFI: Director
1960 *Living Jazz*. BFI: Director
1963 *The Model Millionairess. Tonight*. BBC: Director
1963 *The Solitary Billionaire*. BBC: Director
1963 *West Indians*. BBC: Director
1964 *Death in the Morning. Tonight*. BBC: Director
1965 *Ladies and Gentlemen It Is My Pleasure*. BBC: Director
1966 *Ninety Days*. BBC: Director
1966 *On Top of the World*. BBC: Director
1966 *Wall Street*. ATV: Director
1967 *Dispute*. 2X 60 Minutes. BBC: Director
1967 *Famine*. Rediffusion: Director
1967 *The Lump*. Wednesday Play. BBC: Director
1967 *World of Coppard*. Omnibus. BBC: Director
1968 *Black Campus*. BBC: Director
1968 *The Bofors Gun*: Director
1969 *The Reckoning*: Director
1971 *Dowager in Hot Pants*: Thames. Director
1972 *Stockers Copper*: Director
1973 *Arturo Ui*: Director
1973 *Catholics*: Director
1973 *The National Health*. Columbia Pictures Corporation: Director
1973 *Who?*: Director
1975 *Man Friday*: Director
1975 *The Naked Civil Servant*: Director
1976 *Aces High*: Director
1978 *Thank You, Comrades*: BBC. Director
1978 *The Medusa Touch*: Director
1978 *The Sailor's Return*: Director
1980 *Little Lord Fauntleroy*: Director
1983 *Red Monarch*: Director
1984 *Sakharov*: Director
1984 *The Chain*: Director
1986 *Murrow: Director*
1987 *Escape From Sobibor*: Director
1988 *Jack Gold on the Battle of Algiers: Movie Masterclass*. (Peter West) Third Eye Productions: Writer
1990 *The Schlemiel, the Schlemozzel, and the Doppess*. Bookmark. BBC: Director
1991 *She Stood Alone*: Director
1998 *Goodnight Mister Tom*: Director
2002 *The John Thaw Story*: Director

Further Reading

"The Difference between TV and Film Is That in TV You've Got to Compromise," *Television Today*, April 1979, 17–19.

"A Director Without a Script Is Most Limited of All Vision," *Television Today* December 31, 1975, 10, 4, 1.

Falk, Quentin, "All That Glisters Is Jack, 'National Health,'" *CinemaTV Today* 10060, December 1, 1973, 10–11.

Gold, Jack, and Kevin Brownlow, "The Pressures of Opportunity and Frustration," *Vision* 1 March 1976, 12–14.

Griffin, Sue, "Horror's Tough Going for Gold," *Broadcast, May 8, 1987, 21.*

Harris, Ian, "Names and Faces," *Listener* 106, 2726, September 10, 1981, 270.

"Jack Gold: An Interview," *Framework* 9, Winter, 1978–1979, 38–42.

Littlefield, Joan, "'Capture Reality, Not Create It', Says Jack Gold," *Film World* 5, 1, January/March 1969, 71–72.

Madden, Paul, and David Wilson, "Getting In Close. An Interview with Jack Gold," *Sight and Sound* 43, 3, 1974, 134–137.

McPherson, Don, "'Muffin' Gives Euston Films Another Big Boost," *Screen International* 197, July 7, 1979, 9.

Pascal, Julia, "Dying to Strauss," *City Limits* 292, May 7, 1987, 21.

Spiers, David, "Interview with Jack Gold," *Screen* 10, 4/5, July/October 1969, 115–128.

Summers, Sue, "Jack Gold," *CinemaTV Today*, 10135, May 24, 1975, 18.

Sussex, Elizabeth. *The Rise and Fall of British Documentary*, Berkeley: University of California Press, 1975.

GOLDOVSKAYA, MARINA

Marina Goldovskaya, a prominent Russian documentary filmmaker, gained recognition in the 1970s, 1980s, and 1990s for a series of landmark works documenting Soviet life and history, the collapse of communism, and its turbulent aftermath. Her father, Yevsei Goldovsky, was a cofounder in 1924 of VGIK, the renowned Moscow Film Institute, and a leading Soviet expert in film technology. Goldovskaya graduated from VGIK in 1964 with a degree in cinematography and directing. She spent the first twenty years of her professional life as a newsreel camerawoman and filmmaker for Gosteleradio, the USSR Central Television agency.

Having found a niche in news documentaries and directing more than twenty-five films, besides working on countless others, Goldovskaya developed a style of documentary portrait using techniques similar to those favored by cinema verité and direct cinema in the 1960s: 16mm handheld camera, synch sound, and fly-on-the-wall approach to the material. At this time she had written accounts only of Western documentary pioneers D.A. Pennebaker, Richard Leacock, and Robert Drew.

In her 1981 book, *Chelovek krupnim planom/ Close-up*, Goldovskaya described her method of observation, noting her preference for people obsessed with their professions. She tried this method first in 1968, as a cinematographer in *Tkachihi/Weavers*, a television documentary about seven alienated female textile workers. The hopelessness of their lives was made visible by this method of filming, which avoided narration or any authorial intervention. The film ran afoul of the censors and was banned. In her directorial debut, *Raisa Nemchinskaya, artistka zirka/Raisa Nemchinskaya, Artist of the Circus* (1970), about an old acrobat who does not want to give up the circus, Goldovskaya had the essentials of her method in place. "My films used to be mostly portraits; I was interested in how to grasp a character, how to reveal it, how to uncover an individual's obsessions, motives and moral principles," she wrote in a 1991 article for *Iskusstvo Kino*.

This strategy allowed the filmmaker to find drama outside of politics, thus minimizing clashes with the censors. Her first documentary with a clear political subject was *Vosmoj Director/8th Director* (1981), the profile of a factory manager who fights the system. It was shown on prime-time television, and caused a storm in the press.

The filmmaker's reputation as the leading documentarian of Soviet Russia was secured during *perestroika*. She took up Premier Mikhail Gorbachev's call for reform and transparency in two polemic works: *Archangelsky Mujik/The Peasant from Archangelsk* (1986) and *Vlast' Solovetskaya/ Solovki Power* (1988). Both documentaries tackled with honesty and candor—and at the time, considerable personal risk—the failure of Soviet economic methods and the Leninist origins of the Gulag concentration camp system.

Archangelsky Mujik profiled a farmer, Nikolai Sivkov, who fights to take charge of sixty cows in his own farm. He speaks to the camera, extolling the virtues of private property and deploring the inefficiency of the collective farming system. "In 'the land where socialism has triumphed' it was a truly heroic deed," Goldovskaya wrote in the *Iskusstvo Kino* article. Banned after its first broadcasting, the documentary was later reaired under the policy of *glasnost*. In 1988, it won the top national prize for the best documentary.

The film was a turning point in the filmmaker's career because it showed her ability to turn a simple character into a political metaphor about larger issues. This interweaving of the personal with the political, and the historical, a trademark of the director's work since the 1980s, would reach a higher degree of artistry and complexity in *Solovki Power*.

A 35mm feature-length documentary produced by Mosfilm, the Moscow State studio, *Solovki Power* turns the double meaning of its title, Solovki as Soviet might, into a political metaphor: This medieval monastery on a remote island in the White Sea, operating as a concentration camp between 1923 and 1939, becomes a symbol of the regime's destruction of dissidence. The film skillfully combines the testimonies of survivors and prison guards, with present-day color footage of the location, and a 1927 government propaganda short about the "reeducation" of Soviet citizen in this "model" camp. The sound track counterpoints the sober voice of a narrator with heartbreaking readings from letters found in the camp and the haunting recollections of former prisoners.

Solovki Power became one of the filmic landmark events of *glasnost*. Initially banned, it was later released and won several top awards at the national and international film festivals. This success lead to European and American funding of Goldovskaya's 1990s projects. *Dom s rizariami* (1993)/*The House on Arbat Street*, for example, is another remarkable instance of her ability to capture Soviet history through individual stories. The documentary profiles the Filatov House, a luxurious apartment building of the Romanov era located in Moscow's central Arbat district. With imaginatively edited interviews, old photos, propaganda, and entertainment films, seventy years of the Soviet experiment in communism emerge. These intimate portraits,

laced with vivid recollections, depict a human fresco marked by suffering and loss.

Compelled to record the seismic changes brought about by the breakup of the Soviet Union, Goldovskaya made a series of journals, in video and film, chronicling the first post-Soviet times as they affected herself, her friends in the *intelligentsia*, and ordinary Muscovites. The emphasis is not on the fall of the Soviet regime per se, but on the portrait of individuals caught in the collapse of the system. These video diaries marry the techniques of a verité style with an openly subjective involvement in the subject: Goldovskaya and her ubiquitous camera become an integral part of the films. *Vkus svobodi* (1991)/*A Taste of Freedom,* Oskolki zerkala (1992)/ *The Shattered Mirror—A Diary of a Time of Trouble, Povezlo roditsia v Rossii* (1994)/*Lucky to Be Born in Russia*, and *The Prince Is Back* (1999) cover a decade from the perspective of a passionate observer, who is also a cautious optimist. *A Taste of Freedom* and *The Prince Is Back* profile a television journalist and an engineer of aristocratic origins obsessed with achieving goals such as truth in the news and the restoration of an ancestral palace; these efforts become, once more, a rich metaphor of the times.

Naum Kleiman, director of the Film Museum in Moscow, remarked in 1998 that Goldovskaya's work "presents small individual lives in the larger context of history. In our cinema, we traditionally showed the larger view, with a few figures inside. Her reverse angle is very important. It's as if she's painting a fresco; you can examine each figure by itself, but together they form a panorama of the entire country."

Now living in the United States, Goldovskaya combines a teaching career at UCLA with work on two ambitious projects: an oral history of the documentary cinema and *Russian Chronicles: Diary of Change*, a portrait of her generation, for which she has amassed more than 400 hours of footage.

The artistic and historical significance of Marina Goldovskaya's body of work makes it an indispensable document to examine the life and times of twentieth-century Russia.

MARIA ELENA DE LAS CARRERAS

See also **Documentary Film: Russia/Soviet Union**

Biography

Born in Moscow, Soviet Union, July 15, 1941. Graduated from State Moscow Film Institute (VGIK), with degrees in cinematography and direction in 1964, and a doctorate in Fine Arts in 1987. Worked for USSR Central Television (Gosteleradio), as director, scriptwriter, and cameramen in more than fifty films, 1964–1988. Professor in the Department of TV Journalism, Moscow State

University, 1968–1995. Chief Executive, Department of Video Technology, in the Moscow Research Institute of Film Art, 1988–1996. Since 1990, professor and lecturer of film in several European and American universities. Author of several books in Russian on the art and technique of documentary filmmaking. Her documentaries chronicling the demise of the Soviet system and its aftermath have been awarded many national and international prizes. Interviewed by Chris Marker about directors of the Soviet cinema in his television documentary *Le Tombeau d'Alexandre/The Last Bolshevik* (1992). Currently, head of the documentary program at the UCLA Department of Film and Television, where she created its Documentary Salon series and organizes workshops with documentary filmmakers. Board member of the International Documentary Association. Member of the Russian Academy of Television. Based in Los Angeles, California, Goldovskaya continues to make films about her native country and the art scene of the United States.

Selected Films

1972 *Valentina Tereshkova*: director, writer, cinematographer

1973 *Eto nasha professia/This Is Our Profession*: director, writer, cinematographer

1975 *Arkadi Rajkin*: director, writer, cinematographer

1978 *Ispitanije/The Experiment*: director, writer, cinematographer

1981 *Posle zatvi/After the Harvest*: director, writer, cinematographer

1985 *Zdravstvujte, eto Bedulia govorit/Hello, It Is Beduliya Speaking*: director, writer, cinematographer

1986 *Archangelsky Mujik/The Peasant from Archangelsk*: director, cinematographer

1987 *Chtobi bil teatr/For the Theater to Be*: director, writer, cinematographer

1988 *Tumbalalaika v Amerike/Tumbalalaika in America*: director, cinematographer

1988 *Vlast' Solovetskaya/Solovki Power*: director, writer, cinematographer

1989 *Mne 90 let, esche legka pohodka/I Am 90. My Steps Are Light*: director, co-writer, cinematographer

1989 *Vishe, chem Liubov/More Than Love*: director, writer, cinematographer

1991 *Iz Bezdni/Aus dem Abgrund/From the Abyss—Part1: Liudi Blokadi/The Siege of Leningrad; Part 2: Liudi I vojna/People and War*: director, co-writer, cinematographer

1991 *Vkus svobodi/A Taste of Freedom*: director, cinematographer

1992 *Oskolki zerkala/The Shattered Mirror—The Diary of a Time of Trouble*: director, writer, editor, cinematographer

1992 *Dom s rizariami/The House on Arbat Street*: director, writer, editor, cinematographer

1994 *Povezlo roditsia v Rossii/Lucky to Be Born in Russia*: director, writer, editor, cinematographer

1995 *Etot sotriasajuschijsia mir/This Shaking World*: director, editor, writer, cinematographer

1997 *Deti Ivana Kuzmicha/L'Ecole pas comme les autres/The Children of Ivan Kuzmich*: director, editor, writer, cinematographer

1997 *A Poet on the Lower East Side. A Docu-Diary on Allen Ginsberg*: cinematographer

1997 *The Prince Is Back*: director, writer, editor, cinematographer

2002 *Peter Sellars: Art as Moral Action* (in progress): director, writer, editor, cinematographer

Further Reading

Dyomin, Victor, "Marina Goldovskaya: Close-Up," in *Soviet Life*, May 1988, 5, 380.

Goldovskaya, Marina, *Chelovek krupnim planom* [Close-up], Moscow, 1981.

———, *Tvorchestvo i technika* [Creativity and Technology], Moscow, 1986.

———, "Zenshchina s kinoapparatom," *Iskusstvo Kino*, 6, 1991.

Jennings, Peter, and Todd Brewster, *The Century*, New York: Doubleday, 1998, 506–507.

Menashe, Louis, "Woman with the Movie Camera: The Films of Marina Goldovskaya," *Cineaste*, xxiv, 2–3, 1999.

Ramsey, Nancy, "A Filmmaker's Duty: To Document Her Homeland," *New York Times*, December 6, 1998.

Taubman, Jane, "The Art of Marina Goldovskaia," *Slavic Review*, 54, 4, 1995, 1010–1015.

GOLDSON, ANNIE

Annie Goldson's career offers telling evidence of the predicament of the politically concerned documentary filmmaker in a millennial culture of globalisation, electronic media, and multinational capitalism. Her work mobilises the force of factual information, personal testimony, social commentary against the oppressive realities of social injustice, and human rights abuse. It often mounts a critique of the recording and reporting techniques of the media, thus revealing the ideological basis of their claim to objectivity and truth. From this perspective, documentary provides the means for promoting an awareness of the cultural politics of image production. It gives voice and visibility to the stories of those whose freedom of speech, political beliefs, or legal status is not recognised within the dominant system of representation.

Yet, despite affirming the values of difference and self-determination, Goldson's dependence on a liberal-democratic understanding of documentary's function within the public sphere—as social and moral conscience, arbiter of justice, confessor, advocate, accuser—reinstalls the procedures of address and authority that guaranteed an earlier paternalistic and moderately progressive tradition of documentary filmmaking. Such a position fails to acknowledge the degree to which it participates in the maintenance and revision of those discursive and institutional structures that facilitate the circulation of power and knowledge in a globalised economy of information and media imagery. The inauguration of a postcolonial model of documentary practice, to which Annie Goldson's work contributes, must equally interrogate the vestiges of imperial and instrumental reason that govern its own method and message.

Goldson's development as a documentary filmmaker roughly coincides with New Zealand's steady integration and assumption of the values of a "knowledge-based society." Her films provide an interesting example of the role of documentary in negotiating the transition from ideological state apparatus to the conceptual hegemony of communication as a world system. They also reflect an unresolved conflict between a documentary practice that serves the interests of a local/national community and a global/multinational constituency. In *Framing the Panthers* (black and white) (1991), *Counter-Terror: The North of Ireland* (1990), and *Punitive Damage* (1999), Goldson takes an oppositional position against the processes of global imperialism and media (dis)information, whereas *Wake* (1994), *Seeing Red* (1995), and *Georgie Girl* (2001) establish a range of strategic alliances with the production of a national image and identity that is more in keeping with the restructuring of New Zealand society as a postmodern, postindustrial culture.

Between 1990 and 1993, Goldson produced and directed a number of videos that expose the practices of racism and colonialism in Puerto Rico, Northern Ireland, and the United States. These pieces possess a philosophy of social criticism, political education, and media activism. They provide an alternative source of information, interpretation, and expression for communities and causes that are ghettoised or suppressed, and supply the method and materials for a counter-analysis of historical events and current affairs. Goldson's political agenda also includes a reflexive critique of the media. To this end, she clearly shows how the act of representation is ideologically motivated. For instance, African-American high school students admit their lack of knowledge about the Panthers in strictly staged interviews, the construction of news clips is analysed to reveal how the British authorities "frame" the story of "terrorist" incidents in Northern Ireland.

On returning to New Zealand, Goldson abandoned a direct activist stance. Rather, she assumes a critically reflexive attitude toward personal and public history. The emphasis shifts from issues to ideas, from content to concept. The language of film theory and cultural studies increasingly informs her films. *Wake* examines the conditions of visuality that permit a colonialist politics of looking and naming. The paintings of the early settlers and her father's home movies illustrate the immigrant's reinscription of landscape and community as markers of a displaced identity. Stylistically, the film foregrounds the codes of documentary representation with its use of narrative voice, fictional reconstruction, found footage from the family album, and popular film.

Goldson perfects these techniques of formal and theoretical reflection in *Seeing Red*, a film about the scandal that erupted in 1949 around Cecil Holmes, a young filmmaker with Communist sympathies. Subject matter and cinematic style thoroughly reinforce the critical project of reimagining the tradition of New Zealand documentary and redefining its place in the present. Goldson composes a historical narrative that locates her own work in a political and artistic context. The story of Cecil Holmes acts as a myth for the institution of a new chapter in the development of a national film culture. *Seeing Red* constitutes its subject as a means of authorising its own discourse. Its recuperation of a forgotten cinematic legend parallels the successful effort of the New Zealand Film Archive in recovering and restoring the nation's moving picture heritage. Goldson brilliantly uses archival footage, particularly from *The Coaster*, a film Holmes made for the National Film Unit (NFU), to support her reading of documentary history. The NFU, established with Grierson's advice, promoted the interests of social and national unity. Goldson accommodates for the demise of such an institutional and ideological framework by endorsing the discourse of the academy and the archive. The university and the arts sector lend credibility to the rebranding of New Zealand's past for consumption as a contemporary commodity. In the process, a state-sponsored, civically sanctioned ideal of documentary as a public service is recast as a professionally accredited enterprise in managing and marketing the national imaginary.

Punitive Damage and *Georgie Girl* complete the cycle of legitimation for documentary as a home-grown form of social discourse. They successfully present stories of local interest—a mother's fight for justice after the death of her son in an East Timor massacre, the life and times of the world's first transsexual, Maori MP—according to an international standard of value. An official round of film festivals, conferences, awards and prizes, funding panels, press releases, public talks, and interviews guarantee the quality of the film's documentary veracity. The global resurgence of documentary as a form of serious entertainment fosters an audience and artist with a shared set of moral and political reflexes: cultural tolerance,

emotional empathy, and human understanding. Annie Goldson fits the bill well.

ALAN WRIGHT

Biography

Filmmaker and Associate Professor in the Department of Film, Television and Media Studies at the University of Auckland, New Zealand. Has been producing and directing award-winning documentaries for fifteen years in the United States and New Zealand. Published extensively on a variety of topics such as the documentary, feminism, and experimental video.

Selected Films

1990 *Counterterror: The North of Ireland*: co-producer/co-director
1991 *Framing the Panthers* (black and white): co-producer/co-director
1993 *Death Row Notebooks*: co-producer/director
1993 *A Small War: The United States in Puerto Rico*: director
1994 *Taonga*: director
1994 *Wake*: director
1995 *Seeing Red*: producer/director
1999 *Punitive Damage*: director; produced with Gaylene Preston
2001 *Georgie Girl*: co-director with Peter Wells; producer

GOOD WOMAN OF BANGKOK, THE

(Australia, O'Rourke, 1991)

The Good Woman of Bangkok is a controversial account of the Australian documentary filmmaker Dennis O'Rourke's nine-month involvement with a Thai prostitute named Yaiwalak Conchanakun, called Aoi. Modeled after Bertolt Brecht's *The Good Woman of Szechuan*, which uses the central figure of a prostitute to examine the possibility of living a good life in a corrupt world, O'Rourke's film explores the conjunctions of sex and money in the East-meets-West world of Bangkok and examines the ethical complexity of his multiple roles as client, lover, and director in relation to Aoi. Although O'Rourke remains an off-camera voice through-

out the film, his work is centrally concerned with his intercession into and interrogation of Aoi's life, which culminates in his offer to rescue her from prostitution by buying her and her family a rice farm. O'Rourke provocatively positions his very personal film as "documentary fiction," an antithesis of the objective documentary that rearranges chronology for dramatic effect and self-consciously examines the voyeuristic nature of filmmaking. Although the film centers on the life of Aoi, it indicates the elusive edges of a larger story about the intercultural, interracial, and economic complexity of postcolonial capitalism.

The Good Woman of Bangkok, 1991.
[*Still courtesy of the British Film Institute*]

The film begins after the collapse of O'Rourke's marriage, when he travels to the notorious Patpong region of Bangkok to explore the nature of love and sexual desire. The 43-year-old O'Rourke hires the 25-year-old Aoi for her sexual services and begins to film her as she tells a life story full of victimization and exploitation. The film traces the trajectory of Aoi's life: her birth into a poor peasant family, her parenting by an alcoholic father, and her pain from an untreated birth defect that has left her blind in one eye. She spent her adolescence in servitude before making a bad marriage to a man that deserted her when she was two months pregnant. Aoi eventually moved to Bangkok at the urging of her mother and worked in the Patpong area to support her family and pay off their debt. The camera unblinkingly follows Aoi as she plies her trade at night, tells her story during the day, and performs the intimate acts of eating, sleeping, and tending to her dead father's shrine. Aoi eventually moves to the rice farm that O'Rourke has promised to buy her and her family. *The Good Woman of Bangkok* concludes with an epilogue that reveals Aoi's return to the sex trade underworld, from which O'Rourke attempted to rescue her. The reason for her return to Bangkok is never revealed, suggesting that there is much O'Rourke does not know and perhaps cannot know about Aoi, bound as he is by cultural, economic, and sexual lines that frame Aoi as an ever-elusive subject.

LISA HINRICHSEN

The Good Women of Bangkok (Australia, 1991, 82 mins.). Produced by Dennis O'Rourke and Glenys Rowe. Directed by Dennis O'Rourke. Cinematography by Dennis O'Rourke. Editing by Tim Litchfield. Filmed in Bangkok.

Further Reading

Berry, Chris. *The Filmmaker and the Prostitute: Dennis O'Rourke's "The Good Women of Bangkok,"* Sydney: Power Institute Press, 1997.

Stones, Rob, "Social Theory, Documentary Film and Distant Others: Simplicity and Subversion in The Good Woman of Bangkok," in *European Journal of Cultural Studies*, 2003.

GORIN, JEAN-PIERRE

Jean-Pierre Gorin was initially known for his collaboration with Jean-Luc Godard in the late 1960s and early 1970s. Working collectively under the banner of the *Dziga Vertov Group*, the New Left activist, who later said "I'm a Nietzschean-Marxist . . . certainly more Nietzschean than Marxist" (Walsh, 1976), co-directed a series of formally experimental films strongly influenced by the theoretical debates of the time, questioning bourgeois notions of representation and ideology and exploring alternatives in works such as *Wind from the East* (1969), *Struggle in Italy* (1970), *Tout Va Bien* (1972), and *Letter to Jane* (1972). Godard, whilst ultimately sharing co-authorship for these works, maintains that the majority of the initial concepts came from his younger collaborator. Gorin for his part has insisted that the creative relationship was based on a "constant exchange of ideas."

Poto and Cabengo (1978), his first film after leaving Paris for California in 1975, was a documentary portrait of seven-year-old identical twins, Virginia and Grace Kennedy, who had apparently developed their own private language. Stylistically a departure from the rigours of the earlier work, the project was as much an essay on language and communication as a wry outsider's commentary on the underside of the American dream as reflected in the isolated social circumstances of the German-American family. The second of the Southern California trilogy, *Routine Pleasures* (1986) juxtaposes the singularly unspectacular activities of a club of model train enthusiasts with an exploration of the creative process of carpenter, film critic, and artist Manny Farber (who had originally invited Gorin to the University of California at San Diego). The miniature train sets of the middle-aged men (". . .in [a] hangar on Jimmy Durante Boulevard across from the Bing Crosby Hall") seem to preserve America in a nostalgic microcosm, mirrored by and in contrast to the epic landscapes and movie myths of Farber's paintings. Switching between black and white and colour, the film is a celebration of "Flaubertian dullness," undoubtedly inspired by Farber's dictum on filmmaking that Gorin summarised

thus: "I make films in my backyard. . .the way I define my subject matter is by planting myself on the ground, whirling around my own axis, extending my two arms, and within that square foot radius, defining where my subjects are" (Seidenberg, 1992).

My Crasy Life (1992), which was awarded the Special Jury Prize at Sundance in 1992, looks at the everyday lives of Samoan gangs in Los Angeles. Gorin and his producer Dan Marks wrote the film in close collaboration with the gang members, scripting scenes that were then acted out by the gangsters themselves. The formal compositions of cinematographer Babette Mangolte (who shot *Routine Pleasures*), as well as fictional elements such as a quasi-human talking computer in a patrol car, distance the film strongly from verité and hark back to earlier experimentation with genres.

Although his output has been limited in quantity over the past decade, Gorin's playful exploration of the no-man's-land between documentary, fiction, and the essay form mark him as an influential innovator, one who can no longer be regarded as wholly European or American but perhaps both.

JOHN BURGAN

See also **Blank, Les; Marker, Chris; Vertov, Dziga**

Biography

Born in Paris, France, April 7, 1943, and graduated in philosophy from the Sorbonne in 1964. Collaborated on *Les Cahiers Marxistes-Léninistes* and *Les Cahiers Pour L'Analyse*, also working as literary critic at *Le Monde* (1965–1968). Advisor on Jean-Luc Godard's *La Chinoise* (1967) before co-founding the Dziga Vertov Group with him (1968–1972). Moved to California in 1975 to join Cinema Department of the University of San Diego.

Selected Films

1972 *Tout va bien*: Co-director (with J.L. Godard)
1972 *Letter to Jane*: Co-director (with J.L. Godard)
1978 *Poto and Cabengo*: Writer, director
1986 *Routine Pleasures*: Director, co-writer with Patrick Amos

1991 *My Crasy Life*: Writer, director
1992 *Letter to Peter*: Writer, director

Further Reading

Farber, Manny, *Negative Space*, New York: Da Capo, 1998.
Harvey, Sylvia, *May '68 and Film Culture*, London: British Film Institute, 1980.
MacCabe, Colin, *Godard, Images, Sounds, Politics*, London: British Film Institute, 1998.
Schafaff, Jörn, "*Routine Pleasures* or *All About Eve* or A Point in the Landscape," in Jörn Schafaff and Barbara Steiner, *Jorge Pardo* Ostfildern-Ruit, Hatje Cantz Verlag, 2000, pp. 45–60.
Seidenberg, Steven, "In Search of the Feature Documentary," London: BBC, 1992.
Sobchack, Vivian, "16 Ways to Pronounce Potato: Authority and Authorship in *Poto and Cabengo*," *The Journal of Film and Video*, XXXVI, Fall, 1984.
Ullman, Erik, "Jean-Pierre Gorin" http://www.sensesofcinema.com/contents/directors/03/gorin.html.
Walsh, Martin, "Godard and Me: Jean-Pierre Gorin Talks," in *Take One*, 5, 1, 1976; reprinted in *The Brechtian Aspect of Radical Cinema*, London, BFI, 1981.
Wollen, Peter, *Readings and Writings: Semiotic Counter-Strategies*, London: New Left Books, 1982.

GPO FILM UNIT

See **General Post Office Film Unit**

GRABE, HANS-DIETER

Hans-Dieter Grabe has had a long and varied career in documentary film, as a director, writer, cinematographer, and producer. From 1963 to 2002, Grabe worked at the ZDF (Zweiten Deutschen Fernsehen), the second national German television network, making more than fifty television documentaries during his tenure.

By the beginning of the 1970s, Grabe had found his own style of documentary editing. He produces dialogue-based films, which focus on drawing out the memories and life experiences of the filmed subjects. The film's titles are frequently based on a headline drawn from the news. Grabe looks for and focuses on the real people behind the event, shunning sensationalism.

Grabe has a wide spectrum of themes. He has produced films about the Berlin *Truemmerfrauen* (1968), about a former prisoner at a concentration camp (1972), a *Varietekuenstler*, who lets people shoot themselves (1972), about the wife of a child murderer (1977), the survivors of a mine disaster (1979), a German resistance fighter (1983), a Turkish worker, who has killed her daughter (1986), a ZDF colleague diagnosed with cancer (1987), about the parents of a child with multiple disabilities (1990) and about the victims of war. The films are connected by their focus on the themes of responsibility, guilt, misery, and fear as they stem from individual personal experiences. "Better more than less." With these words, Grabe summarizes his guiding principle as documentary film director (Voss, 2000: 13).

A historical image is usually projected at the beginning of a Grabe film, and a brief commentary provides the necessary background information. Grabe then withdraws the explanatory information, limits the use of voice-over narration, and relies primarily on his principal characters to convey what is essential.

Grabe has worked with the same camera crew repeatedly, including Horst Bendel, Fritz Adam, Per Mustelin, and Carl Franz Hutterer, and with the same editor, Elfi Kreiter. They all refrain from making use of any sensationalistic effects. Camera movements are subtle and limited, and pacing is generally slow and consistent.

Grabe's conversation with his film subjects is a necessary step that directly impacts the outcome of the film. After a lengthy preliminary conversation, he interviews his subjects on-camera, attempting to be friendly while maintaining some degree of distance, which he calls "positive distance." The filmed exchange mimics a therapeutic session, in which people who have repressed their emotional reactions to past events gradually reveal their emotional wounds. Grabe creates spaces full of silence, in which he focuses on the faces of his subjects, to convey the full impact of the words previously spoken. The intense conversation slowly approaches the point at which the emotional cocoon breaks and tears run; it is a cathartic moment.

Grabe achieved the most consequential effect of this emotional close-up in the film *Mendel Schainfelds zweite Reise nach Deutschland/Mendel Szajnfeld's Second Journey to Germany* (1972). The film was shot exclusively on a train. Grabe documented the journey of former Polish forced laborer Szajnfeld from Oslo, where he had lived since his release from camp, to Munich, where he wants to obtain a medical certificate that will allow him to receive a higher pension based on his inability to work, which is a long-term consequence of his time in camp. During this journey, Szajnfeld slowly opens up, until he speaks of a particularly traumatic event: desperately taking a piece of bread from a deceased person. He admits that this memory still tortures him and says "perhaps somebody would have needed it more than me."

Grabe's films expose both psychological and physical wounds. Shots of the film *Nur leichte Kaempfe im Raum Da Nang/Only Light Skirmishes in the Da Nang Area* (1970), were taken in 1970 in the German hospital-ship *Helgoland*. The title comes from a short press report about the Vietnam War, which had been already almost forgotten in Europe. The film shows the effects of "light skirmishes" on the so-called "civil population." It is a pitiless film that is difficult to watch. Grabe shows, in precise detail, bodies destroyed by gunshots, lacerated by mines, and burned by napalm, and lets a doctor explain each of the wounds. By forcing us to look, he gives the victims their dignity back: "[. . .] we had to show the devastation of the body in precise detail—we owed it to those broken people. They offered us their bodies to film them and therefore we felt this was a way to contribute to the ending of war"(Goldsmith, 2003: 50).

Hiroshima, Nagasaki—Atombombenopfer sagen aus/Hiroshima, Nagasaki—Atom Bomb Victims Declare (1985), Grabe's first long documentary film, was made to commemorate the 40th anniversary of the nuclear bombing of Japan by the United States. The central section of the film is a mute sequence, which initially shows parts of American archives material. For example, doctors bend over a boy, whose back is a single bloody and purulent wound, in which they sink their cotton swabs. These images are followed by pictures of the same man in front of Grabe's camera. He shows his deformed body and explains that the skin on his back is dead, he is cold even during the summer because he has no more fatty tissue, and he may never eat until he is full because by doing so, the skin stretches intolerably.

Grabe's interest in his subjects occasionally extends past a single film. For example, Grabe met Do Sanh, a severely wounded Vietnamese boy, while shooting *Nur leichte Kaempfe im Raum Da Nang*. He made five films about Do Sahn over a period of twenty-eight years. *Do Sanh–Der letzte Film/Do Sanh–The Last Film* (1998) was completed after Sanh's death, which resulted from the long-term consequences of his wartime injuries.

Grabe viewed television as the appropriate medium for his political films because it is such a universal and populist vehicle.

BRITTA HARTMANN

Biography

Born March 6, 1937 in Dresden, Germany. In February 1945, after the destruction of Dresden, relocated to Cottbus with his family, where he attended school until 1955. From 1955 to 1959, Grabe studied film direction, specializing in documentary film, at the Deutschen Hochschule fuer Filmkunst (German University for Cinematic Art, today University for Film and Television, "Konrad Wolf") in Potsdam-Babelsberg. From the beginning of 1960 to the end of 1962, worked as a freelancer at Bavarian Televisiont. From the end of 1962 until his retirement in March 2002, worked as an editor with the Zweiten Deutschen Fernsehen (ZDF, Second Channel of German Television) in Mainz. As author and director has contributed to several magazines and made over 50 full-length documentary films. Has been awarded the Special Prize of the Union of Asiatic Broadcast and TV Organizations, the Special Prize of the Film and Television Federation, the Robert-Geisendoerfer-Prize (twice), the Eduard–Rhein-Prize (twice), the Adolf-Grimme-Prize (three times), the ARTE-Documentary Film Prize, the Peace Film Prize of the International Film Festival of Berlin, as well as the Grand Prix of all Categories at the Festival of the Independent Film in Brussels, among others. In 2002, received the Federal Cross of Merit.

Selected Films

1966 *Hoffnung–fünfmal am Tag, Beobachtungen auf einem Zonengrenzbahnhof/Hope, Five Times a Day* (30 min.): writer, director

1966 *Die Helgoland in Vietnam* (28 min.): writer, director

1968 *Die Trümmerfrauen von Berlin/The Women Who Cleared Away the Ruins of Berlin* (40 min.): writer, director

1970 *20 Meilen vor Saigon/20 Miles to Saigon* (44 min.): writer, director

1970 *Nur leichte Kämpfe im Raum Da Nang/Only Light Skirmishes in the Da Nang Area* (44 min.): writer, director

1972 *Mendel Schainfelds zweite Reise nach Deutschland/Mendel Szajnfeld's Second Journey to Germany* (43 min.): writer, director

1972 *Wer schießt auf Ralf Bialla? Warum läßt Herr Bialla auf sich schießen?* (43 min.): writer, director

1975 *Sanh und seine Freunde* (44 min.): writer, director

1977 *Mehmet Turan oder Nioch ein Jahr, noch ein Jahr* (44 min.): writer, director

1977 *Gisela Bartsch oder Warum haben Sie den Mörder geheiratet?* (45 min.): writer, director

1978 *Simon Wiesenthal oder Ich jagte Eichmann* (46 min.): writer, director

1979 *Das Wunder von Lengede oder Ich wünsch' keinem, was wir mitgemacht haben* (44 min.): writer, director

1981 *Bernauer Straße 1–50 oder Als uns die Haustür zugenagelt wurde* (72 min.): writer, director

1982 *Fritz Teufel oder warum haben Sie nicht geschossen?* (53 min.): writer, director

1983 *Ludwig Gehm–ein deutscher Widerstandskämpfer* (55 min.): writer, director

1984 *Dr. med. Alfred Jahn, Kinderchirurg in Landshut* (59 min.): writer, director

1985 *Hiroshima, Nagasaki–Atombombenopfer sagen aus* (90 min.): writer, director

1986 *Abdullah Yakupoglu: Warum habe ich meine Tochter getötet?* (45 min.): writer, director

1987 *Gudrun Pehlke–Statistisch gesehen sind Sie tot* (61 min.): writer, director

1990 *Jens und seine Eltern* (80 min.): writer, director

1990 *Dien, Chinh, Chung und Tung–Lebensversuche in Vietnam* (59 min.): writer, director

1991 *Do Sanh* (56 min.): writer, director

1994 *Tage mit Sanh* (34 min.): writer, director

1994 *Er nannte sich Hohenstein–Aus dem Tagebuch eines deutschen Amtskommissars im besetzten Polen 1940 bis 42* (89 min.): writer, director

1995 *Drei Frauen aus Poddembice* (36 min.): writer, director

1995 *Letzte Stunden in Poddembice–Jakob Rosenkranz und Abraham Ziegler* (72 min.): writer, director

1996 *Frau Siebert und ihre Schüler* (118 min.): writer, director, camera

1998 *Do Sanh–der letzte Film/Do Sanh–The Last Film* (99 min.): writer, director, camera

1999 *Mendel lebt* (99 min.): writer, director, camera

2002 *Diese Bilder verfolgen mich–Dr. med. Alfred Jahn/These Pictures Haunt Me–Alfred Jahn, M.D.* (100 min.): writer, director, camera

Further Reading

Erlewein, Christian, "Annähern, nicht anbiedern. Hans-Dieter Grabe über die behutsame Methode seiner Dokumentarfilme im Gespräch mit Christian Erlewein," in *Medium*, 2, 1992, 42–46.

Goldsmith, David A., *The Documentary Makers. Interviews with 15 of the Best in the Business*. Mies (CH)/Hove, East Sussex (GB): Roto Vision, 2003, 46–53.

Grabe, Hans-Dieter, "Der sprechende Mensch. Mein Weg zum Gesprächsfilm," in *Medium*, 3, 1992, 20–26.

Roth, Wilhelm, *Der Dokumentarfilm seit 1960*. München/Luzern: Bucher, 1982, 151–153.

———, "Mit Fragen einen Prozeß auslösen," in *Süddeutsche Zeitung* (München), 23.01.1986.

Rothschild, Thomas, "Zur Dramaturgie des Dokumentarfilms. *Do Sanh–Der letzte Film* von Hans-Dieter Grabe," in *Filmbulletin*, 41, 2, 1999, 12–17.

Voss, Gabriele (ed.), *Ins Offene . . . Dokumentarisch Arbeiten 2. Christoph Hübner im Gespräch mit Hans-Dieter Grabe [. . .]*. Berlin: Vorwerk 8, 2000, 12–59.

Wetzel, Kraft, "Hans-Dieter Grabe: Oral History als Offenbarung," in *Abenteuer Wirklichkeit. Dokumentarfilmer in Deutschland*, edited by Akademie der Künste Berlin, Abteilung Film- und Medienkunst und Aktuelle Presse ZDF/3sat, Berlin, 1989, 19–28.

GRAEF, ROGER

Roger Graef is a highly acclaimed observational documentary filmmaker renowned for working in "a very austere" direct cinema mode (Winston, 1995: 207). Graef and his long-term film crew, which included cinematographer Charles Stewart, developed a series of work practices through which they hoped to minimise the intervention of the film crew and gain the trust of those being filmed. Their code of practice included no use of scoops, a firm agreement to film only what was previously agreed on, and an agreement to offer a degree of confidentiality on material that the crew might come across during filming, careful consideration of camera angles, no lights, no staging of events, no interviews, but rather observation of events.

Graef's major work included the television series *The Space Between Words* (1972) about interpersonal and public communication; *Decisions* (1975–1976), which observed the decision-making process and workings of powerful institutions, such as The British Steel Corporation and Occidental Petroleum, as well as Hammersmith Council; and, *State of the Nation* (1973–1975), which included two programmes filmed inside the headquarters of the Common Market, in Brussels, and the Department of Industry.

One of Graef's later television programmes made for the BBC in 1981 was to prove controversial and was at the centre of a public outcry on police procedures. *A Complaint of Rape,* an episode from his series *Police* (1981), showed the insensitive handling of a rape victim by three Thames Valley police officers and provoked change in the way that the police deal with rape cases. Twenty years later, Graef returned to make another film about the Thames Valley Police, *Police 2001,* which proved to be less contentious and, in a departure from previous practice, Graef appeared on screen.

Graef's documentary films set out to demystify the power brokers in society and, in doing so, made an informed contribution to the democratic process. Through the use of classic observational filming conventions, audiences were offered insight into the decision-making processes that affect ordinary people's lives.

PAT A. COOK

Biography

Born in New York in 1936. Studied Law at Harvard University before moving to England in 1962. Initially worked in theatre before developing a distinguished career as an acclaimed documentary filmmaker. Appointed as a Governor of the British Film Institute in the mid-1970s and was a founding member of Channel 4 in the United Kingdom. Awards include The British Academy Award, The Television Critics Award, and The European TV Critics Awards at Cannes. Has lectured at universities throughout Europe and the United States, and in January 2000 was appointed as News International Visiting Professor of Broadcast Media at Oxford University. Has written for a number of English newspapers and is the author of several books on law and order, which include, *Talking Blues: Police in Their Own Words* (Paperback, HarperCollins, 1999) *Living Dangerously: Young Offenders Talking in Their Own Words* (Paperback, Harper Collins, 1993).

Further Reading

Rosenthal, Alan, *New Challenges for Documentary*, California: University of California Press, 1988.

Winston, Brian, *Claiming the Real; The Documentary Film Revisited*, London: BFI, 1995.

Sight and Sound, 41, 4, Autumn 1972, 190–191.

Sight and Sound, 45, 1, Winter 1975–1976, 2–7.

Vision 1, 1, Spring 1962, 10–12.

GRANADA TELEVISION

Granada Television has always had a reputation for being one of the more quality-conscious independent television networks, a reputation built mainly on their strong documentary output. This was primarily due to the influences of two men, Sidney Bernstein and Denis Forman (director and chairperson of the company, respectively). Both men were *cinéphiles*: Bernstein had been a member of the first "alternative" British exhibition outlet, the Film Society (1925–1939), whilst Forman had worked in the film department of the COI and had been a director of the British Film Institute before joining Granada. Both men were also concerned with social issues and were left-leaning in their political views. Such a combination of social and filmic values would ultimately feed into the establishment of a strong documentary output.

The television arm of Granada, which was already an established cinema chain, was formally set up in 1954 under the directorship of Sidney Bernstein and his brother Cecil. It was granted the northern weekly license, an area that Sidney Bernstein claims he chose because of its heavy rainfall and high population density. It first began to transmit programmes on May 3, 1956, from its television studio in Manchester. The company broke new ground quickly in the world of current affairs when it transmitted the first political by-election in Rochdale in 1958.

From hereon, Granada continued to consolidate its reputation in the world of current affairs and documentary. In the late 1950s, most current affairs programmes were based around a familiar format: a magazine-type show shot in the studio and based around a few film clips. Granada's *Searchlight* (1959–1960) made an innovation when it began to use 50 percent film material. Produced by Tim Hewat and Jeremy Isaacs, the show took a bolder, more brazen line than previous current affairs programmes and also occasionally used synchronised sound film material (hitherto film clips had been shot silent and used studio voice-over narration).

Hewat would later become the first producer of *World in Action*, Granada's most famous, long-running current affairs series, which ran from 1963 to 1998. *World in Action* extended the stylistic breakthroughs of *Searchlight* in that it adopted an even bolder, sometimes-controversial, style. It was shot entirely on 16mm film and used off-screen narrators and interviewers. It was also rapidly shot, giving it a fast, hard-hitting quality, accentuated by its often opinionated editorial line, which was a daring manoeuvre at a time when most documentaries attempted to take a nonjudgmental, "objective" viewpoint. Its use of 16mm synch sound equipment also meant that it was visually mobile and direct, moving television documentary into more cinematic territory. The production team were heavily influenced by American direct cinema and even got the Maysles brothers and Don Pennebaker to shoot material for some of its programmes in 1964.

Throughout the 1960s and 1970s, Granada produced many acclaimed, pioneering documentary programmes. These include a number of important works from Denis Mitchell, who developed a more personal, impressionistic documentary style. Mitchell had already established himself as a major figure at the BBC and continued to strengthen his profile when he joined Granada in 1963. Mitchell began to innovate by using videotape at Granada, which he used on both *Wedding on Saturday* (1964) and *The Entertainers* (1964). The latter was a particularly interesting experiment in which a number of different entertainers had to share the same lodging house. The programme was a mix of verité observation and stylistic, fictional devices. Mitchell, along with producer Norman Swallow, also produced a series called *This England* (1966–1967, 1977–1980). This series of documentaries was devised as an opportunity for young, talented filmmakers to direct films on contemporary issues, and featured contributions from Mike Grigsby and Dick Fontaine, amongst others.

Grigsby went on to make a number of highly acclaimed documentaries for Granada, which looked at the plight of outsider communities. These included *A Life Apart* (1973) and *A Life Underground* (1974). Grigsby also contributed to the acclaimed series *Disappearing World* (1971–1991). This series was the first regular attempt on television to analyse indigenous cultures that were being eroded by the growth of industrialism. Produced by Brian Moser, the series featured professional anthropologists and a number of reputable filmmakers associated with observational, verité styles of filming. Granada's association with verité television was also evident in the programmes that Roger Graef made for the company. Graef directed a number of meticulous observations of committee meetings in *Decision* (1976) and *Decision: British Communism* (1978), which showed how important decisions were made.

Granada was also influential in developing drama-documentaries. This particular generic hybrid can be traced back to the early days of television (when events had to be reconstructed in studios because of technical limitations) and through to the pioneering work of Loach and Garnett in the early 1960s. Granada developed the form and established a special drama-documentary department in 1977 under Leslie Woodhead. Woodhead had worked on *World in Action* and had used dramatic reconstruction for that series in his account of Soviet dissident General Grogorenko's time spent in a mental hospital. He extended the technique of dramatising unfilmed events (through documentation and eyewitness accounts) in his controversial programme *Three Days in Szczecin* (1976), which portrayed a Polish dock strike. Granada has continued to establish itself in the drama-documentary field, producing such controversial programmes as *Hostages* (1992), which dramatised the kidnapping of, amongst others, Terry Waite and John McCarthy in Beirut.

The drama-documentary has now become a staple of television broadcasting, permeating the schedules in a number of different formats. The rise of the drama documentary has, however, caused controversy, often for the way that it is seen to veer too far into entertainment at the expense of analysis. This development should be related to the changing nature of television, which, with the rise of cable television and other multimedia entertainments, now has to compete heavily for audiences. In line with this, it seems that Granada's reputation for daring and innovative documentaries has waned. The company is now a major media enterprise: it took over LWT in 1994, Yorkshire-Tyne Tees in 1997, and has since taken over Anglia and Meridian. It should not come as a surprise, then, that both *World in Action* and *Disappearing World* ended their long runs in 1991 and 1998, respectively.

JAMIE SEXTON

Further Reading

Aitken, Ian (ed.), *The Documentary Film Movement: An Anthology*, Edinburgh: Edinburgh University Press, 1998.

Bell, Elaine, "The Origins of British Television Documentary: the BBC 1946–1955," *Documentary and the Mass Media*, edited by John Corner, London: Edward Arnold, 1986.

Black, Peter, *The Mirror in the Corner: People's Television*, London: Hutchinson, 1974.

Bonner, Paul, and Leslie Aston, *Independent Television in Britain, Volume 5: ITV and IBA, 1981–92*, London and Basingstoke: Macmillan, 1998.

Buscombe, Edward (ed.), *BFI Dossier Number 9—Granada Television: The First 25 Years*, London: BFI, 1981.

Forman, Denis, *Persona Granada*, London: André Deutsch, 1997.

Godard, Peter, John Corner, and Kay Richardson, "The Formation of *World in Action*: A Case Study in the History of Current Affairs Journalism," in *Journalism* 2, 1, April 2001.

Moorehead, Caroline, *Sidney Bernstein: A Biography*, London: Jonathan Cape, 1984.

Paget, Derek, *No Other Way to Tell It: Dramadoc/Docudrama on Television*, Manchester: Manchester University Press, 1998.

Sendall, Bernard, *Independent Television in Britain, Volume One: Origin and Foundation, 1946–62*, London and Basingstoke: Macmillan, 1982.

Swallow, Norman, *Factual Television*, London: Focal Press, 1966.

GRANTON TRAWLER

(UK, Cavalcanti, 1934)

The shot list of the National Film Archive for *Granton Trawler* is as follows: "The work of a trawler on the Viking Bank in the North Sea.... The trawler Isabella Greig moored at Granton. She sets off. On the outward journey the crew check and prepare the nets. On arrival at the fishing grounds the trawl is lowered. A storm blows up and the trawler has to ride out the rough seas. The seagulls circle the ship. When calm returns the nets are hauled in by the crew and the catch hoisted on board, as the seagulls flock round. The fish are tipped out on the deck. The crew gut the fish and throw them into baskets. The trawler on the homeward run, the pilot at the wheel, sunset over the sea."

Granton Trawler can be thought of as a shorter version of *Drifters*, lyric rather than epic in its intentions and form. Grierson himself shot it on a busman's holiday in the North Sea. Edgar Anstey edited it under his supervision (as he had *Industrial Britain*). Though shot during the EMB period, it was finished after the unit had been transferred to the General Post Office (GPO). Cavalcanti added the sound, one of his first creative acts after arriving at the GPO Film Unit. The sound track is made up of the rhythmic thumping of the ship's engine, the creaking of its rigging, the cries of gulls, the harsh metallic sound of a winch playing out cable, muffled shouts of the men as they pull the nets, a repeated fragment of a plaintive tune played on an accordion and another whistled, and random and mostly unintelligible comments from members of the crew. There is no commentary. The sounds were all post-recorded, simulated in the studio. (One of the "fishermen's" voices is Grierson's.)

The sounds are laid over a succession of impressionistic views of parts of the ship, the fishermen's activities, and the shifting horizon, which becomes vertiginous in high seas. It is as if the makers of the film, and therefore the viewers, were standing on the trawler looking about as their eyes are led to one thing or another while their ears register certain sounds. Simple as it is, the track is a remarkably strong component of the picture. This montage of seemingly natural sounds arbitrarily modified and arranged is what would come to be called *musique concrète*. Not only was it an aesthetic experiment ahead of its time, it represents the kind of poetry that can be achieved by a stylized rendering of reality completely controlled by the creator(s). It has not dated and is still in active nontheatrical distribution.

JACK C. ELLIS

See also **Anstey, Edgar; Cavalcanti, Alberto; EMB Film Unit, GPO Film Unit; Grierson, John**

Granton Trawler (UK, New Era Films for Empire Marketing Board [silent version; sound version completed at GPO Film Unit], 1934, 11 min.). Distributed by New Era Films. Produced and photographed by John Grierson. Editing by Edgar Anstey. Sound direction by Alberto Cavalcanti; sound recording by E. A. Pawley.

GRASS

(US, Schoedsack, Cooper, and Harrison, 1925)

Along with Robert Flaherty's *Nanook of the North* (1922), Ernest B. Schoedsack, Merian Cooper, and Marguerite Harrison's *Grass* (1925) helped to define the explorer-as-documentarist tradition in nonfiction film. Filmed under dire circumstances, as well as financial difficulties, *Grass*, nevertheless, is a unique example of an attempt, in the words of the filmmakers themselves, to "dramatize exploration." That it is not as well known as Flaherty's ethnographic film can be attributed to its filmmakers' hardships in compiling their footage into a cohesive narrative framework. The subject of human beings living and surviving in conflict with their natural surroundings is the primary attraction of these films. In the case of *Grass*, that subject is not an individual, as in the titular hero of Flaherty's film, but a nomadic tribe.

Ernest B. Schoedsack and Merian C. Cooper first formulated the idea of making an epic film set in some little-known region of the world in London. The original plan was to film a nomadic tribe during their annual migration for survival. The Kurdistans was the peoples of choice for their initial film project. Schoedsack had served as a second assistant cameraman for Mack Sennett at Keystone studios and also as a news photographer in Europe during and after World War I. Cooper was a decorated pilot during the war, as well as a worker for the American Relief Association after the war. After a brief stint as a reporter for the *Daily News* and the *New York Times*, Cooper signed on as first officer on the schooner *Wisdom II*. The purpose of the voyage was to collect information on little-known areas of the world for a book, magazine articles, and motion picture films. When the expedition's cameraman left, Cooper contacted Schoedsack, whom he had met on several occasions in Europe. When the expedition ended after the *Wisdom II* was disabled during a storm, Cooper and Schoedsack began making plans for their own epic film.

With a financial capital of $10,000, the two explorer-photographers, now accompanied by Marguerite Harrison, a journalist, made their way to Ankara, Turkey. The plan was to cross Anatolia to Turkestan and join with the Kurdastans to accompany their migratory route. The Turks, who had recently driven both the French and German forces out of Anatolia, were highly suspicious of all foreigners and delayed the intended expedition for several weeks. By the time they had crossed the border into French-occupied Syria, the only nomadic tribe they encountered were the Beduins. A British official, Sir Arnold Wilson, told Cooper about the Bakhtiari tribe in southern Persia. These nomadic people had an annual trek through mountainous terrain for green pastureland. Cooper, Schoedsack, and Harrison met with the khans at Shustar, the capital of Arabistan, and were given permission to join one of their tribes on its annual migration. The Great Trek of the Bakhtiari, accompanied for the first time by foreigners, began on April 17, 1924. The migration involved 30,000 men, women, and children, with herds totaling approximately 250,000 animals including sheep, goats, cattle, horses, asses, and camels. The people traveled along five separate routes; about one-sixth of this number was represented by the Baba Ahmedi tribe, which Cooper, Schoedsack, and Harrison elected to accompany because their route was the most difficult. *Grass*, was the filmed record of that expedition.

Grass is the account of the annual migration of the Bakhtiari people in what is now Iran. The film begins with an opening shot of a camel caravan traveling east. A map of the region denotes Constantinople, Persia, and Arabia. The caravan

Grass, 1925.
[*Still courtesy of the British Film Institute*]

encounters several natural obstacles including a sandstorm and mountains before meeting up with the "Forgotten People," the Bakhtiari and their tribal leader, Haidar Khan, and his son, Lufta. The Bakhtiari are preparing to migrate to the east for more fertile lands. They first encounter the river Karun, which the Bakhtiari cross by constructing rafts supported by inflated goat skins. They also cross through several mountainous terrain and finally come to the dreaded Zardeh Kuh, described by the filmmakers as "twelve thousand feet of defiance in rock and snow and ice." The ascent is accomplished when the Bakhtiari dig a path through the snow and ice, and climb barefoot, because shoes were as "useless as bedroom slippers in a blizzard." The final descent from the mountain top into the fertile valley below ends the epic trek and the film.

The lack of a specific subject for their "natural drama" cost the explorer-filmmakers both time and footage. When Cooper-Schoedsack-Harrison met up with the Bakhtiari, the tribe were making preparations for their journey, and the filmmakers had used a considerable amount of film while they were delayed in Ankara. Much of the footage that was shot of the trek had to be taken during a short time span, as the tribe slept during the hot hours of the day and traveled at night. When the migration ended after the crossing of Zardeh Kuh, Schoedsack had only eighty feet of film left and quickly shot an ending for the film. When the filmmakers were in Paris, they realized that it was far from a finished product. Cooper and Schoedsack decided that one would return to the Bakhtiari to record additional footage, while the other would try to raise more money by writing articles about their expedition. The additional footage would focus more clearly on the tribal chief, Haidar, his two wives, and his son. This film footage was never shot and consequently, the resulting film, according to many critics (as well as the filmmakers themselves), lacks a central human focus.

The economic market for travel films (which necessitated that the filmmakers shoot whatever they thought would make an interesting subject) initiated a hasty and disjointed filmmaking process. Travel films, particularly of exotic places and peoples, were extremely popular in the 1920s. Travelogs or "scenics" were popularized by Burton Holmes, whose short films usually situated a Western adventurer in exotic settings.

Robert Flaherty, with the success of *Nanook of the North* (U.S., 1922), proved that the personalization of a subject for a documentary, could be as exciting as a fiction film. Although it does have some footage of Hadair and his son, Lufta, *Grass*, out of necessity, concentrates on the Bakhtiari tribe itself, primarily in long shots of the migration. These are dramatic, particularly the crossing of both the river Karun and the mountain Zardeh Kuh, but the overall effect is weakened by the lack of human interest.

Once the film was bought for distribution by Jesse Lasky at Paramount Studios, additional footage (of the filmmakers themselves) and inter-titles were added. Though the film was not a huge box-office success, it did allow Schoedsack and Cooper to finance and eventually produce other projects of a more fictive nature, primarily *Chang* (1927), *The Four Feathers* (1929), *The Most Dangerous Game/The Hounds of Zaroff* (1932), and a film in which they lampooned themselves, as well as appeared as biplane pilots in the climatic sequence, *King Kong* (1933). *Grass*, nevertheless, still remains a good example of the early romanticist documentary style, which offered its audiences a glimpse into another culture and its epic struggle for survival.

RONALD WILSON

See also **Anstey, Edgar; Cavalcanti, Alberto; EMB Film Unit, GPO Film Unit; Grierson, John**

Grass: A Nation's Battle for Life a.k.a. *Grass: The Epic of a Lost Tribe* (U.S., Famous Players Lasky, 1925, 69 min) Distributed by Paramount Pictures. Presented by Adolph Zukor and Jesse Lasky. Produced and Directed by Merian C. Cooper, and Ernest B. Schoedsack, and Marguerite Harrison. Photography by Ernest B. Schoedsack and Merian C. Cooper. Music arranged by Hugo Riesenfeld. Editing by Merian C. Cooper. Titles by Terry Ramsaye. Filmed in New York, Turkey, Arabia, Iran. New York premiere at the Paramount Theatre, March 30, 1925.

Further Reading

Barnouw, Eric, *Documentary: A History of the Non-Fiction Film*, New York: Oxford University Press, 1993.

Barsam, Richard M., *Non-Fiction Film: A Critical History*, Bloomington: Indiana University Press, 1992.

Brownlow, Kevin, *The War, the West and the Wilderness*, New York: Alfred A. Knopf, 1979.

Cooper, Merian C., *Grass*, New York: Putnam's, 1925.

Goldner, Orville, and George Turner, *The Making of King Kong*, New York: A.S. Barnes & Company, 1975.

Mould, D.H., and G. Veeder, "The Photographer-Adventurers: Forgotten Heroes of the Silent Screen," in *Journal of Popular Film and Television*, 16, 3, Fall, 1988.

Schoedsack, Ernest B., "*Grass*: The Making of an Epic," *American Cinematographer*, 64, 2, February, 1983.

GREAT ADVENTURE, THE

(Sweden, Sucksdorff, 1953–1955)

Arne Sucksdorff's feature-length debut, his best-known effort, and almost certainly his greatest, most influential achievement, *The Great Adventure/Det stora äventyret* occupies an important yet troublesome spot in documentary history, because it seems like one of his least documentarian films. It has been claimed as founding "the style that stretches the definition of a documentary to its absolute limits. It is held together by a continuous narrative where the images illustrate the voice's narration, and creates a closed world that is built on assumptions about the state of things rather than their reality" (Soila, 1998). The film strikes many as a break in Sucksdorff's work, given its fictional framing story, narrated by an adult voice

as the movingly poetic memory of the elder of two brothers. Sucksdorff, acting for the only time in his films, plays a small role as the father of two boys, Anders and the younger Kjell (played by Sucksdorff's own son Kjell), who capture an otter and secretly try raising it as a pet. Others, however, productively read the film as the summation of Sucksdorff's work up to this point, imposing a slight narrative framework and themes consistent with his oeuvre upon footage essentially documentarian in its shooting, style, and spirit.

The film is justly noted for many individual shots and sequences. Sucksdorff's penchant for water imagery is evident from the early shots of water beads on reeds to those on a spider's web, to later shots of icicles and water ripples evoking nature's vibrant delicacy. The work and the world of humans can be beautiful, too, as with shots of a threshing machine. Most famous, however, are the animal scenes, often presented without narration; the film does not show a human until seven minutes in, and the story of the boys and their pet does not commence until the film is half over. The mating of the wood grouse combines fascinating footage with the careful, foregrounded use of sound typical of Sucksdorff. His legendary patience in seeking shots, many in close-up, shows in shots of an owl swooping down to catch a dormouse, a fox cub tugging at a sibling's corpse, or in the best-known example of a lynx waiting in a tree. One is left to wonder if the boys were indeed close to a lynx as one swish pan seems to indicate. Such effects blend seamlessly into those created by editing, or the stylized montage of spring's return.

The film succeeds remarkably at balancing its documentary and fictional aspects. The extended nature scenes, so rewarding in themselves, never make the story of the boys seem perfunctory or forgotten, while the "adventure" of the boys never imposes itself so strongly as to make one feel that this is not a nature documentary. Given that the division between the world of choice-making humans and that of instinctual animal nature is so important to Sucksdorff (viz., *A Divided World*), perhaps this is why he had such insight into children, those creatures who most closely span the divide, driven more by base desires and impulses. When the boys slide down a snowy hill, we then hilariously see "Ottie" belly-wop as well. At the same time, the interaction between humans and animals is at the heart of his work, whether in the story of the boys and their pet, the nuisance and economic threat the fox presents to farmers, or even a shot of an owl appearing to watch airplanes skywriting. Sucksdorff's flair for simulating point-of-view shots from animal as well as human perspective is on display, lending credence to the nonjudgmental claims he made: "I try to show an acceptance of life and other human beings. After all, one of the main human rights is the right to make mistakes!" (qtd. in Cowie, 1985).

That said, mistakes by animals or humans can prove fatal, and Sucksdorff, in typical form, never flinches from the cruelty of circumstance, the constraints that humanity places on animals, and the harsh ironies of the wild. The most piercing example occurs as the fox escapes with its takings from the henhouse. The dog pulls away from his post and dashes after the fox, who seems doomed, given his size and the burden he carries. Ironically, the dog's dangling chain gets caught on a branch, trapping the dog, who soon falls prey to a lynx. Linking the animals with humans, the film reminds us of the lynx when Anders is startled by suddenly falling snow clumps. The parallels, however, are even richer, for Nature appears to give its replacements. By February "Ottie" is tame enough to know his own name and to follow the boys around like a dog. Still, the otter and the foxes responsible for the dog's death play together, and Ottie, too, pilfering food, becomes a menace to the fishermen. The boys' toughest realization of that lingering division, though, comes near the end. For all of Ottie's apparent bonding with them, he is also content to simply run off and return to the wild. The powers of recovery in nature, however, be they human or animal, are considerable. Kjell's blabbing to others about Ottie's existence is forgiven, and it only takes a flock of cranes on the wing to enchant the boys once again. The gentle narration, highlighting the theme of "life as a great adventure," is not as sentimental as it might first seem: "No happiness of our exists without heartache . . . no love without anxiety. . . In the forest so little time for grief, and joy is short-lived too."

DAVID M. LUGOWSKI

See also **Sucksdorff, Arne**

The Great Adventure (aka Det Stora Aventyret), Anders Nohrborg, 1953, Swedish documentary by Arne Sucksdorff. [*Courtesy of the Everett Collection*]

The Great Adventure/Det stora aventyret (Sweden, Svenska Filmindustri, 1953, 77 min.). Direction, producing, scenario, cinematography and editing by Arne Sucksdorff. Original music by Lars-Erik Larsson.

Further Reading

Cowie, Peter, *Swedish Cinema, from Ingeborg Holm to Fanny and Alexander*, Stockholm: Swedish Institute, 1985.

Cowie, Peter, *Scandinavian Cinema*, London: Tantivy Press, 1992.

Hardy, Forsyth, *Scandinavian Film*, London: Falcon Press, 1952.

Kwiatkowski, Aleksander, *Swedish Film Classics*, Stockholm: Swedish Film Institute and New York: Dover, 1983.

Soila, Tytti, Astrid Soderbergh Widding, and Gunnar Iversen, *Nordic National Cinemas*, London and New York: Routledge, 1998.

Wakeman, John (ed.), "Arne Sucksdorff," in *World Film Directors, Vol. One, 1890-1945*, New York: H.W. Wilson, 1987.

GREAT DAY IN HARLEM, A

(US, Bach, 1994)

A celebration of the famous photograph of nearly sixty jazz luminaries posing in front of a Harlem brownstone apartment-block, taken by Art Kane for *Esquire* magazine in 1958, *A Great Day in Harlem* has some striking parallels with *Jazz on a Summer's Day* (1959). Kane had been a magazine art director hitherto, this being his first photographic assignment; Bert Stern had been an advertising stills photographer before directing his first (and only) film. The photograph was another instance of the interface, in the late 1950s, between commercial art and jazz iconography. Where it differs, however, is in the kinds of iconography deployed. The bustling inner-city backdrop captured in pristine mono-chrome contrasts sharply with Stern's boldly coloured juxtaposition of old money and youthful exuberance.

A Great Day in Harlem pays tribute to as many of the musicians featured in the photograph as can be crammed into its sixty minutes, ranging from veteran stride pianist Willie "The Lion" Smith to then-younger musicians on the rise, including Sonny Rollins and Horace Silver. That it avoids feeling repetitive can be attributed to skillful pacing. It can also be attributed to the different kinds of footage utilised. Jean Bach, the director, conducted contemporary interviews with surviving participants on their reminiscences of the day and of the other musicians featured in the photograph. A sometime journalist in Chicago, later a radio and television producer, Bach had long-standing acquaintance with many of her interviewees. The ensuing mutual respect resulted in a series of engaging interviews, by turns moving, elegiac, hilarious, with musicians whose experiences, in most cases, made them reluctant to talk expansively with the uninitiated.

The somewhat visually bland interview footage is combined with home movie photography, in colour, shot on the day by veteran swing bassist, Milt Hinton, or his wife, Mona. The vibrancy of this material is, again, reminiscent of the quality of immediacy in the cinematography of *Jazz on a Summer's Day*. This, in turn, is interposed with black-and-white archive footage of the musicians being discussed, mostly from 1950s television, characterised by low-key lighting and grainy film stock.

A Great Day in Harlem, 1994.
[*Still courtesy of the British Film Institute*]

In these ways, the effect is of cumulative layers of an artfully constructed authenticity: in the iconography of the photograph, in the other contemporaneous photography capturing the event, and in the direct testimony of those who were there. Hearing the music on the sound track, of which improvisation was an important component, alongside the awareness of the intervention of several decades since its recording, is analogous to the film overall, in its chronological distance from Kane's photograph, and in its fusion of the here and now and the elegiac. Once an artefact of glossy contemporaneity, the photograph now acts as a springboard to a multifaceted oral history. As such, the film is not only an invaluable resource for those wishing to know more about jazz; it is also a nuanced meditation on the nature of time and memory.

JOHN YOUNG

A Great Day in Harlem (U.S., Flo-Bert/Jean Bach/New York Foundation for the Arts, 1994, 60 min). Distributed by Castle Hill Productions. Produced by Stuart Samuels and Matthew Seig. Directed by Jean Bach. Shooting script by Jean Bach, Susan Peehl, and Matthew Seig. Cinematography by Steve Petropoulos, Del Hall, Milt Hinton, and Mona Hinton. Animation camera by Ralph Pitre. Title animations by Michael Bianchi. Edited by Susan Peehl. Interviews by Jean Bach. Narrated by Quincy Jones. Interviews with Robert Altschuler, Robert Benton, Art Blakey, Scoville Browne, Buck Clayton, Art Farmer, Steve Frankfurt, Bud Freeman, Dizzy Gillespie, Benny Golson, Johnny Griffin, Nat Hentoff, Milt Hinton, Mona Hinton, Chubby Jackson, Hank Jones, Taft Jordan, Jr, Max Kaminsky, Mike Lipskin, Eddie Locke, Elaine Lorillard, Marian McPart-land, Felix Maxwell, Paula Morris, Gerry Mulligan, Everard Powell, Sonny Rollins, Horace Silver, and Ernie Wilkins. Archive footage of Henry "Red" Allen, Count Basie, Vic Dickenson, Roy Eldridge, Sonny Greer, Coleman Hawkins, Jo Jones, Gene Krupa, Charles Mingus, Thelonious Monk, Jimmy Rushing, Pee Wee Russell, Zutty Singleton, Stuff Smith, Willie "The Lion" Smith, Rex Stewart, Maxine Sullivan, Mary Lou Williams, and Lester Young.

Further Reading

Bruzzi, Stella, *New Documentary: A Critical Introduction*, London: Routledge, 2000.

Clark, Andrew (ed.), *Riffs and Choruses: A New Jazz Anthology*, London and New York: Continuum, 2001, 448–449.

DeVeaux, Scott, "Constructing the Jazz Tradition: Jazz Historiography," in *Black American Literature Forum*, 25, 3, Fall 1991, 525–560.

Gilroy, Paul, *The Black Atlantic: Modernity and Double Consciousness*, Cambridge, MA: Harvard University Press, 1993, 72–110.

Harlos, Christopher, "Jazz Autobiography: Theory, Practice, Politics," in *Representing Jazz*, edited by Krin Gabbard, Durham, NC: Duke University Press, 1995, 131–166.

Levine, Lawrence W., "Jazz and American Culture," in *Journal of American Folklore*, 102, 403, January-March 1989, 6–22.

Shapiro, Nat, and Nat Hentoff (eds.), *Hear Me Talkin' to Ya: The Story of Jazz as Told by the Men Who Made It*, Harmondsworth: Penguin, 1963.

Stowe, David W., *Swing Changes: Big Band Jazz in New Deal America*, Cambridge, MA: Harvard University Press, 1994.

Walser, Robert (ed.), *Keeping Time: Readings in Jazz History*, New York: Oxford University Press, 1999.

GREAT WHITE SILENCE, THE

(UK, Ponting, 1924)

The Great White Silence was the first feature documentary version of the footage shot by the photographer and cinematographer Herbert Ponting (1870–1935) during the failed attempt to reach the South Pole on foot by a team lead by the naval officer and explorer Robert Falcon Scott in 1910–1912.

Scott was the best known of a group of Polar explorers who mounted expeditions on foot across the Arctic and Antarctic continents during the late Victorian and early Edwardian period. The 1910–1912 expedition—his last, as it would turn out—followed a previous unsuccessful attempt to reach the Pole in 1901–1904, and voyages by others including his arch-rival Ernest Shackleton and the Australian Sir Douglas Mawson. Their work coincided with the rapid growth of still photography as a mass medium and of cinema as industrialised entertainment, hence the reason both Scott and Shackleton enlisted the services of cameramen on their later journeys. Fundraising was always a problem, and advance sales of the distribution rights for both still and moving images provided much-needed income (it took Scott more than a year to raise the £40,000 needed to finance his attempt on the Pole).

Scott's second voyage was an unmitigated disaster. His colleagues were largely inexperienced, and the party relied heavily on untested motorised sledges, all of which broke down at an early stage in the expedition. Scott and his party of five colleagues had to manually haul their supplies almost 800 miles from Ross Island to the South Pole. They achieved this on January 18, 1912, only to discover that Scott's rival, the Norwegian Roald Amundsen, had got there first. As a result of a combination of exhaustion and unusually bad weather on the return trip, Scott's party became stranded and all eventually died.

Despite the expedition not only having been a failure, but one that could have been easily foreseen and prevented (as demonstrated by Amundsen's having reached the Pole with relatively little difficulty), Scott was celebrated as a national hero when news of the expedition's outcome reached Britain in February 1913. A memorial service held the following month characterised Scott's attempt as a "heroic failure," rhetoric that would characterise the commercial exploitation of Ponting's footage over the next two decades.

Herbert Ponting was born in Salisbury in 1870 and emigrated to California in the early 1890s. Within a decade he had gained a formidable reputation as a documentary photographer, largely as a result of his visits to Japan in 1902–1905. It was on the strength of this reputation that he persuaded Scott to hire him to photograph and film the 1910–1912 expedition. Ponting was not among the group of five who died on the return march from the South Pole, and on his return to London he devoted the rest of his life to publicising the work of Scott through the medium of his photographs and films. He presented more than a thousand lectures during the following years, illustrated by both slides and film, and in 1921 published *The Great White South*, the first of many illustrated books documenting Scott's final expedition.

The Great White Silence, released in 1924, was the first of three stand-alone feature versions of Ponting's edited film footage. The continuity is clumsy and relies heavily on inter-titles, and the film was not shown widely (nor is it readily available for viewing today). The second version, *90° South* (1933), featured recorded music and a synchronised commentary by Ponting. It is far more fluently edited and uses animated diagrams to recount the details of Scott's final march (on which, given that Ponting did not take part, no actual footage was shot). A shortened version was released in 1936 as *The Story of Captain Scott*, shortly after Ponting's death the previous year.

The two decades that Ponting spent in tirelessly promoting his Scott footage undoubtedly established the "heroic failure" genre as a mainstay franchise in British documentary and realist cinema, especially in depicting military conflicts with negative outcomes. Its influence can be seen in settings as diverse as the politically controversial account of Edith Cavell's execution in *Dawn* (UK 1927, dir. Herbert Wilcox) and the Arnhem landings in Brian Desmond Hurst's reconstruction, *Theirs Is the Glory* (1946).

The image of Scott as the gallant loser was further cemented in a highly budgeted and publicised biopic (shot in Technicolor and featuring music by Ralph Vaughan-Williams), *Scott of the Antarctic* (UK, 1948, dir. Charles Frend). Though a fictionally re-created account of Scott's last expedition the film appears to have been based heavily on Ponting's work, including staged versions of some of the more memorable scenes in both *The Great White Silence* and *90° South*. With this film, Scott's final expedition took its place alongside the Charge of the Light Brigade or the battles of Trafalgar and The Somme as a distinct strand in the British cultural memory, which the historian Jeffrey Richards argues is characterised by an emphasis on self-belief and on trying rather than succeeding. It is perhaps for this reason that *Scott of the Antarctic* was a box-office failure in the United States. Interestingly, the Ealing version does explicitly note a number of key errors made by Scott as having contributed to the eventual disaster (most notably the decision to rely on motorised sledges); the Ponting films give a more simplistic impression of a visionary battling elements beyond his control.

In this respect, therefore, both *The Great White Silence* and *90° South* have been seen as overtly propagandist in the context of Ponting's largely unproblematic and sycophantic depiction (at times bordering on worship) of his protagonist, and the hindsight of what we now know to be a number of serious errors on Scott's part. That having been said, it must be borne in mind that Ponting (and, for that matter, his counterpart on the 1914–1916 Shackleton expedition, Frank Hurley) was primarily a photographic ethnographer by trade, and did not approach filmmaking with the same institutional and cultural baggage as Grierson's generation of documentary-makers and the "social realist" tradition of British filmmaking that followed.

LEO ENTICKNAP

See also **South**

Great White Silence, The (UK, Ponting, 1924) Distributed by New Era Films. Produced and directed by Herbert G. Ponting.

Further Reading

Arnold, H.J.P., *Photographer of the World: The Biography of Herbert Ponting*, London: Hutchinson, 1969.

Ponting, Herbert, *The Great White South*, London: Gerald Duckworth & Co., 1921.

Ponting, Herbert, *With Scott to the Pole* (2nd ed.), London: Bloomsbury, 2004.

Richards, Jeffrey, *Films and British National Identity*, Manchester: Manchester University Press, 1997.

Savours, Ann (ed.), *Scott's Last Voyage: Through the Antarctic Camera of Herbert Ponting*, New York: Praeger, 1975.

GREECE

In the early decades of the twentieth century, the practice of documentary was hardly thought of as an important aspect of Greece's cinematic output (relatively slim, at any rate). The considerable value that has since been attached to the many newsreels produced in that era is attributable to the country's tumultuous history, whose political and military events are evoked in those documents. These documents were made beyond any notion of adherence to the various evolving international theories and practices of "addressing the real," and being (for the most part) uninformed by formal concerns of an aesthetic or diegetic order.

Nevertheless, Greek cinema actually begins with documentary, arguably via the pioneering work of the Manakias brothers, Greek Vlachs, who inaugurated Balkan cinematography in May 1905 with *Yfantres/The Weavers*, featuring their 116-year-old grandmother in their native Macedonian village. This was the first of sixty-seven films of mainly ethnographic interest. It should be pointed out, however, that the Manakias's output did not belong to the Greek "national cinematography" to start with, given that their work coincides historically with the upheavals that resulted in the formation of Greek Macedonia. The Manakias brothers' story has become familiar to the international viewing public mostly by way of its recent incorporation into the plot of Theo Angelopoulos's 1995 fiction film *To Vlemma tou Odyssea/Ulysses' Gaze*.

Also worthy of mention is the work of Dimitris Meravidis, a Greek based in Istanbul whose earliest (1903) newsreels actually predated those of the more celebrated brothers, but were neither produced nor exhibited on the Greek mainland. From 1905 onward, Meravidis produced several such films, which he sent to the Gaumont and Pathé companies in Paris for exhibition. Later he became the first important Greek director of photography, and, in 1928, he filmed *Prometheas Desmotis/Prometheus in Chains* in Delphi, capturing the attempted revival (by the poet Angelos Sikelianos and his wife Eva) of Delphic Mysteries. That document, funded by a French company for the promotion of ancient drama, was coupled with a later (1930) performance of *Prometheus*, this time in Athens, a pairing that remains of great historical interest, insofar as it constitutes the first full-length film on Greek tragedy.

Particularly notable are the 1917 film *I Katastrofi tis Thessalonikis/The Destruction of Thessaloniki* by an unnamed director (a work that, in 10 minutes 35 seconds, captured by purely cinematic means the fire that ravaged a part of Thessaloniki) and M. Dorizas's *Meteora*, of uncertain date. These films are of special value, insofar as they are among the few of that period that have survived integrally. Of the important early makers of Greek newsreels, the Hungarian Joseph Hepp merits mentioning, as do Costas Theodoridis, the Gaziadis brothers (Dimitris and Michail), and especially the painter Yorgos Prokopiou, with his remarkable films on the campaign to Minor Asia and the 1922 catastrophe that followed, resulting in the expulsion of the Greek community (approximately 1 1/2 million refugees). Many of the episodes captured by Prokopiou reveal a coherence and singularity of purpose that lends them a diegetic quality with strong humanist overtones.

Before World War II, those Greek documentaries that did not fall under the "newsreels" label aimed at capturing the singularities of the indigenous landscape. This continued after the war, notably via the shorts made by Prodromos Meravidis (Dimitris's son), photographed, edited, and produced by himself. Other directors who worked in this field include Elias Paraskeuas and Gavriil Loggos, whose films also registered the spectacle of countryside, by now wounded by the recent wartime experience. It is precisely this factor, as well as the tendency evident in the works of such filmmakers, to focus on the unexpected as opposed to the typical, that often differentiated their work from a facilely picturesque and folkloric treatment of the natural spectacle. The latter ideologically charged option, aiming from the outset at the passive acceptance, consumption, and tourist exploitation of the said spectacle, contrasts sharply with the surprising or disturbing aspects revealed by highlighting the peculiarities of the Greek landscape.

The aforementioned recent experience, of course, included not only the Nazi occupation of Greece, but also the events immediately following its liberation. The country's allegiance to the Western bloc, and the consequent defeat of the Left in the catastrophic 1945–1949 civil war (a matter whose complexity is beyond the scope of this essay), meant that by the end of the 1940s Greece was at once politically divided and materially devastated. At the same time, the conservative political powers that, under various guises, ruled almost uninterruptedly until the advent of the 1967–1974 colonels' junta, imposed, among other things, a Cold War policy regarding freedom of expression.

This overview illustrates the evolution of Greek cinematography, as well as the problems faced by documentary makers in the first decades after the war. Although a number of developing compa-

nies produced innumerable generic fiction films, thereby giving rise to a "tradition" with a popular following, albeit lacking the foundations of a film industry proper (hence the tradition's gradual demise on the advent of television in the late 1960s), the documentary mode was plagued by limitations, both on the level of expression and on production, distribution, and exhibition.

Put simply, the "short" format was deemed nonlucrative by commercial producers and cinema owners alike and useless save for special cases funded for propagandist purposes by the state itself (ministries and public companies). This was a sector in which directors such as Yannis Panagiotopoulos produced some notable work in the early postwar period. This resulted in the majority of documentaries being self-funded and made with few prospects regarding consumption. A Law on Cinematography, which passed in 1961, imposed on all film theatres the obligation of projecting at least four indigenous short films per month, but was never put to practice.

A potential outlet for documentary work appeared in 1960, with the inauguration of the Thessaloniki Film Festival. Yet this type of exhibition (which was much later systematized via the shorts-only annual festival held in the town of Drama) did not guarantee an actual career. Certain directors thus resorted to projects designed for propaganda purposes, such as those promoting Greek tourism. Television's appearance, as well as the 1970 inauguration of the Greek Film Center (E. K. K.), entailed further possibilities that will be addressed later.

One of the earliest important documentaries that appeared after the civil war was *Daphni* (1952) by the art historian Angelos Prokopiou (son of the aforementioned Yorgos), a film unrelated to the country's recent history, albeit of special interest, as it was the first documentary on Greek art. The film explored the mosaics of an eleventh-century Byzantine church near Athens, with an English commentary (translated from Prokopiou's text by Aldous Huxley) and a voice-over featuring Ethel Barrymore and Maurice Evans. It inaugurated a long line of documentaries that dealt with the indigenous cultural heritage and that proliferated in the following decades, notably via several works made especially for TV, from the 1970s onward.

Roussos Koundouros became the first Greek filmmaker exclusively occupied with the documentary mode. In 1953, he founded the Institute for Educative and Scientific Cinematography and went on to produce a multitude of films, many of which corresponded precisely to the "educative" principle, insofar as they dealt with matters of medical and scientific information. Others explored the countryside-centered themes of previous filmmakers. His 1965 film *Aluminio tis Ellados (Aluminum of Greece)*, however, was a formally experimental documentary, focusing on an industrial topic and funded by the aluminum factory, whose construction and function it captured. The film adopted an aesthetic attitude toward its topic by stressing the symmetry of the machines' geometrical shapes beyond any sentimental or social rhetoric and replacing commentary with atonal music. This formal treatment, which suppressed work conditions in favor of abstraction and highlighted a quasi-metaphysical transformation of the machinery into a kind of enigmatic sculpture, coupled an apparent lack of social concerns with a bold experimental tendency, foreign to the history of Greek documentary and actually reminiscent of the Soviet constructivist films of the 1920s.

Leon Loisios directed certain documentaries in 1959–1961, addressing the everyday activities of islanders: *Psarades kai Psaremata (Fishers and Fishing)*, *I Zoi sti Mytilini (Life in Mytilene)*, and *Lesbos*. These films, which purported to readdress the familiar theme of "provincial life," whilst rejecting the option of folklore, were produced and distributed by Loisios's own documentary company and later represented Greece in international festivals. Following John Grierson's dictum on documentary as a "creative treatment of actuality," the films contained prewritten commentaries, albeit informed by experience and thereby aspiring toward a synthesis of aesthetic construction and factual authenticity.

In the early 1960s, Loisios collaborated with Koundouros's institute, which at the time made certain state-funded films. By 1964–1965, however, Loisios also attempted a series of political newsreels on behalf of EDA, Greece's major left-wing party at the time. That series, named *Elliniki Zoi (Greek Life)* and otherwise known as *Ta Epikaira tis EDA (EDA's Newsreels)*, was not completed, but the surviving documents are of prime historical importance, given the era's political upheavals, which would soon culminate in the abolition of the parliamentary system by the junta. Loisios would reemerge in the 1980s via TV work, the series *Panorama tou Aiona (Panorama of the Century)* (1982–1986), a historical project based on old Greek newsreels.

The long-standing tradition of documentaries focusing on the Greek landscape and provincial life informs part of Vassilis Maros's work as well. This exceptionally important director, however,

has also touched on urban themes, as in his first two documentaries, *Uranoxystes/Skyscrapers* and *Rock and Roll stin Athina/Rock and Roll in Athens*, both made in 1957. The second of these films in particular attempted a social approach of the rock and roll phenomenon and its early reception in Greece, while predating the first films of the *nouvelle vague*, which it largely resembled stylistically, while its *semifictional*, diegetic character presaged a tendency developed by later filmmakers, as we shall see.

Maros has expressed his debt to the modernist documentaries of the Dutch filmmaker Joris Ivens and to certain works of the British (griersonian) school. These influences may illuminate his simultaneously social and lyrical tendencies. The latter are mostly apparent in his films of ethnographic aspirations, such as *Hydra* (1958), *Kalymnos, to Nisi ton Sfouggaradon/Kalymnos, the Island of Sponge-fishers* (1963), *Pascha sto Agio Oros/Easter on the Holy Mount* (1966), *Sina: Enas Theos, Treis Prophites/Sina: One God, Three Prophets* (1968), *Criti kai Neoellines Poietes/Crete and Modern Greek Poets* (1978), and *Meteora, oi Katakomves tou Ouranou/Meteora, the Sky's Catacombs* (1992). Maros has also directed numerous portraits of painters, actors, and other public personalities.

Yet Maros's most important work is probably the diptych *I Tragodia tou Aigaiou/The Tragedy of the Aegean* (1961)/*I Ellada xoris Kolones/Greece without Columns* (1964). The former consisted of early newsreels capturing important moments of Greece's history between 1912 and 1945, which Maros synthesized into a seventy-five-minute narrative presenting the tumultuous fate of a small, wartorn, and manipulated country. The commentary used in the film was written by Angelos Prokopiou, the original material having been largely supplied via the archive of Prokopiou's father, Yorgos, whose films on the Minor Asia campaign have been previously mentioned. This montage of historical fragments was highly acclaimed, gaining prizes in various world festivals and later being transmitted by BBC, NBC, and other international TV channels. The film's political aspects, however, resulted in its Greek release being almost jeopardized by state censorship because of its implicitly critical attitude toward the treatment of Greece by those world powers on whose side the country had been firmly placed after the Nazi occupation and the Left's defeat in the civil war.

Greece Without Columns (whose title may as well be cited in English, given that it was a BBC production, not projected in Greece until 1995) was in its way a sequel to the earlier film, albeit with a crucial difference. Rather than a montage of preexistent material, this was an original work of social observation, free of the limitations imposed by censorship and addressing in a pioneering mode several crucial problems of contemporary Greece, such as poverty and unemployment and its side effects, forcibly felt in the 1960s (movement toward the urban centers, bureaucracy, and mass immigration). The film used a kind of poetic irony in its critical treatment of the topic, whereby an impeccably thought out, quasi-musical editing expressed the rhythms of a troubled social body. Here as elsewhere, Maros displayed a directorial clarity of purpose, partly obtained via his long previous experience (as a maker of newsreels) vis-à-vis the treatment of immediate reality, yet also involving a technical and formal sophistication in addressing the inner, perhaps hidden, side of this same reality. Maros's method was thus a combination of the aleatory and the preplanned, in the sense that his abstract principles preclude any resort to facile spectacle, whilst allowing the registration of unpredicted factors occurring in the course of the filmmaking process.

The first female director of Greek documentary was Lila Kourkoulakou, who, having first appeared in the late 1950s with fiction features, went on to direct a number of works on historical themes. Her documentary debut, *Eleutherios Venizelos* (1965), was a portrait of perhaps the single most important Greek political figure of the early twentieth century, based on newsreels from that era. Made in a period of great political instability, Kourkoulakou's film involved an underlying stance in favor of the challenged (and soon to be abolished) parliamentary democracy. In 1973, Kourkoulakou made another documentary, *Dionysios Solomos*, on the most celebrated poet of modern Greece and later went on to produce TV work.

Starting with Takis Canellopoulos's 1960 film *Makedonikos Gamos/Macedonian Wedding*, an innovative and experimental approach would mark the work of several young filmmakers, who made their first appearances in the course of that crucial decade. One could even speak of a clearly modernist tendency, echoing the situation brought about in poetry and the plastic arts by the 1930s generation. Thematically, nevertheless, documentary would continue to verge toward a twofold preexistent tradition, namely, the recording of ritualistic movement within a rural context. There was still a kind of hesitation on behalf of Greek filmmakers toward the complexity of the urban landscape, although the popular districts of cities were filmed with considerably greater ease, albeit seen as metaphors-cum-transformations of village life. Given that such areas, populated by the more destitute portion of the new urban crowd, were themselves gradually transformed by the struggles of their inhabitants, however, these films are situated at a crucial position regarding the documentation of the struggles in their successive stages.

The problem, nevertheless, remains, as to the reasons for which this emphatic preference for rural themes continued to be apparent, as much in the choices of certain documentary makers whose works may be said to promote both research and experimentation, as in those of others, who seem more academic and unquestioning in their approaches. One possible reason is the evocation, through the medium of documentary, of the "Greek-ness" issue, an ideological factor that has marred many discussions of the aforementioned 1930s generation (whose modernist elements are often interpreted in tandem with the "ethnocentric" inclinations of some of its representatives).

At the same time, the survival of ancient, ritualistic forms of collective behavior in the context of agricultural production was open to study, entailing as it did the individual's harmonic incorporation into its particular society, thereby determining (up to a point, as we shall see) the actual character and function of the said society. Herein lies the value of certain ethnographic films by Yorgos Zervoulakos and Nestoras Matsas.

Another factor that may account for Greek filmmakers' reluctance vis-à-vis urban themes is the nature of the Greek urban landscape itself. Rather than being at once an emblem of the industrial revolution and a token of high modernity, thereby encouraging a treatment analogous to that adopted in numerous classic Western European documentaries (but also in Soviet films, such as Dziga-Vertov's *Man with a Movie Camera*), the Greek city is a chaotic, arbitrarily structured space, in whose context those revolutionary developments that shaped modernity are late imports rather than organically evolved features. At the same time, Greece's "modernization" has tended to destroy or obscure the available evidence of the urban centers' historical past.

Takis Canellopoulos, on the other hand, had stressed the *survival* of the ritual in his debut, *Makedonikos Gamos*. By capturing the ancient wedding customs of a Macedonian village, a process of *initiation*, whereby the newlyweds are accepted into the adult world, but also a reaffirmation of the community in its collective and circular function, Canellopoulos internalized in the very filmic *form* the depersonalized nature of social myth. The role of commentary was assumed by folksong, and the recording of the events evaded all intellectualization by its extreme concision and literalness. At the same time, the processes of production (the ritualistic preparation of the wedding banquet) were seen to attain a religious-cum-magical character via their incorporation into an organic whole, whereby myth and social life seemed inextricably linked. This line of documentary would find an echo in the work of another director, Takis Hatzopoulos, who made films such as *Prespes* (1966) and *Gynaikokratia / Women's Rule* (1969), which recaptured the theme of the Macedonian landscape and of the customs surviving therein.

In Apostolos Kryonas's 1973 documentary *Itan Mera Giortis/It Was a Feast Day*, a film thematically similar to *Makedonikos Gamos*, the viewer faces a countryside that has suffered the devastation effected in the course of the 1960s by its population's move toward the cities and the gradual abandonment of the local landscape and architecture to decay. Here, too, the "feast" ritual was seen to survive, albeit this time *in spite* of the factors that challenge a no longer self-evident community. Kryonas (who, like Hatzopoulos, served his apprenticeship as an assistant of Canellopoulos) also directed the lyrical *Anemoi* (*Winds*) (1967), as well as *Entos ton Teihon/Within Walls* (1977), a film that dealt boldly with the custom of circumcision as celebrated by the Muslim minority of Didymoteicho, the town closest to the Greco-Turkish northern border.

Another example of a countryside-set documentary, also made in the midst of the junta, which registers this change in the organic experience of the ritual, while being radically innovative in form, is *O Thiraikos Orthros/The Matins of Thera* (1968) by Costas Sfikas and Stauros Tornes. Focusing on the island of Santorini, the film presented a traditional community alienated by tourism, industrial production, and the exploitation of crops. Here, the ritualistic life of an agricultural society disappeared in the maddening rhythm of sounds and images, wholly deprived of commentary. The form, at once elliptic and dynamic, attained the precision of an essay.

Among the earliest examples of urban documentaries made in the 1960s by younger filmmakers, one may single out those testifying to specific socio-political problems of the era such as *Ekato Ores tou Mai/One Hundred Hours in May* (1963) by Dimos Theos and Fotos Lambrinos. This film deals with the recent assassination of Grigoris Lambrakis, an EDA MP (an event that would later inspire Costa-Gavras' semi-fictional French feature *Z*). *Gramma apo to Charleroi/Letter from Charleroi* (1965) by Lambros Liaropoulos dealt with mass immigration, describing the personal lives of Greek coalminers in Belgium. The same overall topic was addressed by Mily Giannakaki's *Achilleas* (1965), describing immigrants in France, and in Alexis Grivas's *750000* (1965), set in Germany. These three filmmakers were the first to produce, almost concurrently, films on this burning issue, whilst maintaining a modernist attitude in their treatments. On an even more experimental level, Theodoros Adamopoulos' almost surrealistic *I Roda/The Wheel* (1964) focused on bizarre aspects of urban reality, with a tone of sarcastic, rather cynical humor, regarding the city's decay following a wheel's revolutions.

Also of note is *Gazi/Gas* (1967) by Dimitris Stavrakas, a film on the life of workers in the gas factory, with special emphasis on their visible *alienation* vis-à-vis the production procedures. In total contrast both to Koundouros's *Aluminio tis Ellados* (in which the industrial functions were subjected to an aesthetic/abstract treatment) and to Maros and Loisios's ethnographic films on island life (where the community was seen to participate in the double *ritual* of life's cycle and the work process), Stavrakas's documentary at once pointed out the human factor involved in industrial production and implied the transgression of ritualistic integration (as a mythic notion that had here ceased to function) in favor of class solidarity, apparently the sole potential token of community in the context of modern work relations.

A tendency to recapture Greek history in tandem with its contemporary repercussions was evident in two documentaries by Lakis Papastathis. *Periptoseis tou Ochi* (*Instances of 'No'*) (1965), a montage of photographs, drawings, and comments from the World War II era, made in collaboration with Dimitris Augerinos, was complemented by Papastathis's 1972 film *Grammata apo tin Ameriki/Letters from America*, wherein the same method was used to address the first wave of Greek immigration to the United States in the early years of the twentieth century. Apart from the innovative technique of construction used in these films, Papastathis also adopted a semi-fictional approach, harking back to Maros' *Rock and Roll stin Athina*, but also apparent in Liaropoulos' *Gramma apo to Charleroi*. He incorporated documentary evidence into a loose diegetic context by *framing* the nonfictional aspect within an elementary fictional "story." This tendency, whose continuation may be detected in such recent films as *O Dromos pros ti Dysi/The Way West*, also incorporated documentary footage into essentially fictional films, an example of which is the film made by Papastathis in collaboration with Avgerinos, *Odos Ermou 28/28 Ermou St.* (1968).

Finally, with regard to the documentary makers who made their early appearances in the early 1960s let us also mention the work supervised by Roviros Manthoulis in collaboration with Fotis Mesthenaios and Heraklis Papadakis. Between 1958 and 1965, this group made a number of films, either state-funded or in collaboration with Koundouros's institute such as *Acropolis ton Athinon/Acropolis of Athens, Leukada, to Nisi ton Poieton/Leukada, the Poets' Island, Prassino Chryssafi/Green Gold*, and *Anthropoi kai Theoi/Men and Gods*, mostly involving a highly aesthetic treatment of the Greek landscape, with particular emphasis on classical monuments. Manthoulis, also a notable director of fiction features, went into self-exile in France after the colonels' coup d'état, and went on to produce some important documentary work there.

In the course of the seven-year junta, a great deal of material regarding social struggle was filmed clandestinely by certain filmmakers of the younger generation, such as Pantelis Voulgaris and Costas Zirinis. These documents were used after the reinstatement of the parliamentary system in the production of politically engaged works. The latter current, a predictable development given the circumstances, gave rise to numerous films, some of which were even projected commercially as features in the years that followed. These dealt with the regime's rise and fall, its consequences and the experience of its victims, including footage from that period and from its direct aftermath, as well as interviews, filmed extracts from the colonels' trial, and related forms of evidence.

Of particular note are *Martyries/Testaments* (1975) by Nikos Kavoukidis, *Ellas Ellinon Christianon/Greece of Greek Christians* (1976) by Diagoras Chronopoulos, *Megara* (1974) by Yorgos Tsemberopoulos, and the collective work *Agonas/Struggle* (1975), a politically engaged montage of filmed events by a group of six filmmakers. Meanwhile, the almost four-hour film *Parastasi gia ena Rolo/Performance for a Role* (1978) by

Dionysis Grigoratos was an experiment in historical documentary that used newsreels footage to address Greece's recent history within the wider context of the country's positioning vis-à-vis the international events of the twentieth century and its function within the geopolitical developments of the period.

Otherwise, the general thematic tendencies apparent in the first post-1974 efforts of Greek documentary may be roughly divided into the following main categories, with several overlaps and variants: first, a number of films that attempted to extend geographically the ethnographic aspirations of earlier works and second, an increasing presence of social and political issues within a spatial and thematic framework that also acknowledged and developed that of the pioneering works made in the 1960s. Of prime (tone-setting) importance in this context were the documentaries of Dimitris Maurikios and Lefteris Xanthopoulos.

Maurikios made his first appearance with *Polemonta* (1975), a feature-length film on the surviving Greek-speaking community of South Italy. The film depicted the harsh realities of their agricultural life, which transcend ethnic boundaries, as well as their cultural and linguistic suspension between a fading if ancient tradition and their problematic integration into the specificities of time and place. An underlying problem on the meaning of "Greek-ness," as implied by the survival of rituals and challenged by historical change and geographic diversity, echoes the concerns of the earlier ethnographic films addressed previously. The film created a sensation at the Thessaloniki Film Festival, but was never projected commercially.

Maurikios went on to make a number of documentaries, including some important work for the national TV network (ERT)—the latter having evolved into the most prominent factor in matters of documentary production and exhibition after the watershed year of 1974. Amongst the films Maurikios directed for TV in the 1980s and 1990s, it is worth mentioning *Oi Gefyres tou Ioniou/The Bridges of the Ionian Sea*, a series of documentaries made in the early 1980s dealing with the correspondence exchanged between Greece and South Italy. Also worth noting is *Mesogeiako Triptycho gia ta Pathi/Mediterranean Triptych on the Passion* (1986), a comparative study of the rituals pertaining to the Holy Passion in Spain, Italy, and Greece. Finally, *Aenigma Est* (1990) was a feature-length portrait of the Greek-born Italian painter Giorgio de Chirico that was even exhibited on the commercial circuit.

This last film captured de Chirico's cosmopolitanism along with the enigma of his work's and thought's origins, a theme that remained indirectly related to the persistent questioning of Greece's social/cultural past and present, vis-à-vis an increasing acknowledgment of "global" concerns.

Lefteris Xanthopoulos first made his mark with a trilogy of films on the Greek diaspora, the first of which was funded by the community of immigrants whose everyday lives and testimonies it addressed. These films were *Elliniki Koinotita Haidelbergis/Greek Community of Heidelberg* (1976), *O Yorgos apo ta Sotirianika/Yorgos from Sotirianika* (1978), and *Tourkovounia* (1982). The films focused on both the living conditions of immigrant Greeks and the situation of the abandoned provinces that they had left behind (and, rarely, came back to). They also attempted to examine the reasons and consequences of immigration. The persistence and indeed flourishing of these themes attests to the long-term effects of the mass immigration first evoked in documentaries made in the 1960s. Xanthopoulos, also a director of fictional features on related topics, has since worked widely on TV. The 1970s documentary works of filmmakers such as Yorgos Antonopoulos and Yorgos Karypidis have moved along similar thematic lines.

Of the other documentary makers who appeared in that period, Takis Papayannidis has produced films that testify to a special sensibility, starting with *Yorti sti Drapetsona/Feast in Drapetsona* (1977), whereby a local feast was used as a pretext for an attempt to capture the history of a marginal urban district. Papayannidis's feature-length *I Ilikia tis Thalassas/The Sea's Age* (1978) developed this tendency by using the marine element (so obviously pertinent to various notions of "Greekness") as a catalyst between myth and historical experience via the evocation of the major events that had shaped modern Greece in the course of past decades.

Of the filmmakers touching on urban themes, with a social-centered perspective, albeit deprived of a political stance or a standardized formal approach, Gaye Aggeli made two original works, the idiosyncratically structured and purposely fragmentary *Monastiraki* (1976) and the direct and precise in its rough material and perspective *Thessaloniki 6.5 Richter* (1976). With *Karvouniarides/Coalmen* (1977), Alinda Dimitriou created a plain-styled and convincing social portrait. Let us also mention the historical, essayistic in scope, documentaries of Yorgos Dizikirikis,

such as *Ellines Laikoi Zografoi/Greek Folk Painters* (1974).

Tasos Psarras, a politically minded filmmaker who has also directed several fiction features, made a number of documentary shorts in the 1970s, notably *Mellele* (1972), a film on the life of a gypsy community. Using methods of pointed immediacy, such as a handheld camera (not a common practice at the time) and interviews, Psarras provided a prototype for much of his later work in which the ethnographic or biographic perspective contained a latent political element in the shape of detectable social factors and processes. Psarras has worked extensively for TV from the early 1980s onward, and his documentaries touch on topics as diverse as the Greek communities of the former Soviet Union and the lives of celebrated Greek writers, albeit maintaining a consistency in their attempts to register and illuminate the underlying presence of the historical conditions framing the primary subject matter.

The first urban Greek documentary that had the country's capital as its sole topic, while attempting to address it in all its complexity, was made by Theo Angelopoulos, best known in Greece and abroad for his fiction features. *Athena/Athens* (1982), a made-for-TV work, was informed by a tendency, apparent in the early 1980s, toward an increasingly idiosyncratic type of documentary, touching on a set of specialized topics, whose treatment registered an emphatically structural and formal approach. This current, essayistic in scope, addressed reality in its elusive or chaotic aspects, abandoning the certainties of a granted common "mythology," and thereby perhaps also signaling a move away from earlier "rural" and "ritualistic" themes. Thus, Angelopoulos's film had no precedent in its wandering, labyrinthine structure. The various contrasting layers of history (from archeological findings to architectural remnants bearing testament to stages in the development of modern Athens) captured a complex "whole," whose ultimate meaning was suspended over a void, as evidenced by the absence of people and hence of *indices* regarding historical continuity and meaning.

A short while before *Athena* was released, Costas Vrettakos had finished his important documentary *Stroma tis Katastrofis/Layer of Destruction* (1980), which had been three years in the making. Here, the provincial setting entailed an approach somewhat similar in principle, if not in form, to that of Angelopoulos. The film's topic was the archeological search for an ancient town under a village, a town revealed but momentarily, before sinking into the waters of an artificial lake. Again, archeology was used at once as a *link* with the historical past and as a sign of temporal divergence underlying spatial contiguity.

Other directors have used the documentary mode in the last three decades, with notable results. Of the older names, Fotos Lambrinos (former collaborator of Dimos Theos) has made several interesting films, and Lakis Papastathis, having started with documentary, has continued to incorporate elements of that mode in his fictional works. Yannis Smaragdis's TV series *I de Polis elalisen/Thus spoke the City* (1990) revealed a new genre—a cinema deprived of fictional intrigue, rather in the form of an essay. And Menelaos Karamaggiolis, with the feature-length *Rom* (1989), marks a search for new aesthetic principles, while addressing the topic of national definition, identity, and *otherness*, its focus being the relations between ethnic and religious minorities in Greece. This question is touched on in certain previous documentaries, as we have seen, albeit one that will become increasingly crucial in the 1990s and beyond.

Significant work has also been produced by filmmakers such as Eleni Alexandraki, Popi Alkouli, Nikos Anagnostopoulos, Soula Drakopoulou, Yannis Ekonomidis, Kleoni Flessa, Stauros Ioannou, Stavros Kaplanidis, Marios Karamanis, Despoina Karvela, Stathis Katsaros, Yannis Lambrou, Pandora Mouriki, Olga Panagopoulou, Antonis Papadopoulos, Maria Papaliou, Thanassis Rentzis, Yorgos Sifianos, Memi Spyratou, Eva Stefani, Minas Tatalidis, Stella Theodoraki, Yanna Triantafylli, Antonis Voyazos, Dimitris Yatzoutzakis, Layia Yourgou, and others.

Meanwhile, the problems of funding, distribution, and exhibition have never ceased plaguing Greek documentary, albeit not without significant improvements, reflecting the country's political situation and the increasing respectability film culture has attained from the viewpoint of official cultural institutions. The catalytic role played by national TV has already been mentioned. Yet whilst providing a solution in terms of funding, that institution's policy regarding the mode of production (given that from the early 1990s onward, recording on film has been replaced by video) all but precludes the works' consumption beyond the medium of TV, that is, their commercial exhibition and participation in international festivals. The Greek Film Center also evolved into a seminal funding source, albeit at a relatively late stage. But the actual consump-

tion of films not made specifically for TV transmission has remained an unsolved issue. So has the question of adjusting documentary to the demands of a commercially exploitable venture, given the prevalent (after the combined influences of TV production and age-old tradition) tendency to associate that filmic mode with the "short" format.

After the inauguration, in 1978, of the aforementioned Shorts festival in the town of Drama (originated by the local film club, but now an international event sponsored by the Ministry of Culture, as well as by the European Community project *Media*, and involving a wider if brief distribution of prize-winning films), there has been a proliferation of fiction and nonfiction works alike, of which documentaries form a substantial and constantly increasing minority. To this there must be added the Athens festival, "Cinema and Reality," which has been operating for the past twenty-seven years, and the Thessaloniki Documentary Festival, "Images of the 21st Century," which started in 1999.

In recent years, a few feature-length documentaries have been screened commercially with a considerable degree of success. Most notable in this respect was *Agelastos Petra/Mourning Stone* (2001) by Filippos Koutsaftis, already a director of documentary shorts. The film, widely praised as an aesthetic achievement, was actually informed by several precedents in the history of Greek documentary, but was still original in its approach. It focused on Eleusis (a district universally known because of the Eleusinian mysteries) by juxtaposing the still-enigmatic remnants of antiquity with views of contemporary life, thereby revisiting the earlier themes of landscape and the problematic relation of modern Greek society with ancient ritualistic traditions.

Another documentary that met with warm public reception was Stelios Haralambopoulos' *Yorgos Seferis—Imerologia Katastromatos/Yorgos Seferis—Logbooks* (2003), a film on the poet, diplomat, and Nobel Laureate Seferis, addressing its subject's relation both to the landscape and poetic tradition of Greece and to the political events that shaped the country's history in the past century. Finally, let us mention a feature film that may be classified as a semi-documentary, and that is also notable for touching on a topic peculiar to the past decade. Kyriakos Katzourakis's *O Dromos Pros ti Dysi/The Way West* (2003) deals with the problems of illegal immigrants (a community created after the collapse of the Eastern bloc and the mass immigration to Greece from the early 1990s onward), focusing in particular on the female experience and mixing fictional representation with real-life documentation. All these films were either produced or co-produced by the Greek Film Center; whether their success will mean the beginning of a new era for Greek documentary, perhaps entailing a degree of involvement on the part of private producers remains, of course, to be proven.

Greek documentary has registered in various (and still evolving) ways the country's history over the course of the past century, as well as its collective or contrasting concerns regarding self-definition and relations to international processes. The discernible themes, practices, and aesthetic and ideological attitudes reflect a wider network of discourses operating parallel to cinematic production. The open question is the films' international potential—a question pertaining to a combination of the country's geopolitical situation and the extent to which the situation (and/or its images and representations) affects the forms and perspectives of works.

ANDREAS PAGOULATOS AND NIKOS STABAKIS

Further Reading

Dimitriou, Alinda, *Lexiko Ellinikon Tainion Mikrou Mikous 1939–1992 (Dictionary of Greek Short Films 1939–1992)*, Athens: Kastaniotis, 1993.

Mitropoulou, Aglaia, *Ellinikos Kinimatografos (Greek Cinema)* [Private publication], Athens, 1980.

Pagoulatos, Andreas, "Regards sur le Documentaire Grec," in *Le Cinéma Grec*, edited by Michel Dimopoulos, Paris: Cinéma Pluriel (Centre Georges Pompidou), 1995.

Pagoulatos, Andreas, and Eleni Kontogeorgi, *Praktika A' Synantisis gia to Documentaire, Drama 2–4 Apriliou 1993 (Minutes of the A' Conference on Documentary, Drama 2–4 April 1993)* Drama: Ekdosi tou Fetival Tainion Mikrou Mikous Dramas kai tou Dimou Dramas (The Drama Festival of Short Films and the Municipality of Drama), 1993.

Pagoulatos, Andreas, and Vassilis, Spiliopoulos, "Astiko kai Ypaithrio Topio sto Elliniko Documentaire"/ "Urban and Rural Landscape in Greek Documentary," in *Utopia*, 47, November–December 2001, 45–53.

Praktika B' Synantisis gia to Documentaire, Drama 13–15 Maiou 1994 (Minutes of the B' Conference on Documentary, Drama 13–15 May 1994) Drama: Ekdosi tou Festival Tainion Mikrou Mikous Dramas kai tou Dimou Dramas (The Drama Festival of Short Films and by the Municipality of Drama), 1994.

Soldatos, Yannis, *Istoria tou Ellinikou Kinimatografou/History of Greek Cinema*, Athens: Aigokeros, 1982.

GREENE, FELIX

Felix Greene, filmmaker, journalist, and author, played a crucial role in opening the tightly closed doors of Asian society to Western eyes. As a filmmaker, he sought to expose and publicize the realities of life found within the Communist world. Seeing himself as a counterbalance between the prevailing assumptions he believed were often deliberately engendered by Western governments, Greene sought to ease the Western fear of Communism through the documentation of not the Communist government, but the people beneath the governmental shroud.

The driving catalyst of Greene's documentary films formed during his first visit to China in 1957. Armed with Western misapprehensions common to the era, Greene began his Communist venture prepared to see a vast expanse of squalor, disease, and impoverishment; and although those conditions did exist in varying degrees, he did not find a nation of embittered people broken by the rigid coercions of a police state. Instead, he found a buoyancy in the people, an optimism, a tangible vitality that directly opposed the brutalized peasant/oppressive militant binary nurtured within the Western press.

Having walked among, spoken to, and dined with the people of China, Greene found himself bewildered at the contradiction his China experience suggested of his cultural conditioning. His films depict this tension through his continued commitment to focus not on the negatives to be found within a Communist-ruled country, but on the universality of humanity. Armed with a crew of three—himself as photographer, his wife, Elena as sound technician, and his daughter, Ann as production assistant—Greene departed with films that allowed Western audiences to view their political enemy completing the simple tasks of daily life during a time in history when Chinese imports did not exist. His universality in presenting the Chinese to the West pioneered new views on old preconceptions that aided the eventual modification of both general and official attitudes toward China culminating in the 1970s with President Nixon's dramatic reversal of his own anti-China policies, as well as his historic visit to China.

Greene's first visit to China, moreover, awakened an awareness in the filmmaker that China was on the cusp of a momentous social and industrial explosion that was being ignored by the West. Granted, mutual mistrust existed between the Western nations (primarily America and England) and China, but the tragic outcome resulting in a virtual breakdown in communications would only serve to further hinder what he viewed to be a desperate situation. To Greene, this Communist country did not simply encapsulate one fourth of the world's population; it contained the most relevant story in the world, one he was determined to report despite bureaucratic tangles or Western criticism.

Although Greene's concept of documentary film envisaged the role that documentary would play in providing a medium of communication between two states with vastly contrasting political ideologies, he found hardship both in the making of his documentaries and in bringing them to the American public. In China, authorities tried to dictate the subjects and scenes depicted within his films, and government "chaperones" accompanied Greene during filming, often exposing film to the sunlight to destroy the images that might reach Western viewers. In the West, Greene reached an impasse when authorities refused to grant him a license to show the film *China* in Carnegie Hall, which he had rented at his own expense. The legal maneuvering that followed resulted in a remarkable sixteen-week run for the documentary. American audiences filled the theater seven times a day eager for a glimpse into a world previously banned for reasons of national security and found, as Greene did, an enemy with the same basic needs, wants, and joys that combated the same basic struggles. By putting a face to Communism through documentary, Greene humanized political difference.

Although Greene used the documentary as a tool to mediate two diverse cultures, critics charge that his writings, all of which hold sociopolitical themes, served only to further his anti-capitalism beliefs. *The Enemy: What Every American Should Know About Imperialism,* written in 1970, reads as a sharp polemic. Following a lucid and well-documented critique of imperialism, Greene explains how imperialism distorts our thinking, and why— unless the people revolt against it—imperialism will destroy all that is best in humanity and society. Critics assailed the anti-American implications of the book, yet Greene's self-appointed role as apologist for modern China provided him with a "voice" in the Western world. He discovered in the Vietnam War a new plight needing public exposure. His films and writing, however contrary to the American ideology of the time, acted as seeds sown for the emerging peace movement that was to sweep the country. Again, the eyes of the American people were opened to a view beyond the "good propaganda" generated by the government's war machine, and again, the documentary medium served to awaken debate.

CHRISTINE MARIE HILGER

See also **China!**

Biography

Born in Berkhamsted, England on May 21, 1909. Graduated from Sidcot School and attended the University of Cambridge for two years. 1931–1933, served the office of the Prime Minister doing political work. 1932–1940, senior official in London and in United States for the British Broadcasting Corp. 1940–1978 freelance filmmaker, radio and television writer, and lecturer on international affairs. Died June 15, 1985.

Selected Films

1963 *China!*: director, producer
1967 *Inside North Vietnam*: director, producer
1968 *Cuba Va!*: director, producer
1972 *One Man's China*: director, producer
1977 *Tibet*: director, producer

Further Reading

Aiken, Ian, *Film and Reform*, London: Routledge, 1990.
Aiken, Ian, *The Documentary Film Movement: An Anthology*, Edinburgh: EUP, 1998.
Barnouw, Erik, *Documentary: A History of the Non-fiction Film*, New York: Oxford University Press, 1983.
Corner, John, *Documentary and the Mass Media*, London: Arnold, 1986.
Greene, Felix, *Awakened China*, New York: Doubleday, 1961.
Greene, Felix, *A Curtain of Ignorance*, New York: Doubleday, 1964.
Greene, Felix, *Vietnam! Vietnam!*, Palo Alto, CA: Fulton Publishing Co., 1966.
Greene, Felix, *The Enemy: What Every American Should Know About Imperialism*, New York: Vintage, 1970.
Rotha, Paul, *Documentary Diary*, New York: Hill and Wang, 1973.

GREENE, GRAHAM

British novelist, scenarist, and cinema critic, Greene was arguably the most "film-minded" writer of the 1930s. Basil Wright believed Greene developed "a built-in filmic style." Fascinated from the late 1920s with the montage documentaries of Cavalcanti and Ruttmann, Greene was quick to link them with the "cinematic" tendencies of modernist "big city" fictions such as Joyce's *Ulysses* and Woolf's *Mrs. Dalloway*. Exemplified by the cross-sectional structure of *It's a Battlefield* (1934), his early novels and feature films often drew on the techniques and motifs of documentary for their sense of visual dynamism and social reality.

Greene explored cinema as a model for "poetry expressed in images" (*Spectator*, February 26, 1937). It was partly for the fact that documentary was the principal genre through which montage techniques entered British cinema that Greene pronounced "the only important films being made in England today come from Mr Grierson's system of film units" (*Spectator*, December 20, 1935). Despite his initial enthusiasm for the theories of Eisenstein and Pudovkin, Greene came to believe creative editing could be overused. Unrelieved cutting between points of high "tension" came "close to melodrama," because it omitted the merely routine comprising the bulk of social reality (*Spectator*, 27 September 27, 1935). Greene's direct association with Britain's home-grown documentary movement also began in the mid-1930s. His cinema criticism was much exercised by the inauthenticity and lack of social inclusiveness in popular features. However, he saw great potential in the documentary's combination of critical realism and aesthetic form, epitomised for him by Edgar Anstey's *Housing Problems*, Wright's *Song of Ceylon*, and Paul Rotha's *Shipyard* (all of 1935). Anstey's subordination of the aesthetic to the goal of revealing the reality of slum conditions enabled him to use "the camera as a first-class reporter," one "too truthful, too vivid, to find a place on any modern newspaper." (*Spectator*, October 9, 1936). Similarly, Robert Flaherty's calculated pastorals could not compare with the insight into relations between colonial subjects and consumers in *Song of Ceylon*, which closed "with the revolving leaves . . . as if [Wright] were sealing away from us devotion and dance and the gentle communal life of the harvest, leaving us outside with bills of lading and loud-speakers" ("Subjects and Stories," 1937). Greene felt the way ahead for the embryonic TV programming was also marked out by the GPO, where Cavalcanti was "first to realise the enormous possibilities" in sound editing (*Spectator*, January 24, 1936). While championing documentary's potentials, Greene nonetheless criticised its fallacious connotations. In practice, it was neither transparent nor purely objective, but a rhetorical discourse with institutional bases in governmental or commercial sponsorship. Similarly, the BBFC ban on "controversy" drastically limited its scope and approach: "I am getting a little tired of that word 'documentary.'" Its associations of "incomprehensible machinery revolving before the camera eye" and "earnest, expert faces mouthing abstractions" carried "a false air of impartiality." Conversely, "the best documentaries" were *openly* propagandist and personalised. Otherwise, "to call *The River—or* Wright's *Children at School—*documentary is about as meaningless as calling a sonnet documentary: they document the creator's mind that is all" (*Spectator*, May 26, 1939).

In the 1930s Greene contributed more to documentary's evolving critical self-awareness, than personally to specific films as such. By May 1936, he produced the GPO's *Calendar of the Year*, which showed how it contributed to seasonal festivals and activities, and scripted Paul Rotha's 1937 Strand film on the inauguration of the Empire Mail Service, *The Future's in the Air* (1937). Influenced by the aerial panoramas of Auden's early poems, but disappointingly avoiding the scepticism about the social purpose of modern communications systems evident in his own fictions, the latter was *Night Mail* on wings: "As the aeroplane has conquered natural barriers, so radio has conquered weather," the commentary trumpets. Arthur Calder-Marshall criticised it as an aesthetic paean, belying conflicts between capital and labour. Greene shared his reservations in theory, if not always in practice, as his own analysis of the cultural "unrepresentativeness" of other industrial showcases such as *BBC: The Voice of Britain* confirms.

Greene was concerned about documentary's increasingly propagandist tendencies. The hijacking of its techniques to fabricate in Stalinist film was a blatant example, matched only by the British industry's double standard about publicising the facts about Nazi Germany during Appeasement. Greene satirised the belatedness and muddle of early MOI policy in the story *Men at Work* (1940), while simultaneously agitating for the greater realism and social-democratic aims of the *People's War* in filmmaking. Greene advocated a formula like that pursued in broadcasting by J. B. Priestley's *Postscripts* and D. G. Bridson's radio features. His models, for allowing ordinary Britons more authentic representation of their War experience and a voice of their own, were more radical documentaries such as Hemingway and Ivens' *Spanish Earth* (1937), *Shipyard*, or *Housing Problems*. American neutrality was more likely to be swayed by "the rough unprepared words of a Mrs Jarvis of Penge, faced with evacuation, blackouts, a broken home," than "smooth-handled phrases of personalities" (*Spectator*, September 29, 1939). Everything he objected to was encapsulated in the "documentary feature" on the Kiel canal raid, *The Lion Has Wings*. As a declaration of war aims, it left "the world beyond Roedean still expectant" (November 3, 1939). Greene's astute demands for change in accent, style, and content, in his column, were noted and developed by the *Documentary News Letter* group, which eventually gained considerable influence on MOI policy.

Greene's own wartime scripting was relatively scanty, however, and not so exemplary as yet. His commentary for Strand's *The New Britain* (1940), extolled prewar social progress, as if the Depression had little impact on conditions and the welfare state were virtually achieved, threatened only by inter-cutting contrasts with Nazi Germany. This screen pageant avoided the very class conflicts Greene criticised many prewar documentaries for omitting. Its patriotic sentiments were far less radicalised than those established by Priestley's 1940 GPO short *Britain at Bay*. (It is possible that Greene was also involved in scripting Rotha's film on Nazi censorship, *The Battle of the Books* (1941), but this has not been authenticated.)

The popular appeal of Greene's own cinematic style, together with his critical agenda for documentary's role in creating a genuinely national cinema, bore more direct fruit in wartime features (especially Cavalcanti's adaptation of his 1940 short story, "The Lieutenant Died Last," as the "documentarised" fantasy of invasion, *Went the Day Well?* 1942). This was unsurprising considering that Greene spent the period from 1941–1944 in Sierra Leone for the Secret Intelligence Service. Nevertheless, he was crucially responsible for raising the level of debate about documentary's aesthetic standards, in relation to social and ethical values, at a vital stage of its development. Small wonder Grierson dubbed him "the best critic we had" (quoted in Sherry, 1989). Few twentieth-century writers achieved such simultaneous popularity, critical acclaim, generic range (subtly adapting spy thriller and detective forms), and impact on the content and creative direction of filmmaking.

KEITH WILLIAMS

Biography

Born Henry Graham Greene at Berkhampstead, Hertfordshire, October 2, 1904, and educated at its public school, where his father was headmaster. Read History at Balliol College, Oxford. After flirting with espionage and Communism, became a Roman Catholic in 1926, although retaining broadly left-wing sympathies. Both were recurring, if antagonistic themes in his fiction (epitomised by *Brighton Rock* [1938] and *The Power and the Glory* [1940]). Training as a *Times* journalist shaped the reportage style of his writing. Early novels made little impact, until *Stamboul Train* (1932), in which he first consciously cultivated his highly cinematic technique and which was quickly filmed by Hollywood. His Liberian *Journey Without Maps* (1936) and Mexican *The Lawless Roads* (1939) are classics of 1930s travel writing. Greene's output was prolific, as novelist, playwright, screenwriter, essayist, and 1935–1940 film critic for both the *Spectator* and, briefly, *Night and Day* (the latter closed after Twentieth Century Fox's lawsuit against Greene's innuendoes about Shirley Temple's unsavoury appeal). Film script for *The Third Man* (1949) is the most distinguished of his collaborations with director Carol Reed. Its location setting (in a contemporary occupied Vienna of black-marketeering and incipient Cold War frictions) epitomises the documentary visualisation and cosmopolitan topicality of both Greene's writing and films. Continued to map a highly atmospheric, politically unstable and morally ambivalent region known as "Greeneland." More a postwar condition than a specific place, its settings were as diverse as Vietnam (*The Quiet American*, 1955), the Congo (*A Burnt Out Case*, 1961), Haiti (*The Comedians*, 1965), and Argentina (*The Honorary Consul*, 1973). Became a Companion of Honour in 1966 and received Order of Merit in 1986. Died at Vevey, Switzerland, April 3, 1991.

Selected Films

1936 *Calendar of the Year* (Evelyn Spice): producer
1936 *Cover to Cover* (Alexander Shaw): co-writer

1937 *The Future's in the Air* (Alex Shaw): commentary, writer
1940 *The New Britain* (Ralph Keane): commentary, writer
1941 *The Battle of the Books* (Rotha): co-writer?

Further Reading

Falk, Quentin, *Travels in Greeneland: The Cinema of Graham Greene*, revised edition, London: Quartet, 1990.
Greene, Graham, *A Sort of Life*, London: Bodley Head, 1971.
———. *Ways of Escape*, London: Bodley Head, 1980.
———. *Reflections*, London: Reinhardt/Viking, 1990.
Parkinson, David (ed.), *The Graham Greene Film Reader: Mornings in the Dark*, Manchester: Carcanet, 1993.
Sherry, Norman, *The Life of Graham Greene* Vol. I 1904–1939, London: Jonathan Cape, 1989.
———. *The Life of Graham Greene* Vol. II 1939–1955, London: Jonathan Cape, 1994.
Williams, Keith, *British Writers and the Media 1930–45*, Houndmills: Macmillan, 1996.
Wright, Basil, *The Long View*, London: Secker and Warburg, 1974.

GRIERSON, JOHN

John Grierson, the founder of the British documentary film movement, played a pivotal role in the development of British film culture during the 1930s and 1940s. Grierson's theory of documentary film was fashioned against the backdrop of World War I, economic recession, and the build up to war during the 1930s, and his ideas were closely linked to the events and intellectual terrain of the inter-war period. During this time, conservative political convictions on the value of laissez faire free enterprise and limited state intervention in the economy dominated social and political discourse within Great Britain. From 1931 to 1939, however, various strands of intellectual opinion gradually converged to form an emergent social democratic consensus, which eventually achieved political ascendancy in 1945, with the formation of the first postwar Labour government. It is this configuration of political and cultural discourse, designated by its champions as a "middle way" between unfettered capitalism and a nationalizing state socialism with which the documentary film movement, and Grierson in particular, must be associated, and Grierson is best understood as a social-democratic, corporatist reformist, rather than a socialist, or proto-Marxist thinker.

Grierson's theory of documentary film was conceived against a dual context of national and international instability and the growth of social-democratic corporatist thought and was premised on the belief that the documentary film could both play a vital role in preserving social stability and act as an effective medium of communication between the state and the public. Grierson's social democratic corporatist ideology, however, was also influenced by neo-Hegelian ideas, derived from philosophers such as F. H. Bradley and T. H. Green, which asserted the importance of the state and corporate institutions within national life. This influence led Grierson to the conviction that the needs of the individual must be subordinated to the requirements of corporate institutions and structures that possessed an intrinsic historical legitimacy and that guaranteed the unity and progress of society.

The origins of Grierson's conception of "good totalitarianism," whereby the principal role of the documentary film was to promote an understanding of the essentially unified and interdependent character of society, rather than the transient, idiosyncratic conceits of individual filmmakers, can be located in this neo-Hegelian model of the corporate state (Aitken, 1998). Similarly, and closely associated with this, is Grierson's conviction that the documentary filmmaker must be constrained by the "degree of general sanction": the consensual ideological and ethical framework that "imposes a clear limit upon the creative artist" (Aitken, 1990). Such a formulation appears to rule out any fundamental criticism of the status quo. However, in a key distinction—again drawn from Bradley—that he drew between the *agents* and *institutions* of state, Grierson argued that, during the 1930s, the agents of state (the government and ruling class) had turned against the needs of the people and had subverted the institutions of state to promote sectional interest (Aitken, 1990). This led Grierson to argue that the documentary film must both criticize the agents of state and represent the interests of the exploited working classes. Grierson's theory of documentary film, therefore, was motivated by a desire to reshape British society in closer accord with an ideal of ethical social cohesion and unity and was derived from the Hegelian ideas of the "Absolute," and "universal will."

Grierson's theory of documentary film envisaged that documentary would play a role in providing a medium of communication between the state and the people. Although Grierson acknowledged that ideally this should be a two-way process, however, he paid little attention to the means by which the views of the people were to influence the actions of the state. As a consequence, Grierson's theory of documentary film implicitly endorses a hierarchical practice of social ideology production, in which social communication is passed down from a bureaucratic elite, via the documentary film, to the public. Similarly, and despite his belief that democratic representation was the principal means through which the agents of state were to be prevented from recasting a liberal corporate society into "something else" (that is, totalitarianism), Grierson's conception of a society managed by mandarins and public relations experts can only be characterized as "democratic" with some difficulty (Aitken, 1990).

Although Grierson's theory of documentary film was concerned to a considerable extent with the issue of the civic and social purposiveness of film, it was also centrally preoccupied with questions of aesthetic technique and judgment, and many of his ideas can be traced back to aesthetic theories that have their origins within the idealist philosophy of Kant, Hegel, Bradley, and others. Grierson's first systematic elaboration of his theory of documentary film appeared in a memorandum he prepared for his then employers, the Empire Marketing Board (EMB), in 1927. In the second part of this memorandum, "English Cinema Production and the Naturalistic Tradition," Grierson postulated two different categories of film production, one consisting of films between seven and nine reels long, the other of films four reels long. The first of these categories was based on the theory of "epic cinema," which Grierson had elaborated in America in the mid-1920s. Here, in addition to their usual preoccupation with matters of individual characterization and psychological motivation, commercial feature films would also contain representations of national social and political institutions and would demonstrate how individuals were indissolubly connected to such institutions within an overarching social totality.

Grierson initially developed his theory of epic cinema in response to a number of right-wing, anti-democratic theories that he encountered during the 1920s. In 1924, Grierson was awarded a Rockefeller scholarship to study the impact of immigration on the United States. When he arrived in the United States he came into contact with theorists who argued that restrictions should be placed on immigration, and that the voting franchise should be limited to members of the professional classes. Grierson rejected the disavowals of democracy then being promoted by figures such as Harold Lasswell and Walter Lippmann, however, and argued, instead, that film could be used to sustain democracy by providing the public with crucial social information.

Grierson's ambitious model of epic cinema, however, bore little relation to the limited budget and resources available to the EMB, and, in the second part of his 1927 memorandum, he suggested the development of a form of cinema more appropriate to such circumstances. This second category of film production would consist of shorter films, the principal objective of which would be to represent social interconnection in both primitive cultures and modern industrial society. Grierson believed that these films would mark a "new phase" in cinema production, and that, in them, the visual features of often prosaic, everyday subject matter, would be orchestrated into expressive cinematic sequences, through the sophisticated use of montage editing and visual composition (Aitken, 1998). Such an approach would necessarily involve the abandonment of rudimentary documentary naturalism, and many of the processes of narrative construction common to the commercial feature film, as well as the adoption of more modernist stylistic techniques.

Although this original model of the Griersonian documentary emphasized modernist, formative editing technique, the actuality content of the documentary image also remained an important factor for Grierson. This is well illustrated by a key distinction that he drew between the "real" and the "actual." Writing about *Drifters* shortly after it was premiered, Grierson argued that the empirical content (the actual) of the film's documentary images was organized so as to express general truths (the real) that existed at a level of abstraction beyond the empirical, and that could not, therefore, be directly represented (Aitken, 1990). Grierson's definition of the real is not fully theorized, but was essentially derived from the Hegelian notion of *zeitgeist*, or "spirit of the age." From this, Grierson arrived at a conception of the real that consisted of those general determining factors and predispositions specific to a particular historical stage in the development of human society, and argued that documentary imagery should be so organized as to express this underlying reality. Grierson's first definition of documentary film, therefore, was based on the revelation of the real through the manipulation of documentary footage by formative editing technique.

Although Grierson believed that the principal objective of the documentary film was to represent the "real," he also argued that the documentary image was able to signify that underlying reality more profoundly than the image produced within the artificial environment of the film studio because it transcribed the "phenomenological surface of reality," and because, for Grierson, an existential relationship existed between the phenomenal world (the actual) and the real (Aitken, 1998). The origin of Grierson's conceptualization of the relationship between the empirical image of reality and underlying, more abstract realities, can be traced back to his influence by kantian aesthetics. However, it can also be related to models of film theory that emerged in Europe during the 1920s and 1930s, and, in particular, to the ideas of the Hungarian Marxist theorist Béla Balázs.

Grierson's early theory of documentary film consisted of three principal elements: (1) a concern with the content and expressive richness of the actuality image, (2) a concern with the interpretive potential of editing, and (3) a concern with the representation of social relationships. All of these can be found in his early film theory and in his first and perhaps only film as a director: *Drifters* (1929). *Drifters* reveals the influence of idealist aesthetics in its elevation of symbolic expression over more rudimentary forms of naturalistic representation and is replete with impressionistic imagery of natural forces and phenomena. Here, Grierson uses symbolic expression to depict the "real" through the "actual," and to imply the existence of an underlying unity (the real), which bonds the labour of fishermen to a surrounding natural order. Later in the film, this concern with the depiction of wholeness is also extended to include representations of commercial and technological forces within a filmic

"Absolute." The underlying idealist imperative within *Drifters* led to a prioritization of essence over appearance, and Grierson spoke of "exalting" each sequence in the film and "attaching splendour" to the film as a whole (Aitken, 1990). One consequence of this stance is that *Drifters* makes extensive use of metaphor, allegory, and impressionistic suggestion. *Drifters* can best be defined (as Grierson himself did in 1932) as an "imagist" film, influenced by the formalist imperatives of avant-garde film theory and by the philosophical idealist distinction between the real and the phenomenal (Hardy, 1979). *Drifters* was to be Grierson's only major film as a director, however, and, after 1930, he put his energies into the role of producer, rather than director. Nevertheless, the "imagist'" approach embodied in *Drifters* can be observed in a number of important films made by the documentary movement between 1929 and 1936, including *Song of Ceylon* (Wright, 1934), *Granton Trawler* (Grierson and others, 1934), *Coal Face* (Cavalcanti and others, 1935), and *Night Mail* (Wright, Watt, Cavalcanti, and others, 1936).

After 1936, the poetic montage style of films such as *Drifters* and *Song of Ceylon* gradually gave way to a more didactic, journalistic style, and the earlier concern with philosophical aesthetics gave way to a discourse grounded in issues of propaganda and civic education. The preoccupations and concerns of this later period are most clearly expressed in *Grierson on Documentary*, the collection of Grierson's essays first published by his official biographer, H. Forsyth Hardy, in 1946. In "The Documentary Idea: 1942," the essay within this collection that embodies Grierson's later position on the documentary film most uncompromisingly, he argues that the documentary film movement was an "anti-aesthetic movement," and that what was now required was instrumental filmmaking that would abandon depictions of the "beautiful" and that would play a more directive role in processes of social persuasion (Hardy, 1979). Between 1939 and 1945, Grierson was employed as the first Film Commissioner of the National Film Board of Canada and was in charge of the production of documentary series such as *World in Action* and *Canada Carries On*. At the National Film Board, he took every opportunity to champion the more didactic, instrumental style adopted by such films; in "The Documentary Idea: 1942" and elsewhere, he criticized the more "aesthetic" work of earlier colleagues such as Alberto Cavalcanti and Humphrey Jennings.

It is arguable that, not only the 1942 essay, but most of Grierson's writings of the war period, should be considered as uncharacteristic of his true position, and as a temporary and strategic response to the pressing demands of the time. Such an argument is, however, undermined by the fact that what is particularly striking about Grierson is that his general ideology remained largely unchanged from the 1920s to the 1970s. This unusual degree of continuity makes it unlikely that any sort of epistemological shift occurred during the war period and demonstrates the importance of understanding the ideological continuity that underlay Grierson's pre- and post-1936 positions on the relationship between the aesthetic and the sociological.

The radical change of emphasis in Grierson's ideas, from the pre- to the post-1936 period, was influenced by the increasing emphasis he gave to authoritarian tendencies that were always implicit in his ideology, but, that before 1936, were dialectically linked with more progressive tendencies. This change of emphasis can also be explained in terms of a shift from a concern with the phenomenological naturalism of the image to a more directive stance always implicit in Grierson's notion of the creative *interpretation* of reality. In the later period this more directive approach became increasingly allied to the cardinal objective of representing unified social relationships, while the earlier aesthetic of the image was increasingly discarded.

There is evidence to suggest, however, that toward the end of his life, Grierson returned to his earlier concerns and increasingly emphasized the importance of the aesthetic within documentary. In *I Remember, I Remember*, the film he made for BBC TV in 1970, he described documentary almost entirely in terms of its artistic qualities and abandoned the instrumental discourse that characterized his middle period. This indicates that the dialectical tension between the aesthetic and the sociological, a tension always implicit in his ideology and one that was skewed decisively in one direction during the 1937–1967 period, had reverted once again to the kind of balance that had characterized the 1929–1936 period.

IAN AITKEN

See also **BBC Voice of Britain**; **Cavalcanti, Alberto; Coal Face, Crown Film Unit;** *Drifters*; **EMB Film Unit; GPO Film Unit;** *Granton Trawler*; *Housing Problems*; **Industrial Britain; Jackson, Pat; Jennings, Humphrey; National Film Board of Canada;** *Night Mail*; **Rotha, Paul;** *Song of Ceylon*; **Taylor, Donald; Taylor, John; Wright, Basil**

Biography

Born near Stirling, Scotland, April 26, 1898. Graduated from Glasgow University, reading literature and philosophy, in 1923. Served in the naval minesweeping service during World War I. Awarded a Laura Spellman Rockefeller scholarship to study the impact of immigration on the United States, 1924–1927. Assistant Films Officer at the Empire Marketing Board, 1927–1933. Film Officer at the GPO, 1934–1936. Established Film Centre and other independent documentary film production units 1936–1939. First Film Commissioner of the National Film Board of Canada, 1939–1945. Appointed Head of Information at Unesco, 1946. Controller, Film, at the Central Office of Information, 1948–1950. Joint head of Group 3, a production arm of the National Film Finance Corporation, 1951–1955. Presented the Scottish Television Programme *This Wonderful World*, 1957–1967. Died in Bath, February 19, 1972.

Selected Films

1929 *Drifters*: director, writer
1931 *The Country Comes to Town* (Wright): producer
1931/32 *Industrial Britain* (Flaherty): producer, co-editor
1933 *Cargo from Jamaica* (Wright): producer
1933 *Windmill in Barbados* (Wright): producer
1934 *Granton Trawler*: co-director, producer, photographer; Pett and Pott (Cavalcanti): producer
1934 *Song of Ceylon* (Wright): producer, co-writer
1936 *Night Mail* (Wright, Watt, Cavalcanti and others): producer, co-writer
1938 *The Face of Scotland* (Wright): producer

Further Reading

Aitken, Ian, *Film and Reform*, London: Routledge, 1990.
———, *The Documentary Film Movement: An Anthology*, Edinburgh: Edinburgh University Press, 1998.
———, *Alberto Cavalcanti: Realism, Surrealism and National Cinemas*, London: Flicks, 2000.
———, *European Film Theory and Cinema: A Critical Introduction*, Edinburgh: Edinburgh University Press, 2001.
Beveridge, James, *John Grierson: Film Master*, London: Macmillan, 1979.
Ellis, Jack C., *John Grierson*, Carbondale: Southern Illinois University Press, 2000.
Evans, Gary, *John Grierson and the National Film Board*, Toronto: University of Toronto Press, 1986.
Grierson, John, *Grierson on Documentary*, edited by Forsyth Hardy, London: Collins, 1946, New York: Harcourt Brace, 1947; revised edition, London: Faber, 1966, New York: Praeger, 1971; abridged edition, Faber, 1979.
———, *Grierson on the Movies*, edited by Forsyth Hardy, London: Faber, 1981.

Hardy, Forsyth, *John Grierson: A Documentary Biography*, London: Faber, 1979.

Rotha, Paul, *Documentary Diary*, London: Secker and Warburg, and New York: Hill and Wang, 1973.

Swann, Paul, *The British Documentary Film Movement*, Cambridge: Cambridge University Press, 1989.

Sussex, Elizabeth, *The Rise and Fall of British Documentary*, Berkeley: University of California Press, 1975.

GRIGSBY, MICHAEL

Michael Grigsby is an important figure in British documentary, having ploughed a doggedly individual path over the last forty years. Grigsby has worked almost exclusively within television and has managed to retain his commitment to serious documentary work despite the increased commercial restrictions that have come to characterise television during the 1990s. Grigsby's ability to sustain an individual voice over so many years within television can be likened to figures such as Roger Graef and Denis Mitchell. In a sense, Grigsby is a figure who straddles the approaches of these two figures: Graef's rigorous verité style is evident in some of Grigsby's work, whilst Mitchell's attempts to poeticise the margins of everyday life is also apparent in many films he has made.

Although Grigsby's work is not at all homogeneous and does vary in style, it is marked by a number of recurring themes and stylistic approaches. The most striking of these, and the one that Grigsby himself would stress, is his dedication to documenting the working classes and other voices that are usually denied access to the media. He thinks that it is important to give the "voiceless" a voice and to allow the working- and under-classes a chance to speak on their own terms, rather than have another class speak for them.

Grigsby joined Granada as a trainee cameraman after leaving school, a post he found unsatisfactory because it was studio based. In his spare time, with friends, he formed a filmmaking group, Unit Five Seven. After purchasing a Bolex camera, they managed to shoot *Enginemen* (1959), a documentary about the transition from steel to diesel on the railways. The film was shot over two years in spare time and was eventually finished after Lindsey Anderson and Karel Reisz saw rushes and managed to secure money from the BFI Experimental Film Fund to complete the film. A romantic documentary, the film was very much in the tradition of the more poetic films made within the British Documentary Film Movement. It was actually shown on the final Free Cinema programme at the National Film Theatre on March 22, 1959.

Grigsby made one more film with Unit Five Seven, *Tomorrow's Saturday* (1962), before the group disbanded. He then began to make a name for himself within television. At Granada he directed the *Inside* series (1965), which examined prison life. Grigsby was still unhappy with his lack of freedom, however, and at this point managed to persuade Denis Forman to make a film on his own terms. The result was *Deckie Learner* (1965), another film about rail workers, which was nominated for a British Film Academy Award. Grigsby argues that this was his first "proper" television excursion because it was conceived as a film, rather than a piece of television journalism. Grigsby's connection to the cinematic documentary school is betrayed in such comments; whilst his work is investigative, he criticises many television documentaries because they tell stories with words and are too journalistic. For Grigsby, films must tell stories with images; whilst this does not mean that the sound track is of no importance, it does mean that the selection and composition of images should be carefully thought out.

Grigsby's approach to documentary filmmaking is rather different from that of American direct cinema, although he started to make television films when the influence of that style was becoming marked. His methods are not totally removed from such an approach. His dedication to filming on location, his tendency to shoot using only available light, and his belief in an image-driven form of documentary are similar to methods associated with direct cinema. Yet, there are two major areas where Grigsby diverts from such filmmakers. First, he does not claim any position of "objectivity" within his films. He believes films must be made from a specific viewpoint, his being "marginal" interventions within the dominant power structures. Second, he thinks that the form of a documentary should be carefully planned out, so that methods "appropriate" to the subject matter at hand are deployed.

Grigsby commitment to allowing "marginal" figures to speak runs through his work. *A Life Apart* (1973) and *A Life Underground* (1974) expose the isolation of trawlers and miners, respectively. They examine the fragmentation of industrial communities by unlocking the thoughts of community members and, alternately, focusing on their work. *The Silent War* (1990) uncovers the fear and resentment of communities in Belfast living with sectarian violence and the continual presence of the British army. More recently, in *Lockerbie—A Night Remembered* (1998), he looks at the effects of the Lockerbie plane crash of 1988 on the community, revealing how the lives of its residents were turned upside down.

The formal methods that Grigsby used are not so consistent as his themes, but two main approaches mark his work. The first is a rather minimal approach, in which careful, long, static takes of communities predominate. This formal approach can be found in films such as *A Life Apart* and *Eskimos of Pond Inlet* (1976, part of the *Disappearing World* series), the latter depicting the life of an Eskimo community whose traditions have been disrupted by growing consumerism. The second main approach evident in Grigsby's work is a more poetic, montage-based aesthetic. Probably the most impressive example of this style can be found in *Living on the Edge* (1986), an ambitious, collage-style film that cuts between historical moments and uses archive footage to build up a rich, intertextual picture of lost hope. The film is undoubtedly inspired by Humphrey Jennings, even pictorially "quoting" *Listen to Britain* (1943) in one sequence. Jennings' depictions of national unity are replaced, however, with a more pessimistic portrait of social fragmentation. These two approaches certainly do not exhaust Grigsby's formal palette, and he has occasionally worked outside of them, as with the documentary-drama *SS Lutisania* (1967). Yet much of his work can be seen to fall somewhere between the two extremes already outlined.

Grigsby has been criticised in some quarters; his obsession with troubled communities, for instance, has been seen as nostalgic. This nostalgic tendency is not offset by his formal approach, which refuses to supply easy answers to the problems depicted (Grigsby steers clear from using "objective" narration). Grigsby, claims that this would be an arrogant manoeuvre. Whether or not one agrees with him on this issue, it cannot be denied that his body of work is impressive and consistent and is welcome in that he continually airs the views of those who are often left unheard, thus adding a different dimension to events often covered very differently (or not at all) in media journalism.

JAMIE SEXTON

See also **Graef, Roger**; *Listen to Britain*; **Mitchell, Denis**

Biography

Born in Reading, 1937. Educated at Abingdon school. Trained as cameraman at Granada after leaving University. Set up *Unit Five Seven* in 1957. From 1956 freelance producer and director with Granada. Later works for a number of other television production companies.

Selected Films

1959 *Enginemen*: producer
1962 *Tomorrow's Saturday*: director
1965 *Inside* (Granada, series): director
1965 *Deckie Learner* (Granada): director
1967 *Death by Misadventure: SS Lusitania* (Granada) director
1969 *Deep South* (Granada): produced
1970 *I Was a Soldier* (Granada):director
1973 *World in Action: Working the Land* (Granada): producer
1973 *A Life Apart* (Granada): producer
1974 *A Life Underground* (Granada): producer
1976 *Disappearing World: Eskimo's of Pond Inlet* (Granada): director
1979 *Before the Monsoon* (ATV, series): producer
1990 *True Stories: Silent War* (Central): director
1994 *Fine Cut: Time of Our Lives* (BBC): director
1994 *Sound on Film: Pictures on the Piano* (BBC): director
1995 *Fine Cut: Hidden Voices* (BBC): director
1996 *Witness: Living with the Enemy* (Channel 4): director
1998 *Lockerbie—A Night Remembered* (Channel 4): director
1999 *Sound on Film: The Score* (BBC): director
2001 *Lost at Sea: Solway Harvester* (BBC): director

Further Reading

Butler, David, "'Progressive' Television Documentary and Northern Ireland—The Films of Michael Grigsby in a 'Postcolonial Context,'" in *Dissident Voices: The Politics of Television and Cultural Change*, edited by Mike

Wayne, London and Sterling: Virginia: Pluto Press, 1998.

Corner, John, *The Art of Record: A Critical Introduction to Documentary*, Manchester: Manchester University Press, 1996.

Grigsby, Michael, and Nicolas McLintock, "The State We're In," in *DOX: Documentary Film Quarterly*, 6, Summer 1995.

Macdonald, Kevin, and Mark Cousins (eds.), *Imagining Reality: The Faber Book of Documentary*, London: Faber and Faber, 1996.

Orbanz, Eva, *Journey to a Legend and Back: The British Realistic Film*, Berlin: Edition Volker Spiess, 1977.

Petley, Julian, "Living on the Edge," in *Monthly Film Bulletin*, 54, 640, 1987.

GROULX, GILLES

Born into a large working-class family in Montreal, Gilles Groulx worked his way up to the middle class by obtaining an office job. Unhappy in the corporate milieu, he turned his back on the mainstream (a choice to which he remained true all his life) and started moving in artistic and intellectual circles, including Paul-Émile Borduas's radical Automatist group.

He tried his hand at poetry and painting, made a short experimental documentary in 1954, *Les héritiers/Heirs*, (released 1998) and worked as a film editor for the Canadian Broadcasting Corporation (CBC) television news service. He was hired as an editor at the National Film Board of Canada (NFB) after its move from Ottawa to Montreal in 1956. In 1958, he made his directorial debut at the NFB, with his documentary, *Les raquetteurs/Snowshoers*, which he co-directed with Michel Brault. This seemingly simple reportage on a congress of snowshoeing clubs became a landmark in the evolution of direct cinema. The visual style of the film (owing primarily to Brault's camera work and use of a wide-angle lens) and its ironic structure (owing primarily to Groulx's editing) made it a film that revealed a side of French-Canadian culture that had rarely been acknowledged: the mundane but important rituals and customs that make Québec unique.

During the few years after the release of *Les raquetteurs*, Groulx directed a handful of shorts in the direct cinema style, the best of which are *Golden Gloves* (1961) on an unemployed aspiring boxer; *Voir Miami . . . /To See Miami* (1963), which analyzes the Quebecker's fascination with, and resistance against, American culture; and *Un jeu si simple/Such a Simple Game*, (1964) on hockey.

Late in 1963, Groulx was commissioned by the NFB to direct a documentary on how young people spend their time during the winter. Groulx used the budget for this project to make *Le chat dans le sac/The Cat in the Bag* (1964), a feature-length fiction film on the nationalist awakening of a twenty-something French-Canadian and the disintegration of his relationship with an English-speaking Jewish woman. Blending a documentary look with new-wave self-referentiality, and examining contemporary issues such as nationalism, feminism, and Marxism, *Le chat dans le sac* became a model for subsequent *engagé* features and is often acknowledged as marking the beginning of modern fiction film in Québec (Harcourt, 1980).

Groulx moved again from documentary to fiction in *Où êtes-vous donc?/Where Are You?* (1968), an experimental narrative on the evils of consumerism. A similar theme is explored in another experimental fiction, *Entre tu et vous/Between "tu" and "vous"* (1969).

Groulx returned to a more "traditional" mode of documentary with *24 Hours or More . . .* (1973) a passionate study of Québec politics and society in the early 1970s. The film was deemed subversive by NFB's conservative commissioner Sydney Newman and was banned from circulation until 1976. After making a commissioned documentary on education, *Place de l'équation/The Place of the Equation* (1973), he directed a co-production with Mexico in 1977, *Première question sur le bonheur/Primera pregunta sobre la felicidad/The First Question on Happiness*, on the struggle of Mexican farmers against bourgeois landowners.

In all of his films, Groulx remained critical of capitalist society and of the inability of Quebeckers to escape a culture saturated with vacuous images and useless products. As he was finishing his surrealist fiction on a selfish businessman, *Au pays de Zom/In the Land of Zom* (1982), Groulx was involved in a serious accident that put an end to his career. Richard Brouillette made the documentary *Trop c'est assez/Too Much Is Enough* (1995) on Groulx's life.

ANDRÉ LOISELLE

See also **National Film Board of Canada**

Biography

Born May 30, 1931, Montreal, Quebec, Canada. Made a short experimental documentary, *Les héritiers/Heirs* (released 1998), 1954. Worked as a film editor for the Canadian Broadcasting Corporation (CBC) television news service. Hired as an editor at the National Film Board of Canada (NFB) after its move from Ottawa to Montreal in 1956. In 1958, made his directorial debut at the NFB, with his documentary, *Les raquetteurs/Snowshoers*, which he co-directed with Michel Brault. While finishing *Au pays de Zom/In the Land of Zom* (1982),

involved in a serious accident that put an end to his career. Died August 22, 1994.

Selected Films

1958 *Les Raquetteurs/Snowshoers*: (Director, editor
1959 *Normétal/Normetal*: Director, script
1961 *La France sur un caillou/France on a Rock*: Director, editor
1961 *Golden Gloves*: director, Photographer, editor
1962 *Voir Miami . . ./To See Miami*: Director, editor
1964 *Un jeu si simple/Such a Simple Game*: Director, editor
1973 *24 heures ou plus/24 Hours or More . . .* : Director, editor
1973 *Place de l'équation/The Place of the Equation*: Director, script, editor
1977 *Première question sur le bonheur/The First Question on Happiness*: Director, editor

Further Reading

Gilles Groulx. Montréal: Conseil québécois pour la diffusion du cinéma, 1969.
Harcourt, Peter, "1964: The Beginning of a beginning," *Self-Portrait: Essays on the Canadian and Quebec Cinema*, edited by Pierre Véronneau and Piers Handling, Ottawa: Canadian Film Institute, 1980, 64–76.

GUZMAN, PATRICIO

Chilean Patricio Guzman is one of the foremost directors of Latin American and worldwide political documentary cinema. During his ongoing and internationally acclaimed four-decade career, he has directed more than fifteen award-winning documentary feature films and has successfully combined his political militancy as a committed Marxist with his concept of the filmmaker's role. His primary contribution has been to document certain aspects of Chile's political history from 1970 forward, including the country's socialist revolution, Salvador Allende's three-year presidency, the violent coup d'etat by General Augusto Pinochet's army in 1973, Pinochet's seventeen-year reign of terror as a military dictator, his eventual exile in 1992, and the legal proceedings that lead to his arrest in London in 1998.

Guzman has made six films documenting this turbulent period in Chile's history: *Primer ano/The First Year* (1971), *La Respuesta de octubre/*

The October Answer (1972), *La batalla de Chile, Parts I, II, and II/The Battle of Chile* (1975–1980), *Chile, la memoria obstinada/Chile, Obstinate Memory* (1998), *El Caso Pinoche/The Pinochet Case* (2001), and *Salvador Allende* (2004).

In 1971, after making several shorts, Guzman, directed and wrote his first documentary feature, *Primer ano/The First Year*, which covers the first year of Allende's presidency. The film includes topics ranging from land reform to the nationalization of various industries, to the empowerment of workers and peasants, to the state visit of Fidel Castro. In 1972, Guzman directed and wrote *La Respuesta de octubre/The October Answer*, a film about the first management strike against Allende's government. Although both films were not circulated widely outside of Allende's Chile, they were well received by working-class audiences.

In 1973, using stock footage donated by Marker, Guzman began co-producing (with Marker), directing, and writing *La batalla de Chile I, II, and III/The Battle of Chile, Parts I, II, and III*, an epic trilogy that documents Allende's final period, the violent right-wing counter-revolution against his government, and the accession of Pinochet's military junta. Using just one 16mm Éclair camera and one Nagra tape recorder, Guzman, aided by five associates, filmed events during ten weeks immediately before, during, and after the military coup. On the first day of the coup, Guzman was imprisoned in the National Stadium and filming was halted. After his release fifteen days later, he left for Europe and began to live in exile. One by one, four of the other five filmmakers escaped the country, and the film was smuggled safely out to Europe and then Cuba. The last filmmaker, Jorge Muller, was seized by the secret police in 1974 and was never heard from again. Over a period of four years, Guzman completed the film in Cuba with funding and support from the Instituo cubano del arte y industria cinematograficos, the Cuban national film institute. The three parts were released in 1975, 1977, and 1979, respectively, and established and secured Guzman's international reputation as a documentary filmmaker.

In the trilogy, Guzman found and developed his distinct documentary style. He uses a rich mixture of direct cinema observation and investigative reporting. Deciding to use actuality footage, rather than archival footage and the compilation method, he was able to obtain extraordinary footage by skillfully combining his rigorous and disciplined production techniques with his ability to understand, foresee, and immerse himself in the flow of political events. Guzman frequently uses the sequence shot, a cinematic device that allows viewers to see events unfold without breaks in the flow of the images. The four-hour film, a poignant work of historical testimony, conveys both a sweeping drama of the historic events portrayed, and an emotional texture that gives the footage multiple dimensions. While the film strongly favors Allende's efforts and does not pretend to be objective, it does present and convey a high level of information in a balanced manner and is not uncritical of the Left.

Part I, *La insurreccion de la borguesia/The Uprising of the Bourgeoisie* (1975) documents the final days of Allende's presidency through the first day of the military coup. Part II, *El golpe de estado/The Coup D'Etat* (1977) documents the "Popular Unity" period of Allende's government, the tumultuous events leading up to the coup, and Allende's controversial death (some believe he committed suicide and others that he was murdered by Pinochet's henchmen). Part III, *El poder popula/The Power of the People* (1979) documents the thousands of local groups of "Popular Power" that were created during Allende's presidency by ordinary workers and peasants to perform various services in the country. Guzman, following the Marxist concept that views classes as the protagonists of history and conflict as an inherent dimension of class societies, frames events in terms of class conflict. Parts I and II tracks the military's drift to the right and the anti-Allende activities of the legislature, and Part III centers on workers organizing as a class so that they can achieve emancipation from, and the transformation of, the bourgeoisie-dominated world.

The trilogy runs is considered by most international critics, Marxist and non-Marxist alike, to be one of the major political documentaries of the period, and, by some, to be one of the most important political documentary ever made. The film has been screened internationally in more than eight countries, has been shown commercially in more than thirty-five countries, has won seven Grand Prizes in Europe and Latin America, has been distributed in more than twenty countries, and has been televised in more than ten countries.

In 1998, twenty-eight years after the death of Allende, Guzman returned to Chile for the first time and screened *La Batalla de Chile* to students and to those who actually witnessed and/or participated in the battle. Their reactions formed the subject of his next documentary, *Chile, la memoria obstinada/Chile, Obstinate Memory*, which he directed, wrote, and narrated. Guzman's premise is that the memory of those times and events that were captured in the trilogy was largely barred from the collective consciousness of the Chilean people, and the film investigates this political amnesia and the reawakening of memory in the Chilean people.

In 2001, Guzman co-produced, directed, and wrote *El Caso Pinoche/The Pinochet Case*, a film that examines the landmark legal case brought against Pinochet in Spain, both before and after his arrest in London in 1998. In 2004, Guzman directed and wrote *Salvador Allende*, a film that documents the political career of the fallen leader by exploring both his rise to the presidency and the forces that collaborated against him to remove him from office.

Guzman also has made a number of other types of documentaries, including several that have focused on Chilean and Latin American historical and religious concerns. In 1983, he directed and co-wrote *La Rosa de los vientos/The Compass Rose*, a mythological fable about Latin America. In 1985, he directed and wrote *Precolombian Mexico*, a Spanish television series about the ancient times of the Myan and Aztec cultures. In 1987, he produced, directed, and wrote *En nombre de Dios/In the Name of God*, a film about the Catholic Church's fight for human rights in Chile under the Pinochet regime. In 1988, he directed and wrote *El proyecto aclarado de Carlos III/The Enlightened Project of Carlos III*, a Spanish television series about the age of enlightenment in Spain and the United States.

In 1992, he produced, directed, and wrote *La Cruz del Sur/The Southern Cross*, a Spanish television series about the discovery of America and the popular religions in Latin America. In 1995, Guzman directed and wrote *Las barreras de la soledad/ The Barriers of Loneliness*, a film about history and memory in a Mexican village. In 1999, he directed and wrote *Isla de Robinson Crusoe/Robinson Crusoe Island*, a film about Daniel Defoe's novel, and the remote island with the same name that lies off the Chilean coast. In 2001, he co-directed and wrote *Invocacion/Invocation*, and in 2002, he directed and wrote *Madrid*, a film that explores Spain's capital.

Guzman also is a cinematographer, writer, and actor. In addition to working as a cinematographer on several films in the 1960s, he has published four books, several short stories, and numerous articles and has acted in three films: *Vivir al día/To Live a Day* (1996), *El Cobrador/The Collector* (1994), and *Moon Over Parador* (1988). He also worked as the cinematographer on *11'09''01/September 11, 2001* (2002) and *Salvador Allende* (2004).

SUZANNE EISENHUT

See also **Battle of Chile, The; Underground/Activist Documentary: Chile**

Biography

Born Patricio Guzman Lozanes in Santiago, Chile, August 11, 1941. Attended the University of Chile from 1960 to 1965: the Theater School (1960), the Faculty of History (1961), and the Faculty of Philosophy (1962 to 1965). Attended the Film Institute at the Catholic University of Chile (1963 to 1965). Attended the Official Cinematographic School of Madrid (1966 to 1969), where he received a Director-Producer degree (1970). Joined Chile-Films (Chile's national film production company) and headed the Documentary Films Workshops (1970). Formed Grupo del tercer año (Group of the Third Year) to produce *The Battle of Chile*. Presented at numerous conferences and cinema seminars in Canada, Chile, Cuba, Mexico, Spain, and the United States (since 1978). Served as a member of the jury for the

documentary sections of many acclaimed film festivals, including those in Brazil, France, Germany, India, Italy, Mexico, and the United States (since 1993). Received a Scholarship from the John Simon Guggenheim Memorial Foundation (1993). Served as the Director of the International Documentary Film Festival in Santiago (1997 to 1999), and as the Malaga Director of the Documentary Section in Spain (1998 to 1999). Employed as a professor of documentary film at various schools in Europe and Latin America. Currently resides in Paris with Renate Sachse, who also collaborates on the scripts for his films. Father of two daughters, Andrea and Camila, who are also filmmakers and often work on his projects. Production company: Patricio Guzman Producciones, S.L.

Selected Films

1971 *Primer año/The First Year*: director, writer
1972 *La Respuesta de octubre/The October Answer*: director, writer
1975 Part I: *La insurreccion de la borguesia/The Uprising of the Bourgeoisie*
1975–1980 *La Batalla de Chile)/The Battle of Chile*: co-producer, director, writer
1977 Part II: *El golpe de estado/The Coup D'Etat*
1978–1983 *La Rosa de los vientos/The Compass Rose*: director, co-writer
1979 Part III: *El poder popula/The Power of the People*
1985 *Precolombian Mexico*: director, writer
1987 *En el nombre de Dios/In the Name of God*: producer, director, writer
1988 *El proyecto aclarado de Carlos III/The Enlightened Project of Carlos III*: director, writer
1988 *Moon Over Parador*: actor
1992 *La Cruz del Sur/The Southern Cross*: producer, director, writer, production designer
1994 *El Cobrado/The Collector*: actor
1994 *Vivir al dia/To Live a Day*: actor
1995 *Las barreras de la soledad/The Barriers of Loneliness*: director, writer
1997 *Chile, la memoria obstinada/Chile, the Obstinate Memory*: director, writer, narrator
1998 *La barrieres de la solitude/The Barriers of Solitude*: director, writer
1999 *Isla de Robinson Crusoe/Robinson Crusoe Island*: director, writer
2001 *El Caso Pinoche/The Pinochet Case*: co-producer, director, writer
2001 *Invocación/Invocation*: co-director
2002 *Madrid*: director, writer
2002–2003 *11'09''01 – September 11 (2002)/September 11* (2003): cinematographer
2004 *Salvador Allende*: director, writer, cinematographer

Selected Publications by Guzman

BOOKS
Cansancio en la Tierra [*Exhaustion in the Land*], 1961 (short stories).
El cine contra el fascismo, with P. Sempere, edited by Fernando Torres, Valencia, Spain, 1977.
Juegos de Verdad [*Play Tribute*], 1962 (a novel), edited by Luis Rivano, Santiago, Chile.

La batalla de Chile: La lucha de un pueble sin armas, Colec-
cion Libros Hiperion, Madrid, Spain, 1977.
La insurrecciion del la burgesia, edited by Racinante, Car-
acas, 1975.

ARTICLES AND SHORT STORIES

"'Chile' 3: Guzman," and "Chile," in *Framework* (Nor-
wich), Spring and Autumn, 1979.
Interview with Z.M. Pick, in *Cine-Tracts* (Montreal), Win-
ter 1980.
"La Batalla de Chile," interview with Carlos Galiano, in
Cine Cubano (Havana), 91–92, 1978.
"La Bataille du Chili II," interview with Marcel Martin, in
Ecran (Paris), 1977.
"Le Cinema dans la politique de l'Unite Populaire," in
Jeune Cinema (Paris), January 1974.
"Politics and the Documentary in People's Chile," inter-
view with Julianne Burton, in *Socialist Review*, October
1977.
Several short stories published in *Cansancio en la Tierra*
[*Exhaustion in the Land*], 1971.
Short story published in *El Primer Premio* ["The First
Prize"], 1963.

Selected Readings on Guzman

Interview with Patricio Guzman, "El Cine Contra el Fascismo" ["Cinema Against Fascism"]), 1971.

Angry Arts Group, "Battle of Chile in Context," in *Jump
Cut* (Chicago), November, 1979.
"La Batalla de Chile Section," in *Cine Cubano* (Havana),
March 1978.
Delmas, Jean, "La Batalla de Chile, deuxieme partie: La
Coup d'etat," in *Jeune Cinema* (Paris), February 1977.
Gauthier, Guy, "Chili: la premiere annee," in *Image et Son*
(Paris), March 1973.
———. "*La Bataille du Chile*, premiere partie: L'Insur-
rection de la bourgeoisie," in *Image et Son* (Paris),
January 1976.
Mouesca, J., "El cine chileno en el exilio (1973-1982)," in
Cine Cubano (Havana), 109, 1984.
Niogret, Hubert, "La Batalla de Chile: el golpe de estado,"
in *Positif* (Paris), July/August 1976.
Wallis, V., "Battle of Chile: Struggle of People without
Arms," *Jump Cut* (Chicago), November 1979.
West, Dennis, "The Battle of Chile," in *Cineaste* (New
York), 11, 2, 1978.
———. "Documenting the End of the Chilean Road to
Socialism: *La Batalla de Chile*," in *The American Hispa-
nist*, February 1978.

GUZZETTI, ALFRED

American filmmaker Alfred Guzzetti has been a
central figure in the documentary film culture of
the United States from the 1970s up to the present
day. Since the early 1970s, he has examined how
the realm of the subjective and the role of personal
reflection were perceived as challenging obstacles
to established models of documentary form. Guzzetti's interest in the nuances of personal experience
has resulted in a long career of simultaneously
building on as well as dismantling the general
understanding of the roles of filmmaker and audience of nonfiction film. His body of work spans
four decades and is often divided into three distinct
yet interwoven types of nonfiction form: personal
documentary, political documentary, and experimental film and video.

For Guzzetti, the subject and the realm of the
subjective complicate rather than challenge the
potency of the indexical nature of documentary.
His emergence into documentary filmmaking
began at a moment when he saw both American

culture and artistic practices meld aspects of the
personal with the political. The political and social
issues of the 1960s such as the Vietnam War, as well
as the civil rights and the women's movements
helped mark a shift on what had previously been
considered private or personal topics into the political arena. This fusion of the personal and political
also took hold in many arts. Much of Guzzetti's
earlier work and ideas were influenced by well-
known photographers such as Henri Cartier-Bresson and Henry Callahan, as well as revolutionary
and experimental filmmakers such as Jean-Luc
Godard, Peter Kubelka, and Jean Rouch.

In the 1970s and 1980s, Guzzetti made a cycle of
autobiographical documentaries that included private moments filmed by and about his family.
Although it was not commonplace for filmmakers
to combine 8mm archival footage and 16mm contemporary images from their personal lives in their
documentaries, Guzzetti was not alone in this practice. In his catalogue essay for the 1993 Cinéma du

Réel, "The Documentary Gets Personal," he proposes that the personal documentary is not the practice of a single filmmaker but rather a mode that spans decades, social classes, genders, and continents. By evoking examples from a broad range of filmmakers such as the Lumière brothers, Martin Scorsese, Robb Moss, Maya Deren, Ross McElwee, Ed Pincus, and Su Friedrich, Guzzetti demonstrates how private images, although present in nonfiction films, often remain unsung in criticism on documentary film history. This essay provides a much needed historical mapping of the legacy behind the personal and autobiographical cinema.

His model of personal documentary filmmaking challenged filmmakers, not only to interact and observe their subjects but to use their own experiences and relationships with them to guide the filmmaking process. For instance, the second film of Guzzetti's autobiographical cycle, *Scenes from Childhood* (1977–1980), was inspired by a staple of cinema verité film, Jean Rouch's and Edgar Morin's *Chronique d'un été* (1961). Guzzetti chose to use conventions of direct cinema such as synchronized sound, as well as an avoidance of interviews and voice-over narration to convey the intimacy of his personal relationship with the film's subjects, his child and his child's playmates. In this sense Guzzetti's personal documentaries can be seen as both a continuation of and a radical response to what are often considered more social and public issue-oriented modes of nonfiction filmmaking such as direct cinema and cinema verité.

By the late 1980s, Guzzetti became involved in a series of collaborative political film projects. In the 1990s, he also worked on two anthropological projects with Lina Fruzzetti, Ákos Östör, and Ned Johnston: *Seed and Earth* (1994) and *Khalfan and Zanzibar* (2000). Such collaborations reflect the interests and skills of their co-authors, but strong connections can be made between these documentaries and Guzzetti's other nonfiction projects. Many of Guzzetti's sensibilities and preoccupations resurface in his second collaboration with Susan Meiselas and Richard Rogers, *Pictures from a Revolution* (1991), a film that combines cine and still photography to convey the social unrest in postrevolutionary Nicaragua. This film, as in his earlier autobiographical film, *Family Portrait Sittings* (1971–1975) and in many of his later experimental films and videos, uses many formal devices and motifs found in much of Guzzetti's works: the role of the filmmaker and subject as eyewitness, the employment of various techniques that destabilize common assertions about the medium of photography while refusing to flatten out its

power as artistic beauty or relativize its use as historical record, fragmenting and mismatching sound from its image to complicate the audience's sense of temporal order, and a preoccupation with the passage of time.

Guzzetti's writing on documentary positions fiction film as working, in part, to compensate and distract the spectator from the "disruptive forces" of the cinematic medium. In his 1996 critical essay, "Notes on Representation and the Nonfiction Film," Guzzetti asks: "Might it not also be true that it was only through fiction that styles could have been evolved capable of managing the disruptive forces that Lumière let loose? Was fiction among other things a defense erected against all that is disquieting and problematical in the moving image?" This concern for tackling "all that is disquieting and problematical in the moving image" is found not only in his personal and political documentaries but also in Guzzetti's more experimental nonfiction films and videos such as *A Tropical Story* (1998) and *The Tower of Industrial Life* (2000). He posits his later more experimental films and videos as a species of nonfiction consistent with his earlier approach to documentary. He began to use first Hi8 and later digital video formats to convey, in his words, "the daily experience of contemporary life, its assaults on us in public places, in television, our ineffectual refuge in the private and the distant."

Guzzetti's consistent personal vision and diverse approaches to nonfiction form provide insightful ways for individuals concerned with the "disruptive forces" of documentary film to mobilize questions of medium specificity (how cinema represents) alongside questions of identity politics (who gets represented and in what manner). His critical and filmic explorations offer historical records for not only how we lived but what in our lives we choose to document and archive. In his words: "For when future generations try to understand our civilization, it will be films such as these that provide the most vivid record of who we were and how we lived." Such a democratization of history-making places Guzzetti's past and current projects alongside contemporary scholars and filmmakers dedicated to revealing personal experiences seldom told or heard in nonfiction works.

THERESA SCANDIFFIO

Biography

Born in Philadelphia, PA in 1942. Graduated from Harvard College with Bachelor of Arts degree in 1964. Graduated from Harvard University with a doctorate in English literature in 1968. Professor at Harvard University 1968–present. Received numerous National Endowment of the Arts grants, Artists Foundation fellowships and film festival prizes for many of his non-fiction film and video projects. He is a member of numerous panels and groups such as the Academy of Motion Picture Arts and Sciences. He continues to produce and discuss his film and video works at museums, galleries, *cinematheques* and film festivals around the world. He is currently the Osgood Professor of Visual Arts at Harvard University.

Selected Films

1970–1971 *Air*
1971–1975 *Family Portrait Sittings*
1977–1980 *Scenes From Childhood*
1981–1986 *Beginning Pieces*
1984–1985 *Living at Risk: The Story of a Nicaraguan Family*: co-director
1988–1994 *Seed and Earth*: co-director
1989–1991 *Pictures from a Revolution*: co-director
1997 *Under The Rain*
1998 *A Tropical Story*
1999 *Khalfan and Zanzibar*: co-director
2000 *The Tower of Industrial Life*
2002 *Down from the Mountains*
2003 *Calcutta Intersection*

Further Reading

Askew, Kelly, "Khalfan and Zanzibar," in *American Anthropologist*, 103, March 2001, 189–190.

Canby, Vincent, "Pictures from a Revolution," *The New York Times*, November 19, 1992, C26–29.

Charlip, Julie A., and Charly Bloomquist, "Pictures from a Revolution," in *The American Historical Review*, 97, October 1992 1166–1168.

Guzzetti, Alfred, *Two or Three Things I Know About Her: Analysis of A Film By Godard*, Cambridge: Harvard University Press, 1981.

——, "The Documentary Gets Personal/Le documentaire la première personne," catalogue essay for Cinéma du réel, Paris, March, 1993, 90–91 (French translation, 88–89).

——. "Notes on Representation and the Nonfiction Film," *New Literary History*, XXVII, Spring, 1996, 263–270.

Kopkind, Andrew, "Living at Risk: Witness to War," *The Nation*, 241, 15, November 9, 1985, 484–485.

Leighton, Tanya, "Places of Images, Plus Sounds: Alfred Guzzetti's Films and Videotapes," http://www.location1. org/artists/guzzetti/files/text.html.

Rothman, William, "Alfred Guzzetti's Family Portrait Sittings," *The Quarterly Review of Film Studies*, 2, 1, 1977, 96–113.

Sutherland, Allan T., "Family Portrait," in *Sight and Sound*, 48, 1, Winter 1978–1979, 29–30.

INDEX

A

Aadel, Shahaboddin, 620
Abbott, Jennifer, 163
ABC. *See* American Broadcasting Company (ABC); Australian
   Broadcasting Corporation (ABC)
A.BC. Africa, 702–704
ABC of Ethnocide/ABC del Etnocidio, 759
ABC of the Strike, The/ABC da Greve, 214
Abdes-Salam, Shadi, 945
Abel Gance: The Charm of Dynamite, 2
Abel Gance: Yesterday and Tomorrow, 1, 2
Abitia, Jesùs, 876, 877
aborigines. *See* indigenous people
About Britain, 1360
About the Learning Human Being/Vom lernenden Menschen, 683
above-the-line costs, 1063
Abrahão, Benjamin, 132
Abrego, Eugenio, 207
absolute film, 110, 111
Absolute Majority/Maioria Absoluta, 133, 213
abstraction, realism and, 1084, 1085
Abyssinian Flames/Fiamme abissine, 634
Académie du Cinéma, 430
Acadia/Acadia?!?/L'Acadie/l'Acadie?!?, 131, 930, 931, 1026
Acción Chicano, 195, 197
Accordion Dreams, 442
Aces/Asse, 447
Achbar, Mark, 163, 843, 844, 1440, 1441
Achilleas, 500
Acin, Ramon, 744
Ackerman, Chantal, 68
Across the Border/Cruzando Fronteras, 196
Across the Interior of Iceland/Yfir Kjöl, 597
ACT Films Ltd., 120
acting, 4–6
Acting: Lee Strasberg and the Actors Studio, 714
activist filmmaking, 6–9
   Angela: Portrait of a Revolutionary, 40–42
   anti-pornography, 382
   Barclay, 78–80
   Bond, 119–121
   Cinema Action, 209, 210
   Film and Photo League, 394, 395
   Goldson, 479, 480
   Guzman, 515, 516
   Hell Unlimited, 539–541
   Hiroshima-Nagasaki-August 1945, 550–552
   Makavejev, 824–826
   Marxism and, 856, 857
   The Mills of the Gods, 883, 884

   Mita, 887, 888
   Moore, 911, 912
   Near/Middle East, 942, 943
   Obamsawin, 993, 994
   Ogawa Productions, 997, 998
   Rotha, 1134, 1135
   Zilnik, 1495, 1496
Act of God, 2–4
Actualidades de Angola, 267
Actualidades de Moçambique, 267
Actualidades Militares, 267, 268
Actualidades NO-DO para Brasil, 968
Actualidades Portuguesas, 267, 268
Actualités françaises, 975
Actualités Ufa/Ufa Wereldnieuws, 961
actualities, 927–928
   Lumière, 1452–1454
   Near/Middle East, 941
   newsreels, 971
   Scandinavia, 1168
   United Kingdom, 1360
   Vertov, 1377
Adair, John, 347
Adalil, 541
Adam, Fritz, 484
Adam, Kenneth, 1403
Adamopoulos, Theodoros, 500
Adams, Ansel, 1276
Adams, Randall, 1298
Adams, Sam, 186
Adamson, Margaret Ann, 157
Addicted to Solitude, 77, 1171
Adenauer, Konrad, 1489
Adio Kerida, 794
Adolescents, The (A.K.A. *That Tender Age*), 6–9
Adriatic Shipyards/I cantieri dell'Adriatico, 633
Advance, Democracy!, 120, 1093, 1457
Advance of the Tanks, 1464
Adventurer, The (Sinclair), 1212
Adventures on the New Frontier, 766
advertising films, 610
Aenigma Est, 502
Aero Engine, 1356
aesthetics and documentary film: poetics, 12, 13
   Benoit-Lévy on, 109
   Grierson on, 509–512
   Heynowski and Scheumann, 547
   Junge and, 683, 684
   modernism and, 897, 898
   narration and, 929
   New Earth, 952, 953

INDEX

INDEX

INDEX

INDEX

INDEX